# Creative Activities

## for Young Children

# RELATED TITLES IN THE DELMAR EARLY EDUCATION SERIES

- Rosalind Charlesworth and Karen K. Lind, *Math and Science for Young Children,* 1995
- Carol Gestwicki, *Developmentally Appropriate Practice,* 1995
- Judy Herr and Yvonne Libby, *Creative Resources for the Early Childhood Classroom,* 2nd edition, 1995
- Rae Pica, *Movement and the Young Child,* 1995
- LaVisa Cam Wilson, Michael Watson, and Linda Douville-Watson, *Infants & Toddlers: Curriculum and Teaching,* 3rd edition, 1995
- K. Eileen Allen and Lynn R. Marotz, *Developmental Profiles: Prebirth to Eight,* 2nd edition, 1994
- Kathleen Dolinar, Candace Boser, and Eleanor Holm, *Learning Through Play: Curriculum and Activities for the Inclusive Classroom,* 1994
- Robert Schirrmacher, *Art and Creative Development for Young Children,* 2nd edition, 1993

# Creative Activities
## for Young Children

**Mary Mayesky**  5th EDITION

**Delmar Publishers Inc.**

I(T)P An International Thomson Publishing Company

New York • London • Bonn • Boston • Detroit • Madrid • Melbourne • Mexico City • Paris
Singapore • Tokyo • Toronto • Washington • Albany NY • Belmont CA • Cincinnati OH

# NOTICE TO THE READER

Cover illustration by Alexander Piejko
Cover design by Spiral Design Studio

COPYRIGHT © 1995
By Delmar Publishers Inc.
an International Thomson Publishing Company

I(T)P™ The ITP logo is a trademark under license

Printed in the United States of America

**For more information, contact:**
Delmar Publishers Inc.
3 Columbia Circle Drive, Box 15015
Albany, New York 12212-5015

International Thomson Publishing
Berkshire House
168-173 High Holborn
London, WC1V7AA
England

Thomas Nelson Australia
102 Dodds Street
South Melbourne 3205
Victoria, Australia

Nelson Canada
1120 Birchmont Road
Scarborough, Ontario
M1K 5G4, Canada

International Thomson Publishing GmbH
Konigswinterer Str. 418
53227 Bonn
Germany

International Thomson Publishing Asia
221 Henderson Bldg. #05-10
Singapore 0315

International Thomson Publishing Japan
Kyowa Building, 3F
2-2-1 Hirakawa-cho
Chiyoda-ku, Tokyo 102
Japan

  2  3  4  5  6  7  8  9  10     XXX     01  00  99  98  97  96  95

**Library of Congress Cataloging-in-Publication Data**
Mayesky, Mary.
    Creative activities for young children / Mary Mayesky. — 5th ed.
      p.  cm.
    Includes bibliographical references and index.
    ISBN 0–8273–5886–5
    1. Creative activities and seat work.   I. Title.
LB1537.M34  1995                      94–21328
372.5—dc20                        CIP

To my daughter Claire—

You were the beginning. Through your eyes I learned a new way to see the world. Thank you for this and for the person you've become.

In love and appreciation. Momma (MEM)

# Contents

# APPENDICES                                                                       673

# Preface

Day in and day out, dedicated people in the field of early childhood education work tirelessly to perform one of the most important roles in our society—guiding the learning of our youngest citizens. Daily, they face the difficult challenges presented by young children growing up in a world so very complex and confusing. Unfortunately, the size of their task is not often equalled by the size of their paychecks or the regard in which they are held by society.

It is with a deep sense of respect and thanks that this book is presented to these unsung heroes of early childhood education. It is hoped that this book will be an aid and inspiration to their work with young children.

The fifth edition of *Creative Activities for Young Children* has been updated to reflect the unique challenges facing those in early childhood today. Some of the new features of the fifth edition include:

- New field-tested activities in each unit.
- New lists of children's books and teacher's reference books in each unit.
- Updated and additional information on the use of computers with young children.
- Increased emphasis on the use of recycled materials in activities.
- A new section entitled "Think About It . . ." that provides thought-provoking and research-oriented material related to the unit topic.
- Many new "This One's for You!" sections, which expand on some of the text material or touch on a related concept for added interest.
- In the Health and Safety Unit, a new section on allergies and young children.
- Also in the Health and Safety Unit, new research on television viewing and its effects on children's eating habits.
- More sugar-free and sugar-reduced recipes in the Food Unit as well as in other units, designated by the symbol ☺.
- A special section on teaching peace in the Social Studies unit.

- Also in the Social Studies Unit, an enlarged section on blocks and their use in teaching social studies.
- In the Program Basics Unit, a list of unsafe and potentially dangerous art supplies.
- A new section on scissoring in Unit 12, including how to introduce and practice this skill with young children in a developmentally appropriate way.
- An expanded woodworking section in Units 11 and 13, including more specific information on materials, setup, supervision, and specific activities.
- A new section on how to talk with young children about their art.
- A new bilingual/bicultural education section in the Language Arts Unit, including a comprehensive list of references for many multicultural children's books.
- Additional lists of children's books for many ethnic groups: Chinese-American, Latino, Vietnamese-American, African-American, Native American, etc.
- An expanded environmental education section, including a section on ecology.
- Non-sweet alternatives for trick-or-treat in the Halloween Holiday Unit.
- Also in the Halloween Holiday Unit, a Halloween Carnival, with simple games, as an alternative to trick-or-treat.
- In the Winter Holiday Unit, more information on holiday symbols, their origins, and significance.
- New sections on Native American and Hawaiian holidays.
- New activities, recipes, songs, and poems in all holiday and seasonal units.

You will discover these and many other new features as you use the fifth edition of *Creative Activities for Young Children*.

The same purpose remains in this edition as in the first four; it is designed for the person who is dedicated to helping young children reach their full potential. It is written for people who want to know more about creativity, creative children, creative teaching, and creative curriculum and activities.

Most people agree that creativity is natural to young children. However, creativity is a delicate skill that can easily be destroyed. Too few teachers receive instruction in the meaning of creativity or the ways in which creativity can be stimulated in children. This has been particularly true of teachers who work in early childhood education centers. Because these centers are rapidly increasing in number and size, the need for more trained teachers is especially great. Stimulation of children's creativity must be placed high on the list of priorities of all of these centers.

*Creative Activities for Young Children* is written for anyone who is interested in children, but since it is written especially for busy persons who work with children in early childhood schoollike settings, the following points are emphasized:

- The approach to creativity is a practical one. A wide variety of activities is included in each section. All activities have been successfully classroom-tested with young children.
- Information on *why* activities should be carried out as well as on *how* to carry them out is presented. Theory is provided where it is needed.
- Learning activities and skill builders are included to help readers experience their own creativity.
- References for additional reading are given at the end of each unit so students can explore each subject in more depth as desired.
- Each unit begins with carefully worded, easy-to-understand objectives and ends with review questions.

Part 1 presents a general discussion of various background theories relating to child development. Included in Part 1 are units on creativity, aesthetic experiences, social-emotional and physical-mental growth, as reflected in art development theories, and theories on play and encouraging creative dramatics in the early childhood program. Part I sets an appropriate theoretical stage for application of these theories in specific classroom activities presented in Part 2.

Part 2 covers early childhood classroom practices in what are generally considered traditional early childhood settings such as preschools, nurseries, and child care centers. It is organized into three sections: Section 6 (Creative Activities in Other Curricular Areas), Section 7 (Creative Activities Involving Holidays), and Section 8 (Creative Activities Involving Seasons). In the units, the student is given many suggestions for creative experiences for young children in the following areas: music, games, finger plays, creative movement, sciencing, environmental education, poetry, food experiences, math, language arts, social studies, and health and safety. Part 2 also includes photographs of children's artwork, providing further creative ideas to use with young children.

## ACKNOWLEDGMENTS

The author gratefully acknowledges the contributions of the many people who helped make this book possible: Casper Holroyd, for the many wonderful photos of children; the staff of Hayes Barton United Methodist Summer Program, for their cooperation; the Director and Staff at Method Day Care Center, for their continued support and cooperation; Charles E. Merrill Publishing Company, for permission to reprint materials used in Unit 4 and Unit 23; the National Association for the Education of Young Children, for permission to reprint materials in Unit 3, Unit 5, Unit 11, and Appendix F.

Special thanks to Jane Holding, for her technical assistance in the manuscript preparation; as well as to Mr. Eugene Adams, Principal of Brooks Elementary School, in Wake County Schools, Raleigh, North Carolina, for allowing the author to photograph kindergarten classes at Brooks School. The early childhood teachers in Wake and Durham County Schools are gratefully acknowledged for their inspiration, which is reflected in many of the practical ideas and techniques throughout this book. Special acknowledgment is given to the early childhood teachers in the Durham County Schools for the Halloween and Halloween Carnival ideas, as well as for Thanksgiving and fall ideas. A final word of thanks and remembrance for Dr. Rebecca Murray of Meredith College for the woodworking skills information in the text.

## ABOUT THE AUTHOR

Mary Mayesky, author of this fifth edition, is a certified preschool, elementary, and secondary teacher. She is a former professor in the Program in Education at Duke University former director of the Early Childhood Certification Program, and supervisor of student teachers. She has served as assistant director for programs in the Office of Day Care Services, Department of Human Resources, State of North Carolina. She is also the former principal of the Mary E. Phillips Magnet School in Raleigh, North Carolina, the first licensed day care magnet school in the Southeast. She has served several terms on the North Carolina Day Care Commission and currently serves on the Wake County School Board.

Dr. Mayesky has worked in Head Start, day care, kindergarten, and Y.W.C.A. early childhood educational programs and has taught kindergarten through grade eight in the public schools. She has written extensively for professional journals and for general circulation magazines in the area of child development and curriculum design. She is a member of Phi Beta Kappa and the National Association for the Education of Young Children and was named Woman of the Year in Education by the North Carolina Academy of the Y.W.C.A. Her other honors include being named Outstanding Young Educator by the Raleigh Jaycees, awarded research grants by the Duke University Research Council and the American Association of School Administrators Research Award, and being nominated for the Duke University Alumni Distinguished Undergraduate Teaching Award.

# PART 1
# Theories Relating to Child Development

Part I presents a general discussion of various theories relating to child development. Beginning with the concept of creativity, theories, techniques, and basic program components and how they are related to the growth of creativity in young children are presented. Within this theoretical context of creativity, Part I provides basic information on planning and implementing creative activities for young children. Also included is a section on art and how it is related to the physical, mental, and social-emotional development of young children.

Practical information on how to set up an early childhood art program with individual units for both two- and three-dimensional activities is also included. The final section of Part I covers the concept of play and its relationship to a child's overall development as well as development of creativity. Units on dramatic play and puppetry provide numerous ideas and activities to encourage the young child's natural creativity.

At the end of each unit in Part I are many suggested activities designed to reinforce the concepts covered in each unit. A wide variety of field-tested activities for young children are also included in each unit for use in early childhood settings.

The review questions and references for further reading provided at the end of each unit further reinforce the main concepts. In essence, Part I sets the theoretical stage for application of these theories in the more specific subject and classroom areas presented in Part II.

# SECTION 1
# Fostering Creativity and Aesthetics in Young Children

# UNIT 1

# The Concept of Creativity

## OBJECTIVES

After studying this unit, you should be able to

- define creativity.
- list three ways in which children benefit from an environment in which creativity is encouraged.
- list two ways teachers benefit from encouraging creativity in the classroom.
- name five things a teacher can do to help children develop a willingness to express creativity.
- list several characteristics of creative children.

Take a few minutes to watch a four-year-old child in action. At one moment he is building a tower out of blocks. Suddenly he spots one of his friends playing with a homemade finger puppet. He wants to make one, too. A bit later he is playing with a guinea pig, stroking its fur and tickling its chin. Next, he is placing long, wide strokes of color on a piece of paper and getting spots of paint on everything in sight.

What is this? Now he is at the sand table building a sand castle with a high sand tower that keeps falling over. He seems to have discovered something. It is easier to build a tower out of blocks than out of sand; so he is back building with wooden blocks. It looks as though he is back where he started, except that the new block tower does not look anything like the one he started earlier.

It is exciting to watch active young children studying the world around them. A couple of things become clear almost immediately. First of all, children are full of curiosity. They seem to enjoy investigating

and finding out things. Second, they seem quite capable of doing this successfully. They are very creative in finding answers to problems that arise from their curiosity. A child can figure out how to reach a needed block that somehow got thrown behind the piano. Another child selects interesting materials in order to make a finger puppet that is different from all the others.

Young children seem to have a natural ability to come up with creative answers, creative approaches, and creative uses of materials. They must be free to develop all these natural abilities that make each child so uniquely different.

People who are specially trained to work with young children need to understand creativity and have the skills to help and encourage children to express their creative natures. They should realize the importance of creativity for children and for teachers. They should be able to identify creativity in chil-

**FIGURE 1–1 Young children are naturally industrious and involved in learning new skills.**

dren and be able to help them develop a willingness to express this creativity.

Teachers can also promote creativity by modeling creative behavior. Torrance (1970) found that students with more creative teachers produce more creative work than students with less creative teachers. Whether motivation, imitation, or both create this effect is unknown. The important point is that teachers can model creative behavior for children. Thus, children can see "how it is" to be creative.

## WHAT IS CREATIVITY?

Perhaps the most important thing for the student to realize about creativity is that everyone possesses a certain amount of it. Some people are a little more creative, some a little less. No one is totally uncreative.

It should be recognized that young children tend to be highly open and creative. Unfortunately, many adults want children to conform. As outside pressures from adults grow, the children's environment closes in on them. They find it less and less rewarding

to express interest in things, to be curious, to be creative in investigating their world.

One shudders to think about how many creative children have been "forced into line" by well-meaning adults. Even some trained teachers prefer children who are quiet; some even punish children who ask too many questions. It is important to know ways of encouraging a child's creativity in order to avoid these kinds of mistakes. To begin with, one should understand the meaning of the term *creativity*.

There are many meanings for this word. A definition by one writer on the subject, May (1975, p. 39) describes creativity as the "process of bringing something new into being." Paul Torrance (1970), a pioneer in the study of the creative process, suggests

**FIGURE 1–2 Children may use play equipment in unexpected ways.**

that creativity is the ability to produce something novel, something with the stamp of uniqueness upon it.

No matter how creativity is defined or understood, all agree that it is a precious element of human intelligence and life. However, the following definition may help the student understand the concept better. *Creativity* is a way of thinking and acting or making something that is original for the individual and valued by that person or others. What this means is that any new way to solve a problem or to produce a new product, such as a song, a poem, or a new machine, is a creative act. A person does not have to be the first one in the world to produce something in order for it to be considered a creative act.

**The Creative Process.**   When someone is creating something, there are usually two parts to that person's activity. The first part has to do with the discovery of an idea, plan, or answer. The second part has to do with working out, proving, and making certain that the idea or answer works or is possible. The first part, *discovering*, involves using the imagination, playing with ideas, and exploring. The second part, *proving*, involves using learned skills, evaluating, and testing. This is shown in the creative process model in Figure 1–3.

**Thought Processes and Creativity.**   There are two kinds of thinking that produce solutions to prob-

lems. One of these types is called convergent thinking. The other type is called divergent thinking. *Convergent thinking* usually results in a single answer or solution to a question or problem. *Divergent thinking* opens things up and results in many answers to a single problem.

For example, if a child is asked to count the number of fish in an aquarium, there is only one correct answer. This is a question that leads children to convergent thinking. On the other hand, if a child is asked to tell as many things as possible about the aquarium, there are obviously many correct statements that can be made. Questions such as this encourage divergent rather than convergent thinking.

**Variety and Creativity.**   One of the problems in understanding the meaning of creativity is in recognizing the many kinds of creativity that exist. There is the kind of creativity that allows people to express themselves in a way that makes others listen and appreciate what they hear. There are creative abilities that enable human beings to discover meaning in nature—meaning that others had not understood before. In other words, creativity can be of many and

| Part I | Part II |
|---|---|
| Using the imagination | Evaluating ideas |
| Playing with ideas | Testing solutions |
| Exploring alternatives | Judging answers |
| Speculating with possibilities | Analyzing results |
| ↓ | ↓ |
| LEADS TO DISCOVERING | LEADS TO PROVING |
| Ideas | Acceptable ideas |
| Answers | Satisfactory answers |
| Solutions | Workable solutions |

FIGURE 1–3  Creative process model

FIGURE 1–4  Giving children a variety of materials lets them create at their own pace.

varied types. It may result in the production of new inventions. It may lead to new or better designs. It may result in new ideas or new thinking. It may cause better plans to be developed. It may display itself in the production of new and attractive compositions.

Creativity begins in a person's mind. It usually results in some form of expression that can be seen, heard, smelled, tasted, or felt.

## IMPORTANCE OF CREATIVITY

Creativity is the mainspring of our civilization: from the concept of the wheel, through the steamboat, the telephone, the automobile, the airplane, radio and television, computers, automation, the electronics industry, nuclear power, and space travel. All the milestones of great inventions, scientific discoveries, as well as great painting, literature, music, drama, and all forms of artistic expression have depended on creative thinking of the highest order. Thus, the progress of civilization and humanity's present evolutionary stature are essentially due to creative thinking and innovations. Our inherent creativity contributes to the very quality of our lives.

The rapid changes of our present age require that problems be tackled creatively. The technological advances and discoveries during the next couple of decades could surpass all the past accomplishments in human history (Raudsepp, 1980). It is difficult to foretell exactly what knowledge we will need to solve future problems creatively. What the young are learning now will surely become obsolete. Everyone can and must continue to learn throughout life, but knowledge alone is no guarantee that we will meet future problems effectively. Only a strong creative ability will provide the means for coping with the future (Raudsepp, 1980).

Encouraging or discouraging a child's creative nature makes a great deal of difference in the first experiences in a school setting. Children learn early and quickly that there is a reward for certain kinds of behavior. If the rewards they seek result from quiet, uncreative behavior, the children quickly learn to act in a quiet and uncreative way. It may take a teacher a long time to "shape up" the children. But in time, these "different" youngsters can be made to

**FIGURE 1–5 Children enjoy activities in which they can participate freely and openly.**

conform. In the process, however, the children's creative natures may be destroyed. Therefore, one must understand the importance of encouraging a child's creativity.

Children want to express themselves openly. They want to bring out new ideas and have new experiences. They enjoy creativity and benefit from it in many ways, including:

- Learning to feel good about themselves.
- Learning to seek many answers to a problem.
- Developing their potential to think.
- Developing their individuality.
- Developing new skills.
- Experiencing the joy of being different.

Teachers also benefit from encouraging creativity, in such ways as:

- Being able to provide for more and greater variety in the program.
- Learning to recognize children for their unique skills.
- Being able to develop closer relationships with children.
- Having fewer behavior problems.
- Using a minimum of standardized curricula and external evaluation.

## IDENTIFYING CREATIVITY IN CHILDREN

It is important to recognize four main things when identifying creativity in children:

1. All children are creative to some degree.
2. Some children are more creative than others.
3. Some are more creative in one area than another.
4. Creativity can be destroyed by a teacher who does not appreciate the creative act or the child who expresses the act.

With these points in mind, the student should consider the following suggestions for identifying creativity in children:

*Provide free periods when materials are available and children can do whatever they wish with the materials.*  During these periods, observe who gets tired quickly and goes from one thing to another. Identify who becomes deeply involved with the materials. Also observe which children use materials in an unexpected way.

*Question children in ways that permit them to freely express opinions and ideas.*  Some children have set opinions and are closed to new ideas. For them, questions usually have just one answer. Other chil-

dren see many possible ways of answering a question and come up with unexpected ideas and solutions. They also look at problems in many ways.

*Encourage children to share an experience.*  Then ask individual children to create a story about the experience or make a drawing. Some children just stick to the facts. Others are more imaginative in their stories or drawings. Unusual or unexpected relationships may be described by some children.

In other words, when children are being creative, they are flexible, original, confident, and adventuresome. They can redefine situations and are willing to work at things for a long time. They will work hard

FIGURE 1–6 Young children have a natural ability to find creative uses for materials.

| 1. Accepts disorder |
| 2. Adventurous |
| 3. Strong affection |
| 4. Altruistic |
| 5. Aware of others |
| 6. Always baffled by something |
| 7. Attracted to disorder |
| 8. Attracted to the mysterious |
| 9. Attempts difficult jobs (sometimes too difficult) |
| 10. Outwardly bashful |
| 11. Constructive in critism |
| 12. Courageous |
| 13. Deep and conscientious in convictions |
| 14. Defies conventions of courtesy |
| 15. Defies conventions of health |
| 16. Desires to excel |
| 17. Determined |
| 18. Discontented |
| 19. Disturbs organization |
| 20. Dominant (not in power sense) |
| 21. Emotional |
| 22. Emotionally sensitive |
| 23. Energetic |
| 24. A fault-finder |
| 25. Doesn't fear being thought "different" |
| 26. Feels whole parade is "out of step" |
| 27. Full of curiosity |

FIGURE 1–7 Sample characteristics of creative persons (adapted from Torrance, 1962)

# THINK ABOUT IT . . .

No teacher I've ever known became a teacher to stifle creativity in young children. Somewhere along the way, teachers become affected by the "package" syndrome: using "packaged" curricula, using "packages" of ideas, and—worst of all—expecting young children to come to the classroom in neat, tidy, predictable "packages."

To help restore your own joy of teaching, try this:

- List the reasons you became a teacher.
- List what you like about young children.
- List what you like about yourself.
- List what you think is creative about you (in teaching and in your life in general).
- Go over these lists whenever you are making choices that will directly affect young children—choices such as materials, texts, curricula. See how your choices fit your lists.
- Use your lists as a guide to "unpackaging" your life.

and can produce many possible answers to a single question.

This list can be used as a starting point to identify creativity in children. Common sense is also needed to help the identification process. Regardless of the degree of creativity possessed, children should be encouraged to fully develop whatever creative potential they have.

## CHARACTERISTICS OF CREATIVITY

Paul Torrance, a noted expert on creativity in children, has frequently emphasized that the kind of behavior teachers identify as desirable in children does not always coincide with characteristics associated with the creative personality. For example, teachers who think they value uniqueness may find that, when a child has spilled her milk because she tried the original method of holding the cup with her teeth, they don't like creative exploration as much as they thought they did!

*There are certain things that our age needs. It needs, above all, courageous hope and the impulse to creativeness.* Bertrand Russell

This lack of conformity can be inconvenient, but teachers should realize that some creative individuals possess character traits that teachers may not care for. Torrance lists 84 characteristics of highly creative persons, a sample of which is shown in Figure 1–7. Some of the less attractive qualities include stubbornness, finding fault with things, appearing haughty and self-satisfied, and being discontented. Yet it is easy to see that stubbornness might be a valuable quality when carrying through a new idea or that finding fault and being discontented could result in questioning and analyzing a situation before coming up with suggestions for improving it.

In all fairness, we must admit that we do not know at present if these less attractive attitudes lie at the root of creativity or if some of them are the result of mishandling by teachers, peers, and families as the child matures. On the other hand, Torrance also found that creative children possess many likable qualities, such as determination, curiosity, intuition, a willingness to take risks, a preference for complex ideas, and a sense of humor.

We point out these possible problems of encouraging creativity in children not to discourage teachers from fostering such behavior, but to enlighten them so that they will not subtly reject or discourage creative responses out of failure to recognize the positive side of such behavior. Ideally, understanding creativity will result in increased acceptance and valuing of creativity in young children. Acceptance is

# THIS ONE'S FOR YOU!

## ARE YOU A CREATIVE DOER OR A SPECTATOR?

Painter Stanley A. Czurles feels that the modern person has contracted the dreaded sickness called "spectatoritis," which leads to increased feelings of boredom, lack of satisfaction, and apathy. In his view, only the creative person can experience true fulfillment in life. Czurles presents the following comparison of the two contrasting approaches to life. See if you can find yourself in either (or maybe both!) of the following two lists:

### SPECTATOR

- Kills time
- Is an observer
- Has few self-sufficiency interests
- Seeks to have something happen to or for him or her
- Is involved in a merry-go-round of prestructured activities
- Has only temporary enjoyment, with little or no lasting product
- Is swept into activities
- Has fractionated experiences
- Is prone to boredom
- Experiences no deep challenge
- Accomplishes nothing very distinguished
- Curtails self by a focus on pessimistic personal concerns
- Has increased hardening of opinions and attitudes
- Achieves superficial trappings of culture
- Is subject to early spiritual-mental aging
- Experiences primarily what is

### CREATIVE DOER

- Uses time to develop self
- Is involved, experiences personal achievement
- Is rich in self-enriching activities
- Is self-stimulating; is at home and in control of many conditions
- Enjoys selected relevant activities
- Experiences continuous satisfaction, achieves tangible results, and becomes a more efficiently functioning person
- Selects planned participation
- Has completeness and continuity of involvement
- Is stimulated by challenging interests
- Aspires more as he or she achieves new goals
- Grows in potential through unique achievements
- Is enlivened by a recognized freedom to pursue creative interests
- Continues being flexible through continuous new insights
- Experiences the essence of a culture

- Enjoys an extended youthful spirit
- Experiences what might be

(Adapted by permission of The Putnam Publishing Group from *More Creative Growth Games* by Eugene Raudsepp. Copyright © 1980 by Eugene Raudsepp.)

vitally important because it will encourage children to develop their creativity further. Let us now consider some additional ways to encourage creativity in all young children.

## HELPING CHILDREN EXPRESS CREATIVITY

There are at least eight things that can be done for children to help them express natural creative tendencies:

*Help children accept change.*  A child who becomes overly worried or upset in new situations is unlikely to express creative potential.

*Help children realize that some problems have no easy answers.*  This may help prevent children from becoming anxious when they cannot find an immediate answer to a question or problem.

*Help children recognize that many problems have a number of possible answers.*  Encourage them to search for more than one answer. Then they can evaluate all the different answers to see which ones fit the situation best.

*Help children learn to judge and accept their own feelings.*  Children should not feel guilty for having feelings about things.

*Reward children for being creative.*  Let children know that their creative ideas are valued. In fact, the more creative the idea or product, the more greatly they should be rewarded. It is also useful to help children realize that good work is sometimes its own reward.

*Help children feel joy in their creative productions, and in working through a problem.*  Children should find that doing things and finding answers for themselves is fun. The adult should establish the conditions that allow this to take place.

*Help children appreciate themselves for being different.*  There is a tendency to reward children for conforming. This discourages creativity. Children should learn to like themselves because they are unique.

*Help children develop perseverance—"stick-to-itiveness."*  Help children by encouraging them to follow through. Provide chances for them to stick with an activity even if everyone else has moved on to something different.

**FIGURE 1–8 Children find that doing things for themselves is fun.**

## SUMMARY

Creativity is a way of thinking and acting or making something that is original for the individual and valued by that person or others. Young children are naturally creative. This means they behave in ways and do things that are unique and valued by themselves or others. Creativity in preschool children is stimulated when they are allowed to do divergent thinking. In many ways, both the child and teacher benefit from activities that encourage creativity.

Some kinds of creative behavior are not seen by adults as desirable in children. The inconvenience and possible frustration caused by the constantly exploring child are often discouraged by well-meaning adults. Understanding and accepting these behavior traits can go a long way in encouraging creativity in children.

Children are being creative when they are solving problems, redefining situations, demonstrating flexibility, and being adventurous. Adults can help children develop a willingness to express creativity in many ways, such as by teaching them that change is natural in life and that many problems do not have easy answers. When children can go at their own pace and figure out their own way of doing things in a relaxed learning situation, they are likely to become more creative.

# LEARNING ACTIVITIES

### Changing the Known

Although creative thinking can be hard thinking, that does not mean it cannot be fun. This activity is designed to prove it. Try it alone or with a few classmates. When the activity is completed, it may be enjoyable to compare lists with those of others.

A. Materials needed: paper, pencil, wristwatch (or clock).
B. Time allowed: two minutes.
C. Task: List as many uses as you can (not related to building or construction) for a standard brick. Do not worry if some of them may seem silly. The important thing is to think of using something in a new and different way.
D. It might be fun to try exercise C with a number of different objects: a nail, powder puff, paper clip, key, belt, cup, book, or other objects.

### Just Suppose

Creative thinking occurs when one imagines what might be. It is a way of "playing" with the mind. Here is an exercise that allows you to experience this type of creative process. It can be done alone or with a few classmates.

A. Materials needed: paper, pencil.
B. Time allowed: unlimited.
C. Task: From the following eight possibilities choose any number of tasks:
1. "Just suppose" that there is nothing made of wood in the room. What would change? What would things look like? What dangers might exist? What would one be unable to do?
2. "Just suppose" (try this with other people) you cannot use words, either written or spoken, for an hour. How can you communicate? What is frustrating about it? What is pleasing about it? What would it mean if it continued for days?
3. "Just suppose" you receive a million dollars and must spend it within two minutes. Make a list of ways to spend the money and compare it with others'.
4. "Just suppose" you were the first person to meet a man from Mars and could ask him only three questions. What would they be? Compare your questions with those of others in the class.
5. "Just suppose" you were with Julius Caesar when he met Cleopatra for the first time. If you could say only one sentence, what would it be?
6. "Just suppose" you could be any person in the world for one hour. Who would it be? What would you do? Compare responses with classmates'.
7. What would happen if . . .
   all people awakened tomorrow morning to find themselves twice as large?
   everyone could marry as many people as he or she wanted?
8. IMAGINE!
   Create seven sentences for which the seven-letter word "imagine" would be the acronym. All sentences should reflect in some way your thoughts about creative thinking, imagination, and ingenuity from what you have learned by reading this unit.

Example: **I**deas should not be hoarded or hidden.
**M**any small solutions are necessary to solve big problems.
**A**ll people are created creative.
**G**ood ideas drive out bad ideas.
**I**nnovative ideas are resisted by "spectators."

**N**ever mind what others think—use your own judgment.
**E**njoy your fantasies—that's what they are for!
Now, it's *your* turn!

---

## UNIT REVIEW

1. Discuss the following terms briefly.
   a. Creativity
   b. Convergent thinking
   c. Divergent thinking
2. List five things a teacher can do to help children develop a willingness to express creativity.
3. List three ways in which children benefit from engaging in creative activities.
4. List several characteristics of creativity.

---

## ADDITIONAL READINGS

Brittain, W.L. *Creativity, Art and the Young Child.* New York: Macmillan, 1979.

Clemens, S.G. "Art in the Classroom: Making Every Day Special." *Young Children,* 46 (1991):4–11.

Cropley, A.J. *More Than One: Fostering Creativity.* Norwood, N.J.: Ablex Publishers, 1992.

Early Childhood Creative Arts: Proceeding of the International Early Childhood Creative Arts Conference (1991). Reston, Va.: American Alliance for Health, Physical Education, Recreation, and Dance. (Available from the National Association for the Education of Young Children (NAEYC).)

Edwards, L.C. *Affective Development and the Creative Arts: A Process Approach to Early Childhood Education.* Columbus, Ohio: Merrill-Macmillan, 1990.

———, and M.L. Nabors. "The Creative Arts Process: What It Is and What It Is Not." *Young Children,* 48 (1993):77–81.

Grady, M.P. *Whole Brain Education.* Bloomington, Ind.: Phi Delta Kappa, 1990.

Guilford, J.P. *Intelligence, Creativity and Their Educational Implications.* San Diego: Robert R. Knapp, 1968.

Haiman, P.E. "Developing a Sense of Wonder in Young Children: There is More to Early Childhood Education than Cognitive Development." *Young Children,* 46 (1991):52–53.

Herr, J., and Y. Libby. *Creative Resources for the Early Childhood Classroom.* Albany, N.Y.: Delmar Publishers Inc., 1995.

Maxim, G.W. "Creativity: Encouraging the Spirit of Wonder and Magic," *The Very Young.* Belmont, Calif.: Wadsworth Publishing Company, 1985, 359–402.

May, R. *The Courage to Create.* New York: W.W. Norton, 1975.

Murdock, M. *Spinning Inward: Using Guided Imagery with Children for Learning, Creativity, and Relaxation,* revised edition. Boston: Shambhala Publications, 1987.

Raudsepp, Eugene. *More Creative Growth Games.* New York: Perigree Book, G.P. Putnam's Sons, 1980.

Schirrmacher, Robert. *Art and Creative Development for Young Children,* 2nd edition. Albany, N.Y.: Delmar Publishers Inc., 1993.

Severeide, R., and A.E. Sugawara. "The Effectiveness of Creative Experiences in Enhancing Creative Development." ERIC Document Reproduction Service, No. 258–375, November, 1985.

Torrance, E.P. *Guiding Creative Talent.* Englewood Cliffs, N.J.: Prentice-Hall, 1962.

———. *Creativity.* Belmont, Calif.: Fearon Publishers, 1969.

———. *Encouraging Creativity in the Classroom.* Dubuque, Iowa: William C. Brown, 1970.

Torrance, E.P. and P. Torrance. *Is Creativity Teachable?* Bloomington, Ind.: Phi Delta Kappa, 1973.

---

## CHILDREN'S BOOKS—CREATIVITY

Aiken, J. *The Moon's Revenge.* New York: Knopf, 1987. A wildly imaginative tale encouraging creative thinking.

Burningham, J. *John Patrick Norman McHennessy—The Boy Who Was Always Late.* New York: Crown, 1988. The outrageous, creative adventures of a young boy make him continually late.

Caines, J. *Just Us Women*. New York: Harper & Row, 1982.

Field, R. *General Store*. New York: Greenwillow, 1988. The dreams of young children, expressing "Someday I'm going to have . . ." encourages divergent thinking.

Goode, D. *Rumpty-Dudget's Tower*. New York: Knopf, 1987. A mischievous gray gnome about as high as your knee has a thousand and one corners in his tower, all full of creative ideas and adventures.

Howe, J. *I Wish I Were a Butterfly*. San Diego: Harcourt/ Gulliver, 1987. Wishing and dreaming in the animal kingdom.

Joseph, L. *Coconut Kind of Day*. New York: Lothrop, Lee, & Shephard, 1990.

Marzollo, J. and C. Marzollo. *Jed and the Space Bandits*. New York: Dial, 1987. A beginner version of a science fiction tale with all kinds of adventures.

Miller, M. *Whose Hat?* New York: Greenwillow, 1988. A book designed to enrich the game of dress-up and all kinds of imaginative fantasy play.

Patterson, B. *Bun and Mrs. Tubby*. New York: Orchard Books/Watts, 1987. A young elephant invents games and toys of his own.

Tolhurst, M. *Somebody and the Three Blairs*. New York: Orchard Books, 1990.

# UNIT 2
# Promoting Creativity

## OBJECTIVES

After studying this unit, you should be able to
- list three ways to foster a creative situation for children.
- demonstrate four questioning strategies to encourage creative thinking in young children.
- describe five approaches teachers can use to motivate children in creative activities.
- list four conditions in the environment that stimulate creative behavior.

Creative thinking is not a station one arrives at, but a means of traveling. It happens whenever a person comes up with a new answer to an old problem or considers what might happen before it actually does.

Although it is a popular notion that creative thinkers are geniuses, that is not so. The creative process can occur when one has a dream or makes up a fantasy about something. Children do it when they play house, listen to a fairy tale, or make a sand castle. Adults do it when they read a book, plan a trip, or

FIGURE 2–2 Dress-up games encourage young children to "try on" adult roles.

just imagine what they are going to do with the savings in their bank account.

The creative process can also involve discovering and inventing. Whenever something is done or thought about in a new way, that is part of the creative process. It does not matter whether it is done while playing, cooking, gardening, or just rearranging furniture; it is still creative.

There is usually some degree of risk-taking when children are being creative. This does not mean they are in danger of harming themselves. It means that they are probably doing something new and that they are uncertain about how it will turn out. Therefore,

FIGURE 2–1 Playing house is a popular creative activity for young children.

# T H I N K   A B O U T   I T . . .

## WHERE CREATIVITY BEGINS

Creativity begins with YOU. Too many teachers under-emphasize their own creativity. And even worse, many teachers feel that because they find inspiration from suggested activities in books, they really aren't being creative. While you may find creative activities in books, YOU are still the source of creativity in your classroom. This is true for many reasons, and here are the most basic of these reasons:

- YOU choose from the myriad of activity books offered on the market today.
- YOU choose which activities to use with your particular group of young children.
- YOU adapt the activities to suite YOUR own, the group's, and individual children's needs.
- YOU choose whether to use an activity again or not.
- YOU, as an early childhood educator, use YOUR developmental knowledge to make all of the above choices.

Let's expand on the last reason—your knowledge of child development. This knowledge of child development is your best source of creativity in the classroom. Armed with knowledge of child development, you have a wealth of information from which you can develop your own creative activities. For example, knowing what physical skills can be expected to be developing at different ages, you can provide children with opportunities to practice these emerging skills. And *voilà!* you've created an activity. Thus, the teacher who provides lots of plastic cups, pitchers, and bowls at the sand table for the children who are "into" pouring lately has created an activity just for them.

Knowledge of child development also makes you a creative teacher because it helps you be a good *observer* of young children. The teacher who observed the children's interest in a nearby construction site experienced the first stirrings of creativity. Choosing books on buildings for the book corner, adding trucks and cranes to the block area, plastic shovels and pails to the sand table, and hard hats to the dramatic center has created activities especially for her group.

Being creative, then, does not always mean being the first to do something. You don't have to write the activities to use them creatively. Creativity is using YOUR knowledge, YOUR tastes, and YOUR opinions to reflect YOU . . . the source of creativity in your classroom.

---

the children are taking a chance. At such times, they need freedom to explore and plenty of room for mistakes. Judgmental criticism or imposing adult standards of perfection will do them little good. It is important for the teacher to show the children that their work is accepted and that they are "in charge" of where it goes.

Perhaps the greatest challenge for all teachers is to help preserve the sense of wonder that lives within the hearts of those who are very young.

Creative behavior in children has a much better chance of occurring when they are open to more than one way of thinking or doing something. For example, there are many ways to paint, many ways to make a house, and many ways to play with blocks. Children who are encouraged to try new ways of doing the same thing are more likely to be comfortable in creative situations.

Adults who work with young children are in an especially crucial position to foster each child's creativity. In the day-to-day experiences in early childhood settings, as young children actively explore their world, adults' attitudes clearly transmit their feelings to the child. A child who meets with unquestionable acceptance of her unique approach to the world will feel safe in expressing her creativity, whatever the activity or situation.

The following are guidelines on how to help transmit this positive acceptance to children, which in turn fosters creativity in any situation:

• Openly demonstrate to young children that there is value in their curiosity, exploration, and original behavior.
• Allow the children to go at their own pace when they are doing an activity that they are excited about and interested in.
• Let children stay with what they are making until they feel it's done.
• Let children figure out their own ways of doing things if they prefer to do so.
• Keep the atmosphere relaxed.
• Encourage guessing, especially when the answers make good sense.

This last suggestion encourages another important aspect of children's creativity—the art of asking questions. Just the way a question is phrased or asked sets the stage for creative replies. For example the question, "Describe (or tell me about) the sky . . ." would certainly get different answers than "What color is the sky?" In the first, more open-ended question, children are encouraged to share their personal feelings and experiences about the sky. This might be color, or cloud shapes, or even how jets, birds, and helicopters can fill it at times. The second question is phrased in such a way that a one-word reply would do. Or even worse, it may seem to children that there is one and only one *correct* answer!

In asking questions, then, a teacher can foster children's creativity. Let us now consider more specific factors involved in creative questioning.

## CREATIVE QUESTIONING FOR CHILDREN

The activity suggestions that follow deal mainly with specific ways of asking questions and beginning lessons or sessions and are designed to draw out the creative potential in young children. Activities that deal directly with specific arts, crafts, and media are found in later sections of this book.

**1. Making Things Better with Your Imagination.** One way to help children think more creatively is to get them to "make things better with their imagination." Ask children to change things to make them the way they would like them to be. Here are some examples of questions of this type:

• What would taste better if it were sweeter?
• What would be nicer if it were smaller?
• What would be more fun if it were faster?
• What would be better if it were quieter?
• What would be more exciting if it went backwards?
• What would be happier if it were bigger?

**2. Using Other Senses.** Young children can stretch their creative talents by using their senses in unusual ways. For example, children may be asked to close their eyes and guess what has been placed in their hands. (Use a piece of foam rubber, a small rock, a grape, a piece of sandpaper, etc.) Another approach is to have the children close their eyes and guess what they hear. (Use sounds like shuffling cards, jingling coins, rubbing sandpaper, or ripping paper.)

When doing this exercise, the children should be asked for reasons for their guesses. It makes it more fun and a better learning experience for the children.

**3. Divergent Thinking Questions.** Any time children are asked a question requiring a variety of answers, their creative thinking skills are aided. Here are some examples using the concept of water:

- What are some uses of water?
- What floats in water?
- How does water help us?
- Why is cold water cold?
- What are the different colors that water can be?
- What makes water rain?
- What always stays underwater?

Divergent thinking questions using concepts such as sand, ice, smoke, cars, and similar topics are fun for children. They also encourage openness and flexibility of thinking.

## 4. What-Would-Happen-If Technique.

The "What-would-happen-if?" technique has been used successfully by many teachers of young children to spark good thinking-and-doing sessions designed to ignite imaginations. Some of the following questions may be used:

- What would happen if all the trees in the world were blue?
- What would happen if everyone looked alike?
- What would happen if all the cars were gone?

- What would happen if everybody wore the same clothes?
- What would happen if every vegetable tasted like chocolate?
- What would happen if there were no more clocks or watches?
- What would happen if you could fly?

## 5. In How Many Different Ways.

Another type of question that extends a child's creative thinking is one that begins, "In how many different ways . . . ?" A few examples are given to add to one's own ideas:

- In how many different ways could a spoon be used?
- In how many different ways could a button be used?
- In how many different ways could a string be used?

All of these questioning strategies are intended to help an adult encourage creativity in young children. Children may also generate these types of questions once they have been modeled for them. Often, the use of these strategies is enough to begin a long-running and positive creative experience for the child as well as the teacher. They are limited only by the user's imagination.

## MOTIVATING SKILLS FOR TEACHERS

Some children need help in getting started. The fact that the activity is labeled "creative" does not necessarily make the child "ready to go." A child may be feeling restless, or tired, or may feel like doing something else. All teachers, even those with good ideas, face this problem. There are several ways to help children become motivated for the creative process.

*Physical needs.* Make sure children are rested and physically fit. Sleepy, hungry, or sick children cannot care about creativity. Their physical needs must be met before such learning can be appealing.

*Interests.* Try to find out, and then use, what naturally interests the child. Children not only want to do things they like to do, they want to be successful at them. Whenever children feel that they will succeed in a task, they are generally much more willing to get involved. Parents may be good resources for determing the child's interests.

*Friends.* Permit children to work with their friends. This does not mean all the time, nor should it. However, some teachers avoid putting children who are friends together in working situations. They worry that these children will only "fool around" or disturb others. When this does happen, one should question the task at hand, since it is obviously not keeping the children's interest.

*Activities for fun.* Allow the activity to be fun for the child. Notice the use of the word "allow." Children know how to have their own fun. They do not need anyone to make it for them. Encourage child-initiated activities and self-selection of creative materials, and emphasize voluntary participation of the children in the activities presented. Teachers are giving children opportunities for fun if they honestly can answer "yes" to these questions:

- Is the activity exciting?
- Is the activity in a free setting?

FIGURE 2-3 Allow children to set their own pace when involved in an exciting activity.

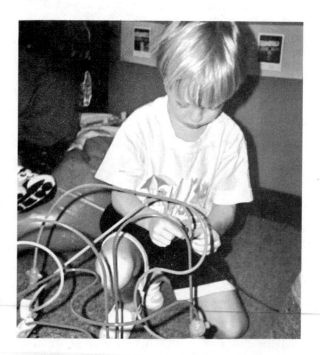

FIGURE 2-4 When given the right materials, children know how to create their own fun.

- Can the children imagine in it?
- Can the children play at it?
- Is there a gamelike quality to it?
- Are judgments avoided?
- Is competition deemphasized?
- Will there be something to laugh about?

*Goals.*   Permit children to set and reach goals. Most of the excitement in achieving a goal is in reaching for it. Children should be given opportunities to plan projects. They should be allowed to get involved in activities that have something at the end for which they can strive. If the completion of an activity is not rewarding to a child, then the value of that activity is questionable.

**FIGURE 2–5 A teacher should question an activity's merits if children seem bored or their attention wanders.**

*Variety.*   Vary the content and style of what the children can do. It is wise to consider not only *what* will be next, but *how* it will be done, too. For example, the teacher has the children sit and watch a movie, then they sit and draw, and then they sit and listen to a story. These are three different activities, but in each of them, the children are sitting. The content of the activity has changed, but not the style. This can, and does, become boring. Bored children are restless children.

*Challenge.*   Challenge the children. This means letting them know that what they are about to do is something that they might not be able to do, but that it will be exciting to try. An example of this is letting the children know that their next activity may be tricky, adventurous, or mysterious. It is the "bet you can't do this" approach with the odds in favor of the children.

*Reinforcement.*   Reinforce the children. The basic need here is for something to come at the end of the activity that lets the children feel they would like to do it again. It could be the teacher's smile, a compliment, reaching the goal, or just finishing the activity. The main thing is that the children feel rewarded and satisfied for their efforts.

*The children's feelings.*   Try to make certain the children feel good about what they are doing. Some teachers feel if a child is working intensely or learning, that is enough. This may not be so. The most important thing is not *what* the children are doing but *how they feel* about what they are doing. If children feel bad about themselves or an activity while doing it, this is a warning. If a child is made to continue the activity, it may be damaging, as it tends to lower self-concept and security. It is a destructive form of learning and must be avoided. This means the teacher must be continually in touch with how the children are feeling. It is done by listening, watching, and being with the children in a manner that is open and caring.

## CREATIVE ENVIRONMENTS FOR CHILDREN

The environment is just as important as the teaching strategies we have listed for fostering creativity in young children. If a safe and stimulating environment that promotes creativity is provided for children, they will routinely seek out all the possibilities in that enviornment. Children are naturally inquisitive and will venture out to learn about their environment. In those ventures, children are very aware of the limits of their world, both positive and negative ones. Limits naturally direct children's energies elsewhere and are a normal part of understanding how the world operates.

The teacher's challenge is to construct a learning environment that welcomes exploration and has

**FIGURE 2–6 Through day-to-day experiences in early childhood settings, young children actively explore their world.**

meaningful and necessary limits, rather than arbitrary limits that inhibit creativity. Maxim (1985) lists the following conditions in the environment that stimulate children's creative behavior:

1. Time limits are removed from activities in which children are deeply involved.
2. A free, open atmosphere is established where open expression is encouraged.
3. Children are allowed to share ideas and to stimulate one another's thinking.
4. Conditions providing stress and anxiety are removed from the environment.

This stimulating environment must also include many and varied concrete materials, since young children need to manipulate materials physically as they learn about their world. A full description of these materials and their placement and use in creative ways appears in Unit 6, "Creative Environments."

## SUMMARY

The creative process involves discovery and inventing. Risk-taking is a natural part of creative behavior. Teachers who allow children to go at their own pace, and be self-directed in a relaxed atmosphere, are fostering creative development.

Questioning strategies encourage creativity in young children. Even with creative activities, there may be motivational difficulties with some children. Appealing to natural interests, giving expectancies of success, reinforcing, and challenging are a few of the many ways to help children get started and keep going.

The learning environment needs to be a welcoming place. It must encourage exploration by its lack of strict time limits and stressful situations. It must be an environment that encourages children's self-expression and sharing of ideas.

# LEARNING ACTIVITIES

## Invention Dice

It has been said that the creative process involves discovery and inventing. Here is a game that provides experience in "making something up" for the first time. Try it with a few friends.

A. Materials needed: a single die, paper, pencil.
B. Time allowed: unlimited.
C. Task: players should sit facing each other or in a circle. A dice point list with directions is posted so that everyone can see it.

## Dice Point List

1. Invent a story in which you experience a huge success.
2. Invent a story in which you experience a terrifying escape.
3. Invent a story in which you experience a moment of beauty.
4. Invent a story in which you experience tremendous fear.
5. Invent a story in which you experience great joy.
6. Invent a story in which you discover something important for the first time.

Each person takes at least two turns (more can be decided upon) throwing the die. If the cube comes up 2, for example, the person who has thrown the die "invents" a story in which the person makes a terrifying escape, perhaps from some disaster. (This game asks one to "pull out all of the stops." Surprise the listeners. Do not be afraid to exaggerate.)

D. After having tried some of these exercises, think about what was done. Notice how necessary it was to "let go" while being creative. How important was it to feel free and relaxed while doing the exercises? What do these exercises make one aware of when attempting to work creatively with children?
E. List three important things you learned as a result of doing these exercises.
F. List three personal experiences that were challenging to you. Consider each and get in touch with the feelings experienced on those occasions.
   1. Was there any chance of failure during these experiences?
   2. What was the motivation?
   3. How did it feel to succeed?
   4. What does this mean for working with young children?

5. How does it relate to creativity?
6. List some of your reactions.

G. "Become" one of the following objects and dramatize its characteristics in class:

Bicycle
Rake
Hose
Wheelbarrel
Tire pump
Beach ball

Describe how you felt. Would children's dramatizations of these be similar? different? Explain.

H. Tape 10–15 minutes of classroom interactions in which you play an instructional role. Analyze your interaction in terms of the kinds of questions you used, the amount of time you waited for children to respond after asking a question, and the way you responded to children's talk.

I. Observe a classroom and note the creative experiences available to children. To what extent do the experiences offered seem to contribute to the development of creativity? Describe your impressions and suggestions for improvement for the curriculum in creative expression.

J. Observe a teacher and describe the kinds of questions used, the amount of time allowed for children to answer, and the kinds of responses the teacher makes to the children. Do you think the communication you observed is effective in encouraging divergent thinking? Why or why not?

K. Read the following scene and answer the questions following it:

Peggy has been standing on top of the jumping board for quite a while. When the teacher walks over to her, Peggy says, "I want to jump off, but my feet might think I'm falling." The teacher suggests she tell her feet she is jumping. Peggy bends down, looks at her feet, and announces, "I'm jumping." Then she jumps off the board and lands on the ground with a smile.

*Questions:* In what other situations might it be helpful for a teacher or parent to assist a child by using this creative approach? Under what circumstances would this type of response be inadvisable? Explain your answers.

# ACTIVITIES FOR CHILDREN

## Shady Characters

A. Area: Classroom
B. Equipment: Overhead projector
C. Set up the overhead projector to shine on one wall. The children should be in single file or with a partner (works better with partners). One at a time, they move in front of the lighted area and respond to challenge statements as listed below.
D. Challenge statements (each child should be allowed to experience each one):
   1. As you pass in front of the screen, stop and look at your shadow.
   2. As you pass in front of the screen, make a curled shape. Then jump up high.
   3. As you pass in front of the screen, move your arms and legs and head at once.
   4. This time, with your partner, one of you make a tall shape while the other makes a short shape.
   5. After you are in front of the screen, make up a dance with your partner.

If any of these are difficult, modify them to make them easier.

## Water Play Activities for Creative Thinking

Water play lends itself to the development of creative thinking in young children. A creative teacher can extend the play of young children by asking thought-provoking, divergent-thinking questions, posing simple problems to solve with water and play objects. Some of these divergent-thinking questions are:

1. Can you make the water in your squeeze bottle shoot out like the water from the hose?
2. Can you make a water shower for the plants?
3. Can you catch one drop of water on something? How many drops of water can you put on a jar lid?
4. Can we think of some words to talk about what we do with water? (sprinkle, pour, drip, trickle, drizzle, shower, deluge, torrent, splash, spank, stir, ripple, etc.)
5. Could we collect some rainwater? How?
6. How far can you make the water spray?
7. Can you make something look different by putting it in water?
8. Can you find some things that float (or sink) in the water?
9. Can you make a noise in the water?

## Designs

A. Equipment: Designs drawn on paper or cut from scraps of cloth.
B. Divide the class into five or six groups with a design for each group. Each group is then asked to form the design assigned to them, using all members in their group. Given a few minutes to decide how, let each group show the others their design. Rotate until each group has done every design. Do not allow a group to form a design in the same way that another group has used. Examples are:

## Space Explorers

A. Have the children pretend they are on a planet in space where they are much *heavier* than on earth. They lift their arms as though their bodies were twice as heavy as they are.
B. Have the children pretend they are on the moon, where their bodies are much *lighter* than on earth. They move body parts as though they were very light and walk as though their bodies were very light.

C. Have the children select a familiar activity such as dancing, moving to rhythms, etc., and do it on the strange planet, using slow motion because of increased weight.

## Day at the Zoo

Before playing, help the children list the animals they know about. It would be helpful to write these down or draw the list in pictures if you are planning to go outside and play the game. Call out the animal's names one at a time while the children act out what they think the animal looks like.

## Zoo Walk

The leader calls on various children in turn to stand up and make sounds and perform actions of an animal one might see at the zoo. When called on, the child says: "I went to the zoo and saw an animal that acted like this _____."

## Mirror Movement

With an instructor (teacher or another child) facing the group, the children should be encouraged to mirror her movements, either moving to the side (step-close-stop), forward (as the "mirror instructor" moves backward), or backward (as the instructor moves toward them).

This kind of activity should precede slower stop-and-go drills, and various children can be chosen to be the next leaders.

## Conversation Cube

Get a photo cube of clear plastic measuring 6″ × 6″ × 6″. Then glue a picture, photograph, or postcard to each side of the cube. Or you may cut them and slide them into the cube as you would a normal photo. Sit across from the child. Roll the cube to him. Have the child tell you about the picture in front of him. Then he can roll the cube back to you, and you can tell him about the picture facing you. Keep rolling the cube and talking. Remember, it is all right to talk about a picture more than once. See if, at each turn, you can say something new and different.

## Creative Jingles

Make up jingles and rhymes any time during the day when the occasion arises. Jingles are word-tinglers: "Taffy is laughy" or "Mrs. Morgan plays the organ." Begin with a line, and then let the child add her ideas:

"I have a frog that is green. Some people think that she is _____."

## Space Ship

A. Children and teacher decide upon an object that will represent the earth, such as a tree, bean bag, circle, base, etc. Children are space ships, and on the countdown, "Five, four, three, two, ONE!" the rockets blast the space ships off the ground; they quickly pick up speed and go into orbit around the earth. After one or more orbits, space ships return and "splash down."

B. Game may be repeated any number of times with space ships flying any number of orbits. To improve endurance, children try to run longer and faster each time.

## Scarf Dance

The teacher gives a scarf to each child or to the child who will start the activity. The teacher explains that the children are to use their imaginations, letting the scarf be anything they want as they move with it in response to the music. Use a record or tape of instrumental music, or put on the radio. Each of the children in turn moves with the music, explaining, if they like, what they are doing.

## Creative Ballooning

Give each child an inflated balloon and have each child find a place to work without bumping into the other children. The children follow the teacher's directions, finding different ways to keep the balloon in the air (for example, with one hand, with one finger, with the head, with one foot, lying down, kneeling, sitting).

## Becoming an Object

The teacher calls out the names of inanimate objects. Children show with their bodies the shapes of the various objects. If the object is moved by an external force, they show with their bodies how the object would move. For instance, they may imitate the movement of:

1. An orange being peeled.
2. A standing lamp being carried across the room.
3. A wall with a vine growing over it.
4. A paper clip being inserted on paper.
5. An ice cube melting.
6. A balloon with air coming out of it.
7. A cloud drifting through the sky, slowly changing shapes.
8. Smoke coming out of a chimney.

9. A twisted pin being thrust into paper.
10. A rubber ball bouncing along the ground.
11. A boat being tossed by the waves.
12. An arrow being shot through the air.
13. A steel bar being hammered into different shapes.

## Poems for Creative Movement

These movement poems are designed to permit creative movement. Encourage the children to listen well and move quietly so they can hear the next line of the poem.

## Movement Poems

Stretch out flat as a mat,
Arch your back like a cat,
Crouch low like a scared rat,
Curl up tight as a kitty cat,
Make your arms long as a bat,

Try your legs just like that,
Pull together round and fat,
Slowly fade like a sleeping bat.

**All in All**
Round your back like a rubber ball,
Sit up straight nice and tall,
Lean back and look at the wall,
Grab your feet, curl up small,
And that is really all.

**Ticky-Tacky-Wacky**
Look at the sky flat on your back,
Draw the clouds with an artist's knack,
Cover the sky so there's not a crack,
Flip over and don't look back,
Point arm and leg, sharp as a tack,
Crouch like a duck, but you can't quack,
Spin around and end in a stack,
Start again on another track.

## UNIT REVIEW

1. List three ways to foster a creative situation for children.
2. Name four questioning strategies that encourage creative thinking in the young child.
3. State five approaches that help children to motivate themselves in creative activities.
4. List four conditions in the environment that stimulate creative behavior.

## ADDITIONAL READINGS

Beaty, J.J. *Preschool: Appropriate Practices.* Ft. Worth, Tex.: Harcourt, Brace, Jovannovich College Publishers, 1992.

Bos, G. *Please Don't Move the Muffin Tins; A Hands-off Guide for Art for the Young Child.* Carmichael, Calif.: The Burton Gallery, 1978.

Bredekamp, S., ed. *Developmentally Appropriate Practice in Early Childhood Programs Serving Birth Through Age 8,* expanded edition. Washington, D.C.: National Association for the Education of Young Children, 1987.

Brickman, N., and L. Taylor. (eds.). *Supporting Young Learners.* Ypsilanti, Mich.: High Scope Press, 1991.

Christoplos, F., and P.J. Valletutt. *Developing Children's Creative Thinking Through the Arts.* Bloomington, Ind.: Phi Delta Kappa Educational Foundation, 1990.

Dodge, D.T., and L.J. Colker. *The Creative Curriculum for Early Childhood.* Washington, D.C.: Teaching Strategies, Mt. Ranier, MD, 1992.

Gestwicki, Carol. *Developmentally Appropriate Practice: Curriculum and Development in Early Education.* Albany, N.Y.: Delmar Publishers, 1995.

Maxim, G.W. *The Very Young.* Belmont, Calif.: Wadsworth Publishing Co., 1985.

May, R. *The Courage to Create.* New York: W.W. Norton, 1975.

Nunnelly, J.C. "Beyond Turkeys, Santas, Snowmen, and Hearts: How to Plan Innovative Curriculum Themes." *Young Children.* (Nov., 1990): 24–29.

Schiller, P.B. *100 Wonderful Things to Keep Kids Busy & Having Fun.* Berkeley, Calif.: Ten Speed Press, 1992.

Torrance, E.P. *Guiding Creative Talent.* Englewood Cliffs, N.J.: Prentice-Hall, 1962.

# UNIT 3

# The Concept of Aesthetics

## OBJECTIVES

After studying this unit, you should be able to
- define aesthetics.
- list three things a teacher can do to help children develop their aesthetic sensitivity.
- list five benefits of aesthetic sensitivity in children.
- list at least three art elements to discuss with children.

*Aesthetics* refers to an appreciation for beauty and a feeling of wonder. It is a sensibility that uses the imagination as well as the five senses. It is seeing beauty in a sunset, hearing rhythm in a rainfall, loving the expression on a person's face. Each person has an individual personal sense of what is or is not pleasing.

Aesthetic experiences emphasize doing things for the pure joy of it. Although there can be, there does not *have* to be any practical purpose or reason. Thus, one may take a ride in a car to feel its power and enjoy the scenery rather than to visit someone or perform an errand. A child may play with blocks to feel their shapes and see them tumble rather than to build something.

Some art specialists believe that since young children are not able to make mature judgments, they are not capable of aesthetic responses at all. Hence, they believe that aesthetics is not an appropriate concern in the early years. Yet early childhood educators know that young children benefit from aesthetic experiences. Children are fascinated by beauty. They love nature and enjoy creating, looking at, and talking about art. They express their feelings and ideas through language, song, expressive movement, music, and dance far more openly than adults. Young children have strong preferences for books, objects, and food. They are creative and inquisitive and delighted by art.

FIGURE 3–1 Children gain an aesthetic sense by doing.

24

The capacity for aesthetics is a fundamental human characteristic. Infants sense with their whole bodies. They are open to all feelings; experience is not separated from thinking. A child's aesthetic sense comes long before the ability to create. All of an infant's experiences have an aesthetic component—preferring a soft satin-edged blanket, studying a bright mobile, or choosing a colorful toy. These choices are all statements of personal taste. As infants grow into toddlers, the desire to learn through taste, touch, and smell as well as through sight and sound grows, too. The capacity to make aesthetic choices continues to grow through preschool. Preschoolers'

ability to perceive, respond, and be sensitive becomes more obvious and more refined. They enjoy creating spontaneously with a wide variety of materials (Feeney and Moravcik, 1987).

To develop an aesthetic sense in children, one must help them continuously find beauty and wonder in their world. This is any child's potential. In fact, it is the potential of every human being. To create, invent, be joyful, sing, dance, love, and be amazed are possible for everyone.

The purpose of aesthetic experiences is to help develop a full and rich life for the child. It does not matter whether an activity is useful for anything else. There does not have to be a product or something that can be eaten or sold. That is why mud pies are still made and probably always will be made.

A child's reason for doing something should not always be to gain adult approval, prizes, grades, or pay. At times, doing just for the sake of doing is enough. Teachers must be careful to allow for and encourage such motivation.

Children sometimes see and say things to please adults; teachers must realize this and the power it implies. Teachers who prefer that children see beauty as they themselves do are not developing good taste in children. They are developing uniformity and obedience. Only children who choose and

FIGURE 3–2 Only children who choose and evaluate for themselves can truly develop their own aesthetic taste.

FIGURE 3–3 Aesthetic development is encouraged through musical activities for young children.

evaluate for themselves can truly develop their own aesthetic taste. The teacher's role is to provide opportunities and guidance, but not to set standards. Each child has a right to a personal choice of beauty, joy, and wonder. Each time a teacher says that something is pretty or makes some similar personal judgment, this influences the children. They must be able to feel that it is acceptable to differ with the teacher in such matters: "What you like is okay, and what I like is okay, too."

Children gain an aesthetic sense by doing. This means sensing, feeling, and responding to things. It can be rolling a ball, smelling a flower, petting an animal, or hearing a story. Aesthetic development takes place in secure settings free of competition and adult judgment. For example, children and their teachers may listen to music. They should all feel that they have a right to hear it for themselves and to create their own experience around it. For one person, it may mean happy memories; for another, it may mean an urge to dance; and for someone else, it may mean only the sound of music.

## AESTHETICS AND THE QUALITY OF LEARNING

Aesthetic learning means joining what one thinks with what one feels. Having feelings about what one reads makes reading a human experience. Through art, ideas and feelings are expressed. People draw pictures and sculpt monuments to show their feelings about life. Art is important because it can deepen and enlarge understanding. All children cannot be great artists, but children can develop an aesthetic sense, an appreciation for art.

Teachers can encourage the aesthetic sense in children in a variety of ways. For example, science activities lend themselves very well to beauty and artistic expression. Since children use their senses in learning, science exhibits with things like rocks, wood, and leaves can be placed in attractive displays for children to touch, smell, and explore with all of their senses. Reading readiness activities, when chil-

**FIGURE 3–4 A happy balance must be established between structured and nonstructured activities.**

dren are learning about things like letters and letter sounds, are another avenue for aesthetic experiences. The imaginative use of color, shapes, sounds, and forms can be incorporated into teaching practices to make these experiences aesthetic, and not rote, boring tasks.

**FIGURE 3–5 Free periods throughout the day are important to a child's aesthetic development.**

# THINK ABOUT IT . . .

So much is written about the difficulty of explaining what "aesthetics" really IS. And when you try to understand it in the context of early childhood education, it becomes even more complex an idea. I like to think about aesthetics as a child's "Bill of Rights" in the early childhood program. Here is my idea of the Aesthetics Bill of Rights:

A child has a right to:

- have many sensitive experiences that make her more sensitive to the beauties and wonders of the physical world around her.
- have her own values and standards of judgment, rather than be judged by others' standards.
- express with eagerness her own uniqueness, which lies dormant unless it is encouraged.
- express what she knows and dreams with honesty and integrity and have these attempts respected and shared by others.
- be assisted in expressing herself in her own unique way, rather than being trained as an artist.
- express joy in simple things and savor the quiet moments as well as those of excitement.

**FIGURE 3–6 For aesthetic sensitivity to grow, young children must be allowed to work without self-consciousness.**

Children must have something about which to paint, sculpt, dance, and sing. This can be provided by stories, exploring the outdoors and the immediate neighborhood, and going on trips. Teachers must allow the children to evaluate and express these experiences. This means talking about what these experiences mean to the children and how they feel about them. It means allowing the children to express those feelings and meanings through paint, clay, collage, dance, or whatever medium each child chooses to use.

The arts are developed best as a whole. After hearing a story, some children may want to act it out. Some may prefer to paint a picture about it. Others may wish to create a dance about it, and some may want to make the music for the dance. These activities can lead to others. There should be a constant exchange, not only among all the art activities, but among all subject areas. This prevents children from creating a false separation between work and play, art and learning, and thought and feeling.

# THIS ONE'S FOR YOU!

## SUGGESTIONS FOR AESTHETIC ENHANCEMENT OF ENVIRONMENTS

For young children, giving special attention to the environment can help develop their aesthetic sense. Here are some suggestions on how to enhance the environment to develop children's aesthetic sense:

**Color**—Bright colors will dominate a room and may detract from art and natural beauty. If there is a choice, select soft, light, neutral colors for walls and ceilings. Color coordinate learning centers so that children begin to see them as wholes rather than as parts. Avoid having many different kinds of patterns in any one place—they can be distracting and over-stimulating.

**Furnishings**—Group similar furniture together. Keep colors natural and neutral to focus children's attention on the learning materials on the shelves. When choosing furnishings, select natural wood rather than metal or plastic. If furniture must be painted, use one neutral color for everything so that there is greater flexibility in moving it from space to space. Periodically give children brushes and warm soapy water and let them scrub the furniture.

**Storage**—Rotate materials on shelves rather than crowding them together. Crowded shelves look unattractive and are hard for children to maintain. Baskets make excellent, attractive storage containers. If storage tubs are used, put all of the same kind together on one shelf. If cardboard boxes are used for storage, cover them with plain-colored paper or paint them.

**Decoration**—Mount and display children's art-work. Provide artwork by fine artists and avoid garish, stereotyped posters. Make sure that much artwork (by both children and adult artists) is displayed at children's eye level. Use shelf tops to display sculpture, plants, and items of natural beauty like shells, stones, and fish tanks. Avoid storing teachers' materials on the tops of shelves. If there is no other choice, create a teacher "cubby" using a covered box or storage tub.

**Outdoors**—Design or arrange play structures as extensions of nature rather than intrusions upon it. If possible, use natural materials like wood and hemp instead of painted metal, plastic, or fiberglass. Provide adequate storage to help maintain materials. Involve children, parents, and staff in keeping outdoor areas free of litter. Add small details like a garden or a rock arrangement to show that the outdoors also deserves attention and care.

(Adapted with permission from S. Feeney and E. Moravcik, "A Thing of Beauty: Aesthetic Development in Young Children," in *Young Children,* Sept., 1987, 11.)

## AESTHETICS AND CREATIVITY

You will remember from Unit 1 that when an individual creates something, there are two factors involved in that creative activity: discovering and proving. The discovery part of the creative process is directly related to a child's aesthetic sense. The child's ability to "toy" with ideas, to "see into" things, and to "make up" more than what is there is needed for discovery. In fact, *more* is the key word. The truly creative person always sees more, feels more, and finds more than the less creative person. That is why the creative person discovers more.

An aesthetic sense does not mean "I see" or "I hear"; it means "I enjoy what I see" or "I like what I hear." It means that the child is using taste or preference. This must occur for discovery to take place. Children should not be too concerned about results or the standards of others. They must choose what they feel is right in order to discover its meaning for themselves. This means that children must learn to work without self-consciousness, as a real artist does; children can be spontaneous and inventive. If they are trying to please the teacher and not themselves, they are denying their own aesthetic sense and hindering the discovery process.

## ENCOURAGING AESTHETIC SENSITIVITY

Teachers can encourage aesthetic sensitivity in children. This in turn encourages the discovery part of the creative process. Teachers can do this by supporting attentive play, avoiding giving answers (having children find their own answers), and setting limits that do not pressure children to learn the one "best way." When answers are given by children in groups, teachers can ask the children to "think over" the response. Sometimes preschool children think the first right answer is the best answer. Teachers can encourage more guessing and trying out hunches to avoid this.

In order to discover, children must "let go" of their minds and their bodies. This is a natural tendency in preschool children. The choice and respon-

FIGURE 3–7 The child's ability to "toy" with ideas, to "see into" things, and to "make up" more than what is there are all needed for discovery.

sibility for allowing children to "let go" rest with the caregiver.

It has been said that aesthetic sensitivity is important for children because it improves the quality of learning and helps the creative process. Aesthetic sensibility in children has many other benefits, too:

- Children are more sensitive to problems because they have more insight into their world. This means they can be more helpful to other children and to adults.
- Children are more likely to be self-learners because they are more sensitive to gaps in their knowledge.
- Life is more exciting for children because they have the capacity to be puzzled and to be surprised.
- Children are more tolerant because they learn that there are many possible ways of doing things.
- Children are more independent because they are more open to their own thoughts. They are good questioners for the same reason.
- Children can deal better with complexity because they do not expect to find one best answer.

For the teacher, children with aesthetic sensitivity become more exciting to be with, to learn from, and to teach.

# THINK ABOUT IT . . .

Teachers need to cultivate *their own* aesthetic sensitivity if they are going to help children develop theirs. And that's not always easy! I always searched for something of beauty to inspire me, especially in the dreary days of seemingly endless midwestern winters.

The following ideas helped boost my aesthetic sense, which in turn benefited the young children in my care:

- The weekly purchase of a single, fresh flower (usually costing under $2), which I displayed on my desk in a small vase. It perked up my and the children's spirits.
- The purchase of a new set of brightly colored markers for *my* use. I made up my lesson plans in several gorgeous colors. I even used some metallic colors and glitter markers for a real spark!
- An inexpensive prism, hung in a sunny window. The light designs cheered all our hearts.
- A borrowed instant camera to take pictures of us in our everyday routine. I posted them all over the room. Our smiling faces couldn't help but inspire us.
- A wallpaper sample book gave me almost a year's supply of placemats. Each week, each child had a new and different placemat for snack time.
- The radio or tapes played during rest time for *my* pleasure. I chose the music that pleased me that particular day: pop, western, rock, rap, and hip-hop.

## AESTHETIC EXPERIENCES

Aesthetic experiences for young children can take many forms. They can involve an appreciation of the beauty of nature, of the rhythm and imagery of music or poetry, or of the qualities of works of art. Far from being a specialized talent, the recognition of aesthetic qualities comes quite naturally to children.

For instance, let us consider art appreciation. What adults have come to regard as strictly a "museum-type" experience—seeing and appreciating good artwork—is an enjoyable experience for young children whose fear of the "intellectual" is not yet developed. Art appreciation can occur in the early childhood program through the combined experiences of learning to look at and learning to create visual arts. Introducing young children to art appreciation should be a series of pleasurable experiences with time to look, enjoy, comment, and raise questions. It is a time when children learn to "see" with their minds, as well as their eyes. They begin to feel with the painter, the sculptor, or the architect, and to explore their ideas and techniques.

School is a place where children are introduced to new experiences. Teachers have a responsibility to provide the very best that our culture has to offer by introducing a range of good art, not merely what is easiest or most familiar. Most children have plenty of exposure to cartoon characters, advertising art, and stereotyped, simplistic posters. These do not foster aesthetic development and are sometimes demeaning to children. Teachers often say, "children like them," but the fact that children like something— for example, candy and staying up late at night— does not necessarily mean it is good for them. Children might never have seen a Van Gogh sunflower, a mother and child by Mary Cassatt, or a sculpture by Henry Moore. Yet, young children can learn to appreciate these as well as arts and crafts from many cultures if introduced to them in the early years.

From such experiences, children also gradually learn the concepts of design. During group discus-

**Colors** can be called by name or hue—red, scarlet, turquoise, magenta—that add richness to children's experience. They can be pure—primary colors (red, blue, yellow), white, and black—or mixed. Different hues have temperature—coolness at the blue end of the spectrum and warmth at the red end. They have different degrees of intensity or saturation (brightness or dullness) and value (lightness or darkness). Colors change as they mix, are related to one another (orange is related to red), and appear to change when placed next to each other. We have enjoyed using Haskin's (1973) book for children, *Color Seems*, as a springboard for talking about color.

*Examples of things to say:*
Hue—I saw a lavender sunset last night.
Intensity—The ball is bright red; the bricks are a duller red color.
Temperature—The blue in your painting makes me feel icy.
Value—The pale green reminds me of jade: it's a soft, misty color.
Relationship—My car looks orange next to the school bus, but yellow by the truck.

**Line** is a part of every work of art. Every line in a piece of art has length, beginning, end, and direction (up/down, diagonal, side-to-side). Lines have relationships with one another and with other parts of the work. They can be separate, twined, parallel, or crossed.

*Examples of things to say:*
Kind—Michael's socks have zig-zags; Thad's have stripes.
Direction—I see wide, heavy lines in the wallpaper.
Length—Mary Ann filled her paper with short lines.
Relationship—The paint strokes cross each other.

**Shape or Form** in art is more than geometric shapes. Artists combine regular with irregular shapes. Some have names. All can be filled or empty, separate, connected, or overlapping. One shape may enclose another. When the boundaries are completed, the shape is closed; if uncompleted (like a U or a C) it is open. Three-dimensional shapes may be solid (like a ball) or incorporate empty space (like a tire). Empty and filled spaces have shape. Shapes can be large or small and be compared (bigger, smaller, rounder, more angular, etc.).

*Examples of things to say:*
Size—You used a necklace of tiny circles to make a pattern.
Name—The ridge of the dragon's back has triangles on it.
Solidity—We can walk through the bead curtain.
Relationship—Zach's picture has a person on each side of the house.
Open/Closed—Can you take one block away and open your structure?

**Space** refers to the distance within or between aspects in artwork. It can be crowded, sparse, full, or empty, creating feelings of freedom or enclosure. Space can have balance with other forms. Boundaries, inclusion, and exclusion are spatial qualities. Space can be solid or permeable.

*Examples of things to say:*
Location—The birds are in the top corner of the picture.
Boundaries—Some animals are inside the house and some are outside.
Feeling—I feel free when I can see such a long way.

**Design** is the organization of artwork. Children initially work without plan; as they gain experience they design. Design includes use of an element (like a circle) repeated or varied. The ways color, line, shape, and form are placed give the work a visual effect. Symmetry, balance, repetition, and alternation are design characteristics.

*Examples of things to say:*
Symmetry/Asymmetry—The wings of the butterfly mirror each other.
Repetition—Every one is filled with circles.
Alternation—There is a stripe after every heart.
Variation—In all of your pictures you used different shades of red—each one a little different.

FIGURE 3–8 Talking with children about art elements. (Adapted with permission from S. Feeney and E. Moravcik, "A Thing of Beauty: Aesthetic Development in Young Children," in *Young Children*, Sept., 1987, 11.)

sions, children should be encouraged to talk about the design qualities of a specific color, the movement of lines, the contrast of sizes and shapes, and the variety of textures. They should be helped to think and feel, as individuals, about a certain art object or piece of music. Their understanding of aesthetics, and their willingness and ability to discuss its concepts, will increase with experience. In Figure 3–8 you will find some helpful suggestions on how to talk with children about art elements, including examples of things to say.

Aesthetic experiences for young children should be chosen according to their interests and level of understanding. Such details as dates and the social-political implications of a piece of art or music have no relevance for a child. Rather, a painting or a piece of music or a dance may appeal to them because of its familiar subject matter, its bold colors or rhythm, or its story. A variety of experiences in appreciation—paintings and sculpture, ballet and jazz dancing, marches and concertos—should be offered.

Art appreciation also includes the development of an awareness of the aesthetic qualities of everyday man-made objects. Children are surrounded daily by an endless number of objects such as furniture, clothing, toys, buildings, and machines and countless images in films, television, newspapers, books, magazines, advertisements, and exhibits. Examples of good and bad design can be found in all areas of the environment. In this program of increasing awareness, children will become more sensitive to their environment and eventually will develop more selective, even discriminating, taste.

## SUMMARY

Aesthetics is an appreciation for beauty and a feeling of wonder. The purpose of aesthetic experiences for children is to help them develop a full and rich life.

Children gain an aesthetic sense by doing, sensing, feeling, and responding to things. As children learn and grow together in the early childhood years, a sense of aesthetics can be developed as they learn to join what they think with what they feel. Such aesthetic experiences allow children to express their feelings about what they are learning and experiencing. In this way, there is no false separation between work and play, art and learning, and thought and feeling. Children with improved aesthetic sensitivity have a greater chance to be creative and receive more enjoyment from learning.

Teachers can help develop children's aesthetic senses by involving them in the arts; introducing them to famous works of art, music, dance, or literature; allowing them to explore their environment; and avoiding single solutions to complex problems.

Children benefit from their aesthetic sensitivity because it generates more excitement in their lives as well as more insight. The ability to use one's taste or to know one's preference, which is basic to an aesthetic sense, can improve the quality of learning. Aesthetic sensibility in children also helps them develop their feelings of sensitivity, independence, and tolerance.

## LEARNING ACTIVITIES

### Being Aware

In order to use one's aesthetic sense, one must pay very close attention to that which is personally interesting. This means being very aware of oneself and one's surroundings.

A. Try to think a new thought or make a discovery by paying closer attention to yourself.
B. Begin by going to a place that is quiet and relaxing. Sit down and take a minute to rest. Then say,

"Now I am aware of . . ." and finish this statement with what you are in touch with at the moment. Notice whether this is something inside or outside yourself.
C. Make the statement again and see what happens.
　1. Has your awareness changed?
　2. Are fantasies, thoughts, or images part of your awareness?
D. Make the statement again, but this time think of a person.

1. Who comes to mind?
2. What does it mean?
E. Try the same sentence, but change your awareness by thinking of different things such as a flower, a picture, someone from the past, a child, your favorite place, and so on.
F. Notice that when thinking of something outside, one cannot think of something inside at the same time.
G. What does this mean for working with children? Compare your answers with classmates, and find out how they feel about this activity.

## Fruit

This is an activity to make new discoveries by paying closer attention to everyday things.

A. Take three different types of fruit. Close your eyes and pick each one up. Feel them with your fingers from top to bottom.
1. How are they different?
2. How are they the same?
B. Place the fruits against your face.
1. Do they feel different?
2. What about the temperature of the fruit?

C. Smell the fruits, being sure to keep your eyes closed.
1. How different are the aromas?
2. Which is your favorite?
D. Open your eyes and look at the fruits.
1. Hold them up to the light.
2. See if you can see anything new about each fruit.
E. What have you discovered from this activity? (Notice you did not taste or eat the fruit.)
1. Could you still receive pleasure from the fruit without eating it?
2. What does this mean for working with children?
F. Compare your answer with that of classmates, and find out how they felt about this activity.
G. Plan a trip to a local museum for a group of young children. Help the children to focus in the gallery with activities such as
- searching for a particularly interesting picture. For example, in a room filled with paintings ask children, "Can you find the painting where there is a bear, a house, a mother, and a baby?"
- asking "What would it feel like to be in the painting?" "Where would you like to go?" "What would you like to do if you were there?"
- asking children to find two pictures that are the same in some way—the same colors, the same subject, the same feeling.

# ACTIVITIES FOR CHILDREN

A. Art Talk
Using Van Gogh's famous painting *Starry Night,* ask young children the following questions about the painting:
What do you see in the painting?
What do you notice about the colors, lines?
Show me in the painting what you think is the most important thing in it.
Why?
How does this picture make you feel?
What do you think the artist was feeling when he was painting this picture?
   Another kind of questioning about *Starry Night* might be to have the children imagine they are in the scene:
If you were in the painting, where would you want to be?
How would that feel?
What kind of things do you think you'd smell?
What kind of animals might live there?
   These questions could be used for any other painting of your choice.
B. Artwork in Children's Books
Children's books provide many opportunities to develop children's aesthetic senses. Beautifully illus-

trated books introduce different art styles and techniques. Picture books are especially good for use in discussing art elements and children's personal preferences. Look for children's books that have been awarded the Caldecott Medal for excellence in illustration.
C. Art at a Touch
Plan a visit to a museum that has outdoor art such as large sculpture. These can be viewed closely and touched, and provide a very meaningful experience for children as they can be freely explored by all the children.
D. Art in Nature
The beauty of nature is also a continuing source of inspiration for young children. It is through nature that many children acquire some of their earliest ideas and concepts of design. A variety of experiences can be planned to help children observe and discover color, line, form, pattern, and texture in natural objects:
- Make a bulletin board arrangement of natural objects and materials.
- Begin a collection of natural objects, such as flowers, weeds, twigs, stones, shells, seed pods, moss, and feathers, for a touch-and-see display.

- Take a walking trip to observe color, shape, and texture in the immediate environment. Share individual discoveries with others during class discussion.

- Show films, conduct dramatizations, or read stories and poems to develop these concepts.

## UNIT REVIEW

1. Define aesthetics.
2. List three things a teacher can do to help children develop their aesthetic sensitivity.
3. List five benefits of aesthetic sensitivity in children.
4. List at least two specific ways to introduce young children to the work of an artist and to involve them in art appreciation in general.
5. List at least three art elements to discuss with children.

## ADDITIONAL READINGS

Broudy, H.S. "The Case of Aesthetic Education." *Report of the Tanglewood Symposium.* R.A. Choate, ed. Washington, D.C.: Music Educators National Conference (1968): 33–42.

———. *Enlightened Cherishing: An Essay on Aesthetic Education.* Urbana, Ill.: University of Illinois Press, 1972.

Eisner, E.W. *Educating Artistic Vision.* New York: Macmillan, 1972.

———. "Why Art in Education and Why Art Education?" *Beyond Creating: The Place for Art in America's Schools.* p. 64–69. Los Angeles: Getty Center for Education in the Arts, 1985.

Clemens, S.G. "Art in the Classroom: Making Every Day Special." *Young Children.* (Jan., 1991): 4–11.

Feeney, S., and E. Moravcik. "A Thing of Beauty: Aesthetic Development in Young Children." *Young Children* (Sept., 1987): 6–15.

Haskins, I. *Color Seems.* New York: Vanguard, 1973.

Schirrmacher, R. *Art and Creative Development for Young Children.* 2nd ed. Albany, N.Y.: Delmar, 1993.

Wolf, A.D. *Mommy, It's a Renoir!* Altoona, Pa.: Parent-Child Press, 1984.

# UNIT 4
# Promoting Aesthetic Experiences

## OBJECTIVES

After studying this unit, you should be able to
- describe three types of sensing and feeling.
- choose materials that have good aesthetic potential.
- list four guidelines to help children work with aesthetic materials.
- list six guidelines to use in talking with children about their artwork.

People search their world for what is important to them. They look for what they need. They see what they want. This is as true of preschool children as it is of adults.

Imagine that a group of people are taken into a room and are asked to look at a table. On the table is some food, a glass of water, and a small amount of money. Those who are hungry are most likely to look at the food. Those who are thirsty will probably look at the water. Those who are in debt are apt to look at the money. And those who need furniture will probably take a closer look at the table.

Children also look for things they need and want. A tired child looks for a place to rest. A lonely child looks for a friend. The point here is that only when children are physically well, feel safe, and sense that they belong can they be ready to develop an aesthetic sense. Beauty is not seen when one is afraid. Children hide their feelings when they do not feel safe.

## LOOKING AND SEEING

Children look in many different ways. Touching, patting, poking, picking, and even tasting are ways of looking for young children. Children look for what they need, but they also see what they find to be stimulating. Something can be stimulating to a child for many different reasons. It can be because it is colorful, exciting, different, interesting, changing, moving, weird, and so on. The list of stimulating things is seemingly endless. However, there are some basic guidelines for preparing a stimulating activity or object:

*Can children experience it with more than one sense?* Children enjoy what they can touch, see, and hear more than something they can only see or hear.

*Can children interact with it?* Children tend to enjoy what they can participate in. For children, the picture of a guinea pig will never replace a live guinea pig.

*Are the children interested in it?* Children relate to what is familiar to them and part of their life. Talking about a television program that children have never seen cannot produce the kind of discussion that comes when they talk about their favorite program.

*Is the activity well paced?* Something that moves too quickly or too slowly eventually becomes boring. When a game slows down, watch how many children drop out.

*Is it colorful?* Flowers, circuses, and animals are popular for this very reason.

*Does it promise to be rewarding?* Is the activity fun, adventurous, or exciting? Does it have something worthwhile at the end? If not, why should the children stick with it? Searching for a piece of a puz-

**FIGURE 4–1 Molding clay with no other purpose than to feel it in their hands gives children the motivation to continue the activity.**

**FIGURE 4–2 Children explore in many different ways. Touching, patting, poking, and even tasting are ways children explore their world.**

zle or looking for a hidden treasure is only fun if the children believe they can find it.

## SENSING, FEELING, AND IMAGINING

There are basically three types of sensing and feeling. The first is contact with the world outside of the person, actual sensory contact with things and events. It is seeing, hearing, smelling, tasting, and touching. The second is what people feel within themselves. This includes what they experience under their skin. Itches, tensions, muscular movements, discomfort, and emotions are all a part of this type of sensing. The third type of sensing and feeling goes beyond the present and reality. It is usually called fantasy, and includes dreams, memories, images, and guesses.

For a child, each of these types of sensing and feeling is very important. All three can take place during the same activity. Any one can become more important than the other two, depending on what the child needs or wants at the moment. Most teachers are concerned about the child's sensory contact with the outside world. Children do many things that involve touching, seeing, and hearing; yet, what they feel inside and what they fantasize about are also important. The teacher must give attention to these two processes as well. They are part of aesthetic sensitivity. Teachers should ask themselves two questions each day when working with preschool children. Both should be answered yes, followed by the question, "How?"

The first question has to do with the inside feelings of the children: *Have the children done something today that has helped them feel good about themselves?* The second has to do with the fantasies of the children: *Have the children done something today that has helped them use their imagination in either the past, present, or future?*

Lesson plans, activities, and trips should be planned and evaluated with these two questions in mind. If teachers are sincere about answering yes to the two questions, their teaching will relate to all the ways children sense and feel.

## FINDING AND ORGANIZING AESTHETIC MATERIALS

Every teacher has many ideas about what materials are best for children. Sometimes the desired materials are too expensive or difficult to find. Schools have limited budgets, and even ordinary items can seem impossible to obtain. There are three resources with great potential: salvage material, commonly known as "junk"; the hardware store; and things the children bring in.

Before describing the organization of these materials, it is helpful to have some guidelines for choosing materials with good aesthetic potential:

- Choose materials that children can explore with their senses (touch, see, smell).
- Choose materials that children can manipulate (twist, bend, cut, color, mark).
- Choose materials that can be used in different ways (thrown, bounced, built with, fastened, shaped).

Children enjoy finding materials because it suggests exploration and discovery. The discovery of materials can be celebrated and shared in a "beauty corner" where newly found leaves, ribbons, and other treasures can be placed (Chandler, 1973). A small collection of colored cloths, a few blocks or boxes, and a screen, pegboard, or tack board to fasten things on, all set in adequate light, can make a beauty corner. Children can develop aesthetic skills in sensing and exhibiting by helping to build such a place. They can learn to ask such questions as, "Does it look better this way?" or "Should we put more light on it?"

Usually, the finding of materials involves more than looking. Children need to play with the found materials to try them out for weight, texture, structure, and so on. After the materials have been tested and shared, they may go into the beauty corner or a classroom collection.

Sometimes the children's search can be focused on something, as in finding things for painting or building. As they find that their discovered materials make their day-to-day work more interesting, they become alert to new possibilities. For the teacher and the children, this can mean a constant supply of materials and new aesthetic experiences.

The experience of selecting, collecting, and using materials can be aided by classifying the materials according to their design possibilities. The number and names of classification should be developed slowly with the children, as they bring in their findings. This may vary with age level and interest.

**FIGURE 4–3 For aesthetic experiences, choose materials children can manipulate and use in different ways.**

## AESTHETIC USE OF MATERIALS

Uses for the materials collected by the teacher and children are unlimited (Chandler, 1973). Space, time, and imagination may form some boundaries on what may be done. However, what is most important is that the materials and what is done with them become personal statements of the children and teacher. This is not done by what is made, but by how it is made—whether it is an art project, a building project, or another activity. The *process* of making and the child's personal involvement in it are the keys here—*not* the finished product.

A common approach to collected materials is to turn them into representations of flowers, animals, dolls, or scenes. The value of these activities depends

# THIS ONE'S FOR YOU!

## PROMOTING AESTHETIC EXPERIENCES: TALKING WITH YOUNG CHILDREN ABOUT THEIR ARTWORK

John Pete, age four, runs up to you with his dripping-wet painting. Beaming with pride, he thrusts his painting of several dark blotches at you and says expectantly, "Look what I painted!"

Just what do you say to him? Should you praise John Pete, encourage more painting, critique his work, or withhold any judgment at all? What is the best way to talk with young children about their art in a way to encourage their individual aesthetic experience? The following suggestions should assist you in answering this question.

1. The next time children show you what they have created, smile, pause, and *say nothing at first*. This serves two purposes. It gives you time to study the children's art and to *reflect* on what you want to say before you speak. It gives you time to think of a better response than an impulsive, stereotypical response like, "That's nice." Second, and more importantly, it will give children an opportunity to talk *first* if they so choose. This provides a lead-in and direction for your subsequent comments.

2. The elements of art (for a description of the art elements, see Figure 3–8 in Unit 3) provide a good framework for responding to children. You can comment on such things as design, pattern, color, line, shape or form, texture, and space. Figure 3–8 provides sample "things to say" to help you here.

3. Do *not* focus on representation in art ("What *is* it?"), but focus instead on the abstract or design qualities ("Look what a beautiful pattern these blue lines make!").

4. Use reflective dialogue in talking with children about their art. "You are so proud of your work, aren't you?" "You spent a lot of time making so many different shapes." "You worked very hard at drawing today."

5. Not all comments need to refer to the artistic elements. Your comments might also refer to other aspects of the project or to the child's specific interests as well. For example, a young artist hands you a drawing and says, "That's my house, and the painter is painting it." You may want to comment on other qualities of the work such as the amount of time and effort spent, how the materials were handled, or the meaning of the drawing to the child. For example, you might respond, "Your drawing really shows a lot of action!" or "How hard you worked to include the paint cans and brushes!" "I can tell by your drawing that you really enjoyed using so many different colors of crayons."

6. Don't attempt to correct a child's artwork or try to improve a child's art by having it more closely approximate reality. Children's art is not intended as a copy of the real world. Child artists may freely choose to add or omit details. Adults' criticism or corrections only discourage children and do not foster aesthetic experiences. Concentrate and comment on what *is* in the child's work and not on what *isn't!*

7. You may even want to simply ask the child "Do you want to tell me about your work?" Of course, with this question, "no" is as acceptable an answer as "yes."

**FIGURE 4-4 A child's personal statement is more important than either the materials or the process.**

## GUIDANCE IN USING AESTHETIC MATERIALS

Some guidance by the teacher in working with aesthetic materials is necessary. This guidance must be very gentle, supportive, and sensitive. If guidance is given in the selection or arrangement of materials, the child is pressured to produce "like everyone else" or like older brothers and sisters. Children need to know they can take chances and be different. The teacher can give guidance in several ways (Chandler, 1973):

*Ask questions aimed at helping the children reach out for and get the "payoff" they are seeking.* A question teachers can ask themselves that will help them ask the right question of children is, "What can I ask the children that would help them better understand what they want?" When the children are working with paints, this question may be something about color. When they are working with paper, it may be something about form, such as "What shape would you like it to be?" Even better, ask how paper feels, as just seeing a shape is only one way of sensing paper.

*Avoid too many ready-made models or ways of doing things.* Teaching children over and over to do something in only one way may ruin their aesthetic sense. Repetition tells them to stop thinking. For example, why always start to draw in the middle of a piece of paper? Why not sometimes draw from the edges or bottom? Or why not change the shape of the paper on which children draw, using paper in the shape of a triangle, parallelogram, or circle?

*Be positive and creative when using models or examples.* In craft activities where models are used, always make it a point to encourage each child to use her own unique approach to the project. Occasional use of models and examples is not uncommon in many classrooms today. Their use need not be a negative experience for children if they are used positively—as a springboard to unlocking each child's

on the quality of individual discovery and the imagination of the child. Again, the important point is not what is made, the product, but rather the process—who planned it and how much of the child's thought and feeling went into it. Children must have the opportunity not only to find the materials but also to try them out. This means much experimenting with the materials to determine what the children feel they need. A question such as, "What would you like to say with these things?" might help both the children and the teacher get started. Checking with the children's moods may be helpful, too. Do they seem to feel happy, dreamy, sad, gentle, aggressive? Such questioning can help the children reach their own purpose based on their experience and interests.

Another important consideration in the creative process is the number of materials. It is important to remember not to give children too many materials too often. Too much to choose from can overwhelm a child. The qualities of one material can be lost in the midst of so many others. An example of this would be to work with a certain color or a single material, such as buttons or paper. In this way, the children can learn more about making their own aesthetic choices, as well as mastering such skills as pasting and cutting.

own creative approach to a shared, common theme (or object). Many times, a brief look at one or two examples (which should *not* then be displayed for "copying" during the activity) can help motivate children to get started on making one of their own. Also, using a model produced by another child of the same age can encourage children in that it is something possible for them to do, too. Teacher comments throughout activities and the use of examples can help encourage each child to be creative in her approach. Statements like, "Claire, I like how you are using so *many* colors," or "Jeremy, you used that paper in a very nice and different way to make your own design," clearly communicate the positive acceptance of different approaches.

*Help children select the materials they prefer.* This may mean asking the children which materials they plan to use first, which materials they may not use at all, and which materials they may possibly use.

*Help children "hunt" for aesthetic qualities.* Help children get in touch with what they feel about differences. For example, ask children to show what they like or think is better. Ask what is brighter, darker, happier, sadder.

*Help children use other senses when only one sense seems necessary.* Children can be asked to hear what they see in a drawing or to draw what they hear in music. Colors can be related to feelings, music, and body movements, as well as to seeing.

*Help children use aesthetic experiences to deepen experiences.* This requires timing, for example, using painting, drawing, or sculpting to express a strong feeling rather than talking about it or, perhaps, talking about the feeling after the painting. It could mean playing music at an especially happy time. In this case, the important question has more to do with when than how. When is a good time to paint, draw, or dance?

Often, children feel that "more" is better. To have more paint, more color, or more buttons seems best to some children. They want the brightest colors, the most crayons, and the loudest music.

FIGURE 4–5 Sharing creative experiences helps children broaden their horizons and begin to relate more actively with others.

A noted child development expert, Jean Piaget, describes this trait of young children to concentrate on bigness and "more is better" as "centering" (Furth, 1970). He feels that centering is quite natural in young children and that gradually, through experiences in their active exploration of life, they can learn to be more selective. (The ideas of Piaget will be discussed at greater length in Unit 9.)

In creative activities, young children can begin to learn about selection by choosing materials they like instead of the "biggest." In this way they can begin to move away from the "more" tendency, or "centering" as Piaget described it. Creative experiences can also help children learn to "follow through something," to share their interests with others, and to learn care of shared materials.

**Displaying Children's Work.** An important part of the teacher's role in developing children's aesthetic sensitivity is showing their work to parents and others. A good rule of thumb is that if the children feel good about their work, let them show it. The work does not have to be complete. It should be displayed at children's eye level so that they, as well as adults, may enjoy it.

Set up displays to show the different ways the chil-

**FIGURE 4–6** Only when children are physically well, secure, and comfortable in their surroundings will they be ready to develop an aesthetic sense.

dren have used a medium, such as painting, collage, clay, and so on. Let the room reflect the children's diversity, their likes, their interests—much the way a well-decorated home reflects the interests and skills of the people who live in it. Children aren't raised to be clones, so we certainly don't expect to see 25 identical works of art with different names on them displayed in the room. How does this reflect the children's diversity?

Take time at the end of the day to show artwork to the children, letting them talk about each other's work. Model for the children how to make a positive comment, using the guidelines presented in this unit.

Be sure to send all artwork home in a way that shows your respect for the artist and the art. For example, paintings folded rather than rolled, or rolled when wet and therefore stuck together, tell children their work doesn't matter (Clemens, 1991, p. 10). (More specific suggestions on displaying children's work are covered in Appendix C.)

**Interpreting Children's Creative Work for Parents.** Parents should be helped to see what the child liked about the creative work. All people have their own ideas of what creative talent is. Parents are

no exception. But it is important that they understand and know that what their children enjoy and feel about what they are doing is much more important than the finished product. Parents, however, may enjoy getting involved in the process by helping their children plan, choose, and evaluate their work. Of course, the evaluation should be a positive sharing on the child's part of her feelings and thoughts about the experiences involved in making the creative work. It would *not* begin with a parent asking, "What is it?" A parent's simple request such as "Tell me about it . . ." may begin this positive sharing between parent and child. Having children take work home to get their parents' reactions and then work on it the next day is another way of doing this. This may be followed by asking parents to help in finding useful materials.

Parents should also know why some materials are used by their children and others are not. And more important, parents should learn to approach their child's making of gifts, art exhibits, and displays as demonstrations of the child's aesthetic sense. With these displays, the child is saying, "This is how it is with me."

Parents want to know their children; children's creative work can help parents know more about their children. Teachers can assist parents by showing these visual examples of the creative *process* and pointing out that they are valuable for the process *alone.*

Very few children will become professional artists, but given encouragement and experience they can learn to work with many media, enjoy beauty, and discriminate with aesthetic understanding. Our arts heritage is open to anyone who can appreciate it. A person naturally responds to a lovely sunrise, painting, or piece of music. These aesthetic experiences help us live fully in the moment. Such responses do not need to be taught, but a child might need education and exposure to appreciate them fully. Aesthetic enjoyment provides an avenue through which people can find focus and achieve balance and tranquility in an increasingly fast-moving world. Moreover, children who learn to love beauty in nature and in the arts are likely to want to support and protect these valuable resources.

## SUMMARY

Children look for things they need and want. They are stimulated by things they find interesting, colorful, and rewarding.

There are three types of sensing and feeling. The first is contact through the five basic senses; the second is what the person feels inside; and the third is fantasy.

Many materials with aesthetic potential can be found. Anything children can explore, manipulate, and use in different ways has aesthetic potential. What is most important is that these materials (and what is done with them) become personal statements of the children.

Teachers and parents can help children explore this aesthetic potential by concentrating on the importance of the *process* and *not* the product in children's creative work. The teacher can give supportive and gentle guidance by asking helpful questions, avoiding too many ready-made models, and helping children "hunt" for aesthetic qualities.

Displaying children's work at their eye level is yet another way to show appreciation for their involvement in the creative process. Parents' appreciation for these displays must also concentrate on the importance of the child's creative process and not on the finished product. The teacher's role is to help interpret children's work for parents.

## LEARNING ACTIVITIES

### Beautiful Things

Everyone has had some experience with beauty and has a special idea about what is beautiful. It can be a very interesting experience to examine this concept with each of the five senses.

A. Write down the three most beautiful things (living or nonliving) that you have ever experienced with each of your five senses.
B. As you write your list, try as much as possible to relive the sensations.
C. Answer the following questions:
   1. Were most of your things living or nonliving?
   2. How many involved people?
   3. Did any of your answers surprise you?
   4. How often do you encounter beautiful things?
   5. Which sense seems to find the most beauty?
   6. How much does beauty in life depend on you?
   7. What does this mean for working with children?
D. Compare your responses with fellow students.

### Amazing Journey

A. Find a quiet place and relax. Close your eyes and think of something that amazes you or produces wonder in you.

B. Think of yourself as that something. (Take some time to get the feel of being it.)
C. Write a description of yourself as this something. (Use plenty of adjectives.)
D. As a result of this experience:
   1. What emotions do you feel?
   2. How are you like what really amazes you?
   3. How are you unlike it?
   4. Would you like to change in any way?
E. Compare your answers with classmates.
F. Do you think children would enjoy using their imaginations like this?
G. Using the material presented in this unit, comment on the following quotation:

Kuroyanagi (1982, p. 88), describing her experiences in a very special school, quotes headmaster Sosaku Kobayashi: "Having eyes but not seeing beauty; having ears but not hearing music; having minds but not perceiving truth; having hearts that are never moved and therefore never set on fire. These are things to fear."

• How does this apply to early childhood education?
• What could you do as a teacher to prevent the situation described in the quote from happening?
• Does anything from your own experience come to mind when you read this quote? Explain.

# ACTIVITIES FOR CHILDREN

## Aesthetic Thinking Through Art

Help the child to think of new ideas to create the following.

A. Say to the child, "If you could invent a new means of transportation, what would it be? Draw or construct how it would look."
B. Ask the child, "If you had a funny-shaped piece of paper, what kind of an animal or automobile or house could you make it into?"
C. Ask, "How do you think the world would look to a giant? Draw a picture (or make a model) of it."
D. Ask, "What could you do with this empty box, this stick, this cardboard (beautiful junk)? How could you place it or arrange it to make something that's your very own idea?"
E. Relate topics given to the child to actual personal involvement or prior study and experience. Take your cues from the child's world. Typical subjects to suggest might include
   - your house
   - your family
   - where you like to play
   - your favorite thing to play with
   - an animal you know
   - how you feel when you're lonely
   - a make-believe place
   - what you want to be when you grow up
   - clothes you like to wear
   - how you help others in your family
   - what you like to do when it is hot
   - your self-portrait
   - things that scare you
   - a friend
   - someone you love
   - a trip you have taken

## Sensory Experiences

### Seeing

A. *Colors.* Have the children look for colors in the room, as "How many red things can you see?" Or play a guessing game, as "I am thinking of something green in this room. What is it?" Colors sometimes tell us important things, as the traffic lights tell us when to go or stop. Red flags on a road mean danger. Red lights in a building mean an exit. We must obey these signals. We can make different colors by mixing them. (Allow children to experiment with mixing colors.) Show a prism to see the colors.

Blow soap bubbles, and look for the rainbow colors in them.
B. *Shapes.* Show blocks or other objects that are circles, squares, rectangles, and triangles. Have children find things in the room that are these shapes. We can see color and shape at the same time. Find a red square, a blue circle, etc.
C. *Sizes.* Compare sizes of children and objects. Develop concepts of big, bigger, biggest; large, small; tall, short; thick, thin; wide, narrow; etc. Play riddles, as "I am thinking of something that is white and round (clock)."
D. *Miscellaneous Activities with Equipment in the Classroom.*
   1. Sorting—for color, shape, color and shape, size, buttons, pegs, blocks.
   2. Lotto—color, shape, object.
   3. Puzzles—simple teacher-made puzzles first, then more difficult ones.
   4. Parquetry.
   5. Stringing beads—to color and then shape.
   6. Cover up and take-away game—a number of objects are placed under a napkin. They are shown to the children, then one is taken away. The children have to guess which is gone. The number can be increased gradually.
   7. Position games—played like the preceding except the position is changed.
   8. Coin recognition.
E. *Tactile Experiences When It's Cold Outside.* When it's too cold to play outside for long periods of time, try some of these outdoor-type activities adapted for indoor use.
   1. Use a summer wading pool for sand or mixed dry beans. Let the children sit on the floor and play as long as they wish—sorting, measuring, or just letting them take off their shoes and walk in! Use a plastic table cloth under the pool for easier clean-up.
   2. Stock up on sand and rice. Have them available for measuring, pouring, and even for gluing onto paper.
   3. Make up a water play table using a baby bath tub or large dishpans at the proper height for children's use. Try food color in the water for a fun variation.
   4. Shaving cream on the table or in trays allows children to finger "paint" and draw as long as they like—and clean-up is easy!

### Listening

A. *Tape Recorder.* The children can listen to their own voices, to voices of others, to classroom sounds. Take the recorder on field trips and record sounds of animals' environments. Replay to review trip and to help children remember sequence of events. Record sounds of environment: cars passing, steps in the corridor or on the street, children skipping, hopping, running. Ask questions like, "Do any of the animals sound alike? Which of the sounds was loudest? How would you describe that sound?"

B. *Street Corner.* Listen to sounds. Identify them: car turning corner, wind blowing past sign, click as light changes, dog barking, rain dripping, wheels on wet pavement, animal footsteps, high heels on pavement, sneakers on pavement, noises from buildings.

C. *Classroom Sounds.* Listen to sounds of different toys, clock ticking, blocks falling. Have children cover eyes. "Where does the sound come from? What is the sound?" Have Mary walk (skip, run) across the back of the room, the front, or along the side.

D. *Stethoscope.* Listen to heartbeats of children, adults, and animals. Listen to stomach after snack. Scratch different objects on a table top (floor, rug, pipe) and listen to sound through the stethoscope.

E. *Rhythms.* Beat out simple and then more complex rhythms with clapping hands. Ask the children to repeat them.

F. *Sound Hunt.* A sound hunt is a delightful way to add the children's "repertoire" of sounds. Have the children find objects in the room that will make interesting sounds to share with the group. Add another dimension to the sounds your students collect by asking them to make the sounds loud or soft and to decide if they have a high sound or a low sound. You can incorporate a sound hunt into an ongoing listening experience when your class moves through school corridors, enters the playground, eats in the cafeteria, or takes a neighborhood walk. Make a point of giving the students a few specific things to listen for on these excursions and then having them add their own observations as well. For example, in the school hallways ask the children to heed footsteps, voices, clothes rustling, or a typewriter clacking. Give the children an opportunity to use some of their new knowledge and skills by having them devise original sound effects for a play or puppet performance in class.

## Taste and Smell

Be sure to teach children proper precautions in tasting or smelling strange substances.

A. *Cooking.* Make puddings, candy, cakes. Smell before, after, and during cooking. Identify what's cooking by smell. Taste brown sugar, white sugar, molasses, corn syrup, maple syrup. Make lemonade with and without sugar. Squeeze tomatoes, apples, oranges for juice. Question children about what smells best, what smells they don't like.

B. *Snack or Lunch.* Talk about differences in taste between hamburgers and bologna, between peanuts and peanut butter, between potato chips and mashed potatoes. (These discussions may also get into sense of touch as well as smell and taste.) Have children guess what they will have for lunch from smells coming from the kitchen.

C. *Street Corner or Classroom.* Identify smells: exhaust of cars, cooking, people, gasoline, sneakers, soap, flowers, trees, animals, smoke, smog, pine needles, leaves, cut grass. Try to decide what causes a particular smell. Talk about smells in other places like the doctor's office, hospital, restaurant, home, park.

D. *Olfactory (Smelling)*
   1. Dramatize agreeable and disagreeable odors.
   2. Identify different household items placed in jars—ammonia, soap, cleaners.
   3. Identify fruits—lemons, apples, bananas—blindfolded or with hands covering eyes.
   4. Guess what is in lunchbox—not peeking.
   5. Utilize field trips and kitchen play.

E. *Gustatory (Tasting)*
   1. Cook simple things with children, emphasizing the taste—sweet, sour, bitter.
   2. Place small portions of fruits on the child's tongue. Have her identify without looking. Reward with a large portion.
   3. The same game as (2) with beverages. Reward here, too.
   4. Distribute foodstuffs on wooden sticks and have child identify without looking.
   5. Recognize differences in taste of bread—white, rye, wheat.

## Smelling and Listening

A. *Popping Corn.* As the children are finishing some other activity, have someone begin popping corn. Be sure that the children do not see the preparation or corn popping. The sound and the odor should arouse their attention. Ask questions such as these: What do you think is happening? What makes you think this is happening? What did you observe first?

B. *Extending the Learning Experience.* Encourage the children's questions. You may want to use analogies and comparisons during the discussion of their questions. The children may be able to reason out answers to some of their questions if they participate in the activities that follow:
   1. Why is there a noise when the corn pops? Blow up a paper bag, and pop it with your hand. The sudden release of pressure as the bag breaks pro-

duces a sound similar to the sound of an exploding kernel of corn.

2. How much bigger does the popcorn get when it pops? Tell the children to line up ten unpopped kernels in a row. Alongside this row, have them line up ten popped kernels. Point out that this is one way of *comparing* the size of popped and unpopped corn.

*Touching (Tactile Awareness)*

A. *Rough or Smooth?* Teacher discusses tactile sensitivity with the children. Objects of varying textures are available, such as silk cloth, burlap, feathers, rope, seashells, mirrors, balls, driftwood, beads, furry slippers, and so on. Children form small groups and each group receives an object. Each child shows how the object makes her feel. For example, a feather may stand in a straight line with arms and legs extended, and then move "softly," with arms waving gently from side to side.

B. *A Collage Made for Touching.* A texture collage is a bulletin board that all students can contribute to and use later for further projects. Have the children bring in materials of different textures—sandpaper, flannel, velvet, burlap, plastic, bottle caps, pebbles, and paper clips—to glue on the board. Once the collage is complete, the children can make "rubbings," using charcoal sticks on newsprint. This board should encourage use of vocabulary-expanding words like "coarse," "smooth," etc.

C. *Creative Movement.* Discriminate between various textures through movements. Have the children feel a texture such as that of silk and interpret it by moving the way it feels. Use a variety of textures that exhibit characteristics such as bumpy, smooth, coarse, prickly.

D. *Tag an Object*
1. Equipment: Several objects: toy car, truck, boat, ball, jacks, erasers.
2. Procedure: Place seven different objects on the floor. Choose seven children and ask each one to cover her eyes (or blindfold them, if they prefer). Whisper the name of the object they are to locate. On the signal "go," send them to the area of the seven objects to try to locate their object. They may look again when they think they have located the proper object.

E. *Outdoor Textures*
1. Words to use: Rough, smooth, bumpy, soft, hard, sharp, cold, warm, wet, dry, same, different.
2. At the beginning of the walk, ask the children, "How do things feel?" Say, "Let's feel this building," or "Let's feel the back of this tree."

3. For the child who does not know the word "rough," say to her while she feels the tree, "The tree bark feels rough. Let's see if we can find something else that feels rough."
4. For the child who knows the word "rough," say, "Can you find something that feels different from this rough tree?" (Example: a smooth leaf.) Or, "Can you find something that feels the same as this rough tree?"
5. As you continue your walk, find new objects to touch, and name their textures. *Note:* For very young children, begin with two simple words such as rough and smooth, soft and hard, or wet and dry.

F. *Hidden Objects in Boxes.* Hide objects inside boxes and have children feel and describe them without seeing them. Have them match a given object by hunting for its mate in the box without seeing it. Have children match objects by size and shape, or only shape, by pulling them out of the boxes. (Some children may be able to do this only if they have felt both objects with the same hand.) Put several objects in the boxes to make the task harder; more similar objects also make the task harder.

G. *Furniture, Objects in Environment.* Feel hardness of different surfaces. Order objects according to fuzziness, roughness, squeezableness, softness, sharpness, and so on.

H. *Animals.* Children can study the human animal. Use songs to learn the names of body parts. Try to challenge the children in a movement exploration program, running, skipping, tiptoeing, jumping. Children bring animals of all kinds to class, including snakes, mice, insects. The teacher should encourage the children to observe, handle (if safe), and talk about these animals. A terrarium or aquarium in the classroom will also bring opportunities to discuss life, birth, death, eating habits, and so on, of animals. Ask questions about how the animal's movements relate to movements the children may also be able to make.

I. *Miscellaneous Activities with Classroom Equipment.*
1. Make a surprise box that the children can put their hands into but cannot see into. Put objects into it such as toys, comb, key, or geometric shapes. The child has to reach in and pick out of the box what she has been shown beforehand.
2. Have the children discriminate between hot and cold.
3. Make a number of cloth boards with one piece of fabric on each one.
4. Classify rough and smooth articles, heavy and light ones, hard and soft.
5. Use a form board and jigsaw puzzles.

6. Manipulate buttons, zippers, shoelaces, and so on. Trace name and patterns in raised outlines with yarn.

*Combined Sensory Experience*
You may wish to bake cookies with your class. Have the children identify the sounds of mixing and beating, the texture and appearance of the dough, the baking odors, and the taste of the dough. Keep one unbaked cookie to show the difference between the unbaked and baked cookies. Throughout the activity emphasize the importance of the five senses for making observations. If this activity is not practical, your children might discuss the senses they use when observing cooking at home.

## UNIT REVIEW

1. List three types of sensing and feeling.
2. Give three guidelines to use in choosing materials that have aesthetic potential.
3. List four suggestions to help children work with aesthetic materials.
4. Discuss how to involve parents in their children's aesthetic experiences.
5. List some points to cover when discussing with parents how to interpret their children's creative works.
6. List some points to consider when displaying children's creative works.
7. List six guidelines to use in talking with children about their artwork.

## ADDITIONAL READINGS

Chandler, M. *Art for Teachers of Children,* 2nd ed. Columbus, Ohio: Charles E. Merrill, 1973.

Clemens, S.C. "Art in the Classroom: Making Every Day Special." *Young Children* (Jan., 1991): 4–11.

Edwards, L.C. *Affective Development and the Creative Arts: A Process Approach to Early Childhood Education.* Columbus, Ohio.: Merrill-Macmillan, 1990.

Edwards, L.C., and M.L. Nabors. "The Creative Arts Process: What It Is and What It Is Not." *Young Children* (March, 1993): 77–81.

Eisner, E.W. *Cognition and Currriculum—A Basis for Deciding What to Teach.* New York: Longman, 1982.

Furth, Hans G. *Piaget for Teachers.* Englewood Cliffs, N.J.: Prentice-Hall, 1970.

Gardner, H. *Artful Scribbles: The Significance of Children's Drawings.* New York: Basic Books, 1980.

Kuroyanagi, T. *Totto-Chan.* Tokyo: Kodansha International, 1982.

Lasky, L., and R. Mukerji. *Art: Basic for Young Children.* Washington, D.C.: National Association for the Education of Young Children (NAEYC), 1980.

Schirrmacher, R. "Child Art." In *Toward a Theory of Psychological Development,* edited by S. Modgil and C. Modgil, 733–762. Windsor, England: National Foundation for Educational Research, 1980.

Schirrmacher, R. *Art and Creative Development for Young Children.* Albany, N.Y.: Delmar, 1993.

Smith, N.R. *Experience and Art: Teaching Children to Paint.* New York: Teachers College Press, Columbia University, 1983.

———. "The Visual Arts in Early Childhood Education: Development and the Creation of Meaning." In *Handbook of Research in Early Childhood Education,* edited by B. Spodek, 295–317. New York: The Free Press, 1982.

Sparling, J.J., and M.C. Sparling. "How to Talk to a Scribbler." *Young Children,* 28 (6) (July, 1973): 333–341.

Taunton, M. "Reflective Dialogue in the Art Classroom: Focusing on the Art Process." *Art Education,* 37 (1) (1984): 15–16.

Taunton, M., and C. Colbert. "Artistic and Aesthetic Development: Considerations for Early Childhood Educators." *Childhood Education,* 61 (1) (1984): 55–63.

Topal, C.W. *Children, Clay and Sculpture.* Worcester, Mass.: Davis Publications, 1983.

Wachowiak, F. *Emphasis Art.* New York: Harper & Row, 1985.

# SECTION 2
# Planning and Implementing Creative Activities

# U N I T   5

# Children, Teachers, and Creative Activities

## OBJECTIVES

After studying this unit, you should be able to

- ask a series of questions to better know and work with young children's developmental levels.
- discuss attention span and activity patterns as they relate to young children.
- discuss three aspects of the teacher's attitude that have an impact on children's creativity.
- explain the teacher's role as facilitator in children's creative activities.
- list the necessary steps in preparing for a creative activity.
- discuss strategies for handling transition times.

Planning creative activities always begins with the child. Each child is unique; each has his own way of being and his own way of responding to the world. The teacher must try to know what each child is like and should be aware of each child's level of development, strengths, abilities, and special personality. With this knowledge, the teacher can relate his own personality and unique skills to those of the young child. Thus, an atmosphere is created in which both adult and child remain themselves in order to help and respect each other.

Watching a child at play helps an adult understand this young person. A teacher is able to see how the child uses materials and relates to other children. Subsequent chapters will more closely relate children's developmental levels to specific activities. In many educational experiences, and especially in creative activities, the teacher's role is incidental to the creative process. This does not mean that the teacher is unimportant; the teacher is, instead, a facilitator. To *facilitate* means to help along, to guide, to provide opportunities, and to be sensitive and caring without interfering. The meaning as used here is that the teacher allows the young child to deal directly with the materials, with the teacher acting as an aide rather than a leader or judge.

Since there is divergent thinking and no single right answer in creative activities, judging is not necessary. Yet, guidance and feedback are helpful. Because creative activities are open-ended, there are no simple standards for evaluating them. The teacher's role, then, is one of encouraging, questioning, and

**FIGURE 5–1 Watching children play may give a teacher a better understanding of each child.**

experimenting. The teacher also tries to help young children to be more comfortable about not being sure of themselves and what they are doing. Young children may have difficulty handling a brush or crayon in art activities. A child may add a color to a picture that changes the picture in a way not intended. Another child may use too much glue or too little glue. These and similar difficulties can cause discomfort for the child. The teacher's patience, calmness, sense of humor, support, and knowledge of children's needs and developmental levels help greatly in these frustrating circumstances.

## CONSIDER THE CHILD

**Developmental Level.** In many early childhood books and journals, we often see the phrase "developmental level." Generally, when we speak of a child's development, we are referring to four major areas of growth: physical, social, emotional, and intellectual. These areas serve as a framework upon which we organize our knowledge and observations of children. These four areas combined make up the

individual child. When the needs of a child are met in each of these areas, in any particular activity, we can be fairly well assured that the overall growth of that child is being encouraged.

Another aspect of a child's development refers to *individual* differences. For example, two children may be exactly the same age but they may be performing at different levels in one or more of the areas of development. Both children may be within the normal range of development.

This is called individual difference. Therefore, a teacher must not only have a knowledge of developmental levels, but must also tune in to the different levels of each child's progress in the four major areas.

A child's ability is closely related to his level of development. If a teacher understands this, failure, frustration, and waste can be avoided when planning creative activities. Answers to the following questions can help adults better evaluate, understand, and work with a young child:

- What is special about the child?
- What are the child's interests?
- What are the child's strengths?
- What abilities and skills are already developed?
- What is the child's home life like?
- How does the child relate to adults?
- How does the child respond to other children?
- What are the motor skills (large and small muscle) of the child?
- How does the child express himself?
- How does the child speak?
- How are problems solved by the child?
- With what materials does the child enjoy working?
- How does the child learn?
- How does the teacher feel about the child?

The last question is most important. Helping children in creative activities is done through the relationship between adult and child. To think one knows a young child without realizing one's own feelings toward the child is a mistake. How the teacher *feels about* a child affects how the teacher *acts toward* the child. An honest understanding of how one feels toward a child must be combined with knowledge of

**FIGURE 5-2 Planning activities that suit the developmental level of each child helps them experience a sense of accomplishment when they are able to complete an activity.**

the child if the teacher is really to help the child be creative.

**Individual Creative Styles.** Children, as well as adults, have a right to their own styles of working, learning, and creating. Individual differences are to be accepted. Sometimes a teacher notices behavior in a child that may be harmful or may prevent the child from being successful or happy in an activity. At such times, a safe approach is to suggest other ways to the child that may increase the choices and show new behaviors from which to select. Some creative styles that may limit children are discussed next. For each there are also some suggestions that may expand choices and create alternatives.

*The highly active/impulsive style.* These children choose too quickly. They appear to do things without thinking or exploring. They tend to jump from one thing to another. They are in the paint, then in the clay, then in the paste. Without punishing them, place the children away from distracting materials for a start. Encourage them whenever possible to stick to activities. Ask them to stay with an activity for a period of time rather than as long as it interests them. Give reinforcement for doing so. Help children see the value of finishing things by displaying their work or honestly complimenting it. Make remarks that help them see the next step toward a goal.

*The rigid/inhibited style.* These children must have things one way. They have difficulty with flexibility and change. They may have difficulty sharing or working with other children. They are often unhappy about trying new things. They need structure and security so that they do not have to change unreasonably. They must not be forced to try new things. No one must make fun of a child for sticking with

| DEVELOPMENTAL CHARACTERISTIC | HOW TO PROVIDE FOR THE CHARACTERISTIC |
|---|---|
| 1. They are extremely active. | 1. Provide opportunities for physical activity; do not expect long periods of sitting. |
| 2. They are egocentric; full of themselves. | 2. Plan a child-centered program that builds the self-image of each child. |
| 3. They are at varying levels of physical maturity. | 3. Expect and plan for individual differences in all activities. |
| 4. They need a feeling of security. They frighten easily. | 4. Give physical and verbal assurances frequently. |
| 5. They are beginners, making many mistakes. | 5. Be patient and understanding. Environment for activities must be safe and relaxed. |
| 6. They want to feel good about themselves. | 6. Provide space and time for many successful activities; build their self-concept. |
| 7. They are easily fatigued. | 7. Alternate between active and quiet experiences and provide space for both. Provide a quiet area for the over-stimulated child. |
| 8. They are easily frustrated. | 8. Begin at the success level for each child; provide suitable materials. |
| 9. They have not fully developed visual and auditory acuity. | 9. Use large pictures and print; speak carefully and distinctly. |
| 10. They develop coordination of the large muscles before they develop fine muscle control. | 10. Use large materials. |
| 11. They are naturally curious if not threatened. | 11. Provide a rich, stimulating environment to explore in a relaxed atmosphere, with a smooth traffic pattern. |
| 12. They do not distinguish play from work; they learn through play. | 12. Include a wide variety of materials to manipulate, discover, and use to facilitate learning. |
| 13. They learn through the five senses; they must experience the concrete before the abstract. | 13. Provide a wealth of concrete material and activities. Verbalize after "doing." |
| 14. They do not always distinguish between fantasy and reality. | 14. Provide dramatic and imaginative activities to allow children to "try on" roles: experiment with and sort out ideas, develop self-concept. |

FIGURE 5–3 Providing for young children's needs in creative activities.

one activity. Trust is the most important thing here. Gentle acceptance and time are needed. If something new is to be started, it should be as simple as possible. Perhaps the teacher can work along with these children until they are comfortable. The better they know what to expect, the greater their chances of getting involved.

*The acceptance/anxious style.* For these children, adult approval is very necessary. They must have their work checked often. They constantly ask for the teacher's attention. The slightest disapproval can bring tears and withdrawal from the activity. It is usually helpful to put these children on a time schedule for looking at their work. If they know the teacher is coming every so many minutes, they can get into their work without worrying about whether the teacher is paying attention or not. Asking the children to finish a certain amount of work before requesting teacher attention is another choice.

In all creative activities, the teacher has two basic questions to ask in helping young children. The first

FIGURE 5–4 Granting freedom to explore materials in her own way aids the child's creative development.

FIGURE 5–5 It is far easier to work *with* children's specific developmental levels, adapting as necessary to meet their changing needs and interest.

is, "How is the child being creative?" The second is, "How does the child feel about it?" Sensitive answers to these questions can show the teacher what to do. Never stop asking these questions.

**Attention Span and Children's Physical Needs.** One must also consider a child's attention span and activity patterns when planning creative activities; it may mean the difference between successful creative learning experiences and creative activities that dissolve into a chaotic classroom and related behavioral problems.

*Attention span.* A general rule to remember on the length of a child's interest (attention span) is this: The *younger* the child, the *shorter* the attention span. It is not unusual for toddlers and two-year-olds to have a maximum attention span of two to three minutes on the average. Attention span gradually increases as a child gets older, and a child of six years of age can be expected to attend for an average of 15 minutes maximum. A teacher may come to expect a longer attention span than is really possible, simply because the child maintains the *appearance* of attention. More often than not, however, young children make it quite obvious when their attention span is waning—by a yawn, a turned head, fidgeting, excess

wiggling, or even by physically leaving—giving clear signs that attention to the task is "turned off."

An early childhood teacher needs to be able to read these obvious signs of lessening (or lost) attention. When they appear, it is time to move on to another topic, suggest a new activity, ask a question, do some "body stretching," or use any other change of pace to get back the child's interest. On the other hand, if a teacher has planned developmentally appropriate activities—those that are not too easy and present just enough of a challenge—even very young children will attend longer. Noting which activities keep the children's interest longer and planning for their frequent inclusion in the program are good ways to work *with* children's developmental needs and interests.

In direct contrast, many teachers feel compelled to "forge ahead" on their lesson plans despite the children's lack of interest or involvement. While it may be difficult to scrap one's lesson plans in midstream, it is even more difficult to try to "make" children pay attention when the activities just don't match the children's needs and interests. As many experienced teachers have found, it is far easier to work *with* children's specific needs and interests, adapting as necessary to meet their changing developmental needs. If, for instance, the interest at the

# THINK ABOUT IT . . .

The following personal story of a first-year teacher provides an excellent example of a developmentally inappropriate activity. Teachers can benefit greatly from reading, re-reading, and sharing this story with other teachers and parents, too!

It was time for the annual Christmas program. Because I doubled as the music teacher, my principal appointed me chair of the program committee. I was excited! This was my first year teaching, my first class of five-year-olds, and the principal wanted me to be in charge of the Christmas program. I decided that the whole school would do *The Nutcracker Suite,* complete with costumes, music, props, and all the embellishments. I was eager to impress the parents and the other teachers, so I decided to teach my kindergarten boys "Dance of the Toy Soldiers." For weeks, I taught these children perfect steps, perfect timing, turn right, stand still, curtsy, and step-and-turn. At first, the children seemed to enjoy it, but as the days and weeks went on, they started resisting going to practice or would actually beg not to have to do "the program" again. On several occasions, some complained of being tired and some were discipline problems . . . disrupting, acting out, hitting, and being generally unhappy; however, we did make it to the big night. The parents loved the performance. We all congratulated ourselves on a wonderful program. I remember talking with a first-grade teacher about how much the children loved it and what a good time they had. The truth is that the children were exhausted. They were fidgety and irritable, tired and pouty.

After a long weekend, the children returned to school and seemed to be the happy, well-adjusted children they had been before I had had this brilliant idea of performing. Young children, as you know, are so resilient. In the weeks that followed, they didn't want me to play music during center time. I would put on a Hap Palmer album, and they would argue about the right and wrong way to "march around the alphabet." Why would kindergartners turn against the sacred Hap Palmer? They didn't want to hear the music from the ballet. Just the mention of the words "dance" or "costume" or "program" would change them into terrors.

It wasn't until years later that I came to know that I had forced these little children to perform (under the name of "creative arts"—specifically, "dance") in ways that were totally inappropriate for children their age. Not only had I involved them in a developmentally inappropriate practice, I had imposed my own ideas of how to be a flower and a toy soldier without regard as to how *they* might interpret or create their own ideas, thoughts, fantasies, or forms of expression. (Edwards and Nabors, 1993, p. 78)

---

art center is waning and children choose to go elsewhere when given the choice, a teacher needs to re-evaluate the activities in that center to see if they are, in fact, a suitable match for the developmental needs of the children.

The children might be ready to move from tearing and pasting to trying out scissors, since their small motor skills are better developed from all the previous tearing experiences. Or they may be ready for colored markers as a change of pace from crayons. The point is that by changing activities and equip-

ment to keep them "matched" to their present developmental levels, you are helping the children attend to activities longer *on their own.*

Another approach to working with short attention spans is to plan *around* the expected attention span of the children in the group. For example, for a 10-minute circle time, a teacher of a group of three-year-olds would plan an average of four activities taking about two to three minutes each. This could be four different finger plays; two poems, one finger play, and one song; or two "Simon Says" games and two

**FIGURE 5–6 An observant teacher knows when a child is ready to move from tearing and pasting to trying out scissors.**

fingerplays. The point is to *work* with what you know about the group of young children with whom you are working.

Another important point about attention span is its highly individual nature. Some young children of three may attend to a very favorite activity for longer than three minutes; or on the other hand, a first grader of six may not be able to attend to a phonics lesson for five minutes! In this case, you need to consider the match between the individual child and the specific activity.

*Activity patterns.* A young child will generally attend better to new activities that are a good match to his present level of development, that is, activities that are neither too difficult nor too easy. It is also important to vary activities so that the new and the old are in an interesting as well as developmentally appropriate pattern for young children. A good activity pattern is one that begins with the familiar (or favorite), reviews some other related activities, then moves on to introduce the new and different. For example, in introducing the letter "B," the teacher may begin with a favorite song about "Buttons, the

Clown." Then he has the children identify picture cards of foods that begin with "B," and later introduces the phoneme "b" and related written words. In a similar activity pattern, a teacher of four-year-olds begins with a favorite finger play about five little monkeys, has five children act out the monkeys, and then introduces a new book he plans to read about monkeys and their babies, which is part of a new animal unit.

An activity pattern for young children also must take into account their physical characteristics. Children develop large muscle skills first and enjoy practicing these skills. They also need practice to develop small motor skills. So, activity patterns should include time for both large and small motor tasks. In the previous example, the teacher of four-year-olds might include a large motor task (jumping like monkeys) with a small motor task (a finger play). Activities planned to include both types of activities in one session also help increase attention span since they include favorite large motor activities.

Creative activities for young children must also have a good balance between active and quiet activities. All of one type activity would not be appropriate for the developmental needs of young children. A good rule to remember here is: The younger the child, the greater the tendency to become overstimulated. So, the amount of activities for toddlers and young two-year-olds should be limited to avoid overstimulation. Activities should be added as the children can handle them.

Also, in a single instructional setting (or lesson), young children of all ages need active as well as quiet activities since they have a difficult time sitting quietly for extended periods. In the previous first-grade example, the teacher could provide an appropriate balance of active–quiet activities by having children go to the board and write a "B" on it, or even walk to an object beginning with the letter "B." This way, children's physical inability to sit quietly is considered in the lesson. In the example of the teacher of four-year-olds, we see similar planning for the active (jumping) and quiet (listening to a story). By following the more active with a more quiet activity, the teacher is working with the physical needs of young children to be active and to rest after exertion.

# THIS ONE'S FOR YOU!

Young children spend an amazing amount of routine time in nonproductive ways. For example, time is wasted while teachers perform managerial classroom tasks, making last-minute preparation for an activity or waiting for children to settle down. These delays are short but, when put together, add up to a great deal of wasted time.

For teachers of older preschool children and kindergarten-aged children, the following are a few ideas that could be used to allow children to develop responsibility while helping with the classroom routine of taking attendence:

- Each child takes his own name tag (with a photo on it, if possible), from a pocket chart when entering the classroom and places it in a basket. Those names left on the chart will indicate absences. This process can be reversed after lunch, thus getting tags back in the pocket chart ready for the next morning, and at the same time making any afternoon absentees obvious.
- Have a clothesline with a marked clothespin for each child which he moves to an "I'm here" line upon arrival.
- Make an attendance chart and teach children to put a mark by their name or photo for each day of the week when present.
- Hang name tags on an "out" hook by the door. Entering children place their name tags on an "in" hook, thus making it easy to visually check who is absent or late.
- Make a cardboard school house and stick figures with the name of each child. When the child comes to school, he puts his stick figure in the school house. Sticks of absentees are easy to check.

(Jennings and Eade, 1990, p. 3).

*Transitions from group times.* Transitions from group times to the next activities can be chaotic if group times are uninteresting, too long, or too demanding. When resentment and discomfort grow, the children's desire to escape focuses not only on the situation, but also on the teacher's domination. If children in a group become wiggly and uncomfortable, you can expect a difficult transition.

Even a short, interesting group time can end with a mad exodus if precautions are not taken. Consider how the teacher in the following scenario took such precautions:

The teacher is showing slides to the children. Between shows, she suggests the children get up to jump and stretch to get their wiggles out. Just as she is about to start the projector again, Christine and three friends come running up to her. The teacher looks at Christine and asks, "What is it?"

Christine reports, "John is bothering us. He didn't get all his wiggles out."

This teacher has a delightful way of labeling the process through which young children settle down and become quiet after active play or after a period of concentration. Getting rid of wiggles on demand is seldom an easy process. Each child has her or his own way and time to achieve quiet, as this scene so nicely demonstrates. A group of young children without wiggles would be cause for concern. Such passivity might indicate a lack of interest or stimulation, or it might indicate an authoritarian regime. None of these situations is suitable for productive or creative activities.

A healthy group of children needs a patient teacher, one who can accept the various ways in which individual children respond to the request for quiet. The children who ran to report that John didn't get all of his wiggles out might be having trouble with their own wiggles!

Another suggestion for preventing chaotic transitions from group times is to share with the children at the beginning of the day the day's schedule. This way they know what will happen. Any special rules may need to be reviewed. Then as each activity begins and ends, reminders will suffice. "Do you remember what we are going to do after our story today?" "When we get ready for our walk we will need to get our coats. How can we do that without bumping into each other when we leave the circle?" When children help with the plans and participate in setting the limits, they are more apt to understand, to remember, and to be willing to help enforce the rules. Don't forget to give positive reinforcement when things go well, not just reminders when someone fails to manage. However, positive reinforcement should not become so automatic or mechanical that children begin to doubt its sincerity. Some genuine response— a smile, pat, or word—is always more effective than a stock phrase.

*Transitions to free choice times.*   A key strategy for avoiding mad dashes at the beginning of free choice times is the assurance that children will have ample time for their favorite activities. If free choice time is too short or few activities are interesting, some children will run to grab their chosen activity. Others will flit about aimlessly and not bother to start anything because they know they will have to stop soon. It is important to have enough interesting things to do and to use a system that allows children to select a second activity if the first is not satisfactory. Children who are bored or frustrated during free choice time are rarely cooperative when it is time to clean up. A free choice time that is too long, on the other hand, will give you tired children who are no longer constructively busy and are ready to misbehave. It takes flexibility and a good eye for the quality of work and play to know the right amount of time for free play.

*Transitions to group times: back together.*   Moving into a group time is often facilitated by a little ad-

vance publicity. It builds interest to have something in a bag and as the children ask about it, say, "I'll show you at group time." Children will look forward to group times in which they have a chance to show their block building or artwork or the book they have drawn and stapled. The morning planning time can give advance notice of exciting things to come, and reminders can keep interest alive throughout the day.

From the first arrival at group time, there should be a teacher or classroom assistant there to be with the children. Trying to control behavior at a distance is always hazardous and never more so than during a transition.

Sometimes teachers let children look at books until all are ready for storytime or music. When the last things are put away at cleanup time, the teacher walks over to the rug and says, "Time to collect the books." Some children have just arrived and have opened the cover of their favorite storybook. Some children are in the middle of reading their favorite book. Some children may resist and some might cooperate, but they will all be left with the feeling that the teacher does not value books except as a tool to keep them quiet.

You might try this different approach: When all the children are seated and looking at books, sit down with the children. You may share books with some of the children or just wait for a reasonable period of time. Then you may give a warning that it will soon be time to put the books away. As children finish, collect their books and allow others to finish while you begin the discussion or possibly a fingerplay to occupy those who are through. When most books have been collected, then you may have your group activity. This process respects children and their interest in books.

## Children's Social-Emotional Needs
*Expressing emotions.*   Creative activities are usually unstructured, allowing for individual freedom and expression. Deep feelings or strong emotions often occur when young children are involved. The important job that the teacher has at such times is to neither stop nor encourage the child's feelings, but to help the child find acceptable ways to express

these feelings. Flexibility and a broad range of available creative activities facilitate this.

If given the chance, free from outside judgment, children usually let the materials and their fantasies take care of the emotions they are feeling. They may pound clay, throw a puppet, or crumple paper to vent anger. Or they may kiss a puppet, stroke the clay figure, or gently paint on paper to show affection. In this way, the children can let go of the feeling when it occurs. They can then go on to create and involve themselves in other productive activities.

If one child interferes with other children when expressing emotions, the other children's responses may be enough to help the child stop and adjust. If the child still cannot stop or adjust, then the teacher may have to help out. The teacher should respect the child's feelings, but show that there are limits to what the child can do. In no way does this mean punishment. It means helping a child to know limits (setting them when necessary), and then helping the child to channel emotions in a more positive direction.

Such behavior problems demand creative responses from the teacher. A disciplinary situation usually requires divergent thinking on the part of the adult. Some guidelines for directing young children's behavior are presented in Figure 5–7.

It is important that young children learn that there is nothing wrong with having personal feelings. It is the expression of these feelings that may cause problems. If children think that feelings are bad or wrong and must not be felt, they are likely to hurt themselves emotionally. They may develop defenses that stop them from feeling good about themselves, being open to others, and trusting themselves or others. A young child should learn that the *expression* of some feelings can hurt others and must understand that it is the means of expression and not the feeling itself that may be harmful. Thus, children learn they have freedom to feel and to accept feelings as part of themselves. They also learn that they do not have freedom to express feelings in any manner without regard for others.

To help you evaluate your own ability to relate to the feelings of young children, consider the self-evaluation checklist presented in Figure 5–9.

1. Establish limits with the children. State rules in positive terms. Involve the children in making rules.
2. Use a signal for attention–bell, piano, flicker of lights, etc.
3. Finger plays can be effective to get attention in a group situation.
4. Use a well-modulated voice. Never try to out-shout a group.
5. Give advance notice when changing activities so children can finish what they are doing; avoid abrupt changes.
6. Keep an eye on all ongoing activities. Do not become totally involved with one activity or child, unless it is a total group activity.
7. Plan with children so they know what to expect.
8. Give the necessary directions for an activity, then stop; check for understanding; be specific and don't talk too long.
9. Follow their interests. (If a bulldozer is outside your window, drop your plans and go watch it.)
10. Be firm, consistent; set clear, reasonable expectations.
11. Have reasonable, predictable consequences. (When a child throws blocks, he is removed from that area.) Involve the children in rule-making.
12. Provide a cleanup system. (Have attractive containers, color-coded items for correct location.)
13. Involve the children in periodic reflection on and evaluation of their activities.
14. Use positive reinforcement when children follow directions, attend to signals, and participate in activities, cleanup, etc.

**FIGURE 5–7 Tips on guiding young children's behavior in creative activities.**

*Competition.* Young children naturally compare their work to others and seek their teacher's approval. However, they do not naturally try to be better than one another, make fun of another child's work, or try to be the best at what they do. This is learned. It may be learned from parents, brothers

**FIGURE 5–8 While playing with other children, a child learns respect for the feelings of others.**

and sisters, or other adults and children. It is not to be learned from their teacher.

At such a young age, creative growth is not helped in a competitive atmosphere where to win or gain approval, a child must learn to meet another person's standards. At this age, children are beginning to learn about themselves. It is harmful for a four- to five-year-old to try to please others in activities meant for exploring and wonderment. It hinders self-growth. It puts pressure where pleasure should exist. Instead of complete involvement in the materials and task, children manipulate the task to gain something outside of it. Discovery is sacrificed for recognition; and insight, for approval. This is too great a cost for a young child.

When confronted with competitive striving in a young child, the teacher is to respect this. Not only is it learned behavior, but it may be a chosen value of the child's parents. Teachers do not have the right to change parents' values in children without the parents' permission. But teachers do have a right to their own values. They do not have to reinforce competition in young children. They can ask the children for their own judgments as well as refer them back to their parents for approval. Children at this age can also grasp the idea that they and their creative works are unique, and therefore it is not fair to compare with others without some qualification.

Put a check in front of all the statements that apply to your working with young children's feelings:

_____   1. Respect the feelings of a child.
_____   2. Do not reject a child.
_____   3. Do not criticize or reprimand a child in front of others.
_____   4. Use a positive approach—encourage at all times.
_____   5. Keep anecdotal records of significant and specific acts. Be objective.
_____   6. Always have a stimulating classroom environment: books, bulletin boards, centers of interest, tools of interest, equipment, and materials.
_____   7. Don't make a crisis of everything.
_____   8. Keep my voice low, clear, and firm. Don't shout or raise my voice.
_____   9. Am fair, unemotional, and calm.
_____  10. Avoid being placed on the "defensive"—don't argue with children.
_____  11. Discuss actions, not personalities.
_____  12. Believe that punishment is not always the answer.
_____  13. Don't show negative feelings toward a child. I try to always let him know that I like him.
_____  14. Don't make quick judgments or diagnoses.
_____  15. Don't accuse or threaten, because I might have to carry out something that is impossible or impractical.
_____  16. Use the principal or center director as a resource person. Make no major decisions without his guidance, suggestion, and approval.
_____  17. Request outside resource help. Don't "do it alone."
_____  18. Listen more than I talk.

**FIGURE 5–9 Self-evaluation checklist: Dealing with the feelings of young children.**

## CONSIDER THE TEACHER/CAREGIVER

**Attitude.** The basic agent for helping the teacher in the role of facilitator in creative activities with young children is attitude. Change a teacher's attitude, and the whole teacher is changed. Some teacher attitudes and ideas that help in facilitating creative behavior in young children are the following:

*Tolerate small mistakes.* When children do not have to worry about being perfect, they have more energy to be creative.

*Avoid telling the child the best way to do things.* To tell a child the best way implies, first, that the teacher knows it; second, that the child does not know it; and third, that the child has to ask the teacher in order to know the next time.

*Be concerned about children doing—not about the final product.* In creative activities, young children are in a process—playing, drawing, painting, building. Although they are interested in mastering tasks and producing things of which they are proud, they are not like adults. The final product may not be as important as experimenting, as using their minds and senses while doing it. That is why young children often build a complex structure with blocks and then take great joy in knocking it over. They want to see what happens!

*Resist the temptation to always have quiet and order.* Silence may not be the spirit of joy. Cleanliness may not be the companion of discovery. Timing and flexibility are all important in these matters. Only one rule is necessary: "When learning stops and respect for other people is lost, then order and direction must come."

*Get involved.* The teacher who is painting, drawing, and working beside the children, or accompanying them on a field trip or a walk, is a companion and friend. To the children, the activity must be worth doing if the teacher is doing it too. This helps motivation and is a legitimate entry into the chil-

**FIGURE 5–10 Teachers encourage creativity by letting children discover their own best way of doing something.**

dren's world. Besides, it's fun! Be careful, however, not to cause the children to copy what you are doing. Be sure to "slip away" before this happens.

## STRATEGIES FOR SUCCESS

An early childhood environment should provide many opportunities for children to express their creativity. Besides providing an environment that encourages self-directed creative activities, teachers should also plan specific activities for young children, activities designed not only to provide the children with opportunities for creative expression, but also to promote their growth in developmental skills. Developing large and small motor skills, increasing vocabulary, fostering self-help skills (and thus, a positive self-image), and reinforcing sharing experiences are just a few of the many ways that children benefit from creative activities. (All of these developmental skills are covered in greater detail in subsequent units.)

Teachers plan creative activities with the children's needs and interests in mind. In addition to assessing whether the planned activity is developmentally appropriate for a particular group of children, there

## FRAGILE! SPEAK TO WITH CARE

The way a teacher speaks to and with a young child can mean the difference between the child's positive feelings of self and those not-so-positive feelings. The following suggestions may be helpful to you as you work with young children, helping them grow, as you cherish their uniqueness.

1. Before speaking to children, get their attention. Putting your hand on a child's shoulder or speaking the child's name helps. Always get on the child's eye level.
2. The younger the child, the simpler your statement should be.
3. Act as if you expect your words to be heeded. Young children are influenced by the confidence in the adult's tone and action.
4. Give children time to respond—their reaction time is slower than yours. Try not to answer your own questions!
5. Tell children what they can do rather than what they cannot do. Use positive rather than negative suggestions or statements.
6. Give only as much help as is needed, and give simple directions. Use manual guidance to aid verbal suggestions with young children.
7. Use encouraging rather than discouraging statements: "You can do it," not "Is it too hard?"
8. Use specific rather than general statements: "You need to put on your socks; now your shoes;" not, "Put on your clothes."
9. Use pleasant requests rather than scolding: "You will need to pick up your materials now"; not, "Get those things picked up."
10. Use substitute suggestions rather than negative comments: "Use that pencil from the drawer over there"; not, "Don't use that."
11. Give a choice between two things when possible. You may say, "Will you wash your face, or shall I help you?" This means the child will be washed in any case. Never give a choice where there is none, such as, "Do you want to wash?" when washing is necessary. Try not to say, "Would you like to _____?" if you do not intend to abide by the child's choice.
12. Remember to show disapproval in what the child *does* when necessary, but never disapproval of the *child.* You can say, "You are a good climber, but you will need to climb on the jungle gym. This roof is not solid enough."
13. Working *with* a child—trying to tell or show the child how to do it alone—is better for learning than doing it *for* the child.
14. Keep your promises to children. For example, if you say you will let someone have a turn later, be sure to offer that turn as soon as you can, even though the child may have found another activity. Let the child decide whether to leave the present activity to take a turn.
15. Encourage children to use language (to replace physical force, crying, whining, etc.) to communicate their problems, needs, and wishes.
16. Children learn through example. Many things, such as manners, are "caught," not always necessarily "taught."

**FIGURE 5–11 An early childhood environment should provide materials that encourage self-directed creative activities.**

are some general guidelines to follow that will help ensure the success of these activities.

**Preparation.** Often, teachers attempt a creative activity that they have not experienced before. They may have read about it in a book, heard about it from a friend, or seen it at a workshop. They try it because they feel it should work and the children should gain something from it. Often it does succeed, but sometimes it does not. The unfortunate part is that when it does not, the teacher may not know whether it was because of the activity itself, or the way it was prepared for and offered. For any activity, especially for a first-time experience, the following suggestions may be helpful:

*Try the activity before presenting it to the children.* (In other words, "try it, you might not like it.") Do this physically, if possible, or else mentally. Sometimes things sound better than they really are. The children should experiment, not be experimented on.

*Make sure all necessary physical equipment is present.* Too few scissors, paints without brushes, and paper without paste can cause a great deal of frustration.

*Read the directions completely.* Any creative activity should have the full chance to succeed. Ignorance about how to do something lessens the opportunity for success.

*Modify the activity, if necessary, to meet the developmental needs of the children.* Few activities are right for all cultures, all situations, or every type of child. All teachers must be sensitive to this.

*Arrange the parts of the activity for easy distribution.* When getting started is more effort than the activity itself, motivation suffers.

*In as little time as possible, explain the activity so that the children know how to begin and proceed.* For this part, rules are not necessary, but understanding is.

*After the children have started, circulate among them.* Offer suggestions where helpful, and answer questions as needed. Try to let the children answer their own questions as well as solve their own problems. The teacher's role remains that of a facilitator.

**Presentation of Creative Activities.** The success of any creative activity is influenced by how it is presented, which in turn is affected by how prepared the teacher is for guiding the children in the activity. In planning for each activity, the teacher should

- identify goals for the activity.
- identify possible learnings from the activity.
- list the materials necessary for the activity.
- determine how to set up the activity.
- decide how to stimulate the children and how to keep their interest alive.
- anticipate questions the children might ask.
- plan ways to evaluate the activity.
- consider follow-up activities.
- consider cleanup time and requirements.

A broad range of creative activities should be included each week. This gives children a variety of choices to suit their many interests. Not only should each curriculum area be highlighted, but certain types of behavior should also be considered. Dra-

**FIGURE 5–12 A young child is always learning new ways to approach materials. Always allow time for children to explore new media and repeat desirable activities.**

matic play, creative movement, singing, outdoor activities, and small group projects should all take place within each week.

Do not move too fast when presenting new ideas or activities for young children. They need time to create and explore with new materials. For the very young child, even more time may be needed. Activities should be repeated so that the children learn new ways of approaching the material and expand their understanding through repetition.

Proper sequencing should be given close attention. Activities should build upon each other. For example, some children may want to taste, feel, and smell an apple before they draw or paint one. Once a child is involved in a creative activity, a few words of encouragement may be all that is needed to keep the child interested. It is always wise to avoid judging a child's work. One can encourage without passing judgment. It is useful to watch for children who are having problems. A little help may be needed to solve

a small problem. Children need enough time to finish an activity. Be sure children are not stopped just when they are beginning to have fun.

At the end of each day, the teacher evaluates the day's activities. Ideas for the next day can be revised or created based on what then appears best. What were the successes of the day? How interested were the children in what they were doing? What did their conversation and play indicate? What does the teacher feel like doing? The key words are *question, think, feel, decide.* A person who works with young children must always be open to new information and feedback.

**Completing a Creative Activity.** The importance of evaluation has already been mentioned. Before the teacher has time to evaluate, however, some other things may be required.

Finishing an activity involves cleanup. Young children can be very helpful with this. It is important to remember that they must learn this behavior. They acquire good habits if the teacher takes time to teach them and serves as a model to them. Reinforcement of the right habits is necessary. Young children usually want to help out and enjoy feeling needed.

A place to start is to encourage the children to be as tidy as possible. This can be done by having towels handy for spills and always keeping cleaning materials nearby. It should be made as easy as possible for the children to be neat and orderly. For example, if they are to take care of their own possessions such as paints, smocks, and paste, then hooks and shelves must be located near where they work. Children can put away materials when they clearly understand where the materials belong.

The teacher may ask different children to be responsible for taking care of items such as the wastebasket and art supplies. This is done on a rotating basis to guarantee fairness. Children think of this as a privilege if the teacher responds with enthusiasm and gratitude for the help. Some confusion is to be expected and must be accepted until a routine is established.

Children need at least ten minutes' notice of the approach of cleanup time, with reminders after five and nine minutes. Teachers can circulate around the room giving quiet notice, which seems more effective than flicking lights or making other signals.

It may seem reasonable to insist that the children who are involved in an activity are the ones who must clean it up, but the result of this may be an early flight from the block corner by those whose grand building used all 500 blocks. Some cleanup tasks are so time-consuming that they may cause children to decide never to play in that area again. These tasks need help from adults and from other children (who will themselves be helped when they play in that area another day). Since blocks take a long time to organize on the shelves, it may take a 15-minute advance warning to get them all put away at the same time that the rest of cleanup chores are completed. Or you may need to allow some adults and children to finish that task after the next activity has begun, waiting to begin anything particularly fascinating until they are finished. The next activity after cleanup should be interesting to the children and anticipated with enthusiasm, or you will have lots of dawdling with the cleanup process!

Completing an activity is important to young children. They finish something with a sense of accomplishment. The teacher has to allow time for individual differences in finishing creative activities. All children cannot be expected to work at the same rate. Sometimes it is fun to leave something purposely undone until the next day. The children are usually excited to return and finish their efforts.

## SUMMARY

Planning creative activities for young children begins with an awareness of the young child. There are many questions to ask about the child, the child's environment, and the teacher's own feelings in order to plan properly. The teacher's plans need to take into consideration: (1) the children's needs and interests; (2) their developmental levels; and (3) the available materials and resources.

Young children have their own individual styles of working, learning, and creating. Three main styles are: (1) the active/impulsive style; (2) the rigid/inhibited style, and (3) the acceptance/anxious style.

Other considerations in planning creative activities are children's attention spans and activity patterns. A teacher should have reasonable expectations of how long young children can be attentive in certain activities and should know how to supervise these activities so that there is a good balance between active and quiet ones.

Although young children naturally compare their work with other children, competition is not necessary or helpful in creative activities. It is important that young children learn that personal feelings are normal and acceptable. Sometimes the expression of these feelings may cause problems and, therefore, may need modification. Sensitive answers to the questions, "How is the child being creative?" and "How does the child feel about it?" can help guide the teacher in facilitating creative behavior.

Teachers also need to consider their own needs, interests, skills, and abilities when planning activities for young children. They must work within the limits of their own skills, knowledge, and available resources. Their attitude is also crucial to the success of any creative activity.

In creative activities, the teacher's role is to facilitate creative expression. This generally means having a knowledge of children's developmental levels and skills, a sensitive and caring attitude toward them, and a willingness to help them interact with materials. It means guidance without interference or judgment.

To ensure the success of creative activities, careful planning is essential. Also, attention and thought must be given to the manner in which the activity is to be presented, the children's interest sustained, and the activity completed. Once the creative activity is finished, its success should be evaluated in terms of individual and program goals.

# LEARNING ACTIVITIES

A. Check the list of attitudes found in this unit that facilitate creative behavior in young children.
1. Choose one example of each from your personal life in which you demonstrate the attitude.
2. Decide whether this is an attitude you already possess or one that you need to work on in order to improve.
3. For those attitudes that need improvement, consider how you plan to go about doing this.
B. There are strategies that teachers use to create a good climate for creative activities. There are other factors that may cause a child's creativity to be hindered by a teacher.
1. Make a list of five do's and don't's for creative activities in the early childgood setting.
2. If possible, compare and discuss your list with those of your classmates.
3. Observe a head teacher who is supervising a creative activity in an early childhood classroom. What does he or she do to facilitate the children's expression of creativity?

# UNIT REVIEW

1. Discuss the ways you can plan activities to match a child's attention span.
2. List at least two ways you can plan activities to match the young child's activity level.
3. List ten important questions that should be asked in order to better know and work with young children.
4. With regard to young children, discuss the difference between having feelings and expressing feelings.
5. Define *facilitator* as it applies to the teacher involved in creative activities for children.
6. List the necessary steps in preparing for a creative activity.
7. Discuss strategies for handling transition times.
8. Discuss the term developmental level.

# ADDITIONAL READINGS

Alger, H.A. "Transitions: Alternative to Manipulative Management Techniques." *Young Children* (Sept., 1984): 16–25.

Edwards, L.C., and M.L. Nabors. "The Creative Arts Process: What It Is and What It Is Not." *Young Children* (March, 1993): 77–81.

Faber, A. and E. Mazlish. *How to Talk So Kids Will Listen and Listen So Kids Will Talk*. New York: Avon Books, 1980.

Jennings, C. and G. Eade. "Managing Classroom Routines." Association for Childhood Education International. *Early Childhood Division Newsletter* (May, 1990): 3–4.

Zavitkovsky, D. *Listen to the Children*. Washington, D.C.: NAEYC, 1985.

# U N I T   6

# Creative Environments

**OBJECTIVES**

After studying this unit, you should be able to
- describe an appropriate physical environment for creative activities for young children.
- discuss the main considerations involved in setting up activity centers.
- list and describe interest centers that encourage children's creativity and developing skills.
- list six factors that are important when selecting equipment to be used in creative activities for young children.
- list five unsafe conditions to be avoided in the early childhood environment.

The setting in which a creative activity takes place is very important. Young children are very aware of mood and environment. A dark room or tight space can have much more of an effect on them than a rainy day. The arrangement of space and the type of equipment provided can also have a dramatic impact on a child's creative experiences.

## THE PHYSICAL FACILITY: GENERAL GUIDELINES

A positive physical environment is a key to the success of the creative activities that take place within it. Some basic guidelines to consider when evaluating the early childhood facility are the following:

- The shape of the room. A rectangular room seems to lend itself more readily to activities than a square one. L-shaped rooms are difficult to supervise with young children.
- Satisfactory acoustics help communication. Therefore, curtains and carpets should be used to help eliminate noise, as well as add beauty and comfort.
- Wall colors should be selected that add to the light available in the room. Yellow and other light colors are good. It is best if walls are washable at least as high as children can reach.
- Floors should be sanitary, easily cleaned, suited to hard wear and comfortable for children to sit on

and should deaden sound. Some suitable floor coverings are linoleum, carpets, and rubber or plastic tiles. A carpeted section of the floor makes possible a comfortable arrangement for group activities without the need for chairs.

- Proper heat, light, and ventilation are important. Remember that children live closer to the floor than do adults, and that warm air rises and is replaced by cooler air. It may be helpful to install a thermostat or thermometer at their level so you can be aware of the temperatures they are experiencing. However, it must also be remembered that children are more active than adults and that they may not feel cool at temperatures that may be uncomfortable for you.
- Running water and sinks are a must for preparing and cleaning up after some creative activities. They should be near the area where they are needed.
- Easy-to-reach storage space for equipment that is in daily use should be provided so that children learn to put their things away.
- Chairs should be light enough for the children to handle and move without too much noise. Since the chairs are used at tables for creative activities, the kind without arms should be used.
- There should be some tables that accommodate from four to six children for group activities. Rectangular tables are better for art activities involving large sheets of paper. Some small tables designed

to be used singly or in combinations are quite versatile. Tables with washable surfaces such as formica are best.

- Shelves should be low and open so that children have a chance to see, touch, and choose materials independently. Sliding doors are preferred for shelves that have to be closed. Shelves that are sturdy, but easy to move, are more flexible in room arrangement and help create interest centers. Bulletin board or peg board backing provides display areas for creative works.

**Safety Factors.** Special consideration should be given the safety of the physical environment. Some important safety checks are the following:

- Be sure that all low window areas are safe.
- Beware of and remove toxic, lead-based paints, and poisonous plants, particularly berry-producing plants.
- Cover hot pipes and radiators. Insert protective coverings over all electrical outlets. A pronged cover, available at hardware and electrical supply stores, is made especially for this purpose.
- Install door knob locks that only adults can use in areas prohibited to young children. These are available at hardware stores. Also, install high knobs on cabinets within prohibited areas.
- Check the facility to make sure that there are no hooks, hangers, or other sharp objects that protrude, especially at child's level.
- Make sure that there are adequate exits provided in the event of a fire or other emergency.
- Check to see that fire exits, fire alarms, smoke detectors, and fire extinguishers are in working order and are placed appropriately in the classroom.

## ARRANGEMENT OF SPACE AND EQUIPMENT

The arrangement of the space within an early childhood facility also has an effect on the safety and success of the creative activities for which it is used. Adults need to consider a number of factors in planning for the arrangement of equipment.

**Children's Age and Developmental Levels.** The age and developmental levels of the children using a room dictate how that room should be arranged. A group of two- and three-year-olds, for example, would do quite nicely in a simple, small, enclosed space. At this age, children may be overwhelmed by too large a space or too much equipment in it. Yet, as their large motor skills are developing rapidly, the space should be big enough for active, large motor activities. Here is where balance is very important. Also, as coordination is not well developed yet, space should be as uncluttered as possible since children aged two to three years fall, stumble, and slip quite a bit.

In contrast, a five-year-old has better coordination due to a more centralized center of gravity and doesn't fall as frequently as a two- or three-year-old. More equipment in a room won't present a space or safety problem for the five-year-old. Yet the space still needs to be large enough to allow for five-year-olds to run, jump, climb, and pretend. In organizing space for young children, then, there should be enough open space for the children to move around safely and comfortably at their level of physical coordination, and to work together cooperatively and freely. Approximately 40 to 60 square feet per preschool child is recommended.

**FIGURE 6–1 Children need space for creative activities.**

**Supervision.** Another consideration in arranging space for young children is the supervision of that space. Open play spaces should not be so large that it becomes difficult to supervise the children properly. A common technique is to divide the space up into interest centers (or activity areas) with limited numbers allowed at each center. When breaking up the space in such a way as to facilitate supervision, using low, movable barriers, such as child-level bulletin boards, bookshelves, or room dividers, provides a clear view of the area and permits a more flexible use of the space itself.

**Flexibility.** Space should be kept as open and flexible as possible so it can be adjusted as the children grow, develop, and change in their needs. Your early childhood program certainly shouldn't look the same on the last day of the year as it did on the first day of the year! The early childhood environment must reflect the young children in it—changing and developing along with them. As the children develop intellectually, socially, and physically, space must be adjusted to fit these changes. In response to children's growing ability to deal with more concepts, additional equipment, supplies, and interest centers need to be incorporated in the room. Conversely, materials, equipment, and even whole centers need to be removed to storage when the children have outgrown them. In a flexible environment, space can easily be rearranged to fit these new centers without major renovations. For instance, an inexpensive child-sized room divider for a center area could be a cardboard, folding, pattern-cutting board displaying children's art on both sides. With this and other movable devices, a different environment can be made with a few minor adjustments.

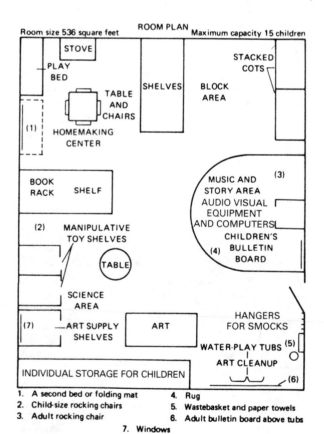

Room size 536 square feet    ROOM PLAN    Maximum capacity 15 children

1. A second bed or folding mat
2. Child-size rocking chairs
3. Adult rocking chair
4. Rug
5. Wastebasket and paper towels
6. Adult bulletin board above tubs
7. Windows

**FIGURE 6–2 Sample classroom arrangement using interest centers.**

**FIGURE 6–3 An early childhood program organized around activity centers encourages creativity by giving children many opportunities to play, experiment, and discover.**

**FIGURE 6–4 Ice cream cartons bolted together make an unusual yet practical wall storage unit.**

**FIGURE 6–5 Plastic milk crates provide an inexpensive and practical storage area.**

**Traffic Flow.** Even when increasing the activity options in a room, space should be as free as possible to allow the traffic to flow between activities. For example, the traffic flow should not interfere with activities that require concentration. A language arts/reading or book corner is more likely to be used by children if it is away from the noise of people coming and going. The block corner, too, will be used more often if it is planned for a space that is free from interruption.

The placement of doors and gates, too, determines some of the traffic patterns; but placement of equipment within the room also determines how teachers and children move from one place to another. For example, large-wheel toys near a doorway would affect traffic flow by blocking or impeding direct access to the room. In a similar way, placement of an art corner across the room from a sink would increase cross-room traffic.

Most important, the flow of traffic should be planned so that the children's safety is assured. An area near the tire swings, for example, should not be used for large-wheel toys. Similarly, climbing equipment should be in a safe, grassy spot or other soft-surfaced space to ensure its safe use.

**Personal Space.** In the early childhood years, children are not only growing physically and intellectually, but are developing their sense of self. For this reason, it is very important to plan space in such a way that each child has a place of her own. Having a place of one's own to keep personal belongings, extra clothes, artwork, and notes to take home helps encourage a child's developing sense of self. A snapshot of the child used to label her personal space is a good way, too, of assisting the growth of her sense of self. A snapshot removes all doubt that the place is "private property" even before a child has learned to recognize her name. Each child needs to be able to count on having a place belonging only to her.

It is only by firmly establishing an understanding of ownership that a young child learns about sharing. Having a "cubby" of one's own helps the child learn about possession and care of self, which are both basic to a growing sense of independence.

If there is not enough space for individual cubbies, labeled dishpans, clear plastic shoeboxes, large round ice-cream containers, or even plastic milk crates can be used. To further encourage the importance of these personal spaces, children can paint or color these containers with their own designs. Making personal space important recognizes each child's personal needs. This says to the child, "You are important." And we know young children need to know that others feel they are important before they feel it themselves.

In developing a positive self-concept, young children also need privacy. Besides respecting a child's private cubby, the space in a center should be arranged so that there are quiet places to be alone. Especially as a child grows intellectually, she needs space and time to reflect and think. Quiet places to be alone encourage this reflection where a child can enjoy her own thoughts, her own mental perceptions of the world.

## ACTIVITY/INTEREST CENTERS

One approach to fostering creative activities and use of materials is to provide as part of the environment *activity,* or *interest, centers* and to identify activities and materials for each, based on the group of children in the class. Learning centers have long been an integral part of the educational scene. Their roots can be found in the work of educators like Pestalozzi, who believed that children learn through direct interaction with other children and their environment; Dewey with his emphasis on learning through doing and the "organic connection be-

**FIGURE 6–6 Activity centers with materials in good condition, neatly arranged, and placed far apart on open shelves, tell a child that materials are valued and important enough to be well cared for.**

tween education and personal experience" (Dewey, 1966, p. 25); and Montessori, with her deep conviction that the young child learns through tasks and carefully prepared teaching materials. The *open education* movement in the 1960s and early 1970s was another step toward opening the schoolroom and the schedule to make room for educational projects and learning activities meaningful to children. This was in contrast to giving them, in a fixed sequence, printed material already prepared *for* them (Myers and Maurer, 1987).

An early childhood program organized around activity centers encourages creativity by giving children many opportunities to play, experiment, and discover as they engage in activities that help them with problem-solving, learning basic skills, and understanding new concepts. Activity centers are carefully designed areas that contain a variety of learning activities and materials. In activity centers, young children can manipulate objects, engage in conversation and role-playing, and learn at their own levels and at their own pace. These centers let children develop independent learning skills because of the self-directing and self-correcting nature of many activity center materials.

For the young child, most educators and experts recommend the following interest centers:

*Art area.* A place for painting, collage-making, cutting, pasting, chalking; it should be located near water and light.

*Housekeeping center.* A place for acting out familiar home scenes with pots, pans, and dishes.

*Block-building area.* A place where children can create with both large and small blocks, tinker toys, logs.

*Manipulative area.* A place to enhance motor skills, eye-hand coordination, and mental, language, and social skills through the use of play materials such as toys, climbing structures, and games.

*Science center.* A place to learn about nature. Here, children can display what they find at home or

**FIGURE 6–7 Art activities work best near a source of water for clean-up, as do cooking and science activities.**

on nature walks, for example. It is a place to explore and ask questions.

*Music center.* A place for listening to records, singing, creating dance, and playing musical instruments.

*Books and quiet area.* A place to be alone quiet in one's thoughts, and to explore the world in books.

*Sand and water play area.* A place to learn through sensory experiences with sand and water, such as floating and sinking experiments; weighing, measuring, and comparing quantities; building boats; drawing letter shapes and numbers in the sand; experimenting with food coloring and water; making buildings in the sand.

*The social studies center: people and places.* This could be a special area to study about families, different cultures, ethnic groups, community awareness, specific occupations, and lifestyles.

*Woodworking center.* An area that provides the opportunity to develop large and small muscles by working with wood in sanding, gluing, fastening, drilling, and sawing.

*Outdoor play area.* A natural learning environment where activities from indoor learning areas can be extended.

Appendix B lists materials for each of these centers. Figure 6–8 shows how these interest areas are related to a young child's developing skills.

A teacher can certainly add other interest centers to this list. The sample room arrangement in Figure 6–2 shows how interest centers can be designed. Again, it is a suggestion, to be adjusted to the needs of the children.

**Decisions About Activity Areas: Where and When.** Before setting up activity centers, you have to make a number of decisions about which centers to use, when to use them, and where they can best be placed in the classroom. Some of the questions you must address include the following:

- Will centers be offered all day, every day; part of the day; or only some days of the week? The ideal choice is to offer activity centers for a large block or blocks of time every day at approximately the same time. This lets children plan ahead, make choices, and get involved in activities. It allows teachers initially to structure learning centers throughout the room and gradually add centers, remove centers, or modify centers during the year. The centers themselves do not often change; the activities available in the centers will.
- What room features offer potential settings for centers? You can make creative use of walls, floor, chalkboards, tables, and nooks and crannies.
- Should there be limits on the number of children using any specific center? If so, how will this be determined, and how will children know what the limits are? Activity centers need to be planned so children can work individually or in small groups of various numbers. The size of a small group of children at any center is determined by the amount of materials available, the purpose of the center,

| DEVELOPING SKILL(S) | ACTIVITY AREA(S) |
|---|---|
| 1. Counting | 1. Math, sand, blocks, water, housekeeping |
| 2. Developing vocabulary | 2. All areas |
| 3. Developing spatial ideas | 3. Physical education, language arts, music, blocks |
| 4. Observing, experimenting, drawing conclusions | 4. Math, water, science, art, sand |
| 5. Developing visual memory and discrimination; developing auditory memory and hearing discrimination | 5. All areas |
| 6. Comparing, graphing, charting, matching, making categories | 6. Math, sand, language arts, science, water, blocks |
| 7. Developing self-expression, sequence, memory, creativity, listening skills | 7. Language arts, music, art, physical education, book area |
| 8. Fine muscle control | 8. Writing area, math, language arts, art, finger plays, pegboards |
| 9. Large muscle control | 9. Blocks, art, water, sand, physical education, movement activities |
| 10. Positive self-concept | 10. All areas |

**FIGURE 6–8 Activity areas for a child's developing skills.**

physical space considerations, and the need to avoid overstimulating confusion. Signs with stick figures and numbers can indicate the number of children who can use a specific center.

- What kinds of centers will provide a workable balance in terms of content? This will depend on the characteristics of the children and staff.
- How free should movement in and out of the centers be? Ideally, children should move at their own pace, guided by the teacher. This allows for more individualization within the program.
- How will children know what to do in each center? Some centers will require more direction than others. You may want to use pictures or symbols for routine directions (hands with a faucet of running water to remind children to wash; aprons on pegs to facilitate art and cooking cleanup without having to mention it).
- Each time a new center is added or a center is modified, you will need to help children understand the rules related to that specific center.

(Myers and Maurer, 1987)

**Placement of Activity Areas.** When organizing a room for young children's use, it is helpful to look at those features of the environment that cannot be changed, i.e., where the sink or source of water is, where doorways enter the room, where light shines in from windows, which areas of the room are dark and more secluded, etc. Where centers are placed in the room is important to ensure a smooth flow of traffic through the room as the children move from one activity area to another. It is also important to place compatible activity areas side by side and to place areas that are potentially disturbing to one another far apart. The book corner should be a quiet area and, therefore, would not go well next to the block or music area. Blocks might go well near housekeeping if the teacher wants the dramatic play possibilities to span both areas. Small cars and wheel toys can be placed nearby, too, to further enrich block play. Art activities go well near the source of water for cleanup, as do cooking and science activities.

Floor surfaces should also be taken into consideration when activity centers are planned so that messy

FIGURE 6–9 In organizing areas for young children, there must be enough open space for children to move around in safely and comfortably at their level of physical development.

FIGURE 6–10 Floors should be sanitary, easily cleaned, suited for hard wear, and comfortable for children to sit on.

activities are conducted in areas with washable floor surfaces. If young children are expected to live all day on a rug-covered floor, it is unrealistic to expect the rug to remain clean, even if it is washable. Pieces of masonite work well as a hard, washable floor covering on top of rug areas where children will be eating or doing artwork.

**Condition and Organization of Materials within the Activity Center.** Activity centers with materials that are in good condition, arranged and placed far apart on open shelves, tell a child that materials are valued and important enough to be well cared for. What kind of message does a child get from crowded, open shelves with a mixture of materials and broken or missing pieces? What kind of message does she get from torn books?

Young children work best in a predictable environment where materials are organized and can be found repeatedly in the same place. Organizing materials can help children develop self-help skills and self-control, as well as helping them learn to respect materials and use them well. For example, cutouts of

tools or other hanging equipment help children learn to identify materials and return them to the proper place. Organizing open storage shelves by labeling them clearly with pictures and words makes it possible for children to find materials they want to work with. When shelves are clearly labeled with few objects on them at a time, putting things back in place becomes an easier task for young children.

Labeling, too, can be done in the block area by

FIGURE 6–11 Equipment for creative activities should encourage children to work together.

# THINK ABOUT IT . . .

If you, like most teachers, are always looking for ways to improve the daily operation of your program, you may want to think about using some of the following general hints:

- For a change of pace, convert an empty shelf in a bookcase into a cute "dollhouse." Just attach wallpaper or giftwrap to the inside walls and glue on a fireplace, doors, windows, and other decorations. Put a carpet square on the bottom of the shelf, add doll furniture, and you're ready. For a two-story house, use two shelves.
- Store small books easily and neatly in plastic napkin holders. These can be found at discount stores and even at gargare sales.
- When odd parts of toys and games turn up around the room during the day, forget trying to return them to their proper place each time they are found. Instead, make a special container just for toy and game parts. A zipper-type plastic bag works well for this purpose. Not only will this save time during the day, but you will always know where to look if a part is missing.
- To preserve posters, pictures, and other items you want to last from year to year, cover them with clear Con-Tact® paper. The items will be easier for the children to handle, and dirt and finger marks can be wiped off easily.
- Spray new puzzles and gameboards with clear varnish (outdoors and away from the children, of course). You'll find they last much longer.
- Empty food boxes used in the housekeeping corner and for other learning games will be sturdier if you stuff them with newspaper and then tape them shut. Be sure to brush all crumbs out first.
- When sanitizing furniture and fixtures with bleach and water, put the mixture into an empty window cleaner spray bottle which has been thoroughly washed and dried. The spray bottle is easy to use, and it will protect your hands from the harsh bleach.
- Instead of using tape to hang paper shapes on a wall with a hard finish, try sticking them on with dabs of toothpaste. The toothpaste can be washed off the wall when you change decorations.
- When a child paints a picture that you want to display on a wall, attach the paper to the tabletop with masking tape. The tape keeps the paper from sliding during painting, and when the child has finished, you can unpeel the ends of the tape from the table and use them to retape the painting to the wall.

cutting out the shapes of the blocks in colored contact paper and pasting them on the back and shelves of the cupboard. Pictures of games and toys can be used to label the containers in which they are kept as well as the shelves on which the containers are stored. If it is not possible to have a picture, a simple shape such as a blue circle or a red square can be used on both the container and shelf to remind the children where the toy is to be returned. Clear labeling of shelves helps even very young children become independent in the use and maintenance of their environment.

Another good organizational technique is to encourage the use of toys on the floor near where they are stored. This encourages children to clean up materials directly after an activity.

# THIS ONE'S FOR YOU!

## TAKE YOUR CUE FROM COLORS: USING COLOR CODING IN ACTIVITY CENTERS

A tried and true method for helping children function independently and successfully with activity centers is the systematic use of color and symbols. Children can quickly learn a color-coding system even if they do not yet know how to read. Colors and symbols can be used to identify activity centers, to manage children's movement in and out of centers, and to let children independently find and replace assigned materials.

Special symbol and color codes help children identify and locate each center. The symbol identifies what is learned in the center. The color code helps children easily locate the center in the classroom. For example, the art center's symbol might be a paintbrush and its color code red. A card would be hung at the entrance to each center with its corresponding symbol and color code.

To manage traffic in and out of the centers, the card at the center's entrance would also indicate the number of children allowed in the center at one time. It could be a number of stick people, or the actual numeral, depending on the children's knowledge of written numbers. That corresponding number of color-coded clothespins would be attached to the bottom of the card. For example, the art center might allow ten children and thus have ten red clothespins. The clothespins are children's "tickets" to the centers. Children must pin on the clothespin when they enter the center, wear it while using the center, and replace it on the card when they leave. When no clothespins are on the card, the center is full, and children must choose another activity until a clothespin is available.

**Organization of Activity Centers in Convertible Centers.** Many early childhood programs operate in multi-purpose facilities. In family day care homes, day care centers in churches, and public school day care programs, equipment must be packed up for storage after school or over the weekend. If materials are packed up and stored frequently, movable shelves that are ready for use as soon as they are rolled into place and unlocked are helpful. If shelves are not available for material storage, tables or boxes may be used. Whatever the arrangement, children should understand the system for selecting toys and replacing them in the right containers. Visual cues, such as putting red oilcloth on the storage tables and white oilcloth on the play tables, help children remember the organizational principles and keep the environment functional.

Convertible or multipurpose environments will have to make use of many portable activity boxes. This is also the case in small classrooms or in day care programs in public schools where space is shared. An individual activity box includes all the materials needed for a particular activity—related books and pictures, reminder cards with relevant questions for the teacher, rhymes, games, and songs. For example, a fire fighter prop box might include fire fighters' hats, hose sections, several books about fire fighters, and a ball. The children would use the props and other items in the box as a mini-center of sorts. The teacher would integrate the center into the program by using the questions, books, reminder cards, and other activities prepared as part of the instructional plans for that particular activity.

Activity boxes can be used outdoors or indoors,

either in response to requests by the children, or as part of the teacher-prepared activities. Activity boxes can be made up with all the materials needed for science experiences, such as a sink-float game, or for a cooking activity. Various objects commonly found in an early childhood center environment, such as blocks and beads, can be organized into sorting, matching, or seriation games and kept in separate boxes.

## SELECTION OF EQUIPMENT FOR CREATIVE ACTIVITIES

The kinds of equipment available to young children can either promote or discourage creative expression. If equipment is to encourage creative activities, it should have certain characteristics.

**Characteristics of Useful Equipment** *Simple in design.* Too much detail destroys the children's freedom to express themselves. Crayons, blocks, clay, sand, paints, and even empty cardboard boxes are examples of simple, but useful, equipment for young children.

*Versatile.* Equipment should be usable by both boys and girls for many kinds of activities.

*Stimulating.* The equipment should be the kind that allows children to do things and motivates them. If adults must supervise children every minute that they are using the equipment, this may hinder creativity. Long explanations on how to use the equipment should not be necessary.

*Large and easy to use.* Because of the growth of muscles during this time, very small equipment can cause young children to become anxious. Big trucks and wagons are just right. Large, hollow blocks are better than small, solid ones.

*Durable.* Breakable equipment soon is broken by two- to five-year-olds. Equipment made of hard wood such as maple is less likely to splinter than equipment made of soft wood such as pine. Rubber-wheeled riding toys are preferred to those with wooden wheels.

*In proper working order.* Nothing frustrates children more than a bicycle with wheels that do not turn or a cabinet with drawers that do not open. Sometimes hinges have to be oiled in order to make equipment operate properly. Other times, care must be taken in the selection of materials. The equipment that costs the least may not be the least expensive in the long run.

*Available in proper amounts.* Too many toys or too much equipment can decrease the effectiveness of those materials. In order to carry out creative play, a child needs room. Of course, it is important to have enough blocks, too, so that a child can finish a building. On the other hand, if there are too many blocks, the child may never start to build.

*Designed to encourage children to play together.* Many pieces of equipment are designed for one child to use alone. This is not considered bad. However, children need to work together and find out what the others are thinking and doing. Therefore, equipment designed to get children together should also be provided. Housekeeping equipment from a grocery store or kitchen often draws children together for play.

*Safe.* Safety is a key consideration in selecting equipment for young children. Among the safety factors to consider are whether the equipment is developmentally appropriate (for instance, you would not select for 1½-year-olds toys that are small enough to be swallowed easily), whether nontoxic and nonflammable materials were used in the manufacture of the equipment, whether the materials have any sharp edges or rough areas that could cause injury, and whether the physical environment allows for the safe use of the equipment. (Appendix E provides more complete information on appropriate toys and equipment for early childhood programs.)

**Pitfalls to Avoid.** In selecting equipment and materials for creative activities, the following pitfalls should be avoided:

- Do not choose a material or piece of equipment because it looks "cute" to you. Instead, select each item with some developmental purpose in mind. For example, ask yourself, "What contribution will the item make to the growth of small or large motor skills of the children? How will it help a child's intellectual growth? Her self-esteem? Will it encourage the growth of social skills?"
- Resist the temptation to buy inexpensive merchandise as a matter of course. Select equipment that is sturdy and durably constructed, as it will get hard use. In the long run, one high-quality, durable item will last longer and be more cost effective over time than an item that is less expensive but poorly constructed. For example, one good piece of climbing equipment, sturdy enough for several years of hard use, is an initially expensive purchase. Yet, it is far less expensive than the cost of repeatedly replacing inexpensive climbing equipment every few years.

**Other Considerations.** In addition to these characteristics of good equipment, consider each new item of equipment in light of what you already have. Work toward a balanced environment, one that permits several types of creative expression: working alone, in pairs, in small or large groups. In addition to equipment for large and small motor skills, select items that appeal to the sensory motor explorations of young children. Equipment should be stimulating to see, interesting to touch, and satisfying to maneuver.

As you plan for equipment, think, too, of the ratio of children to adults in the room. Closer adult supervision is needed when climbers, rocking boats, large blocks, wood working, and similar large muscle equipment is used. Art activities, doing puzzles, and reading books often require direct adult assistance. Be sure there are enough adults to supervise the use of the equipment. Obviously, there is no point in having equipment that may be used dangerously or materials that go unused because adults are not there to help or to supervise.

Purchase all major equipment in child-size, rather than doll- or toy-size. It is also important to have some real-life and adult-sized equipment where appropriate. Real hammers and screwdrivers in a smaller adult-size (and not toy tools) work best in construction projects. Home furnishings, too, should be large enough to provide living, not just pretend, experiences for the children.

Choose equipment with *your* space in mind. You may need to limit the number of large, space-consuming items, or you may need to select equipment that challenges children to use a large, open space more constructively.

Consider the total number of children and how many at a given time are to use the equipment. Ten two- or three-year-olds need a basic supply of equipment. Add several more children, and you may need more blocks, more cars and trucks, etc. Also consider the age of the children in the group. Because young children spend much of their time in egocentric (solitary) play or parallel play (playing *next to* but *not with* another child), there must be enough blocks, people, animals, cars, and dishes to allow several children to engage in similar play at the same time. Yet another strategy is to have duplicate or very similar copies of favorite items on hand.

## SUMMARY

To ensure the proper environment for creative expression in young children, careful attention must be given to safety, amount and organization of space, light, sound, and furniture. Planning the environment in the early childhood program involves knowledge of children's needs, as well as attention to traffic flow in the room, goals of the center, children's developing skills, and safety. Arrangement of personal space for each child also needs to be planned.

A balance between teacher planning and children's self-direction is necessary. Interest or activity centers help children make their own choices. The placement and organization of the various activity centers have an impact on how creative materials within them are used by children, how safe the environment is, and how children's self-help skills are encouraged.

Since creative activities are so important in promoting children's development, careful attention must be directed toward the selection and care of creative materials and equipment. The best equipment is simple in design, versatile, easy to use, large, durable, working properly, available in needed amounts, designed for group play, and above all, safe.

It is also important that equipment be stored properly so that children can reach it easily, thereby developing their self-help skills.

## LEARNING ACTIVITIES

A. Choose one activity center from the list provided in this unit. Design your own unique version of this activity center. Describe it in detail. List the items and activities it would include.

B. Draw an ideal room plan for creative activities. Imagine you have all the money, materials, and space necessary. Be creative. After drawing it, list what you feel is important in it, starting with the most important feature. Share this list with classmates and discuss it.

C. Using small blocks or any other similar object, show how you would arrange space in a room to ensure smooth traffic flow and noninterference among interest centers in the room.

D. Go through a school supply catalog. Find examples of furniture, shelving, and play objects that you would include in planning your "ideal room" in the activity preceding.

E. Obtain a toy and equipment catalog or go to a toy store. Make a list of materials that would be useful for children's play. Imagine that you have $1,250 to spend on equipment. Make a list of items you would purchase. Assume you may not go over the $1,250 amount.

## UNIT REVIEW

1. List 10 items to consider in creating a positive physical environment for young children.
2. Discuss the considerations and requirements involved in setting up activity centers, including convertible centers.
3. List the major considerations involved in arranging space in the early childhood setting.
4. List five interest centers that early childhood experts recommend be available for the creative expression of young children. Describe what skills are developed in each.
5. Name at least five important factors when selecting proper equipment for young children's creative activities.
6. Discuss some safety precautions to consider in choosing equipment.

## ADDITIONAL READINGS

Dewey, J. *Experience and Education.* New York: Collier, 1966.

Kritschevsky, S., and E. Prescott, with L. Walling. *Planning Environments for Young Children: Physical Space.* NAEYC, 1990.

Modica, M. "A Positive Approach to Discipline in an Early Childhood Setting." *Day Care & Early Education* 19 (Summer, 1992): 323–34.

Montessori, M. *The Secret of Childhood.* Translated by M.J. Costello. Notre Dame, Ind.: Fides Publishers, 1966.

Moyer, J. *Selecting Educational Equipment and Materials for School and Home.* Wheaton, Md.: Association for Childhood Education International, 1986.

Myers, B.K., and K. Maurer. "Teaching with Less Talking: Learning Centers in the Kindergarten." *Young Children* (July 1987): 20–27.

NAEYC. *Facility Design for Early Childhood Programs Resource Guide.* NAEYC Information Service, 1992.

Pestalozzi, J.H. *How Gertrude Teaches Her Children.* Syracuse, N.Y.: C.W. Bardeen, 1898.

Rinne, C.H. *Attention: The Fundamentals of Classroom Control.* Columbus, Oh: Charles E. Merrill, 1984.

Sweeney, N. *Do You Ever Wish You Could Change Your Child's Behavior?* Walnut Creek, Calif.: Magic Touch, 1990.

Vergeront, J. *Place and Spaces for Preschool and Primary.* NAEYC Publication, 1990.

Warren, J., ed. *Teaching Tips.* Everett, Wash.: Warren Publishing House, Inc., 1987.

# UNIT 7
# Using Media to Promote Creativity

**OBJECTIVES**

After studying this unit, you should be able to

- state the meaning of the terms *media, software, hardware.*
- list at least five characteristics of developmentally appropriate computer software.
- list four reasons why media should be used with young children.

Media are materials used to enhance learning experience in the early childhood program. Media may be the machines used to see movies or hear records or the materials used in an art project, such as clay or paint. Items that are used with machines, such as films, records, or computer discs, are also considered to be media.

Specific types of media will be explored in specific units within this text. This unit will serve as an introduction to the *hardware* and *software* used as creative media with young children. Because most machines are made of metal, they are collectively referred to as hardware. Films, tapes, printer materials, and computer disks, as well as most other items used in conjunction with hardware, are soft, or flexible, and are called software.

## ABILITY TO USE AUDIO-VISUAL EQUIPMENT

Some teachers may be reluctant to use audio-visual/media equipment, worrying about breaking it. They may also be afraid things will not run right. Some may feel it is easier not to use "fancy gadgets." Yet, someone in each program must learn how to set up and use all the equipment as well as make simple repairs, such as changing a bulb in a projector. If no one in a program is willing to do this, the use of media becomes quite limited. A person knowledgeable in the use of audio-visual/media equipment can further enhance the program by teaching others how to use the hardware and its related software.

## IMPORTANCE OF USING MEDIA

Media serve a number of purposes in the early childhood program:

*They provide variety in the program.* Some children learn best when they view a film or hear a record. The total preschool program must meet the needs of a variety of children. Therefore, the program must have a variety of activities for each child. Using media is one more means of meeting the children's needs.

*They provide children with highly interesting learning experiences.* Media help children learn facts, learn to enjoy the school setting, and develop skills—particularly creative skills.

*They get children involved in the creation of materials.* Some of the software can be made or used by one child working alone or by a group of children working together. This gives the children a chance to handle the materials and to create useful things for their class. "Hands-on" activities are very important for young children. The creation of media software is a hands-on activity.

*They build on and reinforce other activities.* It is important that young children learn and relearn. After learning some information, the child can relearn it through the media. Thus, learning through the use of media can reinforce concepts a child learned earlier.

## ACTIVITIES TO DEVELOP CREATIVITY

As just mentioned, media provide variety, interest, involvement, and reinforcement. One of the most important things they provide is a chance for a child to develop creativity. The creativity comes when a child designs, manipulates, and puts together software for the machines. The activities suggested in this section involve the creation and use of software by children.

**Videotapes and Movies.** It is possible for children to plan and produce videotapes of class activities. They can videotape dramatic presentations, dancing, field trips, and other activities in and around the school.

Movies can be obtained by renting them or on a free loan basis. These movies can then be used to introduce creative activities. Creative dramatics can begin with a movie. The movie can introduce a story and some characters. At the proper time, the movie is turned off, and children take the parts of the characters. The children then create their own ending to the story.

**Slides, Filmstrips, and Snapshots.** Using an inexpensive camera, children can take slides of many activities. They can create a slide show for parents or other children. Creative dance or drama can be the subjects of the show. A children's art show can be the theme of a slide show. Sound can be added by making a tape recording. A click or other signal may be used to tell the person showing the slides to move to the next picture.

Slides can also be used for demonstrating a skill. Creative cooking can begin with a slide show on how to get started. Slides are used to build interest and to entertain. Slides of a trip (for example, to Disneyland or Mount Rushmore) can lead children to new creative interests.

Children can take their own slides, though many times they do not hold the camera steady, and their pictures tend to be blurred. The teacher may avoid this problem by taking pictures of scenes chosen by the children. If sound is desired, children can plan

**FIGURE 7–1 Learning about cameras is an exciting experience for a child.**

the words and record them in their own voices to play along with the slide show.

*Filmstrips* are a series of slides made in a strip of film rather than cut up and placed in slide mountings. A film processor will send 35-millimeter film back in a strip of film; it is necessary to request this when turning in the film for developing.

Snapshots can be used to create a storybook by using a collection of snapshots made by children. Snapshots from home may be used for this, or picture books that tell stories about school experiences can be created. Pictures taken at school can be printed in duplicate so that more than one child may create a story using the same photo. Photos can be used to make a story library of pictures taken by children. Books can be made in which photos are taken by one child and the story created by another.

**Videotape.** Today, fairly inexpensive videotape equipment is available to schools. It is lightweight, easily moved, and easy to use.

Videotape can do all the things that movies and slides do, and it is less expensive to use. Videotape can be reused. Mistakes may be erased. Children see the results of their work right away. Video can be used with theater-arts activities: a play can be video-taped; a children's art show can be recorded. Some children enjoy doing "man-on-the-street" interviews. Playtime games can be created and taped.

Many portable units can be taken on field trips. Tapes made on field trips can be used to spark creative story telling and the creation of new games.

When children get tired of a tape, it can be erased and reused. Thus, although the cost of hardware is high, the cost of software can be relatively low.

**Cassette Tape Recorders.**   Small cassette tape recorders that are inexpensive and easy to use are available to all schools. Young children use these recorders with few problems, recording their own voices just for the fun of it. They can also record common

**FIGURE 7–2 Young children enjoy recording their own voices on a cassette tape and take pride in being able to play back the tape all by themselves.**

sounds, creative plays, and man-in-the-street interviews.

**Overhead Projectors.**   These are lightweight machines that project pictures and words on a screen. Light must pass through the film or plastic being projected. The projectors rest on a tabletop and project onto a screen.

Overhead projectors can be used to help children develop creativity in many ways. The machines can be used to project silhouettes (shadows) on a screen, a creative way for children to learn names of shapes. The children can create their own shapes and project them on the screen. Children can make their own transparencies of pictures and drawings on pieces of clear plastic. The transparencies are made by drawing on a piece of clear plastic with a grease pencil or by using a special copy machine. Pencil line drawings, some pictures, and words are easily copied onto the plastic transparency.

The transparency is placed on the overhead stage and projected on a screen. Creative sketches can be enlarged and shown to groups in this way. Creative stories can be built from pictures shown on the overhead screen; sketches made by a child may be used for this purpose.

**Opaque Projectors.**   With these devices, book pages, photographs, and paintings can be shown directly on a screen. The things to be projected must be quite thin and must lie flat. They are then placed on a stage in the projector and brought into focus in an enlarged size on a screen or blank wall.

Opaque projectors can be used in several ways. Drawings made by individuals can be shown to the whole group. A picture from a book can be used to start children on creative story-telling experiences. Snapshots may be used to begin a creative art experience. Pictures and shapes from a book can be traced onto paper or a chalkboard. The shapes or parts of the pictures can be used to start a creative art or story experience.

**Phonographs and Records.**   Phonographs are so common that many children have a phonograph of their own. Records are available in stores and through material catalogs. Using records helps children develop creativity in many ways:

- Recorded music helps children express and develop creative movement.
- Music helps develop creative imaginations in children. Classical music is very good for this.
- Music that builds feeling in children leads to many creative art experiences. The music sets the mood, then the children create.
- Records that tell stories or parts of stories can help children become creative. The stories build a mood as well as tell a story.

## POTENTIAL VALUE OF COMPUTERS IN EARLY CHILDHOOD PROGRAMS

Computers have found their way into the preschool setting, taking their place beside the finger paints, play dough, books, and other media found within the early learning environment. Computer programs have been developed for young children that allow them to produce colorful graphics, music, and animated (moving) graphics.

Based on recent research, some general conclusions about the value of computers with preschool and kindergarten children may be made:

- *Computers can be used effectively with young children.* Researchers have consistently observed high levels of spoken communication and cooperation as young children interact at the computer. Compared with more traditional activities, such as puzzle assembly or block building, the computer elicits both more social interaction and different types of interaction. For example, young children initiate interactions more frequently and engage in more turn taking (Clements, Natasi, and Swaminathan, 1993).

   "When they use these new (software) programs, children are thinking, doing all the things we would like children to do," says Sue Bredekamp, director of professional development at the National Association for the Education of Young Children in Washington. "And for young children, computers are really a social activity. Children will interact in pairs, even in threes and fours. It's very different from the adult experience of computing." (Mills, 1994)

- *Computers can be interactive.* This means that the computer used with young children provides a vehicle for two types of interaction: child-to-computer and child-to-child. Child-to-computer interaction depends to a great extent on the software. Some software requires children to choose one response, which is then corrected. Some programs have been developed that allow children to use information on the screen to make more than one response.

   Child-to-child interaction at the computer depends on the arrangement of the environment. When children work near each other by the computer, they discuss what they are doing and assist each other as they work. Some software is also designed for, or lends itself better to, participation by more than one child.

   The teacher and the software together also make a difference. For example, the teacher encourages cooperation by placing two chairs in front of the computer, suggesting that children work in pairs,

FIGURE 7–3 In comparison with television viewing, computer use produces far more active, positive, and emotionally varied facial expressions and smiles (Hyson, 1985).

and encouraging them to establish cooperative goals or to converse as they work on projects.

- *Age and computer use.* Age doesn't appear to be a limiting factor in computer use. Even two-year-old children can work proficiently on the computer using age-appropriate software that requires only simple keypresses or pointing with a mouse. Preschoolers can easily start the computer, load disks, type on the keyboard, and understand pictorial cues.

Children of all ability levels show a general interest and motivation for working with computers (Okolo, 1991). High-ability children seem to prefer the challenge of problem-solving software and are bothered by the frequent evaluation provided by drill programs. Low-ability children, in contrast, seem to enjoy programs that provide animation and graphics and are bothered by the lack of structure in problem-solving (Hativa and Shorer, 1989).

- *Children prefer action.* Just as in other aspects of their play, children like action with computers, and they do not necessarily choose to follow the rules of games. They watch what happens when they press new keys, and they purposely may try to squash all the keys at one time. One of the strengths young

**FIGURE 7–4 Listening to a taped story and following along with a book is an excellent audio-visual activity that encourages reading readiness.**

children bring to computer use is their fearless experimentation!

- *Nonreaders may be encouraged to read.* While this is not a skill of focus in the early childhood program, research showed that nonreading children mastered keyboard letter-matching tasks within a few weeks. Within two months most children in the several experiments were easily able to select options from written "menus" on the screen and read prompts (directions) related to the operation of particular programs. These children were reading and, in most cases, they had little or no outside assistance (Anselmo, 1986, p. 26).

- *Computers and social development.* Computers can encourage, rather than discourage, social experiences. For example, children's cooperative interactions increase, and they seek and receive more help both from each other and their teacher as they use computers. They form new friendships because of shared interests, and they identify new leaders—sort of youthful "computer experts." Computer activities may enhance the cognitive (intellectual) level of both play and work such that children engage more in games with rules, reflective problem-solving, and conflict-solving by negotiating with another child. Such interactions may in turn promote later academic achievement and cognitive development. (Clements and Natasi, 1992).

A good environment for young children includes many experiences that involve the senses, adult–child and child–child conversation, and a host of other age-appropriate activities. Computers can supplement, but do not substitute for, experiences in which children can discover with all their senses.

Only after a sound, basic program has been developed should preschool and kindergarten teachers consider buying a computer. First should come blocks, sand and water tables, art materials, books, and all of the other proven elements of a good program for young children.

## Choosing Software for Young Children

Care must be taken to select computer software that is developmentally appropriate for the children

# THINK ABOUT IT . . .

## THE EFFECTS OF SEX AND GENDER ROLE ON PRESCHOOL CHILDREN'S COMPUTER INTEREST

In a study of 82 preschool children, ages 3 and 4, in a heterogenous group representing a mix of boys and girls with different income levels and from varied ethnic groups, little evidence was found for masculine stereotyping of computer use. More specifically, there was no greater male interest nor competence in the use of computers by preschool children. While the boys did view the computer as "masculine," girls in the study viewed it as "feminine." Videotapes of sequences of children's behavior in actual computer-related activities did not support evidence of greater male interest.

No differences were found between boys and girls in the area of computer competence. However, as expected, the older the child, the better the child performed on the computer.

As a result of the study, the researchers advise parents and teachers to encourage computer interest and experience in young girls as much as in boys to combat current gender-biased media portrayal of girls as being afraid of computers. Also, because computers are generally located in school math departments, early computer experience may be especially important for females, considering that math is traditionally perceived as a masculine endeavor. With these early interventions, the potentially negative effects of computer technology on female success may be avoided. (Williams and Ogletree, 1992)

who will use it. The following ten criteria distinguish software that is developmentally appropriate:

1. *Age appropriateness.* The concepts taught and their method of presentation reflect realistic expectations for young children.

2. *Child control.* Children are active participants, initiating and deciding the sequence of events, rather than reactors, responding to predetermined activities. The software needs to facilitate active rather than passive involvement (Olds, 1985). The pace is set by the child, not the program.

3. *Clear instructions.* Since the majority of preschool children are nonreaders, spoken directions are essential (Pournelle, 1985). If printed instructions are used, they are accompanied by spoken directions. Directions are simple and precise. Graphics accompany choices to make options clear to the children.

4. *Expanding complexity.* Entry level is low; children can easily learn to manipulate the software successfully. The learning sequence is clear; one concept follows the next (Vartuli, Hill, Loncar, and Cacamo, 1984). The software expands as children explore, teaching children the skills they are ready to learn. Through the expanding complexity of the software, children build on their knowledge.

5. *Independent exploration.* After initial exposure, children can manipulate the software without adult supervision.

6. *Process orientation.* The process of using the software is so engaging for children that the product becomes secondary. Children learn through discovery rather than being drilled in specific skills. Motivation to learn is intrinsic, not the result of praise, smiling face stickers, or prizes.

7. *Real world representation.* The software is a simple

# THIS ONE'S FOR YOU!

## ARE YOUNG CHILDREN READY FOR COMPUTERS? WHAT RESEARCH TELLS US.

Although questions about the use and effectiveness of computers in education are raised at all levels, these questions are debated most passionately about the early childhood ages (birth through eight). Are young children physically and cognitively ready to use computers? The following short summaries of research in the area of computers and young children will answer some of these questions.

- *How Young?* Although older children may be more interested in using computers, there is little evidence that computers should not be introduced to younger children. No major differences have been found between the way computers are used by younger and older preschoolers (Beeson and Williams, 1985), although three-year-olds take longer to get used to the keyboard than five-year-olds do.
- *Equity: Girls and Boys* A consistent finding is that as early as the later elementary school years, boys have more access to computers, own more computers, and use computers more frequently and with more control (Lieberman, 1985; Picard and Guili, 1985). A pair of studies found that, although children aged five years or older used computers similarly, boys younger than five used the computer more than did girls the same age (Beeson and Williams, 1985). However, other studies have not revealed such differences, and the vast majority of studies report that girls and boys do not differ in the amount or type of computer use (Williams and Ogletree, 1992).
- *Characteristics of Children* Do any characteristics distinguish preschoolers most interested in using computers? They tend to be older and to show higher levels of mental maturity. They show higher levels of vocabulary development, yet they do not differ from less interested peers in creativity and social development (Hoover and Austin, 1986; Haughland, 1992).
- *Social Development* Computers appear to facilitate certain social behaviors, such as helping others, sharing, and teaching one another (Borgh and Dickson, 1986; Clements, Natasi, and Swaminathan, 1993).
- *Attitudes* Observing five-year-olds, Hyson (1985) found that, in comparison with television watching, computer use produces far more active, positive, and emotionally varied facial expressions and more smiling. Also, children working at a computer speak more often either to each other or to observers than children watching television.
- *Language Development* Preschoolers' language activity, measured as words spoken per minute, was almost twice as high at the computer as at any of the other activities: dough, clay, blocks, art, or games (Muhlstein and Croft, 1986; Scott, Cole, and Engel, 1992).

In summary, we know from the research that computers are neither perfect nor a problem. Young children do not need computers any more than they "need" any of the many other learning centers. There is, however, nothing to lose and potentially rich benefits to acquire through appropriate use of computers with young children.

and reliable model of some aspect of the real world, exposing children to concrete representation of objects and their functions.

8. *Technical features.* The software has high technical quality that helps the young child pay attention. It is colorful and includes uncluttered, realistic animated graphics. There are realistic sound effects or music that corresponds to objects on the screen. The software loads from the disks and runs fast enough to maintain the child's interest.

9. *Trial and error.* The software provides children many chances to test alternative responses. Through resolving errors or solving problems, children build structures and knowledge.

10. *Visible transformations.* Children have an impact on the software, changing objects and situations through their responses (Haugland and Shade, 1988).

In this list, it is important to note that software may have a developmental approach to learning without having all of the criteria. Some software has more developmental criteria than other software. You need to choose the software that includes as many of the above criteria as possible.

## SUMMARY

The full meaning of media involves two main things: hardware and software. Hardware includes the machines and instruments—usually made of metal or a hard plastic. It is used to show pictures or reproduce sounds. Software includes the materials that are shown or heard when the machines work. It can be most useful in developing a child's creativity.

Media enhance the early childhood program because:

1. They provide variety in the program.
2. They lead to interesting learning experiences.
3. They lead children to create materials or develop new ideas.
4. They build on other things children have experienced in the preschool program.

Computers are rapidly becoming more common in early childhood programs. It is important to choose developmentally appropriate software that includes ten characteristics: age appropriateness, child control, clear instructions, expanding complexity, independent exploration, process orientation, real world representation, technical features, trial and error, and visible transformations.

## LEARNING ACTIVITIES

### Taking Creative Slides

A. Obtain an inexpensive camera that takes slide pictures. Shoot a roll of color slide film, trying to make each picture creative.
B. Try to get pictures of
   1. a beautiful sunset
   2. an ugly, broken-down house
   3. a beautiful building
   4. interesting-looking people
   5. a flower in bloom
   6. an animal
   7. a brightly colored bird
C. Use the slide pictures to tell a creative story about some experience. The story may or may not be true.

### Using Hardware

Learn how to use each of the following kinds of hardware:

1. a motion picture projector
2. a slide projector
3. a filmstrip projector
4. an overhead projector
5. an opaque projector

### Additional Hardware and Software Activities

A. Using a tape recorder, make tape recordings of interesting sounds. Try to get fellow classmates to recognize the sounds. Try any or all of the following sounds:
   1. a typewriter
   2. a door closing
   3. a car starting
   4. a jet plane taking off
   5. voices
   6. music
   7. popcorn popping
B. Make a list of software materials that could be made

by children. The cost of raw materials for the software should be determined. How much money would be needed for a good supply of materials?
1. Find catalogs that list prices of film, blank tape, and other materials.
2. Contact film processors to figure the cost of developing and printing the film.
3. Decide how materials should be stored and taken care of.

C. Make a list of hardware needed for a program involving media. Figure costs of hardware by checking school supply catalogs, camera stores, and discount department stores. How much money would be needed?

D. Preview a computer software program designed for preschoolers. Does it allow for individual creativity? Is it developmentally appropriate?

E. Choose one of the research references from the list provided at the end of this unit and report on its findings with regard to young children's use of computers. Apply what you have read to your own experience with children.

## UNIT REVIEW

1. Define the term *hardware*.
2. Name three limitations in using media.
3. List four reasons why using media is important to preschool programs.
4. Choose the answer that best completes each statement about media.
   a. An opaque projector shows
      (a) slides.
      (b) images on paper.
      (c) movies in a plastic case.
   b. Overhead projectors
      (a) use slides for projecting images.
      (b) project enlarged images.
      (c) project shadows on a screen.
   c. Videotape is good to use because
      (a) videotape can be reused.
      (b) the hardware is inexpensive.
      (c) it enlarges the image.
5. List at least five factors to consider when evaluating computer software for young children.
6. List four potential values of computers for young children.

## ADDITIONAL READINGS

Anselmo, S. "Activities to Enhance Thinking Skills: Visual Closure." *Day Care and Early Education.* 11 (1) (1983): 36–37.

Anselmo, S., P. Rollings, and R. Schuckman. *R is for Rainbow: Developing Young Children's Thinking Skills through the Alphabet.* Menlo Park, Calif.: Addison-Wesley, 1986.

Beeson, B.S., and R.A. Williams. "The Effect of Gender and Age in Pre-School Children's Choice of the Computer as a Child Selected Activity." *Journal of the American Society for Information Science* 36 (Nov., 1985): 339–341.

Borgh, K., and W.P. Dickson. "Two Preschoolers Sharing One Microcomputer: Creating Prosocial Behavior with Hardware and Software." In *Young Children and Microcomputers,* P.F. Campbell and G.G. Fein, eds. Pp. 37–44. Reston, Va.: Reston Publishing, 1986.

Buckleitner, W. *High/Scope Buyer's Guide to Children's Software 1993.* Ypsilanti, Mich.: High/Scope Press, 1993.

Clements, D.H. "Enhancement of Creativity in Computer Environments." *American Educational Research Journal,* 28 (1) (1991): 173–187.

Clements, D.H., and B.K. Natasi. "Computers and Early Childhood Education." In *Advances in School Psychology: Preschool and Early Childhood Treatment Directions,* M. Gettinger, S.N. Elliott, and T.R. Kratochwill, eds. Pp. 187–246. Hillsdale, N.J.: Lawrence Erlbaum, 1992.

Clements, D.H., B.K. Natasi, and S. Swaminathan. "Young Children and Computers: Crossroads and Directions from Research." *Young Children* (Jan., 1993): 56–64.

Crook, C. "Computers for Preschool Children: The Role of Direct Manipulation Interfaces." *Early Child Development and Care* 69 (1991): 5–18.

Hativa, N., and D. Shorer. "Socioeconomic Status, Aptitude, and Gender Differences in CAI Gains of Arithmetic." *Journal of Educational Research* 83 (1989): 11–21.

Haugland, S.W. "The Effect of Computer Software on Preschool Children's Developmental Gains." *Journal of Computing in Childhood Education* 3 (1) (1992): 15–30.

Haugland, S.W., and D.D. Shade. "Developmentally Appropriate Software for Young Children." *Young Children* (May, 1988): 37–43.

Hohman, C. *Young Children and Computers.* Ypsilanti, Mich.: High/Scope Press, 1990.

Hoover, J., and A.M. Austin. "A Comparison of Traditional Preschool and Computer Play from a Social/ Cognitive Perspective.'' Paper presented at the annual meeting of the American Educational Research Association, San Francisco (ERIC Document Reproduction Service No. ED 270–220), April 1986.

Hyson, M.C. ''Emotions and the Microcomputer: An Exploratory Study of Young Children's Responses.'' *Computers in Human Behavior* 1 (1985): 143–152.

Lieberman, D. ''Research on Children and Microcomputers: A Review of Utilization and Effects Studies.'' In *Children and Microcomputers: Research on the Newest Medium*, M. Chen and W. Paisley, eds. Pp. 59–83. Beverly Hills, Calif.: Sage, 1985.

Mills, J. ''Tots Use Computers Before They Learn to Read.'' *New York Times*. Reprinted in the *Raleigh News and Observer*, Sunday, Feb. 13, 1994.

Muhlstein, E.A., and D.J. Croft. ''Using the Microcomputer to Enhance Language Experiences and the Development of Cooperative Play Among Preschool Children.'' Unpublished manuscript, 1986, De Anza College, Cupertino, Calif. (ERIC Document Reproduction Service No. ED 269–004).

Okolo, C.M. ''Learning and Behaviorally Handicapped Students' Perceptions of Instructional and Motivational Features of Computer Assisted Instruction.'' *Journal of Research on Computing in Education* 24 (2) (1991): 178–188.

Olds, H.F. ''The Microcomputer and the Hidden Curriculum.'' *Computers in the Schools* 2 (1) (1985): 3–14.

Picard, A.J. and C. Guili. ''Computers as a Free Time Activity in Grades K–4: A Two Year Study of Attitudes and Usage.'' Unpublished manuscript, University of Hawaii, Honolulu, 1985.

Pournelle, J. ''A High-Tech Education.'' *Popular Computing* 4 (1985): 46–49.

Scott, T., M. Cole, and M. Engel. ''Computers and Education: A Cultural Constructivist Perspective.'' In *Review of Research in Education*, G. Grant, ed. Pp. 191–251. Washington, D.C.: American Research Association, 1992.

Shade, D.D. ''Computers and Young Children.'' *Day Care and Early Education*. (Summer, 1991): 16–18.

Smith, M.L. ''Cubbies, Coloring and Computers: Learning to Do School in a Day Care Program.'' *Child Education* 67 (Annual Theme Issue, 1991): 317–318.

Vartuli, S., S. Hill, K. Loncar, and N. Caccamo. ''Selecting and Evaluating Software for Use in a Preschool Classroom: From the Young Child's and Researcher's Perspective.'' Unpublished manuscript, Ann Arbor, Mich, 1987. (ERIC Document Reproduction Service No. ED 259–838)

Williams, S.W., and S.M. Ogletree. ''Preschool Children's Computer Interest and Competence: Effects of Sex and Gender Role.'' *Early Childhood Research Quarterly*. 7, (1) (Mar., 1992): 135–146.

# SECTION 3
# Art and the Development of the Young Child

# UNIT 8

# Art and Social-Emotional Growth

## OBJECTIVES

After studying this unit, you should be able to
- define the terms self-acceptance and self-concept.
- describe how the art program can add to a child's self-concept and self-acceptance.
- discuss how the art program helps a child in child-to-child relationships, child-to-teacher relationships, and child-to-group relationships.

The term *social-emotional growth* refers to two kinds of growth. Emotional growth is the growth of a child's feelings, and social growth is the child's growth as a member of a group.

Learning to be a member of a group involves many social skills. Young children, for example, must learn to relate to other children and adults outside the family. Often, a child's first experience of sharing an adult's attention with so many other children occurs in the early childhood setting. Of the social skills involved in learning to work in a group, the child has to learn how to share materials, take turns, listen to others, and how and when to work on her own—and these are just a few of the social skills to be learned!

This unit covers both the social and emotional growth of the child as it occurs in the early childhood art program. While social-emotional growth occurs at the same time as physical-mental growth, the two are covered in separate units within this text for the sake of clarity. *The developmental concepts learned and applied in this and the following two units are applicable to all other creative activities and materials.* The objective

of all creative activities, it must be remembered, is to promote development of the child in all areas, thus maximizing his or her full potential.

This unit is divided into four main sections: (1) self-concept and self-awareness, (2) child-to-child relationships, (3) child-to-teacher relationships, and (4) group relationships.

## SELF-CONCEPT AND SELF-AWARENESS

Self-concept can be defined as the child's growing awareness of his or her own characteristics (physical appearance as well as skills and abilities) and how these are similar to or different from those of others. Self-acceptance is related to the child's feelings of self-regard; this is the opinion we form of ourselves as a person possessed of a unique self.

All children like to feel good about themselves. This good feeling about oneself is called *self-acceptance* or self-esteem. Children who feel that they are good people and can do things well have a good sense of self-acceptance.

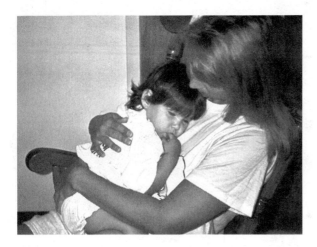

**FIGURE 8–1 Children learn about themselves by the way they are treated by others.**

Children who accept themselves know and accept their strengths and limitations. They must have this good feeling about themselves before they can ever learn to accept others. A good preschool art program helps children develop and improve their level of self-acceptance.

Children learn to accept themselves from birth all the way throughout life. They learn about themselves by the way they are treated by others. The way parents

**FIGURE 8–2 Learning to be a member of a group is an important milestone for young children.**

hold their baby makes the baby feel accepted. A baby who is being held closely with tenderness learns to feel loved and good. The only way babies understand this is by physical touch, since they do not yet understand words.

As babies grow into young children, they continue learning to accept themselves. When toddlers are encouraged and praised for messy but serious attempts to feed themselves, they learn to accept themselves and feel good about what they do. If children are accepted as they are, they learn to accept themselves. This is the only way they learn to feel accepted.

A young child's environment often includes changing family structures, extended experiences outside of the home in a day care or preschool setting, as well as the vivid but often confusing messages presented by television and the media. The child often finds this complex world confusing and is frustrated in trying to understand it.

Many teachers, attempting to assist the confused child, design classroom strategies based solely on the development of such cognitive skills as counting and reading. However, programs based exclusively on these abstract concepts may confuse the child more than ever. Understanding oneself and one's relationship with the environment and feeling positive about oneself are all highly cognitive experiences and crucial to a child's development.

In the preschool art program, children must continue to learn to accept and feel good about themselves. The art program can be of special help in this area. When children feel they can do things well in art, they grow in both self-confidence and self-acceptance.

An early childhood teacher needs to plan the art program in such a way that it gives each child a chance to grow in self-acceptance. To do so, the program should be *child-centered*, which means that it is planned for the age and ability levels of the children in it. The art program should never be adult-centered, or planned to suit only adult ideas of what children should do. The adult-centered program does not consider the age and ability of the children in the group.

A teacher must also understand children's developmental levels in planning the art program. Knowledge of the way children develop helps the teacher plan a setting with appropriate materials and activities for the level of each child in the program.

**Encouraging Self-Acceptance Through the Art Program.** To plan an art program that gives each child a chance to have a good experience with art, a teacher should keep in mind the following points:

*Accept children at their present developmental level.* If the adult accepts the child in a positive way, the child feels this acceptance. This does not mean that the child should not be challenged. Art activities can be planned that are a slight challenge for the

**FIGURE 8–3 Children feel secure when they feel accepted by the adults caring for them.**

child's present level. But they must not be so hard that they frustrate the child. By feeling successful in art activities, children learn to feel more sure about themselves and their skills.

*Provide an environment that is comfortable for the age level of the group.* Plan the room so that it is a place where preschool children can feel at home. It should have small tables and chairs that are the right size for young children. If necessary, there should be covering on the floor and work areas so that the children can work freely without worrying about spills. It is hard for children to feel good about themselves and their work when they are always being told they are "too messy." If sponges and towels are within reach, children can clean up their own mess. A little thing like this is fun for them, as well as a good way to help them develop independence and confidence. By being in charge of keeping their own area clean, children learn to feel good about how they can take care of themselves. This strengthens their self-acceptance and personal pride.

*Provide materials that are age appropriate.* By giving children tools they are able to work with at their age and skill level, the teacher helps them have more success in art projects. Success helps them grow with pride and confidence and know that they can do things well. Success breeds success.

*Plan activities according to the age and ability levels of the group.* Projects should be fun at the child's age, ability, and interest level.

*Provide creative materials and activities that the children can work on and complete by themselves.* Activities that children can finish themselves help them feel more self-assured and confident about their art ability. To do this, teachers need to be good observers to know exactly what materials and activities are developmentally appropriate for each child. This match between children's developmental levels and appropriate activities and materials is an ever-changing one, as children continue to grow and develop in the early years.

*Be a facilitator of the development of self-acceptance and self-concept in young children:*

- Encourage children to try again after mistakes or unsuccessful experiences. Provide many opportunities for them to succeed.
- Compliment children on things that are done well. Avoid false compliments, as they do not encourage a child's best work.
- Inform the parents of their child's success with art activities or materials. Not only does this please most parents, but they are also likely to reinforce the child's self-acceptance through praise of her efforts.

## CHILD-TO-CHILD RELATIONSHIPS

It is only after a child has developed self-acceptance that it is possible for her to accept other children. In the early childhood art program, there are many chances for a child to be with other children of the same age. Children who have had good art experiences are the ones who can honestly accept their own abilities and those of other children.

The art program is a good place for child-to-child relationships, where children can work, talk, and be

**FIGURE 8–4 The early childhood program is a good place to learn how to get along with others of the same age.**

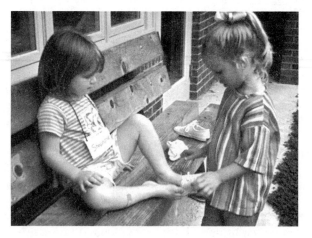

**FIGURE 8–5 Helping others is a joyful learning experience.**

together. If the art activities are right for the children, they provide a relaxed time for exploring, trying new tools, and using familiar ones again. They also allow children many chances to interact with each other.

The freedom of art itself encourages children to talk about their own work or the work of other children. Working with colors, paint, paper, paste, and other materials provides children an endless supply of things to talk about.

**Sharing Ideas and Opinions.** Art activities also provide many opportunities for a child to learn how other children feel about things. For example, a three-year-old boy may hear for the first time how another child his own age feels about his painting. At home, this child may hear mostly adult comments; in the early childhood setting, he can experience the ideas and feelings of another child his own age. An action as simple as putting easels side-by-side encourages this type of social learning.

Although this sharing can be a new and exciting thing for a child, it can also be hard for some children to accept at first. If children have good feelings about themselves and their work in art, however, they can accept these ideas about their work from others.

The chance to share ideas and talk about one's own work or the work of others is the beginning of

**FIGURE 8–6 The early childhood program provides many opportunities for cooperation and idea-sharing.**

a new type of relationship. It is a sharing relationship. The child begins to see that other children have different ideas and feelings. This type of sharing makes the child see that people can have different feelings and ideas and still be friends. A child can learn that everyone does not have to agree all the time and can share ideas and opinions.

**Cooperation and Sharing.** Working together with other children in creative activities gives a child the chance to learn about being with others. Being with others teaches a child the value of sharing and cooperation.

Working with limited amounts of crayons, paint, and paper means that a child has to share. She soon learns that sharing is a part of being in a group. One can of red paint for two young painters is a real-life lesson in sharing.

Cooperation among children is also part of the art program. A child learns the meaning of cooperation while helping another child glue seeds on a paper, clean a brush, or button a painting shirt. This is truly learning by doing.

**Getting Along with Others.** Getting along with other children helps a child feel good about herself. It gives a child a good feeling of belonging and being accepted by others.

By working with other children, a child learns to enjoy people other than those in her own family. This is an important step toward growing up. Being in an early childhood program is often the first time the child is away from home. This is why it is so important for her to have a successful experience. A child's feelings about these first school experiences affect all the other school days to come.

## CHILD-TO-TEACHER RELATIONSHIPS

The teacher in the early childhood program is a very important person in the child's eye. Children look up to their teachers or caregivers and tend to take them very seriously.

A child learns new ways to be with an adult in the early childhood program. The teacher is an adult, but not the child's parent; therefore, a new type of relationship opens up. Of course, it is different in several ways from the adult–child relationship at home.

The school setting is unlike the home situation. Children learn how to be and act in a place other than the home. They learn how it is to be in a larger group than the family and how to share an adult's attention with other children.

The children learn about art as well as about themselves from the teacher. The teacher helps them feel that it is safe to be themselves and to express ideas in their own way. The sensitive teacher lets the child know that the fun of participating in and expressing oneself in art or other creative activities is more important than the finished product. A teacher opens up many new art skills and feelings for the child and is thus a very important person in the eyes of the child.

The teacher may be the first real adult friend for the child. It is, therefore, important for a good child–teacher relationship to develop during the art program. A happy feeling between teacher and child affects the child's school days to come. A child who has a satisfying first experience with a teacher goes on to kindergarten expecting more good things, which makes each new experience easier and more fun for both child and teacher.

**FIGURE 8–7 The teacher in the early childhood program is a very important person.**

**Building Rapport.** Building a warm and friendly feeling, a *rapport*, between teacher and child is not always easy; it may not happen quickly. The best learning and teaching take place, however, when the child and teacher have this feeling for each other.

Beginnings are important for both teacher and child. The following are some ways in which the child–teacher relationship may be enhanced:

• Welcome each child into the room. Make the child feel wanted and special. Have a special place to put each child's clothes.
• When speaking to children, look into their eyes.
• When speaking to children, use their names.
• Understand that children like to feel proud of themselves.
• Talk with and listen to every child as much as possible.
• Use a normal speaking voice.

**Guidelines for Encouraging Social and Emotional Growth.** The teacher is often the first adult the child works closely with outside the home. For this reason, it is important that the teacher do all that

is possible to encourage the child's social and emotional growth. Some basic guidelines to follow in encouraging this social and emotional growth in art activities follow:

*Accept each child's developmental level.* An early childhood teacher must help the child feel accepted. Accepting the child's present developmental level is basic to her feeling accepted. It also helps her feel secure and that her present level of performance is acknowledged positively by the teacher. For example, a three-year-old does not have to feel ashamed if unable to cut very well with scissors; the teacher still accepts the child warmly. The teacher who accepts every child, whatever her ability, helps each child find self-acceptance and grow in skills at her own unique rate.

*Accept children's feelings and ideas.* Encourage children's free and honest self-expression. When children express ideas openly, adults should respect the feelings expressed. By encouraging children's honest expression of ideas, the teacher is encouraging the children to be themselves. And when the teacher respects the ideas expressed, it tells a child that it is all right to be oneself. In other words,

**FIGURE 8–8 Children learn to accept their own ideas and feelings when allowed to express themselves freely in art.**

# THINK ABOUT IT . . .

## ALTRUISM

Why are some children more altruistic than others? The answer is complicated, since altruism is affected by many factors. During the past few decades, researchers have observed hundreds of adults and children in laboratories and in real-life situations to gain insight into three main altruistic behaviors—helping, caring, and sharing.

The beginnings of altruism are present at birth, research shows. In one study, babies only 18 hours old were more distressed by tapes of other infants' crying than by recordings of their own crying and would cry longer and more often when they heard human cries than when they were exposed to other loud noises.

Researchers also report that some people are innately more empathic than others. There are individual differences in temperament, so some children respond more intensely to other people's distress than others. But all children have the ability to be affected deeply by other people's emotional states.

Adults have a great deal of influence on children's altruism, experts say. Here's what you can do to teach children the value of helping, caring, and sharing:

- Make your environment as nurturing as possible. By meeting children's physical and emotional needs, you free them psychologically to meet other people's needs.
- Foster self-esteem by encouraging children to do things for themselves. Acknowledge children's accomplishments, and let them know they don't have to perform to be loved. Children with high self-esteem can behave altruistically because they are not preoccupied with their own perceived inadequacies.
- Talk about the feelings of others. For example, if you see a bus driver snap at a passenger, say: "He seems upset about something. Maybe he's having a bad day today."
- Assist children in defining their own feelings toward others. Ask them if they feel sad because they have to miss a birthday party, or if they are excited about going to their grandparents' house. Research shows that children can't empathize the emotions of others until they understand their own.
- Let children know how much you value helping, caring, and sharing, and model altruistic behavior yourself. In several studies, children exposed to generous models were more inclined to donate money and trinkets to others than children exposed to selfish models.
- Establish clear behavioral standards for children and emphasize how misconduct hurts other people.
- Explain why disciplinary measures are necessary and use emotion so youngsters know you really mean business, but discourage aggressive behavior and avoid spanking and belittling.
- Welcome children's help, and stress how much you appreciate even the smallest effort. This will foster altruism by teaching youngsters to view themselves as caring individuals. But do not give children material rewards for helping, caring, and sharing. They should help because they want to, not because they expect rewards.
- Minimize TV viewing. Behavior experts say most children's television shows encourage aggression, rather than helping, caring, and sharing. Two exceptions are *Mister Rogers' Neighborhood* and *Sesame Street,* which have increased altruistic behavior among preschoolers.

- Talk children through conflicts, step by step. For example, if a child is fighting about a toy with another child, empathize with her distress and ask how she thinks her friend is feeling. Praise her when she takes her playmate's point of view, and encourage her to solve the problem in ways that will benefit both children.
- Encourage cooperation, not competition. Buy toys that foster cooperative play and emphasize that other people are not obstacles to a child's success. Research shows that children who are encouraged to triumph are less generous and emphathetic than their peers (Brody, 1992; Curry and Johnson, 1990; Katz, 1991; Kohn, 1990; Woodhead, Carr, and Light, 1991).

when the child's work seems to say, "This is me and the way I feel," and the work is respected, the teacher is saying to the child, "I accept you and your feelings in your work." In this way, a child learns that it is good to be oneself, which is what self-acceptance is all about.

*Help children accept the ideas of others.*   The only way a child can accept others is by first experiencing self-acceptance; the child who feels accepted is more likely to be able to accept others. As Dorothy Briggs says (1974):

> True, all children need to experience their competence to build self-respect. But each child needs to feel that his person is cherished regardless of his competence. Successful performances build the sense of worthwhileness; being cherished as a person nurtures the feeling of being loved. Every child needs to feel both loved and worthwhile. But lovability must not be tied to worthwhile performance. The more lovable any child feels, however, the more likely he is to perform in satisfactory ways, for then he likes himself.

When the teacher accepts and respects each child's physical and artistic abilities, the children then accept each other. By accepting each other, they learn about ideas, opinions, and feelings different from their own peers. These new ideas make the art program richer and more exciting for the children.

The teacher must always keep in mind that children act as they are treated. Only the child who is treated with respect can treat others with respect. The teacher who respects each child's ideas and abil-

ities is teaching them how to respect the abilities and ideas of others.

*Enrich the child–teacher relationship.*   The teacher can make art a time when the children share ideas and experience new ones. By bringing ideas to the program, a teacher can enrich the lives of the children in the art group.

For example, a teacher can encourage a child who often draws animals to develop new ideas by bringing in toy models or pictures of many different animals. Giving the child a chance to see other animals can be very stimulating; it may encourage the child to draw more detailed animals or to think of more ideas.

As another example, a teacher can plan field trips

**FIGURE 8–9 Learning to dress oneself is a big step in developing self-confidence.**

# THIS ONE'S FOR YOU!

## COLLABORATING WITH CHILDREN: ANOTHER WAY TO BUILD SELF-CONCEPT

Involving young children in decorating their room is a fun, productive way of building their self-concept and improving the room's appearance at the same time! Designing a bulletin board (or wall decoration) can involve many skills and can be a learning experience unlike any other. Here are some tried and true bulletin board ideas to involve children while building their self-concept, too.

- **Hands On**—Cover one wall with brown craft (wrapping) paper. With bright paint (one color for each letter), write the title, "Hands On!" at the top of the paper. Children then place handprints randomly on the board by first pressing hands on a paint-coated sponge and then pressing directly on the paper. Label each print with the child's name and date.
- **Pattern Prints**—Prepare the bulletin board by measuring off horizontal lines on backing paper to create one horizontal stripe/space for each child. At the left end of the stripes, list the children's names. Then, offer the children a variety of materials for printing (cut fruits and vegetables, rubber stamps, printing letters, etc.) and an inked pad (or sponge soaked in tempera paint). Allow the children to create any pattern or design they would like to make.
- **Names**—Cover a large bulletin board with a bright, solid background. Divide paper evenly into a grid design, thus providing each child with a 12-inch-square space on the board. With a marker, print each child's name in large letters at the top of the space, leaving at least 11 inches of paper exposed under each name. First, use the board as a basis for a matching game—children must match namecards to their name printed on the board. Children are then invited to decorate their name with markers, crayons, or paints. As the year progresses, children can copy their names in a variety of (for older preschoolers): yarn, sparkles, macaroni, etc.
- **Artwork**—Children are always being told not to write on the walls, but now they can have the freedom and the fun to write on at least one board in the room. Once again, cover a large bulletin board with craft (or wrapping) paper. (You may want to tack several layers at first so that you can tear off the top layer to expose a fresh piece when needed.) Then, invite the children to draw to their hearts' content. If you share a special story, event, or trip, expose a fresh piece of craft paper to create an instant mural!

Decorating the room with your children develops a sense of pride in them toward themselves and their environment. They will be proud to show off their room and the bulletin boards they all shared in creating! (See Figure 8–10.)

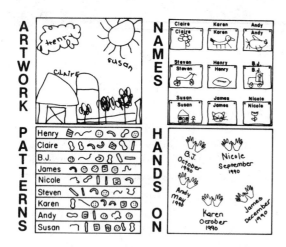

**FIGURE 8–10 Collaborating with children: Decorating bulletin boards.**

to give the children new ideas. The children may use these new ideas in their paintings and drawings. For example, animals seen on a trip to the circus may be made up as hand puppets, drawn in a mural, or painted in tempera colors. Although children have a large supply of their own ideas, the teacher can be a source of many new ones.

*Provide motivation for children's creative experiences.* Another way the teacher can help children develop their creativity is to begin each activity or learning experience with a motivational challenge. The teacher can do this by introducing new materials or conducting discussions and conversations to stimulate and challenge the child's imagination. Basically, the most effective motivation is praise and encouragement, but there are some specific ways to motivate children in creative experiences:

The teacher who hands out materials, then leaves the child to create out of a vacuum, is surely not fulfilling his role, which is one of establishing a wholesome climate for creative work, providing good motivations, introducing sufficient orderly procedure to insure good basic foundations on which to work, and then permitting the child to use his own ideas for the development of his project. (Linderman and Herberholz, 1979)

Beginning creative experiences with a stimulating motivational dialogue is very important to all successful learning experiences. With a motivational introduction by the teacher, the child is challenged to be inventive, imaginative, and to use her own ideas.

Three important points to remember in planning motivational dialogues to introduce art experiences are the following:

1. Hand out all materials before the motivational dialogue begins. This helps maintain interest at the end of the session and stimulates enthusiasm before the motivational dialogue actually takes place.
2. Show enthusiasm and knowledge of the activity as well as a genuine excitement in presenting it. Teachers, of course, should have actually worked with the materials beforehand so they know if the materials are suitable for the children.
3. A motivational dialogue for children should use words at the children's level of understanding. Examples of motivational dialogue starters follow:

Who has walked in the rain with an umbrella? What else did you wear? What color was your raincoat? (Have children show how to open umbrella.) Could you hold the umbrella over your head without bending your elbow? Let's draw a picture of how you look and feel while walking in the rain.

Let's draw a picture (or paint, cut and paste, etc.) about this:

*Preschool and kindergarten:*
If I were a duck . . .
What I look like with measles (chicken pox, mumps) . . .
Looking inside a tunnel, a box, a well, etc.
Getting a shot at the doctor's office . . .
What do I look like on the inside . . .
On horizontal paper: a family of tightrope walkers, a tug of war; a parade; a train or subway

*Early elementary:*
An ant's-eye view of a street scene
Eating my favorite food
How I came to school
What woke me up this morning
Walking in the rain
An imaginary animal composed of three different parts

## CHILD-TO-GROUP RELATIONSHIPS

When taking part in creative activities, a child learns to be in a group. Being in a group at school is not the same as being in a family. In school, the child is a student as well as a member of the group.

As a member of a group, the child learns many things. In the art group, a child learns how to follow, for example, learning to use a paintbrush by following directions. When making a mural with a group of children, a five-year-old learns to follow and work with group ideas in planning the project. Learning to follow rules about cleanup is another way a child learns to follow in a group.

A child learns how to lead in a group, too. For example, a six-year-old who is in charge of her group's paint learns to be a leader with responsibility. Children who can go ahead with ideas on their own are learning the qualities of a leader, too. Thus, in art projects, children have many chances to learn to sometimes be leaders and sometimes be followers.

Being a member of a group is a social learning experience. A group of children engaged in a creative project is a little social group for the child. In society, a group, or an early childhood program, chil-dren learn how to share and cooperate. They learn that being in a social group has advantages, such as being with other children their own age, working, sharing ideas, and having fun with them. Children also learn that it is sometimes a disadvantage having to work with the group's rules and that it is not always easy to take turns or to play with others each day in school.

A child learns to respect the rights and ideas of others by being a member of a social group. Learning to respect others is also a part of the child's life outside the school. The things children learn about being members of a group in school help them as members of social groups outside the school.

## SUMMARY

Well-planned creative activities help children develop good feelings about themselves and their abilities. In these activities, a child learns to be with other children, to be with adults other than parents, and to be in a group. The social skills learned in the early childhood art program help children adapt to other groups outside the school.

## LEARNING ACTIVITIES

A. Your first peer group may have been made up of children in your neighborhood or classmates in school. Can you remember their names? What did they look like? How did they behave toward you? How did you feel about your involvement with this group?

B. During these early years, who were the popular, amiable, rejected, or isolated children with whom you came into contact? How would you rate yourself?

C. What happened to this group? What caused it to break apart? Can you remember how you felt about this change?

D. If you could go back in time and give the child you once were a message, what would you say? Is there some way of communicating this type of idea to children in your classroom? (Adapted from Smith, 1987)

## ACTIVITIES FOR CHILDREN

The following activities can be used with classmates or with children in laboratory situations. Remember them for real-life classroom use.

### "I Can" Book

Show parents of young children the specific skills their children have learned. Make an "I Can" scrapbook using samples of the child's work. Show "I Can Paint," "I Can Color," "I Can Paste" with samples of work. Illustrate "I Know Colors," for example, with samples of the colors the child can recognize and "I Can Count" with drawings of the number of objects that the child can count.

## Teachers Are People, Too

A teacher who was late one day and was explaining to the children that she'd had a flat tire was surprised to hear one four-year-old say: "But don't you sleep here?" A teacher was obviously part of the equipment that came with the room! How much do your children know about you? Do you live in a house, an apartment? Do you come to school by car, by bus? Are you married? Do you have children? Talk with the children about *your* life. It will help broaden their understanding of the world.

## Group Effort Activity

To encourage and develop children's self-esteem, cooperation, and group effort, try this activity. You will need a table, crayons, markers, paper, and tape. Cover the top of the table with paper, attaching it with tape. In the middle of the paper write the title of the picture, for example, "Our Group Art." Allow the children to draw pictures on the paper during group or free-choice time. When the picture is finished (to everyone's liking), take it off the table and tape it to the wall or put it on a bulletin board. As a variation, use different shapes or colors of paper. Use a round table or a rectangular table, or an animal or tree shape. Or try to have a special theme for the group artwork: nature, families, animals, etc.

## Looking in the Mirror

A. Objectives: To admire and feel good about one's self. To learn about one's self. To learn the names for body parts.
B. Equipment: A large, full-length mirror or small individual hand mirrors.
C. Procedure: Let the children look in the mirror and tell you what they see.
   1. Have them name parts of their body.
   2. As they look, ask them such questions as:
      a. "Why do people look in mirrors?"
      b. "Why do people like to look at themselves?"
D. Try gluing or taping a small mirror to the back of each child's "cubbyhole" (storage space) for the child's personal use and enjoyment.
E. Play "Mirror, Mirror, On the Wall." A large hand mirror is shared by a small group of children. As

each child looks into the mirror, the teacher will lead the children in reciting the following verse:
   "Looking in a mirror,
   Guess what I see?
   A *(round)*, *(happy)* face
   That belongs to me.
Together the children will recite the verse, but only the child looking in the mirror will say the last two lines, completing the blanks.
F. To further develop self-image awareness with young children, use the following "body-image" finger play.
   EYE-WINKER
   Eye Winker (Point to eyes)
   Tom Tinker (Point to ears)
   Nose Smeller (Point to nose)
   Mouth Eater, (Point to mouth)
   Chin Chopper, (Tap chin)
   Chin Chopper, Chin Chopper, Chin Chopper, Chin.

## Making a Photo Album

A. Objectives: To see oneself and others. To learn to admire oneself and others.
B. Procedure: Have each child bring in a photo of herself.
   1. Use large pieces of colored paper. Punch holes in the side of each sheet of paper. Tie yarn through the holes to hold the pages together.
   2. Paste each child's photo on a page. Print the child's name under the photo.
C. Leave the photo album out so the children can look at and enjoy the pictures.
D. A personal picture sequence chart can be made for each child using photos taken at different times of the year (birthday, outing, holidays, etc.). Children will gain a sense of time, change, and growth in these photo charts.

## Field Trips

A. Objective: To enrich the child's preschool experience.
B. Procedure: Take the children on a field trip.
   1. Talk about what they are going to see before they go. Use books, records, toys, or other materials to familiarize them with the subject in advance.
   2. After each trip, use follow-up materials. Take pictures for recall or use a scrapbook. If the visit is to a zoo, have the children paste or draw pictures of what they saw and did. Make a book out of their pictures.
C. Some suggested field trips:
   grocery store                    classmate's home
   fire and police stations         office building

library
television studio
neighborhood park
zoo
circus
airport

ride on a city bus
pumpkin farm
dairy farm
any farm
train station
department store

## Activities for Self-Awareness, Self-Acceptance, and Cooperation

### Clothes Encounters

Gather together the spare clothes that were stored at the school for the year or packed away the previous year. Use a full-length mirror for this activity. At the end of the school year, encourage each child to try on his or her old spare clothes and examine himself/herself in the mirror. This activity provides a concrete measurement experience that is full of surprises. Talk about the "tight squeeze" of the clothes now and why this is so.

### Body Shapes

A. Objectives: To encourage children's positive feelings about themselves and their bodies. To encourage cooperation among children.
B. Equipment: Large pieces of brown paper, crayons, and paints.
C. Procedure: Have a child lie down flat on a piece of paper. Another child uses a crayon to trace the first child's body outline on the paper. Then the first child paints or colors in her own body shape outlined on the paper.
D. Encourage the children's self-awareness by having them notice what they are wearing and the colors before they paint their outline.

## Activity to Encourage Group Feelings

### Patty-Cake (For Three-Year-Olds)

A. Objectives: To learn to use body parts. To learn other children's names.
B. Procedure: Teacher begins by singing and clapping:
"Patty-cake, Patty-cake, Baker's Man,
Bake me a cake as fast as you can,
Roll it and pat it, mark it with (use a child's initial)
Put it in the oven for (use a child's name) and me."
  1. Use all the children's names in the song. (Or each child can have a turn to sing the song and name another child in the group.)
  2. Repeat it often so that children learn each other's names.

## Getting Acquainted Song/Poem

A. Objectives: To participate in a group activity. To learn each other's names.

B. Procedure: The teacher or child says the following poem, then points to another child, who answers by saying her own name in the poem. Try it with a whole group.

**Song/Poem**
My name is (Mary, Mary, Mary)
My name is (Mary)
Who are you?

C. To further help children become better acquainted, substitute their names whenever you sing familiar songs. For example, "The Muffin Man of Drury Lane" becomes "Clair Bear of Ridge Crest Street," or "Yankee Doodle" could be "Scott White." This name substitution technique allows each child a chance to be a "star."

## Feelings Wheel

You will need a large "pizza" cardboard, two large buttons, and a length of yarn. Cut from magazines several pictures that reflect emotional states (happy, angry, lonely, scared, tired, proud, nervous, and sad). Divide the cardboard into sections with the crayon. In each section glue one of the pictures and cover the entire cardboard with clear contact paper. Insert a pencil into the middle of the cardboard to create a hole. Insert the yarn through the hole and attach a large button to either end of the yarn. Be sure that the yarn is no longer than the outside edge of the cardboard. The yarn and button will act as a simple "spinner" device. Two or three children take turns "spinning" the button so that it randomly lands on one picture. The child will then make a facial expression that reflects the pictured emotion, name the emotion, or tell about an experience that may produce the emotion.

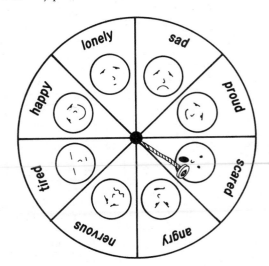

*Fingerplay*
Who feels happy, who feels gay?
All who do, clap their hands this way.
(Follow action as rhyme indicates)

Who feels happy, who feels gay?
All who do, nod their heads this way.

Who feels happy, who feels gay?
All who do tap their shoulders this way.
(All children like to suggest things to do)

## Child–Child and Child–Group Relationships: Making Murals

A. Make up a mural after a field trip. It can be made by all of the children working together on one large piece of paper, or it can be made by pasting separate paintings together on a large piece of paper.
B. Variations: Decorate some windows in the school. Plan and give a puppet show. Have two children make one puppet. Have two children make one mask.

## Activities for Self-Concept Development

### Who Is This? (Three Years Old and Above)

A. Objective: To help children achieve social contact by becoming more familiar with the characteristics of individual group members.
B. Setting: Small group or learning center arrangement.
C. Equipment: One picture of each child in the group (each one mounted on a separate sheet of construction paper); several "screens" cut from a piece of construction paper.
D. Procedure: Make the screens by cutting holes in a piece of construction paper. A screen is then placed over a child's picture. The children are then asked to guess who the child is, examining only what they can see through the "screen." Some examples of screens are shown below:

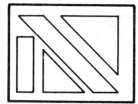 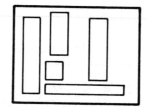

E. Variations: This activity can be made more difficult by placing more than one screen over a picture and removing them one by one as a child tries to guess who it is. If photos are not available, children can draw self-portraits. (Adapted from Smith, 1982)

### Create Your Face

You will need (1) several oval-shaped cardboard pieces that have been covered with felt or flannel (representing a variety of skin shades); (2) facial features cut from felt or flannel. Be sure to include eyes, nose, mouth (smiling and frowning), ears (with and without earrings), hair (realistically accomplished with yarn), eye brows, eye glasses, hearing aids, and teeth (with braces, if possible); and (3) a mirror.

Place items on a small table so that children will individually use the materials. The mirror should be close at hand so that children can refer to it in order to create their own faces. Encourage the children to talk about their work, noting their awareness of detail, expression, and personal accomplishment.

Try the following activity with children three years old and above to help them achieve social contact by becoming more aware of each other's names. The key concept is *name*.

### Name Fame

A. Setting: Group arrangement
B. Procedure:
   1. This activity involves chanting and associating group members with their names. The teacher should move around the outside of the circle while the entire group chants:
      Think real well
      We hope we don't miss
      Think real well
      Now, who is THIS?
   2. Just before the word THIS, the teacher moves directly behind one of the children in the group. After the chant is finished, the group shouts the child's name in unison. This can be repeated until everyone is named.
   3. Once they are familiar with the "rules" of the game, children can be selected to take turns moving around the circle.

### I Like

You will need a tape recorder. Individually ask children to name something they like or are interested in. Record these statements and create a pause on the tape. After the short pause, ask each child to say his or her name and record it. During group meeting time, play the tape for the children, asking them to identify the child after each statement of interest. The children can check their guesses when they hear the name of the child recorded on the tape.

### Object Sharing (All Ages)

A. Working in a small group, bring an object to the group and say, "I would like to share something with you that gives me a good feeling." Explain why the object is meaningful to you. For example, "Here is a necklace that someone I like very much gave to me. Whenever I wear it, I am reminded of that person and I get a good feeling." Then, "I would like to give you a chance to share something with us and tell us how it gives you a good feeling."

B. In the "Magic Circle" in the classroom the teacher asks the children to obtain something to bring back to the circle. One by one, they are given an opportunity to share their object with the group. Sometimes this can take place over several days as children bring sentimental objects from home.

### Me-Mobiles

You will need: (1) a selection of magazines (school and department store catalogs, nature, sports, as well as any popular family magazines); (2) scissors; (3) paste; (4) construction paper; (5) wire hangers; (6) yarn (or string); and (7) name tags large enough to fit in the central triangle of the hanger.

Tie the child's name tag to the central portion of the hanger and allow three strings to dangle from the bar of the hanger. Have the children look through the magazines and cut (or tear) out three pictures that reflect a favorite thing or activity. The children then paste the pictures on the construction paper. The paper can be cut in various shapes (clouds, geometric forms, stars). Tie or staple the mounted pictures to the strings attached to the hanger. Encourage the children to talk about their selections. Hangers can be hung on a "clothesline" in the classroom or in any other appropriate place. If children are not able to tie or staple, it is best to limit the number of children involved in this activity.

### The Missing Person Game (Four Years and Older)

A. Objective: To help children achieve social contact by becoming more aware of the presence of others in the peer group.

B. Setting: Circle formation.

C. Equipment: One large bedsheet.

D. Procedure:

1. Briefly discuss the idea that although sometimes people have problems with each other, everyone in the group is important. Sometimes the group misses someone when he or she is not there. Going around the circle, identify who is (and is not) present. Tell the children that you would like them to do an activity with you in which someone in the group will hide and the rest will try to guess who is missing.

2. Take out the sheet. Tell the children that you will first ask them to close (or cover) their eyes. Then you will go around the inside of the circle and tap someone on the shoulder. That person should

open his or her eyes and crawl under the sheet. Explain that when the selected child gets under the sheet, you will ask everyone else to open their eyes and guess who is the missing person.

3. Begin the activity by crawling under the sheet yourself and allowing the children to identify you as the missing person. Following this warmup, select children who are self-confident and are not likely to feel too uncomfortable under the sheet. This procedure may encourage less confident children to participate. If the group is unable to identify someone, ask the person under the sheet to say something. Children can use this clue to make their guesses. When children make a correct identification, show your approval by clapping and cheering their success.

E. Variation: The difficulty of this activity can be increased by putting two or more children under the sheet (probably no more than five). Children who are identified should remain under the sheet until all are named.

F. Suggestion: *Do not force* any child to go under the sheet if he or she is hesitant to do so. Be supportive and encouraging, but at all times respect the child's feelings. This activity should provide interesting feedback regarding the degree of awareness the group has for its peer members. Some children are, unfortunately, "missing" even though they are present in the group. (Smith, 1982)

### Fingerplays for Self-Awareness

Try these fingerplays to further emphasize children's self-awareness.

*Five Years Old*
Please, everybody, look at me! (Point to self)
Today I'm five years old, you see! (Hold up five fingers)
And after this, I won't be four, (Hold up four fingers)
Not ever, ever, any more!
I won't be three—or two—or one, (Hold up three, then two, then one)
For that was when I'd first begun.
Now I'll be five a while and then, (Hold up five fingers)
I'll soon be something else again.

*Hands on Shoulders*
Hands on shoulders, hands on knees, (Follow action as rhyme indicates)
Hands behind you, if you please;
Touch your shoulders, now your nose:
Now your hair and now your toes;
Hands up high in the air;
Down at your sides and touch your hair;
Hands up high as before,
Now clap your hands, one, two, three, four.

# UNIT REVIEW

1. Define the terms *self-acceptance* and *self-concept*. Describe a child with a good sense of self-acceptance and self-concept.
2. Decide whether each of the following statements helps develop self-acceptance, does not help develop self-acceptance, or does not apply to the situation:
   a. Holding a baby closely with tenderness.
   b. Giving a baby enough vitamin C each day.
   c. Encouraging a baby who tries to feed herself.
   d. Teaching a child to feed herself when the parent wants the child to do it.
   e. Leaving an infant alone as much as possible since too much touching spoils her.
   f. Having early dental care.
   g. Praising a child who dresses herself.
   h. Discouraging the child's messy eating habits.
   i. Getting yearly eye examinations.
   j. Making a child ashamed of an inability to walk well.
3. Describe what each of the following means:
   a. Child-centered program.
   b. Adult-centered program.
4. Choose the answer that best completes each of the following statements about an art program and a child's self-acceptance.
   a. An art program should be planned so that it is
      (a.) adult-centered.
      (b.) child-centered.
      (c.) year round.
   b. With each child in the program, a teacher must
      (a.) encourage the child to do more advanced work.
      (b.) praise only successful work.
      (c.) accept the child's present level.
   c. To challenge children, the teacher must provide activities that are
      (a.) a bit beyond their present level.
      (b.) two or three years advanced.
      (c.) for some children only.
   d. A well-planned art room
      (a.) is best on the north side of the building.
      (b.) has child-sized chairs and tables.
      (c.) has mostly large chairs and tables.
   e. A teacher should choose art materials on the basis of the
      (a.) age group using them.
      (b.) price of materials.
      (c.) type of distributor.
   f. A good reason for buying high-quality art materials is
      (a.) the low cost of the materials.
      (b.) children prefer quality materials.
      (c.) the good results children get with quality materials.
   g. In planning art activities, a teacher must consider each child's
      (a.) ethnic origin and sex.
      (b.) age.
      (c.) age, ability, and interest level.
   h. Success in art projects
      (a.) depends on having high-quality materials only.
      (b.) helps the child's pride and self-confidence.
      (c.) depends on the teacher's daily attitude.
   i. One good guide to help children's self-confidence is to tell children
      (a.) what they are doing right.
      (b.) to improve their drawing.
      (c.) to copy other children's work.
   j. Another good guide to help children's self-confidence is to
      (a.) tell them what they are doing wrong.
      (b.) guide their hands to help improve their drawing.
      (c.) encourage them to try again after mistakes.
5. Complete the statement in column I about child-to-child relationships by selecting the letter of the best choice from column II.

   | Column I | Column II |
   |---|---|
   | 1. A child can accept other children. | A. See that not all people have the same ideas. |
   | 2. Sharing ideas helps children. | B. Affects all the other school days to come. |
   | 3. Helping another child clean a brush. | C. Makes the child feel good about herself. |
   | 4. Getting along with other children. | D. Has no effect on a child. |
   | 5. A good preschool experience. | E. Is an example of learning to cooperate. |
   | | F. Only after she accepts herself. |

6. Discuss why the teacher is so important in the preschool art program or any preschool program.
7. List two ways a teacher can help a child feel accepted.
8. List three things children learn by being part of a group.
9. List some advantages for the child in a group.
10. List some disadvantages for the child in a group.

# ADDITIONAL READINGS

Asher, S.R., and J.D. Cole. *Peer Rejection in Childhood.* Cambridge, Mass.: Cambridge University, 1990.

Briggs, D.C. *Your Child's Self-esteem.* Garden City, N.Y.: Doubleday, 1974, p. 131.

Brody, S., and M.G. Sieger. *The Evolution of Character: Birth to 18 Years—A Longitudinal Study 1992.* Madison, Conn.: International University Press, Inc., 1992.

Curry, N., and C. Johnson. "Beyond Self-Esteem: Developing a Genuine Sense of Human Value." (Booklet) Washington, D.C.: NAEYC, 1990.

Gottlieb, G., and N. Krasnegor, eds. *Friendship and Peer Culture in the Early Years.* Norwood, N.J.: Ablex, 1985.

Harrison, J. *Understanding Children: Towards Responsive Relationships.* Hawthorn, Victoria, Australia: The Australian Council for Educational Research, 1991.

Jenkinson, E.B. *Student Privacy in the Classroom.* Bloomington, Ind.: Phi Delta Kappa, 1990.

Katz, L.G., and D.E. McClellan. *The Teacher's Role in the Social Development of Young Children.* Urbana, Ill.: ERIC Clearinghouse on Elementary and Early Childhood Education, 1991.

Kohn, Alfie. *The Brighter Side of Human Nature.* New York: Basic Books, 1990.

Kostelnik, M.J., L.C. Stein, A.P. Whiren, and A.K. Soderman. *Guiding Children's Social Development.* Cincinnati: South Western, 1987.

Light, P., S. Sheldon, and M. Woodhead, eds. *Learning to Think: Child Development in Social Context.* London: Routledge, 1992.

Linderman, E.W., and D.W. Herberholz. *Developing Artistic and Perceptual Awareness,* 4th edition. Dubuque, Iowa: William C. Brown, 1979.

Peterson, R. *Life in a Crowded Place: Making a Learning Community.* Portsmouth, N.H.: Heinemann Educational Books, 1992.

Smith, Charles A. *Promoting the Social Development of Young Children,* 2nd ed. Palo Alto, Calif.: Mayfield Publishing Company, 1987.

Woodhead, M., R. Carr, and P. Light, eds. *Child Development in Social Context I: Becoming a Person.* London and New York: Routledge, 1991.

———. *Growing Up in a Changing Society: Child Development in Social Context III.* London: Routledge, 1991.

# SELECTED CHILDREN'S BOOKS ABOUT SELF-CONCEPT AND SELF-AWARENESS DEVELOPMENT

Blanchard, A. *The Bear and Henry.* New York: Barron's, 1987.

Brown, T. *Hello Amigos!* New York: Henry Holt, 1986.

Cohen, M. *It's George.* New York: Greenwillow, 1988.

Conover, C. *Sam Panda and Thunder Dragon.* New York: Farra, Straus & Giroux, 1993.

Graham, B. *The Red Woolen Blanket.* New York: Little, 1988.

Harper, A. *It's Not Fair!* New York: Putnam, 1986.

Henken, K. *Sheila Rae, the Brave.* New York: Greenwillow, 1987.

Kurtz, J. *I'm Calling Molly.* Niles, Ill.: L. Albert Whitman & Co., 1990.

Lansky, V. *Koko Bear's New Potty.* New York: Bantam, 1986.

Lionni, L. *It's Mine!* New York: Alfred A. Knopf, 1986.

Omerod, J. *Messy Baby.* New York: Lothrop, Lee & Shepard, 1985.

Polushkin, M. *Baby Brother Blues.* Bradbury, 1987.

Schwartz, A. *Annabelle Swift, Kindergartner.* New York: Orchard Books, 1988.

Simmonds, P. *Fred.* New York: Alfred A. Knopf, 1987.

Stevenson, S. *I Forgot.* New York: Orchard Books, 1988.

Tsutsui, Y. *Anna's Secret Friend.* New York: Viking Kestrel, 1986.

Tyrell, A. *Elisabeth Jane Gets Dressed.* Woodbury, N.Y.: Barron's, 1988.

Warren, J., ed. *Short-Short Stories.* Everett, Wash.: Warren Publishing Co., 1987.

# Art and Physical-Mental Growth

## OBJECTIVES

After studying this unit, you should be able to
- explain how art aids a child's physical (motor) development.
- describe how art aids a child's mental development.
- discuss the place of art in the total early childhood program.

This unit presents the ways in which art relates to physical and mental growth. Physical, mental, social, and emotional growth all occur together in a child, but physical and mental growth are discussed separately here for the sake of clarity.

## ART AND PHYSICAL (MOTOR) DEVELOPMENT

The term *motor development* means physical growth. Both terms refer to growth in the ability of children to use their bodies.

In an early childhood program, activities like dance, drawing, painting, pasting, and other activities that exercise muscles aid a child's motor development. Exercising muscles in creative activities aids both small- and large-muscle development. Before we consider each of these types of motor development, let us look at the overall pattern of growth and development.

**Pattern of Development.** The process of human development follows a general pattern that includes growth in three basic directions. The first of these is called large to small muscle or *gross to fine motor* development. Large (gross) to small (fine) motor development means that large muscles develop in the neck, trunk, arms, and legs before the small muscles in the fingers, hands, wrists, and eyes develop. This is why young children can walk long before they are able to write or even scribble.

The second direction of growth, from head to toe (or top to bottom), is called *cephalocaudal* development. This growth pattern explains why a baby is able to hold up his head long before he is able to walk, since the muscles develop from the head down.

The third pattern of development is from inside

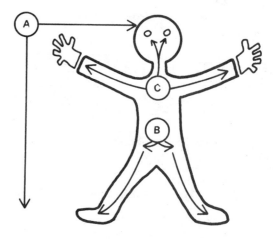

THE BODY DEVELOPS FROM

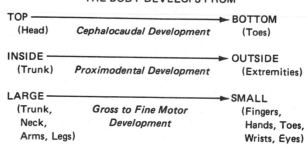

| TOP ————————————————→ BOTTOM |
| (Head) *Cephalocaudal Development* (Toes) |

| INSIDE ————————————————→ OUTSIDE |
| (Trunk) *Proximodental Development* (Extremities) |

| LARGE ————————————————→ SMALL |
| (Trunk, Neck, Arms, Legs) *Gross to Fine Motor Development* (Fingers, Hands, Toes, Wrists, Eyes) |

**FIGURE 9–1 The pattern of development.**

to outside (or from center to outside) and is called *proximodental* development. This explains the ability of a baby to roll over before he is able to push himself up with his arms. Because the inner muscles of the trunk develop first, rolling over comes before pulling or sitting up. Understanding these basic principles of development, especially large to small motor development, is important in planning appropriate art activities for young children. Let us now consider large and small motor development.

**Large-Muscle Development.** A child's proportions are constantly changing as he grows because different parts of the body grow at different rates. Throughout the first year, most of the child's growth occurs in the torso of his body, with a generally increasing chubbiness. From the big-headed, skinny newborn, he changes to the chubby one-year-old. Then he loses his baby fat as he becomes more mobile and learns to walk, then run. Figure 9–2 lists some of the large motor skills developed in the first 18 months of life.

| APPROXIMATE AGE IN MONTHS | LARGE MOTOR SKILL |
| --- | --- |
| 1–2 | Lifts head when lying on stomach |
| 3–4 | Lifts chest when lying on stomach |
| 4–5 | Reaches out and grasps objects; rolls over |
| 5–6 | Sits up if propped |
| 6–7 | Transfers objects hand to hand |
| 7–8 | Sits without support |
| 8–9 | Grasps small objects with thumb and index finger |
| 9–10 | Crawls; creeps on hands and knees; stands with support |
| 11–12 | Walks with support of one hand ("cruising") |
| 13–15 | Walks alone; climbs onto furniture; turns the pages of a book |
| 16–18 | Runs stiffly; feeds self |

**FIGURE 9–2 Large motor skills: 0 to 18 months (Adapted from Weinberger, 1981).**

Physical disproportions are common from birth to approximately age six as the upper body is generally longer and not in proportion to the lower body. As a consequence of these body proportions in which the legs and body are not developed in proportion to the upper body region, toddlers and preschoolers have a high center of gravity and are prone to falls.

By age six, however, body proportions are more similar to those of an adult. When the child has matured to adultlike proportions, his center of gravity is more centrally located so that he achieves a greater sense of physical balance and is able to be more purposeful in his movements.

Since large muscles in the arms, legs, head, and trunk develop first, by the time children reach the preschool age, they are able to use large muscles quite well. They can walk, run, sit, and stand at will. They can use their arms and hands quite easily in large movements like clapping, climbing, and holding. Younger children often are more involved in large motor play activities. Most three-year-olds and many four-year-olds are actively using their large muscles in running, wiggling, and jumping. They are not yet as developed in small motor skills (like cutting) as five-year-olds.

The early childhood art program gives the child a chance to exercise large motor skills in many ways other than just in active games. Painting with a brush on a large piece of paper is as good a practice for large-muscle development as dancing. Whether it be wide arm movements made in brush strokes or arms moving to a musical beat, it is only by first developing these large muscles that a child can then develop small motor skills.

Creative activities in the early childhood program provide many opportunities for exercising large-muscle skills. Activities that exercise large muscles include group murals, tracing body shapes, easel painting, clay-pounding, and crayon rubbings. (See end of unit activities for more specific activities.)

**Small-Muscle Development.** Small muscles in fingers, hands, wrists, and arms are used in art activities such as painting, cutting, and pasting. These small motor art activities and any other activity that

FIGURE 9–3 Small motor skills develop in pasting activities.

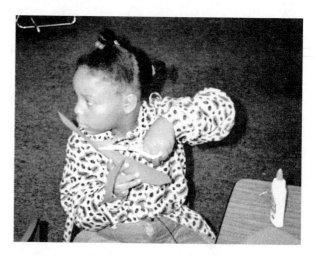

FIGURE 9–4 A child's small muscles are exercised by using blunt scissors in art activities.

requires the use of small muscles all help exercise and develop a child's fine motor control.

A teacher of young children must know that small muscle skills are different for a child at different ages. For example, many three-year-olds do not have good small muscle development, so the muscles in their fingers and hands are not quite strong enough to enable them to use scissors very well.

In the following report, a teacher found out that the planned art activity was, in fact, too difficult a small motor task for some of the children in the group.

Making masks out of paper bags was a good experience for many of the children. However, I found that many other children had difficulty handling the scissors and became frustrated. They were eager to have the masks, but couldn't handle the problem of not being able to manipulate the scissors [easily] enough to make a mask quickly. I tried to overcome this problem by helping them make the first holes, or cutting out part of an eye, and letting the child finish the job. Perhaps many theorists would say that I should have let them do it by themselves completely. But I just felt that their eagerness to make the mask and to complete the cutting once I had helped them was not to be overlooked. The children all wanted to take home their masks and ran to put them in their lockers so they wouldn't forget them. One little girl wore hers all day and had to be convinced that she couldn't eat with it on! (Author's log)

Practice in crushing and tearing paper, and later practice in using blunt scissors, all help small muscles grow stronger. The better the small muscle development, the easier it is to cut with scissors. Small muscles can grow stronger only by practice and exercise. A teacher encourages a child to exercise these small muscles in small motor artwork, such as cutting, pasting, working with clay, making and playing with puppets, and finger painting.

A teacher also encourages a child to exercise small muscles by providing the right small motor tools. The teacher in the following report managed to use clay as the medium for helping children practice small motor skills.

In my activities I wanted to emphasize fine motor development, so I used clay with different-sized soda-straw pieces, toothpicks, buttons, etc., to stick in the clay. The children made animals, designs, and monsters. They kept up a running commentary on how they were making a monster and could smash it if they wanted to. It seemed that the clay was a good means of having them release their fears, ideas, and emotions on many things. This clay activity went over very well. During the day, many different, as well as the same, children came back to play at the clay table. (Author's log)

Small muscles are often better developed in four- and five-year-olds. However, small motor activities

FIGURE 9–5 This child is using the small muscles in her hands, fingers, and wrists.

FIGURE 9–6 Cutting with scissors is an advanced small motor skill for young children.

are still necessary to help the child's small muscles keep growing. Drawing with pencils, crushing paper into shapes, modeling figures with clay, and making mobiles are examples of more advanced small motor activities.

It is important to plan small muscle activities for older children, too, as they will soon enter school programs in which they learn to write or print. Working with small muscles in small motor art activities helps make learning to write much easier for the child. The control over hand and finger movements used for finger painting and clay modeling is the same control the child needs to be able to write. Early childhood art activities give the child a chance to practice and develop the small motor skills needed in schoolwork to come.

**Large and Small Motor Activities.** The preschool art program should have a good mixture of both small and large motor tools and activities. A child needs to develop both large and small muscles, and artwork provides this chance. A small motor activity like cutting is fun as well as serious work for the child. Just as much fun and equally important to the child's growth is painting large brush strokes at an easel. Painting combines both large and small motor skills. Small muscles are used to hold the brush, and large muscles are used for the wide arm movements.

The teacher needs to respect each child's need to develop both large and small muscles at any age. This means a teacher needs the right equipment, but more important, the right attitude, for the level of each child. The right attitude is one that lets the child know it is all right to try many large and small motor activities at any age. In this type of art program, not all four-year-olds are expected to cut well or to button a shirt successfully, or to be able to do either at all. Five-year-olds, as well as younger children, may enjoy pounding clay for no other purpose than the fun of pounding. In an art program with this type of freedom, a child naturally uses creative materials in a way that helps large and small muscles grow.

**Hand–Eye Coordination.** In the early childhood program, as children exercise their small and large muscles, they also improve their hand–eye coordination. *Hand–eye coordination* refers to the ability to use hand(s) and eyes at the same time. Painting is a good example. When children paint, they use their eyes to choose the colors and their hands to hold and use the brush.

Hand–eye coordination is also used in clay modeling, making a mobile, pasting, and finger painting. In all of these art activities, the child is receiving practice in *coordinating* (using together) the hands and eyes.

## Hand–Eye Coordination and Reading.

Hand–eye coordination is important for future schoolwork. Many reading experts feel that good hand–eye coordination helps a child learn to read. They feel that the ability to use hands and eyes together in activities like painting or playing ball helps a child learn the motor skills needed in reading. Holding a book in two hands and using the eyes to read from left to right is simple hand–eye coordination.

Reading experts feel that the growth pattern of large to small muscles affects reading ability. In other words, a child must have a chance to develop large muscles before being able to use small muscles—such as the eyes in the right-to-left movements of reading. The side-to-side or lateral movements developed in such activities as painting and printing are also helpful in developing left-to-right tracking in reading. Thus, art activities are important for future reading as they exercise and develop hand–eye coordination and left-to-right tracking.

## Development of Motor Control.

All that we've discussed thus far about muscle growth and hand–eye coordination falls under the general category of motor control. As a child grows, he gains progressive control over his body. By the age of two, a child can usually feed himself with a spoon; by age three, he can eat with a fork and use a knife to spread food on bread. A five-year-old is relatively skilled in feeding himself and uses a knife and fork when eating. A similar developmental sequence is seen in a child's ability to dress himself. A three-year-old child can put on his shoes but cannot tie his shoelaces; by age four, he brushes his teeth and buttons and zips his clothes. By age five, he can dress and undress himself.

Other examples of a child's developing motor skills can be seen in outdoor play performance such as sliding, swinging (pumping the legs back and forth to create movement), climbing up and down, climbing across and through climbing bars, and walking across a balance board.

To throw a ball, a child must coordinate his arm movements with the rest of his body. Most children are not proficient in throwing and catching a ball until after the age of four and a half. Some do not master this task until age six. But most five-year-old children can run, jump, and climb with some proficiency.

Most children by age four move both feet in a coordinated fashion when riding a tricycle. By age five, some perform such feats as riding backwards and tilting or rearing up on two wheels. By age six, some children can ride a bicycle. A young child generally becomes intrigued by his developing skill and practices diligently until he masters it. He may try new variations on the skill. Soon after this, he may lose interest and move on to master a new skill.

Fine motor skills are developed in such activities as tearing and cutting paper, pasting, drawing, and coloring. By age three, a child can copy a circle. A year later, he can draw a circle and a cross. He can also trace a square and a diamond. The five-year-old is able to print his first name in large, irregularly shaped letters, but there may be some reversing of letters.

Children growing in small and large muscle skills and in hand–eye coordination are growing in total motor control. (Suggested activities for children ages 2 through 6 are found in Figure 9–7.) The child's work in various activities demonstrates this growing motor control. An observant teacher can assess an individual child's motor skills in one activity and make judgments about his likely skill or ability in another area. For instance, when considering art activities, a teacher recognizes that early scribbling is the beginning of motor control. The child holds the crayon and scribbles with very little motor control. As children grow in motor control, they can control the direction of their scribbles, then control lines to make basic forms, and finally draw pictures.

Therefore, a teacher can learn about children's general body control by knowing their artwork. For

| SKILLS AND CHARACTERISTICS | SUGGESTED ACTIVITIES |
|---|---|
| | *The Two-Year-Old* |
| Very active, short attention span | Provide pushing and pulling toys. |
| | Encourage play with pounding bench, punching bags, and soft clay. |
| | Provide opportunities both indoors and outdoors for active free play that involves climbing, running, sliding, tumbling. |
| Interest in physical manipulation, ability to stack several items, pull apart, fill and empty containers. | Provide stacking cups or blocks for stacking and unstacking. |
| | Provide pop-apart toys, such as beads, for taking apart. (Large enough *not* to swallow.) |
| | Provide opportunities for filling and emptying containers with sand, water, rice, beans, rocks, etc. |
| Increased development of fine motor skills | Provide crayons, chalk, paint, and paper for scribbling and painting. Be sure all materials are lead-free and nontoxic. |
| | Allow the child to "paint" the sidewalk, building, wheel toys, etc., with clear water and a brush large enough to handle. |
| | Provide opportunities to play with play dough, finger paint, paper for tearing, etc. |
| Increased development in language skills | Encourage the child to talk with you. Use pronouns such as "I," "me," "you," "they," "we." Encourage the child to use these words. |
| | Talk with the child about pictures. Ask him to point to objects or name them. Always give the correct name for objects. |
| | Give directions to follow: "Close the door," "Pick up the doll." Be sure to make this a fun game. |
| | Teach the child the names of unusual objects such as fire extinguisher, thermometer, screwdriver, trivet. |
| Likes to imitate | Encourage finger plays. |
| | Cite nursery rhymes. Encourage the child to repeat them. |
| | Play "I am a mirror." Stand or sit facing the child and have him copy everything you do. |
| Shows interest in dramatic play | Provide dolls, dress-up clothes, carriage, doll bed, toy telephones for pretend conversations. |
| | *The Three-Year-Old* |
| Increased development of large motor skills | Provide opportunities for vigorous free play indoors and outdoors. |
| | Provide opportunities for climbing, jumping, riding wheel toys. |
| | Play "Follow-the-Leader," requiring vigorous body movements. |

**FIGURE 9–7 Motor skills and characteristics of children, ages two through six years, with suggested activities to encourage physical development (cont. on pages 110–112).**

| SKILLS AND CHARACTERISTICS | SUGGESTED ACTIVITIES |
| --- | --- |
| Greater control over small muscles | Provide opportunities for free play with blocks in various sizes, shapes.<br>Provide a variety of manipulative toys and activities such as pegboard and peg sets, tinker toys, puzzles with 3–8 pieces.<br>Encourage children to dress and undress themselves, serve food, set the table, water the plants. |
| Greater motor coordination | Provide art activities. Encourage free expression with paint, crayons, chalk, colored pens, collage materials, clay, playdough. Be sure all materials are lead-free and nontoxic. |
| Increased development of language skills and vocabulary | Provide opportunities each day for reading stories to children in a group or individually.<br>Encourage children to tell stories.<br>Tape record their stories.<br>Encourage children to talk about anything of interest. |
| Beginning to understand number concepts. Usually can grasp concepts of 1, 2, and 3. Can count several numbers in a series but may leave some out. | Count objects of interest, e.g., cookies, cups, napkins, dolls. When possible, move them as you count. Allow children to count them.<br>Display numbers in the room. Use calendars, charts, scales, and rulers. |
| Enjoys music and is beginning to be able to carry a tune, express rhythm | Provide music activities each day. Sing songs, create rhythms.<br>Move body to music.<br>Encourage children to make up songs. Tape record them and play them back for the children to dance to or to sing along with. |
| Curious about why and how things happen | Provide new experiences that arouse questions. Answer the questions simply and honestly. Use reference books with the child to find answers.<br>Conduct simple science activities: What will the magnet pick up? Freeze water, make ice cream, plant seeds, make a terrarium, fly kites on a windy day. |
| | *The Four-Year-Old* |
| Good balance and body coordination; increased development of small and large motor skills | Provide opportunities each day for vigorous free play.<br>Provide opportunities for the child to walk on a curved line, a straight line, a balance beam.<br>Encourage walking with a bean bag on the head.<br>Games: "See how fast you can hop," "See how far you can hop on one foot," "See how high you can jump."<br>Provide opportunities to throw balls (medium-sized, soft), bean bags, yarn balls. |

**FIGURE 9–7 cont.**

| SKILLS AND CHARACTERISTICS | SUGGESTED ACTIVITIES |
|---|---|
| Small motor skills are developing most rapidly now. Drawings and art express world about him. | Provide opportunity for variety of art work. Encourage child to tell a story or talk about his finished project.<br>Encourage child to mix primary colors to produce secondary colors. Name the colors with him. |
| Increasing hand-eye coordination | Encourage child to unzip, unsnap, and unbutton clothes. Dressing self is too difficult at this point.<br>Encourage child to tear and cut.<br>Encourage child to lace his shoes. |
| Ability to group items according to similar characteristics | Play lotto games.<br>Group buttons as to color or size.<br>Provide a mixture of seeds. Sort as to kind.<br>At cleanup time, sort blocks according to shape.<br>Play rhyming word games. |
| Increased understanding of concepts related to numbers, size and weight, colors, textures, distance and position, and time | In conversation, use words related to these concepts.<br>Play "Follow Direction" games. Say, "Put the pencil beside the big block," or "Crawl under the table."<br>Provide swatches of fabric and other materials that vary in texture. Talk about differences. Blindfold the child or have him cover his eyes and ask him to match duplicate textures. |
| Awareness of the world around him | Build simple bird feeder and provide feed for birds. Record the kinds of birds observed.<br>Arrange field trips to various community locations of interest (park, fire station, police station). |
| Has a vivid imagination; enjoys dramatic play | Provide variety of dress-up clothes. Encourage dramatic play through props such as cash register and empty food containers, tea set, and child-sized furniture. |

*The Five- and Six-Year-Old*

| | |
|---|---|
| Good sense of balance and body coordination | Encourage body movement with records, stories, rhythms.<br>Encourage skipping to music or rhymes.<br>Teach him simple folk dances. |
| A tremendous drive for physical activity | Provide free play that encourages running, jumping, balancing, and climbing. Play tug-of-war. Encourage tumbling on a mat. |
| Development and coordination of small muscles in hands and fingers | Encourage opportunities to paint, draw, cut, paste, mold clay.<br>Provide small peg games and other manipulative toys.<br>Teach sewing with large needle and thread into egg cartons or punched cards.<br>Provide simple carpentry experiences. |

**FIGURE 9–7 cont.**

| SKILLS AND CHARACTERISTICS | SUGGESTED ACTIVITIES |
|---|---|
| Increased hand–eye coordination | Allow children to copy designs of shapes, letters, and numbers. Show a child how his name is made with letters.<br>Encourage catching small balls. |
| Ability to distinguish right from left | Play games that emphasize right from left. Games can require responses to directions such as "Put your right hand on your nose" or "Put your left foot on the green circle." |
| Can discriminate between weights, colors, sizes, textures, and shapes | Play sorting games. Sort rocks as to weight; blocks as to weight or shape; marbles or seeds as to colors. Match fabric swatches. |
| Increased understanding of number concepts | Count anything of interest—cookies, napkins, cups, leaves, acorns, trees, children, teachers, boys, chairs, etc.<br>Identify numbers visible on the calendar, on the clock, on measuring containers, or on other devices. |
| Enjoys jokes, nonsense rhymes, riddles | Read humorous stories, riddles, nonsense rhymes. |
| Enjoys creative, dramatic activities | Move body to dramatize opening of a flower, falling snow, leaves, rain, wiggly worms, snakes, blowing wind.<br>Dramatize stories as they are read. Good stories to use are: *Caps for Sale, Three Billy Goats Gruff, Three Bears.* |

**FIGURE 9–7 cont.**

example, the teacher who knows that a certain five-year-old cannot yet cut with scissors knows how to reply to parents who ask if this child is ready for piano lessons. On the other hand, a teacher would know that a child is ready for more advanced puzzles if the child puts together and pastes objects on paper in a collage. Thus, knowing about each child's motor control in artwork helps the teacher know each child's motor control in other areas as well.

## ART AND MENTAL DEVELOPMENT

As children grow physically, they also grow mentally. This is because young children learn by doing. Jean Piaget, in his work with young children, describes a child's learning by doing as "sensorimotor" development.

The word *sensorimotor* derives from the two words *sensory* and *motor*. Sensory refers to using the five body senses and motor refers to the physical act of doing. Sensorimotor learning involves the body and its senses (sensori) as they are used in doing (motor).

For Piaget, the foundation of all mental development takes place in physical knowledge, the knowledge that comes from objects. Children construct physical knowledge by acting on objects—feeling, tasting, smelling, seeing, and hearing them. They cause objects to move, throwing, banging, blowing, pushing, and pulling them. They observe changes that take place in objects when they are mixed together, heated, cooled, or changed in some other way. As physical knowledge develops, children become better able to establish relationships (comparing, classifying, ordering) between and among the objects they act upon. Such relationships are essen-

**FIGURE 9–8 Young children learn mentally as they do things physically.**

**FIGURE 9–9 Seeking answers and finding new ways to approach old problems are part of the emotional growth in the early childhood program.**

tial for the development of logical, flexible thought processes (Smith, 1987).

**Sensorimotor Learning in Art.** An example of sensorimotor learning in art is modeling with clay. In using clay (the motor activity), children use their senses (sensory), such as feel and smell, to learn about clay and how to use it. A teacher can tell the children how clay feels and how to use it; but children really learn about clay by physically using it themselves. A child needs this sensorimotor experience of learning by doing to truly learn about clay or any other art materials.

In the art program, children learn many things in this sensorimotor way—learning by doing. Many ideas and concepts are learned from different art activities. Just as children exercise different muscles in art activities, they also learn new concepts in many kinds of art activities.

**Concepts Learned Through the Sense of Touch.** Art activities that use the sense of touch

teach children many important concepts. For example, working with clay helps them learn the concepts of hard and soft. The children feel the softness of clay in their hands as they work with it. When the clay is old and needs water, they feel how hard it has become. In using clay this way, children learn not only that clay is soft, but that it can be hard, too.

Concepts like big and small can be learned by making or using clay balls in different sizes, painting on different sizes of paper; and with different sized brushes.

**Improving the Sense of Touch in Art.** Art activities provide many experiences involving the child's sense of touch. For example, in a collage activity, children learn to match scrap materials that have the same feel or texture. They match the ones that are soft and smooth (velvet and corduroy), the ones that are rough (burlap and wool), and the ones that are fuzzy (fur and cotton balls).

Making a collage can be an art activity as well as a touching game, and it helps sharpen a child's sense of touch. A teacher can use this and many other art activities suggested at the end of this unit to help develop children's sense of touch.

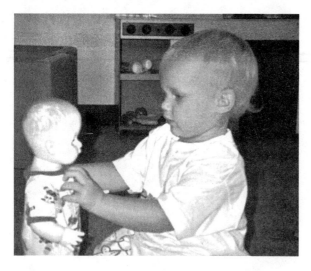

FIGURE 9–10 Young children learn about their world in active ways.

FIGURE 9–11 Physical activity abounds in an early childhood program.

**Concepts Learned Through the Sense of Sight.** Art activities involve the sense of sight as well as touch. A child sees and feels the art material being used. The sense of sight in artwork helps the child learn many important concepts.

The child sees the sameness and the difference in size, color, shape, and texture when working with different materials. He learns concepts like big/small and wide/thin by using many types of art materials. A child sees that different sizes of crayons make different sizes of lines. Wide brushes make paint strokes that look different from strokes made with a thin brush. He learns that a figure drawn with a felt-tip pen looks different from the same figure made with paint and a brush.

Ideas about basic shapes are learned in cutting with scissors, working with clay, painting, and drawing. A child also sees many basic shapes in the scrap materials used for a collage.

In artwork, the child sees that things can look alike but feel different. Sand and cornmeal may look alike, but they feel different to the child as they are glued onto paper. In this way, he learns that the sense of sight alone is not enough to really learn about a material.

*Color concepts.* Concepts about colors are learned in the art program. While painting and drawing, children learn the names of colors, how to mix colors, and how to make colors lighter or darker. In such a sensorimotor experience, the child learns that colors are not set things, but things that the child himself can change. This idea of change is an important thing for the child to know and is a concept that develops slowly.

*Concept of change.* Piaget, in his writings about the growth of intelligence in young children, emphasizes the fact that mental growth is aided by a child's active exploration of the environment. The child, according to Piaget, gradually comes to understand about how things can change as he experiences different materials in various situations in his environment. For example, by using color, mixing colors, and making color lighter or darker, the child learns that things can change. Clay can change from hard to soft. Plaster can change from liquid to solid.

"Learning by doing" in art, thus, helps a child grow mentally, as he grows more flexible in his thinking. The child learns to think of things in the context of change and that not all things are permanent. The ability to think this way is called *flexible thinking* (Figure 9–12).

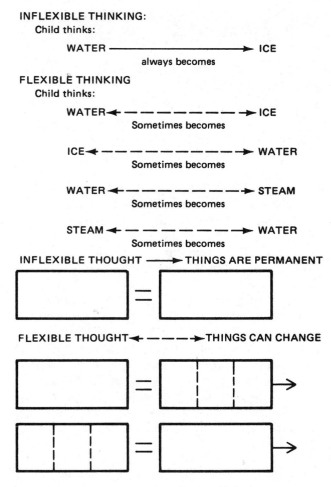

**FIGURE 9–12 Inflexible and flexible thinking.**

**Improving the Sense of Sight in Art.** The sense of sight can be improved in art activities just as can the sense of touch. Learning to see things as clearly as possible, according to Piaget, is an aid to a child's mental growth.

The teacher who encourages children to really look around them for art ideas helps them sharpen their sense of sight. Encouraging them to tell about what they see as they look out the window on a familiar scene is one way to improve looking.

The teacher may ask children to tell about all they see outside the window. This way, the teacher encourages them to really look hard at the everyday scene and not miss a detail. This close-looking exercise teaches children to really see their surroundings—not just to glance at the familiar things.

Seeing the differences among colors is another way in which art helps sharpen mental growth through the sense of sight. Making different shades of red by adding a little bit more white each time is one way to train the eye to become sharper in seeing the fine differences among colors. Picking out and matching colors of paper from a pile of mixed colors is another way artwork can train the eyes to see better. Maria Montessori, a famous physician and teacher, developed many similar color-matching activities to help develop children's eyes for later reading skills. Being able to see small and large differences is an important part of physical and mental growth. Good observational skills help young children develop skills that will be used in academic subjects like science, math, and reading.

Being able to think flexibly helps children become mentally prepared for later school experiences. Math, spelling, and science all require thinking that can deal with change. In science, for example, a cooking lesson involves changes ingredients go through in the process of becoming a cake. In math activities, a child learns how numbers can change by such things as addition and subtraction. In spelling, children learn how words change with plurals, suffixes, and prefixes. Flexibility in thought processes is, therefore, basic to most of a child's subsequent learning experiences.

**Vocabulary and Art.** A child's vocabulary also can grow through working with different materials. For example, in making a collage, a child can learn many new words to describe the feel of familiar things.

The teacher introduces words like *soft* and *smooth* to describe the feel of velvet material. Scraps of burlap are called rough, bumpy, or scratchy. Even the word *texture* is one that can be used with young children. As they feel the different kinds of cloth, the different "feels" can easily be called "textures." Children then put together in their minds the feel

# THIS ONE'S FOR YOU!

## LEARNING ACTIVITIES EVERYWHERE! APPROPRIATE SENSORIMOTOR EXPERIENCES

Including appropriate experiences for young children's sensorimotor learning is not really that difficult to do in the daily schedule. The early childhood program abounds with everyday experiences that are appropriate for sensorimotor development. Consider the following possibilities with painting.

Young children love to paint; they enjoy experimenting with color and can be quite creative in their artistic expression. You can use experiences with painting to heighten children's awareness of colors and color changes. As children become familiar with the primary and secondary colors through painting activities (naming or labeling colors is not necessary at this time), color matching and sorting on the basis of visual comparisons can gradually be introduced. As the children use different colors in their paintings, you can encourage them to match the colors of their paints to the clothes they are wearing or to other objects in the room. Further opportunities for developing color perception can be made available through experience with mixing paints. During painting activities, children may mix paints together and produce a new or different color. You need to help children focus on this color change; the observation that a *change* has taken place, however, is more important at this stage than what combination of colors produced the change. Children can even be encouraged, through the teacher's example, to experiment by mixing different paints to discover what happens. An activity that allows children to combine colors (mixing food colors in water or mixing paints) is an excellent example of observing changes in objects, a type of physical knowledge activity. Tactile (sensory) experiences can also evolve from children's painting. Their dried, finished products may be lumpy or bumpy in some spots and smooth in others. Having children carefully feel their dried paintings enhances their sense of touch and begins to focus their attention on different kinds of surfaces. Appropriate language—smooth, rough, bumpy, scratchy—can be introduced. Thus, an added dimension of an object's properties, that of roughness or smoothness, begins to become part of the child's developing knowledge.

of the velvet with the words soft, smooth, and texture. This is sensorimotor learning—learning through sensing as well as by association.

Learning to notice the different way things feel teaches a child about concepts that are opposite, which are important in subjects like math and science. The difference between hard and soft is similar to the difference between adding and subtracting in math; both ideas are opposites. A child learns in art that soft is not the same as hard. In math, a child

learns that adding is different from, or the opposite of, subtracting. Mastering opposite concepts used in doing artwork thus helps the child learn the mental concepts needed later in other school subjects.

## ART AND THE TOTAL PROGRAM

The early childhood art program helps a young child grow in social, emotional, physical, and mental ways. It gives children a chance to be themselves and grow at their own individual paces.

Art should not be the only part of the preschool program where this growth can occur, however. Freedom for growing at the child's own pace should be part of the whole early childhood program. The exploring, creating, and relaxing parts of artwork should be part of all the other early childhood activities. (Activities in these other program areas are included in subsequent units.)

Art helps a child grow through creative thinking and feeling, not only about art but about all other things. The confidence and good feelings about themselves and their work that children develop in art apply to other things in and out of school.

Seen in this way, art cannot be thought of as a separate part of the program. It is and always must be an approach to learning inseparable from all the rest.

## SUMMARY

Young children learn mentally as they do things physically. In the art program, they learn many important concepts that are used later in other learning experiences. Art activities involve children in sensorimotor learning through the use of the body, senses, and mind. Involving all the senses in art activities helps provide a complete learning experience for young children.

Young children learn important concepts such as hard/soft and same/different by doing artwork. Artwork also helps in developing their mental abilities: learning to think flexibly; being able to see fine differences; being able to hear, listen, follow directions; and learning new words. Finally, art helps them develop a creative mental attitude that will help in all school subjects. The creative aspects of art cannot and should not be separate from the total early childhood program.

## ACTIVITIES FOR CHILDREN

The following activities are designed to help the child exercise both small and large muscle skills and develop hand–eye coordination. Students should try the activities themselves, with classmates, and with children.

### Small Motor Activities

#### Chalk

Fat, soft chalk of different colors mixes with ease and provides a great beginning for small motor, free expression. Chalk discourages tight, inhibited work and makes free expression easy. Covering each piece of chalk with a piece of aluminum foil, leaving about half an inch of the chalk exposed, prevents smearing. It also prevents the transferring of colors from one piece of chalk to another while they are stored. A variation: Try wetting the paper, especially brown paper bags, and then applying dry chalk; the colors will be bright and almost fluorescent.

If a slippery surface is desired, liquid starch may be applied to the paper before the dry chalk. There is less friction with starch, and the paper is less likely to tear.

Soaking pieces of large chalk in sugar water (one part sugar and two parts water) for about 15 minutes and then using the chalk on dry paper is another method of application. Sugar gives the chalk a shiny look when dry.

Let the child experiment with all of these variations for small motor fun.

#### Tearing, Punching, and Stapling

Children love to just tear, punch, and staple. Keep a stack of old magazines and newspapers on hand for this purpose. It is great small motor practice and lots of fun for young children. If you do not have a paper punch or if the child is too young to use it, the child can use the handle of a wooden spoon to punch large holes in the paper.

If a paper punch is used, save the circles that the child punches from white waxed paper and put them in a jar full of water. After you fasten the lid on tightly, he can shake the jar and make a "snowstorm" inside.

Give the child a variety of paper, such as smooth, bumpy, heavy, and tissue-thin, all in different colors. Then ask the child if he can tear a tiny shape, an enormous shape, a wide shape, and so on. Let the child paste or staple all of the interesting, ragged shapes on a long piece of paper for a big, colorful mural. Tape the mural on an empty wall for all to see!

## Additional Small Motor Activities

A. Fine Motor Development and Drawing Practice: Decorate a Shirt
   Using wax crayons, have the children color a picture on a white or light colored shirt. Press with newspaper over the picture and on the ironing board. The picture will stay indefinitely.
B. Fine Motor Development: "Stringing Straw"
   1. Cut different colored plastic or paper straws into various lengths. Use large straws for young children.
   2. The child uses yarn or cord to string the pieces of straw. (Dip the end of the yarn in glue to harden the tip, and knot the end of the string to hold the straws.)
   3. Large macaroni can be used in the same manner. The macaroni may be *painted* first, so the child can string them in color patterns similar to those that the teacher has drawn out on task cards.
   4. Water Colors and Salt
      Children love to water paint, but sometimes the colors seem too subtle and quiet. Once a picture is done (using enough water to make it a moist picture), bring out table salt and sprinkle a little over the still-wet picture. The salt causes the paint to separate and gives the painting a completely new look. This is a good activity to talk about *change* in objects, and to discuss what the child *sees* as a change.
C. Hand Tracing
   1. Equipment: Paper, pencil, ink blot pad.
   2. Procedure: Have the child place his hand firmly in the center of a 9″ × 12″ sheet of paper. Using the other hand, he traces the first one on the paper. Make sure he realizes that the hand must be held firmly. If desired, the child may take each finger, put it in ink, and paint in the corresponding finger on both right and left hands.
D. Tracing
   1. Equipment: Crayons, large manila paper.
   2. Procedure: Child will make a certain letter with one color crayon. Then tell him he can make letter "rainbows" by tracing over the letter. Then have him outline letters and make his name or certain vocabulary words that are giving him problems.
E. Object Identification
   1. Equipment: A variety of objects familiar to the child: bench, button, bead, peg, ball, etc.
   2. Procedure: A leader blindfolds each child or has him cover his eyes. Place an object in his hand for him to feel. Ask him to identify the object. Then put it on a table with two other objects and ask him to find it. Gradually increase the diffi-

culty of the task by adding more shapes and sizes. Example: a round bead and an oval bead, a small ball and a large ball, a square box and a rectangular box.
F. Touch and Feel Box
   1. Equipment: Small familiar objects, box with holes for hands (only large enough for a child to reach into the box).
   2. Procedure: Out of sight of the child, place in the box a well-known object (scissors, crayons, etc.). Have the child place both hands in the box and feel the object with both hands.
G. Foot Designing
   1. Equipment: One or two pans of wet textures of mud, sand, moist clay; one or two pans of dry mixtures of sand, dirt, grit, pebbles.

   2. Procedure: Blindfolded or covering his eyes, the child places his feet in different wet textures and dry textures (dry textures first), and makes basic forms and free designs with feet.
H. Printing with Feet and Hands
   1. Equipment: Finger paint and finger paint paper.
   2. Procedure: Children step in finger paint and print their right feet and left feet, and then their hands. This work could be saved and used in Social Studies for a book "all about me."
I. Temperature Identification
   1. Equipment: Four bowls of water (cold, hot, cool, warm).
   2. Procedure: Blindfolded or covering his eyes, the child uses his elbow to identify hot, cold, warm, and cool water temperatures.
J. Matching Symbols
   1. Equipment: A box with a piece of cloth attached to the front, shapes (two of each), and other symbols (letters, numbers, two of each).
   2. Procedure: The child matches basic symbols inside a cloth-draped wooden box.
K. Fruit Identification
   1. Equipment: Various pieces of fruit (orange, apple, pear, banana). Could use vegetables also.

2. Procedure: One child in the group is blindfolded or covers his eyes. The leader of the group hands the child a piece of fruit. The child tries to guess the name of the fruit.

L. Shaving Cream Art

An easy-to-do favorite is to take shaving cream and put a few squirts of it in an empty water table. Take food coloring and dye the shaving cream the color the children choose. Watching the shaving cream turn color is half the fun; the other half is to finger-paint with the dyed shaving cream and save the design on paper. To save the design, put a clean sheet of white paper over the design drawn by the child, rub the paper, and lift. Hang to dry.

Shaving cream is also great to use when there are a few minutes until cleanup time and the children are bored with what they are doing. Squeeze a little dab of shaving cream on a table in front of each child. Show how it grows, changes, and that designs, mountains, and squeezy-feely shapes can be made from the cream. When time allotted is over, each child can clean up with a sponge. The children and the table will shine and smell good.

M. Creative "Find" Sculpture

On a neighborhood walk, on a field trip, or from a child's weekend trip with his family, collect an assortment of wood scraps such as driftwood, weathered boards, seashells, stones, twigs, dried flowers, pine cones, leaves. Use either a flat stone or piece of wood for the base of the sculpture. The rest is up to the child's imagination; animals, designs, birds, etc., can be created. Simply assemble your creation and glue it together in place on the base. Markers can be used to draw in faces, make decorations or whatever details are necessary.

## Large Motor Activities

A. Crayon Rubbings
   1. Provide large pieces of newsprint and large crayons. Show the children interesting textures such as wood and cement around the room.
   2. When they put the paper over the surface and rub with the side of the crayon, the texture comes out as a design on the paper.
B. Mixing Soap
   1. Children enjoy mixing up a solution of soap and water with egg beaters to make it sudsy.
   2. The water can be colored with food coloring for variety.
C. Sand Painting (Individuals or Group)
   1. Spread glue on a large piece of paper.
   2. Children drop sand onto the glue. (Shake the extra sand off.)

3. The children may make a mural, working together on one large piece of paper.
D. Clay Cookies and Cakes
   1. Have a clay party.
   2. The children pound cookie shapes, dish shapes, cake shapes, and similar items.
   3. Add cookie cutters for more fun.

## Additional Large Motor Activities

A. Create a Body
   1. Collect a variety of materials such as bean bags, boxes, cans, hoops, balls, wands, ropes, etc. Arrange the children in small groups of four to six.
   2. Using the materials made available by the teacher, the children build a body on the floor. "Can you build a human body using the boxes, hoops, etc., you see here?" The children may need advising. "Can you see something we could use for the neck?" Use the same suggestion procedure for other body parts.
   3. When the children have finished, ask them to study the body they created for several minutes. Afterward, take the different parts, stack them in a pile, and see how quickly they can put the body back together again. For added interest, let the children give their body a name.
B. An Art Lesson Using the Theme of Body Image
   Have the children trace their partner's body shape on large pieces of newsprint paper. When they are finished, instruct the children to color a designated part of their own outlined body a specific color. For example: Color the feet yellow, the toes blue, the legs orange, the ankles green, the knees red, etc. Children can give these directions, too. This provides practice in large motor skills, fine motor skills, and in hearing and following directions.
C. Flashlight Call
   Have one child stand in the front of a darkened classroom. The "leader" shines a flashlight beam on different parts of the child standing before the group. When the light shines on the child's arm, the group names it, saying, "arm," "foot," "head," etc.

## Hand–Eye Coordination Activities

A. Water Pouring
   1. Set up a pan filled with water.
   2. Provide different-sized plastic containers, squeeze bottles, funnels, and strainers.
   3. The children enjoy pouring water from one container to another.
B. Bean Bag Toss
   1. Make a large circle on the floor with a rope.
   2. Children aim and toss a bean bag into it.

C. Block Bowling
1. Set up a long unit block on the floor.
2. The children sit in a circle around it.
3. Each child has a chance to knock it down by rolling the ball at it.
D. Music and Painting
1. Play music while the children paint.
2. Suggest that they make their strokes go with the music's rhythm.
E. Ball Rolling
1. Play catch with the children who are able, or roll the ball to the children who cannot catch yet.
2. Notice which ones can catch and return the ball.
3. Compare this ability with their motor control in art.
F. Painting with Water (Outside Activity)
1. Fill a bucket with water and let the children "paint" the building or sidewalk with water.
2. The children should use large "real" paint-brushes (one to two inches wide) and buckets of water small enough to be carried around.

## Activities for Checking Motor Control

A. Artwork Samples
1. Collect examples of artwork from children aged two to six years.
2. Divide up the examples into the degree of children's motor control as seen in the examples.
B. Obstacle Course
1. Make an obstacle course of chairs, tables, or blocks to climb under, over, or around.
2. Notice how easy or difficult it is for children aged three, four, and five.
C. Action Songs
1. Sing an action song, such as, "If You're Happy and You Know It," using different directions: "clap your hands," "clap your hands and tap your head," "clap your hands and shake your head."
2. Notice which children can do the combined actions and which can do the single actions.
3. Note their ages.
D. Rope Games
1. Put a long rope on the floor in a zigzag pattern and have the children walk on it. Note how many of the children can do this and how well they can do it.
2. Put the rope in a straight line and pretend it is a tightrope. The children "walk the tightrope" with a real or pretend umbrella in their hands for balance. Note the balancing ability of each child.
3. Two children take turns holding the rope very high at first and then gradually lower and lower.

The rest of the children go under the rope without touching it.
4. Place the rope straight out on the floor. The children walk across it, hop on one foot across it, hop on two feet across it, crawl across it, jump across it, and cross it any other way they can think of. Note each child's physical control.

## More Large Motor Games

### Building Block
A. Equipment: Building blocks—wood or plastic (one for each child)
B. Procedure:
1. Each child has a block in his own space. Ask, "How many different ways can you find to get around the block?"
2. Have them find a way to get over the block.
3. Can they find other ways to get over the block?
4. Can they get over the block using just two parts of their bodies? Try three parts of the body.
5. Have them find a way to get onto the block and then fly off into space.
6. Have them find other ways to get onto the block and fly off in a different way. Use as many different parts of their bodies as possible. Have them try using different levels and different directions.
7. Can they balance on one foot on their blocks?
8. What other parts of their bodies can they balance on?
9. Have them get on their blocks and make a skinny shape at a low level.
10. Have them make as many shapes as they can think of while on their blocks.
11. Make an obstacle course and let the children find different ways to get through the course.

### Run, Little Bunny
Divide children into groups of three. Two of each group get on their knees, facing each other, and place their hands on each other's shoulders; the third child gets under their arms as though he were in a "rabbit hole." One child in the class acts as Farmer McGregor and one child is a bunny without a home. The farmer chases the extra bunny, which runs into one of the rabbit holes and, as it enters, the rabbit in the hole backs out and is chased by Farmer McGregor until the rabbit finds a new home.

### The Magic Box
1. Equipment: A box with fifteen to twenty different animal pictures; a stool or chair
2. Procedure: Place the box of pictures on the chair to

one side (this is the "magic box"). Children are seated in a circle on the floor. Four to five children are selected by the teacher; one is designated to pick out a picture from the magic box. He shows the picture to the four or five picked by the teacher. After the four or five students have seen the picture, they return to the circle (stand in the center) and imitate the animal they saw in the picture. When the circle players guess the animals, the animal imitators return to the circle formation and another group is chosen. In order to guess what animal is being imitated, children should raise their hands.

3. Variation: Use transportation pictures.

## Activities for the Senses

The following activities are designed to exercise the senses. Students should try the activities themselves, with classmates, and with children.

### Seeing Activities

A. Game with a Magnifying Glass
   1. Provide the children with a magnifying glass and a tray full of different objects—stamps, coins, leaves, and so on.
   2. Use the magnifying glass to look at your fingernail and a child's fingernail, a bug, and the other things in the tray.
   3. Ask the children to look carefully and to tell what they see. Use the magnifying glass outside on a nature walk. Encourage the children to talk about what they see. This helps them to express ideas and learn new words.
B. Paper Towel Telescope and Binoculars
   1. Use rolls from paper towels for making telescopes.
   2. The children look through the rolls out a door or window.
   3. Ask them to tell all about what they can see. Two bathroom tissue rolls can be taped together for binoculars and used in the same way as the telescope.
D. Examining Objects in Different Colors (Silverblatt, 1964)
   1. Use different-colored pieces of transparent plastic or colored cellophane.
   2. The children look at the things around them through transparent, colored material. They can see how the brown table looks through "yellow" or how the blue sky looks through "red," for example.
   3. When the chidren seem to understand how the color of different objects changes when seen through another color and have been satisfied using just a single color, they may look through

two colors at once (superimpose red over blue) and see still another change.
E. Mixing Paints (Silverblatt, 1964)
   1. Six saucers, six teaspoons, and paint (red, blue, yellow, as a start) are needed. Each child may experiment with mixing paints while painting a picture.
   2. A small amount of each color of paint may be placed in each of three saucers—a dish of red, one of blue, and one of yellow. Put a spoon in each and let the child mix the various colors in the three empty saucers.
   3. A styrofoam egg carton may be used for mixing the colors. Prepare three separate juice cans of color (one red, one blue, and one yellow). Put an eyedropper in each can. The child drops the colors into each of the separate cups in the egg carton and mixes them with a tongue depressor or wooden stick. The egg carton can be rinsed out for another child's use.
F. Prism (Silverblatt, 1964)
   1. Hang a prism in an area where it will be in the direct rays of the sun.
   2. Call attention to the different colors seen in the prism itself and to those reflected on the wall.
   3. Relate these colors to the colors seen in a rainbow.
   4. Be on the lookout for a real rainbow and provide pictures of rainbows.

### Feeling Activities

A. Different Objects to Feel—A Feeling Game
   1. Encourage the children to feel cotton first and then a piece of sponge against their skin.
   2. Talk about the hardness and softness of each.
   3. Ask them to feel a rock and then a chair.
   4. Talk about the hardness of each.
   5. Then have them touch the cotton and sponge again.
   6. Encourage them to talk about how these objects feel.
B. Paper Bag with Objects
   1. Fill a paper bag with common objects, such as a pencil, ball, comb, key, wallet, coins.
   2. Each of the children puts one hand in the bag (with eyes closed) and feels one object.
   3. The child must decide what the object is and describe it. (Add more and different items to make the game harder.)
C. Touching Game with Textures
   1. Fill a box with two pieces each of sandpaper, glass, rock, plastic, wood, cotton, corduroy, or velvet.
   2. Take out a piece of sandpaper. Tell the children what it is and how it feels (rough).
   3. Let each of them feel it.

4. Ask a child to find the other piece of sandpaper in the box.
5. Repeat for all the other items. Everyone has a turn to match up the textures.
6. Vary this activity by walking around the room to find things that are hard, soft, smooth, rough. This variation may be done outside, also.

## Hearing Activities
A. Sound Experiments
   1. The children close their eyes and name the different sounds they hear in the room.
   2. Make up noises and sounds (birds singing, blocks dropping, sawing wood, bells, drums and other instruments, tearing paper, water splashing, for example). Have the children guess what they are.
   3. A child closes both eyes while another child speaks. The first child tries to guess who is speaking.
B. Rattlesnake
   You will need a small plastic bottle with beans inside. The group closes their eyes and the "leader" walks around shaking the bottle. The group then points to the direction from which they hear the sound, and identifies the level of sound, i.e., "high" or "low." This can be played with one child as well.
C. Sound Cans
   Place four different substances—a small block, a piece of clay, a piece of cotton, small amount of sand—in four identical cans. When all the lids are on, shuffle the cans. The child guesses what is in each can by the noise made as the can is shaken.
D. Parrot Talk
   Use a paper bag puppet of a parrot, or just use your hands and fingers to look like the mouth of a parrot talking. Discuss with the child how parrots like to repeat everything they hear. Let the child speak first while you are the parrot and repeat everything the child says. Then you speak first and the child repeats. Begin with a single word and build up to a full sentence.

   Nonsensical words may also be used. Variation: Talk with the child about echoes and how they repeat the sounds two or three times. After you have echoed something the child has said or a noise the child has made, by tapping for instance, let the child be *your* echo.

## Smelling and Tasting Activities
A. Tasting Activity
   1. Place small pieces of cheese, apple, carrot, and banana on a tray. Show the tray to the children. Ask them to identify the foods on the tray and tell where they come from.
   2. Give each child a turn to taste each of the foods with both eyes shut. Ask the children to identify each food they eat.
   3. Try the activity again, tasting different drinks, such as milk, water, soda, and orange juice.

## Painted Toast
Make "paint" with ¼ cup of milk and a few drops of food coloring. Paint designs or faces on white bread with a clean paintbrush. Toast the bread in a toaster. The bread can be buttered and eaten or used as part of a sandwich. This is a very popular tasting experience!
A. Smell-o-Gram (Silverblatt, 1964)
   1. Collect items for a smelling game with a group of children. Use a variety of things: perfume, bacon, clay, paint, wood shavings, flowers, chocolate, soap, onions, and spices.
   2. The children close their eyes and try to identify familiar odors of objects held in front of them.
   3. Encourage sensitivity to different kinds of odors, for example, outdoor odors after a spring rain, food cooking, and so forth.
B. Community Fruit Salad
   1. To further experiment with how things taste, the children may help make a community fruit salad. Each child brings a different fruit: apples, peaches, pears, seedless grapes, tangerines.
   2. The children help peel bananas and oranges, wash grapes, and cut the fruit with blunt or serrated knives.
   3. The children should taste each fruit separately as they are preparing the salad. Then they should taste how the fruits taste together.
   4. Talk about how each fruit tastes, looks, and smells different from the others.
C. Fingerplays for Small and Large Muscle Practice

*My Hands*
My hands upon my head I place, (Follow action as
   rhyme indicates)
On my shoulders, on my face;
On my hips I place them, so,
Now I raise them up so high,
Make my fingers fairly fly.
Now I clap them, one, two, three,
Then I fold them silently.

*A Fingerplay for Naptime*
My fingers are so sleepy (Hold hand, palm up, fingers loosely bent)
It's time they went to bed.
So first you, Baby Finger, (Put each finger down in
   palm of hand as rhyme indicates)
Tuck in your little head.

Ring Man, now it's your turn,
And then Come, Tall Man great;
Now Pointer Finger, hurry
Because it's getting late.

Let's see if all are snuggled,
No, here's one more to come
So come lie close, little brother,
Make room for Master Thumb.

*Bedtime*
This little fellow is ready for bed, (Extend index
    finger)
Down on the pillow he lays his head; (Lay finger in
    palm of other hand)
Pulls up the covers, snug and tight, (Close fingers
    over "fellow" in palm)
And this is the way he sleeps all night. (Close eyes)
Quickly he pushes the covers aside; (Open fingers)
Jumps out of bed, puts on his clothes, (Let opposite
    hand dress "fellow")
And this is the way to school he goes. (Walk two
    fingers up opposite arm)

*Toys*
Here is a window in a toy shop. (Make a circle with
    arms)
This is a round balloon that pops, (Clap hands)
This is a top that spins in a ring. (Twirl one hand)

This is a little bird that can sing. (Pucker lips and
    "whistle")
This is a soldier that can walk. (Make two fingers
    "walk")
This is a momma doll that can talk. (Move one finger
    up and down)
This is a funny jumping-jack man. (Swing arms out
    suddenly)
This is a sleepy Raggedy Ann. (Let arms and hands
    go limp, relax head)
And now we will say goodbye to the toys.
And tip-toe away without any noise. (Stand in place
    and then tip-toe out)

*Ten Little Fingers*
I have ten little fingers,
They all belong to me.
I can make them do things,
Would you like to see?
I can shut them up tight.
I can open them wide.
I can put them together,
Or make them all hide.
I can make them jump high.
I can make them jump low.
I can fold them quietly,
And hold them just so.
(Act out each line with hands and fingers)

# UNIT REVIEW

A. Physical Development
   1. Define motor development.
   2. List three examples of locations of small
      muscles.
   3. Define small motor activities and give three
      examples.
   4. Define large motor activities and give three
      examples.
   5. List three examples of locations of large
      muscles.
   6. Tell whether each of the following activities
      helps a child develop a small or a large motor
      skill.
      a. Tracing body forms
      b. Using scissors
      c. Pounding clay
      d. Finger painting
      e. Finger puppets
      f. Painting with a brush
      g. Pounding nails
      h. Clay modeling
   7. Choose the answer that best completes each

statement describing a child's motor development in art.
   a. Most three-year-olds
      (a.) have good small muscle development.
      (b.) do not have good small muscle devel-
           opment.
      (c.) have good small and large muscle devel-
           opment.
   b. One way to check small motor skill is by hav-
      ing a child
      (a.) pound on clay.
      (b.) walk a balance board.
      (c.) cut paper with blunt scissors.
   c. Development of the body goes from
      (a.) small muscles to large muscles.
      (b.) large muscles to small muscles.
      (c.) arms to legs.
   d. In order to be able to use small muscles, a
      child must first be able to use
      (a.) finger muscles.
      (b.) large muscles.
      (c.) eye muscles.

e. By the time children are in preschool, they can use
  (a.) small muscles quite well.
  (b.) both large and small muscles quite well.
  (c.) large muscles quite well.

f. An art activity that exercises large motor skills is
  (a.) painting on large-sized paper with a wide brush.
  (b.) cutting paper with scissors.
  (c.) finger painting.

g. In planning the art program, a teacher should include
  (a.) mostly large motor activities for four-year-olds
  (b.) mostly small motor activities for three-year-olds
  (c.) both large and small motor activities for all ages.

h. The age group that uses mostly large muscle activity is the
  (a.) three-year-old.
  (b.) four-year-old.
  (c.) five-year-old.

i. A teacher in the art program should let children know that they are free to
  (a.) use only small motor activity.
  (b.) try all types of activities.
  (c.) try only large motor activity.

8. Define hand–eye coordination and give two examples of it.

9. Discuss what reading experts say about the importance of hand–eye coordination.

10. Describe how one can see motor control develop in a child's artwork.

B. Mental Development

1. Define sensorimotor learning and give one example of it.

2. Which of the following mental concepts does a child learn in art by the sense of touch?
  a. New words
  b. Hard/soft
  c. True/false
  d. Large/small
  e. Smooth/rough
  f. Names of colors
  g. Feel of clay
  h. Difference in shades of color
  i. Feel of play dough
  j. Sweet/sour

3. Choose the answer that best completes each of the following statements about how art helps mental development.

a. Concepts are
  (a.) phrases.
  (b.) songs.
  (c.) ideas.

b. The mental concept of opposites learned in art is also used in
  (a.) math.
  (b.) finger plays.
  (c.) cooking.

c. Introducing new words in art activity
  (a.) often confuses the children.
  (b.) helps improve the child's vocabulary.
  (c.) has little effect on young children.

d. An example of an activity that improves the sense of touch is
  (a.) a piano lesson.
  (b.) work on a collage.
  (c.) a seeing game.

e. Some concepts of color a child learns in art are
  (a.) how to erase color errors, paint over, and choose colors.
  (b.) how to choose colors, mix colors, and color over.
  (c.) names of colors, how to mix colors, and how to make colors lighter or darker.

f. An important new way of thinking that a child learns in art is
  (a.) flexible thinking.
  (b.) inflexible thinking.
  (c.) permanent thinking.

g. Seeing and learning that clay can have many shapes and textures helps the child develop
  (a.) inflexible thought.
  (b.) flexible thought.
  (c.) permanent thinking.

h. In artwork, very young children often use the senses of
  (a.) touch and sight only.
  (b.) smell, taste, touch, sight, and hearing.
  (c.) touch and smell only.

4. Discuss development of a creative mental attitude as a goal in the art program for young children.

5. Discuss what other aspects of the preschool program should be like the art program.

6. Should art be considered a separate part of the preschool program? Explain your answer.

# ADDITIONAL READINGS

Bergen, D., ed. *Play as a Medium for Learning and Development: A Handbook of Theory and Practice.* Portsmouth, N.H.: Heinemann, 1988.

Clemens, S.G. "Art in the Classroom: Making Every Day Special." *Young Children,* (Jan., 1991) 4–11.

Decker, C.A. *Children: The Early Years.* South Holland, Ill.: Goodheart-Willcox, 1988.

Engstrom, G. *The Significance of the Young Child's Motor Development.* Washington, DC.: NAEYC, 1992.

Gallagher, J.J., and C.T. Ramey. *The Malleability of Children.* Baltimore, Md.: Paul H. Brookes Publishing Co., 1987.

Gorlitz, D., and J.F. Wohlwill, eds. *Curiosity, Imagination and Play: On the Development of Spontaneous Cognitive and Motivational Processes.* Hillsdale, N.J.: Lawrence Erlbaum, 1987.

Healy, J.M. *Young Child's Growing Mind.* Garden City, N.Y.: Doubleday, 1987.

Lasky, L., and R. Mukerji. *Art: Basic for Young Children.* Washington, D.C.: NAEYC, 1992.

Moll, P.B. *Children & Scissors: A Developmental Approach.* Tampa, Fla.: Hampton Mae Institute, 1985.

Piaget, Jean. *The Child's Conception of Reality.* London: Routledge & Kegan, Paul, 1955.

———. *The Child and Reality: Problems of Genetic Psychology,* translated by A. Rosin. New York: Grossman Publishers, 1973.

Siegler, R.S. *Children's Thinking.* Englewood Cliffs, N.J.: Prentice-Hall, 1986.

Silverblatt, I.M. *Creative Activities.* Cincinnatti: I.M. Silverblatt, 1964.

Smith, C.A. *Promoting the Social Development of Young Children,* 2nd ed. Palo Alto, Calif.: Mayfield Publishing, 1987.

Weinberger, H.L., M.D. "The New Baby: Birth to 18 Months." In *Guide for Parents,* Vol. 15. Chicago: World Book—Childcraft International, Inc., 1981.

Zion, L.C., and B.L. Raker. *The Physical Side of Thinking.* Springfield, Ill.: Thomas Publishing, 1986.

# UNIT 10

# Developmental Levels and Art

**OBJECTIVES**

After studying this unit, you should be able to
- define the cognitive, perceptual, perceptual delineation, and psychoanalytic theories of art development.
- describe the scribble stage, including appropriate materials for use in this stage.
- explain the basic forms stage, including appropriate materials for use in this stage.
- discuss the pictorial stage, including appropriate materials for use in this stage.
- discuss appropriate art activities and materials for toddlers, young preschoolers, and older preschoolers and kindergartners.

As children grow older, they change in height and weight and gain new skills. They also develop different abilities in art. The artwork of a three-year-old is different from that of a four- or five-year-old. It is different in the way it looks, as well as in the way it is made.

For many years people have been trying to explain why all children, the world over, draw in the way they do. There are many theories of children's art, each of which offers an explanation for why children produce art and suggests strategies for teachers.

## THEORIES OF CHILDREN'S ART

According to one theory, the *cognitive theory,* children draw what they know. In visual art, the distortions a child draws in size, shape, and form are believed to represent the child's level of thinking. Florence Goodenough developed the Goodenough Draw a Man Test, which supports the idea that the amount of detail and accuracy in children's drawings reflects their thinking (Goodenough, 1926). The cognitive theory suggests that as children gain in understanding, grow, and have more and more experiences, they increase their fund of concepts (ideas), and thus their visual art increases in both detail and accuracy.

The *cognitive development* theory of Piaget relates children's art to their ability to understand the permanent existence of objects. Unless children understand that objects have a permanent existence, they have no image through which to evoke the past and anticipate the future. They must be able to recall what is absent in order to think about it, and this requires a symbol to stand for what is not here and now. Representation of these symbols is the means by which human beings organize their experiences of the world to further understand it (Piaget, 1955).

Another theory, the *psychoanalytic theory,* claims that children draw what they feel and that their art is a reflection of deep inner emotions (Cole, 1966). This theory holds that children's artwork is influenced by emotions, feelings, and inner psychological drives. The reason children draw daddy so tall is not because that is what they know, but because they feel daddy is so powerful and looms so large in their emotions (Lasky and Mukerji, 1980).

Another theory, the *perceptual theory,* suggests that children draw what they see (or perceive), not what they know or feel. Arnheim, one of this theory's supporters, believes that children do not see objects as the sum of observed parts, but that they see wholes or total images structured by the brain. To Arnheim, perception is learned, or at least can be improved, through training in visual discrimination (Arnheim, 1954). Thus, teachers should try to strengthen and improve children's visual perceptions by asking them to look at and observe their environment more closely.

Finally, a more comprehensive theory, the *perceptual delineation theory,* has been advanced by June McFee. McFee (1970) believes children draw as they do, not because of any one factor, but because of several. One such factor is the child's readiness, including her physical development, intelligence, perceptual development, and cultural dispositions. A second factor is the psychological environment in which the child works, including the degree of threat or support, as well as the number and intensity of rewards and punishments present. A third factor relates to how children handle information—the ability to handle details and to organize and categorize information coming from the environment. A final factor deals with how children's drawings are influenced by their ability to manipulate the art materials, as well as their creative and inventive ability.

No one theory is best, and it would be unusual to find an early childhood program based on one theory alone. In fact, the different theories, though varied and distinct, have similar characteristics. No theory suggests that a teacher interfere directly with children's art production, nor does any theory suggest that children follow adult patterns or color in lines drawn by an adult. Each theory recognizes the need for children to express their own ideas and to do their own thinking in a supportive environment. Our discussion will now focus on the developmental theory of children's art.

## DEVELOPMENTAL LEVELS/ STAGES OF ART

One who works with young children must know the different stages children go through in the development of art abilities. These stages are called *developmental levels.* A developmental level is a guide to what a child can do in art at different ages, but it is not a strict guideline. Some children may be ahead or behind the developmental level for their age. Developmental levels tell the teacher what came before and what is to come in the artwork of the young child.

There is no exact pattern for each age level. Not all three-year olds behave alike, nor are they completely different from four-year-olds. But there is a gradual growth process, called *development,* that almost every child goes through.

An understanding of developmental levels helps an adult accept each child at the child's present level, whatever it is. To understand development is to know that forced practice in art is unnecessary and useless.

From 1830, when Ebenezer Cooke first drew attention to the successive stages of development found in children's drawings, to Viktor Lowenfeld's *Creative and Mental Growth of the Child* (1982) and Rhoda Kellogg's *Analyzing Children's Art* (1970), teachers have based their objectives for art activities on the idea that children's art is developmental. Ability in art develops as the child grows and matures. Each stage is a part of the natural and normal aspects of child growth and development. These stages are sequential, with each stage characterized by increasing progress. Even though stages in art have been identified and accepted, the age at which children progress through these stages is highly *individual.* As children's bodies and minds mature, so does their art ability. Children learn to paint, model, and build as they learn to walk—slowly, developing in their own way. They learn each new step in the process as they are ready for it. As a general guide, art development progresses from experimentation and exploration (the scribble stage in drawing), to the devising of basic forms, to the forming of symbolic figures and their naming.

The following discussion of the development of children's drawing is intended to serve as a general guide to the overall process of art development. The basic developmental levels, or stages, apply to all art media. For the sake of clarity, children's drawing will be the primary focus of the discussion.

## CHILDREN'S DRAWING

There are three developmental levels in drawing that are of concern to the early childhood teacher: the scribble stage, the basic forms stage, and the pictorial (or first drawings) stage.

# THE SCRIBBLE STAGE

Most children begin scribbling at about one and one half to two years of age. They will scribble with anything at hand and on anything nearby. Their first marks are usually an aimless group of lines. Yet these first scribbles are related to later drawing and painting. They are related to art just as a baby's first babbling sounds are related to speech.

The crayon may be held upside down, or sideways, or even with the fist or between clenched fingers. Children may be pleased with this scribbling and get real enjoyment from it. However, they do not try to make any definite pictures with these marks. They simply enjoy the physical motions involved in scribbling. It is the act of doing—not the final product—that is important to the child.

If you watch a baby draw or a toddler making art, you know art is a sensorimotor activity. As a child draws or paints, every part of the body moves, all working to move the crayon or brush across the paper. Once the child begins the movement, it's difficult to stop! As a consequence, whatever surface the child is working on often becomes covered with paint and crayon.

**Early Scribble Stage: Disordered or Random Scribbling.** During the early scribble stage, the young child does not have control over hand movements or the marks on a page. The marks are random and go in many directions. The direction of the marks depends on whether the child is drawing on the floor or on a low table. The way the crayon is held also affects how the scribbles look. But the child is not able to make the crayon go in any one way on purpose. There is neither the desire nor the ability to control the marks. (See Figure 10–2 for some examples of random scribbles.)

Because it is the sensory experience of making marks that's important at this stage, the child doesn't even recognize the scribbles that have been created. In fact, these children receive as much satisfaction from just handling the materials—dumping the crayons out of the box, putting them back in again, rolling them across the table or in their hands—that they may not even begin drawing!

Art is such a sensory experience at this age that children may use crayons in both hands as they draw, singing along in rhythm to the movements they are making. They may not even notice the pen they're working with isn't leaving marks on the paper.

Because it is the process that is important to children when they're toddlers, there's no need to label their scribbles with their names, or ask for stories or titles to accompany the scribbles. You will, however, want to save samples of scribbles from time to time to keep a record of the children's progress.

**Later Scribble Stage: Controlled Scribbling.** At some point, children find a connection between their motions and the marks on the page. This may be about six months after the child has started to scribble, but the time will vary with each child. This is a very important step. The child has now found it possible to *control* the marks. Many times, an adult cannot see any real difference in these drawings. They still look like scribbles—but they are different in a very important way.

The child's gradual gaining of control over scribbling motion is a vital experience for the child. She now is able to make the marks go in the direction desired. Most children scribble at this later stage with a great deal of enthusiasm, since coordination between seeing and doing is an important achievement.

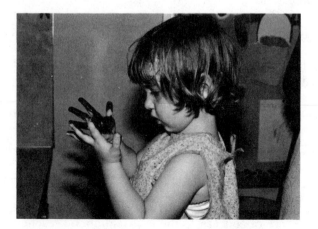

**FIGURE 10–1 Small muscles in the hands are exercised in scribbling as well as finger painting.**

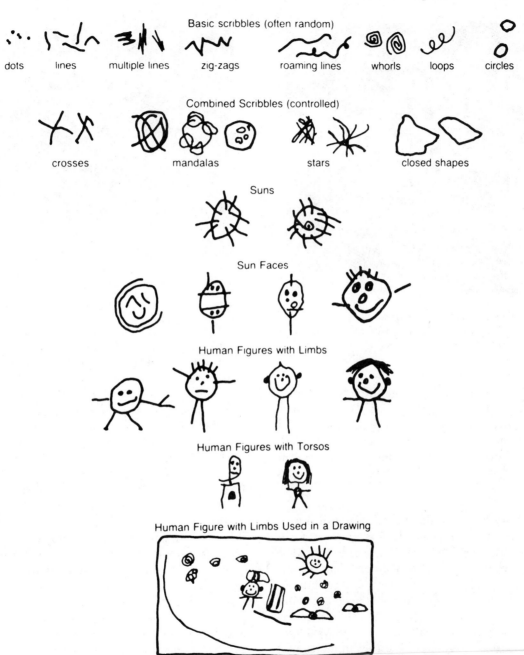

**FIGURE 10–2  Examples of development in children's drawing (from Feeney et al., 1983).**

FIGURE 10–3 In the later scribble stage, children begin to control their scribbles and make marks that go in a desired direction.

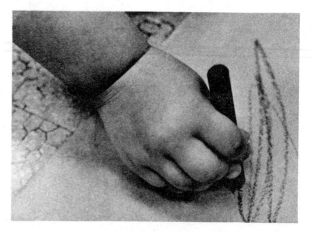

FIGURE 10–4 The ability of children to repeat certain motions in drawings means they are beginning to develop better muscle control.

Because children enjoy this new-found power, they are encouraged to try new motions. They now may scribble in lines, zigzags, or circles. When they repeat motions, it means they are gaining control over certain movements. They can become very involved in this type of scribbling. (See Figure 10–2 for examples of controlled scribbles.)

**The Scribble Stage and Two-Dimensional Media.** The term *two-dimensional* refers to any art form that is flat. Art in two dimensions has only two sides, front and back. Examples of two-dimensional art processes are painting, drawing, collage, and scribbling.

Children just beginning to scribble need tools that are safe and easy to hold and use. For a child between the ages of one and one half and three years, large, nontoxic crayons are good tools for two-dimensional artwork. Pencils are dangerous for the young child and are also too difficult to hold and use. A good-grade kindergarten-type crayon is the best tool. The crayon should be large and unwrapped so it can be used on both the sides and ends. Good crayons are

strong enough to hold up to rough first scribbles. They also make bright, clear colors, which are pleasant for the child to use.

Since motion is the chief enjoyment in this stage, the child should have large blank paper (at least 18″ × 24″). This size allows enough room for wide arm movements and large scribbles in many directions. The paper should always be large enough to give the child a big open space for undirected, random scribbles. Paper should be in a variety of shapes, such as triangular, circular, oval, etc.

If possible, a child in the scribble stage should use large white paper. Crayon scribbles show up better on white paper, so the child can see more easily the results of the scribbling. The want ad section of the newspaper is also appropriate paper for beginning artists. The small print of the advertisements makes a neutral, non-intrusive background for scribbling, and this section of the paper provides a generous supply of material for young scribblers, which encourages the frequency of their scribbling.

The child needs only a few crayons at a time. Because it is important that the child develop motor control in the early period of the scribbling stage, too many different crayons may distract the child in the scribbling process. A box of 32 crayons, for example, would become an object of exploration itself, and hence a distraction from the act of scribbling. This type of interruption breaks up arm movement as well as total physical involvement. New crayons may be added when a new drawing is started.

Painting is another good two-dimensional art activity for children in the scribble stage. Paint brushes for two- and three-year-olds need to have 12-inch handles and ¾-inch to 1-inch bristles. Paint for two- and three-year-old children should be mixed with a dry soap so it is thick enough to control. The paper for painting may need to be heavier than newsprint because children will repeatedly paint the paper until it disintegrates. Toddlers and two- and three-year-olds all enjoy experimenting with paint at the easel

and table. Pasting, tearing paper, and soap and finger painting are also two-dimensional art activities enjoyed by most children of this age. A good deal of monitoring is required with toddlers because they are tempted to taste the materials and carry them about the room. Some toddlers begin to express ideas with the activities suggested here, but the major value for them lies in simple experimentation with the colors and textures.

**Observation of the Scribble Stage.**    The student observer of young children (ages one and one half to three years) should keep in mind the following points in observing scribbling. A copy of the observation sheet (Figure 10–5) may be used to record your observations.

| CHILD | AGE | MOTOR CONTROL | ARM MOVEMENTS | TYPES OF SCRIBBLES | USE OF PAPER | EARLY PERIOD | LATER PERIOD |
|-------|-----|---------------|---------------|--------------------|--------------|--------------|--------------|
|       |     |               |               |                    |              |              |              |

COMMENTS:

**FIGURE 10–5 Scribble stage observation form.**

**FIGURE 10–6 A two-finger grip on the crayon is a sign of emerging motor control.**

*Age.* Note the age of the child. Keep in mind the average range for the scribble stage (one and one half to three years). See how the child fits in the range. There may be an overlap between stages.

*Motor control.* Note how the child holds the crayon: with two fingers, clenched fingers, or a fist. If the child uses a two-finger grip, this is the start of good motor control. The other methods of holding the crayon show less motor control. See if the child can hold the crayon without dropping it during the entire drawing. This also shows good motor control. Note any other things that might show the child's degree of motor control.

*Arm movements.* In scribbling, a child may use one type of arm movement or a variety. Note if movements are wide, long, short, jabbing, or of other kinds. The type of arm movement used affects the basic forms the child will make in the future. For example, if circular scribbles are being made, later these scribbles become circles.

*Types of scribbles.* Note the kind of scribbles the child is making. They may be controlled or uncon-

trolled, circular, lines, or others mentioned earlier. Consult Figure 10–2 for examples.

*Use of paper.* There are many ways of using paper for scribbling. Some are moving across the paper from left to right, moving across the paper from right to left, scribbling on only one part of the page, and moving the paper to make marks in the other direction. See if the child seems to know how to use the paper. Older scribblers often have more control over the paper.

Try these activities, observing and noting what happens:

- Provide the child with some soft, colored chalk. See if this new tool causes any differences in the way the child scribbles. (See Unit 9 for more suggestions on various uses for chalk.)
- Change to smaller paper. See if there are any differences in the child's arm movement, type of scribbles made, and use of paper.
- Place two extra colored crayons in the child's view. See if the child uses them. Then see if scribbles look different when the child uses many colors. Compare an all-one-color drawing with a many-color drawing.

## THE BASIC FORMS STAGE

Basic forms like rectangles, squares, and circles develop from scribbles as the child finds and recognizes simple shapes in the scribbles. More importantly, they develop as the child finds the muscle control and *hand–eye coordination* (use of hand(s) and eyes at the same time) to repeat the shape.

At this stage, the drawings look more organized. This is because the child is able to make basic forms by controlling the lines. A child in the age range of three to four years is usually in the basic forms stage (see Figure 10–2).

During this stage children hold their tools more like an adult and have a growing control over the materials. Children can now control their scribbles, making loops, circular shapes, and lines that are distinguishable and can be repeated at will. Children at this age value their scribbles. By age three or four,

FIGURE 10–7 A child in the three- to four-year-old range is generally in the basic forms stage.

**FIGURE 10–8 The basic forms stage is present in a child's work with clay as well as with crayons.**

children won't draw if their pen is out of ink. The names of the children now can be placed on the scribbles and can be taken home or displayed in the room.

It is important to note, again, that there may be an overlap between developmental levels in art. For example, one three-year-old child may be drawing basic forms and an occasional scribble. Another three-year-old may still be totally in the scribble stage. Developmental levels are meant merely as guidelines, not as set laws on age and ability levels.

**Early Basic Forms Stage: Circle and Oval.** Generally, the first basic form drawn is the oval or circle. It develops as children recognize the simple circle in their scribbles and are able to repeat it. Both the oval and the circle develop from circular scribbles.

Another early basic form in this stage is the curved line or arc. This is made with the same swinging movement of an arm used in the early scribble stage. Now, however, it is in one direction only. This kind of line gradually becomes less curved, and from it come the horizontal and vertical lines.

**Later Basic Forms: Rectangle and Square.** As muscle control of three- to four-year-olds improves in this stage, more basic forms are made in their drawings. The rectangle and square forms are made when the child can draw separate lines of any length desired. The child joins the separate lines to form the rectangle or square.

The circle, oval, square, and rectangle are all basic forms made by the child's control of lines. These basic forms are needed in the next developmental stage of art—the pictorial stage.

**The Basic Forms Stage and Two-Dimensional Media.** Children in the basic forms stage have enough motor control and hand-eye coordination to use different tools. In addition to crayons, the child may now begin to work with tempera (poster) paint.

**FIGURE 10–9 Basic forms drawings might look simple, but they represent a great motor achievement for the child.**

Tempera paint is the best kind for children because it flows easily from the brush onto the page. Large lead pencils are good for children in the later period of this stage; there is less danger of injury with these older children. A variety of papers can be supplied, from newsprint to construction paper. These children should be allowed plenty of time with the basic tools of drawing, painting, modeling, cutting, and pasting and should not be rushed into other media. The basic developmental goal for this age is the control of the media and tasks of drawing, painting, or modeling. (A complete list of proper materials is included in Unit 11 on selecting materials.)

Felt-tip pens are an excellent tool for this stage. They make clear, quick, easily made, and nice-looking marks. In the basic forms stage, when the child really enjoys seeing the marks come out as desired, these pens are best. They require little pressure to make bold marks. Felt-tip pens should be nontoxic and water-soluble so that most spots can be washed out of the child's clothes.

The largest paper size is not as necessary in this stage as in the scribble stage. Because the child now has better motor control, it is easier to keep marks on a smaller space. Room for wide, uncontrolled movements is not as necessary. Make available paper of many sizes and shapes. Figure 10–10 lists some other suggestions for basic art supplies.

Easel
Different kinds, sizes, shapes, textures, and colors of paper
Finger paints, watercolors
Tempera paint (liquid, dry powder)
Colored chalk, pastels, charcoal, pencils
Crayons, marking pens, colored pencils
Materials for weaving, stitchery
Box of materials for collages
Tissue paper
Glue, paste, starch, rubber cement, tape
Bags, socks, papier-mâché for making puppets
Art prints and art objects
Magazines and catalogs
Box of paper scraps and fabric scraps
Wallpaper samples
Cleanup equipment (buckets, sponges, mops)
Drying rack/line
Aprons or substitutes
Newspaper for cleanup
Various containers: cans, cartons, etc.
Clay: natural, playdough, modeling
India ink (printing ink, stamp pad)
Yarn
Paper clips, beads, stapler, staples
"Beautiful junk": spools, toothpicks, aluminum foil, wood curls/chips, leather scraps, miscellaneous small boxes, egg cartons, shingles, paper plates, doilies, styrofoam packing bits, coat hangers, wire, shells/ string/ribbons, wood scraps, used colorful/patterned envelopes, metal scraps, shopping bags, leftover/ used wrapping paper.

**FIGURE 10–10 Basic materials for art activities.**

Also make available different colors of paper and pens. Children in this stage like to make basic forms in many colors as an exercise of their skill.

Student observers should realize that children of this age like to repeat forms and should not try to force them to "make something else" to fill up the paper. It is important that children practice making their own basic forms. The forms may look simple,

# THINK ABOUT IT . . .

## MARKER MAINTENANCE

Markers are wonderful for young artists. But busy artists frequently lose caps from these markers, often resulting in dried-out markers. Replacing dried out markers can be expensive, so here are a few hints on "marker maintenance" to help preserve markers as long as possible:

- Solve the lost cap/dry out problem by setting the caps with *open ends up* in a margarine or whipped topping container filled with plaster of Paris. Make sure the plaster does not cover the holes in the caps. When the plaster dries, the markers can be put into the caps and will stand upright until ready for use again.
- Give new life to old, dry felt markers by storing them *tips down with the caps on.* When the markers become dried out, remove the caps and put in a few drops of water. This usually helps "revive" them.
- Recycle dried-out markers by having children dip them in paint and use them for drawing.
- Make your own pastel markers by adding dry tempera paint (or food color) to bottles of white shoe polish that come with sponge applicator tops.
- Use empty plastic shoe polish bottles, or roll-on deodorant bottles, to make your own markers. Wash the tops and bottles thoroughly and fill them with watery tempera paint (Warren, 1987).

---

but each drawing is a great motor achievement for them. The children may rightly be quite proud of their basic form drawings.

**Observation of the Basic Forms Stage.** The student observer of young children in the basic forms stage should keep in mind the following points when observing children. The points may then be recorded on a copy of the observation form, Figure 10–12. If students are observing children in both the scribbling and basic forms stages, observations of each stage may be compared to help highlight the differences in these two stages.

*Age.* Note the age of the child. Check Figure 10–29 for the average age range for the basic forms stage. See how the child fits in the range. See if there is an overlap between stages.

*Motor control.* See how the child holds the crayon. Note if it is held very tightly or if the child can draw with sureness and ease. Also note if the child draws with a lot of arm movement or uses just the hand to draw. The child who uses more hand movement and less arm movement is showing good motor control. In the basic forms stage, children use fewer unnecessary arm movements.

*Types of basic forms.* Write down the number and type of basic forms mentioned earlier which the child can draw. See if the shapes are well drawn or rough and unclear. Rough, less clear forms are made in the early stage. A child in the later basic forms stage draws clear, easy-to-recognize shapes.

In drawings with a variety of forms, see if one form is clearer than another. Clearer forms are the ones that the child first began to draw. The less clear forms

**FIGURE 10–11 When young children work with new forms or practice new skills, allow enough space and time for their understanding, activity, and involvement.**

are in the practice stage and should soon become clearer.

*Use of paper.* Use the same checkpoints for the use of paper that were used in the scribble stage section. In addition, see if the child fills the page with one or many basic forms. If the same shape is made over and over, it means the child is practicing a new basic form. Practice like this occurs at an early point in the stage.

Try these activities, observing and noting what happens:

• Give the child pieces of cardboard in square, circular, and rectangular shapes. Show how to trace lines around the forms. After the child has traced the forms for a while, see if freehand basic forms improve. Discuss the need for such practice. Consider if it is possible to speed up the development of basic forms by tracing.

• Arrange poster paint and brushes so the children can paint. Mark down the ages of the children who are best able to handle these tools. Are the older children always the best at painting? See if the children who can draw good basic forms are able to do the same with paint. In general, a child who shows good motor control with crayons should be able to paint as well.

## THE PICTORIAL STAGE

With the two earlier stages complete, the children now have the ability to draw the variety of marks that make up their first pictures; this occurs at the next developmental level in art—the pictorial stage. Many four-year-olds and most five-year-olds are at this level.

Pictures or first drawings are different from scribbling in that they are not made by chance. Instead, they are made by the child for a purpose. The basic forms perfected in the preceding stage suggest images to the child that stand for ideas in the child's own mind. A new way of drawing begins. From the basic forms the child is able to draw, only particular ones are chosen. Miscellaneous scribbling is left out. In this way, children draw their first symbol. A *symbol* is a visual representation of something important to the child; it may be a human figure, an animal, a tree, or similar figure. Art in which symbols are used in such a way is called *representational art*. This means there has been a change from kinesthetic, or sheer physical, activity to representational attempts. Children realize that there is a relationship between the objects they've drawn and the outside world and that drawing and painting can be used to record ideas or express feelings.

The ability to draw symbols in representational art comes directly from the basic forms stage. The basic forms gradually lose more and more of their connection to body motion only. They are not put together to make symbols, which stand for real objects in the child's mind. In scribbling, the child was mainly involved in a physical activity, trying out the materials to see what she could do with them. Now the child sees real meaning behind the drawings and names the objects that appear in the artwork. It may seem to be a scribble, but it is now a "man" or a

| CHILD | AGE | MOTOR CONTROL | ARM MOVEMENTS | TYPES OF BASIC FORMS | USE OF PAPER | EARLY PERIOD | LATER PERIOD |
|-------|-----|---------------|---------------|----------------------|--------------|--------------|--------------|
|       |     |               |               |                      |              |              |              |

COMMENTS:

FIGURE 10–12  Basic-forms stage observation form.

"dog"—a definite symbol representing something in the child's life.

The human form is often the child's first symbol. A man is usually drawn with a circle for a head and two lines for legs or body. Other common symbols include trees, houses, flowers, and animals. The child can tell you what each symbol stands for in her work. (Figure 10–2 gives some examples of common symbols.)

Further attempts to make symbols grow directly from the basic forms the child can make. Flowers and trees are combinations of spiral scribbles or circles with attached straight lines for stems or trunks. Houses, windows, doors, flags, and similar objects are simply made up of rectangles and straight lines.

It is a common adult practice to label these first drawings "children's art" because they contain recognizable objects. If children's drawings appear to be mere scribbles to an adult, they are not considered "children's art" because they don't look like "something." Yet being able to identify objects in a child's work does *not* make it "children's art." Art is self-expression and has value in any form and at any stage.

Because art is now representational, children need tools that permit control. Thinner crayons, paintbrushes, and less fluid paints can now be made available so children can express their ideas and feelings with greater realism. Children over age five will want to be able to select representational colors, so a variety of colors of paint and crayons are necessary.

Naming and owning the art produced are also im-

# THIS ONE'S FOR YOU!

## PORTFOLIOS FOR DEVELOPMENTAL ASSESSMENT

Artists generally keep a *portfolio,* or a representative collection of their work. The artist's portfolio usually has samples chosen from various periods, showing how the artist's talent has developed over time. Samples chosen from different media are also included in the portfolio to reflect the artist's versatility and range of talent. For example, you may find works done in pastels, in chalk, fine line drawings, and watercolors in the portfolio.

In the early childhood art program, many teachers find the use of portfolios (or individual art files, as it is more generally called) for young children—most often children four years and older—quite helpful. There are many advantages to this practice for the young child, teacher, and parents.

The most obvious advantage of a portfolio/file is the fact that it is visible evidence of the child's development in art. From the earliest selections in the portfolio to the most recent, one can see the child's progress in art.

A portfolio/file can greatly aid the teacher during parent-teacher conferences, by showing examples of how the child is developing in this area. It reduces the subjectivity of discussions by helping both teacher and parent focus objectively on the portfolio.

Another excellent advantage of the portfolio is that it encourages growth of the child's aesthetic sense of choice. By involving the child in selection of pieces for the portfolio, the child learns about the *process of selection.* Of course, learning to be selective is a very complex skill and will take time for the child to develop. But like any other skill, given the time, opportunity, and guidance to make selections of one's own work for the portfolio (or file), the child will develop his or her own personal preferences.

For all of these reasons, then, using a portfolio in the early childhood art program has definite merits. Alongside these merits are some pitfalls one needs to keep in mind. Most importantly, if you plan to use portfolios for developmental assessment, *stick to it for the whole year.* There is nothing particularly advantageous to having a half-done portfolio. Beginning a portfolio with good intentions and then only sporadically filling it with work reduces its importance as the year goes on—this type of portfolio is best left out of the program entirely. To be of use in developmental assessment, the portfolio needs to be as complete as possible, reflecting the process of artistic development *as a whole.* Many teachers find it helpful to include in their monthly planning a week set aside for portfolio selection. This way, they are sure to have it on their list of priorities. Of course, there should always be time for spontaneous inclusions whenever they occur.

Also keep in mind to include the child in portfolio development, even if it "takes longer that way." Don't ever forget that the development of personal preference is on a par with developmental assessment as a reason for using portfolios.

Finally, in the spirit of "celebrating" one's artwork, be sure to have an attractive place to keep each child's work. Of course, the child should be involved in decorating the file, or box, or whatever other form is used to "house" the collection. Precious art deserves special treatment.

FIGURE 10–13  Good motor control is shown by the child who uses more hand than arm movement.

FIGURE 10–14  Notice how the child puts basic forms together in a drawing.

portant to children in this stage. These children may ask you to record the name of their paintings or drawings as well as write stories to go with their drawings. These children recognize other children's work at this point. They will want to take their work home, as well as contribute some to display in the classroom.

**Early Pictorial (First Drawings) Stage.**  In the early period of the pictorial stage, a child works on making and perfecting one or many symbols. The child practices these symbols, covering sheets of paper with many examples of the same subject. For example, a child may draw windows and doors over and over in each drawing. Also at an early point in this stage, a child's picture may be a collection of unrelated figures and objects. This type of picture is a

sampling of the child's many tries at making different symbols. At this point, pictures are done very quickly.

During this early pictorial stage, the child is searching for new ideas. Symbols change constantly. A picture of a man drawn one day differs from the one drawn the day before. In this stage, there is often a great variety of forms representing the same object. Early first drawings are very flexible in appearance.

**Later Pictorial (First Drawings) Stage: Use of Schema.**  At this point in the pictorial stage, through practice, a child draws symbols easily and more exactly. Many four-year-olds and most five-year-olds perfect to their own liking and take pride in producing a series of many symbols. A child at this point often likes to see these symbols set clearly and

FIGURE 10–15 The three-and-a-half-year-old artist who made this figure is in the early pictorial stage. This figure was called a "man." It was made by first drawing a circle for the head, then adding two lines for legs.

FIGURE 10–17 An animal is a favorite symbol for the child of four or five years of age.

neatly on the page. They are now drawn one at a time with few or no other marks on the page. They are clear and well drawn. If children can draw the letters of their name on the page as well, they may feel this is all that belongs in the picture.

For a while, children are content to make these finished yet isolated examples of their drawing skill, but it is not long before more complex drawings are made. Children four to five years of age are able to use their symbols in drawings to tell a story or describe an event. The naming of these symbols is an important step, in that the artwork becomes a clear form of visual communication. It may not look any different, but the circle is now called a "sun" and represents a specific object.

By five and a half to six years of age, children generally are ready to make a picture of many things

FIGURE 10–16 A child in the early pictorial stage still uses stick figures and few details in a picture.

FIGURE 10–18 Circles with lines heading down are the usual symbols for trees.

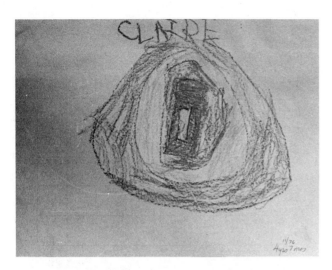

**FIGURE 10–19  Children's early symbols do not always make sense to an adult.**

in their experience or imagination. Their drawings are made up of combinations of symbols they are familiar with and that have meaning to them. Children can also create new symbols as they have new experiences and ideas. However, children at this point can't be expected to make pictures of the unfamiliar or of things they have not personally experienced. Another common error by well-meaning teachers is a misunderstanding of this stage by expecting all children five years old and older to be able to use symbols in their art. This is not a valid expectation since the age at which children begin to use symbols is as highly individual as the age at which they learn to walk. A child uses symbols when she is ready—and no sooner. Creative expression is the goal at this and all ages; a child's art does not have to include specific symbols, like a house, tree, or animals, unless the *child* chooses to include them.

Some teachers find it helpful to keep track of each child's level by keeping occasional samples of their work with a short note on the back indicating what is important about the sample. For example, when Claire first made a scribble that she called ''doggy'' her teacher noted it down on the sample and kept it in Claire's folder. Over the school/program year a collection of these various samples can give quite a graphic story of Claire's progress in art.

In the later pictorial stage, each child has a special way of drawing the human form, houses, and other symbols. This individual way of drawing is called a *schema*. A schema, or individual pattern, often can be

**FIGURE 10–20  This drawing was made by a five-year-old child. Seemingly unrelated figures and objects are drawn together in one picture—common in the early pictorial stage.**

**FIGURE 10–21  First drawings often lack the order of later drawings, as this picture illustrates: The child drew flowers without any attention to order.**

seen in drawings by the age of six. A schema comes after much practice with drawing symbols. Once the child has a schema, symbols become special marks. A schema is special for each child just as a signature is unique for each adult.

*Importance of schema.* The schema drawn by a child represents something important to the child, something that is part of the child's environment and experience. Things of emotional importance to the child are included in the picture.

Children draw schema in a picture not according to actual size, but in a size that shows the emotional importance of the object to them. For example, people and things important to a child might be drawn large and with many details. The psychoanalytic theory discussed at the beginning of this unit suggests that people or things the child dislikes are often drawn smaller. If a tree is drawn, the limbs may be made larger because the tree is used for climbing. If it is an apple tree, the apples may be drawn very large.

Children express other responses to their environment in their drawings. A painting showing a child walking on wet grass may show the feet and toes large in size. This may show how the child felt after a walk in the early morning.

**Importance of First Drawings.** At about the same time children develop their own schemas, they begin to name their drawings. Naming a drawing is really an important step for children. It is a sign that their thinking has changed; they are connecting their drawings with the world around them. This is the beginning of a new form of communication— communication with the environment.

Soon a five-year-old may think: "My daddy is a big man; he has a head and two big legs. My drawing has a head and two big legs. Therefore, my drawing is Daddy." Through drawing, the child is making a clear relationship between father and the drawing. The symbol of a man now becomes "DADDY." Of course, a child will not verbally name all objects every time a picture is made.

In their use of schemas, children express their own personalities. They express not only what is impor-

**FIGURE 10-22 The size of objects relative to each other in a drawing indicates what is important to the child.**

tant to them during the process of creating, but also how aware they have become in thinking, feeling, and seeing. From early drawings to the most complex, they give expression to their life experiences.

**Observation of the Pictorial (First Drawings) Stage.** The student should keep in mind the following points when observing children in the pictorial stage. Observations should be written on a copy of the observation form, Figure 10–23.

*Age.* Write down the age of the child. Check to see what the average age range is for the pictorial stage. See how the child fits in this range. There may be an overlap between stages. For example, the student may see figures as well as simple basic forms in one drawing.

*Combination of basic forms.* See how the child puts basic forms together to make figures. Very sim-

ple combinations mean the child is at an early point in the stage. An example would be a flower made up of a single circle and one-line stem. On the other hand, a flower of many circles with oval petals and a stem of many leaves is a more complex combination of basic forms and would show that the child is at a later point in the stage.

*Size of figures.* A child in both the early and later periods of this stage may use size to show importance. The large figure represents something important to the child. Note, for example, if children draw themselves or other figures such as their mother in a very large size. Extra-large heads on a small body are found mainly in the early period of this stage.

Notice the relative size of certain things in the picture. For a child who likes animals, a dog may be far larger than the human form. Here, too, size indicates that the object is important to the child.

| CHILD | AGE | COMBINATION OF BASIC FORMS | SIZE OF FIGURES | NUMBER OF FIGURES | DETAILS | USE OF FIGURES | NAMING DRAWINGS | EARLY PERIOD | LATER PERIOD |
|---|---|---|---|---|---|---|---|---|---|
| | | | | | | | | | |
| COMMENTS: | | | | | | | | | |

FIGURE 10–23 Pictorial (first drawings) stage observation form.

| AGE | DEVELOPMENTAL CHARACTERISTICS | CHARACTERISTICS AS AN ARTIST |
|---|---|---|
| Birth to two years (infants and toddlers) | Work in creative expression is sensory and exploratory in nature. | Reacts to sensory experience.<br>Explores media through *all* senses.<br>Draws for the first time from 12–20 months.<br>Begins to follow a universal developmental sequence in scribbling (see Figure 10-2). |
| Two to four years (young preschoolers) | Work in creative expression is manipulative and oriented toward discovery and skill development. | Explores and manipulates materials.<br>Experiences art as exploratory play.<br>Often repeats action.<br>Begins to name and control symbols.<br>Views final product as unimportant (may not be pleasing to adults).<br>May destroy product during process.<br>Sees shapes in work. |
| Four to six years (older preschoolers and kindergartners) | Work in creative expression becomes more complex and representational. | Creates symbols to represent feelings and ideas.<br>Represents what is *known*, not what is seen.<br>Gradually begins to create more detailed and realistic work.<br>Creates definite forms and shapes.<br>Often preplans and then works with care.<br>Rarely destroys work during process. |

From Feeney et al., 1983

FIGURE 10–24 The development of art in young children.

*Number of figures.* Mark down the number of figures in each drawing. A drawing with few figures or a single figure means that the child is at an early point in the stage. The child making this type of drawing is working on developing a symbol.

At a later point, the child can draw many types of symbols and figures in one drawing. Also, drawings at a later point look as if they tell a story with the figures.

*Details.* Note the type and number of details a child uses in a drawing. They indicate at what point the child is in the stage.

Figures with only a few details are made in the early pictorial stage. For example, a circular head, round body, and stick arms and legs make up an early human form. A picture of a man with details such as full arms, hands, and fingers is a sign that the child is at a later point in the pictorial stage.

See if certain objects are drawn in greater detail than others. A child's experience with certain objects can cause this increase in detail. As an example, tree limbs may be unusually large in the drawings of children who love to climb trees. Special sense experiences can also cause increase in detail. For example, a child may draw large raindrops in a drawing after a walk in the rain.

*Use of figures.* Note how the child uses figures. See if the paper is filled with many unrelated figures that just fill space and look like practice forms. If there is no real connection between figures, it can mean the child is at an early point in the stage; the child is

| STAGE | AGE RANGE | MOTOR CONTROL | PURPOSE OF ARTWORK | CHARACTERISTICS OF STAGE |
|---|---|---|---|---|
| Scribble Random/ disordered scribbling | One and one half to three years (toddlers) | Lacks good motor control and hand–eye coordination. | Scribbles for pure physical sensation of movement. | 1. Lacks direction or purpose for marks.<br>2. Does not mentally connect own movement to marks on page. |
| Controlled scribbling | Young pre-schoolers | Improving motor control and hand–eye coordination. | Scribbles with control. | 1. Explores and manipulates materials.<br>2. Tries to discover what can be done—explores color, texture, tools, and techniques.<br>3. Often repeats action.<br>4. Makes marks with intention and not by chance. |
| Basic Forms | Three to four years | Has more developed motor control and hand–eye coordination.<br>Has control over direction and size of line. | Enjoys mastery over line. | 1. Masters basic forms: circle, oval, lines, rectangle, and square.<br>2. Discovers connection between own movements and marks on page. |
| Pictorial Stage (First Drawings Stage) | Four to five years and up | Has most advanced motor control and hand–eye coordination. | Communicates with outside world through drawing. Expresses personality and relationship to symbols drawn. | 1. Combines basic forms to create first symbols.<br>2. Names drawings as a form of true communication. |

**FIGURE 10–25 Developmental levels in children's art.**

practicing a symbol and is not yet ready to tell a story with it.

If there seems to be a connection between figures, the child is at a later point. This type of drawing is a narrative drawing, one that tells a story. It is a visual form of communication for the child.

*Naming drawings.*  Be sure to listen to the child who wants to talk about a drawing. Note if the child names certain things, figures, or the whole thing, but never force the child to tell you "what it is." Naming must come only through the child's own idea. It is an important step in the child's ability to communicate with the environment. It is only worthwhile if the child sees the meaning in the work and *wants* to name it.

Try the following activities, observing and noting what happens:

- Read a story about animals to the children before art period. Do not tell them what to draw. See how many children draw animals. Do this with other types of stories and discuss the results with classmates.
- Display prints of famous artworks. Examples: Mondrian's *Composition with Red, Blue, and Yellow,* Pollock's *Detail of One (#31, 1950),* and Van Gogh's *Cypress Trees.* See if these examples affect the children's choice of colors, type of figures made, and amount of details in their pictures.
- Play a record during part of the art period. Compare the drawings made with music to those done without music.

# THIS ONE'S FOR YOU!

## COLORING BOOKS AND YOUNG CHILDREN

Young children are often provided with coloring books because they are relatively inexpensive and readily available. Parents, grandparents, and even some teachers feel that a child must learn to stay within the lines, and a child who cannot do this is often made to feel inadequate. Yet, when you know how children develop (from large to small muscles) you realize that to color within lines requires a level of physical (small-motor) development far beyond what is normal for young children.

The pictures in most coloring books are not very good artistically and serve as poor models for the development of children's aesthetic tastes. The images in coloring books are usually cartoonlike, stereotyped images of the world. How much better to provide young, budding artists a supply of blank drawing paper, felt-tip markers, crayons, and the encouragement to "do his own thing."

If you have ever had the chance to glance at a coloring book given to a young child, you will usually find that the blank inside covers are usually scribbled in a free style, which is characteristic of how young children *should be* using colors! It seems that young children have the good sense to use the coloring books in the right way—scribbling in many colors on the space provided (and often even scribbling over the printed images).

Your guideline when choosing art materials for young children needs to be this: Choose materials that suggest *multiple* uses. For example, when choosing records for children, records with *specific* instructions (for instance, calisthenics) suggest one "right" use. On the other hand, records with suggestions for many types of improvisation, with a variety of music forms, would be a material suggesting multiple uses.

Coloring books and step-by-step art activities suggest one right answer to the child. Easels, paints, markers, crayons, finger paint, and paper suggest multiple uses.

When you are tempted to buy a coloring book for a young child, try to remember the following quote from Piaget before you do:

The goal of intellectual education is not to know how to repeat or retain ready-made truths (a truth that is parroted is only a half-truth). It is in learning to master the environment by oneself at the risk of losing a lot of time and going through all the roundabout ways that are inherent in real activity.

(Piaget, 1973, p. 106)

# SUMMARY

There are many theories about children's art, each of which offers an explanation for why children produce art. According to the *cognitive theory,* children draw what they know. The distortions a child draws in size, shape, and form are believed to represent the child's level of thinking. The *psychoanalytic theory* claims that children draw what they feel and that their art is a reflection of deep inner emotions. The *cognitive development* theory of Piaget relates children's art to their ability to understand the permanent existence of objects. Unless children understand that objects have a permanent existence, they have no image through which to evoke the past and anticipate the future. Finally, the more comprehensive theory, the *perceptual delineation theory,* believes that children draw because of several factors. These factors are a child's readiness, psychological environment, how children handle information, and their ability to manipulate the art materials.

As children grow older and change in height and weight, they also develop different abilities in art. There are three developmental levels in art that are of concern to the preschool teacher: the scribble, basic forms, and pictorial stages.

The scribble stage ranges from about one and a half to three years of age. It covers the time from the child's first marks to more controlled scribbles. The child enjoys the pure motion involved in scribbling.

Wide, good-quality crayons are the best tools for the scribble stage. Large paper should be given to the child to allow room for wide arm movements. Age, motor control, use of paper, and type of scribbles should be noted in scribble stage observations.

The basic forms stage covers approximately ages three to four years. The child develops more muscle control and hand-eye coordination through scribbling. Basic forms come when children can see simple forms in their scribbles and are able to repeat them. The oval or circle is usually the first basic form, followed by the rectangle or square. Children now enjoy seeing forms emerge out of their own will.

A wider variety of art materials can be used with children in the basic forms stage. Age, motor control, use of paper, and basic forms used should be noted in observations of the basic forms stage.

The pictorial stage generally occurs from ages four to six. Basic forms made in the prior stage are put together to make up symbols. The human form, birds, flowers, and animals are examples of some symbols. Naming drawings is an important part of first drawings. Children can now communicate outside themselves and with their environment. A child's artwork is very individual and expresses the child's own personality.

In the pictorial stage, children make the most varied and complex drawings. Points to note in observing this stage are the age of the child and figures and details in the drawings.

These basic stages of art development parallel the overall development of children at particular periods. In planning the early childhood art program, the teacher must choose appropriate activities for the ability and interest levels of the age group of children in the program. Each age group has its own special considerations that must be included in a teacher's planning.

# LEARNING ACTIVITIES

### Selecting Appropriate Materials for Art Experiences

A. Examine the tools that are available for the children to work with in a preschool classroom—paintbrushes, scissors, crayons, to mention but a few. Inventory these in terms of how many are available, the condition of the various tools, their suitability in terms of design and quality for young children.

B. Using toy and equipment catalogs that can be cut up, compile a catalog with classmates that pictures appropriate materials in terms of the many areas covered in this unit. Select and annotate each entry in each category in terms of age level, appropriateness, appearance, versatility, durability, and safety.

## Scribble Stage Experiences for the Student

A. Exercise 1. Goal: To experience some of the lack of motor control of a young child in the scribble stage.
1. The student is to use the hand opposite the writing hand to "draw" a crayon picture. Using a large crayon in the hand that is not usually used for drawing, the student should experience difficulties like those of the young child.
2. Consider and discuss the following:
   a. Clumsy feeling of the crayon in hand.
   b. Lack of good control over finger and hand movements.
   c. Inability to draw exactly what is desired.
   d. Difficulty in controlling crayon, paper, and hand movements all at once.
3. Try painting on your knees at an easel. Discuss how it felt and how it may have affected your painting. After this experience, what would you change about your approach to easels and painting for young children?

B. Exercise 2. Goal: To experience the pure motor pleasure of scribbling.
1. The student is to close both eyes and do a crayon scribbling.
2. To experience feelings similar to the young child, consider and discuss the following:
   a. Difficulty of overcoming the adult need for seeing as well as doing.
   b. How it feels to move hand and fingers for movement's sake alone.
   c. What forms are seen in the scribbles.
   d. Feelings about how the drawing looks.

## Recognizing and Evaluating the Three Art Stages

Obtain samples of drawings from children one and a half to five years of age. Separate the samples into three groups (one for each stage). Give reasons for the stage selected for each sample, especially for the samples that are not clearly defined.

A. Note and explain the differences in scribble stage examples:
1. Early or later scribbling period.
2. Type of scribbles (circular, jagged).
3. Control of crayon.
B. Note and explain the differences in basic forms examples:
1. Type of basic forms used.
2. How clear and exact the forms are.
3. Control of crayon.
4. Early or later basic forms period.
C. Note and explain the differences in pictorial examples:
1. Early or later period.
2. What basic forms are combined into symbols.
3. Observable symbols.
D. Use the same drawings and see if you can determine why some people believe children draw what they feel, know, and see.
E. Make a list of children's books with outstanding illustrations that could be used to introduce children to the concept of the artist as well as to different techniques and a wide variety of art materials.
F. Work with a small group of children (or even one child) to try to motivate art with a firsthand experience, such as touching a tree or kitten or observing a moth. Then ask the children to draw a picture. Identify how this experience influenced the drawings.

# ACTIVITIES FOR CHILDREN

## Some Variations on Easel Painting

- Use a number of shades of one color.
- Use colored paper—colored newsprint comes in pastel shades, or the backs of faded construction paper can be used.
- Use the same color of paint with same color paper.
- Use black and white paint (fun at Halloween and wintertime).
- Use colors that are traditionally associated with the particular holiday season.
- Use various sizes of brushes, or both flat and floppy ones, with the same colors of paint.
- Paint objects the children have made in carpentry, or paint dried clay objects.
- Paint large refrigerator-type boxes.
- Work on a long piece of paper (computer paper) together to produce murals.
- Paint the fence with water and large brushes.
- Draw firmly on paper with crayons, and paint over it to produce "crayon resist" art.
- Paint with undiluted food coloring (expensive but lovely).
- Use all pastel colors (start with white and add color a bit at a time when mixing).

- Set up a table with many colors of paint and encourage the children to select the colors they prefer.
- Paint to music.

## Young Preschool Children (Two to Four Years)

### Crumpled Paper Designs
A. Bits of different colored tissue or newspaper can be crumpled up by the children.
B. The paper wads can then be dipped in school paste and pasted onto colored construction paper to make a design.
C. Paper shapes can be filled in with crumpled paper for Christmas ornaments, Valentine hearts, and Thanksgiving turkeys.
D. A group of children can work together to make a cooperative collage for the room. Choose a theme like toys, holidays, friends, seasons, or likes and dislikes.

### Using Finger Painted Pictures
Save the children's finger painted pictures. These may be sprayed with a plastic coating and used for covering books, wrapping gifts, or making wastebaskets. A round ice cream carton or coffee can may be covered with finger painting to make a wastebasket for the room.

### Painting with Soft Objects
A. Dip a cotton ball in a shallow dish of wet paint. Smear it or squish it on paper or another surface.
B. Dip a cotton ball into dry powdered paint. Rub it across dry paper to create an interesting soft effect.

### Cotton Swab Painting
Dip cotton swabs into the paint, and use as brushes, pens, or sponges.

### Marshmallow Painting or Printing
A. Use marshmallows of different sizes for painting or printing.
B. If desired, they can be stuck onto the picture with paint to make a collage. A good use for hard marshmallows!

### Button Printing
Glue buttons onto small wooden dowels, and have the children use the buttons for printing. Vary the sizes, shapes, and designs of buttons.

### Spool Painting
A. Attach empty wooden thread spools to a handle made from an old coat hanger or other wire.
B. Make small nicks on the ends of the spools to create various designs.
C. Dip each spool end in paint and print on paper.

### Screen and Toothbrush Painting
A. Hold a piece of screen above a sheet of paper.
B. Dip a toothbrush into paint and brush it across the screen.
C. If desired, leaves, twigs, or different shapes of paper may be placed on paper, paint spattered over them, and the objects removed. (A design is made this way.)

### Sponge Painting
A. Cut sponges into different shapes.
B. Dip each shape in paint. Then dab, press, or rub it on paper.

### Paper Towel Painting
A. Wad a paper towel into a ball.
B. Dip it in paint. Then dab, press, or rub it on paper.

### Crayons
A. Surfaces for Crayon Drawings
   Children may draw with crayons on these surfaces for variety:
   fabric              wood scraps
   egg cartons         sticks amd stones
   paper towel rolls   spools and clothespins
B. Crayon Shavings Designs
   1. Make shavings by scraping the side of a crayon with the blade of blunt scissors. Sprinkle shavings between sheets of waxed paper (folded in half).
   2. An adult can then press the paper with a warm iron, protecting the iron with an old cloth. The shavings melt and the sheets of paper stick together.
   3. For variety, bits of tissue paper, colored cellophane, or fall leaves can be put between the pieces of waxed paper.
C. Candle Stub Resists
   1. For paint resist, instead of using crayons, use a candle stub to draw a picture.
   2. Paint over the design with thin paint.

### Printing
A. Toy Prints
   1. Dip the wheels of an old toy car, truck, or other toy in paint.
   2. Make tracks on the paper.
B. Plastic Alphabet Letters and Numbers
   1. Dip plastic alphabet letters and numbers in paint.
   2. Then print them on paper.
C. Paper Cup Printing
   1. Dip the rim of a paper cup into paint.
   2. Press the rim on paper to make a design.
D. Comb Printing
   1. Dip the teeth of a comb into paint.
   2. Print with it by drawing it along the paper.

E. Printing with Clay
1. Children pound the clay into small flat cakes about an inch thick.
2. Then they carve a design on the flat surface with a bobby pin or popsicle stick.
3. The design is either brushed with paint or dipped in paint and pressed onto paper to print the design.

## Drawing

Draw on 2″ × 2″ blank slides with small felt-tip pens and have a slide show. Draw on larger transparencies and have a transparency show using an overhead projector.

Use permanent magic markers to draw on fabric. Use the fabric to make curtains, aprons, skirts, or other items to give as gifts or for use in the room.

Draw with yarn. Dip yarn in liquid starch or heavy white glue that has been diluted with a bit of water. Then draw with the yarn, draping it in shapes on the paper.

## Puppets

A. Paper Plate Puppets
1. A plain paper plate can be made into a face with crayons, paint, or glued-on colored paper pieces.
2. A popsicle stick is then stapled to the bottom of the plate to make a handle.
3. The plate can be moved along a table edge as a puppet or used as a mask.
4. A hole can be made for a mouth, through which the child uses one finger as a tongue to make the puppet "talk."
B. Cylinder Puppets
1. Roll a piece of 9″ × 12″ × 18″ drawing or construction paper into a cylinder. Staple or glue it together. This is the head of the puppet.
2. Using paper, scissors, and paste, make a face on the tube.
3. Hats of paper, yarn hair, and scrap ribbon bows can decorate the puppet.
4. The puppet is slipped over the child's finger. If desired, a body, skirt, or suit can be cut out and pasted or stapled to the tube.
C. Food Puppets
1. Fruits and vegetables make good heads for puppets. A potato or an apple may be used, with a clothespin inserted as a handle.
2. Buttons, pins, or old jewelry pieces can be used to make a face.
3. Yarn can be used for hair.
4. Bits of cloth or an old sock may be used as a dress or suit.

## Older Preschool Children and Kindergartners (Four to Six Years)

### Yarn-on-a-Metal-Can Painting
A. With strong glue, glue yarn or string to a small metal can.
B. Brush paint over the yarn or string.
C. Roll the can over a surface.

### Fabric Printing
A. Wrap small pieces of burlap, nylon netting, or other textured fabrics (2½″ to 3″ inches square) over a sponge that has been attached to a clothespin or secured to a dowel with a piece of string or elastic.
B. Dip fabric into paint and press onto a surface.

### Pinecone Printing
A. Roll whole or pieces of pinecones in paint. The large ones with flat bottoms can be dipped into paint.
B. Use them to make impressions on surfaces.

### Blot Painting
A. Fold a piece of paper in half.
B. Drop a small amount of paint with either a spoon or an eyedropper into one inside half.
C. Fold the paper over and the halves are blotted together.

### Plaster of Paris Molds
Plaster of Paris can be bought at hardware stores or hobby shops. Follow directions on the package for adding water.
A. Hand or Foot Prints
1. Pour wet plaster into a mold, such as a food tray, or try pouring it into a plastic bag or rubber glove.
2. Place a hand or foot in the wet plaster; leave it until the plaster begins to harden. The impression may be painted when dry.
B. Nature Design
1. Gather together assorted objects from nature, such as shells, weeds, stones, and sticks.
2. Pour plaster in the bottom of the food tray. Quickly, before the plaster hardens, arrange the objects in the plaster.
3. This design may be painted when dry.

### Fingerprint Art
A. Using ink pads let children make thumbprints/fingerprints on a piece of construction paper.
B. They then can turn into animals, stick people, flowers, etc. (Or just make designs with them.)

*Salt Dough Hands*

A. Equipment: Salt dough (see recipe in Unit 13).
B. Procedure: Provide child enough salt dough to make a plaque-type form (¼″ to ½″ thick), larger than the child's hand size. Child presses hand into dough forming a handprint. On an ungreased cookie sheet, bake in 200-degree oven until hard. Or leave out to harden on an ungreased cookie sheet for one to two days.
C. Hint: Hardened handprints make great spoon rests for parents, friends, and family. Be sure to have the child put her name on the back and date it before it dries!

*Combination Painting*

A. Thicken paint with liquid starch. Prepare the paint in individual servings.
B. Have children make their paintings first.
C. Sprinkle any of the following over the wet paint for attractive combination paintings: salt, sand, coffee grounds, eggshells, glitter, colored rice, tiny Styrofoam balls, seeds, cornmeal, sequins, tiny beads. The media dry in the paint for interesting effects.

*Small-Grained Pasting Activities*

A. Have the child paint an area of paper with either a white glue mixture or liquid starch.
B. The child then shakes on any small-grained media such as sand, salt, flour, or cornmeal. These can be put into shakers with large or small holes. (Dry tempera can also be added to granular material.)

*Spice Pictures*

A. The kitchen shelf offers many smells and tastes for this activity. Prepare shakers with such things as instant coffee, cloves, cinnamon, dried parsley, savory, salt, nutmeg, thyme, etc.
B. Thin white glue with water, or use liquid starch.
C. The child paints an area of the paper with the glue and then shakes spices onto the paper.

*Marble Painting*

A. Equipment: Pie or cake pan, paper cut to fit pie pan, food coloring (or watercolor paint), marbles.
B. Procedure: Line the pan with the paper. Child dips marble in small amount of food coloring (or watercolor) and moves pan to make a design.
C. Hint: Dipping different marbles in different colors makes this even more fun.

*Clothes Designs*

A. Equipment: Scrap pieces of fabric, white glue, scissors, paper.
B. Procedure: Child cuts up fabric scraps into designs, animal shapes, or any other creation desired. The pieces are then glued onto paper.

*Tie-Dyeing*

A. Tie-dyeing techniques can be used to decorate a piece of old sheet. Wrap rubber bands or string around bunches of the fabric, or gather up a section of the fabric around a few stones and then tie it.
B. Put the fabric into a dye solution. (The brands that require hot water, but not boiling water, are safer.)
C. When the fabric is the color desired, remove it from the solution and take off the string or rubber bands.

*Masks: Scrap Art*

Face masks made from paper bags usually inspire make-believe activities. Children love them and can do all the decorating once an adult has cut out the holes for the eyes, nose, and mouth.

A. Mark the spots for the features while the bag is on the child's head so that the holes are in the right places.
B. Remove the bag, cut the holes, and let the child decorate it. Some children enjoy pasting on yarn or fringing paper for hair.

# UNIT REVIEW

1. Choose the answer that best completes each of the following statements describing the theories of children's art development.

a. The cognitive theory supports the idea that
   (a.) children draw what they see.
   (b.) children draw what they feel.

(c.) children draw at their level of thinking.

(d.) children draw at their level of feeling.

b. The cognitive development theory of Piaget related children's art to their ability to

(a.) speak.

(b.) speak, feel, and manipulate objects.

(c.) manipulate objects.

(d.) understand object permanence.

c. The perceptual theory suggests that

(a.) children draw what they see.

(b.) children draw what they feel.

(c.) children draw what they know.

(d.) children draw what they have experienced.

d. The perceptual delineation theory suggests that children draw as they do

(a.) because of genetic factors.

(b.) not because of any one factor, but because of several.

(c.) not because they have the concept of object permanence.

(d.) because of perceptual factors.

2. Describe a young child in the scribble stage in the following areas:

a. Age.

b. Degree of motor control.

c. Reason for scribbling.

3. List three basic forms that a child in the basic forms stage may be able to draw.

4. Describe a schema.

5. Give four examples of symbols.

6. Discuss the importance of children's naming their pictures.

7. Define the term *two-dimensional media* and give an example of a two-dimensional process.

8. List the materials that are right for children in the scribble stage and basic forms stage.

a. For the scribble stage, what are the best (a) crayon size and type; (b) paper size and type?

b. For the basic forms stage, what are the best (a) tools for drawing; (b) paper size and type?

9. Give an example of an early and a later combination of basic forms.

10. In the following, decide which period of the pictorial stage best shows each listed characteristic.

| Period | Characteristics of Drawing |
|---|---|
| 1. Early pictorial stage | a. Few, unrelated figures |
| | b. Greater degree and amount of detail |
| 2. Later pictorial stage | c. Narrative or story drawings |
| | d. Greater size to show importance |
| | e. Larger head size for figures |

11. Choose the answer that best completes these statements about the basic forms stage.

a. The child with good motor control

(a.) drops the crayon often.

(b.) uses a clenched grip.

(c.) uses more hand than arm movement.

b. An early type of basic form is

(a.) well drawn.

(b.) a less clear form.

(c.) combined to make a symbol.

c. In the later period of basic forms, a child

(a.) cannot draw good basic forms.

(b.) easily draws clear forms.

(c.) fills the page with practice forms.

# ADDITIONAL READINGS

Allen, E., and L. Marotz. *Developmental Profiles: Pre-birth to Eight.* Albany, N.Y.: Delmar Publishers, 1994.

Arnheim, R. *Art and Visual Perception: The Psychology of the Creative Experience.* Berkeley, Calif.: University of California Press, 1954.

Cataldo, C.Z. *Infant and Toddler Programs: A Guide to Very Early Childhood Education.* Reading, Mass.: Addison-Wesley, 1981.

Clemens, S.G. "Art in the Classroom: Making Every Day Special." *Young Children* (Jan., 1991): 4–11.

Cole, N.R. *The Arts in the Classroom.* New York: The John Day Co., 1966.

Edwards, L.C. *Affective Development and the Creative Arts: A Process Approach to Early Childhood Education.* Columbus, Ohio: Merrill-Macmillan, 1990.

Forman, G.E., and D.S. Kushner. *The Child's Construction of Knowledge: Piaget for Teaching Children.* Washington, D.C.: NAEYC, 1983.

Gardner, H. *Artful Scribbles: The Significance of Children's Drawings.* New York: Basic Books, 1980.

Goodenough, F. *Measurement of Intelligence by Drawings.* New York: Harcourt Brace Jovanovich, 1926.

Goodnow, J. *Children Drawing.* Cambridge, Mass.: Harvard University Press, 1977.

Kellogg, R. *Analyzing Children's Art.* Palo Alto, Calif.: National Press Books, 1970.

Lasky, L., and R. Mukerji. *Art: Basic for Young Children.* Washington, D.C.: National Association for the Education of Young Children, 1980.

Lowenfeld, V. *Creative and Mental Growth of the Child,* 7th ed. New York: Macmillan, 1982.

McFee, J. *Preparation for Art,* 2nd ed. Belmont, Calif.: Wadsworth Publishing Co., 1970.

Piaget, J. *The Child's Conception of Reality.* London: Routledge and Kegan Paul, 1955.

Piaget, Jean. *The Child and Reality: Problems of Genetic Psychology,* translated by Arnole Rosin. New York: Grossman Publishing, 1973.

Warren, J. (ed.) *Teaching Tips.* Everett, Wash.: Warren Publishing House, Inc., 1987.

# SECTION 4
# The Early Childhood Art Program

# UNIT 11

# Program Basics: Goals, Setting Up, Materials, and Strategies

## OBJECTIVES

After studying this unit, you should be able to
- discuss goals for the early childhood art program.
- describe the basic setup for the early childhood art program.
- list the basic materials, equipment, and strategies required in the early childhood art program.

Art experiences are an essential part of the early childhood curriculum in which young children have the chance to work with many kinds of materials and to use many techniques in expressing themselves creatively. Yet, creative experiences don't just happen. They are the result of careful planning. This unit covers three major areas of concern in planning for children's creative art experiences: (1) program goals; (2) setting up for art activities; and (3) strategies for using basic art materials and equipment.

## BASIC GOALS OF THE EARLY CHILDHOOD ART PROGRAM

The early childhood art program provides the time and place to express thoughts, ideas, feelings, actions, and abilities in a variety of media and activities.

**Process, Not Product.** The main goal in all art experiences is not how the end product looks, but the process of making it. It is in the process that the child expresses experiences and feelings. The ex-

pression of one's self is what is important here, not what the finished product looks like.

Another reason that it is better to emphasize the process is that young children are not skillful users of materials. Much of their creative effort is expended in the manipulative experience of trying these out and becoming acquainted with them. Also, little children are more interested in doing than in producing and rarely, if ever, betray a planned intention when they take up their paintbrushes or select collage materials. This sort of advance planning belongs to children on the verge of kindergarten age or even older.

Children take paints, bits of cloth, clay, wood, and stone and put them together into products that express their own ideas. In the art program, emphasis must be on continued satisfying experiences with many kinds of materials and a continued involvement in the process of making. Creative activities provide opportunities for self-expression by allowing children to construct something that is uniquely their own.

**Needs of the Children.** A second major objective of the art program is to meet the needs of the children in it. This means that it must be designed for their age, ability, and interest levels. Thus, a program for three-year-olds is set up to have the right material and activities for a group with a limited interest span and limited motor control. It has material and activities that interest them and that they can use without a lot of adult help. Two-year-olds, in contrast, need to be carefully supervised when using round-edged scissors, while scissors can be available on open shelves for three- and four-year-olds to use independently. The same applies to art activities for four-, five-, and six-year-olds. In a mixed age group, the program must be set up with a variety of materials and activities available to all children in the group.

**Originality and Independence.** A third important objective of the early childhood art program is to give each child the chance to think originally and to learn to work independently. In artwork, a child can use and explore all kinds of materials. This encourages original thought. Also, giving children material that they can control at their physical level encourages independent work. These two things (originality and ability to work on their own) are basic to children's creativity.

**Creative Thinking.** Another goal in the early childhood art program is for children to be creative thinkers. Creative children work freely and flexibly. They attack each problem without fear of failure. Children in an art program that is right for their level are able to work creatively, freely, and flexibly. They can handle the material in the setting, which helps them feel more sure of themselves.

**Individualized Progress.** Finally, the art program must allow children to grow at their own speed. Activities may be planned to stimulate children, but true growth comes only at their own pace. Just as children learn to walk on their own, they learn to paint by painting in their own way.

Respecting each child's rate of growth helps them feel good about themselves. Children who feel good about themselves can be successful in the art program and in other learning situations, too.

## SETTING UP FOR ART ACTIVITIES

Whether setting up an art center or an entire room for art experiences, there are certain basic guidelines for arranging the environment. Of course, the age of the group will always be a major consideration in planning, as each age group has varying abilities and interests requiring different arrangements. Specific requirements for different age groups are covered in Unit 6. At this point, our discussion covers basic guidelines that cross age levels. The following are basic to setting up art activities:

*General considerations.* The art area needs to be arranged for ease in cleaning up and dispensing materials. Wet materials such as paint and clay and sharp materials such as scissors must be placed out of reach of children who have not yet mastered handling them independently and safely. Usually such materials are dispensed from a teacher-height counter placed in a location convenient to children's work tables, the easels, and the sink that is used for preparation and cleanup of the area. Easels are placed out of the way of casual traffic so that children can work without being jostled. Next to the easels are places for children to hang paint aprons and a rack to drape paintings to dry; a place for children to wash after using wet materials is also nearby. A plastic

**FIGURE 11–1 Materials must be readily available to the children so they can work independently.**

kitchen tub half filled with water and placed on a low stand next to the paper towels and wastebasket works well. Dry materials such as paper, crayons, chalk, and collage materials are displayed on low shelves from which children can help themselves.

In the creative art area, unlike other areas, teachers play a major role in dispensing materials and cleaning up; therefore, the convenience of these activities for teachers becomes an important consideration in how the area is arranged. Particularly useful is a central counter or table on which materials needed for separate activities may be grouped: paint and brushes together near the easel, paste and collage materials near the table used for pasting, and clay near both tables and where completed objects are put to dry. The counter also holds sponges for wiping up spills. The rack where children's paintings are hung to dry is situated so that the teacher does not carry wet paintings through areas where children are working or walking; clean sheets of easel paper are hung on the drying rack, too, on a top rung so the teacher can hang a wet painting and get a new paper for the easel in a single movement.

*Set up art materials so that children have daily art experiences.* A teacher should make sure every day that there are set places, equipment, and materials for art experiences. For example, the teacher should have easels set up with paper and paints ready for children's use. This way, there would be a smooth movement through the easel area instead of the teacher rushing around to get paint ready amid waiting children.

A supply of paper, crayons, and clay should also be available in a set place every day for the children's use. Cutting and pasting supplies should be ready and easily available, too. (Specific suggestions on supplies and their care follow later in this unit.) As part of this preparation, the teacher should help the children learn the necessary use and care of all equipment as it is set up.

Being prepared in all these ways ensures that children will have the supplies they need and know where to get them and how to use them—which certainly helps them pursue independent, creative activities on a daily basis.

*Set up for weekly art activities.* To enhance children's creative experiences, the teacher should plan for and set up weekly art activities in addition to the children's daily experiences. For example, a teacher might plan a unit on printing (see Unit 12 for more information on printing), using each week to introduce a specific technique of printing. This, of course, would be in addition to and *not* in place of the children's regular art experiences. The teacher would have to plan in advance to set up a table or other area with printing supplies and equipment. Scurrying around for "things to print with" at the last minute can be avoided in this planned weekly approach.

Work of the previous week should be evaluated before new plans are prepared. Even though plans have been carefully thought through, a teacher must be prepared to make changes due to unexpected events. For example, a sudden snow storm extends the amount of time the children will play outdoors. Or one morning the road outside the building is being repaired and huge machines appear on the street. The teacher of young children recognizes this scene as a good opportunity for learning and arranges time for children to observe the workers.

In weekly plans, a teacher plans for a balance between the familiar and the new as she makes decisions about how materials and equipment are to be used. The teacher need not be concerned that children may lose interest if the same activities are offered week after week. If children have freedom to use materials in their own ways, they do not tire of playing with the same ones. After a child has gained success in using a material, she has a special interest in repeating the experience. Phillip has learned how to roll clay into a smooth, round ball. It took him several days to accomplish this feat. He now pounds the clay into a flat piece and remakes a smooth ball, repeating the process many times. He will probably wish to repeat this accomplishment for many days before trying something new, so the teacher will be certain that the clay is there for him.

Since some activities require more supervision than others, a teacher needs to consider how many activities will be available for a given period. The number of activities chosen that require close supervision depends upon the number of adults assigned to the room. After a teacher has made careful observations and has decided upon the activities for the week, he must think through what would be the best use of his time—for example, whether to give special attention to the block area or to the art area.

In weekly and monthly planning, consideration must be given to the time of the year and to the developmental levels of the children. At the beginning of a school year, too many choices and too much open space may be upsetting to children because they are not yet familiar with the room or the school. At a time when a teacher's goal is to help children feel comfortable in the school, too many new and exciting materials can be overwhelming and distracting. Therefore, the materials offered at the beginning of the year should be those that are familiar to most children. For example, even a very shy child can feel secure at a table with crayons and paper. As children begin to know each other, feel more comfortable in the room, and become aware of the daily routines, additional materials can be introduced and activities can be expanded.

**FIGURE 11–2 Although some children may occasionally enjoy working on the floor, it is important to have a table set up for regular art activities.**

*Set up the art area so that it facilitates children's creative experiences.* While specific materials and their use are discussed individually later in this unit, there are some general ideas that apply to the use of all materials for young children.

Children work better in art activities in a predictable, organized environment where materials can always be found in the same place. For example, art materials on open storage shelves at child-level make it possible for children to find the materials they want to use easily and independently. Also, when materials such as paper or paste are spaced far apart on shelves, putting things back in place becomes an easier task for young children. There also should be cabinets for storage of materials near the art area. (More information on setting up centers is found in Appendix C.)

Art activities in the early childhood program work best on child-level tables. Although some children may occasionally enjoy working on the floor, it is important to have a table set up for regular art activities. It is also a good idea to have this area near a water source if at all possible. Another good idea is to have a limit on the number of children for each art activity/area to ensure the proper space for children as well as sufficient materials for each child. And in each area set up for art activities, it is important that all the required materials be readily available for the children's use. A teacher encourages both independence and creativity when he teaches the children how to begin, end, and clean up after each activity.

## Setting Up for Art Activities—Specific Considerations

In addition to the general considerations discussed earlier, there are some specific, age-related considerations for setting up art activities for young children.

**Planning Art Activities for Toddlers.** Very young children benefit from a program divided into well-defined areas in which they have freedom to move, explore, and make decisions about activities and materials. However, when planning for this age range, special considerations must be kept in mind.

Since toddlers and young two-year-olds are very active and instinctively want to explore everything, the materials they use must be sturdy, practically indestructible, and should not include tiny pieces that might be swallowed.

Put only a few materials out at a time so that young children are not overwhelmed with too many choices. Materials should be rotated often, and children should learn to work on the floor or table area nearby and not carry materials across the room.

Art materials, such as crayons, play dough, felt pens, chalk, and paint, as well as materials such as sand and water, should be frequently available to children of this age. These materials are presented under the supervision of an adult so that appropriate use is encouraged. Also, since children of this age have difficulty sharing, duplicates of materials will help cut down on competition for the same materials.

Traffic patterns and the children's distractibility also need to be considered when art or any other interest areas are arranged in the room. Place activities requiring running water, such as play dough and painting, convenient to sinks. Walking babies and younger toddlers are prone to falling, grabbing, and running; therefore they need clear, open spaces. They are also easily distracted by other activities, making task completion or cleanup difficult unless areas are visually divided. (See Appendix C for more information on dividing the room into centers.) The need for occasional solitude and quiet is especially important at this age. Toddlers can easily become overstimulated if exposed to too many activities at once. In view of all these considerations, dividing and organizing a room becomes an art in itself. Several arrangements should be tried to determine which one best fits the children's needs.

Some of the following interest areas may be considered when planning art and art-related centers for toddlers.

*Construction center.* Learning to put things together with blocks provides toddlers with a fun activity and introduces them to making an original design. A shelf or cabinet with a small set of blocks identifies the construction area. Units, double units, ramps, and a few semicircular blocks are just right for toddlers to use with cars and people on the floor. Smaller, colorful cubes, connecting blocks, and small foam blocks are appropriate on tables. Large Tinker Toys®, Lego® blocks, Bristle® blocks, and other varieties of construction toys help toddlers create different types of structures. Sorting sizes and putting together pieces teach the toddlers to discriminate and to develop control over small muscles in the fingers and hands. Imaginative caregivers may need to work along with toddlers to build enthusiasm for using their own ideas in creating simple constructions of houses, stores, zoos, and other things. All of these projects aid in developing the child's sense of design.

*Curiosity corner.* Toddlers begin to appreciate more than infants the unusual objects to be found in the curiosity corner (with less mouthing and throwing). Plants, leaves, shells, magnets, pumpkins, nests, gourds, pine cones, tree bark, magnifiers, and many other natural objects and examining implements delight the curious toddler, who observes carefully, touching and feeling these objects. The assortment can be changed with each season. All of these experiences contribute to very young children's understanding and knowledge of the world and may help them develop an enduring curiosity. They also help develop a child's appreciation of color, texture, size, and shape.

*Sensory corner.* An area with playthings rich in a variety of textures, shapes, sizes, sounds, weights, and colors can be an exciting spot for toddlers. Floors, walls, and the sides of cabinets can be used to mount textures. Bells, sound canisters and multisized balls, animals, cups, bowls, and similar sensory toy objects can be placed in containers together. All the sensory experiences contribute to the development of perceptual skills basic to all art activities. Shapes and visually detailed toys, for example, will improve the toddler's visual perception. It is a challenge for toddlers to enjoy new playthings using the senses, such as soft rings and snakes made up of differently textured squares, fabric quilts, and wall hangings, or painted or covered sets of blocks with varying textures, colors, and sizes.

## Finger Paint Recipes*

1. *Starch and Soap Finger Paint*

   1 cup starch
   1½ cups boiling water
   ½ cup soap flakes (not soap powder)

   1 tablespoon glycerine (optional, makes it smoother)

   Method: Mix starch with enough water to make smooth paste. Add boiling water and cook until glossy. Stir in soap flakes while mixture is warm. When cool, add glycerine and coloring (powder paint, poster paint, or vegetable coloring).

2. *Flour and Salt Finger Paint, Cooked*

   2 cups flour
   2 teaspoons salt

   3 cups cold water
   2 cups hot water

   Method: Add salt to flour, then pour in cold water gradually and beat mixture with egg beater until it is smooth. Add hot water and boil until it becomes glossy. Beat until smooth, then mix in coloring.

3. *Flour and Salt Finger Paint, Uncooked*

   1 cup flour
   1½ teaspoons salt

   1 cup water

   Method: Combine flour and salt, add water. This has a grainy quality unlike the other finger paints, providing a different sensory experience.

4. *Argo Starch Finger Paint*

   ½ cup boiling water
   2 tablespoons Argo starch

   6 tablespoons cold water

   Method: Dissolve starch in cold water in cup. Add this mixture to boiling water, stirring constantly. Heat until it becomes glossy. Add color.

5. *Wheat Flour Finger Paint*

   3 parts water

   1 part wheat flour

   Method: Stir flour into water, add food coloring. (Wheat flour can be bought at low cost in wallpaper stores or department stores.)

6. *Plastic Starch Finger Paint*

   liquid plastic starch (obtainable in grocery store, approximately 25¢ per quart)
   powder paint in salt shakers

   Method: Spread liquid starch over dry paper. Shake powder paint on paper and spread with hands.

7. *Tempera Finger Paint*

   dry tempera paint

   ½ cup liquid starch or ½ cup liquid dishwashing detergent

   Method: Mix the tempera paint with the starch or detergent, adding starch gradually until desired thickness is reached. Paint extender can also be added to dry tempera paint.

8. *Easy Finger Painting*

   clear liquid detergent      dry tempera paint

   Method: Mark off sections on a table with masking tape the size of the paper to be used (newsprint works fine). Squirt liquid detergent on this section and add about 1 teaspoon of dry paint. After the picture has been made, lay the paper on the finger paint and rub. Lift off carefully.

9. *Cold Cream Finger Paint*

   Dry tempera paint can be mixed with most brands of cold cream. This is good for a first experience with a child reluctant to use colored paint with his fingers.

10. *Chocolate Pudding Finger Paint*

    Mix instant chocolate pudding according to the directions on the package. Paint on wax paper.

## Paste Recipes

1. *Bookmaker Paste*

   1 teaspoon flour
   2 teaspoons salt
   ¼ teaspoon powdered alum

   1 heaping teaspoon oil of cloves
   1 pint cold water

   Method: Mix dry ingredients with water slowly, stirring out lumps. Slow fire; cook over double boiler until it thickens.

2. *Hobby Craft Paste*

   ¾ cup water
   2 tablespoons light Karo syrup
   1 teaspoon white vinegar

   ½ cup Argo starch
   ¾ cup water
   ¼ teaspoon oil of wintergreen

   Method: Combine first ¾ cup water, corn syrup, and vinegar in a medium-sized saucepan; bring to a full boil.

*Interesting smells can be obtained by adding different food flavorings (mint, cloves) or talcum power to finger paint if desired.

**FIGURE 11–3 Classroom recipes.**

Stir cornstarch into second ¾ cup water until smooth. Remove boiling mixture from heat. Slowly pour in cornstarch–water mixture, stirring constantly until smooth. If lumps form, smooth them out with back of spoon against side of saucepan. Stir in oil of wintergreen. May be used immediately but will set to paste consistency in 24 hours. Store in covered jar. Keeps two months. Makes about 2½ cups.

3. *Flour Paste*
   Mix together: ¼ cup flour
                 cold water—enough to make creamy mixture

Method:  Boil over slow heat for 5 minutes, stirring constantly. Cool. Add cold water to thin if necessary. Add a few drops of oil of peppermint or oil of wintergreen.

4. *Co-op Paste*
   | 1 cup sugar | 1 cup flour |
   | 1 tablespoon powdered alum | 1 quart water |
   | | oil of cloves |

Method:  Mix and cook in double boiler until thick. Remove from heat and add 30 drops of oil of cloves. This mixture fills a juice container (8–10 oz.) about ¾ full. Needs no refrigeration.

## Recipes for Dough and Other Plastic Materials

1. *Cooked Dough*
   | ½ cup flour | 2 cups boiling water |
   | ½ cup cornstarch (blend with cold water) | ½ cup salt |

   Method:  Add salt to boiling water. Combine flour with cornstarch and water. Pour hot mixture into cold. Put over hot water and cook until glossy. Cool overnight. Knead in flour until right consistency, adding color with flour.

2. *Cooked Dough*
   | 4 tablespoons cornstarch | ½ cup boiling water |
   | ½ cup salt | |

   Method:  Mix cornstarch and salt. Add color if desired. Pour on boiling water, stir until soft and smooth. Place over fire until it forms a soft ball. In using, if it sticks to fingers, dust hands with cornstarch.

3. *Sawdust and Wheat Flour*
   | 4 parts sawdust | 1 part wheat flour |

   Method:  Make paste of wheat flour and water. Add sawdust. Presents interesting sensory appeal.

4. *Uncooked Play dough*
   | 3 cups flour | 1 cup water |
   | ¼ cup salt | 1 tablespoon oil |
   | coloring | |

   Method:  Mix flour with salt; add water with coloring and oil gradually. Add more water if too stiff, add more flour if too sticky. Let the children help with the mixing and measuring. Keep dough stored in plastic bags or a covered container.

5. *Salt Dough*
   | 1 cup salt | ¾ cup cold water |
   | ½ cup cornstarch | |

   Method:  Combine all ingredients in a double boiler placed over medium heat. Stir the mixture constantly; in about two to three minutes it should become so thick that it follows the spoon in mixing it. When the consistency is similar to bread dough, place on wax paper or aluminum foil to cool. When dough is cool enough to handle, knead for several minutes. It is then ready to use. To store for up to several days, wrap in wax paper or place in plastic bags.

6. *Ornamental Clay* (Suitable for Dried Objects)
   | 1 cup cornstarch | 1¼ cups water |
   | 2 cups baking soda | |

   Method:  Cook ingredients together until thickened, either in double boiler or over direct heat—*stir constantly*. When it is cool enough, turn it out and let children knead dough and make it into whatever they wish. If used for ornaments, make hole for hanging ornament while dough is still moist.

7. *Baker's Dough* (Suitable for Dried Objects)
   | 4 cups flour | 1 to 1½ cups water |
   | 1 cup salt | |

   Method:  Mix ingredients to make a dough easy to handle. Knead, and shape as desired. Bake at 350° for 50 to 60 minutes. Material will brown slightly, but baking at lower temperatures is not as successful.

**FIGURE 11-3 Classroom recipes—cont.**

**FIGURE 11–4 For children unfamiliar with the use of art materials, begin with the most basic equipment, such as crayons and paper.**

*Sand table.* A low table containing sand, vehicles, animals, shovels, and assorted cups and spoons is a standard fixture in the early childhood program. Toddlers gain a good deal from the endless sorting, measuring, classifying, and sensory experiences they have with sand. Scooping, patting, smoothing, pushing, piling, and packing are examples of activities with sand, all of which contribute to the child's developing coordination and perception. Vocabulary is also developed when adults explain actions and changes everyone notices. As with water and play dough, the props should be changed occasionally, except when particular toddlers have strong preferences for some plaything.

*Special space.* An area of the toddler room can be devoted to unique projects and specially planned ac-

tivities. Such activities might include specific experiences (such as cooking) for holiday events. Holiday events should be kept simple and concrete for toddlers. Special projects conducted a few times a week on a regular basis may be encouraged in this area, especially when the toddlers seem to need an interesting experience or when teachers wish to try something new and different.

**Art Activities for Young Preschoolers, Age Two to Four Years.** Most young preschoolers two to four years of age have a limited span of interest and attention. Many activities, even the most interesting, hold their interest for only 10 to 15 minutes. Even less time, in fact, is more usual. However, it should be remembered that each child is different and interest spans may be shorter or longer for each individual child.

The point is that the teacher must, first of all, plan activities that appeal to the interests of the young preschooler. Simple, basic art activities are of most interest to the child of this age group. Second, the

**FIGURE 11–5 When working on a collage, a child may concentrate more on pasting than on the materials being pasted. This, however, is all part of a child's enjoyment of the process.**

teacher must be prepared to accept the fact that the activity may hold the child's interest for only a short time. It helps to remember that a period of time that seems short to an adult may be quite long to the young preschool child. Finally, alternative and extra activities should be available for those children who may not be interested in the first activity planned.

With this young preschool group, it is usually best to use only the basic materials at first. This helps keep the art program from being too confusing for the child. Using only a few crayons or paints or pasting one or two kinds of things at first is a good idea. It encourages children to experiment with each new tool and medium. They learn to use the basic tools and materials first. When they have acquired the basic skills, more colors and variety can be added. Let us consider now specific activities for the interest, ability, and skill levels of young preschool children.

*Collage.* (For more information on the techniques of collage, see Unit 12). Making a collage is a good activity for young preschoolers, as it can be completed quickly and within the interest span of most young preschoolers. It helps them grow physically in their ability to use small muscles as they cut, tear, and paste. Young preschoolers can also benefit mentally since they learn in collage activities to choose items and to arrange them into a design. As they paste together a collage, they learn about the feel, shape, and color of many things and develop the ability to use things in unusual ways.

At times, it may seem as if young preschoolers focus more on the paste than on the items being pasted, but that is part of the fun. The teacher must be sure that the objects available are suitable for the child who is using them. For example, it is good to keep tiny, inedible objects away from children who still put things in their mouth.

Young preschoolers who are new to this activity should begin with just one thing to paste. A good idea is for them to make a tear-and-paste collage. To do this, they are given pieces of newspaper, colored tissue, or any colored scrap paper that tears easily. The teacher shows them, if necessary, how to tear large and small pieces. Then they paste these torn bits of paper into a design on colored construction

**FIGURE 11–6 Putting one's name on artwork is an important part of the artistic process.**

paper. This is a good activity for young preschoolers who do not want or are not yet able to use scissors. Some scissors should be available for children who want to try cutting the pieces to paste on the collage. Children should not be forced to practice cutting, however.

As the children master the basic technique of pasting, more objects can be added to the collage. Some good things to add are large buttons, bits of cloth and paper in different colors, textures, and shapes, and bottle caps. Care must be taken to be sure the materials are not sharp, not painted with lead paint, and not small enough to swallow.

For a change of pace, different materials may be used for the backing of the collage. The children may use Styrofoam meat trays to paste things on, or shoe box lids, or even pieces of burlap. The teacher and children use their imaginations to come up with new ideas for the arts and crafts materials.

*Painting.* Young preschool children also get much satisfaction from working with paint at the easel. They like to experiment with color and form, making designs, and later simple pictures. Young preschool-

**FIGURE 11–7 When a child gets involved in finger painting, she often uses more than just her fingers.**

ers will also paint one color on top of the other and enjoy the effect. But most of all, they enjoy the movement involved in painting.

Using finger paint gives young preschoolers a chance to use their bodies freely and to arrange the paint at will. In work with finger paint, a child of this age feels a sense of relaxation that often leads to communication with others. A child communicates best when relaxed.

Finger paint is an especially good medium for this age group, as it can be arranged over and over again. In this way, the process is stressed, not the product. This is very important for children, who at this age are learning the basic ways to use paint. This age group enjoys the feel (and sometimes even the taste) of the paint. They sometimes even use their upper arms and elbows to help them in their designs.

To save on the cost of finger paint paper and to try something new, adults can sometimes let the children finger paint on a formica table top, an enamel-top table, a sheet of smooth formica, or even linoleum. When this is done, a print can be made from the child's finger painting by laying a piece of newsprint paper on the finger painting and gently rubbing it with one hand. The painting is transferred in this way from the table top to the paper. More finger paint activities are suggested later in this unit.

There may be some preschool children who do not like the feel of finger paint. If this is so, the child should never be forced to use it. Instead, another art activity can be found that the child will enjoy.

*Printing.* Printing with objects is an art activity that is appropriate for the age, ability, and interest level of young preschool children. In a basic printing activity, the child learns that an object dipped in or brushed with paint makes its own mark, or print, on paper. Children use small muscles in the hand and wrist as they hold the object, dip it in paint, and print with it on paper. They learn that each object has its own unique quality since each thing makes its own imprint.

For the young preschool child, stick prints are best to start with. In this type of printing, children dip small pieces of wood of various sizes and shapes into a thick tempera paint and press them onto a piece of paper. Twigs, wooden spools, wood clothespins, and bottle caps are objects suitable for three-year-olds to use in printing.

After stick printing is mastered, printing with vegetables is good with this age group. Green peppers, carrots, turnips, and potatoes are some vegetables to try. The vegetables are sliced in half, making two smooth surfaces for printing. A good way for young preschoolers to begin printing is to "walk" the inked vegetable across the paper in even "steps." When it gets to the other side, they walk it back again. By making three or four lines, or walks, the child has made a pattern.

After one color is used, the vegetable can be wiped clean and another color used. Three-year-olds like to try many colors with the same printing object. They may even print over their first prints in a different color. More printing actvities for young preschool children are found in Unit 12 and at the end of this unit.

*Crayons.* Crayons are the most basic, most familiar, and easiest tool for young preschoolers to use. Large crayons are easy to hold and can be used to make attractive colored marks on paper. Most young preschoolers have crayons, but often drawings on paper are the only use made of them. There are, however,

FIGURE 11–8 Although children have a relatively short attention span at three years of age, certain activities might hold their interest for longer periods of time.

several other ways to use crayons that the teacher might try to vary the program for young preschoolers.

- *Crayons and a Variety of Materials.* Crayons can be used to draw on many surfaces. Cardboard in any form (including corrugated cardboard, paper gift boxes, and food trays) is a good surface for crayon drawings, as is Styrofoam. Crayon drawings on sandpaper have an interesting effect.
- *Crayon Rubbings.* Drawing pictures with crayons is only one of the uses for crayons. Crayon rubbing is a technique that young preschool children can easily master. To make a crayon rubbing, the child puts a piece of paper over a textured surface, and rubs the sides of a peeled crayon over the paper.

    The crayon picks up the texture on the paper in a design. Some surfaces that can be used are bumpy food trays, bark, leaves, the sidewalk, bricks, and corrugated cardboard. This is a good activity for developing both small and large muscles.
- *Crayon Resist.* Another way to use crayon is in crayon resist drawings. To make a resist drawing, the child first draws a picture on paper with cray-

ons, pressing hard. She then paints over and around the crayon drawing with thin paint (tempera paint diluted with water). A dark-colored paint works best. The dark color fills in all the areas that the crayon has not covered. In the areas covered with crayon, the crayon "resists," or is not covered by, the paint. Crayon resist gives the feeling of a night picture. It is a thrilling experience for the child to see the changes that come when the paint crosses the paper.

See Unit 12 for additional activities and techniques for using crayons.

**Art Activities for Older Preschoolers and Kindergartners (Four to Six Years).** Just as in the case of the younger preschool child, there are preferred and suitable materials and activities for older preschoolers. Although there may be considerable overlap, children in this age group generally differ significantly from younger preschool children.

There are some general traits of preschoolers and kindergartners four to six years old. Small muscle development in the fingers, hands, and wrists is much improved. Whereas younger preschool children may have great difficulty buttoning their clothing or using scissors, most in this older group do not. Use of crayons, magic markers, and, in some cases, pencils and pens is quite possible. With their vocabulary now expanded to over two thousand words, they are quite capable of speaking in sentences of four and five words. Their ability to converse, coupled with their increased attention span (15 to 30 minutes), now allows for some small-group activities in the art program.

Since these children are very interested in life beyond home and school, art activities including outside environments (television characters, for example) can be stimulating. Youngsters of this age paint and draw with more purpose. Designs and pictures are within their abilities. These will probably be somewhat simple, but nonetheless fun and exciting for the children to do.

*Painting, music, and literature.* Older preschoolers and kindergartners usually are very interested in music. They enjoy dancing and performing to musical accompaniments. This is a good age group for art activities with musical stimulation. "Accidental watercolor" is an example of such an activity. Each child is given a large sheet of paper and instructed to apply water to the entire sheet with a brush. Then the teacher announces that the children may try watercolor experiments that fit their mood or fantasies. Music can be used to create or influence the children's moods.

The first mood might be a happy one. The children are asked to decide which colors are "happy" and to moisten each of them in their watercolors. When the chosen colors are wet, the children are asked to pick one with their brushes and to put it on their paper any way they want. They then choose another color and apply it, being very careful not to cover one color with another. They continue in this way until the entire paper is covered with colors that should combine in unusual ways to create a variety of brilliant "accidents."

Different moods can be attempted while the previously painted pictures are drying. The children must not pick up the paintings while they are still wet, or all the colors will mix into a drab gray. After the paintings have dried, children may talk about them and the mood or fantasy they express. Black watercolor or India ink can be used to outline the brilliant colors. This adds a dramatic touch to the work.

This same method can be used with tempera paints. They are very rich and even better for over-painting. When watercolors and tempera paint are both available, they may be used together. This provides variety and another form of expression.

The child of this age is able to listen for longer periods to stories with wider content. Thus, making art activities relate to story presentations is a good tool to help motivate children.

It is also quite possible for children of this age group to build elaborate block structures. They are not only capable of naming these creations but also can tell interesting stories about them. Block building can be a cooperative activity for several children working together. Very often, pictures of these block creations occur in the paintings and drawings of children of this age.

Whereas younger preschoolers should use only the basic materials, older preschool children and kindergartners can explore with more materials. They need not be restricted to a few crayons or paints. Generally, in familiar activities such as drawing, painting, and pasting, a wide variety of resources can and should be used.

*Mosaics.*   Mosaics are surface decorations made of small pieces of colored glass, stone, or other inlaid materials. The young child can make a very simple mosaic using torn or cut colored paper. This can be a very exciting project because it combines the elements of drawing, cutting, pasting, and putting a puzzle together. It may be a group project.

The children begin by cutting colored paper into half-inch square pieces. They keep the colors separate by placing the pieces in different small boxes or containers. When enough pieces have been cut, the group can try a mosaic picture. An art book with illustrations of mosaics can be shown to give children a better idea of the meaning of this project.

Pictures of animals, flowers, and many other things are possible. The main idea is to keep the project simple. A cat, a car, and a tree are just a few of the many possibilities.

After the children have decided what they want to do, they select the colors that satisfy the idea they have in mind. They should apply the bits of paper by starting with the central figure or object and working toward the edges. Mosaics are more attractive if they are pasted on a background of colored paper or cardboard. Interesting variations can be made from books of wallpaper samples, which are often discarded by wallpaper stores.

Some children may be able to make slightly more complex mosaics by combining a variety of materials. Gravel, pebbles, seeds, pods, and various types of grains make unique mosaics when combined in imaginative ways. However, these materials require a stronger glue than library paste. There are several milk-white liquid glues that are satisfactory for this activity. They are completely safe and nontoxic for children of any age.

Let us now consider some specific art activities and the required materials and strategies for each.

# BASIC EQUIPMENT, MATERIALS, AND STRATEGIES

What follows are lists of basic art materials needed in the early childhood art program and related strategies for their use. Figure 11–3 gives instructions for making many of the materials discussed in this section. In choosing from the lists, the teacher must keep in mind the motor control and coordination of the children in the group.

## Drawing Materials

1. Sturdy sheets of paper (manila or newsprint, 8″ × 12″ or 12″ × 18″). Spread the paper on a table or on the floor, or pin it to a wall or easel. Paper of different shapes may also be used for variety.
2. A basket of jumbo crayons about three quarters of an inch in width. These are a good size for the muscle control of small fingers. Unwrap the crayons so they can be used on both the sides and the ends.
3. Felt-tip markers in many colors and tip widths. (Be sure they are not permanent markers.)

Felt-tip markers do come in beautiful, clear colors. Compared with paint, they have the additional advantage of staying bright and unsullied until the children use them up.

Most schools set out crayons or pens jumbled together in a basket. However, you might try assembling them in separate boxes so that each user has an individual, complete set. This cuts down on arguments and means that all the colors are available to each child as the children require them.

Another alternative is to store crayons in wide-mouth containers according to color—all red crayons in one container, all blue in another, etc.

*Strategies.* Crayons are an ideal medium for children; they are bold, colorful, clean, and inexpensive. They consist of an oily or waxy binder mixed with color pigments. They are of various types, some soft, some semihard, some for general use with young children (kindergarten or "fat" crayons.) Crayons work well on most papers. They do not blend well; if attempts are made to do this, the wax often "tears." New crayons won't break as easily if you wrap them with masking tape before letting the children use them.

## Chalking Materials

1. A blackboard and eraser, and/or a stack of wet or dry (or both) paper.
2. A container full of colored and white chalk.

*Strategies.* Chalk is inexpensive and comes in pretty colors. Its most typical use is with chalkboards, but little children do not seem to use it very effectively there. They do better if they can mark on the sidewalk with it—perhaps because the rougher texture of the cement more easily pulls the color off the stick, and the children seem more able to tell what they are doing as they squat down and draw. It is, of course, necessary to explain to them that they may "write" with chalk only on special places.

Some young artists apply chalks in separate strokes, letting the color blending take place in the viewer's eye. Others are not reluctant to blend the colors and do so successfully, although there is danger of the colors being muddied. Of course, there is no need to caution children against this; they should be encouraged to explore by rubbing with fingers, cotton swab, anything available. Most children will select and use chalks easily.

Chalk drawing is best done on a paper with a slightly coarse, abrasive surface. This texture helps the paper trap and hold the chalk particles. Many papers have this quality, including inexpensive manila paper.

Chalks are brittle and easily broken. They are also impermanent, smearing very easily. Completed works should be sprayed with a "fixative" (ordinary hairspray works well); this should be done with proper ventilation.

Chalk strokes can be strengthened by wetting the chalk or paper. Various liquids have also been used with chalks for interesting results. These include dipping the chalk sticks in buttermilk, starch, and sugar water. Liquid tends to seal the chalk, so teachers must occasionally rub it on a piece of old sandpaper in order to break this seal and allow the color to come off readily.

### Brush Painting Materials

1. Two easels (at least) with two blunt-tipped nails sticking out near each upper corner to attach the paper. (Or paper can be held on the board with spring-type clothespins.) Easels must be at the right height so that a child can paint without stretching or stooping.
2. Sheets of paper (18″ × 24″ plain newsprint), white or in assorted colors.
3. Three or four jars of tempera (poster) paint. These may be mixed with powdered detergent for proper consistency.

4. Paint containers. These must have flat bottoms so they will not tip over easily. Quart milk cartons (cut down) are good since they can be thrown away after using. Also, plastic fruit juice cans with lids work well when unused paint needs to be stored.
5. Large, long-handled brushes in each jar. Those with 12″ handles and ¾″ bristle length are easy for young children to use. Soft, floppy, camel-hair brushes allow the child to swoop about the paper most freely. The stiff, flat kind of brush makes it harder to produce such free movements.
6. Smocks. An old shirt with the sleeves cut to the child's arm length makes a practical smock. Oil-cloth or plastic aprons are also good.
7. A place to dry finished paintings.

*Strategies.* Painting should be done near running water. Floors, tables, or anything that must be kept paint-free should be covered before starting any messy activity. Each child should wear a smock to prevent soiling clothes. Painting should be done in an

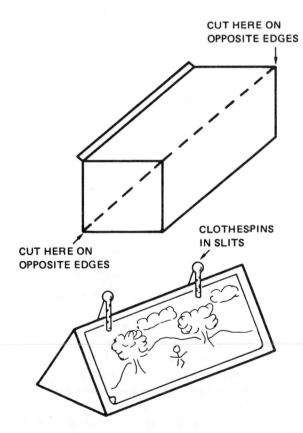

FIGURE 11–9 Cardboard box easels.

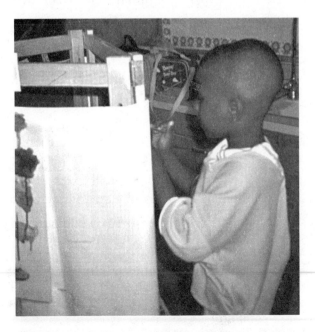

FIGURE 11–10 An easel set up at the appropriate height ensures a child's successful experience at painting.

area away from large-motor games, toys, or activities like blocks, rocking boats, and climbing toys.

*Mixing paint.* Although mixing paint in large quantities saves teacher's time, the children enjoy making it so much, and this is such a good learning experience for them to do, that mixing a fresh batch each day with one or two children helping stir is generally preferred. A surprising amount of tempera is needed in relation to the quantity of water to make rich, bright, creamy paint; thus it is best to dump the tempera into a pint container first and then add water bit by bit. Instead of water, some teachers prefer using liquid starch because it thickens the paint mixture. However, it does increase the expense. It is also helpful to add a dash of liquid detergent, since this makes cleaning up easier.

At the easel, it may help children to see that if they wipe the brush on the side of the jar the paint does not drip or run. An adult can show the children that keeping each brush in its own paint jar keeps the color clear. Children can be shown that colors can be mixed on paper by brushing one color over another.

It will expedite matters if several pieces of paper are clipped to the easel at once. Many teachers prefer to write the child's name on the back of the paper to avoid the problem of having him paint over it. If a developmental file is kept at school for each child,

dating a few paintings and saving them delights parents at conference time because it enables them to see how the child's skills have developed during the year.

The children must be shown where to put their paintings and where to get a cloth to wipe up. If necessary, they should be reminded to wash their hands before taking off their smocks.

*Easel painting procedure.* Easel painting requires running water, a work-shelf area, and paint supply shelves at child height. In some centers, a stool or steps are needed so children can reach an adult-height sink.

Sometimes teachers like to start with only the three primary colors (red, blue, and yellow) in the beginning of the year and then add others in the second month or so. Each jar of blue tempera (poster) paint should be labeled with a strip of blue paper clearly printed BLUE. (Use the same label idea for each color.) Brushes should be thoroughly washed and in good condition. This makes the need for their care and washing more obvious to the children. Children must be shown how to mix the dry paint into a liquid. The teacher must also show them the kind of wiping up and washing needed in cleanup.

At the end of each day, all paintbrushes are washed thoroughly in running water and dried before being put away. Easels and aprons are washed with a wet

# THINK ABOUT IT . . .

The following hints may be both helpful and motivating to the children's art experiences:

- Make exciting finger paint by adding food coloring to vanilla pudding for a great lesson on the senses.
- If you add soap flakes to tempera paint, it will wash out more easily; you can also paint on window glass with this mixture and it will come off very easily.
- Add a drop of the following to tempera paint to prevent it from smelling sour: oil of cloves, oil of peppermint, lemon juice, vanilla. (A drop or two of bleach will also prevent it from spoiling.)
- A wooden or aluminum clothes-drying rack and pinch clothespins are great for drying children's paintings. Paintings can be hung on the line to dry in the same manner as clothes.

# THIS ONE'S FOR YOU!

Painting supplies can eat up a large part of your budget. The following ideas may help your budget (and maybe your creativity, too!):

1. Individual watercolor sets can be made by pouring leftover tempera paint into egg carton cups. Set them aside to dry and harden. Use the paints with water and brushes just as you would ordinary paint sets.
2. Paint containers need to be sturdy and inexpensive. Here are some ideas for different types of paint containers:
   - Cupcake or muffin tins are excellent for painting with several colors at a time.
   - Egg cartons work well when children are painting with cotton swabs. Cut cartons in thirds to make four-part containers, and pour small amounts of paint into each egg cup.
   - Store liquid tempera in recycled glue or dishwashing liquid bottles. Paint can be squirted quickly and neatly into paint cups from these bottles.
   - Use baby food jars as paint containers. Make a holder for them but cutting circles out of an egg carton lid. An empty 6-pack soft drink carton also makes a great tote for baby food jars of paint.
   - When using paint cups, make a non-tipping cup holder from an empty half-gallon milk or juice carton. Cut holes along the length of the carton and pop in the cups.
   - Sponges can be good paint holders, too. Cut a hole the exact size of the paint jar or cup in the center of the sponge, then fit the jar/cup in the hole. Besides keeping paint containers upright, the sponges also catch drips.
   - Cotton-ball painting is more fun (and neater) when you clip spring-type clothespins to the cotton balls. Children use the clothespins like handles. The same clothespins can also be used when printing with small sponge pieces.

cloth and soap if necessary. Paint containers are washed and put away. Leftover paint must be covered with a tight lid or aluminum foil. Aprons and smocks are hung up.

*Economy measures.* Putting a small amount of paint at a time in a can is one way to avoid waste. Ordering paint in quantity once a year is another way to make money go as far as possible, and if schools combine their orders, sometimes an even lower cost per can is offered. Children should be taught some practical techniques for handling paint to avoid waste, such as wiping the brush on the edge of the can and returning paintbrushes to the same color paint each time.

## Finger Painting Materials

1. Paper that has a shiny surface. This can be butcher paper, shelf paper, special finger paint paper, freezer wrap, or glossy gift wrap paper.
2. A water supply to make the paper damp. A damp sponge or rag works best. Water may also be sprinkled directly onto the paper.
3. Finger paint. This can be special finger paint or dry tempera paint mixed with liquid starch or liquid detergent to make a thick mixture.
4. Racks to dry the finished work. Cake-cooling racks work well for this.
5. A smock for each painter.
6. A nearby sink and running water for washing hands and cleaning up.

*Strategies.* For finger painting, the tables should be covered with linoleum, formica, or plastic, and children should wear aprons. The sink area should be nearby. Plenty of paper towels and clean rags should be provided. Smooth-surfaced paper is dipped in a pan of water and spread flat on a table.

The quickest, simplest way to make fingerpaint is to combine liquid starch with dry tempera. This may be done by pouring a generous dollop of starch onto the paper and then sprinkling it with dry tempera. Alternatively, some teachers like to stir the dry pigment into an entire container of starch base. No matter how the paint is originally prepared, you need to be ready to add more ingredients as the children work. The results to strive for in mixing are rich, brilliant color and sufficient paint to fill the paper completely if the child wishes. Children must be allowed to experiment with the paint as they wish, using their fingers, the palms of the hands, or wrists.

Prepared finger paints may be used, or the children may help mix the recipe in Figure 11–3. If the recipe is used, the mixture may be separated into three or four parts and coloring added—either food color or the powdered paint used for easel painting. Children like to add their own color; they may use salt shakers containing powdered paint and mix in the color with their fingers. Adding soap flakes (not detergents) to the paint mixture increases variety.

*Variations.* Another method of fingerpainting is to cover a table with white oilcloth and let the children work on the oilcloth. The mixture can later be washed off with a hose or under a faucet. This activity is good for all ages.

Use waxed paper for a change, instead of regular finger painting paper, because of its transparent quality. A combination of any liquid dishwashing detergent and a dark-colored tempera paint (one part paint, one part soap) can be applied onto waxed paper. Cover the surface evenly so the painter can make a simple design with his fingers.

Finger painting without paper is another variation. The children finger paint directly onto plastic trays. When each child finishes, place a piece of paper on top of the finger painting and rub across the back of the paper. Lift the paper from the tray and a print

of the finger painting is made. The trays are easily rinsed off in the sink.

**Pasting Materials**

1. Small jars of paste. (Or give each child a square of waxed paper with a spoonful of paste on it. This prevents waste.) A wooden tongue depressor is a good tool for spreading the paste, or paste can be spread with the fingers.
2. Sheets of plain or colored manila or construction paper in many sizes.
3. Collage materials. Some of these can be paper shapes in different colors, scraps of cloth, feathers, yarn, tinfoil, string, beans, sawdust, bottle caps, buttons, Styrofoam packing pieces, rock salt, bits of bark, and any other things that look interesting.
4. Blunt scissors, for both left- and right-handed children.

*Strategies.* Pasting should be done away from climbing toys, building blocks, and similar large motor activities. All the materials for pasting should be on a shelf at child level. Collage and pasting materials should be placed on a separate table and sorted into

**FIGURE 11–11 Pasting is an art activity that requires sufficient space as well as materials to be a successful experience.**

shallow containers, such as baskets, so that children can readily appraise the kinds of things that are available and consider how they will look when arranged together. Some children will enjoy tearing and pasting, while others will prefer cutting and pasting. Of course, the children should learn about safety rules for using scissors early in the year. The teacher must also be sure that all young children have only blunt scissors.

Paste should be kept in small plastic containers or jars. To help children learn to keep lids on jars, mark the bottom and top of each jar with a number or a colored X. The children are shown how to match up the jar with its lid by matching colored X's or numbers. In this way, children learn to keep the lids on the jars and to recognize numbers and colors.

Children should be shown how to rinse out paste brushes and where to return all pasting material. A place to put finished work to dry should be set up.

Using common recycled household disposables will make cleanup easier. Aluminum pie tins and frozen food trays are both excellent for holding paint, paste, or glue for table activities. At the end of the activity, you may want to recycle the aluminum. Another way to make cleanup easier after pasting is to fold over the top edges of a large paper bag, then tape the bag to one end of your work table. When the children have finished their projects, scraps can easily be swept off the table into the bag. Then, just toss the bag in the trash.

## Puppet Materials (Age 4½ and Up).
1. Paper bags in any size.
2. Scissors, colored papers, paste, paints or crayons, tape, and stapler.
3. Sticks for stick puppets. Some kinds are yardsticks, twigs, wood scrap sticks, and tongue depressors.
4. Cardboard rolls for tube puppets.
5. Socks or mittens for sock and mitten puppets.
6. Styrofoam balls for heads.
7. Miscellaneous material to make faces: buttons, pins, old jewelry, and yarn.

## Scrap Art Materials.
1. Paste, glue, tape, and stapler.
2. Colored tissue paper.
3. Colored sticky tape, gummed circles, stars, and designs.
4. Tempera paint, chalk, crayons, and felt-tip pens.
5. Odds and ends of scrap material—egg cartons, Styrofoam pieces, plastic containers and lids, pine cones, feathers, and buttons.

*Strategies.* For puppets and scrap art activities, all material must be in good order. This is because both activities require a large supply of materials. A special place is needed for all supplies within the child's reach and eye level.

Scraps of cloth may be kept in one box with scrap pieces glued on the outside to show the child at a glance what is in the box. Buttons may be kept in a muffin tin, feathers in a plastic bag, and old bits of jewelry for puppets in a plastic shoe box. The point is to keep each material in a specific place so that it is ready for planned or spontaneous projects.

Organizing material in this simple, easy-to-find way helps children learn to work on their own. Having glue, scissors, paper, and all other materials on shelves at the child's height also encourages independent work. Cleanup time is much easier, too, when the children can see "what goes where" and can reach the places where materials are supposed to go.

When painting puppets or scrap artwork, the suggestions in the painting section can be used. The im-

FIGURE 11–12 A variety of materials must be readily available for the child's use in the art program.

portant thing is to prepare the room and the child for a messy activity. This preparation makes painting more fun and relaxing because neither the teacher nor the child has to be concerned about the mess. (See Unit 15 for more suggestions on making puppets.)

## Potter's Clay and Play Dough Materials.

1. Potter's clay or play dough (mixed from the recipe in Figure 11–3) kept in an airtight container.
2. Clay or play dough table. Use a table with a formica top or any table that is easy to clean. (Or use large pieces of plastic spread out on the table, or cut one for each child's use.)
3. Tools for clay work like toy rolling pins, cookie cutters, spoons, and blunt plastic knives.

*Strategies.* Working with clay and play dough requires a place away from all active centers such as building blocks, wheel toys, and climbing toys. The tables should be covered with formica or oilcloth to make cleaning easier. Young children also enjoy working with clay on individual vinyl placemats, Masonite boards, burlap squares, or brown paper grocery bags. Newspaper doesn't work well because when it gets wet, bits of paper may mix with the clay. For clay projects that are meant to be hardened and possibly painted later, a good place for drying must be set up. Since these objects may take a few days to dry, this place must also be away from frequently used areas. The basement, coatroom, windowsill, or a special rack are all good places for drying.

Before starting any three-dimensional projects that require several stages such as molding, drying, and then painting, the teacher must be aware of the children's interest spans. Some of these projects take longer than other art activities, and some children may lose interest and not finish the project. The teacher must also consider the time needed for preparing the material, making the objects, drying them, and painting them. Then it must be decided if the children's interest is strong enough to last through the time needed for the whole project. It is an unpleasant experience for both teacher and children when a project is too rush d. This takes the joy out of the activity for all involved.

*Potter's clay.* Potter's clay may be purchased at any art supply store in moist form. This is much easier to deal with than starting with dry powder. It is available in two colors—gray and terra cotta. (Terra cotta looks pretty but stains clothing and is harder to clean up.) Clay requires careful storage in a watertight, airtight container to retain its malleable qualities. When children are through with it, form it into large balls, press a thumb into it, and then fill that hole with water and replace in container. If oilcloth table covers are used with potter's clay, they can simply be hung up to dry, shaken well, and put away until next time.

*Making play dough.* Children should participate in making dough whenever possible. If allowed to help make the dough, children learn about measuring, blending, and cause and effect, and also have the chance to work together to help the school.

The doughs that require no cooking are best mixed two batches at a time in separate deep dishpans. Using deep pans keeps the flour within bounds, and making two batches at a time relieves congestion and provides better participation opportunities. Tempera powder is the most effective coloring agent to add because it makes such intense shades of dough; adding it to the flour before pouring in the liquid works best. Dough can be kept in the refrigerator and reused several times. Removing it at the beginning of the day allows it to come to room temperature before being offered to the children—otherwise it can be discouragingly stiff and unappealing. The addition of flour or cornstarch on the second day is usually necessary to reduce stickiness.

*Dough variations.* All the dough recipes in Figure 11–3 have been carefully tested and are suitable for various purposes. In preschool centers where process, not product, is emphasized, the dough and clay are generally used again and again rather than the objects made by the children being allowed to dry and then sent home. For special occasions, however, it is nice to allow the pieces to harden and then to paint or color them. Two recipes included in Figure

11–3 serve this purpose particularly well: ornamental clay and baker's dough.

Once made, dough is easy to get out and simple to supervise. Usually all the children have to remember is to keep it on the table and out of their mouths. It is a pleasant material to bring out toward the end of the morning or in late afternoon when children and teachers are tired and cleanup needs to be quick and easy.

For dough to be truly satisfying, children need an abundance of it rather than meager little handfuls, and they should be encouraged to use it in a manipulative, expressive way rather than in a product-oriented way.

*Cleanup.* For clay cleanup, sponge off tables, mats, and boards. Burlap squares can be stacked and shaken when dry, and grocery bags can be thrown away. Clay-caked hands and tools should never be washed in the sink because clay can clog the drain. Instead, have the children wipe off their tools and hands with paper towels, then wash them in a basin filled with soapy water. When the clay particles settle, you can let the soapy water down the drain and throw the sediment in the trash can. Children may rinse their hands in the sink, and the tools may be left to dry on paper towels.

The cooked cornstarch recipes are the only ones that are particularly difficult to clean up because they leave a hard, dry film on the pan during cooking. However, an hour or two of soaking in cold water converts this to a jellylike material that is easily scrubbed off with a plastic pot-scrubbing pad. If pans are soaked during nap time, the children will be quite interested in the qualities of this gelatinous material when they get up. You might even have one or two of them work on scrubbing the pot clean!

## Woodwork Materials.
1. A bin of soft lumber pieces (leftover scraps of lumber).
2. Supply of nails with large heads.
3. Wooden spools, corks, and twigs.
4. Wooden buttons, string, and ribbons to be nailed to wood or tied to heads of nails already hammered into the wood.
5. Bottle caps.
6. Small-sized real tools. Hammer and nails are best to start with. Saws, screwdrivers, a vise, and a drill may be added later.
7. Workbench.
8. Sandpaper.
9. A vise or C-clamp placed near the corner of the workbench, flush with the table top.

*Strategies.* Carpentry needs to be done in a special area away from other activities. Children should be provided with plenty of good wood and satisfactory tools. A sturdy workbench of the right height is helpful.

The most basic woodworking tools are hammers and saws. The hammers should be good, solid ones—*not* tack hammers. The saws should be crosscut ones so that they can cut with or across the grain of the wood, and they should be as short as possible. A well-made vise in which to place wood securely while sawing is invaluable. Preferably, there should be two of these, one at each end of the table. (C-clamps can also be used for this purpose and are less expensive, or a board can be nailed to the table while the child saws it, but this leaves the troublesome chore of removing the nails afterward.)

Very young children enjoy sawing up the large pieces of Styrofoam that come as packing for electronic equipment. Hammering into such material or into plasterboard is also quick and easy and does not require more force than two- and three-year-olds can muster. Older children need plentiful amounts of softwood to work with.

Cabinet shops are a good source for scrap lumber. Only smooth lumber should be used. Pieces of various lengths and sizes add interest. The greater the variety of wood, the greater the challenge for building. An old tree stump is great fun for children to pound countless nails into.

Woodwork needs careful adult supervision, since children can easily hurt themselves or each other with a hammer and saw. General guidelines for adult supervision include the following:

• Stay very close to the woodwork activity. Be within reach of each child.

- There should be no more than three or four children for one adult to supervise. Only one child at a time should use a saw.
- Show the children how to saw away from their own fingers and from other children. Show them how to avoid hitting their fingers with the hammer.
- Hand out nails a few at a time.
- Never turn your back on the activity for even a few seconds.
- Make a wall-mounted toolboard to store frequently used tools. (Less used tools can be stored in a cupboard.) The outline of each tool can be marked on the board so children can figure out where to hang each tool. (More woodworking information is found in Unit 13.)

*Some variations for woodworking.*
- Remember to vary the tools the children use as their skill (and self-control) increases.
- Purchase a variety of nails by the pound, not by the little box, from a hardware store. Children love an assortment of these. They can be set out in small foil pie plates to keep them from getting mixed up. Some schools nail these pie plates to a long board to prevent spilling.
- Offer various kinds of trims to go with woodworking, such as wire, thick, colorful yarn, and wooden spools (with nails long enough to go through the spool).
- Offer round things for wheels, such as bottle caps, buttons, or the lids of 35 mm film containers.
- Provide dowels of various sizes that will fit the holes made by the different sizes of bits.

**Unsafe Art Supplies.**   For all the activities in this unit, and in any art activities for young children, be sure that you aren't using any unsafe art supplies. Potentially unsafe art supplies include the following:

- Powdered clay. It is easily inhaled and contains silica, which is harmful to the lungs. Instead, use wet clay, which can't be inhaled.
- Paints that require solvents such as turpentine to clean brushes. Use only water-based paints.

- Cold-water or commercial dyes that contain chemical additives. Use only natural vegetable dyes, made from beets, onion skins, and so on.
- Permanent markers, which may contain toxic solvents. Use only water-based markers.
- Instant papier-mâché, which may contain lead or asbestos. Use only black-and-white newspaper and library paste or liquid starch.
- Epoxy, instant glues, or other solvent-based glues. Use only water-based white glue (Clemens, 1991).

## SUMMARY

The early childhood art program is a part of the early childhood curriculum in which children have the chance to work with many kinds of materials and techniques to make an original end product. It provides a time and place for children to put together their thoughts, ideas, feelings, actions, and abilities into their own creations. Art activities also have real application to other areas of the curriculum, including science, social studies, and reading readiness.

Toddlers are very active and want to explore everything. For this reason, they need materials that are sturdy, practically indestructible, and do not include tiny pieces that might be swallowed. Only a few materials should be put out at a time so toddlers are not overwhelmed by too many choices. Art materials, like crayons, playdough, chalk, and paint, need to be frequently available to toddlers. These materials should be presented under the supervision of an adult to encourage their appropriate use. In setting up art (and all other) centers for toddlers, a teacher should arrange lots of space and clear traffic patterns, since toddlers are prone to falling, grabbing, and running.

Young preschool children, two to four years of age, have a limited interest span. Even the most interesting activities hold their interest for only 10 to 15 minutes on the average. Thus, the teacher must plan several activities and alternative activities for this age group. Some appropriate art activities for children of this age are easel and finger painting, printing, collage, crayoning, play dough, making simple puppets, and object sculpture.

# THIS ONE'S FOR YOU!

## TEACHER TIPS

The way a teacher sets up her own materials, supplies, and space can make or break the children's and teacher's successful experiences in art. The following are suggestions on how to arrange teacher supplies for art experiences, as well as how to organize children's supplies.

1. *Scissors Holders.* Holders can be made from gallon milk or bleach containers. Simply punch holes in the container and place scissors in holes with the points to the inside. Egg cartons turned upside down with slits in each mound also make excellent holders.
2. *Paint Containers.* Containers can range from muffin tins and plastic egg cartons to plastic soft drink cartons with baby food jars in them. These work especially well outdoors as well as indoors because they are large and not easily tipped over. Place one brush in each container; this prevents colors from getting mixed and makes cleanup easier.
3. *Crayon Containers.* Juice and vegetable cans painted or covered with contact paper work very well.
4. Crayon pieces may be melted down in muffin trays in a warm oven. These, when cooled down, are nice for rubbings or drawings.
5. Printing with tempera is easier if the tray is lined with a sponge or paper towel.
6. A card file for art activites helps organize the program.
7. *Clay Containers.* Airtight coffee cans and plastic food containers are excellent ways to keep clay moist and always ready for use.
8. *Paper Scrap Boxes.* By keeping two or more scrap boxes of paper, children will be able to choose the size paper they want more easily.
9. To color rice or macaroni, put two tablespoons each of rubbing alcohol and food coloring into a jar. Cap and shake well. Add rice and macaroni and shake again. Turn out onto paper towels and let dry approximately 10 to 15 minutes.

Older preschool children and kindergartners (four to six years of age) have begun to develop better small muscle control in the fingers, hands, and wrists. For this reason, they enjoy cutting with scissors, using smaller paint brushes, and trying out a wide variety of felt-tip pens. In addition to the basic two- and three-dimensional activities, older preschoolers and kindergartners enjoy watercolor painting experiences with music and making mosaics.

The objectives of the art program must consider the interest, age, and ability levels of the children. An important goal of the art program is the growth of a child's creativity and ability to work independently. But the main goal is to let children grow at their own individual rates.

Teachers play an important role in the success of the early childhood art program. They must choose the right materials, as well as know the right way to set up and use the materials for each activity.

# LEARNING ACTIVITIES

A. It is hard to really appreciate the individual merits of the dough recipes unless they are actually available for inspection and experimentation. As a class project, have volunteers make them up and bring them to class to try out.

B. Suppose a bad fairy has waved her wand and ruled that you could only select three basic types of creative self-expressive activities to use for a whole year in your preschool. Which three would you select and why?

C. Suppose that same bad fairy has waved her wand again, and now you are allowed to *purchase* only paint and glue (no paper even!) for your creative activities. How limiting is this? What self-expressive activities would you actually be able to offer under these circumstances? How might you go about acquiring the necessary free materials to make them possible? Be specific.

D. Visit one or possibly several preschool programs and observe the arts and crafts activities. Keep in mind these points in observing:
1. Are the equipment and activities right for the age, ability, and interest levels of the children?
2. Is the area well planned for each activity?
3. Are the children free to make what they want with the material?

E. Set up a classroom, real or imagined, for one or more of the following activities:
Fingerpainting
Collage
Making puppets
Consider the following in setting up the activity:
Location of water source
Preparation of area

Preparation of materials
Preparation of children
Teacher preparation
Activity itself
Cleanup
Drying and storage space for work in progress or finished

F. Draw up a plan of a room setup for arts and crafts for three-, four-, and five-year-olds.
1. Include the following areas:

Brush and finger painting
Clay
Puppetry

Papier-mâché work
Crayon and chalk work
Woodwork
Scrap art

2. Show on the plan where the following areas would be found:

Storage space
Child-level shelves
Drying areas

Water source(s)
Light source(s)

G. Ask young children what they think is the hardest part about cleaning up. Record their answers. See if there is one thing that is mentioned more than others. Check on the problem to see if it is caused by room setup, supply setup, water source, or something else.

H. Go on an odds-and-ends hunt.
1. See how many different kinds of things can be found for use in art projects. Things to look for include spools, Styrofoam, feathers, buttons, and foil.
2. Sort the material and store it in the best way possible. Label each container so that children will know what is inside.

# UNIT REVIEW

1. Is the product or the process more important in the art program? Explain your answer.
2. Choose the statements that describe an important purpose of art in the early childhood program:
   a. Art gives the child a chance to try new materials and techniques.
   b. Art helps the child make perfect artwork.
   c. The child has a chance to express experiences and feelings.
   d. The emphasis in art is on continued good experiences with many kinds of materials.
   e. In art, the child learns how to copy models.
   f. Learning to judge one's own work and other children's work is very important in art.

   g. Being successful in art helps develop a child's self-confidence.
3. Select the items that should be included in a list of equipment for each of the following activities:
   a. Crayoning
      (a.) Newsprint or manila paper, 8″ × 12″ or 12″ × 18″
      (b.) Lined white paper
      (c.) Colored tissue paper, 18″ × 24″
      (d.) Felt-tip pens in many colors
      (e.) Jumbo crayons, unwrapped
      (f.) Jumbo crayons, all wrapped
   b. Chalk work
      (a.) Colored chalks, white chalks

  (b.) Colored tissue paper
  (c.) Paper, wet and dry
  (d.) Chalkboard
  (e.) Eraser
  (f.) Pencils
c. Brush painting
  (a.) Easels
  (b.) Lined 9″ × 12″ paper
  (c.) Newsprint, 18″ × 24″, plain or pastel
  (d.) Construction paper
  (e.) Tempera paint
  (f.) Finger paint
  (g.) Glue
  (h.) Brushes, long (12″) handles and ¾″ bristles
  (i.) Smocks
  (j.) A place to dry finished paintings
d. Finger painting
  (a.) Dull, porous paper
  (b.) Shiny-surfaced paper
  (c.) Water supply
  (d.) Crayons
  (e.) Finger paint
  (f.) Colored tissue paper
  (g.) Smocks
  (h.) Racks to dry finished work
e. Pasting
  (a.) Glue in small jars
  (b.) Paste in small jars
  (c.) Lined 9″ × 12″ paper
  (d.) Colored tissue paper
  (e.) Plain or manila construction paper
  (f.) Scissors, blunt, left and right types
  (g.) Collage materials
  (h.) Stapler and staples
f. Puppets and scrap art
  (a.) Paper bags
  (b.) Boxes
  (c.) Scissors, paper, paste, paints
  (d.) Sticks
  (e.) Play dough
  (f.) Colored sticky tape
  (g.) Cardboard rolls
  (h.) Odds and ends
  (i.) Airtight container
  (j.) Socks and mittens
g. Clay and play dough
  (a.) Plasticene
  (b.) Real clay
  (c.) Open containers
  (d.) Airtight containers
  (e.) Formica-top tables
  (f.) Oilcloths
  (g.) Paint
  (h.) Scissors

  (i.) Tools for clay work
  (j.) Play dough, purchased
  (k.) Play dough, made with help from the children
h. Woodwork
  (a.) Paint
  (b.) Workbench
  (c.) Supply of soft lumber pieces
  (d.) Bottle caps
  (e.) Sandpaper
  (f.) Wooden spools, corks, twigs
  (g.) Clay
  (h.) Supply of nails
4. Choose the answer that best completes each of the following statements describing the basic objectives of the early childhood art program:
a. The most basic objective of the art program is to
  (a.) produce the best artists possible.
  (b.) meet the age, ability, and interest levels of the children.
  (c.) fit into the total preschool program.
b. Learning to be a creative thinker is
  (a.) more important in the elementary grades than for younger children.
  (b.) not an objective in art.
  (c.) an important objective in art.
c. The art program must allow children the freedom to
  (a.) grow at their own individual paces.
  (b.) do anything they please.
  (c.) go against safety rules.
5. Choose the answer that best completes each of the following statements describing techniques for using material in arts and crafts:
a. With very young children, it is best to begin with
  (a.) a great variety of materials.
  (b.) the basic essentials.
  (c.) only small motor activities.
b. A teacher must avoid
  (a.) making models for the children to copy.
  (b.) helping the children with the material.
  (c.) giving suggestions at cleanup time.
c. Painting work should be done
  (a.) in an area near the quiet activities.
  (b.) in an area away from climbing toys.
  (c.) only if sunlight is available.
d. Finger painting works best with
  (a.) dull, porous, dry paper on wood tables.
  (b.) shiny paper on the floor.
  (c.) shiny paper on a table covered with formica or oilcloth.
e. It is best to keep pasting supplies
  (a.) out of child's reach.
  (b.) on a shelf at child-level.
  (c.) in a locked cabinet.

f. Puppets and scrap art activities require
   (a.) a good deal of organization of supplies.
   (b.) no special order in supplies.
   (c.) a small amount of supplies.
g. Woodwork is an activity that
   (a.) needs very little supervision.
   (b.) needs careful adult supervision.
   (c.) is too dangerous for young children.
h. In woodwork and all art activities, it is important to encourage children to
   (a.) copy the teacher's models.
   (b.) copy the ideas of the other children.
   (c.) do what they want with the materials.
6. List some special considerations for setting up art and art-related areas for toddlers.
7. Describe several appropriate art and art-related centers for toddlers, including
   a. materials in the center.
   b. arrangement of materials.
   c. skills developed in the center.
8. List the skills, interests, and abilities of older preschool children and kindergartners.
9. List appropriate art activities for older preschool children and kindergartners.
10. Choose the answer that best completes each of the following statements describing the skills and abilities of the young preschool child (aged two to four).
   a. The young preschool child often has
      (a.) better small than large muscle development.
      (b.) better large than small muscle development.
      (c.) good large and small muscle development.
   b. The interest span for a young preschool child is usually
      (a.) long, more than 20 minutes.
      (b.) short, not more than one minute.
      (c.) short, between 10 and 15 minutes.
   c. In lesson plans for young preschool children, the teacher plans
      (a.) only one main activity for the whole group.
      (b.) alternative activities for those who have different interests.
      (c.) only challenging activities to stimulate interest.
   d. Some good art materials for young preschoolers are
      (a.) blunt scissors, wide brushes, and large crayons.
      (b.) narrow brushes, ball-point pens, and clay.
      (c.) Plasticene, play dough, and felt-tip pens.

## ADDITIONAL READINGS

Beaty, J.J. *Preschool: Appropriate Practice*. Ft. Worth, Tex.: Harcourt, Brace, Javonovich College Publishers, 1992.

Christoplos, F., and P.J. Valletutti. *Developing Children's Creative Thinking through the Arts*. Bloomington, Ind.: Phi Delta Kappa Educational Foundation, 1990.

Clemens, S.G. "Art in the Classroom: Making Every Day Special." *Young Children* (Jan., 1991): 4–11.

Dodge, D.T., and L.J. Colker. *The Creative Curriculum for Early Childhood*. Washington, D.C.: Teaching Strategies Distributors, Mt. Rainier, Md., 1992.

"Early Childhood Creative Arts: Proceedings of the International Early Childhood Creative Arts Conference," 1991. Reston, Va.: American Alliance for Health, Physical Education, Recreation, and Dance. (Available from NAEYC).

Gestwicki, C. *Developmentally Appropriate Practice*. Albany, N.Y.: Delmar Publishers, 1995.

Kohl, M.F. *Scribble Cookies*. Bellingham, Wash.: Bright Ring Publishing Co., 1985.

Miller, S.A. "Messy Play." *Scholastic Pre-K Today*. (Feb., 1993): 32–40.

Moffit, M.W. *Woodworking for Children*. New York: Early Childhood Education Council of New York.

Skeen, P., A.P. Garner, and S. Cartwright. *Woodworking for Young Children*. Washington, D.C.: NAEYC, 1992.

Sunderlin, S., and N. Gray (eds.). *Bits & Pieces: Imaginative Uses for Children's Learning*. Washington, D.C.: Association for Childhood Education International, 1984.

Torre, F.D. *Woodworking for Kids*. Garden City, N.J.: Doubleday, 1987.

## CHILDREN'S BOOKS

Adoff, Arnold. *Black Is Brown Is Tan*. New York: Harper, 1973.

Becker, Edna. *900 Buckets of Paint*. Nashville, Tenn.: Abingdon Press, 1949.

Brown, Margaret. *The Color Kittens*. New York: Golden Press, 1967.

Crews, Donald. *Freight Train*. New York: Greenwillow, 1978.

Emberly, Ed. *Green Says Go.* Boston, Mass.: Little, Brown, 1968.

Florian, D. *A Carpenter.* New York: Greenwillow, 1991.

Gibson, M.T. *What Is Your Favorite Thing to Touch?* New York: Grosset & Dunlap, 1965.

Grossman, Barney, and Gladys Broom. *Black Means . . .* New York: Hill and Want, 1970.

Johnson, Crockett. *Harold and the Purple Crayon.* New York: Harper and Row, 1955.

Klamath County YMCA Family Preschool, Klamath Falls, Oregon. *The Land of Many Colors.* New York: Scholastic, 1993.

Levitin, Sonia. *A Single Speckled Egg.* New York: Parnassus, 1976.

McGovern, Ann. *Black Is Beautiful.* New York: Four Winds, 1969.

Miles, Miska. *Apricot ABC.* Boston, Mass.: Little, Brown, 1969.

O'Neil, Mary. *Hailstones and Halibut Bones.* Garden City, N.Y.: Doubleday, 1961.

Showers, Paul. *Find Out by Touching.* New York: Thomas Y. Crowell, 1961.

Tester, Sylvia R. *A World of Color.* Elgin, Ill.: The Child's World, 1939.

# UNIT 12

# Two-Dimensional Activities

## OBJECTIVES

After completing this unit, you should be able to

- describe the tools, materials, techniques, and strategies involved in the two-dimensional activities of picture making, print making, and collage.
- discuss some ways a teacher may help motivate children in activities involving picture making, print making, and collage.
- define collage.
- discuss both psychological and environmental motivation.
- discuss scissoring skills and related materials and techniques.

Using as a framework the basic information presented thus far on developmental levels, creativity, aesthetics, and the planning and implementing of creative activities, let us now take a closer look at the general processes of picture making, print making, and collage. You will note that this unit has a different format from preceding units. This is because this and all of the activity units within this text are designed to be *used with children,* not only as a reference. Since the entire unit is meant to be used as a guide to activities for children, no separate unit-end activities are included. Also, specific ages are not listed for the activities, since all of the activity units are designed to be springboards for art experiences and not strictly limited to certain age groups. You will, however, find the developmental information provided in the previous sections helpful in determining which activities to initiate with children. Children's reactions to the suggested activities will determine the appropriateness of the choice. Their interest, enthusiasm, and ability to do the activity should be your guide to each activity's appropriateness.

## PICTURE MAKING

The term *picture making* in this unit refers to any and all forms of *purposeful* visual expressions, beginning with controlled scribbling. A common error as-

sociated with picture making is to equate it with artwork that contains recognizable objects or figures. Yet children's pictures (artwork) may take any form, just as long as the child is expressing herself visually in a nonrandom way.

To the young child, the act of drawing and painting comes naturally. It is a means by which she communicates visually her ideas and feelings about herself and her world. She may work in paint, crayon, or chalk; each material has its own distinct characteristics for the child to explore.

The sensitive teacher understands and appreciates the charm and freshness of children's early drawings and paintings. He motivates children by helping them recall their experiences and record these in art media. Because he respects her individuality, the teacher inspires and encourages each child to express her own personal reactions about the world as she understands it. In this way, she discovers and builds her own unique style of expression. Her picture is different from the others in the class, just as her appearance and personality are different.

**Motivation for Picture Making.** When properly motivated the child eagerly examines the materials and looks forward to proceeding with the lesson. A successful lesson occurs when each child is inspired to her own ideas and when those ideas are carried through in visual expression.

*Psychological motivation.*   Brittain (1979) believes that teachers must provide the psychological motivation that makes creating possible. If children do not feel secure, safe, and comfortable with you, other children, and themselves, they will not be able to risk or meet the challenge art offers. They must know that they and their work will be accepted and respected.

Freedom and choice are also involved in children's psychological safety. Children have to know they are free to choose the materials they wish to work with, as well as how they use the materials. Giving children the freedom to choose and the time to create helps affirm children as individuals who are important, worthy, and creative. A great deal of time is required for psychological safety. Children need time to spend simply exploring and manipulating the materials. What may seem like aimless play with the media is actually a necessary prerequisite. They need to find out how the materials feel, what they can do with them, and how to control them. Once past the manipulative stage, children still need time to complete their projects. Large blocks of time should be planned so children can work on a project as long as they wish.

*Environmental motivation.*   Psychological safety, freedom, and time are not enough for motivating art experiences. Eventually children deplete their store of ideas. What can children paint, draw, or construct if they have no ideas or they have nothing to express? The opportunity to reflect on firsthand experiences motivates like nothing else.

According to Dewey (1944), we experience all the time. But a true experience involves both an active and a passive element. The child, rather than just walking in the rain or stepping on the grass (the active experience), must have the opportunity to reflect on the experience (the passive experience). Teachers need to help children make the backward and forward connection Dewey speaks of as they experience their environment. Teachers should encourage children to really observe, to use all of their senses to look at a raindrop or a spider, or to think about and describe their experiences.

Experiences are not always direct, and sometimes vicarious experiences are needed. A familiar Mother Goose rhyme or a poem from a contemporary author might be chosen for vicarious motivation.

Reading a familiar story or singing a song can stimulate art. Literary stimulation is usually more successful when children are able to associate themselves with the story, poem, or song. They might be asked to think about the character they liked the best, a new ending for the story, or the part that frightened them or pleased them the most, and to draw or paint what they thought.

There are many ways of motivating that awaken the child to the world of color, shape, size, texture, action, and mood:

- a walking trip employing careful observation
- a "show-and-tell" period
- a collection of objects for a "touch-and-see" display
- an interesting bulletin board or case display of artwork
- dramatization of stories, animals, birds, etc.
- listening to music, hearing a story, or describing events from everyday life
- demonstration of the use of materials

The child's growing awareness is gradually reflected in her picture as the ability to interpret her environment increases.

Before working, the teacher can direct children's thinking about what makes a successful drawing or painting by discussing the following points:

- What is the picture going to be about?
- What will be the most important thing in the picture? Where will it be placed on the paper? Will it be large or small?
- Where is the action taking place? Outdoors? In school? On the street? How many related things will be needed to complete the picture?
- What can be done to make the picture easily seen? A successful drawing or painting usually includes some light and some dark colors. A painting that has contrasting colors is easy to see from a distance.

As the lesson continues, the teacher and children can evaluate their progress and consider how the pictures may be improved.

**Suggestions for Picture-Making Topics.** Suitable topics for drawings and paintings come from children's daily life experiences: home, school and community, family and friends, holidays and happenings, and the world of make-believe. Subjects should be broad in scope, of general interest, and ones in which all children have had some experience. Each child's interpretation of the subject should be individual and unique. The source of topics is endless, but some topics to help get you started might be the following:

| | |
|---|---|
| My Family | Self-Portrait |
| Where I Live | Helping at Home |
| My Neighborhood | My Favorite Story |
| Community Helpers | Shapes |
| We Like to Play Games | Colors in My World |
| Playing with My Friends | Beautiful Things |
| How I Get Ready for School | Textures |
| How We Observe Holidays | Love |
| The Changing Seasons | Happiness |

---

Don't tell children what to paint and avoid asking what the painting is. Comment instead on what *you* experience in the painting. Be a learner like the child in her creative process. Asked what their paintings are, children often create stories to please those who ask.

(Clemens, 1991, p. 6)

---

**Painting with a Brush.** Painting with a brush encourages the spontaneous use of color. Finger painting, which was covered in Unit 11, is another form of painting that is enjoyable for children.

*Materials.* Basic materials for painting with brushes include the following:

• Semimoist watercolor paint sets. These are actually dehydrated tempera colors in concentrated cakes; they provide easy and convenient paint for individual use or group activity in the classroom. *To use*

*paints in cakes:* Place a few drops of water on the surface of each cake of color to moisten the paint. Dip brush in water and brush surface of moistened cake of paint to obtain smooth, creamy paint. *To use powder paint (tempera):* Fill a can one-fourth full of paint. Add water slowly, stirring constantly until the paint has the consistency of thin cream. A small amount of liquid starch or green soap may be added to the mixture as a binder. Use enough paint to make good rich colors. For best results, prepare paint when needed; large amounts kept over a period of time have a tendency to sour. Containers for use with powder paint include milk cartons, juice cans, baby food jars, coffee cans, plastic cups, and cut-down plastic bottles. A set of paints can be carried easily if containers are placed in tomato baskets, soft-drink carriers, boxes, or trays.

FIGURE 12–1 **A variety of brush sizes needs to be available for children's use.**

- A set of paints and a brush for each child. The paints are opaque when used with a little water, transparent when more water is used. (See Unit 11 for information on making paint sets.)
- Individual pieces of paper, at least 12″ × 18″: roll paper, manila paper, newspaper, wallpaper, newsprint.
- Water containers for painting and rinsing brushes: coffee cans, milk cartons, juice cans, cut-down plastic bottles, or plastic dishes. Half-gallon plastic containers with handles (the kind used for liquid bleach) are light and can be filled to carry water during the painting lesson.
- Paper towels or scrap paper for blotting brushes while painting.
- Newspapers to protect painting area. Painting may be done on paper placed on tables, desks, pinned to a bulletin board, fastened to a chalkboard, or on the floor if protected with newspaper.
- Moist sponge for cleanup.

See Figure 12–2 for additional hints on painting materials.

*Care and storage of materials.*
- Lay paintings horizontally to dry before stacking. An unused floor space along the wall is suitable for this purpose.
- Wipe paint sets clean with paper toweling. They can be stored conveniently in a cardboard carton.
- Rinse brushes in clean water, blot, gently point bristles, and leave to dry standing upright in a container.
- Clean brushes after each use. Neglect will cause the brush to lose its shape. Never rest a brush vertically on its bristles. Suspend it, if possible; if not, rest it on its side.

*Processes.* In presenting a painting activity, it may be necessary to demonstrate and teach the following:

- How to prepare paint trays for use. A drop or two of water should be placed in each paint color to moisten it.
- How to use a variety of brush strokes. Encourage children to paint directly, using full free strokes without first drawing in pencil. Use the point, side,

and flat surface of the brush. Try wide lines, thin lines, zigzag lines, and dots and dabs.
- How to mix colors on the paper as they paint. Try dipping one side of the brush in one color, the other side in a second color to blend paint in one stroke.
- How to create textures. Paint with bits of sponge, crushed paper or cloth, cardboard, string, sticks, or an old toothbrush. A stiff brush with most of the paint removed creates interesting textural effects.
- How to handle excess paint or water on a brush.
- How to clean paint trays.
- How to rinse and dry burshes.

Other painting activities include illustrating stories, painting murals, and painting scenery for puppet stages and dramatizations.

*More painting hints.*
- Thicken easel paint with liquid starch to cut down on drips.
- To help paint stick better to slick surfaces such as foil, waxed paper, Styrofoam, or plastic, mix dry tempera with liquid soap.
- To keep paints smelling fresh and sweet, add a few drops of mint extract or oil of wintergreen or cloves.
- For an added sensory experience, try adding lemon flavoring to yellow paint, mint to green, vanilla to white and peppermint to red paint. You might want to caution the children not to taste the paint, especially with younger children.
- For a glossy look, mix condensed milk with tempera paints.

*Evaluation.* Dated examples of each child's work should be kept through the year to enable the teacher to study her growth and development in creative art expression. The child will experience success and satisfaction when she sees her progress in the ability to control paints and express ideas. (See Unit 11 for further information on tempera paint.)

**Crayons.** Most young children are introduced to the common crayon before starting school. In the classroom, a lesson in crayon drawing should be a

### Art Tool Holder

Heavy paper, folded several times, will make a holder that keeps tools from rolling.

### Drying Rack

Drying racks for wet artwork are ideal if space is at a premium. A number of wooden sticks of the same size tacked or stapled to pieces of corrugated cardboard of the same size will make a drying rack. If pieces of wood are not available, substitute two, three, or four pieces of corrugated cardboard taped together. Tape stacked pieces to the cardboard base.

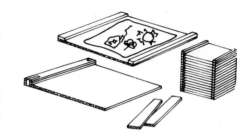

### Paint Container

Paper milk cartons stapled together (with tops removed) and with a cardboard handle make an ideal container for colored paint and water.

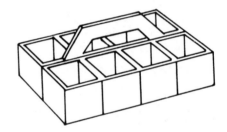

### Paint Dispensers

Plastic mustard or ketchup containers make good paint dispensers. An aluminum nail in the top of each will keep the paint fresh. In some cases the plastic containers can be used for painting directly from the container. Syrup pitchers make good paint dispensers and are ideal for storing paint.

### Plastic Spoons

Keep plastic spoons in cans of powdered tempera for easy paint dispensing.

FIGURE 12–2 Some helpful hints for storing and handling painting materials.

**FIGURE 12–3 Crayon drawings are one of the most popular two-dimensional art activities with young children.**

creative picture-making experience that encourages the child to tell a story visually as she feels it. (See Unit 11 for further information on crayons.)

*Materials.* Crayon drawings may be done on a wide assortment of surfaces, such as newsprint, wrapping paper, newspaper, construction paper, corrugated board, cloth, wood. This is an ideal medium for young children; it is bold, colorful, clean, and inexpensive. Crayons work well on most papers. They do not blend well; when attempts are made to do this, the wax often "tears." Thus, most drawings are linear in character. Crayons can be scraped thin to produce semitransparent layers of subtle color, and they can be coated with black and scratched through for crayon etchings.

*Motivation.* The general guidelines for motivating children in picture-making projects apply to the use of crayons, too.

*Processes.* Encouraging children to experiment with crayons and to explore the use of different parts of the crayon leads to their discovery of new methods that satisfy the needs for expression. The wax crayon has great versatility and can be used in many different ways:

- Make thin lines with the point of the crayon, heavy lines with the blunt end or side of the crayon.
- Vary the pressure to create subtle tints or solid, brilliant colors.
- Make rough texture by using broken lines, dots, dashes, and other strokes with the point.
- Create smooth texture by using the flat side or by drawing lines close together in the same direction with the point.
- Twist, turn, swing the crayon in arcs, and move it in various ways to achieve different effects.
- Repeated motions create rhythm.

Avoid small pieces of paper and "tight" drawing of the type outlined with pencil and colored with crayon. Children enjoy working with broad, sweeping lines, drawing directly with their colors. As they mature, they can sketch lightly with white chalk or yellow crayon, then fill in with other colors.

When used in combination with other materials, the crayon offers several new areas of creative interpretation:

- Use crayon and white chalk on colored construction paper.
- Make a crayon rubbing by placing shapes or textures under paper and rubbing over the surface.
- Make a crayon resist by first drawing in brilliant color, then cover drawing with watercolor paint.
- Paint a colorful background, allow to dry, then draw directly over painted surface with chalk or crayon.

*Further suggestions for projects using crayons.*
- Illustrate experiences about life at home, in school, in the neighborhood, including friends and pets.
- Read and illustrate stories and poems.
- Correlate with another school subject by making and illustrating a booklet about a unit being studied.
- Design and make greeting cards for birthdays and other special days.
- Make a mural consisting of separate cutout figures arranged in a composition.
- Make decorative wall masks.

FIGURE 12–4 A group mural can be made by pasting individual crayon drawings onto a long sheet of paper.

- Design a colorful headband.
- Make a movie to illustrate a series of events.

*Evaluation.*
- Was the topic for illustration selected with the children's interests in mind?
- Did they express their own ideas freely?
- Did children have opportunities to explore the uses of crayons and discover new techniques?

**Using Cut and Torn Paper in Picture Making.**
The use of cut and torn paper provides another dimension for young children in creative picture making. Their talents for direct thinking and use of a fresh approach lead them naturally to a satisfying experience with this technique. Without the use of exact directions or patterns, children are free to work imaginatively. They can experiment with the medium and explore combinations of original shapes and colors to express feelings and ideas. When satisfied with the arrangement in the design or picture, they can paste it in place.

**Scissoring Skills.** The use of scissors is in itself a separate skill that children must master. For a comprehensive discussion of scissoring as a developmental skill see *Children and Scissors: A Developmental Approach* (Moll, 1985). This section is based on this excellent source. The skill of using scissors is actually made up of a sequence of skills, beginning as early

as age two, in a child's first attempts at tearing. Tearing is a necessary pre-scissoring skill. Young children require lots of experience with random tearing in order to develop the necessary fine motor skill for controlled tearing. Controlled tearing is quite different from random tearing, requiring more fine motor control and purpose than simple random tearing. To aid young children's tearing activities, provide a variety of lightweight papers, as well as other materials like old cloth, packing materials, lettuce, and leaves.

Before actually teaching scissor cutting, a review of each child's skill level is necessary. Informal observation of children during routine activities can give clues about their readiness for scissoring. The following skills and knowledge are all required for cutting with scissors:

1. *Knowledge of body parts.* This includes not only knowing the names for parts of the body, but also the position of body parts (hand and fingers go together) and the position of body parts in space (head above shoulders).
2. *Bilateral integration.* The ability to perform activities requiring both sides of the body working together, such as hopping, skipping, and walking on a line.
3. *Use of hands in three ways.* The use of hands unilaterally, reciprocally, and bilaterally.
   a. *Unilateral. One* hand is required to do the job. (Examples: patting, reaching, grasping.)

# THINK ABOUT IT . . .

## MOTIVATION . . . . INSPIRATION . . . . OBSERVATION

Ideas to get those creative juices flowing are really all around us. For example, photo books provide many wonderful examples of the beauty of our world. The work of Ansel Adams is an excellent example. Nature books and magazines that feature good photos (like *National Geographic*) are an endless source for creative beginnings. Seeing nature through the eyes of a good photographer provides an aesthetic viewing experience that is different from seeing with one's own eyes.

Use a magnifying glass to add a different perspective to children's observations when looking at:

- Slabs of wood for grain patterns
- Concrete or asphalt for walk surfaces
- Leaves from different trees for vein patterns, shapes, textures, and edges
- Shells for shapes, swirls, colors, and textures.
- Tree bark with different textures
- Windows covered with steam, frost, or rain

---

b. *Reciprocal. Both* hands are required to do the task. Each hand is doing the same task. (Examples: pulling up, hugging, and clapping.)

c. *Bilateral.* The use of *both* hands is required. Each hand is performing a separate task for a common outcome. (Examples: buttoning, cutting, and shaking hands).

4. *Prehension.* The development of a preferred hand grasp. This means a definite preference for right- or left-handedness.

5. *General motor development.* This includes both fine and gross motor control.

6. *Eye-hand coordination.* The eyes and hands work together at levels of both fine and gross motor coordination.

When all of the above requisites are observed to be present in the child, learning the art of cutting with scissors can begin.

In learning scissoring, the quality of the tool plays an important role. Poor-quality scissors present unnecessary frustrations to children learning to cut. Quality scissors are made of forged steel, have an adjustment screw, and may have rubber-coated handles.

Plastic scissors with reinforced metal blades will cut some paper, while allowing a child with underdeveloped muscle strength to cut more easily. The flexibility of the plastic allows either right- or left-handed children to use the scissors.

For initial cutting experience, use 5″ blunt-nosed scissors. Be sure to have left- and right-handed scissors. As children gain control over the tool, they may move to 5″ clip-point scissors. Frequently check blade sharpness and screw adjustments. The ease with which scissors cut makes a great difference in a child's success in cutting activities.

Safety should be an initial concern when teaching the use of scissors, and should be thoroughly discussed. Children must learn to hold scissors safely when walking or handing them to another. Scissors should be held firmly by the closed blades, with the points sticking out of the closed fist just enough to prevent jabbing the body, and yet far enough out to prevent jabbing the hand in case of a fall. Children should also learn to be aware of where their scissors

FIGURE 12–5 Scissoring is a developmental skill.

FIGURE 12–7 Mastering the use of scissors is a complex developmental task.

FIGURE 12–6 Children need good-quality scissors when they are working on scissoring skill development.

are in relation to their bodies. Incidental waving or pointing should be considered a misuse of the scissors.

Children need to realize the dangers involved when using scissors and have a respect for the proper use of the tool. When this is understood by a child, his self-concept becomes more positive in two ways. First, knowing he is trusted to use the tool properly gives him a "grown-up" feeling. Second, the doors to self-expression are opened wider for him when using this "grown-up" creative tool.

During initial cutting practice, the scissor hand's major movement should be an open/close motion. The other hand holds the paper, moving it slowly into an easy cutting position. When children are given scissors at the appropriate developmental level and presented with an appropriate cutting task, they will assume a naturally relaxed sitting or standing position, with elbow bent and hands and forearms almost perpendicular to the body. The child who contorts his body and tenses his muscles while cutting needs either to return to a simpler task and/or return to the related activities that develop the necessary skills for learning to cut. He should not be required to cut in such opposition to his body.

Ample paper should be provided for young children learning to cut. Scrap paper donated by offices, friends, and local printers can be recycled to provide enough for scissoring.

For first snipping practice, a fairly stiff paper that will not bend over the blades—like construction paper—is the most desirable. As the children's skills increase, lighter papers like newsprint, magazine pages, and computer paper, as well as cloth and other materials should be provided. Scissors appropriate for cutting these materials also should be made available to the children.

About every three months, have a scissors cleaning time. Wash the blades with soap and dry them; then put a drop of sewing machine oil at the screw joint to insure a smoother and longer cutting life. Cutting through a fine grade of folded sandpaper with the scissors will help sharpen the blades (Moll, 1985).

**Pasting.** Paste serves a functional purpose, and its properties also make it a valuable medium for creative expression. The stickiness, texture, odor, and changes that take place as paste is used provide children with opportunities for many discoveries. When a child picks up paste in her hands, she will almost automatically spread it over her fingers and squeeze it or roll it between her fingers and feel its stickiness. Before long, she spreads paste over her hands, sometimes even rubbing it into her palms. As paste dries, a child feels a different sensation. When she begins to wash her hands, the paste is transformed from hard to sticky to slimy, a phenomenon of great interest to a child. Paste is a medium that can stimulate her to repeated explorations of the properties of matter.

Given sufficient paste and a piece of paper, a child almost invariably smears the paste on the paper as though it were fingerpaint. She moves her hand across the page with sweeping motions. In some places on the paper she smooths the paste until it is slick and shiny. In other places she forms lumps of paste and then enjoys pressing down on the lumps to smooth them out. The paste-smeared paper becomes an artistic creation for her.

Having explored paste in this manner, a child reaches for small pieces of paper and pastes piece upon piece, using large quantities of paste in the process. She is excited by what she can accomplish with the medium. When she attempts to lift the mound of paper she has created, very often the paper tears. She discovers that paste is heavy.

Adults should avoid instructing children on the uses of paste and allow them to make their own discoveries. Eventually a child will begin to create a collage, arranging random shapes of varied colors on large paper. At first she pays no attention to design but carefully arranges the pieces, achieving a balance that is pleasing to her. A child will create patterns later.

By adult standards, it may appear that the amount of paste children use is exorbitant, but their explorations are limited if they cannot have as much paste as they need. Although most paste for children is nontoxic, a teacher should be certain that the commercial paste used in the classroom is safe, because children will put paste in their mouths. Paste can also be made by the teacher (see Unit 11 for paste recipes).

*Materials.*
- Kinds of paper: construction paper, wallpaper, gift wrappings, metallic paper, tissue paper, newspaper, illustrated magazine pages
- For mounting: newsprint, construction paper, cardboard, back of wallpaper, newspaper (classified ad pages), cardboard box lids
- Paste, glue, scissors, brushes

*Motivation.*
- Demonstrate cutting and tearing paper shapes, visualizing the outlines without preliminary drawing.
- Ask several children to cut and tear paper shapes. They may take turns working with the pieces until satisfied with the arrangement.
- Show a variety of papers different in color and texture and encourage children's suggestions on how to use them.
- Demonstrate pasting the papers to the background, emphasizing the sparing use of paste.

*Processes.*
- Torn paper creates a textured edge. Cut edges appear smooth.
- In tearing paper, greater control of the paper is achieved by tearing slowly with fingers close together.
- Encourage children to choose light and dark colors for interesting contrast and different sizes or shapes and a variety of papers for textural effects.
- Paper shapes can be overlapped or grouped to produce new shapes and new combinations of colors and textures.
- Cut paper can be textured by wrinkling, crumpling, slitting, and folding out.

*Suggested projects.*
- Paper collage: Use papers of various textures, colors, sizes, and shapes to create a design or picture. See section on collage later in this unit.
- All-over design: Cut or tear related shapes of different sizes and colors to form a decorative design. This may be used as a place mat, wrapping paper, or booklet cover.
- Cut-paper mural: Select a topic. Each child may cut shapes and combine them in a group mural.
- Paper mosaic: Make a picture composed of tiny pieces of cut or torn paper fitted together.
- Three-dimensional picture: Parts of the picture may be modeled, curled, fringed, or fastened only at the edges to allow them to protrude from the background. Objects can pop out of the picture by attaching a paper spring on the back.
- Related activities: Greeting cards, posters, story illustrations, decorated gift boxes.

See Figure 12–9 for ideas on using torn or cut tissue paper.

*Evaluation.*
- Did the children's compositions show originality?
- Did the children experiment with a variety of shapes, textures, and color combinations?

**Murals.** A story-telling picture or panel intended for a large wall space is called a *mural,* another form of picture making. A suitable topic for a mural may

**FIGURE 12–8 An example of a crumpled paper design.**

come from children's personal experiences at home, at school, or at play, or it may relate to other school subjects. In the classroom, mural making is a versatile art activity; it may involve a large group or just a few children, depending on the size of the mural. It may require a variety of materials or just one or two. With young children, it should be a simple, informal, spontaneous expression with a minimum of preplanning. Tedious planning destroys much of the intuitive quality and reduces interest.

*Materials.*

| | |
|---|---|
| kraft paper | paste |
| roll paper | newspapers |
| wallpaper | collage materials |
| crayons | brushes |
| paint | scissors |
| water and container | colored construction paper |

*Motivation.*
- A mural usually begins with a group discussion of a theme and related ideas. The subject may be in-

**Tissue Twists or Wads**

This activity can be used as an individual or small group experience. Teacher cuts tissue into strips (a paper cutter saves teacher time). Size of strip could range anywhere from 2 to 4 inches in length to ½ to 1 inch in width. If tissue squares are to be wadded, cut 2″ × 2″ or 3″ × 3″ squares. Children twist or wad pieces of tissue and then paste them onto paper. A large piece of butcher paper can be filled by several children for a mural project.

**Tissue and Starch Pictures**

Teacher cuts or children cut tissue into pieces. Containers of liquid starch are made for each child. Children paint an area with liquid starch and apply pieces of tissue to the starch.

**Geometric Shapes Tissue**

Children are presented with pre-cut tissue in squares, circles, triangles, and rectangles to use in their tissue creations.

**Flower Vase**

Teacher and/or children tear tissue into small pieces. Paint some liquid starch on a bottle or jar. Stick on paper and paint over with starch. When bottle is dry, spray with shellac or varnish.

**Tissue Paper Collage**

Lay a piece of plastic wrap on a 9″ × 12″ piece of newsprint. Paint the plastic with a mixture of equal parts of glue and water. Tear tissue paper into irregular shapes. Lay tissue on glue-covered wrap. Overlap tissue paper until entire piece of wrap is covered. Allow to dry overnight. Peel wrap from tissue paper. Hang finished products in the window.

**FIGURE 12–9 Some tissue paper experiences.**

**FIGURE 12–10 Example of a use for hand printing: A Get-Well mural.**

spired by dramatization, use of visual aids, trips, or other experiences.

- Planning also includes selecting the part of the mural each person wants to make, size of figures, and materials to be used.
- The amount of preplanning depends on the maturity of the children.

*Processes.*

- Watercolor paint allows for spontaneous bold design and brilliant color, ideal for murals. Young children do best by painting their ideas directly on the paper without preliminary sketches. Usually the background is simple with few details. Painting should be done on a table or the floor with newspaper for protection.
- Cut or torn paper is a flexible medium suitable for murals, permitting many changes and parts as the mural progresses. Children with little experience may begin by making simple flat figures without preliminary sketches. Other techniques for manipulating paper are folding, curling, pleating, twisting, fringing, and overlapping. Place background paper on a bulletin board, then plan, pin, and move parts before attaching. Various papers, such as tissue, wallpaper, illustrated magazine pages, and metallic paper, add interest.
- The composition of the mural may be:
  *Figures.* A parade may be depicted with large characters and fantastic costumes on a simple background.
  *Panel.* Storybook panels may be made and used in a series without the problem of unifying the different backgrounds.
  *Scenic.* A "city-scape" mural is scenic and may show many points of interest: people, homes, stores, factories, streets, cars, and buses.

*Suggested topics.*

| | |
|---|---|
| How We Feel | What Our Mothers Do |
| Playground Fun | What We Do in School |
| My Father's Work | How We Communicate |
| We Build a Snowman | Trips to the Park, Zoo |
| A Trip in Space | Shopping Centers |
| Our Neighborhood in Different Seasons | |

How Things Feel—Textures
How Things Look—Shapes and Colors
How We Look

*Evaluation.*

- Is the mural original?
- Does the project represent the planning of all the children in the project?
- Does the mural tell the story and fill the purpose originally planned?
- Are the sizes and shapes in the mural well related to the space?
- Have children grown in their ability to plan and work together?

## PRINT MAKING

Long before they enter the classroom, most children have already discovered their footprints or handprints, made as they walk or play in snow or wet sand. *Relief prints* are created in a similar manner. An object is pressed against a flat surface to create a design that may be repeated over and over again. Generally, the process of relief printing consists of applying paint to an object and pressing it onto the paper. Techniques range from a simple fingertip printing to carving a potato and printing with it. Emphasis should be on the free manipulation of objects and experimentation with color, design, and techniques.

The teacher may begin by encouraging children to search for objects from the home or classroom. Household items, kitchen utensils, hardware, discarded materials, and many objects of nature are useful in relief printing. Gradually, the child learns to look and discover textures, colors, and patterns that exist all around her.

In their first attempts to organize shapes into a design, young children usually work in a random fashion. Preliminary experiments help them develop a better understanding of the print-making process and of the possibilities for variety of design.

**Helping Children Get Started in Print-Making Activities.** The following suggestions are some ways to introduce print-making activities:

# THIS ONE'S FOR YOU!

## TALKING WITH CHILDREN ABOUT THEIR ART

There is a *right* way to respond to children's art—whether it be painting, crayon drawings, or any other medium. A correct response is one that stimulates more and complex uses of the medium. Comments should focus on the use of the various elements of the artwork as well as on the feeling, mood, and ideas evoked.

*Descriptive, nonjudgmental* remarks are best:

- Right Way: "Claire is using color on all parts of the paper, while Mark is keeping big spaces around his colors."
- Wrong Way: "I like how Claire's painting is neater than Mark's."

Do *not* ask, "What did you paint?" This question implies that the only purpose of art is to communicate verbally a story or piece of information. The only logical answer to such a questions is "I painted a painting."

Another caution: Don't ask children in advance what they plan to create. Painting and drawing are visual thinking. Asking children to verbalize their ideas just prior to the art of creating is an interruption and an inhibitor of their visual thinking.

A further caution, especially with very young children: Refrain from asking them the names of the colors they are using in their artwork. Colors are important only in how they act upon one another and upon other elements within the artwork. To quiz a child on color names during a creative painting session transforms the *aesthetic* experience into an *academic* experience. Such an intrusion is as inappropriate as interrupting an exciting conversation to ask the child how to spell a word.

As a final caution, refrain from undue emphasis on neatness, either in the process or the product. Neatness is not a requirement for aesthetically pleasing work and, if stressed inappropriately, may become a hindrance to creativity. (Christopolus and Valletutti, 1990)

---

- Children may observe and discuss examples of repeat design in clothing, wrapping paper, and wallpaper in which objects appear again and again, up and down, across the whole material.
- The teacher may demonstrate printing repeat designs using found objects, such as sponge, rubber eraser, stick, and bottle cap, or natural materials, such as leaves, twigs, stones, and bark.
- In potato printing, the teacher demonstrates carving a section of the potato, making simple designs on the flat surface by notching the edges or carving holes with dull scissors, split tongue depressors, or a small plastic knife.

- The object must be painted each time it is printed; print by pressing slowly and firmly.
- The creative teacher demonstrates processes of using materials and tools without dictating what the final product will look like. Instead, she provides stimulation and guidance in the use of children's original ideas and encourages children to experiment with various objects and techniques.

Gradually, through their print-making experiences, children discover for themselves the following:

- The amount of paint needed to obtain clean edges.

- The amount of pressure needed to get a print.
- How the shape and texture of an object determine the shape and texture of the print.
- How to repeat a print over and over to create a design.

**Print-Making Materials.** Materials for print making may include the following:

- *Paint.* Any of the following are suitable: tempera paint in sets of eight colors, powder paint in thin mixture, food coloring, water-soluble printing ink.
- *Stamp Pad.* Place discarded pieces of felt or cotton cloth inside a jar lid, cut-down milk carton, frozen food tin, or similar waterproof container and saturate with color.
- *Paper.* Absorbent papers suitable for printing include newsprint, manila paper, wallpaper, tissue, construction paper, want-ad pages of the newspaper, plain wrapping paper.
- *Cloth.* Absorbent pieces of discarded cloth can also be used to print on, such as pillow cases, torn sheets, men's handkerchiefs.
- *Other Items.* Newspaper for covering tables, brushes for applying paint when not using stamp pad, cans for water.

**Print-Making Techniques.** The following are some of the techniques commonly used in print making for children.

*Found object printing.* With a few familiar objects, such as forks, spools, sticks, buttons, bottle tops, some paper, paint, and a brush, the child can learn to print her own designs. Objects of nature, such as leaves, weeds, seeds, and stones can be used similarly. With experience, she can make decorative papers, greeting cards, booklet covers, and border designs on fabrics. Found objects are used effectively in relief printing.

*Fingerprints.* Get a sheet of newsprint. Press one of your fingers onto a stamp pad or onto a tray filled with thickened tempera. Press your finger onto the newsprint. Experiment. Use different fingers, singly or in combinations, etc. Add details with magic markers and crayons.

*Vegetable printing.* Cut a potato, carrot, or other firm vegetable into sections that facilitate handling. Keep the design simple, avoiding thin lines. Draw the design on the flat cut surface and carve the design about ¼-inch deep, leaving the area desired to be printed. Paint the raised part of the design and press on paper or cloth.

*Monoprinting.* Apply paint to paper. Carefully place a sheet of paper over the painting and rub smoothly from the center out to the edge. If desired, children can draw in crayon on the top sheet of paper, pressing the lines into the paint on the bottom sheet. Pull the print gradually, starting from one corner.

*Styrofoam prints.* Get a Styrofoam tray. Draw a picture or design using permanent magic markers. These markers will dissolve the foam. Use a brush or sponge to apply a thin layer of tempera to the surface of the tray. Place a piece of construction paper over the tempera. Rub.

Styrofoam meat trays can also be used as printing plates by cutting them into shapes and pasting them on a background. The same applies to heavy cardboard.

*Paper stencils.* The four- to five-year-old can begin to use stencils in a most creative manner. Paper stencils are good because they do not require many materials.

Each child is given four or five pieces of drawing paper about four inches square. With scissors, the child cuts holes of various sizes and shapes in the center of each piece. It is a good idea to cut more than one hole per piece. When the holes have been cut, each child is given a cleansing tissue, small piece of cotton, or patch of cloth. This is rubbed on a piece of colored chalk to pick up enough dust to stencil. Then the child selects a shape and places it on the paper on which the design is to go. The child rubs the tissue across the hole, making strokes from the stencil paper toward the center of the opening. This is continued around the edge of the opening until the paper under the stencil has a clear print. The

**FIGURE 12–11 Hand-tracings and cutouts are good practice of scissoring skills.**

same shape can be continued across paper, or other shapes and colors may be added according to the child's preference. Visual rhythms and themes can be printed without boring repetition.

A child can choose the shapes and combinations desired. Holiday cards, programs, and classroom decorations may be made in this manner. The same technique can be used with wax crayons instead of chalk. The crayons are rubbed directly on the stencil. If unbleached muslin or cotton material is used to print on, attractive door and wall hangings can be produced.

*The spatter technique.* Simple spatter or spray printing is both fascinating and fun for the young child. It also has the advantage of allowing for a wide variety of patterns and shapes. Children can work individually or with partners on this project.

Several of the children bring in old toothbrushes. Besides toothbrushes only a small amount of watercolor paint and paper is needed. The method is to "spray" the paint with a toothbrush. This is done by dipping the brush in paint and gently pulling a straight-edged object (ruler, emery board, or tongue depressor) across the ends of the bristles. This causes the bristles to snap forward throwing small particles of paint onto the paper.

The children create designs by placing small, flat objects on the paper. When the bristles snap the small particles of paint forward, the object prevents the spray from striking the paper directly under the object. This leaves the shapes free of paint spray while the rest of the paper is covered with small flecks of paint.

This technique has endless possibilities. Not only can a variety of shapes be used, but colors can also be superimposed on one another. Natural forms such as twigs, leaves, and grass are excellent for this activity. Several forms can be combined, leading to interesting arrangements with unlimited variety. A field trip to a vacant lot is a way to find new print forms and shapes, thus encouraging children to find and learn about beauty in their own environment. Another strength of this project is that it avoids stereotyped designs and ready-cut patterns. The children create beauty for themselves.

As children progress in the use of this technique, they can make their own stencils from cut paper. Two stencils may be cut simultaneously when a design unit is cut from the center of a piece of folded paper. The unit cut out is the positive design; the hole in the paper is the negative design. Actual living leaves and flowers may be used as a positive unit. Shapes can be arranged and rearranged in a pleasing design on background paper. Paint of rather heavy consistency is then spattered over the design by rubbing a paint-filled toothbrush over a piece of window screen. Designs are more interesting when contrasting colors are used.

*Stencil rubbings.* Flat objects are placed under paper, then rubbed over with the side of a crayon to reveal the pattern. Objects can be moved into different positions as the all-over design progresses. Texture rubbings can be made with such objects as leaves, pieces of wood, tree bark, sandpaper, and corrugated cardboard.

# THIS ONE'S FOR YOU!

## BITS OF HISTORY—ART MATERIALS

You might like to know a little about the history behind some of the familiar art media you use with children. Here are bits of history on these everyday materials:

*Chalk*—The original chalks for drawing, some still in use today, were pure earth, cut and shaped into implements. The addition of a binder created a fabricated chalk that we know today as a pastel chalk. Chalks used by the early master painters were generally limited to reds (sanguine), black, and white.

*Crayons*—Of the many art materials, probably none is more familiar than wax crayons. The fact that most of us were introduced to them at a tender age may influence us to think that they are beneath the dignity of more mature artists. Such is not the case; examples abound of distinguished drawings executed in this humble medium (Miro and Picasso, for example). Examples of the use of crayons begin in the nineteenth century.

Crayons consist of an oily or waxy binder impregnated with pigments or color. Records exist of a variety of prescriptions for binders, involving soap, salad oil, linseed oil, spermaceti, and beeswax.

*Ink*—The earliest ink known, black carbon, was prepared by the early Egyptians and Chinese. This was followed by iron-gall (made from growths on trees), bistre (burnt wood), and sepia (a secretion from cuttlefish). Today, there is a wide variety of inks available, but the best known is India ink, which is really a waterproof carbon black.

*Pens*—Those of us who take for granted our familiar metal pen points of various kinds may not realize that they are fairly new, not having been successfully developed until the last century. Until that time, the reed pen had been the pen of the ancients, and the quill pen the principal instrument from the medieval period to modern times. Most of us probably remember the use of quill pens in the drawings of Rembrandt and in the historical documents drawn up by the founders of our Republic.

*Brushes*—Bristle is obtained from the body of hogs and boars found in Russia, Japan, Formosa, Korea, France, and Central and Eastern Europe. While all animal hair has "points," bristle has "flags." The individual bristle splits into two or three tiny forks on the end, which are called "flags."

**Suggestions for Experimentation.**
*With color.*
- Alternate thin transparent watercolor with thick opaque tempera paint.
- Use a light color to print on dark paper or vice versa.
- Use transparent paint on colored paper or cloth so that the color of the background shows through.
- Combine two sizes of objects of the same shape.
- Combine objects of different sizes and shapes.
- Use one object in various positions.
- Try overlapping and grouping objects.

*With texture.*
- Vary the amount of paint used in printing.
- Use objects that create different textures, such as sponges, corrugated paper, wadded paper or cloth, stones, vegetables, and sandpaper.

*With background paper.*
- Try using a variety of shapes and sizes of paper.
- Paint background paper and allow to dry before printing.
- Paste pieces of tissue or colored construction paper onto background paper, allow to dry, then print.
- Print a stippled design on background with sponge, allow to dry, then print with a solid object.

*With pattern.*
- Print a shape in straight rows or zigzag pattern. Repeat design to create an all-over pattern.
- Use different shape for each row and add a second color in alternate rows.
- Group shapes in units of two or three and print rhythmic designs. Move shapes to alternate position and print in a second color.
- Print in a border design with a single shape or group of shapes in a regular repeated manner.

**Suggested Uses for Prints.** There are several possible uses for the products of print-making activities. Some of them are the following:

- Book covers for stories, poems, pictures, notes
- Designs for greeting cards, place cards, murals, simple posters, gift wrapping, covering for gift container
- Border for writing paper, place mats, napkins

As they mature, children grow in their abilities to handle tools and to control paint and begin to develop design concepts. Older children gradually progress to more complex printing processes using a greater variety of materials and techniques.

## COLLAGE

*Collage,* a French word meaning "to paste," is the product of selecting, organizing, and arranging materials of contrasting color and texture and attaching them to a flat surface.

One way a child becomes aware of things around her is by touching. Through manipulation of everyday objects, she grows in sensitivity to shapes and textures and discovers ways to use them in creating new forms and images. With added experience, the tactile

**FIGURE 12–12  Examples of cloth figures.**

***Seed Collage.*** Press a ball of play dough or clay into a plastic lid. Arrange seeds, beans, and other grains on top of the dough/clay. Press into the dough. Allow to dry.

***Patchwork Collage.*** Divide a piece of cardboard into several rectangular spaces using a pencil and ruler. Fill each rectangle with one type of "beautiful junk." Glue on with white glue.

***Texture Collection.*** Select a texture theme (soft, hard, smooth, rough, etc.) Find objects at home and in the classroom that have that texture. Glue the collection onto cardboard or heavy construction paper. Display in the classroom.

**FIGURE 12–13 Additional collage ideas.**

sense becomes an instrument of knowledge and a tool of expression. Unlike the *imitation of texture* in drawing and painting, the textural materials in collage are *real.*

**Helping Children Get Started in Collage Activities.** The following suggestions are designed to help motivate children in their initial collage activities:

- Arouse children's awareness of texture by passing various materials for them to touch and examine. Discuss the qualities of various textures by asking, How do these materials feel? Are they smooth? hard? soft? fuzzy? sharp? round? How can we use these materials?
- Arrange a "touch-and-see" display.
- Discuss sources of collage materials and encourage children to collect them.
- Demonstrate making a collage, selecting and arranging materials on a background, and ways of fastening, using paste, thread, and staples.
- Assess qualities of materials in relation to ideas to be expressed: Gold paper is bright and "shiny like the sun"; cotton is soft and white "like snow."

*Materials.*
- *Background:* Manila paper, construction paper, cardboard, and shirtboard
- *Collage materials:* Paper and cloth scraps, magazine pages, yarn, string, ribbon, lace, and other discarded fragments
- *Natural materials:* Leaves, twigs, bark, seed pods, dried weeds, feathers, beans, ferns, sands, small stones, and shells
- Scissors, brushes, paste, stapler, and staples

Sort and keep materials of similar nature in boxes to facilitate selection.

*Processes.*
- When working with beginners, limit the number of collage materials; this lessens the confusion in selection.
- Encourage children to use materials in their own way. Instead of giving exact directions, suggest ways of selecting materials for variety of shape, size, color, and texture.
- Materials may be cut, torn, or left in their original shapes.
- As children arrange and rearrange the shapes on the background, they may form a representational picture or compose an abstract design.
- Throughout the work period, emphasize thoughtful use of space by overlapping and grouping shapes, trying different combinations of colors and textural surfaces.
- Create three-dimensional effects by crumpling flat pieces of material and attaching them to the background in two or three places. Other techniques include overlapping, bending, folding, rolling, curling, and twisting paper.
- Include buttons, braids, tissue, or yarn for added interest and accent.
- Use glue or staples to fasten heavy materials and plastics.
- A collage may be displayed in a shadow box, using a box lid as a frame; it can be mounted in an old picture frame or on a sheet of colored construction paper.

- A collage may be abstract, emphasizing contrasts of materials; others may suggest representational themes.
- Topics may be related to other school curricular areas.
- Use of man-made materials suggests correlation with science or social studies.
- Natural materials combine to create a nature collage.
- Make a paper or cloth collage, exploring a variety of one kind of material.

*Evaluation.*

- In experimenting with varied materials, did the child develop a knowledge of texture?
- Did the experience with collage help develop the child's perceptual awareness and sensitivity to texture in her immediate environment?
- Did all the children share the responsibility and contribute found objects toward this experience?
- Did the children's work show sensitivity in the arrangement of materials, in the use of colors, patterns, and textures?

# UNIT REVIEW

1. Discuss both psychological and environmental motivation and their importance in children's artwork with two-dimensional media.
2. Describe how to motivate children for two-dimensional picture-making activites.
   a. Give specific examples of motivating activities and questions.
   b. List some topics that are good starters for picture-making activities.
3. Discuss how to mix, store, and use paint for picture making.
4. List some variations to include in crayon pictures.
5. Explain how to introduce children to torn-and-cut pictures.
   a. List some materials needed.
   b. List some possible demonstration strategies.
6. Discuss the importance of murals as two-dimensional art activities.
   a. List some topics for murals.
   b. List some materials for murals.
7. Discuss the various printing techniques.
8. List the basic materials needed for each technique.
9. Give some examples of questions and activities that would help children get started in print making.
10. Define the word *collage* and give specific examples of collage activities.
11. Discuss ways of motivating children in collage activities.
12. List specific materials and techniques used in collage activities.
13. What are the six areas of skill/knowledge required for cutting with scissors?
14. Discuss the basic points of scissor safety.
15. Describe the type and quality of scissors and paper required for children's initial cutting experiences.
16. Define the terms *unilateral*, *bilateral*, and *reciprocal*, and give examples of each.

# ADDITIONAL READINGS

Baer, G. *Imaginative Art for Kids and Their Teachers.* West Nyack, N.Y.: Parker Publishing Co., 1982.

Brittain, W.L. *Creativity, Art and the Young Child.* New York: Macmillan Publishing Co., 1979.

Christoplos, F., and P.J. Valletutti. *Developing Children's Creative Thinking through the Arts.* Bloomington, Ind.: Phi Delta Kappa Educational Foundation, 1990.

Clemens, S.G. "Art in the Classroom: Making Every Day Special." *Young Children* (Jan. 1991): 4–11.

Dewey, J. *Art and Experience.* New York: Macmillan Publishing Co., 1944.

Lasky, L., and R. Mukerji. *Art: Basic for Young Children.* Washington, D.C.: NAEYC, 1980.

MacStravic, S. *Print Making.* Minneapolis, Minn.: Lerner Publishing Co., 1973.

Moll, P.B. *Children and Scissors: A Developmental Approach.* Tampa, Fla.: Hampton Mae Institute, 1985.

Rockwell, H. *Printmaking.* Garden City, N.Y.: Doubleday & Co., 1983.

Smith, N.R. *Experiences and Art: Teaching Children to Paint.* New York: Teachers College, Columbia University, 1983.

# UNIT 13
# Three-Dimensional Activities

**OBJECTIVES**

After studying this unit, you should be able to
- describe how young children work with clay.
- define modeling and describe its benefits for children.
- discuss some guidelines to follow for successful modeling activities.
- define assemblage and give specific examples of assemblage activities for children, including the necessary materials and tools.
- discuss how cardboard may be used for three-dimensional activities, and describe the materials and tools used in constructing with it.
- discuss some motivational strategies for getting children interested in cardboard construction projects.
- discuss woodworking supplies and strategies, and its benefits for young children.

The term *three-dimensional art* refers to any art form that has at least three sides. Three-dimensional art is "in the round," which means that one can look at it from many sides. Modeling with clay, working with play dough, making creations with paper boxes, and creating other sculpture forms are examples of three-dimensional art activities.

Just as in drawing, there are basic stages of art development in working with three-dimensional material, much the same as for two-dimensional media. Therefore, this unit applies the information previously presented for two-dimensional media. While the names of stages in two-dimensional art do not apply (a child does not "scribble" with clay), the same process of growth and basic ideas for each stage applies.

## DEVELOPMENTAL LEVELS AND THREE-DIMENSIONAL MEDIA

When young children first learn to use a three-dimensional material like clay, they go through much the same process of growth as in the scribble stage.

*Random manipulation.* At first, clay is squeezed through the fingers in a very uncontrolled way comparable to the early scribble stage. With both clay and crayons, the child in this age range has little control over hand movements. The feel of the clay in hand while squeezing, the kinesthetic pleasure alone, is what the child enjoys about the clay.

Just as children make early scribbles in many directions, they also make early clay forms in many ways. A child of this age beats and pounds clay for no special purpose, just like scribbling in all directions. The child does not try to make anything definite with the clay. What is made depends on whether the child pounds, flattens, or squeezes the clay.

Although a child may occasionally identify a mound of clay as a house, a ball of clay as a car, or, pushing her fist through the top of a chunk of clay, call it a bowl, she is usually more interested at this point in the manipulation of the material and discovering what she can do with it than she is in the object she has created.

Potter's clay is a very good three-dimensional material for young children. It is easy to use because it is soft and elastic. It is best bought in moist form,

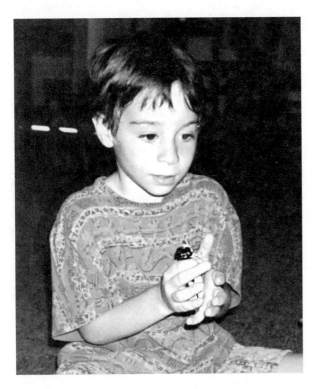

FIGURE 13–1 Potter's clay is an excellent three-dimensional material for young children.

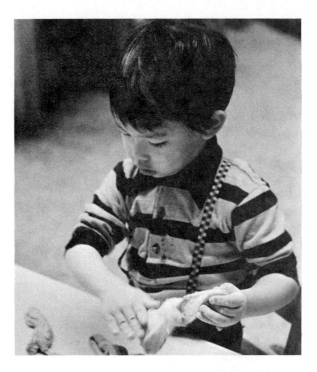

FIGURE 13–2 Salt dough is more durable than clay, and children enjoy its flexibility and texture.

because the dry powder is difficult to prepare and the silica dust is unhealthy for children to inhale. Plasticene, a plastic-type clay, is more expensive and is much harder for the young child to use because it is not as soft and elastic as real clay. To make it easier for young children to use, warm and soften cold or hard plasticene by rolling it between your hands.

To make the play dough and clay area satisfying for toddlers, use a small, low table and add play dishes. While many different props can be used (animals, cookie cutters), most of the activity with these media can come from the use of hands and fingers. Squeezing, patting, pulling apart, and rolling all help develop muscles and make the experience relaxing and successful for toddlers. Many young children like to watch and vocalize to their friends while they use dough. If the playhouse area is nearby, the toddlers may even initiate simple imaginative games around themes of cooking, eating, and birthday parties. Play

dough can be made from water, flour, and salt; the colors can be varied each time. (See Unit 11 for recipes for various doughs for three-dimensional activities.) Toddlers appreciate helping to mix the dough, which can be refrigerated for storage. Adult supervision prevents toddlers from eating or throwing the material.

*Patting and rolling.* When children's muscle control gets better, they begin to pat and roll the clay. This matches the controlled scribbling stage. In both scribbling and clay work, the children now enjoy seeing the effects of their movements. They find that they can use their hand movements to make the clay go in desired ways. At this point, a child may roll the clay into thin lengths (ropes), pound it, or shape it into balls. Lines drawn with crayon and rope lines made of clay are both proof of the child's growing muscle (motor) control.

*Circles and rectangles.* An older preschool child who can draw basic forms can also make clay into similar forms. Rolling clay to make balls is an example of a basic form (circle) in clay. Boxes made of clay are examples of basic forms (rectangles) in a three-dimensional material.

In drawing and in clay, the circle is one of the first basic forms made. In both two- and three-dimensional media, the child is able to make this form by controlling the material.

The rectangular form usually comes after the circle. Just as in scribbling, the rectangle is made with clay when the child can shape it into whatever length desired.

*Forming clay figures.* Many children aged four to five can put together basic clay forms to make up figures. This is equivalent to the pictorial stage in two-dimensional media.

Most children in this age range like to make definite things with clay. They combine basic forms to build objects that are like figures in drawing. They begin by making simple things out of basic forms. The child working with clay puts together a round clay ball (circle) for a head and a clay stick-type line or lump for a body. This is an early combination of

**FIGURE 13–4 An abundance of materials encourages a child's creativity in three-dimensional art forms.**

**FIGURE 13–3 As their muscle control improves, children begin to have better control over the shapes they form with clay.**

**FIGURE 13–5 This clay stick figure is similar to a stick figure in the basic-forms stage of drawing.**

basic forms in clay. It is a lot like the stick figure made in early first drawings.

Later, in working with clay, children five years and older may put these forms together in more complex ways. They may make a person with legs, arms, fingers, and feet. This is like the later pictorial stage when a child draws more details.

Children of this age do not make the same forms over and over again for practice as in the stage before. This is because a child of four or five has the muscle (motor) control and hand–eye coordination to easily make any form desired. The clay is now used to make a definite object, a symbol for something important to the child. Children make human figures, animals, houses, pies, and many other things with clay. The forms are made in the child's own special way, just as in drawing.

*Schema.* This special way (schema) of working with clay is the same for two- and three-dimensional media. It comes from much practice in making symbols and is the child's own special way of making these symbols.

**FIGURE 13–7  Just as with their drawings, children may make figures that are important to them larger than those objects that are less important.**

*Symbols.* Just as in drawing, children may make things that are more important to them (symbols) bigger than things that are less important. They may use more details for an important clay figure, too. At this stage, these details may be made by putting other pieces on the clay, like buttons for eyes, straws for legs, and cotton for hair.

*Naming objects.* Children start to name their clay objects at about the same time they start to name their drawings. This is just as important with clay as with drawing. In both cases, it means the children are expressing their ideas in art. The children now can tell other people just what these ideas are by naming their work.

## THE VALUE OF CLAY

At all ages, work with clay gives the child many chances for creative experiences. Most children like the damp feel of clay. They like to pound it, roll it, poke holes in it, pull it apart. Just as in drawing, it is the fun of working with the clay that counts. The end

**FIGURE 13–6  A detailed clay figure, such as this, can be compared to a child's later first drawings.**

product is not as important as using it; a child becomes really involved in the process.

The scene below from an early childhood program emphasizes this value of clay experiences:

> In my activities I wanted to emphasize fine motor development, so I used clay with different sizes of soda straw pieces, toothpicks, buttons, etc., to stick in the clay. The children made animals, designs, and monsters. They kept up a running commentary on how they were making a monster and could SMASH it if they wanted to. It seemed that the clay was a good means of having them release their fears, ideas, and emotions on many things. This clay activity went over very well. During the day many different children, as well as the same children, came back to play at the clay table. (Author's log)

Most children like to do messy things with their hands, and clay gives them a chance for this experience. Working with clay can be a social experience, too. Sitting around a table in small groups, children enjoy trading and sharing lumps of clay.

Children who perceive clay as "messy" or "slimy" however, may not want to work with it. Never force the issue! Be patient and give these children lots of time and plenty of opportunities to see the fun others have with clay. Some teachers find that involving timid children first in a "cleaner" aspect of clay work, such as mixing up play dough, helps involve them on a gradual basis. Hesitant children might feel more comfortable sitting near you as you pat the dough and describe how it feels. Acknowledge these simple participations. Eventually, when hesitant children feel more comfortable, they may try patting gently with you or a friend (Miller, 1993).

## STRATEGIES FOR WORKING WITH CLAY

Since using clay is messy, it requires planning and forethought. However, working with clay is no fun for the children when the teacher always has to remind them about the right use. Proper setup will make this unnecessary. Some tips for clay setup are:

- The tables used for working with clay should be placed away from wheel and climbing toys. They should be covered with linoleum or formica to make cleaning easier. If the tables in the room are plastic coated, covering is not usually needed.
- The number of children at a table at one time should be limited.
- Each child should be given a lump of clay about the size of a large apple or a small grapefruit. The clay may be worked with in any way the child wants. However, the clay should not be thrown on the ground, and no child should interfere with another child's work.
- The teacher may sit at the table and play with the clay, too; this adds to the social feeling. But the teacher should not make objects for the child to copy. This discourages the child's creative use of the clay.
- When the children are done, the clay is put away. It is best to make it into balls, each about the size of an apple. A hole filled with water in each ball helps keep the clay just right for use the next time. It should be kept in a container with a wet cloth or sponge over the top of the clay. The container should be covered with a tight-fitting lid. (Margarine tubs with clear plastic lids work well.) Clay becomes moldy if it is too wet and hard to handle if it becomes very dry. If clay should dry out, it can be restored to a proper consistency by placing the dried-out clay in a cloth bag and pounding it with a hammer until it is broken into small pieces. After soaking this clay in water, it can be kneaded until it is the proper consistency again. If clay does become moldy, there's no need to throw it away. Simply scrape off the moldy area and drain off any water collected in the bottom of the container.

## MODELING

*Modeling*—manipulating and shaping flexible materials—has many benefits for young children. It helps them develop tactile perception, the understanding and appreciation of the sense of touch. Modeling also helps develop the child's adaptability to change, by use of an ever-flexible material. In modeling three-dimensional objects, the child's concepts of form and proportion are strengthened as he learns to make objects with his hands. With older children, the appreciation for sculpture and pottery

# THIS ONE'S FOR YOU!

## MORE SCULPTURE IDEAS

Here are some more ideas to encourage young children's experiments with three-dimensional media. You will probably have many more of your own.

**Bread Dough Sculpture**

Ingredients: White glue, bread, lemon juice, paint, brushes, plastic bag.

Procedure: Remove the crusts from four slices of bread. Tear the bread into small pieces (children love to do this), mixing them thoroughly with three tablespoons of white glue and one or two drops of lemon juice. Model or cut as desired, allowing one or two days for complete drying. Pieces may be painted with tempera paint. The clay can be preserved for modeling by wrapping in plastic and placing in a refrigerator.

**Foil Sculpture**

Supplies: Foil, gummer tape, brush, liquid detergent, tempera paint.

Procedure: Crumple the foil into individual forms, shapes, or creations that when assembled will create a piece of sculpture. Join these forms together, if desired, with tape. Color can be added to the surface by painting with a drop or two of liquid detergent mixed in the tempera paint.

**Natural Object Sculpture**

Supplies: Natural materials (seeds, twigs, pine cones, seed pods, stones, driftwood, etc.), quick-drying glue, clear quick-drying spray, paint, construction paper, felt.

Procedure: Collect a number of natural objects of various sizes and colors. Arrange several of these items to create a small piece of sculpture. When satisfied with the creation, glue it together. Paint or colored paper can be added to enhance the design. Spray with clear spray to preserve the finish. Spray with optimum ventilation, preferably outdoors.

Glue a piece of felt to the bottom to prevent scratching.

**Spool Sculpture**

Supplies: spools (a variety of sizes are useful), assorted fabric pieces, glue, anything that will serve to stimulate children's imaginations as decorations.

Procedure: There is no prescribed procedure in this project, as each of the spool sculptures is made differently, according to the imagination of the artist. Basically, the procedure involves "dressing" the spool, which serves as a body. The materials are contrived to serve as clothing and are glued onto the spool. If desired, a child may use the spool purely as a base; it does not have to be a figure to dress. Details can be made with drawing materials, and bits and pieces of yarn, ribbon, etc., can be glued on for interest.

as they appear in our environment may also be enhanced as they have experiences modeling their own original sculpture and simple pottery.

**Materials.** The soft, plastic quality of natural clay has a strong appeal for children at any age. In addition to the types of clay referred to earlier in this unit, *salt clay* may be substituted for modeling; it is quite a suitable modeling material for young children. To prepare salt clay, mix together ⅔ cup of salt, ½ cup of flour, ⅓ cup of water. Add a small amount of dry powder paint or food coloring, if desired, while mixture is moist. When the clay is left white, the dried piece has a crystalline sheen or "snow" effect caused by the salt. Finished objects dry to a durable hardness.

*Paper pulp* (papier-mâché), another clay substitute, is easy to work with, does not crack or break readily, and is inexpensive. The texture of paper pulp lends itself to the bold, spontaneous quality of a child's expression. To prepare paper pulp:

- Tear newspaper into tiny pieces and soak overnight.
- Squeeze out excess water and add powder paste and a few drops of oil of wintergreen to prevent mold.
- Knead mixture until texture is smooth and pliable.

When you would like to add variety to clay activities, introduce the children to some tools for modeling. Sticks, tongue depressors, toothpicks, popsicle sticks, paper clips, nails, and even combs make interesting tools for modeling. Of course, any tools small enough to put into the mouth should not be used with toddlers or any young children who like to put things in their mouth. All young preschoolers need to be supervised in their use of modeling tools.

**Motivational Strategies.** The following suggestions are intended to help you get children involved in modeling activities:

- Clay interests and absorbs children. As with painting, use clay with young children for the process—the feelings it generates, the pleasure of discovery, putting one's mark on it, making it change. Very rarely should clay be used to make something permanent. Rather, clay is to work with at a table with others and to make back into a ball once you're through, storing it for the next time.
- Give each child large amounts, at least grapefruit-sized chunks, so they can work with the mass of it.
- If, during any of these activities, children say, "I don't know what to do," they are trying to find out how to do the activity right. You might tell them, "Just play with it and see what happens." What we must fight here is a stereotype children often adopt: that there is a right way to draw, or paint,

or model—which, of course, there isn't (Clemens, 1991).

**Processes**

- Some children find satisfaction in manipulating a modeling material without making anything. Others, in the symbolic stage, give names to objects such as balls, pancakes, and coils that appear unreal to adults. The teacher, recognizing different stages of growth, encourages children's efforts on all levels.
- One child may pull, pinch, or squeeze the material into a desired shape with head, arms, and legs extended. Another may make each part separately, then put them together into the whole figure. Some children may combine the two ways of working. It is best not to block the child's thinking by diverting him from one method to the other.
- When children are ready for other techniques, the teacher may demonstrate how to
  – Moisten both parts when joining pieces of clay together, then pinch and work them together so they will not separate when the object has dried.
  – Avoid delicate parts that break off.
  – Smooth the material to prevent cracking.
  – Create texture using fingernails or carving tools.
  – Depict action by bending the head or twisting the body.
- Or, if a child has difficulty with this method, you might demonstrate how to "pull" a smaller piece of clay out of the larger mass, rather than add an attachment. Just be sure your suggestion helps the child accomplish his own goal for his clay.
- Unfinished clay work may be wrapped in plastic bags or aluminum foil or placed in covered cans with child's name attached.
- Oil-base clay cannot be painted but may be exhibited when finished (away from the sun).
- A small lump of modeling material can be used as a magnet to pick up crumbs at cleanup time.

**Evaluation**

- Did children find satisfaction in modeling?
- Does their work show evidence of growth in understanding the concept of form in working with a three-dimensional material?

# THINK ABOUT IT . . .

## CORNSTARCH!

Believe it or not, a fascinating modeling medium is plain old cornstarch. Use the following recipe to mix up cornstarch for children's three-dimensional play.

**Cornstarch and Water**
2 cups warm water
3 cups cornstarch
Put ingredients in bowl and mix with your hands. This mixture will solidify when left alone, but turns to liquid from the heat of your hands. Magic!

Involve the children in making the above cornstarch recipe. Have them feel the dry cornstarch. Encourage their reactions to it, using their senses of sight, smell, touch, and even taste. Add a little water, and then let the children mix it and feel it again. It is lumpy. After this lumpy stage, you can add a little more water until it's all moist. Wet cornstarch forms an unstable material, which is fun because of its unexpected behavior—it breaks, but it also melts. It doesn't behave like glue, or like milk, or like wood; it's a liquid, and it's a solid, too. If you rest your fingers lightly on the surface of the cornstarch-water mix, it will let your fingers drift down to the bottom of the container. If you try to punch your way to the bottom, it will resist.

Cornstarch works well in a baby bathtub set on a table, with a limit of two or three children using the entire recipe. If you leave it in its tub overnight, by morning it's dry. Add some water, and it becomes that wonderful "stuff" again. Be sure to invite the children to watch this event.

It's a clean sort of play: the white, powdery mess on the floor can be picked up easily with a dustpan and brush or a vacuum cleaner.

Children come back to this cornstarch and water mix again and again, because it feels good and behaves in an interesting way. (Clemens, 1991)

- Was each child's work accepted with praise and encouragement?
- Has the child acquired new knowledge of the medium?

## ASSEMBLAGE

As an art form, *assemblage* refers to placing a number of three-dimensional objects, natural or man-made, in juxtaposition to create a unified composition. Discarded materials are combined in a new context to express an abstract, poetic, or representational theme. Assemblage makes use of three-dimensional space, resembling a still-life arrangement as objects are first selected, then grouped and regrouped.

Assemblage can be a reflection of our urban environment, depicting everyday habits in the selection of food, clothing, and objects for household use. For example, every meal is an assemblage, creating order in arrangements of food, tableware, and linen that vary according to the type of meal and the occasion.

**FIGURE 13–8 A child may sometimes require an adult's assistance in an assemblage activity.**

The daily act of dressing requires assembling cloth and leather, metal and plastics in relation to a particular purpose and meaning.

Objects collected for comfort and use in the home indicate discriminating taste or the lack of it in the area of environmental assemblage. Obviously different environments produce particular kinds of objects, each with a special kind of assemblage. All human beings are natural assemblers; assembling is a process of life.

These are some other environmental assemblages:

- Stores and marketplaces
- neighborhoods and cities
- bands and orchestras
- parades and processions
- interiors and exteriors
- fairs and circuses

**Motivational Strategies.** Try some of the following suggestions to introduce children to an assemblage activity:

- Display and discuss collected items from our environment.

- Arrange a bulletin board with illustrations of assemblage in daily living.
- Encourage children to bring objects from their environment and containers for assemblages.
- Demonstrate ways of arranging various objects emphasizing variety of shapes, sizes, colors, textures, and methods of fastening the objects.
- Demonstrate ways of making items for an assemblage.

**Materials.**
- *Containers:* Wooden boxes, cardboard boxes, cigar boxes, match boxes, suitcases, egg cartons and crates, packing cartons. Containers may be painted or covered with paper, cloth, magazine illustrations.
- *Mounting boards:* Pasteboard, corrugated cardboard, wood, crates, picture frames.
- *Objects:* Wooden forms or scrap lumber, driftwood, screening, corks, cardboard boxes, discarded toys, household items; articles of nature such as seeds, weeds, stones, twigs.
- *Adhesives:* Paste, glue, staples.
- *Tools:* Scissors, stapler, knife, hammer, nails, pliers.

**Processes.** Children should be encouraged to collect objects that are meaningful to them. Almost any area of interest or everyday experience is a possible theme for assemblage.

- Objects may be selected according to an idea, topic, size of container, or variation in line, form, color, and texture; use multiple items for repetition of shapes.
- Three-dimensional forms may be altered or transformed so that they lose their original identity and take on a new meaning. They can be bent, twisted, stretched, crumpled, or painted.
- Objects also can be made by cutting out pictures or illustrations and pasting them over cardboard, wood, or other substantial material.
- Select a box, container, or mounting board and cover it with paint or paper. Divide the box into compartments with vertical and horizontal shelves, or use a variety of smaller boxes, grouped together and glued in place.

- Arrange and rearrange objects until the desired composition is achieved.
- Objects can be glued, stapled, or nailed.

### Evaluation.
- Did this project help increase children's awareness of their environment?
- Did children learn more about the possibilities of design in trying various combinations of colors, shapes, and textures in collage and assemblage?
- Did this project increase children's sensitivity to the design and form of commonplace objects?
- Did children acquire an ability to arrange shapes and forms into a unified composition?

## CARDBOARD CONSTRUCTION

Cardboard, an indispensable material for construction projects, stimulates and challenges the imagination of children on all levels. It is readily available in various forms. Such commonplace objects as milk and egg cartons, apple-crate dividers, toweling tubes, and assorted sizes of boxes offer unlimited possibilities for creative art projects. (See Appendix E for specific art project suggestions with these materials.)

### Materials.
- Assorted cardboard boxes and cartons, corrugated cardboard, paper cups and plates
- Discarded materials: paper bags, soda straws, yarn, string, buttons, feathers, cloth, tissue paper, and construction paper
- Paste, glue, tape, crayons, paint, brushes, scissors, and stapler

**Motivational Strategies.** Most topics of interest to young children can be adapted to cardboard construction projects. Some of these are holidays, seasons, community, stories, transportation, sports, animal life, home and family, designs, shapes, and other individual "creations."

- While exploring the cardboard objects collected, stacking them, or combining them in different arrangements, children should be encouraged to

**FIGURE 13–9 Construction paper family.**

explore the possibilities for carrying out their ideas.
- Teacher and children should discuss and demonstrate ways of fastening boxes together, covering them with paint or construction paper, and adding other parts or features.
- Children can make their selection of objects needed for the construction.

### Processes.
- Fasten cardboard together with glue, masking tape, gummed tape, paper fasteners, or staples.
- Boxes with waxed surfaces can be covered with a layer of newspaper and wheat paste and allowed to dry before painting. Powder paint mixed with

starch adheres well to box surfaces. Boxes may also be covered with construction paper or even painted with tempera.

- Textured surfaces can be created by using corrugated cardboard, shredded packing tissue, or crinkled newspaper.
- Shapes and sizes of cardboard objects may suggest ideas for a project, such as using an oatmeal box for the body of an elephant, a milk carton for a tall building.
- Use a variety of discarded materials to complete the design, such as pieces of ribbon, buttons, sequins, spools, etc.

**Suggested Activities.**
*Buildings.* A variety of round and rectangular cartons may be painted or covered with paper. Add cut-paper windows and doors, chimneys and balconies. Arrange buildings to create a city, small town, or farm. Store windows can have merchandise painted on, cut out, or pasted on.

*Animal cages.* Cut a large window on each side of a box. Paint the box or cover with paper. Attach several strips of construction paper in the windows for the bars. Paste a paper animal inside the cage. If wheels are desired, cut circles of cardboard and glue in place.

*Box characters.* Cardboard boxes of assorted sizes can be used to form the body of the figure. Divide the space according to the parts of the body—the neck and the waist. Arms may consist of a paper strip attached to either side of the box. Create costumes with cut-paper scraps or felt. Add bits of cloth, rickrack, feathers, yarn, string, or ribbon for color and texture. Features can be created with buttons, beads, or sequins.

*Costumes.* Select a cardboard carton large enough to fit over the child's body. Remove the box, also the top if the child is to wear a hat. Cut out arm holes on the sides. Two pieces of rope put through holes from front to back form shoulder straps. If the costume consists only of the box, without a hat or mask, cut a window near the top for the face. The box may

**FIGURE 13–10 Three-dimensional art paper farm for spring unit on animals.**

be painted or decorated with cut paper. A child should never be forced to wear a costume if he does not wish to.

*Imaginary animals.* Collect boxes of various sizes and shapes. Children can stack them one on another and rearrange them until they are satisfied with the combination. Shapes and sizes of boxes may suggest certain animals, such as an oatmeal box for an elephant, a long narrow box for a giraffe's neck. Smaller boxes or toweling rolls can be used for legs or a head. Fasten boxes together with glue, masking tape, brown gummed tape, or paper fasteners. Boxes with waxed surfaces can be covered with a layer of newspaper and wheat paste and allowed to dry before painting. Textured surfaces can be created by using corrugated paper or egg cartons for bodies of animals. Wood shavings, bark, or wrinkled-paper scraps can be glued to boxes to create interesting texture. Exaggerated features help create dramatic effects, such as large buttons for eyes, frayed string or rope for a mane or tail, or pieces of cloth for ears.

**FIGURE 13-11 A cutout paper animal decorated with crayons and cut-paper ears.**

*Cars, trucks, and trains.* Assemble boxes and stack in desired shapes. Fasten with glue or tape. Ribbon spools, spools of thread, or circles cut from flat cardboard make wheels. Cover boxes with paint, wrapping paper, or construction paper.

*Totem poles.* Collect a number of medium-sized boxes; glue or tape them shut. Paint or cover boxes with construction paper. If three-dimensional features are desired, use parts of egg cartons, toweling rolls, buttons, spools. For flat features, use cut paper scraps. Stack finished "heads" to desired height.

*Mask.* Make sure the box fits the child's head. Cut a window in one side for the face. Decorate the box according to the characterization. Never force a child to wear a mask if he does not wish to.

## WOODWORKING

Woodworking involves a range of activities from hammering nails, to sanding, gluing, and painting wood. As with other three-dimensional activities, woodworking can be an excellent medium for fostering a child's creativity if the *process,* and not the product, is emphasized.

There are many valuable reasons for including woodworking in the early childhood art program:

- Woodworking provides opportunities for children to strengthen and control their large muscles through participating in vigorous activities such as sawing and nail-pounding.
- Through participation in woodworking experiences, children improve social and communication skills as they share ideas, talk over problems, or help one another handle tools.
- Woodworking provides opportunities for children to release tension. They soon discover that pounding wood causes less trouble than pounding another child! Experiences that allow a child to work off his tension, either consciously or unconsciously, help build an emotionally healthy child.
- The satisfaction and feeling of accomplishment children experience in the woodworking area contribute substantially to a child's sense of self-esteem. Usually, the woodworking products children produce provide tangible evidence of their accomplishment. For some children, the woodworking product is not nearly as important as the process by which it was made.
- Skills a child learns in the woodworking area may carry over into other classroom activities. The child may use tools to measure, repair, or construct something for use in other areas of the room. This additional experience provides the child an added demonstration of competence.
- Skills learned through woodworking furnish the basis for developing scientific thinking. Woodworking materials provide opportunities for young children to investigate, experiment with, and develop problem-solving skills. Through fitting, fastening, connecting, and cutting, children learn basic mechanics—the foundation for understanding math and physics.
- Woodworking provides children with opportunities to become aware of textures and forms. Senses are sharpened as children explore the field of construction. Fingers explore many textures, ears pick out the sounds of different tools, noses test the different smells of various woods, and eyes see the many hues of wood.
- Working with tools and materials allows the child to express herself. What a child chooses to play with, and how the child uses her play materials,

reflects her feelings about and reactions to the people around her.

## Planning for the Woodworking Experience.

Planning for the woodworking area and related experiences is the key to success. Thought needs to be given to time allotment, location of the woodworking area, limits, number of children working at one time, and the role of the teacher. The following criteria need to be considered:

- Enough time should be allotted for children to explore materials without feeling rushed and complete a simple project. If the woodworking area is a popular one, the teacher may find it necessary to set up time allotments to give all children a chance to participate.
- The workbench should be situated so that several children can move around and work without bumping into one another. It should be located out of major traffic patterns to avoid interruptions and accidents. It should be located away from quiet areas, so the noise will not disturb others. Weather permitting, and with adequate supervision, woodworking can be provided out of doors.
- A specific limit should be set in advance regarding the number of children working at one time. Usually, one teacher can comfortably supervise three or four children. No more children than the set limit should be allowed in the woodworking area at one time. Teachers can enforce this limit by requiring all children who are woodworking to wear an apron.
- Tools and materials should be geared to the ability level of the children using them, and must be safe, workable, and suitable for the planned activities.
- The teacher needs to familiarize herself with the use of woodworking tools and materials in order to give effective guidance and set reasonable limits. To create enthusiasm in the children for woodworking, it is important that the teacher be excited about its possibilities herself. The carpentry area must be constantly supervised to avoid accidents and to forestall the children's frustration with using unfamiliar tools.

## Guidance in the Woodworking Area.

In guiding children in woodworking activities, the teacher must first help them become familiar with the tools. In introducing the saw, for example, show the children how to hold the saw at a 45-degree angle and gently move it back and forth rhythmically. Instruct children that they do not have to use a great deal of force or power for sawing; the saw will do the work on its own. Demonstrate how to fasten the wood in a vise, hold the wood with the left hand and saw with the right hand, or vice versa for left-handers.

The rules of saw safety must be emphasized, including where to keep the hands, how to carry the saw, and where to lay it down.

In introducing the hammer, show the children how to set a nail by gently tapping it into the wood. It can be driven using more vigorous strokes while holding the hammer by the end of the handle. Make a series of holes in various pieces of wood, showing how to set nails into these premade holes.

Avoid too many detailed instructions, or making models or patterns, because all of these things limit the children's initiative, independence, and creativity.

To prevent children from becoming frustrated, show them how to make handling wood easier by laying it flat and securing it with a vise. Allow the child to try out his own ideas, but guide him in choosing the proper tools to use for carrying out those ideas.

Providing woodworking experiences for young children can contribute to their total development. Feeling good about woodworking builds a child's self-confidence and encourages him to continue to explore his creativity through woodworking.

## Selecting Tools for Woodworking Experiences.

When buying tools and equipment for woodworking, choose adult-type tools of good quality to withstand hard use. Tools should also be able to be resharpened, reconditioned, and have broken parts replaced.

- *Saws.* Three types of saws are generally sold for woodworking purposes: the rip saw, the crosscut saw, and the coping saw. The rip saw has coarse teeth for cutting wood in the direction of the grain. The crosscut saw is designed to cut across the grain, while the coping saw is designed for use on thin wood and for cutting curves. Of the three saws available, the crosscut saw is the easiest for young children to manage. An 8- or 10-point saw (teeth per inch) is the most satisfactory size for children's use.

- *Hammers.* A 10- to 13-ounce clawhammer, with a broad head, is the most satisfactory for use by young children.
- *Plane.* A plane may be provided for children's use. If it is available, the blade should be adjusted to make small cuts, and children should be cautioned to use it only on surfaces free from nails, screws, or knots.
- *Workbench.* The workbench used must be strong, sturdy, and stable. An old door or heavy packing box are ideal for homemade workbenches. Or a pair of sawhorses connected with a heavy board can be easily set up. All workbenches should be about 16″ to 18″ high, just under a child's waist height, for the most convenient work.

*Optional tools.*
- Pliers for holding nails as children are "setting" them
- Scissors for cutting sandpaper and string
- Screwdriver
- Rasp for smoothing a rough or splintered edge against the grain and for rounding corners on wood
- One-foot rule, yardstick
- Pencil
- C clamp

**Storage and Care of Tools.** A special wall-mounted tool board is essential for storing frequently used tools, while infrequently used tools can be stored in a cupboard. Paint the outline of each tool on the board so children can see where to put them away.

Saws should be professionally sharpened and oiled once or twice a year and wrapped in newspaper for long-term storage. Tools should be kept free from dust and rust; lightweight machine oil will remove any rust that forms.

**Choosing and Using Woodworking Materials.**
*Woods.* The wood provided for young children in the woodworking area should be unfinished, smooth, and porous enough for children to pound or saw. Pine, balsa, poplar, and basswood are good, soft woods for children's use. Children work best with small pieces of wood of varying sizes, shapes, and thicknesses. Lumberyard scraps of doweling, molding, and mill ends offer endless possibilities when provided along with basic wood pieces.

Wood should be stored in a container that allows visibility and accessibility to the child. Plastic vegetable bins work well for this.

*Nails.* Nails are supplied in pennyweights (d's), which refers to the length of the nail. Common nail sizes are 2d or 1″; 4d or 1½″; 6d or 2″; 8d or 2½″; and 10d or 3″. At first, most children have trouble pounding nails without bending them, so 1½″ nails with large heads are best for starters. Nails should be stored in small jars according to size, to allow children to select them easily.

*Glue.* Glue can be used by children who have not mastered the skill of pounding nails well enough to fasten wood pieces together. A quick-drying, all-purpose glue can be used for this purpose. Glue can also be used to make wood sculptures, attach accessories, and strengthen joints.

*Screws.* Screws may be provided in the woodworking area but are often difficult for children to handle. They can be made more manageable to children by making a guide hole with a nail first.

**Additional Materials for Woodworking.**
- Sandpaper in four weights: coarse, medium, fine, extra fine. Sandpaper should be mounted on wooden blocks and used in a back-and-forth motion.
- Brushes of medium and narrow widths.

- Tempera paint for painting completed creations.
- Accessories such as string, rubber bands, small pieces of rubber, scraps of leather, pieces of cloth and carpeting, bottle caps, pieces of Styrofoam, and metal gadgets like cuphooks, staples, paper clips, etc.

## SUMMARY

Three-dimensional art refers to any art that has at least three sides. It is "in the round," which means one can look at it from many sides. Examples of three-dimensional art are modeling with clay and play dough, assemblage, cardboard construction, and other forms of sculpture.

Just as children have different drawing abilities at each age, so do they work with clay in different ways at each age. When young children first learn to use a three-dimensional material, like clay, they go through much the same process as a child using crayons in the scribble stage. In work with both crayons and clay, children at this age have little control over their hands or the material. They enjoy the feel of the clay but do not have good control in working with it.

Older preschool children who can draw basic forms like circles or rectangles can also make clay into similar forms. Balls and boxes are examples of basic forms in clay. Children's muscle (motor) control helps them make these forms. Children in this age group can also put together basic forms in clay to make up figures. This is similar to making figures in the pictorial stage of two-dimensional media.

Children name their clay objects at about the same time that they name their drawings. Naming is an important form of communication in both two- and three-dimensional media.

A teacher needs to set up the room for the enjoyable use of three-dimensional materials by children. Proper tables, number of children, and care of materials are all points to keep in mind when planning for clay work.

Modeling refers to the manipulation and shaping of flexible materials. Modeling activities help children develop their sense of touch, their adaptation to change, their concepts of form and proportion and, especially in older children, their sense of aesthetics.

Assemblage is a creative activity that involves placing a number of three-dimensional objects together to create a unified composition. Discarded materials and everyday materials found in the school or home environment are media for this type of activity.

Cardboard is also a suitable material for construction activities for young children. The potential uses of cardboard in the art program include the construction of buildings, puzzles, dioramas, costumes, imaginary animals, and masks, to name a few.

Woodworking, another three-dimensional activity, involves a range of activities from hammering nails, to sanding, gluing, and painting. Woodworking experiences for young children contribute to their total development. These experiences must be planned so that appropriate, good-quality tools are provided for the children's use. Close supervision is required in woodworking.

## LEARNING ACTIVITIES

### Exercise 1

Goal: To experience how a child aged one and a half to three years works with clay.

A. Use your hand opposite your writing hand.
B. Use a piece of real clay about the size of a large apple.
C. Squeeze the clay in one hand only.
D. Keep these points in mind:
   1. How it feels to lack good muscle (motor) control.
   2. How hard it is to make an exact object.
   3. How the clay feels in the hand.

### Exercise 2

Goal: To feel the differences in clay.

A. Prepare large balls of real clay, plasticene (oil-based) clay, and play dough.
B. Use the hand opposite the writing hand to squeeze and feel each of the three clay balls. (This should help you experience both the child's lack of muscle control and different materials.)
C. Consider the following points while working with each of the three balls of clay:
   1. Which is the easiest to squeeze?

2. Which feels the best?
3. Which is the most fun to use?
4. Is the type most fun to use also the easiest to use?
D. Try the above activity with children aged one and one half to three years. Ask them the above questions. Compare answers.

## Exercise 3

Goal: To practice analytic and synthetic ways of working with clay.

A. Use two balls of clay.
B. Make two clay boxes—one in the analytic way and one in the synthetic way.
C. Ask other students to identify which box is the analytic example and which is the synthetic example.
D. The two sample boxes should look different. Discuss how each box is different in the way it looks because of how it is made.
E. Variation: Form a clay figure of a man in the analytic and in the synthetic way. Use the same procedure as above for discussion.
F. Obtain some samples of children's (aged three to four years) clay objects. See which are synthetic examples and which are analytic examples. Discuss how they look.
G. Observe children as they work with clay. See how they make their objects. Note if they work in the synthetic or analytic way.
H. Obtain samples of children's clay objects. Look for these points:
1. Which basic forms are made.
2. Which forms are made the most.
3. Whether there are practice forms or definite objects.

## Exercise 4

Goal: To help you understand how children feel when they are given a model to copy.

A. Obtain and display small glass or porcelain figures. These could be decorative birds, glass dolls, or any other finished figure from the dime store or other source.
B. Provide all the students with small balls of clay. Have each student try to copy the model.
C. Look at and discuss the finished objects.
1. How did it feel to copy such a difficult model?
2. Was it a pleasant or frustrating experience?
3. Did this copying exercise make you feel happy about working with clay? Did it make you like to copy?

4. How do you think children feel about trying to copy models the teacher sets up?
5. Why is it undesirable for a teacher to have children copy a model?

## Exercise 5

Obtain some pictures of modern sculpture. (Henry Moore's are good examples.)

A. Show the pictures to the children before they work with clay.
B. See if there are any effects on their work in relation to the following:
1. Kinds of objects made.
2. New shapes made.
3. More or less clay work done.
4. Change in the way objects are made.
5. Change in the way child works with clay.

## Exercise 6

Read an exciting story to the children before they work with clay. For example, try M. Sendak's *Where the Wild Things Are* or Dr. Seuss' *To Think It Happened on Mulberry Street*.

A. Do not tell the children what to make.
B. See if their work with clay shows any influence from the story, regarding the following:
1. Type of figures made.
2. Size of figures made.
3. Details of figures made.

## Exercise 7

To add variety to play dough activities, try one of these variations:

A. Work a drop of food flavoring and a drop of food coloring into your play dough recipe. Match scents with colors, such as mint flavoring with green and lemon flavoring with yellow.
B. It won't matter if young children put their three-dimensional masterpieces in their mouths if you let them use pie dough or thawed bread dough as play dough substitutes.
C. Use a tasty mixture of peanut butter and powdered milk as playdough for another three-dimensional taste treat.
D. Make your play dough recipe slippery by adding a little vegetable oil.

# UNIT REVIEW

1. Define three-dimensional art and give two examples.
2. Choose the answer that best completes the following statements about three-dimensional activities and the child first learning to use clay.
   a. Children first learning to use clay
      (a.) make basic forms with clay.
      (b.) combine basic forms to make objects.
      (c.) squeeze the clay in an uncontrolled way.
   b. Children using clay for the first time work with clay in a way similar to the way they draw in the
      (a.) scribble stage.
      (b.) basic forms stage.
      (c.) pictorial stage.
   c. For children first learning to use clay the most important thing about working with clay is
      (a.) what they can make with it.
      (b.) how it feels.
      (c.) how they can control it.
   d. The best kind of clay for children first learning to use clay is
      (a.) potter's clay.
      (b.) oil-based, plasticene.
      (c.) ceramic, nonelastic clay.
3. Decide which answer best completes each statement about three-dimensional activities and the child who can draw basic forms.
   a. A child who can draw basic forms
      (a.) cannot make similar forms in clay.
      (b.) can make clay into similar forms.
      (c.) combines these forms to make clay objects.
   b. Rolling clay to make balls is an example of
      (a.) lack of motor control.
      (b.) uncontrolled movement like scribbling.
      (c.) a basic form in clay.
   c. Children can make basic forms in clay because they
      (a.) can name their clay objects.
      (b.) now have better motor control.
      (c.) do not have enough motor control.
   d. Some simple basic forms that children can make in clay are
      (a.) balls, boxes, and coils.
      (b.) flowers, houses, and animals.
      (c.) triangles, hexagons, and octagons.
5. Choose the answer that best completes each statement about three-dimensional activities and the child in the pictorial stage of drawing.
   a. Most children like to make
      (a.) nothing in particular with clay.
      (b.) just balls and boxes with clay.
      (c.) definite things with clay.
   b. When working with clay, a child in the pictorial stage can
      (a.) combine basic forms to make a definite object.
      (b.) make only basic forms in clay.
      (c.) make only uncontrolled hand movements with clay.
   c. A simple combination of basic forms in a clay object is a
      (a.) house with four floors of clay and a four-part chimney.
      (b.) clay box.
      (c.) man made of a round ball head and a stick-type body.
   d. When children in the pictorial stage name their drawings, they
      (a.) have no motor control.
      (b.) also name their clay objects.
      (c.) are not yet ready to name their clay objects.
   e. When children name clay objects, it means they are in the related two-dimensional stage called the
      (a.) scribble stage.
      (b.) basic forms stage.
      (c.) pictorial stage.
   f. A more complex combination of basic forms in clay is a
      (a.) man made of a round ball head and a stick-type body.
      (b.) clay man with feet, fingers, hands, and arms.
      (c.) clay ball.
   g. When a child makes a clay figure with many more details than another figure, it means
      (a.) nothing of any particular importance.
      (b.) that it is an important figure for the child.
      (c.) that it is a simple combination of basic forms.
   h. When a clay object is made large, it means the object
      (a.) is a basic form.
      (b.) is not very important.
      (c.) stands for something important.
6. Describe the right room setup for clay work, in regard to
   a. table type
   b. location of clay tables
   c. number of children at table
   d. amount of clay for each child
   e. kind of storage container for clay
7. List the types of modeling materials and tools appropriate for young children.

8. Discuss how modeling benefits young children.
9. Describe the different ways children may use clay and how a teacher must work with each.
10. List several suggestions to make working with modeling materials a successful experience for young children.
11. What is *assemblage?* Give examples of assemblage activities.
12. What are the processes involved in assemblage activities?
13. List the materials and tools needed for assemblage activities for young children.

14. What are some appropriate topics for cardboard projects for young children?
15. Describe ways you might get children started on cardboard construction projects.
16. List appropriate materials and tools for cardboard construction units.
17. Discuss the value of woodworking in the early childhood art program.
18. List some specific equipment required for woodworking experiences for young children.
19. Describe the role a teacher must play in woodworking experiences for young children.

# ADDITIONAL READINGS

Bryant, J.C. *Why Art, How Art.* Seattle: Special Child Publications, 1983.

Clemens, S.C. "Art in the Classroom: Making Every Day Special." *Young Children* (Jan., 1991): 4–11.

Florian, Douglas. *A Carpenter.* New York: Greenwillow, 1991.

———. *A Potter.* New York: Greenwillow, 1991.

Hawkinson, J. *A Ball of Clay.* Chicago: Albert Whitman & Co., 1974.

Langstaff, N., and A. Sproul. *Exploring with Clay.* Washington, D.C.: NAEYC, 1979.

Leavitt, J.E. *Carpentry for Children.* New York: Sterling Publishing Co., 1959.

———. *Easy Carpentry Projects for Children,* 2nd ed. New York: Dover Publications, 1986.

Lillegard, D. *I Can Be a Carpenter.* Chicago: Children's Press, 1986.

Lowenfeld, V., and W. Brittain. *Creative and Mental Growth,* 7th ed. New York: Macmillan, 1982.

Miller, S.A. "Messy Play." *Scholastic Pre-K Today,* (Feb., 1993): 32–40.

Price, C. *Arts of Clay.* New York: Charles Scribner & Sons, 1977.

Renfro, N. "It's in the Bag." *Instructor 93* (1993): 18–20.

Skeen, P., A.P. Garner, and S. Cartwright. *Woodworking for Young Children.* Washington, D.C.: NAEYC, 1992.

Torre, F.D. *Woodworking for Kids.* Garden City, N.Y.: Doubleday, 1978.

Val Baker, D. *The Young Potter.* New York: Frederick Warne Co., 1963.

Walker, L. *Carpentry for Children.* Woodstock, N.Y.: Overlook Press, 1982.

# SECTION 5
# Play, Development, and Creativity

# UNIT 14

# The Role of Creative Play in Development

## OBJECTIVES

After studying this unit, you should be able to
- name and discuss the four kinds of human growth that are influenced by play.
- describe differences in the way infants, toddlers, preschoolers, and school-age children play.
- define solitary, parallel, associative, and cooperative play.

Some children are busily involved in activities in a school for young children. One group of children is removing the wheels from the wooden trucks in the room. Now they are having races by pushing the wheelless trucks along the floor. One child notes the scraping sound being made, while another discovers that the trucks without wheels make marks on the floor.

One child is preparing a tea party for three friends. The child has baked an imaginary cake and has just finished putting on icing. Now the table is being set and the chairs arranged. Another group of children is carefully observing several small furry animals on the other side of the room. While petting one of the animals, a child notices an unusual bump on the animal's back. Several more children join this group to see why everyone seems so excited.

Are these children working? Are they playing? Is there a difference between work and play for a young child? Must children be involved in games in order to be playing? Must toys be involved? Is play natural or can children be taught to play?

The answers to these questions are important. They help define the meaning of the word *play*. The answers lead to an understanding of how children benefit from creative play. They give direction for the purchase and placement of creative materials that guide children's play. They help adults plan activities that help children grow through creative play. (For a review of the characteristics of creativity refer to Unit 1.)

## WHAT IS PLAY?

For adults, play is what they do when they have finished their work. It is a form of relaxation. For young children, play is what they do all day. Playing is living, and living is playing.

Young children do not differentiate between play, learning, and work. Children are by nature playful. They enjoy playing, and will do so whenever they can latch onto the opportunity. Challenges intrigue them. They can concentrate for long periods to per-

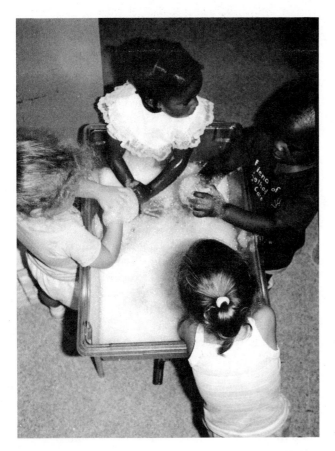

**FIGURE 14–1 Free play with water is always a popular choice for young children.**

fect a skill. Good feelings spur children on to try something new. Why do children love to play? Because play is intrinsically motivated—that is, no one else tells them what to do or how to do it. An activity ceases to be play, and children's interest dwindles, if adults structure or even interfere inappropriately with play.

For older children and teenagers, learning may be a chore. When they complete their chore, they can play. For young children, mental development results from their play. Growth of their ability to deal with the problems of life—social development—results from play. Growth of their imaginations results from play. Muscles develop in play, too.

Play is an activity. It does not necessarily result in a product. It may involve one child or groups of chil-

dren. It may be built around toys and tools or may involve nothing more than the child's imagination. A play period may last a few minutes or go on for days.

Most people who have studied play agree on one thing about its meaning: No single definition or statement can describe the true meaning of play. Therefore, the best way to define play is not to define it at all, but to look at its characteristics.

**Characteristics of Play.**
*A natural part of a child's life.* Adults do not have to tell children how to play.

*Self-directed.* Adults should not interfere because play is determined by the personality of the player, not the desires of adults.

*A creative activity, not a production.* Adults should not concern themselves with what the children might produce during play. The outcomes are never certain. The play is dominated by the players.

*A total activity.* Children become completely involved as they play. Thus, play may last a long time or it may end quite suddenly.

*A sensitive thing for children.* Play may sound noisy, and children may seem deeply involved, yet it can be easily destroyed by interference from other children or suggestions from adults. There is no blueprint for play—no right way or wrong way to play. It is a highly creative and highly individualized activity requiring *active* involvement of the players.

**Types of Play.** There are two main types of play: free (or spontaneous) play and organized play. In either type, children may work alone or in a group. Each type may involve materials and equipment, or it may not. Basically, *free play*, as its name suggests, is flexible. It is unplanned by adults. It is a self-selected, open exercise. The scene below depicts free play.

Two teachers I know regularly take their class to a park where there is no equipment. At first the children were disoriented, thinking there was nothing to do. The adults purposely got busy preparing food, and in time the children began to lead each other into forays of discovery. They climbed trees and fences and hills; hid from each other in the bushes; chased each other; collected sticks and squashed bugs; and discovered pine cones, pebbles, feathers, and wonders of all sorts. They brought treasured items back, and came for help when others got stuck in hard-to-get-out-of places. The adults limited them to a large, but visible, area. This was excellent teaching, nonintervention to let children find their own fun.

*Organized play* may also be open and flexible. However, some structure is provided in terms of materials and equipment or directions given by teachers. Play may be further subdivided according to the age of the child, whether it is imaginative, or whether it involves the use of specialized materials or equipment.

*Dramatic play.* Children act out the parts of one or more characters who may be real or imaginary. Additional information on this type of play will be provided in Unit 15.

**FIGURE 14–2 A young toddler often engages in solitary play.**

*Play involving other children, materials, or equipment.* Children may use materials alone or in groups. Sometimes equipment is used in dramatic play.

*Games.* Games can be invented by the children on the spot, or they can be existing games known to most children or adults. Only somewhat older children can engage in games that are played according to rules.

**Sequence of Play.** The nature of play at various age and developmental levels will be discussed in more depth later in this unit. There is, however, a sequential order of play activities that may be observed in young children. These types of play activities, as with all areas of development, may be classified according to stages.

In early toddlerhood, a child generally plays alone at first, or with adults. This stage is termed *solitary play.* Using all of their senses, children explore long before they put any objects to use in their play. They touch, smell, see, and listen. Manipulating and handling materials are important parts of play experiences. In the earliest months and years, children are more involved with the manipulation of materials than they are with the uses of them. Gradually, as the

**FIGURE 14–3 Group time activities offer opportunities for associative play.**

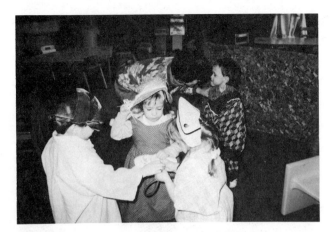

**FIGURE 14–4 In cooperative play, children talk about, plan, and carry out play activities.**

## IMPORTANCE OF PLAY IN CHILD DEVELOPMENT

Creative play activities influence children's total growth, including physical, mental, emotional, and social growth.

**Physical Growth.** Play contributes to muscle development in many ways. Throwing a ball or lifting objects helps children's muscles develop. Placing an object on top of another and grasping tools also add to a child's muscle development and hand-eye coordination. Another type of physical growth involves developing the senses through creative play activities. Play that requires children to look for objects, feel textures, smell various odors, hear sounds, and taste substances help them develop their senses.

Children spend hours perfecting such abilities in play and increasing the level of difficulty to make the task ever more challenging. Anyone who has lived or worked with one-year-olds will recall the tireless persistence with which they pursue the acquisition of a basic skill like walking. In older children, this repetitious physical activity is also a major characteristic of play. It is evident on playgrounds, where we see children swinging, climbing, or playing ball with fervor.

As a child gains control of her body, her self-concept is enhanced. When a child runs, she feels exhilarated. When she uses her last bit of strength to accomplish a goal she herself has set, she gains a better sense of self. As the child discovers her own strength, she develops a concept of herself as a competent individual. A young child is quite physical in her play, playing with her whole being. As she plays, she decides what to do and how to do it; she does her own planning and implements her plans in her own ways.

When children have a chance to be physically active, they continually gain strength. As they become more adept, they become more adventurous and learn to take reasonable risks to test their strength. When children set their own challenges, they are less likely to have accidents. Without predetermined

toddler's social realm expands beyond parents, she will engage in *parallel play*. Parallel play occurs when a child plays side by side with other children, with some interaction, but without direct involvement with them.

As the number of relationships outside the home increases, the child's ability to play with other children develops further. At this point, the child may engage in *associative play*. This type of play may take the form of a child merely being present in a group. For example, a child who participates in fingerplays during circle time or group time would be said to be engaging in associative play. Common activities occur between children. They may exchange toys and/or follow one another. Although all the children in the group are doing similar activities, specific roles are not defined, and there is no organized goal (such as building something or playing a game with rules). Eventually, as they grow more comfortable with their social ties, young children will begin to talk about, plan, and carry out play activities with other children. This type of play, marked by mutual involvement in a play activity, is called *cooperative play*. Children cooperate with others to construct something, produce dramas with coordinated roles, or play games with rules. Group membership is defined, usually by one or two leaders.

FIGURE 14–5 Play activities like climbing promote the development of large motor skills.

FIGURE 14–6 Play can also foster a child's mental (or cognitive) development.

goals, they can pace themselves and discover what they can and cannot do. But physical motor development is only one purpose that play serves.

**Mental Growth.** Play helps children develop important concepts. Through play activities, a child learns the meaning of up and down, hard and soft, and big and small. Play contributes to a child's knowledge of building things and arranging things in sets. Children learn to sort, to classify, and to probe for answers.

Piaget (1962) feels that imaginative play is one of the purest forms of symbolic thought available to the young child. According to Piaget, it permits the child to fit the reality of the world into her own interest and knowledge of the world. Thus, imaginative play contributes strongly to the child's intellectual development. Some researchers even maintain that symbolic play is a necessary part of a child's development of language (Dyson, 1991; Kagan, 1990; Monighan-Nourot, 1990).

Play also offers the child opportunities to acquire information that sets the foundation for additional learning. For example, through playing with blocks a child learns the idea of equivalents (that things can be equal) by discovering that two small blocks equal one larger one; or through playing with water or

sand, she acquires knowledge of volume, which eventually leads to developing the concept of reversibility.

A child gains an understanding of her environment as she investigates stones, grass, flowers, earth, water, and anything else around her. Through these experiences, she eventually begins to make her own generalizations: Adding water to earth makes mud. A puddle of water disappears in sand. The inner part of a milkweed pod blows away in the wind. Wet socks can be dried out in the sun.

As a child plays, she develops spatial concepts; as she climbs in, over, and around the big box in the yard, she clarifies concepts of "in," "over," and "around." She hears someone call the box a "gigantic" box and "gigantic" becomes a new word for her. In the sandbox, words such as "deep," "deeper," and "deepest" begin to have meaning.

**Research on Cognitive Development and Play.** Research and theory about how young children learn show us that play contributes to learning and intellectual (cognitive) maturity in a number of specific ways:

1. Play provides the opportunity for children to practice new skills and functions. As they master these activities, they can integrate or reorganize them into other task-oriented sequences. Babies learn to turn the pages of a book and begin to sense a sequence to the story. Books become lifelong friends when children begin to learn about them in a playful manner.

2. Play offers numerous opportunities for children to act on objects and experience events—it gives children a wide repertoire of experiences. Each field trip, each friendship built with children and adults, including some from different cultures, each experience in building with blocks builds understanding of the world.

3. Play is an active form of learning that unites the mind, body, and spirit. Until at least the age of nine, children's cognitive structures function best in this unified mode. Watch how intense children are when they paint at an easel, work on a puzzle, or gaze into another's eyes.

4. Play enables children to transform reality into symbolic representations of the world. For example, children may be bowling and decide to keep count of how many pins each knocks down. Tokens or paperclips may be kept in a pile, or older children may want to write the numbers on paper.

5. Through play children can consolidate previous learning. Much of what we learn cannot be taught directly but must be constructed through our own experiences. We all know the feeling of "Ah-ha!" when something finally clicks.

6. As they play, children can retain their playful attitude—a learning set that contributes to flexibility in problem solving. Children are open to a variety of solutions. They are amazingly inventive in solving problems, such as how to get an enormous Halloween pumpkin from the bus to their room—roll it, pull it in the wagon, find someone strong enough to lift it, use a derrick, drive the bus up to the door and push the pumpkin in, carve it first to make it lighter, or chop it up and give everyone a piece (solutions don't always have to be workable!).

7. Creativity and aesthetic appreciation are developed through play. When children work with clay, they can appreciate the efforts involved in sculpture and pottery. As they play with words, they develop a sense for the rhythm of poetry and prose.

8. Play enables children to learn about learning—through curiosity, invention, persistence, and a host of other factors. Children's attention spans are amazingly long when they are interested. They are entranced as they watch an anthill; they keep trying until the puzzle is solved; they delight in having recognized their own name for the first time! Children become self-motivated learners.

9. Play reduces the pressure or tension that otherwise is associated with having to achieve or needing to learn. Adults do not interfere, and children relax. Play provides a minimum of risks and penalties for mistakes. Have you ever seen a child who wanted to stop playing? (Rogers and Sawyers, 1988)

**Emotional Growth.** One of the keys to the quality of children's emotional health is how they feel about themselves. Creative play activities help a child develop a positive self-concept. In play activities, there are no right or wrong answers. Children are not faced with the threat of failure. They almost always are successful to one degree or another. They learn to see themselves as capable performers. Even when things do not go well, there is little pressure built into play. Thus, young children learn to view themselves as successful and worthwhile human beings through creative play. This is an important first step in developing a healthy outlook on life.

Children also learn to express and understand their emotions in creative play experiences. They may be observed almost anyplace in the early childhood setting expressing their feelings about doctors by administering shots with relish or their jealousy of a new baby by walloping a doll, but creative play is not necessarily limited to the expression of negative feelings. The same doll that only a moment ago was

**FIGURE 14–7 In creative play, the same doll that only a moment ago was being punished may next be lulled and crooned to sleep.**

being punished may next be lulled and crooned to sleep in the rocking chair.

Another emotional value of creative play is that it offers the child an opportunity to achieve mastery of her environment. When she plays, she is in command. She establishes the conditions of the experience by using imagination and exercises her powers of choice and decision as the play progresses.

Play is a safe and acceptable way to test out the expression of feelings. Through play a child can recreate experiences that have been important to her and elaborate on experiences that have special meaning. She can relieve anxiety or stress through play activities and feel perfectly safe in doing so. For example, Susan gets pleasure out of hammering on a piece of wood. She feels strong as she swings the hammer and sees the deep indentations she is making in the wood. Woodworking, thus, is providing a medium through which she can release tension or aggression in an acceptable way.

**Social Growth.**  Children learn social skills as they relate to others during play. As a child becomes proficient in his social relating, he learns to deal with more than one person at a time. As a group partici-

pant, he finds not everyone behaves in the same way and that some forms of behavior are not acceptable. When Claire takes a block from Jimmy's building, Jimmy pushes her away. Next time, she does not try that. In one situation, Claire learns that crying will get her what she wants, while in another it does not work at all. Children also establish social relationships as they sit side by side playing with clay, dough, and other manipulative materials. A child discovers that he can make some decisions about what he will or will not do. If a child does not wish to push a wagon, he can play somewhere else. He cannot, however, always be the one to tell others what to do. Sometimes he takes the role of leader and sometimes he finds the role of follower satisfying.

When children play together, they learn to be together. The development of common interests and goals takes place among children during creative play. They must learn to "give a little" as well as "take a little" when involved in creative play activities. Whether two small children are arguing over the possession of a toy or a group of children are playing together on a jungle gym, play helps children grow socially.

Psychologists feel that three- to five-year-olds need

**FIGURE 14–8 Social growth occurs when children play together and learn to share space and equipment.**

# THINK ABOUT IT . . .

## SETTING THE STAGE FOR PLAY

Considering all the discussion in this unit about the pure, spontaneous nature of children's play, you may be led to believe all a teacher needs to do is step back and "let it happen." Yet, the teacher's role in *setting the stage* for play is highly active and multifaceted. In fact, everything the teacher does is an *intervention*. Researchers tell us that we can think of intervention on a range from direct to indirect. Preparing the room and scheduling the day are at the indirect end, while intervening as an artist assistant, matchmaker, peacekeeper, parallel player, spectator, or coach are all examples of more direct interventions necessary to children's play.

Teachers assume many roles as they intervene during play. For example, as "artist assistant," the teacher helps remove clutter around an ongoing play episode so that children can maintain the focus of their play. As "peacemaker," the teacher helps children resolve disputes by suggesting alternative roles or materials, or by interpreting children's motives. As "guardian of the gate," a sensitive teacher can help a child gain access to play without violating the rights of the players in an ongoing episode. As "matchmaker," the teacher deliberately helps particular children play with one another. In the role of "parallel player," the teacher uses similar material and plays next to the child, thereby suggesting new variations. As "spectator," the teacher helps children extend their play by commenting on it from "outside" the play theme, e.g., "Are you using the fireman's hat today?" Finally, teachers can also act as play "participants" by taking active roles in children's play. ("Yes, I would love some of your rice cakes.")

Teachers, in less direct interventions, schedule the day to be conducive to children's play. The day needs to have a lengthy free-choice time, allowing children enough time to move from the exploration of objects into play with them and to construct, elaborate, and refine the products of their imaginations. (Ervin-Tripp, 1991; Kagan, 1990; Smilansky and Shefatya, 1990)

to do things together and to talk about what they are doing. Children in this age group seem to see the world from only their own point of view. They must learn to realize that other people see the world differently and that these other people can be correct in their views. They can begin learning this for themselves through the experiences they have with other children. Play activities provide these needed experiences by drawing children together and providing them with chances to listen to each other's ideas.

Smilansky, one expert on children's play, speaks of two kinds of play: *dramatic* and *sociodramatic*

(1990). Dramatic play involves imitation and may be carried on alone, but the more advanced sociodramatic play involves verbal communication and interaction with two or more people, as well as imitative role playing, make-believe in regard to objects, actions, and situations, and persistence in the play over a period of time.

Sociodramatic play also helps the child learn to put herself in another's place (Bruner, 1975; Ervin-Tripp, 1991), thereby encouraging the child's growth of empathy and consideration of others. It also helps define social roles: the child learns by ex-

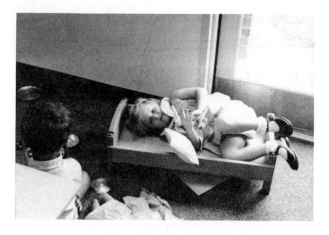

FIGURE 14–9 Children like to pretend in their play activities, sometimes being a "baby" again.

periment what it is like to be the baby or the mother or the doctor or nurse. And it provides countless opportunities for acquiring social skills: how to enter a group and be accepted, how to balance power and bargain with other children so that everyone gets some satisfaction from the play, and how to work out the social give-and-take that is the key to successful group experiences.

FIGURE 14–10 A make-believe friend is also a part of creative play.

## STAGES OF PLAY

The kinds of creative play activities enjoyed by young children are different at various age levels.

**Infants and Toddlers.** Play activities for infants and toddlers, especially in group settings, come from a variety of sources. In one sense, there is really very little mystery about how to play with a baby. Appropriate play activities are very much like the activities of an attentive, responsive parent who is able to help the infant busily enjoy each day. Some play activities, however, are particularly good for building intellectual and sensorimotor skills.

Play activities for infants and toddlers also derive from traditional preschool programs. Play dough, water, music, puzzles, climbers—all of these have always been suggested as appropriate for young children, and research findings and developmental theories have shown that they are good for toddlers as well.

Play activities for infants are often tied to developmental markers or age- and stage-determined abilities and interests of the child. Games and play opportunities that are intended to enhance an emerging skill or interest are suggested. Young infants, for example, love face-to-face talking and grasping rattles, partly because they are trying to recognize people and voices and partly because they are building their touching and grasping skills. Older infants love peek-a-boo games and manipulative toys; they are at a developmental stage when these are challenging and satisfying.

Age categories can, however, create problems in the selection of play activities for infants and toddlers. Inappropriate activities can restrict or pressure children by creating false expectations. For example, any activity that is incorrectly determined to be too easy or too difficult may not be attempted when it could have satisfied the child's needs for challenge or for practice. Books, water play, and simple nesting toys, for example, may be postponed to toddler ages, but they can also be enjoyed by younger infants. On the other hand, complex puzzles, art projects, or group story times may be attempted too early, which

FIGURE 14–11 Older two-year-olds enjoy dramatic play. They often pretend to be a member of a family and act out a specific role of mother or father.

will frustrate the young toddler. Age definitions, here or elsewhere, should be evaluated by the teacher and adjusted for individual children and programs.

**Older Two- and Three-Year-Olds.** Children in this age group enjoy dramatic play. They often pretend to be another member of their own immediate family when they are involved in this kind of play. They may act out the part of their mothers or fathers, by cooking, cleaning, caring for others (dolls), driving an imaginary car to the store, or mowing the lawn. Three-year-olds also like to pretend they are television characters. They find it difficult to separate real people from "pretend" people when they are playing. Therefore, they often become convinced that they really are some imaginary person. They may even become angry when an adult uses their real name rather than their imaginary one. However, children of this age shift their roles very quickly, often from moment to moment. They may be a horse one minute and a jet pilot the next.

Three-year-olds collect anything that is attractive to them or to others in their group. They like to col-

lect such things as books, puzzles, and toys. They repeat games or play activities over and over, never seeming to tire of repetition.

**Four-Year-Olds.** Four-year-old children are generally more imaginative than three-year-olds. Their play often reflects more aggressive activity. Playing monster or ghost characters is one of their favorites. Dramatic play involving aggressive television characters is also common. There is a tendency to act out male or female roles to an extreme. They like to wear costumes that show the strength of the character.

Four-year-olds are better coordinated in using tools and equipment than three-year-olds. An interesting trait at this time is that of hiding things. Toys, tools, and blocks are often buried in the sandbox. The children delight in playing hide-and-seek.

Four-year-olds differ most from three-year-olds in their ability to distinguish the real from the imaginary. They are beginning to know the difference between playing a character and actually being the character.

**Five- and Six-Year Olds.** Children of this age group begin to play games that have rules. They start to understand the need for rules. They also understand the meaning of games that have certain objectives.

Children of this age play out their fears and sometimes relieve their aggressions through dramatic play. Rather than hit another child, a five-year-old pretends to be a ghost who frightens that child. Dramatic play becomes more complicated in the roles children play and characters they become. Some characters are taken from everyday life (a fire fighter or nurse), and some are made-up characters (a space adventurer or queen).

Five-year-olds become interested in their bodies and sometimes play "doctor" with children of the opposite sex. They also show some interest in romance by playing bride-and-groom games.

Improved coordination enables these children to play with more complicated toys. Some are able to ride two-wheel bicycles. Muscle development helps them handle smaller tools. They can hold a paint-

# THIS ONE'S FOR YOU!

## DIFFERENCES BETWEEN ADULTS' AND CHILDREN'S PLAY

From the child's point of view, play is something you don't have to do well; it is just fun (Caldwell, 1985). Until the ages of seven or eight, children are much more interested in what they are doing (the process) rather than how it turns out (the product). It appears that children engage in play for the pleasure of the activity itself until they become relatively skilled. Then they alter the activity to create new challenges. Play offers a multitide of risk-free opportunities to match skills and challenges.

As adults, we rarely allow ourselves the luxury of engaging in real play. We tend to limit our pursuits to the things we do well, afraid to take the risk of trying something new and failing. Perhaps the closest we come to play as children know it is when we take up a new game or attempt a new craft. As beginners, we are willing to suspend or bend the rules a little, until we perfect the skill. If we win or succeed in our first attempts, we attribute it to beginner's luck. Adult play (such as bridge, tennis, or fishing) has aptly been described as having the following characteristics: not fun; lacking spontaneity; deadly serious; and focused on doing it correctly and well (Caldwell, 1985). In other words, adults tend to view play as a means to an end, whereas children ignore the end in order to explore, enjoy, and toy with the means (Fagan, 1984).

---

brush so that it begins to respond to their wishes. The five-year-old can build tall block towers and interesting block castles.

## SUMMARY

Play is a central part of the lives of young children, not something to do when work is finished. Play may be organized (structured) or spontaneous (free). It may involve dramatics or special equipment, or it may take the form of a game. Play usually develops in a natural sequence that evolves from a child's level of socialization. The sequential stages of play include solitary, parallel, associative, and cooperative play.

The needs of children are met through creative play. They learn about themselves, others, and the world around them through their play activities. Creative play has specific purposes in the early childhood program—to promote physical, mental, social, and emotional growth. Observation of children engaged in creative play will reveal some differences (stages) of play. Play is quite different for three-year-olds than it is for five-year-olds. Three-year-old children often cannot separate the real from the pretend. They prefer to be characters about whom they know something. Four-year-olds tend to be aggressive and play characters that enable them to display their aggressive feelings. Five-year olds can separate the real world from the world of their imaginations. They are better able to control their emotions.

## LEARNING ACTIVITIES

A. Observe children of various ages at play. Without letting them know you are watching, observe one or more children from each age group at play for periods of at least ten minutes for each group. How are the play activities similar? How are they different?

B. Select one play activity and discuss how it contributes

to a child's growth in each of four areas of development discussed in this unit (physical, mental, social, emotional).

C. Observe the dramatic play of a group of three-year-olds and a group of five-year-olds. In what ways is their play different? How is it similar?

D. A game to try is called the Animal Cracker game. It is an example of a game that children enjoy and one that helps the student develop a better understanding of the creative possibilities of games.
1. Obtain a box of animal crackers. Stand before a full-length mirror and, without looking, take one of the crackers from the box. Look at and then eat the cracker. With that action, you "become" the selected animal for two minutes. Observe your behavior as that animal. Do this a number of times.
2. Answer the following questions about this activity:

   a. How did you feel about doing this?
   b. How is creativity different from silliness?
   c. How do games help people develop creativity or become more creative?

## ACTIVITIES FOR CHILDREN

### Body Parts Game

A. Note to teacher: Sing the song "If you're happy and you know it," using body part movements as your verses.

B. Example:
1. If you're happy and you know it, shake your head.
2. Repeat.
3. If you're happy and you know it and you really want to show it—
4. If you're happy and you know it shake your head.

C. Other ideas:
1. Clap your hands.
2. March your whole body.
3. Shake your hips.
4. Touch your toes.
5. Roll your head.
6. Wiggle your nose.
7. Smile really big.

D. Children like very much to make up their own verses.

### Imagination Exercises

Children enjoy "being" animals or other "pretend" things. These activities are good for large muscle development as well as for creative play. In these activities, encourage children to move slowly and quietly. Once they interpret the object or animal in their own way, suggest that they hold the positions while continuing to breathe slowly.

A. *Tree.* Together, close your eyes and think about different trees you've seen. Then stand up and raise your arms to look like a tree. Breathe slowly in and out and try to hold the pose for about 30 seconds.

B. *Mountain.* Begin by sitting on the floor, legs crossed, or sitting in any position that's comfortable. Then, slowly raise your arms to create a mountain peak. As you hold the position, ask the children to pretend they are a huge, quiet mountain. You, or someone in the group, can describe the peaceful scenes you might see below.

C. *Cat.* Find a comfortable way to curl up like a cat and pretend to be sleeping in a warm, comfy place, like near a fireplace or in a sunny place. Then wake up and stretch.

D. *Turtle.* Pretend you are a turtle by rounding your back like a shell and tucking your head, arms, and legs under the shell. Hold this pose for a bit, then very slowly stretch out your neck, arms, and legs (Church, 1993).

### Old McDonald Game

A. Note to teacher: The children sing the tune, "Old McDonald," using a new format. Use the children's names and different body parts. Prepare the children ahead of time for the part of the body they will sing about.

B. Example:
Suzy, Suzy had a body, e-i-e-i-o
and on her body she had a foot, e-i-e-i-o
with a (stomp), (stomp), here and a (stomp), (stomp) there
Here a (stomp), there a (stomp).
Everywhere a (stomp), (stomp).
Suzy, Suzy had a body, e-i-e-i-o.

C. Repeat, using various body parts.

### Suggested Activities for Large-Muscle Development

Besides these common large-muscle activities, the following are some creative play activities that require the use of large muscles and that promote large (gross) motor skills.

## Follow the Leader
The leader child moves about freely. She may imitate animals—a rabbit hopping or a fish swimming. The others must follow the leader.

## Guess What I Am
Without saying a word, a child tries to act out the movements of some object. This may be an airplane making a landing, a rooster strutting around the barnyard, a cement truck dumping its load, a clock telling the time of day. The child may think up things to do, or the teacher may whisper suggestions.

## Water Play
A water table or a large tub is filled with water and used for creative water play. Children pour, mix, and stir the water. Soap may be added so they can create suds, too. They may also enjoy using water and a large paintbrush to "paint" a fence or the school building. A variety of objects can be put together to make a boat that floats. (Aluminum foil works well for this.) Creative cleanup can be developed by children as they find how water, tools, and materials can help them clean up messes.

## Playing with a Hose
A child enjoys playing with a hose connected to an outlet with the water on strong. The children learn about what happens when they put their thumbs over the nozzle. They discover the push effect as water leaves the hose. They make rain by sprinkling water into the air. They create a rainbow. They hear different sounds as the water strikes different materials.

For a realistic gas-pump hose to use outdoors with riding toys, fit an old piece of garden hose with a pistol-grip nozzle. These nozzles are available at hardware stores.

## Driver's Licenses
Make "driver's licenses" for children to use on their riding toys. String cards on loops of yarn for children to wear when riding toys. Have the children pass their "driver's test" by showing how they can safely ride the toy, bike, etc. Once they have passed, they then wear their "driver's license" when playing with the riding toys. They'll be more likely to follow safety rules if they know that their licenses can be "suspended" for "reckless driving."

## Building with Sand, Mud, and Clay
Children use large muscles to build sand mounds with moats around them. Sand pies and sand forts can be built in a sandbox, on a sand table, or at the seashore. Children use mud to make large structures. Clay is also used to create structures and shapes.

## Creative Play with Blocks
Large, hollow blocks can be used to build a city, grocery store, beauty parlor, bridge, tall tower, and many other structures.

## Using Empty Cartons
Many children receive toys that come in large cartons. After a short time, many of these children put aside the fancy toys and play with the empty cartons. In view of this, it makes sense to provide such boxes for children to play with. The boxes can be used in many creative ways—they can be arranged into trains, they can serve as houses and stores; they can be used as a cave or hideaway. Children can paint the outsides and insides.

## Using Children's Literature
Poetry and stories are other good sources of creative play for children that promote large motor development. Poems should be read to the children first, allowing them to hear the rhyme. Then the children can act them out, either as the teacher repeats them or as the children themselves say them. Some poems suitable for developing large muscles are presented below.

**Balloon**
I'm a bright red balloon that is little and flat,
I'm being blown up, what do you think of that?
Away I will fly,
Up to the sky,
Pop—now I'm small,
It was fun being tall.

**Weather**
*Swish* goes the wind,
It makes the leaves *fly*.
Whoops, there's *thunder* and *lightning* up *high*.
*Down* comes the *rain*,
In buckets so *big*.
In a near farm, it's just cleaned a *pig*.
Out comes the *sun,* so yellow and bright.
It's drying the wetness with all of its might.

## Suggested Activities for Small-Muscle Development
Many of the following activities may be used most effectively with older children three to five years old.

## What Can You Make?
Given some nails, wood, a small saw, and a hammer, a child can create a new toy or a game. The child can create something that serves a special purpose, such as a toothbrush holder or a stand to support a broom.

*Using Sand and Water*
Building a city out of sand, using different cookie shapes, is a creative way to play. Lakes and roads can be added around and in the city, using waxed paper or aluminum foil. Children can then try to draw a picture of their city, using crayons or felt-tip pens.

## UNIT REVIEW

1. List the four areas of development that are enhanced by play activities.
2. Explain the sequence in which play develops and the characteristics for each stage.
3. Describe and compare the characteristics of play for an infant, toddler, two-and-a-half-year-old, and four-year-old.

## ADDITIONAL READINGS

Bruner, J.S. "The Ontogenesis of Speech Acts." *Journal of Child Language* 2 (1975): 1–19.

Caldwell, B.M. "Parent-Child Play. A Playful Evaluation." In C.C. Brown and A.W. Gottfried, eds, *Play Interactions: The Role of Toys and Parental Involvement in Children's Development*. Pp. 167–178. Skillman, N.J.: Johnson & Johnson, 1985.

Church, E.B. "Moving Small, Moving Quiet." *Scholastic Pre-K Today.* (Feb., 1993): 42–45.

Dyson, A.H. "The Roots of Literacy Development: Play, Pictures, and Peers." In B. Scales, M. Almy, A. Nicolopoulou, and S. Ervin-Tripp, eds, *Play and the Social Context of Development in Early Care and Education*. Pp. 98–116. New York: Teachers College Press, 1991.

Eisner, "The Role of Art and Play in Children's Cognitive Development." In E. Klugman and S. Smilansky, eds., *Children's Play and Learning: Perspectives and Policy Implications*. Pp. 43–56. New York: Teachers College Press, 1990.

Ervin-Tripp, S. "Play and Language Development." In B. Scales, M. Almy, A. Nicolopoulou, and S. Ervin-Tripp, eds., *Play and the Social Context of Development in Early Care and Education*, pp. 84–97. New York: Teachers College Press, 1991.

Fagan, R. "Play and Behavioral Flexibility." In P.K. Smith, ed, *Play in Animals and Humans*. Pp. 159–173. New York: Blackwell, 1984.

Garvey, C. *Play: The Developing Child Series*. Cambridge, Mass.: Harvard University Press, 1990.

Jones, M. *Understanding Your Child Through Play*. New York: Prentice Hall, 1989.

Kagan, S.L. "Children's Play: The Journey from Theory to Practice." In E. Klugman and S. Smilansky, eds., *Children's Play and Learning: Perspectives and Policy Implications*. Pp. 173–185. New York: Teachers College Press, 1990.

Koplow, L. *Where Rag Dolls Hide Their Face: A Story of Troubled Children*. New York: E.P. Dutton, 1990.

Monighan-Nourot, P. "The Legacy of Play in American Early Childhood Education." In E. Klugman and S. Smilansky, eds., *Children's Play and Learning: Perspectives and Policy Implications*. Pp. 59–85. New York: Teachers College Press, 1990.

Piaget, J. *Play, Dreams, and Imitation in Childhood*. New York: W.W. Norton, 1962.

Rogers, C.S., and J.K. Sawyers. *Play in the Lives of Children*. Washington, D.C.: NAEYC, 1988.

Sawyer, J.K., and C.S. Rogers. *Helping Young Children Develop Through Play: A Practical Guide for Parents, Caregivers, and Teachers*. Washington, D.C.: NAEYC, 1991.

Smilansky, S., and L. Shefatya. "Facilitating Play: A Medium for Promoting Cognitive, Socioemotional and Academic Development in Young Children." Gaithersburg, Md.: Psychosocial and Educational Publications, 1990.

Stoy, M.C. *Spontaneous Play*. Albany, N.Y.: Delmar Publishers, Inc., 1990.

Zavitkovsky, D. *Listen to the Children*. Washington, D.C.: NAEYC, 1985.

# UNIT 15
## Dramatic Play and Puppetry

### OBJECTIVES

After studying this unit, you should be able to
- give the objectives of creative dramatics.
- list guidelines for working with young children in creative dramatics.
- list the items needed to assemble at least five kinds of puppets.
- discuss appropriate ways to use puppets in the early childhood program.

A disturbing sight in some early childhood settings is a small group of children tensely acting out a play. The lines are memorized and said in a stilted, artificial manner. The children feel and look out of place in the costumes they are wearing. They may be excited, but many are also frightened—afraid of tripping or spoiling the show. Adults can be found looking on and making remarks like ''Isn't that cute?'' Adult anxiety for the children is hidden by nervous laughter. An even more common response on the child's part is to say and do nothing, the safest way to avoid making a mistake in front of one's parents. This is not creative dramatics; it is a mistake. The error is made because the play is meant to please adults rather than to relate to children. It is a ''show-off'' when it should be a ''happening.''

Dramatic play is an excellent means for developing the creativity and imagination of young children, who have instinctive ways of dealing with reality. They need no written lines to memorize or structured behavior patterns to imitate to fantasize their world. What they do need is an interesting environment and freedom to experiment and be themselves.

One of the best ways children have to express themselves is through creative *dramatic play*. Here, they feel free to express their inner feelings. Often, teachers find out how children feel about themselves and others by listening to them as they carry out dramatic play. The pretending involved in such dra-

matic experiences, whether planned or totally spontaneous, is a necessary part of development. In the home center, with dramatic kits, and in other such activities children can act out feelings that often can't be expressed directly. For example, the child who is

**FIGURE 15–1 For young children, dramatic play might involve toys and equipment, or just the power of their imaginations.**

**FIGURE 15–2 Children enjoy many different types of creative dramatics, such as hand puppets.**

afraid of the doctor can express this fear by giving shots to dolls or stuffed animals in the home center. In a like manner, a child can act out with a friend a visit to the doctor. Thus, children can learn to deal with their anxieties as well as act out their fantasies through creative dramatic play.

**FIGURE 15–3 For creative dramatic play, children do not need very elaborate equipment to enjoy themselves.**

Through the imitation and make-believe of dramatic play, children sort out what they understand and gain a measure of mastery and control over events they've witnessed or taken part in—making breakfast, going to work, taking care of baby, going to the doctor. The logic and meaning of these events often escapes young children, but dramatic play helps them enter and begin to make sense of the exciting world of adults.

Many times creative dramatics begins with one child, and others soon join in. Playing store with a storekeeper and a number of customers is a form of creative dramatic play. Speaking on a toy telephone to a friend is another form. Puppet shows in which children use finger puppets and make up a story as they go along is still another form. By pretending that a coaster is a car, a train, or an airplane, children can take an imaginary trip. They can make up and act out stories for other children as part of creative dramatics. They can listen to music and tell what they see in their mind as they hear the music. They can even make up a story about the music. Then each child, in turn, can add to the story.

The use of simple props, costumes, and puppets can enhance children's dramatic play. Figure 15–4 contains several suggestions on child-made hats which are fun props for dramatic play. Although an audience can heighten children's enjoyment of drama, the emphasis has to be on their personal creativity.

Dramatic play occurs daily in the lives of young children. It is one of the ways that children naturally learn. They constantly imitate the people, animals, and machines in their world. They begin to put on their parents' slippers at 20 months of age. They enjoy re-creating the exciting experiences of their lives. Dramatic play is their way of understanding and dealing with the world.

The dramatic play of most children progresses through three themes. The first theme is domestic scenes. Children in the home living center who cook, clean, and care for the dolls are exploring domestic situations. They are role-playing from experience. The second theme is rescue. The "family" is busy in the housekeeping center when suddenly the doll becomes sick or the daddy has a flat tire and cannot

## BUNNY HAT

Cut strips of construction paper into rabbit ear shapes. Staple to paper band and fit to child's head. Children can color and decorate ears with crayons and markers.

## PARTY HAT

Use a small paper bag. Gather the bottom of the bag with a string, after the child has decorated the bag with crayons and markers.

## KING OR QUEEN HAT

Cut crown shape out of 8″ × 11″ construction paper. Have children decorate. Add "King John" (child's name) or Queen Suzie, if desired, on the crown.

## PAPER BAG ANIMALS

Cut ears out of construction paper. Using a large paper bag, cut out a space for the child's face. Glue ears to the bag.

## EASTER BONNET

Use a paper plate to decorate with ribbon scraps, flowers, and decorations of every and any kind. Attach pieces of yarn or ribbon to the sides of the paper plate so the child can tie on the hat.

## FIREMAN HAT

Using an 18″ × 24″ sized piece of red construction paper, cut out an oval shape. On the inside, cut an inner circle, which will be the front of the hat. It might help to trace the circles and have the child cut them out. Child's head size determines the size of the inner circle, which should fit the child's head.

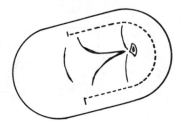

**FIGURE 15–4 Child-made hats for dramatic play props.**

VALENTINE HAT
Glue hearts onto a construction paper band, then fasten it at the size that will fit the child's head.

CLOWN HAT
Cut a slit in a paper plate from the center to the edge. Decorate the plate with crayons and markers. Paste (or tape or staple) into a cone shape. Attach yarn or ribbon pieces to the ends to tie on as a hat.

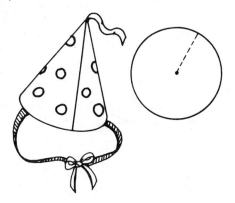

**FIGURE 15–4 (cont.)**

get to work. The children have to solve the problem. Often the most socially mature children will introduce the conflict and solve it as the rescue theme begins to emerge in role-play. The third theme is sudden threat. Monsters come out from under beds as the mother is sweeping, or a mean animal chases the children as they play outside (Kostelnik, Whiren, and Stein, 1986).

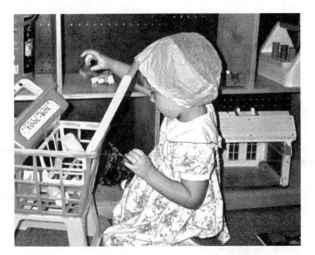

**FIGURE 15–5 In dramatic play, children play a variety of roles.**

Once children have played through these themes, they go back and forth through them to satisfy their play needs. One theme may interest them more, and they may spend a great amount of time engaging in that role-play situation. Children's age does not influence the themes they play out as much as opportunities they have had to engage in any dramatic play. One of the best ways to stimulate spontaneous drama is to provide young children with some simple props and the freedom to experiment.

## MATERIALS FOR DRAMATIC PLAY

Teachers of young children can help encourage children's dramatic play by providing kits containing "props" for them to use. Dramatic play kits are created by assembling a variety of available everyday items into groups that have a common use or theme. Children can select the props and use them in groups or alone to play roles or create games. Just letting the children know about the use of these kits is often enough to get them started. Materials for these dramatic kits can be kept together in shoe boxes or other containers. Some common types of dramatic play kits follow.

**FIGURE 15–6 Dramatic play may begin with the addition of special props such as a playhouse.**

*Supermarket.* Old cash register, play money, paper pads, pencils or crayons, punchers, paper sacks, empty food cartons, wax food, grocery boxes, cans with smooth edges.

*Post office.* Index card file, stamp pads, stampers, crayons, pencils, old Christmas seals, old envelopes.

*Beauty parlor.* Plastic brushes, combs, makeup, cotton balls, scarves, clip-on rollers, colored water in nail polish bottles, empty hair spray cans, wigs, and play money.

*Cooking.* Pots pans, eggbeaters, spoons, pitchers, salt and flour shakers, medicine bottles with colored water, tablecloth, aprons.

*Cleaning.* Small brooms, mops, cake of soap, sponges, toweling, plastic spray bottle, plastic basin, clothesline, clothespins, doll clothes to wash.

*Doctor.* Tongue depressors, old stethoscope, satchel, adhesive bandages, cotton balls, uniforms, discarded plastic hypo syringes without needles (available from clinics and should be boiled).

*Mail carrier.* Hats, badges, envelopes, mail satchel.

*Fire fighter.* Hats, raincoats, badge, boots, short lengths of garden hose.

*Farmer.* Shovel, rake, hoe, seeds.

*Plumber.* Wrench, plastic pipes, tool kit.

*Gas station attendant.* Shirt, hat, tire pump, boxes for cars.

*House painter.* Paint cans full of water, brushes of different sizes, drop cloth, painter's hat.

*Grocer.* Paper bags, toy cash register, shelves, empty cans, food boxes and cartons, balance scale, apron, and either hand bell or buzzer. (A bell lets people in for a visit, calls a store clerk for service, or announces a sale!)

*Entertainer.* Records, record player, musical instruments, costumes, makeup.

Many more dramatic play kits can be added to this list. It is important to encourage both boys and girls to assume a variety of roles. Imagination can also be used to transform regular classroom items into "new materials." Chairs can become trains, cars, boats, or a house. A table covered with a blanket or bedspread becomes a cave or special hiding place. Large cardboard cartons that children can decorate become houses, forts, fire stations, and telephone booths.

## GUIDELINES FOR PROMOTING DRAMATIC PLAY EXPERIENCES*

Young children's dramatic play may be encouraged even more by keeping in mind the following guidelines for dramatic play experiences:

*Adapted from *Learning Activities for the Young Preschool Child* by Rita Watrin and Paul Hanly Furfey. Copyright © 1978 by Litton Educational Publishing, Inc. Reprinted by permission of Wadsworth Publishing Company, Belmont, California 94002.

# THIS ONE'S FOR YOU!

## ADD SOME VARIETY WITH THESE IDEAS

Add some variety to the housekeeping or dramatic play center. Remodel this center as a post office.

A discarded box can be cut for a mailbox. In addition to the slot to insert the mail, be sure to add a door near the bottom of the back side for the mail to be retrieved.

Delivery bags can be made from paper grocery bags. Cut a strip about two inches wide from the top of the bag. Split this strip across the narrow part and staple each end to the top of the bag to form a strap. The bag may be decorated and personalized with crayons or markers.

Supplies to collect are newsprint in a variety of sizes, rubber stamps, and pencils. If the contents of "junk" mail have been saved, you will have a wonderful collection of printed envelopes and colorful stickers at no cost. This activity provides many opportunities to use language and develop several fine motor skills. The children will be writing, folding, licking, and sticking their special letters. A trip to a real post office is a good addition to this activity. As a follow-up, children can mail their own "letters" to their families. These can be drawings, designs, and anything the child would like to send home via the mail.

1. *Select a simple idea for the dramatic play of a particular child from the child's past experiences.* To pretend to do something, the child must have already experienced first hand (or on television or through stories and pictures) the concepts and roles used in dramatic play. His *everyday life* is the best source of such ideas.

2. *Do not allow too much time to elapse between the original experience and the follow-up dramatic play.* If the experience is not repeated often in the child's everyday life, help the child recall the original experience before introducing the activity. Appropriate pictures or a story are often helpful in refreshing the child's memory not only of an experience but also of his original interest in and enjoyment of it.

3. *Set the stage with a few simple but fairly realistic props.* Elaborate, expensive toys are not the key to success. Their charm is usually lost on children. A box with a homemade doll's pillow and a piece of terry cloth will do just as well as a fancy toy crib and bed clothing.

4. *Do not overplan.* Remember the key words *flexibility* and *freedom.* The child must be free to introduce his own ideas into the role playing. You must be flexible enough to follow his leads. Moreover, spontaneous ideas often work better than rehearsed ones. And don't be afraid to humor things you might find ridiculous. In other words, relax, enjoy the activity yourself; that helps the child enjoy it, too.

5. *Start the role playing by taking part in it.* Keep your part simple so that the child (especially very young children) can at least imitate your ideas. It is even more important for him to use these ideas as stepping stones to spontaneous role playing of his own. Avoid telling the child directly and specifically what he should pretend to do, but use role playing to make suggestions. For example, in playing family roles, as the "daddy" you might say, "Should Daddy put the baby to bed now?" or "It is time for baby's nap. Mommy, do you have time to put baby to bed?"

6. *Once the playing gets going, reduce your participation.* The more the child takes over and the more you can stand back, supplying adult support and an

appreciative audience for the child, the more effective is the activity in promoting the values of spontaneous dramatic play for the child. If the child runs out of ideas, you may then want to step back into your role and come up with another idea.

7. *In general, keep the dramatic play and game activities short,* especially for young children, whose attention may last for only a few minutes. If the children show considerable interest, continue the activity longer, but always cut it off at the first sign of disinterest or fatigue. If the children show no interest in a proposed activity or simply become your audience, stop and try the same idea or another idea at a later time.

8. *In both dramatic play and game playing, do not force a child to participate.* If you are working with a small group of children, let an unwilling child watch from the sidelines. He may change his mind when he sees the fun or builds up his own confidence. So after a few minutes of play, invite him again to join the group or tell him he can join the group whenever he is ready.

## DRAMATIC PLAY AND LANGUAGE LEARNING

Dramatic play is an important medium for language learning, helping children develop fluency in language. A child who is reluctant to speak in other situations is almost compelled to speak in order to be included in dramatic play. As play becomes elaborate, a child's language becomes more complex. When children talk with each other in a nondirective setting, like the housekeeping center, it is possible for the flow and quality of language to develop. If others are to understand her role, a child needs to explain what she is doing so that her friends will respond in appropriate ways. If she is to understand what they are doing, she must listen.

When children become involved in complex make-believe, they need to listen and respond to each other. A child speaks convincingly to others when she wants them to change the nature of the play. If they still do not understand, she may try to

find other ways to persuade them. When she needs to elaborate on her ideas, she is likely to use a longer sequence of words and move from two words to more complex syntax. It was not too many months ago when Barb said, "Baby hungry," as she prepared food and fed her doll. Now she says, "I am making eggs for baby's breakfast."

As children play together they learn new words from each other. At their make-believe restaurant, Maria prepared tacos and Justin ordered fruitcake from the menu. Justin liked the sound of the new word, "tacos." He pretended he was eating one, even though he did not know what a "taco" was.

As children play, they repeat words and phrases they have learned and enjoy saying them. They name objects, talk about what they are doing, and plan as they go along. They begin to recognize the importance of planning and take time to formulate more detailed plans for their dramatizations.

## DRAMATIC PLAY IN THE HOME (OR HOUSEKEEPING) CENTER

One of the best places for children to express themselves in creative, dramatic play is the housekeeping or home center. Here, in a child-sized version of the world, children are free and safe to express how they feel about themselves and others. While they carry out dramatic play in the housekeeping center, they can pretend to be many different kinds of people, "trying on," so to speak, many social roles. (Figure 15–7 presents a summary of basic home center activities and equipment.)

The home living (housekeeping) and creative dramatics center provides endless opportunities for the teacher as a facilitator of learning to broaden a child's horizon. The center can be decorated and rearranged to represent an area that pertains to a specific content. Possibilities include creating a home, hospital, post office, grocery store, and more. The change of seasons as well as certain holidays can be easily incorporated in this center. For example, during fall, a child's rake, batons, sweaters, and pom-poms might be included in the center. During the winter months, mufflers, mittens, a child's shovel, a

Activities in this center afford the child experiences in the following:

- Clarifying adult roles.
- Trying out social skills.
- Getting along with others.
- Sharing responsibilities.
- Making group decisions.
- Controlling impulsive behavior.

- Recognizing cause and effect.
- Developing positive attitudes about one's self and others.
- Enjoying the fantasy of the grown-up world.
- Using oral language spontaneously.
- Practicing the use of symbols, which are subskills in reading.
- Learning social ease and confidence in his own strengths.

---

Materials:*

| | | |
|---|---|---|
| Full-length mirror | dustpan, pail, sponge, rags, duster) | Postman's bag with letters |
| Stove | | Postman's hat |
| Refrigerator | Playdough | A variety of hats, dresses, shirts, |
| Sink | Bed (doll), doll carriage, baby | ties, belts, scarves, shoes, pock- |
| Closet or rack of clothes | highchair | etbooks, and jewelry |
| Cooking/eating utensils | Rocking chair | An old suitcase (for "trips") |
| Table and chairs | Empty cans, food boxes | A nurse's cap (hypodermic nee- |
| Tea set | Mirror/hand mirror | dles—minus needles—pill bot- |
| Telephone | Carriage | tles, a play thermometer) |
| Stethoscope | Dolls/doll clothes | Play money |
| Props for cleaning (broom, mop, | Iron/ironing board | An old briefcase |
| | Puppets | |

*Add objects as needed for special emphasis

**FIGURE 15–7 Suggested experiences and equipment for the home center.**

holiday apron, candles, candlesticks, and bells may be additions to the center. For spring, the teacher may add baskets, plastic, colored eggs, plastic or silk flowers, and variety of bonnets and hats. (See Figure 15–4 for suggestions on child-made hats.) The supplies in the housekeeping center should reflect the activities in the classroom and extend the skills being taught elsewhere in the room, as well as introduce new skills. Be sure to include clothing, dishes, and dolls that are familiar and represent each of the ethnic groups in your classroom.

It is important to emphasize a nonsexist approach in teaching, especially in the housekeeping area. For example, boys' dramatic play must be encouraged in an early childhood program as much as the girls'. A good tactic to encourage boys' participation is to change themes of the dramatic play corner to topics that interest the boys, such as restaurant, doctor, boat, etc. An observant teacher, sensitive to both sexes' dramatic play and developing sex-role concepts, even gives cues that encourage *all* children to play in *all* centers. "John, I'm sure that coffee you're making will be *delicious.* Be sure to serve me some, too." Entering into the child's dramatic play in this way, the teacher gives subtle instruction in a nonintrusive way, respecting the child's dramatic experience at that moment.

In the home center dramatic experience often begins with one child, and others soon join in. In observing dramatic play in the home center, with children of various ages, you can see definite age differences in their dramatic play. Younger children two to four years old generally are involved in such dramatic play for a much briefer period of time than children five years and older. Before the child is two years old, for example, he may say "Nice baby" when he hugs a doll and then move on. After the age of two, the child's dramatic play may begin to combine several ideas, in contrast to the single-idea dramatization of the younger child. The older child may hold a doll and pretend to feed the "baby" his cookie, perhaps saying, "Eat, baby. Eat, nice baby." Or he may decide to put the baby to bed, covering the doll with a blanket because it is time for "baby to take a nap." This process of imitating what has been observed is called modeling (Smith, 1982).

Instances of such modeling behavior in the home center and elsewhere are even more prevalent in older children. For example, a five-year-old will feed the baby, discussing why milk was good for him, telling him it was nap time, and that children must "be good" and listen to their parents. This dramatization is in marked contrast to that of the two-year-old.

**Equipment in the Home Center.** In the early stages of dramatic play, the child is apt to need fairly realistic props. He experiences the world as it is. Whereas an older, more experienced child might simply use "pretend food" to feed the "baby," the younger child usually needs the real object to spark the imagination. (Suggested materials for the housekeeping center are found in Figure 15–7.) To distinguish between real and pretend may also be difficult for the young child. For example, early first experiences with pretend cookies made from play dough may include actually trying to eat them.

Children involved in dramatic play also use materials from various parts of the room to support their play. For example, a child who needs some pretend money to put in her purse may decide to make some in the art area, or she might go to the manipulative area to gather beads, chips, or even puzzle pieces to use as money.

Whether they are searching for materials or on their way to another related location, it is perfectly natural and appropriate for children involved in dramatic play to move about the entire space as part of their play. Confining role players and pretenders to one area or part of the room frustrates rather than supports their intentions. When their use of space

and materials conflicts with other children's use of space and materials, the opportunity for group problem-solving arises.

Remember also to provide outdoor materials and equipment for pretending and role play. With more space and fewer boundaries, outdoor dramatic play is often robust and highly mobile. Children will make use of anything available—wagons, tricycles, and other wheeled toys for cars, buses, trains, and boats; large packing boxes, boards, sheets, ropes, and tires for houses, stores, forts, and caves; sand and sand utensils for cooking, eating, and building. They may also enjoy the addition of some "indoor" materials (hats, scarves, baby dolls, dishes, chalk) to their outdoor dramatic play.

## PUPPETS*

Puppets can be used for almost any of the dramatic experiences that have been described here. They offer the child two ways to express creativity: (1) the artistic experience of making the puppet, and (2) making the puppet come to life. Many kinds of puppets are suitable for use by young children.

Puppets fascinate and involve children in a way that few other art forms can, because they allow children to enter the world of fantasy and drama so easily. In this magic world, children are free to create whatever is needed right then in their lives. Children enjoy puppets because they provide this variety and because puppets put a little distance between the children and roles that may be too frightening for them. Because puppets often reveal the inner world of the child, a great deal can be learned through puppetry.

**Using Puppets.** The use of puppets usually begins in the nursery or preschool, where they are invaluable when readily available for dramatic play. Teachers can teach fingerplays with simple finger puppets;

---

*Portions of this section adapted from the book *The Magic of Puppetry: A Guide for Those Working with Young Children*, by Peggy Davison Jenkins. © 1980 by Prentice-Hall, Inc. Published by Prentice-Hall, Inc., Englewood Cliffs, N.J. 07632. Used with permission.

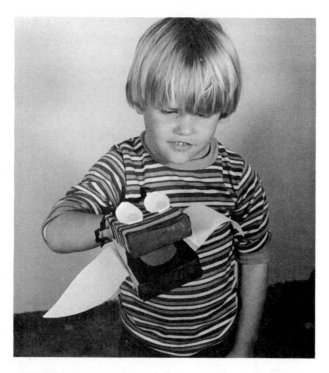

FIGURE 15–8 A hand puppet can help a child express feelings in a safe, nonthreatening way.

FIGURE 15–9 Making finger puppets "come to life" is one dramatic play activity that helps children express their creativity.

hand puppets can act out familiar nursery rhymes. Music time is enhanced by a puppet leading the singing and other puppets joining in. The shy child who is reluctant to sing often will participate enthusiastically through a puppet. Puppets are also excellent for concept teaching and can help clarify abstract concepts and demonstrate concrete concepts. For instance, in the preschool the concepts of "above," "below," "behind," "in front of," and so on can be clearly shown with the puppet. With older children, puppets can help illustrate concepts such as self-esteem, friendship, and creative thinking. The more important an idea is, the more the teacher might consider using a puppet to get it across.

Puppetry, as a form of dramatic play, is a sure means of stimulating creative storytelling in younger ones. Some teachers tape-record spontaneous puppet skits and, by writing them down, show the children how they have created a story.

In a room with a climate of flexibility and freedom, the children are bound to come up with countless other ideas for using their puppets, in addition to the following:

- Put together a puppet center—Puppet Stuff Box, prop box, and theater for children to use during free time.
- If some children enjoy making puppets more than using them, or vice versa, allow for such individual preferences. All children do not have to be doing the same thing.
- Provide a home for each child's puppet, a box in which the puppet can have additional costumes and props. Let the child fix it up to his or her own satisfaction.
- Consider having a specific puppet for each center area. This puppet could remind the class that it's music time, for instance, and be used to give directions and explain new concepts. If the puppet has trouble in an area, the children could teach it and straighten out its confusion. Through such dra-

matic experiences, self-confidence and skills are strengthened.

- Puppets are used for praise in various ways by teachers. In one room, "Fanny Tastic" chooses one child each day to honor in some special way. In others, the praise puppet is an astute observer and ends the day with statements like, "I especially liked the way Rick helped Johnny clean up after painting today" (Jenkins, 1980).

- Self-introductions in the first days of school are more comfortable when they are done through a puppet. Children choose a puppet from the box, and then the puppet and child talk together to get aquainted. Then, going around the room, the teacher calls on the puppet to introduce its new friend to the class.

- Puppets are very popular with teachers as mood indicators. A kindergarten teacher uses paper-plate stick puppets with the following expressions for many of her "feeling" activities:

HAPPY    MAD    SURPRISED    SAD

The child chooses a puppet to use and then tells why he is feeling that way. "How do you feel when . . . ?" situations are proposed, and a child chooses a puppet to respond with. In some classrooms every child has a "happy" and "sad" puppet at his or her desk. It has a happy face on one side of the paper cup or plate head and a sad face on the other. Feelings are indicated by the side that is revealed.

- A Surprise Box Puppet is popular in one classroom. Each week it is responsible for bringing something new and interesting to its surprise box. Sometimes the "Twenty Questions" game leads up to revealing the surprise (Jenkins, 1980).

- Felt boards and puppets work well together. A puppet with hands can effectively help the adult or child put pieces on or take them off the felt board. One teacher who was teaching toddlers the parts of the face used a rather "stupid" puppet that kept making mistakes by putting the parts in the wrong place. The children had a lot of fun correcting it.

- Phonics puppets are good to use in kindergarten classrooms. The teacher can have one for each letter, and the puppet can only say words beginning with its letter or eat foods starting with its letter. For example, "Larry Lion loves licking licorice lollipops." Andy Alligator brings an apple, avocado, and asparagus for the children.

- Puppets enliven science experiments by discussing them or performing simple ones. Puppets can be used in the natural sciences to represent the elements in a particular environment, such as air or water.

- In teaching music, teachers find that puppets help students develop a feeling for rhythm and music interpretation by moving the puppets to the beat. They also encourage reluctant children to sing, since the puppet does the singing and not the child. Puppets with moving mouths are most effective but not necessary. One preschool teacher had great success getting shy children to sing through decorated toliet-paper tubes that represented the mouths of animals (Hunter, 1977).

- Social studies is a natural area for puppets; it presents countless opportunities to dramatize holiday customs, represent particular cultural groups being studied, or portray the roles of various community helpers.

- Reading via a puppet brings results. One special-education teacher found that her students who disliked reading were able to read a little more easily and a lot more happily with a puppet on the hand (Hunter, 1977).

These suggestions are simply intended to be idea starters. The use of puppets in the classroom is limited only by your attitude and imagination.

**Kinds of Puppets.** Some of the most common and easiest puppets to make are stick puppets, shadow puppets, hand puppets, finger puppets, people puppets, wooden spoon puppets, mitten and sock puppets, paper-plate puppets, play dough puppets, Styrofoam ball puppets, vegetable (fruit) puppets, Ping-Pong ball puppets, and cylinder puppets.

*Stick puppets.* The simplest of all puppets, stick puppets are controlled by a single stick (any slim, rigid support) that goes up inside the puppet or is attached to the back of it.

Stick puppets are fun and easy to make. The teacher can use some sticks from the lumber yard, large twigs, or wood popsicle sticks. With this type of puppet, the child puts a bag or piece of cloth over the stick and stuffs the bag or cloth with wads of newspaper or cotton. The child then ties the top of the bag to the stick, making a head. A rubber band may be used instead of string to form a head.

The child can then paint the head or make a face with crayons or colored paper and paste. Scrap yarn, wood shavings, and buttons are also good materials for the puppet's face. A body can be made by adding a dress cut out of paper and stapled to the stick. Scrap pieces of fabric can be used to "dress" the puppet; wallpaper samples are an inexpensive material for puppets' clothes.

With the stick, the puppet is moved around the stage or turned from side to side. It has the advantage of being a good first puppet for preschoolers, since a stick can be attached to any little doll, toy animal, cutout figure, fruit, or vegetable, and the puppet is easy to operate.

*Bag puppets.* The common paper bag in any size makes a good puppet for young preschoolers. The bags are stuffed with wads of newspaper and stapled or glued shut. A body is made with a second bag stapled to the first, leaving room for the child's hand to slip in and work the puppet.

A face can be made with paint, crayons, or colored paper and paste. Odds and ends are fun to use for the face, too. Buttons make eyes; crumpled tissue, a

**FIGURE 15–10 A stick puppet is a good prop for dramatic play.**

**FIGURE 15–11 A puppet is easy to make out of everyday items like a paper bag, some bits of cloth, yarn, ribbons, and buttons.**

nose; yarn, hair. The search for the right odds and ends to make the puppet is as much fun as using the finished puppet later.

*Shadow puppets.* These puppets are figures that appear on a screen due to the arrangement of light behind them. They are usually flat, cutout figures made of cardboard or other heavy material. Usually they are attached to a stick like a stick puppet, dangled from a stick by means of a thread, or moved by a wire attached at right angles to the puppet. Hand shadows also make a type of shadow puppet. Shadow puppets have great appeal, and a single puppet can take on many sizes and shapes through a change in the position of the light or the puppet.

*Hand puppets.* Frequently called glove or mitten puppets, these are the most popular for young children. There are many types of hand puppets, but most can be classified into two general groups: (1) those with moving mouths, and (2) those with moving hands.

**FINGER-LEG**

**FINGER-CAP**

**FINGER-FACE**

**FIGURE 15–13 There are many different kinds of finger puppets.**

**FIGURE 15–12 Paper bag hand puppet.**

The first (with moving mouths) is any sort of hand covering—a handkerchief, a sock, a mitten, a paper bag—inside of which one's fingers open and shut, forming the mouth of the puppet. The second kind has a head and two hands and is operated by putting one or two fingers in the head and one in each hand. This kind of puppet can freely pick up objects and make hand motions, thus putting more realism into a performance. The moving-mouth hand puppet, however, has the advantage of being able to "talk." (Recycle small plastic detergent bottles for a hand puppet rack. Bolt these small detergent bottles to scrap lumber and your puppets will have a "home."

# Detergent Bottle Puppet Rack

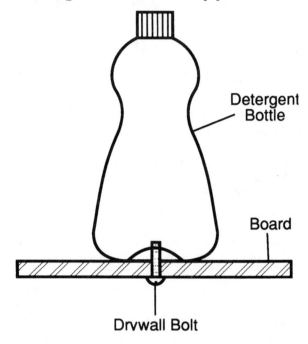

**FIGURE 15–14 Detergent bottle puppet rack.**

*Finger puppets.* The three general types of finger puppets are the following:

- *Finger-leg.* Finger puppet in which two fingers (usually the index and middle fingers) serve as the puppet's legs.
- *Finger-cap.* Finger puppet that slips over an individual finger.
- *Finger-face.* Puppet made by drawing a face on a finger with a felt pen. Usually, one can perform with quite a few puppets of this type at one time. They are great for fingerplays! (See end of unit for fingerplay suggestions.)

Some advantages of finger puppets include the following:

- They are easy to manipulate, even by a toddler.
- They encourage small-muscle action.
- They are inexpensive to make.

- One child alone can put on a performance with an "entire cast."
- They maintain interest because they are always easy and quick to make.
- They can be made in spare moments, since materials are small and mobile.

*Wooden spoon puppets.* You will need wooden spoons, yarn, string, material scraps, glue, and construction paper. Draw a face on the wooden spoon. Glue on yarn, string for hair, and scraps of material for clothing.

*Two-faced (paper-plate) puppets.* Draw a face on the back of each paper plate. Add features with various types of materials. Insert a stick between the paper plates and glue it into place. Staple edges together.

*Milk carton puppets.* Cut through the center of a half-pint–sized milk carton. Cut three sides only. Do not cut the fourth side. Fold the carton in half (the uncut side becomes the hinge). Cut facial features from colored paper and paste them to the carton. Add string or yarn for special emphasis. To operate the puppet, place four fingers in the top section and the thumb in the lower section. Spreading and closing the hand makes the puppet's mouth open and shut.

*Play dough puppets.* Place a small amount of play dough onto a finger. Mold play dough into a face shape covering the finger. Add raisins, cereal, toothpicks, etc., for facial features and added emphasis.

*Styrofoam ball puppets.* Insert a stick into a Styrofoam ball. Cover the Styrofoam ball with fabric. Tie the fabric around the stick. Glue on buttons and felt scraps for facial features.

*Ping-Pong ball puppets.* Cut an X shape out of a ball. Place a piece of lightweight fabric on finger. Cover the area of the ball with sturdy glue. Force ball at the X onto the fabric on finger. While the glue is drying, draw or paste face onto puppet.

*Sock puppet.* Pull sock over hand. Glue, sew, or paint facial features onto toe of sock, or decorate as desired.

*Finger Puppets from gloves.* Recycle stray gloves. Cut off the fingers and use them for finger puppets. To keep the ends from unraveling, lightly coat them with white glue, or use a commercial product called Fray-Check®. Fray-Check is available at craft or hobby stores. Recycle old rubber gloves, too, by drawing features on rubber glove fingers with marking pens.

*Paper towel hand puppets.* Thick, spongy paper towels can be cut out and sewn into mitten shapes for hand puppets. Slip cardboard inside the mitten before decorating them with markers so color won't soak through.

*Vegetable puppet.* Force potato, turnip, or carrot onto a stick or dowel. Pin, glue, or paint characteristics onto the vegetable.

*Cardboard cylinder puppet.* Place a cardboard cylinder, from paper towels or toilet tissue, over the fingers. Decorate with desired features. The cylinder could be used for the body, and a Styrofoam ball or Ping-Pong ball could be placed on the top for the head. Decorate as desired.

*Old mitten puppets.* A child can slip his hand into an old mitten and make the puppet "talk" by moving his thumb up and down against his four fingers. You might sew or glue on two buttons near the top for eyes, another for the nose, and a slip of colored paper for the mouth.

*People puppets.* Also called "humanettes," these are half person, half puppet. The easiest people puppet for children is a large paper sack put over the head. Holes are cut out for the eyes, and facial features and decorations are added with paint or paper and paste. The bags can be turned up slightly above the shoulder or cut away on the sides for arm holes. People puppets make a natural transition from puppetry to creative drama. Also, shy children generally feel more protected behind this kind of puppet than all the other types (Jenkins, 1980). Be sure not to force a child to use this type of puppet if he doesn't like his head covered!

**FIGURE 15–15 People puppets, or humanettes, are half-person, half-puppet.**

## ROLE PLAYING

One final technique to encourage the development of young children's imagination in dramatic play is through role playing.

Pictures can be an excellent starting point for experiments with role playing. A picture showing action or conversation between two or more people can be used, and it is helpful if one of them is a child.

Show a picture of a doctor talking with a young child. While showing the picture, ask questions to create a thinking atmosphere. "Who are the people? (doctor, patient) Where are they? What are they doing? What is the child saying? How does the child feel? What is the doctor saying? What do you think happens next?"

Choose volunteers to be the doctor and the child. The children take the places of the people in the picture. They almost "step into the picture" as they begin to speak and act the roles of the doctor and the child. When these volunteers have finished, other children can demonstrate their views of the same scene. Some children may think the child in the picture is sick. Some may see the doctor as the child's father. Some may think the doctor is telling the child about a brother or sister. All interpretations are new creative opportunities.

The teacher can change the pictures used to create more role-playing situations, but a picture is not always needed for role playing. The reading of a story can be stopped midway, and the children can act out its finish. Children can role-play their dreams. Television programs and movies are other good stimulators.

Role playing is also a way to help children see the viewpoints of other people. When feelings and emotions come out, sensitive and open discussions after the role playing can offer new insights and learning experiences. This is a good way to help young children explore their feelings and find ways to handle their emotions and their relationships with others.

## SUMMARY

Drama is an excellent means for developing creativity and imagination in young children when it is related to the child's personal sense of reality without imposed adult standards. Dramatic play kits are easy to make and help develop opportunities for creative play. Role playing helps children explore their feelings. The use of puppets provides opportunities for creative movement, dramatics, and language development.

Other uses of puppets in the early childhood program include helping shy children express themselves, having children introduce themselves, and teaching new concepts in various areas. Types of puppets appropriate for use with young children are stick, shadow, finger, hand, people puppets (humanettes), vegetable, Ping-Pong ball, and Styrofoam puppets.

## LEARNING ACTIVITIES

A. Create two dramatic play kits not listed or suggested in this unit.
1. Try to make one that no one else might think of making.
2. Compare wih those of classmates.
B. Have some fun. Each class member is to bring in a picture of two people (in any situation). Put all the pictures in a common pile. By random selection, have class members in sets of two select a picture and role-play it for five minutes.
C. Make up a play kit of "props" children might use in one of the listed activities.
1. Playing mail carrier.
2. Playing dentist.
3. Playing airline pilot.
4. Playing waitress/waiter.
D. Make one of the types of puppets discussed in this unit. Demonstrate its use to your classmates before you use it with children. Describe how you plan to use the puppet with children in the future.
E. If you had $50 to spend for drama equipment in setting up a new room in your first year of teaching, what would you buy and why? Itemize each purchase, and give at least three uses for each item. You may use a school supply catalog for assistance in your purchasing.

F. Field Work Assignment:
Observe in two early childhood rooms. What roles did you observe children playing in dramatic activities? How do you think these roles are related to children's real-life experiences? Explain.

Consult the teacher in each of the two rooms you observed to learn how information obtained through observing children's dramatic play is utilized (if at all) in guiding children or in making future plans. Give examples.

In each of the rooms you observed, what limits were placed on children during dramatic play? How do you think these limits would change in an outdoor dramatic activity?
G. Make plans for bringing in new pieces of equipment, new props to help extend children's dramatic roles in each of the situations you observed. Bring them in, and then observe how children use these materials.
H. Use the children's book, *The Land of Many Colors* (New York: Scholastic Books, 1993), written by the Klamath County YMCA Family Preschool, as a starting point for a role-playing activity (both for you and the children). Written by a preschool class, the story of fighting among the purple people, green people, and blue people, and their eventual peace, all pro-

vide great scenarios for role playing. (Art activities are a natural tie-in with this book as well.)

I. Fingerplay for finger puppets

The following fingerplays are fun for you and the children to act out with their finger puppets.

### The Family
This is my father (Point to thumb)
This is my mother (Point to index finger)
This is my brother, tall (Point to middle finger)
This is my sister (Point to ring finger)
This is the baby (Point to little finger)
Oh! How we love them all! (Clasp hands)

### People
Big people, little people, (Hold thumb and index fingers apart horizontally, then close together)
Fat people, skinny. (Hold index fingers apart vertically; then close together)
Grumpy people, happy people, (Make appropriate facial expressions)
People who are grinny.
Rushy people, slow people,
(Walk fingers of one hand up and down other arm as rhyme indicates)
Walking up and down.
Babies in their carriages,
(Move one fist slowly up and down other arm)
Being pushed through town.

### Ten Little Firemen
Ten little firemen
Sleeping in a row; (Extend both hands, fingers curled, to represent sleeping men)
Ding dong goes the bell, (Pull bell cord with one hand)
And down the pole they go.
(Close both fists, put one arm on top of the other, slide them down pole)

Off on the engine, oh, oh, oh.
(Steer engine with hands)
Using the big hose, so, so, so.
(Make nozzle with fist)
When all the fire's out, home so-o slow.
(Steer engine with hands)
Back to bed, all in a row. (Extend both hands, fingers curled)

### Miss Polly's Dolly
Miss Polly had a dolly,
Who was sick, sick, sick.
(Rock dolly)
She called for the doctor to come
Quick, quick, quick. (Use telephone)

The doctor came with his bag (Swing arm)
And his hat (Touch forehead)
And he knocked on the door with a rat-atat-tat (Knock in air)

He looked at the dolly and he shook his head.
He said, "Miss Polly, put her right to bed." (Shake head and finger)
He wrote on his paper for a pill, pill, pill.
(Use hand and finger to write)
And said, "I'll be back in the morning with my bill, bill, bill!" (Wave goodbye)

### Five Little Girls
Five little girls woke up in their beds (Curl fingers of one hand loosely in palm)
This little girl jumped right out of bed. (Starting with thumb, let each finger pop up for one girl)
This little girl shook her curly head.
This little girl washed her sleepy face.
This little girl got all her clothes in place.
This little girl put on her shoes and socks.
And they all ran down to breakfast when the time was eight o'clock.
(All fingers run behind back)

# UNIT REVIEW

1. List the objectives of creative dramatics.
2. What are dramatic play kits? Give specific examples of some you would use in your classroom and what they would contain.
3. Discuss what you consider the early childhood teacher's role in children's dramatic play.
4. Do you feel that it is appropriate for the teacher to make special plans for children's dramatic play? Give examples in your explanation.
5. What are some important guidelines to remember when working with young children in creative dramatics?
6. List the items needed to make puppets for young children.
7. Discuss how to use puppets with young children.

# ADDITIONAL READINGS

Edwards, L.C. *Affective Development and the Creative Arts: A Process Approach to Early Childhood Education.* Columbus, Oh: Merrill-Macmillan, 1990.

Frazier, N., and N. Renfro. *Imagination: At Play with Puppets and Creative Drama.* Austin, Tx.: Nancy Renfro Studio, 1987.

Hohmann, M. *Young Learners in Action: A Manual for Preschool Education.* Ypsilanti, Mich.: High/Scope Preschool Curriculum, 1993.

Hunter, Lynn S. "Piscataway's Puppet Program." *School Library Journal* (May 1977): 89–97.

Jenkins, P.D. *The Magic of Puppetry: A Guide for Those Working with Young Children.* Englewood Cliffs, N.J.: Prentice-Hall, 1980.

Klamath County YMCA Family Preschool. *The Land of Many Colors.* New York: Scholastic, Inc., 1993.

Kostelnik, M.J., A.P. Whiren, and L.C. Stein, "Living with He-Men." *Young Children* 4 (1986): 3–9.

McCaslin, N. *Creative Drama in the Classroom.* New York: Longman, 1980.

Smilansky, S. "Sociodramatic Play: Its Relevance to Behavior and Achievement in School." In E. Klugman and S. Smilansky, Eds., *Children's Play and Learning.* Pp. 18–42. New York: Teachers College Press, 1990.

Watrin, R., and P.H. Furfey. *Learning Activities for the Young Preschool Child.* Belmont, Calif.: Wadsworth Publishing Co., 1978.

# P A R T   2

# Theory into Practice: Creative Activities for the Early Childhood Program

Infusing a creative approach into every area of early childhood curriculum is the focus of Part 2. Building and expanding on the theory presented in Part 1, the units in Part 2 cover several other phases of the early childhood curriculum in which a creative approach is appropriate. These curricular areas include movement, music, language arts, science, math, food experiences, social studies, and health and safety. Also included in Part 2 are numerous seasonal and holiday units containing a wealth of art activities, games, fingerplays, songs, and group projects.

All of the activities presented in Part 2 are based in developmental theory, yet are simple to reproduce and expand upon. All are presented in the hope that they will be adapted to children's individual needs, abilities, and interest levels. They are designed in this way to be springboards to many learning experiences limited only by the child's and teacher's imagination and creativity.

Unlike simple manipulation of media, such as pounding clay and finger painting, the activities offered in this section generally require more skill on the part of the children and more instruction (at least initially) by the teacher. They tend to have a more definite focus and direction, even though the teacher may meticulously avoid providing an actual model. In using these activities, there must be considerable latitude allowed for individual ideas to be expressed. For example, children might be left free to arrange their flowers in the May baskets any way they wish, or to stamp the Christmas paper in any pattern that appeals to them. To be successful, these activities usually require repeated presentation so that children can practice and gain skills in their manipulation of the materials. These activities should not be isolated attempts for special occasions only! These are valuable activities that provide opportunities for purposefulness and challenges to skills that children will appreciate. They also increase the variety of experiences available to young children in full-day centers.

In all units in Part 2 the teacher should *always* consider the development level of a child or a group of children before initiating any activitiy. The activities presented are appropriate for children three to six years of age, unless otherwise indicated. These activities should allow opportunities for direct involvement of the children with the materials. There should always be room for them to express their intentions and feelings (their own personal, creative selves), and they should not be concerned with *how* to use the materials above all else.

Finally, while guidance of a child's activities is appropriate, ***each child should be given the freedom to adapt these activities and the processes used to his or her own creative needs.*** In other words, the approach should not be "What is it?" but "Tell me about what you've made/drawn.'' Most important, emphasis in all activities should be on the *process* and not the end product. Thus, while diagrams and illustrations are given for many of the activities, it is *not* appropriate to assume that all of the children's (or *any* of the children's) finished products need to look like the examples given. The examples merely provide further clarification for the activity and serve as starting points for teachers and children to begin their creative process.

Rather than displaying a model or sample product at the beginning of an activity, have the children talk about their own ideas and plans for the activity. The beginning, middle, and end of every activity is the child—unique and singular in her own way.

**Section 6    Creative Activities in Other Curricular Areas**

**Section 7    Creative Activities Involving Holidays**

**Section 8    Creative Activities Involving Seasons**

# SECTION 6
# Creative Activities in Other Curricular Areas

# UNIT 16

# Creative Movement

## OBJECTIVES

After studying this unit, you should be able to
- discuss the importance of creative movement activities for young children.
- list creative movement activities that help children develop large and small muscles.
- discuss guidelines for providing creative movement activities for young children.

Young children learn by doing. They are immensely active and energetic. Movement activities are natural avenues for this energy.

Physical movement is the young child's first means of nonverbal communication. Closing her eyes, crying, shaking—a nonverbal infant very clearly communicates her need for attention! Physical movements provide one of the most important avenues through which a child forms impressions about herself and her environment.

For many years, movement has been a part of the curriculum for young children, often disguised by terms such as "rhythm." It continues to be an integral part of the total curriculum, reinforcing and extending concepts of math, language arts, science, social studies, and other basic areas. Movement can serve as a unifying factor and can enhance the interrelated nature of the curriculum (Sullivan, 1982, p. 3).

Movement activities contribute to the total physical, mental, social, and emotional growth and development of the child. Movement activity for children is as vital as art or music, for in movement activities, a young child acquires skills, knowledge, and attitudes that help her discover and understand her body and how it works, her physical abilities, and her limitations. Movement activities concern the whole child and not just physical fitness and recreation. And through creative movement activities a child is able to express her creative self in a very natural way.

## THE IMPORTANCE OF MOVEMENT ACTIVITIES FOR YOUNG CHILDREN

To adults, the word "exercise" calls to mind ominous visions of doing calisthenics and other unpleasant actions. Yet to a child, physical exercise is one of the activities nearest and dearest to her heart.

This is because the young child is busy acquiring all sorts of large and small motor skills during the early years of life. Her main learning strategy is through physical manipulation of her world. Movement activities, more than any other type of activity, offer children rich opportunities for the development of their total selves.

FIGURE 16–1 Movement activities contribute to the total physical, mental, social, and emotional growth and development of the child.

FIGURE 16–2 Painting to music is a popular movement activity.

There is usually no planning or forethought on the part of children in creative movement. They forget about themselves and let the music's rhythm or an idea carry their bodies away. There is no pattern of movements to be practiced or perfected. Young children are free to move about in any mood which the music or rhythm suggests to them.

Two main types of movement are *personal creative movement* and *functional/physical movement*. Personal creative movement is movement that reflects the mood or inner state of an individual, while functional/physical movement is movement which serves a practical purpose, such as fine muscle development (Lynch-Fraser, 1982). This unit focuses on both creative movement and functional/physical movement activities for young children.

**Creative Movement.** In creative movement, children are free to express their own personalities in their own style. They do not have an example to follow or an adult to imitate. Creative movement can occur in any situation where children feel free and want to move their bodies. It can be done to poetry, music, rhythm, or even silence. By feeling a pulse, beat, idea, or emotion, children's bodies become instruments of expression. They are musical notes running along a keyboard or wheat waving in the wind. They are anything they want to be. Their movement is an expression of that being.

The following scene depicts a good example of a creative movement experience:

In a room of three-year-olds, the teacher plays a tape of Debussy's "Children's Corner" during center time. The topic of the week in the class is "Butterflies and Other Things that Fly." At large group time, when teacher and all the children are sitting down together, the teacher tells the children she has a magic wand that can help them move and dance just like butterflies and other things that fly. She tells the children she will touch each of their heads with her magic wand and then they will become (pretend to be) butterflies, birds, bees, or anything else they want to be. The teacher reminds them that everything moves in its own special way. "Listen to the music and see how you can fly just like the butterflies and other things that fly, that we have been learning about this week." At that moment, she has the children stand and wait for the touch of the magic wand. She turns up the volume on the tape player so that it is a bit louder, and moves about, touching the children with her magic wand (Edward and Nabors, 1993).

The teacher in the preceding example taps into the children's imaginations as they move about the room in ways that feel good for them. She has given the children freedom to be expressive in personally meaningful ways. This teacher understands that creative movement experiences must be compatible with children's own basic knowledge of the world and their own basic ways of knowing how butterflies and other things that fly move about in space. This freedom to respond, which is basic to creative movement experiences, engages the children's imaginations and allows them to be flexible, fluent, and original. These children are engaged in their own uniqueness (Edwards and Nabors, 1993).

If creative movement is a regular part of the young child's curriculum, a number of objectives may be reached:

- Relaxation and freedom in the use of the body.
- Experience in expressing space, time, and weight.
- Increased awareness of the world.
- Experience in creatively expressing feelings and ideas.
- Improvement of coordination and rhythmic interpretation.

**Functional/Physical Movement.** In *functional/ physical movement* activities, the child's body benefits as both large and small muscles get lots of exercise in activities specifically designed to promote their healthy growth. In this unit, you will find many activities and strategies to help children work on physical skills in a positive, creative way. In contrast to creative movement activities, these activities are directed toward the development of specific muscles as well as overall body coordination. Yet, just as with creative movement activities, the emotional self of the child benefits as well, since the child learns to feel competent by acquiring new skills. These functional/ physical movement activities also are a good outlet for aggressive feelings, as well as an opportunity to explore a wide range of movements and skills.

Creative and functional/physical movement activities are both of great value to the young child and should be included in the early childhood program. In both types of movement activities, the teacher must first know the developmental level of the children.

## PLANNING FUNCTIONAL/PHYSICAL MOVEMENT ACTIVITIES TO MEET YOUNG CHILDREN'S NEEDS

All movement activities best serve young children's needs when they address their current developmental levels. An appropriate physical movement activity for a three-year-old, for example, would be quite different from that of a five- or six-year-old. Three's are a lot more likely to be interested in simple climbing skills and riding tricycles than in catching balls or skipping rope, which are more popular with five's and six's. (Appendix A presents a general measure of the *average* ages at which young children acquire various physical skills.)

In functional/physical movement activities, as in all activities for young children, a teacher must know each child's level before using or planning any activities. The information presented in Appendix A can only be used as a starting point. A teacher will know through daily observation and work with each child just exactly what is the child's level of large and small motor development. The *child* is the measure, *not* any chart of developmental skills.

The teacher's role in functional/physical movement activities is to provide a series of activities that challenge the child and lead to the development of greater skill and expression. Activities must be presented in a developmental sequence, that is, teaching easier movements before more difficult movements. The order of presentation is determined by the needs of the children. For example, preschoolers are not mentally or physically ready for sports. These children need freedom to express themselves in a different way through movement and dance. Their large muscles have not been fully strengthened, and teachers need to provide creative activities to develop these large muscles.

**Kinds of Movement Activities.** Physical (functional) movement activities are generally divided into two types—gross motor and fine motor. Both fine and gross (large) motor activities need to be encouraged with young children. Gross motor skills develop in young children prior to fine motor skills.

Young children, for example, will be quite good at walking and running when they enter preschool. Skipping, galloping, and hopping develop thereafter. The fine motor skills are, however, most often far less developed in young children; the movement program can be quite effective in working on these skills in a fun, positive way.

Since young children really enjoy physical activities, the wise teacher can incorporate practice in fine motor skills in a pleasurable way. When movement activities become overly academic and dull, it is due to an overconcentration on isolated, rote skills practice. The following general teaching suggestions include activities for both fine and gross motor skill development. Of course, the skill level of the children will determine which of these suggestions to incorporate in the movement program.

*Gross motor activities.*

1. Encourage *climbing* activities (within reason, but a child is usually more capable than overly cautious adults give her credit for).

**FIGURE 16–3 Even an old tire can be used for outdoor play equipment.**

2. Encourage *jumping* activities: hopscotch, jumping rope, broad jump, hop-skip-jump activities, etc.
3. Encourage *running* activities.
4. Encourage proper *walking* activities; stress and emphasize arm movement with legs and chest "out," chin up.
5. Encourage *throwing and catching games:* ball, balloons, objects, etc. Use different sizes and weights.
6. Encourage other *physically oriented games:* tag, hide-and-seek, Simon Says, Captain-May-I, follow the leader, etc.
7. Encourage *skipping* activities.
8. Encourage *dancing* activities.
9. Encourage *calisthenics.*
10. Encourage the *walking of steps;* some suspect that "one-level" homes without stairs contribute to poor perceptual-motor development.
11. Encourage the development of *muscular strength.* Pushing and pulling activities will help.
12. Encourage *kicking* activities.
13. When choosing equipment, look for various types of equipment that can be used both indoors and outdoors. An old tire swing is an inexpensive playground toy. Also consider barrels, ropes, pipes, boxes, etc.

*Fine motor activities.*

1. Encourage *balancing* activities: walk on a board, walk on a line, stand on one leg, walk heel-to-toe, etc. You can also have the child balance something on her head, hand, etc.
2. Encourage *eye movement* activities: tracking from left to right, pointing, eyes following a moving object, "flashlight writing" (consult an eye specialist if eyes don't seem to be working together).
3. Develop the *ability to stop an action* as in games of "statue" or "freeze." This helps promote general as well as specific motor control and coordination.
4. Promote both *near point* and *far point* vision, changing frequently.

**Related Activities.**

1. Encourage the *identification of body parts;* don't be too technical, but a child should know where her

toes, knees, hips, ankles, shoulders, elbows, etc., are located.

2. Provide areas and opportunity for *physical catharsis,* or release of physical energy, and learn to identify times when it is most needed.
3. Provide an opportunity for *rest* and *relaxation;* learn to identify times when it is *most* needed. Learning to be "immobile" is as important as learning to be mobile.
4. At kindergarten level and beyond, encourage knowledge of left and right.

It is not enough just to know what activities encourage muscle development. In working with young children, it is important to know how to go about conducting physical/functional movement activities in a way that encourages children's active participation.

## CONDUCTING PHYSICAL/FUNCTIONAL MOVEMENT ACTIVITIES

There are some basic guidelines on how to work with young children in all types of movement activities to encourage their gradual development of skills. The following guidelines are important to keep in mind so that children's movement activities don't degenerate into either chaotic, undirected movement or boring, overly planned exercises.

Here are some "do's" for a successful physical/ functional movement program:

• Be sure you have the children's attention when presenting a new skill or game. One teacher, for example, got the group's attention and signaled the beginning of movement time by having all the children stand up and join hands, forming one big circle. Then she directed all the children to drop hands and sit down. In this way, the children were not only aware that "movement time" was starting, but they were also in the appropriate formation the teacher used for the activity.

• Give the name of the game or skill and explain it clearly and concisely, using as little of the play time as possible. Be sure you use words that are at the children's level. To ensure young children's com-

An adequate amount of teaching supplies is essential if children are to have the chance to accomplish the learning tasks planned for them. Much of the equipment and supplies can be made or improvised. A central storage area for supplies and equipment is recommended.

**Supplies for Movement Activities**

*Plastic cellophane* (with rule that the plastic cannot be put up to the face)
*Scarves, drapery material, or pieces of lightweight fabric*
*Ribbons, pieces of string or yarn, strips of crepe or tissue paper*
*Balloons*
*Balls* (of various sizes): beach balls, playground balls, Nerf footballs, tennis
*Jump ropes*—individual, 7'–8' long
*Long jump ropes* (14'–16' long)
*Boxes* (cardboard, various sizes)
*Feathers*
*Tubes* (inside of waxed paper or paper towel rolls, decorated as desired)
*Bean bags*—different shapes and colors
*Playground balls*—rubber, mostly 8½", may be plastic
*Wands*—mop or broom handles, 36" long
*Cones, rubber*—to use as boundary markers for outside play (detergent bottles or milk containers)
*Hoops*—may be made from plastic water tubing (See Appendix E.)
*Yarn balls* (See Appendix E for instructions on making these.)
*Tambourine*—can be made by using tinfoil pans
*Paddles*—wooden
*Scoops*—(See Appendix E for instructions on making these.)
*Record player*
*Individual mats*—carpet or carpet squares can be used
*Ball inflator with gauge*
*Stretch ropes*—can be made from clothing elastic

**FIGURE 16–4 Basic supplies for movement activities.**

# THIS ONE'S FOR YOU!

## MORE POSSIBILITIES: SUGGESTED MOVEMENT INTERPRETATIONS

The following are some suggested movement interpretations. Movement explorations and creative movement experiences can be used to interpret nearly every experience, thing, or phenomenon. This list, then, can be expanded with endless possibilties:

1. Life cycle of butterfly
   a. Caterpillar crawling
   b. Caterpillar eating grass
   c. Caterpillar hanging very still from branch or twig
   d. Chrysalis hanging very still
   e. Butterfly emerging from chrysalis
   f. Butterfly drying its wings
   g. Butterfly flying
2. Piece of cellophane or lightweight plastic
   a. Item is put into teacher's hands without children seeing; children encouraged to guess what item might be, interpreting their guesses through movement.
   b. Teacher's hands are opened, children watch plastic move, and then interpret what they see through movement.
   c. Piece of plastic is used for movement exploration.
3. Shaving cream
   a. Spurting from aerosol can
   b. Foaming up
   c. Spreading on face
   d. Being used for shaving
4. Airplane sequence
   a. Starting motor
   b. Taking off
   c. Flying
   d. Arriving
   e. Landing safely
5. Popcorn
   a. Butter melting
   b. Popping
   c. Everyone ending in a ball shape on the floor, all "popped"
6. Water
   a. Dripping
   b. Flooding
   c. Flowing in a fountain
   d. Freezing

e. Melting
f. Spilling
g. Sprinkler
7. Laundry
  a. Inside washing machine
  b. Inside dryer
  c. Being scrubbed on a washboard
  d. Being pinned to clothesline
  e. Drying in a breeze
8. Fishing
  a. Casting out
  b. Reeling in
  c. Pretending to be a fish
  d. Fly fishing
  e. Pretending to be a hooked line
  f. Frying and eating fish

prehension, let them repeat the information back to you in their own words. Demonstrate, or have the children demonstrate, each step, skill, or technique necessary. Remember, lengthy explanations cause interest to wane. Use visual aids whenever possible.

- Have all needed equipment ready *before* the session begins. (Figure 16–4 lists some basic equipment for many movement activities.) Because young children's attention span is limited, don't waste the short time you have their attention in noninstructional scurrying around for supplies!

- Discuss with the children and agree on a signal to be used when it is time to stop and listen.

- When a piece of equipment is involved, indicate what the children are to do as soon as they get the item. Immediate involvement is preferable to waiting until every child has his or her rope, ball, or bean bag before beginning the activity.

- Remind the children to avoid collisions with one another when they are working in the general or shared space. This requires constant attention and good body control. It is, therefore, a better learning condition than having the children always move in the same direction.

- Encourage children to wear comfortable clothing that does not bind or impede free movement of any body part. Barefoot participation is highly recommended if the floor surface is splinter-free. The muscles of the feet work more efficiently and tactile sensation is enhanced when walking barefoot.

- Avoid demonstrating the movement to prevent preconceived notions about the solutions. Once the children are involved, the children themselves will provide good examples of the activity.

- Allow time for practice and creativity. Free choice of any activity for a given time will allow the teacher to observe and suggest individual problems to be solved. Encourage children to make up games or activities to use with the equipment. Children thus become responsible for their own challenges.

- Allow the children to choose a partner (or assign one, if this is necessary) with whom they can work during the movement activity session. Change partners often (each week, at least) so that children have a chance to work with different people.

**Using Poetry and Music to Stimulate Creative Movement Activities.** Thus far in this unit, we have discussed physical/functional activities that involve large- and small-muscle development in traditional ways such as running, jumping, and playing with balls and other such equipment. Let us now consider how music and poetry can encourage children's creative movement in the classroom.

*Music.* Listening to music is a natural way to introduce creative movement. Distinctive types of music or rhythm should be chosen for initial movement experiences. There are many ways and numerous books that can give teachers ideas on this topic. See the suggested additional readings at the end of this unit for books on this topic.

In order to provide the music or rhythm for creative movement, only a few items may be necessary. A phonograph and some records along with a drum, sticks, and bells may be more than enough. Depending on the circumstances, hand clapping can be a rhythmic addition or a last resort.

Some basic concepts for the teacher to remember when using music for creative movement are:

- The teacher should make it clear that anything the children want to do is all right, as long as it does not harm them or others.
- The children should understand that they do not have to do anything anyone else does. They can do anything the music or an idea "tells" them to do.
- The child should be allowed to "copy" someone for a start if desired.
- The children should understand that each child is different and all people move in different ways.
- The children should have help in realizing the experiences of freedom of movement, the relationship of movement to space, and the relationship of movement to others.

The teacher may begin the experience by playing music on a phonograph. A record should be chosen that has a strong and easily recognized beat or rhythm. The children should not be told what to listen for. The teacher should let them listen and then ask them to think what the music is saying to them.

While the children are listening, the teacher may turn the music down a bit lower and ask them to

**FIGURE 16–5 Musical games are excellent movement experiences for young children.**

form a circle facing inward. The teacher should talk with each child about what the music is saying. Some of the children probably are already moving to the music by this time, and the teacher may join in. The children may go anywhere in the room and do anything that the music "tells" them to do. For this exercise, clapping, stomping, and even shouting are all

**FIGURE 16–6 Helping children with props helps them begin their creative movement activity.**

# T H I N K   A B O U T   I T . . .

## CREATIVE MOVEMENT FOR TRANSITION TIMES

Whenever young children move from activity to activity (in transitional times), they often lose their focus and may even get a bit confused and disruptive. The following hints may help children move more easily from one activity to another:

- Pretend you are a train, with the teacher as the engine and each child a car in the train. Assign one child to be the caboose, to turn off the lights and close the door.
- Turn your jump rope into a dragon, worm, caterpillar, or other animal by attaching a head at one end of the rope and a tail at the other end. Have the children make the body and legs by holding onto the rope with one hand and walking down the hall and out to the playground.
- Imagine you are a tired puppy; yawn and stretch and roll on the floor. Then lie very still. (Suggested for the beginning of rest time.)
- Construct a "feel" box or bag or a "look" box or bag. Place an item in the bag or box that will suggest the next activity or topic for each child to feel or look at.
- To help children quiet down between activities, clap a rhythm for them to copy. Start by clapping loudly, then gradually clap more softly until your hands are resting in your lap.
- Pretend to be a bowl of gelatin and shake all over.
- Pretend to lock your lips and put the key in a pocket.
- Pretend to put on "magic" ears for listening.
- Pretend to walk in tiptoe boots, Indian moccasins, or Santa's-elf shoes.
- To make lining up more fun and to enhance motor skills, make a balance-beam "bridge" for the children to cross. Cut two 5″ wide strips from a carpet sample and tape them together end to end with duct tape. Place the "bridge" on the floor alongside a smiling paper alligator for children to walk across, being careful not to let the alligator "nip" their toes. (Church, 1993; Hohmann, 1993)

possible and helpful. When appropriate, a quieter piece of music may be played to allow the children to rest and to give them a sense of contrast.

As children become involved in movement explorations, try to redirect, challenge, and stimulate their discoveries by suggestions such as "Do what you are doing now in a slower way," or "Try moving in a different direction or at a different level," or "Try the same thing you were doing but make it smoother or lighter."

Some creative movement activities with music can also be done with a partner. Some possibilities are:

- Face your partner and do a "mirror dance" with your hands and arms. Can you do a mirror dance with your feet and legs? How about with different facial expressions?
- Hold hands with your partner and slide, leap, gallop, etc., until you hear the signal; then find a new partner and continue to move to the music.
- Move the same way your partner moves until you hear the tambourine; then move in a different way.
- What interesting body shapes can you and your partner make? Can the two of you create an inter-

esting design in the space you share? Practice until you and your partner can make three different designs to music.

This general approach can be adapted to movement with dolls and puppets; movement of specific parts of the body, such as hands, feet, or toes; and movement in different kinds of space or groups. The imaginations of the children and the teacher are the only limits. These ideas are discussed in greater detail in Unit 17.

*Poetry and prose.* For creative movement, poetry has rhythm as well as the power of language. It is not necessary to use rhyming verses at all times. In the beginning, poems that rhyme may help to start a feeling of pulse and rhythm. Poems should be chosen that fit the young child's level of appreciation. By adult standards, they may be quite simple. They are often short, vivid, lively descriptions of animals or motion, but children should not be limited to these, as there are many books and collections available with a wider variety. The local library is the best resource for this.

A suggested beginning may be to ask the children to listen to the reading of a poem. After they have heard it, they may pick out their favorite characters in it. The teacher should encourage some discussion about who those characters are and what they do. The poem should be read a second time; teachers can suggest that the children act out their characters as they listen to the poem. Anything goes—the children may hop like bunnies, fly like planes, or do whatever they feel. An example of a good poem for a movement exercise follows:

### Poem to Develop Awareness of Self and Teach Body Parts

I use my brain to think, think, think—
(Point finger to brain)
I use my nose to smell—
(Point to nose)
I use my eyes to blink, blink, blink—
(Point to eyes)
And I use my throat to yell—
(Point to throat and yell!)
I use my mouth to giggle, giggle, giggle—
(Point to mouth and giggle)
I use my hips to bump—
(Point to hips and "bump" them)
I use my toes to wiggle, wiggle, wiggle—
(Point to toes and wiggle)
And I use my legs to jump—
(Point to legs and jump)

Encourage each child to move in his own way, and encourage as many variations as you see! (Other suggestions are at end of unit.)

As the readings continue, more complex poems can be selected. They may contain a series of movements or simple plots. The same general idea can also be carried through with prose.

As children become more comfortable in acting out poetry read aloud, they may become more sensitive to the less obvious actions or emotions described by the poetry. When stories or poems that have several characters and more complex interaction are read, the entire selection should first be read for listening only. Then it can be discussed to get some idea of the children's understanding and appreciation. If the children are interested, several readings may be necessary.

**FIGURE 16–7 A children's story can be the inspiration for later dramatic and creative movement.**

The procedure of reading/listening, picking roles, and acting out what is read can be used over and over. Children may ask to "play the story" whenever they enjoy something that is read to them. Costumes and scenery may be added. Notice how much the wearing of hats can stimulate imagination and involvement. (See Unit 15 for suggestions on child-made hats for props.) You will find more poems for use with movement activities at the end of this unit.

*Fingerplays and creative movement.* Fingerplays provide an endless supply of creative movement opportunities. Keep fingerplays used for creative movement experiences open-ended. You might start by asking, "I wonder how many different ways there are to move your fingers?" Then try it! By using open-ended, divergent questions, you invite children to get actively involved right from the beginning. You might also encourage children to invent movements when learning a new fingerplay or ask them to suggest variations to revitalize a well-loved rhyme you've repeated often. Don't forget that it isn't necessary for all children to make the same motions during fingerplays. Always accept individual interpretations.

For example, the words to the song "My Hand Says Hello," sung to the tune of "The Farmer in the Dell" invite children to wave their hands in their own ways as they sing:

My hand says hello, my hand says hello,
Everytime I see my friends,
My hand says hello.

After singing this a few times, children can take turns choosing different body parts to sing about and move. How does your head say hello? Your foot?

Other favorite fingerplays include funny or silly actions that give children the chance to giggle and wiggle without losing control. "Open, Shut Them," about moving hands, grabs children's attention and provides just the right amount of silliness:

Open, shut them, open, shut them.
Give a great big clap.
Open, shut them, open, shut them.
Put them in your lap.
Creep them, creep them, creep them, creep them,
Right up to your chin.

Open wide your little mouth, but . . .
Do not let them in!

Surprise endings often bring smiles, such as those in "Ten in a Bed," "Five Little Monkeys," and "Thumbkin." (See Section 7 for these and other fingerplays.) Invite children to act out their favorite fingerplays.

## SUMMARY

Young children learn by doing, and movement activities are a natural avenue for children's learning. Movement activities contribute to the total development—physical, mental, social, and emotional—of young children. Movement activity is as vital for children as are art and math, for in movement activities a young child acquires, skills, knowledge, and attitudes that help her discover and understand her body and her physical abilities and limitations.

Two main types of movement are *personal creative movement* and *functional/physical movement*. Personal creative movement reflects the mood or inner state of an individual, while functional/physical movement is movement that serves a practical purpose, such as muscular development.

Creative movement usually requires no planning or forethought on the part of children. They can forget about themselves and let the music's rhythm or an idea carry their bodies away. There is no exact pattern of movements to be practiced or perfected.

The child's body benefits in physical/functional movement activities as large and small muscles (and overall coordination) get lots of exercise to promote their healthy growth. In planning these movement activities for young children, the developmental level of each child is the starting point. The information provided in developmental skill charts (such as Appendix A) for young children can be used to get some idea of what to expect of children physically at different ages. Yet, the most important thing to remember is that the individual *child* is the measure, not any chart of developmental skills.

Physical movement activities are generally divided into gross (large) motor and fine (small) motor skills. Both gross and fine motor activities should be encouraged with young children. Climbing, running, throwing, catching, dancing, and skipping are some examples of large motor movement activities. Small motor movement activities include digging, pointing, and using the eyes to follow moving objects.

It is not enough to know which are gross and fine motor activities. In working with young children, a teacher needs to know how to conduct these movement activities in a way that encourages children's participation and creativity. Guidelines or "do's" for a successful movement program are suggested in the unit to accomplish these goals.

Poetry and music can also be used to encourage children's creative movements. Listening to music is a natural way to introduce creative movement. Distinctive types of music with clear rhythmic patterns should be used for the initial creative movement experiences. Poetry also has rhythm as well as the power of language. Poems that rhyme are good to begin with, as they help children get the feel, pulse, and rhythm of the words. (There are rhythm poems at the end of this unit, as well as in Unit 18.) Fingerplays also provide many opportunities for creative movement activities. Whether movement activities occur with music, poetry, ropes, or hoops, they benefit young children by developing their relaxation, freedom of expression, and increased awareness of their own bodies.

## LEARNING ACTIVITIES

A. Make a list of five do's and five don't's for creative movement in the classroom.
B. If possible, compare your list with lists made by other people.
C. Observe a group of children involved in movement activities of any kind. Record evidence of each of the following situations:
   1. A child discovers a new way to move.
   2. A child uses small and/or large muscles in the activity.
   3. A child discovers what other children are like as a result of the activity.
D. There are things that teachers do to help create a good climate for creative movement to their classes. There are other things that teachers do that keep children from becoming involved in creative movement activities. Describe both these situations. Share these descriptions with others and compare your results.

## ACTIVITIES FOR CHILDREN

### Pantomiming a Specified Object or Action

1. Explain to the class that putting a finger over your mouth means to be quiet and that holding a hand out means to stop. Then say some words and use your hands to demonstrate what the words mean. For example: sun, ball, eating, sleeping, hot, bathing, cold, climbing, counting.
2. Demonstrate ways of walking. For example: tiredly, quietly, happily, sadly.
3. Whisper a word and have a child describe the word with her body without speaking. The rest of the class can guess what the word is. (Flash cards can be made and given to the children.) Examples: rain, cutting (with scissors), painting, cold, giant, fairy, tired, sleepy.
4. Imitate animals.

### "Become" One of the Following

Have children dramatize the features/characteristics of bicycle, rake, hose, wheelbarrow, tire pump, beach ball, any other familiar play objects children come up with.

### Stop and Go

Children walk around doing whatever they want to with their arms and bodies. When the teacher says "stop," the children must freeze and hold that position until the teacher says "go." Children who lose their balance while the game is stopped must sit down. Children move creatively and assume interesting positions.

## Jump Over the River

Two long sticks can serve as the banks of the river. Children jump from one bank to the other. The sticks can be moved further apart at times to make a wider river. Children can find ways to get from one side of the river to the other, like sliding, crawling, rolling, etc. Encourage any and all creative attempts to "cross."

## Call and Roll

Children sit in a circle. Two large rubber balls are used. The balls are handed to two children on opposite sides of the circle. Each child with a ball must call out the name of another child in the circle and roll the ball to that child.

## Seeing Jack-in-the-Box

Have a small group of children (approximately five) stand in a circle. Ask them to pretend they are jack-in-the-boxes. Have them tuck their bodies up tight and cover their eyes with their hands. Ask them to remember what they see as soon as they pop up out of their boxes. When the children are crouched close to the ground repeat the following poem:

"I'm jack-in-the-box,
All shut up tight.
Not a breath of air,
Not a ray of light.
It's dark in here,
I cannot see.
Open the cover—
Up jumps me." (Teacher claps hands)

After the children have jumped up, have them tell what they saw first. *Related Activities:* Rotate the children and repeat the activity. After hearing the children's responses, ask them why they saw something different.

## Copycats

Gather children in a small circle. Select a body part to emphasize (hands, feet, head, etc.) and ask children to think of a way to move that part of their bodies. All the children will then have a chance to demonstrate their ideas and the group will copy the movement. When all ideas for moving one body part are exhausted, go on to another part of the body. Teachers should par-

ticipate and join in the uninhibited activity of the children. *Related Activities:* Combine two movement ideas using two different parts of the body. This will add complexity and develop coordination.

## Body Roll

Each child will need a large ball. Have them place and/or roll the ball on different parts of their body. For example, direct the children to roll the ball from their toes to their waist. Roll your ball up your arm. Can you find a way to hold your ball without using your hands? If a rather small ball is used during this activity, it will take a long time to cover the length of the body. *Related Activities:* Collect all but one of the balls (a smaller one) and direct the children to pass the ball to the next child without using their hands. Children solve this problem using their necks, upper arms, and legs.

## Going for a Walk

Chant these lines, allowing the children to name what they see on the "walk" as well as the motions they want to make of the things they see.

"We're going for a walk, a walk, a walk,
We're going for a walk
And we see _____. (Example: child chooses a lion, and roars and crawls around like a lion.)

## Body Sounds

Many children are aware of the familiar sounds of hand clapping and feet stamping. Using the production of these sounds as a starter, encourage children to experiment with their bodies in order to create other body sounds (such as knee knocking, finger snapping, tongue clicking, body rubbing, head scratching, teeth chopping, etc.). As a child discovers new sounds, have her share it with others so that all can have the pleasure of producing the unique sound. *Related Activities:* Record each "body sound" on tape so that the children can later listen to the sounds and try to guess what each sound is and how it was made.

## Hula Hoops

Each child has a hula hoop. Have the child place it on the floor, leaving enough space so movement around it will be safe.

A. Have the children:
   1. Move around their hoops. When the teacher calls out a part of the body, the children stop and put that part (hand, foot, elbow, etc.) in the hoop.

2. Go over the hoop as many different ways as they can.
3. Go around the hoop as many different ways as they can.
4. Touch the hoop with as many parts of the body as they can at the same time: hand, foot, knee, etc.
5. Make the hoop twirl in as many ways and with as many different parts of their body as they can.
6. Roll the hoop and run beside it.
7. Roll the hoop and run past it.
8. Roll the hoop and go through it.
9. Roll the hoop in a circle.

B. Ask the children if they can:
1. Jump in and out of the hoop? Front, side, and backward?
2. Hop in and out of the hoop? Front, side, and backward?
3. Run around the outside of the hoop? Change directions?
4. Put both hands inside the hoop and both feet outside the hoop? Circle around the hoop in this position?
5. Put both feet inside the hoop and both hands outside? Circle around the hoop in this position?
6. Roll the hoop and keep it from falling over?
7. Spin the hoop away from you so that it will return?
8. While the hoop is rolling, make it turn without having to stop it? Spin the hoop like an egg beater?
9. Throw the hoop into the air and catch it before it hits the ground?
10. Jump the hoop like a rope? Make your hoop turn around your neck? Around your waist? Around your arm?

C. Ask the children:
1. How many different things can you do with the hoop while you are walking the balance beam?
2. What can you do with two hoops?

## Tin Can Stilts

(Simple to construct—children love them!)

A. Materials: two no. 10 tin cans, nylon cord, four nails
B. Procedure:
1. To secure the cord to the cans, punch two holes in the top of the cans.
2. Tie the cord to the middle of the nails and insert through the hole in the can. The nail will keep the cord from pulling out of the can. Do this in all four holes (two cans).

## Shoe Box Walkers

Punch holes in the sides of shoeboxes and put 36-inch strings in each box. Tie knots in the strings. The children can use these shoe box "monster feet" or "giant's toes" for walking, using the strings like reins, and other fanciful things!

## Rope Skills

A. Procedure:
1. With the rope laid in a straight line on the floor, can you walk it as if it were a tight rope? Can you do this while moving backward?
2. Who can walk the "tight rope" with their eyes shut?
3. Can you jump from side to side across the rope without touching the rope?
4. Can you hop from side to side without touching the rope?
5. Can you straddle the rope, jump in the air, turn around, and land on your feet straddling the rope?
6. Lay your rope in the pattern of a circle. Can you get inside the circle, taking up as much space as possible, without hanging over the edges?

**FIGURE 16–8 Rope skills.**

7. Make several little circles with the rope. Can you put one body part in each circle and balance?

8. If your rope were shaped as the letter "V," could you jump over the "V" without touching the rope? See how close you can come to jumping or leaping over the widest part of the "V."

9. Can you go over your rope by placing both hands on one side and swinging your legs across? How high can you swing your legs as you bring them across?

10. Place the rope on the floor in a long curved shape. Can you begin at one end and travel to the other end by kicking your feet in the air and doing most of the traveling in the air?

11. Take one end of the rope in each hand (step over the rope so that it is behind you). Now, pull the rope over your head and see if you can jump it as it comes down to your feet. Can you jump it one time? Two or three times without stopping? How many can you do without having to stop?

## More Rope Skills

A. Give each child a short rope. Find an empty space in the classroom. To the child: Pull hard on both ends of your rope. See how many places you can take your stretched rope in your own space. Try to keep moving your rope all the time: up, down, front, forward, back, side to side. How far from the middle of your body can you stretch your rope? How far in front? How far behind you? Keep pulling and stretching. Can you bend your body sideways and keep stretching the rope? Bend backward? Feel how strong your muscles are as you pull on the ends of your rope.

B. Variation: Try standing with your feet wide apart. Then, with your feet close together, which way can you get a stronger and longer bend in your body and stretch on your rope? Sit down and see how many places you can stretch your rope: high over head and down near the floor. Try kneeling. How far to the side can you bend your body and still keep moving the rope? Can you feel the tightness of the muscles when you pull hard on the rope?

## Circles

A. With chalk, make four groups of circles on the floor, with six to eight short ropes in each circle. Have one child to each rope.

B. The teacher asks the children if they can move forward, backward, and sideways over the ropes, or go over each rope in some other different way. How high can they get into the air as they go over the rope? How softly can they land? The teacher then changes directions on the call. Everyone forward over two ropes in different ways; everyone backward over three ropes in as many ways as they can; then forward. Can everyone turn halfway around as they jump over each of the three ropes? And so on.

## Partners

A. Pick partners who have about the same level of skills.

B. Procedure:

1. How many can face their partner holding the end of the rope in one hand and turn it slowly? When they can do this, try the same thing with the other hand.

2. Have partners facing each other across the rope. While each partner holds the other partner's hands, can they both jump at the same time so that they land straddling the rope? How many can give a bigger jump and land on opposite sides of the ropes while still holding hands?

3. Can the partners do the same thing from a stoop position?

4. Have partners facing each other across the rope again. Can they jump across the rope, turn and jump again, doing this at the same time? If successful, they can try the same routine with hopping and leaping.

## The Box

A. Find a large cardboard packing box, large enough for children to crawl in and out of. Cut four openings, one on each side, in the shape of a triangle, a square, a rectangle, and a circle. Make openings large enough for the children to crawl in and out of the box.

B. Set up problems for the children to solve such as:

1. Identify all openings.

2. Crawl in the box head first through the circle, and come out feet first through the square.

3. Crawl in head first through the rectangle. Now head out of the triangle, then the square, and then the circle.

## I Can

Here's an action poem that leads to a lot of fun and movement.

Like a bunny I can hop
I can spin like a top.
I can reach way up high

And I almost touch the sky.
In a boat I row and row
Sometimes fast and sometimes slow.
Now a bouncing jumping jack
I pop up and then go back.
Then sway gently in the breeze
Like the little forest trees.
Make silly faces like a clown
And then I quietly settle down.

## Three-Quarter Time

Bring in some old and new dance records—a waltz, a tango, a foxtrot, ragtime, the twist, and some popular songs. Let the children make up their own dances to suit the way the music makes them feel. Then sit in a circle and clap to the dance rhythms.

## Creative Movement with Music

When the music plays slowly, the children should move slowly; as it speeds up, so should they. Begin this activity with a drum. Each time you beat it, the children should take a step. At first, the beat will be slow and even. Later, it should be faster and the children should be running. Then, musical pieces of increasing complexity can be introduced as the children gain the ability to interpret tempo in music into a corresponding tempo in movement.

## How Do You Feel?

Many children know only a few verbal expressions for their feelings, for example, happy, sad, mad. A good way to sharpen their awareness of emotions and increase their vocabulary is to have them pantomime stories. Tell a story about a commonplace activity, such as going to the store or riding the bus. Be sure to introduce incidents that produce different emotions. As you get to each incident, name the emotion (puzzlement, frustration, joy, weariness, annoyance) and have the children act it out.

## It's How It's Said

Have the children act out the following phrases as they would be said by different people: "I'm thirsty," as said by an athlete who has run a mile, by Count Dracula, and by a whiny child. "Oh," as said by someone in pain, in surprise, in admiration, in disbelief.

## Use the Tube

Long cardboard tubes, like the ones used for wrapping paper, can be imaginative props for pantomime.

Have each child use a tube in a way that suggests an action. As each child performs the pantomime, have the others guess what is being done. Some obvious uses are a telescope, cane, sword, etc., but children can come up with such variations as a straw for a "giant soda" or a dispenser for paper cups.

## Ring Around the Rosy-Leader

This game is a combination of "Ring Around the Rosy" and "Follow the Leader." The group joins hands in a circle. The leader says, "Circle left" or "Circle right." As they walk around they sing "Ring around the rosy, a pocket full of posies. Ashes, ashes. Leader, what do we do?" After the words "Ashes, ashes," everyone stops to see what the leader will do. Everyone follows the actions of the leader. A new leader is chosen by the previous leader each time.

## Keep the Basket Full

A. Take a basket of balls and pour them out on the floor. The children, who are scattered around the room, run after the balls, bring them back, and put them in the basket. The teacher should keep pouring them out for a few minutes to give all the children an opportunity to get one or more balls.
B. This active game helps develop space awareness, quick change of direction, and moving in a straight line.

## Can You Do This?

The children are standing scattered around the floor. Have them cross their legs (Indian style), cross their arms, and try to sit down without uncrossing either arms or legs. Then ask them to stand up without uncrossing either arms or legs or touching knees to the floor. Suggest that they keep their feet as flat as they can if they are having trouble standing up. Have them try the exercise several times during this activity period, and frequently throughout the year. It is an excellent way to develop coordination and a sense of balance.

## Follow the Ropes

A. Give each child a rope and make sure each is positioned so there is plenty of space between children. Say, "Pull on the rope as hard as you can and move the stretched rope as many places as you can." (For example, they may extend their arms overhead with the rope stretched in their hands; try to get the rope behind their back, etc.)
B. Lay out the ropes and ask the children to follow you

and do as you do. As you go over each rope, do something different, such as hop.

## Unwinding

A. Children pretend they are wind-up toys, such as dolls, dogs, monkeys, rabbits, clowns. The teacher winds up the toys and the children begin moving at a brisk pace, getting slower and slower until they are completely "run down" and stop or collapse to the floor. Teacher or a child rewinds the toys and sequence is repeated.

B. Children explore moving in the manner of many kinds of wind-up toys, using both locomotor and nonlocomotor movement. For example, a child may be a toy monkey who hops up and down and claps her hands together, a toy bear who beats a toy drum, or a toy soldier who marches a few steps with her gun on her shoulder. Children might bring their wind-up toys to school to stimulate other ideas.

## Collapsing

A. Teacher explains that "collapsing" means relaxing a body part or the whole body, allowing gravity to pull it down to earth. Children stand and stretch tall, then slowly collapse (relax) one part at a time, first the fingertips, then the wrists, elbows, arms, head and shoulders, and so on, until they are left collapsed on the floor.

B. Children lie on floor with eyes closed. Teacher slowly and quietly tells them that they are sawdust dolls with a hole in the toe, and the sawdust is slowly running out of each part of the body; first the hands, then the arms, head, shoulders, chest, hips, and so on until the children are completely collapsed on the floor. Children try a first collapse, starting from a sitting position and falling to the floor, then from the knees to the floor, and finally from a standing position to the floor.

C. Children move around the room, and on the teacher's signal they stop and collapse one body part.

## Balloon Fun

A. In a gym or large classroom have the children scatter around, spaced evenly in the general area. Give one ballon per child.

B. Challenges:
   1. Can you tap your balloon and keep it up in the air?
   2. Can you hit your balloon and keep it up in the air?
   3. Can you hit your ballon up by using another body part?
   4. Can you tap your balloon up with your foot?
   5. Can you tap your balloon up, turn around, and then catch it?
   6. Can you tap your balloon up and clap five times before it comes down?
   7. How long can you tap your balloon and keep it in the air?
   8. Get a partner (Put one balloon away). Tap your balloon to your friend by using your shoulder.

## Rhythm Poems

Repeat these as many times as needed, allowing the children to supply appropriate actions.

### Little Birds

All the little birds
All asleep in their nest;
All the little birds
Are taking a rest.
They do not even twitter;
They do not even tweet.
Everything is quiet
All up and down the street.

Then came the mother bird
And tapped them on the head.
They opened up one little eye,
And this is what was said:
"Come, little birdies; it's time to learn to fly.
Come, little birdies; fly way up to the sky."

Fly, fly, oh, fly away, fly, fly, fly.
Fly, fly, oh, fly away, fly away so high.
Fly, fly, oh, fly away, birds can fly the best.
Fly, fly, oh, fly away—now fly back to your nest.

### Flower Seeds

All the little flower seeds sleep in the ground,
Warm and snuggly and tucked in all around,
Sleeping, oh, so soundly the long winter through.
There really wasn't very much else for them to do.
There really wasn't very much else for them to do.
(Repeat above five lines.)
Now their eyes they opened and they peeked all
   around.
And started to grow right up through the ground.
They grew so very slowly, but they grew straight and
   tall.
And their leaves they unfolded and waved at us all.
And their leaves they unfolded and waved at us all.

Then the sun shone down and made the flowers
   smile.
And they swayed and swayed in the breeze for
   awhile.
Until a big wind came and blew them all away.

And there were no more flowers that day.
And there were no more flowers that day.
Blow, blow, blow away, flowers. Blow, blow away.

### Worms Are Crawling

Worms are crawling, crawling, crawling.
Worms are crawling, crawling, all around

*or:*

Making tunnels in and out of the ground.
Wiggly, wiggly worms are squirming all around
Wiggly, squiggly, swiggly worms
Crawl in and out of the ground.
(This can be sung to "The Farmer in the Dell"
   tune.)

### Bobby Snake

Oh, Bobby Snake is crawling, crawling, crawling.
Oh, Bobby Snake is crawling, crawling right to
   meeeee.
(Substitute the name of the child for meeeee)

Wiggly, wiggly, wiggly snake
Is crawling, crawling all around.
Slithery, slippery, flippery snake
Is crawling, crawling on the ground.

### Turtle

(Tune: "Twinkle, Twinkle, Little Star")
Tur-tle, tur-tle, where are you?
Oh, you are so slow, slow, slow.
First one hand and then the other,
That's what makes you go, go, go.
Hide your winky little head,
And you cannot see, see, see.
Tur-tle, tur-tle, peek-a-boo!
Peek-a-boo at me, me, me.

### Snails

(This is the same as turtle song, but change "turtle"
   to "snail.")
Change third and fourth lines as follows:
You have no hands and you have no feet;
I wonder what makes you go, go, go?

### Baby

Now the little baby is learning how to walk,
Little, tiny baby that cannot even talk.
See the little baby, see how he walks so slow.
Walking little baby, now show us how you go, "Maa-
   maa."

Now the little baby is learning how to run,
Little tiny baby that wants to have some fun.
(Repeat third and fourth lines.)

### Little Man—Big Man

The little, tiny man
Takes little, tiny steps.
Oh, the little, tiny man

Takes little, tiny steps,
      little, tiny steps,
      little, tiny steps.
The little, tiny man
Takes little, tiny steps.
VARIATIONS: Funny crooked man takes funny,
   crooked steps.
Big, tall man takes long, fat steps.
Great tall man with long, giant steps.

### I Wiggle My Fingers

I can wiggle my fingers, I can wiggle my toes.
I can wiggle my shoulders, and I can wiggle my
   nose.
Now no more wiggles are left for me.
So I will be as still as can be.

## Fingerplays for Creative Movement Activities

Use these fingerplays with the children, allowing
them to make whatever motions comes to mind to
match the lines.

### An Airplane

If I had an airplane,
Zum, zum, zum,
I would fly to Mexico,
Wave my hand and off I'd go.
If I had an airplane,
Zum, Zum, Zum.

### Auto, Auto

Auto, auto, may I have a ride?
Yes, sir; yes, sir; step right inside.
Pour in the water,
Turn on the gas,
Clug-away, chug-away,
But do not go too fast.

### The Circus

Going to the circus to have a lot of fun;
The animals parading, one by one.
Now they're walking two by two,
A great big lion and a caribou.
Now they're walking four by four
A stripey tiger and a big old boar.
Now they're walking five by five
Makes us laugh when they arrive.
Now they're walking six by six,
Little dogs jump over sticks.
Now they're walking seven by seven,
Zebras stamping on to Devon.
Now they're walking eight by eight,
Running and jumping over the gate.
Now they're walking nine by nine,
Scary rabbit and porcupine.
Now they're walking ten by ten
Ready to start all over again.

# UNIT REVIEW

1. List at least six activities that help children develop large motor skills. Make a similar list for small motor skills.
2. List four points that teachers should remember when planning and carrying out creative movement activities for young children.
3. List some objectives of creative movement. On your list, indicate some activities you would use to accomplish each of these objectives.
4. List three things to avoid in creative movement activities with young children.
5. How would you select music and poetry and fingerplays to use with young children in creative movement activities? What would be your criteria?
6. Define the terms *personal creative movement* and *functional/physical movement*. Give examples of each.

# ADDITIONAL READINGS

Bergen, D., *Play as a Medium for Learning and Development: A Handbook of Theory and Practice*. Porstmouth, N.H.: Heinemann, 1988.

Block, S.E. *Me and I'm Great: Physical Education for Children Three Through Eight*. Minneapolis: Burgess, 1977.

Carlyle, S. *Move to Learn: Physical Activities for Young Children*. Norfolk, Va.: Bleecker Street Publishing Corp., 1983.

Cherry, Clare. *Creative Movement for the Developing Child*. Rev. ed. Belmont, Calif.: Fearon Publishers, 1977.

Church, E.B. "Moving Small, Moving Quiet." *Scholastic Pre-K Today* (Feb. 1993): 42–44.

Doray, Maya. *Make Believe Movement*. Long Beach, N.J.: Kimbo Educational Recording, 1976.

Edwards, L.C., and M.L. Nabors. "The Creative Arts Process: What It Is and What It Is Not." *Young Children* (Mar., 1993): 77–81.

Gabbard, E., E. Leblanc, and S. Lowy. *Physical Education for Children: Building the Foundation*. Englewood Cliffs, N.J.: Prentice-Hall, 1987.

Hall, Tom. *Academic Ropes*. Norfolk, Va.: Front Row Experience, 1981.

Hohmann, M. *Young Children in Action*. Ypsilanti, Mich.: High Scope Press, 1993.

Kamii, C. *Group Games in Early Education*. Washington, D.C.: National Association for the Education of Young Children, 1980.

Lynch-Fraser, D. *Dance Play—Creative Movement for Very Young Children*. New York: Walker and Co., 1982.

Pica, Rae. *Poetry in Motion: Poems and Activities for Moving and Learning with Young Children*. Norfolk, Va.: Bleecker Street Publishing Corp., 1986.

Stangl, Jean. *Holiday Movement Activities*. Norfolk, Va.: Front Row Experiences, 1984.

Sullivan, M. *Feeling Strong, Feeling Free: Movement Exploration for Young Children*. Washington, D.C.: Association for the Education of Young Children, 1982.

Weikert, P.D. *Movement in Steady Beat*. Ypsilanti, Mich.: High Scope Press, 1990.

Wilt, J., and J. Watson. *Rhythm and Movement*. Waco, Tex.: Creative Resources, 1977.

# BOOKS FOR CHILDREN ABOUT MOVEMENT

Brown, Marc. *D.W. Flips!* New York: Joy Street/Little, 1987.

Cole, Joanna. *Norma Jean Jumping Bean*. New York: Random, 1987.

Holabird, Katharine. *Angelina and Alice*. New York: Crown/Potter, 1987.

Marshall, James. *The Cut-Ups Cut Loose*. New York: Viking Kestrel, 1987.

McMillan, Bruce. *Step by Step*. New York: Lothrop, 1987.

Ormerod, Jan. *Bend and Stretch*. New York: Lothrop, 1987.

# UNIT 17

# Creative Music

## OBJECTIVES

After studying this unit, you should be able to

- outline some basic goals for music activities for young children.
- list guidelines for planning music activities for young children.
- describe four types of songs suitable for young children.
- suggest various teacher-made rhythm instruments appropriate for use with young children.

Lisa sang to herself in a sing-song way while drawing with crayons: "One purple, two purple, three purple, four purple." Next to her, William was humming the jingle for a fast-food restaurant advertisement and keeping rhythm with his coloring strokes.

Out on the playground, Drew chanted, "I-am-going-to-be-a-lawn-mo-wer." And as he slid down the slide, he made a sound like a lawn mower. Picking up his cue, Claire and Christy slid down after him, each on their stomach making motor-growling sounds.

Musical experiences like these are a common occurrence in a young child's life. Making up original chants and songs, moving rhythmically to musical beats are quite natural to a young child, for whom music is a natural avenue for creative expression. In contrast, an adult finds it more difficult to be as spontaneous as children in the inclusion of music in everyday life. Consider how your peers would react to your chanting as you read this paragraph, "One paragraph, two paragraph, three to go—yeah, yeah, yeah." Unlike William's humming in our opening scenario, your musical monologue probably would not go unnoticed by your peers as they hummed to themselves!

This is the challenge in early childhood education—overcoming an "adult" approach to music so you can share musical experiences with young children in a way that preserves and encourages their innate spontaneous and open attitude. You are challenged in this unit to put aside any self-consciousness

and fears about your own musical talents and to try returning to the openness of a young child experiencing music. You don't need to know how to play a musical instrument or even be able to read music to plan and conduct creative music experiences for children.

Music is created so naturally and easily every day in many forms—by voice, by instruments, even by nature in the rhythm of the rain, the sound of a waterfall. Children are introduced very early to music through radio and television. Music sends commercial messages for everything from cars to breakfast food. Shoppers shop to piped-in classical music, meant to ease frazzled nerves and encourage purchasing. Sitting in a dentist's chair, the patient is treated to music designed to calm, soothe, and even more important, distract attention from the event at hand!

The child's world, too, is filled with music—even his toys make musical sounds. Infants' wind-up musical teddy bears, crib mobiles, and go-to-sleep lullabies are just a few examples of early introductions to music. Young children respond quite naturally to music by rhythmic movement, and they also create their own musical patterns in original chants and songs as well as in unaccompanied rhythmic movements such as swinging, tapping, and even rocking in a chair. Activities that make up the natural beginnings of musical learning right in the home can be extended by the early childhood teacher to classroom music activities.

| AGE | BEHAVIORAL CHARACTERISTICS | MUSIC EXPERIENCES |
|---|---|---|
| Newborn to 1 month | Responds to stimuli by moving entire body. | Quiet singing and rocking soothe the baby. Scary sounds avoided. Sound stimuli important. |
| 1 to 4 months | Changes from hearing to listening. Turns head toward stimulus. Follows moving objects with eyes. | Same as for newborn. |
| 4 to 8 months | Involved in purposeful activity. Reproduces interesting events. Develops hand-eye coordination. | Hits suspended bells again and again to reproduce the sound. |
| 8 to 12 months | Anticipates events, shows intention. Knows that objects have functions. Imitates actions. | Hits drum or xylophone with stick. Claps hands to music. Hits instrument to produce a sound. Understands purpose of instrument. |
| 12 to 18 months | Invents new actions. Uses trial and error to solve problems. | Experiments by hitting instrument in different ways with different objects. |
| 18 to 24 months | Creates new actions through prior thought. Imitates actions after person leaves. | Continues music activity after adult stops. Listens to radio, dances to it. |
| 2 years | Steps in place. Pats. Runs. Increases language. Has limited attention span. Attends to spoken words a few at a time. Develops independence, is very curious. Tendency to tire easily. | Enjoys action songs and moving to music. Can learn short, simple songs. Enjoys activities with short, simple directions. Many opportunities to experiment with instruments and sound. Likes phonograph because he can watch it turn. Opportunity for frequent rest breaks in strenuous rhythmic experiences. Avoid prolonged activities. |
| 3 years | Jumps, runs, and walks to music. Has self-control. Attentive, has longer attention span. Uses more words. Compares two objects. Participates in planning. Initiative emerges. | Special music for special movements. Can wait for a turn. Longer songs or small group experiences can be planned. Experiments with sound comparisons. Suggests words for songs or additional activities. Can recognize several melodies and may have several favorites. Choices important along with an opportunity to try out own ideas. |

FIGURE 17–1 Developmental characteristics and music experiences.

| AGE | BEHAVIORAL CHARACTERISTICS | MUSIC EXPERIENCES |
|---|---|---|
| 4 years | Has better motor control.<br>Interested in rules.<br>Plans ahead with adults.<br>Likes to imagine. | May begin skipping.<br>Rule songs and games appropriate.<br>Can make suggestions for music activities.<br>Adds words to songs.<br>Creates songs on instruments.<br>Dramatic movements.<br>Likes to experiment with the piano.<br>Likes to play phonograph records over and over.<br>Can identify simple melodies. |
| 5 to 6 years | Has good motor control.<br>Likes to have rules.<br>Vision not yet fully developed; eye movements slow; likely to have trouble seeing small print or making fine linear distinctions when music staff is not enlarged. Heart in stage of rapid growth. | Able to sit longer.<br>Enjoys songs and dances with rules.<br>Can follow specific rhythm patterns.<br>May pick out tunes on the piano.<br>Likes musical movies but may become restless.<br>Strenuous activity periods should be brief. |
| 7 to 8 years | Begins to read written symbols.<br>Concerned with rules.<br>Cooperation and competition.<br>Logical thought processes emerge.<br>Can compare more than two objects after first object removed (seriation).<br>Thoroughly enjoys group play, but groups tend to be small. Boys and girls play together. | May be able to read words to songs.<br>Rule dances and songs especially valued.<br>Better able to tell reality from fantasy.<br>Can compare three or more sounds or pitches.<br>Likes duets and doing anything musical with a friend.<br>May want to take piano or dancing lessons.<br>Likes group activities including singing games, playing informal instruments, phrase games. |

**FIGURE 17–1 Developmental characteristics and music experiences (cont.)**

Anthropologists and historians have studied a great number of societies, those living and those long gone. Virtually every society that we have ever studied has placed at the center of its priorities music and art (Hollander, 1991, p. 125).

As with other areas of the curriculum, appropriate music activities can be planned only if the teacher understands the developmental levels of the children involved. Although individual rates of development vary widely, the sequence of development follows a particular pattern. Figure 17–1 shows some important behavioral characteristics for each stage of development, along with their effect on a child's experiences with music. This material is based on the theories of Piaget (Wadsworth, 1979) and Erickson (1963) and the writings of Todd and Heffernan (1977). Figure 17–1 should be used as a guide for choosing from the musical activities for children listed at the end of this unit.

**FIGURE 17–2 Musical activities with simple instruments are appropriate for young children.**

## MUSIC EXPERIENCES FOR YOUNG CHILDREN

From preschool age through approximately age eight, children's physical growth rate slows markedly from the earlier period of rapid growth. Increase in body length is the most noticeable physical growth characteristic of this age group. Since large muscles are developed first at this age, music activities that emphasize free movement to rhythms involving these large muscles are most appropriate.

Young children's running, jumping, chasing, and dodging games are also well suited to music activities and rhythmic experiences involving the *whole* body in creative, interpretive rhythms and in active singing games.

Music activities must also be suited to the young child's naturally high activity level, which makes sitting still an effort and wiggling a noticeable sign of this effort. Music activities can meet the young child's need for activity by providing frequent chances for getting up and moving about. Such musical activities are marching, skipping, galloping, etc., with songs and playing informal instruments. And because young children, while active, do tire easily, there should be opportunities for frequent rest breaks in strenuous rhythmic experiences, avoiding prolonged activities that lead to exhaustion.

## GOALS FOR YOUNG CHILDREN'S MUSIC EXPERIENCES

As we have seen, music is a common and enjoyable occurrence in a young child's life. One of the main goals of musical activities for young children is to maintain this natural appreciation of musical experiences. Focusing and then building on this natural enjoyment of music will help you produce the most successful and joyous music program for young children. As in all early childhood activities, it is the *process* that teaches and enriches a young child and not the finished *product*.

Other goals of the early childhood music program include the following:

- Numerous opportunities to sing a wide variety of songs.
- Frequent exposure to various forms of music with wide ranges of rhythms, tempos, and moods.
- Opportunities to hear and learn about music from different cultures and ethnic groups.
- Endless opportunities to express feelings and emotions in song, rhythm, and movement.
- Experience in playing simple instruments, moving to rhythms, and expressing emotions in motion during musical activities.
- Learning to identify some basic musical concepts and terms, such as loud and soft, fast and slow, and high and low.

# THINK ABOUT IT . . .

As you and the children become more accomplished musically, the following hints will add to your musical enjoyment:

- Keep on hand a list of songs you have taught the children. They really enjoy singing old favorites, and it's easy to forget which songs they know. You may want to post the list with some associated picture words so that the children can choose their favorites to sing from this list.
- Try using the Suzuki method when introducing children to a musical classic such as "Peter and the Wolf." Before actually introducing the classic to the children, play the piece as background music for several weeks, during center time, for example. Then, when you tell the story of Peter and the Wolf, the children already will have learned to distinguish the various melodies in the piece and will be able to anticipate what comes next. Follow up with another few weeks of just listening to the piece. Using the Suzuki method, children will never forget the music they learned.
- While playing music, tell stop-and-start stories about characters who wake up, dance around, then fall asleep again. For example, tell a story about dolls that come alive at night in a toy store, then quickly fall asleep when the storekeeper returns. Another one would be jelly beans that roll around in their jar when the cupboard is closed, then stop when the cupboard is open. Or even gelatin, which shakes all around when the refrigerator door is closed, but "sets" when the door is opened. During these stop-and-start activities, vary the volume and tempo of the music to match the characters' actions.

## PLANNING MUSIC ACTIVITIES

In using the suggested activities in this unit and the ones you design yourself, there are some basic guidelines to help ensure your and the children's successful musical experiences.

1. Provide short selections of a variety of kinds of music for the child's listening pleasure. Include both simple children's music and more complex adult music. Include some from each of these categories: spirituals, folk and country, popular contemporary songs, classical and semiclassical, jazz.

2. When you are selecting music for an activity, try to use music that you enjoy. Your enjoyment is apt to be picked up by the child.

3. Schedule musical activities carefully. Intersperse free or spontaneous activities with structured ones. Remember, too, that the structured sessions demand careful and concentrated attention by the child. Too much for too long may create a dislike of music rather than enjoyment. Avoid musical activities requiring concentration when the child is tired, and stop activities at the first sign of fatigue. By the same token, follow strenuous musical activities with a quiet time, such as listening to restful music or to a relaxing story.

4. Do not be concerned about the quality of your singing voice or your gracefulness when dancing. Here is your chance to enjoy being a star. After all, you have a captive, uncritical audience who will think you are great!

5. Make musical activities a shared experience. Through music you can often teach such social skills as sharing, taking turns, and enjoying the company and talents of others. Participate in the activities yourself whenever you can.

6. If you are working with a small group of children, do not expect or insist on full or the same kind of participation by all the children. Some may respond immediately to your plans. Others may

**FIGURE 17–3 Build musical enjoyment on what children already find enjoyable.**

**How to Present a Song to Children**

The method you choose to present a song to children will depend on the mood and the nature of the song itself.

1. *Phrase-wise method.* Introduce the song with a brief story, discussion, or question. Sing one phrase and ask children to repeat. Then sing two phrases and so on.
2. *Whole-song method.* Present the whole song in a variety of ways, rhythmic moving, dancing, playing instruments, or dramatizing to make repetition interesting and meaningful.
3. *Combination of phrase-wise and whole-song method.* The teacher sings and presents the whole song, but asks the children to respond to the easiest part of it—with voices, hands, or an instrument.
4. *Teaching songs from recordings.* The whole-song method is used, responding to the music rhythmically, dramatically, and with instruments. The teacher can use his own voice to clarify the words after several playings.

The songs in the "Activities for Children" section of this unit are good choices for presenting songs to young children. You may, of course, have many other songs of your own choice to teach the children in your group. The songbooks listed at the end of this unit contain numerous other songs appropriate for young children.

**FIGURE 17–4 Some tips on introducing new songs to children.**

need time to listen and observe before deciding to join the group, and still others may not be ready for the activity and will join the group only at a later time (Watrin and Furfey, 1978).

The key to success in all your musical endeavors is flexibility. You should be able to accept more than one kind of response to a music activity and adapt the activity accordingly. If, for example, the child in a planned clapping activity chooses to pat the rug or his leg, accept the response and imitate it as you continue the activity. In fact, the child may interpret your imitation of his response as a form of praise, thus making the enjoyment of what he is doing even greater. Or if the child is more interested in just listening to music than in dancing to it, accept that too. Try to catch him for your dancing activity at another time when he is in a dancing mood. In other words, take your cues from the children and build enjoyment and learning on what they already find enjoyable. Build, don't tear down, the joyful world music naturally creates for young children.

With these guidelines in mind and with an understanding of the developmental needs of children at different ages, a teacher may plan appropriate musical activities for young children. Let us now consider some examples of specific musical experiences appropriate for young children.

**Songs and Singing.** Listen to the sounds of young children playing in the housekeeping corner, on the playground, in the sandbox, in the building block area—you will often hear young children in these everyday situations singing, humming, or chanting familiar songs. Songs and singing are a common occurrence in the everyday life of a young child. Songs—from the earliest lullabies a baby hears to group renditions of the "Happy Birthday" song, holiday carols, and songs from popular children's television shows—are all a familiar part of the pattern of a young child's life. Therefore, teaching songs and singing are a natural part of the early childhood program. The way in which you teach songs and singing to young children must reflect the same natural and enjoyable place music holds in a young child's life.

The following suggestions are intended to help you present songs and singing experiences in the early childhood program in a way that maintains the young child's natural musical interest.

- Choose songs that have a natural appeal for young children. Popular topics include the children themselves, family members, animals, seasons, toys, holidays, etc. Be sure to include songs for all ethnic and cultural groups represented in the class, as well as in the larger community group.
- Choose songs with a clear, strong melody. If the melody is easy to hear, it will be easier to remember.
- Try out all songs yourself first. If, in the process of trying out a song, you find you don't really like it, choose another. Children will surely sense it if you don't really enjoy the song and will reflect your feelings.
- Once you've chosen a song, learn it yourself—and learn it *well.* Nothing is less inspiring to eager songsters than a teacher who has to check her notes while teaching a song. It is important to be spontaneous when you sing with children, and this takes work beforehand.
- Based on the length of a song, you may want to teach it in sections, by verses, or even in short phrases. Often, a song's wording may be a bit tricky, and you may want to practice key words a bit more. Whatever method you choose, remember to be light on practice and heavy on praise. Don't make learning a song work; instead, give children lots of verbal encouragement during singing activities.
- Visual aids can help add to the pleasure of singing and song activities. Pictures of key characters in the song, or a series of pictures on key song events, add interest to song activities. For example, a flannel board with farm animals for "Farmer in the Dell" helps add interest to this old favorite song.
- Encourage *all* attempts at singing. Just as with other

developmental skills, each child will perform at his own unique level. Thus, there is never any reason to compare children's singing or encourage children to compete with one another. If you've ever had the experience of hearing a group of children attempting to out-shout one another in a choral performance, you will know firsthand the results of encouraging competition between young children in singing.

- In the first stages of teaching a song, use a recording. But be careful not to use tapes or recordings too often in the process of teaching songs, to avoid causing a dependence on audio equipment over the human voice for both you and the children. You and the children can sing without them!
- Add movements, gestures, and props when appropriate for the song and for the children. A too heavy emphasis on gimmicks to teach a song is unnecessary if you have chosen a song that interests the children and is of an appropriate level of difficulty for them to learn. Added devices need to be thought of as "spices" and used as such: a few appropriately placed hand gestures in a song is like a dash of cinnamon in the applesauce. An entire routine of cute gestures and too many props adds too much "spice" to the recipe. Let preserving the integrity of both the song and the children be your guides in the use of all "extras" in teaching songs to young children.
- Show your enjoyment of singing. Young children will see it in your eyes, your gestures, and your movements.
- Include the new song in other areas of the curriculum by playing the song softly during center time or rest periods.
- Write key or new words from the song on the blackboard or poster board together with pictures of the word. Read these words aloud to the children. Ask them where they've heard them. Talk and sing the words together.
- Introduce new books related to the song's topic in the language-arts area.
- Include art activities related to the song's topic throughout the week's activities.
- Tape the children singing the song. Have the tape available in the listening center for the children to

enjoy (with earphones or without). Play the tape during your next musical activity session. You may want to retape the next version—with rhythm instruments, with a "solo" performance by one of the children, or with any other new variation you and the children prefer.

- Make rhythm instruments like the circle embroidery hoop, egg shaker, and small plastic bottle rattles (instructions found on page 282) as an activity in the arts and crafts center. Have the children use these as a rhythmic accompaniment to the song.

- Make "flutes" out of paper towel or tissue paper rolls. (See page 282 for instructions.) Have the children decorate them with crayons, colored markers, and stickers, and use their "flutes" to "hum along" to the song.

- Humming through difficult sections of a song is a good way to learn it. Play a "hum-along" game, using the new song. You may begin by humming parts of the song (or the whole song) for the children. Then hum it all together as a group. Then hum a part, and have a child (or several children) hum the next part. Have different children continue until you've hummed the whole song.

**Varying the Rhythm of the Program.** Just as variety is the spice of life, variety provides the same spark for the early childhood music program. Al-

**FIGURE 17–5 Rhythm instruments are fun to use as children sing their favorite songs.**

though young children enjoy the stability that routine provides, it is important to vary these routines to prevent lessening their, and your own, interest in music. Consider how many people can't remember the words to our national anthem, even though they've heard it innumerable times: it has become so routine that people don't really *hear it* anymore. They've heard it so often, they don't actively listen to it anymore. The same thing can happen in your early childhood music program if you have too rigid a routine.

Variety can be provided in your choice of music, your method of presentation, and your lesson planning.

*Variety in choice of music.* In choosing music for young children, your own interests as well as the children's can improve the variety of your music program. Children's music need not be exclusively from music resource books. In an early childhood classroom, music selections can include classical, jazz, rock, American Indian, South American, and African music, to name only a few. Young children are very interested in what's new and different, and enjoy hearing popular music. In fact, most preschool children can name their favorite pop singers and their latest hits. Although music experiences should expose young children to a wide variety of musical styles, a music program including popular songs gives young children a familiar sound, a friendly starting point. Developmentally, it is appropriate to begin with the familiar, using it as a base for the introduction of new concepts to the child.

Variety in choice of music can also be provided by the families of the children. A teacher may find a rich source of musical variety by asking families to share the names of their favorite music, or even to share tapes, records, or compact discs with the class for special activities. In preparing for special ethnic and cultural holidays, for example, you might find families willing to share favorite holiday music with your group. Some parents may be willing to sing for the group, or bring in special instruments for the children to see and hear. The key is to go beyond *your* likes and the dictates of curriculum guides into the children's lives, their parents' lives, and the community at large, where a variety of music awaits you and your group.

*Variety in presentation.*  We've already discussed several basic methods of presenting a song (See Figure 17–3). In addition to these basics, you need to consider other ways to add variety to your presentation of songs and musical experiences for young children.

- Vary the time of day you have musical activities. Switch from afternoons to mornings and vice versa. Also, don't neglect the spontaneous inclusion of a song during the day. Mixing up a recipe together is an excellent time to vary your program by singing as you work with the children. Singing a song on a nature walk is another. Swinging and singing on the playground is fun. And who can refrain from a song ("The Wheels on the Bus" is an obvious example) on a bus trip? In essence, *plan* for the unexpected occasion to sing, and have a mental repertoire of songs to sing with the children. Singing can make an ordinary event joyous, so start making a list of favorites for this very reason.
- Vary your presentation by having the children choose the songs they want to sing and how they want to present them. Be sure to have available puppets, pictures, rhythm instruments, and audiovisual or other necessary equipment for their creative choices.
- Play games with music. Musical chairs is only one of these games. Games can focus on voice recognition. For example, a child is challenged to guess who is humming the song, or who sang the last verse. A "name that tune" game is also a way to vary the presentation of songs. Play, sing, or hum a few bars of a song for the children to guess. Charades, or acting out a song, is an appropriate musical game for older children.

*Variety in lesson planning.*  The key to variety in lesson planning is *cross-curricular planning.* More specifically, music need not be planned for only one area of the curriculum. Music should cross all curricular areas, and this can be accomplished by specifically planning for it to do just that. Here are some suggestions for this specific planning:

- When making lesson plans for the week, include music in at least two other curricular areas. For example, plan to play music during art activities, and note which selections you will use and on which day. Be sure to make a note to have the tape ready and the tape player set up for the days required. Then, plan to read a book at group time that relates to the new song(s) introduced that week. Plan to locate the book *early.*
- Use music as your cue to adding new materials and props to the housekeeping and dramatic centers. For example, engineer hats, trains, and railroad signs are natural additions when you've planned to teach "I've Been Working on the Railroad" to the children. Putting the book *The Little Engine That Could* (Piper, 1986) in the book corner is another example of a music-inspired topic used in another curricular area.
- Review past lesson plans to assist you in your future planning. We are creatures of habit and often tend to get in a rut when making lesson plans. Review past plans to see what kinds of music you have been introducing, the method of presentation, and curricular coverage. If a pattern is obvious, then you need a change! Make a conscious effort to find new types of music or methods of presentation, or plan a new schedule of times/days for music. If you are bored with the lessons and the planning of music lessons, the children will reflect this as well.

**Songs for Children.**  Thousands of songs have been written especially for young children. Listed below are several kinds of songs appropriate for use with young children. There are many other kinds of songs, such as ballads, rounds, and story songs, which are not included in this list but are covered in the books referenced at the end of this unit.

*Nursery rhyme songs.*  Many young children have already heard nursery rhymes either on television or on children's tapes, or have read to them from nursery rhyme books. Nursery rhyme songs are very simple, well-known rhymes put to music. The melodies are simple, catchy, and easily remembered. References at the end of this unit contain many books with nursery rhyme songs appropriate for young children.

*Lullabies.* Lullabies are another form of music that many young children have heard and enjoyed earlier in their lives. Young children also use lullabies they create themselves as they rock their "babies" to sleep in the drama corner. Lullabies are soft, slow, and soothing. You will find many appropriate lullabies for young children in K. Roth's *Lullabies for Little Dreamers* (Random, 1992), as well as in many other books referenced at the end of this unit.

*Expandable Songs.* An expandable song is one which the child helps to "build" by his own suggestions for further verses. The familiar song "The Wheels on the Bus" is an example of a popular expandable song for young children. Suggesting new movements can also expand a song. For example, a child can make up his own suggested movements as well as new words for the song, "Wheels on the Bus." Expanding songs by using suggestions from young children is an exercise not only in singing, but in creativity. Because it is a creative activity, there are no right or wrong ways to expand on a song: the limit is set only by the children's imaginations. (If the bouncing up and down gets out of hand when using the expandable song favorite, "The Wheels on the Bus," combat this by having the children pretend to "buckle-up" before they begin singing. This reinforces the safety habit of seatbelt use and helps moderate the bouncing to a more acceptable level of energy.)

*Folk and Traditional Songs.* These songs are part of our heritage, sung by children for centuries. Songs such as "Bingo," "I'm a Little Teapot," "Yankee Doodle," and "Where Is Thumbkin?" have been favorites of young children for generations. There are hundreds of these folk songs to choose from, and the traditional and folk music songbooks suggested at the end of this unit will aid you in your selection.

**Rhythm Activities.** Rhythm is present from life's earliest moments, when a baby hears its mother's heartbeat. Infants continue to enjoy rhythms in many everyday situations, such as the soothing ticking beat of a wind-up swing, or the soft sounds and smooth rhythms of a lullaby.

In an early childhood program, one of a child's earliest musical experiences is clapping and moving to rhythmic music. The addition of rhythm instruments is another traditional practice in early childhood music programs. Young children, who love movement and motion in general, are naturally drawn to the use of rhythm instruments. Listening first to the music for its rhythmic pattern and then matching the beat with rhythm instruments is the most familiar method of introducing rhythm instruments. Having young children listen to the music and clap out the beat with their hands or tap it out with their feet is another appropriate, traditional rhythm activity.

To use rhythm instruments, children must learn to listen for a pattern of sounds in the music. In beginning rhythm activities, it's a good idea to choose music with a clear, easy-to-hear beat or rhythm. Marches and many types of ethnic music are excellent choices for this strong beat.

Some children may have difficulty hearing rhythms and/or reproducing them. This can be handled in the same way you would handle a reluctant singer. Specifically, do not force the child to copy your pattern or to use a rhythm instrument or practice this activity. Your emphasis should be on the child's natural enjoyment of music. Whether he can reproduce a rhythm or not is not essential to his enjoyment of music. As many an adult can attest, not being able to sing or reproduce rhythms does not affect one's enjoyment of music.

**Teacher-Made Rhythm Instruments.** Creating rhythm instruments from found objects gives young children another opportunity for self-expression. They receive satisfaction and pleasure from beating rhythmic sounds and keeping time to music on the radio or record player.

*Materials:*

| | |
|---|---|
| paper plates | plastic egg-shaped |
| empty spools | containers |
| pebbles | small plastic bottles |
| nails | sticks |
| toweling rolls | old Christmas bells |
| embroidery hoops | bottle caps |

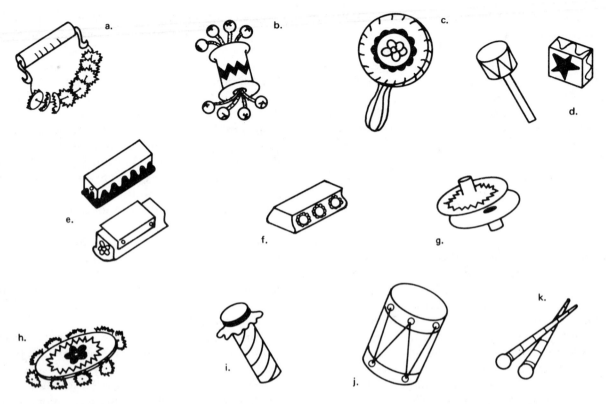

**FIGURE 17–6** Rhythm band instruments: (a) bottle cap shaker, (b) spool shaker, (c) plate shaker, (d) box shaker, (e) sandpaper blocks, (f) clappers, (g) cymbals, (h) tambourine, (i) hummer, (j) drums, (k) drumsticks.

small boxes or cartons     peas or corn
dried beans     wire

*Note:* Some of the instruments discussed below are illustratated in Figure 17–6.

*Bottle cap shaker.* Remove plastic from inside bottle caps. Punch a hole in the center of bottle cap. String on a string and attach to a package handle. Paint if desired.

*Spool shaker.* Paint designs on a large spool. Force four pipe cleaners through the center of the spool. Attach a Christmas bell to the end of each cleaner by bending.

*Plate shaker.* Decorate two paper plates with crayons or paint. Put pebbles, dried corn, peas, or beans between them and staple or sew the plates together with bright yarn or string. Bend wire as shown in Figure 17–5. Fit the ends inside with a loop protruding to form a handle.

*Box shaker.* Place small pebbles, beans, or seeds in a small box or empty clean milk carton to make a shaker. It can be used with or without a handle. Decorate as desired.

*Flute.* Use a paper towel or tissue paper roll. With a pencil, punch three or four holes (about one inch apart) in the cardboard tube. Cover one end of the roll with a piece of waxed paper, as described later in the instructions for the Hummer. Hum a tune in the open end, moving your fingers over the holes.

*Sandpaper blocks.* Paint two small wooden blocks. Place a strip of sandpaper on the surface, allowing

# THIS ONE'S FOR YOU!

## ORGANIZE WITH MUSIC: SONGS FOR INTEREST CENTERS

To add a new, interesting feature to your room, try a song for each area in your room to help direct children to an area as well as provide new ideas for play. First, list the songs you (and the children) are familiar with, then sort them according to the classroom area. For example, have the children lay "miles of track" in the block area to the tune of "I've Been Working on the Railroad." Then build boats with blocks to the tune "Row, Row, Row Your Boat."

Next door in the dramatic area, as the children are "cooking" cakes, they can be encouraged to sing the "Happy Birthday Song." "The Wheels on the Bus" can be acted out with chairs arranged in rows, with a cap for the driver, and even a cardboard steering wheel.

"If You're Ready and You Know It" (a handy version of "If You're Happy and You Know It") can signal time to assemble on the rug for group time. Or start singing a familiar song like "I'm a Little Teapot" at the beginning of cleanup time and see if, after two verses, cleanup time is ended.

Your book corner probably holds a number of nursery rhymes and storybooks already set to music. Why not use "Jack and Jill" one week, then "Hot Cross Buns" another. These nursery rhyme books will become very popular as the children try to match words and pictures to the songs you sing.

Art projects are easy to organize in the art corner to songs like "Frosty the Snowman," which can inspire cotton-ball creations on a painted background. "Old MacDonald" is a great springboard for animal pictures, murals, designs, etc. Cows, horses, pigs, chickens, goats, and ducks are just a few of the ideas in this popular children's song.

"Jingle Bells" can be a year-round favorite. Sing it complete with bells, triangles, drums, and xylophones. "The Ants Go Marching" is another good tune for active participation as children march in time to the music.

Keep a song in your heart in your classroom. Use singing to help organize space and activities. Singing will draw you together at circle time, as well as help foster group cooperation. Try it for variety and fun!

---

an overlap on each end for fastening with thumbtacks. Sandpaper may replace carpet on old eraser blocks. Rub together to make a sound.

*Clappers.* Nail bottle caps to a painted eraser block.

*Cymbals.* Decorate two lids from tin cans. Fasten a small spool or block of wood on for a handle.

*Tambourine.* Tie bottle caps by thin wire, pipe cleaners, or string to a decorated paper or tinfoil plate.

*Hummer.* Decorate a tube from waxed paper or paper toweling roll. Fasten a piece of waxed paper over one end of the tube. Humming through the waxed paper is fun.

*Circle shakers.* Stretch two layers of plastic cloth with uncooked rice or tapioca between them over one half of an embroidery hoop. Fasten with the other half of the hoop to make a circle shaker. (When making any shaker-type toys, be sure that the small objects used are sealed securely inside. Small objects like beans, peas and even rice can pose a serious choking risk to young children.)

*Egg shakers.* Fill plastic egg-shaped containers (either panty hose containers or plastic Easter eggs) with dried beans. Tape the halves together and use them as maracas.

*Bottle shakers.* Collect empty small plastic bottles. Fill with rice, beans, or nuts until half full. Seal bottles that don't have childproof lids with tape. These are excellent shakers for tiny hands.

*Drums.* Glue lids to salt boxes, cereal boxes, or ice cream boxes and decorate with paint to use as drums. Older children may make drums from restaurant-size tin cans with canvas or heavy paper stretched and laced to cover the ends.

*Drumsticks.* Mold balls of paper pulp on the end of two sticks. When this is dry, paint the sticks and use them for drumsticks.

*Clinkers.* Use two coconut shells. Play by hitting shells together.

*Gong.* Use an old license plate (the older the better). Strike with a mallet to play. Describe the sounds.

*Jingle instrument.* Use a set of metal measuring spoons. Play by slapping them into your hand.

*Wrist or ankle bells.* Lace two or three bells through a shoestring. Tie to wrist or ankle. Move to shake your bells.

*Kazoo.* Use a piece of waxed paper over a clean comb. Play by pressing your lips against the paper and humming.

*Box stringed instruments.* Make a round, fairly large hole (3 inches in diameter) in the center of a cardboard box. Stretch rubber bands around the box and over the hole. Pluck the rubber bands like strings to make musical sounds.

## SUMMARY

Music is a common occurrence in a young child's life. Making up original chants and songs and moving rhythmically to musical beats are quite natural to a young child. Music is a natural avenue for a young child's creative expression. Appropriate musical experiences for young children must take into account the child's developmental level and need for self-expression. Careful planning is essential in providing successful learning experiences for children. In this planning, the teacher must consider many things. First, the teacher must plan for the developmental level of the group. Next, it is important to include activities from each area of music—singing, rhythm, instruments, movement, listening, and musical concepts, such as loud and soft. It is equally important to be flexible and happy when presenting musical activities to children. You must enjoy yourself as much as the children. Presenting songs to children may be done by either the phrase-wise method, whole-song method, a combination of these, or teaching songs from recordings. Rhythm instruments may also be used with songs, and these instruments may be teacher- and child-made.

## LEARNING ACTIVITIES

A. Form a group of three or four children from your center, your neighborhood, or local school. Spend at least 15 minutes with them singing songs they know and new ones you teach them. Following this session, write an anecdotal record for each child, commenting on (a) participation in singing, (b) attitude, and (c) knowledge of songs. Compare and contrast the children and comment on the likenesses and differences you found in each anecdotal record.

B. Select from additional sources provided at the end of this unit an appropriate song for each of the following groups of children: four-year olds, six-year olds, two-year olds. Justify each choice using the criterion and information provided in this unit.

C. From your own childhood, recall several popular singing games and action songs that you have not found in this unit. Tape each song along with clear directions on how to play the game or move to the song. Share the activities with your classmates.

D. Choose one of your own favorite songs (popular, rock, country). Teach it to your fellow classmates, using one of the methods discussed. Discuss your experience, including the following points: How well did your "class" learn by the method you chose? Did you feel comfortable using this method? Discuss how you would feel teaching a song you didn't especially like. Would it make any difference in your effectiveness?

E. Using a box of animal crackers and one of the suggested rhythm instruments (preferably a drum) or a hand-clapping accompaniment from your classmates, try the following creative/interpretive movement to rhythm activity:
1. Take out one animal cracker and note what animal it is.
2. "Become" that animal, acting it out by walking, hopping, sliding, etc.
3. Have one (or several) of your classmates pick up your rhythm and beat or clap, accompanying your movement.
4. See who can guess what animal you are. Whoever guesses correctly gets the next opportunity to "become an animal."

F. Using a concept song like "Round the Mulberry Bush" (describing a daily routine), make up several verses and accompanying motions. Share your song and actions with your classmates for comments and improvements. Tape your song to use later with a group of young children. Examples of other concept songs: "Old MacDonald Had a Farm," "If You're Happy and You Know It," "The Wheels of the Bus."

G. Make a drum (tin coffee can with plastic lid, empty oatmeal carton with lid) for the following rhythm activity:
1. Beat a rhythm on the drum for walking, running, skipping, and hopping movements.
2. Beat out a pattern of rhythm and have your peers repeat it by clapping hands (or by using their own handmade drums!).
3. Imitate a pattern clapped (or made on a drum) by one of your peers in the class.
4. Sing a song (your own creation, if you like) to accompany a rhythm you make on your drum.

H. Begin a card file of songs for young children. Use your school library to locate songbooks for young children and choose at least two songs for each of the following categories:

| Category | Sample Songs |
|---|---|
| Emotions | "If You're Happy and You Know |
| Actions | It" |
| Holidays | "Here We Go Looby Loo" |
| Birthdays | |
| Concepts | |

I. Obtain a music supply catalog. Choose $75.00 worth of teaching materials. Explain why you chose each item, for what age group, and how you plan to use it.

J. Make a set of simple rhythm instruments as suggested earlier. Use these instruments in a demonstration lesson on rhythm for your classmates.

## ACTIVITIES FOR CHILDREN

### Suggested Songs to Use with Young Children

#### One, Two, Three, Four, Five

Ella Jenkins

One, two, three, four, five, I caught a fish alive. Six, seven, eight, nine, ten, I let him go again.
Why did I let him go? 'Cause he bit my finger so. Which finger did he bite? The little one on the right.

## Mary Mack

Ella Jenkins

Mary Mack, dressed in black.  Buttons all up and down her back. (Hi Yo 4x)
Give me a nickle, give me a dime.  See my sugar baby all the time. (Hi Yo 4x)
Went to the river, couldn't get across.  Got into trouble with my boss. (Hi Yo 4x)

## The Man in the Moon

The man in the moon looked out of the moon, looked out of the moon and said,
" 'Tis time for all children on the earth to think about getting to bed!"

## See My Pony

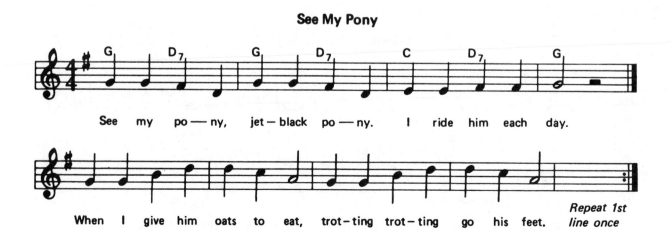

See    my    po — ny,    jet — black    po — ny.    I    ride    him    each    day.

When    I    give    him    oats    to    eat,    trot — ting    trot — ting    go    his    feet.

*Repeat 1st
line once*

## Fingers Are Very Smart

Did you know your fin — gers can tap tap tap? Did you

know your fin — gers can clap clap clap? Yes they can, yes they

can, 'cause your fin — gers are ver — y smart. | Wiggle, wiggle, wiggle, | *Make up*
Jiggle, jiggle, jiggle | *your own*

## My Tambourine

Shake shake, knock knock, shake shake, knock knock. I

play on my tam — bou — rine.        rine.

## Tic Toc

Tic toc tic toc goes the clock. Tic toc tic toc tic tic toc.

### Clap Your Hands

Clap your hands, count one, two, three;
Pull your ear, and slap your knee;
Stamp your feet, one two, three, four;
Wiggle your fingers and touch the floor.

Raise your hands up to the skies;
Touch your nose, then touch your eyes;
Stamp your feet, one, two, three, four;
Wiggle your fingers and touch the floor.

Elbows out, now be a bird;
Touch your mouth without a word;
Softly clap and stamp your feet;
Tip-toe quietly and take your seat.

*Note:* These verses may be used alone or to a steady march tempo as accompaniment, such as "Turkey in the Straw." The value of these verses is in identification of body parts, counting, and diversionary activity.

### Washing Hands and Face
(To the Tune "Skip to My Lou")
Plenty of soap and lots of water,
Plenty of soap and lots of water,
Plenty of soap and lots of water,
Wash, oh, wash your hands.

CHORUS:
Wash, wash, wash your hands,
Wash, wash, wash your hands,
Wash, wash, wash your hands,
Make them clean and neat.

Plenty of soap and lots of water,
Plenty of soap and lots of water,
Plenty of soap and lots of water,
Wash, oh, wash your face.

CHORUS:
Wash, wash, wash your face,
Wash, wash, wash your face,
Wash, wash, wash your face,
Make it clean and shiny.

### The Ants Go Marching One by One

The ants go marching one by one
Hurrah! Hurrah! (Repeat)
When the ants go marching one by one
The little one stops to suck his thumb
And they all go marching down to earth
—to get out of the rain—
Boom, boom, boom, boom, boom, boom, boom, boom!

The ants go marching two by two
Hurrah! Hurrah! (Repeat)
When the ants go marching two by two
The little one stops to tie his shoe
And they all go marching down to earth
—to get out of the rain—
Boom, boom, boom, boom, boom, boom, boom, boom!

The ants go marching three by three
Hurrah! Hurrah! (Repeat)
When the ants go marching three by three
The little one stops to climb a tree
And they all go marching down to earth
—to get out of the rain—
Boom, boom, boom, boom, boom, boom, boom, boom!

Verses:
The ants go marching four by four
The little one stops to shut the door.

The ants go marching five by five
The little one stops to kick a hive.

The ants go marching six by six
The little one stops to pick up some sticks.

Eight by eight—shut the gate
Nine by nine—pick up a dime
Ten by ten—shout THE END.

### If You're Happy and You Know It

If you are happy and you know it
Clap your hands (Clap, clap). (Repeat)
If you are happy and you know it
Then your face will surely show it.

If you are happy and you know it
Clap your hands (Clap, clap).

If you are angry and you know it
Stamp your feet (Stamp, stamp). (Repeat)
If you are angry and you know it
Your face will surely show it.
If you are angry and you know it
Stamp your feet (Stamp, stamp).

If you are sad and you know it
Shed a tear (Sniff, sniff). (Repeat)
If you are sad and you know it
Your face will surely show it.
If you are sad and you know it
Shed a tear (Sniff, sniff).

If you are weary and you know it
Heave a sigh (Whee-you).
(Repeat refrains)

If you are joyous and you know it
Click your heels (Click, click).
(Repeat refrains)

## Mime and Music

When you mix mime with upbeat music, the children will have a chance to exercise creativity and expend energy, too. Make a set of flash cards, including words for objects, actions, sensations, and emotions. Some examples are "wash a dog," "hot," "spaghetti." Play some music and after every eight or 16 bars, hold up one of the cards. The children can do whatever movements the words and music suggest to them.

### Tambourines

A. Young children or those with poor fine motor skills can make a simple tambourine from egg cartons and bottle caps. Simply put a few bottle caps in each egg carton, tape the carton closed, and you have an instrument that players can shake or hit. Or staple together two paper plates, face to face. Leave a small opening to pour in uncooked macaroni, noodles, popcorn kernels, beans, or any available dry material that will rattle. Staple the edges closed and glue or staple fabric scraps or crepe paper all around the outside. This instrument sounds like a maraca, but looks like a tambourine. Children will love playing it both in rhythm and creative movement activities.

B. For an unusual set of musical instruments, assemble an assortment of large nuts, bolts, and washers. Young children will get excellent practice in fine finger movements when they create musical rattles out of these. All you have to do is place several washers on each bolt and loosely turn the nut onto the bolt. Place these inside empty adhesive bandage boxes, tape shut, and use as interesting sound instruments (rattles).

## Music—Your Servant

Music can be your "servant" many times. When you are waiting in the classroom for your turn to join the cafeteria line, sing during those three to five minutes one of the children's favorite songs. It will solve the discipline problems and will bring the children to a happy mood, so necessary at mealtime. When you draw the assignment for the P.T.A. program, present your youngsters in a "musicale." Have the class sing, accompanied by rhythm instruments made by the children. The possibilities are unlimited.

## Music and Art

Have the children paint as they listen to music. The paintings are then cut into giant musical notes and mounted on a bulletin board or taped onto the wall. Be sure to tell the children that their paintings may be cut into notes before beginning this activity. If the child prefers that you *not* cut her painting into a note-shape, respect her wishes and simply mount it on a note-shaped paper backing.

## Sample Listening Activities

A. *Listening for specific sounds and being able to tell what they are* (auditory discrimination).
   1. Have a child play a musical instrument such as a bell, tambourine, drum, triangle, wood block. Another child must close his eyes and identify the object.
   2. A variation of the same game is to have two sounds played, and both must be identified. The number can gradually be increased to see how many can be identified at once.
   3. A child can go to the piano or some other instrument and hit a high or low note. The children in the classroom can show with their hands, arms, or body whether the note is high or low.
   4. Listen for the sound of a bell, drum, etc., from some specific position in the room. The children must have their eyes closed and identify where the sound came from. They also must identify the instrument and tell whether the tone was loud or soft.
   5. Children can identify instruments by comparing two different tones, such as large and small horns, large and small bells, wood blocks, and play blocks.
   6. Children can distinguish the sound effect created by tapping of objects around the room such as

window glass, door, vase, fish bowl, or blackboard. They can compare the tapping of the teacher's pointer with the bouncing of a ball, playing of the piano with the playing of the xylophone or other instruments.

B. *Listening for sounds of nature.* The children must close their eyes and listen for the rain, leaves rustling, the wind, birds, hail, snow, etc.

C. *Listening for school sounds.* Children walking, people laughing, bells ringing, etc.

D. *Listening for outdoor sounds.* Whistles, trucks, cars, train, airplane, etc. You can also listen for occupational sounds, home sounds, etc. Children should be encouraged to use descriptive words for the sounds, such as "It is like a bang, buzz, knock, crash."

E. *Identifying sounds in a series.* The teacher can increase the number of sounds as the class's ability improves. Many records for children are excellent for this type of activity. *Sound Around Us* (Scott Foresman & Co.) is an excellent three-record album for prereading classes.

F. *Listening for a series of high or low notes.*
1. Children listen for a series of high or low notes and identify them by raising or lowering their hands or using the words "higher" or "lower." Children enjoy identifying a series of notes when they actively participate. They might like to raise and lower their bodies and arms as you play.
2. The teacher might have a picture of a painter's ladder or house steps on the blackboard. One child will point to the rung or step as notes go up and down. As their ability to identify improves, you can mix the order of identification.
3. Children enjoy playing "Elevator," a game similar to the one mentioned previously, which starts off simply by having the child going up and down stopping at different floors as the notes are played. Later on this game can be changed to a word game. A simple elevator can be made by cutting out a cardboard square, which can be run up and down on a string.

G. *Rhythms to loud and soft music.* Stamping for loudest, walking for medium, tip-toeing for softest. Clapping and tapping can be used in the same manner.

H. *Huckle-buckle beanstalk.* An object is hidden in the room while one child is in the coatroom. He returns when the class claps. They clap loudly when he is close to the object and softly when he is far away. The game continues with another when the object is found.

## Music and Auditory Discrimination

To help develop children's auditory discrimination (the ability to hear and distinguish the differences among sounds), play a piece of music, occasionally changing the volume from loud to soft, the tempo from slow to fast. Have the children accompany the music with rhythm instruments, adjusting their playing whenever they hear a change on the tape.

## Musical Games

### Where Is the Bell?
A. Equipment: Two or three little bells.
B. Procedure: Seat the children in a circle. Have one child leave the room. Give one of the children in the room a bell that is small enough to hide in his hand. Ask the child who left the room to come back in. When the child has returned, have all of the children stand and shake their fists above their heads. You may use more than one bell when the children become accustomed to the game. The player who is "it" will have three chances to locate the bell.

### Warm-Up (15 minutes)
A. Procedure: A child is blindfolded (or covers his eyes with his hands) and seated. Other children are stationed at different places in the room. On a signal by the teacher, a designated child talks, sings, or plays an instrument. The blindfolded child must identify the child or the instrument.
B. Variations:
1. The instrument is sounded and the blindfolded child must tell if it is near or far away.
2. The instrument is sounded and the blindfolded child must say if it is loud or soft.
3. Children are placed at various points in the room with the same instruments. The teacher indicates which children are to play loudly and which are to play softly. As each is heard, the blindfolded child must point to the place from which the sound came and tell if it was loud or soft.

### "It Is I"
A. Procedure: Play this game when the children know one another fairly well. One child sits in a chair with his back to the class. Another child comes up behind the seated child and knocks three times on the back of the chair. The seated child asks "Who is knocking at my door?" and the other child replies, "It is I." The seated child tries to guess who is knocking by identifying the child's voice. The teacher sets the number of guesses permitted.
B. Variations:
1. Teacher claps his hands or raps on the table in a rhythmic pattern, e.g., short, short, long; long, pause, long, pause; short, short, short. The child repeats the pattern. As soon as the children understand the procedure, they may take turns pro-

ducing rhythmic patterns for the others to imitate.

2. Use rhythm sticks, blocks, or drums to do the same thing.

## Making Music with Bottles

Gather a collection of bottles with both small and large mouths, soft drink bottles, ketchup bottles, quart canning jars, mayonnaise jars, etc.

Blow across the various openings to show the children how different sounds can be made with different-sized bottles. Let the children listen for high and low sounds. Stand the bottles on a table and gently tap them with a spoon. Let the children explore the different sounds the bottles make by blowing across them and by tapping them with a spoon.

## Musical Hugs

As a variation to "Musical Chairs," play "Musical Hugs." Clear a large space in the room for the children to move about freely. Play the music while the children move freely with the music. When the music stops, everyone hugs someone nearby. If several children are close together, they can have a group hug. (This is also a good activity for more grown-up students, like you!)

# UNIT REVIEW

1. Discuss what you consider the greatest obstacles to overcome in order to be an effective music teacher. Relate these to your own personal situation.

2. Describe some examples of how the child spontaneously approaches music. How early do children become involved in musical experiences? Who initiates these activities?

3. What are some basic ways to teach young children new songs? Give an example of each way from your own experience.

4. Discuss what you consider to be one of the most important teacher characteristics in a successful early childhood music program. Give additional characteristics you feel are also necessary.

5. How necessary is it to accompany the singing of young children? If you can't play the piano, how would you conduct a singing activity with young children?

6. How would you introduce a new song to young children? Use an example of a specific song.

7. Discuss some ways rhythm instruments can be used in music activities. What are some general guidelines for both the introduction and use of rhythm instruments with young children?

8. What advice would you give a teacher who is afraid to teach music because she can't play an instrument and doesn't know anything about musical notation, theory, etc? Be specific in your reply, giving suggested activities.

9. What would you do when instead of clapping the rhythm as directed, a child bounces up and down to the beat? How important is your handling of this situation?

# ADDITIONAL READINGS

Erickson, F. *Childhood and Society*. New York: W.W. Norton, 1963.

Todd, V.E., and Heffernan, H. *Years before School: Guiding Preschool Children*, 3rd ed. New York: Macmillan, 1977.

Wadsworth, B. *Piaget's Theory of Cognitive Development*, 2nd ed. New York: Longman, 1979.

Watrin, R., and P.H. Furfey. *Learning Activities for the Young Preschool Child*. Belmont, Calif.: Wadsworth Publishing Co., 1978.

## Selected Children's Books About Children's Music

————. *This Old Man*. New York: Grosset and Dunlap, 1974. Charming illustrations of the folk song. Holes in page emphasis number. Curriculum area: Math.

Adams, Pam, illustrator. *There Was an Old Lady Who Swallowed a Fly*. New York: Grosset and Dunlap, 1973. This book is a "must." The holes in the pages grow larger and larger to show what the old lady swallowed. Children love it! Teaches sequencing, too.

Child, Lydia M., and Brinton Turkle (illus.). *Over the River and Through the Wood*. New York: Scholastic Book Services, 1974. Lovely, "old-fashioned" pictures illustrate the song.

Emberly, Barbara, and Ed Emberley (illus.). *One Wide River to Cross*. Englewood Cliffs, N.J.: Prentice-Hall, 1966. Beautiful woodcuts illustrate the folksong about Noah. Music included.

Fish, Helen D., and Robert Lawson (illus.). *Four and Twenty Blackbirds*. Philadelphia: J.B. Lippincott, 1965.

Nursery rhymes of yesterday recalled for children of today. Some music included.

Hogrogian, Nonny, illustrator. *The Cat Who Loved to Sing.* New York: Knopf, 1988. A story about a regular Pavarotti of a cat. A fine read-aloud book with the words and music to ''Cat Song.''

Keats, Ezra Jack, illustrator. *The Little Drummer Boy.* New York: Macmillan, 1968. This book should be part of every child's Christmas. Mr. Keats has created a ''drummer boy'' that could be of any race. Music included.

Kuskin, Karla, and Marc Simont (illus.). *The Philharmonic Gets Dressed.* New York: Harper and Row, 1982. The 105 members of the Philharmonic Orchestra get ready for a performance. Original, fabulous story accompanied by an abundance of humorous illustrations.

Langstaff, John, and Feodor Rojankovsky (illus.). *Frog Went A-Courtin.* New York: Harcourt, Brace, and World, 1955. Caldecott winner. Color and charm give individuality to Mr. Frog and Miss Mouse. Music included.

————. *Over the Meadow.* New York: Harcourt, Brace, and Co., 1957. Caldecott winner. Realistic pictures that every child should see. Presents a contrast to illustrations in text *Experiences in Music for Young Children.* This should stimulate interest. Music included.

Lionni, Leo. *Geraldine, the Music Mouse.* New York: Pantheon Books, 1979. Geraldine accidentally discovers music and shares this gift with the other mice. Charming story and pictures.

Mill, Eleanor, illustrator. *My Schoolbook of Picture Stories.* New York: Holt, Rinehart and Winston, 1967. No words or music, but every one of the large multiethnic pictures could be used to illustrate a song and stimulate music and discussion. One of the author's favorite books!

Petersham, Maud, and Miska Petersham, illustrators. *The Rooster Crows.* New York: Macmillan, 1945. Caldecott winner. The classic Petersham illustrations portray several well-loved songs and games.

Politi, Leo. *Songs of the Swallows.* New York: Charles Scribner's Sons, 1949. Caldecott winner. Lovely story. Illustrates ''La Golondrina,'' which is good for rest time. Music included.

Prokofiev, Serge, and Frans Haacken (illus.). *Peter and the Wolf.* New York: Franklin Watts, 1968. Stylized, interesting pictures to illustrate the musical story. Effective contrast to the Palazzo illustrations.

Prokofiev, Serge, and Tony Palazzo (illus.). *The Story of Peter and the Wolf.* New York: Doubleday, 1961. Large, modern, realistic pictures to illustrate the classic. Effective for use with children.

Roach, Marilynne R., and Joseph Low (illus.). *The Mouse and the Song.* New York: Parents Magazine Press, 1974.

Based on fact, the story is about a man (H.D. Thoreau) and a mouse who lives in his cellar and shares his lunches. The mouse loves hearing the man's flute music and, later, makes music of his own. Lovely illustrations.

Schackburg, Richard, and Ed Emberley (illus.). *Yankee Doodle.* Englewood Cliffs, N.J.: Prentice-Hall, 1965. Interesting woodcut illustrations for words of the song. Music included.

Walker, M.L. *The Frog's Party.* Albany, N.Y.: A Gentle Wind Publishers, 1989.

Weimer, T.E. *Animal Friends for Sale.* Pittsburgh: Pearce-Evetts Productions, 1991.

Yashima, Taro. *Umbrella.* New York: The Viking Press, 1958. A three-year-old Japanese child who lives in New York City hears the ''music'' on her umbrella. Aesthetic illustrations for adults as well as the very young. Appealing story!

## Music Texts

Bayless, Kathleen M., and Marjorie Ramsey. *Music: A Way of Life for the Young Child*, 3rd ed. Columbus, Ohio: Merrill Publishing Co., 1987.

Boswell, Jacquelyn, ed. *The Young Child and Music.* Washington, D.C.: Music Educators National Conference, 1985.

Chosky, Lois, et al. *Teaching Music in the Twentieth Century.* Englewood Cliffs, N.J.: Prentice-Hall, 1986.

Haines, B.J., and Linda L. Gerber. *Leading Young Children to Music*, 3rd ed. Columbus, Ohio: Merrill Publishing Co., 1988.

Irwin, Phyllis, and J. Nelson. *The Teacher, the Child and Music.* Belmont, Calif.: Wadsworth, Inc., 1986.

McDonald, D.T., and G.M. Simons. *Musical growth and Development.* New York: Schirmer, 1990.

Moomaw, S. *Discovering Music in Early Childhood.* Boston: Allyn & Bacon, 1984.

National Dance Association. *Early Childhood Creative Arts: Proceedings of the International Early Childhood Creative Arts Conference.* Washington, D.C.: NAEYC, 1990.

## Music Resource Books/Song Books

Birkenshaw, Lois. *Music for Fun, Music for Learning*, 3rd ed. Toronto: Holt, Rinehart and Winston of Canada, Ltd., 1986.

Bley, Edgar S. *Best Singing Games for Children of All Ages.* New York: Sterling, 1976.

Burton, Leon, and Kathy Kuroda. *120 Singing Games and Dances for Young Children.* Englewood Cliffs, N.J.: Prentice-Hall, 1981.

Chosky, Lois, and Davis Brummitt. *Music for Very Little People: 50 Playful Activities for Infants and Toddlers.*

(Book and optional cassette.) Farmingdale, N.Y.: Boosey & Hawkes, 1987.

Feierabend, John, and Gary Kramer. *Music, Rhythm & Movement.* Evanston, Ill.: Summy Birchard Publishing Co., 1987.

Hollander, L. "Music, The Creative Process." *The Educational Forum.* (Winter, 1991): 123–133.

Jarrow, J. *All Ears: How to Choose and Use Recorded Music for Children.* New York: Penguin Books, 1991.

Jenkins, E. *The Ella Jenkins Song Book for Children.* New York: Oak Publications, 1966.

Jack, D. *Dance in Your Pants.* Leucadia, Calif.: Ta-Dum Publications, 1988.

McDonald, D.T. *Music in our Lives: The Early Years.* Washington, D.C.: NAEYC, 1990.

Palmer, Hap. *Getting to Know Myself.* (Songbook.) Freeport, N.Y.: Activity Records, 1974.

————. *Learning Basic Skills: Music by Hap Palmer.* Baldwin, N.Y.: Educational Activities, 1984.

Peery, J.C., I.W. Peery, and T.W. Draper, eds. *Music and Child Development.* New York: Springer-Verlag, 1987.

Regner, Hermann, ed. *Music for Children.* Orff-Schulwerk American ed., Vol. 2, Primary. Princeton, N.J.: European-American Music. Corp., 1977.

Reilly, Mary Louise, and Lynn Freeman Olson. *It's Time for Music.* Sherman Oaks, Calif.: Alfred Pub., 1986.

Roth, K. *Lullabies for Little Dreamers.* New York, Random House, 1992.

Weikart, Phyllis. *Movement Plus Music, Activities for Children Ages 3–7.* Ypsilanti, Mich.: High/Scope Press, 1985.

Weimer, T.E. *Folk Songs for Children.* Pittsburgh: Pearce-Evetts Productions, 1992.

Yolen, Jane. *The Lullaby Songbook.* New York: Harcourt, Brace & Jovanovich, 1986.

# RECORDS

Alsop, Peter. *Take Me With You!* Topanga, Calif.: Moose School Records, 1986.

Atkinson, Lisa. *I Wanna Tickle the Fish.* Albany, N.Y.: A Gentle Wind Records, 1987.

Bailey, Charity. *Music Time with Charity Bailey: More Music Time and Stories.* Folkway Records, 43 West 61st, New York, N.Y. 10023.

Barlin, Paul, and Anne Barlin. *Dance-a-Story.* (Albums with books.) Ginn & Co., R.C.A. Records, Educational Dept., 1133 Avenue of Americas, New York, N.Y. 10036.

Berman, Marcia. *Rabbits Dance: Marcia Berman Sings Malvina Reynolds.* B/B Records, 570 Arden Blvd., Los Angeles, Calif. 90004.

Dallas, Patti, and Laura Baron. *Good Morning, Sunshine! Songs for a Day Full of Wonder.* Golden Glow Recordings, 317 Pleasant Street, Yellow Springs, Ohio 45387.

Haber, Jim. *Baby Road.* Golliber Records, 9219 Independence Loop, Austin, Texas 78748.

Hintz, Randy, and Diane Brunengo. *Sing a Song of Sunshine.* Vols. 1 & 3. American Teaching Aids, Covina, Calif.

Jackson, Isaiah. *My First Concert: Isaiah Jackson Conducts the Rochester Philharmonic Orchestra.* Rochester Philharmonic Orchestra, 108 E. Ave., Rochester, N.Y. 14604.

Jenkins, Ella. *Adventures in Rhythm; Call and Response Rhythmic Group Singing; Counting Games and Rhythms for the Little Ones; Early, Early Childhood Songs; Rhythm and Game Songs for the Little Ones; You'll Sing a Song and I'll Sing a Song; and others.* Folkway Records, 43 West 61st St., New York, N.Y. 10023.

Reynolds, Malvina, et al. *Artichokes, Griddle Cakes and Other Good Things.* Pacific Cascade Records, American Education Films, 331 N. Maple Dr., Beverly Hills, Calif. 90210.

Seeger, Pete. *American Folk Songs for Children; Birds, Beasts, Bugs and Little Fishes; Song and Play-Time; and Others.* Scholastic, 904 Sylvan Ave., Englewood Cliffs, N.J. 07632.

————. *Sounds I Can Hear.* (4 albums with graphics.) Scott, Foresman and Co., Glenview, Ill. 60025.

Staton, Barbara R. *Move into Music*, Vols. 1 & 2. Silver Burdett Company, Morristown, N.J.

## Record Libraries/Related Materials/Catalogs

Children's Book and Music Center, 2500 Santa Monica Blvd, Santa Monica, Calif. 90404.

Children's Record Guild/Young People's Records. Fransom Corporation, Institutional Trade Division, 225 Park Ave., South, N.Y. 10013.

Disneyland Records, 800 Sonora Ave., Glendale, Calif. 91201.

Educational Activities, Inc., P.O. Box 391, Freeport, N.Y. 11520.

Folkways Records & Service Corp., 632 Broadway, Ninth Floor, New York, N.Y. 10012. (Charity Bailey, Ella Jenkins, and others.)

Scholastic Records, 904 Sylvan Ave., Englewood Cliffs, N.J. 07632. (Pete Seeger and others.)

# U N I T   1 8

# Creative Language Experiences

**OBJECTIVES**

After studying this unit, you should be able to

- disuss speaking and listening skills in young children.
- define "emerging literacy" (reading readiness) and the various skills it involves.
- explain how to choose and use children's books for teaching young children.
- list some guidelines to follow when reading to young children.
- discuss the importance of poetry for young children's language development.
- discuss the needs of bilingual/bicultural young children.
- discuss the anti-bias curriculum.

## THE DEVELOPMENT OF LANGUAGE

On a warm, sunny, fall afternoon the store was filled with shoppers, many browsing the racks of women's sale-priced clothes. Among them were a grandmother and her daughter, who pushed a pretty toddler along in a stroller. The child wore a large patch over her right eye. Soon, she filled the air with pleading cries, "Off, off!" Her mother simply responded, "The doctor said you have to wear the patch, honey. We can't take it off." When the child continued to cry "Off, off!" in a plaintive voice, the grandmother took a more direct approach, saying, "Now, I'll have *no* more of that. You can't take the patch off." The little girl looked at her grandmother, then resumed her cries, "Off, off!" But this time, when she received no response from her cries, she tugged on the arm of her coat, saying, "Off, off!" She wanted her coat off, *not* her eye patch!

This scene demonstrates the power of a young child's language, both verbal and nonverbal. It also demonstrates very clearly the fact that adults often assume they know exactly what young children are saying and respond to them on this basis. Yet, communicating can be a more complicated process than this, as the preceding scene should emphasize. Two points can be made from this scene: (1) we can never *underestimate* the ability of a young child to get her message across, and (2) we should never *overestimate* our understanding of a young child's message. In this unit we will explore the many facets of language development.

Language is part of a child's total development. As with physical growth, there is a definite developmental pattern to a child's use of language. There are four distinct skills involved in the development of language: speaking, listening (in the sense of comprehending or understanding speech), writing, and reading. Each of these, in turn, has its own pattern of development.

Ability in one language skill is not always directly related to competence in another. For example, many young children are far better speakers than listeners!

In the early childhood program, language experiences must take into consideration the developmental levels of children in each of these four distinct parts of language development. Emphasis in the early childhood program, however, is not on teaching writing and reading. Developing skills that are *related to* reading and writing help prepare a child for more formal instruction in these skills in later years. Thus, reading and writing skills will be handled as "emerging literacy" skills. The term *reading readiness* is also used to describe these skills.

# THIS ONE'S FOR YOU!

## GROUP TIME TECHNIQUES

The value of shared experiences during group time in the early childhood program has been a long accepted fact. Yet, there probably isn't a teacher in existence who hasn't had problems with group time. Here are some tips to help smooth out potential group time problems:

- To establish how long "fair turns" should last, use a sand-filled, hourglass-type egg-timer. When the children learn to use the timer themselves, you won't be the constant judge of when a turn is up.
- To help children get into a circle formation (not always easy), put large colorful paper circles on the floor for them to sit on during group time. When it's time to collect the circles, reinforce color recognition by calling all the reds to bring up their circle mats, then all the blues, and so on, until all circle mats are collected.
- Make simple seating mats for the children to use at group time by writing their names on cardboard squares. Have the children decorate their mats with markers or crayons. Not only will the mats help with name recognition, they'll also allow you to seat the children where you wish.
- Padded seating mats can be made by cutting out two 11″ × 12″ sheets of vinyl wallpaper and punching holes about one inch apart around the edges. Place a magazine or a folded newspaper between the wallpaper sheets to make a cushion. Then, let each child lace the sheets together with yarn. (A bit of tape around the ends of the yarn to form a "needle" will help with the threading.) Write the children's names on the finished mats and place them on the floor before group time begins. This eliminates a mad rush to find one's seat.
- Sharing time will go more smoothly if you limit the number of children who share each day. Listeners will be more attentive and polite to a selected group. This practice also encourages children to take greater care in deciding what to bring for sharing on their own special day.
- Make a special drawstring bag with the words "Show and Tell" written on it, along with your school's name. When it's a child's turn to share, let her take the bag home and bring back something that fits in the bag for "Show and Tell" time.
- To schedule "Show and Tell" times, divide your class into five groups and assign one day of the week to each group as its sharing day. For each group, make a Sharing Day Chart that includes the name of the day and the names of the children. Use a different color of paper and matching ink for each chart and cover the finished charts with clear contact paper. When the charts are displayed on the appropriate days, they will remind the children of special sharing times as well as aid in color and name recognition.
- As an alternative to "Show and Tell" during group time, set up a corner or table in the room for displaying items brought in for sharing. Have a special time for the children to go by the corner or table to see what's on display and to listen to those who have something to share.

satisfy needs by speaking, they gain confidence in their abilities to speak and begin to value language.

Interaction is an important part of communication. Children speak and listen as they play with clay, dough, paint, pegs, blocks, sand, and water. If they feel comfortable when they talk, they are more likely to experiment with language. In a housekeeping area, children talk to each other as they re-enact familiar roles. Formal or informal midday snack arrangements provide natural settings for conversations.

When a teacher relates experiences outside a classroom to children's interests, it gives children new things to talk about and thus enriches language development. If a teacher tells children what to do as they play, she denies them the opportunities for language explorations. They become more involved in following instructions than in talking about what they are doing. They are likely to limit themselves to words the teacher uses, rather than experimenting with words they hear playmates use. A teacher's talk is very important, however, because through spontaneous conversations with children she stimulates their use of language as they interact with her. Children have a need to hear and to be heard by others. In an informal setting they can talk to themselves, to peers, and to adults, getting different kinds of reactions and stimulating further language explorations. A child may communicate without words as he uses a nod, smile, or other nonverbal sign to indicate what she plans to do.

*Language experiences in small-group activities.* In small groups children are more likely to talk to each other and to the teacher and have less anxiety than when they are expected to respond in large groups.

Sharing time in an early childhood program can involve a small group of three to five children talking or 18 or more children being directed in a group discussion. A group of 15 children is too large for a child to speak to. In a large group, it is necessary to limit each child's conversation so that several children have an opportunity to speak, and this limitation tends to discourage children from talking. A group of three to five is a more natural situation for a child.

Formal discussion periods are neither as interesting nor as meaningful as informal conversations in a small group. A child who takes a treasured item out of his pocket to share with two or three friends is probably enjoying a very personal experience. But when "Show and Tell" time is made into a daily ritual in which many children are expected to participate, the personal excitement may disappear for the speaker. The telling supersedes the sharing, and the personal reactions of peers are not part of the experience. When incorporated into a program at an appropriate time, "Show and Tell" can be valued by all as a sharing experience. When it is structured as a language lesson, its values are likely to be lost.

Sharing experiences and ideas in a group situation is a natural phenomenon. At arrival time, some children may have very exciting information they wish to share with their friends—an excellent way for them to use language in a meaningful context. At departure, a few words from the teacher about what a child has done during the day stimulates recall and provides mother and father with something to share with the child as they talk on the way home.

## UNDERSTANDING BILINGUAL/ BICULTURAL YOUNG CHILDREN'S LANGUAGE DEVELOPMENT

Although this book is not designed to be directed specifically to bilingual teachers and children, the population growth of the last decade clearly indicates that language-minority students comprise an increasing proportion of our youngest learners (DeSoto, 1991). The number of non–English-language children, aged birth to 4 years, rose steadily from 1.8 million in 1976 to 2.6 million in 1990, while the number of bilingual children aged 5 to 14 is projected to rise from 3.6 million to 5.1 million by the year 2000 (Oxford, 1984). Demographic evidence also points to "minority" enrollments, including culturally diverse learners, ranging from 70 percent to 96 percent in the nation's 15 largest school districts (Hodgkinson, 1985).

Young, immigrant children from diverse, developing nations such as Haiti, Vietnam, Cambodia, El Salvador, Guatemala, Honduras, and Laos are entering early childhood classrooms usually unprepared to receive them. Experts estimate that two-thirds of young language-minority children may not be receiving the language assistance needed to succeed in school. All of these facts point to the importance of including bilingual/bicultural children in our discussion of language development in the early childhood program (LaFontaine, 1987).

The early childhood teacher plays a critical role in the lives of linguistically and culturally diverse young children. The early childhood setting becomes a home-away-from-home, the first contact with non-family members, the first contact with culturally different people, and the first experience with non-native speakers. A teacher's attitude and knowledge base is crucial in making the early childhood program accepting and appreciative of diversity (Ramsey, 1987).

The possibilities are endless for teachers of young children who, as role models, are in a unique position to establish the tone or "classroom climate" through decision making, collaboration, interactions, and activities.

Teachers of young children are currently implementing a variety of educationally sound strategies for this special population. In addition, based upon recent research (DeSoto, 1991) and what we know about young children, we can do the following:

- Accept individual differences with regard to language-learning time frames. It's a myth to think that young children can learn a language quickly and easily. Avoid pressures to "rush" and "push out" children to join the mainstream classroom. Young children need time to acquire, explore, and experience second-language learning.
- Accept children's attempts to communicate, because trial and error are a part of the second-language learning process. Negotiating meaning and collaborating in conversations are important. Children should be given opportunities to practice both native and newly established language skills.

Adults should not dominate the conversations; rather, children should be listened to. Plan and incorporate opportunities for conversation within dramatic play, storytime, puppetry, peer interactions, social experiences, field trips, cooking, and other enriching activities.

- Maintain an *additive* philosophy by recognizing that children need to acquire new language skills instead of replacing existing linguistic skills. Afford young children an opportunity to retain their native language and culture. Allow young learners ample social opportunities to practice emerging linguistic skills.
- Provide a stimulating, active, diverse linguistic environment with many opportunities for language use in meaningful social interactions. Avoid rigid or didactic grammatical approaches with young children. Children enjoy informal play experiences, dramatizations, puppetry, telephone conversations, participation in children's literature, and social interactions with peers.
- Incorporate culturally responsive experiences for all children. Valuing each child's home culture and incorporating meaningful, active participation will help children develop interpersonal skills and contribute to eventual academic and social success.
- Use informal observations to guide the planning of activities, interactions, and other conversations for speakers of other languages.
- Provide an accepting classroom climate that values culturally and linguistically diverse young children. Young children are part of today's natural resources, capable of contributing to tomorrow's multicultural/multilingual society (DeSoto, 1991).

**The Anti-Bias Curriculum (ABC).** Creative teachers promote an *inclusive environment*, one which addresses both the daily-life realities of cultural diversity as well as the potentially biased attitudes and behaviors that are part of this reality. The early childhood teacher creating an inclusive environment plans the curriculum to address the cultural differences represented by the children in her group and in the society in general. This inclusive curriculum reflects a sensitivity to all cultural groups in all areas of the curriculum. Related inherently to the inclusive environment is the concept of an *anti-bias curriculum (ABC)*. The anti-bias curriculum (ABC) developed by the National Association of Young Children's ABC Task Force and Louise Derman-Sparks (Derman-Sparks, 1990), is an excellent starting point for planning an inclusive, anti-bias curriculum. This booklet, as well as other references at the end of this unit, contain many excellent suggestions on anti-bias curriculum planning, working with parents, suggested books and materials—all essential in preparing an inclusive environment for young children of all cultural groups.

## DEVELOPMENT OF LISTENING

Just exactly how a child learns to listen and understand (comprehend) language has been studied by many researchers and language experts. Some argue that language and thought grow somewhat independently, at least in the early stages of language development. This view does make sense when you consider the fact that young children are often able to learn words and phrases that have no meaning for them. (Remember how three-year-old Drew could sing popular love songs yet didn't understand the words?)

Consider, too, the following scene as another example of young children's development of the understanding of words and their specific meanings:

"Excuse me" or "Thank you"?
Megin, who has been at the center for less than a week, is just beginning to learn the language, routines, and expectations of her new world. She sits close to the teacher. As she eats, she watches the other children, all of whom are relaxed and comfortable. When she finishes eating her lunch, she turns to the teacher and says, "Thank you."
The teacher replies, "You're welcome."
Megin repeats, "Thank you," and the teacher repeats, "You're welcome." Megin appears to be uncertain about what to do next. The teacher observes her distress and asks Megin, "What is the matter?"
Megin explains that she wants to go outside to play. She thought "Thank you" was what she was supposed to say when she had finished eating and wanted to leave the table. (Zavitkovky, p. 4)

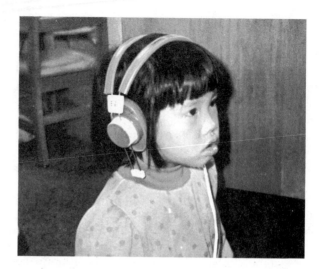

**FIGURE 18–2 Learning to listen is one of the language arts skills.**

Megin has obviously learned more than words in this scene. She also learned that she need not be afraid of making "mistakes" at her center and that eating is a pleasant experience. The teacher notices her concern right away, finds out what Megin is attempting to communicate, and explains the use of the two phrases. Her teacher is a helpful language model, not a critical one.

Young children also *act* as if they have developed concepts at a level that they cannot yet express in words. The best evidence for this is how young children use the rules of grammar (using the past participle "go-ed") long before they have acquired enough language understanding to explain what they are doing (using the past tense).

Because young children think in simple, basic ways, they have difficulty comprehending adult language that is abstract or too complex. Abstraction is beyond the thinking capabilities of the young child in preschool and early elementary years. The teacher or child care worker who is not aware of these language limitations of young children can easily lose their attention. For example, a visiting fire fighter who described the firehose as "a supplementary anti-incendiary device" obviously was unaware of the language level of her audience and more accustomed to addressing adults! In the same manner, a teacher who directs a child pulling another's hair to "be nice" is too general and abstract in her directions. A more appropriate, direct, and less abstract request for a young child would be "Don't pull Jane's hair."

Physical conditions affecting the listener (deafness, hunger, fatigue, illness, and physical environment) can impair the listening process or influence the quality of listening. However, listening is not largely a matter of intelligence. We listen with our experience, not with our intelligence. The child who has had rich and varied experiences will be interested in many facets of living; he will have words in his vocabulary to help him comprehend more of what he hears; and thus he will be better equipped to listen.

The environmental climate or atmosphere in the early childhood program should motivate listening. The atmosphere needs to be one in which children are free to express their ideas; they should feel that their contributions will be accepted and respected.

We listen for different reasons, but generally listening may be said to be of three types: (1) appreciative listening to any kind of stimuli pleasing to the sense of the listener; (2) discriminative listening to informative speech for the purpose of comprehension; and (3) critical listening to persuasive speech for the purpose of evaluating the speaker's argument and evidence.

The progressive stages in developing listening skills and behavior are the following:

- *Little conscious listening.* The child listens only when he is the center of interest and is easily distracted by people and things.
- *Half-listening.* The child is more interested in his own ideas and waits to break in.
- *Passive listening.* The child just sits, with little or no reaction.
- *Sporadic listening.* The child shows interest if the conversation is closely related to his own experience but terminates his attention when the conversation turns away from him.
- *Listening.* The child reacts through comments or questions.

- *Responsive listening.* The child exhibits indications of sincere emotional and intellectual response.
- *Highest level of listening.* The child completely understands what is being said.

Children listen at one or more of these levels throughout the day. Each year the child should be nearer the highest level of listening as a communication skill. Young children will vary in their ability to listen, but every young child can learn basic listening skills as a part of the speech situation. There are many activities at the end of this unit that will enhance a young child's listening skills.

## EMERGING LITERACY SKILLS/READING READINESS

**Readiness for Formal Reading.**  If reading is defined as the interpretation of symbols, it could be said that a child begins reading the day she is born. A baby gets excited when she sees her bottle. She stops crying when mother enters the room and smiles at her. She gurgles with pleasure when members of the family stop to play with her. She is responding to what *she* reads into the actions of others. These experiences precede understanding the printed word.

**FIGURE 18–3 Long before children can read words, they can "read" pictures.**

Not all children should be expected to learn to read in the same way, at the same rate, or at the same age. Children begin by reading pictures, taking great delight in recognizing objects with which they are familiar. As adults read to children, thereby exposing them to words in the books they read, children begin to understand that printed words say something. Some children come from homes where their parents read; others never see a book at home.

Reading involves total development—emotional, social, physical, and intellectual readiness. A child who has not yet acquired large muscle control will not be able to develop more refined skills, such as matching shapes and recognizing patterns needed for reading. Some children are not interested or physically ready to read until they are six, seven, or even eight years of age. When children are forced to engage in reading activities before they are physically, intellectually, or emotionally ready, reading can become a burden. Vision, hearing, diet, and physical coordination are all factors to be considered. Eye–muscle development is necessary and cannot be rushed. Speaking skills are needed for success in reading. And motivation is a primary factor for success.

A child who perceives herself as a reader is more likely to have success than one who does not. When

**FIGURE 18–4 Developing an interest in books is one way to develop a child's future reading ability.**

she sees a reason for decoding and has developed the necessary visual and auditory skills, she is ready to read. This stage of development is most commonly called "reading readiness" but has recently been termed "emerging literacy." Both terms can be used interchangeably and describe not only the time immediately before a child learns to read printed symbols, but also the continuous development of pre-reading skills that begins at birth. Each set of new skills readies the child for more complex reading.

**Factors in Emerging Literacy (Reading Readiness).** The following six factors affect readiness for reading: physical, perceptual, cognitive, linguistic, affective, and environment/experiental conditions:

*Physical readiness.* A child who is in poor general health, whose needs for proper nutrition and rest have not been met, may have difficulty learning to read. Children who have hearing or visual impairments, or those with delayed speech or some other physical problem, may require special attention before tackling the process of reading.

*Perceptual readiness.* In order to read, it is necessary to associate printed language with spoken language. That association requires the child to discriminate among letters and sounds. Though children may be able to see and hear without difficulty, they may have problems in distinguishing similarities and differences in sounds and words. Some children may need practice focusing their attention, attending to details, and developing observation skills.

*Cognitive readiness.* Reading is a cognitive or intellectual process, and such components as comprehension, problem solving, and reasoning require intellectual capacities. Severely retarded people do not learn to read. However, a high IQ is not a prerequisite for the process. At one time it was determined that children should have a mental age of six and a half before being introduced to reading. But other studies indicate that it is the *type* of instruction that is more important than a specific mental age.

| Goals | Methods* Samples of suggested teacher behavior that fosters realization of goals. The teacher's ways and "talk" must build the child's faith in her ability to learn and take into account her unique way of learning and feeling. |
|---|---|
| 1. To discover that who you are, your name, can be said and written down. | 1. Using letters at least ¾ of an inch high, print each child's name on the upper left-hand corner of her paintings, above her cubby or on her box, perhaps on her block building—certainly on the daily chores and birthday charts. Teachers will facilitate children's learning if each letter is consistently formed and a sample name given to each child's parent. |
| 2. To discover that your spoken and written name is different—you can tell it from others. | 2. When a child recognizes her own cubby or box, point out that the cubby holds her sweater, her treasures, and her name. |
| 3. To discover that sometimes you share the same letter with a friend. | 3. If the teacher always arranges names in alphabetical order, some children will discover that Terry and Tony begin and end with the same letter, that Marcella and Mark begin with the same sound. (No word is as important as your name . . . or the names of your friends.) |
| 4. To discover that whatever is spoken can be written down and then shared with others. That when a teacher has written down the words that you spoke a week ago, she can read it today or a month from now. Written words keep experiences alive. | 4. If teachers write down children's personal experiences—like getting new shoes or seeing a dentist—and group experiences that children have enjoyed—like a trip to the farm—then she can assemble these in a book with children's illustrations and photographs and read them aloud from time to time. |
| 5. To discover that the world is full of symbols—shape symbols, word symbols, color symbols—and each symbol has its own special significance. | 5. Teachers responding to readiness levels of individual children use symbols to record weather, birthdays, changes in activities, stopping and going, the day's plan. |
| 6. To discover that words help you tell others about your feelings, your thinking. | 6. Teachers can help children: (a) Develop from grabbing and hitting to the telling level by using expressions like: "Ask him, don't grab it from him." "People don't like grabbing. Ask, and then listen to his answer." "Tell him. Tell me. Use words you know. I know how you feel, and it's alright to feel angry. But you may not hurt other people here. Tell him with words." (b) Dignify their dramatic play by making printed signs, e.g., identifying block constructions, menus for restaurant play, "specials" for store play, signs for transportation play. |

*More activities are at the end of this unit.

FIGURE 18–5 Reading readiness in the early childhood program: Goals and methods.

| Goals | Methods* |
|---|---|
| 7. To discover that words flow from left to right and from top to bottom. | 7. If a child sits beside and not across from a teacher as she writes, her eyes will naturally follow the teacher's pen marks. Each day offers many opportunities to practice systematic eye movements—"reading" pegs on a board, beads on a string, children in a row, paints on an easel, pictures in a book. |
| 8. To discover that new words come through listening to others and then playing back over and over again what you have heard. | 8. Teachers need: (a) To use new words like "triangle," "eight," "cashier," "the same as," "different from," over and over and in many different relevant situations. (b) To ask questions that offer the child the chance to "play back," to use new words. |
| 9. To discover that teachers will take time to listen to what you have to say. | 9. Use every opportunity to listen to the child. An attentive ear and readiness to enter the child's world encourage a child to talk, teach her to listen. |
| 10. To discover that stories and your own experiences follow sequences: and then . . . and then . . . and then . . . | 10. Words are the basis for thinking, problem solving, reasoning. Teachers foster mental growth when they help children recall sequences—in their school day, on a trip, in the bus ride to the center, in a familiar story, in the cycle of seasons or a finger play. |
| 11. To discover that words and pictures in books tell you about things you want to know, and make you wonder about things you never thought of before. | 11. It is important that teachers keep a variety of books and stories to meet the various and changing interests of young children. If books are to "come alive" for children, the teacher must be sensitive to the idea behind the story, the rhythm of words, and the elements of suspense. Continued involvement with books contributes to the teacher's feeling for books. This is caught by the children. |
| 12. To enjoy a story at home with someone you love is to build a desire to read. | 12. Loan books to children to take home and help parents to see how their reading aloud at home builds the child's readiness. |

*More activities are at the end of this unit.

**FIGURE 18–5 Reading readiness in the early childhood program: Goals and methods (cont.)**

**FIGURE 18–6 Language arts are part of all curriculum areas.**

*Linguistic readiness.* Preschoolers are usually skillful users of oral language. This skill is important, as it serves as the basis of the child's understanding of the printed word. Some of the children will have less advanced language fluency, since they may not have had the opportunities for speaking and listening that other children have had. Before these children become involved in the reading process, they may need more opportunities to develop speaking and listening skills.

*Affective readiness.* Just as a child's physical well-being and cognitive development must be considered, one must not overlook the child's affective development. Children may be linguistically capable, intellectually ready, and physically capable, but still have difficulty adjusting to the task of reading. How children feel about themselves, school, and others can have an affect on their ability to read.

*Environmental/experiental readiness.* In order to give meaning to what they are reading, children need experiences relating to those concepts. Many children come to an early childhood program with a rich background of experiences—parents have read to them a great deal, taken them on trips to the zoo and to visit relatives, and so on. Parents have interacted with and related to their children as they walked around the house, explaining what they are doing and why. Children from homes like these already have many clear concepts based on their experiences.

Other children may enter a program with limited experiences. Experiences designed to extend their concepts through trips to the community, books, films, pictures, cooking, play, and special art, music, science, or social studies projects will be necessary.

## PRE-WRITING SKILLS

Another skill that is part of a child's emerging literacy is writing. In the preschool and early childhood period, a child is developing the physical skills needed to write later on in school. It is not the goal to have young children ''practice'' letters and words in the early childhood language arts program. Instead, the goal is to provide young children with opportunities to practice the hand–eye coordination and small-muscle skills needed to be able to write.

For preschoolers, writing is a part of the total language experience, preceded by many fine-motor control activities. Writing begins when children first become interested in making their own marks, and it continues to be a part of their everyday experiences. When children show an interest in writing, large pieces of paper are made available along with crayons, felt-tip pens, and pencils.

For preschoolers, reading and writing are closely related. Writing can be part of the language experience of children when children dictate stories for the teacher to write down.

Although young children often cannot control a pencil well enough to print their names or other words at first, there are many other ways to ''write.'' Of course, children must be willing and interested in such writing-type activities and never forced to become involved against their wishes. Specific activities to enhance emerging literacy skills are found at the end of this unit.

## POETRY EXPERIENCES

Poetry is part of the magic that motivates children to love reading. The educational benefits of including poetry in the early childhood program are many. Exposure to poetry raises children's level of general language development and vocabulary development and whets their appetite for reading, too!

Some other benefits of including poetry on a regular basis in the early childhood program include:

- Poetry's often playful approach to language helps children think about language forms as well as meaning. The predictable rhymes of Mother Goose rhymes naturally segment speech sounds and expose and highlight phonetic similarities and differences in a way that normal speech does not.
- By listening to poetry children can learn that we all share some common experiences such as this one:

*The Drinking Fountain*

When I climb up
    To get a drink,
It doesn't work
    The way you'd think,

I turn it up.
    The water goes
And hits me right
    Upon the nose.

I turn it down
    To make it small
And don't get any
    Drink at all.

- Children take pride in learning to recite short poems. Thus, poetry can be used to stimulate the development of memorization skills, which will aid in future learning. Knowing poems enhances feelings of competence, which is important for young children. Young children who continually hear poetry read effectively, and those who have the opportunity to join informally in reciting it will soon have quite a repertoire of memorized poetry without any effort. It is quite appropriate to expect three- and four-year-old children to happily chant finger plays, Mother Goose rhymes, and short poems such as those found at the end of this unit.

**FIGURE 18–7 Children learn many language arts concepts in art activities.**

- Fingerplays, or poems recited and accompanied by appropriate body movements, help develop coordination and muscle tone. Asking children to invent their own movements helps them develop problem-solving abilities. Some of these poems also help in learning to name body parts (Hokey Pokey, for example). Piaget (1971) saw imitation, such as the movement in fingerplays and action poems, as a means of giving a concrete image of something. This type of symbolic play, he said, attaches related meanings to words. Conversely, capitalizing on the fact that children learn best through their bodies and their senses and through doing things, connecting movement with poetry can encourage enjoyment of poetry; children already enjoy moving!
- Acting out poetry can be a fun and beneficial drama and speech activity. By allowing children to organize and act out poems using props and costumes, the teacher encourages the development of creativity and positive self-concept as well as of language.
- Children can be encouraged to illustrate favorite poems to display in the classroom or to take home, thus stimulating artistic expression and develop-

**FIGURE 18–8 To accompany a poem about animals, a good art activity is to make an animal bean bag from found items, such as pieces of burlap, felt, and yarn.**

ment while aiding language development. Using colored chalks, paint, markers, and crayons, many young artists will illustrate the mood of the poem more movingly than we ever could have imagined!

- Smooth, natural transitions from one activity can be made through the use of carefully selected poems. The poem below, for example, is a perfect choice when the teacher wishes to move from an energetic activity to a quiet one like storytime or a group discussion:

Touch your ears.
Touch your ears.
Touch your nose.
Now bend down and touch your toes.
Wiggle your fingers.
Turn around.
Now bend down and touch the ground.
Clap your hands—1, 2, 3.
Now see how quiet you can be.
(Janice Hayes Andrews)

**Selecting Appropriate Poems.** Using poetry in the classroom will, of course, be much more valuable and enjoyable if the poem selection is made carefully with the children's interests and needs in mind. Not all children have the same needs. And by no means are all children in the three- to six-year age range at the same developmental level. Think about each individual child.

Another important criterion for selecting poetry to present in any classroom is that the teacher should like it, too. It is not possible for a teacher to read a poem well or generate much enthusiasm for it if she does not enjoy it herself.

- When selecting poems, think about what the children are likely to find appealing. From approximately three to six years old, young children like things that seem relevant to them. In order for something to be relevant to children, it must somehow relate to the world as they know it, if not directly to them. By selecting poetry about familiar objects, events, and feelings, the teacher takes a major step toward making poetry interesting and enjoyable for young children.
- Focus on popular topics. There are certain subjects that almost all young children enjoy. For this reason, these subjects are traditionally dealt with in most early childhood programs—self-awareness, the senses, the family, feelings, transportation, seasons, holidays, animals, plants, water, earth, sky. By selecting poems that deal with these subjects as they are being emphasized in class, you can capitalize on the interest generated by other classroom activities: science, social studies, music, and so on. Many children's poetry books classify poems according to these categories, making it easy to find appropriate poems. There are several good collections of children's poetry listed in the references at the end of this unit.

## CHILDREN'S BOOKS

Children's books are a traditional part of the language arts program in most early childhood programs. These books must be chosen with care for young children's use. They must be right for the de-

## USING POETRY WITH YOUNG CHILDREN—A DAILY EXPERIENCE!

A teacher I know sets up a Poetry Corner in her classroom for two- and three-year-olds. She describes it this way:

"Our small Poetry Corner is the second place visited in the center each Monday morning. (Whisper, the rabbit, is first; I run a poor third!) Each Monday, we spotlight a new verse, a poem, or favorite fingerplay complete with illustrations, drawings, a collage of pictures from magazines that relate to the poem, or even a collection of items that make us think of the words of the poem. Because it is ever changing and always exciting, the Poetry Corner is one of our favorite centers.

"Children are much more receptive to poetry than most adults think they are. Since infancy, they have been familiar with fingerplays, rhymes, and short verses. They love the rhythm and cadence of poetry, and they love words that have interesting sounds, even if these words are unfamiliar or nonsensical. It is only a small jump to go further and talk about poetry and poets and even write original verse.

"Here are some of our favorite poetry selections and ideas:

"Young children laugh with Shel Silverstein and love his drawings in the poem 'The Sitter' where an absurd babysitter thinks she is supposed to sit *on* the baby! This poem is found in *A Light in the Attic* (Harper and Row).

"Another funny book of poems that my children love is *The New Kid on the Block* by Jack Prelutsky (Greenwillow Books). We have a favorite 'mouse' song and some pictures of field mice and newborn mice, so the poem 'Boing! Boing! Squeak!' from the book was quoted by lines and words for a long time after the poem had been replaced in the Poetry Corner.

"One of our favorite fingerplays is 'Ten Little Monkeys Jumping on the Bed.' (Can it be because our children would never jump on their beds?) I lettered it broadside on a posterboard, and at circle time everyone helped me decorate and illustrate it. Then, several children got to 'act out' the monkeys!

"Animal poems are always favorites. Sometimes we use imaginary animals, sometimes real ones. 'The Elephant' by Hilaire Belloc is popular:

*The Elephant*
When people call this beast to mind,
They marvel more and more
At such a *little* tail behind,
So LARGE a trunk before.

Because the poem pointed out the obvious and the ridiculous, the children loved it and were happy to help illustrate it in their own unique ways with crayons, paint, and even play dough creations.

"You may want to consider including poetry in your program plans for fun and learning in a different way. All it takes to make your own Poetry Corner is a small section of wall, a corner, a table, or even a large cardboard carton. A screen or pegboard can also be used. Bring in a favorite poem to share with the children. If the poem is about a rose or a daffodil, try to bring one in. This way the children will get an opportunity to see, touch, and smell the poem. If the poem is about a snake, a picture (unless you are braver than I) or two will make the poem come alive."

velopmental level of the child. The pictures should be easily seen, the story easily understood by young listeners. Books also must be at the child's level of interest. The following research report on children's books shows just how important it is to choose the right books for young children.

*Research Report: Sometimes Children Miss the Moral*
Children who read stories about bad boys and girls who learn to be good often pick up the *bad* habits the books are designed to cure, researchers say. This was discovered as a result of a two-month study on what children learn from story books.

The researchers chose for the study 11 popular books that had a moral issue or lesson. They included "Noisy Nancy Norris," "Contrary Woodrow" and "The Toughest and Meanest Kid on the Block." Each of the books is designed to show bad children improving their behavior. But in real life, after children were read these books, it didn't always work that way.

When they read (or were read) a story describing a naughty girl who had a habit of sticking her tongue out, for example, they noticed later that a lot of the children were sticking their tongues out at each other. The effect was especially noticeable in preschool children. Yet, children who read books showing only good behavior did *not* mimic the characters.

The researchers said parents and teachers should look for books with good or neutral behavioral content. The findings of the study concluded that it proves the idea that we must be very sensitive to how books can affect children. (Latzker and Latzker, 1981)

Other research shows that children's books can positively influence a young child's sharing behaviors (Cagan, 1980) and that children's books can even help children better understand death (Godwin and Davidson, 1991; Davis, 1993). Other experts feel that children's books can (and should) help children solve their problems by presenting stories of interest to young children with solutions to problems they present. Other experts believe that books can also help young children better understand and accept handicapped and other exceptional children (Heine, 1991; Saccardi, 1993/1994).

Children's books also give young children some very clear messages about sex roles, family life, and many other important social ideas. (The "Additional Readings" section at the end of this unit lists books that deal with these issues.) It is very important, then, to be sure that the books young children are exposed to in the early childhood program are not biased and present a wide range of social experiences.

**Using Children's Books in Language Arts Lesson Plans.** In language arts, books should be a natural part of the whole program and not only of story time or the book corner. Children's books can be a good starting point for lessons and units. The following two teaching reports are examples of how teachers can use children's books for fun-filled and interesting lesson plans.

*Teaching report #1—using children's books to teach size, shape, and color discrimination.* This teacher used the book *The Carrot Seed* by Ruth Krause (New York: Harper and Row, 1945) to begin her lesson plan. In the book, a boy believes his carrot seeds will produce real live carrots, despite the fact that all his friends and family doubt it. Every day he waters the seeds and watches for signs of growth. His patience pays off one day, when his garden is filled with giant carrots.

The teacher used the children's interest in the idea of a big carrot growing from a speck of a seed to make up a lesson on visual discrimination and plant growth. To prepare for this activity, she collected apple, orange, grapefruit, pepper, carrot, and marigold seeds, which are all different sizes, shapes, and colors. Then she arranged them in groups on a piece of tagboard according to the particular vegetable, fruit, or flower. Covering the tagboard and seeds with clear self-sticking paper kept everything in place.

Next, she set out live examples of each kind of plant and asked the children to match the fruit, vegetable, or flower with its seed. (If the fruits, vegetables, and flowers are out of season, you might want to use a photograph instead.) This gave the children a chance to touch and smell the "real thing."

As a follow-up activity, and in keeping with the carrot theme, she cut the top off a carrot and placed it in a pie pan filled with water. She explained that, besides planting seeds, this is another way to grow

# T H I N K   A B O U T   I T . . .

## HOW TO SHARE A BOOK WITH YOUNG CHILDREN

We know how important books are in the development of language skills for young children, and we know how important reading to children is in the early childhood program. Now here are some hints from a reading expert on how to share a book with young children:

- *Begin with a quality book.* Use a resource such as the children's book review in the journal "Young Children" or in "Children's Editors' Choices," published by the American Library Association. Make a list of several that sound interesting, based upon the annotated bibliography. Then go to the library.
- *Review several books.* Begin by locating several of your choices. Skim through each book by looking at the pictures. This is what children will see, so the visual impression is important. If the pictures in a book appeal to you, go back through and read the text. If the text of the book is appealing as well, go back through and read the text and pictures together. Consider how you would present it to children and imagine what their responses are likely to be.
- *Select a book that both you and the children enjoy.* We sometimes assume that stories we enjoyed as children are the best selections. Your childhood favorites, however, may not be well suited to the developmental level of the children in your group. Many books published before 1970 include stereotypes about women and minorities. There is also the possibility that the books you heard as a child were selected more on the basis of availability than on the basis of quality.
- *Consider the curricular implications.* Look for books that are suitable for storytelling and dramatization, seasonal books, and books that tie in with specific content. Make notes about when and how to share these stories with children. Discuss several of your long-term projects with the librarian and ask for recommendations. There are many resources to help you quickly locate stories on a particular topic or theme.
- *Practice presenting and reading literature aloud.* Consider how you will introduce the book to the children. One teacher showed her preschool class several eggs of different shapes, sizes, and colors before reading *Chickens Aren't the Only Ones* (Heller, 1981). Another teacher used a small toy mouse to introduce *Frederick* (Lionni, 1970).

  When reading aloud to children, remember that your voice is an important tool. It can be used to differentiate among characters or to emphasize an important story element.

  But don't get overly dramatic: a preschooler who heard a particularly chilling rendition of *The Three Billy Goats Gruff* handed the book to her mother and said, "Here, burn this." It *is* possible for adults to get carried away and "perform" a book rather than share it. The human voice should be used far more subtly and effectively.
- *Develop questioning skills.* Although children need to understand that the book is the focus of the conversation, recognize that the child's "agenda" usually differs from an adult's. When the adult-child interaction about a book becomes stilted and predictable, the adult is being too directive.

When teachers share stories with groups of children, there is a limit to the amount of discussion that can transpire before a story begins to lose momentum. Experienced teachers use professional judgment to decide when the children's attention needs to be redirected to the book. As children acquire additional experience with literature, they will become more skilled at focusing discussions on the story or on personal experience related to the story.

Talking about picture books becomes far more pleasurable when adults ask questions without obvious right and wrong answers, questions that challenge children's thinking. When teachers use open-ended discussion techniques (see Unit 1 for more information on open-ended questions), children have opportunities to talk about literature in more meaningful ways. Some recommended questions and comments are the following:

What do you think?

Why? Why did . . .?

What would happen if . . .?

Tell me more about . . .

Do you mean that . . .?

I wonder how . . .?

Maybe we act a little bit like _____ when he or she . . .

Did you ever . . .?

Dialogue about literature need not be children parroting back details recalled from the story. Instead, it can and should be a window on each child's thought process, a means of developing communication skills, and a way for teachers and parents to glimpse children's growth in literacy. (Jalongo, 1988)

vegetables. Checking on the sprouting roots was one of the first things the children did each morning. Throughout the year the teacher planned to root other plants in water, such as a potato, a grapefruit, and an avocado.

*Teaching report #2—using children's books to teach about the seasons.*   This teacher used the book *Frederick* by Leo Lionni (New York: Pantheon, 1970) to help the children recognize the changing seasons in an amusing and poetic way.

The children loved the story of Frederick the mouse. Even though he doesn't gather "corn and nuts and wheat and straw," he does collect beautiful images from the lazy summer and shares them with his friends by reciting a poem: "One is the Spring-mouse who turns on the showers./Then comes the Summer who paints in the flowers./The fall-mouse is the next with walnuts and wheat./And Winter is last . . . with little cold feet."

On a sheet of tagboard the teacher traced the four seasonal mice and designated what season each represented by drawing a small circle above their heads. Inside the circle was a symbol of the particular season. For example, the spring mouse was represented by an umbrella. After stapling these pictures on the bulletin board, she showed the children pictures she had collected of seasonal activities, clothes, holidays, and weather. Their assignment was to pin each picture under the correct seasonal mouse. For example, a picture of a tulip belonged under the spring mouse; an ice skate went under the winter mouse.

Just like these two teachers, when you read a story to young children, or they tell you about a book they love, think about lesson plan possibilities. You may be surprised at the number of fun approaches you can plan with children's books as the starting point. (For further information on choosing children's books, see the references at the end of this unit.)

**The Book Corner.** Create a place where children can explore the world of books. A library or book corner is an important part of every early childhood classroom. As you use books during circle time, children will realize the "magic" of books, that they have good make-believe stories or are full of facts and have pretty pictures. Children will then want to explore those books on their own, so they need to have a well-organized place where they can go and read.

Think about the physical space first and be sure you find a place that is away from the more "active" goings-on in the room, a place where the child can quietly explore books. Gather together a table, some chairs or soft cushions, and shelves for books, records, and magazines. When covering some units, you might want to create an unusual seating place, such as making an airplane out of a large box as you talk and read about types of transportation.

Take time to decorate the nearby bulletin boards or tops of shelves with book jackets, pictures, flowers, and special collections related to the books you have in the book corner.

Place certain kinds of books on the shelves so that they are readily available at all times—Mother Goose books; poetry books; a children's simple encyclopedia (there are some two- and three-volume sets); "sense" books where children can touch, scratch, and smell as they look; some of the classic stories with which children are already familiar, such as *Goldilocks and the Three Bears, The Little Engine That Could, The Three Little Pigs, The Cat in the Hat.* Books reflecting ethnic diversity should always be available for children's use. Books portraying ethnic diversity of children in the group as well as those not represented in the group need to be on the shelves.

As concepts—the alphabet, numbers, animals, families, and transportation—are introduced, provide a special bookshelf or display area where children can find books on those subjects and expand their knowledge about each concept.

You can begin to introduce the organization of a real library by color-coding the different types of books with a colored dot fastened to the bottom edge of each book. Then, use paper strips on the shelves so that children can replace the books where they belong just by matching the strip on the shelf with the mark on the book.

Help children determine what rules should be followed as they read in the book corner; these should relate to behavior, care of books, and removal of books from the areas.

Encourage frequent use of the book corner. This means that you need to change the displays and what books are available so that children will want to explore continually to see what is new. It's hard to be interested in a shabby collection of books casually tossed on a table in the corner of the room!

You may also want to include other media in the book corner, such as records, tapes, and books with tapes or records.

Involve the children in decorating the book corner. They can help you change the display or make pictures for use on the library corner bulletin board. Then the book corner will be a place where they feel they belong.

Just as important as *what* you read is *how* you read it to young children. The following section gives some guidelines for storytelling to help you read to young children in the best possible way.

**Reading to Young Children.** Reading to young children has a few very general requirements. For instance, it is best to work with children's short attention span by choosing books that are not too long. Young children's visual discrimination also requires books that have pictures large enough for them to see. (Remember, the small muscles of the eyes are the last to develop to maturity.) A book with a story that is simple, yet interesting in its wording, is also good for young children. Consider, too, the following suggestions to help you read stories to young children more effectively.

*Guidelines for story groups.*
1. Select a suitable spot—one that is quiet, away from distracting noises and activities. In the quiet corner, have books displayed at children's

eye level. Have books already read out for children to look at and "reread" themselves.

2. See that everyone is seated comfortably. Avoid crowding. Be sure that you as storyteller can see all the children's faces and that they can see yours. Rugs on the floor or ground in a semicircle facing the teacher make a good seating arrangement. Sitting in chairs is uncomfortable for young children and causes a distraction whenever a child falls out of one (which is often!).

3. If using a book, be sure to hold it so that all can see it. Do not hold the book in your lap. The best plan is to hold it out to one side up beside your cheek. This means that you must be able to read the story out of the side of your eye without turning the book toward you.

4. Before you begin to read or tell the story, provide opportunities for the children to look at books on their own. This is a good prereading experience in getting meanings from pictures.

5. Get the children's attention before you start to read. Collect the books they have been looking at and keep them in a pile by you. If the children are restless, some conversation about the book or a familiar fingerplay or song will help draw their attention to you.

6. Be sure you like the story you read, otherwise you will put little enthusiasm into the telling of it.

7. Know your story well! If you do not, you will focus too much of your attention on the book. You must be free to notice the reactions of the children. Also, knowing the story well means that you will be able to tell it with appropriate enthusiasm, expression, and emphasis. Sounds are better made than read. For example, crow for "cock-a-doodle-do" and bark for "bow-wow" instead of just reading the words.

8. Read the story unhurriedly with an interesting, well-modulated voice. Read naturally—do not "talk down" to the children or have a special "storytelling" voice.

9. Do not comment so much throughout the story as you read it or point out so many things in the pictures that you break the thread of the story and spoil its effect.

10. Encourage comments and questions, but not to such a degree that it interrupts the flow of the story.

Practice reading a book to a group of children. Then go back to these guidelines to check to see if you used them effectively with children. It takes a good deal of practice to achieve mastery of the skill of story reading. If you make the experience a fun learning experience for yourself with the children, you are halfway there!

## SUMMARY

Language is a part of the child's total development. Similar to physical growth, there is a definite pattern of development related to a child's growth of language, involving four distinct skills: speaking, listening, writing, and reading. Each of these four skills can develop at different rates in each individual child. This is why one child can be better at speaking than a peer who listens better than she speaks. A teacher of young children needs to understand each child's developmental level for each of these language skills in planning appropriate language arts experiences. For young children of non–English-language background, the early childhood teacher must create an environment which is accepting and appreciative of diversity. For non–English-speaking children, a teacher needs to accept individual differences with regard to language-learning time frames and give young children the time needed to acquire, explore, and experience second-language learning.

There are great differences among children in the age at which they begin to speak and the rate at which they achieve competence. Yet young children can communicate very effectively with a minimum of vocabulary. The ability to speak is not always directly related to the ability to understand. This is why young children can repeat words to a song without understanding what the words mean. Young children may also *act* as if they understand what is said, when in fact, they do not. The teacher or child care worker who is not aware of these language limitations of young children can easily lose their attention. This is because young children are really just learning how to listen. This is also why the teacher must be careful to give young children directions that are at their level of understanding.

Readiness for reading is also termed "emerging literacy." Both terms refer to the time immediately before a child learns to read printed symbols as well as to the continuous development of prereading skills that begins at birth. The factors involved in emerging literacy are physical readiness, perceptual readiness, cognitive readiness, linguistic readiness, affective readiness, and environmental/experiental readiness.

Pre-writing skills are also considered a part of a child's emerging literacy. Learning to write involves fine motor skills and much hand–eye coordination. While actual writing practice is not appropriate in the early childhood program, activities that allow young children to practice these skills, such as paint-ing, cutting, and working with clay, are practice writing skills.

Just as the child develops physically in a gradual process, reading skills also develop gradually. Early experiences at home and in the early childhood program can positively influence a child's reading readiness.

The use of children's books and poetry in the early childhood program is one very good way to help develop young children's reading readiness. Children's books must be appropriate for the developmental level of the child. This means that the pictures must be easily seen and the story easily understood by the young listeners. The way a teacher reads books to young children is just as important as choosing the right books. Guidelines for story groups are designed to help teachers be effective story readers.

## LEARNING ACTIVITIES

A. Observe an early childhood program and describe the language development of the children. Record at least three statements from the children to share with your classmates. Discuss your findings in class.

B. Visit a library and ask a librarian to recommend two good books for each of the following age levels: two-year-olds, three- and four-year-olds, five-year-olds. Compare each of the books on the following points:
   1. Number of pages
   2. Average number of sentences per page; average number of words per sentence
   3. Theme of the book
   4. Number of illustrations and size
   Discuss how the books were similar and different for each age group. If possible, bring your books into class. Share your ideas on them with your classmates.

C. Give examples from your own experience with young children of the various language skills discussed in this unit. For example, do you know any children who are better talkers than listeners? Better listeners?

D. Study the language development of a child three to six years of age and compare it to Figure 18–1. What similarities do you find? What differences do you find? You may wish to make comparisons with an-other child of approximately the same age.

E. Based on the information given in this unit for selecting appropriate books, begin a story file with at least five excellent books for children three to six years of age. Make a card for each book. On the card, include the title of the book, author, illustrator, publisher, copyright date, age level the story is appropriate for, and a brief summary of the story.

F. Go to the drugstore or variety store and look over the inexpensive books offered there for children. Select and purchase a desirable and undesirable one and bring them to class. Be ready to explain their weak and strong points.

G. Observe groups of children at play to collect examples of their language. Group examples according to the ages of the children. What similarities and differences do you observe? Use the chart provided in this unit to group your examples.

H. Observe in a classroom where young children have free-choice activities. Select three activities and, for five minutes during each activity, record children's language as they play. During which activity was there the most talking? Why do you think this was so? How would you change the activities to encourage more talking? Explain.

# POEMS FOR YOUNG CHILDREN

## Animals

### The Animal Store
If I had a hundred dollars to spend,
    Or maybe a little more,
I'd hurry as fast as my legs would go
    Straight to the animal store.
I wouldn't say, "How much for this or that?"
    "What kind of a dog is he?"
I'd buy as many as rolled an eye,
    Or wagged a tail at me!
I'd take the hound with the drooping ears,
    That sits by himself alone,
Cockers and cairns and wobbly pups
    For to be my very own!
I might buy a parrot all red and green,
    And the monkey I saw before.
If I had a hundred dollars to spend,
    Or maybe a little more.

### My Rabbits
My two white rabbits chase each other
With humping, bumping backs.
They go hopping, hopping
And their long ears
Go flopping, flopping
And they make faces
With their noses up and down.
Today I went inside their fence
To play rabbit with them
And in one corner under a loose bush
I saw something shivering in the leaves.
And I pushed
And I looked
And I found
There in a hole in the ground,
Three baby rabbits hidden away
And they made faces
With their noses up and down.

### Baby Kangaroo (Action poem, fingerplay)
Jump, jump, jump goes the big kangaroo.
    (Make jumping motion with index and middle
        fingers; other fingers and thumb are folded)
I thought there was one, but I see there are two—
The mother and a baby. See his head pop out
    (Thumb comes between index and middle
    fingers)
Of her cozy pocket, while he looks about.
Yes, he can see what's going on
As his mother jumps along.

(Repeat jumping motion with thumb showing)
Jump, jump, jump,
Jump, jump, jump,
Jump, jump, jump.

### If You Find a Little Feather
If you find a little feather,
A little white feather,
A soft and tickly feather
    It's for you.
A feather is a letter
From a bird
And it says,
"Think of me,"
"do not forget me."
"Remember me always."
"Remember me at least until
    the little feather is lost."
So—if you find a little feather,
A little white feather,
A soft and tickly feather,
    It's for you.
Pick it up, and put it in your
    Pocket.

### Duck Song
(Tune: "Bell Bottom Trousers")
Six little ducks went out
    for a swim,
Tall ones, short ones, fat
    and thin—
Four little ducks that I
    once knew,
Went out walking two by two—
Down to the river, they did go,
Wiggle, wobble, wiggle, wobble,
    to and fro—

Chorus:
But the one little duck with
    the feathers on his back,
He led the others with his
    "Quack, quack, quack."

### There Once Was a Puffin
Oh, there once was a puffin
Just the shape of a muffin
And he lived on an island
In the
    Bright
        Blue
            Sea!

He ate little fishes,
That were most delicious,
And he had them for supper
And he
    Had
      Them
        For tea.

But this poor little puffin,
He couldn't play nothin',
For he hadn't anybody
To
    Play
      With
        At all.

So he sat on his island,
And he cried for awhile, and
He felt very lonely,
And he felt
    Very small.

Then along came the fishes,
And they said, "If you wishes,
You can have us for playmates,
    Instead
      Of
        For tea."

So they now play together
In all sorts of weather
And the puffin eats pancakes
Like you
    And
      Like me.

### Caterpillar

A fuzzy, wuzzy caterpillar
On a summer day
Wriggled and wriggled and wriggled,
On his way.

He lifted up his head
To get a better view.
He wanted some nice green
Leaves to chew.

He wriggled and he wriggled
From his toes to his head
And he crawled about until
He found a comfy bed.

He curled up tight
In a warm little wrap
And settled himself
For a nice long nap.

He slept and he slept
And he slept until

One day he awoke
And broke from his shell.

He stretched and stretched
And he found he had wings!
He turned into a butterfly
Such a pretty-colored thing.

Oh, how happily
He flew away,
And he flew and he flew
In the sun all day.

### Polliwog

Little Mister Polliwog
You swim to and fro,
When you turn into a frog
You'll hop where'er you go.

### Mice

I think mice
Are rather nice.
Their tails are long,
Their faces small.
They haven't any
Chins at all.
Their teeth are white,
They run about
The house at night.
They nibble things
They shouldn't touch
And no one seems
To like them much.
But I think mice
Are nice.

### The Snail

The snail is very odd and slow,
He has his mind made up to go
The longest way to anywhere,
And then won't let you help him there.

### The Woodpecker

The woodpecker pecked out a little round hole
And made him a house in a telephone pole.
The day when I watched, he poked out his head
And he had on a hood and a collar of red.

### Ducks

A pillow's good for somersaults
Or a softa, or a bed.
But when a duck stands upside down
He likes a puddle for his head.

### The Goldfish

My darling little goldfish
Hasn't any toes;
He swims around without a sound
And bumps his hungry nose.

He can't get out to play with me.
Nor I get in to him
Although I say, "Come out and play."
And he, "Come in and swim."

## Elephants at Work and Play (Action poem, fingerplay)
Five gray elephants marching through a glade
    (March the fingers of the right hand)
Decide to stop and play they are having a parade.
The first swings his trunk and announces he'll lead.
    (Make a trunk of arms and swing back and forth)
The next waves a flag which of course they need.
    (Hold right arm up, bend hand to represent flag,
    wave)
The third gray elephant trumpets a song.
    (Make a trumpet of fists and blow)
The fourth beats a drum as he marches along.
    (Use right fist in drum-beating gesture)
While the fifth makes believe he's the whole show
And nods and smiles to the crowd as they go.
    (Smile and nod to right and left)
Five gray elephants marching through the glade
Have a lot of fun during their parade.

*Suggestion:* At the conclusion let children do an elephant walk, with heads down and arms swinging to resemble the motion of elephants.

## Elephant Hunt
Boom! Boom! Boom! Boom!
The jungle drums are beating.
    (Use the flat of the hands on a flat surface to
        suggest jungle drums)
Boom! Boom! Boom! Boom!
Calling chieftains to a meeting.
    (Use the jungle-drum effect throughout)
They'll plan to have an elephant hunt
And sell their catch to a trader.
He'll put the elephant in a cage
And take him to the zoo later.
Boom! Boom! Boom! Boom!
The jungle drums are still beating.

## Mrs. Peck-Pigeon
Mrs. Peck-Pigeon
Is picking for bread,
Bob-bob-bob
Goes her little round head.

Tame as a pussycat
In the street,
Step-step-step
Go her little red feet.

And with her little round head,
Mrs. Peck-Pigeon
Goes picking for bread.

## If I Were a Fish
I like to play in water
And if I were a fish,
I'd have water all around me
In a big glass dish.

My tail would make it splatter
'Til it splashed the sky,
And the mother fish would only say,
"No, don't get dry!"

## Bird
Once I saw a little bird
Come hop, hop, hop.
So I cried, "Little bird,
Will you stop, stop, stop?"

And as I was going to the window
To say, "How do you do?"
He shook his little tail,
And far away he flew.

## Tiny Tim
I had a little turtle.
His name was Tiny Tim;
I put him in the bathtub
    To see if he could swim.
He drank up all the water;
He ate up all the soap;
And woke up in the morning
    With bubbles in his throat.

## Bugs
I like bugs!
Black bugs
Green bugs
Bad bugs
Mean bugs
Any kind of bugs!

A bug in a rug
A bug in the grass
A bug on the sidewalk
A bug in a glass
I like bugs!

Round bugs
Shiny bugs
Fat bugs
Buggy bugs
Lady bugs
I like bugs!
                    —Margaret Wise Brown

## Legs
Two legs for birds
And you and me
Four legs for dogs
And for squirrels in a tree.

Six legs for beetles—
Away they go.
Eight legs for spiders
What do you know!
      —Aileen Fisher

### The Grasshoppers

High
Up
Over the top
Of feathery grasses the
Grasshoppers hop.
They won't eat their suppers
They will not obey
Their grasshopper mothers
And fathers, who say:
"Listen, my children
This must be stopped—
Now is the time your last
Hop should be hopped;
So come eat your suppers
And go to your beds—"
But the little green grasshoppers
Shake their green heads.
"No, no—"
The naughty ones say
"All we have time to do
Now is to play.
If we want supper we'll
Nip at a fly
Or nibble a blueberry
As we go by;
If we feel sleepy we'll
Close our eyes tight
And snooze away in a Harebell
All night
But not now.
Now we must hop.
And nobody,
NOBODY,
Can make us stop."
      –Dorothy Addis

### Jump or Jiggle

Frogs jump
Caterpillars hump

Worms wiggle
Bugs jiggle

Rabbits hop
Horses clop

Snakes slide
Sea gulls glide

Mice creep
Deer leap

Puppies bounce
Kittens pounce

Lions stalk—
But
I walk!

### Buttercup Cow

Buttercup cow has milk for me
I drink in my silver cup at tea.
Buttercup cow is speckled and white,
She lives in the meadow from morning
   Till night.

Buttercup cow hasn't got any bed,
But the moon and the stars look into her shed.
Buttercup cow, I'm glad to be me,
Drinking your pretty white milk for my
   Tea.

### Bigger

The cow is big
Her eyes are round.
She makes a very scary sound.

I'm rather glad the fence is tall—
I don't feel quite so weak and small.
And yet I'm not afraid. You see,
I'm six years old—and she's just three.
      —Dorothy Brown Thompson

### The Dragon Fly

A dragon fly upon my knee
Is sitting looking up at me.

He has a scarlet tail and six
Little legs like jointed sticks.

With two of them he rubs his head.
His eyes are brown, his mouth is red.

His wings are colored like the rain;
He lifts them, and flies off again.

### My Pony

I have a little pony,
He is very nice and plump.
And he always nuzzles me,
For a sugar lump.

The smell of clover makes him stop
Much quicker than a Whoa:
That's why we named him Clover Top
He likes to eat it so.

### Slow Pokes

Turtles are slow,
As we all know
      But
   To them

It is no worry,
    For
Wherever they roam,
They are always at home,
    So
    They do not
    Have
    To hurry.
      —Laura Arlon

### Fuzzy Wuzzy

Fuzzy, wuzzy,
Creepy, crawly,
Caterpillar funny—

You will be a
Butterfly
When the days are sunny.

## Seeds and Plants

### Mister Carrot

Nice Mister Carrot
Makes curly hair,
His head grows underneath the ground—
And early in the morning
I find him in his bed
And give his feet a great big pull
And out comes his head!

### The Apple

Within its polished universe,
The apple holds a star,
A secret constellation
To scatter near and far.

Let a knife discover
Where the five points hide.
Split the shining ruby
And find the star inside.

### This Man Had Six Eyes

I met a man that had six eyes
And still he could not see.
He lay in bed and hid his head
And would not look at me.

I pulled him up and took him home
(I don't think I did wrong).
And I let him stay, and day by day
I saw his eyes grow long!

I saw them grow out of his head.
I saw them turn to me.
I saw them grow a foot or so.
And *still* he could not see.

"I think he could see the sun," I said,
So I put him on the sill,

And I gave him a drink. But, what do you think?
His eyes kept growing still.

They grew as long as I was tall.
They grew like a sleepy tree.
They grew to the floor and out the door,
And still they could not see.

Now what do you think has eyes that long?
You may tell me now—if you know.
Or, look in the pot: there, like as not,
You will find Mr. Pot 8 oh!
      –John Ciardi

### Seed

In the heart of a seed,
Buried deep so deep,
A dear little plant lay fast asleep.
"Wake," said the sunshine
"And creep to light."

"Wake," said the voice of raindrops bright.
The little plant heard
And rose to see
What the wonderful world
Outside might be.

### Spring

I like March, the soft wind blows,
The tree buds swell,
The white crocus grows.
I like March.

### Dandelions

On dandelions as yellow as gold,
What do you do all day?
I wait and wait in the tall green grass
Til the children come out to play.

Oh dandelion as yellow as gold,
What do you do all night?
I wait and wait in the tall green grass
Till my yellow hair turns white.

And what do the little children do
When they come out to play?
They pick me up in their hands
And blow my white hair away.

## Birthdays

### Five Years Old

Please, everybody look at me.
Today I'm five years old, you see.
After this, I won't be four,
Not ever, ever, anymore;
I won't be three, or two, or one,
For that was when I'd first begun.

Now I'll be five awhile, and then
I'll soon be something else again!

### The Birthday Child
Everything's been different
All the day long.
Lovely things have happened,
Nothing has gone wrong.

Nobody has scolded me,
Everyone has smiled.
Isn't it delicious
To be a birthday child.

### When I Was One
When I was one,
I had just begun.
When I was two,
I was nearly new.
When I was three,
I was hardly me.
When I was four,
I was not much more.
When I was five,
I was just alive.
But now I am six,
I'm as clever as clever
So I think I'll be six now
For ever and ever.

### My Birthday Candles
My mother made a birthday cake,
She says it is for me.
She put six candles on the top
For everyone to see.

When I have a party
This is what I'll do—
I'll make a wish and blow real hard
And hope my wish comes true!

## Action Poems

### Riding
Rumble, rumble, ro
A-riding we will go.
Down the sunny street we ride
Out into the world so wide.
Rumble, rumble, ro
A-riding we will go.

### A Swing Song
Up, down
Up and down,
Which is the way to London Town?
Where? Where?
Up in the air,
Close your eyes, and now you are
    There.

### Swinging
Hold on tightly, up we go
Swinging high and swinging low.

### See-Saw
See-saw Margery Daw,
Jack shall have a new master.
He shall have but a penny a day,
Because he won't work any faster.

### Trains
Over the mountains,
Over the plains,
Over the rivers,
Here come the trains.

Carrying passengers,
Carrying mail,
Bringing their precious loads
In without fail.

Thousands of freight cars,
All rushing on,
Through day and darkness
Through dusk and dawn.

Over the mountains,
Over the plains,
Over the rivers,
Here come the trains.

### Planes
Whenever I hear
Up in the sky,
Zzz zzz uuu mmm
I know an airplane
Is flying by,
Zzz uuu mmmmm mmmmm.

### Marching
See, here comes the big procession
Marching, marching
Down the street.

Dennis and Charles are
    Marching, marching,
    Marching, marching
    Down the street.

### The Ball
Bounce the ball and catch the ball
One, and two!
Bounce the ball and catch the ball,
And I throw it back to you.

Bounce the ball and catch the ball,
One, two, three!
Bounce the ball and catch the ball,
And toss it back to me.

**Blocks**

Blocks will build a tower tall,
Blocks will make a long, long wall,
Blocks will build a house or plane,

A truck, a tunnel, or a train.
Get the blocks, so we can see
What they'll build for you and me.

**Soap Bubbles**

Fill the pipe!
Gently blow;
Now you'll see
The bubbles grow!
Strong at first,
Then they burst,
Then they go to
Nothing, oh!

## About You

**Hiding**

I'm hiding, I'm hiding
And no one knows where;
For all they can see is my
Toes and my hair.

And I just heard my father
Say to my mother—
"But, darling, he must be
Somewhere or other."

"Have you looked in the inkwell?"
And mother said, "Where?"
"In the inkwell," said father.
But I was not there.

Then "wait" cried my mother—
"I think that I see
Him under the carpet."
But it was not me.

"Inside the mirror's
A pretty good place,"
Said father and looked, but saw
Only his face.

"We've hunted," sighed mother
"As hard as we could.
And I am afraid that we've
Lost him for good."

Then I laughed out loud
And I wiggled my toes
And father said—"Look dear,
I wonder if those

Toes could be Ben's.
There are ten of them. See?"

And they were so surprised to find
Out it was me!

**Choosing**

It must be dull to be the street
And just see feet, feet and feet.
It must be dull to be the sky,
But of the two I think that I
Would rather be a slice of sky
Than a sidewalk or a street;
Stars when they go skipping by
Must be prettier than feet.

**All Excited**

I wondered and I wondered
When I could go to school.
They said I wasn't old enough
According to the rule.

I waited and I waited
I was patient as could be.
And now—I'm all excited
It's time for school for me!

**Nose**

It doesn't breathe;
It doesn't smell;
It doesn't feel so very well.

I am discouraged with my nose;
The only thing it does, is blows.

**Daddy**

When Daddy shaves and lets me stand and look
I like it better than a picture book.
He pulls such lovely faces all the time
Like funny people in a pantomime.

**Lunch Time**

I have my own table,
And my own little chair.
And my own little spoon,
And my own bib to wear.

There's always milk
In my own little cup
And I always, always
Drink it all up!

**Mouths**

I wish I had two little mouths
Like my two hands and feet,
A little mouth to talk with
And one that just could eat.

Because it seems to me mouths have
So many things to do,
All the time they want to talk
They are supposed to chew!

**The Train**

My train runs on a track
Chug-a-chug, chug-a-chug
Slow at first, then faster,
Chug-a-chug, chug-a-chug,
Chug-a-chug-chug!

Round and round the wheels go
Just listen to the whistle blow,
Toot-toot-toot!
Chug-a-chug, chug-a-chug,
Toot-toot-toot!!

**Bumps**

Hurrah, for Bobby Bumble
Whenever he gets a tumble
Up he jumps
And rubs his bumps
And doesn't even grumble.

**Toys**

See the toys on my shelf?
I can count them by myself.
One, two, three, four, five.
Here's an airplane, zoom, zoom,
And a drum, boom, boom,
A ball that bounces up and down.
A top that spins round and round.
A telephone, so I can say,
"Come and play with me today."

**Raggedy Ann**

Raggedy Ann is my best friend
She's so relaxed, just see her bend.
First at the waist, then at the knee
Her arms are swinging, oh so free.
Her head rolls around like a rubber ball,
She hasn't any bones at all.
Raggedy Ann is stuffed with rags,
That's why her body wigs and wags.

**The Cupboard**

I know a little cupboard
With a teeny tiny key.
And there's a jar of lollipops
For me, me, me.

It has a little shelf, my dears,
As dark as dark can be,
And there's a dish of Banbury Cakes
For me, me, me.

I have a small flat grandmomma
With a very slippery knee,
And she's the keeper of the cupboard
With the key, key, key.

And when I'm very good, my dears,
As good as good can be,

There's Banbury Cakes, and lollipops
For me, me, me.

**If I Were**

If I were an owl,
At night I'd prowl.
If I were a bear,
At night I'd growl.
If I were a sheep,
At night I'd bleat.
But since I'm a child,
At night I sleep.

## Personal Hygiene

**New Shoes**

I have new shoes in the fall time.
And new shoes in the spring.
Whenever I wear my new shoes
I always have to sing.

**Shoe Lacing**

Across and across the shoe we go,
Across and across, begin at the toe.
Criss and cross us over and then,
Through the hole, and across again!

**Loose Tooth**

I had a little tooth that wiggled
It wiggled quite a lot;
I never could be sure if it
Was coming out or not.

I pushed it with my tongue
To see if it would drop;
But there it stayed and wiggled
Until I thought I'd pop.

My auntie tied it with a string
And slammed the kitchen door!
And now I haven't got a tooth
That wiggles anymore.

**But Then**

A tooth fell out
And left a space
So big my tongue
Can touch my face.

And every time
I smile, I show
A space where something
Used to grow.

I miss my tooth,
As you can guess.
But then, I have to
Brush one less!

**A Good Thing**

When I've finished with my tub
I always play about
With my little sponge and then
I pull the stopper out.

And every day I'm very glad
That I am big and tall;
To slip down through the stopper hole
Would not be funny at all!

**Bed Time**

This little boy is going to bed,
Down on the pillow he lays his head.
Wraps himself in the covers so tight,
This is the way he sleeps all night.

**Washing**

With soap and water,
I rub my hands;
With the bubbly suds,
I scrub my hands,
Rubbity, scrubbity scrub!

Rub my hands
And scrub my hands,
Til no more dirt is seen!
Rub and scrub;
Rub and scrub
And then my hands are clean!

**Naughty Soap Song**

Just when I'm ready to start
    On my ears,
That is the time that my
    Soap disappears,
It jumps from my fingers, and
    Slithers and slides,
Down to the endof the tub
    Where it hides,
And acts in a most disobedient
    Way,
And that's why my soap's
    Growing thinner each day.

**Winking**

It would be fun to wink, I think.
But when I try to shut one eye
The other closes too!
It won't stay open
No matter what I do.

When Daddy winks, it's easy—
Seems like there's nothing to it.
So I'll keep trying very hard
And one day I shall do it.

# ACTIVITIES FOR CHILDREN

## Language Activities

### Name Games

Play with children's names can build a sensitivity to the sounds of language and the use of words. The pure silliness of songs and poetry based on names—"John Jacob Jingleheimer Schmidt, That's My Name Too" or A. A. Milne's "James, James, Morrison, Morrison, Weatherby George Dupree" (1924)—are enjoyable introductions to the sounds, patterns, and fun of language.

- The patterns and rhymes found in children's names can be explored. Begin by clapping the rhythm of children's names: Ste′pha′nie′, Rich′ard′, Al′li′son′. Children can use rhythm sticks, drums, or triangles to follow the beat of their names and find ways to jump, step, hop, or slide to the rhythm of their names. These activities will attune children to the sound of words.
- Children's names can also be used to further understanding of the connection between the spoken and written word. Children's names are spoken and then written over cubbies, on paintings and artwork, and on other personal objects. Use lists of children's names whenever possible so the similarities and differences between names can be observed. You might list all of the children who have a birthday during each month, or those voting to name the guinea pig Christina and those voting to name it Andrea. Other lists might name each child who has brown, black, or blond hair.
- Another language experience that uses names involves constructing two sets of name cards using heavy index cards. Five-year-olds will enjoy using the double set of name cards without direction. They will pick out the two cards with their name, sort and classify names that look alike, begin alike, or end alike. They might pick out all of the names they can read, the names of their friends, or all of the girls' and boys' names. Children can also use these identical sets of name cards to play simple card games. They can match pairs of names, pick a card from a partner's hand and read it, or play other games of their making.

### Outdoor Language Experiences

Outdoor play materials can be used for language experiences. These can promote print awareness in young children. Tricycle paths can have traffic signs (commercial or teacher-made). The work bench can have rebus charts to describe something to build. Animal cages and insect containers can have rebus instructions for care. In addition, seed packages can be used to label plants in the garden, graphs of plant growth can be created, and collections of nature objects can be gathered and labeled. Charts of pictures of safety rules can be on display.

The outdoor classroom provides a variety of avenues for teacher–child and child–child interactions. The teacher should be ready to provide props, label activities, and create charts to enhance print awareness as children enjoy the out-of-doors.

### Recycled Materials for Language Experiences

- *Mail order catalogs.* These are a comfortable hand size for young children and have more pictures and fewer words than regular magazines. Use them to find categories of colors, objects, beginning sounds, etc. Be sure to screen them first for any inappropriate pictures.
- *Purse story.* Fill old pocketbooks with assorted items such as tickets, keys, lists, snacks, make-up, combs, and so on. Have the child examine the contents of the purse and tell about the owner. List the ideas. Draw pictures of how the owner of the purse might look. Tape stories about the owner.
- *Original picture books.* Photograph events throughout the year and have the children use these pictures to tell stories. Place photos and children's stories in a self-sticking photo album to become a permanent part of the book corner.
- *Name game.* Make two 3″ × 5″ name cards for each child in the group. Put cards face-down in random order. Children take turns choosing two to see if they match. If they do, the child takes another turn. If not, play passes to another child. This helps with name recognition, as well as with memory development.

### Language Experiences in the Housekeeping Center
*Materials:* Some materials that encourage reading and writing behavior include note pads; paper and envelopes for writing letters; recipe cards; a pencil holder with a variety of pencils, pens, crayons, markers; catalogs, newspapers, *TV Guides,* magazines, old telephone books; cookbooks; a noteboard or chalkboard; a mailbox with junk mail; blank checks (many banks give away their old ones); and a briefcase with legal pads and pens.

The teacher can encourage children to use these print materials by "setting" the environment. For example, writing "milk" or "Call Sue" on the chalkboard, having mail in the mailbox, stationery on the table, or a cookbook opened with cooking utensils laid out. In addition, teacher comments and questions can facilitate young children's use of print materials. "I see you are going out. Have you written down your phone number so the sitter can call you?" "Why don't you look in the yellow pages of the phone book to see where you can order a pizza?"

### Language Experiences in the Block Center
*Materials:* Use written labels to help children identify their constructions, such as "Fire Station," "Dunkin' Donuts," "Krogers" "Open," "Closed," "Exit." Use written words plus illustrations to define storage space—"large, long blocks" (with a picture of this), "small, square blocks" (picture provided), or "short blocks."

### Language Experiences in the Writing Center
*Materials:* Provide paper for writing letters, notes, envelopes; blank books made of newsprint, computer printouts (backs), typing papers; various pencils, crayons, felt-tip pens; small chalkboard and chalk; printing stamps and ink pads; magnetic letters; an old typewriter; and a message board.

## Visual Discrimination Activities

### Shape Go-Fish
*Equipment:* Construction paper circles, triangles, and squares cut 4″–5″ wide; paper clips; a small horseshoe magnet

*Procedure:*
1. Cut several circles, triangles, and squares from construction paper (preferably of several different colors).
2. Attach a paper clip to each shape.
3. Put one triangle, one circle, and one square on table or floor in front of children (shapes should be of *same* color).
4. Present another circle of the same color as those shapes already out. Say, "Who can catch another fish the *same shape* as mine?"
5. Child "catches" by placing magnet over paper clip on the correct shape (more dexterous children can use "fishing pole"—stick with magnet attached by string).
6. Compare outlines of the two shapes and let children decide if catch is the same. If not, "Throw it back in and try again."
7. As children get more adept at matching shapes, increase the number of paper shapes to choose from and vary the color.

*Variations:*

1. Tape a large circle, large triangle, and large square on floor. Teacher or child holds up shape; other children find matching shape on the floor.
2. Use shape index cards for sorting shapes.
3. *At home:* Glue or color in triangles, squares, and circles on paper plates or sheets of paper. Cut triangles, squares, and circles of paper. Have child sort into paper plate.

### Toy Sort
*Equipment:* Different colors and sizes of balls, toy cars, blocks, and dolls; any category of toys that have obvious differences in form and are familiar to children in the classroom; several boxes and one large box

*Procedure:*

1. Put one of each toy in each of the smaller boxes.
2. Put the rest of the toys in the large box.
3. Show children what is in each of the smaller boxes (have them name the item).
4. Have each child pull a toy from the large box and put it into the small box where it belongs.
5. If child makes a mistake, pull incorrect toy from box and compare it with other toys in box. Comment, "Look, this is a car. What are all these?" "Bells?" "Right." "Can you find the box that has a bell in it?"

*Variations:*

1. Keep crayon stubs in a large canister. Have children sort into boxes by color.
2. Organize art materials so that paints, aprons, brushes, and paper have specific places. Children return materials after use.
3. *At home:* Mix together several pairs of socks that vary in size, texture, and/or color. Have child pair up socks.
4. Mix two kinds of toys together (pop beads with blocks, for example). Have child sort back into proper containers.

### Footprints
*Equipment:* Sheets of construction paper; magic markers; scissors; crayons

*Procedure:*

1. Trace each child's footprints and your own (with shoes on) on construction paper.
2. Have children cut out (teacher may do this if necessary) prints and draw in and color their shoes.
3. Take one of child's prints. Write name on back.
4. Let children compare the sizes of the different prints; then line them up in order of size.

*Note:* If you have a large group of children, divide prints into groups of four or five that have obvious size differences. If prints are all very similar, use one teacher, one child, and one baby print.

5. Prints can be thumbtacked to bulletin board. *Note:* You may want to save one of each child's prints for several months; then repeat the tracing exercise so that children can compare prints and see how much they have grown.

### Apple Half
*Equipment:* Apples; a sharp knife; toothpicks

*Procedure:*

1. Have child close her eyes, hand her apple.
2. Ask her to turn it around while holding it in both hands and guess what it is.
3. After talking about the shape of the apple with the child, say, "Now, let's cut it into two pieces."
4. After cutting the apple, show the child how to put the two pieces together again.
5. Ask the child to show you how to put the apple back together.

*Note:* May stick toothpicks in one half of apple; then stick apple back together.

*Variations:*

1. At snack time cut sandwiches, fruit, or soft cookies in half, let child put two pieces back together. Be sure child eats whatever she has handled.
2. Have plastic barrels or other two-part toys that child can fit together at playtime.

### Play Dough Shapes
*Equipment:* Several different shapes of cookie cutters; play dough or clay; rolling pin

*Procedure:*

1. Have children help you roll dough into relatively flat pieces.
2. Have them take turns cutting out dough with cookie cutters.
3. Try stacking pieces of different shapes.
4. Have children trace around holes in flattened dough.
5. Talk about the different shapes using simple terms. "This one is round. This one has many edges. This one is a heart (like a valentine). See, it is round at the top, pointed at the bottom."
6. Let each child use each shape of cookie cutter.

*Variations:*

1. Have cookie cutters for use in sandpile or clay during playtime.

2. Have shapes (circle, square, triangle) cut from sand-paper for finger tracing.

3. Make cookies or biscuits of different shapes, letting child help you.

### Simply a Bingo Game!

*Equipment:* Lotto cards or picture Bingo game

*Procedure:*
1. Give each child a card (card should have four to eight pictures on it).
2. Draw a picture from the deck of lotto pictures.
3. Describe the pictures: "Here I have a red cat drinking milk. Who has the card of the red cat?" Show the picture to the children.
4. Child who has that picture on her card raises hand and gets the picture to place on card.
5. Play until all children have filled their cards.

*Variations:*

1. Have lotto boards available for children to play with.
2. Have Old Maid card sets.

## Receptive Language Activities

### Treasure Hunt

*Equipment:* 10 pieces of construction paper (8½″ × 11″) with large, clearly defined arrows, e.g.,

package of balloons

*Procedure:*
1. Lay pattern of arrows on classroom floor.
2. Place one balloon ("treasure") at end of pattern.
3. Children are chosen one at a time and directed by teacher: "The arrows will lead you to a treasure. Start here. Follow this arrow to the next. Now, to the next, now to the next," etc. (Child pauses for each of the teacher's directions.)
4. When child reaches balloon, she claims her "treasure." *Optional:* Have child name color of her balloon.
5. Repeat for each child.
6. Teacher may change pattern to go in any direction, going around or under objects in classroom.

*Variation:*

Children blow up balloons. Teacher attaches tape to each balloon. Teacher calls each child by name and color of his/her balloon and directs the child to stick balloon on wall or chalkboard forming a pattern: "John, tape your red balloon on the wall. Bill, tape your yellow balloon next to the red one. Sue, tape your green balloon next to the yellow one," etc.

### Geometric Figures

*Equipment:* Sets of blocks and rings. Set of large blocks and rings, different colors. Set of small blocks and rings of different colors but same colors as large blocks.

*Procedure:*
1. Play with the large blocks. Talk about how they are the same size, how they are different (color).
2. Play with the small blocks. Show how they are the same (size) but different (color).
3. Put the large and small blocks together.
4. Have the children show you the large red block, the small green block, etc.
5. Do the same with the rings.
6. When children are ready, add the rings and blocks together. The children will have to discriminate three characteristics (color, roundness, size).

### The Mystery Bag

*Equipment:* Grocery bag; blindfold; 20 or so common objects (e.g., blunt scissors, blocks, shoes, buttons, cup, pencil, book, etc.)

*Procedure:*
1. Display "Mystery Bag" with objects already inside. Tell children they will all be detectives and each will choose a mystery object by reaching into the bag with their eyes blindfolded or shut.
2. If child guesses object immediately, go on to next child. If she cannot guess, you may supply appropriate "clues." Example: If object is a pencil, say: "This can help you write a letter."
3. Continue around the group, giving each child several chances.

*Variations:*

1. Children can play "Mystery Bag," on their own during independent time. Suggestion: Groups of two or three.
2. In pairs, children can use mystery bag by having one child turn her back while second child chooses object from bag and gives first child a clue to help in guessing object.

## Help the Bunny

*Equipment:* Puppet of bunny (or other character); 15 to 20 objects that are function oriented

*Procedure:* Introduce the bunny and tell the children that he is just a baby and has many new things to learn. They can help bunny by telling him what all the objects are and what he can do with them. Encourage children to tell whether or not object can be used for more than one function. Example: Ball—we can throw it, bounce it, etc.

*Variation:* Encourage children to use puppets. In pairs one child can hold up an object and have puppet ask other child what we do with it, or tell what object can do and have other child's puppet locate object.

## Expressive Language Activities

### Nursery Rhyme Activity

1. Have the children sit on the floor around you. Use familiar short nursery rhymes, e.g., "Jack Be Nimble," "Old Mother Hubbard."
2. Tell the children that you want them to help you tell nursery rhymes. "I will tell you a nursery rhyme and then I want you to tell it."
3. Tell the nursery rhyme; then repeat the first word or two ("Jack be . . .") and ask the children to say the rest.
4. Children love this. They may say only a word or two and you will have to give another key word; e.g., you say "Jack be . . ." The child may say only "nimble." Then you will need to say, "Jack be . . ." She may say only "quick." Then you will say "Jack jumped . . ."
5. Children should be able to repeat 12–13 syllables from familiar nursery rhymes.

### Rainbow Experiences

*Note:* This activity extends ability in repetition to repeating names of colors. Teacher should predetermine that children can identify some basic colors.

*Equipment:* 1" × 12" strips of construction paper in a variety of colors.

*Procedure:*
1. Place strips of colored paper on table.
2. Tell children that they will make a rainbow of colors by listening to the colors teacher says, repeating them, and then picking up correct colors from table.
3. Giving each child a turn, say two colors: Red, blue. Child must repeat in correct order. Then pick up one red and one blue paper strip.
4. Go around group several times until each child has 10 or 12 strips in a variety of colors.
5. Provide each child with a large piece of paper and paste. Encourage children to paste their strips of paper on paper in any design they choose.
6. Children may hang pictures for display if they choose.

*Variation:* Using a cassette recorder with two children, have one child record two sounds or words; then second child repeats into recorder. They then play back two sets of sounds or words to see if they match.

### Match the Sound Game

Make cards with pictures of simple objects (such as a fish, a broom, or a hat) on one side, and the letter the object starts with on the other. Make about 30 cards with each letter of the alphabet represented. Then make another set of cards with a letter of the alphabet on each card. Spread out the alphabet letter cards in rows between the players (four players at the most). One player begins the game by placing one of the picture cards in the middle, and tries to put the right alphabet letter card with it. To check if the letter is correct, the player turns over the picture card to see if the right letter was matched with the right picture. If the cards were matched correctly, the player gets the picture card. The next player tries to match the next picture card with the correct letter of the alphabet, and so on until all the picture cards are won. The winner is the one with the most picture cards.

### The Letter Game

A. In this simple but helpful game, the teacher says, "I went to the store and bought butter, beans, and blocks." The child then adds a word beginning with the same letter.

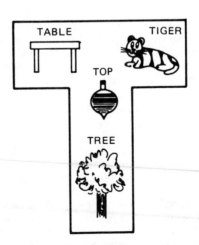

**FIGURE 18–9 Letter "T" of the letter game.**

B. To reinforce letter sounds in an art activity, cut large letters out of paper. Talk about each letter and its sound. Then have the children list all the things they can think of that start with that letter. The large paper letter can then be filled in with pictures or the words suggested by the children. Or the children can draw the objects inside the letter. Over the course of a month, semester, or year, the room can be decorated with these large alphabet letters filled with pictures of objects with that sound.

### What Did I Do?

Make a sound and have the children guess what you did. For example, while the children hide their eyes or look the other way, move a chair, stir something in a bowl with a spoon, close a door, etc.

### Tap Out Rhythms

Use a pencil or coin to tap out a short, simple rhythm on the table. Ask the children to tap out the same pattern. This helps train children to listen carefully and to remember what they heard. These skills are necessary for learning the phonics and sounding patterns of reading.

### Ask Children to Tell a Story

After the teacher has read or told a story, ask the children to help tell a story. The teacher starts with a sentence and lets each child continue it, in turn, from there. For example, "There was once a brown dog running along a country road and all of a sudden he barked at a _____." The child makes up the rest of the story.

### Find the Missing Parts

Old pictures from magazines or coloring books, or even torn reading books, can be used. Parts of the pictures are removed and the child is asked what is missing. Some things to remove: tails of animals, the engine of a train, wheel of a car, etc.

### Simple Verbal Directions

Give the children simple directions. At first, ask the child to perform one familiar task. Then, gradually add another and another until each child is able to remember them and do them in order. This develops alert listening and auditory memory. For example, you can say, "David, please close the door." When he can perform one direction, give him two. "Please close the door and then bring me the paper." When he can perform three directions in the correct order, the child has developed his auditory memory to the level of the average beginning reader.

### Restaurant

The teacher sits at the table and lets one child be the waiter or waitress. The teacher gives the order verbally and makes sure that the "food" served is the same as ordered. Pictures of food cut from magazines or even "play food" from the doll corner can make this activity more fun. Inexpensive props for this activity about food can be made by gluing pictures of food onto paper plates and covering them with clear contact paper to help them last longer.

## Poetry Activities

### Poem of the Week

Use large newsprint to print the poem of your choice. Use illustrations. Try substituting pictures for words in the poem. Have them point to the pictures when you read the poem to them.

### Cluster Poems

Select a subject of interest to young children—animals, seasons, weather. Read several poems, each by a different poet. See if the children like one more than another. Have them talk about why.

### Musical Poetry

Locate a short piece of instrumental music to play as background music to a poem that you read to the children.

### Rhyming Nonsense

Although poetry doesn't have to rhyme to be effective, children do enjoy making their own rhymes. Allow them to create a poem using six rhyming words of their choice. The words do not have to make sense. Write them on paper for the child.

### Descriptive Poem

Have the children select a subject that will be the title of the poem. Encourage them to give you two words that tell something about the subject, for example, *cat*—furry, soft; *broccoli*—green, yucky.

## More Activities for Reading Readiness

### Children's Seeing Ability

In order to learn to read, children must be able to distinguish small differences in the objects they are looking at—differences in size, shape, position, and color.

A. *Provide picture puzzles.* Start with very simple puzzles for the younger children. The pieces should be large and easy to fit together.

B. *Play color detective.* To sharpen the children's sense of color, ask them to point out all red objects in the room, all blue objects, and so on.

## Helping Children Learn to Speak Fluently

A. *Encourage conversation on the toy telephone.* If a child mumbles, the teacher can say, "Speak more clearly, sir. We seem to have a bad connection!" The teacher plays announcer; the children can give a weather report or report the "news."

## Sam Smith's Suitcase

*Procedure:*

1. The first time, the teacher is the leader. The leader says, "My name is Sam Smith. I'm going to take a trip and take along a suitcase. I'll take some of you with me, but only if you take the right thing with you. Remember, I'm going to take a suitcase."
2. Each of the young players is then asked what they will take along. Thomas says, "My name is Thomas and I will take along ties." "You may come," says the teacher. Janes says, "My name is Jane. I'll bring along a ribbon." "I'm sorry," says the leader, "you must stay home this trip." (It may be necessary to tell the children that the only ones who can go on the trip are those who name objects that begin with the first letter of their name.) Be sure to go on a second trip so that those who couldn't go on the first trip get a chance to go.

## Auditory Memory Exercises

Both the teacher and the children are sitting on the floor. The teacher says sentences similar to the following: "Birds fly," "Cows swim under water," and "Snakes drive cars." If the children think the statement is true, they sit still; however, if they think the statement is false, they imitate what the subject of the sentence really does.

## Dog and Bone

One child is selected to be the dog. This child sits on a chair facing away from the other children, who are sitting at their desks. The "dog" closes both eyes. The dog's bone (which is an eraser or any small article) is placed near the dog's chair. Another child, selected by the teacher, tries to sneak up to the dog and get the bone. The child who tries to get the bone then barks, with a disguised voice. This player returns to her seat, and the dog has three tries to guess who has the bone. If the dog does not guess correctly within three tries, the player who has the bone becomes the dog.

## Echo

The teacher claps out a simple rhythmic pattern and the children repeat it. Progress from short rhymes to more complex and longer patterns.

## Listening Exercises

### What Is It?

*Equipment:* Glass, bell, block, tin can, glass of water, book, paper clip to strike a comb with, and drum
*Procedure:* Place a number of objects on a table. Tap these objects so that the children become familiar with the sounds produced. Have the children put their heads down. Tap an object and ask "What is it?" After the children have become familiar with the objects, tap several of the objects and ask which one was tapped first, which second, and so forth.

### Where Is the Bell?

Seat the children in a circle. Have one child leave the room. Give one of the children in the room a bell that is small enough to hide in one hand. Ask the child who left the room to come back in. When the child has returned, have all of the chldren stand and shake their hands above their heads. You may use more than one bell when the children become accustomed to the game. The player who is "it" will have three chances to locate the bell.

### Guess the Animal!

Have the children imitate various animal noises (dog, cat, cow, sheep, etc.). Make sure the noises they make are recognized by the other children. Then blindfold one child or have her cover her eyes while others are positioned around the room. Have one child make an animal noise. The child who is blindfolded must identify the sound and the direction from which it comes. When the blindfolded child gets three right, another child becomes "it."

### What Is It?

*Equipment:* Something one can stand behind and not be seen, a pin, a paper clip, a rubber ball, a pencil, a blown-up paper bag, a tin pan, a rattle, a pebble, castanets, etc.
*Procedure:* Ask children to close their eyes. Stand behind the screen and drop one of the articles on the floor. Ask, "What did you hear?" The performance may need to be repeated several times. Children may take turns dropping the object. Without a screen, children should close their eyes while an object is dropped and then replaced on the table.

## Whose Voice Is It?

Form a circle of several children. Blindfold one child or have her cover her eyes and have this child stand in the middle. Have the children regroup so that each will be in a different place in the circle. Then have each child make a simple statement, such as "I like to play games." The child in the center then points to one child and identifies this child or asks questions (up to three) that must be answered in a sentence. If the child who is "it" guesses correctly, or fails to after three times, "it" returns to the circle and another child becomes "it." To make the game more difficult, have children disguise their voices. (The class can be divided into two or more circles instead of one big circle.)

*Variation:* Blindfold one child (or have her cover her eyes) and point to another who taps several fingers on the table, floor, etc. The child who is blindfolded says "Who's knocking at my door?" The child who knocked says, "It is I." The person who is "it" has three turns to guess correctly. This game, too, may be made more difficult by having children disguise their voices.

## Miscellaneous Activities

### Flannel Board Tips

Flannel boards are excellent for language development activities. Consider the following hints when using a flannel board:

- For easy-to-store flannel boards, purchase old fold-up gameboards at garage sales and cover them with flannel. The boards are sturdy and will stand up by themselves. Make several different backgrounds to use for favorite stories and activities.
- If your room has a storage container on wheels, you can use it as a flannel board as well as a room divider by attaching flannel securely to the back with a staple gun.
- A carpet sample or piece of indoor-outdoor carpeting can be used as a flannel board. Both are available at carpet stores and are relatively inexpensive.
- When making a flannel board, slip a piece of wire screen between the flannel and the backing, and you can use it with magnets.
- Create flannel board shapes easily and inexpensively by making them out of paper towels. Thick, white, rather spongy towels work best. You can use felt markers to decorate the shapes, and the children will love playing with them.
- Save used, sponge-type dryer fabric softener sheets to cut into pieces and use as backing for paper flannel board shapes.
- Other materials that can be used for flannel board

shapes or for backing are felt, flannel, flocked wallpaper, sandpaper, and fabric interfacing.

### Touch Me Box

Cut holes in opposite sides of a cardboard box—large enough for a youngster to put a hand through. Each day place a variety of things inside the box and ask the children to touch the objects. Ask them to describe what they have touched. When selecting objects for the box, try for a good mix of textures—hard, soft, rough, smooth, squishy. Also strive for varied textures that inspire colorful descriptions—velvet, bark, a sponge, sandpaper, cotton, a powder puff, a feather.

### Tick Tock

Many children first learn about time through television. They may know the hour of a favorite television program long before they know when school begins. Ask the children what television programs they watch. Make a wall chart and draw a clock face beside each program showing the time it begins.

### Togetherness

Help children sort objects by like qualities. Ask them: "In what way is this table like that table?" "In what way is this chair like that table?" (They are both made of wood. They both have four legs.) Have the children suggest things that are alike in some ways. Ask: "How many things in the room are made of wood?" "Which are made of plastic?"

### Sorting Practice

Glue different buttons into the bottom sections of egg cartons. Have several extras of each button so the children can place matching buttons in the right cup.

### Classification

Introduce the concept of classification, using everyday objects in the classroom. After explaining that things can be classified in any number of ways, ask the children for suggestions on things they can classify. Accept all suggestions. Start with simple objects—blocks, coins, colored paper—that the children can classify using just one criterion (size, shape, color, etc.). Gradually move into two criteria, such as size and color. Make circles, squares, and triangles from construction paper. First ask the children just to name shapes, then add color, size, and so on.

### Are You Listening?

Fill eight margarine tubs (with plastic lids) with different materials: for example, two with flour, two with buttons, two with nails, two with pins. Have the children find the two that sound alike by shaking them.

## Tape That

Tape a story all of the children have read—but make some mistakes, changing words here and there. Have the children listen to the tape and pick out the errors.

## Character Collage

Instead of wondering how much your children are getting out of the stories you read together, you can enrich their reading experience with a cut-and-paste activity that could generate imaginative thinking and discussion.

Have on hand some old magazines, catalogs, sheets of paper, scissors, and paste or stick glue. First talk a little with the children about a book you have recently read together. Ask the children to identify their favorite character and make this character the subject of a picture collage.

The idea is to think carefully about the character as you all thumb through the magazines, cutting (or tearing, as the case may be) out pictures that in some way represent or remind you of the character. For example, a Winnie-the-Pooh collage may include pictures of a honey jar, a teddy bear, and someone looking thoughtful because, as the children may have observed, "Pooh always sits and thinks before he does anything." After the collage is completed, encourage the children to make up stories about their pictures.

## What's in the Bookstore?

Is there a bookstore in your neighborhood? Take the children on a trip there. (Call ahead to arrange the best time.) Show them some of the most interesting books, especially inexpensive paperbacks. If there is no bookstore nearby, is there another store that sells books? Find out about different book clubs for children.

## Following Directions

Divide the class into pairs. Have one member of each pair give directions to the other to get to the front door; the other member of the pair should follow the directions exactly.

## I Can Read Pictures

Gathering information from pictures is a useful skill. Have the children look at some pictures in a book. How much can they learn about the characters without reading any of the words? Do the words and pictures always agree? Could the children make up a different story to go with the pictures?

## Learning the ABC's

Help children learn to recognize the letters of the alphabet by giving them each a 26-page scrapbook to use as an "Alphabet Book." Each time they learn a new letter, have them glue a lowercase and an uppercase version of the letter in their books along with items or pictures of things whose names begin with that letter. For example, their "B" page might contain a bear cut from fuzzy material, a deflated balloon, a picture of a boat they have colored and cut out, and a sticker with a ball on it. Your children are sure to be very proud of their finished books.

When introducing a new letter of the alphabet, make a special container for the children to fill with items that begin with that letter. For example, put "H" items in a "Hocus-Pocus Hat," or "J" items in a pair of jeans with the legs stitched or tied closed at the bottoms.

## Library Lessons

Do all of the children in the class have a library card? Plan a trip to the public library and ask the librarian to speak to them about all the services the library offers. When the children return to class, ask them to tell about all the services they remember and to explain how to join the library.

## Not Alike

Ask the children to tell how things in the room are not alike. "How is a table different from a chair?" "How is this block different from that block?" Use colored construction-paper shapes and ask: "Find two triangles that are different colors," or "Find three different shapes."

## Who Is That?

Tape voices; radio and television are good sources as well as people you know. Tape voices of people the children know: the custodian, the principal, other children. Tape singers, news announcers, political figures, comedians, cartoon characters, movie stars. Play the voices back and have the children identify them.

## Sound Idea

Use a tape recorder and some imagination to create activities to stimulate children's perceptions and imaginations. Tape all kinds of sounds for the children to identify and describe. Tape individual sounds, such as an alarm clock, a police siren, a piano, a flute, a baby crying, a cat meowing, a dog barking. Play the tape and ask the children to identify the sounds and describe the sound makers.

## Nonverbal Communication

Not all language is verbal. Have the children act out the following phrases silently: "Stop!" "Just a minute!" "Yes!" "No!" "I'm tired." "I have a headache." "That smells good." "What a surprise!"

## Rhyming Game

Children are seated in a circle. The teacher says to a child, "Say, may, day, play. Do these words sound the same?" (Yes)

*Note:* At first, the child may have difficulty understanding the concept of rhyme. In the beginning, it might be easier to offer two choices. Once several children understand what a rhyme is, a game can be made out of it. The first player says a word. The second player says the first player's word and another word that rhymes with it. Continue around the circle in this manner. The third player has to repeat the first two players' words, plus make up a third word that rhymes with the first two. The last child left is the winner.

## Textures

*Equipment:* Various items with different textures, such as salt, flour, rice, beans, water, or ice; several small bowls

*Procedure:* The child places a hand in the first bowl and feels what is inside. The teacher says, "How does the flour in this bowl feel?" The child may answer that it feels "fine." The teacher says "Doesn't it feel soft and smooth?" After two or three different things are felt and described, ask the child to close both eyes. Place one of the three bowls in front of the child. Say, "Let's play a touching-guessing game. What does this feel like?" The child may be able to remember, from the feel of it, what is in the bowl and be able to describe it. If the child has trouble, give some hints. Let the child try the guessing game with the teacher. The teacher closes both eyes and the child places a bowl under the teacher's hand, for the teacher to guess the contents. More items can gradually be added to the game. The children can play the guessing game with each other, too.

## Touch and Tell Game

Ask a child to sit down, close her eyes, and open her hands in front of her. Place an object (stone, pencil, leaf) in her open hands. Ask questions about the object: "What does it feel like? Is it hard or soft? Is it thick or thin? What is it used for? Where is it found? What does it do?" The last question should be "What is it?" The goal of the game is for the child to figure out what the object is without opening her eyes. Let each child take turns holding an object and answering questions about it.

*Note:* This game can be played anywhere, indoors or out. Play it with one or more children. Once they learn the game, the children can play it with each other.

## Colors

*Equipment:* Five or six colors of construction paper cut into shapes (circles, squares, triangles), one piece per child

*Procedure:* The children are seated in a circle. Each places a marker in front of him/herself. The teacher calls out one of the colors. All children having that color run around the circle in the same direction and back to their places. The first one seated upright and motionless is the winner. Different kinds of movements can be specified (skipping, galloping, walking, hopping, etc.).

*Variations:* Use shapes instead of colors.

## Footprints and Handprints

*Equipment:* Finger paint and finger paint paper

*Procedure:* Children step in finger paint and print their right feet and left feet, and then their hands. This work could be saved and used in social studies for a book "all about me."

## Fruit Guess

*Equipment:* Blindfold and various pieces of fruit (orange, apple, pear, banana); vegetables can also be used.

*Procedure:* One child in the group is blindfolded or covers her eyes. The leader of the group hands the blindfolded child a piece of fruit. The child tries to guess the name of the fruit.

## Identifying Body Parts

*Equipment:* Blindfold for each child (tear up an old sheet); a jump rope for each child. (If you have a child who doesn't like to be blindfolded, let her wear a stocking cap pulled down over her eyes. Wearing a cap this way helps the child feel more in control.)

*Procedure:*

1. Children will identify body parts while blindfolded or covering their eyes.
   a. Touch your toes.
   b. Touch your knees.
   c. Touch your elbows.
   d. Touch your shoulders.
   e. Touch your ankles.
   f. Touch your heels.
2. Blind crawl using ropes
   a. Can you crawl over the rope blindfolded or with your eyes closed?
   b. Can you jump over the rope blindfolded or with your eyes closed?
   c. Can you crawl up and down the rope blindfolded or with your eyes closed?
   d. Can you crawl on your back up and down the rope?
   e. Can you hop over the rope blindfolded or with your eyes closed?
   f. Can you jump rope blindfolded or with your eyes closed?

# UNIT REVIEW

1. Describe ways by which children develop language skills. Explain the pattern of growth.
2. Discuss guidelines to follow when reading to young children.
3. Why can some children speak more easily than other children? Why are some children better listeners than others?
4. Why is it important for adults to speak with children at their level during their daily activities?
5. What are some things to consider when choosing books for young children? Why is it necessary to consider these things?
6. Much is said about being "ready" to read. What exactly does "reading readiness" mean? How can a teacher help young children develop readiness for reading?
7. Why are teaching reading and writing not appropriate in the early childhood program? What is taught instead in these two areas?
8. Discuss how to work with bilingual/bicultural young children in language development.

# ADDITIONAL READINGS

## General

Barrow, M. *I Learn to Read and Write the Way I Learn to Talk. A Very First Book about Whole Language.* New York: Richard C. Owen Publishing, Inc., 1990.

Bauer, Caroline. *Handbook for Storytellers.* Chicago: American Library Association, 1977.

Bloom, L. "Language Development Review." In *Review of Child Development Research*, vol. 4, edited by F.D. Horowitz, and E.M. Hetherington, S. Scarr-Salapatek, and G.M. Seigel. Chicago: University of Chicago Press, 1975. Pp. 129–131.

Bruner, J.S. "Learning the Mother Tongue." *Human Nature* 1 (1978): 42–49.

Burke, E.M. *Early Childhood Literature: For Love of Child and Books.* Boston: Allyn & Bacon, 1986.

Cagan, E. "Children's Books and Generosity: An Exploratory Study." *Child Study Journal* 10 (3) (1980): 165–177.

Chenfeld, M.B. *Teaching Language Arts Creatively*, 2d ed. San Diego: Calif.: Harcourt Brace Jovanovich, 1987.

Comer, D. *Growing Up with Literature.* Albany, N.Y.: Delmar Publishers Inc., 1990.

Davis, J.R. "A Lesson on Life . . . and Death." *Learning 93* 22 (1993): 72–78.

Derman-Sparks, L. "Understanding Diversity: What Young Children Want and Need to Know." *Pre-K Today* (Nov.–Dec., 1990): 44–50.

———, and the ABC Task Force. *Anti-bias Curriculum: Tools for Empowering Young Children.* Washington, D.C.: NAEYC, 1989.

Durkin, D. *Getting Reading Started.* Boston: Allyn and Bacon, 1981.

Filmore, Lily Wong. "Language and Cultural Issues in the Early Childhood Education of Language Minority Children." *National Social Studies Education.* 90th Yearbook, Part 1 (1991): 30–49.

Geller, L.G. *Wordplay and Language Learning for Children.* Urbana, Ill.: National Council of Teachers of English, 1985.

Genishi, C., and S.H. Dyson. *Language Assessment in the Early Years.* Norwood, N.J.: Ablex, 1987.

Godwin, C., and P.M. Davidson. "A Child's Cognitive Perception of Death." *Day Care and Early Education* 19 (1991): 21–24.

Heine, P. "The Power of Related Books." *Reading Teacher* 45 (1991): 75–77.

Hodgkinson, H. *All One System: Demographics of Education, Kindergarten through Graduate School.* Washington, D.C.: Institute for Educational Leadership, Inc., 1985.

Hynds, S. and D.L. Rubin, eds. *Perspectives on Talk and Learning.* Urbana, Ill.: National Council of Teachers of English, 1990.

Jalongo, M.R. *Young Children and Picture Books.* Washington, D.C.: NAEYC, 1988.

LaFontaine, H. *At-Risk Children and Youth—The Extra Educational Challenges of Limited English-Proficient Students.* Washington, D.C.: Summer Institute of the Council of Chief State School Officers, 1987.

Latzker, John, and Sandra Latzker. "Research Report: Sometimes Children Miss the Moral." *United Press International* (October 26, 1981): p. 13.

Lukens, J. *A Critical Handbook of Children's Literature*, 3rd ed. Glenview, Ill.: Scott, Foresman, 1986.

Machado, J. *Early Childhood Experiences in Language Arts*, 4th ed. Albany, N.Y.: Delmar Publishers Inc., 1990.

Meek, Margaret. *Opening Moves: Work in Progress in the Study of Children's Language Development.* Portsmouth, N.H.: Heinemann, 1988.

Oxford, C., et. al. *Demographic Projections of Non-English*

*Background and Limited English-Proficient Persons in the United States in the Year 2000.* Rosslyn, Va.: Inter-America Research Associates, 1984.

Personke, C.R., and D.D. Johnson. *Language Arts Instruction and the Beginning Teacher: A Practical Guide.* Englewood Cliffs, N.J.: Prentice-Hall, 1987.

Piaget, J. *Play, Dreams and Imitation on Children.* New York: W.W. Norton, 1971.

Ramsey, P. *Teaching and Learning in a Diverse World.* New York: Teachers College Press, Columbia University, 1987.

Saccardi, M. "Children Speak: Our Student's Reactions to Books Can Tell Us What to Teach." *Reading Teacher* 4T (1993/1994) 318–324.

Strickland, D.S., and L.M. Morrow, eds. *Emerging Literacy: Young Children Learn to Read and Write.* Washington, D.C.: NAEYC, 1989.

Sutherland, Z. *Children and Books.* Glenview, Ill.: Scott, Foresman, & Co., 1985.

Tarrow, Norma Bernstein, and S.W. Lundsteen. *Guiding Young Children's Learning.* New York: McGraw-Hill, 1981.

Teale, W., and E. Sulzby, eds. *Emergent Literacy: Writing and Reading.* Norwood, N.J.: Ablex, 1986.

U.S. Office of Educational Research and Improvement of the U.S. Department of Education. *Becoming a Nation of Readers: What Parents Can Do.* Washington, D.C.: Office of Education, March, 1988.

White, Dorothy. *Books Before Five.* Portsmouth, N.H.: Heinemann, 1988.

## Children's Language Experience Books

Arnold, T. *Mother Goose's Words of Wit and Wisdom.* New York: Dial Books, 1990.

Auerbach, S. *The Alphabet Tree.* Mt. Desert, Me: Windswept House Publishers, 1986.

Chorao, Kay. *The Baby's Good Morning Book.* New York: Dutton, 1986.

de Paola, Tomie. *Tomie de Paola's Favorite Nursery Tales.* New York: Putnam, 1986.

Fowler, Richard. *Mr. Little's Noisy Boat.* New York: Grosset & Dunlop, 1986.

Heller, R. *Chickens Aren't the Only Ones.* New York: Grossett & Dunlop, 1981.

Kellogg, Steven. *Aster Aardvark's Alphabet Adventures.* New York: Morrow, 1987.

Kitamura, Satoshi. *Lily Takes a Walk.* New York: Dutton, 1987.

Krause, R. *The Carrot Seed.* New York: Harper & Row, 1945.

Lester, Alison. *Clive Eats Alligators.* Boston: Houghton, 1986.

Lionni, L. *Frederick.* New York: Pantheon, 1970.
———. *Six Crows.* New York: Knopf, 1988.

Macaulay, David. *Why the Chicken Crossed the Road.* Boston: Houghton, 1987.

Mahy, Margaret. *17 Kings and 42 Elephants.* New York: Dial, 1987.

Mayer, Mercer. *There's an Alligator Under My Bed.* New York: Dial, 1987.

McPhail, David. *Fix-It.* New York: Dutton, 1984.
———. *Pig-Pig and the Magic Photo Album.* New York: Dutton, 1986.

Meddaugh, S. *Martha Speaks.* New York: Houghton-Mifflin, 1992.

Ormerod, Jan. *Our Ollie.* New York: Lothrop, 1986.

Oxenbury, Helen. *The Helen Oxenbury Nursery Rhyme Book.* New York: Morrow Junior Books, 1987.

Plotz, Helen. *A Week of Lullabies.* New York: Greenwillow, 1988.

Tafuri, Nancy. *In a Red House.* New York: Greenwillow, 1987.

Van Allsburg, Chris. *The Z Was Zapped.* Boston: Houghton, 1987.

Warren, J., ed. *Short-Short Stories: Simple Stories for Young Children Plus Seasonal Activities.* Everett, Wash.: Warren Publishing House, Inc. 1987.

Westcott, Nadine B. *The Lady with the Alligator Purse.* Boston: Little Brown, 1988.

## Special Books for Young Children

*Poetry Books*

Belloc, Hilaire. *The Bad Child's Book of Beasts.* New York: Knopf, 1965.
———. *Poetry for Fun.* New York, Knopf, 1989.

Booth, D. *Voices on the Wind: Poems for All Seasons.* New York: Morrow Junior Books, 1990.

Carlstrom, N.W. *Wild Wild Sunflower Child Anna.* New York: Macmillan, 1987.

Ciardi, John. *The Man Who Sang the Sillies.* Philadelphia: J.B. Lippincott, 1961.

Ginsburg, Mirra. *Four Brave Sailors.* New York: Greenwillow, 1987.

Hayes, Sara. *Clap Your Hands: Finger Rhymes.* New York: Lothrop, Lee & Shepard, 1988.

Livingston, Myra C. *Sea Songs.* New York: Holiday House, 1986.

Lear, Edward. *The Jumblies.* Boston: Waine, 1907.

Mahy, Margaret. *17 Kings and 42 Elephants.* New York: Dial, 1987.

McCord, David. *Every Time I Climb a Tree.* Boston: Little, Brown, and Co., 1967.

Milne, A.A. *Now We Are Six.* New York: Dell, 1975.
———. *When We Were Very Young.* New York: Dutton, 1966.

O'Neill, Mary. *Hailstones and Halibut Bones.* New York: Doubleday, 1961.

Prelutsky, J. *The New Kid on the Block.* New York: Greenwillow Books, 1984.

Silverstein, S. *A Light in the Attic.* New York: Harper & Row, 1981.

## Books on Special Topics

*Compassion*

Anderson, Hans Christian. *The Ugly Duckling.* New York: Charles Scribner's Sons, 1965.

Blue, Rose. *Wishful Lying.* New York: Human Sciences Press, 1987.

Estes, Eleanor. *The Hundred Dresses.* New York: Harcourt, Brace, and World, 1944.

Saunders, Lowell. *The Kitten Who Was Different.* New York: T.S. Denison, 1966.

Terry, Berger. *I Have Feelings.* New York: Human Sciences Press, Inc. 1987.

Girard, L.W. *Jeremy's First Haircut.* Niles, Ill.: Whitman, 1986.

Wright, Dare. *The Lonely Doll.* New York: Doubleday, 1957.

*Coping*

The following books can be used to help a student understand a new situation.

Berger, Terry. *A New Baby,* Oshkosh, Wi.: Advanced Learning Concepts, 1974. Through photographs and writing this book deals with the feelings—especially the fears—of a child about to become a brother. It is designed to alleviate the fears of a child in such a situation. By using open-ended questions, it helps a child realize that having a baby sibling will not cause him/her to lose parental attention and that he/she will remain important.

Greenfield, Eloise. *She Come Bringing Me That Little Baby Girl.* Philadelphia: J.B. Lippincott, 1974. An excellent story about having a new sibling. It deals with the feelings of jealousy and the loss of parental attention that accompany the arrival of a new baby.

Hines, Anna Grossnickle. *Don't Worry, I'll Find You.* New York: Dutton, 1986.

Rockwell, Harlow. *My Doctor.* New York: Macmillan, 1973. A nicely illustrated book designed to eliminate a child's fear of the doctor's office. All the instruments of the office are illustrated and explained, though there is not much writing.

Shay, Arthur. *What Happens When You Go to the Hospital.* Chicago: Reilly and Lee, 1969. Photographs illustrate all aspects of a surgical stay in pediatrics. The book is easy to read.

*Divorce*

Ewing, Kathryn. *A Private Matter.* New York: Harcourt, Brace, and World, 1975. The author deals with the thoughts and emotions of a young girl who lives with her mother. She becomes attached to a kind man next door.

Ewing, Kathryn. *Things Won't Be the Same.* New York: Harcourt Brace Jovanovich, 1980. Upset by her mother's coming remarriage, ten-year-old Marcy is upset further when she learns she'll be staying with her father, whom she's never known.

Goff, Beth, and Susan Pearl (illus.). *Where Is Daddy? The Story of a Divorce.* Boston: Beacon Press, 1969. Through Janeydear's eyes, the author reveals the emotions a child experiences in parents' divorce.

Stein, Sara Bonnett. *On Divorce.* New York: Walker and Co., 1979. This book contains separate texts for parents and children exploring various emotions resulting from a divorce.

*Emotions*

Cole, William, and George MacClain (illus.). *I'm Mad at You.* Evanston, Ill.: William Collins and World Publishing Co., 1978.

de Saint-Exupery, Antoine. *The Little Prince.* New York: Harcourt, Brace, and World, 1943.

Howe, James. *There's a Monster Under My Bed.* New York: Antheneum, 1986.

Simmonds, Posy. *Fred.* New York: Knopf, 1987.

## Books About Dreams

Alexander, L. *Scared of the Dark.* Racine, Wis.: Western Publishing, 1986.

Babbit, N. *The Something.* New York: Farra, Straus & Giroux, 1970.

Hayward, L. *I Had a Bad Dream: A Book About Nightmares.* Racine, Wis.: Western Publishing, 1986.

Hill, S. *Go Away Bad Dreams.* New York: Random House, 1985.

Litowinsky, O. *The Dream Book.* New York: Coward, McCann & Geoghegan, 1978.

Mayer, M. *There's a Nightmare in My Closet.* New York: Dial, 1968.

Mayle, P. *Sweet Dreams and Monsters: A Beginner's Guide to Dreams and Nightmares and Things That Go Bump Under the Bed.* New York: Harmony Books, 1986.

McPhail, D. *Adam's Smile.* New York: Dutton, 1987.

Sendak, M. *In the Night Kitchen.* New York: Harper & Row, 1970.

————. *Where the Wild Things Are.* New York: Harper & Row, 1964.

Wahl, J. *Humphrey's Bear.* New York: Henry Holt, 1987.

Wiesner, D. *Freefall.* New York: Lothrop, Lee & Shepard, 1988.

Winthrop, E. *Maggie and the Monster.* New York: Holiday House, 1987.

## Specialty Books

Aseltine, Lorraine, Evelyn Mueller, and Nancy Tait. *I'm Deaf and It's Okay*. Niles, Ill.: Albert Whitman, 1988.

Drescher, Joan. *My Mother's Getting Married*. New York: Dial, 1986.

Fassler, Joan. *All Alone with Daddy*. New York: Human Sciences Press, Inc, 1987.

Flora, James. *The Fabulous Firework Family*. New York: Harcourt, Brace, and Co., 1955. A captivating story that introduces Mexican culture and some Spanish vocabulary. A fun and effortless way for young children to learn Spanish.

Smith, Lucia B. *My Mom Got a Job*. New York: Holt, Rinehart and Winston, 1979. Describes the differences in one girl's life when her mother begins to work. Discusses the girl's sadness because of the changes but also includes the changes that are happy and overall stresses; the girl is very happy with the situation, but it is just different.

Vigna, Judith. *She's Not My Real Mother*. Chicago: Albert Whitman and Co., 1980. Deals with a father's divorce and remarriage. Tells how the child did not accept his father's new wife, but eventually learns that she does not want to take his mother's place but just be his friend. Could be very useful when a child's parents remarry.

## Ethnic Diversity Topics

### African American

Abrahams, R.D. *Afro-American Folktales*. New York: Random House, 1985.

Adoff, A. *Black Is Brown Is Tan*. New York: Harper, 1973.

Banks, V.J.R. *Kwanza Coloring Book*. Los Angeles: Sala Enterprises, 1988.

Clifton, L. *The Boy Who Didn't Believe in Spring*. New York: Dutton, 1973.

————. *The Black BC's*. New York: Holt, 1970.

Dumas, A. *Golden Legacy*. Seattle: Baylor, 1982.

Feelings, M. *Majo Means One*. New York: Dial, 1971.

————. *Jambo Means Hello: Swahili Alphabet*. New York: Dial, 1974.

Freeman, D. *Corduroy*. New York: Viking, 1968.

————. *A Pocket for Corduroy*. New York: Viking, 1978.

Giles, L.H. *Color Me Brown*. Chicago: Johnson Publishing Company, Inc., 1982.

Giovanni, N. *Spin a Soft Black Song*. New York: Hill and Wang, 1985.

Greenfield, E. *She Come Bringing Me That Little Baby Girl*. Philadelphia: Lippincott, 1974.

————. *Daddy Is a Monster . . . . Sometimes*. New York: Dial, 1980.

————. *Daydreamers*. New York: Dial, 1985.

————. *Me and Nessia*. New York: Methuen, 1981.

Havill, J. *Jamaica's Find*. Boston: Houghton, 1986.

Hudson, W., and V. Wilson-Wesley. *Book of Black Heroes from A to Z*. Orange, N.J.: Just Us Books, 1988.

Keats, E.J. *Whistle for Willie*. New York: Macmillan, 1971.

Leslau, C., and W. Leslau. *African Proverbs*. White Plains, N.Y. Peter Pauper Press, Inc., 1985.

Lowery, L. *Martin Luther King Day*. Minneapolis: Carolrhoda Books, Inc., 1987.

McGovern, A. *Black Is Beautiful*. New York: Scholastic, 1969.

McKissack, P.S. *Flossie and the Fox*. New York: Scholastic, 1986.

Musgrove, M. *Ashanti to Zulu: African Traditions*. New York: Dial, 1976.

Nolan, M.S. *My Daddy Don't Go To Work*. Minneapolis: Carolrhoda Books, Inc., 1978.

Sealy, A.V. *Color Your Way into Black History Book*. Brooklyn, N.Y.: Association for the Study of Family Living, 1980.

Steptoe, J. *Mufaro's Beautiful Daughters*. New York: Lothrop, Lee & Shepard, 1987.

————. *Baby Says*. New York: Lothrop, Lee & Shepard, 1988.

Thomas, I. *My Street's a Morning Cool Street*. New York: Harper, 1970.

————. *Lordy, Aunt Hattie*. New York: Harper, 1973.

Udry, J.M. *What Mary Jo Shared*. Chicago: Albert Whitman, 1966.

### Alaskan/Eskimo/Inuit

Robinson, T. *An Eskimo Birthday*. New York: Dodd, Mead, 1975.

Rogers, J. *Runaway Mittens*. New York: Greenwillow, 1988.

Steiner, B. *Whale Brother*. New York: Walker, 1988.

### Chinese-American

Fogel, J. *Wesley Paul: Marathon Runner*. New York: Lippincott, 1979.

Pinkwater, M. *Wingman*. New York: Dodd, Mead, 1979.

### Hawaiian

Feeney, S. *A is for Aloha*. Honolulu: University of Hawaii Press, 1980.

————. *Hawaii is a Rainbow*. Honolulu: University of Hawaii Press, 1985.

Mower, N. *I Visit My Tutu and Grandma*. Kailua, HI: Press Pacifica, 1984.

### Japanese-American

Bang, M. *The Paper Crane*. New York: Morrow, 1985.

### Jewish

Avni, F. *A Child's Look at . . . What It Means to be Jewish* (Recording). Waterbury, Vt.: Alcazar.

————. (1986) *Mostly Matzah* (Recording). Waterbury, Vt.: Alcazar.

Greene, J.D. *Nathan's Hanukkah Bargain*. Rockville, Md.: Kar-Ben Copies, Inc., 1986.

Hirsh, M. *I Love Hanukkah*. New York: Holiday House, 1984.

### Korean-American

O'Brien, A.S. *The Princess and the Beggar: A Korean Folktale*. New York: Holt, 1993.

————. *I Don't Want to Go*. Board Book Series Books for Young Readers, New York: Holt, 1986.

Pack, M. *Aekyung's Dream*. Chicago: Children's Press, 1978.

### Latino

Atkinson, M. *Maria Teresa*. Carrboro, N.C.: Lollipop Power, 1979.

Marten, C. *Yagua Days*. New York: Dial, 1976.

### Native American

Bales, C.A. *Kevin Cloud: Chippewa Boy in the City*. Chicago: Reilly & Lee, 1972.

Baylor, B. *Hawk, I'm Your Brother*. New York: Scribner's, 1976.

Blood, C., and M. Link. *The Goat in the Rug*. New York: Macmillan, 1980.

Cameron, A. *Spider Woman*. Madeira Park, B.C.: Harbour, 1988.

Hayes, J. (1989) *Coyote and Native American Folk Tales* (Recording). Santa Fe, N.M.: Trails West.

Hoyt-Goldsmith, D. *Totem Pole*. New York: Holiday House, 1990.

Jeffers, S. *Brother Eagle, Sister Sky*. New York: Dial Books, 1991.

Locker, T. *The Land of the Gray Wolf*. New York: Dial Books, 1991.

Martin, B. Jr., and J. Archambault. *Knots on a Counting Rope*. New York: Henry Holt, 1987.

New Mexico People and Energy Collective. *Red Ribbons for Emma*. Berkeley, Calif.: New Seeds Press, 1981.

Shor, P. *When the Corn Is Red*. New York: Abingdon, 1973.

Smith, M.M. *Grandmother's Adobe Dollhouse*. Santa Fe, N.M.: New Mexico Magazine, 1984.

### Spanish Language

Ada, A.F. *Abecedario de los Animales*. Madrid, Spain: Espasa Calpe, 1990.

Baden, R. *Y Domingo, Siete* (And Sunday Makes Seven). Niles, Ill.: Albert Whitman, 1990.

Blue, R. *I Am Here/Yo Estoy Aqui*. New York: Franklin Watts, 1971.

Gra???, J.S. *La Ratita Presumida* (The Little Conceited Rat). Barcelona, Spain: Ediciones Hymsa, 1989.

Pomerantz, C. *The Tamarindo Puppy and Other Poems*. New York: Greenwillow, 1980.

Rosario, I. *Idalia's Project ABC: An Urban Alphabet Book in English and Spanish*. New York: Holt, Rinehart & Winston, 1987.

Simon, N. *What Do I Do/QUE HAGO*. Niles, Ill.: Whitman, 1974.

Suarez, M. *Los Colores (Colors)*. Mexico City: Editorial Grijalbo, 1989.

### Vietnamese-American

Constant, H. *First Snow*. New York: Knopf, 1974.

Macmillan, D., and D. Freeman. *My Best Friend Duc Tran: Meeting a Vietnamese-American Family*. New York: Julian Messner, 1987.

Shalant, P. *Look What We've Brought You From Vietnam: Crafts, Games, Recipes, Stories, and Other Cultural Activities from New Americans*. New York: Julian Messner, 1988.

# UNIT 19

# Creative Sciencing

## OBJECTIVES

After studying this unit, you should be able to

- state the meaning of sciencing and why it is important to the development of young children.
- name and describe three general kinds of sciencing.
- describe three creative sciencing activities that can be done in these places: school, school grounds, and school neighborhood.
- discuss environmental education and its place in the early childhood program.
- discuss how water play can be used as a creative sciencing experience in the early childhood program.

## SCIENCING AND THE YOUNG CHILD

When considering creative activities, it is not possible to skip the area of science. This is because true science is a highly creative activity. There is a purpose in using the word "true" with the term science. Most of the science learning that takes place in schools is not true science. Instead, it is the learning of science history—learning about facts that others have discovered in the past. Learning facts is not very creative, but learning science is.

## THE MEANING OF SCIENCE

There are twenty young children in a classroom. Each has just been given a small box wrapped in brightly colored gift paper. There is a big ribbon around each box. There are some objects inside each box. Each child is trying to find out what is in a box without taking off the ribbon and paper.

Some children are shaking their gift boxes. Some are holding them up to their ears and listening very carefully. Others are squeezing them. A few are punching the boxes. The children are interested in finding out what is in their own wrapped-up box.

Is this a game? It may seem so, but it is not. It is a way in which children make creative discoveries. In many ways, it is also the way that scientists make creative discoveries. The little gift box is somewhat like the world in which the children live. The children study their own little "worlds" by shaking the box, smelling it, squeezing it, and looking at it. Each child makes some discoveries but cannot find out everything because the box cannot be unwrapped. The children may be able to make some good guesses after studying the boxes, however. Some things are open to the children's discovery; some things are not. Scientists are faced with the same problems. They, too, study the world. They, too, can observe some things and only guess about others.

There are two things, then, that both the child and the scientist do. They *investigate* (carefully study the world around them) to discover *knowledge* (find answers to questions or problems about that world). Science consists of two phases, or parts, that cannot be separated: investigation and knowledge.

## WHAT IS SCIENCING?

If science is investigating in order to gain knowledge, then what is sciencing? In dealing with young children, it has been found that investigating is much more important than the knowledge that comes from investigating. To help people understand that

**FIGURE 19–1 In science activities, children are free to explore, investigate, and experience the process of finding answers to questions about the world.**

exploring is more important for children than the information turned up, the term *sciencing* is used. Science is a thing; sciencing is an action. Young children need a lot of action, not a lot of facts. This does not mean that understanding the world is put aside completely for young children. It just means that learning *how to find* answers is considered more important than the answers themselves. However, investigation and knowledge are a team. They cannot be completely separated from one another. To provide the experiences children need to develop scientific creativity, teachers must understand the meaning of sciencing. They must help children investigate in order to find answers to questions about the world. How can a teacher do this?

There are three types of activities that provide the experiences children need: formal sciencing, informal sciencing, and incidental sciencing. Each of

these terms will be explained in detail later. In general, however, *formal sciencing* is a teacher-organized, skill-building activity. *Informal sciencing* is nondirected, free investigation by the child. *Incidental sciencing* is a happening. (That is, incidental sciencing takes place when something happens to one or more children that is of interest to the group. It is usually unplanned and often is unexpected.)

## IMPORTANCE OF SCIENCING

Sciencing is important to young children in a number of ways. First, it is well known that some children are very able thinkers but are not good at talking about their thoughts. Those children who express themselves well are almost always noticed by teachers and other adults. They are usually rewarded for their ability. Nonverbal children (those who do not speak very well or very often) are usually considered to be less able thinkers. Somehow this information is passed on to the nonverbal children, who start to believe they are less able. They act the part they think they ought to act, thus confirming the suspicions of teachers and other adults—a kind of self-fulfilling prophecy.

This is a tragic chain of events that takes place too often. What is most tragic is that many of these children are good thinkers. They merely have trouble

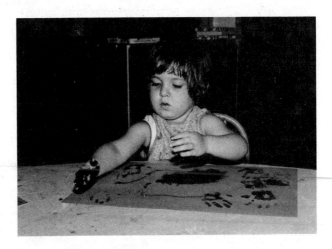

**FIGURE 19–2 Exploring the world with the sense of touch is part of the sciencing process.**

expressing their thoughts. If only they could be given a chance to show their skill without having to talk about it! Sciencing is a way of doing this. When children investigate, they learn by doing, not by speaking or listening. Moreover, a teacher can see what the child is doing. The children do not have to speak about results unless they want to. Thus, the teacher may be able to discover bright but nonverbal children by watching them during sciencing activities. Somehow, the teacher will let these children know they have been discovered.

Second, sciencing activities are designed to help children develop skills in using their senses. Use of these skills is not limited to sciencing. These skills can be used every day throughout a person's lifetime.

Educators use the term *transfer of learning* to describe knowledge and skills that are gained in one area and used in many other areas. Sciencing skills are particularly important because they are so highly transferable. Skills in seeing, feeling, and tasting are not limited to sciencing even though they do represent the basic skills that are taught.

Third, children with creative potential must be given a chance to show off their creativity. Activities that give them this chance are needed in the curriculum. Sciencing is designed to let children show off

their skills. Activities are also needed that help creative children develop their skills further. They need a chance to "play" with ideas and materials. They need openness—the freedom to do things without fear of being "out of line." Sciencing is designed for this.

## TYPES OF SCIENCING ACTIVITIES

In order to carry out sciencing in the classroom, the teacher must understand the three phases of sciencing: formal, informal, and incidental. Figure 19–3 explains each phase.

**Formal Sciencing.**   Only this phase of sciencing is planned by the teacher. Activities are planned that develop children's observational skills. Other activities are planned that give children a chance to use these skills. Children then apply the skills to some basic areas of knowledge.

Thus, children first learn how to be better observers. Then they apply these skills to observing properties, observing similarities and differences, and observing changes. Children can also learn words to help them describe their observations.

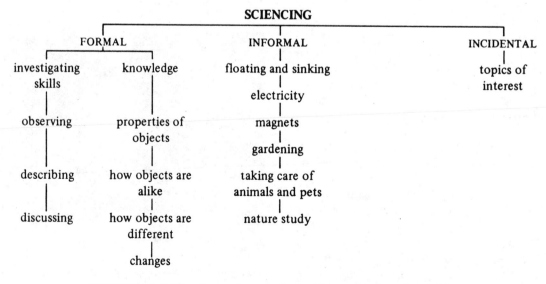

FIGURE 19–3 The three phases of sciencing and selected activities.

# Creative Activities in Other Curricular Areas

Creative Movement and Music

The poster in the image reads:

1. We see with our eyes, we hear with our ears.
2. We smell with our nose, we taste without our mouth.
3. We reach with our arms, we jump with our feet.
4. We have ten toes on our feet, We have ten fingers on our hands.
5. We listen with our ears, we watch with our eyes.
6. We draw with our hands, we dance with our ... mouth, we sneeze thr... ...s, we clap with our ...fingers, we lick with... ...with our lips, we tap wi...

# Creative Language Experiences

Stegosaurus

# Creative Sciencing and Mathematics

**Creative Food Experiences**

# Creative Social Studies

Creative Art Programs

**Informal Sciencing.** Unlike formal sciencing, the informal phase calls for little or no teacher involvement. Children work on their own, at their own rate, and only when they feel like it. They select the kinds of activities that interest them. They spend as much or as little time working at a given activity as they desire. It is when this sort of openness is available to children that creative potential begins to show up. A need to explore and a willingness to deal in the unknown are signs of a creative child. The ability to keep at a task is another sign that a child is creative.

When a child shows signs of interest and creative skill, the informal sciencing activities become important. Materials provided for children can encourage them to continue their quests to discover. Materials and equipment should be available in large enough numbers that several children can investigate at the same time. Care must be taken that dangerous materials and broken equipment are kept away from children. If materials are available, the only other thing that a child may need is a word of encouragement.

**Incidental Sciencing.** Incidental sciencing cannot be planned, even by a clever teacher. It sometimes does not take place once a week or even once

FIGURE 19–5 Matching games can be used in the sciencing process.

a month. It does not always appeal to every child in a class. Just what is incidental sciencing?

A city or town may be struck by a violent windstorm. Limbs of trees are knocked down; whole trees are uprooted. Great sheets of rain fall and streets become flooded. Children are scared by the great noise and wild lightning as the storm passes. Finally the storm is over.

Is this the time for an incidental sciencing experience? Of course it is! This is the time for children who are interested to learn many things. They can study the roots of trees; they may have the chance to observe growth rings. They are able to examine tree bark. They can observe what happens to water as it drains from a flooded street. Some might want to talk about their feelings as the lightning flashed and the thunder crashed. Some may wish to create a painting about the experience.

A teacher cannot plan such an experience. A good teacher can, however, take advantage of such an opportunity by letting children explore and seek an-

FIGURE 19–4 In the formal phase of sciencing, activities are planned that exercise a child's observational skills.

**FIGURE 19–6** An incidental sciencing session can result from a storm, when teacher takes the children outside to see what changes the storm has caused.

**FIGURE 19–7** Children get started better if they can work at tables or on the floor.

swers to questions. A teacher can encourage children to be more inquisitive and creative.

The following sections provide ideas for formal and informal sciencing. Creative activities and materials are suggested. Creative teachers can, of course, think of many more activities to help children be creative.

## FORMAL SCIENCING ACTIVITIES

These activities have been tested with young children. They work well if a few simple suggestions are followed:

- All equipment and materials needed for an activity should be on hand and ready to go. Nothing kills an activity faster than the child having to stop in the middle because one key item is missing.
- Children should be free to learn for themselves if possible. Teachers who talk too much destroy children's creative interest in the process.
- All of the children should not be expected to carry out all of the activities at the same time. Children need freedom to move around in order to be cre-

ative—they need freedom to move ideas around. They need to try out hunches when they are working with sciencing materials. Directions that leave no room for individual discovery destroy rather than foster creativity.
- Children get started better if they can work at tables or on the floor. They need plenty of room to move and spread out their equipment. A room with running water is desirable.
- Children may want to work with a partner at times, but the most creative discoveries take place when children work alone. Arguments are avoided if children have similar equipment when starting an activity. Additional things can be provided on an individual basis.
- Some formal sciencing sessions may hold a child's interest for only a few minutes. There are other times when children wish to work with materials for as long as 30 or 40 minutes. They should not be forced to work on an activity if they are not interested.
- Above all, children should never be made to feel that they have failed in a sciencing activity. All chil-

dren should feel they have done something right and have learned something of value. If they feel they have failed, the teacher is doing something wrong.

• Classrooms become noisy. This is to be expected when children are busy at work.

**Process Skill-Building Activities.**  The following are two examples of the many activities that can be used to help children learn to investigate.

*Observing color changes.*  In this activity, children mix paint and food coloring to see how many new colors they can create.

• Objectives: At the end of this activity, children should be able to
  1. Mix red and blue to get purple; mix blue and yellow to get green; mix red and yellow to get orange.

**FIGURE 19–8 Children enjoy watching food coloring and paint mix in water; they also learn how two colors mix to form a third color.**

  2. Identify and name the colors red, orange, yellow, green, blue, and purple.
• Materials: Each child receives
  1. Eight small plastic pill bottles, each of them half-filled with water.
  2. Red, blue, and yellow tempera paint.
  3. Red, blue, and yellow food coloring.
  4. Three eyedroppers.
  5. Eight wooden stirrers.
  6. Waxed paper and newspaper.
• Procedure:
  1. Distribute all the materials to the children.
  2. Make sure that the newspaper is spread out on the table or on the floor.
  3. Let children mix colors as they wish at first.
  4. Later, ask children if they can make the colors green, orange, and purple from any of the colors they have been mixing.
  5. An interesting follow-up is to let children mix a variety of colors in larger containers. They can use plastic cups or gallon containers and food coloring for this. Many colors can be created in this way.

*Making colors with a water prism.*  Another way to observe the color changes described previously is through a water prism.

• Objectives: At the end of this activity, children should be able to
  1. Identify colors.
  2. Use a mirror and sunlight to project colors onto the ceiling.
• Materials:
  1. Small, shallow pan.
  2. Mirror.
• Procedure:
  1. Fill the pan with water.
  2. Place the mirror inside the pan, leaning it against one side.
  3. Place the pan so that full sunlight shines on the mirror. Banks of color—red, orange, yellow, green, blue, indigo, and violet (always in that order) will reflect on the ceiling.
  4. Encourage children to talk about what they find most interesting in this activity.

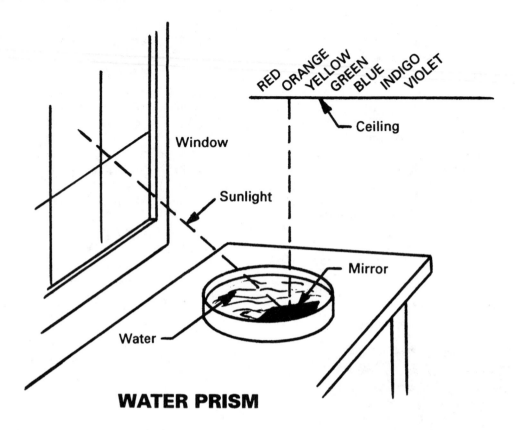

**WATER PRISM**

5. To extend this activity, invite children to paint or crayon the colors they see on the ceiling onto paper.

*The blindfolded teacher.* In this activity, children discover ways to describe objects and their positions to a blindfolded teacher.

- Objectives: At the end of this activity, children should be able to
  1. Describe three characteristics of some common objects.
  2. Describe the position or location of those objects.
- Materials:
  1. One master set consisting of
     a. Construction paper circles: two red, two green, two blue, two yellow, two orange.
     b. Construction paper squares: two brown, two black, two purple, two white.
     c. Photographs of each child in the class mounted on a large piece of tag board.
     d. Cork board or felt board for mounting circles and squares.
     e. Blindfold for the teacher.
  2. One set for each two children with
     a. Ten construction-paper rectangles: two red, two green, two blue, two yellow, two orange.
     b. Ten paper triangles in four colors: brown, black, purple, white.
     c. Felt board or other surface for placing colored shapes.
     d. Blindfold for child.
- Procedure: Demonstrate the need to communicate information in a very careful way.
  1. Explain to the children that their teacher cannot see.

2. Put on the blindfold.
3. Someone is asked to place the various shapes on a cork board or on a felt board.
4. The blindfolded teacher does not know where the shapes are. A "helper" is selected.
5. The "helper" must direct the blind teacher to the location of the colored shape—up, down, this way or that way, until all the shapes have been removed from the board.
6. Repeat the activity using a blindfolded child (or have the child cover his eyes), another helper, and photographs of children in the class mounted on tagboard.
7. Volunteers name children and the helper directs the blindfolded child.
8. Children can then receive their own sets of equipment and play the game in pairs.
9. They can try to create their own game using the materials.
10. Children then try to communicate the rules of their game to the teacher or another group of children.

**Content Activities.** The following activity is presented as one example of the many content activities that can be used in formal sciencing.

- Objectives: At the end of this activity, children should be able to
  1. Identify materials that are liquids.
  2. State that some liquids mix and some do not.
- Materials: Each child receives
  1. A set of five pill bottles with screw-on caps. Each set contains the following liquids: water, baby oil, liquid hand cream, liquid starch, dishwashing detergent.
  2. Five eyedroppers
  3. Plastic wrap
  4. Wooden stirrers
  5. Newspapers
  6. Three or four plastic mixing cups (5 ounces)
- Procedure:
  1. Distribute materials to each child.
  2. Cover tables or other work areas with newspapers. It might be wise to have children wear smocks.

**FIGURE 19–9 Children can learn about the properties of liquids by dropping beads of water, baby oil, etc., on a piece of waxed paper, and using a stirrer to investigate the liquids (for example, to see if they mix).**

3. Ask children to mix and match liquids to see what happens to the combinations.
4. Help children identify the liquid materials in their sets.
5. Talk with individuals about which liquids mix and which ones do not.

**Other Formal Sciencing Activities.** Figures 19–10 and 19–11 list activities that can be used in formal sciencing. Lesson plans are not provided, but such plans would follow a format similar to the three lessons outlined earlier. Other related sciencing activities are at the end of this unit.

## INFORMAL SCIENCING ACTIVITIES

Informal sciencing activities are designed to be carried out by individual children. Little or no information is provided by the teacher. Experience has

| PROCESS | ACTIVITIES | MATERIALS SUGGESTED |
|---------|-----------|---------------------|
| Observing | Using the senses of sight, smell, hearing, tasting and feeling to improve observations. | Paints, crayons, color chips (paint chips), seeds, rocks, leaves, cloth of various textures, sandpaper. |
| | Observing smells to identify objects. | Perfumes, room fresheners, flowers. |
| | Increasing the accuracy of observations by using more than one sense. | Tape recorder, bells, musical instruments, sound effects. |
| | Increasing awareness of sound and smells in the environment. | |
| Communicating, Describing | Building child's ability to describe objects in terms of one observable property. | Colors: felt material, paint chips. |
| | Developing skill in describing objects in terms of more than a single property (such as soft and red). | Textures: swatches of material of various textures, sandpaper of many grades. |
| | | Shapes: 3D wooden shapes. |
| | Developing a child's vocabulary related to describing words: colors, textures (roughness/smoothness), size (large/small), odors (sweet/sour), sounds (high/low pitch, loud/soft), shapes | Size: large and small corks, cups, cutout figures, shells, stones. |
| | | Odors: room fresheners, perfumes, colognes, vanilla, almond extract, coffee. |
| | | Sounds: musical instruments, pop bottles filled with water, noisemakers. |
| | | Shininess: foils, papers, paint samples, coins. |

**FIGURE 19–10 Investigative processes.**

shown that informal sciencing works best when these suggestions are followed:

- A section of the classroom should be provided for the storage of materials. The materials should be easy for children to reach and are best stored in color-coded boxes such as shoe boxes. It is easy for a child to take the equipment needed from a green box and return it to a green box. If possible, a work area should be provided for informal sciencing.
- Open periods should be provided during the school day when children can feel free to play with sciencing materials. If possible, children should be encouraged to try things out.
- A teacher should not hover over the children. The teacher should watch those who are working, however, to make sure they are not hurting themselves or others.

- A wide variety of attractive materials should be available for the children.
- If children become upset when working with materials, they can be given small clues to help them move along. The adult should not do the work for the children. A good approach is to give clues by saying "I wonder what would happen if . . .?"

**Informal Sciencing Materials.** The following materials can be used to help children develop their creativity in sciencing. Materials that are carefully selected and organized help children make discoveries.

- Floating and sinking
  1. Plastic containers: one-gallon aquariums, shoe boxes, large freezer containers.

| CONTENT AREA | ACTIVITIES | MATERIALS SUGGESTED |
|---|---|---|
| Properties | Reviewing words that name properties. | Use many of the same materials used in building communicating skills. |
| | Sorting objects on the basis of one property. | Sets of buttons, shells, rocks, leaves, seeds, toys, dolls, pictures of animals, dowels. |
| | Finding objects that have a particular property. | Sets of materials that may all be related, such as a set of crayons.<br>Sets of materials that are not related in some obvious way. |
| Comparing | Using all the senses to observe how some objects are alike. | Sets of objects with similar properties, such as color, shape, size, texture. |
| | Using all the senses to observe how some objects are different. | Sets of objects with some similar properties but one obvious difference, such as: a set of buttons of the same size and shape but all of different colors; a set of buttons of same size and color but with a different number of holes. |
| | Counting the number of objects that are alike in a set; counting the number that are different. | Set of objects: half float in water, half sink; set of shapes: some are triangles and some are circles, or some are red and some are green. |
| Changes | Observing common objects change in shape. | Salt or sugar dissolving in water; ice cubes melting; sawing a square into 2 triangles or 2 rectangles; building blocks; cutting material (patterns).<br>Pouring sand from one container into another. |
| | Observing changes in properties and states of matter (gas to liquid, liquid to solid). | Melting sugar; dissolving materials such as salt; melting ice; ice to hot water to steam. |

FIGURE 19–11 Content activities.

2. Various objects that float and sink: paper clips, aluminum foil, corks, rocks, screws.
3. Oil-based clay that can be formed into boat shapes.
4. Baby-food jars, capped and filled with different amounts of sand.
5. Salt water versus tap water.
• Small animals and fish in the classroom
  1. Terrariums that contain woodland plants and animals, or desert plants and animals.
  2. Aquariums with goldfish, guppies, tropical fish, various plants.
  3. Small animals in cages: guinea pigs, rabbits, mice. (Children can handle some animals. They can observe the living and eating habits of others.)
• Magnets
  1. Magnets of various sizes and shapes.
  2. Iron filings and paper.
  3. Variety of magnetic and nonmagnetic objects.
  4. Various materials through which magnetic force passes.
• Simple electricity
  1. Energy sources such as D-cell battery or dry cell.

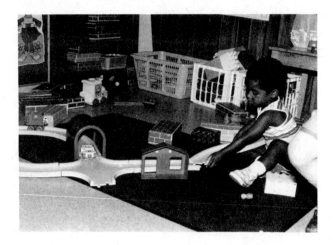

**FIGURE 19–12 "Open moments" to experiment with objects are crucial to a child's development.**

2. Wires, lights, and sockets.
3. Small DC motors.
4. Switches.
5. Clips for connecting wires at terminals. (Children can connect one light to a cell using two

**FIGURE 19–13 Discovering the properties of materials is part of the sciencing process.**

wires. Using additional wires, they can add a switch. Then they can add more lights, a motor, and more switches.)

• Indoor gardening
1. Small wooden flats filled with soil.
2. Variety of seeds.
3. Gro Lux light (if available).
4. Absorbent paper toweling. (Children can watch seeds germinate and discover conditions that make plants grow. Seeds can sprout on moist paper toweling. These activities work best in the fall or spring of the year when the heat is not on in the classroom.)

• Outdoor activities. (Later in this unit there is a section on children exploring their environment.)

**Finding Sciencing Materials.** The keys to children's success in sciencing are the amount and kind of materials available. There must be enough materials to provide them with a creative challenge. Much of the equipment needed is simple and can be homemade. Materials that cannot be made at home may be obtained from other sources. Several suggestions are included here to help a teacher increase the number and variety of materials in the classroom.

• All needed materials often can be obtained in junk shops, resale shops, yard sales, rummage sales, and barn sales.

• Often, material discarded by local industrial plants is just the kind of equipment that is needed for sciencing.

• Scrap bins in lumber yards are a source of inexpensive wood products.

• Hospitals, nursing homes, and drugstores may be contacted for pill bottles and other discarded material that can be useful.

• Materials may be bought from discount stores when they have sales. Remnants are available at department stores. Store catalog sales offer savings on equipment.

• Donations from children's parents and friends provide many needed materials.

• As a last resort, needed equipment may be purchased from a science supply catalog. This is, however, the most expensive way to obtain materials.

FIGURE 19–14 One informal sciencing experience involves using magnets with several magnetic and nonmagnetic objects. Children experiment with each of the objects to discover which types are attracted by the magnet.

> Environmental education for young children is about wonder; it's about enjoyment of the outdoors; and it's about teaching responsibility and caring for the child's immediate environment and gradually widening circles of the Earth. It's about feeling moss, picking up a Coke can, and watching ants. It's an essential part of the early childhood curriculum just because we—children and adults—are a part of the Earth. (Dighe, 1993, p. 63)

## ENVIRONMENTAL EDUCATION

A four-year-old child stands at the sink gazing at the water pouring down over his fingers. After a while, he reaches for the soap and slowly turns the lathery bar over and over as the water flows in a column from faucet to drain. Finally, he rinses away the suds and turns from the sink. The waste basket is filled with slightly crumpled towels. For him, as for most of us, endless streams of clean water and inexhaustible supplies of convenience products are taken for granted.

Ecologists have varied estimates on how much time is left before we will have wasted natural resources and polluted the Earth to the point where we can no longer survive. Some fear the damage is already irreversible. Others believe that there is still time— provided a profound change in attitude and behavior occurs. For adults, it means finding new values. For children, it means growing up with an understanding of the environment and a desire to conserve

FIGURE 19–15 In sciencing activities, children can often investigate the materials on their own, making discoveries for themselves.

| | | |
|---|---|---|
| Collection of objects (many of which the children can bring—rocks, shells, insects, etc.) | | |
| Things to classify | Collection of books | Color paddles |
| Magnifying glass | Science kits | Flashlight |
| Objects that float and sink (an old washtub works well to hold the water) | Magnets (horseshoe, bar) | Binoculars, telescope, periscope |
| | Iron filings | Rope, fibers |
| | Prisms | Sponges |
| Different kinds of soil | Tuning forks | Batteries |
| Seeds to plant and classify | Aquarium | Rubber tubing |
| Shapes | Terrarium | Animals/animal cages |
| Compass | Vivarium | Stethoscope |
| Simple machines | Tactile board/box | Food coloring |
| Things to take apart and put together (old clocks, toys, motors, etc.) | Plants | Electric bell |
| | Bug house | Dry/liquid measure containers |
| | Thermometer (Celsius) | Pendulum frame/bobs |
| Objects to smell, taste, hear, touch, and see | Kaleidoscope, scanoscope | Scales (kitchen, balance, spring) |
| | Hourglass, clocks, stopwatch | Assorted balancing materials |
| Filmstrips about science | | |

FIGURE 19–16 Basic science materials and supplies.

and protect those things essential for continued life on this planet.

If children are to grow up in a world fit for human survival, the environment must be protected. Children should learn about nature from their earliest years on. Nature is not the only part of a child's environment, however. Home, school, and neighborhood are all parts of the child's environment. In fact, everything that contributes to children's experiences—good or bad—is part of their environment. Can a child learn creativity by learning about the environment? Can a child learn to improve the environment? Can young children learn about ecology? The answer to these questions is "yes." Most of all, learning about these things can and must begin when a child is young.

## ECOLOGY AND THE ENVIRONMENT

Their environment is one of the most important influences in the lives of children. They need an environment full of love. They need an environment that provides for their other basic needs: water, food,

clean air. Children need an environment that provides for their safety, that helps them grow intellectually, that they can understand and control.

In other words, children need to learn about their environment because their lives depend on that environment. This learning can be done in a very creative way. Activities that help children understand their environment can also help them become more creative thinkers.

**Environments.** For the purposes of this unit, the term *environment* refers to two things: man-made and natural things that children meet in their surroundings. Streets, houses, and schools are examples of man-made things in the environment. Trees, grass, and birds are parts of nature. Street lights, cars, and buildings are man-made. Animals, clouds, and snow are natural things. Noise, light, and smells may be man-made or a part of nature.

Children have many environments in which they live. Home is one. It may be a pleasant part of a child's life, or an unpleasant one. School is another environment that influences a child's life, and it, too,

**FIGURE 19–17 Care for the environment begins with care for the immediate classroom environment.**

may be an enjoyable experience or an unpleasant one. The neigborhood environment may be friendly and safe, or it may be hostile and dangerous. There are also many people who are part of a child's environment: parents and neighbors, grocers and police officers, teachers and doctors. The people who make up the communities in which children live may make the children feel very good about their lives, or they may make the children feel unhappy.

In these environments, there are also natural things and natural happenings: grass, trees, and flowers; rain, wind, and earthquakes; cats, rats, and beetles. All these things are parts of a child's environment. They all affect one another. Nature influences people; people influence nature.

**Ecology.** Ecology is the study of all elements of an environment, both living and nonliving, and the interrelation of these elements. The term comes from two Greek words; *ecos* meaning the "place to live" or "home," and *ology* meaning "study of". By way of further definition, some experts refer to ecology as "living gently," a phrase that brings together the ideas of respecting life, not wasting resources, and not harming the planet (Herman, 1991).

If we stop to consider our work with young children, we have probably touched on the subject of ecology frequently. For example, we notice the changes in the weather and discuss how these affect plants, birds, animals, and ourselves. When we plant seeds, hatch eggs, or care for a pet, we notice those things that are necessary for life and growth—nourishment, light, heat, nurturing. We like to examine and observe many organisms, but if we remove an insect from its home we take care to restore it unharmed to its place after our observation is finished. Consequently, children learn that all life is precious, and no creature is more or less worthwhile than another.

Those of us in early childhood education are also old hands at recycling materials and using up discards. Bits of paper left over from cutting shapes find their way into the collage box instead of the wastebasket. Empty boxes evolve into constructions, large and small. The blank sides of printed sheets of paper are used for drawing. Old newspapers are used for many art projects. We all think twice before throwing anything away, and with a little encouragement children and their parents soon catch the saving habit.

By our example, we can teach other ways of living a more ecologically sound life-style. For example, using durable dishes for food service rather than disposable dishes is an ecologically sound practice. When food and beverages for snacks and meals come in bottles or cans, these containers should be cleaned and the cans flattened and deposited at a recycling center. The use of personal cloth towels instead of paper towels is another good ecological practice. To encourage parents to recycle, you might consider establishing a collection site at your school, perhaps making it a cooperative project run by the parents.

To truly grasp the concept of ecology, young children need more opportunities to observe the total process rather than just a portion of it, or only the finished product. For example, by combining a field trip, pictures, a movie, and samples a teacher can help children understand the steps that go into bringing their glass of milk to the snack table. The series could begin with a farmer planting seeds in the field, cultivating and harvesting the grain, feeding the cow, milking the cow, then transporting the milk to the dairy. You could show how the milk is sterilized and packaged before it is transported to the store. Finally, you could show where it is purchased and how it is brought to home or school to drink.

Help children understand the total process when you want to explain the need for conservation. Describing how the paper-making process begins with the cutting down of a tree in the forest and ends with the paper products that we use every day helps children understand why it is important that they use only one paper towel to dry their hands.

Incorporating the subject of ecology into an early childhood curriculum is not so much a matter of information, knowledge, or method, as it is an *adult attitude*. Attitudes lead to habits and habits structure our routines—like switching off lights and shutting doors. It's the little things we do every day that make a difference in our lifestyle and our impact on the environment (Dighe, 1993; Holt, 1990; Nuebebaur, 1992; Sherwood, Williams and Rockwell, 1990).

## ACTIVITIES IN SCHOOL

A child first learns about caring for the environment by caring for his most immediate environment, that is, home, school, playgrounds, and parks. In the early childhood years, the teacher can use everyday experiences to point out to children the importance of caring for the environment.

**Getting Started.** Getting young children outdoors to touch and experience nature is the starting point for learning about ecology and the environment. Unfortunately, a visit to many early childhood classrooms reveals the obvious: indoor time and space are given far more priority than outdoor. Many early childhood programs allot only a short daily period of outdoor time for children's energy release and motor development.

Increased time for outdoor learning experience can be worked into the daily routine without difficulty, however, at least in good weather. Music, movement, and art acquire new dimensions outside; there is often plenty of space for construction with large blocks, boxes, tires, and boards; and snack and lunch times become picnics. Best of all, the outdoors provides a natural setting, complete with props for dramatic play.

Even if the outdoor play space is a concrete-covered square, children experience more of nature than they would inside. They know the warmth of the sun, the power of the wind, and the coolness of shade; they find plants that spring up in cracks and insects that crawl or fly; they experience weather in its many forms.

Obviously, the more natural an environment, the better. Slightly unkempt spaces are more interesting to investigate than blacktop or grassy lawns. In many areas, the edges of property lines where the mower doesn't reach hold the greatest promise for exploration.

Just by being outside, children not only begin to feel comfortable in the outdoor environment, they learn about nature the way young children learn best—by experiencing it. Outdoor experiences are the only authentic foundation for environmental education. Television, computers, films, and books can give only two-dimensional experiences and images that cannot be touched, smelled, or seen in their relative size—"tinier than my fingernail" or "so much bigger than me." (Dighe, 1993)

**Teacher's Role.** The teacher's most important role is sharing enthusiasm, curiosity, and wonder. Adults can best do this by using their legs—stopping and getting down to see what has caught a child's attention. Just the focusing of attention, perhaps with an expression of wonderment—"Look how pretty!" or "Great, you found something amazing!"—can encourage exploration and child-adult conversation. When we share our own ideas and feelings with a child, it encourages a child to explore his own feelings and perceptions.

**Art and Ecology.** Art, music, dance, movement, and storytelling all provide opportunities for children to express their interests and discoveries developed through environmental education.

Setting up easels outdoors may inspire children to paint trees or their feelings about trees. Modeling clay outdoors may encourage children to create their own versions of natural objects in their outdoor play space. In movement activities, children may reflect the wiggle of caterpillars they observed on the playground. Or in music, the sounds of birds and crickets can be reflected with rhythm instruments or their own voices. They may dance the story of birds, flowers, and animals awakening to the Earth's springtime sun. Children's books are also excellent for further expanding a child's understanding and appreciation of the Earth. (See lists at end of this unit for suggestions.)

The above are all general ideas on how to incorporate environmental education and ecology into your early childhood program. The following are some more specific activities on environmental education and ecology for young children:

- When someone in the classroom breaks a toy, use the opportunity to talk with the children about the consequences—that no one can play with the toy until it is repaired; that if the toy cannot be repaired no one can ever play with it again. Have the children discuss ways of preventing accidents with toys, e.g., keeping them off the floor when not in use, sharing willingly with others, using them for the purpose for which they were intended.
- Help children (and by your own example) use materials—paint, paper, crayons, etc.—conservatively, by saving scraps, storing unused paint, completing a picture before starting another, and keeping pencils and crayons off the floor.
- Encourage children to help care for and clean classroom furniture. Provide cleanup materials for washing off tables and chairs and cleaning up spills.
- Before looking at books, discuss with the children the importance of caring for them. Suggestions might include: washing hands, turning pages at the corner, putting them in a special place away from pets and younger brothers and sisters. Remind them of their disappointment over a missing page in a story.
- Snack time offers an opportunity for children to learn to conserve. Persuade them to take only what they will eat, to eat all they take, and to refuse what they do not want. Each child should frequently have the opportunity to clean up after snack.

In all these experiences, the emphasis should be on exploring and learning through the senses, not on rote or memory learning. Learning how to care for the environment is an approach to life and more than a subject to learn.

Children should be given the responsibility of feeding and caring for classroom animals and plants. Also discuss care of pets at home. During the winter let the children make some arrangements for feeding the birds by putting out feeders and houses or stringing popcorn and cranberries on the Christmas tree and putting it out after Christmas.

The following teaching suggestions include many other activities that promote environmental awareness:

- Have a "Litter Bug" Party. The children may be familiar with the Litter Bug idea from television. Take the class to the playground and pick up all the paper on the ground.
- Before going on a class picnic, remind the children to pick up their trash in the park, and let them discuss why this is important.
- During the year encourage appreciation for the jobs of the school janitor and the garbage man, etc. Have these helpers talk with the children about what they do and how the children can help make their job easier.
- Avoid frightening children with threats about results of things they cannot control (Example: What will happen when there is no clean air left?). Concentrate instead on the things they *can do,* such as keeping their own yards and school grounds neat, putting their own waste in proper receptacles, having a litter bag in the car, avoiding open burning, keeping pets clean, etc.

# THIS ONE'S FOR YOU!

**SELECTED BOOKS FOR CHILDREN ON ECOLOGY AND ENVIRONMENTNAL THEMES:**

*Play With Me.* (M. H. Ets, 1955) One has to be quiet and receptive to experience what the Earth has to offer.

*Gilberto and the Wind.* (M. H. Ets, 1963) The wind as a playmate.

*Mirandy and Brother Wind.* (McKissack, 1988) Fun with the wind.

*The Biggest House in the World.* (Lionni, 1968) Bigger is not necessarily better.

*Nicholas, Where Have You Been?* (Lionni, 1987) Nature provides food for all creatures. We must not disturb nature's balance.

*Wild, Wild Sunflower Child, Anna.* (Carlstrom, 1987) Fun in the outdoors.

*A House of Leaves.* (Soya, 1986) Fall fun in the leaves.

*Come to the Meadow.* (Hines, 1984) Fun in the meadow.

*Once There Was a Tree.* (Romanova, 1985) The tree's place in ecology.

*Hello, Tree.* (Ryder, 1991) A child's relationship with a tree.

*The Hidden Jungle.* (Henwood, 1992) Urban blight.

*The Legend of the Indian Paintbursh.* (DePaola, 1988) Native American reverence for nature.

*Owl Moon.* (Yolen, 1987) The Moon, its phases, and its place in nature.

*The Sun's Asleep Behind the Hills.* (Ginsburg, 1982) Cycle of the moon.

*The Goodnight Circle.* (Lesser, 1984) Cycle of the moon.

*Racoons and Ripe Corn.* (Arnosky, 1987) Animals in nature.

*Chipmunk's Song.* (Ryder, 1987) Chipmunks and their lives.

*Hey, Get Off Our Train.* (Burningham, 1989) Endangered species.

*Somewhere Today.* (Kitchen, 1993) Unusual happenings in nature.

**ENVIRONMENTAL ACTIVITIES FOR YOUNG CHILDREN:**

*Hug a Tree and Other Things To Do Outdoors with Young Children.* (Rockwell, Sherwood, and Williams, 1983)

*Earthways: Simple Environmental Activities for Young Children.* (Petrash, 1992)

*Earth Child: Games, Stories, Activities, Experiments and Ideas About Living Lightly on Planet Earth.* (Sheehan and Waidner, 1991)

*Naturewatch.* (Katz, 1986)

*The Kid's Nature Book.* (Milord, 1989)

**Our Interesting and Changing Weather.** One of the first natural observations a young child makes is about the weather. To help children become more aware of weather, teach them to be observant. Outdoors, or from the classroom if windows permit, let the children watch the clouds while you discuss their shape, their effect on the sun, and their role in the phenomena of rain and snow. Discuss the sun (but avoid having the children look directly at it). They can hold out the back of a hand and feel its warmth, feel the sidewalk in the sun and shade. Invite them to go to the windows and watch the rain, see the splashes on the streets and in the puddles. If feasible, let them see the water gush down a storm sewer. Take them out in a snowfall and let them catch the snowflakes on their mittens. Discuss the wind, fog, mist rising from a stream on a cold day, frost or dew on the ground. Call their attention to the ice crystals on a puddle after a frosty night.

For young children, who can neither understand

# THIS ONE'S FOR YOU!

## THE SEASONS: HELP CHILDREN EXPERIENCE THE CHANGING SEASONS THROUGH ALL OF THEIR SENSES

The change of seasons brings many sensations and experiences that relate to our senses. For each new season, hang a piece of chart paper with the heading, SPRING (SUMMER, FALL, WINTER) IS HERE! Make five columns with the headings: "I Can Smell It," "I Can Hear It," "I Can See It," "I Can Feel It."

Have the children help you to list everything they can think of for each category. Let them illustrate the mural with their own drawings or designs, or with pictures cut out from magazines.

Extend your discussion of the mural with a focus on how and what you can feel with each season. Try the following activities:

### SPRING

- During the spring months, we feel the wind. Your art activities may include a pinwheel, a kite, or streamers. Have the children imagine (and even act out!) what it would be like to be a kite.
- Birds appear in the spring. Talk about how they move when they fly and when they search for food. Let children try their wings and move like birds.
- Spring is the time for planting. Let children imagine that they are a seed sleeping under the soil. As the warm sun and spring rains come, they begin to grow up through the soil slowly until they are a flower or a plant.

### SUMMER

- Ask the children to be a thunderstorm. Could they make themselves into thunder, lightning, or rain?

### FALL

- Fall is the time that school begins for many children. Ask your group to pretend they are doing the things they like best in school. See who can guess what each activity is.
- Falling leaves are a part of the fall season. Ask your children to show you how they could be leaves that are falling from the trees, swirling to the ground, and then blowing away in the wind. Have them imagine a pile of leaves and how they could make believe that they are jumping into that pile.

### WINTER

- For many children, winter means cold weather. Have children tell you with their bodies that the weather is cold. Ask them to walk in the wind and then in deep snow.
- Make a snow person! Let children pretend to roll the snowballs until they are bigger and bigger, heavier and heavier! Place one on top of the other. Add the eyes, nose, hat, scarf, or anything else.
- Let's pretend with winter sports. Ask the children to pretend to skate, ski, make snow angels, sled ride. . . .

Your activities can emerge from the ideas of the children. What they choose relates to where they live, their own special interests, and their unique observations of nature.

nor remain interested in long explanations, the best approach is an informal conversation, a "pointing out," a sharing of your enthusiasm and appreciation for the beauty, variety, and many moods of weather.

To keep a record of the weather conditions:

- On a large calendar, paste symbols to represent the predominant weather for that day. Children can take turns doing this. (Let the children help choose and make the symbols for a sunny day, cloudy day, rainy day, etc.)
- Make a chart similar to the one illustrated. Have the children select the appropriate cards for the day. Cards have tabs on each end for inserting in slits in the pocket charts used in many classrooms.

Read poetry, stories, and nursery rhymes dealing with weather. Examples are Robert Louis Stevenson's "The Wind," Christina Rossetti's poem that begins, "Who has seen the wind?," the nursery rhyme "Rain, Rain, Go Away," and Roger Duvoisin's *White Snow, Bright Snow.*

The weather on a given day can inspire dramatic play. Have the children act out the type of day it is— or choose at random a type of weather condition and act it out. Examples: Snowy—shoveling snow, walking in snow, slipping, building an imaginary snowman, etc. Windy—climbing a hill with the wind blowing hard against you, being blown down a hill with the wind behind you. Encourage the children to act out the weather conditions in their own way. Figure 19–18 summarizes science experiences for each season of the year.

**Pets in the Classroom.** The best way for young children to learn about animals is to have them in the classroom. Through observing and caring for pets in the classroom, children can:

- Grow in understanding the needs of animals for food and water, as well as safe, clean housing and attention.
- Grow in appreciation for the beauty, variety, and functional physical characteristics of animals; for example, the protective shell on a turtle, the webbed feet on a duckling, the sharp teeth and claws on a hamster.
- Grow in compassion for and humane treatment of animals.
- Obtain inspiration for many language experiences and creative activities.

Good classroom pets are (be sure no children have allergies to any of the pets) guinea pigs, rabbits, parakeets, white mice, hamsters, turtles, salamanders, gerbils, and goldfish.

Good short-time classroom pets are chicks, ducklings, puppies, a setting hen, kittens, and turkey poults.

Children can help plan for the pet in advance by building the cage or preparing the terrarium or aquarium. The necessary food and water pans can be obtained, a food supply can be stored up, bedding can be prepared, and the handling of the pet can be discussed. A trip to a pet shop would be an excellent experience.

Children should help with the care of the pet once it is obtained, but in the final analysis the teacher is responsible for seeing that the pet is treated well. Children should learn that pets are not toys; that they have feelings; that when provoked, some of them defend themselves by biting. Children should not be allowed to handle pets excessively or without supervision. It is cruel to let them "wrap pets up in blankets and take them for walks in a doll buggy" or to allow any other activity foreign to the pet's nature— and children should be helped to understand why. Neglected or mishandled pets give a negative message about responsibility and respect for life.

Besides caring for pets, some other activities that

| AUTUMN | SPRING |
|---|---|
| 1. Harvest Time | 1. Weather |
| 2. Food |    Rain, fog, hail, wind |
|    Eating and life |    Lightning, thunder |
|    Storing for winter (people and animals) |    Thawing |
|    Cooking and preparing |    Warm sun |
| 3. Seeds |    Effect on clothing we wear |
| 4. Changes in Plants and Animals | 2. Animals |
|    Caring for plants for winter |    Baby animals |
|    Falling leaves |    Growth |
|    Changing colors |    Changes in trees and plants |
| 5. Animals Preparing for Winter |    Flowers and buds |
|    Birds leaving | 3. Water, Sand, and Mud |
|    Nests |    Evaporation |
|    Changes in fur |    Absorption |
|    Caterpillars |    Flow and forces of water |
| 6. Weather |    Mixing, dissolving, combining |
|    Cooler days | 4. Smells |
|    Effect on clothing we wear |    Damp things |
|    Frost |    Flowers |
| | 5. Machines and Their Uses |
| |    People working after the winter |
| |    Construction (streets and buildings) |
| |    Tree-trimming and spraying |
| |    Tools used on lawns, gardens, fields |
| |    Weights and balance |
| |    Aids to moving things |
| **WINTER** | **SUMMER** |
| 1. Cold Weather | 1. Weather |
|    Melting and freezing |    Hot sun, shade, breezes |
|    Ice, snow, sleet, fog |    Heat, rain, thunder, hail |
|    Clothing necessary |    Effects on body (light clothing, resting, need for |
| 2. Animals |      water, perspiration) |
|    Resting and shelter/protection | 2. Animals |
|    Pets that need care |    Providing food, water, shade |
|    Bird feeding |    Discovery of worms, insects, spiders (how they live) |
| 3. Plants |    Growth of baby animals born in spring |
|    Need for warmth and light | 3. Plants |
|    Freezing/resting outside |    Growth |
|    Winter bulbs and flowers |    Need for sun, water, some shade |
| 4. Heat and Light |    Development and ripening of foods |
|    Short days and darkness |    Preparing fresh fruits and vegetables |
|    Awareness of moon and stars | 4. Machines |
|    Warmth of sun on some days |    Heavy machinery |
|    How buildings are heated |    Construction |
|    Drying and evaporation |    Concepts of levers, wheels, pulleys |
| 5. Light and Color |    Continued use of sand, mud, water |
|    Bubbles | |
|    Prisms | |
|    Flashlights | |
|    Lenses | |
| 6. Electricity | |
|    Clinging elements of static electricity | |
|    Used for heat and light | |
|    Helps us with our work | |

**FIGURE 19–18** Seasonal science activities.

might be inspired by the presence of pets in the classroom are the following:

- Discuss the way pets feel, how they look, the sounds they make, the way they move, the purpose of various parts of the body, the need for food, their homes, reproduction, habits, etc.
- Write experience charts about their care and characteristics.
- Tell original stories based on the pet.
- Draw, paint, or model the pet out of clay.
- Dramatize the pets' movements.
- Take a trip to a pet shop or zoo.
- Show pictures of animals. Have children tell which are tame and which are wild; which fly, hop, swim, etc.; and which live in water, on land, etc.
- Tell animal stories, recite animal poems, and sing animal songs.

*Small animals.* Mice, gerbils, guinea pigs, frogs, turtles, snakes, salamanders, ants, bees, and meal-

**FIGURE 19–19 An aquarium is a good source of beauty and learning for a young child.**

worms can be kept alive in a classroom. Children can observe them and find answers to such questions as: What and how do these living things eat? Do they seem happy or unhappy? How can their environment be changed to make them happier? How do they move? What makes them move?

*Aquariums.* Fish tanks are a source of beauty and learning for a young child. The tanks can be simple or very fancy. Care must be taken that an aquarium does not become too crowded with fish and plants. If it does become overcrowded, many fish and plants may die. The easiest fish to keep in an aquarium are guppies and goldfish. Either type is hardy and inexpensive to buy.

Children can study the eating habits of fish. They can see how fish move and how they are affected by other fish. Children can look for changes in fish over a period of time. They can also see what happens if the water gets too cold, if too much food is added to the aquarium, or if new fish are added to the tank.

*Terrariums.* A terrarium is a glass-enclosed tank without water. Usually dirt or sand is placed on the bottom and plants are added. A terrarium can be made to look like the desert when sand, cactus plants, and desert lizards are used. This kind of terrarium is placed in a warm part of the room and given plenty of sun. A terrarium can also be made to look like a forest. It can be made to look like a grassy area. Insects, small snakes, frogs, and small lizards may be added.

To help children learn about the terrarium environment in a creative way, they should do two things. First, the children should build the terrarium. They should choose the plants and animals and know what types and how many they start with. Second, the children should watch for changes in plants and animals. Are they growing? What are they eating? Which one eats first? Are they disappearing? What changes should be made?

Figure 19–20 gives some further suggestions on other small animals and insects to include in young children's sciencing experiences.

| ANIMAL | WHERE TO FIND THEM | WHAT THEY EAT | HOW TO CREATE A MODEL |
|---|---|---|---|
| ants | • They find you if you put out a little sugar water. • in ant holes • in sidewalk cracks | • sugar water • diluted honey • nuts | 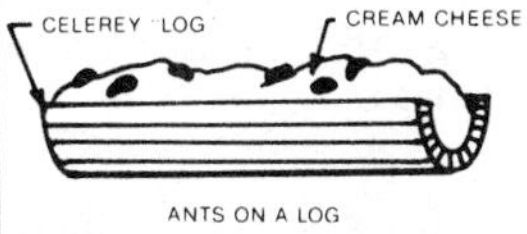 CELEREY LOG   CREAM CHEESE   ANTS ON A LOG |
| caterpillars | • in parks on trees in late spring and early summer | • leaves from the plant on which you found it | 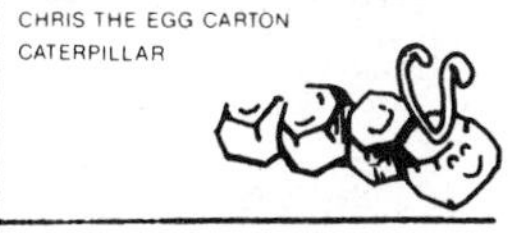 CHRIS THE EGG CARTON CATERPILLAR |
| moths | • in the summer at night near lights • in corner of garages | • sugar water | 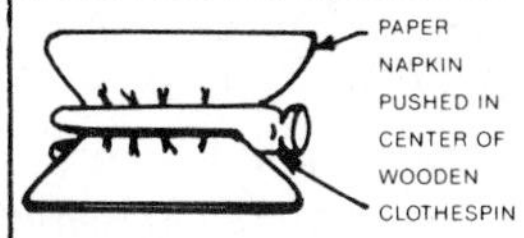 PAPER NAPKIN PUSHED IN CENTER OF WOODEN CLOTHESPIN |
| butterflies | • in parks, near flowers | • thick, fresh sugar water solutions | Same as for moths, but color the napkin first. |
| spiders | • in dark, damp places • on their webs in corners on the ceiling | • flies | 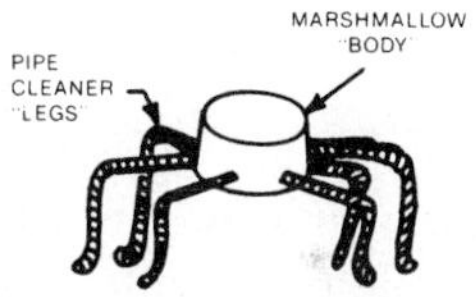 MARSHMALLOW BODY PIPE CLEANER LEGS |
| frogs | • in the country • near ponds | • live insects • worms |  PAINT OBLONG SHAPED ROCKS GREEN DECORATE WITH BLACK FELTTIP MARKERS |
| turtles | • in the country or in parks near or in ponds | • meat pieces • vegetables |  TELLY THE WALNUT SHELL TURTLE |
| tadpoles | • in the country or park in ponds | • water plants • watercress • bits of lettuce • cooked oatmeal | 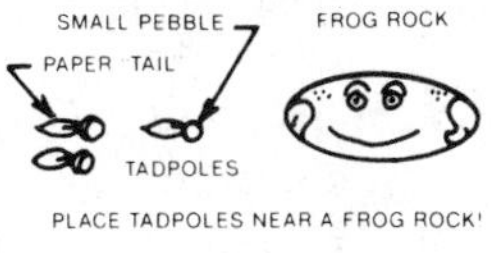 SMALL PEBBLE   FROG ROCK PAPER TAIL TADPOLES PLACE TADPOLES NEAR A FROG ROCK |
| worms | • in the dirt (Dig in the ground.) • on the ground after a rainfall | • dirt | Make playdough worms. |

FIGURE 19–20 Small animals for creative sciencing.

## ACTIVITIES ON THE SCHOOL GROUNDS

Many activities work well inside the school. Others are more suited to the area around the school building. The following are suggested activities for the outside grounds of the school.

**Gardening.** Common vegetables or flowers can be used. Seeds from fruits can be used or seedlings can be transplanted. In order for children to be creative gardeners, they should be given some choices: Where is the best place to plant seeds? What seeds should be planted? How far apart should they be planted? How much water do they need? When is the best time of the year to plant seeds? How much plant food or fertilizer is needed? In some ways—perhaps by tape recording—the children's decisions about these things should be recorded. The children should be allowed to dig up plants to see what is happening as growth takes place. They should compare the growth of their plants with the growth of other children's plants. Is there a difference? If there is, why?

**Bird Feeders.** Children can try to design bird feeders and build them in some way; or they can design the feeders and their parents can help them build the structures. Professionally built bird feeders can also be used.

Children can try to discover what kinds of food attract various kinds of birds. Where is the best place to put a bird feeder? When is the best time of year to watch for birds? What time of day is best for bird watching at a feeder?

**Cloud and Sky Watching.** On a mild, partly sunny or cloudy day, children can learn much about their environment. They can lie on the ground and look up at the sky. They may see clouds of many shapes. Clouds may join together. The sun may disappear. It may get cool very suddenly. Birds may fly past.

The children may have many different feelings as they lie still and watch the sky. Questions may arise. How do clouds seem to move? What do they look like? Are there many colors in the clouds? What do clouds look like just before a storm? Ask the children if they can make up a story about the clouds.

**The Sounds of Nature.** Walking in the woods or along a busy street can be made exciting by listening to the sounds. In the area next to a school, there are many sounds, too. When most of the children are indoors, one or two supervised children may want to go outside and just listen. They can take a cassette tape recorder along and record sounds, too.

How many different sounds can they hear? Can they hear sounds made by birds? By animals? What do the leaves in the trees sound like? How do trees without leaves sound? What other sounds can be heard? How do noises made by cars differ from noises made by trucks? How does a person feel if there is too much noise?

**What Happens to Rain Water?** After a rainstorm, children can try to follow the paths taken by the water. Does all of the water flow into a sewer? Does some of it go into the ground? What happens in paved areas compared to grassy areas? What happens in dirt areas compared to grassy areas?

**Bubbles.** Young children love bubbles—and they provide many an excellent sciencing activity. Colors are a natural topic, but air, soap, and water are other topics involved in bubble making.

To make good bubbles use a top quality brand of liquid detergent. Mix together one gallon of water, one cup of liquid detergent, and 50 drops of glycerine, which you can buy at the drugstore.

Anything with a hole will make wonderful bubbles. The plastic holders that link six-packs of soft drinks together make six big bubbles. Plastic berry baskets make lots of little bubbles. For giant bubbles, use a hula hoop in a wading pool filled with bubble liquid. The child steps into the hula hoop and, as you pull it up, she finds herself enclosed in a bubble. (For safety in the slippery glycerine-soap mixture, put a towel on the bottom of the pool.) (Clemens, 1991)

**Smells Around the School.** Children can search for different smells around the school. Some are good smells. What things give off good smells? What

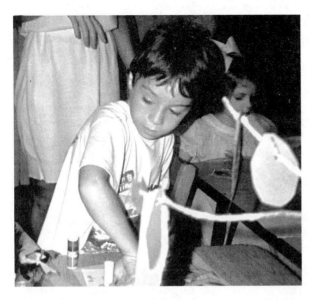

FIGURE 19–21 After a walk around the outside school area, children may want to make a collage out of the objects they discovered.

things have an unpleasant smell? Can any cause for bad smells be found? Can any reasons be found to explain why some things smell good and others do not? Does everyone agree on what smells good and what does not?

It is stimulating for children to compare their feelings with those of others. Are leaves changing colors in the fall beautiful? Are flowers beautiful? What about weeds? Can a cloud formation be beautiful? What about a rainbow? Is there beauty in a swing set or a slide? Can a bicycle be thought of as beautiful? How many words can the children think of that make them feel or see beauty?

**Animal Hiding Places.**   There may be a small hole in the ground or a sand hill in a crack on the playground. Thick grass or bushes serve as hiding places for animals. Under a large rock or near the foundation of the school, there may be places for living things to hide.

Children seek answers to many questions about animals. Why do animals need hiding places? Can a child create a place where an animal will choose to hide? How many natural hiding places can be found? Can children create hiding places for themselves? How do they feel when they are in their hiding places?

If creativity is to be a part of activities such as these, decisions must be left to the children. Help from the teacher should not take the form of orders on what to do and what not to do. Advice is good; orders or carefully worded "cookbook" directions are not.

## ENVIRONMENTAL ACTIVITIES IN OTHER AREAS

There are places other than the school building where children can learn about their environment. There are places outdoors for learning about the environment besides the playground. It is important for adults to know about these other places and to think about how they can be used with children.

**A Trip to the Zoo.**   Creative learning at a zoo is certainly possible if some care is taken in advance. Children should be given something definite to look for. They might be encouraged to watch how animals pace back and forth in their cages or what the large animals eat. Do the animals seem happy? Do they play together? Why are animals different colors?

**A Trip to a Nature Study Area.**   Often, a nature study site has a naturalist to take groups around, but young children need to participate in activities; they do not need a long-winded guide. A nature area is a good place to go to listen to natural sounds. How many sounds can be heard? What might the sounds mean? What is making the sounds? Where are they coming from? A nature area is also ideal for observing beauty. Natural beauty can be seen everywhere. The children can be asked to find a beautiful thing in the nature area. They can be asked to describe it—to tell why they like it. Many nature sites have shallow rivers flowing through them. It is a new experience for most children to wade in the river. They can take off their shoes and socks and roll up their pants. They can then explore under rocks, and feel the flow of water and mud oozing between their toes.

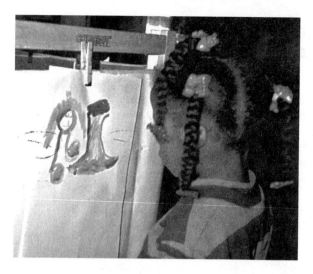

**FIGURE 19–22 A walk in the park inspired this child to paint a picture of her experience.**

What can the children find out about river life? What things live in a river? How do they live? Where do they find food? Are there animals that live both on the land and in the river?

If possible, return to the same spot or walk the same trail often. Go in the spring when the leaf buds are unfurling, after a rain to see the drops glistening on leaves and feel the sogginess underfoot, and in the winter to note the starkness of the branches and wonder where the birds live.

**Neighborhood Polluters.** A walking trip in the area around a school can be interesting. Children can use their senses to find people or places that make life unpleasant. Noise is one form of pollution children can observe. What is making the noise and how? How can the noise level be reduced?

Dirt, ugliness, and a run-down appearance are other forms of pollution. So are foul smells. Children can observe these, find who or what is causing them, and suggest solutions.

It is in the solving of problems that a young child can show creativity. It might even be possible that simple cleanup campaigns can be started by chil-

dren. At the least, the children can suggest ways that neighborhoods can be cleaned up.

**Safety to Make Life Better.** In many neighborhoods, hazards to the health and safety of children can be seen. Children know about them but do not realize the full danger. Old houses about to be torn down attract young children who are curious. Abandoned refrigerators are another safety hazard in many areas. The exhaust from cars that have been left running in the street, broken glass, and leaded paints are other sources of danger. Exposed electrical wires and hungry animals roaming the streets are still other dangers. When learning about the environment, children begin to think about ways to make life better.

**Plants in the Environment.** Probably the best way to observe the magnificent color and variety to be found in plants is to visit the places where they can be seen firsthand. The school grounds are the closest source. Children can hunt with you for the tallest tree, the one with the roughest bark, the ones with needles, pine cones, or smooth leaves. They can hunt for plants that are growing in cracks in the sidewalk, for plants that have been eaten by insects, for seeds, berries, galls, and roots that are exposed.

Going beyond the schoolyard, trips can be made to the grocery store, supermarket, or farmers' market to examine firsthand the potatoes, carrots, onions, eggplants, peas, cabbages, beets, and others. Vegetables represent great beauty in almost every color, shape, and size. If one of each kind could be brought back to the classroom, what a great opportunity for making comparisons they would offer!

The same kind of observations can be made with fruits, or with flowers at a greenhouse, shrubs at a nursery, or plants in an arboretum or small neighborhood garden or truck farm.

The plants can be looked at, cooked, taken apart, tasted, felt, counted, smelled, and weighed.

They could be compared for color, texture, juiciness, shape, kind of leaf, aroma, size, and outside covering.

They could be classified by the above characteristics cited or as nuts, seeds, fruits, roots, leaves, stems, vegetables, usually eaten raw, or usually eaten cooked.

**FIGURE 19–23 Children can learn a great deal about the environment from a trip to the farm.**

If excursions are not feasible, each child could be asked to bring one fruit, vegetable, or other plant to school, or the teacher could supply the necessary items from the school budget. Some other suggestions:

- Pictures of vegetables and fruits can be cut from magazines by the children and enjoyed as they are or pasted on a poster or in a scrapbook.
- Seed catalogs can be made available in the library or book center.
- Seeds can be planted in pots by the children, or better yet, if a small garden plot is available, they can be planted and cared for there. Seed dealers can advise you on types that germinate quickly and what care they need.
- Press a stick such as a tongue depressor down into the soil by the seed when it sprouts. Have each child mark the height of the sprout each week as

it grows. The date and name of the plant can be put on the stick.
- If the seeds in some pots don't grow, dig them up to see what happened to them.
- Help the children build a model greenhouse in the block center, using planks, large blocks, and packing boxes. They can put their plants in the greenhouse, as well as small trowels, watering cans, a bag of potting soil, and experience charts.
- Plants can be started from seeds, cuttings, bulbs, roots, and tubers. Sweet potatoes, placed in glasses so that half the potato is under water, will produce roots and a luxuriant vine. (Try to find potatoes that aren't bruised.) Bulbs of all kinds can be started. Geraniums and philodendron will produce roots from cuttings placed in water and can then be potted. Pussy willow twigs will grow roots in water.
- Top gardens can be made by cutting off about an inch from the top of root vegetables, such as carrots. Place the cut end in water, and new leafy growth will shoot up.
- Seeds of various kinds can be broken or cut open and studied to observe the small plant inside. Then have a plant tasting party. Examples: Seeds—sunflowers; roots—carrots; stems—celery; leaves—lettuce; flowers—cauliflower.
- Seeds can be sprouted in such a way that their growth can be studied. A satisfactory way to do this is to cut up blotting paper or paper towels. Place a couple of layers in the bottom of a saucer, moistening the paper thoroughly. Drop six to ten radish seeds on the blotter. Smear a little Vaseline around the edge of the saucer and cover with a piece of window glass. Tiny white root hairs will develop.
- To see roots, stems, and leaves form, make a plastic bag greenhouse. Place folded paper towels inside a plastic, self-locking bag, then staple a line across about 2″ from the bottom. Children fill bags to just below the line of staples with water, then drop in seeds. Seal the bags and display on a bulletin board to observe growth and development. Children will be able to see the roots, stems, and leaves form.

**Water Play Experiences.** No matter in what quantity or container water is available—in a pool or basin, in a puddle or cup—there are ways to take advantage of its learning potential! A wading pool or large basin lends itself to pouring, sprinkling, and mixing with water, while a cup or a puddle is ideal for floating tiny objects like foil boats or cork stoppers and for dissolving small quantities of sugar or drink mix. Whatever facilities can be provided, water is a marvelous science experience for young children.

Organizing the play space for water play is a matter of selecting and arranging suitable containers and appropriate equipment. A laundry tub or plastic wading pool can be placed outside with a bench or table nearby to hold objects. If water play is to take place inside, the floor covering must be water repellent, and a shelf can be used for equipment storage; a plastic tablecloth can waterproof even a carpet, and a small card table can substitute for the shelf. Plastic aprons are ideal for clothing protection, but garbage bags with neck and arm holes cut serve well, too.

Objects that lead the child to sciencing experiences might include the following:

- Sponges, corks, and light pieces of wood.
- Funnels, strainers, colanders, plastic tubing and siphons.
- Spray containers, sprinkling cans, squeeze bottles, water guns, and rubber balls.
- Plastic pitchers, margarine tubs, plastic cups, and yogurt containers.
- Paint brushes, paint rollers, and wash cloths.
- Spoons, dippers, plastic syringes, and plastic medicine droppers.

Occasionally, bubble bath, corn starch, food coloring, or other mixables can be added to vary the appearance and physical properties of the water.

*Safety tips.* Always have an adult with the children in any water play situation. Never leave a child unattended. Use only unbreakable materials for water play activities. Never use glass, ceramic, porcelain, pottery, china, or other breakable materials. Always gather materials ahead of time, so you do not have to leave the children unsupervised.

Develop water play rules with the children. Discuss and generate a list that is appropriate to your situation and revise them as needed. For example, you will need one set of rules when the children are playing at the water table and other rules for the outdoor pool.

Some ideas for rules might include:

- No splashing.
- Keep the water in the containers.
- Mop up spills immediately.

Specific activities for water play are included at the end of this unit.

## SUMMARY

Sciencing is an activity in which children gain knowledge about the world around them by investigating that world. In sciencing, the emphasis is on investigating; the knowledge gained is less important. Sciencing is important for children because it gives them all an opportunity to succeed.

Formal sciencing activities are divided into two general categories. First, there are activities designed to help children become better investigators. These are called process skill-building activities. The second category consists of activities that help a child apply the process skills.

Informal sciencing is made up of a number of open activities that children may choose to use or to ignore. Informal sciencing is less structured than formal sciencing. Creativity is therefore better served by informal than by formal sciencing.

There are two keys to a child's success in sciencing: (1) the willingness of a teacher to let children investigate, and (2) the availability of equipment. Equipment is available from many sources. Some is free or inexpensive, while other equipment is more expensive. It is important for a teacher to know about and use every source of material that is available.

Ecology is the study of all elements in the environment, both living and nonliving, and how these elements are interrelated. The term comes from two Greek words: "ecos" meaning "place to live" or "home," and "ology" meaning "study of."

Children should begin to understand that all forces in the environment affect one another. Animals influence other animals. Plants affect animals.

The climate has an effect on the environment. People can make the environment pleasant or very unpleasant.

Children should have experiences with both the natural and man-made environments. These experiences take place in the school building and in the play area around the school. They also take place in the community in which the children live. Playing with water is another excellent way for young children to experience the natural environment.

# LEARNING ACTIVITIES

## Sciencing Activities for Young Children

1. Take a field trip around your home or your college. Walk within one square block of the home or school. Identify all of the plant life in this area. How many trees, plants, shrubs, and weeds can you observe?
2. Create a file of resources in the community that could be used to foster children's concepts of their environment and the world around them.
3. Observe in a classroom where there is a living pet or pets. Record the children's conversations as they watch the pet. Discuss how much they have learned about the animal from direct observation. What did their questions/conversations tell you about their experiences with the pet? Be specific in your answers.
4. Using a pail of water, create a puddle on a playground in order to observe children's reactions as they approach it. Record the ways in which they play.
5. Plan a sciencing table where children can be involved in making discoveries. List the objects you might include and describe the types of involvement each object might stimulate. Discuss your list with others in your class.
6. Visit a playground. List natural phenomena that seem to be of interest to children. As you observe children at play, describe behavior that indicates they do take an interest in these phenomena. Compare what interested you at the playground to what interested the children. Discuss the differences between your interests and those of the children.

## Making Some Observations

The ability to make many accurate observations is an important skill for both children and adults. The following activity is designed to test one's ability to make observations and use all of one's senses (hearing, smelling, tasting, touching, and seeing).

A. Materials: One package of peppermint Life Savers, one ruler, one book of matches, one small nail, one sheet of sandpaper, a glass of water, waxed paper.
B. How many observations can be made about a package of peppermint Life Savers? Can as many as 40 observations be made? Try doing this with one or two partners, if possible. Do it for each of the items listed in part A.
C. List all the observations and write down the sense or senses that were used to make each observation (seeing, hearing, etc.).

## Finding Objects for Making Observations

A. Find 10 objects that can be used for making observations. Each object should provide opportunities for an observer to use all five senses. For instance, an ice cube can be one of the objects.
B. After finding the ten objects, try the following:
   1. Decide what other materials would help in making observations of this thing. A ruler or magnifying glass may be needed. Make a list of these materials.
   2. Collect all materials needed for observing each item and place them in small packages or boxes.
   3. Choose a partner. Make observations of three of the partner's objects using materials provided by the partner. Then let the partner try out your objects and materials.

## Describing Shapes

A. Draw three shapes on a piece of paper. The shapes should not be something everyone recognizes.
B. Choose a partner. Try to describe each of the shapes in such a way that the partner can draw pictures of them without seeing them. This is a difficult task.

## Making an Electromagnet

A. Materials: D-cell battery and battery holder or a dry cell; four feet of thin wire; one iron nail; 30 or 40 tacks or paper clips.
B. Make an electromagnet with the materials. This approach has been proven successful with children. Time and patience are needed for discovery learning to take place.
C. Find out how these materials can be put together to make a stronger electromagnet (one that will pick up more tacks or paper clips).

D. Find other things that can be picked up by the electromagnet. Find uses for an electromagnet.
E. Try this investigation with a four- or five-year-old child. See how the child goes about these tasks. Compare the child's investigating methods with the way adults try to solve these problems.

## Finding Materials

A. Visit rummage sales, farm auctions, store sales, and secondhand stores. Look for materials that could be used by children in sciencing.
B. Make a list of things that can be bought, how much they cost, and where they can be purchased. Compare lists with two or more other students.
C. Prepare a master list of these materials.

## Miscellaneous Activities

A. Spend three hours of one day with a group of fellow students, but do not speak to any of them. They may not speak either. Try to do something with two or more people without communicating in any way: no words, no hand signs, no head nodding.

B. Find an area around the school or the neighborhood that needs cleaning up. Organize a cleanup committee. Take pictures before, during, and after the cleanup.

## Nature

An area in the community should be found where nature can be studied. Try any or all of the following activities.

A. In a 15-minute period of time, how many birds can be seen? How many different kinds of birds are observed?
B. In an area three feet by three feet and six inches deep, how many living things can be found?
C. How many living things can be found under a small rock?
D. In a five-minute period of time, how many different sounds can be heard?
E. How many different kinds of plants can be found in an area 50 by 100 feet?

# ACTIVITIES FOR CHILDREN

## Water Play Activities

In all of the following activities, be sure that an adult is *always* present when children are playing with water.

### Activities for Three- and Four-Year-Old Children
### Pouring and Mixing Water Colors
A. Materials: Cups, plastic pitchers, spoons, water, squeeze bottles of red, yellow, and blue food coloring, paste food coloring in red, yellow, and blue, a shallow pan to catch spills (if indoors), assorted construction paper.
B. Procedure: Place a dab of paste food coloring on some of the spoons. The child squeezes a couple of drops of one color of food coloring into each cup. The child pours a small amount of water into each cup and stirs the liquid to create evenly colored water.

### Squeezing Activities
A. Materials: Dishpan half-full of water, clear plastic squeeze bottles (large, medium, and small, clean), plastic basters (the kind with a bulb on the end).
B. Procedure: The child selects a large, medium, or small squeeze bottle. He unscrews the lid and holds it underwater in the dishpan until it is full and then

replaces the lid. The child then empties the bottle by squeezing the water back into the dishpan.

### Spray Art—Mural Making
A. Materials: Spray mist bottle with trigger handle, squeeze bottle of food coloring, large white butcher block paper or a white sheet, scissors, tape, large towel or plastic mat, water, table top.
B. Procedure: Spread the towel or plastic mat on the floor. Cut a large square of butcher block paper. Tape the paper or the sheet to the table top, or outside to a wall or fence. Fill the spray bottle with water. Squeeze 10–15 drops of food coloring into the spray bottle. Secure the top of the spray bottle. Prepare several spray bottles of water with different colors of food coloring mixture.

The child shakes the bottle, standing next to the paper or sheet. Holding the spray bottle, the child sprays the colored water onto the paper to make a mural. When the children are finished spraying the colored water mural, the teacher removes the tape and dries the mural.

### Going Fishing—Catch a Shape
A. Materials: Different colored sponges cut into different shapes; a bucket for each shape cut.

B. Procedure: Tape a different-shaped sponge on the front of each bucket. Put the buckets next to the water table, basin, sink, or any container that is used for water play. Place all of the cut-up sponges in the water. The child picks up the specific shaped (or colored) sponge when so directed. He then squeezes the water out of the sponge "fish" and puts the "fish" in the correct "fish" bucket.

## Ping-Pong Push

A. Materials: Large wooden spoons, Ping-Pong balls/plastic eggs, ribbon, tape.
B. Procedure: The children push Ping-Pong balls or plastic eggs in the water from one side of the water table to the other with a wooden spoon. The teacher can tape or tie a ribbon down the middle of the water table, water tub, sink, bucket, etc. Two children can stand on either side of the ribbon.

## Sprinkler Fun—Looby Loo

A. Materials: Sprinkler.
B. Procedure: The children form a circle around the sprinkler. They play the game "Looby Loo," and put the named body part into the sprinkler.

**Looby Loo**

Here we go looby loo.
Here we go looby li.
Here we go looby loo—
All on a Saturday night!

I put my right foot in.
I put my right foot out.
I give my foot a shake, shake, shake,
And turn myself about.

## Miscellaneous Water Play Ideas

A. Straws are great for blowing bubbles during water play. To prevent children from sucking up the soapy water by mistake, poke holes near the tops of the straws first.
B. Make soap bubbles last longer by adding a few tablespoons of sugar to the soapy water.

## Water Play Activities for Five- and Six-Year-Olds
## Pump Art Chalk Designs

A. Materials: Colored chalk, plastic pump bottles in different sizes, water.
B. Procedure: Fill the plastic pump bottle with water. The child colors the sidewalk with colored chalk. The child presses the pump top and lets the water splatter over the chalk on the sidewalk, making a water design on the chalk. Use different-sized pump bottles, comparing the different water marks made by each bottle.

## Spray Art—Designer T-Shirt

A. Materials: Spray mist bottle with trigger handle, food coloring, large white butcher block paper, scissors, tape, large towel or plastic mat, water, T-shirt.
B. Procedure: Spread the towel or plastic mat outdoors, on the floor, or under a table. Place another towel or mat on the table. Tape a white T-shirt to the towel, mat, or to the towel on the table. Fill the plastic squeeze spray bottle with water. Squeeze 10–15 drops of food coloring into the plastic spray bottle and secure the top. Prepare several plastic spray bottles of water with different colors of food coloring. Shake the bottles.

The child shakes the bottle. Standing next to the table with the spray gun bottle in one hand, the child sprays the colored water onto the T-shirt. Add more food coloring if the color is too light. If you want to be sure of permanent color, use liquid dye instead of food coloring and water. When the child is finished with his design, remove the tape, and hang the T-shirt to dry.

## Rocky Road to Knowledge

Rocks, stones, and pebbles are not only interesting, abundant, and free for the taking; they also provide a rich source of knowledge about matter and are a means of sharpening powers of observation, description, and classification.

A. Some of the things that can be done with rocks are
   1. sorting by size, color, texture, and surface.
   2. identifying them by name.
   3. taking a walk to see the many ways stone is used in buildings.
   4. looking for fossils in limestone.
   5. taking a field trip to hunt for interesting rocks.
B. Equipment that is useful in carrying out such a study includes scales of various types, magnifying glasses, boxes (or egg cartons) for sorting.

## Plastic Bottle Space Helmets

Children will be prepared for unlimited flights of fancy after they design their own plastic bottle space helmets. You make the basic shape by cutting away the bottom and a face-sized part from one side of a plastic milk or bleach container. Be sure you've washed it thoroughly to remove all previous liquid contents. Cover any sharp or rough edges with masking tape. The children personalize the helmets by gluing on pieces of felt or other cloth, buttons, sponges, pipe cleaners—whatever decorations they can think of. They can also draw and write on the helmets with felt-tip markers.

**FIGURE 19–24 Plastic bottle space helmet.**

## Sun Prints

Obtain large sheets of blueprint paper. The child lies in a sunny spot on the paper for a few minutes. When he or she gets up, a body print will be left. The print may be colored or decorated if the child prefers.

Variation: If the child can't lie still long enough, use objects instead for the sun prints.

## Explore the Powers of the Sun

Explore the power of sunlight—what it will pass through and what blocks it. Using different materials (clear glass, soda bottles of various colors, thin paper, construction paper), sort the items as to those sunlight can pass through and those it will not pass through. Talk about shadows, too.

## Bubble Fun

Children of all ages, but especially toddlers, take great delight in blowing bubbles. To make colored bubbles—the ultimate in bubble activities—do the following:

Combine ¼ cup of glycerine, ½ cup water, and 1 tablespoon liquid detergent in a jar. Mix and pour into individual cups for each child. Ask the child the color bubble he or she prefers, then let each child add and mix the colors. Add food coloring for the color preferred. Use a straw or bubble pipe to blow bubbles. Be sure the children know how to blow *out* with straws!

## More Bubble Fun

Here is a way to make a special bubble mix that will make more beautiful, lasting bubbles:

Fill a quart jar two-thirds full of soap bubble flakes. Add 1 teaspoon of sugar and 4 teaspoons of glycerine. Fill the jar to within a half inch of the top with lukewarm water. For colored bubbles, add a few drops of cake coloring. Screw the lid on tight and shake the jar very hard. Pour the mixture into a saucer. (Put the remaining mixture in the refrigerator to use another time. However, when using the mixture, it will make better bubbles if it is at room temperature or warmer.)

Use an empty spool for a soap pipe. When you have a big bubble on the spool, swing the spool gently, and the bubble will fall on the floor. Let it fall on a woolen rug and it will last a long time. Sometimes it can be made to dance by blowing gently on the rug near the bubble.

Experiment with blowing bubbles outside on a very cold day.

## Insect Cage

Cut openings in small plastic or cardboard cartons. Cover the opening with fine netting, taping it into place. Fine netting can also be taped over the top of any plastic container to provide a temporary home for insects. The children can observe insect life more easily if the insect cages are made from clear plastic containers.

A clean, empty, half-gallon milk carton also makes a good insect-viewer. Simply cut rectangular holes on two sides of the milk carton. Slip a nylon stocking over the carton and fasten at the top with a rubber band. Insects can be held inside for temporary viewing.

## The Science Center

Arrange a science table or shelf in the classroom upon which children can display their treasures. Permanent equipment in the center might include a hand lens or magnifying glass, color wheel, scales, magnets, some reference books pertinent to the current topic of interest, a viewer, and slides. Additional items that could be placed on the table at various times are a prism and a tuning fork; and from the children themselves, rocks, shells, feathers, leaves, seeds, etc. Change exhibits often!

A simple bulletin board for mounting signs, pictures, or photos can be made from a cardboard carton. Cut the ends out of the carton, slit the box down one corner, and fasten the box in the shape of a triangle. Corrugated cardboard will take pins. It can be painted or covered with wallpaper. But remember, a science corner should be for touching as well as looking.

## Observing Worms

Make an earthworm observatory with a large glass jar (a large peanut butter jar is good), worms, garden soil, and black construction paper.

Place a layer of small rocks or sand in the bottom of the jar so water will drain. Place 2 inches of moist soil and sand in the jar. Have children pick up worms and place them in the jar. Cover them with more soil. Keep the soil moist. Seal, using a lid with holes punched in it.

Wrap black construction paper around the jar. After 24 hours, remove the paper. The children should be able to see the worms tunneling through the soil.

Encourage children to talk about what interests them about worms.

## Activities That Teach About Plants

To teach some basic facts about plants, try some of these activities:

A. Concept: Roots grow down, while the plant pushes upward toward the light.
   Activity: Cut a piece of blotting paper to fit a glass jar. Put a little water into the jar, then put grass or radish seeds between the blotter and the jar. The seeds will sprout quickly and the roots can be seen pushing upward. Turn the jar any way and the roots will turn also—always going downward.

B. Concept: Plants need warm air.
   Activity: Place a wet sponge in a pan with a little water to keep it wet. Scatter grass seeds over the sponge. Place it in the refrigerator for a week, then put it in the sunshine. The seeds will soon sprout.

C. Concept: Plants get water through their roots.
   Activity: Cut off the lower end of a fresh stalk of celery and put it into a glass of water that has been colored with food coloring or ink. Observe how the colored water pushes up through the stalk and out to the leaves.

D. Concept: Plants get food from the soil through tiny root hairs.
   Activity: Plant grass or radish seeds on a wet paper towel or blotter. Turn a pan or dish over it. In a few days tiny root hairs can be seen. These absorb food from the soil and help to make the plant healthy. Look at them through a magnifying glass.

E. Concept: Sunlight affects the color of plants.
   Activity: Plant two begonias or other cuttings. Place one in the sunlight and the other in a dark place. Observe that the one grown in the sunlight has a deep green color, while the one grown in the dark has little green.

F. Concept: Seeds of many plants are found in the fruit.
   Activity: Cut open an apple, orange, grapefruit, and other fruits to observe the seeds. Show various kinds of nuts that are also seeds.

G. Concept: Some plants need more water or more sunlight than others.
   Activity: Notice the effect of too much water on begonias, geraniums, African violets, etc. (Plants will rot.) Observe the effect of too little water on ferns. Put a blooming plant in the sunshine and another like it in the shade. Observe how sunlight is necessary to profuse blooming. Place a fern, which likes shade, in direct sunlight. Notice how the leaves turn light.

H. Concept: A seed has food on which a baby plant grows.
   Activity: Soak several lima beans in water overnight. Split open one bean. You can see the tiny new sprout coming, while all around it is the food on which it lives as it grows. Pumpkin or squash seeds are also good for this.

## Other Experiences with Plants

A. Make a carrot basket: Hollow out a large carrot. Tie a string on it to hang it in the window, and fill the hollow with water. It will soon grow lovely greenery.
B. Plant morning glory seeds in a window box. Watch the vine grow up the string. Observe growth of bud to flower, and how the flower opens in the sunlight and closes in the shade.
C. Plant bulbs both in water with pebbles and in soil. Split open a bulb to show the baby plant inside.
D. Soak lemon, orange, or grapefruit seeds overnight, then plant them and watch growth and blooms.
E. Make a terrarium.
F. Make a dish garden.

## Grow It Again!

A. Pineapple. Cut off the top and trim three rows of bottom leaves. Let dry for three days. Plant one inch deep in soil. Keep moist and sunny.
B. Carrot. Cut off the top and trim off all leaves. Place in a layer of pebbles in a flat dish. Keep well watered.
C. Onion. Find an onion that is already sprouted. Plant in soil. Keep watered and sunny.

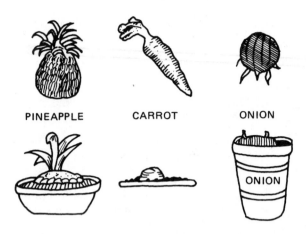

**FIGURE 19–25 Grow it again! Eat these vegetables and fruits and use different parts to grow new plants.**

## Sky Gazer

Save the cardboard tubes from paper towel rolls. Punch two holes at one end of each tube and loop an 18-inch piece of yarn through them (make one for each child). Hang your telescope around your neck. Go outside on a nice, warm day and lie down on the grass. Using your telescope, look up into the sky. What do you see? Look some more. What else do you see? Tell each other.

## The Magic Jar

Give a baby food jar to each child in the group. Have them half fill the jars with water. Then, fill the rest of the jar with vegetable oil and a few drops of food coloring. Attach the lid with waterproof glue and let the children shake their magic jar and watch the oil and water separate! It will keep them busy for a long time and is a wonderful way to discuss the properties of water and oil.

## Vegetable Critter

There are many fresh vegetables. Let the child pick out a potato at the store or from the garden. Talk about its color and how it grows. Let the child make a critter with the vegetable. Use the potato for the body, and using his imagination, cut the eyes, tail, nose, and mouth from any other vegetable that you have around (cucumber pieces, squash tidbits, carrot slices), then attach to the potato with toothpicks. The child can name his "critter."

## Build a Bird Feeder

Treat a bird to lunch. Cut windows and doors into an empty milk carton or plastic soda bottle. Decorate it in such a way that birds will want to visit. Paste on colored pictures of big juicy worms! Glue on twigs, leaves, seeds, and other outdoor things with nontoxic glue. (Keep decorations to a minimum so as not to frighten the birds.) Tie it to a tree branch and fill it with birdseed. Watch and see how many birds and what kinds of birds use the feeder.

## Observations

A. Draw on the chalkboard a large chart similar to the one shown. Ask a child to choose an item in the room. Then let everyone describe characteristics under the appropriate headings. If a ball is selected, one child might say, "I see that it is red." Write "red" under the picture of the eye. When another student says, "It feels soft," write "soft" under the picture of the hand. The children will enjoy seeing their own suggestions written on the board, but do not allow the activity to become a vocabulary lesson. Maintain a focus on the process of observing.

| ITEM | 👁 | 👂 | ✋ | 👃 | 👄 |
|------|---|---|---|---|---|
|      |   |   |   |   |   |
|      |   |   |   |   |   |

B. Some children may wish to bring interesting items from home for observation.

## Science Poetry

### Coffeepot Face

I saw
   my face
   in the coffeepot.
Imagine,
   a coffeepot face!
My eyes
   were small
   but my nose was not,

And my mouth
    was . . . every place!

## Hinges

I'm all made of hinges
    'cause everything bends
    from the top of my neck
    way down to my ENDS.

I'm hinges in front
    and I'm hinges in back;
    but I HAVE to be hinges
    or else I would crack.

## Little Seeds (A Fingerplay)

I put some little flower seeds
    (Pretend to hold seed between thumb and index
    finger)
Down in the warm, soft ground;
    (Stoop down, pretend to plant the seeds in the
    ground)
I sprinkled them with water
From a sprinkling can I found.
    (Pretend to water the ground)
The big, round sun shone brightly,
    (Make a large circle with hands above your
    head)
We had some soft rain showers:
The little seeds began to grow.
Soon I had lovely flowers.
    (Flutter fingers downward)
    (Stoop down, get up slowly)
    (Spread hands outward and smile)

## Think-And-Do Puzzle

Coffee, milk, bread, and tea,
One doesn't belong. Which could it be?

Mothers, fathers, flowers, brothers—
Take one away, but leave the others.

A rose, a dandelion, a daisy, a face,
One could never be put in a vase.

A fly, a bee, a cricket, a toad—
One doesn't belong on the insect road.

A fish, robin, crow, or parakeet,
Which one travels without any feet?

Carrots, potatoes, tomatoes, a hoe—
One of these will never grow.

## Air Riddle

You cannot see it, but it is all around you.
It touches the floor, the ceiling, the walls;
it is between your fingers and toes, inside
your mouth and between the pages of a book.

It is always pushing on you with great force.
But usually you do not feel it pushing.

Sometimes it moves very fast. Sometimes it
stands still. Sometimes it is warm.
Sometimes it is cold. It is worth more to
you than gold, but it costs nothing at all.

What is it?—Air

## Solids, Liquid, Gas

Solids we bump into.
Liquids we jump into.
Solids can crash.
Liquids will splash.

Solids we can grab
and grip.
Not liquids—
they drip.

But air is a gas—
Not solid like brass
or liquid like juice.
Air is all loose!

## Tools and Machines

A. To practice using everyday items to reinforce science concepts, give children opportunities to use simple tools and machines. Direct experience with them at this age leads to later understanding of such abstract concepts as force, balance, momentum, and friction, as well as the funtion of the level, gears, etc.

B. Collect some tools and machines that should be available for young children's use:

| | |
|---|---|
| blunt scissors | pliers |
| paper punch | nails (large heads) |
| scales | a vise |
| typewriter | screwdriver |
| outdoor thermometer | screws (large heads) |
| hammers | hinges |
| saws | dust pan and brush |
| shovels | hoes |
| trowels | spades |
| timer (such as is used in cooking) | wagons |
| | trikes |
| cooking thermometer | cars |
| large room thermometer | dump trucks |
| rakes | wheelbarrow |
| record players | viewer |
| tape recorder | |

C. In using simple tools with children, ask questions such as "What makes it work?" "What is it made of?" "What else is like it?"

# UNIT REVIEW

1. Name the five senses on which observations are based.
2. What are the two phases of formal sciencing? Which phase is more important for young children?
3. List three ways in which children benefit from sciencing.
4. Choose the answer that best completes each statement about sciencing.
   a. The teacher is most involved in planning for
      (a.) formal sciencing.
      (b.) informal sciencing.
      (c.) incidental sciencing.
   b. The teacher cannot plan for
      (a.) formal sciencing.
      (b.) informal sciencing.
      (c.) incidental sciencing.
   c. Observing skills are taught to children in
      (a.) formal sciencing.
      (b.) informal sciencing.
      (c.) incidental sciencing.
   d. Free investigation is used most often in
      (a.) formal sciencing.
      (b.) informal sciencing.
      (c.) incidental sciencing.
5. Define ecology and discuss its place in the early childhood program.

# ADDITIONAL READINGS

## General Science

Clemens, S.G. *"Art int he Classroom: Making Every Day Special." Young Children* (Jan., 1991): 4–11.

Dighe, J. "Children and the Earth." *Young Children* (March, 1993): 58–63.

Forman, G., and M. Kaden. "Research and Science Education for Young Children." In *The Early Childhood Curriculum*, C. Seefeldt, ed. New York: Teachers College Press, Columbia University, 1986, pp. 97–104.

Harlan, J. *Science Experiments for Early Childhood Years.* Columbus, Ohio: Merrill, 1976.

Holt, B. *Science with Young Children.* Washington, D.C.: NAEYC, 1990.

Iatridis, M.D. *Teaching Science to Children: A Resourcebook.* New York: Garland, 1986.

James, J.C., and R.F. Granovetter. *Waterworks: A New Book of Waterplay Activities for Children Ages 1 to 6.* Lewisville, N.C.: Kaplan Press, 1988.

Levenson, E. *Teaching Children About Science: Ideas and Activities Every Teacher and Parent Can Use.* Englewood Cliffs, N.J.: Prentice-Hall, 1985.

McIntyre, M. *Early Childhood and Science: A Collection of Articles.* Washington, D.C.: National Science Teachers Assoc., 1984.

Nuebebaur, B., ed. *The Wonder of It: Exploring How the World Works.* New York: Little Brown, 1992.

Sherwood, E.A., R.A. Williams, and R.E. Rockwell. *More Mudpies to Magnets: Science for Young Children.* Mt. Ranier, Md.: Gryphon House, Inc., 1990.

Sisson, E. *Nature with Children of All Ages.* Englewood Cliffs, N.J.: Prentice-Hall, 1982.

Woodard, C., and R. Davitt. *Physical Science in Early Childhood.* Springfield, Ill.: Thomas, 1987.

## Children's Books on General Science Topics

Barton, Byron. *Machines at Work.* Crowell, 1987.

Bond, Felicia. *Wake-Up Vladimir.* New York: Harper, 1987.

Brandt, K. *Air.* Mahwah, N.J.: Troll Associates, 1985.

————. *Sounds.* Mahwah, N.J. Troll Associates, 1985.

Branley, F. *Air Is All Around Us.* New York: Scribner's, 1986.

Ehlert, Lois. *Planting a Rainbow.* Harcourt, 1988.

Fisher, Aileen. *When It Comes to Bugs.* New York: Harper, 1986.

Gibbons, Gail. *Tool Book.* New York: Holiday House, 1982.

————. *Trains.* New York: Holiday, 1987.

————. *Weather Words and What They Mean.* New York: Holiday House, 1990.

Griffith, Helen V. *Grandaddy's Place.* New York: Greenwillow, 1987.

Hadithi, Mwenye. *Crafty Chameleon.* New York: Little Brown, 1987.

Hankes, Kevin. *Bailey Goes Camping.* New York: Greenwillow, 1985.

Hansen, Ron. *The Shadowmaker.* New York: Harper, 1987.

Hoban, T. *Exactly the Opposite.* New York: Greenwillow, 1990.

Ivenson-Ivenson, J. *Your Nose and Ears.* New York: The Bookwright Press, 1986.

Knutson, Barbara. *Why the Crab Has No Head*. Minneapolis: Carolrhoda, 1987.

Kramer, Stephen P. *Getting Oxygen: What to Do If You're Cell Twenty-Two*. New York: Crowell, 1986.

Livingston, M.C., and L.E. Fisher, illustrator. *Earth Songs*. New York: Holiday House, 1986.

Maris, Ron. *Is Anyone Home?* New York: Greenwillow, 1986.

McCord, David. *All Small*. Boston: Little, Brown, 1986.

McMillan, Bruce. *Becca Backward, Becca Frontward: A Book of Concept Pairs*. New York: Lothrop, Lee & Shepard, 1986.

McNulty, Faith. *The Lady and the Spider*. New York: Harper, 1986.

Mitgutsch, A. *From Wood to Paper*. Minneapolis: Carolrhoda Books, 1986.

Narahashi, Keiko. *I Have a Friend*. McElderry, 1987.

Pluckrose, H. *Think About Hearing*. New York: Franklin Watts, 1986.

Richter, B., and D. Wenzel. *The Museum of Science and Industry Basic List of Children's Science Books, 1973–1984*. Chicago: American Library Association, 1985.

Robbins, K. *A Flower Grows*. New York: Dial Books, 1990.

Rockwell, Ann. *Fire Engines*. New York: Dutton, 1986.

————. *Things That Go*. New York: Dutton, 1986.

Turkle, Brinton. *Deep in the Forest*. New York: Dutton, 1987.

Williams, Vera B. *Stringbean's Trip to the Shining Seas*. New York: Greenwillow, 1988.

World Wildlife Fund. *Snow Leopard*. Illustrated by Lynne Cherry. New York: Dutton, 1987.

————. *Grizzly Bear*. Illustrated by Lynne Cherry. New York: Dutton, 1987.

————. *Orangutang*. Illustrated by Lynne Cherry. New York: Dutton, 1987.

Yolen, Jane. *Owl Moon*. New York: Philomel, 1987.

## Children's Books on Science

### Ecology and Environment Picture Books

Bartlett, Margaret. *The Clean Brook*. New York: T.Y. Crowell, 1960.

Carrick, Carol. *Swamp Spring*. New York: Macmillan, 1969.

Clymer, Eleanor. *A Big Pile of Dirt*. New York: Scholastic Book Service, 1972.

Fisher, Aileen. *We Went Looking*. New York: T.Y. Crowell, 1968.

Freschet, Berniece. *The Old Bullfrog*. New York: Charles Scribner's Sons, 1972.

Garelick, May. *Where Does the Butterfly Go When It Rains?* New York: Scholastic Book Service, 1970.

Hurd, Edith. *Wilson's World*. New York: Harper and Row, 1971.

Keats, Ezra. *The Snowy Day*. New York: Viking Press, 1962.

Keith, Eros. *A Small Lot*. New York: Bradbury Press, 1968.

Lionni, Leo. *Inch by Inch*. New York: Astor-Honor, 1962.

Lubell, Winifred, and Cecil Lubell. *The Tall Grass Zoo*. Chicago: Rand McNally, 1960.

McCloskey, Robert. *Time of Wonder*. New York: Viking Press, 1977.

Mendoza, George. *The Hunter I Might Have Been*. New York: Astor-Honor, 1968.

Miles, Miska. *Apricot ABC*. Boston: Little, Brown and Co., 1969.

————. *Hoagie's Rifle Gun*. Boston: Little, Brown and Co., 1970.

————. *Nobody's Cat*. Boston: Little, Brown and Co., 1969.

Mizumura, Kazue. *If I Build a Village*. New York: T.Y. Crowell, 1971.

Peet, Bill. *Wump World*. Boston: Houghton Mifflin, 1970.

Piatti, Celestino. *The Happy Owls*. New York: Atheneum, 1964.

Schoenherr, John. *The Barn*. Boston: Little, Brown and Co., 1968.

Udry, Janice. *A Tree Is Nice*. New York: Harper and Row, 1956.

Zolotow, Charlotte. *Storm Book*. New York: Harper and Row, 1952.

### Ecology and Environment Nonfiction

Bendick, Jeanne. *A Place to Live: A Study of Ecology*. New York: Parents, 1970.

Bloome, Enid. *The Air We Breathe*. New York: Doubleday, 1971.

————. *The Water We Drink*. New York: Doubleday, 1971.

Busch, Phyllis, *Puddles and Ponds: Living Things in Watery Places*. Cleveland, Ohio: Collins, William, and World, 1969.

Goetz, Delia. *Rivers (How Pollution Develops)*. New York: William Morrow and Co., 1969.

Guilcher, Jean, and R.H. Noailles. *A Tree is Born*. New York: Sterling, 1960.

Haley, Gail. *Noah's Ark*. New York: Atheneum, 1971.

Henwood, S. *The Hidden Jungle*. New York: Farrar, Straus, Giroux, 1992.

Hoover, Helen. *Animals at My Doorstep*. New York: Parents, 1966.

McCord, David. *Every Time I Climb a Tree*. Boston: Little, Brown and Co., 1967.

Parnall, Peter. *The Mountain*. New York: Doubleday, 1971.

Podendorf, Illa. *Every Day Is Earth Day*. Chicago: Children's Press, 1971.

Selsam, Millicent, and Betty Morrow. *See Through the Sea*. New York: Harper & Row, 1955.

Tresselt, Alvin. *The Beaver Pond*. New York: Lothrop, 1970.

Webber, Irma. *Bits That Grow Big*. Reading, Mass.: Addison-Wesley, 1949.

*Air*

Berger, Melvin. *The New Air Book*. New York: Crowell, 1987.

Boegehold, Betty. *What the Wind Told*. New York: Parent's Magazine, 1987.

Cebulash, M. *The Ball That Wouldn't Bounce*. New York: Scholastic Book Services, 1972.

Ets, M.H. *Gilberto and the Wind*. New York: Viking Press, 1963.

Falk, N.M. *Matthew Blows Bubbles*. New York: McGraw-Hill, 1964.

Freeman, M. *When Air Moves*. New York: McGraw-Hill, 1968.

Garrison, Christian. *Little Pieces of the West Wind*. New York: Bradbury, 1987.

Hatch, Shirley. *Wind Is To Feel*. New York: Coward, McCann, and Geoghegan, 1987.

Keats, E.J. *Whistle for Willie*. New York: Viking Press, 1964.

Mizumura, K. *I See the Wind*. New York: T.Y. Crowell, 1966.

Nodset, J.L., *Who Took the Farmer's Hat?* New York: Scholastic Book Services, 1970.

Piltz, A. *What Is Air?* Chicago: Benefit Press, 1960.

Pine, T.S. *Air All Around*. New York: McGraw-Hill, 1960.

Ruis, Maria. *Air*. New York: Barron, 1987.

Scarry, R. *The Great Big Air Book*. New York: Random House, 1971.

Sharp, C., and M. Sharp. *Let's Find Out About the Air*. New York: Watts, 1963.

Stone, A. Harris, and H. Spiegel. *The Winds of Weather*. New York: Prentice-Hall, 1987.

*Light*

Bernstein, Margery. *The First Morning: An African Myth*. New York: Scribner's, 1987.

Blough, G. *After the Sun Goes Down*. New York: McGraw-Hill, 1956.

Bradbury, R. *Switch on the Night*. New York: Pantheon, 1973.

Bulla, C.R. *What Makes a Shadow*. New York: Scholastic Book Services, 1962.

DeRegneirs, B. *The Shadow Book*. New York: Harcourt, Brace, 1960.

Goudey, A. *The Day We Saw the Sun Come Up*. New York: Charles Scribner's Sons, 1961.

Highland, H. *The How and Why Wonder Book of Light and Color*. New York: Wonder Books, 1963.

Hoban, R. *Bedtime for Frances*. New York: Harper and Row, 1960.

Kinney, J. *What Does the Sun Do?* New York: Young Scott Books, 1967.

Lobel, Arnold. *Frog and Toad All Year*. New York: Harpers, 1987.

Schneider, H., and N. Schneider. *Science Fun with a Flashlight*. New York: McGraw-Hill, 1975.

*Magnets*

Branley, F. *Mickey's Magnets*. New York: T.Y. Crowell, 1956.

Freeman, M. *The Real Book of Magnets*. New York: Scholastic Book Services, 1967.

Holden, R. *Magnetism*. New York: Golden Press, 1962.

Keen, M. *The How and Why Wonder Book of Magnets and Magnetism*. New York: Wonder Books, 1963.

Pine, T., and J. Levine. *Magnets and How to Use Them*. New York: Scholastic Book Services, 1963.

Podendorf, I. *True Book of Magnets and Electricity*. Chicago: Children's Press, 1972.

Reuben, G., and G. Archer. *What Is a Magnet?* Chicago: Benefit Press, 1959.

Wyler, R., and G. Ames. *Prove It*. New York: Scholastic Book Services, 1963.

*Rocks*

Baylor, B. *Everybody Needs a Rock*. New York: Charles Scribner's Sons, 1974.

Bradfield, R. *Hello, Rock*. Racine, Wisc.: Western Publishing Co., 1965.

McGovern, A. *Stone Soup*. New York: Scholastic Book Services, 1971.

Podendorf, I. *The True Book of Pebbles and Shells*. Chicago: Children's Press, 1972.

————. *The True Book of Rocks and Minerals*. Chicago: Children's Press, 1972.

Steig, W. *Sylvester and the Magic Pebble*. New York: Simon and Schuster, 1969.

*Time*

Holl, A., and S. Reit. *Time and Measuring*. New York: Golden Book Educational Series, 1963.

*Water*

Dempsey, M., and A. Sheehan, eds. *Water*. New York: World Publishing, The Danbury Press, 1970.

Holl, A. *The Rain Puddle*. New York: Lothrop, Lee and Shepard Co., 1965.

Lionni, L. *Fish Is Fish*. New York: Pantheon, 1970.

Pine, T., and J. Levine. *Water All Around*. New York: Whittlesey House, McGraw-Hill, 1959.

Rosenfeld, S. *A Drop of Water*. Irvington-on-Hudson, N.Y.: Harvey House, 1970.

Simon, S. *Wet and Dry*. New York: McGraw-Hill, 1969.

## Books About Animals

Abolafia, Y. *Fox Tale*. New York: Greenwillow, 1991.

Aliki, J. *Overnight at Mary Blooms*. New York: Greenwillow, 1987.

Baker, Leslie. *The Third-Story Cat*. New York: Little, 1987.

Breslow, S., and S. Blakemore. *I Really Want a Dog*. New York: Dutton, 1990.

Brown, R. *Our Cat Flossie*. New York: Dutton, 1986.

Dabcovich, L. *Ducks Fly*. New York: Dutton, 1990.

Fox, M. *Hattie and the Fox*. New York: Bradbury Press, 1987.

Graham, Bob. *First There Was Frances*. New York: Bradbury, 1986.

Gretz, Susanna. *Roger Takes Charge*. New York: Dial, 1987.

Hearn, M.P. *The Porcelain Cat*. New York: Little, 1987.

Herriot, James. *Bonny's Big Day*. New York: St. Martin, 1987.

Kay, Chorao. *George Told Kate*. New York: Dutton, 1987.

Kellogg, Steven. *Prehistoric Pinkerton*. New York: Dial, 1987.

Khalsa, Dayal K. *I Want a Dog*. Crown/Potter, 1987.

Kraus, Robert. *Where Are You Going, Little Mouse?* New York: Greenwillow, 1986.

Krause, U. *Nora and the Great Bear*. New York: Dial, 1989.

Kitchen, B. *Somewhere Today*. New York: Candlewick, 1993.

Lester, Helen. *A Porcupine Named Fluffy*. Boston: Houghton Mifflin, 1986.

Lionni, Leo. *Nicolas, Where Have You Been?* New York: Knopf, 1987.

Maris, Ron. *I Wish I Could Fly*. New York: Greenwillow, 1987.

Marzolla, J. *Pretend You're a Cat*. New York: Dial, 1990.

Parkinson, Kathy. *The Farmer in the Dell*. Niles, Ill.: Whitman, 1987.

Rayner, Mary. *Mrs. Pig Gets Cross and Other Stories*. New York: Dutton, 1987.

Ryder, J. *Chipmunk Song*. New York: Lodestar, 1990.

Seligson, Susan, and H. Schneider. *Amos: The Story of an Old Dog and His Couch*. New York: Joy Street/Little, 1987.

Simmons, Posy. *Fred*. New York: Knopf, 1987.

Sis, Peter. *Rainbow Rhino*. New York: Knopf, 1987.

Stanley, Diane. *Captain Whiz-Bang*. New York: Morrow, 1987.

Tafuri, Nancy. *Junglewalk*. New York: Greenwillow, 1988.

## Books About Clouds

Battan, Louis J. *Harvesting the Clouds*. New York: Doubleday, 1987.

DePaola, Tomie. *The Cloud Book*. New York: Holiday House, 1985.

Horwitz, Elinor L. *When the Sky Is Like Lace*. Lippincott, 1987.

## Garden Books and Books About the Farm-to-City Market Process

Back, C., and B. Watts. *Bean and Plant*. Morristown, N.J.: Silver Burdett, 1986.

Braithwaite, A. *Life Cycle Books: Flower*. Essex, England: Longman, 1977.

Horwitz, J. *Night Markets Bring Food to a City*. New York: Harper & Row, A Torch Publication, 1984.

Jordan, H. *How a Seed Grows*. New York: Harper & Row, A Torch Publication, 1961.

Lenski, L. *The Little Farm*. New York: Walck, 1942.

Root, B. *Usborne First Nature: Flowers*. Tulsa, Okla.: Educational Development Center, 1982.

## Fish Books

Braithwaite, A. *Life Cycle Books: Fish*. Essex, England: Longman, 1983.

Cole, J., and J. Wexler. *A Fish Hatches*. New York: William Morrow, 1978.

Cole, J. *Shells, When the Tide Is Low*. New York: Lothrop, Lee & Shephard, 1985.

Cook, B. *The Little Fish That Got Away*. New York: Scholastic, 1962.

Cook, D. *Ocean Life*. New York: Crown, 1983.

Lane, M. *The Story of the Stickleback*. New York: Dial, 1981.

Lionni, L. *Swimmy*. New York: Pantheon, 1963.

Morris, R. *Mysteries and Marvels of Ocean Life*. Tulsa, Okla.: Educational Development Center, 1983.

Myers, A. *Sea Creatures Do Amazing Things*. New York: Random House, 1981.

Palmer, H. *A Fish Out of Water*. New York: Random House, 1961.

Posell, E. *Whales and Other Sea Mammals*. Chicago: Children's Press, 1982.

Roux, C. *Nature's Hidden World: Animals of the Seashore*. Morristown, N.J.: Silver Burdett, 1984.

Ruis, M. *Let's Discover the Seaside*. New York: Barron's, 1986.

Schmitz, S. *Fish Calendar*. Morristown, N.J.: Silver Burdett, 1986.

Sharples, A., and A. Bielecki, *Usborne First Nature: Fishes*. Tulsa, Okla.: Educational Development Center, 1982.

## Children's Books for Ecology and Environmental Education Activities/Units

Arnosky, J. *Raccoons and Ripe Corn*. New York: Lothrop, Lee & Shepard, 1987.

Burningham, J. *Hey! Get Off Our Train*. New York: Crown, 1989.

Carle, E. *The Very Quiet Cricket*. New York: Philomel, 1990.

Carlstrom, N.W. *Wild, Wild Sunflower Child, Anna*. New York: Macmillan, 1987.

Carson, R. *Sharing Nature with Children*. Nevada City, Calif.: Ananda, 1956.

DePaola, T. *The Legend of the Indian Paintbrush*. New York: G.P. Putnam's Sons, 1988.

Eta, M.H. *Play with Me*. New York: Viking, 1955.

Ginsburg, M. *The Sun's Asleep Behind the Hill*. New York: Greenwillow, 1982.

Goff, P. *Nature, Children and You* (Rev. Ed.). Athens, Oh.: Ohio University Press, 1981.

Graham, M.B. *Be Nice to Spiders*. New York: Harper & Row, 1967.

Herman, M.L., J.F. Passineau, A.L. Schimpf, and P. Treuer. *Teaching Kids to Love the Earth*. Duluth, Minn.: Pfeifer-Hamilton, 1991.

Hill, D. *Mud, Sand, and Water*. Washington, D.C. NAEYC, 1977.

Hines, A.G. *Come to the Meadow*. New York: Clarion Books/Ticknor & Fields, Houghton Mifflin, 1984.

Hopkins, S., and J. Winters, eds. *Discover the World: Empowering Children to Value Themselves, Others and the Earth*. Philadelphia: New Society Publishers, 1990.

Katz, A. *Naturewatch: Exploring Nature with Young Children*. Menlo Park, Calif.: Addison-Wesley, 1986.

Lesser, C. *The Goodnight Circle*. San Diego: Harcourt, Brace, Jovanovich, 1984.

Lionni, L. *Frederick*. New York: Pantheon, 1973.

———. *The Biggest House in the World*. New York: Pantheon, 1968.

———. *Nicholas, Where Have You Been?* New York: Alfred A. Knopf, 1987.

McDermott, G. *Anansi the Spider: A Tale from the Ashanti*. New York: Holt, Rinehart, Winston, 1972.

McKissack, P.C. *Mirandy and Brother Wind*. New York: Alfred A. Knopf, 1988.

Milord, S. *The Kid's Nature Book*. Charlotte, Vt.: Williamson, 1989.

Petrash, C. *Earthways: Simple Environmental Activities for Young Children*. Mt. Rainer, Md.: Gryphon House, 1992.

Rockwell, R.E., E.A. Sherwood, and R.A. Williams. *Hug a Tree and Other Things to Do Outdoors with Children*. Mt. Rainer, Md.: Gryphon House, 1983.

Romanova, N. *Once There Was a Tree*. New York: Dial, 1985.

Ryder, J. *Chipmunk's Song*. New York: Dutton, Lodestar, 1987.

Sheehan, K., and M. Waidner. *Earth Child: Games, Stories, Activities, Experiments and Ideas about Living Lightly on Planet Earth*. Tulsa, Okla.: Council Oak, 1991.

Soya, K. *A House of Leaves*. New York: Philomel, 1986.

Udry, J.M. *A Tree Is Nice*. New York: Harper & Row, 1965.

Waters, M. *The Victory Garden Kids' Book*. Boston: Houghton Mifflin, 1988.

Yolen, J. *Owl Moon*. New York: Philomel, 1987.

# U N I T   2 0
# Creative Mathematics

## OBJECTIVES

After studying this unit, you should be able to:
- discuss the developmental pattern of learning mathematical ideas.
- define rote counting and rational counting.
- explain the young child's concept of number.
- discuss classification and sorting.
- discuss comparing and ordering.
- describe the young child's understanding of shape and form.
- discuss how block building can help teach mathematical concepts.

Early childhood teachers face the challenging responsibility of opening young children's eyes to the world of mathematics. We may provide creative, stimulating, and manipulative (hands-on) experiences that can initiate long-term positive feelings about mathematical inquiry and activity. Or we may provide a boring stream of workbook pages and dittos. In such a situation, where children are required to sit down, quiet down, and write it down, excitement about math may never ever have a chance to emerge.

Everything we know about young children tells us that early math programs must be hands-on, filled with play and exploration. We know that young children love to move, use as many of the senses as possible, sort, pile, and arrange things, try things out firsthand, and experiment with and manipulate materials. They are not good at sitting still, working within rigid confines of spaces on pages, writing small signs in small answer boxes, coloring in someone else's drawings of sets, or understanding written exercises involving time and monetary value. They should have the experience of turning the hands on a real clock, or trading two nickels for a dime.

In this unit, the emphasis is on *active* exploration of mathematical concepts as a natural part of the early childhood program.

## DEVELOPMENTAL PATTERN OF LEARNING MATHEMATICAL IDEAS

Long before children formally use numbers, they are aware of them through daily experiences. For example, children become aware of sequences in events before they can talk about what is first, second, or third. At the age of two or three they know that one block on top of another is two blocks, and they know that if they add more they will have three, even though they may not know the words "two" and "three." When they lift objects, they experience lightness or heaviness. Cuddling up in their mother's lap, they feel themselves small and her big. They know all this by the reality of their experience through living and doing. Thus, children are able to tell differences in sizes of people, animals, and toys before they have any idea about measurement. They recognize, too, the difference between *one* and *many* and between *few* and *lots* before they acquire real number concepts. And they develop a sense of time long before they can tell time by a clock. Their ideas of time grow out of hearing things like, "It's time for lunch." "It's time to go to bed." "We're going for a walk today." "We went to the park yesterday."

This pattern of early use of numbers is similar to

the general-to-specific pattern of physical growth (see Part I). In these early stages of mathematical thinking, the child has a *general* understanding of numbers which will gradually move toward a more *specific* understanding as the developmental process continues. Thus, a general understanding of time ("It's time for lunch") develops in a gradual process to a more *specific* understanding of time ("Twelve o'clock is lunch time"). The child gradually associates 12 o'clock with the time of day of lunch time. They learn with their senses, with their whole bodies. Their understandings become parts of themselves. Only after this has happened can they name these experiences. By the time they learn the words "big," "small," "light," "heavy," or the names of numbers, they will know by their own senses what these words mean.

Children, then, become aware of numbers early in life, since daily experiences involve various uses of numbers. But understanding the meanings of those number words comes later as the child matures, experiences, and develops.

Before children come to an early childhood program, they already have had many other types of experiences with mathematics in their homes and neighborhoods. They may know where the hands of the clock are when they want to watch their favorite TV program. When they want to go to the store to buy ice cream, they might know that they need a quarter or 25 cents. They know they have a choice of the various kinds of things there are to buy. Some children help their parents cook. They watch and perhaps help their parents measure with cups and spoons before putting the ingredients carefully into the bowl for mixing. Children who are allowed to help their parents unpack the family's groceries see and handle many containers of different shapes, sizes, and weights. Their toys, balls, cups, and shoes also have various three-dimensional shapes, as do their beds and bedrooms. Children experience these properties and come to the early childhood program with many pieces of knowledge that they will explore further in their play.

Young children also have had the experience of hearing numbers as names. A child may know the number of his house but think that it is the name of the house. One child knows that he takes the #30 bus to visit his grandmother. When he climbs stairs, his mother will often say, "one, two, three, four, five, six." He soon learns that his mother is very pleased when he can recite these numbers himself. But the numbers don't, as yet, have any meaning to him in any mathematical sense. Number words are some of the many things that children pick up by imitation from the adults around them. Yet if you observe the way children use these words, you will see that the number names do not carry the same meaning for them as they do for adults.

As the children come into your program, you will probably hear them saying things that show their lack of real understanding of number words and mathematical concepts. Work and play in different curriculum areas will extend and support children's understandings and provide opportunities to develop these mathematical concepts.

**The Language of Mathematics.** There is a language distinctive to the discipline of mathematics, and basic to any work a child will do in mathematics is an understanding of its terminologies. A child develops mathematical language the way he does other language—as he uses it, he gains facility with it. He begins to use number names as he talks. "One Little, Two Little, Three Little Indians," "Rub-a-Dub Dub, Three Men in a Tub," and "Two Little Blackbirds" are among children's favorites long before they comprehend what the numbers represent.

It is important that adults use number terms correctly in their own vocabulary, while listening for any misconceptions children may have in their own striving to understand.

The child acquires a vocabulary of number names (numerals) and quantitative words quite naturally, as part of daily life. In working with young children, the following terms should be part of the daily routine:

| | | |
|---|---|---|
| big and little | few | bunch |
| long and short | tall and short | group |
| high and low | light and heavy | pair |
| wide and narrow | together | many |
| late and early | same length | more |
| first and last | highest | most |

middle          lowest          twice
once            longer than

It is important not only to use these words but also to demonstrate their meanings. For example, in cooking activities, explain to the children that you will use a *dozen* eggs, a *quart* of milk. Let them hear you use these terms often. When they play in the housekeeping area, there will be many opportunities to build their mathematical vocabularies. Play games that encourage children to think of the largest thing they know, the smallest, the highest, the heaviest. This lets children practice using their mathematical vocabularies.

**Numbers.** Children learn numbers by rote. A child often has no comprehension of what these abstract terms mean, but as a result of relevant experiences, he begins to attach meaning to numbers. Children talk about monetary values in their play, usually without any comprehension of what a dime or a quarter is. While playing store Irene glibly sold the apple for a dollar and later sold the coat and hat for ten cents.

Before the child is three years old, she often can count to ten in proper order. Such counting (called *rote counting*), however, may have little specific meaning for the child. The words may be only sounds to her, sounds repeated in a particular sequence like a familiar song. This rote counting is similar to the stage in the development of speech (see Unit 18) when a child can repeat words without really understanding their meaning.

Quite different from and much more difficult than rote counting is understanding the numerals as they apply to a sequence of objects: that each numeral represents the position of an object in the sequence (button 1, button 2, button 3, and so on). Equally or more difficult to understand is the idea that the last number counted in a sequence of objects represents all the objects in the sequence, the total number of objects counted. This is called *rational counting*. For example, in counting six buttons, the child must grasp the idea that six, the last number counted, tells her how many buttons she has—that she has six buttons *in all.*

Rational counting, a higher-level number understanding, develops slowly for most children. However, carefully structured activities that take one idea and present it to children one step at a time help them grow from a general to a more specific understanding of numbers.

Young children frequently hear counting—as steps are being climbed, objects are being stacked, foods are being distributed, fingerplays are being played, familiar nursery rhymes and songs are being enjoyed, and during many other activities. This repetition helps the child memorize the sequence and sounds of numbers, even before the meanings of these numbers are understood. Songs, fingerplays,

**FIGURE 20–1 Dramatic play often involves mathematical concepts in a natural way.**

**FIGURE 20–2 Counting objects is a basic beginning one-to-one correspondence activity.**

**FIGURE 20–3** One-to-one correspondence is one of the most basic mathematical concepts learned in the early childhood mathematics program.

and nursery rhymes using the fingers as counting objects should be common practice in early childhood programs to help young children practice the sounds and sequence of numbers.

True counting ability (rational counting) is not possible until the child understands one-to-one correspondence. In other words, to rote count (to say the number sequence) is one thing; but to count items correctly—one number per item—is more difficult. Very often when a young child is given a series of things to count, the child counts two numbers for one item or two items while saying only one number. Thus, as rote counting develops, teachers should also encourage the skill of one-to-one correspondence.

Having the child touch each object as she counts is one way to encourage one-to-one correspondence. Repeating this exercise in various experiences throughout the day reinforces the concept of one-to-one correspondence.

Young children should be asked to count only with number names that are meaningful to them, i.e., *cardinal numbers* (the numbers one, two, three, etc.). Young children just learning numbers often have difficulty in understanding the relationship between counting and number. For example, Claire may count, "One, two books." Later, when asked to bring two books to the table, she may count, "one, two" and bring only the second book. *Ordinal number* refers to the *place* of an object in a series of numbers. The *second* book in the example above is an *ordinal* number. (The cardinal number is two.)

Activities such as the following help children grasp the mathematical concept of counting:

- In counting activities, begin by having the child touch each object. Count only with number names meaningful to the child. Repeat this in various settings until touching or pointing to objects is no longer necessary. Provide for many manipulative counting experiences with beads, buttons, cookies, napkins, children, chairs. Match beads to boxes, children to chairs. Determine the number of places, quantity of milk, silverware, napkins, and so on needed at the table.
- Use buttons, bottle caps, or similar objects. Have children practice counting *three* and putting *three* in a box and taking *three* (vary the number) out of a box. When you are finished, child can use the buttons or bottle caps and glue them onto a piece of paper to make a picture.
- Bean Bag Toss: Have a large target and give each child a turn to try to get a specified number of bean bags into the hole. Teacher tells the child to choose the specified number of bean bags and counts them again as she throws.
- Animal Four Hop: Make a large square on the floor and divide it into four parts. Have the children jump like kangaroos from one square to the next, counting each square. Another alternative is to place four nearly circular pieces of paper on the floor, each within jumping distance of the one next to it. The children can be frogs jumping from one lily pad to another. Again, count each pad. Vary this activity with different numbers.

In the sample lesson plan in Figure 20–4, the teacher used several activities in one lesson plan to practice counting up to three. Additional activities are at the end of this unit.

**Classification and Sorting.** In order to arrive at the true concept of number, all young children need rich and varied experiences in classification and sort-

TITLE: "The Three Bears"
OBJECTIVE: Reinforce counting up to three objects
MATERIALS: Flannelboard
Pictures for story of "The Three Bears" or book of the story of "The Three Bears"
PROCEDURE:
1. Tell the story of "The Three Bears." Have the children count the bears, the bowls of porridge, the chairs, and the bed.
2. Have the children act out the story. Before acting out the story, have them help you count the props (three chairs, etc.).
3. After the story is over, they can make a picture of "The Three Bears."
VARIATIONS:
1. Make sure the children can count to two. Give them two blocks and have them count. Then add a third block and demonstrate counting all three blocks. Have the children count them with you. Then tell each child to get three blocks and count them. If some child has trouble, help her count the blocks as she selects them.
2. Have the children make a picture of a snowman out of three circles or three marshmallows.
3. Stories such as "Three Billie Goats Gruff" and "The Three Little Kittens."

**FIGURE 20–4 Sample lesson plan—counting.**

ing. Classification and sorting activities are the beginnings that help children perceive a variety of relationships that are interesting to them. This is how mathematical thinking begins. All mathematical thinking involves relationships of increasing complexity.

*Classification.* Putting together things that are alike or that belong together is one of the processes necessary for developing the concept of number. In order to classify, children must be able to observe an object for likenesses and differences, as well as for attributes associated with purpose, position, location,

or some other factor. Children progress through the following stages as they develop the skill of classifying:

1. Sorting into graphic collections without a plan in mind. Children may put all of the blocks with a letter on them together and then, ending with a blue letter, continue by putting all blue blocks with the group. When the grouping is complete, they won't be able to tell you why the blocks belong together, only that they do.
2. Grouping with no apparent plan. When asked why all the things go together, children respond with some reason, but one not immediately clear to the adult: "Well, all these are like George's."
3. Sorting on the basis of some criterion. Children proceed to being able to sort a group of ojects on the basis of one criterion. All of the green things or all of the round things go together, but not all of the green *and* round objects go together in a group.
4. Next, children can create groupings on the basis of two or more properties, putting all of the green *and* round objects together in a group.
5. Finally, children sort objects or events according to function, use, or on the basis of a negative concept, such as all of the things that are not used in the kitchen.

Before children can classify and sort, they must have some concept of "belongingness," "put together," "alike," and "belong together." Concepts and labels for identities, attributes, purposes, locations, positions, and so on are required. The acquisition of these concepts and verbal labels (names) for them becomes an essential part of the early childhood program.

Your role as a teacher is to help children gain these ideas through a variety of experiences and materials. Time for play, too, with a wide variety of materials selected specifically for classifying and sorting activities needs to be provided.

Materials for children's classifying and sorting may be kept together on a shelf in the manipulative toy or game area of your room. Boxes or sorting trays (common plastic dishpans and muffin tins work well) are kept with the materials. Sorting trays can be constructed by either attaching a series of metal jar lids onto a board or piece of cardboard; mounting a number of clear plastic cups onto a board; dividing a board or tray into sections with colored pieces of tape; or by mounting small, clear plastic boxes onto a board. Egg cartons, plastic sewing boxes, tool boxes (such as those for storing nuts and bolts), and fishing boxes are also useful for sorting trays and stimulate children to use materials mathematically. Provide children with the following:

- Boxes of scrap materials—velvet squares, tweeds, and net cut into uniform sizes and shapes for feeling, sorting, and classifying according to texture. A large enough collection of materials may lead children into setting up and playing store.
- A box or shelf of bells—cow bells, Christmas bells, decorative bells, sleighbells—all inviting children to sort and classify on any basis they decide, perhaps size, color, shape, or sound.
- A box of greeting cards—Easter, Valentine's Day, Chanukah, birthday, get well, Christmas. Children use the pictures, symbols, size, shape, color, or texture to decide which cards go together.
- An old-fashioned button box, with many buttons too large to be stuffed into ears or noses. Children sort buttons into groups on the basis of the characteristics they choose.
- A box of various textured papers, cut into uniform shapes and sizes for the younger children and then into a variety of shapes for older children. Smooth papers, watercolor paper, textured papers, and others can be obtained from a local print shop.
- Individual boxes of shells, beans, macaroni, seeds, beads, or rocks. Again, all should be large enough not to be put into the nose or ears.
- Collections of nuts, nails, screws, and bolts to classify and sort according to shape, size, or functions.

If children lose interest in sorting and classifying, put some of these materials away for a while and bring out others. Or you might motivate classifying activities by putting some items in a basket on the top of a shelf along with a sorting board. The basket might contain items of clothing, which could be sorted according to color or function, or it might contain seashells, leaves, or other items that reflect the children's current interest.

*Classifying and sorting in the daily routine.* Daily life in the classroom contains many opportunities for experiences of sorting. Cleanup is an obvious example. The children bring the things they have played with to their designated places and put them away. They bring the trucks to one corner, hats to the dress up area, books to the library corner. Occasionally, the teacher uses the mathematical language that the situation naturally gives rise to in order to allow children to learn the words that go with their understandings. "Are *all* the toys put back on the shelf?" "There are still *some* left on the floor, aren't there?" "Oh, you put away a *lot* of things today!" "*How many* books did you put back on the shelf? Can you count them?" Here, counting is included as it now becomes a part of broader experience. Quantitative comparison and ordering, so vital to real concept formation, can happen when children arrange their books in size order.

Mathematics is always with us. It is there as the children sort out what they brought back from their trip to the park, what they collected at the building site or what they brought back from the store. Mathematics is not isolated from their lives inside or outside of school. But the teacher has to make mathematical use of situations when she feels they come up in a natural and joyous way.

By providing time and opportunities for children to play with their collections, organize them in various ways, and discuss their reasons for doing so, you show the children the natural place of mathematics in our lives. For instance, some children might want to arrange the leaves they collected by size (big and little), others by color, while others still will become aware of the differences between oak, maple, and birch leaves.

## COMPARING

Children seem to make comparisons easily and naturally, especially when it is a personal comparison. "My shoes are newer than yours." "I've got the biggest." "My sister is little." "You've got more." When children build with blocks, they may be asked to make additional comparisons: "Which tower is the tallest?" "Pick up the heaviest blocks first." "Build something as tall as this." Have children identify parts of their buildings using the vocabulary of comparison.

When different size and shape containers are used in sand and water play, children can make comparisons based on volume. In the early childhood program, these are informal and related to children's actual experiences. "How many blue cups of water will it take to fill this bucket?" "How many red?" "Which is the heaviest?" "This doesn't hold as much."

Stories and poems, often the folk tales children are already familiar with, offer other opportunities for informal comparisons. "The Three Billy Goats Gruff," "The Three Bears," and others offer comparisons on the basis of differing attributes.

Throughout the preschool years, ask children to observe and note differences in the objects of their environment, to name them, and to discuss them with one another. The following materials can be used to aid children in comparing:

- String, ribbon, pencils, rulers, clay snakes, lines, or strips of paper. Ask children which is longest, longer, shortest, shorter.
- Buttons, dolls, cups, plastic animals, trees, boats. Have the children identify the biggest one or one bigger than another.
- Containers and coffee cans filled with various materials and sealed, buckets or bags of items. Ask which is the heaviest or the lightest, which is heavier than another.
- Toy cars, trucks, swings. Ask which is the fastest, slowest, which is faster than another?
- Paper, cardboard, books, pieces of wood, food slices, cookies. Have children make or find one that is thick, thicker, thickest, or thinnest.
- Voices, musical instruments, drums, or other noise makers. Pick out the loud and soft sounds, the loudest or softest. (Charlesworth and Radeloff, 1978)

Additional activities are given at end of this unit.

## ORDERING (SERIATION)

Another mathematical idea that is a vital part of a complete number concept formation is the idea of order: Two is more than one, and three is more than two. Number sequence (one, two, three, four) is not the easiest example for young children to start with, since it has the very specific relation of each succeeding number being exactly one more than the preceding number. But before children begin to really understand the relationship of numbers to each other, they must have many concrete experiences of ordering things in different situations in their world.

Ordering the environment into series begins when children are very young and continues throughout adult life. The child begins by perceiving opposite ends of a series:

big————————little
heavy————————light
cold————————hot
long————————short

The intervention of an adult, suitable materials, and appropriate language lead to refinement of these early basic concepts. The comparison of the height of two children is beginning ordering, as is the comparison of two sets of things as more or less. Ordering sticks, blocks, or nesting cups in a sequence that leads gradually from the smallest to the biggest helps children see ordered size relations.

When children line up to go outdoors, they meet another idea of order: Juan stands in front of Claire, and Yvonne stands in back of Drew. They may use their understanding of sequence when they say, "I want to be first," or "Jimmy is last."

After listening to the story of "The Three Bears," their observations may become more refined as they discuss the story. The story contains big–little and one-to-one relationships, in addition to its many other enjoyable qualities.

The idea of ordering in size also appears naturally in other classroom areas. The teacher can make ordering a part of natural discussions in relation to the children's play and activities: sets of cans, bottles, and books can also be used for practicing ordering of size. With younger children, only two objects are compared at first; this will be extended to three or more objects for older children.

Children enjoy ordering activities and do so spontaneously. Many table toys provide ordering experiences, as do ordinary objects like measuring spoons and cups.

# THIS ONE'S FOR YOU!

## USING CHILDREN'S BOOKS TO TEACH MATH

You will find that children's books can be used to launch many interesting math learning activities. There are many excellent sources of children's books for math (see lists at end of this unit). An example of using the book *The Very Hungry Caterpillar* by Eric Carle, which describes the life cycle of a caterpillar through the use of vibrant college-like designs, will give you an idea of how to include books in math experiences.

*Teaching Comparisons.* Size comparison is the most obvious prenumber concept that can be drawn from this book. The caterpillar changes from a tiny egg laid on a leaf to a small, hungry caterpillar to a big brown cocoon and finally, to a large, beautiful butterfly. After reading the book, discuss the size relationships. Later, children can compare cutouts of these items and arrange them from largest to smallest.

*Teaching Ordering.* The prenumber skill of ordering can be related to both the days of the week and the life cycle. Ask children to tell the order of the days of the week or stages of the life cycle told in the book. Ordering the days of the week in this way can promote an interest in the calendar for daily record keeping of days gone by. The life cycle can be used in a game-like situation in which children order the pictures of the cycle. This can be made self-correcting by placing the numerals 1 through 4 on the back of the pictures.

*One-to-One Correspondence.* The fact that the caterpillar ate through a variety of foods one by one can be used to emphasize the one-to-one correspondence. A learning center follow-up could require children to match pompom caterpillars to plastic fruits to see if there is an equal match or if there are more caterpillars or fruit.

*Rational Counting.* Children can also be asked to rationally count the number of pieces of food the caterpillar ate in the story by counting the number of fruits and then the number of other foods eaten. They might also count the number of days of the week and the life cycle changes. A later concrete learning activity would be to have children count out pieces of fruit or other similar foods eaten by the caterpillar for their own particular snack time. Learning center games could involve the counting of food cutouts found in plastic containers.

*Cardinal Number.* Use the story to emphasize the prenumber skill of recognizing cardinal numbers. As the children look at the book, ask them, "How many things did the caterpillar eat on Saturday?" "How many on Monday?" Later, they can work with a learning center activity that involves counting holes made by the hungry caterpillar in card-stock leaves to determine how many bites the caterpillar took. A self-correcting feature can be included by simply writing the answer on the backs of the leaves.

Your role is to provide materials and sufficient time. When children find the existing materials too easy, you can awaken their interest by encouraging them to use the toys differently, by asking them questions, and by providing additional materials.

Ordering activities can include length (sticks), height (bottles), total size (bowls and shoes), weight (stones), color (from light to dark), and other endless possibilities.

Some things you might also have children try are:

- Find the shortest or longest rod or tinker toy.
- Pick from three objects of differing heights the one that is shortest, and describe the remaining two objects.
- Describe how the objects in a series, arranged from shortest to longest, differ from one another.
- Collect nesting materials, such as a set of measuring spoons or measuring cups. Ask the child to arrange the objects in correct order so that they will properly "nest" together, one object fitting inside the other. Be sure to have the children set the objects on the table in order from smallest to largest after they have finished "nesting" them.
- Using three cans of different sizes and three bean bags in the three sizes, arrange the cans from smallest to largest in a row. Ask the child to line the bean bags up next to the cans, putting the smallest by the smallest, etc. Shuffle the cans and the bean bags. Let the child order the cans from smallest to largest this time and then match the bean bags to the cans.
- Cut out three fish. Make each fish large enough to totally conceal the next smaller fish when placed over it. Tell the children that the fish go in order, with the biggest fish first leading the others. Have them find the largest fish and then the fish that will follow. Check to see if the largest fish covers the fish that follows. For self-checking, the child places each fish on top of the next to see if the next fish is smaller. Variation: Order from the smallest fish to the largest fish.

Additional activities are found at the end of this unit.

---

## SHAPE AND FORM

As early as three weeks of age, children begin to distinguish patterns of shape and form (Rogers, 1969). By the age of five or six, children can see differences among squares, triangles, and circles (Scott and Garner, 1978, pp. 26–27).

In teaching young children about shape and form, it is important to include more shapes than the common geometric shapes of a circle, triangle, rectangle, and square. Since shapes aid in, or are sources of,

FIGURE 20–5 Mathematical concepts, such as geometric shapes, develop naturally in playing with blocks.

identification, limiting instruction to the "basic shapes" excludes from the learning environment important aspects of recognition of shapes in general.

Yet familiar shapes must be taught before uncommon ones. Most of these unfamiliar shapes depend on previous shape identification and recognition. From the basis of understanding simple shapes, the child is able to build more complex structures.

As with the teaching of any ideas, shapes can be found throughout the child's environment. Words defining shapes should be used often. For example, everyday language should include such statement as: "That is a square box," rather than "That is square"; "The clock is round," rather than "This is round"; "Put the book on the square table," rather than "Put it over there." With these phrases, the object *and* its characteristic shape are made clear to the child. Later on, more characteristics, such as color, size, texture, and number may be added.

When unfamiliar shapes are introduced, a review of already familiar ones should precede the new introduction. Then the children's thinking can be stimulated with such questions as "How is this new shape the same as . . . ?" or "How is this new shape not the same as (or different from). . . ?" Such comparisons reinforce and review shapes already learned.

Young children need many experiences with shapes and making comparisons between shapes before they focus on naming shapes. Too often we begin with naming shapes. This is also true of letters: children need experiences and opportunities to observe and compare before learning the names of letters.

Usually, it is enough to introduce one new shape at a time. As the new shape is understood, other shapes may be added. The basis for building new meanings on former learning is thus strengthened.

Some ideas for teaching about shape and form are:

- Make a shape collage. Variously shaped pieces of paper may be pasted on a background. Then matching shapes that have been cut smaller than the first shapes are distributed to the children. As a shape is matched, it is pasted onto the background.
- Provide shapes cut from colored construction paper. Allow the child to make objects or designs by gluing them on other sheets of paper.
- Let the children go through old magazines to find objects with obvious geometric shapes. Children can then cut these pictures out and make a shape book with a page or pages for each shape.
- On 3″ × 5″ cards, draw two to five shapes, either all alike or with one or two different. The children sort these cards into two piles—one of cards with all the shapes the same and one of cards with shapes that are different.
- Cut various shapes (geometric or objects) in different colors and sizes from cloth. Have the children classify or sort the items according to shape (all the squares together, all the rabbits, etc.).

Additional activities are at the end of this unit. Let us now consider how the block area can be used for teaching mathematical concepts.

## MATH AND BLOCK BUILDING

Math, like reading, is a basic skill that is used in many ways in and outside of school. It is not a skill isolated from everyday life. It is only natural, then, to teach young children math not only in a math center, but in several areas.

---

*Goals:*

Activities in this center afford the child experiences in:

- Creating real and imaginary structures
- Differentiating between sizes and shapes
- Classifying according to size and shape
- Selecting according to space
- Conceptualizing about space, size, shape
- Defining geometric shapes
- Developing perceptive insight, hand-eye coordination, imagination, and directionality

*Materials*

Set of solid wooden unit blocks (approximately 200)
Wheel toys
Puppets (to use with puppet stage or theater)
Dolls (from housekeeping center)
Dress-up clothes, especially hats
Set of hollow blocks (varying in size)
Miscellaneous construction sets: Tinkertoys®, Lego® blocks, Lincoln Logs®, Bristle-blocks®, Connectos®, etc.
Rubber animals (zoo, farm)
Small plastic/rubber people (family, farmer, policeman, etc.)
Planks, tiles
Old steering wheel
Packing crates, boxes, ropes
Traffic signs
Books related to building
Pulleys and ropes
Large quantities of ''junk'' construction materials, egg cartons, milk cartons, rods, spools, small rectangular boxes, etc.

**FIGURE 20–6 Suggestions for a block center.**

The block area is a perfect place for math experiences. Blocks are especially good for learning math because they are real-life examples of geometric shapes and solids. The block center is usually set up in preschool rooms, but it is just as important in the early elementary classroom. Figure 20–6 lists some suggested block materials to make this center as complete a learning place as possible.

The younger the children, the larger their first blocks should be. Smaller blocks can come later, when children feel the need to supplement larger blocks. If you give too many small blocks to the children early in the year and insist that they reshelve them neatly, the children may come to dislike blocks, defeating your purposes in having them at all. Aside from this, block-building is a tremendously satisfying activity that nourishes minds, imaginations, and the development of mathematical concepts.

If your block area is popular and children must wait for turns, make a waiting list—printed neatly for children to read—and set a timer. When you use a timer, children discover that turns are coming around in a fair way. You may also want to post stick-figure pictures indicating how many children can be in the area at one time. Using these objective symbols—pictograph, waiting list, and timer—rather than your say-so, puts attention on the problem of crowding, not on the teacher's power (Clemens, 1991).

A child building with blocks has many experiences related to math, such as classification (grouping by the same size, for example) and order (putting blocks in order of largest to smallest). There are many other basic math ideas learned through block building, such as length, area, volume, number, and shape. Both small and large motor skills are also developed as children play with blocks. Figure 20–7 lists the many math and physical skills developed in building with blocks.

Cleanup in the block center is another good chance to practice math skills. The following suggestions can help you make this cleanup a true learning experience:

- Ask children to pick up all of the blocks that are curved.
- Ask children to pick up blocks of three different lengths.
- Ask children to pick up blocks according to size.

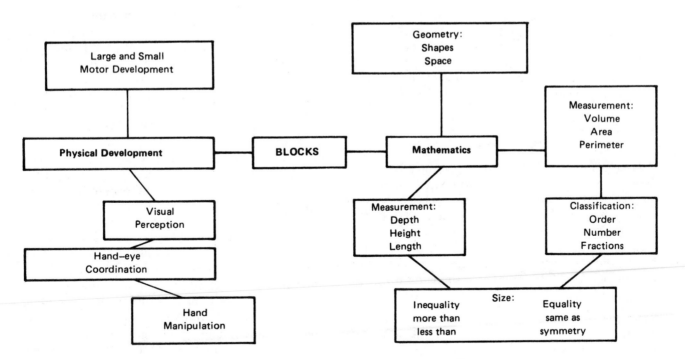

**FIGURE 20–7 Skills developed in block building.**

- Ask children to pick up blocks similar to a specific block that the cleanup director names.*
- Ask children to pick up blocks different from a specific block that cleanup director names.
- Ask children to put away all of a particular shape or size block and ask how many of that block she/he used.
- Ask children to stack all of the blocks that go in the lower left section of the blocks shelf. Then stack the lower middle shelf, etc.
- Ask children to put away blocks in groups of twos, threes, fours, etc.
- Ask children to put away one dozen long unit blocks.
- Ask children to put away blocks according to size beginning with biggest or longest and ending with the smallest or shortest.
- Select certain people to put away certain shapes, e.g., rectangles, cylinders.
- Select certain people to collect blocks according to weight.
- Have children put away a certain unit of blocks and all of the blocks that are a fraction of that unit block.
- Use an assembly line to put away blocks. This encourages cooperation among the children.
- Ask children to pick up a number of blocks that are greater or less than the number of blocks the cleanup director is holding (Hirsch, 1984).

---

## SUMMARY

Long before a child formally uses numerals, she is aware of them through daily experiences. For example, a child becomes aware of sequences in events before she can talk about what is first, second, or third (ordinal numbers). She recognizes, too, the difference between one and many and between few and lots before she acquires real number concepts. The pattern of early uses of number, is similar to the gen-

---

*The teacher need not always be the cleanup director. Children can make up ideas and take turns being director. Also, the teacher can make a list of block cleanup ideas and put it on the wall in the block corner.

eral-to-specific pattern of physical growth. In these early stages of mathematical thinking, the child has a general understanding of number, which will gradually move toward a more specific understanding as the developmental process continues. Thus, a general understanding of time ("It's time for lunch") develops in a gradual process over time to a more specific understanding of time ("Twelve o'clock is lunch time").

It is important that adults use number terms correctly in daily experiences with the child. Demonstrating their meaning in daily activities is just as important as using the right words.

Counting by rote (memory) is common for young children aged three and up. Counting with understanding (rational counting) does not occur until a child understands the one-to-one correspondence of number. At this point, even though the child is not yet able to recognize the numeral, when an object is placed or pointed to, the child can correctly ascribe a number to it. For example, as blocks are stacked in a tower, the child correctly counts 1, 2, 3, 4, 5, respectively, with each block.

Classification, or putting together things that are alike or that being together, is one of the processes necessary for developing the concept of number. In order to classify, children must be able to observe an object for likenesses and differences, as well as for other common factors. Sorting things according to ways they "belong" together is an excellent activity for classification skill practice in the early childhood program.

Comparing is another mathematical process that is appropriate in the early childhood program. Children seem to make comparisons easily and naturally, especially when the comparisons involve them personally.

Another mathematical idea that is a vital part of a complete number concept is the idea of order. Putting things in a series or in order is a process that is appropriate for early mathematical experiences. The comparisons of two objects is usually the beginning for young children with such concepts as big–little, cold–hot, heavy–light, and long–short.

Block building is an excellent activity to reinforce mathematical skills. A child building with blocks has many experiences related to mathematics, such as classification and ordering. The entire cleanup process after block play in itself can be a mathematical exercise for children.

## LEARNING ACTIVITIES

A. Use one of the activities suggested in this unit with a group of young children. Evaluate your experience. Share your evaluation with your classmates.

B. Make up some of your own activities for the mathematical concepts discussed in this unit.

C. Choose at least two of the children's books listed in the Additional Readings at the end of the unit. Explain why you chose them and how you would plan to use them with young children. If possible, use them with a group of children and discuss your results.

D. Using a school supply catalog, choose three pieces of mathematical equipment appropriate for teaching each of the following: seriation, geometric shapes, size.

E. Imagine that as a teacher you have $75 to spend on mathematical equipment. Using a school supply catalog, spend this sum for your class of children. Explain how you spent your $75 as follows:
1. Developmental reason for choice
2. Purpose(s) for item

F. Choose one or two children from each of these age groups: three-year-olds, four-year-olds, five-year-olds. Assess each child's ability to count. Write up your results on each of the children in these age groups. Discuss what math activities would be developmentally appropriate for these children based on your findings.

G. Observe and talk with a preschool child, listening for comments and understanding related to numbers. If possible, ask the child such questions as "How old are you? What is your favorite number? How far can you count? Where do you see numbers?" Now make a comparison. Observe and preferably talk with a child between five and six years old and ask some of the same questions. You will want to ask more questions such as "Show me how you can add some things. Here are three pencils, and what will you have if you add two more pencils?" Challenge the child with number questions and problems. Now compare the differences in the two children you observed, keeping in mind the differences in their ages.

## ACTIVITIES FOR CHILDREN

### Numbers and Snacks

Number concepts can be reinforced easily and in everyday routines. Snack time is an excellent time for teaching about numbers. Once or twice a week, prepare snacks to reinforce mathematical concepts. Discuss the characteristic of each snack at service time. Then let the children eat while they learn from the special snack you have prepared.

A. Choose a number such as "four" and serve snack items in groups of four (four raisins, four carrot sticks, four banana slices, four crackers, etc.)

B. Choose a geometric shape such as a circle and serve round snack items (round crackers, cucumber slices, round cereal, carrot slices, banana slices, etc.)

### Concept of Number and Counting

A. Cut face cards in half (make the cutting lines different on the separate cards so that only the two correct halves will fit together). Then the cards are matched together as puzzles.

B. On a piece of plastic or canvas, paste or draw numerals. This material should be large enough for a child to perform the following instructions: "Place your foot on the numeral 4." "Put your hand on the numeral 5." If the children are older, add right foot, left foot, right hand, left hand, elbow, knee, etc.

C. Play "Bounce." On 9″ × 12″ cards, place different pictures, such as a house, two cars, three boys, four dogs, and so on, until there are ten cards, with ten objects on the last card. (Use stickers, if desired.) The child is given instructions to bounce a ball once for every object on the card. Then the child is told to go to various cards: "Go to the cars," or "Go to the house." The cards are placed around the room so the child must move about, bouncing the ball the number of times indicated by the number of objects on the cards. (Let her tap the ball if she cannot yet bounce it.)

1. Variation: Instead of pictures, draw shapes—a triangle, circle, square, or rectangle, on each card. This game helps strengthen recognition of the names of shapes as well as one-to-one correspondence.
2. Variation: Place numerals from 1 to 10 around the room. Show the child a card with objects on it, and ask her to find the numeral that tells how many objects are on the card.
D. Make a number book by pasting the correct number of beans, pieces of macaroni, or colored squares next to written numerals.
E. Take out two pages from a calendar. Leave the numerals on one of the pages intact. Separate the numerals on the other page. The separate numerals are then matched to those on the whole page.
F. A line with numerals in the proper sequence is made or drawn (or laid down with tape) on the floor. The child stands on a numeral and is directed to "move ahead four numerals—now move back two. What numeral are you standing on?"
G. Set up at the math center a numeral recognition and numeration activity such as "Counting Marbles." Provide ten paper cups and label them with the numerals 1 through 10. Provide a box with lots of marbles. Place these on a table for a minimath center. Two children work together. One child examines the numeral printed on each cup and drops in the appropriate number of marbles. The child then gets her partner to check each cup and count the marbles to see if the correct amount was put in it. The marbles then go back into the box.

## Junk Box Count

A. Collect a different number of various familiar objects, such as one building block, two pencils, three rubber erasers, four paper clips, five rubber bands. Place all of the objects in a large box labeled "junk box." Prepare 3" × 3" tagboard cards, each with a numeral from 1 to 10 on it.
B. The children take the objects out of the junk box and group identical objects into sets. They then take a tagboard numeral and place it under the set it corresponds to.
C. The teacher or center director should be available to check the child's work once the activity has been completed. Ask questions such as: "How many rubber bands did you count?" "Do you have more rubber bands or more paper clips?" "Are there fewer pencils or fewer blocks?"

## Number Necklace

A. Cut long pieces of string or yarn, and tie a button at one end of each piece. Make sets of tagboard squares with numerals from one to ten. Cut drinking straws into half-inch pieces. Glue a section of drinking straw to the back of each numeral square (for stringing). Put many wooden beads in a box.
B. The children string the number "one" card on the yarn, followed by one bead. The number "two" card is strung next, followed by two beads. The children continue in this way, stringing each numeral in sequence, followed by the appropriate number of beads. When they finish (having strung ten beads at the end), help them make a loop at the end of the yarn to hook over the button. They may take their necklaces home.

## Placemats with Numbers

You will need large sheets of construction paper, ruler, felt-tip markers, clear contact paper, index cards, crayons, game markers (dried beans, cereal, etc.), patterned wrapping paper, scissors, tagboard, tape.

Make gameboards on large sheets of construction paper and cover them with clear contact paper. Use the gameboards as placemats, and let the children play games on them before snacktime or lunch.

A. *Number placemats.* Divide large sheets of construction paper into six or more squares and write different numerals in the upper left-hand corners. Set out a large bowl of dried beans, raisins, etc., to use as markers. Let the children place corresponding numbers of markers in the squares on their gameboards.
B. *Shapes.* Make a gameboard for each group of two or three children. In the upper left-hand corner of a large piece of construction paper, draw a circle and write "Start" inside it. Draw a pathway of geometric shapes (circles, squares, triangles, etc.), in random order, winding around the paper. End with a circle in the lower right-hand corner marked "Finish." Make three or four game cards for each shape by drawing the shapes on index cards. Put the deck of cards face down and give each child a different kind of game marker to place on the "Start" circle. As each child turns up a card, have her move her marker to the next shape designated by the index card.

## One and One More

A. Objective: Choose one and then one more.
B. Equipment: One special container; a set of ten objects for each child in the group
C. Procedure:
1. Make sure that each child has a set of ten objects such as blocks, buttons, pennies, poker chips, pegs, etc. You may not have enough of the same type of object for each child to have the same set as every other child. Therefore, one child might have a set of small trucks, another might have a

set of blocks, etc. However, the objects in a child's set should be the same.

2. Have each child come up and put one of her objects into a special container. Then have them add one more.
3. This activity can be done several times as long as the children are interested. The children may want to trade sets between turns.

D. Variations:
1. Make a mural using paper, material, yarn, stars, etc. Each child selects something to put on the mural and then selects one more to put on the mural.
2. Give each child a set of blocks to build a tower or a building. Have each child start to build using two or three of their blocks; then ask them to add one more to the tower.

## Just One More

A. Objective: Choose one and then one more.
B. Equipment: Matching card for each child with two drawn rectangles. Set of three to five blocks for each child; set for teacher (demonstration set).
C. Procedure:
1. Each child has a card that has two rectangles drawn on it. The size of the rectangles should be exactly the same as wooden or cardboard rectangles available in your room. (Circles may be used instead of rectangles.)
2. Each child should have a set of three to five blocks.
3. The teacher should have a demonstration set.
4. Ask the children to pick up one (stress *one*) block and make it fit on one of the blocks on their paper. Demonstrate.
5. Then ask the children how many empty spaces they have on their paper. Have them point to it and count, "One."
6. Ask them how many blocks they need. Just one more!
7. This can be played as a game several times. At other times you may want to vary shape and color.

D. Variations:
1. Use a fairly large picture of a clown holding balloons. Have just the right number of different-colored balloons made from construction paper and identical in size to balloon spaces on the picture. Have each child add one more balloon.
2. Each child should have a picture of a squirrel with two nuts. One of the nuts is already colored in or pasted on. The child must then paste on one more nut for the squirrel. This activity can be altered by having the teacher select one central character (such as the squirrel) with two objects (nuts).

## Little Kitten Has Four Legs

A. Objective: Count four objects.
B. Equipment: Flannelboard or something similar. Pictures: mother cat, little kitten, cow, horse, dog, sheep, pig, and goat.
C. Procedure:
1. Tell the following story, embellishing it so that it is interesting and relevant to your children. Make sure they all join in counting four whenever it is appropriate in the story.
2. "One day the little kitten was getting a bath; her mother was licking her all over so that she would be clean. Mother cat said, 'Let's wash this leg, and this leg, and this leg, and this leg. Now, little kitten, how many legs do you have?' (Have the children help you count the legs.) The little kitten thought it was neat to have four legs, but she wondered how many legs her friends had. So, she went to visit them."
3. Continue the story talking about little kitten's animal friends and the number of legs they had: cow, horse, dog, sheep, pig, and goat. All of little kitten's animal friends had four legs just like she did. How many legs did each animal have?
4. After the story the children could make or color pictures of the animals in the story and count their legs.

D. Variations:
1. Have the children make a building using four blocks, boards, boxes, etc. Have them count the parts of the building.
2. Divide each piece of paper into four sections. Have each child count each section. Then let each child choose four treasures from the treasure box and glue or paste one thing into each section. Then count the pictures. The treasure box could be made up of scraps of material, spools, macaroni, beads, yarn, trinkets from a gum machine, buttons, keys, sticks, and anything else you can dream up.

## Wearing Numbers

Purchase a supply of white paper hats—the kind restaurant workers wear—through a restaurant supply house. (Check with a restaurant manager to find out where to buy them locally.) Use these hats to reinforce number concepts.

A. Write a number on each hat. Have the children glue different sets of items that go with that number onto their hat. For example, three buttons on the hat with a "3" on it; four stickers on the hat with "4" on it; etc.
B. As a variation, make paper crown hats out of construction paper and have the children be Number

Kings and Queens, using the same method as described previously.

C. Choose a geometric shape such as a triangle. Cut various colors and sizes of triangles out of construction paper and let the children glue them onto their hats (or crowns).

## The Squirrel and His Nuts

A. Objective: Count four objects (vary the number of objects).

B. Equipment: Stuffed squirrel; nut box full of nuts still in the shell.

C. Procedure:

1. Most of the other activities have given the child only four objects to count. In this activity, the purpose is to teach the child to select *only* four objects when there are five or more objects.

2. Story: The little squirrel wanted some lunch. His mother told him that he could only have *four* nuts. There were lots and lots of nuts in the nut box. How would Little Squirrel know if he had four nuts? That's right, he would have to count them. Let's help Little Squirrel choose only four nuts. We will have to help him count.

3. Have the children count all together and then let them take turns counting four nuts and taking them from the nut box.

4. Later in the day the children could make or color a picture of the little squirrel eating his four nuts.

D. Variations:

1. Have the children sort objects into groups of four.

2. During snack, have several children select and pass our four napkins, cups, or cookies to four children.

## Number Books

Make a book for each child by stapling four sheets of white paper together with a colored construction paper cover. Title the cover according to a selected learning concept (Number Book, Matching Book, Shape Book, etc.). Have the children look through magazines and catalogs to find pictures that illustrate that learning concept. Have them tear out the pictures and glue them into their books. (Let younger children choose from precut pictures that have been placed in a box.)

A. *Number books.* Number the pages of each book from 1 to 8. Have the children glue pictures of one thing on page one, pictures of two things on page two, etc.

B. *Shape books.* Choose a geometric shape, such as a circle, and have the children glue pictures of circular things throughout their books. Or, label the pages of the books with different geometric shapes (circles, squares, triangles, etc.) and have the children glue correspondingly shaped pictures onto the appropriate pages.

## Number Sticks

Turn a shoebox upside down and cut two parallel rows of slits in the top. Decorate the ends of two sets of popsicle sticks with shape stickers, numbers, objects of different sizes, or any other concept you want to reinforce. Insert one set of popsicle sticks in one of the rows of slits and let the children insert matching popsicle sticks from a second set in the appropriate slits in the other row.

A. *Number sticks.* Write different numerals on one set of popsicle sticks and attach corresponding numbers of stickers to another set.

B. *Shape sticks.* Attach stickers cut into different basic shapes to one set of popsicle sticks and matching shaped stickers to another set.

C. *Variations.* Make popsicle sticks for sorting colors or shapes (circles in one row, squares in another row, etc.). Use unmarked sticks to play counting games.

## Number Wheel

A. Cut a 12″ circle out of tagboard. Divide the circle into eight sections and draw shapes, numbers, objects of varying sizes, etc., in each section. Draw matching shapes, numbers, etc., on eight clothespins. Have children clip the clothespins around the edge of the wheel on each matching section.

B. *Number wheel.* Draw a different number of dots or small pictures in each section of the wheel. Write corresponding numerals on eight clothespins.

C. *Shape wheel.* Draw a different basic shape in each section of the wheel. Draw matching shapes on eight clothespins.

## Magnetic Numbers

Make a magnet board (out of a cookie sheet, a pizza pan, a refrigerator door, etc.) Cut shapes out of tagboard or make shapes with play dough. Attach small magnets or strips of magnetic tape to the back of each shape. Have the children place the shapes on the magnetboard as you give directions.

A. *Number magnetboard.* Cut five squares out of tagboard and number them from 1 to 5. Ask the children to line up the numerals on the magnetboard in the proper sequence. Or, place sets of shapes (two hearts, three hearts, etc.) on the magnetboard and ask the children to place corresponding numerals next to them.

B. *Shape magnetboard.* Cut geometric shapes out of tagboard. Have the children place only squares on the magnetboard, or only triangles, etc. Or, place different geometric shapes on the magnetboard and have the children place matching geometric shapes next to them.

### Number Trivia

Save those magnetic memo holders you receive from merchants as free advertising, and add them to your collection. The holders can be used with your magnet-board for sorting and classifying games, for likeness and difference, and for counting and matching.

A. Use the following materials for matching and classification games: labels from canned goods; brand names and logos cut from food boxes; picture postcards; matchbook covers (with matches removed); colorful brochures.
B. To make cards for number-matching games—or faces on paper-plate clocks—cut numbers out of old calendars.

## Size, Seriation, and Ordinal Numbers

A. Materials such as buttons, gummed stars, lids, beads, feathers, and nails can be used as collage material or to seriate in order of size. Also, size comparisons between two or more of the objects can be made.
B. Boxes or cans can be seriated or ordered from smallest to largest by placing them inside one another.
C. Children can roll balls of various sizes from clay or play dough. They can then seriate these balls according to size.
D. Pie Angles. Draw a picture of a pie cut into five slices of different sizes (use felt or cardboard cutouts as a variation). Arrange the pie slices so that they fit together as a whole pie. Tell a child that the pie has been cut into pieces. Take the pie slices and lay them in a mixed order in front of the child. Tell her to lay the pie slices in a row on the table from the smallest to the largest. Next have her try to put the pie back together.
E. Lollipops. Cut circles into three sizes. Assemble popsicle sticks, paste, or a stapler. Have the children choose a circle of each size. Show them a finished "lollipop" and ask them to tell you which shape is the largest, middle, and smallest. Have them stack and then paste their circles on top of each other. Paste or staple the "lollipops" onto the sticks.
F. Growing Neighborhoods. Make felt or cardboard cutouts in three or more sizes of different heights; for example, trees, houses, hats. Select one set of cutouts and lay them in a mixed order in front of a child. Have the child arrange them in a given order beginning with shortest or tallest. (Variation: Have the child arrange trees in order of height.) Next have the child match the houses to the trees in order of relative height.

### Stair Steps

A. Objective: Arrange from smallest to largest.
B. Equipment: Blocks of different sizes; boxes; cardboard tubes cut into different lengths (toilet tissue tube, paper towel tube, wrapping paper tube)
C. Procedure:
1. Say, "Let's make stairs with these tubes. Who can find the first step, the shortest tube?" Stand the tubes on end.
2. "Now look at the other two; which of these is shorter?" Have a child choose and stand it on end next to the first one.
3. Take the longest tube and ask the children where it should go to finish the stairs.
4. Switch to a set of tubes with smaller differences in length but still at least three inches. Give a child three tubes and ask her to make stairs.
5. Give each child a set of three tubes of graduated sizes to build her own set of stairs.
D. Variations:
1. Have size sequence puzzles available.
2. Have Cuisenaire rods available for children to play with.
3. At home: Use paper towel rods cut to different lengths. Line them up according to length in different ways. Roll marbles through them. Whisper through them. Talk about the size differences.

### Big and Little Circles

A. Objective: Stack rings on a peg in order of size (vary the number of rings).
B. Equipment: Heavy cardboard; two tempera paints; sharp scissors or artist's knife.
C. Procedure:
1. Cut four circles from the cardboard: two with a diameter of 12″ painted red, two with a diameter of 2″ painted white.
2. Put one large and one small circle near child.
3. Pick up the large circle and place near the center of the table while saying, "Put the *big* circle here."
4. Place the small circle on top of the big one while saying "Put the *little* circle on top of the *big* one."
5. Take the little circle back off and say to child, "Now *you* put the little one on the big one."
6. If the child has trouble:
   a. Sit across the table from child.
   b. Put one big and one little circle in front of each of you.
   c. Model putting the little circle on top of the big one and have the child copy your actions.
D. Variations:
1. Have child glue empty spool on top of metal jar lid to make "cookie cutter" for play dough or sandpile.

2. Have simple form boards with shapes of two sizes to be fit into holes.

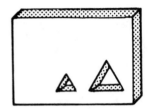

3. At home: Have child stack unbreakable plates and saucers (one saucer on top of one plate).

### Buttons and Math Activities

Ask parents to furnish buttons in all shapes and sizes. Use these for sorting by color and by size. Older children (four- and five-year-olds) can even make graphs showing how many buttons of each color have been collected.

Make at least five different designs by gluing buttons to cards. Give children the same size cards and let them use buttons from the classroom supply to duplicate the designs on their cards.

### Building a Skyscraper

A. Objective: Stack blocks in order (vary the number of blocks).
B. Equipment: three to four blocks or containers of graduated size
C. Procedure:
   1. Demonstrate to child the stacking of two blocks—largest first, then smallest. Say, "Look, I can make a house."
   2. Give the child the two blocks and ask, "Can you make a house like mine?"
   3. If child has trouble, model the placement of the blocks—small on top of large again.
   4. If the child does not have trouble, introduce the middle block and say, "Now, I'll build an apartment building" (or some large building with which the child is familiar).
   5. Demonstrate the stacking in order of size; then ask child to do it alone.
   6. If child has trouble, stack the three blocks together.

7. If she does not have trouble, say, "Now, let's build a skyscraper," and introduce the fourth and smallest block. Follow previous format.
D. Variations:
   1. Have blocks of many sizes available for children in block center.
   2. Have stacking barrels (Kitty in the Barrel) in play area.

### First and Last

A. Objective: Touch first, then last, object in row of five on request (vary the number of objects).
B. Equipment: Five Sesame Street characters: Big Bird, Oscar, Cookie Monster, Bert, Ernie (puppets, pictures, or stuffed animals).
C. Procedure:
   1. Line up the characters. Have the children point to the first one, the last one, and the one in the middle. (Review.) If the child knows the name of the character, that is fine. However, the purpose of the activity is to *point* to the first, last, and middle characters, not to be able to name all of the Sesame Street characters correctly.
   2. Change the positions of the characters and have the children take turns pointing to the one in the middle.
   3. For those children who are having difficulty, find out if they are having trouble with (a) first, (b) last, (c) middle, (d) two of the three, (e) all three. Work with them individually at another time, going back over some of the activities and adding additional activities that begin by giving the children clues; then gradually reduce the clues.
D. Variations:
   1. Have the children stand in a line and identify the person who is first, the person who is last, and the person in the middle. (Review.)
   2. Use five identical objects. Have the children point to the first one and the last one.
   3. Set up five openings in a row for the children to crawl through (boxes with both top and bottom cut out). Tell the children to crawl in the first, come around, and crawl out of the last one.
   4. Use five objects such as forks. Ask child to point to the first one, then the last one, and then the middle one. (Review.) Do the same activity with five spoons or five knives or five spools.

### Cookie Monster Is First

A. Objective: Touch first, then last, animal in row of five on request.
B. Equipment: Cookie Monster (picture, puppet, stuffed animal); four animal creatures that are the same. (Note: If Cookie Monster is a stuffed animal, then the other four animal creatures should be stuffed animals.)

C. Procedure:
1. Position the stuffed animals (pictures or puppets) so that the Cookie Monster is first.
2. Ask the children to look at the animals carefully and describe what they see. Give the children plenty of opportunity to respond. If no one notices, point out the following:
   a. There are five animals.
   b. One of the animals is the Cookie Monster.
3. Ask one child to point to the Cookie Monster. Ask, "The Cookie Monster is standing _____?" (Wait to see if any of the children supply the appropriate answer): First in line (beginning of the line or leader). If not, tell them that the Cookie Monster is standing *first* in line.
4. Discuss the concept or meaning of "first":
   a. before any others
   b. beginning
   c. leader
   d. number one
5. Make sure the children use the word "first" and identify the Cookie Monster as first several times.
6. Then play a game in which the children close their eyes while you move the animals to change their positions, putting the Cookie Monster first at least half of the time. Always ask if the Cookie Monster is first.
7. For children who are having trouble, have the animals stand on colored circles—first circle one color (bright yellow), the other four circles another color (a duller color such as dark blue). This color coding may help.

D. Variations:
1. Have the children stand in line and practice identifying who is first (any time the children line up during the day to go outside, to lunch, etc.). Help them identify who is first. Remember to discuss what "first" means or how to tell who is first.
2. Make a coloring sheet with Cookie Monster first. Have children give him a cookie and color him. Then make a special mat for him to stand on because he is first. They may color the other four animals a different color but make sure you emphasize that Cookie Monster is first.
3. At home: Use four forks and a knife. Place the knife first. Ask child to show you which one is first. Show that first means the beginning. Do this same activity again (several times if desired), using other objects found around the home and of interest to your child.

*Oscar Is Last*

A. Objective: Touch first, then last, animal in row of five on request.
B. Equipment: Oscar from Sesame Street (picture, puppet, stuffed animal); four animal creatures that are the same. (Note: If Oscar is a stuffed animal, then the other four animals should be stuffed animals.)

C. Procedure:
1. Position the stuffed animals (pictures or puppets) so that Oscar is last.
2. Ask the children to look at the animals carefully and describe what they see. Give them plenty of opportunity to respond. If no one notices, point out the following:
   a. There are five animals.
   b. One of the animals is Oscar.
   c. Oscar is on Sesame Street and lives in a garbage can. He likes trash!
3. Tell the children or let someone point to the first of the line. Ask one child to point to Oscar. Ask, "Where is Oscar? Oscar is _____?" Wait to see if any of the children supply the appropriate answer: Last (or at the end). If not, tell them that Oscar is standing last in line.
4. Discuss the concept or meaning of "last":
   a. at the end
   b. everyone is in front of him and no one is behind him.
5. Make sure the children use the word "last" and identify Oscar as being last several times.
6. Then play a game in which the children close their eyes while you move the animals to change their positions, putting Oscar last at least half of the time. Always ask if Oscar is last.
7. For children who are having trouble, have the animals stand on colored circles. The last circle should be one color (bright yellow) and the other four circles another color (dark blue). This color coding may help.

D. Variations:
1. Have the children stand in line and practice identifying who is last. Any time the children line up during the day to go outside, to lunch, etc., help them identify who is last. Remember to discuss what "last" means or how to tell who is last.
2. Make a coloring sheet with Oscar last. Have the children give (draw) him some trash and color him. Then make a special mat for him to stand on because he is last. They may color the other four animals a different color, but make sure you emphasize that Oscar is special because he is last.
3. At home: Use four sticks and an adhesive bandage. Put the bandage last. Show child where the first thing or object is. Then ask child to name and point to the one that is last. Show that "last" means the end. Do this same activity again (several times if desired), using other objects found around the home and of interest to your child.

*Where Is Oscar's Garbage Can—Last?*

A. Objective: Touch first, then last, object in row of five on request.
B. Equipment: Oscar (character from Sesame Street); one large garbage can; four small wastebaskets; four small animals that will fit in the four small wastebaskets.
C. Procedure:
1. Line the wastebaskets and garbage can up so that the garbage can is last. Place a small animal in each of the small wastebaskets. Then talk about how Oscar loves garbage (trash) and ask if everyone knows where he lives. Answer: in a garbage can.
2. Talk about the garbage cans. Ask one of the children to put Oscar in the *last* garbage can. Give several children a turn to put Oscar in the last garbage can.
3. If you want, you can take Oscar and his garbage can away and ask the children to put Oscar and his garbage can last.
4. Be sure to identify where first is at the beginning and then again periodically throughout the lesson because ''last'' is always dependent upon where ''first'' is.
D. Variations:
1. Use wastebaskets or garbage cans that are all the same size; after indicating which garbage can is first, ask which one is last. Children can pretend they are Oscar and crawl in.
2. Make a sheet for each child of five predrawn garbage cans (all the same size). Have each child put Oscar in the last garbage can by drawing a picture in the last can.
3. At home: Line up five different things to eat. Show child which one is first; then have her point and name, if possible, the food that is last. If she does so correctly, she may eat it. Have child close her eyes. Add another food so that there are five once again; move the food to different positions; have child point to the last one again. Some examples of things you might use: small candies, marshmallows, grapes, corn chips, nuts, etc.

## Individual Math Concept Gameboards

Draw pictures on the insides of file folders to make gameboards and cover them with clear contact paper. Make game cards by drawing matching pictures on tagboard or index cards; cover them with clear contact paper and cut them out. Tape squares of tagboard to the front of the file folders to make envelopes for holding the game cards. Have the children use the folders to play matching and sorting games.

A. *Number folders*. Draw eight apples, suns, stars, etc. on the inside of each file folder and write a different numeral inside each picture. Draw matching pictures that contain corresponding numbers of dots on tagboard and cut them out. Children match the numbers by placing the cutouts on top of the corresponding pictures on the file folders.
B. *Shape folders*. Draw eight basic shapes (circle, triangle, square, star, rectangle, etc.) on the inside of each file folder. Draw matching shapes on tagboard and cut them out. Children match the shapes by placing the cutouts on top of the corresponding shapes on the file folders.
C. *Classification folders*. Choose a subject such as ''Mothers and Baby Animals'' and label one side of an open file folder ''Mother'' and the other side ''Baby Animal'' (or draw pictures to indicate the labels). Draw pictures of mother and baby animals on tagboard and cut them out. Children sort the pictures by placing them on the appropriate sides of the file folder.

## Shape and Form

A. While building with blocks, show a child a circle and let her find another circle. Do the same with other shapes.
B. Give the child many opportunities to sort objects, such as laundry items, buttons, and shaped blocks. Egg cartons make excellent sorting trays for small items; muffin tins are good for larger items; and cottage cheese cartons work well for still larger items.
C. Shape Board. On a large piece of tagboard, make (draw) shapes. (You may want to trace block shapes.) Make block shapes on cards to match the drawn shapes. Distribute the cards with shapes on them to the children. Place blocks of these shapes in a pile in a center area. Each child takes a turn at choosing a block and placing it on the geometric shape it matches. Say, ''Can you choose a block and place it on the shape it matches?''
D. With masking tape, jump ropes, or chalk lay out shapes on the floor of the room or out in the hallway. Show the children the shapes on the floor. Have a child say, ''Shape goes around the outside,'' while walking along a shape. Each child may be given a chance to ''make a shape'' for another child to walk along. Variation: Slide along, march on, or walk backwards on the shapes.

*Simple Shape Discrimination*

A. Objective: Match sample circles, squares, triangles.
B. Equipment: 2 yellow circles (3″ diameter); 1 yellow triangle (3″ sides). Plastic or wooden shapes would be ideal. If not available, use heavy cardboard.

C. Procedure:
1. Put three shapes on table in front of child.
2. Have the child trace her finger around the edges of the two circles, then the triangles.
3. Point out to her that the circles are round, but the triangle is pointed.
4. Pick out two circles. Say, "Look, these have the *same* shape." Then put one circle on top of the other.
5. Put the triangle on top of the circles. Ask the child, "Is this one the same shape?"
6. If she seems confused about the shapes, roll the circles on edge on the table; then try to roll the triangle. Have the child try.
7. Put one circle and one triangle back on the table in front of the child.
8. Give the child the second circle. Say, "Put this on the one that is the same shape." or "Find the one like this one."
9. Compare edges to check the child's answer.

D. Variations:
1. Have templates of triangles, square, and circle, which child can trace.
2. Have different shaped blocks for building with.
3. Have heavily outlined triangles, squares, and circles for coloring.

## UNIT REVIEW

1. What is the developmental pattern in a young child's mathematical skills? Give examples and related activities in your reply.
2. What would you consider basic equipment and materials for a math center? Discuss the reasons for your choices.
3. How does building with blocks assist a child's development of mathematical skills? Give examples in your reply. How can block cleanup time be used to help young children in their development of mathematical skills?
4. What is rote counting? What is rational counting? How can you tell when a child is capable of either of these skills?
5. What does it mean to develop the skill of seriation? Give examples of activities that would help a child learn this skill.
6. How would you introduce shapes to a young child?
7. What are some ways to teach classification? Give specific activity examples in your reply.

## ADDITIONAL READINGS

Baroody, A.J. *Children's Mathematical Thinking: A Developmental Framework for Preschool, Primary, and Special Education Teachers.* New York: Teachers College Press, Columbia University, 1987.

Burton, G.M. *Towards a Good Beginning: Teaching Early Childhood Mathematics.* Menlo Park, Calif.: Addison-Wesley, 1985.

Charlesworth, R., and K. Lind. *Math and Science for Young Children.* Albany, N.Y.: Delmar Publishers Inc., 1990.

Clemens, S.G. "*Art in the Classroom: Making Every Day Special.*" *Young Children* (Jan., 1991): 4–11.

Cooney, T.J., and G.R. Hirsch. *Teaching and Learning Mathematics in the 1990s.* Reston, Va.: National Council of Teachers of Mathematics, 1990.

Copeland, R.W. *How Children Learn Mathematics: Teaching Implications of Piaget's Research.* New York: Macmillan, 1984.

Cruikshank, D.E., D.L. Fitzgerald, and L.R. Jensen. *Young Children Learning Mathematics.* Boston: Allyn & Bacon, 1980.

Davis, G.E., and M. Pepper. "Mathematical Problem Solving by Pre-School Children." *Educational Studies in Mathematics* 23 (Aug., 1992): 397–415.

Hirsch, Elizabeth S., ed. *The Block Book,* rev. ed. Washington, D.C.: National Association for the Education of Young Children, 1984.

Kamii, C. *Number in Preschool and Kindergarten: Educational Implications of Piaget's Theory.* Washington, D.C.: National Association for the Education of Young Children, 1982.

Leeb-Lundberg, Kristina. *Mathematics Is More Than Counting.* Wheaton, Md.: Association of Childhood Education International, 1985.

McCracken, J.B. *More Than 1, 2, 3: The Real Basics of Mathematics.* Washington, D.C.: National Association for the Education of Young Children, 1987.

National Council of Teachers of Mathematics. *Soviet Studies in Mathematic Education, Vol. 4: The Development of Elementary Concepts in Preschool Children.* English translation. Chicago: University of Chicago Press, 1991.

————. *Soviet Studies in Mathematic Education, Vol. 3:*

*The Development of Spatial Thinking in School Children.* English translation. Chicago: University of Chicago Press, 1991.

————. *Soviet Studies in Mathematics Vol. 5: Mathematics in Preschool: An Aid for the Preschool Educator.* English translation. Chicago: University of Chicago Press, 1991.

Richardson, L., N. Goodman, N. Hartman, and H.A. LePique. *Mathematics Activity Curriculum for Early Childhood and Special Education.* New York: Macmillan, 1980.

Rogers, D. *Child Psychology.* Belmont, Calif.: Brooks-Cole Publishing Co., 1969.

Scott, L.B., and Garnar, J. *Mathematical Experiences for Young Children: A Resource Book for Kindergarten and Primary Teachers.* New York: McGraw-Hill, 1978.

Stevenson, H.W., M. Lummis, S. Lee, and J.W. Stigler. *Making the Grade in Mathematics, 1990.* Reston, Va.: National Council of Teachers of Mathematics, 1990.

Stoessinger, R., J. Edmunds. *Natural Learning and Mathematics.* Portsmouth, N.H.: Heinemann Educational Books, 1992.

Warren, Jean, ed. *Teaching Toys.* Everett, Wash.: Warren Publishing House, Inc., 1985.

## General Math Books for Children

Anderson, L.C. *The Wonderful Shrinking Shirt.* Niles, Ill.: Albert Whitman, 1983.

Anno, M. *Anno's Counting Book.* New York: Crowell, 1977.

Bang, M. *Ten, Nine, Eight.* New York: Greenwillow, 1983.

Barton, B. *Building a House.* New York: Greenwillow, 1981.

Brown, M. *Once a Mouse.* New York: Scribner's, 1961.

Chalmers, Mary. *Six Dogs, Twenty-three Cats, Forty-five Mice and One Hundred and Sixteen Spiders.* New York: Harper, 1986.

Charlip, Remy. *Handtalk Birthday: A Number & Storybook in Sign Language.* New York: Four Winds, 1987.

Crews, D. *Ten Black Dots.* New York: Greenwillow, 1986.

Dalgliesh, A. *The Little Wooden Farmer.* New York: Macmillan, 1968.

Emberly, B. *Drummer Hoff.* Englewood Cliffs, N.J.: Prentice-Hall, 1967.

Ets, M.H. *In the Forest.* New York: Viking, 1972.

Feelings, M. *Moja Means One: Swahili Counting Book.* New York: Dial, 1971.

Freeman, D. *Corduroy.* New York: Viking, 1968.

Gardner, Beau. *Can You Imagine . . .? A Counting Book.* New York: Dodd, 1987.

Hoban, T. *Circles, Triangles and Squares.* New York: Macmillan, 1974.

————. *Count and See.* New York: Macmillan, 1972.

————. *Is It Red? Is It Yellow? Is It Blue?* New York: Greenwillow, 1978.

————. *Shapes, Shapes, Shapes.* New York: Greenwillow, 1986.

————. *All About Where.* New York: Greenwillow, 1991.

Hughes, S. *Lucy and Tom's 1, 2, 3.* New York: Viking, 1987.

Hutchins, T. *The Door Bell Rang.* New York: Greenwillow, 1986.

James, B. *Natalie Underneath.* New York: Dutton, 1990.

Kitamura, S. *When Sheep Can Not Sleep? The Counting Book.* New York: Farrar, Straus & Giroux, 1986.

Kitchen, Bert. *Animal Numbers.* New York: Dial, 1987.

Lionni, L. *Frederick.* New York: Pantheon, 1967.

————. *Inch by Inch.* New York: Astor-Honor, 1960.

Martin, Bill, and John Archambault. *Knots on a Counting Rope.* New York: Holt, 1987.

Rockwell, Anne. *Bear Child's Book of Hours.* New York: Crowell, 1987.

Russo, Marisabina. *The Line Up Book.* New York: Greenwillow, 1986.

Seuss, Dr. *One Fish, Two Fish, Red Fish, Blue Fish.* New York: Random House, 1960.

Sis, Peter. *Waving: A Counting Book.* New York: Greenwillow, 1988.

Tafuri, N. *Who's Counting?* New York: Greenwillow, 1986.

Wahl, J., and S. Wahl. *I Can Count the Petals of a Flower.* Reston, Va. National Council of Teachers of Mathematics, 1976.

## Children's Books

### Counting

Baum, A. *One Bright Monday Morning.* New York: Random House, 1962.

Blegvad, L. *One Is for the Sun.* New York: Harcourt Brace Jovanovich, 1968.

Bright, R. *My Red Umbrella.* New York: William Morrow & Co., 1959.

Brown, M. *One, Two, Three: An Animal Counting Book.* Boston: Little, Brown and Co., 1976.

Carle, E. *1, 2, 3 to the Zoo.* New York: World Publishing Co., 1968.

Clark, E. *Understanding Numbers.* New York: Golden Book Educational Series, 1963.

Ehrlich, A. *The Everyday Train.* New York: The Dial Press, 1977.

Francoise, J. *Marie Counts Her Sheep.* New York: Charles Scribner's Sons, 1963.

Hoban, T. *Count and See.* New York: Macmillan, 1972.

Hoberman, M.A., and N. Hoberman. *All My Shoes Come in Twos.* Boston: Little, Brown and Co., 1970.

Holl, A. *Let's Count.* Reading, Mass.: Addison-Wesley, 1976.

Ipcar, D. *Brown Cow Farm.* New York: Doubleday, 1959.
Keats, E.J. *Over in the Meadow.* Bristol, Fla.: Four Winds Press, 1972.
Kitchen, B. *Animal Numbers.* New York: Dial, 1991.
Langstaff, J. *Over in the Meadow.* New York: Harcourt, Brace and World, 1967.
McLeod, E. *One Snail and Me.* Boston: Little, Brown and Co., 1961.
Miller, C. *The Sesame Street Book of Numbers.* Boston: Little, Brown and Co., 1961.
O'Neill, M. *Take a Number.* New York: Doubleday, 1968.
Pierce, R. *The Counting Book.* New York: Random House, 1970.
Rand, A., and P. Rand. *Little 1.* New York: Harcourt, Brace and World, 1962.
Reiss, J.J. *Numbers.* Scarsdale, N.Y.: Bradbury Press, 1971.
Rowan, D. *Everybody In.* Englewood Cliffs, N.J.: Bradbury Press, 1968.
Slobodkin, L. *Millions and Millions and Millions.* New York: Vanguard Press, 1955.
True, L. *Number Men.* Chicago: Children's Press, 1962.
Tudor, T. *1 Is One.* New York: Henry Z. Walck, 1956.
Wildsmith, B. *1, 2, 3's.* New York: Franklin Watts, 1965.

*Size and Seriation*
Berkley, E. *Big and Little, Up and Down.* Reading, Mass.: Addison-Wesley, 1950.
Brenner, B. *Mr. Tall and Mr. Small.* Reading, Mass.: Addison-Wesley, 1966.
Clure, B., and H. Ramsey. *Little, Big, Bigger.* Glendale, Calif.: Bowmar Publications, 1971.
Kaufman, J. *Big and Little.* New York: Golden Press, 1966.
Kohn, B. *Everything Has a Shape and Everything Has a Size.* Englewood Cliffs, N.J.: Prentice-Hall, 1971.

Krasilvsky, P. *The Very Little Boy.* New York: Doubleday, 1962.
————. *The Very Little Girl.* New York: Doubleday, 1952.
Krauss, R. *The Growing Story.* New York: Harper and Brothers, 1947.
Lenski, L. *Cowboy Small.* New York: Henry Z. Walck, 1959.
Shapp, C., and M. Shapp. *Let's Find Out What's Big and What's Small.* New York: Franklin Watts, 1959.
Spier, P. *Fast-Slow, High-Low.* Garden City, N.Y.: Doubleday, 1972.
Ward, L. *The Biggest Bear.* New York: Scholastic Book Services, 1975.

*Shape and Form*
Budney, B. *A Kiss Is Round.* New York: Lothrop, Lee and Co., 1954.
Emberly, E. *The Wings on a Flea.* Boston: Little, Brown and Co., 1961.
Hoban, T. *Shapes and Things.* New York: Macmillan, 1970.
Kessler, E., and L. Kessler. *Are You Square?* New York: Doubleday, 1969.
Martin, J. *Round and Square.* New York: The Platt and Munk Co., 1965.
Schlein, M. *Shapes.* New York: William R. Scott, 1967.
Thoburn, T. *Discovering Shapes.* New York: Golden Book Educational Series, 1963.
Yodell, L.D. *Make a Face.* Boston: Little, Brown and Co., 1970.

# UNIT 21
# Creative Food Experiences

## OBJECTIVES

After studying this unit, you should be able to
- describe four ways in which food activities develop children's skills.
- list several ways to help make food experiences more creative.
- give an example of a creative food experience and the necessary steps involved.
- describe at least two creative food experiences in other curriculum areas.

Children learn best when they experience the world firsthand—by touch, taste, smell, sight, and hearing. If you wish to make the most of any food experience, children must be *directly* involved with real food and given as much responsibility as possible for growing, selecting, preparing, and eating the food.

Activities involving foods are included in most programs for young children. However, many of the food activities are under the complete direction of the teacher. The children sit and watch the teacher do the work. Sometimes the children are given spoons and told to stir a mixture, or are allowed to pour liquids from one container to another. Sometimes they are given the job of listening for a timer to "ding." Rarely is the child allowed to decide what foods to use, how to use them, in what order to mix them, or for how long to stir things.

The use of foods in a classroom can be one of the most creative parts of the program. Foods are a part of each child's experience. Foods and cooking are interesting to children. All of their senses are used in food activities. They see the foods. They smell them, touch them, and taste them. The children can even hear many kinds of foods boiling, popping, or frying. Other learning is enhanced by food activities, too. Art, sciencing, and aesthetics are all related to cooking in some way.

**FIGURE 21–1 Children enjoy food activities at any age.**

## IMPORTANCE OF FOOD EXPERIENCES TO THE TOTAL PROGRAM

Foods are well known to all children. They are a part of every child's basic needs. Children come into contact with foods many times each day. They ex-

**FIGURE 21-2 Preparing food is a pleasant activity for young children.**

perience foods in the school, at home, and in stores. Foods are highly interesting to them. Activities involving foods can be used to help children learn new information and gain new skills.

**Building Information.** Food activities help children understand new concepts:

*Children learn to describe things.* Children experience many shapes, sizes, and colors. They see that some things start out in a round shape and become long and flat during the cooking process. Many foods change in size when they are heated; some change in texture and color. Foods come in many colors, and the colors sometimes change with mixing, heating, or cooling. The child thus learns to name shapes, compare sizes, and describe colors.

*Children learn about tastes.* Children find out how heating or mixing changes taste. They learn that some things, such as salt or sugar, can change the taste of foods. They discover that some foods taste good when they are mixed together and that others do not. They also learn that a change in the outward appearance of some foods does not mean that the foods taste any different. Apple juice has the same flavor as a whole apple. Frozen orange pops taste like orange juice and a frozen banana tastes just like banana ice cream.

*Children observe changes.* As they did in sciencing, children observe that foods change from liquids to solids and from solids to liquids. They also see steam (a gas) rising from liquids that are heated. In addition, they sense odors—some good and some bad—as foods change from solids to liquids to gases.

*Children learn to express themselves.* Language develops as a result of food experiences. Words like bitter, sour, sweet, and salty have real meaning. Hot, cold, warm, and cool are part of the food vocabulary. Children may learn the words delicious and tasty. They learn a more complete meaning of terms like liquid and solid, freezing and boiling, smelly and odorless. When the words relate to direct experiences, the child's vocabulary grows.

The following scene is an example of how all these skills are developed in a simple food experience:

> The making of pudding went over quite well, as do all food-oriented activities. My organization ahead of time helped it to be a pleasant and not too disorganized activity! We used instant pudding and it required a specified amount of milk to be added. This fact helped us discuss the number of cups of milk we would need, as well as the concept of milk and nutrition, etc. They poured out the milk, measuring the amounts, and all had a chance to use the hand rotary beater to beat the pudding. This

**FIGURE 21-3 Tasting different snack foods helps broaden a child's vocabulary as well as food experience.**

**FIGURE 21–4 Planning for a group cooking activity involves both adult and child input.**

was good small motor exercise for them all. They poured out the pudding (a bit messy!). Then we had to wait for five minutes for it to set, and this helped introduce the idea of time, and where the clock's hands would be when five minutes went by. All these things were discussed in making the pudding, so I feel that it was a true learning experience for all. However, I'm sure the children enjoyed eating the pudding at the end of the learning experience the best!

Many concepts can be discussed in an informal situation such as this. I hope to use many more such situations when I assume my role as a teacher of young children. Learning under such a natural and relaxed atmosphere was a pleasure for both myself and the children (author's log).

**FIGURE 21–5 Cutting out pictures of one's favorite foods is both a small-motor and food-related activity.**

**Building Skills.** There are a number of skills that children can learn from working with foods. These skills can be developed during other parts of the program also, but working with food is an excellent way to build skills in fun and popular activities.

*Small-muscle coordination.* Mixing foods and pouring liquids from one container to another are ways in which children develop coordination. The small muscles in the hands develop so that a child can hold a large spoon and help in the mixing process when using a recipe. The measuring, pouring, and mixing of foods all require the use of small muscles as well as hand-eye coordination. Thus, food activities provide excellent small motor activities for young children.

*Simple measuring skills.* By using cups and spoons that have marks showing amounts, a child begins to understand measurements. A three- to five-year-old is not expected to read a recipe. Nor is the child expected to measure exactly one cup or one tablespoon. The child is, however, able to observe that a tablespoon is larger than a teaspoon and that a cup holds more than a tablespoon.

The child can also begin to realize that by using too much flour, water, or salt, recipes don't turn out quite as well as if the correct amounts are used. The child begins to understand that the amount of each ingredient used makes a difference in the final product. This realization leads the child to look for ways to figure out amounts. This is when measuring tools are discovered.

*Social skills.* Food experiences are a natural avenue for social learning. Mixing, measuring, decorating, and eating all provide many opportunities for talking with others, exchanging ideas, sharing likes and dislikes, and learning about each other. You will find that in preparing food, children many times will talk more freely about themselves and their lives in the homey, routine nature of this type of activity.

In cooking, a child may need help in holding a pan steady while pouring something into it. He may need help in carrying ingredients or finding certain foods. He may need some new ideas for a special

**FIGURE 21–6 Cooking with young children provides a pleasant combination of social, math, and science experiences.**

frosting. One child may need an "expert" opinion on how much lemon to squeeze into a drink. These things call for some working together. As children work together, social skills develop in the natural give-and-take of group experiences.

**Health and Safety.** As children are involved in food experiences, they learn some basic information on routines and cautions about food and cooking necessary to good health and safety. This information is best learned in the process of working with food, and not as a "lecture" type lesson.

For example, learning that cleanliness is important in all food preparation can be taught as children work with food. Both children and adults always wash their hands with soap and water before beginning any food experience. Aprons or other cover-ups may

**FIGURE 21–7 Donning a smock, this child is prepared to actively participate in a cooking activity.**

also be necessary, especially if you are preparing foods that stain easily.

Young children often need encouragement to keep fingers and utensils out of their mouths while preparing food. If they do lick fingers or spoons, simply and calmly ask the children to wash them before proceeding. This is a good opportunity to teach chil-

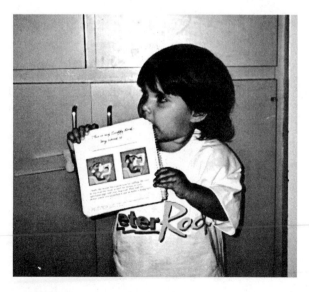

**FIGURE 21–8 Putting things into the mouth is a natural occurrence with toddlers.**

dren about germs and how they are transmitted. Tasting is also a good opportunity to help children learn about how foods taste at various stages of preparation and to observe changes in texture. However, no products containing dried egg should be eaten before being fully cooked. Dried egg is a source of salmonella bacteria and can cause digestive problems for young children.

Any cooking adventure involving heat, sharp knives, or operating appliances should be carefully supervised. Sharp knives are rarely needed, since plastic serrated knives will slice most produce and are much safer for even very young children. Children will need to be cautioned when observing food in the oven or on the range burner; utensil handles should be turned toward the center of the range at all times. Since electric burners don't always appear to be hot, children will need to learn how to identify when the burner is on, by recognizing the position of the switch or by reading "on," "off," "high," or "low," and be made aware that the burner remains hot for a while even after it has been turned off. All of these are important health and safety learnings for young children in food experiences.

Finally, food allergies are very common among young children, and before planning any experience, you will need to know which children are allergic to specific foods. Some children may also have ethnic food restrictions that prohibits their eating certain foods as well. Every adult participating in food activities, whether teacher, cook, parent, or community volunteer, must have this information. If fresh produce is to be used, adults must know what parts of plants are poisonous. Children should learn that these parts and any other wild plant must never be eaten.

## FOOD ACTIVITIES THAT HELP CHILDREN'S CREATIVITY

The following are some guidelines to use to ensure that food experiences for young children are planned to enhance their creativity:

1. *Activities should be open.* If all children must follow the same directions at the same time, they will not become creative. In fact, just the opposite will happen. The children will be conformers and do only what the teacher tells them to do. To some adults, this may sound like a good thing. It is—if the only concern of a teacher is a quiet, orderly class. Teachers who want to help children be creative must help them be open. The teacher must let the children create their own directions and work at their own pace.

2. *Activities should be challenging, but not too difficult for the children.* If food activities are too hard, children will give up and quit. If they are too easy, the children will not be challenged. It is important to start with easy things. It is also important to increase the possibilities, so children will do harder things as they go on.

3. *Activities should be varied.* Children get bored if they do the same thing day after day. Variety is needed. Children should work with foods they know. They should also work with new foods they have not seen or tasted before. Some activities should be very short. Others should take a longer time to finish. In some activities, children should use just one type of food. In others, they may mix in several ingredients.

4. *The process is more important than the product.* Emphasis should not be placed on what the children create, but on how they have done it. If only the final product is considered, then many children will fail. Things do not always taste good—especially when children create new recipes. But if children are rewarded for the way they create, then what they have created does not seem so important.

5. *Inexpensive materials and small amounts should be used.* No child should feel heartbroken if a recipe does not work. If, however, a great deal of money is spent on foods, it is hard to justify wasting the food. If ingredients are inexpensive, there is less chance that children will be made to feel guilty because something they made did not taste very good.

6. *Dangerous foods must be kept away from children.* Only those things that are safe for people to eat are used. Make certain that available foods are safe when mixed together. Some foods are safe when

eaten by themselves, but can produce illness when mixed with other foods. The teacher controls this by being careful about the foods made available to the children.

7. *Activities should be carried out in a variety of places.* Food activities do not have to be limited to the indoors. They can also be done outside the classroom. They work well on the school grounds or in a nearby woods. *Note:* An important restriction for outdoor cooking is for the teacher to see and inspect all food before it is used. Poison mushrooms and berries are sometimes gathered by children. These foods must be avoided.

## GETTING STARTED

**Planning.**   Careful planning is crucial to successful food experiences. All ingredients (in sufficient quantities) need to be purchased, utensils assembled, and objectives for the activity established.

Children's abilities should be matched to the food experience so that the adult does not carry out the preparation while the children watch. Confident adults can lead very difficult experiences, especially if the group is composed of a small number of children who are capable of learning the skills involved.

Depending on the complexity of the recipe, the number of children, and the time available, it may at times be necessary for the adult to complete some tasks or to use prepared foods such as peanut butter. Keep in mind, however, that *the more the adult does, the less the children learn.* The extra time children take learning is well spent.

Objectives for the children's learning will help focus the activity for the adults involved. Do you want children to successfully cut celery into finger-sized strips? Is your objective to have the children sample a variety of food textures and discuss the differences? Will children try less familiar foods? Is your goal to facilitate cooperative work in a small group?

Common goals for food experiences for young children include strengthening their manipulative skills, expanding their knowledge about nutrition, and trying new foods. You will want to develop your own objectives for each recipe you choose based on your knowledge about the children in the group.

Goals for very young or inexperienced children will be different from those for more advanced food preparers. Initially, try to plan food preparation ac-

**FIGURE 21–9 In food experiences, children learn while having fun.**

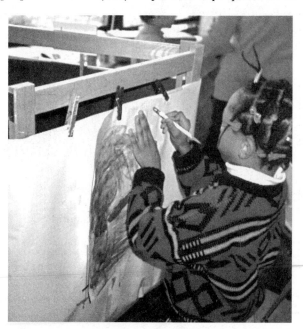

**FIGURE 21–10 Painting one's favorite food is a natural follow-up to a food experience.**

### Using Food in Science Activities

- Plant an outdoor or indoor garden.
- Have a tasting party.
- Arrange unusual foods on a science table.
- Place carrot, beet, or pineapple tops in a shallow bowl of crushed stones or pebbles covered with water.
- Cut off the top third of a sweet potato and put it in water. Allow sprouts to vine at the top. Hold the potato part way out of the water.
- Examine a coconut. Break it open.
- Examine and cut a fresh pineapple.
- Taste baby foods.
- Place seed catalogs on the reading shelf.
- Make a food dictionary.
- Draw pictures of your favorite foods from each food group. Make a meal: Draw a picture of a plate and cup and fill them with your foods to make a nutritious meal. Make sure you label each food.

### Creative Art Activities with Food

- Macaroni or dried bean collage
- Fruit-colored play dough
- Stringing Cheerios/Fruit Loops
- Potato printing
- Stringing macaroni
- Printing with cabbage, lemons, oranges, celery, carrots, onions, peppers
- Seed collage
- Gelatin or pudding finger painting
- Rice and felt collage (color rice)
- Broken eggshells on paintings
- Child-made food books
    Foods I Like
    Fruits I Like
    Foods My Daddy (or Mommy, Sister, etc.) Likes
- A mural made of pictures of foods
- Salt trays (place salt in shallow box, child may write with finger in it)
- Creating flannelboard pictures (have foods cut from flannel for child to arrange on table, on plate, in basket)
- Food pictures cut from newspaper or magazine ads to paste on colored paper
- Colored cornmeal (mix cornmeal and dry tempera; sprinkle on glue designs)
- Have children paste pictures of foods on a chart with area for fruits and vegetables, breads, milk, meats.
- Make picture charts of favorite recipes (see Figures 21–14 and 21–16).

### Table Activities—Food Experiences

- Sewing cards with food pictures
- Teacher-made "move forward" games (ice cream store, hot dog stand)
- Lotto games—teacher made or store bought
- Set out dishpans of beans with funnels, cups.
- Food scale with beans for weighing
- Balance with beans

### Field Trips—Food Experiences

- Grocery store
- Vegetable garden
- Fruit orchard
- School kitchen
- Bakery
- Restaurant
- Pizza parlor
- Ice cream store
- Fruit and vegetable stand
- Bottling company
- Dairy
- Canning factory
- Hatchery
- Cornfield, strawberry or melon patch
- Kitchen of one of the children's family

### Games for Cooking Experiences

- Farmer Plants His Seeds (corn, oats, beans, carrots, etc.)
- Farmer Picks His Corn (beans, radishes, turnips, etc.)
- Can You Remember? (display foods on a tray, cover, try to remember where each is)
- How Many? (different foods, etc.)
- Which? (foods that can be eaten raw, foods that are yellow, etc.)

FIGURE 21–11 Activities to reinforce learning in other areas.

- Grouping (those that are yellow, those that are eaten for breakfast, etc.)
- Touch and Tell (place food in a bag; have child feel and try to identify)
- Smell and Tell (have child close eyes and try to identify food by smelling)
- Guess What? (describe the characteristics of food, children try to identify)

- Hot Potato (choose an object that is light and easy to pass; pretend it is a hot potato; have children sit in a circle; pass the hot potato quickly around the room; ring a bell to catch someone with the hot potato)

**FIGURE 21–11 Activities to reinforce learning in other areas (cont.).**

tivities that involve only one or two skills and a limited number of ingredients. Squeezing orange juice involves one ingredient and two skills, squeezing and pouring. Washing vegetables or fruits (in a basin to conserve water, rather than under running water) and possibly then cutting them into convenient pieces is also a good beginning activity. For children who are just becoming competent in balancing, pouring, or cutting, these tasks are a real challenge. The following list is a summary of things to keep in mind when planning a food experience.

*Things to remember when planning cooking activities:*
1. Work out ahead of time a sequence of steps for the activity.
2. Plan a series of activities that are gradually more complex.
3. Encourage the children to talk about what they are doing.
4. Relate the activity to home experiences.
5. Give the names for new foods, processes, and equipment used.
6. When appropriate, involve the children in getting supplies for the activities.
7. Encourage discussion of what has been done. Allow a good amount of time for tasting and touching.
8. Use follow-up activities to reinforce the learning. (See Figure 21–11 and the end of this unit for suggestions.)

## ACTIVITIES TO TRY AS STARTERS

The following are a few suggestions of creative food activities that may be used with groups or by a single child. These are meant to be just starters since the kinds and varieties of food activities appropriate for young children are endless.

**Group Activities.** A small group of four to five children usually works best with a food activity. Some activities work best with a larger group. Some work best with small groups. But 15 children or the whole group together are too many for one cooking activity. If step-by-step recipes are needed for any of the activities, a good cookbook may be used.

*Community fruit salad.* Each child may select one fruit to add to the salad. A large bowl is needed. Children decide the way they add their fruit to the salad (crushing, slicing, whole). This same basic activity can be varied by using different raw vegetables.

*Topless popcorn.* Children sit around a hot-air type popcorn popper. Popcorn is added, but the top of the popper is left off. Interesting results follow. Of course, the children would first be involved in getting the popcorn into the popper and in any other related activities in making it. (Don't let kids sit too close.)

*Making ice cream.* A hand-operated ice cream maker is needed. Children can turn the crank in re-

FIGURE 21–12 Picture recipe—Magic Three Ice Cream.

lays. Flavorings can be the creation of the children involved. Coffee beans or vanilla beans are interesting to use. Sugar-free syrups of other flavors can also be created. Directions for making ice cream usually come with the maker. Children can suggest creative uses of materials that go into the cream container.

*Creative gelatin or pudding.* Using clear gelatin and a variety of other foods for flavoring, children can be creative. They can select a variety of flavorings to add. They can whip gelatin into sponges and puddings. They can make or select their own molds. In cold climates, gelatin or pudding sets in a short time on a window ledge as children watch. Bavarian cream types, fruit-flavored gelatins, or puddings can be created by children as they experiment. *Note:* As a precaution, an adult must provide the boiling hot water (heat and pour). The children direct this part of the activity, but must never be permitted to do it themselves.

*Creative use of a blender.* An activity that is both fun and valuable for creative learning is making a cocktail juice. The children can select the vegetables

FIGURE 21–13 Picture recipe—Pumpkin Pie.

# THINK ABOUT IT . . .

## RECYCLING AFTER FOOD ACTIVITIES

Creative food activities can lead to even more creative *recycling* experiences. After you have made your recipe, try recycling some of your discards into science experiences by planting seeds and other parts of vegetables and fruits to make classroom plants. Here are some ideas:

*Carrots.* Cut off a carrot with shoots growing at the top about 1 inch from the top. Plant the top shallowly in a soil-filled 3-inch pot. After a time, the carrot will grow more greens, and may produce even a flower that looks like Queen Anne's lace. (You can also grow a carrot in water only.)

*Peaches.* Wash a peach pit and let it dry for a few days. Bury it in an inch of soil in a 4″ pot.

*Citrus seeds.* Wash orange, grapefruit, or lemon seeds with water and dry for a few days. Plant a few seeds about an inch deep in soil in a 4″ pot. In a few weeks, they will sprout. Once the seedlings are about 4 inches tall, plant each in its own 4″ pot. After a few years, these plants may flower, producing very sweet-smelling blossoms.

Note: To produce bushy plants, pinch back tip of the main stem every now and then to make side stems grow. Citrus plants will need repotting every two or three years.

*Pineapple.* Slice off the top, leaving a tiny bit of the crown or top of the fruit attached— about ½ inch. Barely bury the crown of the pineapple in soil in a shallow 5″ pot.

*Radishes.* Find a radish with sprouts. The sprouts will become leaves if you plant the radish to about half its depth in a 4″ pot.

*Avocado.* Plant an avocado seed, flattened end down, to about half its depth in a 4″ pot with holes in it for drainage. Lightly pat the soil to get rid of any air pockets. Repot when the roots begin to poke through the bottom of the pot. To make the avocado branch out, pinch back the tip of the main stem when it gets about 7 inches tall.

You can also sprout an avocado seed in water. Gently stick three nails or toothpicks into the seed. Suspend it in a jar of water with the broad end pointing down. Once the roots thicken and the stem gets leafy, transplant the avocado to a pot of soil. The seed should be planted at the same depth it was in the water, half above soil, half below.

*Sweet potatoes.* Gently stick nails or toothpicks into a sweet potato that has begun to sprout. Suspend one-half of it in water. Vines will grow from most of the eyes. Pinch off the weaker vines and allow the strongest one to grow.

*Potatoes.* Find a potato with sprouting eyes. Cut a ½″ thick slice containing a sprouting eye. Plant the slice, covering the eye with ¼ inch of soil. In a few days, roots will develop from the potato and the eye will grow a vine.

Note: These plants from vegetables will live for only a few months.

*Final note:* You might want to discuss with older children (five-year-olds and older) where these vegetables and fruits *first* originated:

| Fruit | First Grown in |
|-------|----------------|
| pineapple | South America |
| potato | South America |
| peaches | Asia |
| oranges | Asia |
| carrots | Europe |

for their own drink. A variety of flavors results when certain vegetables are added to or omitted from the juice. Soups can be started in a blender. Peanut butter can also be created, using about two tablespoons of vegetable oil per cup of peanuts. Other nuts, such as almonds or walnuts, might make an interesting butter.

Fruit drinks are delicious when made in a blender. Start with strawberries or bananas, add a small amount of milk, and blend for a fruit shake. Be adventurous and try adding pineapple, cantaloupe, or any other fruit available.

For a further variation (and to teach about how liquids can change), you may want to freeze the fruit malt in an ice cube tray with popsicle sticks in each cube for individual frozen fruit-shake treats.

*Making fancy bread.* Children can make the bread dough, or you may begin with a prepared bread dough. Children then add other foods to make creative bread. Nuts, fruits, cinnamon, and a variety of other foods can be used. Baked breads can be topped with creative frostings or other toppings. Various containers can be used to bake the bread in unusual shapes. Tasks such as placing breads in and removing them from an oven should be done by adults—never by the children.

**Individual Activities.** Some of the activities suggested for groups can also be done by one child. Likewise, some of the individual activities mentioned here may also be carried out in groups, if desired.

*Collecting and using seeds.* Seeds that are edible as well as those that are not can be used. Children may be provided with a variety of seeds, or they may

be asked to find the seeds. Pumpkin, watermelon, orange, cherry, and green pepper seeds are usually available. Many creative uses for seeds can be found. Edible seeds can be baked or cooked in a variety of ways. Lima beans can be planted as well as cooked.

*Creative decorating.* Creating an "ideal" frosting or cookie topping is a good activity for children. Cupcakes or cookies can be baked in advance. Materials for making frosting or decorating can be provided. Children should be encouraged to try out foods. When they have created their "ideal" topping, they can frost their own cupcakes or decorate their own cookies.

*Creative snack time.* In place of a teacher-planned snack for the entire group, the children each create their own snack. Materials from which to choose are provided by the teacher. Choices are left up to individuals. A homemade soup, a special milk shake, or a peanut butter sandwich (homemade peanut butter) might be selected. A special fruit juice may be created. Other good suggestions for snacks include the following:

- Cheese spreads work on anything, from crackers to raw apple, potato, and turnip slices.
- Chinese celery is less stringy and more tasty than Pascal celery.
- Use flattened (rolled with a rolling pin—by the children, of course!) hamburger bun halves or refrigerator biscuits instead of English muffins for pizza.
- Peanut butter is easier for young children to spread if it has been whipped with butter or margarine: use two parts of peanut butter to one part of margarine.

# THIS ONE'S FOR YOU!

## INDIVIDUAL COOKING ACTIVITIES IN INTEREST CENTERS: ANOTHER FREE CHOICE ACTIVITY

It's John's turn to "cook" during free activity choice time. First, he washes his hands; second, he puts on a white paper chef's hat, and third, begins cutting fruit into bite-sized pieces with a plastic knife. He is following a picture recipe and will eventually put the fruit on a skewer to make a fruit kabob for his snack to be eaten later with his classmates. And, he made his snack all by himself! Independent snack preparation can easily be set up in the classroom with some basic equipment and recipes designed for individual portions.

Below are ideas and recipes to help you get started cooking independently in your classroom.

Cut off one of the end flaps of a sturdy cardboard box and cut the box apart at the side seam so it will stand up using the other end flaps as supports. This will be your instruction "board." Cover the entire box with colorful contact papers. The box can be set up on a table to designate your snack and work area. Sequential picture recipes can be clipped to each section of the box-board. For example, the pictures in sequence would indicate to (1) wash hands, (2) cut fruit into pieces, (3) put fruit on skewer, and (4) place on paper plate with name on plate. Basic equipment for your snack activity center would include measuring cups, small bowls, tongue depressors, small wire whisks, five-ounce paper cups, plastic serrated knives, electric skillet, blender, and paper chef's hats. AN ELECTRIC APPLIANCE IS OPERATED BY ADULTS ONLY.

After you've designated your snack area and gathered your equipment, you're ready to begin with the recipes that follow. Before each child actually begins their snack preparation, gather the children in a group, tell them briefly about the recipe, and remind them of any specific directions. For example, a direction might be that each child may cut up only one slice of melon. While one or two children are working in the snack area, the teacher always needs to be available for assistance as the children need it.

**Peanut Butter Pudding for One**
You'll need: 2 tablespoons dry milk; 2 tablespoons instant vanilla pudding mix; ⅓ cup water; 1 tablespoon fresh peanut butter (no sugar added)
What to do: 1. Using a tongue depressor for leveling dry ingredients, measure dry milk and pudding mix in 5-ounce paper cup. 2. Add water and stir using a small whisk, 1½ minutes. 3. Add peanut butter and whisk until smooth. 4. Chill.

**Lettuce Wrap Arounds**
You'll need: lettuce leaves; any combination of luncheon meats or cheese slices, or spreads such as cream cheese, peanut butter, or egg salad
What to do: 1. Lay lettuce leaf flat on cutting board. 2. Place meat and/or cheese slice on lettuce leaf. 3. Add a spread or other filler and roll up the combination securing with a toothpick. These may be eaten rolled up or can be cut into bite-sized pieces with a serrated knife.

**Banana Shake Bag**

You'll need: ¼ cup chopped peanuts; 1 banana

What to do: 1. After peeling banana, cut in one-inch chunks. 2. Place peanuts in a plastic baggie. 3. Put a few banana chunks at a time in the bag and shake. Serve bananas on paper plates.

**Pineapple Mix-Up**

You'll need: ¼ cup plus 1 tablespoon instant nonfat dry milk; ½ cup pineapple juice, chilled; ½ cup cracked ice

What to do: 1. For cracked ice, wrap some ice cubes in a towel and pound with a hammer. 2. Combine all ingredients in a blender and blend on high 30 seconds until thick and foamy.

Watch the food disappear at snack time because the children love these activities. Don't forget the paper chef's hats (available at a party store) or you can make your own hats! The hats make the children feel even more special, like "professional" chefs.

---

- Use Grapenuts® or wheat germ in or on top of "everything" instead of nutmeats.

*Flavored butter.* Whipping cream, interesting flavors, and a chilled bowl and beater are needed. Placing the butter in a creative container is an added touch. (This makes a nice gift for children to take home.) Lemon, orange, or honey are just a few flavors that can be added to the butter. It is best for the children to make the butter, then warm it and add the flavorings.

**Activities for Toddlers and Two- and Three-Year-Olds.** Even though more food preparation activities are being included in the early childhood program for children three years and up, adults are often inclined to think that children under the age of three would just make a mess. For example, many cooks in early childhood centers do not want to be bothered, and of course young children underfoot in a kitchen increase the risk of accidents and injuries. An alternative is to bring the foods and the appropriate utensils for cooking activities to the children's room. The term *cooking activities* in this instance includes all the steps necessary in the preparation and serving of foods, with or without the use of heat. The cooking-related activities that follow are listed in progressive order, from the simple to the more involved. Many toddlers and two-year-olds are able to master many of these activities, and most three-year-olds are capable of mastering them all.

1. Exploring cooking utensils (banging, nesting, putting away)
2. Exploring cooking utensils with water (cups, bowls, beaters, spoons, funnels)
3. Pouring dry ingredients (corn, rice)
4. Pouring wet ingredients (water)
5. Tasting fresh fruit and vegetables
6. Comparing tastes, textures, colors of *fresh* fruits and vegetables
7. Comparing tastes, textures, colors of *canned* vegetables and fruits
8. Dipping raw fruits and vegetables in dip or sauce
9. Scrubbing vegetables with brushes
10. Breaking or tearing lettuce; breaking or snapping beans; shelling peas
11. Stirring and mixing wet and dry ingredients
12. Measuring wet and dry ingredients (use rubber band to mark desired amount on container or measuring cup)
13. Placing toppings on pizza or snacks; decorating cookies or crackers that have been spread
14. Spreading on bread or crackers
15. Pouring milk or juices to drink
16. Shaking (making butter from cream or coloring sugar or coconut)
17. Rolling with both hands (peanut butter balls, pieces of dough for cookies)
18. Juicing with a hand juicer
19. Peeling hard-cooked eggs, fruits
20. Cutting with dull knife (fruits, vegetables, cheese)

21. Beating with fork or egg beater
22. Grinding with hand grinder (apples or cranberries)
23. Kneading bread dough
24. Cleaning up

---

## REDUCING SUGAR IN CHILDREN'S DIETS

Research on the human infant shows that even infants prefer sweet over bitter or sour taste (Ausubel, 1980). This preference posed no problem when early human diets consisted of natural fruit and vegetable sources of sweetness. However, when refined sugar came into our diets, the total amount of sugar consumed at one time increased. The consumption of sugar in the United States is about 104 pounds per person per year (U.S. Dept. of Agriculture and Health and Human Services, 1980). Although we do not know what proportion of all of this sugar is consumed by children, we do know many parents and teachers are trying to limit children's sugar consumption for two main reasons: the danger of tooth decay and a diet with too many empty calories.

*Tooth decay.* If teeth are not brushed frequently, sugars can cause tooth decay—dental caries or what are more commonly called "cavities." One way to avoid dental caries is to avoid foods that are high in sugar. However, some of the foods that are most likely to cause cavities (because they are high in fruit sugar or fructose) are very nutritious. Another sugar, lactose, is contained in milk. Obviously, it would not be appropriate to eliminate all sugar-containing foods. A more preferable goal is to eliminate those foods that are high in sugars and low in nutritional value.

In addition, children should brush their teeth within 30 minutes after eating the nutritious foods that are most likely to cause cavities.

*Empty calories, the prevention of obesity.* For many years, a fat baby was thought to be healthy and cute rather than a cause for concern. Today, nutritionists and pediatricians concur that infantile and childhood obesity should be prevented. Not all fat children are destined to become fat adults. Conversely, not all fat adults were fat children. However, there is evidence that obesity that begins in childhood is difficult to reverse (Goodnow and Collins, 1991).

The best plan to prevent obesity in children is to balance their caloric intake with the number of calories they expend through exercise. Children who are overweight may also have a tendency to overeat, so they may need to reduce their consumption of empty calories as well as the size of their portions.

The best way to reduce obesity is to limit empty calories—foods high in fat or sugar but low in protein, vitamins, and/or minerals. Sugar is not the only source of empty calories. High-fat and/or high-salt snacks should also be eliminated. Good choices then for snacks and meals, will include vegetables, fruit, and protein-rich items.

Because young children have a limited capacity for food intake, and because 22% of their caloric intake comes from snacks, it is important that empty calories be avoided. If between-meal snacks containing sugar are allowed, you should not be surprised when children refuse to eat more nutritious foods at mealtime. Snacks, as well as meals, must center around foods that contribute to children's need for a balanced diet.

*How to limit children's sugar intake.* There are four primary ways to limit children's sugar intake: (1) avoid obvious sources of high-sugar foods, (2) avoid "hidden" sugars, (3) find alternative sources of sweetness or reduce the amount of sugar, and (4) find other ways to celebrate special events.

Avoid high-sugar foods. The term "sugar" is generally used to refer to "sucrose," which is refined sugar from sugar cane or beets. The most common form of sucrose is white, granulated table sugar. This type of sugar is an ingredient in cakes, cookies, doughnuts, pies, candy, and soft drinks. One obvious way to reduce sugar intake is to reduce the intake of these foods. Another method is to use one half or less of the sugar called for in a recipe.

Other common forms of sugar are fructose, dextrose, lactose, and maltose. Read the list of ingredi-

# T H I N K   A B O U T   I T . . .

## LOW FAT FOODS

The American Academy of Pediatrics recommends in its *Pediatrics* journal, that all American children over the age of two years follow the lower-fat diet now recommended for adults, to prevent heart disease and obesity. In issuing the guidelines, the nation's leading organization concerned with children's health in effect adopted the advice given a decade ago by the American Heart Association.

In a statement in *Pediatrics,* the academy says all children over the age of two years should consume a daily diet containing approximately 30 percent calories from fat and no more than 300 milligrams of cholesterol.

In addition, it says, no more than 10 percent of daily calories should come from artery-clogging saturated fats, like butter and beef fat, that are solid at room temperature. Saturated fats tend to raise cholesterol levels in the blood, and elevated blood cholesterol is widely considered the leading underlying factor in heart disease.

The pediatrics group warns against overzealous restrictions in the fat content of children's diets, however, noting that some children have failed to grow normally because their parents restricted their fat intake too much. The academy emphasizes that the main goal of dietary recommendations for children is to maintain proper growth and development.

American children now derive an average of 35 percent of their total calories from fat, with 14 percent to 15 percent of calories coming from saturated fats, the academy notes. The average American child already consumes fewer than 300 milligrams of cholesterol a day, it says. (Brody, 1992)

ents on prepared foods and watch for words ending with "ose," which indicates that some form of sugar is present. These different forms of sugar have varying degrees of sweetness. For example, "lactose" (milk sugar) is the least sweet per unit. Fructose is nearly twice as sweet as sucrose, and invert sugar is about 30% sweeter than sucrose. All, however, provide basically empty calories.

Avoid hidden sugars. Most parents and teachers are aware that foods like candy, cake, and soft drinks contain sugar and are low in nutritional value. Very few people are aware, however, that sugar is also present in catsup, peanut butter, luncheon meats, hot dogs, pork and beans, nondairy creamer, fruit-flavored yogurt, and canned vegetables. Although these foods do contain nutrients, the addition of sugar is usually unnecessary. Shop for foods that contain *no* sugar.

Find alternative sources of sweetness. Snacks and desserts of unsweetened foods can be emphasized at home and school. Examples include unsalted popcorn, cheese, vegetables with dip, and no-sugar-added peanut butter on apples and celery.

Fresh fruits and vegetables should be given priority. When you must use canned fruits, look for fruits canned in their own juices or in the juices of other fruits. Avoid fruits canned in heavy syrup, and accept those canned in light syrup only if fresh or water-packed fruits are not available.

Find other ways to celebrate special events. What treats are sugar-free and calorie-free? Anything that is nonedible! Because children attach more value to foods when we offer them as special treats, adults should use their creativity to think of nonfood rewards and treats for Halloween, Valentine's Day celebrations, birthday party favors, and other holidays.

Young children enjoy small favors like barrettes, finger puppets, combs, small wind-up toys, and stuffed animals.

You might try to plan parties around an event other than food. Puppet or clown shows, a treasure hunt, group singing, gift making, or a trip to the park might be just as exciting to young children. Those of us who are responsible for the diets of young children can limit sugar consumption by avoiding obvious sources of sucrose and hidden sugars. Instead, we can use natural sources of sweetness, reduce the focus on sweetness, and find other types of treats for young children.

## FOOD AND SENSORY EXPERIENCES

Cooking and other food-related experiences provide children with many naturally fun experiences for their five senses. Young children take great pleasure in exploring with their five senses: seeing, tasting, smelling, touching, and hearing. While they can easily *see* that a carrot and a marshmallow are not alike, they find it far more exciting to close their eyes and taste, feel, or even hear the differences between them (as someone bites into each or drops them onto the table). Intriguing guessing games can be played on the spur of the moment with ordinary objects and foods, while waiting for the bus to arrive, awaiting the arrival of a guest, or while waiting for their rides home. And while playing such games, the children will be delighted to discover how useful a nose or a tongue can be!

In many cases the children can do most of the preparation themselves. Searching the room for the objects or materials needed can be almost as much fun as playing the game. In choosing activities, keep in mind the skills and preferences of the children, modifying them when necessary. Frequently the use of a blindfold is suggested. Some children prefer to pull a knitted hat over their eyes rather than have a cloth tied around their heads. Other children choose to close their eyes instead.

The following suggested activities include many food activities designed for emphasizing the senses as well as just plain "yummy" play experiences.

**Suggested Activities: Tasting**

*What is it?*   Without looking, the child tries to guess what familiar food he is eating. For the young child, offer him a chance to look at the foods first. Then, one at a time, offer him such foods as:

| | |
|---|---|
| apple slices | raisins |
| orange slices | bread |
| marshmallows | pickles |
| dry cereal | bologna |
| banana slices | olives |
| cooked spaghetti | grapes |
| granola | |

Or give him a bite of whatever you are preparing for snack! If he can't guess by tasting, let him feel and smell a piece of each food. Talk about the way it feels and smells. "Is it salty?" "Is it hard?"

*Tasting opposites.*   Assemble a few foods that have opposite tastes, such as:

sweet vs. sour; honey vs. lemon juice
salty vs. not salty: salted cracker vs. graham cracker, or pretzel vs. carrot stick

Let the child taste the opposites, compare them, and talk about which is salty, sweet, bitter, etc.

*Texture tasting.*   Compare foods with opposite textures, such as:

crunchy vs. soft (hard vs. soft): celery vs. banana; raw carrot vs. cooked carrot
smooth vs. rough: piece of spaghetti vs. pretzel

Can the tongue and teeth, as well as the fingers and eyes, tell you which is smooth, which is hard, etc.?

*Which is which?*   Gather together a few foods that look alike but are really quite different, such as:

flour and confectioner's sugar
salt and sugar
vanilla and soy sauce
instant coffee and unsweetened cocoa (add a little sugar to both to make them less bitter)

# T H I S   O N E ' S   F O R   Y O U !

## SNACK TIME EXPERIENCES

Snack time is an obvious time for food experiences. But snack time also provides a natural opportunity for both social and small motor physical experiences. Consider these ideas:

**Small muscle development**
- Let children pour their own milk or juice. For a pitcher they can handle, use a clear plastic 8-ounce measuring cup with a small amount of milk or juice in it.
- Before pouring liquids, have children practice pouring dry things such as rice or salt with the measuring cup first.
- To help children pass out eating utensils, use small serving trays. (Like those used in elementary school cafeterias.) Line the trays with sheets of paper towels, colorful tissue paper, or colored construction paper. Lay out the spoons, forks, and napkins on top. The children will find the trays easier to hold when moving around the table.
- Use muffin tins as trays when passing out cups of juice or milk. The individual muffin cups keep mugs from tipping over.

**Social skills**
- To help young children remember to sit close to the table during snack time, try saying, "Tummy to the table, girls and boys." The saying helps the children understand what they are to do in words they can understand. You'll find they'll use it among themselves at snack time as a reminder of proper seating.
- Placemat "cues" help young children remember the correct placement of utensils when setting the table. Make placemats out of vinyl window shades. On each mat, use a permanent felt marker to draw a large circle for a plate and a smaller circle for a cup in their proper places. Placing the cup or glass circle above the plate circle (closer to the center of the table and away from the side of the plate) cuts down on accidental spills at snack time.
- Encourage children to make new friends in the group. Make place cards for each child, and let children take turns setting the cards out on the table at snack time. You may also use paper cups with children's names written on them as place cards.
- For further social learning, make personal placemats for each child. Cut out squares, rectangles, and oval shapes from heavy paper. Let each child choose a shape for her placemat. In the center of the paper shape, glue a photo of the child, either brought from home, or taken at school. Write the child's name under the photo in large letters and let the child decorate the rest of the placemat with markers, crayons, glued-on fabric pieces and trims, bits of shiny paper, etc. Laminate the placemat or cover it with clear contact paper.
- These placemats provide natural topics of conversation as they are laid out at snack time: children learn their own and other children's names, discuss letters in each other's names, hair/eye colors, clothes shown in the photo, how much one has grown and changed since the photo was taken, and so on.

Let the child look carefully at a small amount of the "look-alikes" (on a plate or in a baby food jar, for example). Can he guess what they are without tasting? Then let him taste them to see whether his eyes were right. (Only the tongue can tell for sure!)

## Suggested Activities: Smelling

*Smell collection.* Assemble a group of containers that look more or less alike, such as baby food jars, pill bottles, small tea containers, etc. Put a small amount of each smelling substance into a container (one substance per container). Possibilities include:

| | |
|---|---|
| cinnamon | coffee grounds |
| vanilla | tea leaves |
| cloves | black pepper |
| tobacco | vinegar |
| perfume | talcum powder |

chocolate (powder or chips)
mint leaves (dried or fresh)
lemon (dried, grated peel keeps longer than fresh)
orange (dried peel keeps longer than fresh)
rubbing alcohol
onions or garlic (can be used for a while, but will soon get moldy)

Let the child try to guess what each substance is by smelling it. Young children often prefer not to be blindfolded, whereas older children may enjoy the blindfold. Either way, it's fun.

Variation: Instead of putting "smells" into special containers, simply let the child sniff the foods you are preparing, such as onions, soy sauce, lemon juice, vanilla, cinnamon, etc. Or reach into the refrigerator and pull out a few foods with different smells. When possible, offer the child a taste after he does the smelling.

*Matching smells.* Dip cotton balls into various liquid "smells," such as lemon juice, rubbing alcohol, vanilla, perfume, vinegar, etc. Glue each onto a small square of cardboard. Make two of each smell. Or pour a little of each into small containers, again making two of each. Let the child try to match the smells by sniffing (but not by drinking, unless the liquid is edible!).

*Traveling smell experiment.* Put a small container of a strong-smelling substance at one end of the room. Try, for example, perfume, vinegar, slice of onion, or ammonia. Or spray a bit of room freshener, perfume, or even bathroom cleaner on one side of the room. How long does it take before the people on the other side of the room can smell it? At lunchtime, can the children guess what's for lunch without peeking or even going into the kitchen?

## SUMMARY

Foods can be used in activities that help children become more creative in their approach to the world. Food activities help young children learn new information and skills. They develop knowledge about names of shapes and colors; tastes; changes in shape, size, color, and taste; and new words. Food activities also help young children develop skills in hand–eye and small-muscle coordination, simple measuring, and socialization.

In order to ensure that food experiences for young children are planned to enhance their creativity, they must include the following basic guidelines: They must (1) be open-ended, not like a cookbook; (2) be challenging, but not too hard for three- to five-year-olds; (3) be varied, giving children choices; (4) emphasize the doing, not the end product; (5) involve inexpensive materials; and (6) not be dangerous to children.

Food activities can be done in groups or by children working alone. It is important that children be allowed to make decisions for themselves about what foods to use and how to use them. Adults responsible for the diets of young children must limit sugar consumption by avoiding obvious sources of sucrose and hidden sugars. Using natural sources of sweetness, reducing the focus on sweets, and finding other types of sweets for young children are all essential ways to reduce sugar in children's diets.

# LEARNING ACTIVITIES

A. Try testing the sense of taste of some fellow students by making "creative cocktail juice."
1. Materials and ingredients:
Blender
Common vegetables: cucumber, carrots, tomatoes, cabbage, celery, green pepper, and parsley root
Salt
Sugar
Lemon juice
2. Begin with any two vegetables. Add one-half cup of cold water or crushed ice and blend. A pinch of salt and sugar and a small amount of lemon juice will improve the flavor. Taste a small amount. (It may not taste good.)
3. Add a third vegetable to the mixture. Taste. Keep track of the vegetables and amounts used. Continue to add vegetables, one at a time. Try to make:
a. A tasty vegetable juice
b. A juice whose vegetables no one can identify
c. A mystery juice
d. A bad-tasting juice. Then try to improve the taste using ingredients suggested above.
B. Observe a group of children experiencing a type of food for the first time—perhaps eggplant, squash, or beef tongue.

1. What kinds of expressions do they make when they taste the food?
2. How do they react when they find out what the food was that they tasted?
3. What can be said to make a child more willing to taste new foods?
C. Experiment with the taste sense of adults and children.
1. Each person who tastes a food in this experiment must wear a blindfold or cover his eyes.
2. Use small slices of baking apples or potatoes and a freshly sliced onion or garlic.
3. Hold the onion under the blindfolded person's nose. Slip a small piece of apple or potato into the person's mouth. Have the person chew up the food and tell what it was.
4. Try this holding other strong-smelling foods under the nose of the blindfolded person.
a. Are children or adults better at discovering what it really is they are chewing?
b. Try telling adults that they are chewing onion. Hold garlic under their noses, and place pieces of potato into their mouths.
c. Ask children and adults what this experiment tells them about the sense of taste.
D. With a group of children, try out at least one of the food experiences listed in this unit. Evaluate the ex-

| Supermarket | Grocery boxes, cash register, play money, paper pads, pencils, paper sacks, empty food cartons, grocery carts, grocery aprons, cans with smooth edges, food posters, food scale, bread sacks stuffed with paper, plastic foods, number stamps and stamp pads, telephone. |
|---|---|
| Dairy store or milkman | Plastic bottles, milk cartons, wagon or cart, white hat and coat, ice cream cartons, ice cream scoop, ice cream cones, ice cream posters, malt/milk shake cups, sundae dishes. |
| Restaurant | Order pads, dishes, tablecloth, silverware, chef's hat, cash register, hot dog stand, menus, napkin dispensers, aprons, waitress hats, disposable containers, paper bags from drive-ins. |
| Cooking | Pots, dishes, egg beater, toy toaster, aprons, spoons, pitchers, rolling pin, flour sifter, empty spice containers, funnel, salt boxes, empty food containers, skillet, pancake turner, ice cube tray, pictures of food mounted on cardboard, TV dinner trays, plastic foods, measuring cups, cookie cutters. |

FIGURE 21–14 Learning centers related to food experiences.

perience. Would you use this recipe again? Would you organize the experience in the same way next time? If not, what changes would you make?

E. Try out at least two of the cooking experiences suggested in this unit. Where materials are suggested, prepare the materials. Evaluate each experience.

F. Develop your own additional food-related activities.

G. Prepare a lesson plan on a food theme. Try to include at least one food experience during the week.

## ACTIVITIES FOR CHILDREN

### Songs, Fingerplays, Poems Related to Cooking and Food Experiences

Some well-known poems to use:

Pat-a-Cake
Muffin Man
Little Jack Horner
Mulberry Bush
Cats, Peas, Beans and Barley
To Market, To Market
Peas Porridge Hot
Little Tommy Tucker

**Two Little Apples**
Two little apples hanging on a tree
  (Arms out with hand turned down)
Two little apples smiling at me
  (Turn hands up)
I shook that tree as hard as I could
  (Shaking motion)
Down came the apples. Mmmmmm—
Were they good!
  (Falling motion: rub tummy)

**Pumpkins**
A pumpkin is big
  (Circle arms over head)
A pumpkin is round
  (Circle arms in front)
A pumpkin has a great big smile
  (Outline smile on mouth)
But doesn't make a sound.

**My Pumpkin**
Here's my orange pumpkin
  (Have hands outspread)
Big and fat and round
  (Hold hands above one another, outspread and extended; then make circle with hands)
It's the very best one
I could find downtown
  (Point in that direction)

Now I need to make a nose
A mouth, some eyes
  (Pretend to cut)

Or mother'll want to use it
  (Motion to remove)
To cook and bake some pies
  (Act like stirring)

See my jack-o-lantern
Smiling right at you
  (Smile)
You don't need to be afraid
  (Look frightened)
He can't holler "Boo!"

**Making Cookies**
I am making cookie dough.
Round and round the beaters go.

Add some flour from a cup.
Stir and stir the batter up.

Roll them; cut them; nice and neat;
Put them on a cookie sheet.

Bake them; count them; one, two, three.
Serve them to my friends for tea.

**Hot Cross Buns**
Hot cross buns,
Hot cross buns,
One-a-penny, two-a-penny,
Hot cross buns.

**I'm a Little Teapot**
I'm a little teapot, short and stout.
This is my handle,
This is my spout,
When I get all steamed up, then I shout.
Just tip me over and pour me out.

**Bananas**
When I first saw bananas grow
  (Bend and stretch fingers of both hands)
I couldn't help but frown.
I thought I was mistaken, but
The fruit hung upside down.
  (Make hands into cluster, holding the fingers down)

When I first saw potatoes grow,
  (Form a potato with both hands)

I had a big surprise—
I found them growing underground
How could they use their eyes?
   (Point to eyes)

**Five Currant Buns**

Five currant buns in the baker's shop.
Big and round with sugar on top.
Along came *(name of child)* with a penny one day,
She/he bought one and took it away.

**Lickety-lick**

Lickety-lick, lickety-lick,
The batter is getting all thickety-thick.
What shall we bake?
What shall we bake?
A great big beautiful, chocolate cake!

**Pancakes**

Mix a pancake,
Stir a pancake,
Pop it in the pan;
Fry the pancake,
Toss the pancake,
Catch it if you can.

**Apple Tree**

This is the tree
With leaves so green
   (Make leaf with hand; fingers outstretched)

Here are the apples
That hang in between.
   (Make fists)

When the wind blows
The apples will fall
Here is the basket to gather them all.

## Original Recipes

Ask each child to dictate a recipe to you that is made in his home. Write it down *exactly* as he tells you (mistakes and funny parts, too). Put the recipes together in a little booklet for parents. It will be a treasure to save and enjoy for years to come.

## Great Grapes

Give young children the opportunity to make choices and be creative by concocting their own snacks using only one harvest food—grapes! Set out an assortment of red, purple, and green grapes. Discuss the many grape products we eat or drink (jelly, juice, etc.). Suggest that children brainstorm new ways to prepare and eat grape snacks.

Here are a few suggestions for great grape snacks. A grape cookbook, with each recipe signed by the cook, would be a wonderful follow-up activity.

*Frozen Grapes* ☺

Place washed grapes on a cookie sheet with spaces between each one. Cut them in half to avoid choking. Freeze. When frozen, place in a plastic bag. Eat frozen.

*Grapes to Raisins* ☺

Wash and dry a large bunch of green grapes. Place in a basket in a warm sunny spot for four to seven days. You will then have raisins!

*Grape Fruit Cocktail*

Slice grapes in half with plastic kinves. Add sliced grapes to a can of fruit cocktail. Add fresh fruit chunks as desired.

*Grape Surprises* ☺
A. Ingredients:
   ½ cup peanut butter
   ½ cup nonfat dry milk powder
   2 tablespoons honey
   grapes
B. Procedure:
   1. Mix peanut butter, milk powder, and honey until a soft, non-sticky "dough" is formed.
   2. Knead dough, then press out pieces into 2-inch circles.
   3. Place a grape in the center. Wrap dough around grape and seal well.
   4. Variation: Place grapes inside cream cheese balls, then roll in chopped nuts.

*Grape Clusters*
A. Ingredients:
   6 ounces chocolate chips
   1 tablespoon shortening
   small bunches of grapes
   chopped nuts or crisp rice cereal
B. Procedure:
   1. Melt chocolate and shortening in double boiler.
   2. Dip tips of bunch of grapes in melted chocolate.
   3. Immediately dip into nuts or cereal. Let set.

*Grapes and Yogurt* ☺
A. Ingredients:
   small bunch of grapes
   1 cup yogurt or sour cream
B. Procedure: Slice grapes with plastic knife and add to yogurt (or sour cream).

## Recipes for Cooking Experiences

### Cheesy French Fries ☺
A. Ingredients:
1 package (9 ounces) frozen french fried potatoes
½ teaspoon salt
dash pepper
½ cup grated sharp cheese
B. Procedure:
1. Preheat oven to 450°F.
2. Arrange potatoes on cookie sheet.
3. Sprinkle with salt and pepper.
4. Bake uncovered 15 minutes.
5. Sprinkle cheese over potatoes.
6. Bake 2–3 minutes longer or until cheese is melted.

### Turtle Cookies
A. Ingredients:
⅓ cup margarine
2 beaten eggs
1 cup flour
2 squares chocolate
¾ cup sugar
1 teaspoon vanilla
B. Procedure:
1. Melt butter and chocolate in a pan. Let cool.
2. In another bowl, mix the eggs, sugar, vanilla, flour; then add the melted chocolate mixture.
3. Bake in waffle iron, 1 teaspoon batter for each turtle. Bake 2–3 minutes.

### Cocoa Mix
A. Ingredients:
4 cups dry milk
1 cup cocoa
1½ cups sugar
pinch of salt
B. Procedure:
1. Stir until well mixed.
2. Pour mix into a jar or can with a lid.
3. When ready to use, fill glass about ¼ full of cocoa mix.
4. Pour hot or cold water over cocoa and stir until mixed.

### Chocolate Milk Shake
A. For each serving:
½ cup cold milk
3 tablespoons chocolate syrup
2 scoops vanilla ice cream
B. Mix just to blend.

### Lemonade
A. For each serving:
juice of 1 lemon (about ⅓ cup)
1 cup water
5 teaspoons sugar
B. Combine; pour over ice in tall glass.

### Apple Sauce
A. Ingredients:
2½ pounds apples, cooking variety
½ cup water
½–⅔ cup sugar
B. Procedure:
1. Peel apples, cut into quarters, and remove cores.
2. Put in metal saucepan, add water, and cover.
3. Cook over medium heat until it boils, then simmer over low heat for 20 to 25 minutes until the apples are tender. (May be necessary to add more water.)
4. Beat apples until smooth with spoon.
5. Stir sugar in until it dissolves. (It may require more sugar depending on the tartness of the apples.)
6. Serve warm or cold. Makes 10 servings.

### Orangeade
A. For each serving:
⅓ cup fresh orange juice
2 tablespoons lemon juice
2 cups water
1 tablespoon sugar
B. Combine. Pour over ice.

### Limeade
A. For each serving:
juice of 1 lime
1 cup of water
5 teaspoons sugar
B. Combine. Pour over ice.

### Stuffed Baked Apples ☺
A. Ingredients:
4 tart tapples
¼ cup crunchy breakfast cereal
¼ cup chopped walnuts
¼ teaspoon cinnamon
1 cup raisins
2 tablespoons honey
B. Procedure:
1. Core apples.
2. Combine ingredients and spoon equal amounts into each apple cavity.

3. Place apples in shallow baking dish and add ¼ cup of water.
4. Bake uncovered for 40 minutes at 300°F.

*Banana Breakfast Split* ☺
A. Ingredients:
    1 banana, sliced lengthwise
    ½ cup cottage cheese
    1 tablespoon wheat germ
    1 tablespoon raisins
    1 tablespoon chopped nuts
B. Procedure:
    1. Place banana slices in a bowl.
    2. Put scoops of cottage cheese on top.
    3. Sprinkle with wheat germ, raisins, and nuts. Makes one serving.

*Pear Bunnies* ☺
A. Ingredients:
    ripe pear, cut in half lengthwise
    1 lettuce leaf
    1 teaspoon cottage cheese
    1 red cherry
    raisins
    almond slivers
B. Procedure:
    Place pear half on lettuce leaf, rounded side up. Decorate, using cottage cheese for "cottontail," cherry for nose, raisins for eyes, and almond slivers for ears.

*Pretzels* ☺
A. Ingredients:
    1 cake yeast
    1¼ cups warm water
    ¼ teaspoon salt
    1½ teaspoons sugar
    4 cups flour
    1 beaten egg
B. Procedure:
    1. In large bowl, dissolve yeast in warm water.
    2. Add salt, sugar, flour, and knead mixture into a soft dough. (Children *love* to do this.) DO NOT LET THE DOUGH RISE.
    3. Cut unrisen dough into small pieces and roll into ropes. Do not make ropes too thick, because they will swell during baking.
    4. Let children twist the ropes into pretzel shapes and place them on a foil-covered cookie sheet dusted with flour.
    5. Brush with beaten egg. Bake at 400°F until golden brown. Makes 4 dozen pretzels.

*Fruit Leather* ☺
This recipe reinforces the concept that fruits like apricots, peaches, raspberries, apples, etc., can be changed and used in new ways.

A. Ingredients:
    1 quart or 2 pounds of fresh fruit
    sugar
    cinnamon
    plastic wrapping paper
B. Procedure:
    1. Help children break open, peel, and seed or pit fruit.
    2. Puree prepared fruit in blender until smooth.
    3. Add 2 tablespoons sugar and ½ teaspoon cinnamon to each 2 cups of puree.
    4. Pour mixture onto sheet of plastic wrap that has been placed on a large cookie sheet. Spread mixture thinly and evenly.
    5. Cover mixture with a screen or a piece of cheesecloth and place in the sun until completely dry— about one or two days. It can then be eaten, or rolled and stored.

*Peanutty Pudding* ☺
A. Ingredients:
    1 package regular pudding
    2 cups milk
    peanut butter
B. Procedure:
    1. Prepare pudding as directed on package. (You may choose to use the sugar-free type.)
    2. Pour cooked pudding into individual bowls.
    3. While still warm, stir in 1 tablespoon peanut butter to each bowl.

*Fruit Kabobs* ☺
A. Ingredients
    1 cup vanilla or lemon yogurt (low-fat, low-sugar variety)
    2 cups fresh or canned fruit (chunk-style)
    pretzel sticks
B. Procedure:
    1. Thread fruit chunks onto pretzel sticks. Talk about how colors and sizes look next to each other.
    2. Dip each end piece into the yogurt before eating, or spoon yogurt over the entire kabob.

*Strawberry Yogurt Shake* ☺
A. Ingredients:
    ½ cup frozen unsweetened strawberries, thawed
    2 tablespoons frozen orange juice concentrate, thawed

½ banana (optional)
1 cup vanilla or lemon yogurt
B. Procedure:
1. Puree strawberries in blender.
2. Add remaining ingredients to blender and mix until frothy.
3. For holidays or special occasions, stick straws through colorful paper shapes and serve with shakes. Makes two servings, ¾ cup each.

*Peanut Butter Banana Smoothie* ☺
A. Ingredients:
1 cup vanilla yogurt
1 to 2 tablespoons peanut butter
1 banana
B. Procedure:
1. Combine all ingredients in blender.
2. Whip for 30 to 60 seconds or until smooth.
3. Serve in custard cup or small bowl to eat with a spoon, or pour into cups to drink.

*Broccoli Trees and Snow* ☺
A. Ingredients:
¾ cup small-curd cottage cheese
½ cup plain yogurt
¼ cup fresh minced parsley
1 bunch broccoli
B. Procedure:
1. Mix cottage cheese and yogurt in blender until smooth.
2. Add parsley and refrigerate until cool.
3. Cut broccoli into "dippers." (Cucumbers, zucchini, celery, carrots, radishes, and green peppers make good "dippers," too.)
4. Dip vegetables into yogurt mix and enjoy.

*Fruit Sun* ☺
A. Ingredients:
grapefruit, sections
muskmelon, balls
cherries
raisins
B. Procedure:
1. Arrange grapefruit sections in a ring around muskmelon balls.
2. Cherries and raisins may be used to make a face.
3. Amounts depend on the number to be served. ½-cup servings are appropriate.

*Pigs in a Blanket* ☺
A. Ingredients:
frankfurters
bread slices
American cheese

butter
mustard
B. Procedure:
1. Spread butter on bread.
2. Place bread slices on ungreased baking sheet and top each with a slice of cheese.
3. Place frankfurters diagonally on cheese.
4. Fold bread over to form triangle. Brush with butter.
5. Set broiler at 550°F.
6. Broil about 2 minutes.

*Muffins*
A. Ingredients:
2 cups flour, sifted
3 teaspoons baking powder
1 egg beaten
½ teaspoon salt
1 cup milk
¼ cup fat, melted, or cooking oil
¼ cup sugar
B. Procedure:
1. Sift dry ingredients together into a large bowl; make a well in the center.
2. In another small bowl, beat the egg until foamy; add the milk and melted fat.
3. Add the liquid ingredients to the well in the dry ingredients. Stir until the dry ingredients are moist, but still lumpy. *Don't overmix.*
4. Fill greased muffin tins ½ full.
5. Bake at 400°F for 15–20 minutes. Makes 12.
6. To vary, add ½ cup chopped nuts, ¾ cup fresh blueberries, ½ cup halved cranberries, or ¾ cup cut-up dates.

*Fruit Tapioca*
A. Ingredients:
2 cups fruit
2 cups water
4 tablespoons minute tapioca
½ cup sugar
B. Procedure:
1. Place ingredients in saucepan.
2. Put over low flame. Stir frequently.
3. Boil until clear.
4. Use tart fruit: apples, apricots, cherries, rhubarb, pineapple, raspberries.

*Bread Pudding*
A. Ingredients:
6 slices day-old bread
2 cups milk
¼ cup sugar
3 tablespoons butter

| | | | |
|---|---|---|---|
| Toast | Cinnamon, orange, honey and butter, variety of toppings. | Vegetables | Make stew. Scrub potatoes or carrots. Shell peas. Snap beans. Cook vegetables and compare with uncooked. Clean radishes. Clean and stuff celery with peanut butter, cheese. |
| Fruits | Fresh fruit salad, apple crisp, baked apples. Prepare orange juice. Peel oranges and count segments. Pomegranate—cut open and examine the seeds. Put coconut in a "feel bag." Open the coconut and share the milk. Bring in shredded coconut for comparison. Peel bananas. Compare dried, canned, and fresh. Cut apple cross-wise. Count the seeds. good lesson in fractions. Make lemonade, orangeade, limeade. Clean and hull strawberries. Make jam. Plant seeds of any fruits. Make apple sauce. Bake pumpkin seeds with butter and salt. Cut and taste fresh pineapple. Cut and serve melons. | Soup | Canned soup. Packaged dehydrated soup. Add noodles and macaroni. Clean vegetables for soup. |
| | | Pudding | Tapioca, chocolate, rice, bread. |
| | | Pancakes | Mix batter and use electric skillet. Spread with jelly and roll up to eat. |
| | | Gelatin | Add fresh fruit or tiny pieces of celery, carrots or other favorite raw vegetables or fruit. |
| | | Special Projects | Make butter using churn or by simply shaping cream in covered jar. Make popcorn. Freeze ice cubes or popsicles of fruit juice. Make blueberry muffins. |
| Sandwiches | Many varieties! Let each child make a small open-faced sandwich. Try peanut butter, pimento, cheese, etc. | Crackers | Spread crackers with cheese, peanut butter, or butter. Spread graham crackers with frostings, peanut butter. |
| Icings | Start with basic white icing made from soft butter, powdered sugar, milk, and vanilla. Let each child add his own food coloring to a small amount of icing in his own paper cup. Add raisins or chocolate bits. Spread on cookies or graham crackers. | Cottage Cheese | Mix with pineapple tidbits, raisins, sunflower seeds. |
| Instant Puddings | Add chocolate bits, raisins, small pieces of peppermint candy, pieces of canned fruits. | Milk | Add chocolate or carob flavoring. Make milk shakes, cocoa. |

FIGURE 21–15 Cooking ideas for preschool and early childhood classrooms.

½ teaspoon salt
3 eggs
1 teaspoon vanilla
½ teaspoon nutmeg
B. Procedure:
   1. Place day-old bread in buttered baking dish.
   2. Scald milk.
   3. Add butter, sugar, and salt.
   4. Beat eggs and slowly pour milk over eggs. Mix thoroughly.
   5. Add flavoring.
   6. Pour mixture over bread.
   7. Bake at 350°F for 1 hour.

## Meatballs ☺

A. Ingredients:
   1 pound hamburger
   1 cup bread crumbs
   1 or 2 eggs
   ¾ teaspoon salt
   ⅛ teaspoon pepper
   ¼ cup milk
B. Procedure:
   1. Mix ingredients well.
   2. Shape into small balls.
   3. Brown until cooked through in electric skillet.

## Carrot and Raisin Salad ☺

A. Ingredients:
   3 cups shredded carrots (teacher)
   ¾ cup raisins
   juice of one lemon
   3 tablespoons sugar
   dash of salt
B. Procedure:
   1. Mix ingredients thoroughly.
   2. Serve immediately.

## Double Orange Pops

A. Ingredients:
   1 package (3 ounces) orange gelatin
   2 cups water
   ½ cup sugar
   2 cups orange juice
B. Materials: ice cube tray, small paper cups, frozen pop molds, wooden sticks, plastic spoons
C. Procedure:
   1. Dissolve gelatin and sugar in boiling water.
   2. Add orange juice.
   3. Pour into trays, cups, or molds.
   4. Insert wooden sticks or plastic spoons diagonally in each ice cube section, or at an angle in molds or cups for handles. Freeze until firm—2 to 3 hours. Makes 20 to 24 pops.

## Banana Bake ☺

A. Ingredients:
   1 banana, peeled
   butter, melted
B. Procedure:
   1. Place peeled banana in shallow baking dish and brush with melted butter.
   2. Bake in moderate oven (375°F) from 10 to 15 minutes (until tender).
   3. Serve hot as a vegetable.
   4. Yield: 1 serving.

## No-Cook Peanut Butter Fudge

A. Ingredients:
   1 cup peanut butter
   1 cup Karo syrup
   1¼ cups nonfat dry milk solids
   1 cup sifted confectioners sugar
B. Procedure:
   1. Blend peanut butter and syrup in large mixing bowl.
   2. Measure nonfat dry milk solids and sifted confectioners sugar and add all at once.
   3. Mix all together—first with a spoon and then with the hands; knead in dry ingredients.
   4. Turn onto board and continue kneading until mixture is well blended and smooth.
   5. Press out with the hands or a rolling pin into square.
   6. Dough should be ½" thick.
   7. Cut into squares.
   8. Top with nutmeats, if desired. Makes about 2 pounds.

## Muffins

A. Ingredients:
   2 cups self-rising flour
   2 cups softened vanilla ice cream
   1 egg and 2 tablespoons cooking oil (optional)
B. Materials: muffin tins, mixing bowl
C. Procedure:
   1. Combine in mixing bowl self-rising flour and softened vanilla ice cream. Beat until smooth.
   2. Fill lined muffin tins ¾ full.
   3. Bake at 425°F for 20 to 25 minutes, or until golden brown.
   4. Yield: 12 large or 24 small muffins.
   5. For richer muffins, add egg and cooking oil.

## Honey Balls ☺

A. Ingredients:
   3 tablespoons honey
   4 tablespoons peanut butter (freshly made)
   ½ cup nonfat dry milk
   ¼ cup dry cereal flakes, crushed

B. Procedure:
1. Mix honey and peanut butter.
2. Gradually add nonfat dry milk; mix well.
3. Form into balls with greased hands.
4. Roll in dry cereal flakes.
5. Chill until firm. Makes 18 balls.

## French Toast ☺
A. Ingredients:
8 slices bread
4 eggs
¼ tablespoon salt
2 cups milk
B. Procedure:
1. Beat eggs slightly. Add salt and milk.
2. Dip slices of bread in egg mixture and fry in electric skillet.
3. Serve hot with jelly, honey, or syrup.

## Carob-Nut Snack ☺
A. Ingredients:
1 cup dry-roasted unsalted peanuts
1 cup unsweetened carob chips
1 cup unsweetened dried banana chips
1 cup unsweetened cereal
B. Procedure:
Children can take turns shaking ingredients in a plastic container with lid to mix. Serve in small cups, or carry in plastic bags on field trips. Can be stored in container for several weeks.

## No-Bake Brownies ☺
A. Ingredients:
1 cup fresh peanut butter (no sugar added)
1 cup nonfat dry milk
¼ cup soy protein powder (plain, no dextrose or other sugar substitutes)
1 teaspoon vanilla
2 tablespoons carob powder (or cocoa if you don't mind the caffeine)
½ cup fructose
¾ cup water
½ cup raisins (optional)
coconut or chopped nuts (optional)
B. Procedure:
1. Mix peanut butter, dry milk, carob (or cocoa), fructose, and vanilla with mixer or pastry blender.
2. Add water, a little at a time, mixing after each addition. At first it may seem too wet, but the water will be absorbed.
3. Add raisins. Add more water if needed.
4. Press mixture into 8″ × 8″ pan sprayed with non-stick coating.
5. Sprinkle coconut or chopped nuts on top.
6. Cut into squares. Refrigerate unused portion.

## Chow Mein Crunchies
A. Ingredients:
1 package chocolate chips (or 1 package butterscotch chips)
1 can chow mein noodles
1 cup salted peanuts
B. Procedure:
1. Melt chocolate chips in a double boiler or in a saucepan over very low heat.
2. Add chow mein noodles and salted peanuts.
3. Stir until the noodles are coated with chocolate mixture.
4. Drop by spoonfuls on waxed paper.
5. Place in refrigerator until cool.

## Jam Brown-n-Serve ☺
A. Ingredients:
6 brown-n-serve rolls
1 teaspoon melted margarine
6 teaspoons apricot preserves
B. Procedure:
1. Brush butter over top of rolls.
2. Make lengthwise cuts in top of roll.
3. Insert 1 teaspoon of preserves.
4. Bake in greased shallow pan at 200°F for 10 to 12 minutes.

## Cottage Cheese Cookies
A. Ingredients:
¼ cup butter
½ cup sugar
½ cup cottage cheese
1 teaspoon vanilla
1 cup flour
¼ teaspoon salt
1 teaspoon baking powder
B. Materials: fork, cookie sheet
C. Procedure:
1. Mix butter and sugar.
2. Add cottage cheese and vanilla.
3. Add flour, salt, and baking powder.
4. Stir. Smooth into balls.
5. Put on greased cookie sheet. Flatten with fork. Bake at 375°F for 10 to 15 minutes.

## Stir-n-Drop Cookies
A. Ingredients:
2 eggs
⅔ cup cooking oil
2 teaspoons vanilla
¾ cup sugar
2 cups flour, sifted
2 teaspoons baking powder
½ teaspoon salt
B. Materials: cookie sheet, fork

C. Procedure:
1. Break the eggs. Beat with a fork.
2. Stir oil and vanilla into egg mixture.
3. Blend in sugar until mixture thickens.
4. Add baking powder, flour, and salt to egg and sugar mixture. Stir.
5. Drop by teaspoonfuls 2 inches apart on ungreased cookie sheets.
6. Press round with bottom of a glass dipped in sugar.
7. Bake at 400°F for 8 to 10 minutes.

## Scrambled Eggs ☺
A. Ingredients:
eggs, one per child
milk, salt, pepper as desired
B. Materials: fry pan or electric skillet
C. Procedure:
1. Permit each child to break an egg into a bowl.
2. Beat the egg with a fork.
3. Add milk, salt, and pepper as desired.
4. Cook in fry pan or electric skillet.

## Uncooked Fondant
A. Ingredients:
2⅓ cups confectioners sugar
½ cup sweetened condensed milk
1 teaspoon vanilla
food coloring
walnut pieces
B. Procedure:
1. Put sugar into bowl.
2. Slowly add milk and vanilla.
3. Mix until smooth.
4. Tint with food coloring.
5. Drop on flat pieces on waxed paper.
6. Press walnut piece on top of each.

## Ice Cream
A. Ingredients:
4 eggs
2½ cups sugar
6 cups milk
4 cups light cream
2 tablespoons vanilla
½ teaspoon salt
B. Procedure:
1. Beat eggs until light.
2. Add sugar gradually, beating until mixture thickens.
3. Add remaining ingredients; mix thoroughly.
4. Freeze in ice cream freezer. Makes 1 gallon.

## Flavored Milk Drinks
For each serving, add the following syrups, fruits, or flavorings to a tall glass. Fill glass with cold milk and stir thoroughly. Serve.

Maple: 2 tablespoons maple syrup
Caramel: ½ to 2 tablespoons caramel syrup
Berry: 2 teaspoons strawberry or raspberry jam or ice cream topping or thawed frozen berries, and 2 to 3 drops red food coloring

## Peanut Butter Balls ☺
A. Ingredients:
½ cup fresh peanut butter
1 tablespoon jelly
½ cup dry milk powder
1 cup bran or corn flakes
⅓ cup bran or corn flakes (crushed)
B. Procedure:
1. Mix the peanut butter and jelly in bowl.
2. Stir in milk powder and 1 cup bran or corn flakes. Mix well.
3. With your hands, roll the mix into small balls. Roll the balls in the crushed flakes.

## Peanut Butter Apple Rolls ☺
A. Ingredients:
1 8-ounce can refrigerated crescent rolls
2 tablespoons fresh peanut butter
1 apple, peeled and finely chopped
B. Procedure:
1. Separate dough into 8 triangles
2. Spread a thick layer of peanut butter on each triangle.
3. Top with 1 tablespoon of apple.
4. Start at the shortest side of each triangle and roll to other side. Place on cookie sheet.
5. Bake at 350°F for 10–15 minutes.

## Peanut Grahams
A. Ingredients:
graham crackers
fresh peanut butter
one or more of the following toppings—nuts, sunflower seeds, raisins, chocolate chips, sliced bananas, sliced apples
B. Procedure:
1. Break each graham cracker in half.
2. Spread some peanut butter on one half.
3. Place your favorite topping on the peanut butter.
4. Spread some peanut butter on the other graham cracker half.
5. Press the two halves together to make a sandwich.

*Peanut Logs* ☺
A. Ingredients:
    1 cup creamy peanut butter
    1 cup honey
    1 cup instant nonfat dry milk
    1 cup raisins
    1 cup graham cracker crumbs
B. Procedure:
    1. Blend peanut butter, honey, and dry milk.
    2. Add raisins and mix well.
    3. Stir in graham cracker crumbs.
    4. Roll teaspoonfuls of mixture on waxed paper to shape into logs.
    5. Refrigerate one hour. Makes about 50.

*Nutty Swiss Cheese Spread* ☺
A. Ingredients:
    2 cups Swiss cheese, shredded
    ½ cup fresh peanut butter
    ½ cup sour cream
    ¼ cup raisins
B. Procedure:
    1. Mix all ingredients well.
    2. Use spread on bread or crackers.

*Graham Cracker Bananas* ☺
A. Ingredients:
    4 bananas
    ¼ cup evaporated milk
    ½ cup graham cracker crumbs
    ¼ cup butter or margarine, melted
B. Procedure:
    1. Peel bananas and cut in half lengthwise.
    2. Roll bananas in milk, then roll in graham cracker crumbs.
    3. Place in greased baking dish. Pour melted butter over top.
    4. Bake at 450°F for 10 minutes.

*Chocolate Oranges*
A. Ingredients:
    2 or 3 oranges
    ½ cup chocolate chips
    3 tablespoons butter
B. Procedure:
    1. Carefully peel the oranges by hand, and separate them into segments.
    2. Melt butter and chocolate chips over low heat.
    3. Dip half of each segment into the chocolate and place on a plate covered with plastic wrap.
    4. Refrigerate right away for at least 15 minutes before serving. You can use strawberries and bananas, too.

*Rice Pudding* ☺
A. Ingredients:
    4 tablespoons uncooked rice
    4 cups milk
    1 tablespoon butter
    3 tablespoons sugar (optional)
    ½ teaspoon vanilla extract
    nutmeg
B. Procedure:
    1. Combine all ingredients except nutmeg in buttered casserole.
    2. Sprinkle nutmeg on top.
    3. Bake at 300°F for 1½ hours.

*Devils Food Cookies*
A. Ingredients:
    1 box devil's food cake mix
    2 eggs, slightly beaten
    1 tablespoon water
    ½ cup vegetable shortening
    ½ cup pecans, chopped
    powdered sugar (optional)
B. Procedure:
    1. Mix cake mix, eggs, water, and shortening until well blended.
    2. Stir in pecans.
    3. Shape into small balls, then roll each ball in powdered sugar.
    4. Place on greased cookie sheet. Bake at 375°F for 8–10 minutes. Makes about 48 cookies.

*Baked Popcorn Treat*
A. Ingredients:
    ½ cup butter
    ½ cup brown sugar
    3 quarts popped corn
    1 cup peanuts
B. Procedure:
    1. Mix butter and sugar until fluffy.
    2. Combine corn and peanuts. Stir into butter-sugar mixture.
    3. Place in baking dish and bake at 350°F for 8 minutes. Pour into bowl and serve.

*Crunchy Fruit Munch* ☺
A. Ingredients:
    3 quarts popped popcorn
    2 cups natural cereal with raisins
    ¾ cup dried apricots, chopped
    ¼ teaspoon salt
    ⅓ cup butter or margarine
    ¼ cup honey

B. Procedure:
1. Preheat oven to 300°F. Combine first four ingredients in large baking pan; set aside.
2. In small saucepan, combine butter or margarine and honey. Cook over low heat until butter or margarine is melted.
3. Pour over popcorn mixture, tossing lightly until well coated.
4. Place in oven. Bake 30 minutes, stirring occasionally. Makes 3 quarts.
5. Store in tightly covered container up to 2 weeks.

### Popcorn with Peanut Butter
A. Ingredients:
2 quarts popped popcorn
1 tablespoon fresh peanut butter (creamy or chunky)
2 tablespoons butter or margarine
B. Procedure:
1. In small saucepan, melt butter or margarine and peanut butter until smooth.
2. Pour over popped corn and mix well.

### Popcorn Cheese Snacks ☺
A. Ingredients:
2 quarts popped popcorn
½ cup butter or margarine
½ cup grated American or Parmesan cheese—or both
½ teaspoon salt
B. Procedure:
1. Spread freshly popped popcorn in a flat pan; keep hot and crisp in oven.
2. Melt butter and grated cheese and add salt.
3. Pour mixture over popcorn. Stir until every kernel is cheese flavored.

### Peppermint Popcorn
A. Ingredients:
3 quarts popped popcorn
½ cup butter or margarine
1 cup sugar
½ teaspoon salt
¼ cup light corn syrup
½ teaspoon peppermint extract
¼ teaspoon green food coloring
B. Procedure:
1. Turn popcorn into large shallow baking or roasting pan.
2. Melt butter in 2 quart saucepan.
3. Stir in sugar, salt, and corn syrup.
4. Cook, stirring constantly, until mixture comes to a boil. Boil, without stirring, 5 minutes. Remove pan from heat.

5. Add peppermint extract and green food coloring.
6. Pour over popcorn in pan and stir to mix.
7. Bake in 250°F oven for 1 hour, stirring 3 or 4 times during baking. Cool completely. Makes about 2½ quarts.

### Turtle Pancakes ☺
A. Ingredients:
pancake or biscuit mix
⅓ cup nonfat dry milk
2 cups milk
B. Procedure:
1. Follow package directions. (For extra nutrition, add ⅓ cup nonfat milk to the standard recipe calling for 2 cups milk.)
2. The batter should be in a bowl rather than in a pitcher; the child puts the batter on the griddle by spoonfuls, sometimes deliberately dribbling for effect.
3. A turtle is made by adding four tiny pancakes (the legs) around the perimeter of one round pancake about 3 inches in diameter.

### Raisin Cornflake Cookies
A. Ingredients:
2 eggs
⅓ cup sugar
⅔ cup walnuts, chopped
⅔ cup raisins
salt (pinch)
½ teaspoon vanilla
corn flake crumbs
B. Procedure:
1. Grease a baking sheet.
2. Beat eggs until foamy.
3. Stir in sugar.
4. Fold in corn flake crumbs, nuts, raisins, salt, vanilla. Stir until well blended. Let mixture stand for 30 minutes.
5. Preheat oven to 350°F.
6. When mixture has been standing for 30 minutes, drop by teaspoonfuls onto greased baking sheet; bake 10 minutes or until delicately browned.
7. When still warm, remove the cookies from the pan. Cool.

## One Step Cookbook

These are one-process recipes. They require some preparation but the actual recipe uses one method that demonstrates what happens when food is prepared in that manner.

## Carrot Curls ☺

For this activity, you will need carrots, a vegetable peeler, and ice water. Show the children how to use a vegetable peeler safely. When peeling carrots, the peeler should be pushed down and away from the body, rather than towards the body or face.

Help children peel off the outside skin of the carrot, then make additional carrot peels. Place peels in ice water in the refrigerator until they curl. Use the carrot curls for a snack.

## Apples with Cheese ☺

Halve and core apples. Fill hollowed center with smooth cheese spread. Chill for 2 to 3 hours before serving.

## Yogurt and Cereal Parfait

In a tall glass, layer lemon, vanilla, or fruit-flavored yogurt with a favorite breakfast cereal.

## Banana Breakfast Bites ☺

Peel bananas and cut into bite-sized pieces. Dip each piece in yogurt, then drop into a plastic bag filled with wheat germ. Shake to coat. Serve as finger food.

## Fruit Cubes

Make frozen cubes with fruit juice, placing a small piece of fruit in each cube before it freezes. Add a popsicle stick to each cube to make individual fruit treats on a stick.

## Banana on Ice ☺

This is a tasty, low-calorie treat—only about 85 calories per banana. Simply peel a banana and wrap it in plastic wrap. Place it in the freezer for several hours, or until hard. (Don't leave it in the freezer too long.) Eat frozen. It tastes exactly like banana ice cream.

## Smiling Sandwich ☺

Spread peanut butter on a rice or corn cake. Use two raisins for eyes and a banana or apple slice for a smiling mouth.

## Ants on a Log ☺

Fill celery sticks with peanut butter, cream cheese, or pimento cheese. Use raisins or nuts as the "ants."

## Apple Bake ☺

Place a cored apple in a dish with a small amount of water. Cover with foil (for oven) or cover loosely with plastic wrap (for a microwave) and bake at 350°F for 20 minutes (oven) or on HIGH for 5 minutes (microwave). Add a sprinkle of cinnamon if desired.

## Juice Freeze ☺

Fill a 6-ounce paper cup with sugar-free fruit juice, cover with plastic wrap, and push a plastic spoon through center of wrap. Freeze. Tear away cup to eat.

## Dried Banana Chunks ☺

Slice bananas into ¾-inch thick slices. If desired, roll in chopped nuts. Place on baking sheet in 150°F oven with oven door open about 2 inches. Dry until shriveled, or about 12 hours.

## Cheese Melt ☺

Cut Monterey Jack cheese into small cubes. Place far apart on baking sheet and place in 375°F oven for a few minutes until cheese melts and spreads wafer thin. Cool and remove.

## Milk Mix

Pour cold milk into an almost empty jelly or jam jar. Shake vigorously. Drink.

## Peanut Butter ☺

Place 1 cup shelled roasted peanuts and 1 tablespoon oil in blender and blend to peanut butter.

## Popcorn ☺

Pour a handful of popcorn kernels into heavy pan with 1 tablespoon oil. Cover and heat until popcorn is popped.

## Snacks That Count

### Peanut Banana Lollipops

A. Ingredients:
     4 small firm ripe bananas
     8 ice cream sticks
     ¾ cup peanut butter flavored baking chips
     3 tablespoons milk
     ¾ cup coarsely crushed cereal flakes
B. Procedure:
   1. Peel bananas; cut each in half crosswise; insert stick lengthwise into each half. Place on tray; freeze until firm.
   2. Combine peanut butter pieces and milk into saucepan; heat slowly, stirring often until mixture is melted and smooth; remove from heat.
   3. Working with one banana at a time and holding by stick, quickly frost with peanut mixture, then roll in crushed cereal to coat well. Return to freezer until coating is firm.

### Chili Con Popcorn

Give an old-time treat a new and different taste. Instead of making popcorn with salt and butter, try other flavorings. Some people like to sprinkle on Parmesan cheese. In the Southwest, popcorn fans add a little chili powder. Encourage the children to make their own suggestions and try them out. While everyone's involved in this popcorn experience, read *The Popcorn Book*, written and illustrated by Tomie de Paola (Scholastic Books, 1978). It's bursting with information about why popcorn pops, where the top popcorn-eating cities in the United States are, and where we first got popcorn.

## Cooking Soup

A. Before starting this activity, put some instant, dehydrated soup and water into a covered container without letting the children see what you are doing. When you are ready to begin the activity, slowly heat the soup where the children cannot see it. Someone will probably comment, "I smell soup cooking." Encourage the children to talk about why they think soup is being cooked.

B. Open a package of instant, dehydrated soup and let the children compare it with the cooked soup in color, texture, smell, and taste. As you spoon some uncooked soup into one of the children's containers, discuss the sound that it makes. Let the children taste both the cooked and the uncooked soup and compare them. Observations like these may be expected:

> Uncooked soup feels rough.
> Cooked soup feels smooth and slippery.
> Uncooked soup looks like sand.
> Cooked soup doesn't look shiny.
> Uncooked soup tastes very salty.
> Cooked soup tastes just right.

C. Point out to the children that they are making observations in several different ways: by describing what they see, what they feel, what they smell, and what they taste.

## Mr./Ms. Munch

Let the children have fun planning their meals with Mr./Ms. Munch. Draw a face on a lunch bag (or cut out a face from a magazine and paste it on the lunch bag). Look through magazines for all types of food pictures. Cut them out and put them in a box. Talk about each picture with the children, then let them have fun feeding Mr./Ms. Munch that food. Combinations of foods can be put in and others left in the box.

Variation: Sort out from the box: snack, lunches, favorite foods, vegetables, fruits, various drinks.

## Nutrition Games

### Floor Mat with Food Pictures

You will need: 2 yards heavy, clear plastic (this plastic is usually bought from a roll at a variety, carpet, or fabric store); clear pictures of healthful foods drawn or cut out from magazines; clear, self-adhesive plastic; permanent marker.

Divide the plastic into eighteen squares. Draw lines with marker. Use clear self-adhesive plastic to attach pictures of foods onto each plastic square. You can put a label under the food if you like. Games children can play with the floor mat:

1. Hopping onto a named food (Hop into the box with an orange).
2. Hopping onto one example of a named food group (Hop into a box with something that is a fruit).
3. Stepping on or touching two foods that could make a snack.
4. Beanbags can be tossed onto named foods.
5. A second set of pictures, real foods, or clean, empty food containers can be matched to the pictures on the mat.

### Food Lotto Board with Cards

Materials:
gardening seed and plant catalogs
poster board
clear self-adhesive plastic
glue

1. Cut out pictures of fruits and vegetables from catalogs. Cut out two pictures of each food. For example, two pictures of tomatoes, of corn, of broccoli, and of strawberries. Catalogs like Burpees seed catalog usually show several pictures of each plant.
2. Glue one of each pair of pictures onto a piece of poster board or file cards. Cover with clear contact paper.
3. Glue the second of each pair of pictures onto a large piece of poster board to make a lotto board. Cover with clear contact paper.

Games children can play with lotto board and cards:

1. One or two children can match food picture cards to lotto boards.
2. Each player uses one lotto board. Shuffle and turn picture cards face down. A child or adult can hold up pictures, one at a time, and the child who has the same food on his board claims the picture and places it on the correct place. Continue until all boards are covered.

# UNIT REVIEW

1. Name several ways in which food activities help children learn information.
2. Name several skills that develop from activities with foods.
3. Decide which of the following statements are true:
   a. Teachers should give detailed directions to children during food activities.
   b. Children should work at their own pace.
   c. Food activities must be very easy so that no child feels challenged.
   d. Food activities should be varied.
   e. Children should work with new kinds of foods—things they have never tasted before.
   f. The end product is all that counts in food activities.
   g. Foods used in food activities should be inexpensive, if possible.
   h. Children must be warned never to throw foods away.
   i. Food activities should always be done in a kitchen.
   j. Food activities can sometimes be done in groups.

4. Decide which of the following statements are true or false:
   a. Research shows that human infants must learn to prefer sweet over sour.
   b. The average American consumes about 104 pounds of sugar per year.
   c. To avoid cavities, it is essential to eliminate all fructose from the diet.
   d. To avoid cavities, children should brush within 50 minutes after eating.
   e. The best way to reduce obesity is to limit empty calories.
   f. Empty calories are foods that are low in calories but high in protein.
   g. Hidden sugars are found in things like catsup, hotdogs, pork and beans, and canned vegetables.
   h. The most common form of sucrose is milk sugar or lactose.
   i. Approximately 12 percent of a young child's caloric intake comes from snacks.

# ADDITIONAL READINGS

Ault, R. *Kids Are Natural Cooks.* Boston: Houghton Mifflin, 1974.

Ausubel, D.P. "Enhancing the Acquesitionof Knowledge." In *National Society for the Study of Education Yearbook 1979,* part 1. Pp. 227–250. Chicago: The Society, 1980.

Baker, S., and R.R. Henry. *Parents' Guide to Nutrition: Healthy Eating from Birth Through Adolescence.* Reading, Mass: Addison-Wesley, 1986.

Brody, J.E. "Lower-Fat Diet Advised After Age 2." New York Times News Service (Sept. 5, 1992).

Carey, D., and J. Large. *Festivals, Family and Food.* Gloucestershire, England: Hawthorn Press, 1982.

*Cook and Learn: With Pictorial Single Portion Recipes.* Walnut Creek, Calif.: 1978. (Order from: A Child's Cook Book, 656 Terra Calle, Walnut Creek, California.)

Debnam, B. *The Mini Page Rookie Cookie Cookbook: Everyday Recipes for Kids.* Kansas City: Andrews & McNeely, 1989.

Endres, J., and R. Rockwell. *Food, Nutrition, and the Young Child.* St. Louis: C.V. Mosby, 1980.

Goodnow, J.J., and W.A. Collins. *Development According to Parents: The Nature, Sources, and Consequences of Parent's Ideas.* Hillsdale, N.J.: Erlbaum, 1991.

Goodwin, M., and J. Pollen. *Creative Food Experiences for Children.* Washington, D.C.: Center for Science in the Public Interest, 1980.

Lansky, V. *The Taming of the C.A.N.D.Y. Monster.* New York: Bantam, 1982.

Marotz, L., J. Ruseh, and M. Cross. *Health, Safety and Nutrition for the Young Child.* Albany, N.Y.: Delmar, 1985.

Ontario Science Centre. *Foodworks: Over 100 Science Activities and Fascinating Facts That Explore the Magic of Food.* Reading, Mass.: Addison-Wesley, 1987.

Rogers, C., and S.S. Morris. "Reducing Sugar in Children's Diets." *Young Children,* 41 (5) (July 1986): 11–16.

U.S. Department of Agriculture Yearbook. *What's to Eat? And Other Questions Kids Ask About Food.* Washington, D.C.: U.S. Government Printing Office, 1979.

U.S. Departments of Agriculture and Health and Human Services. *1980 Annual Report.* Washington, D.C.: U.S. Government Printing Office, 1980.

Wainwright, A. *Girls and Boys Easy-to-Cook Book.* New York: Grosset & Dunlap, 1979.

Wanamaker, N., K. Hearn, and S. Richarz. *More Than Graham Crackers. Nutrition Education and Food Preparation with Young Children.* Washington, D.C.: National Association for the Education of Young Children, rev. ed., 1984.

Warren, J. *Super Snacks*. Everett, Wash.: Warren Publishing House, 1982.

Wright, P., and M. Packett. *A Pot, a Pan and a Wooden Spoon*. Fort Worth, Tex.: 1976. (Order from: P.O. Box 16276, Wedgewood Station, Fort Worth, Texas.)

## Children's Books

Arnold, Pauline. *Food Facts for Young People*. New York: Holiday House, 1968.

Bayle, Louise. *Picture Books for Preschool Nutrition Education: A Selected Annotated Bibliography,* 1987. Lexington, Mass.: Louise, 73 Meriam St., Lexington, Mass. 02173.

Beck, Barbara. *The First Book of Fruits*. New York: Franklin Watts, 1967.

Berenstein, Stanley. *The Big Honey Hunt*. New York: Beginner Books, 1961.

Best, Allena. *Eating and Cooking Around the World. Fingers Before Forks*. New York: John Day Co., 1963.

Brown, Marcia. *Stone Soup*. New York: Charles Scribner's Sons, 1947.

Brown, Myra. *Company's Coming for Dinner*. New York: Franklin Watts, 1959.

———. *Ice Cream for Breakfast*. New York: Franklin Watts, 1963.

Bueher, Walter. *Bread, the Staff of Life*. New York: William Morrow, 1959.

———. *Food from Farm to Home*. New York: William Morrow, 1970.

de Paola, Tomie. *The Popcorn Book*. New York: Scholastic, 1978.

Dunbar, Joyce. *A Cake for Barney*. New York: Watts, 1988.

Eberle, Irmegarde. *Basketful, the Story of Our Foods*. New York: T.Y. Crowell, 1947.

Fenton, Carroll L. *Fruits We Eat*. New York: John Day Co., 1961.

Goldman, Ethel. *I Like Fruit*. Minneapolis: Lerner, 1969.

Graham, Ada. *The Great American Shopping Cart*. New York: Simon and Schuster, 1969.

Green, Mary. *Everybody Has a House and Everybody Eats*. New York: Young Scott Books, 1961.

Hoban, Russell. *Bread and Jam for Frances*. New York: Harper and Row, 1964.

Hutchins, Pat. *The Doorbell Rang*. New York: Greenwillow, 1986.

Johnson, Lois S. *What We Eat: The Origins and Travels of Foods Round the World*. Chicago: Rand McNally, 1969.

Krauss, Ruth. *The Carrot Seed*. New York: Scholastic, 1945.

Leonni, Leo. *Swimmy*. New York: Pantheon, 1963.

Lerner, Sharon. *I Like Vegetables*. Minneapolis: Lerner, 1967.

Rothschild, Alice. *Fruit Is Ripe for Timothy*. New York: Young Scott Books, 1963.

Selsam, Millicent. *Plenty of Fish*. New York: Harper, 1960.

Sendak, Maurice. *In the Night Kitchen*. New York: Harper, 1970.

Stewig, J.W. *Stone Soup* (Retold). New York: Holiday House, 1991.

Trisselt, Alvin. *Autumn Harvest*. New York: Lothrop, Lee and Shepard Co., 1966.

Watson, Aldren. *My Garden Grows*. New York: Viking Press, 1962.

Weldsmith, Brian. *Fishes*. New York: Franklin Watts, 1968.

Wild, Jocelyn. *Florence and Eric Take the Cake*. New York: Dial, 1987.

Wise, William. *Fresh, Canned and Frozen: Food from Past to Future*. New York: Parents Magazine Press, 1971.

Zim, Herbert. *Your Food and You*. New York: William Morrow, 1957.

# UNIT 22

# Creative Social Studies

## OBJECTIVES

After studying this unit, you should be able to

- describe some of the first things a young child learns about herself in a social sense.
- discuss how to use appropriate activities involving a child's name, voice, and personal appearance.
- discuss the importance of teaching about peace in the early childhood program.
- discuss personal and/or ethnic/cultural celebrations.
- discuss ways to include information on community workers in social studies learning experience.
- describe some points to remember in planning field trips for young children.

As we begin this unit on social studies, consider these two examples of young children in social situations.

*Situation 1*
Kim is waiting at home for her son Billy, who is playing next door. When he arrives 20 minutes later than scheduled, she asks what happened. "Well, Mom," he begins in a grown-up fashion, "Claire's doll broke and I wanted to help her."

"I didn't know you knew how to fix dolls," is his mother's somewhat surprised reaction.

"Oh no, Mom. I *don't* know how. I just stayed to help her cry."

*Situation 2*
Greg and Marc are building together with blocks. Marc gets angry because Greg takes a block from him. They fight. The teacher intervenes and talks with Marc about using words instead of fists. She tells him to try talking to Greg instead of hitting him—to tell Greg what was making him angry. Finally, believing she has made her point, she asks Marc, "Now, what would you like to do?" Marc answers with hesitation, "Hit him!" And he does!

These incidents, while a bit amusing to the adults involved, both demonstrate the funny, unpredictable nature of young children in social settings. They also illustrate clearly the fact that learning to be part of a social group is not something that is natural or inborn in human beings. Young children, like those

above, often react in a socially unpredictable way by their very spontaneous reactions to life. Yet, young children can be very sensitive to the feelings of others, even though they are direct and uninhibited in many situations. The fact is that learning about oneself, about others, and how to act with others is a long process.

Social studies is the study of human beings in their environment and of the concepts, skills, and attitudes that are needed in order to become social beings. Both the content and the processes of social studies can be integrated into activities in which even very young children can participate. As boys and girls reenact the roles of adults known to them, as they build houses, farms, airports, stores, and parks that they have seen, or dramatize past experiences that have special meaning for them, they learn the content of social studies. As children become aware of community services such as fire and police protection, or library and post office facilities, they incorporate them into their play.

Social studies are an important part of a child's education; they help the child understand the complex world in which she lives and enable her to be productive and happy within society's framework.

Education for facing social problems cannot be delayed until the child is older. The early years are very

FIGURE 22–1 Even the youngest child can learn to care about and appreciate the feelings of another.

important, and instruction must begin then. By their content, social studies are designed to develop intelligent, responsible, self-directing individuals who can function as members of groups—family, community, and world—with which they become identified. The social studies of the preschool child must focus on the experiences of the child in her immediate environment.

How should a teacher plan and teach in the social studies area in order to achieve the desired results?

A teacher aware of the major areas of social studies and appropriate concepts for young children can find many opportunities for helping them develop desirable habits, attitudes, and skills to be productive and happy within their social world.

## LEARNING ABOUT ONESELF

A child's universe begins with himself, extends to his family, and then to the larger community. The development of a child's self-concept, his awareness of self, is the important beginning point in social studies for young children.

To know oneself in a social sense involves learning such things as one's name, one's ethnic background, family grouping, and occupations in one's family. In the early childhood years learning about oneself is at a basic level; that is, young children are learning about how their lives fit into the larger social group.

Children learn about where they live—in a house, an apartment, or a condominium—and how it is like and unlike the residences of their peers. They learn

FIGURE 22–2 A child learns to relate to adults other than her parents in the early childhood program.

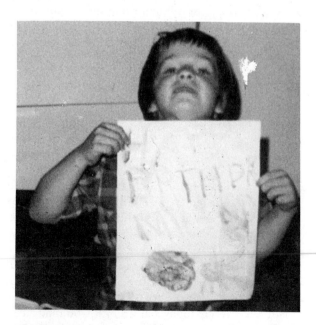

FIGURE 22–3 The child's growing sense of humor develops in appropriate social studies experiences.

the similarities and differences among families in form, style of living, and values.

Those who work with young children from preschool through the early elementary years can help them discover and appreciate their own uniqueness by beginning with a positive acceptance of each child. It is very important that children learn about themselves in a positive way so that they will learn to be positive in accepting themselves.

Yet young children learn about themselves through more dynamic ways than merely being talked to. In the early childhood years, they need opportunities to live important experiences, to learn in an *active* way.

The following sections contain suggestions for active ways to involve children in learning about themselves.

**Who Am I?**    One of the things a young child first learns about self is to recognize her name. In the early childhood program, this recognition is developed even more by teachers' and peers' recognition of this name.

A good strategy for developing children's self-knowledge as well as helping them understand their own uniqueness and that of others is to concentrate on the individual names of children in the group in planned activities. The following activities are designed to develop the idea that each person is a unique individual.

*Suggested activities.*
1. Adults should use the child's name as much as possible when speaking to her and *not* endearments like "honey," "dear," and the like.
2. Write a child's name on her work in the upper left-hand corner to teach the left to right sequence. While writing the child's name, the adult should say it. This provides an auditory and visual model.
3. At transition times the child is called by name to go to another activity or to tell the teacher which activity he wants to go to. "Johnny Jones, you may ride the tricycle today. Sally Smith, you may clean off the table."
4. Children are instructed to go tell another child

something. "Jim, please tell Mary it is time to come inside." Here the child is not only hearing his name, he is beginning to be able to say the other child's name and a sentence as he follows the teacher's direction.
5. When the children are in a group for a story, the teacher can go around and say each child's name. This can then progress to letting the other children, as a group, say the child's name as the teacher places her hand in front of the child. Then each child can say her own name when she is indicated.
6. The teacher may describe a child's clothing, size, coloring, or say the beginning sound of his name, and the class must guess whom she is describing. Later the children may do the describing.
7. Sit in a circle and place a small blanket loosely over a child's head. Then sing, "Who, oh, who, is under the blanket?" to the tune of "Ten Little Indians." After singing the first three lines, stop and let the other children in the circle name the child who is under the blanket. Continue around the circle until every child has had a turn. Do not force a child to sit under the blanket if he is reluctant to participate.

Additional activities are at the end of this unit.

Concentrating on the child's voice, which is as individual as each child's name, is another good way to help develop young children's awareness of self. Here are some suggestions on how to *actively* involve young children in learning that they each have a unique voice.

*Suggested activities—voice.*
1. Compile a tape of all the members of the class. Discuss how each person has a different voice tone. Children speak into the tape recorder, listen to the voices, and guess whose they are.
2. Record children telling their favorite stories ("The Three Bears," "Three Billy Goats Gruff," "Little Red Riding Hood"), emphasizing voice inflections for the different characters.
3. Play the game "Who Am I?" One child is in the center of the circle and is "it." "It" tries to guess who says "Who Am I?" The speaker disguises her

voice after the children have mastered the game with their natural voices.

4. Have the children feel objects of various textures. Another day, discuss voices using familiar comparisons. "Is your voice grating? High? Low? Soft? Hard? Scratching?" Have a box or chart of textured objects for the children to feel, such as steel wool, corrugated metal, silk, velvet, cotton puffs, wool, small mirror.

Birthdates are another topic that can be used to teach self-awareness. Some suggested activites for using birthdays to develop an awareness of self follow.

*Suggested activities—birthdays.*
1. Positive self-concept can be extended by focusing on the child's birthday. Children enjoy singing birthday songs to each other and feel special when they are sung to.
2. Children may participate in birthday fingerplays. The teacher may motivate the fingerplay through presentation of a paper cake. The birthday child places the correct number of candles on the cake or watches as the teacher writes her name (or the child writes it if she can).
3. The teacher may allow the child special privileges for the day, such as helping with snack, playing with a special toy, making first choice at activity time.
4. Encourage the birthday child to share her ideas with the class. She may describe her favorite birthday cake and favorite gifts. Point out that "gift" is another word for "present."

Additional activities are at the end of this unit.

**Self-Awareness—How Do I Look?** A positive awareness and acceptance of one's own appearance is part of the social aspect of learning "Who am I?" In the room, for example, a full-length mirror in a safe, but clearly visible, place at child-level is one way for children to see themselves and each other. Some children have few opportunities to see their reflections because mirrors in their homes are too high. Providing an unbreakable hand mirror in the room is another way to encourage children to see them-

selves. Magnifying makeup mirrors also produce interesting reactions from the children when they see their enlarged images.

The following suggested activities are designed to develop a young child's awareness and appreciation of the uniqueness of her physical appearance.

*Suggested activities.*
1. The use of an unbreakable mirror will be helpful to many children. Bring out the idea that we are more alike than different. Discuss color, size, and shape of eyes, hair, nose, mouth, ears, etc. Children may draw pictures of their faces. Pictures are cut out, mounted on a low board, and labeled.
2. Supply children with pictures of people with missing body parts. The children must describe what part is missing.
3. Put flannelboard cutouts of a boy and girl on the flannelboard. The teacher deliberately places body parts in the wrong area, such as an arm in the leg's place. Have children be detectives to discover what is wrong and place parts in the right location.
4. Play the game "Policeman, Where Is My Child?" One child is the policeman, another the mother. Mother describes the physical appearance of her missing child (dress, hair, eyes). All the children become involved as they look at themselves to see if they're being described. The policeman tries to guess which child in the room belongs to the mother.

Additional activities are at the end of this unit.

## THE BLOCK CENTER

The block center is an excellent place for exploring ideas about the community and neighborhood. Using play models of various members of the family, of people from various races, ethnic groups, industries, and professions, as well as small wheel toys with the blocks, all encourage true social play in the block center.

When children play together in the block corner, they learn to share, communicate, and resolve conflicts. Children see that cleanup is easier when they cooperate with one another, and even toddlers engaged in parallel play learn to compromise and negotiate as they make space and leave blocks for others. Building with blocks builds friendships, too, as children create structures together and role-play events from daily life or their imaginations. Dramatic play using blocks also helps young children work through important emotional issues. Because there is no right or wrong way to play, building with blocks helps boost a child's self-esteem. And knocking down block structures helps children feel powerful and in control.

Young children of about 4 or 5 years of age often add dramatic play to their block building. They name their structures and play "Let's pretend." For example, they may build a fire station and fire engine and add wooden or plastic figures that are firefighters. Children may ask you to help them make a sign for their building.

By age five, group cooperative play is common. Children decide beforehand what they want to build, and they may reproduce or symbolize structures familiar to them. Often, dramatic play centers around their building, and the addition of props and accessories further stimulates creative play. One group of children may want to build their neighborhood, using blocks to make streets, bridges, or subways. They may add a map, street signs, and people; they may locate where they want to go on the map, and buy bus (or subway) tickets to make the trip to their destination. Children may ask to leave their structure standing and may play with it again the next day, adding to it or making changes.

Both boys and girls enjoy the block area. The notion that the block area is the boys' domain and the housekeeping area the girls' is outdated as children and teachers learn that men and women can do all kinds of jobs. You may, however, notice differences in the ways boys and girls play with blocks. Boys tend to be active and adventurous block builders, creating outdoor scenes that take up large areas. Their play themes often include travel and heroes. Most girls, in contrast, tend to be quieter domestic block builders. Their play may be confined in space and physical movement as they take on the roles of family members and pets.

Although their play themes may differ, girls enjoy playing with blocks just as much as boys do. And it's not uncommon to find boys and girls working together. However, if the boys seem to be monopolizing the block area, here are some ways to encourage more cooperative play:

- Locate the block and housekeeping areas side by side, so children can combine activities.
- Provide props and accessories that appeal to girls as well as boys. Boys may prefer tools, transportation toys, and uniformed block figures. Girls often prefer accessories, like scarves, fabric pieces, carpet samples, and an assortment of colored paper bits and pieces, and family block figures. Usually, both boys and girls like to play with animal figures.

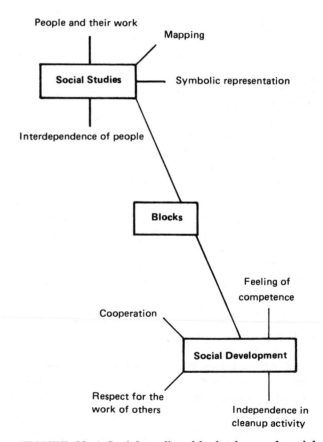

FIGURE 22–4 Social studies, block play, and social development (Adapted from Hirsch, 1984).

**Encouraging Block Play.** You can inspire block builders by providing interesting props and accessories to help children expand their play themes. Here are some ways to spark children's interest:

*Decorate block-corner walls.* Hang pictures, photos, posters, and blueprints of buildings, bridges, towers, and roadways. If children enjoy drawing their own pictures of construction sites, hang those up, too. Include pictures of men, women, and children of all races doing a variety of jobs, to let children know that blocks and construction are for everyone.

*Visit a construction site.* Young children benefit from direct experiences. If possible, visit a construction site several times so children can see the building's progression.

*Read books with construction themes.* Young children enjoy stories about construction and equipment, such as *Kathy and the Big Snow* and *Mike Mulligan and His Steam Shovel*, both by Virginia L. Bur-

ton (Houghton Mifflin). *The Big Book of Real Fire Trucks and Fire Fighting* by Teddy Slater (Grosset & Dunlap, 1987), *The Big Book of Real Trucks*, by Walter Retan (Grosset & Dunlap, 1990), and *How Many Trucks Can a Tow Truck Tow?* by Charlotte Pomerantz (Random House, 1987) are also excellent for this purpose.

*Other possible block accessories.*

- Animals: everything from zoo and farm animals to dinosaurs.
- People: families (various ethnic groups) and community workers (nonstereotypic).
- Trucks of all varieties, cars, airplanes, fire engines, ambulances, boats, etc.
- Puppets
- Rocks
- Batteries and bulbs, pulleys, string, tape, paper, and magic markers for descriptive signs, road signs, water, scenery

FIGURE 22–5 Summary chart—social studies and block play.

- Intervene when you observe gender bias—if you hear Sam and Anthony telling Mary she can't play with them because they're building a firehouse and girls can't be firemen, let children know that in your room everyone can play with everything that's available. You might introduce the term "firefighter," instead of "fireman," or read books about adults having careers traditionally held by the opposite sex.
- Post pictures of boys and girls enjoying block activities together (Burkhardt, 1993).

Figures 22–4 and 22–5 summarize the social studies ideas developed through block play.

## PEOPLE IN THE COMMUNITY

Since a child does not exist in isolation, he is dependent upon people in the community. Many peo-

ple provide services for him—the shoemaker, the bus driver, and the baker, for example. As a child meets people in the community, he learns about the many roles people play and tests some of these roles in his dramatic play. He takes his tool kit and goes to fix the telephone. He becomes involved in relationships in which adults play varied roles and people depend upon each other. He is exposed to different sets of values that people hold. His mother bakes bread or cake at home, but when he visits a bakery he sees that bread, cake, rolls, and cookies are mass-produced. He passes a firehouse in the neighborhood and sees where the firefighters are stationed. His mother washes clothes in the washing machine; other parents take their clothes to a laundromat. Although the concept of producer–consumer cannot be entirely comprehended, a child is the receiver of goods and services and as such experiences producer–consumer relationships. Children gain a sense of respon-

**FIGURE 22–6 An exercise in guessing "Who Am I?" is a way to increase a child's social awareness of others.**

sibility as they learn that what they do makes a difference. Others help them, and they help others.

A good place to begin a discussion about understanding others in the child's world then is to learn about people in the child's most immediate environment. This includes the people who serve the school and community. It is a good idea to focus on these individuals in the school rather than ask the child to think about those people who help her at home. It is good to raise the child's awareness about the importance of all individuals in the community: Each member helps to make the whole community or where we live and go to school what it is; all jobs are important.

*Suggested activities—community workers.*

1. Find out when the garbage is collected at the school. Be there when the truck comes. Talk to the workers about their job, the service they perform, the truck and its operation and care, and possibly how citizens can help get the garbage ready for the collector. Don't overlook the fact that these helpers are also people with personal lives. Children should be assisted to understand that the men and women in our labor force also have spouses, children, hobbies, pets, and so on, just like the rest of us.

2. Follow the preceding procedure for postal workers, grocery store clerks, mechanics, painters, laundry workers, bus drivers, cooks in the cafeteria, and custodians.

3. Follow the preceding procedure for professional and semiprofessional workers—secretaries, principal, nurse, music teacher, librarian, and others. Such activity should follow careful planning with the children as well as with the people you may visit. Preparing the adults beforehand for the kind of questions they can expect will give them a chance to organize their thinking. Discussing courteous and safe behavior with the children is also important. If the people you talk to can be persuaded to visit the classroom informally, the experience will be all the more effective.

4. Prior to a holiday, try the following activity to help bring out the importance of all kinds of workers throughout the year. Ask: "Does anyone have to work on holidays?" The children may guess police officers and firefighters, but list some of the others, too, explaining why each one has to work: hospital employees, toll collectors, telephone operators, radio and television announcers, transportation workers. Ask: "Why do these people work on holidays?" "What would happen if they didn't work?"

5. Use art activities (similar to the following) to help teach about the community.

*Teaching suggestions: art and social studies (community and community workers).*

1. *Carton City.* Assorted cardboard cartons varying in size and shape suggest an imaginary city when grouped together. Square, rectangular, and circular boxes can be combined to create unusual structures; or boxes may be cut in various ways for desired results, then painted or covered with paper. Children should be encouraged to add as many details as they consider necessary. Doors, windows, porches can be made of cut paper fastened with paste. Cardboard tubes, plastic bottles, spools, or egg cartons may suggest smokestacks, chimneys, and other additions. Carton City, arranged on a table or shelf, can be an imaginary

"dream town" or resemble a familiar scene in the community.

2. *Be a Worker.* Dramatization can be a useful teaching technique to reinforce learning; it can be used to help children learn more about community helpers and workers in the city. Costumes for use in the classroom can be simple, with only a hat, a mask, or an object to carry suggesting the characterization. Some children may want to bring an article of clothing to serve as a costume. Workers include people in industry, education, service, politics, entertainment, recreation, or any other area familiar to children. Play acting in the role of adults may take the form of a parade, a guessing game, pantomime, or play. Such experiences help broaden the child's understanding of life in the local community.

*Excursions into the community.* Every school is located in a community. And you can safely assume that every community has members who care about the well-being of its children and who possess talents, hobbies, and resources that can enrich children's learning experiences.

An excursion into the community may help young children gain new information and clarify other information, and can enhance and extend children's experiences. After one trip around the block, a group of five-year-olds arranged a barber shop and kept up their dramatic play as barbers for several days. Even the teacher sat in a chair as the children pretended to cut her hair using their fingers as scissors.

Often the comment is heard, "Why take children to a fruit and vegetable store when they shop there every week with their parents?" A visit to a store with a teacher and a group of peers is a very different experience from the same trip with mother. When a teacher takes a group to a store, the purpose of the trip is to give the children a specific experience. The event focuses on them and their purposes. When children go to a store with their families, ordinarily they are hurried along and the child's experience is not the major consideration of the trip. Thus, because the purposes are different on a school excursion, the experience is different.

Any planned excursion should be either an outgrowth of children's experiences or meet a specific need. A teacher helped a group of children order carrot and radish seeds from a catalog for the school garden. Then they took a trip to the corner mailbox, a meaningful excursion because they were carrying an important letter.

Within the same group of children, needs will differ. For instance, a teacher taking four children to the zoo found that for three of them the short bus trip back and forth was the exciting part of the trip because they had never been on a bus before. For the other child, the bus ride was an everyday event, and the giraffe was the highlight of the trip. When a teacher took two children to a department store to buy burlap for a bulletin board, the ride on the escalator was the event most remembered.

A short trip, such as a visit to the school office, can be a special event for a young child. In some programs, where children live in the immediate vicinity of the school, a teacher may take a small group to a child's house for morning juice and crackers. The child whose house is visited has an opportunity to be a host or hostess. The other children have a chance to see his valued possessions, and the parents see their own child in a different light. Parents enjoy having part of the school come to them, since they are the ones who usually go to the school. Although the visit may last for only 30 minutes, the children remember the experience for a long time. A picnic in a school yard or nearby park can make morning snack a special event, too.

Children enjoy walks around the neighborhood. They notice leaves changing colors, squirrels running about, ice on the branches of trees, and birds feeding their young.

While most trips are planned in advance, sometimes a teacher must do on-the-spot planning. When the children heard new and different noises outside, the teacher took them out to watch the repairmen at work.

A local garage is an interesting place to visit. Children can observe a tire being changed, a car going up on a lift, and a radiator being flushed.

Regardless of where a trip is planned, children should have some background knowledge. They feel

# THINK ABOUT IT . . .

## MORE ABOUT FIELD TRIPS

Let's Go! Here are some ideas for appropriate field trips for young children:

- Down the block to see a flower in bloom
- Around the corner to sit and watch how many cars and trucks pass by
- To a neighborhood grocery shop
- To the public library to browse or hear a story
- To a construction project (houses, roads, bridges, or a new porch on a home)
- To a shady tree, a huge rock, or wall to sit on like birds
- To see pets and animals in a quiet environment (a small farm, a parrot in a cage, a pond where turtles can be seen sunbathing, or a mother cat with her kittens)
- To a hill that is safe for children to run down and climb up again
- To a tree that is safe to try to climb
- To visit the shoe repair shop
- To mail a letter home to be received the next day
- To visit a parent at work
- To look for a specific thing—kinds of wheels, seeds, signs of spring/fall/winter/summer— or a certain shape or color.
- Some other types of field trips could be visits to a bottling company, airport, fish market, and bus or train stations. The list is practically unlimited—look around your community.

In spring and summer, field trips are especially nice. Because children see different kinds of fruits and vegetables, a farmer's market is both interesting and educational. A good follow-up would be to plant some seeds that the children can watch grow.

Spring is the time to plan a trip to help the birds build their nests. While walking, children can collect bits of string, small twigs, leaves, and grass. Place all in a small mesh bag (such as an onion or lemon bag from the grocery store). Tie the filled bag onto a tree branch; children love to watch birds select what is needed for their nest building.

Plan a visit to a dairy farm. If that is not possible, take the children to a dairy processing plant. Later, children can make cows that "move" by using rectangles and squares held together with brass fasteners.

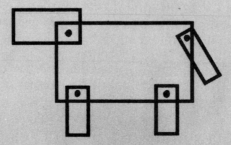

The week before Labor Day is a good time to recognize community helpers. You might want to feature pictures of police officers, postal workers, firefighters, milk delivery persons, and others on the bulletin boards. Plan to tell stories about these community helpers, and let the children tell of some of their experiences with community workers.

The week before Valentine's Day is a good time for a visit to the post office. Before going, each child can make a valentine and stamp it. While on the visit, the child can mail it to his parent(s). A follow-up chat with the postal worker who comes to the center makes the experience a valuable one for the children.

A final safety idea for field trips: Use a woven rope that has knots tied in it at about 4' foot intervals. Each child holds onto his own knot as you walk. The children are able to daydream, yet still have the security of holding onto the rope. The teacher can see at a glance if any child is missing and who he or she is.

good about extending their knowledge in an area that is familiar to them. Unless some item is of special interest to children, a visit to a museum should be left for later years.

*Planning for trips.* A teacher needs to do a good bit of planning for a trip. The purpose of a trip is to provide children with firsthand experiences. A child should not only be able to see, hear, and smell, but he should be able to touch and taste as well. A teacher also needs to know the children and their special interests and concerns.

You should not consider any trips until you are certain that you know the children well enough to anticipate any potential disruptive behavior. In many classrooms, some children may become overstimulated by the interruption of their daily routines.

You will need to familiarize yourself with the community in which the school is situated before planning excursions—become familiar with street signs, working people who come and go from the school, shops, business establishments, buildings, and service. Talk with people in the community. As you plan, try to anticipate the children's reactions, remember-

ing that you are planning for *young* children. This means that you will need to keep in mind these basic guidelines in planning all excursions:

- Keep it simple.
- Discuss, read about, and organize play around the places to be visited in advance.
- Encourage close observations while on the outing.
- Give small amounts of information if children are interested.
- Provide time, materials, and enthusiasm for follow-up plans and projects.

Figure 22–7 summarizes the considerations necessary for planning excursions into the community with young children.

*Understanding transportation.* Those who operate transportation systems are an important part of a community. In a highly complex culture such as ours, people are especially dependent upon transportation in their daily lives. A child's environment is filled with cars, planes, trains, buses, and subways. In dramatic play he incorporates many modes of transportation, including the experiences that have

In selecting a site for a field trip, a teacher should consider:

*Children's interests:* As a teacher listens to what children say, the questions they ask, and their dramatic play, she becomes aware of the knowledge and attitudes they gain and the values they place on certain types of experiences.

*Community resources:* In a walk around the building and the playground, a teacher might discover many places of interest. A survey of the neighborhood can reveal additional places and activities that might be of interest.

*Time needed to reach destination:* Although there are exceptions, a teacher should plan for no more than 20 minutes of travel time each way.

*Mode of transportation:* Walking is usually the best means of travel. When private motor transportation is needed, attention must be given to the competence of the driver, insurance coverage, and safety seats for children. If public transportation is to be used, a teacher must know procedures, cost, and arrival and departure schedules.

*Number of children taking the trip:* Where possible, no more than three or four children should be included on a field trip for each adult.

*Supervision:* When three-year-olds leave the premises, one adult should be responsible for no more than two children. With four- and five-year-olds, one adult should be available for four children.

*Safety:* A teacher needs to determine the safest route. She needs to feel confident that the group can be controlled and that she can cross streets with them and help them on and off conveyances. A teacher should always carry a small first-aid kit.

*Length of visit:* For most trips, 20 minutes at the site is enough for young children. If more time seems appropriate, the trip can be repeated.

*Nature of visit:* A teacher needs to take the trip herself and be sure that anyone else involved understands the purpose of the trip. There should be only one focus for a trip. Too much stimulation defeats the purpose of the trip and causes disruptive behavior.

**FIGURE 22–7 Considerations for field trips.**

meaning for him. He plays the roles of bus driver, taxi driver, engineer, and ticket taker. He creates a bus with chairs, or boxes, or blocks, or pieces of portable playground equipment. He parachutes down from the climbing equipment; then he climbs back up, stretches his arms out wide, and flies down again. After he goes on a trip, he re-creates subway stations or bus stops. He builds an airport in the block area. He becomes interested in the picture of a bus that the teacher placed on the bulletin board. He finds a story about an airplane. A teacher helps extend the children's concept of transportation as she helps them make a pulley so that they can move objects up and down and from side to side.

**Celebrations.** Celebrations should be part of a child's life. A child becomes more sensitive about his

**FIGURE 22–8 Talking with friends after a field trip is almost as much fun as the trip itself.**

**FIGURE 22–9 Through play experiences, children learn about each other.**

own feelings and of the feelings of others when he rejoices with them in celebration. He feels himself in the stream of the ongoing life process and sees himself as part of the larger group. Through celebrations, a child in his own way can be part of a group and acknowledge a special day or event.

Birthdays are special events for the child, and they should be treated according to his individual needs. All the children in the room need not join his birthday celebration. Sometimes they will, but often only a small group joins a child in honoring his birthday. In many schools, parents are invited for the occasion. The parents' presence at the party is welcome, but if parents are unable to attend, this should not be allowed to detract from the celebration. Many parties given in honor of a child's birthday are overstimu-

lating. For some children, a large crowd of people and too much confusion are upsetting. For John, baking his own cake or helping to prepare ice cream may give his birthday special meaning. Young children are happy with small recognitions; a child counts the candles on his cake and then blows them out—a very exciting event for him.

*Religious and national celebrations.* In our diverse society, religious celebrations rest appropriately in the domain of the family and not in publicly supported institutions. Acknowledgement of some holidays based on religions such as Christmas, Hanukkah, and Ramadan, however, help show children that people celebrate in different ways. In response to the questions, "Where is Marlene today?" a teacher may say, "Marlene isn't coming today. She and her family are going to temple." In a multi-ethnic society, teachers and parents can enrich children's experiences by sharing customs. Tara's mother made a piñata for her class. Ms. Andersen wore her Norwegian dress to school so that the children could see that special outfit.

If you decide to celebrate traditional holidays such as Columbus Day, Presidents' Day, Thanksgiving, or Halloween, it is important to select those aspects of the holiday that can have meaning at a child's level—for example, the pleasure of eating a special meal together at Thanksgiving or the excitement of dressing up at Halloween. The deeper meanings of these holidays can be developed later. Drawing a cherry tree, cutting out a jack-o-lantern, or making pilgrim hats are activities that are not likely to give meaning to events or stimulate feelings of any depth; they are not celebrations. It is important to keep this in mind, especially when using the activity units for seasons and holidays that follow in this book.

*Ethnic/cultural celebrations.* The topic of bicultural education for young children was covered earlier; you may want to refer to the teacher's references and children's books listed at the end of Unit 18 for more information on specific ethnic groups.

In using information on various ethnic groups, beware of developing a "tourist curriculum" or teaching about cultures only through such artifacts as

# THIS ONE'S FOR YOU!

## FOLKTALES: LEARNING ABOUT OTHER CULTURES

Children's literature offers young children another way to identify and empathize with others. Over the centuries, all people have told stories. Introducing young children to the folktales of other cultures may help them feel better connected to people far away in time and space—a far cry from tourist curriculi.

You may find that reading different versions of the same folktale helps children see that people the world over share the same feelings, hopes, dreams, and concerns. An example is *The Three Billy Goats Gruff* (Blair, 1964) and the Mexican tale *Borrequita and the Coyote* (Aardema, 1991), which have similar themes.

You may find that fables can also help teach young children about values. *Carmine the Crow* (Holder, 1993) conveys more about why people should be kind to the elderly than any number of more obvious tales about nice little children visiting nursing homes:

Carmine the crow lives alone with his tinfoil collection and his little habits: a cup of tea to drink and old ballads "to cheer himself up." After rescuing a gorgeous swan, he is given a small box of stardust with which he can fulfill his dreams. As he hurries through the meadow, however, he discovers a mouse, a frog, and a rabbit all in need of wishes answered. He gives away his stardust and heads home to his old-man chair and his little bed of nettles. Although the story has a happy ending, it will haunt the reader with its sensitive depiction of being old and set in one's ways.

An authentic Navajo legend, *Ma'ii and Cousin Horned Toad* (Begay, 1993), teaches the importance of generosity. The story details how the lazy coyote Ma'ii tries to outwit his industrious toad cousin. The coyote finds out that small and generous is not necessarily stupid. A true sense of the Southwest is intertwined by the Navajo poems woven throughout the story.

*The Fortune-Teller* (Alexander, 1993) tells the story of a lucky young carpenter who desperately wants more out of life than nails and elbow grease in his village in Cameroon, Africa. Through a series of happy accidents, he ends up rich and blessed. But what makes the folktale so memorable is the expressive African faces, the rich hues of the villagers' garb, and the pictures that convey a true sense of tribe and extended family.

food, traditional clothing, and household implements. *Multicultural activities,* in contrast, are special events in the child's week, separate from the ongoing daily curriculum. A tourist curriculum is both patronizing and trivializing, emphasizing as it does the "exotic" differences between cultures and dealing not with the real-life, daily problems and experiences of different peoples, but with surface aspects of their celebrations and modes of entertainment (Derman-Sparks, 1989, p. 7).

*Personal celebrations.* In the life of any child, there are events that deserve celebrations. When a teacher observes that a child, through his glee or sadness, is moved by a situation, the experience is worth emphasizing with a small but *personal* celebration. For example, a child ties his shoes by himself for the first time. For many children, this is a very special event. The teacher may take time to say, "Great! You did it," or "Show me how you did it!" or "How does it feel to do it all by yourself?" You might want to

FIGURE 22–10 Being able to do things for oneself is basic to developing a positive self-concept.

share a new accomplishment of your own at a time like this. "I just learned how to drive a car and I feel so good when I can go out in the car and drive all by myself!" Share good feelings with children, and a child begins to learn that feelings are important and worth celebrating. When a child ties his shoes, the teacher's knowing glance the next day reaffirms his positive feelings about himself.

## TEACHING YOUNG CHILDREN ABOUT PEACE

*Preventing conflicts is the work of politics; establishing peace is the work of education.*
—Maria Montessori

This quote very simply outlines a very complicated mission for early childhood teachers—teaching about peace. The National Association for the Education of Young Children, in 1991, also challenged early childhood teachers to teach peace, reminding us that of all the lessons we hope to teach young children, the ability to act *in peace* is one of the most important.

This is a complicated idea—this teaching peace—for many reasons. First, many adults don't understand the meaning of peace. For purposes of our discussion, peace is defined as a "state of tranquility or quiet; a freedom from civil disturbance, a state of security or order within a community provided for by law or custom" (Bernat, 1993, p. 36). Another reason peace is such a difficult topic to teach is that most adults have not been able to maintain peace in their own world. Finally, we certainly must ask a basic question—how can we teach young children about peace in a world so filled with strife and conflict?

Many early childhood experts have written about this challenge of teaching young children about peace. You will find references at the end of this unit covering the writings of these experts. They address the many issues related to peace, such as cooperation, democratic behavior, respect for others, peer acceptance, social competence, and trust. To sum up the core idea of these writings, peace begins with a basic attitude, made up of trust, respect, and consideration toward everyone. When the attitudes of trust, respect, and consideration are present in the environment, it is a safe place for people to be themselves. In a safe environment, people have a sense that it is acceptable to be unique; it is acceptable to disagree; and it is *expected* that disputes are settled without hurting one another. Every interaction in a safe environment reflects consideration and respect for individual differences (Bernat, 1993; NAEYC, 1991).

We can choose to create an environment that teaches children how to live peacefully with one another. In every action we have with another person, we can cause hurt or not. It is our choice. It is the responsibility of a teacher to realize that this choice exists and to teach children about their choices. If we realize this, we will choose carefully.

If we value one another, we will not choose to harm each other. In turn, we must help young children understand their choices. For example, an increase in rowdiness results in an increase of people getting hurt. Children must learn to make choices about their style of play, and they must learn that they share responsibility for the results of their actions. They also need to learn that they can choose to stop upsetting behavior in the future, to slow the pace before someone gets hurt.

One expert in teaching peace, Valerie Bernat, suggests that this process of teaching young children about their choices begins with the implements of two simple rules:

- Don't hurt anybody
- Use words to settle problems (Bernat, 1993, p. 36)

*Don't hurt anybody.*  This is a simple rule—on the surface. Yet, just think of how many ways there are to hurt other people. Physical blows hurt. But so do unkind words, gestures, teasing, and exclusion. All of these are harmful and can interfere with a child's ability to learn in general, as well as learning how to act in peace.

*Use words.*  Disagreements are a natural part of life, and they will occur in the lives of young children. The key to peaceful settlement is to maintain harmony in stressful situations. It is sometimes difficult for a child to take a deep breath and clearly express the feelings of the moment. At stressful times, times of conflict or disagreements, it is important for the teacher to be with the children—but to show, not to tell. Steady the children in whatever way you can. Holding them closely in your arms or on your lap often helps a child gain focus in a stressful situation. Help the child express herself. But don't put words in the child's mouth. And make sure that conflicting children listen to one another. Asking them to repeat, or retell, what each has said to the other is one way to see if they are listening to each other.

**A Teacher's Role.**  It is not necessary (or possible) for you to find solutions for ever child's problems. You need only create an atmosphere in which children can work out their own solutions. It is the teacher's job to give children the tools they need to define

and settle differences. Teaching children how to use words to express themselves instead of actions to express emotions is one of the most important of these tools.

Childhood classrooms are very special places, and they must be focused on the child. In these classrooms, there are many different personalities, different needs, different styles of behavior, and different ethnic and family backgrounds. Common to all these groups is the need to feel safe. Only on this basis can we begin to build a framework of trust and respect. And it is within such a framework that each child has a chance to grow and learn. It is in the preschool class that the teaching of peace must begin. If young children do not learn it from us, will they learn it at all?

The following best summarizes the importance of teaching peace in the early childhood program:

Teach peace? Peace emerges from our actions. Teach your children not to hurt in any way. Teach them to use words to settle disputes. Help them understand their choices and the effects their choices have on others. Encourage understanding and the ability to comfort. These are strategies that build peace.
(Bernat, 1993, p. 39)

## SUMMARY

Knowing how to be part of a social group is not natural or inborn in human beings. Learning about oneself and others and how to act with others is a long learning process. Social studies are an important part of a child's learning; they help the child understand the complex world in which she lives and enable her to be productive and happy within a social framework.

Teaching children to face social problems should not be delayed beyond the early years, which are very important; instruction must begin then. The social studies of the preschool child must focus on the experiences of the child in her immediate environment.

Learning about oneself in a social sense includes learning one's name, one's ethnic background, and such things as family grouping and occupations in one's family. In the early childhood years, learning about oneself is at a basic level; that is, young children learn how their lives fit into the larger social group.

Those who work with young children from preschool through the entire period of early childhood can help them discover and appreciate their own uniqueness by beginning with a positive acceptance of each child.

Teaching young children about peace begins with a basic attitude of trust, respect, and consideration toward everyone. Two basic rules make up the basis of teaching about peace: (1) Don't hurt anybody and (2) use words.

Appropriate social learnings and related activities for young children are learning that each person is a unique individual; learning self-awareness; learning about the immediate community and its workers; and taking appropriate excursions into the community. The block area provides young children with many opportunities to actively experience many of these ideas.

## LEARNING ACTIVITIES

A. List specific ways to enhance a child's understanding of self, other than those in this unit.
B. There are many activities and experiences appropriate for teaching children concepts of self and other people. Think of at least three ideas other than those in this unit.
C. Prepare a unit plan on one of the following: family, self, or a specific community worker such as a firefighter. For your unit plan, include a section titled "Children's Books" and include stories and other appropriate language arts activities.
D. Child Study:
   1. Select three children of different ages (e.g., three, five, and seven years) and ask each separately to describe things like what fathers do, what the children can or cannot do when they grow up, or what happens when they are afraid.

Do not contribute your own opinions until you are sure the children have said all they would like to about the matter.
   2. What changes in ideas do you notice as you listen to children of different ages? Did any of the children have a definite misunderstanding about some aspect of the issue you discussed? If so, how did you respond? How should parents respond when this happens?
   3. Observe a dispute between children in an early childhood setting. Record how it was settled. Then compare this method of settlement with the information presented in this unit on teaching about peace. How did the real-life settlement compare? Did it help the children involved learn about peace? Why or why not?

## ACTIVITIES FOR CHILDREN

### Suggestions for Excursions Appropriate for Young Children

*Supermarket*
As eager as young children are, they have a limited attention span, so do not try to do too much. Make several trips to the supermarket, each with a different focus. Watch the goods being delivered. Watch the boxes being unpacked and merchandise being stamped. Look at all the different kinds of machines in the store.

*Produce Department*
What are some things displayed on special cardboard or wrapped in individual papers? Why are some things displayed on crushed ice or refrigerated? See if you and the children can name the fruits and vegetables.

*Dairy Department*
What kinds of things are sold here? Why are they kept cold? Where do the various products come from?

*Meat Department*
Watch the butcher cut and package meat. Why is the meat kept cold? Is it cold in the back, too? See how many varieties of meat you can name.

*Bakery Department*
Compare the ovens with the ovens at home and the size of the flour sacks with the sacks that you buy. Notice the quantities of baked goods and the process of baking. What kinds of clothes do the bakers wear? Why?

## Shoe Repair Shop

Watch the repairman make repairs. Try to give him something that needs fixing. What kinds of machines does he have? What kinds of materials does he use? Try to get some scraps to take back for making collages.

## Dry-Cleaning Shop

What kinds of smells are in the air there? What kind of machine does he use for ironing? How does the cleaner know which clothes are yours?

## Pet Store

What kinds of pets does this store have? Are there any unusual ones? What do the various pets eat? What kinds of houses do they provide for the various pets?

## Florist's Shop

Visiting this shop is an especially good activity on a cold winter's day when everything outside is barren and bleak. A walk through the greenhouse may bring many questions to mind: Why are the flowers growing inside the greenhouse and not outdoors? What kinds of plants are there? What kinds of smells are there? How does the florist keep cut flowers from dying? Buy a plant and learn how to take care of it. The workroom, where bouquets, baskets of flowers, and corsages are assembled, will be of interest to children.

## The Police Officer and Crossing Guard

Within walking distance of your school there is probably an intersection or a school where a police officer or crossing guard is on duty. Watch what she does. How does she tell the vehicles and pedestrians to go? To stop? The children enjoy talking to the officer and getting a good look at her uniform. The police station is of interest to the children, too; perhaps the desk sergeant on duty will spend a few minutes visiting with the children. (You will plan this in advance, of course.) He may show the child the inside of a police car, show them the radio, and give the children a short safety speech.

## Mail Delivery

Make arrangements to meet your own letter carrier at your mailbox and then at the nearest pick-up box on the corner to watch her gather the mail. Buy a stamp and mail a letter at the post office. Children are not usually allowed in the back of most post offices, but they can see a good deal if they look through the window of the parcel-post counter. Watch the packages being weighed and mailed.

## Bus Driver (Conductor)

Sit near the driver of the bus. Watch what he does. Look at his uniform.

## Fire Station

Some fire departments have open-house days. If yours does not, make an appointment for a visit ahead of time. Do not insist that the children get on the equipment, even if invited to do so. Climbing on an engine can be a frightening experience for some young children. Usually the child is invited to try on a fire fighter's hat, watch a fire fighter slide down the pole, and inspect the engine. Find out how the fire alarm works, where the different fire fighters stand on the truck, and what each of them does at a fire. Later look at fire hydrants and fire escapes in buildings. Point out fire doors and fire extinguishers or sprinklers in various buildings.

## Library

Take the children to the children's section of the library. Let them browse. Show them that all the books have letters or letters and numbers written on the bindings. Why? Perhaps your library has a storybook time that you can attend. How does the librarian know which book you take out? Take out some books so the children can see the procedure.

## Sanitation Workers

Be aware of the sanitation workers, street sweepers, or snowplow drivers in action and how they are dressed. Why do they wear gloves?

## Demolition Site

Why is this building being knocked down? How? What will go up on the empty lot?

## Construction Site

What kind of building is going up? What are the girders for? What kinds of machines can you see? What do they do? How do the workers dress? Why?

## Repair Site

Observe surface or underground repair site. What is being fixed? What equipment is in use? How are the workers dressed? Why? What is under the street or sidewalk? Where did the rocks and soil come from? Try to explain to the children that the site of the city was once countryside.

## Food-Processing Plant

Any such plant is of interest to the children, whether it produces ice cream or soup. In large plants there are often guided tours and samples to taste. Call the company and ask.

## Printing Plant or Newspaper Plant

Call ahead of time and find out if tours are available and when the presses are operating. Remember to bring some paper remnants back for the children's artwork.

## What Mommies Do

More and more mothers of young children are working outside the home. Ask the children to ask their mothers about their jobs. Perhaps some of the mothers might be able to come to school and talk about their jobs.

## Names

A. Ball rolling indoors or ball throwing outdoors gives the teacher a chance to use names and to give practice in following directions. "Sue Smith, you roll the ball to John Jones."
B. A tape recorder may be used to record a child's full name, have the child listen to it, then record it herself. Her name may be used in a full sentence describing her or telling something she likes to do.
C. Put name tags on cubbies, lockers, desks, and activity boards. Use the child's name with a picture of an animal beside the name. As the children learn to identify their names without the picture, give them new labels and tags without the picture. Later add the last name.
D. Prepare a bulletin board with a large paper shoe in the center. Children pin their pictures on the board around the shoe, with their names written under them. Children could begin learning the nursery rhyme "Old Woman in the Shoe" at this time.

## Birthdays

A. The children may make a picture of a birthday cake on one side of drawing paper and a picture of the gift each child would like to give on the other. The pictures are presented to the birthday child.
B. Read birthday stories to the children and discuss how they feel at their own parties, when they give someone a gift at a birthday party, etc.
C. Children adore surprises—both those giving and those receiving them. Have the children tape their singing of "Happy Birthday." Individual birthday messages might also be taped for the birthday child at the close of the school day. Children will probably want to join in and sing with their tape.
D. The birthday child may make a crown from tagboard and old jewelry to wear all day at school and take home.
E. Instead of having a parent bring the "snack" needed for the birthday celebration, select a small group of children (including the birthday child) to make cupcakes for the whole class. Cake mixes are easily prepared by children and are almost foolproof. Children can individually ice their own cupcakes using a tongue depressor and prepared icing. Try filling flat-bottomed ice cream cones (about half-way) with the cake batter, and bake as you would

**FIGURE 22–11 A bulletin board for birthdays—a personal celebration for everyone.**

cupcakes. If a stove is not available, instant pudding can be a good substitute.
F. Children can draw a picture and "mail" it to the birthday child through a special classroom post office box.
G. A photo of the child taken on his/her birthday can be added to a class birthday book or bulletin board display.

## Self-Awareness Activities

### All About Me

A. From magazines, children can cut pictures that they like or that remind them of themselves.
B. Draw body images of the children. The children lie on a sheet of butcher paper while a teacher (or other child, if older) draws around the body shape. After being decorated, the images are displayed around the room so that the size and shape variations of the children can easily be observed.
C. Make a puzzle of each child's name, using both first and last names.
D. Make up "Guess Who" riddles describing individual children. Suggest clues that reflect the child's positive characteristics.
E. Make a set of flash cards or similar cards with pictures of community workers. The children could be encouraged to bring pictures of their parents at their jobs or wearing clothing appropriate for that job. An additional game could be collecting pictures of tools or items related to various jobs and having the children sort them.

F. Interviews with community helpers could be taped on a recorder if the workers cannot visit the classroom. Children will be especially proud to hear their parents tell about their professions and jobs.

## How Do I Look?

A. Discuss differences in sex. Ask: "Do girls look different from boys? How? Dresses? Hair? What else? Do men look different from ladies? How? Do they sound different?" If a child brings out the difference in sex organs, accept it very matter-of-factly.

B. Read and dramatize the following poem with the children:

> Mirror, Mirror meet today
> David who is here to play.
> Mirror, Mirror, can you tell
> How to get to know him well?
>
> Here he is. What does he wear?
> Tell us if he's dark or fair?
> Tell us, tell us, is he tall?
> Do you see him? Tell us all.

C. Have the children take turns looking at themselves in a mirror and answering the poem's questions. Have the class explore the possibilities for completing the following:

The color of Jerry's shirt is _____.

The color of Jean's hair is _____.

Anne's eyes are the color of _____.

We call Marc's shoes _____.

If you are wearing Marc's kind of shoes, stand up.

Raise your hand if you have the same color hair as Joan does.

D. Read the poem "My Shadow" by Robert Louis Stevenson. Discuss shadows and go outside to observe shadows, especially those of the children. Let them mark around each other's shadow with chalk on the sidewalk. Compare mirror (reflection) and shadow (for an outline).

E. Take snapshots of the children, alone or in groups and mount them on a bulletin board or in a scrapbook with the names of the children printed beneath the pictures. These pictures are an excellent starting point for a discussion about how we all have the same body parts, even though we all look different. In this and other such activities, the teacher can bring out that we are more alike than different. Natural points in such a discussion are color, size, and shape of eyes, hair, nose, mouth, etc.

F. On a more personal level, try the following self-study activity to see how you look to the children you work with.

*Self-study: How children see you*

Select one or two children who are at least four years old. Seat them individually at a table with paper and crayons (or felt-tip pens) and ask them to draw a picture of you. Encourage them to take their time and include as much as they want. When they are finished give them another sheet of paper and ask them to draw a self-portrait.

When both pictures are completed cut them out and paste them side by side. First look at each child's drawing of you. What features appear to be most important to the children? Did they overlook any important characteristics, such as a beard, long hair, or glasses? Compare the drawing of you with the self-portrait. How are they similar? How are they different? Is there more detail in your picture or in the self-portrait? Is one bigger than the other? Is there a difference in emotional expression? Do these drawings reveal anything about how these children view themselves and you? Treat these ideas as speculation rather than fact since we cannot be absolutely sure of what these drawings mean. (Smith, 1982, p. 30)

G. A variation on self-portraits is to make finger- and handprints on sheets of paper. (In the warm weather, footprints of bare feet are also fun.) These prints are very personal and interesting in their similarities and differences in shapes, sizes, and skin patterns. They also provide a means to sharpen the children's awareness of their physical body, its uniqueness, and its shared likeness with other children.

## Emotion Sorter

*You will need:* two pictures of children's faces that show happy and sad emotions (mounted on stiff cardboard); a collection of pictures that may stimulate the expression of these emotions (birthday party, family outing, eating ice cream, broken toy, etc.); two containers large enough to hold a number of the pictures (gift boxes, dishpan, etc.).

*Procedure:* Introduce the pictures showing a happy and sad child. Be sure the children participating in this activity can identify the difference between the two pictures.

1. Have the children select a picture that would make them happy and have them place their selection in the container beneath the appropriate pictured facial expression. Repeat this introduction for the sad emotion.

2. Have children continue sorting the pictures. The backs of the pictures can be color coded so that the adult can quickly identify pictures that should lead to further discussion.

3. One teacher was surprised to discover that a child had placed a picture of a broken toy truck in the "happy" category. She failed to realize that any truck, even a broken one, stimulated a positive emotional reaction for this child.

## Happy/Sad Books
*You will need:* drawing paper, crayons or markers, brads.
*Procedure:* Give each child drawing paper and crayons/markers and ask them to think of something that makes them happy. Have them draw a picture of themselves when they are happy. Repeat this activity, only this time ask them to draw a sad portrait. Be sure to include the child's name on each drawing. Compile each group of pictures and construct two books for the class. Place a snapshot of the whole group smiling or frowning on the cover of each book.

Instead of creating a class book, the self-portraits can be used to make a bulletin board display.

## Picture Stories
*You will need:* a sample of pictures of people (children and adults) that show various emotional expressions; tape recorder (optional).
*Procedure:* Individually ask each child how the person in the picture is feeling and what could have happened to the person. Write down the child's response or record them on tape. These "stories" can be shared at group time. Later, children may enjoy listening to the tape and selecting pictures that match the "stories."

The pictures can be mounted on cardboard and laminated with clear contact paper and then cut into pieces to form "emotion" puzzles. It is wise to mount each picture on different colored backings so that the pieces can be easily sorted if they become mixed.

## Me-Boxes
*You will need:* a shoe box for each child; a selection of magazines; scissors; paste or glue.
*Procedure:* Have children bring in shoe boxes from home or collect them from a number of shoe stores. Children cut out pictures of their favorite things and activities from magazines (or tear them, if appropriate) and paste/glue them onto the shoe boxes. Be sure to place the child's name on the box in a place where it won't get pasted over. Boxes can be used to store the child's "extra" clothing, art projects, or secret treasures. Teachers may want to add a photo of the child to the box so that other children can easily identify the owner of the box.

## Framed Clothing
*You will need:* several old wooden picture frames (minus the pictures); old shirt (that buttons); old jacket (that snaps or zips); heavy duty stapling gun and staples.

*Procedure:* Cut out the fronts of the shirts and jackets (be sure you cut extra material at the sides to wrap around the frames). Staple the sides of the shirt to two sides of the frame. The sides that button/snap should be flexible and easy to manipulate. It is best to fasten the shirt/jacket before stapling. Introduce one frame at a time (usually beginning with buttoning) to the children and allow them to become fairly proficient at it before introducing another task.

To practice lacing, nail an old men's shoe to a large piece of wood. Attach two different colored laces to the inside base of the shoe to minimize confusion and to help clarify any verbal instructions you may use when talking with the child about lacing and tying.

## The Best Gift in the World
*You will need:* a carton/box (one with a flip top); gift wrapping; a bow; a mirror large enough to fit in the bottom of the carton.
*Procedure:* Cover the carton with the gift wrap (making sure that the top is easily lifted off). Place a bow on the lid of the box. Place the mirror inside the carton. Gather a small group of children and have them sit comfortably on a rug. Introduce the wrapped box to the children by explaining that the box contains "the most wonderful gift in the whole world." Explain that they will have a turn to look in the box, but they are not to tell what they see inside. Pass the box from child to child. After all the children have had a turn, encourage them to talk about their feelings and thoughts.

## Personalized Placemats
*You will need:* selection of wallpaper patterns cut into rectangles; crayons; clear contact paper.
*Procedure:* Have each child select a different pattern from the wallpaper rectangles. Ask them to make a drawing on the printed side of the wallpaper. Encourage the child to draw a picture of herself, a pet, a favorite toy, etc. Print the child's name on the mat (or if the child can write his name, allow the child to do this). Laminate both sides of the mat with clear contact paper. Mats can be used during snack time, play activities, or fingerpainting. Placemats of this kind make excellent gifts for parents, grandparents, etc., during the holiday season.

## "I Can" Can
*You will need:* a juice can covered with contact paper and labeled "I can"; several wooden tongue depressors.
*Procedure:* Draw on each tongue depressor a symbol of a skill appropriate to the age and developmental level of the children you are working with. For example, a picture of a button (or real button affixed to the depressor) will be a symbol for the ability to button a shirt. Other symbols may include snap, lace, toothbrush, boots,

broom, shovel, hanger, dishtowel, fork and knife, scissors, egg beater, paintbrush, staple, hairbrush and comb, etc. Introduce the materials to the children by reviewing the symbols associated with the activity or skill.

Have the child place the tongue depressors that reflect an acquired skill into the "I can" can. The teacher/parent may want to help the child recognize all of the achieved skills as well as identify one or two skills the child may want to practice.

### I'm on TV

*You will need:* a large carton/box; a sharp knife (to be used only by the teacher); paint and brushes.

*Procedure:*
1. Using the sharp knife, the adult cuts the top off the box, then cuts a screen shape out of the bottom of the box.
2. The children then paint the front and sides of the box, adding dials to the front portion.
3. Place the TV box on a table, and the "actors" are ready to sing, make faces, use puppets, or present their favorite commercial.
4. This piece of equipment can be replaced with the frame of a large console television. Be sure to remove the equipment inside as well as the back, checking for any sharp edges.

### Animal Zoo

*You will need:* large carton/box; pictures of animals; glue; a paper strip (large enough to stretch across the front of the carton); a marker.
*Procedure:* Many small children have a "special" stuffed animal that is slept with and held during times of stress. Children enjoy sharing these favorite pets with friends but cannot tolerate having them touched, petted, and poked by others. Establishing an "animal zoo" where special pets can be left and viewed provides an excellent solution to this problem.

A simple zoo can be constructed out of a large carton. Cut the top off the carton and lie it on its side. Have the children transform the carton into a zoo by pasting pictures of animals (cut from magazines or drawn) onto the carton (inside and out). The adult can post a sign cautioning the children "Do not feed or touch the animals."

### Old McDonald

*Procedure:* The children sing the tune "Old McDonald," using a new format. Use the children's names and different body parts.
*Example:*
Suzy, Suzy had a body, e-i-e-i-o.
And on her body she had a foot, e-i-e-i-o.
With a (stomp), (stomp), here and a (stomp), (stomp), there
Here a (stomp), there a (stomp),
Everywhere a (stomp), (stomp),
Suzy, Suzy, had a body, e-i-e-i-o.

Repeat the song using various body parts.

### If You're Happy

*Procedure:* Sing the song, "If You're Happy and You Know It," using body part movements in the verses.

Example: If you're happy and you know it, shake your head.
(Repeat)
If you're happy and you know it and you really want to show it,
If you're happy and you know it, shake your head.

For other ideas, instead of "shake your head," substitute the following:

1. Clap your hands.
2. March in place.
3. Shake your hips.
4. Touch your toes.
5. Roll your head.
6. Wiggle your nose.
7. Smile really big.

The children really enjoy making up their own verses.

# UNIT REVIEW

1. Discuss art activities appropriate for the following units: community helpers, self-awareness, learning one's name.
2. What areas of the curriculum (e.g., art, music, language arts) would you use to help children learn their own and others' names in various ways? Give some examples of activities you would use in each of these areas.
3. Relate incidents similar to the opening scenes in this unit, demonstrating young children's level of social awareness. Explain why you think the children acted the way they did. Explain how an adult (or older child) would react in the same situation.
4. What community/school "helpers" would you invite to your room to aid children's understanding of their community? What would you have these visitors talk

about; bring with them to class; and do with the children (if anything)?

5. What are some ways the block area can be used to teach social studies ideas?

6. What are the two basic rules for beginning to teach young children about peace?

# ADDITIONAL READINGS

## General—For Teachers

Bernat, V. "Teaching Peace." *Young Children* (Mar., 1993): 36–39.

Billman, J. "The Native American Curriculum: Attempting Alternatives to Teepees and Headbands." *Young Children* 47 (6) (1992): 22–25.

Blackburn, L.B. *The Class in Room 44: When a Classmate Dies.* Omaha, Neb.: Centering Corp., 1991.

Brady, P. "Columbus and the Quincentennial Myths: Another Side of the Story." *Young Children,* 47 (6) (1992): 4–14.

Burkhardt, D.H. "Building Blocks, Building Skills." Scholastic Pre-K Today (April, 1993): 42–49.

Buzzelli, C.A. "Research in Review: Young Children's Moral Understanding: Learning About Right and Wrong." *Young Children* 47 (6) (1992): 47–53.

Carlsson-Paige, N., and D.E. Levin. *Helping Young Children Understand Peace, War, and the Nuclear Threat.* Washington, D.C.: NAEYC, 1989.

———. "Making Peace in Violent Times: A Constructivist Approach to Conflict Resolution." *Young Children* 48 (1) (1992): 4–13.

Cartwright, S. "Cooperative Learning Can Occur in any Kind of Program." *Young Children* 48 (2) (1993): 12–14.

Cassidy, J., and S.R. Asher. "Loneliness and Peer Relations in Young Children." *Child Development.* 63 (1992): 350–365.

Cech, M. *Global Child: Multicultural Resources for Young Children.* Ottawa, Ontario: Child Care Initiatives, 1990.

Charney, R.S. *Teaching Children to Care: Management in the Responsive Classroom.* Greenfield, Mass.: Northeast Foundation for Children, 1991.

Clark, L., S. DeWolf, and C. Clark. "Teaching Teachers to Avoid Having Culturally Assaultive Classrooms." *Young Children* 47 (5) (1992): 4–9.

Corbett, S.M. "A Complicated Bias." *Young Children* 48 (3) (1993): 29–31.

Curry, N., and C. Johnson. *Beyond Self-Esteem: Developing a Genuine Sense of Human Value.* Washington, D.C.: NAEYC, 1989.

Daniels, H.A., ed. *Not Only English: Affirming America's Multilingual Heritage.* Urbana, Ill.: National Council of Teachers of English, 1990.

Derman-Sparks, L. *Anti-Bias Curriculum: Tools for Empowering Young Children.* Washington, D.C.: NAEYC, 1989.

———. "Understanding Diversity: What Young Children Want and Need to Know. *Pre-K Today* (Nov./Dec. 1990): 44–50.

Ennew, J., and B. Milne. *The Next Generation: Lives of Third World Children.* Philadelphia: New Society, 1990.

Fabes, R.A., and N. Eisenberg. "Young Children's Coping with Interpersonal Anger." *Child Development,* 63 (1992): 116–128.

Gonzalez-Mena, J. "Do You Have Cultural Tunnel Vision?" *Child Care Information Exchange* No. 80 (July/Aug., 1991): 29–31.

———. Multicultural Issues in Child Care: 1993, Mountain View, Calif.: Mayfield Publishing Co., 1993.

Greenberg, P. "Educational Leadership and the Crisis of Democratic Government." *Educational Researcher* 21 (4) (1992): 4–12.

———. "Ideas that Work with Young Children: How to Institute Some Simple Democratic Practices Pertaining to Respect, Rights, Roots, and Responsibilities in Any Classroom (Without Losing Your Leadership Position)." *Young Children,* 47 (July, 1992): 10–17.

———. "Ideas that Work with Young Children: Teaching about Native Americans? Or Teaching About People, Including Native Americans?" *Young Children* 47 (6) (1992): 27–30; 79–81.

———. "Why Not Academic Preschool? Part 2. Autocracy or Democracy in the Classroom?" *Young Children* 47 (3) (1992): 54–64.

Hendrick, J. "Where Does It All Begin? Teaching the Principles of Democracy in the Early Years." *Young Children* 47 (3) (1992): 51–53.

Hirsch, E.S., ed. *The Block Book,* Rev. Ed. Washington, D.C.: NAEYC, 1984.

Holder-Brown, L., and Parette, H.P., Jr. "Children with Disabilities Who Use Assistive Technology: Ethical Considerations." *Young Children* 47 (6) (1992): 73–77.

Jervis, K., ed. *Separation.* Washington, D.C.: NAEYC, 1990.

Kemple, K.M. "Research in Review. Pre-school Children's Peer Acceptance and Social Interaction." *Young Children* 46 (5) (1991): 47–54.

Little Soldier, K. "Working with Native American Children." *Young Children* 47 (6) (1992): 15–21.

Luvmour, S., and J. Lavmour. *Everyone Wins: Cooperative*

*Games and Activities.* Philadelphia: New Society Publishers, 1990.

Miller, D. *Positive Child Guidance.* Albany, N.Y.: Delmar Publishers, Inc. 1995.

National Association for the Education of Young Children. "Enriching Classroom Diversity with Books for Children, In-Depth Discussion of Them and Story-Extension Activities (A Bibliography)." *Young Children* (Mar., 1993): 10–16.

National Association for the Education of Young Children. "Guidelines for Appropriate Curriculum Content and Assessment in Programs Serving Children Ages 3 through 8." *Young Children* 46 (3) (1991): 21–38.

National Task Force On School Readiness. *Caring Communities: Supporting Young Children and Families.* Washington, D.C.: National Association of State Boards of Education, 1990.

Neugebauer, B., ed. *Alike and Different: Exploring Our Humanity with Young Children (Rev. Ed.).* Washington, D.C.: NAEYC, 1991.

Oken-Wright, P. "From Tug of War to "Let's Make a Deal": The Teacher's Role." *Young Children* (1) (1992): 15–20.

Ramsey, P. *Teaching and Learning in a Diverse World: Multicultural Education for Young Children.* New York: Teachers College Press, Columbia University, 1987.

Raver, C.C., and E.F. Zigler. "Three Steps Forward, Two Steps Back: Head Start and the Measurement of Social Competence." *Young Children* 46 (4) (1991): 308.

Riley, S.S. *How to Generate Values in Young Children: Integrity, Honesty, Individuality, Self-Confidence, and Wisdom.* Washington, D.C.: NAEYC, 1991.

Saracho, O.N., and B. Spodek. *Understanding the Multicultural Experience in Early Childhood Education.* Washington, D.C.: NAEYC, 1990.

Seefeldt, C. "Social Studies: Learning for Freedom." *Young Children* (Mar., 1993): 4–9.

Smith, C.A. *Promoting the Social Development of Young Children: Strategies and Activities.* Palo Alto, Calif.: Mayfield Publishing Co., 1982.

Solter, A. "Understanding Tears and Tantrums." *Young Children* 47 (Mar., 1992): 64–68.

Walling, D.R. *Meeting the Needs of Transient Students.* Bloomington, Ind.: Phi Delta Kappa, 1990.

Walter, M.P. *Habari Gani?* New York: Lothrop, Lee & Shepard Books, 1989.

Wasserman, S. "Louis E. Raths: Theories of Empowerment." *Childhood Education* 67 (4) (1991): 235–239.

Wenning, J., and S. Wortis. *Made by Human Hands: A Curriculum for Teaching Young Children about Work and Working People.* Cambridge, Mass.: The Multicultural Project for Communication and Education, Inc., 1984.

York, S. *Roots and Wings: Affirming Culture in Early Childhood Programs.* St. Paul, Minn.: Redleaf Press, 1991.

## Children's Books (See end of Unit 18 for books on specific ethnic groups)

Aardema, V. *Borrequita and the Coyote.* New York: Alfred A. Knopf, 1991.

Abolafia, Yossi. *Yanosh's Island.* New York: Greenwillow, 1988.

Alderson, Sue Ann. *Ida and the Wool Smugglers.* New York: McElderry, 1988.

Alexander, L. *The Fortune-Teller.* New York: Dutton, 1993.

Andrews, J. *Very Last First Time.* New York: Atheneum, 1986.

Bailey, D. *Nomads.* (Where We Live Series) Austin, Texas: Stech-Vaugh, 1990.

————. *Cities.* (Where We Live Series) Austin, Tex.: Stech-Vaugh, 1990.

————. *Australia.* (Where We Live Series) Madison, N.J.: Stech-Vaugh, 1990.

————. *Hong Kong.* (Where We Live Series) Madison, N.J.: Stech-Vaugh, 1990.

————. *India.* (Where We Live Series) Madison, N.J.: Stech-Vaugh, 1990.

————. *Trinidad.* (Where We Live Series) Madison, N.J.: Stech-Vaugh, 1990.

Balterman, L. *Girders and Cranes: A Skyscraper Is Built.* Morton Grove, Ill.: Albert Whitman, 1991.

Baylor, B. *Hawk, I'm Your Brother.* New York: Charles Scribner's Sons, 1976.

Begay, S. *Ma'ii and Cousin Horned Toad.* New York: Scholastic, 1993.

Birch, D. *The King's Chessboard.* New York: Dial, 1988.

Birdseye, T. *Airmail to the Moon.* New York: Holiday, 1988.

————. *A Song of Stars: An Asian Legend.* New York: Holiday, 1990.

Blair, S. *The Three Billy Goats Gruff.* New York: Holt, Rinehart & Winston, 1964.

Blos, J. *Old Henry.* New York: Morrow, 1987.

Brown, Marc. *Arthur's Baby.* New York: Joy Street/Little, 1987.

Brown, M.W. *A Child's Goodnight Book.* New York: William R. Scott, 1950.

————. *The Runaway Bunny.* New York: Harper and Row, 1977.

Burton, V. *Katy and the Big Snow.* Boston: Houghton Mufflin, 1943.

————. *Mike Mulligan and His Steam Shovel.* Boston: Houghton Mifflin, 1939.

Byers, B. *Go and Hush the Baby.* New York: Viking Press, 1971.

Clure, B., and H. Ramsey. *Me.* Glendale, Calif.: Bowman Publications, 1968.

————. *Things I Like to Do.* Glendale, Calif.: Bowmar Publications, 1968.

————. *Where Is Home?* Glendale, Calif.: Bowmar Publications, 1971.

Cohen, M. *The New Teacher.* New York: Macmillan, 1972.
———. *Will I Have a Friend?* New York: Macmillan, 1967.
Cohn, J. *I Had a Friend Named Peter.* New York: William Morrow, 1992.
Corcos, L. *Joel Gets a Haircut.* New York: Abelard-Schuman, 1952.
Couzyn, J. *Bad Day.* New York: Dutton, 1990.
Davison, Brian. *Looking at a Castle.* New York: Random, 1987.
Day, Niki. *Not So Fast Songololo.* New York: Atheneum, 1985.
Delton, J. *Two Good Friends.* New York: Crown Publications, 1974.
Eichler, M. *Martin's Father.* Chapel Hill, N.C.: Lollipop Power, 1971.
Ets, M.H. *Just Me.* New York: Viking Press, 1965.
———. *Play With Me.* New York: Viking Press, 1955.
Fisher, A. *Going Places.* Glendale, Calif.: Bowmar Publications, 1973.
Francoise, A. *The Things I Like.* New York: Charles Scribner's Sons, 1957.
Gantschev, Ivan. *The Train to Grandma's.* New York: Picture Book, 1987.
Gay, Z. *Who's Afraid?* New York: Viking Press, 1965.
Gerstein, Mordicai. *The Mountain of Tibet.* New York: Harper, 1987.
Gordon, S. *Girls Are Girls and Boys Are Boys.* New York: The John Day Co., 1975.
Green, M. McB. *Everybody Has a House and Everybody Eats.* New York: Young Scott Books, 1961.
Griffith, Helen V. *Granddaddy's Place.* New York: Greenwillow, 1987.
Harvey, Brett. *Immigrant Girl: Becky of Eldridge Street.* New York: Holiday House, 1987.
Hedderwick, Mairi. *Katie Morag and the Big Boy Cousins.* New York: Little, 1987.
Hendershot, Judity. *In Coal Country.* New York: Knopf, 1987.
Henkes, Devin. *Grandpa & Bo.* New York: Greenwillow, 1988.
———. *Sheila Rae, The Brave.* New York: Greenwillow, 1987.
———. *When Grandpa Came to Stay.* New York: Greenwillow, 1986.
Hoban, R. *A Baby Sister for Francis.* New York: Harper & Row, 1964.
Holder, H. *Carmine the Crow.* New York: Farra, Straus, & Giroux, 1993.
Hooks, William. *Moss Gown.* Boston: Houghton, 1987.
Jaynes, R. *Friends! Friends! Friends!* New York: Pantheon, 1973.
Jeffrey, S. *Who Lives Here?* New York: Dandelion Press, 1979.
Keates, E.J. *Peter's Chair.* New York: Harper & Row, 1967.
———. *Whistle for Willie.* New York: Harper & Row, 1964.
Keller, H. *Goodbye, Max.* New York: Greenwillow, 1987.
Kent, J. *Just Only John.* New York: Pantheon, 1972.
Keyworth, C.L. *New Day.* New York: Morrow, 1986.
Kimmel, E.A. *Baba Yaga: A Russian Folktale.* New York: Holiday, 1991.
King-Smith, D. *Farmer Bungle Forgets.* New York: Antheneum, 1987.
Korth-Sander, I. *Will You Be My Friend?* New York: Henry Holt, 1986.
Kratka, S. *Hi, New Baby.* New York: Simon & Schuster, 1970.
Krauss, R. *The Happy Day.* New York: Harper & Brothers, 1980.
———. *Leo the Late Bloomer.* New York: Windmill Books, 1971.
Leaf, Margaret. *Eyes of the Dragon.* New York: Lothrop, 1987.
LeTord, Bijou. *My Grandma Leonie.* New York: Bradbury, 1987.
Mandelbaum, P. *You Be Me, I'll Be You.* Brooklyn, New York: Kane/Miller Book Publishers, 1990.
Martin, Charles E. *Sam Saves the Day.* New York: Greenwillow, 1987.
Marzollo, J. *Close Your Eyes.* New York: Dial Press, 1978.
Mayer, M. *There's a Nightmare in My Closet.* New York: Dial Press, 1968.
———. *You're the Scaredy Cat.* New York: Parents' Magazine Press, 1974.
Nixon, J.L. *Fat Chance, Claude.* New York: Viking Kestrel, 1987.
Pomerantz, C. *How Many Trucks Can a Tow Truck Tow?* New York: Random House, 1987.
Provensen, Alice and Martin. *Shaker Lane.* New York: Viking-Kestrel, 1987.
Retan, W. *The Big Book of Real Trucks.* New York: Grosset & Dunlap, 1990.
Rice, Eve. *City Night.* New York: Greenwillow, 1987.
Rich, G. *Firegirl.* New York: The Feminist Press, 1972.
Rylant, Cynthia. *Birthday Presents.* Orchard Books, 1987.
San Souci, R.D. *The Enchanted Tapestry: A Chinese Folktale Retold.* New York: Dial, 1987.
Schlein, M. *The Way Mothers Are.* Chicago: Albert Whitman, 1963.
Seeger, Pete. *Abiyoyo.* New York: Macmillan, 1986.
Sharmat, M.W. *I'm Terrific.* New York: Holiday House, 1977.
Siekkinen, Raija. *Mister King.* Los Angeles: Carolrhoda, 1987.
Slater, T. *The Big Book of Real Fire Trucks and Firefighting.* New York: Grosset & Dunlap, 1987.
Slobodkin, L. *One Is Good, But Two Are Better.* New York: Vanguard Press, 1955.
Small David. *Paper John.* Indianapolis: Farrar, 1987.

Synder, Dianne. *The Boy of the Three-Year Nap.* Boston: Houghton, 1988.

Steig, W. *Sylvester and the Magic Pebble.* New York: Simon & Schuster, 1969.

Surowiecki, S.L. *Joshua's Day.* Chapel Hill, N.C.: Lollipop Power, 1972.

Torre, B.L. *The Luminous Pearl: A Chinese Folktale Retold.* New York: Orchard Books, 1990.

Udry, J.M. *Let's Be Enemies.* New York: Harper and Brothers, 1964.

Viorst, J. *Alexander and the Terrible, Horrible, Not Good, Very Bad Day.* New York: Atheneum, 1972.

Waber, Bernard, *Funny, Funny, Lyle.* Boston: Houghton, 1987.

Whitney, A.M. *Just Awful.* Reading, Mass.: Addison-Wesley, 1971.

Williams, B. *Albert's Toothache.* New York: E.P. Dutton, 1974.

————. *Someday, Said Mitchell.* New York: E.P. Dutton, 1976.

Wood, Audrey. *Heckedy Peg.* San Diego: Harcourt, 1987.

Zolotow, C. *Big Brother.* New York: Harper & Row, 1960.

————. *Big Sister and Little Sister.* New York: Harper & Row, 1966.

————. *William's Doll.* New York: Harper & Row, 1972.

# U N I T   2 3

# Creative Health and Safety Experiences

## OBJECTIVES

After studying this unit, you should be able to
- discuss the basic health practices that need to be stressed with young children in the early childhood program.
- describe the approach a teacher of young children must take in all health matters.
- list the three major areas of health and safety concerns in the early childhood program.
- discuss traffic safety, fire safety, and poison safety in the early childhood curriculum.
- suggest how topics about health and safety can be incorporated into other curriculum areas.

## HEALTH AND SAFETY IN THE EARLY YEARS

Health is a physical state in the here and now. Safety is also a present state. Young children don't think in terms of the distant future. It's the *now* that interests them, not a talk on how a bad health or safety habit can hurt a person in the future.

Preaching, lecturing, and rote learning of health facts are all ineffective techniques in the early childhood classroom. What should be stressed is a positive, fun, but most of all *natural* approach to health and safety in the classroom.

Good health and safety practices should be modeled by adults as much as they are included in actual lesson plans. Emphasis in this unit will be on presenting basic concepts of health and safety in simple classroom activities that do not require special equipment or curriculum guides. Common sense and daily experiences form the basis of the following activities.

In the area of health and safety, your actions surely speak louder than words. For example, your own shining hair, clean body, neat clothing, and fresh smell "tell" children so much more about personal hygiene and good health practices than any lesson plan. With this emphasis, this unit contains some basic health and safety ideas and how to use these ideas in classroom activities.

## HEALTH PRACTICES

Good health is often not appreciated until the later years in life, when one doesn't always have it. It is important in the early years of life, when we least appreciate health, to learn practices that will extend our health long past those early years.

Good health practices include simple ones such as brushing one's teeth and hair, bathing regularly, and a general interest in cleanliness. Getting enough sleep and good food are also basic to good health at all ages. All these ideas and tasks are first taught at home and need to be reinforced in the classroom. This can be done in many ways, but informal talks, rather than pointed lessons, work best with young children just learning to really care for themselves physically.

Unlike for you and other adults, daily personal hygiene tasks are not yet routine for children. For in-

459

stance, when a six-year-old gets up and ready for school, he often may forget to brush his teeth or comb his hair. He doesn't automatically do these tasks but has to "remember" them every morning. And since it's not always easy for a child to remember, he may often forget. His peers may forget in the same way, too. Thus, he suffers no great social embarrassment. In this situation an adult's gentle (confidential) reminder can help prod the memory of a forgetful child. Yet in no way should learning personal hygiene be a cause for shame or negative comments.

**Dental Care.** Many early childhood teachers make a task such as toothbrushing an enjoyable group activity. Either with individually marked brushes from home or those provided by the school, toothbrushing becomes a fun group activity—after lunch or snack—whenever it fits the daily schedule.

Children learn good dental care in daily routines. The simple practice of daily toothbrushing, rinsing with water after sweets, and frequent use of detergent foods that clean the teeth (such as apples) in snacks all promote good dental health.

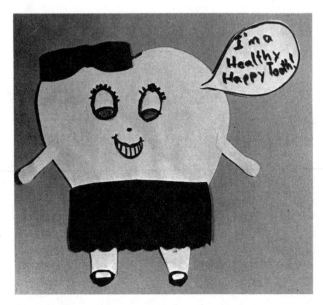

**FIGURE 23–1  In art activities, children can draw about the effects of good dental hygiene.**

Be sure each child's toothbrush is in an individual toothbrush holder to prevent the spread of disease. These are inexpensive plastic containers widely available in drug and variety stores. To help children find their own toothbrushes, put masking tape on the back of each holder and write each child's name on the tape. After brushing, have the children dry off their toothbrushes and replace them in their holders. Be sure to check at the end of each week to see if the holders need cleaning. Put masking tape on each brush and write each child's name on the tape.

Brushing teeth often leads to discussions of teeth or to naming of mouth parts. A nurse, dental hygienist, or dentist might visit and demonstrate correct toothbrushing and flossing techniques to the children. Or you might take the class to visit a dentist's office and examine the chair, mirror, and other equipment. You can also have the dentist demonstrate how to brush and care for teeth and gums.

Follow up routine toothbrushing and visits to the dentist by reading books, role playing, and finding out more about how teeth grow and develop. Provide children with props that will foster dramatic play. A flashlight, white shirts, and a simple chair are all that are necessary to stimulate dental play.

Losing a tooth is an occasion to focus on concepts of growth and development. The lost tooth can be examined and discussed: "Why did the tooth come out?" "What will happen next?" "How else will you grow and change next year?"

In art activities, children can draw about the effects of good dental hygiene. They can sing songs about these ideas, too.

**Positive Approach to Health and Hygiene.**  In any health or personal hygiene matter, emphasis must be on the *positive* view of self. How can a child learn to value others if he doesn't feel valued by the teacher and doesn't care for his own body in a way that preserves its value?

This is true for the various health and hygiene tasks young children learn in the early childhood classroom. In all these tasks, the teacher needs first of all to model good health and hygiene practices himself and to allow time and space in the room for the children to practice them. A large mirror at children's eye level, a sink easily reached and operated by young children, soap in a form that children can easily handle—these are but a few examples of arrangements and equipment that help children "practice" good personal hygiene. To be sure that children always have soap available for handwashing, place a bar of soap in a old knee-high nylon stocking. Tie the stocking to the faucet of the sink. This prevents the soap both from landing on the floor and leaving a soapy mess in the soap dish.

The routines of dressing, washing, eating, and resting will take up a great deal of time when working with young children. In fact, you will sometimes think of yourself as a caregiver and not a teacher. You will need to develop the understanding that these everyday activities, while essential for good health, are equally essential for *teaching* about health. All of these daily routines serve as the basis for teaching children concepts of body functions and parts, as well as the habits of caring for themselves.

Each program will have routines for body care. If you're working with children under age five, it's probably mandated that child-sized toilets, sinks, and mirrors be available. If these are not, arrange for the use of platforms or small sturdy benches or stools so children will be able to reach sinks, get their own toothbrush, and turn on faucets for themselves.

Washing hands before and after using the toilet and before eating, as well as washing faces and brushing teeth after eating, are routines that should be established and followed. When children participate in routines, you introduce them to the purpose and objective of these activities.

Dressing and undressing routines, just as toothbrushing, can be used to introduce vocabulary concepts and ideas of growth. To help children grow in independence in self-dressing, break dressing and undressing into small steps. Offer children help with the first button on a coat or sweater: "I'll do the first. See if you can do the rest." "I'll put the boot over the toe of your shoe, then you can pull it over the rest."

Help with learning to become independent needs to be supportive and informative. As you begin a task, offer explanations on how the children can complete it independently. Give them the opportunity to strug-

gle for a while and accomplish it for themselves, but be observant and ready to step in should frustration occur. Don't do for the child what they can do for themselves. It's ridiculous to see a five-year-old with an easily handled fat zipper being zipped by an adult.

**A Healthy Environment.** Children need to be actively involved in keeping their classroom orderly. A

In your classroom check to see if you have:

( ) Storage shelves and cupboards: low, open shelf space accessible to children and cupboard space for storing supplies. Most shelf space should be movable to permit rearranging the room.

( ) A peg rack or cubbies for children's coats.

( ) Screen dividers or other means to create specific play areas and to provide picture display space.

( ) Enough wastebaskets, preferably of plastic or other washable material.

( ) Dust brush, dustpan, whisk broom, sponges, small mop, and plastic pail.

( ) Paper or cloth towels.

( ) Small bars of soap for hand washing, toothbrush containers.

( ) Bulletin board for emergency numbers, first-aid procedures.

( ) File cards and box of parents' home and work phone numbers, child's doctor, and other authorized adults responsible for child.

( ) A fix-it box: a carton in which to put things that need attention. (Be sure that they are fixed!)

( ) Adequate space for storing items that are not being used as well as expendable items, such as paper and paints.

( ) At least one drawer/cabinet with a childproof latch for storing potentially dangerous material.

**FIGURE 23–2 Checklist of equipment for keeping space clean and in order.**

**FIGURE 23–3 Since young children spend so much of their time on the floor, it is important that all areas are easily cleaned.**

clean and orderly room also mirrors the importance of good hygiene practices. Figure 23–2 contains suggestions on how to involve children in keeping the room neat and orderly. When using this checklist, remember that even the smallest child can pick up and put away a toy after playing with it. Maria Montessori, a famous Italian child developmentalist and physician, felt that whenever *you* do for a child something the child can do for himself, you are *actually harming the child.*

The child's involvement in room maintenance helps his growing sense of responsibility, as well as keeping the play area uncluttered and pleasant looking. It is much easier to teach children about health and hygiene when the classroom reflects an adult's concern for cleanliness.

## EARLY CHILDHOOD HEALTH CONCERNS

Children in the early childhood program learn basic health practices in many simple, daily routines (such as hand washing after toileting to prevent germs). Besides these daily learning experiences, common health concerns for children in the early childhood years fall into three major areas:

1. Infectious diseases (those that can be spread to others) such as chicken pox and measles. The additional readings at the end of this unit include many excellent, easy-to-use handbooks on identifying and dealing with childhood diseases.
2. Injuries. The additional readings also include several books on first aid and emergency treatment designed for teachers' and parents' use.
3. Health problems that are not evident and must be looked for by screening and observing children (such as vision or hearing problems).

Constant daily observation of children is a necessary part of all three main areas of health. For example, every teacher checks the look on a child's face to determine whether or not he is "getting through" to the youngster. A good health practice in that process is to go one step further and consider whether there may be a *health* reason for a child's frequent lack of attention or understanding.

The teacher can call for health service assistance to rule out or correct a possible health reason for failure to perform on a normal level. This may be the school nurse or any other appropriate assistance. Together they help each child perform on the highest level possible for that child.

**Prevention.** While a teacher can often do very little to prevent the *illnesses* children bring to school, he *is* in a position to do a great deal about preventing *injuries* at school. Figure 23–4 presents some basic ideas about accident prevention for children from two to six years of age.

When it becomes necessary to deal with injury or illness, it is important to remember that a teacher is neither the child's doctor nor parent. Other than providing simple first aid and large doses of comfort, the teacher's primary responsibility is to notify the parent according to instructions on the child's emergency card. The teacher can also make the child comfortable until someone who *is* responsible arrives to take over.

Fortunately, real medical crises are rare, considering the number of hours and the number of chil-

# THINK ABOUT IT . . . .

## YOUNG CHILDREN AND ALLERGIES

Have you ever seen or experienced any of these situations?

- Drew complains that his eyes are itchy and his nose is stuffy.
- Claire keeps wiping her runny nose, and she had some trouble breathing when outside.
- Both children seem uncomfortable and irritable.

You might at first suspect that these children are showing the early signs of a cold. But because these events occurred in April, these children are actually exhibiting signs of allergies, since April is the beginning of the allergy season. The following information is intended to help you recognize the signs of allergies and how to deal with them and the young children suffering from them.

**The Causes of Allergies.** A person has an allergy when she reacts abnormally to a substance that doesn't bother most other people. These substances, known as allergens, may be swallowed, inhaled, or touched. The most common allergens include dust; pollen; mold; venom from bees and other stinging insects; foods such as fish and shellfish, eggs, nuts, cow's milk, chocolate, wheat, corn, and certain fruits; and perfumed soaps and creams.

**Treatment of Allergies.** The most effective way to treat allergies in children is prevention. Be aware of which allergens cause a reaction and then try to avoid exposing children to them. Some allergies can be treated with medications, either taken regularly (every day or during certain seasons) or when the child experiences allergic symptoms. Allergy shots may be used with those children who have severe allergies and/or asthma.

**The Symptoms of Allergies.** Different allergens can cause different reactions, and symptoms may differ from child to child. Also, it's possible for a child to be allergic to more than one substance. The most common symptoms are itchy eyes, a stuffy or runny nose, and wheezing. Allergic reactions to insect bites can show up as redness, swelling, and itchiness around the bite. In severe cases, insect bites may cause low blood pressure resulting in shock. Reactions to food include itchiness, wheezing, headaches, hives, and occasionally—but rarely—shock. Perfumes may make skin itchy and red.

**What to Do During an Allergic Attack.** If you can identify the allergen, remove the child from the allergic environment or remove the substance containing the allergen from the child's environment. If you can't identify the allergen and the child's symptoms continue, comfort him or her while another staff member calls the child's parent. In the case of a severe reaction, call 911 or your local emergency number and the child's parent.

**Helping Young Children with Allergies.** You can help children with allergies feel more comfortable, so they can enjoy your program fully, by taking the following steps:

*Maintain up-to-date medical histories.* Be sure all staff members, especially those involved in preparing food, know which children and adults are allergic and to what. Also, if a child needs medication, make sure you have written permission from the child's parent to administer it and written directions that clearly explain the exact dosage and how often the medicine should be given.

*Be sure you have a bee-sting kit on hand and know how to use it.* Available at pharmacies, this kit contains epinephrine, which is used to help block the allergic reaction. You'll need to check with a child's parent for permission to use it.

*Keep the environment as clean and dust-free as possible.* Make sure there is adequate ventilation. If you use a humidifier, clean the system frequently to avoid a buildup of mold. Remember that rugs, stuffed animals, and feather pillows collect dust and can also be the cause of allergic reactions.

*Choose classroom pets wisely.* Because one out of every six children is likely to have some kind of allergy, be sure you check each child's medical record in order to select a pet least likely to cause allergic reactions.

| AGE | CHARACTERISTICS | ACCIDENT HAZARDS | MEASURES FOR PREVENTION |
|---|---|---|---|
| 2–3 years | Fascinated by fire; moves about constantly; tries to do things alone; imitates | Traffic | Keep child away from streets and driveway with strong fence and firm discipline. Teach rules and dangers of traffic. |
| | Runs and is lightning fast; impatient with restraint | Transportation | Demonstrate safety; use belts, etc. Maintain vehicles including safety equipment and mechanical condition of brakes, suspension, tires, etc. |
| 3–6 years | Explores the neighborhood, climbs, rides tricycles; likes and plays rough games | Tools/equipment | Store dangerous knives, sharp scissors, and garden equipment out of reach. Teach safe use of tools and kitchen equipment; careful supervision when using. Guards on fans. |
| | | Water | Even shallow wading pools are unsafe unless carefully supervised. |
| | | Play areas | Guard against children involving selves in play beyond physical capabilities (climbing up something, unable to come down) |

**FIGURE 23–4 Accident prevention.**

| AGE | CHARACTERISTICS | ACCIDENT HAZARDS | MEASURES FOR PREVENTION |
|---|---|---|---|
| | | Toys | Large sturdy toys without sharp edges or small removable parts are safest. Close supervision when equipment with small parts in use. |
| | | Burns | Guards for radiators, hot pipes, and other hot surfaces. Temperature of water not to exceed 120° F. Minimize and properly store all combustible material. |
| | | Poisoning | Store all medicines and poisons in locked cabinet. Store cleaning products out of reach. Store kerosene or gasoline in metal cans and out of reach. Screen windows to protect against insect bites, food contamination. Use proper sanitation procedures in all food preparation. Never use lead-based paint. |

List specific policies of your center for prevention of accidents. It is recommended that the staff review their "minute-by-minute" accident prevention policies periodically in order to evaluate what changes are needed and to include changes in listed guidelines for substitutes and volunteers. The center's accident log should be consulted in such an evaluation. The same applies to the classroom teacher: Consistent accident prevention policies should be followed as well as reviewed on a regular basis.

Based on information provided by the American Academy of Pediatrics in "Standards for Day Care Centers," 1980.

FIGURE 23–4 Accident prevention (cont.).

dren involved in routine school days. And even when a child is hurt or ill, the truly critical factors are not likely to be the time required to decide what to do and the way in which the decision should be implemented. The crisis is far more likely to rest in the psychological effect on the staff, the child, and the parent.

Another area of prevention concerns poisonous plants. Knowing which plants are poisonous, a teacher can avoid an accident involving a child eating a poisonous plant. Figure 23–5 lists several common plants and which parts, if any, are toxic. It also lists treatment for a child who may have eaten part of a poisonous plant.

## SAFETY EDUCATION

Accidents are the leading cause of death for children under age 14. Thus, the importance of providing children with an environment prepared for their experimentation and exploration cannot be understated. Accidents most frequently occur to children who have had little opportunity to explore, to find out for themselves, or to experience minor scrapes and bumps—children who feel no responsibility for their own safety. (See Figure 23–4 for the listing of the most common accidents and methods of prevention.)

When children do not have a safe environment in

| COMMON NAME | BOTANICAL NAME | TOXIC PART | TREATMENT CODE |
|---|---|---|---|
| African Violet | *Saintpaulia ionantha* | Probably none | A, B |
| Azalea | *Rhododendron* | All parts | A |
| Begonia | *Begonia spp.* * | Probably none | A, B |
| Buttercup | *Ranunculus spp.* | All parts | A, C |
| Castor Bean | *Rincinus communis* | Chew seeds, leaves | A |
| Christmas Kalanchoe (or Flaming Katy) | *Kalanchoe bloss Feldiana "compacta"* | Probably none | A |
| Christmas Pepper | *Capsicum annum* | Fruit—causes burns | C |
| Daffodil | *Narcissus spp.* | All parts, especially bulb | A |
| Dandelion | *Taraxacum officinale* | Probably none | A, B |
| Dogwood | *Cornus florida* | Probably none | A, B |
| Dumbcane | *Dieffenbachia spp.* | Leaves | A, C |
| English Ivy | *Hedera helix* | Leaves, berries | A |
| Hemlock | *Conium maculatum* | All parts, especially seed | A |
| Holly | *Ilex* | All parts, especially berries | A |
| Hyacinth | *Hyacinthus orientalis* | Bulb | A |
| Hydrangea | *Hydrangea arborescens* | Leaves and buds | A |
| Impatiens | *Impatiens spp.* | Probably none | A |
| Jack-in-the-Pulpit | *Arisaema triphyllum* | Roots (in quantity) | A, C |
| Jerusalem Cherry | *Solanum pseudocapsicum* | Leaves, unripe berry, possibly unripe fruit | A |
| Jimson Weed | *Datura stramonium* | All parts | A |
| Lily-of-the-Valley | *Convallaria majalis* | All parts | A |
| Mayapple | *Podophyllum peltatum* | All parts, except ripe fruit | A |
| Mistletoe | *Phoradendron spp.* | All parts, especially berries | A |
| Mockorange | *Philadelphus spp.* | Probably none | A, B |
| Mountain Laurel | *Kalmia latifolia* | All parts | A |
| Nightshades | *Solanum dulcamara, S. nigrum* | All parts | A |
| Philodendron | *Philodendron spp.* | All parts | A, C |
| Pokeweed | *Phytolacca americana* | Berries, leaves if cooked improperly | A |
| Poinsettia | *Euphorbia pulcherrima* | Sap in plant | A |
| Pothos | *Scindapsus aureus* | All parts | A, C |
| Privet | *Ligustrum vulgare* | Berries, leaves | A |
| Pyracantha | *Pyracantha coccinea lalandi* | Probably none | A, B |
| Rhododendron | *Rhododendron maximum* | All parts | A |
| Rose | *Rosa spp.* | Probably none | A, B |
| Wandering Jew | *Tradescantia fluminensis* | Probably none | A, B |
| Water Hemlock | *Cicuta masculata* | All parts, especially roots | A |
| Wild Strawberry | *Fragaria vesea* | Probably none | A, B |
| Yew | *Taxus spp.* | All parts | A |

*spp.: includes all species of the plant
*Treatment Codes:*
A. Call the local poison information center to report ingestion and verify plant. Post this number near the phone.
B. No treatment necessary.
C. Give milk immediately and then call the local poison center.

Based on information provided by the American Academy of Pediatrics in "Standards for Day Care Centers," 1980.

**FIGURE 23–5 Poisonous plants and treatment for their ingestion.**

which to practice or the opportunity to face challenges, they're more likely to be involved in some type of accident. They have no idea of the consequences and no experience in making decisions or judging hazards.

A safe environment is not only free from hazards, but contains the presence of a diligent, observing, and supervising adult. Even though you have safety checked the play yard and play room prior to the time the children arrive, you should be continually alert for potential hazards. As children play you must reinforce safety rules that have been decided by you and the children. You might even post them as a reminder. But you will have to keep on reminding young children, in a positive yet firm way, as they play: "Ride your bike here." "Climb the tree with your hands free." "Remove the truck from under the swings." Being prepared means looking over both your indoor and outdoor play areas for all potentially dangerous areas. For example, if swing seats are too slippery, cover them with a coat of paint to which you have added some fine sand. The sand will give just enough traction, yet it won't scratch the children. Or, cover swing seats with pieces of foam rubber to prevent slipping.

For any other potential emergencies, you, other adults who work with you, and the children all need to practice a prepared emergency plan.

Being prepared is a must. The plan should be written and posted. Decide who will stay with the children, what the children will do, and what the other adults will do. Teach children how to use the phone. Have them practice dialing the emergency number, and teach those age two or under how to obtain the operator should the need arise. Even very young children can find the "0" for operator, especially if a red dot is painted over the number.

Think ahead. Who will transport an injured or ill child to the doctor or hospital? Have parents record the numbers of their preferred doctor and hospital, but inform them that in an emergency you may call the health facility nearest to the school. Written permission from the parent needs to be on file, giving the teacher permission to take the child for any emergency medical care.

Decide about the precautions required for special needs children. Who will stay with the child with a visual or hearing impairment, or how will you handle the child in a wheelchair if you need to evacuate the building?

Keep a first-aid kit ready, freshened periodically and within easy access in the room and the play yard. The kit should include the following:

FIGURE 23–6 **Because toddlers are often unsteady in their movements, sufficient room is necessary for their activities.**

- A box of assorted adhesive bandages
- A box of 3″ sterile gauze squares
- Sterile gauze bandages, both 2″ and 1″ sizes

- A roll of 1″ wide adhesive tape
- Absorbent cotton
- Antibacterial spray
- Petroleum jelly
- Cloth or absorbent sanitary pads for application of pressure

For occasional bumped foreheads and cut lips, keep on hand some form of cold pack in the freezer. An easy-to-hold, dripless cold pack can be made by half-filling a small plastic vitamin bottle with water and putting it in the freezer. Or keep a wet sponge or washcloth in the freezer to use as a cold pack; they're easier for little hands to hold than an ice cube.

At least one permanent staff person should be trained in first aid and cardiopulmonary resuscitation (CPR). Your local Red Cross or other health agency will offer free courses in accident preparedness and first aid. This training needs to be updated regularly.

All children should have a feeling of being responsible both for their own and the group's safety. Plan to include content from the guidelines of traffic, fire, and poison safety in your curriculum, since these are the three leading causes of injury and death among children.

**Traffic Safety.** You share in the responsibility of helping children learn to cope in traffic. Real experiences are the best way to teach young children about traffic.

The most common cause of traffic accidents involving young children is darting out in front of cars. Children, intent on their play or crossing the street to join a friend, dart into traffic midblock. Drivers, unable to see a small child and unprepared for a pedestrian in that location, simply do not see the child in time to stop. Most of these accidents happen on residential streets. The traffic is usually moving slower than 35 miles per hour, the child is within a few blocks of home, and the weather conditions are usually good. The goals of traffic safety, therefore, should address the midblock or "dart-out" accident and include these points:

- Stop before entering any street.
- Listen and look for traffic before crossing the street.
- Walk across residential streets cautiously.
- Be able to interpret traffic signs and signals correctly.

(Ross and Seefeldt, 1978, p. 69)

*Stop before entering any street.* For children under age five, or those who have not yet learned traffic safety, the first lesson should be on stopping before entering any street. Two-year-olds begin by going outdoors and identifying the different surfaces of the school and play yard and stopping every time the surface changes. Next, children are taken to a quiet, residential street or on a walk around the block and are asked to identify places where the surfaces change, stopping at each place.

The curb is another place to stop since the surface changes here. Learning and practicing stopping in this way establishes the habit of stopping before entering a street. Parents should also be involved in practicing this habit.

*Listen and look for traffic.* Once children learn to stop at the curb, they must learn to look and listen for traffic before crossing the street. With adequate adult supervision, take the children on a field trip to learn these precautions. Children under age five are confused as to whether traffic is traveling toward or away from them. They'll need to practice observing traffic and identifying direction as well as the speed at which cars are traveling.

*Crossing a residential street.* Construct a pretend street with crosswalks and corners, using masking tape or chalk on the play yard surface. Have children use their tricycles or other vehicles to role-play pedestrians and drivers. Using this street, children practice crossing. They are first reminded to stop when the surface of the yard changes and the street begins and to listen and look for oncoming traffic. Additional practice can be structured using a table-top street with toy cars and people.

# THIS ONE'S FOR YOU!

## YOUNG CHILDREN'S COPING WITH ANGER

Personal safety and well being are daily concerns in the early childhood program. Just as young children are learning the basics of health and hygiene, they are also learning how to deal with their own emotions. Children's anger can be an area of constant concern for early childhood teachers. A recent study of preschool children and how they handle their anger sheds some light on this interesting area. You may find this information helpful in your work with young children.

The researchers studied preschoolers (average age 4½ years) during free-play periods. They observed and recorded the causes of preschoolers' anger and how they reacted to these provocations. They also measured the children's social competence and popularity in the group. They found that boys and girls differed in how they dealt with anger. For example, boys tended to vent more than girls, whereas girls tended to actively assert themselves more than boys. Moreover, the research findings supported the conclusion that socially competent and popular children coped with anger in ways that were mostly direct and active and that minimized further conflict and damage to social relationships.

Conflict over possessions was the most common cause of anger, with physical assault the second most frequently observed cause. Young children's anger-related responses varied according to the cause of the anger.

In most types of anger conflicts, children's coping responses to anger frequently involved the venting of angry feelings (particularly for boys) or active resistance, whereby children attempted to defend themselves in nonagressive ways (particularly for girls).

Children who were popular and socially competent were less likely to be involved in anger conflicts. Also, the causes of children's anger were related to their measures of social functioning: popular and competent boys were less likely to become outwardly angry due to physical assaults or social rejection.

Popular and socially competent children were more likely than children less popular or socially competent to deal with anger in ways that addressed the conflict more directly and nonaggressively. These children were likely to use their social status to deal with anger provocations (e.g., they threatened not to like or play with the instigator). In contrast, children who were relatively low in social competence were likely to utilize aggression or other coping responses that did not directly address the social conflict (e.g., venting, adult seeking, "tattling"). (Fabes and Eisenberg, 1992)

With trained and adequate adult supervision, you may be able to take a group of children to a corner and practice crossing the street. When you focus on crossing, children often get the idea that this is a very dangerous business, and it's best to run across the street as fast as they can. Running to cross is another major cause of traffic deaths. Children, who are generally less coordinated than adults, trip and fall in front of oncoming traffic. Teach children to walk with deliberate speed as they cross. Ask them to focus on the task of crossing, not playing, thinking about anything else, or running.

*Interpreting traffic signals and signs correctly.* Instead of easing the task, traffic signals and signs make crossing streets more difficult for children. Often children will elect to cross midblock in order to avoid the signs and signals that they do not understand.

Children should be taught the meaning of the lights and signals found at intersections. First, they need to learn that red is used to symbolize danger and means "stop." Use a red on objects that may be hazardous in the room and play yard. Ask children where red flags should be placed.

Play "follow-the-leader" games, with children stopping whenever a leader holds up a red flag. Once children understand the meaning of red, play the same games using green and yellow flags. Practice crossing a pretend playground street, following the signals given by one of the children with others role-playing pedestrians and drivers.

Do not attempt to practice crossing streets at an intersection without the aid of a police officer and other well-prepared and trained adults. Police officers can take small groups of children to the intersection to explain the traffic signal lights and to practice crossing with them. Children should be at least five years of age before exposure to this activity.

Protecting children in traffic is the role and responsibility of teachers, parents, and the community alike. All adults and older children will serve as models and thus should practice traffic safety themselves at all times. The community should take action to arrange for traffic signs, signals, or crossing guards wherever needed. (Seefeldt and Barbour, 1986)

**Fire Safety.** Project Burn Prevention (1978), funded by the U.S. Consumer Product Safety Commission, is a program designed to provide schools with fire prevention information. It conducts a nationwide campaign on preventing injury from burns to children. The program instructs children on what to do in case of a fire. Some goals for fire safety include:

- Teaching children to approach fire with caution and respect.
- Involving children in practice fire drills.
- Teaching young children to "drop and roll" should they be involved in a fire.
- Teaching young children where the fire extinguisher is and how to use it, as well as how to call the fire department.

Invite a firefighter to the classroom to introduce the children to fire safety practices. The firefighter can teach children the habit of dropping and rolling should they, or their clothing, catch on fire. They can also demonstrate precautions to take when using fire or heat. Follow this demonstration with a lesson on respect for fire. Even if it's only the candles on a birthday cake, teach them to keep a bucket of sand and water nearby whenever handling fire. You don't have to frighten the children; just teach them the potential dangers of fire.

While the firefighter is visiting, show the children where the fire extinguishers are and how they are used. Have them practice dialing the number to reach the fire department, and hold a fire drill. A fire marshal in Georgia (Collins, 1977) has developed the following questionnaire to assist early childhood educators in training children and staff for fire emergencies:

- Do I have a written plan for a fire drill?
- Do I conduct monthly drills based on the plan?
- Have I had the plan reviewed by the fire department?
- Have I held a meeting with the other staff to discuss the plan?
- Does everyone know where the fire extinguisher is and how to operate it?
- Have I practiced fire drills during nap and mealtimes?
- Do I have an assembly location outside of the building?
- What method do I have for accounting for the children once outside?
- Have I held fire drills with different exits blocked?

**Poison Safety.** Over 117,589 children a year experience accidental poisoning in our country, and these are only the cases reported to poison control centers in 45 states. The development of the poison

# THIS ONE'S FOR YOU!

## TRY THESE! SAFETY ACTIVITIES FOR FUN AND LEARNING

You might find the following safety activities helpful in teaching young children the importance of traffic safety:

### Signs of Safety

Make two sets of traffic signs out of cardboard. Place one set in a "feeling box" and the other on a table next to the box. Have the children select a sign from the table and try to find the same one in the "feeling box" using only their sense of feel to identify the sign's shape.

### Tell Me About It!

Instead of a show and tell time, set aside one day to have children tell how they come to school. Have them name one safety rule they followed and describe hazardous or unsafe practices they've observed as they travel to school either walking, riding the school bus, or in a private car.

### This Is My Neighborhood

Construct a learning center called "Streets and Sidewalks" from two cardboard box lids. Label one box "STREETS" and the other "SIDEWALKS." Cut a number of pictures of various vehicles from magazines—bicycles, toy cars, wagons, tricycles, trucks, cars, and so on. Mount these on cardboard. Place a red dot on the backs of those that are to be driven in the street, a blue dot on the backs of those to be driven on the sidewalk. Children then sort the pictures into appropriate boxes and discuss their choices.

### Safe Corners

As an at-home activity, ask children to count the number of streets they cross between home and school. Construct a class graph with the information. Tape numerals to the top of the edge of a table, i.e., 1, 2, 3, 4, 5, 6, and 7. Have each child place a small block over the numeral that represents the number of streets between home and school.

### Follow These Signs!

Reinforce outside sign and signal traffic experiences with this game. Make simulated traffic signs and signals and play "Follow the Sign." Children march around the room, stopping to follow the sign the leader holds up.
(Seefeldt and Barbour, 1986)

control centers and placing the "Mr. Yuck" sticker on dangerous substances has helped to eliminate many cases of accidental poisoning. Yet children in an early childhood setting are just as susceptible to poisonings as children in a home setting. In the school, it becomes your responsibility to protect children from possible poisoning accidents. Your goals with regard to the children's poison safety need to include:

- Recognize "Mr. Yuck" symbol and understand what it means.
- Take medications only from adult family members, parents, physicians, or health personnel.
- Understand that some things are to eat, while others are not.

Using food for art confuses children on this point. Food is to eat; other substances—berries found on the playground, art materials, toys, leaves, flowers—are not for eating.

When you work with children under age five, you must supervise them carefully, preventing them from putting anything into their mouths. You can't expect babies not to put things into their mouths, as this is their way of learning about their world. However, you are responsible for observing the children, freeing the environment from poisonous substances, and removing nonfood objects that do find their way into the children's mouths. (See Figure 23–5 for a list of poisonous plants and materials. Also see Unit 11 for list of unsafe art supplies.)

Check your room and play yard for all poisonous substances, and remove all that you find. Decide which cleaning supplies and other toxic materials are stored in a place that children might encounter accidentally. If you serve meals, be certain that food items are stored separately from nonfood items. There have been tragic mistakes by hurried cooks or teachers who confused a bag of flour with a cleaning product.

Keep the number of your nearest poison control center posted by the phone. If you don't know this number, write to the U.S. Government Printing Office, Washington, D.C., and obtain a complete listing from the Director of Poison Control Centers in the United States (Seefeldt and Barbour, 1986).

## HEALTH AND SAFETY IN OTHER CURRICULUM AREAS

It is important that children learn good habits of health and safety. In school, children are taught how to cross streets safely, to eat a healthy breakfast before going to school, to keep themselves clean, and to help keep their environment clean and attractive. These lessons are clarified and become more meaningful and lasting when accompanied by creative art experiences. Children are more aware of the importance of practicing safety at the crosswalk when they can create a puppet show and dramatize a safe practice (such as helping the safety patrol person) or when they can make a picture on how to stop, look,

**FIGURE 23–7 In daily experiences, such as breakfast, children learn good health habits.**

and listen before crossing streets. Suggested art activities follow.

**Cross with Safety.** Figures of a safety patrol person and children at a corner can be made of toweling rolls. The children use the figures in play-acting, to show how to cross a street safely. They can thus learn the correct safety practice through a fun activity.

Toweling rolls can be painted to depict the characters. Arms may be made by cutting a narrow strip of paper and attaching it to the back of the figure. For rounded arms, use pieces of soda straws, inserted into holes made on both sides of the toweling roll. Mark streets on a table-sized piece of paper. Then the figures can be arranged and moved as they dramatize the safe way to cross the street.

**Food Montage.** Good eating habits can be illustrated by creating a montage. Cut out random illustrations of healthful foods from magazines, or cut

**FIGURE 23–8 Collages on favorite foods, as well as on the basic food groups, fit well into the health curriculum.**

out foods that are only from certain categories (dairy, meat, etc.), or special meals. Arrange cutouts in a pleasing design on a paper or cardboard background, and paste them down.

**Toothful Tommy.** Puppets can be useful in dramatizing the importance of dental care. Fold a paper plate in half to create a large "mouth." Cut two strips of heavy paper to act as straps in order to operate the puppet. Fasten one at the top and one at the bottom of the plate on the outside, leaving room for four fingers to slip into the strap at the top, and the thumb at the bottom. Add cut-paper eyes and a nose along the top edge of the plate. Paper teeth and tongue can be attached along the inner edge of the "mouth." Use a long sock with a slit in the toes allowing room for the hand to slip through and operate the paper plate puppet.

**Posture Silhouette.** Using a projector, children can easily check their posture. Stretch some white roll paper along an empty wall space. As one child stands in the beam of light, another traces his silhouette. Using a number of silhouettes is a good way to create a group portrait. Later, these outlines can be colored with crayons or tempera paint.

**Set a Healthful Table.** Oiled clay, salt clay, and crumpled paper are suitable for modeling three-dimensional objects, such as meats, fruits, and mashed potatoes or other vegetables. Crumpled-paper objects can be painted in appetizing colors. White paper cups may suggest glasses of milk. Children can create a decorative table by printing colorful designs on napkins and placemats made of white roll paper. Cardboard is suitable for plates and silverware. In this way, children learn how to set the table; they can arrange and rearrange the "food" in various combinations and enjoy learning good health habits at the same time.

**Further Variations:**

• To help children learn how to properly set a table, make plastic-covered placemats with cutouts of

# THINK ABOUT IT . . . .

## TELEVISION AND CHILDREN'S EATING HABITS

The influence of television food advertising on young children is a well-researched area. A review of major research has shown that long-term exposure to commercials for low-nutrition foods (i.e., sugary snacks) has a significant influence on children's eating behavior (Libert and Sprafkin, 1988). Commercials for sugary food products (a risk factor in a number of diseases and dental problems) comprise approximately 80 percent of children's televised advertising (Barcus, 1987). Studies of the effects of this type of advertising on children suggest that these ads substantially affect the attitudes and behavior of children with respect to nutrition and food selections. Studies have shown that young children (four- to seven-year-olds) do not understand that sugary foods are detrimental to health, nor are the disclosure portions of these commercials effective in their caution that they should be part of a balanced meal (Liebert and Sprafkin, 1988).

Studies of children's actual food selection as influenced by television commercials underscore the power of television's impact on this type of child health behavior. Studies of children's exposure to commercials of low-nutrition foods reveal that children choose more low- and fewer high-nutrition foods (Gorn and Greenberg, 1982), especially boys (Jeffrey, McClerran, and Fox, 1982). However, pronutritional programming combined with positive evaluative comments by an adult co-viewer can be effective in reducing three- to six-year-old children's consumption of low-nutrition foods (Galst, 1980). Together, these studies suggest, at least, the powerful potential of televised messages as an influence on children's health-related behavior.

Television has another type of effect on children's health behavior that goes beyond program influence. Television has been demonstrated to alter time use and activity choices in families (Robinson, 1972). In another study (Hei and Gold, 1990), it was found that children who watch television two to four hours a day had dramatically higher cholesterol levels than children watching television less than two hours per day, probably caused by insufficient exercise and improper diet. Thus, this impact of television on children's health derives from its substitution for a more health-promoting type of recreational behavior: exercise.

In summary, television appears to have significant effects on several aspects of children's health-related attitudes and behavior.

knives, forks, spoons, cups, plates, and napkins glued on in their proper places.

- It is also fun to make napkin rings by cutting cardboard tubes into sections and covering them with giftwrap paper or foil.
- Have children decorate placemats for each season or special holidy. Use a simple design such as a tree for spring, summer, fall, and winter. The children decorate the tree as they like, reflecting the particular season or holiday. Laminate the mats or cover with clear contact paper. All of these placemats can be sent home at year's end.

**Action Poem: Toothbrush Routine**
Up and down and all around
That's the way I brush my teeth. (Use right index finger to pantomine using toothbrush.)

I brush my gums and the shining fronts.
Then I reach up underneath. (Pantomine action—outside the mouth, of course)
I rinse my brush and hang it
In an airy place to dry. (Pretend to turn on water faucet with left hand, hold imaginary brush under "water." Hang up the brush.)
And put the cap on the toothpaste tube—(Pantomine)
At least I always try. (Pretend to drop cap and hunt for it; find it, rinse it, put it on the tube; sigh with relief)
Then I look into the mirror and grin
To show myself how good I've been. (Pretend to look in mirror and admire clean teeth)

**Stop! Look! Listen!**
Stop! Look! Listen!
Before you cross the street.
Use your eyes; use your ears;
Then use your feet.

**Stop and Go**
The traffic lights we see ahead
Are sometimes green and sometimes red.
Red on top and green below,
The red means stop, the green means go.
Green below, go—go—go,
Red on top, stop—stop—stop!

**Stop! Yield!** Most traffic signs have their own distinctive shapes. Cut out the shapes from construction paper in appropriate colors and have the children fill in the words. Ask them to note traffic signs on the way home and duplicate as many of them as they can remember the next day.

**Walkabout to Reinforce Safety Habits.** There are many interesting spots in your school, the playground, or the neighborhood that teacher and children can visit. The children may enjoy seeing the school's library, the nurse's and principal's offices, the kitchen, and the gym. (Arrange each visit beforehand.) Is there a tree, a big rock, or a view of interesting traffic near the playground? Is there a bakery store, a supermarket, a pet store, a construction site, trees to watch in various seasons, a vacant lot with weeds and bugs to collect, or gardens to look at nearby?

Some additional suggestions for art activities on health and safety:

- Safe Places to Play
- A Healthful Breakfast
- How I Keep Clean and Neat
- Helping Clean House
- At the Doctor's Office

## SUMMARY

Health and safety are physical states of being in the here and now. Young children don't think in terms of the far-distant future. It's *now* that interests them, not a lecture on how a bad health or safety habit can hurt a person in the future. Preaching, lecturing, and rote learning of health and safety information are all ineffective techniques in the early childhood health program. Instead, a positive, fun, but most of all *natural* approach to health and safety in the classroom should be emphasized.

Good health practices include brushing one's teeth and hair, bathing regularly, and a general interest in cleanliness. Getting enough sleep and good food are also basic to good health at all ages. All these ideas and tasks are first taught at home and need to be reinforced in the classroom. This can be done in many ways, but informal talks, rather than pointed lessons, work best with young children just learning to really care for themselves physically.

In all health or personal hygiene matters, emphasis should be on the positive view of the child. Even more important, the teacher must model good health and hygiene himself.

Other areas that need to be included in the early childhood curriculum are traffic safety, fire safety, and poison safety. When teaching concepts in these areas, young children need real, concrete experiences instead of more abstract lessons.

In the early childhood program common health concerns for children fall into three major areas: (1) infectious diseases such as chicken pox and measles; (2) injuries; and (3) health problems that are not evident and must be looked for by screening and observing children.

A teacher is in a position to do a great deal about preventing injuries at school. Knowing what to expect from children six years of age and younger helps a teacher prevent accidents. Knowing which plants are poisonous can also be an excellent preventive measure in the early childhood classroom.

Finally, health and safety can be reinforced in other curriculum areas, such as in language arts (stories and fingerplays), artwork, and songs.

## LEARNING ACTIVITIES

A. Interview children to find out what they know about the traffic system. Ask them what traffic lights mean and where, how, and why they should cross streets. Design a lesson to promote traffic safety based on their responses.

B. With the children, demonstrate their growth from birth weight to present weight by stacking hardwood blocks on a bathroom scale to equal the two weights for each child. Children may want to enter the following information in books they make up called *ALL ABOUT ME.* When I was a baby, I weighed as much as _____blocks; now I weigh as much as _____ blocks. Each child can feel good about her present state of growth when compared with past growth.

C. Choose one of the health and safety activities suggested in this unit and use it with a group of children. Report on your results as follows:

   Age of Group _____
   Rate lesson success on the following scale:

   Well above average—5
   Above average—4
   Average—3
   Below average—2
   Well below average—1

   Explain your rating.
   Describe the most successful part of the experience. The least successful.
   What would you change to improve the activity?

D. Do the following activity with several three-year-olds and several six-year-olds.

*Cereal Necklaces*
Children delight in stringing dry cereal on a piece of wire to make a necklace. Choose any kind of cereal with a hole in it. If no wire is available, try putting a piece of tape around the end of a string. When the cereal is on, twist or tie the ends together. Wear and eat!
Describe your two experiences as follows:
1. Describe the differences you observed in small motor development between the two groups.
2. Describe the differences in attention span.
3. Was this activity more suited to one group than the other for fine motor practice? Explain.

E. Design several safety-related activities of your own. Use them with a small group of children. Evaluate your experience. Share the results of your activity in class.

F. Consult a local dental hygienist. Obtain any information you can on fluoride and other preventive dental measures for young children. Obtain brochures and other printed materials on dental health for young children. Make a display (or bulletin board) using the materials you receive.

G. Choose one of the finger plays or songs in this unit on safety. With a small group of children, introduce the fingerplay or song. Evaluate your experience. Share your results with your classmates.

H. Assemble a list of local resources you could invite into the class to speak on health and safety issues. Make enough copies of your list to share with each of your classmates.

## ACTIVITIES FOR CHILDREN

### Health

*Are You Sleepy?*
Check the number of children in your group who have siblings who are younger than they, and those who have siblings older. Find out how long babies sleep, the children sleep, and how long the older brothers and sisters sleep. Discuss why the infants sleep longer than older children.

*All About Me Book*
Make a scrapbook for each child called an *ALL ABOUT ME BOOK.* Include the height and weight of the child in the book, as well as pages for the child to describe (draw) his or her physical features in words and pictures.

*Clothes Make the Person*
Collect pictures of different types of clothing—work, play, winter, and summer. Have children categorize these pictures according to when they wear them. Discuss why they wear the clothing they do.

*Dirty, Dirty*
Have children wash their hands. Then take small pieces of cotton dipped in rubbing alcohol. Rub the

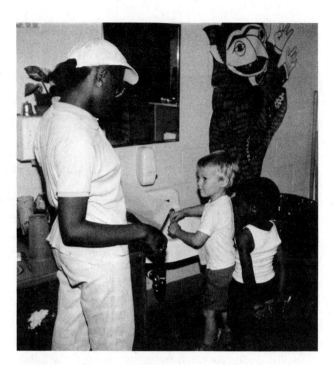

**FIGURE 23–9 Washing hands before eating is a health practice learned in the early years.**

back of each child's hand with the moistened cotton. Look at the dirt on the cotton and discuss what it means. Even when you think you've washed your hands, there still may be dirt present.

*Homemade Toothpowder*

Have each child mix 1 part of salt to 3 parts of baking powder. Put a few drops of wintergreen extract into this mixture and let it dry. Then try it out. Compare this toothpowder with commercial toothpaste. Which do the children like the best and why? Which does the best job and why?

*Our Health Helpers*

When the children arrive at school in the morning, give them name tags that resemble little Red Cross badges. Then have them explore the different areas you have set up in the room:

• Area with collections of books about community helpers
• Housekeeping area with hospital arrangement (bandages, small pillows, adhesive bandages, empty spray cans, gauze, syringes, and tape)
• Art area, constructing nurses' or doctors' hats from available materials
• Dentist's office, complete with magazines, reception

desk, phone, office chair, teeth models, white shirts, cloth to go over patients, tongue depressors

This activity enables children to examine tools used by medical helpers and to experience some role playing. Books that have safety ideas and hints are available for children to examine themselves.

*Group Health Activity*

Take a large freezer box and decorate it so that it looks like an ambulance. Make a siren noise and have the children "hook" onto the teacher's back like a train. Go around the room to collect everyone, and then go to the circle area. After reading a book about community helpers and safety, have a short discussion about the ambulance, doctors, nurses, and dentists. Stress the point that they are available to help—and not to harm—us. Pull out a bag and begin taking items (bandages, thermometer, antiseptic spray, etc.) out of it. Discuss what each item is and how to use it.

## Health Walking Food

Wearable snacks are great for walks and nature hikes.

1. String cereal on yarn for edible necklaces.
2. Core apples and string them on ribbons for the children to wear around their necks.
3. Have each child wear a bagel on a string around their necks for snacking on the walk.

*How Tall Am I?*

A. *Equipment:* Masking tape, ball-point pen or heavy pencil.
B. *Procedure:* Paste a strip of masking tape on a blank wall, reaching from the floor to about five feet in height. Each child will need a separate strip. For additional writing space, you may wish to paste several strips edge to edge. To help children grasp the concept of growth:
1. The child stands against the wall in front of the tape. Place a mark on the tape at the top of his head. The child stands back and sees how tall he is. Mark the date next to the line. Repeat this activity periodically so that the child can see how much he has grown.
2. By using a yardstick or tape measure, you may also wish to mark the child's height in feet and inches. Say, "Today you are three feet and four inches tall." Show him the three-foot mark on the ruler and count off the inches with him.

*How Much Do I Weigh?*

A. *Objective:* To help children grasp the concepts of measurements, growth, and weight (heavy and light).
B. *Equipment:* Bathroom scale.
C. *Procedure:* The child stands on the bathroom scale. Point to the numbers on the scale and say, "See, you

weigh 35 pounds. The three and the five mean 35." Print "35 pounds" on the wall tape next to the child's height. This activity can be done periodically following the "How Tall Am I?" activity, so that the child can see himself growing taller and discover that his weight is changing, too. Explain that he is getting heavier.

*But I'm Not Sleepy Yet!*

With a small group of children, ask: "Do you ever get out of bed in the morning feeling tired? Why do you suppose that happens? Did you go to bed early enough the night before? Who decides when you should go to bed? Does your mom or dad decide, or do you go to bed when you feel tired?" Point out that children usually need help in deciding when it's bedtime.

Then ask the children: "Are there some times when you are allowed to stay up later than usual? Is it when there is a special show on television? When you have company? When you are traveling? What happens if you stay up late and then have to get up early for school? Do you ever feel grouchy?" Explain that our bodies need lots of rest, and it is important to go to bed before we get too tired or when our parents tell us it's time.

*Colds and Germs*

A. *Equipment:* Atomizer from an empty perfume bottle or sprayer from window cleaning fluid.

B. *Procedure:*
1. Ask the children: "Have you ever had a bad cold? Did you go to the doctor or get medicine to take? Were you allowed to go to school or play with friends when you had a fever? Why not?" Explain that people can give someone else their cold or other sickness just by being around them. The germs they have can be carried in the air or on their hands.
2. Let the children spray water into the air and watch how it disappears. Explain that in coughing we can easily spray germs we can't see onto others.
3. Say to the children: "Sometimes we have to be by ourselves when we're sick so that others won't get sick, too." Point out that if they cough or sneeze, they should cover their mouth and nose and use a handkerchief.

*Why Can't I Open the Medicine Chest?*

A. *Equipment:* A variety of empty containers from a medicine chest.

B. *Procedure:* Ask, "Are you allowed to open your medicine chest at home and take out pill bottles or other medicines? Why do you suppose you aren't allowed to do this? Could some of these things hurt your body?"

Say, "Let's look at some things you might find in a medicine chest—aspirin, nosedrops, jars, tubes.

Have you ever been given any of these? Do you know what could happen if you took any of these things without your parents' permission? You could get very, very sick. Maybe the aspirin tastes good, and you might like to eat all of them, but you would be sorry and very sick if you did." Explain that each of these medicines can help us if we need it, but we must let our parents or the doctor decide when or how much we should take.

*What Does the Doctor Do?*

A. *Equipment:* Toy doctor equipment to be used for role playing.

B. *Procedure:* Ask, "How many of you have visited a doctor? All of you have been to a doctor's office, haven't you? What does the doctor do when you go for a checkup? Does he feel your legs? Does he check your ears and throat and eyes? Does he listen to your heart with a stethoscope? Here are some instruments like ones the doctor uses. Let's use them now to play doctor. Be very careful as you pretend to listen to each other's hearts and check ears and throats. Why does the doctor do these things? Can he tell by what he does whether you are in good health?" Explain that the doctor uses these things to help people stay healthy. Arrange for a doctor to visit the class and bring some of his real instruments for the children to see and touch. This may help them overcome any fears they might have of a doctor and the equipment he uses. Help the children understand that a doctor's job is to help us maintain healthy bodies.

## Dramatic Play Ideas

*Hospital play.* Add paper towel tubes to the props provided for hospital play so that children can listen to heartbeats. Add discarded plastic syringes (sterilized, needles removed) to allow children to take the role of shot-giver.

*Grocery Store.* Compare the ways that children arrange the food replicas provided for a play store before and after a lesson on food groups.

*Restaurant.* Make picture menus from manila folders, using illustrations of wholesome foods marked with large numeral prices. Provide restaurant workers with pads of paper, pencils, a toy cash register, trays, and food replicas (or pictures cut from cardboard food cartons).

*Make-believe medicine.* If young children are required to take vitamins (or medicine) while at school, make a game of it by playing "Who are You Today?" While handing out the vitamins, ask the children who they want to be—"Wonder Woman," "Santa Claus," "Bat Man," etc. Children usually can't wait to take their medicine this way.

## Safety

*What's in the Bottle?*

A. *Equipment:* Examples of things that children should not drink—bleach, shampoo, cleaning fluid, liquid detergent, and others; circles cut from peel-off adhesive paper; crayons.

B. *Procedure:* Show the children the containers listed above. Say: "Here are some things that I brought from my house today. Can you tell me what this is? What do you use shampoo for? What is in this bottle? Does your mom use bleach in the washer?"

Ask, "What would happen if you were to drink from any of these bottles? Are you supposed to drink from them? No, you could get very sick. It's important to ask your mom or dad before you put anything new in your mouth."

After you have discussed the danger presented by these common household fluids, say, "Here are some circles I've cut out for each of you. Draw a sad face on each one to remind you that you'd be very sorry if you tasted something in these bottles. When you're done, take the circles home and ask your mom or dad to stick them on the bottles that have things in them you shouldn't drink."

*Is It Safe?*

A. *Equipment:* Pictures cut from magazines or drawn freehand that show both safe and unsafe situations—untied shoelaces, child near stove, spilled paint, etc.

B. *Procedure:* Say, "We have learned a lot about how to keep our classroom, our homes, and our bodies

**FIGURE 23–10 Included in safety practices is the proper use of scissors.**

safe. Today we're going to play a guessing game with pictures. As you look at a picture I hold up, tell me if it shows a safe situation or an unsafe one." Continue by showing the pictures, discussing each, emphasizing why each situation is safe or unsafe. Because a preschooler's attention span is short, it may be wise to discuss only a few of these pictures on one day.

*How Should I Carry Scissors?*

A. *Equipment:* Scissors (blunt and sharp), screwdriver, hammer, pliers, and other tools.

B. *Procedure:* Ask, "Do you like to cut things with scissors? Have you ever used sharp-pointed scissors like these? Has your mom ever asked you to find them for her and bring them to her? Can you feel the difference between these two kinds of scissors? How do you carry sharp scissors?" Demonstrate how to walk slowly with the scissor points down, then supervise closely as the children take turns carrying the scissors. Discuss what could happen if the scissors were carried improperly. Let the children hold and talk about the other tools. Ask how each one should be carried for safety.

*Why Can't I Stand in Front of the Swing?*

A. *Equipment:* Swings and a stuffed toy.

B. *Procedure:* Ask, "Do you like to swing on swings? It's fun, isn't it! Sometimes when you want to swing, the swings are full and you must wait your turn. Where should you stand while you wait? Why must you keep away from the swings when they are moving? Could you get knocked down or hit hard? Did that ever happen to you?"

Say, "Let's use this stuffed toy to show just what can happen if we're not careful around the swings." Have a child start swinging, then place the stuffed toy in his path. Ask: "What happened to the toy? It really got knocked, didn't it? Where is the best place to wait for a swing?"

*Why Can't I Light the Match?*

A. *Equipment:* A visit from a local fire fighter or a carefully planned demonstration of the danger of fire.

B. *Procedure:* Ask, "Do you like to see candles on a birthday cake? Who lights them? Are you allowed to? Why not?"

Say, "I'd like you to sit in a wide circle around this old metal bucket and I'll show you what a little light from this candle can do." (Be sure the room is ventilated or demonstrate outdoors.) "Here is an old pair of pajamas, perhaps like some you have worn. I'll light this candle and then let the light touch the pajamas. What happens? Is there anything left of the pajamas? If someone had been wearing them, that person could be badly hurt. It can be very dangerous to play with matches or get close to fire. Always let your parents light matches.''

## Hygiene

- To clean stuffed toys, rub or shake them in a bag half-filled with cornmeal. Let the toys stand for a while before brushing them off.
- When game cards get sticky from too much handling, shake them in a bag filled with talcum or baby powder.
- To remove felt marker ink from skin, try rubbing on toothpaste, then rinsing with water. Repeat the process until the ink disappears.

## Helping Children Dress Themselves

- When boots won't go over a child's shoes, use a plastic bread bag (or any other plastic bag) over the shoes first; boots slip over the shoes easily.
- When young children are learning to button up their own coats and sweaters, have them start at the bottom. They'll be more likely to get all the buttons in the right buttonholes this way.
- When zippers stick, rub them with a lead pencil to get them gliding smoothly again. Or, rub the zipper with petroleum jelly or spray it with WD40 (an aerosol lubricant), being careful not to get it on the fabric.
- Use old leg warmers or old socks with the toes cut off for extra warmth for children playing in the snow. When dressing to play in the snow, slip the legwarmers or toe-less socks over their arms after pulling on their snowsuits and mittens. The legwarmers (or socks) prevent snow from getting between mittens and sleeves and keeps wrists warm and toasty.

## Health and Safety Communications for Parents

Whenever you have important information on health and safety practices (or any other area of the program for that matter), place it on a Parent Bulletin Board by the entrance of your room to ensure greater visibility.

- Important notices and letters for parents often fall off cubby shelves and are lost. To solve this problem, use a shoebag to make an attractive parent ''mailbox.'' Label each pocket in the shoebag with a parent's name and have mothers or fathers check daily for their ''mail.''
- If your notices to parents regarding suitable dress for outdoor play don't seem to be getting the message across, try sharing a poem, such as the following, with them.

Now, when outside we do swarm,
Make my clothes old, soft, and warm.

Soft old pants and an old hooded sweater
So I can get dirty—what could be better?
Comfy old sneakers, not my best pretties,
So I can go play in the dirty old gritties.
All my clothes will be easier to claim
If in each thing, you please put my name.
Spring is here—time to laugh, jump, and run.
Please won't you dress me to share in the fun?

—Sally J. Horton

## Music Activities

- Fred Rogers, host of ''Mister Rogers' Neighborhood,'' has written and recorded many songs about the concerns of young children. The following extend the learning about the human body: from his album *You Are Special,* the title song; from his album *Won't You Be My Neighbor?* ''Everybody's Fancy'' (teaches acceptance of one's physical makeup); from his album *Let's Be Together Today,* ''Everything Grows Together.''
- The *Inside Story,* an album written and sung by John Burstein, is an excellent resource. The narrator, ''Mr. Slim Goodbody,'' has songs about nutrition, toothbrushing, the heart, and exercise.
- ''Here We Go 'Round the Mulberry Bush'' provides a good pattern for improvising a song about health care. Children can sing, ''This is the way I take care of myself . . . so I'll be strong and healthy.'' Add verses such as ''This is the way I (brush my teeth, take my bath, wash my hands, go to sleep, eat good meals) . . . so I'll be strong and healthy.''
- Young children like to contribute to a simple song about foods they enjoy. Use the tune to Ella Jenkins's song ''I Like the Animals in the Zoo,'' from her album *Seasons for Singing.* Each verse is a favorite food suggested by a child, such as Mary likes scrambled eggs, yum, yum, yum! Mary likes scrambled eggs in her tum.
- Listen to ''What Foods Should We Eat Everyday?'' and ''How Does a Cow Make Milk?'' sung by Tom Glazer on the *Now We Know* album.

*Sources:*

Burstein, John. *The Inside Story.* J. Burstein, Canal Street Station, Box 773, New York, N.Y. 10013.

Glazer, Tom. *Now We Know. (Songs to Learn By).* Columbia Records, CL670, c/o CBS Records Inc., 51 W. 52nd St., N.Y., N.Y., 10019.

Jenkins, Ella. *Seasons for Singing.* Folkways Records/Scholastic Records, #7656, 906 Sylvan Ave., Englewood Cliffs, N.J., 07632.

Rogers, Fred. *Won't You Be My Neighbor?* Columbia Records, CC24516.

———. *You Are Special.* Columbia Records, CC24518, c/o CBS Records Inc., 51 W. 52nd St., N.Y., N.Y., 10019.

# UNIT REVIEW

1. In teaching young children about health, what is the best approach and teaching strategy to use? Describe activities you would plan to use in teaching young children about health.
2. Why is it important to know about childhood diseases in the early childhood program? Give specific examples in your reply.
3. What do you feel are some of the most basic health and other types of information you should have on hand for each child in case of emergency? Explain.
4. Discuss several ways you can prevent accidents with children six years old and younger.

5. How important is dental hygiene in the early childhood program? Describe how you would include it in your program.
6. What are some other areas of the curriculum in which to include health and safety ideas? Give specific examples of activities.
7. What are the three major areas of health and safety concerns in the early childhood program? Give examples for each area.
8. How would you teach young children about fire, traffic, and poison safety in concrete ways? Give specific examples in your reply.

# ADDITIONAL READINGS

## Health and First Aid

American Academy of Pediatrics. *Standards for Day Care Centers.* Evanston, Ill.: The Academy, 1980.

Aronson, M.D., S. Nelson, and H. Nelson. *Health Power: A Guide to the Health Component of the Early Childhood Program.* Department of Community and Preventive Medicine, Medical College of Pennsylvania, 1981.

Aronson, M.O., S. Pizzo, and P. Pizzo. "Health and Safety Issues in Day Care." FIDCR Appropriateness Study, State of the Art Paper. Washington, D.C.: HEW Office for Planning and Evaluation, 1977.

Barcus, F.E. *Food Advertising on Children's Television: An Analysis of Appeals and Nutritional Content.* Newtonville, Mass.: Action for Children's Television, 1987.

Cassidy, J., and S.R. Asher. "Loneliness and Peer Relations in Young Children." *Child Development* 63 (1922): 350–365.

Collins, R.H. "Planning for Fire Safety." *Young Children* 32 (1977): 22–33.

Comer, D. *Developing Safety Skills with the Young Child.* Albany, N.Y.: Delmar Publishers Inc., 1987.

Fabes, R.A., and N. Eisneberg. "Young Children's Coping with Interpersonal Anger." *Child Development* 63 (1992): 116–128.

Galst, J.P. "Television Food Commercials and Pronutritional Public Service Announcements as Determinants of Young Children's Snack Choices." *Child Development* 51 (1980): 935–938.

Gorn, G.J., and M.E. Greenberg. "Behavioral Evidence of the Effects of Televised Food Messages on Children." *Journal of Consumer Research* 9 (1982): 200–205.

Hei, T.K., and V. Gold. Paper presented at the Annual Meeting of the American Heart Association, Dallas, 1990.

Humphrey, J.H. *An Overview of Childhood Fitness: Theoretical Perspectives and Scientific Cases.* Springfield, Ill.: Chalres C. Thomas, 1991.

Jeffrey, D.B., R.W. McClerran, and D.T. Fox. "The Development of Children's Eating Habits: The Role of Television Commercials." *Health Education Quarterly* 9 (1982): 78–93.

Jorgensen, E.C. *Child Abuse: A Practical Guide for Those Who Help Others.* New York: Continuum, 1990.

Kendrick, A.S., R. Kaufmann, and K.P. Messenger. *Healthy Young Children: A Manual for Programs.* Washington, D.C.: NAEYC, 1991.

Liebert, R.M., and J. Sprafkin. *The Early Window: Effects of Television on Children and Youth,* 3rd ed. New York: Pergamon, 1988.

McCracken, J.B. *Children Riding on Sidewalks Safely.* Washington, D.C.: NAEYC, 1990.

National Association for the Education of Young Children. *Walk in Traffic Safely.* 1990.

———. *We Cross the Street Safely: A Preschool Book on Safety.* 1992.

———. *When We Cross the Street: A First Book on Traffic Safety.* 1992.

Peterson, P.E., D.G. Jeffrey, C.A. Bridgwater, and B. Dawson. "How Pronutrition Television Programming Affects Children's Dietary Habits." *Developmental Psychology* 20 (1984): 55–63.

Pringle, Sheila M., and Brenda E. Ramsey. *Promoting the Health of Children.* St. Louis: C.V. Mosby, 1982.

Project Burn Prevention. *Protect Someone You Love.* Washington, D.C.: Consumer Product Safety Commission, 1978.

Robinson, J.P. "Television's Impact on Everyday Life: Some Cross-National Evidence." In E.A. Rubinstein, G.A.

Comnstock, and J.P. Murray, Eds., *Television and Social Behavior: Vol. 4, Television in Day-To-Day Patterns of Use.* Washington, D.C.: Government Printing Office, 1972.

Russell, R.D. *Education in the '80s.* Washington, D.C.: National Education Association, 1981.

Ross, S., and C. Seefeldt. "Young Children in Traffic: How Can They Cope?" *Young Children* 33 (1978): 68–74.

Seefeldt, C., and N. Barbour. *Early Childhood Education: An Introduction.* Columbus, Ohio: Charles E. Merrill, 1986.

Tinsley, B.J. "Multiple Influences on the Acquisition and Socialization of Children's Health Attitudes and Behavior: An Integrative Review." *Child Development.* 63 (1993): 1043–1069.

U.S. Department of Health, Education, and Welfare, Office of Child Development. *A Guide for Project Directors and Health Personnel.* Day Care Series 6, HEW Publication No. (OCD) 73–12. Washington, D.C.: Government Printing Office, 1983.

Winshon, P.M. *Student Obesity: What Can the Schools Do?* Bloomington, Ind.: Phi Delta Kappa, 1990.

## Children's Books

Bang, M. *The Gray Lady and the Strawberry Snatcher.* New York: Four Winds, 1980.

Berenstein, Stan and Jane. *The Berenstein Bears and Too Much Junk Food.* New York: Random House, 1985.

Bridwell, N. *Kangaroo Stew.* New York: Scholastic, 1980.

Cherry, Lynne. *Who's Sick Today?* New York: Dutton, 1988.

de Brunhoff, L. *Babar Learns to Cook.* New York: Random House, 1978.

Dutton, C. *Not in Here, Dad!* New York: Barrons, 1990.

Hoban, Lillian. *Arthur's Loose Tooth.* New York: Harper and Row, 1985.

Le Guin, Ursula K. *A Visit from Dr. Katz.* New York: Atheneum, 1988.

Pinkwater, M. *Fat Elliot and the Gorilla.* New York: Four Winds, 1974.

Robinson, B. *The Fattest Bear in the First Grade.* New York: Random House, 1969.

Sabin, Francene. *Human Body.* Mahwah, N.J.: Troll Associates, 1985.

Solor, M.H. *The 100 Hamburgers: The Getting Thin Book.* New York: Lothrop, Lee and Shepard, 1972.

Sterling, Barbara. *I'm Not So Different.* New York: Golden Books, 1986.

# SECTION 7
# Creative Activities Involving Holidays

# UNIT 24

# Halloween

More than any other holiday except birthdays, Halloween remains a children's day with all the fun of dressing up and carving pumpkins. If well handled, it can also help children learn to cope with half-delicious fears! To young children, Halloween means dressing up in colorful costumes and playing trick or treat. The fantasy and tradition of Halloween have more meaning for children when they understand how this yearly festival began. The tale of how the Druids observed Halloween many centuries ago will unfold as a fascinating story.

"All Hallow's Even," as it was called, was the night when the Lord of Death called together the souls of the wicked who had died during the past year. The Druids believed that on this night, ghosts, fairies, and witches appeared from their hiding places to harm people. They thought that cats had once been human beings but were changed as punishment for evil deeds. An Irishman named Jack, who walked the earth at night carrying a pumpkin lantern, is credited with the origin of the "jack-o-lantern." From these early beliefs comes our tradition of using witches, ghosts, cats, and pumpkins as Halloween symbols.

The transition period from autumn to winter was thought in ancient times to include the return of the souls of the departed to the warmth and light they remembered from their former lives. Not only ghosts

were anticipated, but general mischief, witchcraft, magic, and hobgoblins of every sort. As a Christian festival, Halloween was first proclaimed within the Benedictine Order in the year 998, and later recognized by Pope John XIX in 1006. It was called the Eve of Hallowmass, now known as All Saints' Day, which also honors and remembers the dead, particularly the saintly.

## SOME GENERAL HALLOWEEN ACTIVITIES

Allow the children to draw the features on the jack-o-lantern, but you should do the cutting. Knives coated with pumpkin pulp are dangerously slippery. The children, however, can scrape out the seeds. They can also light the candle inside if long, fireplace-type matches are used.

Eat at snacktime by pumpkin light; serve an orange and black snack (perhaps oranges and raisins and toasted pumpkin seeds, or orange-colored pancakes with raisin faces, made by the children, of course). Use an additional pumpkin to make pumpkin cookies or cake.

If you are fortunate enough to have access to a pumpkin field, bring back a vine with flowers and green fruit still attached, or grow and harvest your own pumpkin. Keep one jack-o-lantern and place it in a shallow pan and allow it to deteriorate. The mold is beautiful if examined with a magnifying glass, and digging the remains back into the soil helps children understand how the life cycle produces more plant life.

Some schools have a tradition of a Halloween parade. If you do this, remember to keep the parade short, and do not make the children wait too long before participating in it. Make certain every child has a costume (this usually requires extra adults around to help dress the children), and do not rely on paper costumes, as they are too delicate for little children to wear successfully.

After Halloween is over, provide Halloween paraphernalia for imaginative play so that children can play through their feelings about this event. Plan a quiet day afterward if Halloween comes on a school evening.

Motivated by this exciting background and their own experiences, children will have individual ideas and feelings to express the weird, spooky fun of Halloween. They will welcome the opportunity to be inventive and do not need patterns to trace. Some suggested topics for picture making and other art activities include the following:

- Halloween Spooks
- Shining Jack-o-Lanterns
- We Play Trick or Treat
- Happy Goblins
- Flying Witches
- A Halloween Party

In addition to these suggested topics for picture making and art activities, the following Halloween related concepts may be taught in art as well as in other curriculum areas:

- Black and orange are common Halloween colors.
- Pumpkins harvested during autumn are carved into jack-o-lanterns.
- Children dress in costumes and go trick-or-treating from door to door.
- Scary creatures, costumes, and stories associated with Halloween are only fantasy and are not to be feared.

**FIGURE 24–1 Pumpkin calendar for October.**

- Safety and having fun without harming other people or property are important aspects of the Halloween holiday.

In these suggestions as well as in the following art activities, the small and large motor development of the child should be one of the primary goals. Of course, another equally important goal is for the child to express herself creatively in these experiences. Therefore, in all of these activities, the *process* should be stressed, *not the end product.*

## ART ACTIVITIES

### Paper Plate Masks.

Materials: Lightweight paper plates, crayons, yarn, paper and fabric scraps, glitter, rubber bands

Procedure:
1. Outline on paper plates holes for eyes, nose, and mouth, and cut these out. You may need to help children by starting these holes for them.
2. Children then can color and/or paste colored paper, yarn, felt, glitter, etc. on the paper plate to create a mask of their own design.
3. To wear the mask, take a large rubber band, cut it so you have one straight piece, and staple one

end to each side of the mask. Then bend the end of the rubber band and staple again to secure.

## Tissue Ghosts.
Materials: White facial tissues, rubber bands, popsicle sticks, cotton balls, magic markers

Procedure:
1. Wrap cotton balls into two white facial tissues, forming a rounded section.
2. Wind a rubber band around the covered cotton balls to form the ghost's head on a popsicle stick.
3. Use a black magic marker to make the ghost's features.

## Painted Pumpkins.
Use a real pumpkin for display prior to this activity.

Procedure:
1. Cut out a pumpkin shape on a large (18″ × 24″) piece of brown wrapping paper, manila paper, or construction paper.
2. Have the children color their paper pumpkin according to how they observe the real pumpkin.

## Sack Jack-o-Lantern.
Stuff paper bags with newspapers, twist the tops, and tie. Have the children paint the bags orange. When they are dry, the children can add faces if they like. These can be hung on a clothesline until time for the Halloween party.

## Pumpkin Accordion People.
Use the pumpkins painted in the previous activity.

Procedure:
1. Cut thin (1½″ × 12″) strips of black construction paper—four for each pumpkin.
2. Have the children accordion pleat the strips.
3. Attach two of the accordion strips for arms and two for legs.
4. Shoes and hands (or gloves) cut from bits of construction paper may be added for fun. A cut-paper hat makes an attractive addition.

## Funny Face Vegetables.
Use squash, potatoes, turnips, or gourds. Make jack-o-lantern faces with felt-tipped pens, felt, yarn, and buttons. For added appeal, string Christmas lights around several "funny faces" placed in a row.

**FIGURE 24–2 Painted pumpkin.**

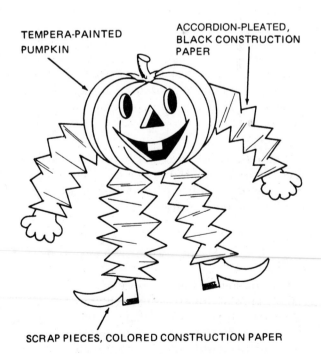

TEMPERA-PAINTED PUMPKIN

ACCORDION-PLEATED, BLACK CONSTRUCTION PAPER

SCRAP PIECES, COLORED CONSTRUCTION PAPER

**FIGURE 24–3 Pumpkin accordion people.**

Foot
Ghost

## String Painting Ghost.

Procedure:
1. Dip string in white paint.
2. Place the end of the string at the top of a dark-colored piece of construction paper.
3. Pull the string downward on the paper, wiggling as you pull. Or, hold the string at the top of the paper, and pull the string back and forth across the paper.

**Foot Ghost.** Have the child step onto a piece of paper. Trace around the child's shoe. Then let her use crayon or felt-tipped pens to make a face or decorate it in anyway she chooses.

## Clothespin Ghost.

Procedure:
1. Paint round-top clothespins white.
2. Make two dots for eyes with a felt-tipped pen.
3. Glue two sleeves cut from paper to the body. The prongs of the clothespin will fit over the side of a nut cup filled with treats.

**Ghostly Pop-Out Card.** (Teachers can make these for children's place cards.)

Procedure:
1. Fold a piece of black paper in half for the card.
2. From white paper, cut a ghost almost as tall and half as wide as the card.
3. Lay the ghost inside the card, matching folds. The folds should bend in opposite directions.
4. Tape the sides of the ghost to the card.
5. When the card is opened, the ghost pops out. These are also nice to use for parents' names when they are "invited guests" at your Halloween party.

Clothes
Pin
Ghost

## Ghost Pop-Up Card

**Witch Mobile.**

Procedure:
1. Cut three orange circles and one black triangle from construction paper.
2. Use strips of yarn for hair.
3. Draw the witch's face on one circle.
4. Glue the hair and triangular hat to the face.
5. Place the witch's head face down on the table. Place the remaining circles below the head approximately 1 inch apart.
6. Place one end of the string in the center of the bottom circle. Extend the string through the center of all circles and triangle. Tape the string to each shape.
7. *Variation:* Instead of yarn, use construction paper hair. Fold a piece of paper accordion-style, and cut folded paper into narrow strips.

## Witch Mobile

**Spooks and Goblins.**  Who knows what spooks and goblins look like? Children do! They can make many fantastic three-dimensional figures with paper and paste.

Procedure:
1. Odd shapes of paper from the scrap box can be used for the body and head.
2. Paper strips for arms and legs can be curled, folded, twisted, crumpled, rolled, or cut to express movement.
3. For variety of design, add a poncho, wings, antennae, floppy hat, or boots. Goblins may be attached to a stick (like a rod puppet), to do a goblin dance to recorded music.

**Scary Night.**

Procedure:
1. Use crayons to draw a Halloween picture. Press down hard with crayons and use bright colors.
2. Use a sponge or brush to "wash" over the picture with diluted tempera.

**Spider Web.**

Procedure:
1. Line a round cake tin with a piece of black construction paper.
2. Place a tablespoon of white glue in the center of the paper.
3. Put a marble in the pan. Roll the marble around to create a spider web effect.
4. After they are dried, these could be hung as mobiles to decorate a Halloween party.

**Ghost Print.**

Procedure:
1. Spread a tablespoon of white tempera on a washable surface. Smooth out the paint with your hand.
2. Use fingers to create eyes and a mouth.
3. Cover with a sheet of black paper. Rub across the back of the paper with your hand. Lift off paper.

**FIGURE 24–4 "Hand"-made ghosts for Halloween.**

## Bouncing Spiders.

Procedure:
1. Tie four 6″ pieces of black yarn in the middle with a 12″ piece of black yarn.
2. Wrap a ball of clay around the center, covering the knot with clay. Let the short ends of the yarn stick out of the clay to form the spider's legs.
3. Allow to dry. Bounce the spider from the 12″ piece of yarn.

## Pinecone Owl.

Procedure:
1. From felt or construction paper, cut beak, feet, and large round eyes.
2. Glue these to a pinecone to create an owl. The children may want to make another type of bird or animal with pinecones as well, so let their imaginations be the guide in using the pinecones and felt pieces. You'll love the results!

## Paper Towel Dip Painting.

Procedure:
1. Fold a paper towel several times.
2. Have the children dip the paper towel into red-colored water and then into yellow-colored water.
3. The child opens the towel carefully (you may

need to assist younger children with this). Allow it to dry. Red, orange, and yellow designs will appear on the paper towel.
4. Mount this design on construction paper for a "finished" look.

**Moon Painting.** Use any circular-shaped objects, such as a lid, spool, or sponge cut into half-circles or crescent shapes. Have children dip these shapes into orange, yellow, or white tempera paint and press onto dark paper.

## Rattles and Noisemakers.

Procedure:
1. Use discarded crayon boxes or similar small boxes filled with seeds, beans, or tiny pebbles. Tape the box shut at both ends.
2. To depict a Halloween character, paint the box or decorate with pieces of cut paper. A tongue depressor or lollipop stick taped to the back of the rattle serves as a handle.

**Stand-Up Paper Pumpkins.** Using a basic round shape, almost any kind of animal, bird, or face may be constructed.

Procedure:
1. Fold a 12″ × 18″ piece of construction paper in half. While still folded, turn up open edges about 3 inches, then turn down so that the crease can be seen.
2. Starting at the fold on both sides, draw a curved line down to the crease and then follow it to the edge of the paper. With the paper still folded, cut along the lines.
3. Add cut-paper features and details. It is easier to paste them in place while the paper is still flat.
4. Fold both bottom strips to the inside and paste one over the other.

## Halloween Mobiles.

Procedure:
1. Have each child cut the shape of a pumpkin, cat, witch, ghost, or goblin out of construction paper or tagboard.

**FIGURE 24–5 Stand-up paper pumpkins.**

2. Decorate both sides with cut-paper features. Small pieces of metallic paper, aluminum foil, or glitter add interest.
3. Punch a hole in the top of the object and thread with black thread.

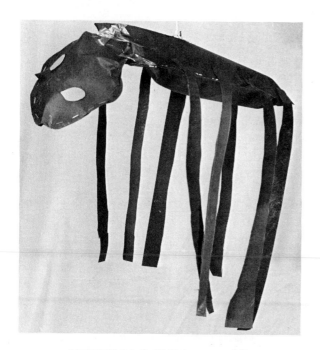

**FIGURE 24–6 Halloween mobile.**

4. Hang on a wire across the room. Some children can tie two objects together (such as making a witch with a cat tied to her skirt).

**Papier Mâché Jack-o-Lantern Group Project.** Inflate and tie the end of a round balloom. Soak strips of newspaper in liquid starch. Apply these strips to the balloon until it is completely covered. Smooth out as many wrinkles as possible, and allow the balloon to dry for two or three days. Paint it orange and decorate it as a jack-o-lantern. Variations:

• To use as a piñata, leave a small area at the top uncovered. After the papier-mâché dries, pop the balloon and fill with treats.
• Instead of a jack-o-lantern, make a witch face. Attach a witch hat (see page 495 for instructions on how to make a witch hat).

**Halloween Mural Group Project.** Cover a table or floor with a large piece of butcher paper. Make available different colors of tempera paint, and have the children paint a mural about Halloween. Work in shifts with a small group of children—three or four—at a time.

**Paper Pumpkin Chains.** As an addition to regular paper chains, add orange construction paper pumpkins to a black and orange paper chain. Alternate pumpkins to every third link for an attractive party decoration.

**Haunted Houses.**
Materials: Paper, scissors, glue or stapler, crayons

Procedure:
1. Discuss with the children what they think a haunted house might look like and what might be found in it. List their ideas on the board.
2. Distribute large pieces of paper and have the children draw haunted houses. In the space for the windows and doors, ask them to draw surprising or scary things that might be found in a haunted house.
3. From other paper, cut out window shades, shutters or curtains, and a door. Glue these on the house so that they can be folded back. Behind

these glued-on sections are the children's drawings of ghosts, witches, and apparitions. Each child can then fold back the doors and shutters and show the class what is in the haunted house.

**Paper Bag Vests.** Use a large grocery bag. Cut arm holes in the side. Then cut down the front of the bag. Let the children decorate their vests with their own Halloween designs. This vest also makes a good Indian or Pilgrim costume for Thanksgiving.

**Holiday Window Decor.** Cut a holiday shape from a sponge. A jack-o-lantern would be good for Halloween, for example. Spread craft glue on the front of your shape, and then dip the shape in glitter. Glue-on or push-in sequins would also give your window decoration a special sparkle. Now attach a string to the top of the shape (thread and needle work well) and put in your window for the world to see! (Not for children under five.)

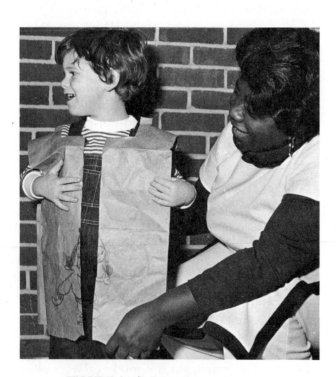

**FIGURE 24–7 Paper bag vest.**

**Ghost Walkers.** A rectangular sponge is perfect for tying on a child's feet right under her shoes. You can use a piece of ribbon, yarn, or string about 22 inches long. Lay the string horizontally on the floor, and place the sponge vertically in the middle of it. The child then steps onto the sponge with one foot and pulls the string over the top of her foot; the teacher ties the ends in a bow. Now the child can go for the "ghostliest" walk—for a silent tip-toe about, for an indoor game of "Ghosts and Witches" (later in this unit), or for quiet creative movement acting out a ghost's walk.

**Witch on a Stick.** Paint or decorate a paper bag with cut paper. (Children may want to add hair, a funny hat, or a bright color.) Stuff the bag with crumpled newspaper and attach it to a stick to be carried on Halloween night. Other Halloween figures may be made using the same method.

**Exploring the Jack-o-Lantern.** Each child should have an opportunity to feel, lift, thump, and smell the pumpkin before, during, and after carving. Weigh the pumpkin on a scale. If more than one pumpkin is involved, make weight, size, shape, and color comparisons.

Other activities centered around the jack-o-lantern include the following:

- Allowing children to scoop out the seeds.
- Telling a story or singing songs about Halloween while carving the pumpkin.
- Passing out small cubes of raw, washed pumpkin for the children to taste.

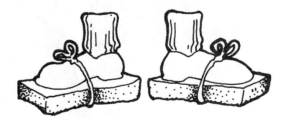

**FIGURE 24–8 Ghost walkers.**

- Baking small cubes in a buttered baking dish and serving them warm.
- Washing and drying the seeds.

**Real Jack-o-Lantern.** Carving a real pumpkin to make a jack-o-lantern is a project in which both children and teachers can participate.

Procedure:
1. The children can draw the features on the pumpkin. The teacher should do the carving.
2. Seeds can be roasted or fried, then salted for a tasty treat at home or left to dry in the classroom and used later for making necklaces or bracelets.
3. Another use for pumpkin seeds is to save them until early spring when children can plant them in individual containers, such as milk or cottage cheese cartons. Later, in warmer weather, the small plants can be placed outdoors.

**Paper Plate Faces.** This is an old standby but a great project for younger children who love to cut, color, paste, and paint.
Materials: Paper plates (the lightweight paper ones will do, but the heavy-duty ones will work better), construction paper, tempera paints, markers or crayons, yarn, string, pipe cleaners, glue, scissors, tape

Procedure:
1. Have children design elaborate facial features on paper plate, using materials at hand. Some tips for making faces: Wrap stiff paper around a pencil to make curls for eyelashes, hair, and feathers. The masks will be more three-dimensional if layers are built up to create cheeks, noses, ears, hair, or hats.
2. Punch holes about two-thirds of the way to the top for ribbon or strings to tie on face.

**Trick or Treat in Reverse.** One way to combat the "gimme" attitude at Halloween is to go trick or treating in reverse. Rather than asking for treats, the children can give treats to others. The children should help decide what the treats will be and to whom they will be given. One idea is for the children to make an excess amount of whatever they are preparing for their own party, such as popcorn, cookies, or cupcakes. The extra food could be wrapped in a party napkin or small, decorated sack, and secured with a ribbon, string, or rubber band. This food would then be delivered around the school or neighborhood. On the package there could be a tag saying something like, "For your afternoon coffee. (signed) The Kindergarten." The children usually take particular delight in hanging the small package on a doorknob, knocking, and then crouching as if to hide until the occupant comes to the door, at which time they jump up and call, "Surprise!"—a voluntary action that seems to come naturally.

**Lining Them Up for Halloween.** Have each child make two sheets of striped paper by pasting strips of orange on black. Using one striped sheet as the background, paste on a Halloween figure cut out of the other striped sheet. Place the figure so that its stripes contrast with those of the background.

**Making Costumes.** Dressing up for Halloween offers children an opportunity to exercise their imaginations. Halloween should be a fun time, free from the experiences that often frighten small children. The costumes they wear should be safe, simple, and amusing rather than gruesome and grotesque.

**FIGURE 24–9 A simple hat and shirt can be a costume for a young child.**

# THIS ONE'S FOR YOU!

## NONSWEET HALLOWEEN TREATS

Candy is frequently received as a Halloween treat. Yet, considering how we try to emphasize good nutrition for young children, this practice really isn't appropriate in the early childhood classroom. The following are some suggestions for treats to be given in place of candy:

- *Stickers.* Give Halloween stickers, scented stickers, stars, notebook reinforcement holes, or shapes cut from gummed paper.
- *Play Dough Pumpkins.* Make orange play dough (See Unit 11). Roll into a small ball. Place the ball in a plastic bag. Tie open end with green yarn or ribbon. Attach a label saying "play dough." (Recipe for the playdough can be included on the label.)
- Unsharpened pencils.
- Penny Jack-o-Lanterns: Cut pumpkins from orange construction paper. To make jack-o-lantern, tape two pennies for eyes and three for the mouth.
- Jack-o-Lantern Crayons: Preheat oven to 375°F. Place crayon chips in a paper-lined muffin tin. Turn oven off, and place muffin tin in oven for five minutes or until chips melt. Remove from oven and allow to harden. Remove paper lining. Place the crayons in plastic bags. Tie the open end with green yarn. Glue paper features to bag for the jack-o-lantern face.
- Small magnets.
- Purchased small party favors.
- Plastic finger rings.
- Small balls.
- Scratchpads.
- Toothbrushes.

Any items not given out can be saved for the following Halloween.

When children make their own costumes, it becomes a wholesome, creative activity. To stimulate the children's imaginations, the teacher should have a variety of supplies available. On one shelf might be various pieces of colorful cloth, and on another a box of old jewelry, some feathers, artificial flowers, ribbons, laces, bits of fur, scraps of construction paper, grocery bags large enough to fit over a child's head, paper plates and cups, yarn, and string. On a third shelf might be scissors, tape, paste, glue, safety pins, crayons, rubber bands, a stapler, and paper fasteners.

The fun the children have in assembling their own costumes is part of the Halloween celebration. As children finish their work, they can join a group for storytelling and perhaps describe their costumes.

### Pumpkin and Cat Costumes.
Materials: Two large sheets of brown wrapping paper for each costume; pencil; staples or paste; crayons or paints

Procedure:
1. Put two sheets of paper together and fold them lengthwise.
2. Draw half the design against the folded edge (Figure 24–11).

FIGURE 24–10 Young children enjoy making their own Halloween costumes and decorations.

3. Cut out the design.
4. Unfold it.
5. Decorate with crayons, or paste on pieces from cutouts.
6. Staple or paste each costume together at the shoulders and sides. (Or make paper straps for the shoulders and sides.) Wear over jeans or leotards.

**Pillow Case Costumes.**

Materials: A plain pillow case, chalk, rubber bands, markers, scissors, bells and bows

Procedure:
1. Pull up corners opposite the pillowcase opening and secure with rubber bands to make ears or jester hats. Use scissors to cut two arm holes.
2. While case is on the child, use chalk to indicate where the face is. Remove the case and cut out a circle for the face opening.
3. Use markers to add features on the pillowcase to individualize each costume. The children love to do this! They can also glue on bells, bows, glitter, and any other details to their costume. (See Figure 24–12.)

**Greasepaint.**   If some children do not like wearing Halloween masks or you're concerned about the

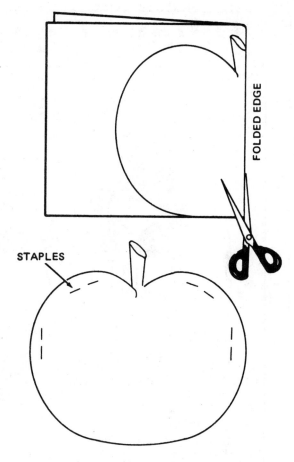

FIGURE 24–11 Pumpkin costumes.

safety of masks, you might find this nontoxic paint a fun solution!

2 teaspoons white shortening
5 teaspoons cornstarch
1 teaspoon flour
Water or glycerin to thin
Food coloring

Mix cornstarch and flour into shortening. Thin a bit with water or glycerin. Add food coloring, mixing well. *Note:* To get brown, add 1 extra teaspoon of shortening and 2½ teaspoons of unsweetened cocoa before thinning.

**Hats.**   Various kinds of hats can be made for use in the Halloween parade and for costumes in general:

# Pillow Case Costumes

Materials:

Rubber bands

Glue

Markers

Scissors

Chalk

Poster board

A plain pillow case

Procedure:

**Step 1.** Pull up corners opposite opening and secure with rubber bands to make ears. Use scissors to cut two arm holes.

**Step 2.** While case is on child, use chalk to indicate where face is. Remove case and cut out a circle.

**Step 3.** Use markers to add features to individualize each costume. Cut petals and tails out of poster board and glue to pillow case.

**FIGURE 24–12 Pillow case costumes.**

- *Paper plate hats.* Paper plate hats work best if a smaller paper plate is stapled to the back of a larger plate so that they are back to back. Punch a hole on each side of the smaller paper plate and attach ribbons or yarn to make ties. The smaller plate fits around the child's head and is not decorated. The larger paper plate will have the appearance of sitting on top of the head and can be decorated with collage paper flowers, cotton balls, pieces of material scraps, tissue, etc.
- *Crowns.* Cut a crown pattern for each child out of heavy paper such as poster paper. The paper can be decorated by the child by painting, collaging, or printing. Add such items as gummed stars, glitter, aluminum foil, or old jewelry stones. Attach ties to the crown, staple on bands of heavy paper, and then staple the two band ends together to fit the child's head.
- *Spring hats or bands.* Make a band of paper about 1½" wide and long enough to extend about three-quarters of the way around the child's head; attach string or ties to the ends. Paper flowers can be cut out and glued on. Flowers can also be made by crushing 1" squares of colored tissue papers and gluing them onto the hat.
- *Wigs.* A brown paper bag is used to make a wig. Cut a face hole in one side of the bag, and then cut the rest of the bag into strips. The strips can be crushed on the ends or rolled on a pencil to curl them.

**Costume Box.** Prepare a box with masks, costumes, and accessories, so the children can experiment with the items. This may ease the fears of some children regarding Halloween. The following can be made for the costume box:

- *Basic cone hat.* Fold 12" × 24" paper in half and cut out a quarter circle. Open and roll the half-circle into a cone. Adjust to fit the child's head. Staple or tape together. Make into a clown hat by adding pom-poms, yarn, or paper designs.
- *Witch hat.* Make the Basic cone hat from black construction paper. Cut out a large circle for the brim. Place the cone hat in the center and trace around the bottom of the cone. Draw tabs inside the circle and cut out the inner circle, leaving tabs. Tape the tabs to the inside of the cone.
- *Basic mask.* Fold a 3" × 8" piece of construction paper in half. Starting at the fold, draw the shape of half of a mask. While the mask is folded, cut mask from paper and cut holes for eyes. Open the mask. Tie string through holes punches in the sides of the mask.
- *Owl mask.* Fold a plastic holder from a six-pack of soda in half and staple at center. Wrap pipe cleaners around each side of the mask. Bend the pipe cleaners to fit around the ears. Tape a construction paper nose to the mask.
- *Paper bag wig.* Use a large paper bag that fits over the child's head. Cut a large rectangle from the front section of the bag for the face. Fringe the bottom of the bag for hair. Curl the fringe by rolling it tightly around a pencil.
- *Mustache.* Fold construction paper. Starting at fold, draw half a mustache shape. Cut the shape from paper. Tape the mustache above the upper lip.
- *Beard.* Fold a piece of construction paper in half and fringe the bottom edges. Curl fringe by rolling tightly around a pencil. Punch holes in each side and tie strings through holes.
- *Master disguise.* Cut two sections from plastic six-pack holder. Wrap pipe cleaners around each side of the glasses. Bend pipe cleaners to fit around ears. Staple an egg carton cup to the bottom of the "eyeglasses" for a nose. Staple a mustache (see above) to the bottom of the "nose."

**Halloween Promenade.** Most children enjoy getting dressed in costumes and playing make-believe. They need to make only those parts of the costume considered important; their imaginations can fill in the rest.

Procedure:

1. A partial costume may include an oatmeal box for a phantom's hat, a paper bag ghost mask, a paper tie for a pumpkin man, some yarn for a witch's hair, or a cape of white roll paper for a spook who is getting ready to fly in the wind.
2. The Halloween "characters" may go for a walk around the school or make a brief visit to another classroom.

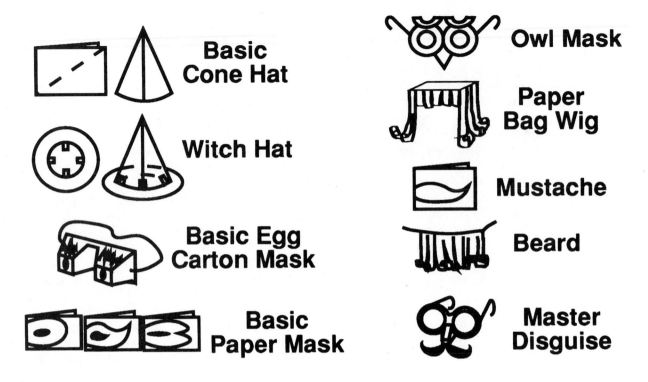

Basic Cone Hat

Witch Hat

Basic Egg Carton Mask

Basic Paper Mask

Owl Mask

Paper Bag Wig

Mustache

Beard

Master Disguise

**My Funny Skeleton.** Around Halloween the children may see skeletons displayed in shops and in school. This might offer the teacher an opportunity to capitalize on children's natural curiosity to provide an awareness of body structure. As they pursue this interest the teacher might:

- Make available a picture of a real Halloween skeleton.
- Have children feel the bones in their body, e.g., the skull, cheekbones, jaw, the bones in the fingers and forearms, ribs and backbone, wrists, elbows, knees, and ankles.
- Discuss the purpose of bones and joints.
- Have children dramatize what they think it would be like if we had no bones or joints (like an earthworm).
- Mention foods that strengthen the bones, such as milk, potatoes, cheese, ice cream, cottage cheese; possibly collect pictures of them from magazines for sharing or for a health chart. Some of the foods could be tasted during the day.

- Arrange a field trip if the community is fortunate enough to have a museum where mounted skeletons can be seen.

## GAMES

**The Old Witch and the Cat.** The children sit on the floor in a half-circle. They are the cats. One child, the witch, stands a short distance away, facing away from the cats. One of the cat meows. The witch turns quickly and tries to guess which cat it was. If the guess is correct, the cat who meowed becomes the witch. If not, the witch hobbles around the circle while the cats meow. A new witch is then chosen. (See Figure 24–13 for a sample art activity to follow up this game.)

**Ghosts and Witches.** Divide the group in half. Have the children line up on opposite sides of the room. These are the ghosts. Two children, one from each side, are selected to be witches. They are blind-

**FIGURE 24–13 Egg-carton head witch.**

her stew. Listen and tell what objects are in the brew from the noises they make." Teacher makes noises behind the poster board, and children guess what makes each noise. Examples are beaters beating, hands clapping, a bell ringing, or blocks hitting.

**Skala Kazam—Witch Magic.** Pretend to be a witch and perform magic. Display pictures related to Halloween. Discuss each picture. Place a "magic" scarf over the pictures. Remove one picture when lifting the scarf and say, "Skala Kazam!" Players tell which picture disappeared. *Variation:* Use objects instead of pictures.

**Mystery Bag.** Explain what a mystery is. Put a number of objects without sharp edges in a large bag. Examples are unsharpened pencil, bead, block, and sponge. One player reaches into the bag for an object and tries to describe it without looking. He then guesses what the object is and removes it to see if the guess was correct. Repeat until all have had a turn. *Variation:* Adult describes the object in the bag, and players try to guess what it is.

folded (or cover their eyes with their hands) and stand in the center of the room. The ghosts, one at a time, cross over to the opposite side. If a witch hears a ghost from the other side crossing, the witch calls, "I hear a ghost." If the witch is correct, the ghost drops out of the game. If the witch is wrong, a ghost from the witch's own side drops out. The side whose witch catches the most ghosts wins.

**What Time Is It, Mrs. Witch?** One player is Witch, who stands in center of room. Remaining players form a line on one side of room. Teacher asks, "What time is it, Mrs. Witch?" If Witch says, "Midnight," players run across to other side of the room. Those tagged by Witch stay in center to help Witch tag other players. Repeat until all but one child is tagged. Last child then becomes the Witch.

**Witch's Brew.** Draw a large pot on poster board, and stand it upright on a table. Children sit on floor in front of table. Teacher explains, "The witch is boiling some brew. A witch uses a variety of things in

**What Is a Shadow?** Discuss shadows. Go outdoors and discover your own shadow. Recite the following verse as the children make actions to go with the words:

If I walk, my shadow walks.
If I run, my shadow runs.
And when I stand still, as you can see,
My shadow stands beside me.
When I hop, my shadow hops.
When I jump, my shadow jumps.
And when I sit still, as you can see,
My shadow sits beside me.

Try to change shape and length of shadow. Discuss other ways shadows can be made, either in bright light or at night when the moon is shining bright. Discuss fears about shadows, and give explanations for shadows to help remove children's fears.

**Shadow Chase.** Go outside on a sunny day and chase each other's shadows.

**Pass the Pumpkin.** Sit in a circle. One player sits, with eyes closed, in the center of the circle. When the music starts, the remaining players pass a small pumpkin or ball around the circle. When the music stops, the player holding the pumpkin (or ball) conceals it in his hands. The other players pretend to be holding the pumpkin (or ball). The player in the center is given three turns to guess who has the pumpkin. The child holding the pumpkin then goes to the center of circle. Repeat.

**Spiders and Flies.** A group of 10 to 20 can play this game. Choose three to four "spiders" and the rest of the group becomes the "flies." The spiders stand in a line, a good running distance from the flies. (The distance depends on the age of the group. A greater distance is needed for older children.) The game begins when the spiders say, "We are the spiders," to the group of children playing the flies. The flies respond, "We are the flies." Then the spiders say, "We're going to catch you," and the flies say, "You just try!" When the flies say this, the spiders begin running toward the flies, trying to tag them. Once tagged, the flies are out. The spiders have to tag all the flies before the game ends. The flies can only run toward the "safe" boundary in one direction. (No running back and forth.) The last three or four flies tagged become the new spiders for the next round.

**Popcorn Vendor.** Children sit in a circle. Choose one child to be the "popcorn vendor." The child chosen bounces a ball in front of three children saying, "Popcorn," while bouncing the ball. After three are chosen, the popcorn vendor says, "Start," or "Begin to pop." To "pop," the three children chosen by the popcorn vendor hop, bouncing the ball, too. They must tag each child separately with the ball. The last child tagged with the ball is the new popcorn vendor. The circle of children represents the boundary. If one of the children steps out of the circle, the child is out.

**Ghost, Ghost, Witch.** (A variation of Duck, Duck, Goose) Have the children sit on the floor in a circle. Choose one child to be "it." The child who is "it"

walks around the outside of the circle, lightly tapping the head of each child in the circle saying, "Ghost" to each child. When the child who is "it" taps a child's head and says, "Witch," the child named "witch" must get up and chase after "it." If "it" gets back to the proper place on the floor, then the "witch" becomes "it" and the game continues.

**Halloween Shapes.**

Materials: A set of Halloween shapes, such as a pumpkin, a ghost, a witch's hat, etc.

Procedure: Distribute the shapes to the children and sing them this song. They should respond to the directions in the song (sung to the tune of "Muffin Man").

> O, do you have the spooky ghost? The spooky ghost, the spooky ghost?
> If you have the spooky ghost, please stand up. (Or hold it up high)

Continue singing about the other shapes the children hold. Use descriptive adjectives to encourage language development.

Variation: This song and activity can be adapted to any holiday and set of holiday symbols.

**Ghost Card Game.** Make two matching sets of cards with pictures of Halloween themes. Spread all

**FIGURE 24–14 Examples of shape cards.**

cards face down on the table. Players take turns turn-ing two cards at a time. The first player to see two matching overturned cards says, "Boo!" and then takes both cards. Play until all cards are matched. *Variation:* Make pairs of cards that are associated. Ex-amples are pumpkin/jack-o-lantern, witch/broom, cowboy/cowboy hat, owl/tree, and princess/crown. The first player to recognize association says, "Boo!" He then explains how the two are associated.

**Pumpkin Throw.**  Place a plastic pumpkin con-tainer on the floor. Stand a designated distance from the pumpkin and attempt to throw bean bag or small ball into the container.

**Jack-o-Lantern Catch.**  With felt-tipped pen, make jack-o-lantern features on an inflated orange balloon. Place the balloon in a kitchen funnel, which is held in the hand. Toss the balloon into air and catch it with the funnel when it falls.

**Witch's Broom.**  Use a broomstick or stick that is at least 3 feet long. Hold the stick in front of the body with both hands. Step over the stick with one foot and then the other. Lift the stick behind the body until it is above the head. Move the stick in front of the body to starting position. Repeat.

**Witch's Broom Relay.**  Divide group of children into two lines. The first player in each line places a broom between his legs and rides it to a designated location. He turns around and rides it back to the next player in line. Repeat until all have had a turn.

**Ghost Trap.**  (A variation of Mousetrap) Select five or six children to be ghosts. The rest of the class forms a circle by joining hands (the ghost trap). When the arms of the ghost trap are *up*, the trap is open and the ghosts can run in and out as they go around the circle. When the teacher says, "Snap," the children who make up the ghost trap will lower their arms to catch the ghosts in the trap. The ghosts who are caught go to the center of the circle and have to stay there. The game continues until all the ghosts have been caught. The last one caught is the winner.

**Bean the Pumpkin.**  This game is a Halloween variation of bean bag. The target can be created by the children. The opening could be in the shape of a big jack-o-lantern on heavy posterboard or ply-wood. Secure the target at an angle so that the bean bag can go through the opening. Each child has a chance to throw from one to three bean bags at the jack-o-lantern. No score needs to be kept, but if the children decide to do so, they could get a point each time they hit the target. Hand–eye coordination is developed through this activity.

The game can be played with partners or with four or five players. Variations of the game can be made for other holidays; for example, a wreath for Christ-mas, a four-leaf clover for St. Patrick's Day, an egg for Easter, and a heart for Valentine's Day.

**Pepper the Pumpkin.**  Cut a large pumpkin face out of cardboard. Draw and cut out features. Paint and prop it against a wall. Children try to throw bean bags through the pumpkin's eyes, nose, or mouth.

A large pumpkin can also be drawn on the chalk-board and a damp sponge used. If the sponge touches any part of the eyes, nose, or mouth, the child scores.

**Black Cat and Ghosts.**  One child is selected to be the cat. The cat hides behind the teacher's desk or sits on a stool with her back to the players, who sit in their seats. The teacher chooses four or five ghosts; she beckons or signals quietly to the children se-lected. They sneak up to the cat's hiding place and scratch on the desk or stool. The scratching is the signal for the cat to start chasing them; they are "safe" only by reaching their holes (seats). Any ghost who is tagged by the cat before reaching her hole becomes the cat. If more than one ghost is tagged, the first one tagged becomes the cat. The cat must be "it" again if she does not tag anyone. The teacher selects other children to be the ghosts and the game begins again.

Teaching suggestions: Choose only one ghost from any row of seats to avoid collisions in the chase. En-courage ghosts to get as close to the cat as they dare before scratching. As for all running games played in the traditional classroom, do not allow the children to cut through vacant seats. They must run around rows of seats, using the aisles. Also, continually remind the children to keep their feet under their chairs when others are running to avoid tripping a player.

## SONGS

**The Goblin in the Dark.**   Use the melody for "A Farmer in the Dell."

The goblin in the dark,
The goblin in the dark,
Hi, ho, on Halloween,
The goblin in the dark.

Repeat, using Halloween creatures, such as: The goblin takes a witch; or the witch takes a bat; or the bat takes a ghost; or the ghost says, "Boo!" Children particularly enjoy one final chorus of:

They all scream and screech,
They all scream and screech,
Hi, Ho, on Halloween,
They all scream and screech.

**Here We Go 'Round the Jack-o-Lantern.**   Use the tune for "Here We Go 'Round the Mulberry Bush." The children form a circle, holding hands, and walk around an imaginary (or real) jack-o-lantern. Everyone sings the chorus:

Here we go 'round the jack-o-lantern,
Jack-o-lantern, jack-o-lantern.
Here we go 'round the jack-o-lantern
So late on Halloween night.

Children stop walking, drop hands, and begin doing this action and singing: "This is the way we take out the seeds."
Repeat the chorus and then another verse, substituting any action suggested by the children, such as carve the face, put in a candle, etc.

**I'm a Jack-o-Lantern.**   Use the tune for "I'm a Little Teapot."

I'm a jack-o-lantern, look at me!
I'm as happy as I can be.

Put a candle in and light the light,
I'll scare you because it's Halloween night!
Boo-oo——!!

**Once I Had a Pumpkin.**   Use the tune for "Did You Ever See a Lassie?")

Oh, once I had a pumpkin,
A pumpkin, a pumpkin,
With no face at all.

With no eyes and no nose,
And no mouth and no teeth,
Oh, once I had a pumpkin,
With no face at all.

So I made a Jack-o-Lantern,
Jack-o-Lantern, Jack-o-Lantern,
So I made a Jack-o-Lantern,
With a big funny face.

With big eyes and big nose,
And big mouth and big teeth,
So I made a Jack-o-Lantern,
With a big funny face.

**Three Little Pumpkins.**   (Sung to the tune "Ten Little Indians")

One little, two little, three little pumpkins,
Rolled down the lane like funny bumpkins.
Had their faces carved and thought they were somethin's,
Funny Halloween jack-o-lanterns.

**Three Little Witches.**   To the tune ("Ten Little Indians")

One little, two little, three little witches,
Flying over haystacks, flying over ditches,
Slide down the moon without any hitches.
Heigh ho, Halloween's here.

**One Little Goblin.**   (Use the tune for "Mary Had a Little Lamb")

One little goblin hopping up and down,
Hopping up and down, hopping up and down.
One little goblin hopping up and down,
For this is Halloween.

*Second verse:* Two little skeletons walking down the street . . .
*Third verse:* Three little witches flying through the air . . .
*Fourth verse:* Four little pumpkins rolling to and fro . . .

**The Great Pumpkin.**   Sung to the tune ("Did You Ever See a Lassie?")

I am the Great Pumpkin, Great Pumpkin, Great Pumpkin.
I am the Great Pumpkin. Come dance with me.
For your friends are my friends, and my friends are your friends.
I am the Great Pumpkin. Come dance with me.

(Dance as the verse is sung)

**Witch on Halloween.**   (Use the tune for "Farmer in the Dell")

The witch on Halloween, the witch on Halloween,
Heigh ho, let's trick or treat, the witch on Halloween.
*Second verse:* The witch chooses a goblin
*Third verse:* The goblin chooses a bat.
*Fourth verse:* The bat chooses a cat.
*Fifth verse:* The cat chooses a ghost.
*Sixth verse:* The ghost says, "Boo!"
*Seventh verse:* They all screech and scream.

Stand in circle. Players hold hands and move clockwise while singing first verse. Teacher chooses witch who stands in center of circle. At the end of the second verse, the witch chooses a goblin, who joins him in the center of the circle. Continue until all characters are chosen.

**Hookey Spooky.**   (To the tune "Hokey Pokey")

Put your right hand in, take your right hand out.
Put your right hand in and shake it all about.
Do the Hookey Spooky and everybody shout,
"That's what it's all about. Boo!"

Stand in a circle. Players do motions for the first two lines. As the third line is sung, the children turn around. As the fourth line is sung, players slap thighs twice, clap hands twice, and raise hands above head. Repeat, using other parts of the body.
*Variations:*

- Instead of the last two lines, use: "Do the Hookey Spooky and hoot like an owl, That's what it's all about. Hoot!"
- Give each child a black or orange crepe paper streamer to wave throughout the song.

## CREATIVE MOVEMENT ACTIVITIES

In a discussion with the children at Halloween time, make a list of feelings and objects that describe the holiday. Then have the children use movement to express these ideas. Encourage creativity.

Several ideas for children to act out are:

- black cat arching its back
- witch riding a broomstick
- owls and bats
- tricks
- full moon
- happy
- excited
- mysterious

Such words might also be used to stimulate creative art, stories, poetry, and songs.

**Halloween Skits.**   Using some of the topics from the previous activity, divide the children into three or four groups. Give each group a topic to act out for the rest of the class. As each group performs, the rest of the class is the audience.

**Halloween Faces and Feelings.**   Facial expressions can reveal feelings to others. Make faces in front of a mirror that suggest feelings and appearances related to Halloween. Examples are spooky, scary, ugly, sad, happy, and angry. Halloween masks also depict feelings. Wear different masks and look into the mirror.

**A Visit to a Haunted House.**   Pretend to visit a haunted house. Huddle together and tiptoe quietly through the woods to the house. " 'Whoo-whoo!' Who made that strange noise? Don't be afraid. It's only an owl." Slowly open the door to the haunted house. "Creak!" Enter and push away the cobwebs. "Look! There's a staircase. Let's climb the stairs. There's a door at the top." Open it carefully. "Ah-h-h! There's a Ghost!" Close the door. Run down the stairs. Open the front door. Scamper through the forest. Run home and lock the door. "Whew, safe at last."

**Halloween Walk.**   Form a line on one side of the room. Cross the room in the following ways:

- Fly like a bat.
- Gallop like a cowboy on a horse.
- Hop like a bunny.
- Roll like a pumpkin.
- Dance like a princess.
- Creep like a cat.
- Walk like a skeleton.
- Float like a ghost.
- Stomp like a monster.

**Let's Be Witches.**

> The witch rides on her broom,
> Going here and there—zoom, zoom.
> Sometimes she rides fast and sometimes she rides slow,
> Watching Halloween fun below.
> Oooooooooooooooo!

Place a yardstick or broom between legs and pretend to be a witch flying while the verse is recited. Encourage conversation to describe how it feels to fly, what the speed of the flight is, and what might be seen on Halloween night.

**Halloween Chatter.**   Make the following sounds: cackle like a witch, screech like a cat, hoot like an owl, and make a spooky noise like a ghost.

**Shadow Theater.**   Hang a sheet and place a bright light behind it. One child goes behind the curtain and pantomimes a character or a simple act. Others guess what character he is portraying or what he is doing. The teacher can help the child decide what to do if necessary. *Variation:* Players shut their eyes while the teacher selects someone to go behind the sheet. Remaining players guess to whom the shadow belongs.

**Paper Bag Owl.**   From construction paper cut nose, eyes, and wings. Glue features to a brown paper lunch sack to make an owl. Use the owl for a hand puppet for use with fingerplays, poems, and songs about Halloween.

**Paper Bag Owl**

**Finger Puppets.**

- *Jack-o-lantern.* Draw and cut out jack-o-lanterns about the size of a quarter. Attach these to narrow paper rings that will fit the top part of the children's fingers. Children use them for fingerplays about jack-o-lanterns and Halloween.
- *Peanut shell ghost.* Use elongated half of peanut shell. Draw face on the shell with a felt-tipped pen. The children place the shells over the tips of their fingers. Develop creative stories about these "nutty" puppets.

**Flashlight Goblin.**   Cut facial features from the bottom of a paper bag. Line the inside base of the

**Flashlight Goblin**

bag with orange crepe (or tissue) paper. Insert a flashlight into the bag. Twist open end of bag around the flashlight's handle, leaving switch uncovered. Secure with rubber band. Turn on flashlight. The children can wave the lighted goblin in a darkened room to appropriate background music.

## FINGERPLAYS AND POEMS

### Fingerplays

**Halloween Witches**
One little, two little, three little witches;
   (Hold up one hand; nod fingers at each count)
Fly over haystacks.
   (Fly hand in up-and-down motion)
Fly over ditches.
   Slide down moonbeams without any hitches,
(Glide hand downward)
   Heigh-Ho! Halloween's here!

**The Friendly Ghost**
I'm a friendly ghost—almost!
   (Point to self)
And I can chase you, too!
   (Point to child)
I'll just cover me with a sheet.
   (Pretend to cover self, ending with hands covering face)
And then call, "Scat" to you.
   (Uncover face quickly and call out "Scat")

**Witch**
If I were a witch
   (One fist rides on top of water, waving through air)
I'd ride on a broom
And scatter the ghosts
With a zoom, zoom, zoom.

**My Pumpkin Round and Fat**
See my pumpkin round and fat.
   (Make circle with fingers)
See my pumpkin yellow.
Watch him grin on Halloween.
   (Point to smiling mouth)
He's a very funny fellow.

**My Friend Jack**
Do you know my friend Jack? (Point to friend)
When I wave to him (Wave)
He doesn't wave back. (Shake head)
But he has a friendly grin on his face so bright,
   (Smile)
Which makes it seem less dark on Halloween night.
Before we adjourn, I'd like you to learn (Point to friend)
Jack's last name is O'Lantern! (Form circle and smile)

**I Have a Jack-O-Lantern**
I have a jack-o-lantern (Form circle with hands)
With a candle in, he's a very happy fellow.
See his jack-o-lantern grin.
   (Narrow circle to half circle)

**Jack-o-Lantern, Jack-o-Lantern**
Jack-o-lantern, jack-o-lantern,
(Form circle with fingers)
You are such a funny sight.
As you sit there in the window,
   (Form square with fingers)
Looking out at the night. (Point to eyes)
You were once a yellow pumpkin,
Growing on a sturdy vine.
Now you are a jack-o-lantern.
   (Form circle with fingers)
See the candle light shine. (Place finger in center of circle)

**I Made a Jack-o-Lantern**
I made a jack-o-lantern for Halloween night (Form circle)
He has three crooked teeth, but he won't bite.
   (Point to teeth and shake head sideways)
He has two round eyes, but he cannot see. (Circle eyes)
He's a jolly jack-o-lantern, as happy as can be.

**I Am a Pumpkin**
I am a pumpkin, big and round. (Form circle)
Once upon a time, I grew on the ground.
Now I have a mouth, two eyes, a nose. (Point to features)
What are they for, do you suppose? (Shrug shoulders)
When I have a candle inside shining bright,
I'll be a jack-o-lantern on Halloween night.

**I Am the Great Pumpkin**
I am the great pumpkin. Wow, what a sight!
I have teeth, but I won't bite.
   (Point to teeth and shake head)
I have eyes so I can see (Point to eyes)
To spread Halloween happiness.
Ha, ha, giggle-ee!

**A Funny Old Woman**
A funny old woman in a pointed cap,
   (Hands form a pointed cap above head)
On my door went rap, rap, rap. (Knock)
I was going to the door to see who was there, (Fingers walk)
When off on her broomstick, she rode through the air.
   (Move hand through air)

## An Old Witch on Halloween Night

An old witch on Halloween night,
Knows how to scare. Oh, what a fright!
BOOOOOOOOOOOOOOOOOOO (Clap)
Then do you know what I do?
SKIDOO! (Jump and fall on floor)

## Witch's Cat

I am the witch's cat,
Meow, meow, meow.
My fur is black as darkest night.
My eyes are glaring, green, and bright. (Point to eyes)
I am the witch's cat,
Meow, meow, meow.

## Coal Black Cat

Coal black cat with humped-up back, (Hump back)
Shining eyes so yellow. (Point to eyes)
See him with his funny tail: (Make tail)
He's very funny fellow.

## Waldo White, the Ghost

A cute little ghost named Waldo White (Signify small)
Gave all the children a terrible fright. (Act frightened)
"Why," said Waldo, "Are you scared of me? (Shrug shoulders)
"I'm a friendly ghost, as friendly as can be."
The children knew that he was right. (Shake head vertically)
When he danced and sang—that Waldo White!
   (Dance)

## One Little Witch

One little witch did a dancing jig. (Raise respective fingers)
Two little witches wish they were big.
Three little witches jumped up and down.
Four little witches went to town.
Five little witches on Halloween night.
Jumped on their broomsticks and flew out of sight.

## An Owl in a Tree

An owl sat watching in a tree, (Sit with thumbs under arms)
Just as wise as he could be, (Point to side of forehead)
Watching tricksters from door to door run, (Make fingers run)
Trick-or-treating and having fun. (Pretend to knock)
After he had watched the whole scene, (Encircle eyes with fingers)
He said, "Whoooo, it's owl-o-ween!"

## Mr. Owl

Mr. Owl perched in a tree. (Place hands under arms)
"Whooo goes there?" he said to me. (Point to self)

I looked high up in that oak, (Look upward)
But could not find the owl that spoke. (Shake head sideways)
In the sky I saw that bird. (Pretend to fly)
"Whoo, whooo, whoooo," was all I heard. (Place hand behind ear.)

## Witches, Ghosts, and Goblins

Witches, ghosts, and goblins:
What a scary sight! (Act frightened)
See the happy jack-o-lantern (Form circle)
It must be Halloween night. (Shake finger)

## A Pretty Princess

A pretty princess wears a crown. (Form circle above head)
Bunny's ears flop up and down. (Place hands above head, move hands up and down)
A beautiful ballerina dances to and fro. (Move arms above head)
A funny clown laughs, "Ho, ho, ho."
Two green eyes shine from a cat. (Form circles around eyes with fingers)
A scary witch wears a pointed hat. (Form point with arms above head)
Jack-o-lanterns shine so bright. (Form large circle)
Happy children on Halloween night!

## Goblins and Spooks

Goblins and spooks, ghosts and witches,
Go door to door giving their pitches, (Pretend to knock)
"Trick to treat,
Trick or treat,
Trick or treat."
Show me a trick, (Do trick)
And I'll give you a sweet. (Hold out hand)

## Heigh Ho for Halloween!

Heigh Ho for Halloween!
Scary creatures can be seen:
An old witch with a crooked hat, (Form point with arms above head)
Wings flap quickly on a bat, (Pretend to fly)
A spider walking with eight feet, (Raise eight fingers)
While ghosts and goblins quietly creep. (Whisper and place finger over lips)
Tiptoe, tiptoe, BOO!

## Mr. Pumpkin

I am Mr. Pumpkin, big and round
   (Use arms to show size of pumpkin)
Once upon a time I grew on the ground.
   (Point to the ground)

Now I have a mouth, two eyes, a nose,
    (Point to each feature on own face)
What are they for, do you suppose?
    (Right forefinger to forehead—thinking gesture)
When I have a candle inside shining bright,
    (Hold up right forefinger)
I'll be a jack-o-lantern on Halloween night.
    (Thumbs in armpits—bragging gesture)

**Five Little Jack-o-Lanterns**
Five little jack-o-lanterns sitting on a gate
    (Put up five fingers)
First one said, "My, it's getting late!"
    (Touch thumb)
Second one said, "It's cold out here."
    (Touch index finger)
Third one said, "There's witches in the air."
    (Touch middle finger)
Fourth one said, "Let's go away from here."
    (Touch fourth finger)
Fifth one said, "It's only Halloween night."
    (Touch fifth finger)
In came the wind, out went the light.
    Now the fun is over for this year's Halloween night!

**Mr. Pumpkin**
Smiling Mr. Pumpkin
With your great big shining eyes,
Will you be my jack-o-lantern
Before we make you into pies?

I'll put you in my window
To watch the children come,
And when they see your shining face
Oh, how they will run!

**FIGURE 24–16 Simple construction paper jack-o-lanterns are fun for young children to make for Halloween.**

**Halloween**
Tomorrow night is Halloween!
Many creatures will be seen
Wearing orange or black or green,
Some quite funny, some quite mean.
I'll be having lots of fun,
As from house to house I run.
It's a secret what I'll be,
But tomorrow night you'll see!

## Poems

**What Am I?**
They chose me from my brothers;
"That's the nicest one," they said.
And they carved me out a face
And put a candle in my head.

And they set me on the doorstep,
Oh, the night was dark and wild;
But when they lit the candle,
Then I smiled.

**Halloween Time**
Halloween's the time for nuts,
And for apples, too,
And for funny faces that
Stare and stare at you.
Right behind them is a friend,
Jack or Bob or Bess,

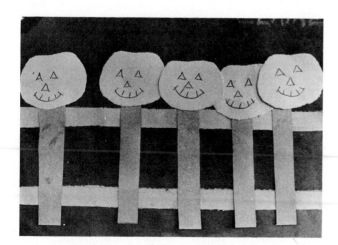

**FIGURE 24–15 Five little jack-o-lanterns.**

Isn't it the greatest fun
When you try to guess?

## Mostly Jolly Jack-o-Lanterns

The following Halloween poem could be read by the teacher with the children acting out the five characters in the poem (Barney, Freddy, Chester, Harry, and Reuben).

Five little jack-o-lanterns
Lighted by a fairy,
Most had funny faces,
Some looked scary.

These little jack-o-lanterns
Shining yellow bright,
Made some ghostly shadows,
All through the night.

Jack-o-lantern Barney
Had a nose that wiggled,
When children looked at Barney,
They jiggled as they giggled.

Jack-o-lantern Freddy
His front teeth out,
Made those who saw him,
Holler and shout.

Jack-o-lantern Chester
Eyes stared at the night,
As children looked at Chester,
They laughed at the sight.

Jack-o-lantern Harry
His mouth with scowls would bend,
When children gazed at Harry,
Their hair would stand on end.

But jack-o-lantern Reuben
With kindly face aglow,
Brought smiles from all the children,
Because he loved them so.

## What Is It?

It will make a jack-o-lantern
Or a big Thanksgiving pie,
It's a big, round, yellow something,
You can guess it if you try.

## Halloween Friends

On Halloween my friends and I
Dress up in frightening clothes,
We each put on a funny face
With an enormous nose.

We ring our neighbors' doorbells
And they get an awful fright,
To see such scary creatures
Standing there at night.

**FIGURE 24–17 Talking about a Halloween costume is a fun part of the experience.**

## Five Little Ghosts

(See related art activity, "Tissue Ghosts," page 485.)

Five little ghosts dressed all in white,
We're scaring each other on Halloween night.
"Boo!" said the first one. "I'll catch you!"
"Wooooo," said the second. "I don't care if you do."
The third ghost said, "You can't run away from me!"
And the fourth one said, "I'll scare everyone I see!"
Then the last one said, "It's time to disappear,
See you at Halloween this time next year!"

## How Does a Goblin Go?

How does a goblin go?
Let me see.
He goes flip, flap, flip, flap, and floggle.
That must be

The way a goblin goes
With his leather heels and flat-top toes,
Flip, flap, flip, flap, floggle.

Down in the marsh
Where bullfrogs goggle,
That's where he goes,
With a sway and joggle,
Flip, flap, flip, flap, flip, flap, floggle.

**Black and Gold**
Everything is black and gold,
Black and gold tonight.
Yellow pumpkins, yellow moon,
Yellow candlelight.
Jet-black cat with golden eyes,
Shadows black as ink.
Firelight blinking in the dark.

With a yellow blink.
Black and gold, black and gold,
Nothing in-between . . .
When the world turns black and gold,
Then it's HALLOWEEN!

**The Magic Vine**
A fair seed I planted
So dry and white and old,
There sprang a vine enchanted,
With magic flowers of gold.

I watched it, I tended it,
And truly, by and by,
It bore a jack-o-lantern
And a great Thanksgiving pie.

**Pumpkin**
A roly-poly pumpkin
Went traveling down the street.
It couldn't walk,
It couldn't run,
It hadn't any feet.

It rolled along
Till out of breath,
It stopped beside our door.
Cook spied it,
And alas, alack,
The pumpkin is no more.

**Little Jack Pumpkin Face**
Little Jack pumpkin face
Lived on a vine
Little Jack pumpkin face
Thought it was fine.

First he was small and green,
Then big and yellow,
Little Jack pumpkin face,
Is a fine fellow.

They chose me from my brothers,
"That's the nicest one," they said.
And they carved out a face
And put a candle in my head.

They set me on the doorstep
And the night was dark and wild,
And when they lit the candle,
Then I smiled and smiled and smiled.

That is the night of Halloween,
When all the witches can be seen,
Some are small and some are lean,
Some are tall as a castor bean.

**The Popcorn House**
   (For related cooking activity, see "Popcorn Balls,"
page 508.)

A mole, a rabbit, and a little gray mouse,
All lived together in a popcorn house.

The mole chose the cellar,
With its nice dirt walls.

The rabbit took the center,
With its cupboards and hall.

The attic was chosen
By the little gray mouse.

And all were very happy
In the popcorn house.

---

# COOKING EXPERIENCES

**Roast Pumpkin Seeds.**   A natural follow-up activity to the carving of a Halloween pumpkin.

Ingredients: Pumpkin seeds, 1 tablespoon butter for each cup of seeds, salt

Materials: Measuring cup, measuring spoons, large saucepan, mixing spoon, cookie sheet

Procedure:
1. Wash the pumpkin seeds and let them dry.
2. Heat the oven to 300°F.
3. Melt the butter in the saucepan over low heat.
4. Add the seeds to the saucepan and mix.
5. Spread the pumpkin seeds on the cookie sheet.
6. Sprinkle with salt.
7. Bake in the oven until crisp and slightly brown.

8. After this activity, see the "Mr. Pumpkin" finger-play for a fun language art experience, page 504.

**Spooky Spiders.** These creepy crawlers are fun to make and are ready much faster than the usual fruit gelatin.

Ingredients: 2 packages unflavored gelatin, 1 box (3 ozs.) blackberry-flavored gelatin, 2 cups boiling water, licorice whips

Procedure:
1. Combine unflavored gelatin with dry blackberry gelatin in a medium bowl.
2. Pour in boiling water and stir until gelatin is completely dissolved.
3. Pour into a 9-inch pan. Chill until firm.
4. Cut into circles using a 2-inch biscuit cutter for the body and a ½-inch cutter for the head. Remove with a spatula.
5. Attach licorice whips cut into 2-inch lengths for legs and 1-inch lengths for antennae. These do not melt at room temperature. Makes 9 spiders.

**Jack-o-Lantern Sandwich.** A simple but fun snack to make for Halloween is a cheese jack-o-lantern sandwich. Spread a piece of whole wheat bread with mayonnaise, lay on a slice of cheese, and top with another slice of whole wheat bread on which you have cut out a face.

**Sand-Witch.** Spread filling between two square slices of sandwich bread. Cut crust from two adjacent sides for face. For hair, place lettuce on filling and extend beyond bread. Decorate with carrot nose, pickle for mouth, and cross-sections of green or black olives for eyes.

**Haystack Salad.** Ingredients: 2½ cups grated carrots; 15 ounce garbanzo beans, drained; and 2 tablespoons plain yogurt.

Procedure: Mix together. Serve chilled.

**Jack-o-Lantern Fruit Cup.**
Ingredients: 1 orange, a bowl of cut fruit pieces (a can of fruit cocktail works fine)
Materials: Toothpicks, felt-tip marker, spoon, bowl, a knife for cutting. Use a plastic, serrated knife for the children's safety.

Procedure:
1. Cut off the top of the orange. Scoop out the insides and put into a bowl.
2. Using the plastic knife, cut up fresh fruits.
3. Fill the scooped-out orange with the cut-up fruits. Replace the top of the orange and stick it together with a toothpick.
4. Draw on a face with a marker. (See Figure 24–18.)

**Popcorn Balls.**
Ingredients: 1 popcorn popper full of prepared popcorn, 1 pound marshmallows, 1 stick margarine, 1 teaspoon vanilla

Procedure:
1. Melt marshmallows and butter, and add vanilla.
2. Pour over popcorn.
3. Have each child rub margarine on both hands and shape the mixture into individual popcorn balls.

**Monster Toast.**
Pour milk into four plastic, see-through cups. Add food coloring to each cup, using red, blue, yellow, and green separately in each cup. Use a clean paint brush to paint a "monster" face on a piece of white bread. After the face is finished, toast the bread. Butter the bread lightly and munch the monster.

**Octopus Bubbles.**
Pour ½ cup of pineapple juice into a large plastic glass. Add some club soda. Stir. *Variation:* Create another bubbly beverage by mixing club soda with a different fruit juice. You may want to rename this beverage with a "Halloween" name.

**Pumpkin Decorated Straw**

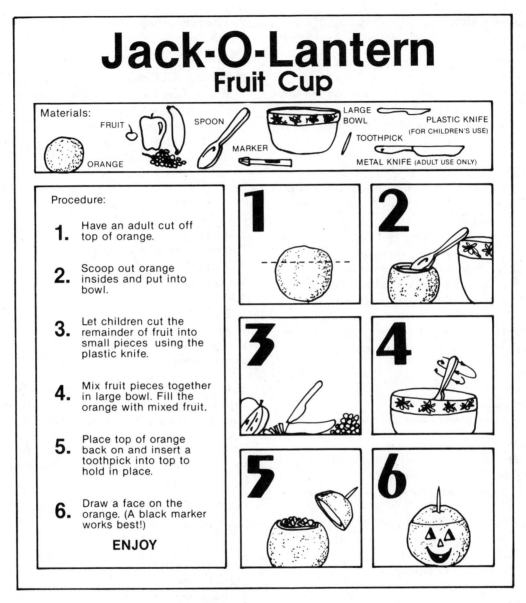

**FIGURE 24–18 Jack-o-lantern fruit cup.**

**Orange Brew.**

Ingredients:

1 cup milk

10 to 12 ice cubes

1 cup water

1 teaspoon vanilla

6 ounces concentrated orange juice

Procedure:

1. Whip ingredients in blender until frothy. Note: If desired, drink with straw decorated with pumpkin cut-out.

2. Slit the pumpkin cutout in two places and insert straw through the slits. Variation: Use the same ingredients to make popsicles.

## Spiced Apple Cider.

Procedure:

1. Pour 10 cups apple cider or apple juice into percolator coffee pot.
2. Place in coffee pot basket 1 cinnamon stick, 2 whole cloves, 2 whole allspice.
3. Perk cider. Serve warm. Decorate with apple wedge.

## Witches' Brew.

Pour 1 gallon cranberry juice into a large bowl. Add 1 gallon apple cider. Stir in 12 ounces. thawed orange juice concentrate.

Children may enjoy making up "recipes" for another witches' brew, including things like spider legs, bat's blood, etc. You can write it down as they recite it. Writing it on a large chart and adding pictures for the ingredients is a good activity at Halloween time.

## Orange Fluff.
Orange Fluff is a great quick dessert or snack with only natural sweetening.

Ingredients:
1 cup water
2 envelopes plain gelatin
6 ounces can orange juice concentrate.

Procedure:

1. Put ¼ cup water into a bowl and sprinkle on gelatin. Stir and let set 5 minutes.
2. Add ¾ cup boiling water and stir until the gelatin is dissolved.
3. Pour mixture into a blender and add orange juice concentrate. Blend and pour into small drinking cups.
4. Refrigerate about 15 minutes.

## Orange Sherbet
Ingredients:
12 ounces can orange juice concentrate
¼ cup apple juice concentrate
1 cup nonfat powdered milk
3½ cups water

Procedure:

1. Blend ingredients thoroughly in a blender, then pour into a baking dish.

2. Place in freezer.
3. Stir thoroughly every hour for 6 to 7 hours.

## Pumpkin Muffins.

Save the cut-out parts of the pumpkin from when you made the eyes, nose, and mouth. Wash these parts and put them on a cookie sheet and bake them at 350°F until they are soft (about 30 minutes). Let them cool, then peel and mash them.

Mix:
¾ cup flour
¼ cup honey
¼ teaspoon salt
1 teaspoon baking powder
¼ teaspoon cinnamon
¼ teaspoon nutmeg
Add:
1 egg
2 tablespoons of milk
¼ cup mashed pumpkin
⅛ cup butter

Mix until smooth and spoon into muffin tins. (Use cupcake paper liners to make them easy to remove.) Bake at 400°F for 20 minutes.

Variation: Do the pumpkin preparation (cutting, cooking, and mashing) one day. Do the muffin mixing another day.

Double the recipe to make a loaf of pumpkin bread. Bake for 50 minutes.

## Orange Muffins.
Ingredients:
1 cup orange juice
1 package yeast
1 tablespoon honey
1 cup whole wheat flour
1 egg
⅓ cup salad oil
⅔ cup honey
1 cup flour
½ teaspoon salt
1 teaspoon vanilla

Procedure:
1. Warm juice to 110 degrees.
2. Add yeast, 1 tablespoon honey, and flour. Set in warm place until bubbly (10 to 15 minutes).
3. Beat the egg.
4. Combine remaining ingredients with the egg.
5. Stir egg mixture into yeast mixture.
6. Fill cups of muffin tin half-full.
7. Place in 150°F oven for 40 minutes. Remove.
8. Preheat oven to 350°F. Bake 20 minutes.

## Honey Balls.

Ingredients: 3 tablespoons honey, 4 tablespoons peanut butter, ½ cup nonfat dry milk, ½ cup dry cereal flakes (crushed)

Procedure:
1. Mix honey and peanut butter. Gradually add nonfat dry milk. Mix well.
2. Form into balls with greased hands.
3. Roll in dry cereal flakes.
4. Chill until firm. Makes 18 balls.

## No-Cook Peanut Butter Fudge.

Ingredients: 1 cup peanut butter, 1 cup corn syrup, 1¼ cups nonfat dry milk solids, 1 cup sifted confectioner's sugar

Procedure:
1. Blend peanut butter and syrup in large mixing bowl.
2. Measure nonfat dry milk solids and sifted confectioner's sugar, and add all at once. Mix all ingredients together—first with a spoon, then with the hands; knead in dry ingredients.
3. Turn onto a board and continue kneading until the mixture is well blended and smooth. Press out with your hands or a rolling pin, making squares. Dough should be ½″ thick.
4. Cut into squares. Top with nutmeats, if desired. Makes about 2 pounds.

## Cheese Pumpkins.

Ingredients:
8 ounces cream cheese
16 ounces American cheese

Procedure:
1. Cut cheeses into ½ inch cubes and let stand at room temperature until softened.
2. Blend together.
3. Shape into 1-inch balls. Place a raisin or slice of green pepper on top of each for pumpkin stem.

## Cheese on Crackers.

Cut American cheese slices into round shapes and place on a cracker. If desired, cut small features from cheese or use raisins to make jack-o-lantern faces.

## Ghost Pancakes.

Ingredients:
½ cup whole wheat flour
1½ cups rolled oats
1 tablespoon baking powder
1 teaspoon salt
1 egg (beaten)
1 teaspoon oil
1 tablespoon honey
1½ cups milk

Procedure:
1. Stir dry ingredients together in a large bowl.
2. Beat egg and honey with fork.
3. Combine with oil and milk. Add to dry ingredients.
4. On hot griddle, pour batter in long streaks to form ghosts. Batter will be thin.
5. When cooked, ghosts will puff up.
6. Serve, decorated with applesauce, bananas, raisins, or blueberries.

## Caramel Apples.

Ingredients: 1 pound small caramels, 1 stick margarine, 10 to 12 small apples, 10 to 12 popsicle sticks

Procedure:
1. Melt a stick of margarine in a 3-quart pan.
2. Add caramels. Melt caramels and margarine over boiling water. Keep stirring.
3. Push popsicle stick squarely into center of each apple.
4. Have the children dip apples into the caramel and place on waxed paper to dry.

# AN ALTERNATIVE TO TRICK-OR-TREAT— A HALLOWEEN CARNIVAL!

Instead of trick-or-treating on Halloween, plan a carnival. When entering the carnival, each child donates a bag of sugarless gum, wrapped popcorn balls, peanuts in shells, or Halloween favors. These are used as prizes for the following games. Give each child a trick-or-treat bag to collect prizes. Start groups at different booths and move clockwise around the room.

**Bats Fly.** Make fishing pole by attaching string to wooden dowel. Tie a magnet to loose end of string. Attach paper clip to black paper bats. Place bats in a tub. Player fishes for bat and makes it fly into a sack.

**Worm in Witch's Brew.** Use a large kettle holding 4 inches of water which contains a small amount of black tempera paint. In the kettle, place rubber worms (sold at sporting goods stores), colored rubber bands, or s-shaped styrofoam packing pieces. Player reaches into kettle, grasps a handful of "worms," and counts them. A treat is received for each "worm" counted.

**Feed the Jack-o-Lantern.** Make a jack-o-lantern on the outside of a box. Cut out a large mouth. Player tosses bean bags into mouth. A treat is received for each bag that enters Jack's mouth.

**Search for Pirates' Treasure Chest.** Player searches for treasure by completing an obstacle course. Examples for course are walking the plank on the balance beam, climbing steps, wiggling through chairs, and crawling through a tunnel made by covering a table with a sheet. Player receives a treat from the treasure chest located at the end of the obstacle course. Note: String yarn for children to follow through the obstacle course and ending at the treasure chest.

**Rat in His Hole.** Player stands beside a quart jar and drops clothespins or rubber rats into a jar. A treat is received for each rat in hole.

**Witch's Ring Toss.** Stand broom between two chairs or in a pail. Make rings from a plastic bleach bottle by cutting bottom from bottle with a knife, and then cutting 1 inch above bottom opening to form a ring. Make several. Player tosses rings at the broom from a designated distance (established according to the ability of the children). A treat is received for each ring on the broom handle.

**Squirt Jack.** Place plastic tarp under and behind a jack-o-lantern. Light candle inside Jack. Player uses squirt gun to extinguish flame, and a treat is received when Jack is "in the dark!" (Keep a pail of water nearby to refill squirt guns and extra candles to replace soaked ones.)

**Bob for Apples.** Attach whole or sliced apple to a string suspended from climbing equipment or broomstick held by two adults. Player holds hands behind back and catches apple with teeth. Apple is given for treat.

**Trick or Treat.** Adult stands behind a door. Child knocks on door and adult opens it. Child says, "Trick or treat." Adult has child do a trick before he receives a treat. Examples of tricks are jump, hop, make an animal noise, or count to a number.

**Shave Jack.** Inflate and tie the end of an orange balloon with a jack-o-lantern face painted on it. Cover the balloon with shaving cream. Player shaves Jack with a bladeless razor. A treat is received if Jack does not break.

**Catch the Ghost.** Inflate a white balloon for the ghost. Do not tie end. Player releases balloon and tries to catch the ghost before it touches the ground. A treat is received for catching the ghost.

**Pumpkin Push.** Place an inflated, round orange balloon at the starting line. At a signal, the player kicks the balloon to the finish line. A treat is received for crossing the finish line.

Even if you do not have a Halloween Carnival, these games are good physical/motor development games for young children during the Halloween season.

# ADDITIONAL READINGS

## General

*13 Great Ways to Celebrate Halloween.* This is a 32-page consumer information booklet written for adults. It is available from the Halloween Celebration Committee, comprised of the toy industry trade association, Toy Manufacturers of America, Inc., and manufacturers of Halloween-related products.

Filled with safety and consumer tips, recipes, and party ideas, the booklet is a comprehensive guide to safe, innovative, and fun-filled Halloween celebrations for families, schools, groups, and communities. For more information, write: Halloween Booklet, P.O. Box 746, Madison Square Station, New York, N.Y. 10159.

## Children's Books for Halloween

Anderson, Lonzo. *The Halloween Party.* New York: Charles Scribner's Sons, 1974.

Anglund, Joan W. *Nibble, Nibble, Mousekin: A Tale of Hansel and Gretel.* New York: Harcourt, Brace, Jovanovich, 1962.

Bowen, Irene. *Suddenly—A Witch.* New York: J.B. Lippincott, 1970.

Bright, Robert. *Georgie.* New York: Doubleday, 1959.

Bunting, Eve. *Ghost's Hour, Spook's Hour.* New York: Clarion/Houghton, 1987.

Calhoun, Mary, and Robert Duvoisin (illus.). *Wobble the Witch Cat.* New York: William Morrow, 1958.

Carey, Valerie Scho. *The Devil and Mother Crump.* Boston: Harper, 1987.

Child Association of America. *Holiday Storybook.* New York: TY Crowell, 1952.

Cole, Babette. *The Trouble with Gran.* New York: Putnam, 1987.

Coleridge, Ann. *The Friends of Emily Culpepper.* New York: Putnam, 1987.

Eager, Edward. *Half Magic.* New York: Harcourt, Brace, Jovanovich, 1970.

Evans, Dilyn. *Monster Soup and Other Spooky Poems.* New York: Scholastic, 1993.

Fox, Mem. *Possum Magic.* New York: Abingdon, 1987.

Garfield, Leon. *Mister Corbett's Ghost.* New York: Pantheon, 1968.

Glovach, Linda. *Little Witch's Halloween Book.* Englewood Cliffs, N.J.: Prentice-Hall, 1975.

Hallinan, P.K. *Today Is Halloween.* New York: Ideals Children's Books, 1993.

Helmrath, Marilyn Olear. *Bobby Bear's Halloween.* New York: Oddo Publishing, 1968.

Karlin, Nurit. *The Tooth Witch.* New York: Lippincott, 1985.

Lystad, M. *Halloween Parade.* New York: G.P. Putnam's Sons, 1973.

Miller, E. *Mousekin's Golden House.* Englewood Cliffs, N.J.: Prentice-Hall, 1972.

Mitchell, Lucy Sprague. *Another Here and Now Story Book.* New York: E.P. Dutton, 1937.

Norton, Mary. *Bed-Knobs and Broomsticks.* New York: Harcourt, Brace, Jovanovich, 1975.

Sauer, Julia. *Fog Magic.* New York: Archway, 1977.

Sendak, Maurice. *Where the Wild Things Are.* New York: Harper and Row, 1963.

Titherington, Jeanne. *Pumpkin, Pumpkin.* New York: Greenwillow, 1986.

Venturi-Pickett, S. *The Halloween Activity Book.* New York: Ideals Children's books, 1993.

Warren, Jean, ed. *Short-Short Stories: Simple Stories for Young Children plus Seasonal Activities.* Everett, Wash.: Warren Publishing House, Inc., 1987.

# UNIT 25

# Thanksgiving

Thanksgiving originated in the Plymouth Colony in the autumn of 1621. At that time and place, the Pilgrims and Native Americans joined in giving thanks for the year's harvest. To this day, people gather in the family circle for Thanksgiving celebrations at home. It is a time of merriment, hospitality, and gratitude for the day-to-day joys often taken for granted. Many families attend religious services, and in some places people of different religions worship together. All over the nation, parades take place on Thanksgiving. Some are patriotic or historic; others are more spectacular Thanksgiving Day parades or even Santa parades.

While the historic background of Pilgrims, Native Americans, and the Plymouth Colony are often too abstract and distant ideas for young children to grasp, the general idea of being thankful is quite appropriate for young children. Teachers can help children learn the true meaning of Thanksgiving by making them more aware of the many things for which to be thankful and how to be helpful to others. The children can learn human values in everyday living by being involved in such creative art experiences as painting pictures, making cut-paper family portraits, or constructing models of their homes. During the discussion, the teacher helps students recall their own experiences and feelings about Thanksgiving and clarifies their thinking about the experiences.

The primary values of Thanksgiving are the pleasures of families gathering together and sharing food together as a social experience—appreciating and being grateful for the earth's plenty.

At Thanksgiving, it is important not to overemphasize how much everyone expects to eat, not to rely mainly on a discussion of Pilgrims and Native Americans to make the day meaningful.

Children can make something at school to bring home and share on Thanksgiving Day, such as cran-berry bread (see page 526), pumpkin bread, or a seasonal decoration.

Children can be encouraged to bring an assortment of fruits and vegetables from home, which they can handle and talk about and then prepare together to share as a wonderfully varied Thanksgiving snack. Or they can be taken to a large market to buy one of every kind of fruit and vegetable they find there for the same purpose.

As follow-up activities, ask the children to talk about the family and guests who came to share the holiday or tell where their family went to be with others. Children also enjoy picking out a variety of flannelboard family members (including pets, of course) who attended; a few older children may wish to attempt to describe how these people are related to each other, but this is usually too difficult for children under five.

The subject of Thanksgiving is broad enough to include a variety of topics for picture making:

- Some Things I Am Thankful For
- Eating Thanksgiving Dinner
- The Thanksgiving Day/Santa Parade
- Getting Ready for Thanksgiving
- My Family on Thanksgiving
- Helping at Home with Thanksgiving Dinner
- A Visit with Friends

The following ideas are designed to focus on the concepts involved in the Thanksgiving holiday, as well as to give children the opportunity to use small muscles in constructing various objects. Of course, hand–eye coordination is also involved in art experiences as well as the chance to express oneself creatively. While specific projects are suggested, they by no means encourage "production line" art in which all children's work turns out looking the same. The Thanksgiving art ideas should be expanded as the children's and teacher's imaginations see fit.

# THIS ONE'S FOR YOU!

## THE FIRST THANKSGIVING: WHAT WAS IT REALLY LIKE?

We know a few basic historic facts about the Pilgrims, their journey, and the First Thanksgiving:*

- The *Mayflower* was not a passenger ship. Before the Pilgrims hired her, she had been used to carry wine and fish.
- There were 102 passengers on the *Mayflower,* and about 40 of them were actually Pilgrims. The others were colonists hired by English businessmen to help start a new colony. Today, we call the entire group "Pilgrims," even though this is not completely accurate, historically speaking.
- We know the *Mayflower's* crossing took 66 days and that one passenger—William Butten—died at sea, and another—Oceanus Hopkins—was born at sea.

**Facts About the Feast.** We know from historical writings that the Pilgrims held a feast to celebrate their good harvest. It was not a religious occasion, but more than likely they said a blessing.

Although we don't know the *exact* date of the feast that became known as the First Thanksgiving, we know it was held sometime between September 21 and November 9, 1621. The feast lasted for three days.

**The Food Served.** We know that only four adult married women survived the first winter in the New World. More than likely, they were in charge of preparing the food. We don't know for certain all of the foods the Pilgrims served at the feast, but we do know that many of the foods we serve at Thanksgiving were *not* on the Pilgrims' table because they were not available in the New World at that time. They did *not* serve: potatoes, sweet potatoes, cranberry sauce, celery, apples, pears, tea, or coffee.

We know by records left behind by two Pilgrims that codfish, sea bass, ducks, geese, turkeys, swans, corn meal, and venison were served.

**Who Was Present at the Feast?** There were 140 people at the feast. There were 90 Native American braves and 50 Pilgrims. About 50 of the 102 Pilgrims who arrived on the *Mayflower* died during the first winter.

*Source: Plimoth Plantation. Plimoth Plantation re-creates the life and surroundings of the Pilgrims' settlement. It is 3 miles from the first site in Plymouth, Massachusetts.

## ART ACTIVITIES

**Handful of Thanks.** Use bright-colored construction paper. Trace around your hand with a crayon. On each finger draw something for which you are thankful.

**Seed Necklace.** Wash the seeds from a honeydew melon or a canteloupe. Put the seeds into a bowl. Add food coloring. Let them sit for a while to soak up as much color as you like. Remove the seeds from the food coloring and allow them to dry overnight on a paper towel. These seeds can be strung on dental floss using a large, darning-size needle.

**Thanksgiving Mural.** Working with a small group of children, create a mural about all the things the children are thankful for at Thanksgiving time. Use a long sheet of butcher paper. Figures and objects can either be painted, crayoned, or cut from magazines and pasted on the paper. If the children are interested, you might record a statement underneath the specific objects the child wishes to "tell

**FIGURE 25–2 Native American paper bag masks.**

about." *Variation:* Draw a large turkey or cut one out of construction paper and place it in the middle of the paper. Each child glues his picture around the turkey.

**Native American Headdress.** Cut a two-inch strip of heavy paper or cardboard long enough to fit around the child's head. Staple the ends together. Add colorful cut-paper feathers or feathers painted or drawn in crayon. The headband may be decorated with Native American symbols. Feathers can be added to note accomplishments, as is the Native American custom. Bands may be decorated, but usually these are decorations only and not symbols.

**Thanksgiving Table.** Turn a cardboard box upside down. Draw and cut legs at the corners. Benches or chairs can be made by folding small strips of paper or cardboard. Make a tablecloth with white roll paper or paper napkins. Plates may consist of jar lids, with food of clay or salt clay. Figures of Pilgrims and Native Americans can be drawn on paper or cardboard and bent into a sitting position.

**Necktie Turkeys.** Old, colorful neckties provide wonderful feathers for turkeys. The children draw the turkey head and body on a large piece of construction paper. The ties can be attached with craft

**FIGURE 25–1 Construction paper Native American.**

glue (or stapled) to make the turkey's tail feathers. An attractive Thanksgiving bulletin board can be made by displaying all these necktie turkeys!

**Paper Bag Turkeys.** Pinch one corner of the bottom of a flat paper bag. Shape it into a head and tie. Stuff the bag half full with crumpled newspaper and tie, leaving the open end fringed and cut for tail feathers. Additional feathers can be attached to the body.

Staple cardboard feet at the base to allow the bird to sit upright. Accordion-pleat a strip of red paper for the wattle. The turkeys make an attractive table centerpiece and may be combined with crumpled paper fruits and vegetables.

**Fabric Turkeys.** Use old scraps of fabric to make a colorful turkey. Glue the pieces of fabric, cut up to make the turkey's body, onto a piece of construction paper. Children can color any other details around the turkey as they desire.

**Toothpick Turkey.** Use an orange, apple, or potato; toothpicks; raisins; marshmallow (for head); and jelly beans (cut for eyes and beak) to make a turkey. Use toothpicks to secure the head to the

**FIGURE 25–4 Fabric turkey.**

body, to secure the features to the face, and inserted below the body for legs. Children can make tail feathers by sticking raisins on toothpicks.

**Turkey Puppet.**

Materials: Paper sandwich bag; yellow, red, and orange construction paper, pencil, scissors, glue

Procedure: Fold a piece of yellow paper in half. With pencil, draw a circle for eyes, a triangle for beak and a foot. Cut them out. Glue on beak—one triangle on top of the flap edge, one under the flap. (Do not glue them together.) Glue on eyes and feet. Cut wiggly red shape and glue next to beak. Cut wings from brown paper and glue on sides. Cut out lots of feathers and glue on brown circle for tail. Glue on the feathers where they will show the most! (See Figure 25–5.)

**Thanksgiving Table Decor.** Have child trace turkey-shaped cookie cutter or his hand on colored construction paper. Child can color feather area if desired and then write name across body of turkey. Use on the table for place cards at Thanksgiving dinner.

**Pinecone Turkey.**

Materials: Pinecones, white craft glue, construction paper, colored felt-tip pens, scissors, plastic foam or clay, pipe cleaners

**FIGURE 25–3 Making a paper bag turkey for the Thanksgiving feast involves many fine motor skills.**

Fold piece of paper in half. Draw a circle for eyes, a triangle for beak, and a foot.

Glue on beak
—one triangle on top of flap
—one triangle under the flap
Cut out wiggly red shape and glue next to beak.

Cut wings from brown paper and glue on sides.
Cut lots of feathers and glue on brown circle for tail. Glue on feathers where they will show the best.

FIGURE 25–5 Turkey puppet.

Procedure: Lay the pinecone on its side. Insert a piece of pipe cleaner for the head and the neck. Make the tail out of construction paper and color with the felt-tip pens. Insert the tail between the petals of the pinecones. A little glue will help hold it in place. Insert short pieces of pipe cleaner on the bottom of the body for legs. Push the legs into plastic foam or a piece of clay to support the turkey. Adjust the size of the tail to the size of the pinecone.

**Large People.** Although drawing people can be done any time of the year, making Pilgrims is good to start with. Be sure children are familiar with Pilgrim dress. Talk about how people look. Start with a

FIGURE 25–6 A Thanksgiving cut and paste mural is a group project.

discussion of the head, which the children can see is not round; then talk about the neck and shoulders. The body gets smaller at the waist. When standing, the elbows come to the waistline and the hands do not reach the knees. The arms come from the shoulders.

Now the children can begin to make their people. The head and the neck are made first, then the clothing, bodies, arms, and legs. When finished, the figures are cut out and tacked to a bulletin board.

**Egg-Face Pilgrims.** Glue hard-boiled eggs into nut cups with rubber cement or paste. Children can decorate the eggs with yarn or curled paper as hair. Cut paper makes faces, and hats.

**Paper Bag Puppets.** Draw or glue paper on the bottom of a bag to make a face. Insert one hand in the bottom fold of the bag to make the face move. It's fun to glue a felt or paper tongue under the flap and a tail on the back of the bag.

**Pilgrim Mobile.** Let each child trace a Pilgrim pattern on a piece of construction paper. Decorate both sides with cut-paper features. Punch a hole in the top of the object and thread it. Hang it on a wire across the room.

**Handkerchief Puppets.** Draw a face on a handkerchief. Put it over your hand to make it move. Or

# THINK ABOUT IT. . .

## PILGRIM CLOTHES

We often think of the Pilgrims in dark-colored clothes, yet historic records show that they really wore many colors, including red, yellow, purple, and green. Black or gray was usually worn by important persons, such as the church pastor or officials.

Children and servants often dressed in blue. People who worked in the fields wore reddish-brown.

Men and women both wore long white shirts under their clothes. The men's were down to their knees, and were tucked into the outer clothing. Both boys and girls wore long white gowns until they were about 7 years old.

Contrary to popular belief, Pilgrims did not wear buckles on their hats and shoes. Buckles were not really worn at all at this time.

Use these facts in your discussions with young children about Thanksgiving. Be sure to provide the above-mentioned colors of tempera paint at the easel during the Thanksgiving season for children's painting.

(Source: Plimoth Plantation tour information)

---

draw a face in the center of a handkerchief, stuff cotton or cloth inside, and tie it with string or ribbon around the neck. (These also make great ghost puppets!)

**Thanksgiving Menu.**
Materials: Paper and pencils

Procedure: Have the children make up a menu for a feast using each letter of the word "Thanksgiving" to name a food; for example, T for turkey, H for ham, A for apple, and so on. Children can draw the pictures for each of the words, then cut them out and arrange them on the table before pasting them onto a large piece of colored construction paper.

**Paper Bag Tepees.**
Materials: Paper sacks, crayons, toothpicks, glue, tempera paint

Procedure:
1. Soak the sacks in water until the seams open. Then crumple up and squeeze out the excess water. Carefully smooth the sack out and let it dry.

2. After the sacks have dried, cut out semi-circle shapes and draw on designs with crayons. Be sure to press hard! Paint over the designs with a thin coat of brown tempera paint.

3. When the paint has dried, glue toothpicks in the center. Fold over the semi-circle to form a cone, and staple or glue the edges near the top. Fold over the bottom flap to give the appearance of a door.

**Play Dough Indian Beads.**
Materials: 2 cups flour, 1 cup salt, 1 cup water, 1 teaspoon cooking oil

Procedure: Mix ingredients together until smooth. Shape into small balls or ovals. The children love doing this at free-choice time in the art area. Push a toothpick or pencil through the beads to make holes. The teacher may help the children do this. Let these dry for several days. Turn them several times while they are drying. Paint them with tempera paint. String with yarn or twine.

**Styrofoam Cup Puppets.**  Draw a face on a cup, or glue on facial features using colored paper, felt, etc. Or make an animal, gluing ears to the top of a cup and a tail to the back, using a pipe cleaner or a strip of paper.

**Styrofoam Ball Puppets.** Make a face with felt-tip pens or by gluing eyes, nose, and a mouth made of paper to the ball. Insert a pencil in the bottom of the ball or make a hole to put a finger in.

## GAMES AND MOVEMENT EXPERIENCES

**Turkeys, Trot.** The children stand and face a child selected as the leader. The leader says, "Turkeys, trot," and runs in place. The class is to copy this motion. If the leader says, "Desks, run," "Rabbits, run," or "Turtles, run," the players stand still. Those who keep running must sit down. A new leader may be chosen by the old leader after a while.

**Hit the Turkey.** Form four lines of children behind a foul line. Put a wastebasket decorated with a picture of a turkey in front of each line, about 8 to 10 feet from the foul line. Each team has three balls or bean bags. The team that throws the most balls into the basket wins.

**Be a Turkey Relay.** Divide the class into equal teams. The first person on each team puts a book on his head (pretending to be a turkey) and walks to the front of the room and back to the second person in line who repeats the act. The first team to finish wins the relay.

**Motion.** Players sit or stand in a circle around the room. The one who is "it" closes both eyes as the teacher points to a leader, who stays in place and all players clap. The player who is "it" stands in the center so it is not possible to see everyone at once. The leader changes the motion from clapping to another motion, and the rest of the class follows. "It" has three guesses to find the leader. Change "it" and the leader for a new game. Hint: Players should not show they know who the leader is by staring. Indoor desk exercises can also be used as motions, and the game may be played from the desk.

**Gobble Goes the Turkey.** Sing the following song (to the tune "Pop Goes the Weasel") one time. Explain to the children that the next time you sing it, they are to jump when they hear the word "gobble."

Round and 'round the mulberry bush,
The turkey chased the Pilgrim.
The Pilgrim thought it was all a joke.
GOBBLE goes the turkey!

**Thankerchief.** Sit in a circle. Pass a handkerchief around the group while saying the poem below. The children pass it along till the end of the poem. When it stops, have that child tell the group what he is thankful for.

Thankerchief, thankerchief
Thankerchief, round you go
Where you stop nobody can know
But when you do someone must say
What she is thankful for this day.

## FINGERPLAYS AND POEMS

**I'm Glad I'm Me**
No one looks
The way I do,
I have noticed
That it's true;
No one walks
The way I walk.
No one talks
The way I talk.
No one plays
The way I play.
No one says
The things I say.
I am special.
I am me.
There's no one
I'd rather be.

**Thanksgiving**
The year has turned its circle.
The seasons come and go,
The harvest is all gathered in,
And chilly north winds blow.

Orchards have shared their treasure.
The fields, their yellow grain,

So open wide the doorway,
Thanksgiving comes again!
—Dee Lelegard

### Thanksgiving Feast

Thanksgiving table? This is it;
   (Hands side by side, palms down, resting on
   thumbs)
And a chair where each may sit.
   (Left hand up, right hand bent, fingers of right
   hand touching palm of left hand)

For each, a plate, a cup,
And spoon,
   (Make circle with thumbs and forefingers for
   "plate," cup the right hand for "cup," lay
   forefinger on table for "spoon")
We'll eat and eat till
Afternoon.
   (Eating gesture)

And everyone will chatter,
   ("Chattering" motion with first two fingers and
   thumb of each hand)
The turkey will rest on a platter,
   (Hands together, palms up, for "platter")

The gravy will be in a boat-shaped bowl,
   (Cup two hands together for "bowl")
And I will have a drumstick—whole!
   (Make "drumstick" with left fist and right index
   finger)

I'll drink milk from a pretty glass
   (Indicate shape of glass with two hands)

**FIGURE 25–7** Drawing about "My Family At Thanksgiving" captures the attention of many young children.

And only let the celery pass.
   (Show shape of celery with index fingers and
   thumbs touching)
And then I'll have a piece of pie,
   (Make pie wedge shape with index fingers and
   thumb)
I can eat it if I try!
   (Rub tummy with right hand)

### The Baby Brother

I am the sister of him
And he is my brother.
He is too little for us
To talk to each other.

So every morning I show him
My doll and my book,
But every morning he still is
Too little to look.

### Grandma's Glasses

These are Grandma's glasses
   (Bring index finger and thumb of both hands
   together and place against eyes as if wearing glasses)
This is Grandma's hat,
   (Bring fingertips together in a peak over head)
This is the way she folds her hands
   (Clasp hands over head)
And lays them in her lap.
   (Lay hands in lap)

### Houses

This is a nest for Mr. Bluebird
   (Cup both hands, palms up, little fingers together)
This is a hive for Mr. Bee,
   (Both fists together, palm to palm)
This is the hole for bunny rabbit,
   (Fingers clasped together to make a hole)
And this is a house for me.
   (Fingertips together to make a peak)

### Our House

Our house is like no house I know
On any street in any row;
For brick or shingle, tall or wide,
A house is yours when you're inside.

### This House So Good

This is the roof of the house so good,
   (Make peaked roof with both hands)
These are the walls that are made of wood.
   (Palms vertically parallel)
These are the windows that let in the light,
   (Join thumbs and index fingers—two windows)

This is the door that shuts so tight.
  (Palms together)
This is the chimney so straight and tall
  (Arm up straight)
Oh, what a good house for one and all!
  (Arms at angle for roof above head, one hand
  extending for chimney)

**The Turkey**
Our turkey is a great big bird (Circle arms in front of
  stomach)
Who wobbles when he walks. (Rock from side to side
  on feet)
His chin is always hanging down. (Drop hands down
  under chin)
He gobbles when he talks. (Make gobble sound)
His tail is like a spreading fan (Spread out hands with
  thumbs touching)
And on Thanksgiving Day
He sticks his tail high in the air
  (Push hands formed as fan up on head)
And swish, he flies away.
  (Open out arms and lower to side)

---

# COOKING EXPERIENCES

**Hardtack.**  Hardtack, often called "seabread," was taken on long voyages, because not having any yeast in it, it lasted for a long time without spoiling. The Pilgrims had hardtack on their long trip to their new land. Hardtack is delicious with any variety of spreads, including peanut butter!

Ingredients:
¼ teaspoon cream of tartar
⅛ teaspoon baking soda
3 tablespoons buttermilk
1 cup flour
4 teaspoons maple syrup
⅛ teaspoon salt
1½ tablespoons shortening

Procedure:
1. Mix baking soda, cream of tartar and buttermilk.
2. Stir together flour, syrup, and salt.
3. Cut shortening into flour mixture until it looks like coarse crumbs.
4. Stir in buttermilk/baking soda mixture.
5. Roll out very thin. Place on baking sheet. Score into rectangles and prick with fork.
6. Bake at 425°F until golden (5 to 10 minutes).

**FIGURE 25–8 One of the important concepts of Thanksgiving is sharing a meal together.**

**Initial Crackers (Serves 6–8).**  With the emphasis on family at Thanksgiving time, making crackers for each person using their initials is a good seasonal activity. Begin with a discussion of initials: What are your initials? Your Mom's? Dad's?

Ingredients:
½ cup flour
⅛ teaspoon garlic salt
2 tablespoons sesame seeds
3 tablespoons cold butter
2 tablespoons ice water

Procedure:
1. Mix flour with garlic salt and sesame seeds.
2. Cut in butter until crumbly.
3. Sprinkle ice water over mixture and gather it into a ball.
4. Roll pieces of dough into "snakes" and shape them into initials on ungreased cookie sheet. Flatten them a bit.
5. Bake at 350°F for 15 minutes.

**Turkey Crackers.**  Make cracker dough as shown. Roll out the dough on a floured surface and cut with a turkey cookie cutter. Poke holes with a fork to make features—feathers, feet, eye. Bake and serve plain or let the children spread the crackers with peanut butter.

**Chappatis Fry Bread.**
Ingredients:
1 cup whole-wheat flour
1 cup white flour
½ teaspoon salt
2 teaspoons baking powder
2 tablespoons oil
½ cup cold water

Procedure:
1. Mix together dry ingredients.
2. Stir in oil and add ¾ of the water and stir. Add remaining water if needed to make a soft dough.
3. Knead 5 minutes. Let stand ½ hour.
4. Break into 12 small balls.
5. Let the children roll them out with a rolling pin. Flat circles should be approximately four to five inches wide.
6. Fry in hot fat (medium setting) for 15 to 20 seconds, each side. If fat is the right temperature, the bread should puff up while frying.
7. Drain on paper towels, then cut open and fill with fruit puree or other spread.

**Thanksgiving Cornbread.** Native Americans gave the Pilgrims their first corn. Making cornbread is a traditional activity in many early childhood programs. This would be great to eat at a Thanksgiving feast!

Ingredients:
½ cup cornmeal
½ cup flour
1 tablespoon maple syrup
1 teaspoon baking powder
½ teaspoon salt
2 tablespoons shortening
1 small egg
½ cup milk

Procedure:
1. Mix cornmeal, flour, syrup, baking powder, and salt until well combined.
2. Add shortening, egg, and milk.
3. Pour into buttered loaf pan.
4. Bake at 400°F for 25 minutes.

**Cranberry Delight Drink.**
Ingredients: One 5½-ounce can cranberry juice, ½ cup vanilla ice milk, 1 cup plain low-fat yogurt

Procedure: Mix all ingredients in a blender at high speed for 30 seconds. Serves 3.

**Turkey Fruit Cup.**
Ingredients:
½ orange
¼ apple
¼ banana
celery leaves
lettuce leaf
carrot round

Procedure:
1. Cut an orange in half, scoop out the center. (It helps to cut first along the inside of the rind.)
2. Dice the orange center and place it in a small bowl.
3. Dice and combine the other fruits. You can also add some chopped nuts or a crunchy-type cereal if you wish.
4. Fill the orange cup with the diced fruit.
5. Add a toothpick for a neck, a carrot round for a head, and half a toothpick for a beak. Stick celery leaves in the back of the cup for feathers.
6. Set on a lettuce leaf on a plate to complete the fruit cup turkey.

**Pilgrim Bread Pudding.**
Ingredients:
4 slices whole-wheat bread
¾ cup milk
⅓ cup apple juice concentrate
2 eggs
1 teaspoon cinnamon
½ teaspoon ginger
¼ cup molasses
dash of salt

Procedure:
1. Dice up four slices of bread. (Stale bread works especially well for bread pudding.)
2. Place a few pieces in a blender at a time and crumble. Place the bread crumbs in a bowl.
3. Next, blend together ½ cup milk, apple juice con-

centrate, eggs, cinnamon, ginger, molasses, and salt.

4. Pour the liquid mixture over the crumbs and mix together.
5. Pour into a greased baking dish.
6. Bake at 350°F for 30 minutes.
7. Pour ¼ cup milk over the top and bake for 25 more minutes. Makes 6–8 small servings.

**Pudding Cookies.**  This recipe is so easy that, once familiar with it, children can make these cookies all by themselves.

Ingredients:
1 cup Bisquick®
1 small package instant pudding—any flavor that appeals to the cooks!
¼ cup salad oil
1 egg
chocolate chips, raisins, shredded coconut, or ⅓ cup peanut butter (all optional, use if desired)

Procedure:
1. Mix ingredients together.
2. Roll the dough into balls and put them on an ungreased cookie sheet.
3. Dip the bottom of a glass in sugar and press it on each ball until flattened. If making plain dough, cookies may be decorated with red cinnamon candies or chocolate chips before baking.
4. Bake at 350°F for 8 minutes. Makes 2 to 3 dozen cookies.

**Good Potatoes.**

Ingredients: Baking potatoes, butter, sour cream, parsley or chives

Equipment: Baking dish, fork, knife for cutting potatoes

Procedure:
1. Heat oven to 425°F.
2. Wash potatoes and let them dry.
3. Grease potatoes with butter.
4. Bake potatoes in baking dish for 40 minutes to 1 hour.
5. When they are half-cooked, prick each one with a fork to let out the steam. Then, finish baking.

6. When the potatoes are done, help the children cut a cross in each potato and push the potato open.
7. Into the opening in each potato, put some sour cream or butter with salt and pepper.
8. Sprinkle with parsley or chives.

**Sweet Potato Pudding.**
Ingredients:
¼ cup apple juice concentrate
2 cups cooked sweet potatoes
⅓ cup orange juice
1 banana, sliced
1 teaspoon cinnamon
2 eggs

Procedure:
1. Blend ingredients together in a blender and pour into a greased baking dish.
2. Bake for 40 minutes at 350°F. Serve warm or cold. You may want to top with a bit of milk if desired.

**Sweet Potato Pie.**  Bake the pudding recipe given above in an 8- or 9-inch unbaked pie shell. Bake at 350°F for approximately 40 minutes.

**Candied Sweet Potatoes.**

Ingredients:
6 sweet potatoes
salt
paprika
⅓ cup maple syrup
1½ teaspoons lemon juice
½ teaspoon grated lemon rind
2 tablespoons butter

Equipment: Grater, measuring cup, measuring spoons, mixing spoon, small mixing bowl, large saucepan, baking dish, fork, knife for cutting sweet potatoes in half

Procedure:
1. Grate the lemon rind.
2. Boil the sweet potatoes in covered saucepan. Use enough water to cover the sweet potatoes.

## THIS ONE'S FOR YOU!

Be THANKFUL for these food tips:

- When making breads for snacks during Thanksgiving season, double the recipe and bake half of the batter in a loaf pan and the other half in small metal juice cans. The large loaf can be eaten at snack time, and the miniature loaves can be taken home by the children as gifts, or for their own contribution to the family's Thanksgiving Dinner.
- When making molded gelatin shapes for special occasions, add a teaspoon of white vinegar to the gelatin and water mixture. The shapes will hold up better when you take them out of the molds.
- Frozen snacks on sticks are a real favorite, but they're messy to eat because they melt so quickly. To catch drips, poke the sticks through the centers of small paper plates.
- Use ice cream cones for fun—and edible—snack containers.
- For Thanksgiving (and other holidays), use cookie cutters to cut sandwich bread into Thanksgiving shapes.
- Children really enjoy frosting their own cookies or muffins. To make the job easier and more fun, put the frosting into empty mustard or catsup squeeze bottles for them to use.

3. When the potatoes are a little soft, prick them with a fork, and pour off the water.
4. Heat the oven to 375°F.
5. Let the sweet potatoes cool.
6. Take off the skins.
7. Help the children cut each sweet potato in half.
8. Put potatoes in a baking dish and sprinkle with salt and paprika.
9. Mix the maple syrup, lemon juice, and lemon rind in a small mixing bowl.
10. Pour the mixture over the sweet potatoes.
11. Dot with small pieces of butter.
12. Bake uncovered for 20 minutes.

**Orange Nut Bread.**

Ingredients:
2½ cups sifted flour
⅔ cup sugar
1 teaspoon salt
2½ teaspoons baking powder
½ cup chopped walnuts
1 egg

1 cup milk
1 tablespoon grated orange peel
¼ cup orange juice
2 tablespoons cooking oil

Equipment: Flour sifter, grater, measuring cup, measuring spoons, large mixing bowl, small mixing bowl, egg beater, loaf pan

Procedure:
1. Help the children sift the flour.
2. Grate the orange peel.
3. Butter the loaf pan.
4. Mix together the flour, sugar, salt, and baking powder in the big mixing bowl.
5. Stir in the chopped nuts.
6. Beat the egg in the small mixing bowl.
7. Add the milk, orange peel, orange juice, and oil to the egg.
8. Add the egg mixture to the flour mixture. Do not stir too much, just until everything is wet.
9. Pour into loaf pan.
10. Bake in oven for one hour and 15 minutes at 350°F.

**Banana Bread.**

Ingredients:

½ cup raisins
¼ cup apple juice concentrate
1 egg
¼ cup vegetable oil
1 ripe banana, sliced
1 teaspoon vanilla
1 cup whole-wheat flour
½ teaspoon baking powder
½ teaspoon baking soda
¼ teaspoon salt
2 teaspoons cinnamon
½ cup chopped nuts (optional)

Procedure:

1. Heat raisins and apple juice concentrate for 3 minutes over high heat, then place in a blender and puree.
2. Leave the raisin puree in the blender and add egg, oil, banana, and vanilla.
3. Mix dry ingredients together in a bowl and add liquid mixture from blender.
4. Stir together.
5. Add nuts if you wish, then pour into a greased loaf pan or muffin tins.
6. Bake at 350°F, 40–50 minutes for bread and 25–30 minutes for muffins.

**Cranberry Bread.**

Ingredients:

1 cup sugar
½ teaspoon salt
1½ teaspoons baking powder
2 cups flour
½ cup orange juice
½ teaspoon baking soda in 2 tablespoons hot water
2 tablespoons melted butter
1 egg
1 cup cranberries
1 cup chopped pecans

Equipment: Measuring cup, measuring spoons, large mixing bowl, small mixing bowl, mixing spoon, egg beater, small pan for melting butter, loaf pan

Procedure:

1. Grease the loaf pan.
2. Melt the butter in a small pan.
3. Heat the oven to 325°F.
4. Dissolve the baking soda in the hot water.
5. Beat the egg in the small mixing bowl.
6. In the large mixing bowl, mix the ingredients in the order they are listed—all except the cranberries and nuts.
7. Mix well.
8. Add the cranberries and nuts, and mix again.
9. Pour mixture into loaf pan.
10. Bake in oven for one hour and 15 minutes.

**Vegetable Stone Soup.**   Start this cooking experience with a trip to the grocery store. Let the children choose one each of the many different kinds of vegetables—one carrot, one celery, one turnip, one potato, one onion, one zucchini, one tomato, etc. When you return, let them help you wash and chop the vegetables.

Next, read the story *Stone Soup* to your children. When you have finished, find a smooth round rock, scrub it clean, and boil it for 5 minutes.

Fill a pot with 2 quarts water, drop in the stone, and the rest of the vegetables. Bring water to a boil and then cook at a low boil for at least 1 hour. Watch the water and add more if it boils down. Add stock or bouillon to the water and season to taste. When the soup is almost ready, small pieces of cooked meat or fowl can be added.

# ADDITIONAL READINGS

## Children's Books for Thanksgiving

Child, L.M. *Over the River and Through the Woods.* New York: Coward, McCann & Geoghegan, Inc., 1974.

Dalgliesch, A. *The Thanksgiving Story.* New York: Charles Scribner's Sons, 1954.

Estes, Eleanor. *Ginger Pye.* New York: Harcourt, Brace and World, 1951.

Janice, J. *Little Bear's Thanksgiving.* New York: Lothrop, Lee and Shepard Co., 1967.

Rogers, Lou. *The First Thanksgiving.* New York: Follett Publishing, 1963.

Spinelli, E. *Thanksgiving at the Tappleton's.* Reading, Mass.: Addison-Wesley, 1982.

# UNIT 26
# December Holidays

December is a month of holidays, a time for lighting candles, feasting, giving and receiving gifts, and caroling. Whether children look hopefully for Santa Claus, Father Christmas, Pere Noel, or Saint Nicholas, people of many countries anticipate the season in much the same spirit. Various customs have developed throughout the world, such as the celebration of Christmas in Mexico beginning on December 16. Children participate in fiestas and play "breaking the piñata" for candies and good luck charms. In Norway, even the birds have their own Christmas trees. On Christmas morning, children tie sheaves of wheat or other grain to poles or spruce trees for the winter birds to eat. In England, under lofty arches of great cathedrals, children join processions at Christmas Eve services to sing carols and hymns.

Children in Germany begin looking forward to Christmas around the end of November. They use Advent calendars to count the number of days until Christmas. On the night of December 5, the children wait for a visit from Saint Nicholas, a tall bearded man who wears a bishop's robes and hat. Saint Nicholas makes his rounds riding on a white horse and carrying a bag filled with cookies, fruits, and nuts. Sometimes the children fill their shoes with hay and leave them out with a bowl of water for Saint Nicholas's horse. In the morning they find small toys and other treats inside their shoes.

Christmas customs also vary in different parts of the United States. In Williamsburg, Virginia, the old English tradition of bringing in the Yule log and lighting it is carried on as it was in the time of George Washington. Fireworks fill the skies the night before Christmas over states farther south. In New England towns, caroling is done in neighborhoods on Christmas Eve. Homes throughout the nation are decorated with greens.

While Christian children light their Christmas candles, Jewish children gather with their families around the Hanukkah candles and attend services in the synagogue (temple). Hanukkah, often called the Festival of Lights, symbolizes religious liberty. It lasts eight days and is celebrated each night by placing a lighted candle in the Hanukkah lamp (called the menorah), until all eight are burning on the last day. After the lighting of the menorah, the children usually receive presents, one on each night of the Hanukkah celebration. Evenings are festive with story telling, gift giving, and feasting. Children play a game with a top called a dreidel, which has four Hebrew letters on it, "nun," "gimel," "hay," "shin." They stand for the Hebrew words "Ness Gadol Haya Sham," which mean, "A great miracle happened there." This refers to the restoration of the Holy Temple in Jerusalem by the Macabees when one day's supply of oil for the holy lamps miraculously lasted a whole week. As it spins around, the children sing a song about the dreidel. Clubs and groups celebrate with plays, concerts, and parties.

**FIGURE 26–1 December holidays involve many different symbols.**

# THIS ONE'S FOR YOU!

## SOME CHRISTMAS "TRIVIA"

Did you know that. . . .

. . . the first Nativity scene had real people and animals in it? The first nativity scene was assembled in Graccio, Italy, sponsored by St. Francis of Assisi. After that, people began setting up miniature scenes in their homes, vying to see who could make their crèche the most unique. Moravian families around Bethelehem, Pennsylvania, have room-sized scenes called *putzes.* At Christmastime, they go visiting from house to house to see the *putzes.*

. . . the tradition of hanging stockings from the mantel started long ago from a legend about St. Nicholas? The story is that St. Nicholas dropped bags of gold down the chimney for three girls who had no dowry. The bags landed in their stockings that were hanging on the mantel to dry.

. . . the Germans first carried an evergreen tree indoors and decorated it with apples, toys, candies, and goodies? They named it the *Tannenbaum.* The practice of decorating the tree with "edibles" was very popular with the Victorians. Eggshell halves were a favorite ornament for holding greens, glitter, and little goodies. Victorians also gathered around the fireplace to string popcorn and cranberries. If the tree came in stiff as a board from spending a month out in the carriage house, they would hang big fat apples all around to bring the boughs down. Candy cherries on wires, fruits, nuts, popcorn balls, and candy canes were all found on Victorian trees.

. . . Ireland has one of the most charming of Christmas customs—they place a lighted candle in the window as a guide to welcome wanderers? They take them in, feed them, give a night's lodging, and send them away in the morning with a bit of money jingling in their pockets. Christmas Eve is *"Oidhche na ceapairi,"* Gaelic for "Nights of Cakes," since everyone has a special cake of his own. On December 26, St. Stephen's Day, another Irish custom is "Feeding the Wren." The children place a wren in a cage on a furze bush and go about from house to house collecting coins for charity.

. . . in Spain on Christmas Eve the streets are alive with singing and dancing to the tune of tambourines, Spanish guitars, and castanets? An old Spanish custom is "The Urn of Fate." Names of friends are placed in a bowl and then are drawn to decide who shall be devoted friends until the following season.

. . . weeks before Christmas, the Norwegian housewife cooks the *lutefisk, lepse,* cheese, sausages, and even food for the birds? For the birds, a sheaf of wheat and suet is mounted on a long pole (where the cats can't get at it). They even prepare a dinner for Julanissen, an invisible, mischievous, gnomelike elf who causes all the minor mishaps like spilled milk, broken pottery, etc. On Christmas, the children dress up in outlandish costumes and go about from house to house asking for goodies, in a way that is very similar to our Halloween trick-or-treat.

# T H I N K   A B O U T   I T . . .

## THE SYMBOLS OF CHRISTMAS AND THEIR SIGNIFICANCE

During the Christmas holidays, we are surrounded with decorations that we simply take for granted. Some of the most common holiday decorations have an historical significance that you might find interesting.

**Poinsettia.**  In 1828, Dr. Joel Roberts Poinsett brought the first poinsettia to this country from Mexico. He was serving as our first ambassador to that country. The legend is that a Mexican boy had no gift for the Christ child. As he knelt to pray, a beautiful flower appeared at his feet. This flowering plant, the pointsettia, became his present to the Child.

**Evergreens.**  Since ancient times, evergreens have been used for winter decorations, symbolic as they are of life when all other plants appear dead. The Romans, for example, used evergreens in honor of Saturn, god of plant life and agriculture. Mistletoe, holly, and ivy were held in special regard because they bore berries in the winter.

**Holly.**  The holly tree is known in Norway and Sweden as the "Christ-thorn" and in Denmark as the "Kristdorn." Some say the English word "holly" may well be derived from "holy," and that the prickly leaves remind us of the Crown of Thorns, and the red berries of drops of blood when the Crown was worn by Jesus.

**Mistletoe.**  We usually hang mistletoe up at Christmas and kiss under it, but mistletoe once hung in the house throughout the year and was a sign that guests greeted under it were safe in that house. It was endowed with the power to ensure peace and friendship. This may be traced to an old Norse legend. Baldur, son of Odin, was the god of light and peace, and as such the other gods deemed that nothing should harm him. Water was not to drown him, by their order. Arrows, swords, and poisons were not to touch him. But they forgot about the mistletoe, and the evil Loki sharpened a mistletoe branch, placed it in the hand of the blind Hodur and guided his hand such that it struck, pierced, and killed Baldur. The other gods brought Baldur back to life, making the misteltoe promise never to harm anyone again, but to stand as protector instead (Carey and Large, 1982).

**Cards.**  The custom of sending printed cards started in England in the 1840s. The artist, John Horsely, created the first Christmas card design and about 1,000 cards were printed. Today, more cards are sent at Christmas than at any other time of the year.

**Wassail.**  Years ago, many English people held Christmas feasts. As they drank a hot punch, they would say "Wassail," which means, "To your health." Today, many people serve a hot punch called wassail.

**Santa Claus.**   The picture we have of Santa Claus as a round, rosy-cheeked, white-bearded man was first drawn by Thomas Nast in 1872. He drew a series of cartoons that gave us this image of a uniquely "American" Santa. Santa Claus is only one example of the many gift bringers who deliver presents around the world. For example, in Italy gifts are delivered by an old fairy called Befana.

**Trees.**   There are many stories about how the first Christmas tree was trimmed. One is that the famous German preacher, Martin Luther, started this custom. As he was walking home one starry Christmas Eve, he cut down a tree, took it home, and trimmed it with candles. Much later, Germans brought the custom to this country.

**Yule Log.**   People of long ago believed that burning a big log drove away evil spirits. Through the years, a custom grew to cut down a big tree several weeks before Christmas. There was a belief that anyone who helped would have good luck. Today, some people burn a special big log, called a "yule log," at Christmas.

The primary values of these holidays lie in doing thoughtful and loving things for others, participating in various craft activities, and sharing in family customs and festivities. This is a particularly good time for children to learn about and share the customs of other families. Remember that not everyone celebrates Christmas; be sensitive to the needs of children who do not, and discuss this with their parents, asking for their suggestions and point of view.

Try to avoid starting these holiday activities too soon and doing too much with the children. Young children also will not benefit from long recitals of what they want Santa to bring. Remember, time is not the same for young children as it is for adults. A week seems more like a month or two to young children!

Some general ideas for gifts that encourage individual self-expression:

- Red and green fingerpaintings, suitably framed
- Lumps of clay or play dough with dried grasses, seed pods, and so forth stuck in them, dried, dipped in white paint, and sprinkled with glitter. This makes a handsome though somewhat fragile holiday decoration

- A Christmas or Hanukkah card made from a small fingerpainting, with the child's offer of things to do to help his family during the holiday season printed inside
- Some kind of bread or store-bought, wholesome cookies decorated by the children
- Various kinds of tree ornaments such as strings of colored, dyed macaroni or bits of Styrofoam, each string marked with the child's name and age. These are often treasured by families long after the child has grown up. Again, if sprayed with acrylic spray in a well-ventilated area and rolled in glitter, they will look especially festive.
- Holiday wrapping paper can be made by stamping plain paper in red and green, using holiday cookie cutters or handprints, or children can stick inexpensive Christmas stickers all over the paper. (Specific activity suggestions follow.)

Afterward, reminisce with the children about the joys of this holiday, encouraging children to discuss a variety of happy events rather than just what they received for gifts. If weather permits, plant a living Christmas tree outdoors.

**FIGURE 26–2 [top & bottom] Star-shaped Santas—Decorated with cotton balls and construction paper details.**

## PICTURE MAKING FOR DECEMBER HOLIDAYS

In picture making, children will have many ideas to paint about their own holiday experiences when they are inspired. Some ideas are:

- Lighting the Menorah
- Six-point Star of David
- Elephants Used by Syrian Armies Who Fought the Jewish Soldiers
- Playing with a Dreidel (or Top)
- Characters from Ancient Scriptures: Jewish Soldiers, Syrian Soldiers, Jewish Leader (Judas Maccabaeus)
- A Beautiful Christmas Tree
- Christmas Angel
- Decorating Our House at Holiday Time
- A Trip to See Santa
- Lighting the Hanukkah Candles
- The Holiday Feast
- Playing Hanukkah Games

As in all holiday activities, young children are often too young to grasp the entire religious significance of the event. The abstract concepts involved in far distant historical events are beyond the cognitive level of preschool children. However, their involvement in holiday festivities can still be meaningful, if it is kept at their level. This would mean using the symbols or representations of the holiday, such as the menorah, Christmas tree, and Santa Claus, in art activities, games, and songs. In all of these activities (including those in this unit), the emphasis should be on the process, not the product. It is also important to choose activities that use small and large muscles, as well as those that encourage hand–eye coordination. These skills are the focus of the following suggested activities.

## ART ACTIVITIES

**Holiday Greeting Cards.** Techniques for making greeting cards may include cutting and folding, stenciling, or printing. Holiday designs are as varied as the number of children in the class.

Children should be encouraged to explore the scrap box for sparkling materials such as metallic foil, gum wrappers, wrapping paper, old greeting cards, and bits of discarded ribbon.

**Holiday Frames.** Recycle empty facial tissue boxes by cutting off the tops to use as picture frames.

Glue paper to the back of the boxtop, turn over, and have the children draw or paint inside the frames. *Variation:* Have the children decorate around the opening on the boxtop for a decorative matting. Glue a photo of the child onto a piece of paper, and glue this paper onto the decorated boxtop.

**Popsicle Stick Frame.** Color, paint, and decorate wooden popsicle sticks using felt-tip pens, crayons, tempera paint, or even white glue with glitter. When they are completely dry, glue the sticks together in square shapes for picture frames. (*Note:* If you like to use glitter in holiday projects, try using plastic bottles with perforated lids, such as those in which food seasonings or cookie sprinkles come, for applying glitter to projects. When young children use these glitter-filled bottles for projects, their hands stay cleaner and less glitter is wasted.)

**Glittery Baubles.** Children make decorative holiday objects for use as tree ornaments, mobiles, bulletin board displays, and party favors. A variety of found objects can be used, such as nonflammable pie tins, detergent bottles, plastic squeeze bottles, metal jar lids and bottle tops, and discarded pieces of Styrofoam.

Procedure:
1. Tins and plastic bottles may be used in their original shape or cut and bent into desired forms.
2. If objects need a covering, use construction paper, wallpaper, metallic foil, or newspaper.
3. Sparkling trimmings include beads, buttons, glitter, sequins, and discarded holiday decorations. Baubles can be hung with ornament hooks or thin wire.

**Toy Shop Window.** A bright holiday bulletin board brings the color and spirit of the season into the classroom.

Procedure:
1. Arrange strips of construction paper over background paper on the bulletin board to indicate windowpanes.
2. For a three-dimensional effect, pull the paper strips out to the head of the pins. Colorful toys

**FIGURE 26–3 Making holiday cut construction paper ornaments involves children in holiday preparations in a real-life way.**

made from children's drawings, paintings, or cut paper can be placed in the windows.
3. A brightly painted paper awning may protrude from the storefront by fastening it in several places to strips of cardboard pinned at right angles to the background.

**Christmas Characters.** Figures such as Santa and his elves, dolls, and toys decorate tables for holiday parties.

**FIGURE 26–4 Paper stockings hung by a paper "fireplace."**

Procedure:

1. Use cardboard boxes of various sizes to form the foundation.
2. Decorate boxes with scraps of construction paper or felt for clothing.
3. Add bits of cloth, braid, feathers, yarn, string, or ribbon for color and texture.
4. Elflike features can be created with buttons, beads, or sequins.

**Holiday Door Decorations.** Bend a thin wire coat hanger to form a desired shape, such as a Christmas tree, Santa Claus, fanciful angel, toy head, or wreath. After covering the coat hanger with construction paper, complete the design with a variety of paper scraps, ribbon, yarn, metallic foil, felt.

**Paper Plate Wreath.** A simple wreath can be made from a paper plate and colored construction paper. Cut out the center of the paper plate, or have the children do the cutting if their small motor skills allow it. Next, have the children cut or tear pieces of green construction paper for the greenery of the wreath and paste them all around the plate. Pieces of red construction paper cut or torn into circles are glued around the wreath for holly. If desired, glitter can be glued on for an added touch of glamour.

**Paper Chains.** Give young children who are just beginning to make paper chains strips from the colorful pages of glossy magazines. The slick paper is easier to paste than construction paper, and it is even more colorful than solid color construction paper. It encourages recycling, too.

**Hand Print Christmas Wreath (Five years and up).** With green construction paper and a pencil, the child traces her hand print six or seven times. These are then cut out and arranged in a circle on a paper plate (with the center cut out) to make a hand print wreath.

**Free-Hanging Snowmen.** Materials: Heavy paper, scissors, colored paper, coloring materials, string, glue. Cut three circles of varying sizes for the head and large parts of the body. (Jar lids of various

**FIGURE 26–5 Paper plate Christmas wreath.**

**FIGURE 26–6 Paper chains tree decorations.**

**FIGURE 26–7 Hand print Christmas wreath.**

sizes can be used to trace the circles.) Hands, facial features, hat, pipe, scarf, and buttons can be cut from colored paper and glued on. If colored paper is not available, draw these parts on white paper and color them.

Punch holes in the top of each snowman and pull a string through. A hat can also be hung with string so that the snowman will be mobile. A free-hanging Santa Claus can be made in the same way.

**Simple Gift Wrapping Paper (Ages two to five).** Holiday gift wrap created by the children is a gift in itself. Stamping shapes onto paper using various objects dipped into tempera paint (See Unit 12 for more print-making information) creates attractive gift paper. Or, have the children press their handprints in tempera paint over a sheet of paper to make yet another attractive and unique gift wrap paper.

You may also want to invest in an assortment of rubber stamps in animal, flower, or toy shapes. Children can use them year after year for making gift-wrap. Rubber stamps don't have to be fancy to be fun to use. Ask businesses to donate old or outdated office stamps they may have on hand; mixed in with other stamp shapes, they make an interesting design.

**Gift Wrappings (Five years and up).** Materials: Kraft paper or newspaper, scissors, coloring materials.

*Stencil method.* Create a stencil by first cutting a holiday symbol out of heavier paper. Place the cutout design on the kraft paper and color or trace around the edges. Repeat this all over the paper.

The cut-out form can also be used as a stencil by tracing it on the kraft paper and filling in the empty space.

*Doodle method.* Tell the children to place their pencils in the middle of the butcher paper and then to look away from the paper. Ask them to move their pencils around on the paper in full swings. After a short time have them examine the designs they have made and look for areas to fill in with colors or textures. This will create an interesting wrapping paper.

*Rubbing method.* Rubbing crayons over objects with rough, uneven surfaces gives a textured feeling to the wrapping paper.

*Printing method.* Halve or quarter fruits or vegetables. Dip pieces into thickened tempera. Press onto white kraft paper. Repeat until an overall design is created.

*Dyeing method.* Fold a piece of white kraft paper into a small rectangle. Dip corners into food coloring or watercolor paint. Allow colors to bleed and mix. Open paper carefully and allow to dry.

**Miniature Trees.** A number of techniques for making miniature Christmas trees are suitable for young children.

*Cone-shaped tree.* This consists of a rolled piece of construction paper stapled firmly in place. Several cones, graduated in size, can be stacked one on top of another and fringed along the edges.

*Three-sided tree.* First fold three pieces of construction paper in half, then paste them back-to-back. Cut in the desired shape, leaving enough space at the base for standing.

*Flat cardboard tree.* To make this a free-standing tree, sink the base in a lump of clay or piece of discarded Styrofoam.

**FIGURE 26–8 Cone-shaped Christmas trees from green construction paper.**

*Tree branch.* A tree branch can be anchored in a small flowerpot, box, or milk carton filled with clay or Styrofoam.

*Decorations.* A variety of odds and ends left over from previous holidays can be used for decorations, but unusual materials make the most interesting trees. Children can collect found objects such as feathers, yarn, sequins, metallic foil, felt, and shells. They may want to make a candy tree using gumdrops or marshmallows.

**Christmas Gift Wishes.** Give children box-shaped paper. The children then draw what they hope to receive for Christmas. An attractive bulletin board can be made by displaying all the Christmas gift boxes.

**Holiday Placemats.** Decorate paper placemats with paint, crayons, or markers. Cover with clear contact paper and trim edges with pinking shears.

**Light Switch Cover.** Choose a cookie cutter with a holiday theme: snowman, star, reindeer, Christmas tree, etc. Trace on lightweight cardboard. In the middle of shape, cut out rectangle for light switch. Using felt, rickrack, paste, markers, paint or crayons, decorate cover (do not cover up cut-out hole for switch!). Use double-stick tape or make a loop with regular tape to put on the back of your cover, and slide onto light switch.

**Snowflake Shakers.**
Materials: Small jars with wide lids (one per child), plastic stand-up Christmas decorations such as Christmas trees, Santas, reindeer, elves, etc., super glue (teacher will need to do the gluing), soap flakes, water.

Preparation: Have child decide which decorations they want in their shakers. The teacher glues the base of the decorations securely to the inside of the jar lid. The child almost fills the jar with water and then adds about a teaspoon of the soap flakes. The teacher puts plenty of glue on the inside rim of the lid and then screws it on. Wait for the glue to dry before turning the jar over. When the jar is shaken and set down, it looks like it's snowing on the Christmas decorations.

**Snow Scene (Five years and up).**
Materials: Baby food jar, paint, glue, small piece of artificial pine tree, molding clay, moth crystals.

Preparation: An easy art idea for the winter season is to make a snow scene in a baby food jar. First, paint the lid of the baby food jar with gold enamel. Allow it to dry overnight. Glue a small piece of artificial pine on the inside of the lid so that when the lid lies upside down the pine stands up like a tree. (Molding clay can also be used to adhere tree to lid.) Put 1 teaspoon of moth crystals in the jar. *(Be sure to provide adult supervision at all times.)* Fill jar with water. Put

SNOW SCENE

**FIGURE 26–9 Snow scene.**

lid on jar. As the jar is turned over and back onto its lid again, snow falls into the pine tree.

## More Decorations.

*Spirals.*  The spiral is made by cutting a circle of paper round and round from the edges toward the center. Variations of the spiral are squares or triangles cut in the same way. Spirals may be hung from ceilings or on trees; two of them may also be glued together at the widest ends and an ornament hung through the center.

*Bird cage.*  Foil paper or poster paper should be used for this decoration since they are easier to cut when folded. The paper is first cut in squares about 6″ × 6″ or larger. A square is folded three times to form a triangular shape. Cuts are made from one

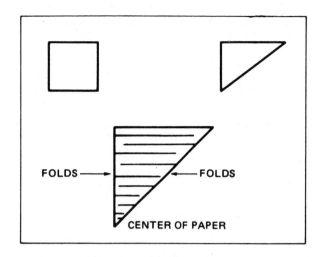

**FIGURE 26–11  Bird cage ornament.**

fold almost all the way over to the opposite fold, alternating from one side to the other, down to the tip of the triangle. Open carefully and pull the center upward to form a cage. Hang the decoration by the center from the ceiling or a tree branch.

*Balls.*  Cut five circles all the same size from construction paper or foil paper. Fold them in half both ways. Cut another small circle, about half the size of the others. Cut a slit across the center of the five circles and slide them on the smaller circle, making a ball. Glue the sides of the circles together, string them, and hang them on a tree or from the ceiling. Interesting variations of this decoration can be made

**FIGURE 26–10  Spiral decorations.**

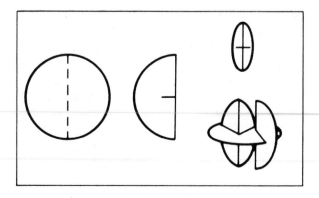

**FIGURE 26–12  Balls.**

by using square shapes, diamond shapes, and so on, instead of circles.

*Pinwheel.* The pinwheel is made from a square piece of paper. Crease the paper from corner to corner. Cut the creases almost to the center. Then glue all left or right corners to the center of the paper. A pinwheel can be hung from one of its points, or a series of them strung through the center and graduated in size. Glitter, cotton, yarn, sequins, and other decorations make the pinwheels attractive.

*Star fan.* Make two fans out of two long pieces of paper, the length at least three times the width of the paper. Cut notches along the folded sides to make a pattern. Cut one end to a point to make pointed edges. Unfold and glue the sides of the two fans together to make a circle. The centers may be sewn together to keep the folds tight. The star fan is then strung and hung from the ceiling or a branch of a tree.

*Dough.* Use up modeling dough as it begins to dry out. Form it into balls and have the children stick small pebbles, beads, buttons, or sequins into the surface of the balls. Make a hole with a toothpick for hanging. Hang them as mobiles or holiday decorations.

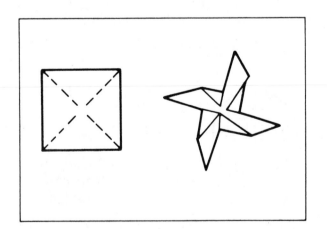

**FIGURE 26–13 Pinwheel.**

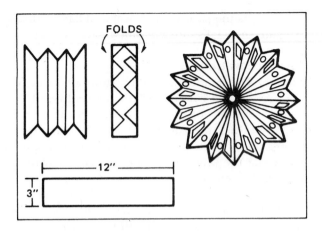

**FIGURE 26–14 Star fan.**

*Snowflakes.* Snowflakes are easy to make and may be used as mobiles, window decorations, or bulletin board decorations.

Procedure:
1. Cut foil paper, tracing paper, poster paper, or any decorative wrapping paper into squares of many sizes.
2. Fold the squares in half, then in half again, making a smaller square, then fold to make a triangle. Keep in mind where the center of the paper is.
3. Cut a "V" shape into the open edges, to get the points of the snowflakes.
4. Cut notches of different sizes along the two folded edges. The more pieces cut out, the fancier the snowflakes will be.

*Santa on a stick.* Rows of Santas in the window box or stuck in mounds of clay are creative room decorations.

Procedure:
1. Double heads and bodies of Santas are cut from heavy tagboard and painted.
2. Cut-paper and cotton faces, beards, hats, buttons, boots, and mittens are added.
3. The figures are then glued back-to-back with a thin, flat stick or piece of No. 4 reed between them.

4. Christmas trees, snowmen, or other figures can also be made the same way.

*Balloon ornaments.* Blow up a balloon. Pour white glue into a dish, adding a little water to thin it. Dip one-yard pieces of yarn, string, or twine in the glue and wrap around the balloon at many different angles. Let dry. Pop the balloon, then spray paint in a well-ventilated area. Or paint with tempera paint. Glitter may be added by brushing on glue and sprinkling glitter on the glue.

*Foam cup bells.* Brush foam cups with white glue. Roll in glitter. Let dry. Decorate with bits of trimming. Use small balls from ball fringe or bells for clappers. Hang by yarn or ribbon in groups of three or four.

*Styrofoam bells.* Cut individual egg cups from the bottom of a Styrofoam egg carton. Make a hole in bottom center of each "bell" and place 2″ piece of pipe cleaner through the hole. Secure with loop on inside end, and make a half loop on other end for hanging. Dip the rim portion in glue, and then in glitter. These bells make very attractive Christmas tree decorations.

*Plastic bell decorations.* Cut bell shapes from plastic meat trays, using a cardboard pattern. Have the children trim these with crayon designs or sprinkle with glue, then glitter. Make a hole, tie a long strand of ribbon through the hole, and tie the bells to the Christmas tree.

*Cup cover ornaments.* Save either margarine lids or carry-out drink cup covers. Trim off rims. Spread white glue on both sides and dip in glitter. Glue on Christmas card pictures or bits of fabric. Put the child's signature or name on the other side. Trim with bits of ribbon or rickrack. Hang by yarn or thread.

**Gift Making.** Gifts are fun to make and give. Children can participate in planning and creating presents for others. An example of what happened in one kindergarten follows:

**FIGURE 26–15 One present a child can make is a cut-paper wreath.**

Teacher: (Reading from a chart upon which the children's plans for holidays have been written) Our third plan says, "We can make holiday presents for other people." Who could we make presents for?

Mary: Our mothers.

Sue: Our fathers.

John: I could make one for my brother.

As the children talk, the teacher makes a list of the people they suggest.

Teacher: That's a good list. What kinds of things do we have in our class that we could use to make gifts for these people?

Jill: We have paper.

Teacher: What could we make out of paper, Jill?

Jill: We could make a picture for our mothers.

Teacher: (Nodding) That's a good idea. (Under the title, "Kinds of Presents We Could Make," she writes, (1) We could make pictures.) The list continues as the children and teacher think of things that could be made out of the paper, clay, lumber, cloth, and waste materials that are available.

Some possibilities for presents include:

- Drawing, painting, or chalking a picture. Give children a variety of kinds, colors, and sizes of paper to choose from. Have them sign and date their pictures. Mount each picture on another sheet or on cardboard for stiffness.
- Making booklets of various sizes for writing memos, notes, telephone numbers, or grocery lists. Books can be made in various ways, by folding single sheets in half and stapling or fastening with a paper fastener. The children can discover different shapes and ways of folding them together. They can then complete the books by designing the cover. It might have a title or a design made of colored paper, paint, or crayon.
- Making bowls, paperweights, candle holders, or pencil holders out of clay. The children decide what they will do and how to do it. Dried objects may be fired if a kiln is available. The objects can be painted with tempera paints, varnished, or shellacked by the children.
- Making hot-dish stands or spindles out of lumber. Each child can saw a piece of soft pine, ¾″ thick, into a shape that they like and paint it in a solid color or a design. For a spindle, drive a large nail up through the center. For safety while taking it home, have the child cover the nail with a sheaf made by rolling corrugated cardboard into a coil, securing it with tape, and pressing it over the nail.
- Boxes and cans of all shapes and sizes can be painted or covered with cloth or decorative paper. Contact paper and shelf paper are good for this. The containers can be used to hold yarn, knitting, buttons, pencils, paper clips, jewelry, or handkerchiefs. They can also be used as drawer organizers.

**Recipe Books.** A recipe book entitled, "My Favorite Food and How My Mother (or Father) Makes It," makes a wonderful gift for parents. Each child dictates to an adult what his favorite food is and how, in his own words, he thinks his mother makes it. All of the ingredients are compiled, along with directions for making this favorite recipe. The child's version of ingredients, amounts and procedures of preparation are often fantastic! These books are cherished for years to come.

**Gift Planters.** Half-pint milk cartons filled with potting soil and planted two weeks in advance of giving with marigold or other fast-growing seeds make beautiful planters for children to take home as gifts. As a finishing touch, punch holes in the sides of the cartons and tie with colorful yarn.

As the children construct these gifts, the teacher should tactfully channel their thinking along workable ideas, while at the same time encouraging their creative talents and active participation in the planning.

To prevent the children from becoming discouraged, the teacher might send a tactful letter to parents explaining how to understand and accept a child's gift. An example of such a letter follows:

Dear Parents,
   Your child will soon be bringing home holiday presents for the family. To you, they may look different than the item usually looks—after all, they are the work of a very young child. But no matter how they appear, your child has put her best efforts into planning and making the gifts, and they are all her own creation.
   When you receive the gifts, you might ask how to use them if they are not immediately identifiable. Point out something of special interest to you and actually make some use of these gifts. This will be the best kind of encouragement that you could possibly give.
   Happy holiday!

**Greeting Cards.** Greeting cards are usually sent to friends and relatives to celebrate holidays, birthdays, anniversaries, births, and other memorable occasions. Making such cards offers children an opportunity to do something thoughtful for others; to plan, organize, and complete a piece of work; and to exercise creative self-expression.

Children can make birthday cards for classmates, Thanksgiving greetings, Christmas cards, Mother's

**FIGURE 26–16 Sample Christmas tree card with glued-on glitter.**

Day cards, Father's Day cards, Saint Patrick's Day greetings, valentines, Easter greetings, sympathy cards, thank-you notes, get-well cards, congratulations cards, and so on. To construct and illustrate the cards, children can use paper of different types, chalk, paint, crayon, scissors, paste, clear tape, paper punch, stapler, ribbon, collage material, paper fasteners, and similar materials.

The following are some of the techniques that are used.

*Finger painting.* Have each child make a large painting, then cut up the painting to use as individual cards.

*Collage.* Arrange scraps of paper, cloth, and so on, in a colorful design.

*Spatter painting.* Child cuts a shape, places it on a background sheet of paper, and spatter paints it by rubbing a toothbrush dipped in paint over a screen. When the shape is removed, its outline remains.

*String painting.* String, yarn, or rope is dipped in paint and dragged across paper, making a colorful design.

*Straw painting.* Blobs of paint are dripped on paper; the child blows through a straw into the blobs to create interesting shapes.

*Block painting.* Wooden blocks or shapes cut from vegetables such as potatoes or carrots are dipped in paint and transferred to paper.

*Crayon resist.* Draw a design with crayon and then paint over it with thin watercolor.

*Rubs.* Put paper on a patterned surface such as a piece of wire netting, a leaf, or an arrangement of strings. Color with the side of a crayon or chalk, pressing down hard on the paper. The design from underneath will come through.

*Chalk on wet paper.* Dip a piece of paper in a pan of water. (Any paper will do; even newspaper looks interesting with chalk colors added.) Spread the wet paper on a flat surface and draw designs with chalk. Hang up to dry. If the paper wrinkles, press with a hot iron. If the chalk is likely to rub off, set it with hair spray.

For the greeting or message the card carries, children might dictate appropriate thoughts to the teacher, who could type them on a primer typewriter or write them in script and duplicate a copy for the children to paste or staple to the card. The more mature children can copy their own messages if the messages are kept very short and simple. "Hi!" is an easy word for even the youngest. "Hello," "Mom," "Dad," and "Love" are meaningful words that many children might like to copy.

### Easy, Decorative Christmas Trees.

Procedure:

1. Cut quarter-circles from colored construction paper. Glue the sides together to form cones, and

place over dowels stuck in spools to make tall, slim trees.

2. Spirals may be added for decoration. To make a spiral, start with a circle slightly larger than the base of the cone and follow directions for spirals, page 537. The center of the spiral is placed on the point of the cone and the rest circles around the cone. Glue at the top and bottom.

3. A small cone placed over the top of a large cone will help hold the spiral in place until the glue dries. Or add glitter, cotton, foil paper, yarn, and so on, as decorations for these easy-to-make, attractive trees.

### Button Jewelry.

Materials: Buttons saved from shirts, coats, sweaters, etc., needle, thread or, for younger children, twine.

Procedure: Making button jewelry requires nothing but a button collection and endless imagination

**FIGURE 26–17 Button jewelry.**

(something children have plenty of). Buttons can be strung into necklaces, bracelets, etc. Smaller ones even can be made into rings. (See Figure 26–17.)

**Stone Paperweight.** Have everyone bring to class medium-sized stones of interesting shapes. Paint them with tempera, making unusual designs, faces, or figures suggested by the shape of the stone.

When the paint is dry, shellac the stones. A felt base may be glued on the bottom, if desired. The stones make useful and decorative paperweight gift items for parents.

**Gift Boxes.** Read the following poem aloud once to the children. Discuss how they "see it" in their minds. Read it again. Then have the children draw and color what they "see" in the poem.

> Big boxes, little ones,
> Some in between;
> All holding presents that
> Cannot be seen.
> Boxes with ribbons,
> Boxes with string;
> Boxes with wrappings
> That don't tell a thing!
> Boxes with lids on,
> Boxes that fold;
> Boxes that whisper
> Of treasures they hold.
> Green boxes, red boxes,
> Silvery ones, too;
> Under the Christmas tree, (Hanukkah lamp/
>    menorah)
> Waiting for you!

**Paper Batik.** Here's an interesting variation of the "resist" technique. After completing a drawing with crayons, soak the paper in water and crumple into a ball. Then uncrumple the paper, flatten it out, and blot off the excess water.

Flow a watercolor or a diluted tempera over the surface with a wet brush. Because the color will be more intense in the creased area, the finished drawing will have dramatic contrasts.

**Holiday Gift Plaque.** Stain a piece of scrap lumber with liquid brown shoe polish. Arrange dried flowers, leaves, and other natural materials on wood. Glue on with white glue.

Optional: Spray with white paint in a well-ventilated area and sprinkle with glitter.

**Holiday Gift Vase or Pencil Holder.** Tear small pieces of masking tape and stick them onto a small can or jar. Completely cover the jar or can with tape pieces. Cover with liquid brown shoe polish to create a leathery effect. When dry, spray with clear varnish or shellac to preserve finish.

**Holiday Candles.**

Caution: There must be adult supervision at all times during the wax melting.

Materials: Baby-food jars, colored tissue, liquid starch, heavy string (cord) for wicks, bar of paraffin, colored dye power.

Procedure:
1. Decorate baby-food jars with pieces of colored tissue. Attach to jar by brushing on liquid starch.
2. Let jars dry.
3. Candles are simple to make using household paraffin wax gaily colored with dye powder. (Do not use liquid dye as this will not mix with the wax.)
4. For larger candles, insert the wick before adding the wax. Punch a hole in the center of the bottom of the mold, no larger than the cord. Run the cord through the hole and up through the mold. Tie the end to a pencil or stick placed across the top of the mold. Pull the cord taut and secure the outer end by knotting and taping. For wicks in smaller candles, dip the cord (which is cut one inch longer than the depth of the mold) into the melted paraffin and set aside to harden.
5. To make colorful candles, melt paraffin wax in top part of a double boiler. Never use direct heat as the wax is flammable. Add dye powder, using about 2 teaspoons for each pound of paraffin. Remove the pan from the boiling water, stir thoroughly for two to three minutes, and let stand. Since dye is made to be soluble in water, not wax, some residue will remain in the pan after pouring. Simply discard. Pour wax carefully into molds from a height of one to two inches.
6. When the wax begins to harden in the small molds, push in the prepared wicks. Remove the tape holding the wicks for larger molds when the molds have hardened. To unmold, dip metal molds quickly in very hot water to loosen; then shake out. Peel off cardboard from carton molds.

**Spatter Printing on Fabric.** Create and design unique and original fabric for use as wall hangings or for covering and decorating items such as wastebaskets, screen, and lamp shades.

Procedure:
1. Begin with a washable fabric—an old sheet, piece of burlap, or unbleached muslin.
2. Place material on a flat surface with protective paper around the work area.
3. Mix ¼ cup liquid dye or ½ package of dye in 1 pint of hot water.
4. Spatter the dye solution onto the fabric with a brush. Use two or three colors for interesting patterns.
5. Allow the fabric to dry.
5. If the fabric is to be used as a covering, a protective coat of clear shellac should be brushed or sprayed on.
7. Note: Do not use spatter-dyed fabric for articles that come in direct contact with other articles (for example, pillow covers), because of possible rub-off from the dye.

**A Gift for the Birds.** String cranberries and cereal on yarn. Drape on trees and bushes for the birds.

**Rope Tricks.** Make colorful jump ropes by dunking ordinary clothesline, cut the proper length, in a solution of dye. Finish the ends by tying on empty thread spools that have been tinted matching or contrasting colors.

**Colorful Animals.** Dye socks following directions on dye container.

Fit ball snugly into toe of sock, making sure that fabric covers the ball smoothly. Secure the ball with string or needle and thread. Leave body limp. Finish raw edges as desired.

Make animal faces with embroidery thread, or paint in features. Use yarn in loops or pieces of bias tape to make ears, mane, or other animal features.

## Play Clay.
Ingredients:
1 cup cornstarch
2 cups baking soda (1-pound package)
1¼ cups water

Procedure:
1. Combine cornstarch and baking soda thoroughly in a saucepan.
2. Mix in water. Bring to a boil over medium heat, stirring constantly, until mixture reaches a moist, mashed-potato consistency.
3. Remove immediately from heat. Turn out on a plate and cover with a damp cloth until cool.
4. When easy to handle, knead like dough. Shape as desired or store in a tightly closed plastic bag for later use.
5. Note: For solid-colored play clay, add a few drops of food coloring or tempera paint powder to water before it is mixed in with starch and soda. Objects may be left white or painted when dry.

## Play Clay Creations.
*Holiday ornaments.* Roll out play clay to ¼-inch thickness on waxed paper. Cut out shapes with cookie cutters of all sizes, bottle tops, or a knife. Use a sharp needle or pin to make a hole for string or yarn to hang on the Christmas tree.

*Beads.* Shape the play clay into small balls or ovals. Using a long pin or wire, make a hole through each bead for stringing.

*Sculpture.* Use as a clay, shaping into all sorts of objects.

*Pendants, pins, and buttons.* Roll out play clay. Cut into circles or other designs, moistening each piece slightly so the pieces will stick together, or glue in place when dry. For buttons, glue a safety pin on the back when dry.

To dry: Play-clay objects will dry and harden at room temperature in approximately 36 hours, depending on thickness. To speed drying heat oven to 350°F; turn oven off and place objects on a wire rack or in a cardboard box on the rack. Leave in the oven until the oven is cool.

To finish: Paint dried play clay with watercolors, poster paints, or felt-tip pens. Spray with clear plastic, dip into shellac, or coat small pieces with clear nail polish.

## Decorating Dough Ornaments.
(See Cooking Experiences section in this unit for recipe for decorating dough.)

*Candy cane and wreath dough ornaments.*
- Add red food coloring to some decorating dough.
- Pinch off equal amounts of red and white dough.
- Roll dough into "snakes" or sticks about six inches long, one red, one white.
- Twist sticks together, red over white and white over red.
- Bend top into a hook for a candy cane ornament.
- For a wreath, add green food coloring to some decorating dough and twist. Use red dough for the bow.
- Bake at 300°F for 1½ hours. Or allow to dry for several days.

*Gingerbread house ornament.*
1. Add enough instant coffee to some decorating dough to make it brown.
2. Roll out dough or flatten it with your hands.
3. Draw a house shape on dough with a pencil. Cut it out with a plastic, serrated knife.
4. Press in small candies, raisins, and nuts for decorations.
5. Roll out some white dough and put it on the roof edge for "snow."
6. Press a paper clip or hairpin into back and allow to dry.

*Molded ornaments.* Place a little dough at a time on waxed paper to mold any ornament shape the child wishes to make. Paint with tempera paint. Put a hairpin hanger or paper clip on the back before letting ornament dry for several days.

*Cutout ornaments.* Roll out dough on waxed paper to about ¼″ thick. Press a cookie cutter into dough. Remove with spatula and allow to set. Press hairpin holder into back. Let dry and paint.

**Mosaics.** Here's a good way to use leftover stubs and pieces of crayons instead of discarding them.

Procedure:
1. Peel off the wrappers of crayon stubs and arrange the stubs in designs and patterns.
2. Use them as they are, or cut them to fit.
3. Glue the pieces to a stiff cardboard backing. The result: a beautiful mosaic.

**Moving Paper Santas.** Cut out from red construction paper a Santa figure, all the pieces separate. Join the pieces with brads to make a moving Santa. Use cotton for Santa's beard and other details. Hang these from string or yarn in the classroom or on windows.

## WHAT IS HANUKKAH?

Hanukkah celebrates the first battle for religious freedom fought more than 2,000 years ago. The Jews fought against the king of Syria who attempted to eliminate the Jewish way of life. The temple in Jerusalem was destroyed, but after the Jews emerged victorious in battle, they came to rededicate the temple. They found only one sealed, undefiled container of oil—just enough to last one day—with which to light their eternal flame. This oil lasted eight days—long enough to get a new supply—and, therefore, Hanukkah is celebrated for eight days. It is primarily a home holiday. Members of the family light one candle a night (in an eight-arm candelabra called a menorah) until all eight candles are lit. Special blessings are said, songs are sung, in some families gifts are exchanged, and a special dish, potato pancakes (called *latkes*), are eaten. (See recipe for *latkes* in the recipe section of this unit.)

Different people spell Hanukkah differently. Here

How to make a
**DREIDEL**

You need:
Cardboard   small jar cap   pencil   magic markers   scissors   pin, and round toothpick.

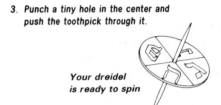

1. Put jar cap on the cardboard and draw circle.

2. Cut out the circle and decorate it.

3. Punch a tiny hole in the center and push the toothpick through it.

*Your dreidel is ready to spin*

**FIGURE 26–18 How to make a dreidel.**

are some different spellings of the word: Hanukhah, Chanukah, Hannukah, and Hanukah.

**How to Make a Dreidel.** See Figure 26–18 for instructions.

**Star of David.** Cut out two blue triangles from construction paper. Paste one over the other to form a Star of David. Glue to construction paper or hang from string.

**Menorah.** Roll out an 8-inch snake from play dough. Press snake down on a 1″ × 8″ strip of cardboard. Put one tall candle in the center. Put four small candles on each side.

## GAMES AND MOVEMENT EXPERIENCES

In a discussion with the children at holiday time, make a list of feelings and objects that describe the holiday. Then have the children use movement to express these ideas. Encourage creativity.

| Christmas: | Hanukkah: |
|---|---|
| opening packages | candles |
| reindeer | menorah |
| shopping | dreidel |
| making a snowman | seder |
| Santa Claus | temple |
| trimming the tree | |
| toys | |

**Story Plays.** Some ideas to stimulate imaginations: bringing home a Christmas tree; activities in Santa's toyshop; lighting the menorah candles; falling snowflakes; winter sports such as skiing, skating, sledding; shoveling snow; carrying in firewood for the fireplace; going for a ride in a horse-drawn sleigh. Let children develop these ideas through rhythmic movements, pantomimes, or simple one-act plays.

**Here We Go 'Round the Christmas Tree.** (Variation of "Here We Go 'Round the Mulberry Bush.") Several verses that can be used for this song include "Here we go 'round the Christmas tree"; "This is the way we hang a star (icicle, ball, candy cane, light, etc.)"; and "This is the way we light the candle."

**Rug in the Center.** A small rug is placed in front or in the center of the room. Individuals take turns dramatizing characters in a familiar holiday song or story. Children guess who is being depicted. For variation, select children to pantomime zoo animals. Then have an animal parade.

**Santa's Toy Shop.** One child, "Santa Claus," comes in at midnight to inspect his toys. All the toys wake up. At Santa's request, the different toys perform. (Give each child the name of a toy or let all children act out all toys.) Examples:

1. Jack-in-the-box—knee bend, spring up quickly.
2. Monkey climbing a stick—bend knees upward alternatively and stretch arms upward as though climbing.
3. Dolls—walk, when wound up, with jerky steps; keep the knees stiff and the arms bent at the elbows; bow stiffly; bend over at waist stiffly and say "Mama."
4. Wooden soldiers—march stiffly; salute.
5. Bicycle—run in place; lift the knees high in front and stretch the arms out in front for handlebars; ring a bell.
6. Jumping Jacks—jump with the feet apart and clap hands over heads; jump with the feet together and return the hands to the side.
7. Trains—slow step-hop around a circle, getting faster and faster; "choo-choo" softly; slow down to a slow step-hop and stop with a long "s-s-s-sh."

**Tommy Tucker's Land.** Equipment: ten bean bags. One child is "Tommy Tucker" and stands in the center of a fifteen-foot square (approximately) within which the bean bags are scattered. Tommy is guarding his land and his treasure. The other children chant "I'm on Tommy Tucker's land picking up gold and silver." The children attempt to pick up as much of the treasure as they can while avoiding being tagged by Tommy. Any child who is tagged must bring back the treasure and retire from the game. The game is over when there is only one child left or all the bean bags have been successfully stolen. You may wish to call a halt to the game earlier if it reaches a stalemate. In this case, the child with the most treasure is the new Tommy.

**Christmas Carol Relay (5 years and up).** Equipment: Chalk and blackboard. Divide the group into three or four teams. One person from each team comes forward, and the leader whispers to them the title of a Christmas carol. Those three people immediately go to the board and try to draw something that will aid their team in guessing the carol quickly. The first team to guess the carol scores a point. Three new people come forward, a new carol is whispered, and the game continues. Variation: Instead of giving a point, the team may be allowed to put up two letters toward spelling Merry Christmas. Me...rr...y C...hr...is...tm...as. The first team to spell Merry Christmas wins.

**Christmas Tree Relay (5 years and up).** Equipment: chalk and blackboard. Before playing the relay, discuss with the children items that can be found on a Christmas tree. Then divide the group into three or four teams, depending on the space you have in the room. They can be sitting in single file on the floor or in rows at their desks facing the blackboard. The first child in the row has a piece of chalk. On the signal, the first child runs toward the blackboard and draws a stand for the tree, the second child draws a Christmas tree, the rest of the team draws ornaments, and the last person draws a star. When the last child is seated, the relay is over.

## POEMS, FINGERPLAYS, AND SONGS

**Little Green Tree**
(Sung to tune of "I'm a Little Teapot.")
I'm a little green tree, short and sparse
Here is my trunk and here is my bough.
Decorate me all up with bright lights
Then plug me in and watch me shine!

**Around the Corner**
Christmas is coming,
Around the corner.
It's time to be good,
Like little Jack Horner.

**Christmas Is A-Coming**
Christmas is a-coming
The geese are getting fat. (Cup hands, palms facing
    each other)
Please to put a penny in the old man's hat.
(Hold one palm open, join thumb and index finger of
    other and lay in open palm)
If you haven't got a penny, (Tap palm)
A ha' penny will do.
(Tap palm)
If you haven't got a ha'penny,
(Tap palm)
Then God bless you.
(Point to child)

**Christmas Morning**
At last it's Christmas morning!
So I'm up and ready for fun.
And I think, as I greet my family,
"Merry Christmas to everyone!"

**A Package**
If you see a package
Gaily wrapped and tied,
Don't ask too many questions
Cause the secret's inside!

**Waiting**
We've hung our Christmas stockings,
They look so long and thin;
And now we're waiting in our beds,
For morning to begin.

It's black outside the window,
It rattles at the door;
Oh, will tomorrow ever come?
Or won't it anymore?

**Christmas Goodies**
It's hustle and bustle at our house,
So I try to keep out of the way.
But I sniff with delight at the goodies
That are baking for Christmas Day.

**A Jolly Time**
Oh, Christmas is a jolly time
    No matter where you're living—
A time for songs and lights and fun
    And getting gifts—and giving.

**Just for You**
Do you know what I'd like to do
When Santa Claus comes knocking?
I'd like to squeeze up a little
And hide behind my stocking.

And then when he opened his pack,
I'd say, "Boo," just for fun,
And maybe it would scare him so
He'd drop his pack and run.

Now wouldn't that be fun?

**Christmas Toys**
A ball, a book, and a tooting horn
    (For ball, make ball shape; for book, put palms
    together as for a prayer gesture; for horn, put fists
    together)
I hope I'll get on Christmas morn.
A ball to bounce,
    (Pretend to bounce an imaginary ball)
A book to read,
    (Put palms together and then open like a book)
And a horn to toot.
    (Hold fists up to mouth like a horn)

When I see Santa I'm going to say,
"Please bring me these toys on Christmas Day."

## Santa's Visit

When you are fast asleep in bed
Santa comes in his suit of red;
From his heavy bag he takes
A doll, a ball, a pair of skates.

Then up with his pack and out of sight.
Away he goes into the night.
If you want Santa to visit you,
These are the things that you must do:

Always listen to daddy and mother,
Be kind to your sister and brother.
And at the end of a busy day,
Pick up your toys and put them away.

If all these things you really do,
Santa Clause will visit you.

## What Santa Brought

Vacation time went by on wings,
Santa brought me lots of things.
A drum to beat,
    (Pretend to beat a drum and to spin a top)
A top to spin,
A puzzle to fit pieces in.

A telegraphic key to click
    (Use index finger of hand to make "clicks")
And best of all, a pogo stick!
    (Pretend to grasp pogo stick and jump)

Next Christmas I hope I get
    (Pretend to type on imaginary typewriter and to
    press with hand stamp)
A typewriter and a printing set.

An easel and palette of paint.
    (Hold imaginary palette in left hand, imaginary
    brush in right; pretend to paint on canvas set on
    imaginary easel)
Oh, dear! It seems so long to wait.

## Pine Tree—Christmas Song

(To tune of "I'm a Little Teapot")
I'm a little pine tree tall and straight
Here are my branches for you to decorate.
Don't forget to put the star on top
Just be careful the balls don't drop.
Now be sure to plug in all the lights
So I will look very gay and bright.
Then put all the presents under me
I'm all set for Christmas as you see.

## S—A—N—T—A

(Sung to the tune of "BINGO")
I know a man with a long white beard
And Santa is his name—O

S—A—N—T—A, S—A—N—T—A, S—A—N—T—A
And Santa is his name—O.

He slides down the chimney with a pack on his back
And Santa is his name—O.
S—A—N—T—A, S—A—N—T—A, S—A—N—T—A
And Santa is his name—O.

Eight little reindeer pull his sleigh
And Santa is his name—O.
S—A—N—T—A, S—A—N—T—A, S—A—N—T—A
And Santa is his name—O.

## Peanut Butter Song

(See related food experience, Peanut Butter, page
    550).
Peanut, peanut butter
and JELLY (In a deep voice)
Peanut, peanut butter
and JELLY (In a deep voice)

First, you take the peanuts and you pick 'em, pick
    'em, pick 'em, pick 'em (Picking gesture)
Then you smash 'em, smash 'em, smash 'em, smash
    'em, smash 'em (Smash hands together)
Then you spread 'em, spread 'em, spread 'em, spread
    'em, (Spreading on bread gesture)
Peanut, peanut butter
and JELLY (In a deep voice)

Then you take the berries and you pick 'em, etc.
    (Picking gesture)
Then you smash 'em, etc. (Smash hands together)
Then you spread 'em, etc. (Spreading on bread
    gesture)
Peanut, peanut butter,
    and JELLY (In a deep voice, two times)

Then you take the sandwich and you bite it, bite it,
    bite it, bite it, bite it (Biting gesture)
Then you chew it, chew it, chew it, chew it, chew it.
    (Hum Peanut Butter chorus)
    (Hum in a deeper voice, the JELLY part)

## I'm Giving Some Presents

I'm giving some presents for Christmas,
And I know I'll receive more than one.
It's not what I get that makes Christmas,
But the things that I give, that make fun.

## A Present for Me

When Santa comes down our chimney
With presents for under our tree,
I hope he'll remember I live here
and leave a nice present for me!

## When Santa Claus Comes

A good time is coming, I wish it were here,
The very best time in the whole of the year.

I'm counting each day on my fingers and thumbs,
The weeks that must pass before Santa Claus comes.
Then when the first snowflakes begin to come down.
And the wind whistles sharp and the branches are
    brown,
I'll not mind the cold, though my fingers it numbs,
For it brings the time nearer when Santa Claus comes.

## COOKING EXPERIENCES

**Decorating Dough.**    (This is the dough you will
need to make the ornaments covered in this unit.)

Ingredients:
4 cups self-rising flour
1 cup salt
1½ cups water

Procedure:
1. Mix flour and salt in a large bowl.
2. Slowly add water, mixing to form a ball. Use a fork
   or your hands.
3. Knead the dough with your hands for 5 to 10
   minutes.
4. Add a little water if dough is too stiff. Add flour if
   it is too sticky.
5. You can store dough wrapped in plastic paper in
   the refrigerator for up to 5 days. The dough may
   be dried at room temperature for several days to
   harden, or baked at 300°F for 1½ hours.
Remember: Decorating dough is *not* to eat!

**Christmas Stocking Treat.**  Put each child's
breakfast or snack in a Christmas stocking instead of
candy. With a little imagination, it's possible to put
together a nutritious meal or snack.

**Reindeer Sandwich.**   Use a triangle of bread for
the head and spread with peanut butter. Antlers
could be pretzels; eyes, raisins; and the nose, a cherry
tomato or radish.

**Apricot Goodies.**   Give the children some dried
apricots to fill. Have them squeeze the edges to
soften and open the apricots. Fill the apricot halves
with a mixture of mashed banana and peanut butter
combined with chopped nuts, rolled oats, wheat

germ, or other dry ingredients to bind the banana
and peanut butter together so they can be rolled into
a small ball and pressed into the apricot half.

**Carrot Balls.**
Ingredients:
One 3 ounce package of cream cheese, softened
½ cup finely shredded cheddar cheese
1 tablespoon apple juice concentrate
1 cup finely grated carrots
½ cup finely chopped walnuts

Procedure:
1. Cream together the first three ingredients.
2. Stir in carrots.
3. Roll into small balls and roll in nuts.

**Candle Salad.**   Place a pineapple ring on leafy lettuce. Place a half or whole peeled banana (depending on the size of the banana) in the center of the
pineapple ring. (It should stand up by itself.) Cut off
the pointed end of the banana. Make a flame for
your candle by peeling off a piece of carrot with a
potato peeler. Roll the carrot strip into a circle, overlapping the two ends. Stick one end of a toothpick
through the ends of the carrot strip and the other
end down into the top of the banana. Pinch the carrot ring to make it more pointed. Children may eat
the salad as it is, or you can decorate the candle with
nuts, fruit, or raisins.

**Uncooked Fudge.**   This makes a good gift to give
at Christmas.

Ingredients:
¼ cup butter
¼ cup sweetened condensed milk
1 teaspoon vanilla
1 pound confectioners' sugar
¾ cup cocoa
¼ teaspoon salt

Procedure:
1. Melt butter in a saucepan (or in the microwave
   for 10 seconds on HIGH).
2. Stir in milk and vanilla.
3. Gradually add mixture of sugar, cocoa, and salt.

4. Mix until soft and creamy.
5. Press into buttered pan. Chill and cut into squares.

## Potato Pancakes (Latkes) for Hanukkah

Ingredients:
6–8 medium potatoes
2 eggs
½ cup flour
1 onion
1 teaspoon salt
oil for frying ¼-inch deep

Procedure:
1. Pare potatoes and grate, along with onion, and mix in a large bowl.
2. Squeeze out all the liquid (you will be amazed at how much water the potatoes have—just squoosh it with hands, like a sponge).
3. Add beaten eggs, flour, and salt. Stir to make batter.
4. Heat oil to very hot in skillet and drop in batter by spoonfuls.
5. Brown on both sides and drain on paper towels. Should be puffy and crisp.

## Christmas Trees

Ingredients:
3 tablespoons butter
3 cups miniature marshmallows
½ teaspoon vanilla
½ teaspoon green food coloring
4 cups Cheerios
wax paper
gumdrop slices

Procedure:
1. Melt butter and marshmallows in a large pan over low heat.
2. Remove from heat and add vanilla and green food coloring.
3. Fold in Cheerios. Cool.
4. Butter hands. Shape ⅔ cup of the mixture into a tree shape on a piece of waxed paper.
5. Add gumdrop slices and a star on a toothpick.
Note: Cool mixture well before shaping.

## Gingerbread People.

Ingredients:
1 cup shortening
¾ cup honey
1 egg
1 cup molasses
1½ teaspoons baking soda
½ teaspoon salt
2 teaspoons ground ginger
1 teaspoon cinnamon
1 teaspoon ground cloves
5 cups flour

Procedure:
1. Mix shortening, honey, egg, and molasses.
2. Sift soda, salt, ginger, cinnamon, cloves, and flour together.
3. Mix wet and dry ingredients together.
4. Roll ¼-inch thick on a floured surface.
5. Cut with a gingerbread person cutter. Decorate with raisins, nuts, licorice, and tiny candies.
6. Bake at 375°F for 10 minutes.
Note: Dough works best when chilled before rolling. Put each child's cookie on foil, with the name in the corner.

## Chocolate Walnut Balls.

Ingredients:
1½ cup ground walnuts
⅔ cup confectioners' sugar
1 egg yolk
3 ounces semisweet chocolate, grated
1 teaspoon grated orange peel
2 egg whites

Materials: Measuring cup, measuring spoons, large mixing bowl, small mixing bowl, grater, egg beater, mixing spoon

Procedure:
1 Grate the chocolate and the orange peel. The children can do this well if supervised.
2. Separate the eggs.
3. Beat the egg yolk in the small mixing bowl.
4. In the large mixing bowl, mix 1 cup walnuts with the sugar, egg yolk, chocolate, and orange peel.

5. Roll the mixture into balls about the size of walnuts.
6. Beat the egg whites until foamy.
7. Dip the balls into the egg whites.
8. Then roll them in the remaining ground walnuts.
9. Let them dry two hours before serving.
10. Read Robert Dahl's, *Charlie and the Chocolate Factory,* as a natural ending to this activity. Do this as the children are tasting their work.

**Peanut Butter.**   (Put in baby food jars, with a bow on top—Makes a great child-made Christmas gift).

Ingredients:
fresh or salted peanuts
1½ to 3 tablespoons corn oil to 1 cup peanuts
If nuts are unsalted, use ½-teaspoon salt for each cup

Materials: Measuring spoons, measuring cup, blender

Procedure:
1. Shell the peanuts.
2. Put all ingredients in the blender and turn on at low speed until the peanut butter is smooth.
3. The "Peanut Butter" song would be an enjoyable enrichment activity after making the peanut butter, or while it is being made.

**Santa Apple.**   Santa apples make excellent table decorations, party favors, and gifts.

Materials: Toothpicks, large red apples, marshmallows, gumdrops

Procedure:
1. Five marshmallows, stuck to the apple with toothpicks, make the head, arms, and legs.
2. A large red gumdrop is stuck to the head for a hat, black gumdrops make boots, red are hands.
3. Small bits of gumdrops make other features.
4. A small bit of cotton makes Santa's beard.
5. Use tiny bits of toothpicks to hold things in place.

## ADDITIONAL READINGS

### Children's Books for December Holidays

Briggs, R. *Father Christmas.* New York: Coward, McCann & Geoghegan, Inc., 1973.

Brunhoff, Jean De. *Babar and Father Christmas.* New York: Random House, 1981.

Buck, Pearl S. (illustrated by Anna Marie Magagna). *The Christmas Ghost.* New York: John Day Co., 1960.

Budbill, D. *Christmas Tree Farm.* New York: Macmillan Publishing Co., 1974.

Carey, Diana, and J. Large. *Festivals, Family, and Food.* Gloucestershire, England: Hawthorn Press, 1982.

Carroll, Latrobe, and Ruth Carroll. *Christmas Kitten.* Portland, Maine: Walck, 1970.

Devlin, Wende, and Harry Devlin. *Cranberry Christmas.* New York: Parents' Magazine Press, 1976.

Duvoisin, Roger. *Christmas Whale.* New York: Knopf, 1945.

Ets, Marie Hall, and Aurora Labastida. *Nine Days to Christmas.* New York: Viking Press, 1959.

Hyman, Trina Schart. *How Six Found Christmas.* Boston: Little, Brown and Co., 1969.

Kent, J. *The Christmas Piñata.* New York: Parents' Magazine Press, 1969.

Knight, Hilary. *The Twelve Days of Christmas.* New York: Macmillan, 1981.

Lenski, Lois. *Lois Lenski's Christmas Stories.* Philadelphia: J.B. Lippincott, 1968.

Lipkind, William, and Nicholas Mordvinoff. *Christmas Bunny.* New York: Harcourt, Brace, Jovanovich, 1953.

Moore, Clement C. *The Night Before Christmas.* New York: Random House, 1962.

Spier, P. *Christmas!* New York: Doubleday & Co., 1983.

Tazewell, Charles. *The Littlest Angel.* New York: Children's Press, 1966.

Vincent, Gabrielle. *Merry Christmas Ernest and Celestine.* New York: Morrow/Mulberry, 1984.

Warren, Jean, and E. McKinnon. *Small World Celebrations: Around the World Holidays to Celebrate with Young Children.* Everett, Wash.: Warren Publishing Co., 1988.

Wilson, R.B. *Merry Christmas: Children at Christmastime Around the World.* New York: Philomel Books, 1983.

# UNIT 27

# Valentine's Day

The ancient Romans believed that at the first hint of spring, around the middle of February, birds chose a mate. Valentine's Day began in the days of the ancient Romans with a festival called the Festival of Lupercalia. At this celebration, the single men would choose their special girlfriend, drawing her name out of a cup or bowl. The couples would give each other gifts and court for the next year. Around the year 500, the festival was given a religious meaning by changing the name to Saint Valentine's Day in honor of two men named Valentine, and the date was set as February 14.

According to legend, there were two saints named Valentine. Both lived in Rome about 200 A.D. Some say St. Valentine was a priest who married couples against the wishes of the Roman emperor. Others say that he was a kindly priest who loved children. He was put in prison because he would not worship the Roman gods. Children would throw him loving notes through the bars in his cell. Before he died, he sent a farewell message to a little girl signed, "Your Valentine."

In the United States, Valentine's Day became popular during the nineteenth century. Many valentines of that period were handpainted and elaborately decorated with ribbons and lace. Some had dried flowers, feathers, tassels, imitation gems, and even seashells. People displayed their valentines and saved them among the family keepsakes.

In 1988, about 850 million store-bought valentines were sent. Valentine's Day is the second most popular card-sending holiday in the United States (Christmas is the first). Teachers get more valentines than any other group. Next come mothers, wives, and girlfriends. (1988 Universal Press Syndicate)

Young children can understand the idea of caring for others, which is the general message of Valentine's Day. Though some adults feel that Valentine's Day is irrelevant to young children, it is hard for children to ignore (or not be curious about) all the valentine cards, candy, and toys displayed around them. The teacher can set the appropriate tone in planning Valentine's Day activities by emphasizing caring for others and giving valentines in this spirit. In such a way, the teacher reduces the possibility of making Valentine's Day a competition over who gets the most valentines.

Valentine's Day calls for pretty collage materials—white lace, red hearts, and so forth. Although costs of mailing can be prohibitive if the school must bear the expense alone, it *is* possible to ask each family to provide a postage stamp. Then encourage the children to make a valentine that they can mail at the post office to their families.

For even more fun, after your children make valentines for their families, put their cards in addressed, stamped envelopes. Place all the cards in one large envelope and mail it to: Postmaster, Loveland, CO 80537. If your valentines arrive in Loveland by February 6, they will be remailed with a Loveland postmark and arrive in time for Valentine's Day.

In this and all Valentine's day activities, be sensitive to all of the families in your group. For example, for some children, making two Valentines (one for each set of parents, or one for each separate parent) can help alleviate hurt feelings and confusion.

It can be fun to carry out the holiday theme by having an all red and pink day, including easel paints, play dough, snack, and even lunch.

Children do love dramatic play involving sending and receiving mail. It can be worth the investment to have lots of inexpensive envelopes in the housekeeping corner that the children can use for making and mailing valentines.

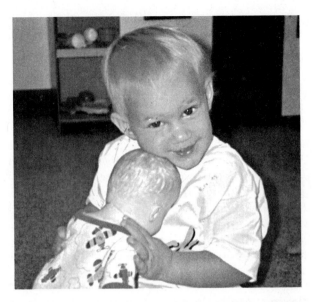

**FIGURE 27–1 Even very young children can understand the idea of caring for others, which is the general message of Valentine's Day.**

## ART ACTIVITIES

Making valentines and other activities as suggested in this unit are especially good for small motor development. Using scissors, pasting, and coloring all involve fine motor skills. In choosing from the Valentine's Day art activities that follow, be sure to consider the motor development, interests, and needs of the children in your group. And most important of all, concentrate on the fun of *doing* and not on the finished product!

Making pictures, one of the most basic art activities for young children, can easily be included in Valentine's Day activities. Some suggested topics for picture making include:

- I Like to Make Valentines
- Fun at a Valentine Party
- Mailing my Valentines
- Making a Valentine Box
- My Valentine Friends
- A Valentine Surprise
- Painting a Valentine

**Valentines.**
Procedure:
1. Design hearts using cut paper, crayon, and paint. Use brilliant colors, or pastel shades of yellow, pink, or blue.
2. Some hearts may have faces or a pattern of stripes or dots to be pierced by Cupid's arrows.
3. Hearts can either be used alone or combined to form animals, people, and flowers.

**Heart-Shaped Valentines.**
Procedure:
1. To cut a heart shape, first fold paper in half.
2. Then, keeping the center of the heart along the fold, cut both sides of the heart at the same time.
3. Hearts attached to background paper may be decorated with bits of ribbon, yarn, paper lace, sequins, and discarded cloth flowers.
4. Valentine cards can be folded at the side, top, in accordion style, or in three parts to form a window. The folding technique depends on the shape desired, such as a house, basket, flower, or bird.

**Lovable Animals.**  Make a caterpillar, fish, bunny, and mouse with heart-shaped cutouts. Show the children how to trace around heart patterns. Then let children cut them out, combine them into lovable animals, and paste them on white sheets of paper.

**Lacy Valentines.**  Cut a heart-shaped valentine out of red or pink construction paper. Use white gummed reinforcement circles for the "lace." Let the children lick and stick the white reinforcement circles around the outlines of their heart shapes to create fancy "lace-edged" valentines.

**FIGURE 27–2 Lovable animals.**

**Valentine Families.**   This activity will encourage children to explore freely, make designs, and practice sorting by size, color, and texture.

Materials: Felt, fabric, wallpaper, foam, sponge, sandpaper

Procedure: Prepare several sets of hearts using a variety of materials. Have the child arrange them in order from small to large (or vice-versa) or according to color or material. Ask the child to describe choices to justify decisions made in sorting.

**A Shiny Valentine.**   Mix white glue with dry red tempera. Cut a three-inch square of oaktag paper. Cover the square with foil. Paint a valentine picture on the foil with glue. Frame or glue on a large red heart.

**Bleeding Heart.**   Use black magic marker to draw a heart outline on paper towels. Brush water onto the outline. Watch the colors bleed.

**Paper Lace.**
Procedure:
1. Cut-paper lace can be made of tissue paper, paper napkins, or other thin paper.
2. Fold the paper into four or eight parts.

**FIGURE 27–3 Young children enjoy creating their own, very special valentines.**

3. The lacy design is created by cutting shapes here and there along the folds; the more cuts, the finer the design.
4. Outside edges may be scalloped or cut in a zigzag pattern.
5. Small figures of birds, flowers, or stars can be added to complete the design.

**King and Queen of Hearts.**   For the figure of the king, use a toweling roll covered with construction paper and crowned with little paper hearts.

A piece of paper rolled into a cone shape forms the queen's body. Make a tiny slit at the top to hold a heart-shaped head, with paper lace for the crown.

Royal robes may be made of paper or cloth, trimmed in sequins, hearts, metallic foil, or paper lace.

**Playing Mail Carrier.**  Young children enjoy dramatizing everyday experiences. They can play-act mailing valentines and delivering them by a mail carrier. To speed the process of "delivery" the teacher can print children's names on a ditto master in proper manuscript form and run off copies of all names for each child. The children then cut out the names and paste them on their envelopes for their friends.

Procedure:
1. A sturdy cardboard box with half the top closed and the other half folded back makes a good mailbox when painted appropriately.
2. A mail carrier's bag may consist of a large paper sack with an old belt for the shoulder strap.
3. Half an oatmeal box painted with a visor of construction paper can serve as the mail carrier's hat.

**Valentine Containers.**
Procedure:
1. Begin the project with a large cardboard box, tin can, or basket.
2. Decorate the containers with bits of ribbon made into bows or cut-paper hearts, paper lace, and discarded trimmings such as flowers, feathers, and sequins.
3. Boxes can be made into a house, truck, or train loaded with valentines.

**Valentine Tree.** A decorative centerpiece may be a group project. The tree consists of a small tree branch set in sand or clay. Trim the tree with paper flowers, hearts, birds, and ribbons.

**Valentine Clown.** Combine different sizes of red and white valentines to make a happy clown. You draw the hearts, then let the children cut them out and paste them together. You may also show the children how to fold a paper in half, draw half a heart, then cut the folded paper to get a heart the same shape on both sides.

### How Do You Say "I Love You" to a Giraffe?

As an alternative to a one-sided focus on human beings at Valentine's time—for the fun of it—introduce the idea of saying "I love you" to animals by giving them some of their favorite foods. You will need to cut out pictures of animals and paste them to cardboard. Or you might have an animal storybook to use (with large pictures that are easy to see).

Many humans will say "I love you" with flowers or a box of candy. Here are some special treats for zoo animals—a way of saying "I love you" to them!

**FIGURE 27–5 Gumdrops and marshmallow tree.**

- A giraffe would be delighted with fresh lettuce.
- A toco toucan would cherish a bowl of blueberries.
- A leopard would love an ox bone.
- A baby rhinoceros would adore a mud puddle.
- A walrus would be happy with a huge herring.
- A brown bear would be pleased with honey on bread.

You might want to read up on various other zoo animals and find out other "ways to say 'I love you.'"

### Party Ideas.

- Fasten little red gumdrops to a small twig stuck into a marshmallow.
- Paste paper hearts onto a toothpick and insert it into a marshmallow or gumdrop.
- Create little heart figures with gumdrops and toothpicks.
- Use a heart-shaped lollipop for the head and body of a valentine figure. For dresses, use paper lace fastened with pipe cleaners at the base of the heart. Paste little paper hearts to the ends of the pipe

**FIGURE 27–4 Valentine clown.**

**FIGURE 27–6 Paper heart, toothpick, and marshmallow decorations.**

**FIGURE 27–7 Gumdrop and toothpick animals.**

**FIGURE 27–8 Painted valentine decorated with cut paper.**

cleaners for hands. The lollipop may be set into a gumdrop for a base.

**Love Your Pet.**    Celebrate Valentine's Day by discussing ways to say "I love you" to your pets. Here are some tips:

• Groom your pets. For example, cats groom themselves with their tongues. The more hair you remove through brushing, the less your cat will have to do.
• Some pets need exercise. Some need playtimes.
• Give your pets food and water and spend some time with them.
• Pets are alive and have feelings. They respond to the same things children respond to, such as good care. They want to please you. If you are not happy, then the animals are not happy either.
• Do not overfeed your fish, and keep their water clean.
• While gerbils tend to bite, they will do well if they are handled a lot and are well cared for. Guinea pigs are bigger and easier to handle, and they rarely bite.
• Birds need to be gently handled so that when they get sick, they are used to being picked up.

**For a Party Table.**

• Decorate the edges of paper plates with hearts or flowers from cut paper.
• Make place mats of white roll paper decorated with valentine designs.
• Use one of the candy treat ideas for place cards.

• Make candy cups from egg cartons, match boxes, paper cups, or frozen pie tins.

**Painted Valentines.**    Cut a large heart from a piece of brown wrapping paper. Have the children paint these large hearts red. Colored construction paper scraps may be pasted on for decoration.

**Valentine Greeting Cards.**    For making valentine cards, use the basic techniques for making holiday greeting cards at the beginning of Unit 26.

## PERSONALIZED VALENTINE GIFTS

**Have a Ball.**    Have the children make their own balls from old socks filled with rags or packing materials. Seal them with masking tape.

**Hands and Feet.**
Procedure:
1. Place a large sheet of paper on the floor.
2. Have the children dip their hands in finger paint and make handprints on the paper.
3. Label each pair of hands with the child's name.
4. Have the children take off their shoes and socks and make prints with their feet.

5. Make sure a pail of water and paper towels are available for cleanup.

**Mosaics on the Roof.**   Here's a unique, yet easy to obtain, raw material that can liven up mosaics.

Procedure:
1. Tiny granules that have fallen off roofing shingles are available in many colors from roofing and construction supply companies.
2. Have the children draw designs, put glue on the area to be covered, and sprinkle on the granules. They look great on valentines.

**Cleanup Paintings.**   One art form can lead to another. Did you ever think of cleaning up excess paint from a dripped paint mural with a blotter? If the paint is thick, it will not dry quickly. Use a large blotter to soak up the excess paint from the mural. Then cut the blotter into smaller panels.

## VALENTINES YOU WILL LOVE TO MAKE

**Heart Mailbag.**   Here's something to put your valentines in.

Materials: A brown grocery bag, paper, scraps, scissors, yarn or heavy string, crayons

Procedure:
1. Hold the top of the bag together. Draw the top of a heart shape on the bag and cut it out. (The front and the back will be heart-shaped.)
2. Cut out hearts, using colored paper, doilies, or felt. Glue them on the bag.
3. Print your name with a crayon or marker.
4. Glue or staple on yarn handles.

**3-D Valentine.**

Materials: Shoebox lid, paper scraps or old Valentine cards, glue, scissors, string, paper doilies, crayons or markers

Procedure:
1. Color the inside of the lid with crayons or markers.

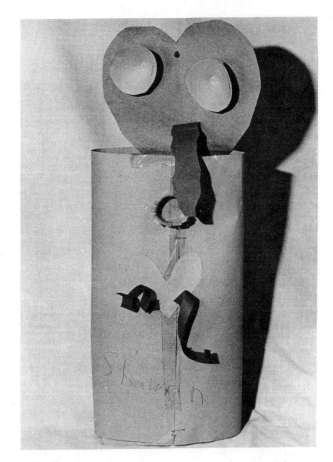

**FIGURE 27–9 Valentine "creatures"—a three-dimensional object.**

2. Cut out letters, words, or hearts and glue them to the inside.
3. Make a frame of paper hearts or use doilies glued to the back.
4. Use glue or staples to hang hearts from the top of your lid.

(See Figure 27–11 for illustrations of the Valentine Heart Mailbag and the 3-D Valentine.)

**Sponge Print Valentines.**   Add natural sponges to your printing supplies.

Put primary colors in two pie pans, and have each child dip a sponge in one and then the other color.

Print on construction paper. The sponges will mix

the colors and print interesting, irregular patterns on a paper heart of any size.

**Decorated Doilies.** Materials: Paper doilies (which can be purchased inexpensively in a dime store), coloring materials, red construction paper, paste

Procedure:
1. Distribute the doilies.
2. Let the children decorate them with color. The intricacy of the doily lends itself to beautiful color designs.
3. For a variation, a red paper heart may be pasted in the center before coloring the doily.

**Love Puzzles.**
Materials: Heavy paper, scissors, coloring materials

Procedure:
1. Draw fairly large hearts.
2. Have the children decorate them.
3. On the back, draw lines to create a jigsaw-type puzzle. Cut along the lines to make the puzzle.

**Valentine Creatures.**
Procedure:
1. Cut one large red construction paper heart for the body and a smaller one for the head.
2. Use thin (½ inch) strips of 3 inch long black construction paper for arms and legs.
3. Accordion pleat (fold) these strips and attach them at the sides and bottom of the body for arms and legs.

**Word Designs (Five years and up).** Materials: Paper, coloring materials. Discuss with the children words connected with Valentine's Day, such as sweetheart, love, Cupid, heart, arrow, and so on. List these on the board, using pictures next to each word for preschoolers. The children can use these words as the basis for their designs. They may use one word or many. The words (written or printed) should be placed in varying directions on the paper; they can be repeated or overlapped, or the letters can be distorted or varied in size. Then, with color, the chil-

**FIGURE 27–10 Valentine creatures.**

dren may fill in letters, parts of letters, or spaces, or they may outline parts of letters.

If these designs are to be used as cards, have the children work on smaller paper. Designs on large paper make a very effective mural. For this activity, the children take turns writing their words.

**Love Symbol Designs.** Materials: Paper, coloring materials. Discuss with the children symbols of Valentine's Day, such as hearts, arrows, Cupid, and flowers. For their own cards the children can work in the same way as for word designs above. For a mural, they can make their designs at their desks, cut them out, and then decide where to place them on a big paper.

## GAMES AND MOVEMENT EXPERIENCES

In a discussion with the children, make a list of objects that describe Valentine's Day. Have the children use movement to express these ideas. Encourage creativity. Some ideas that could be used are:

- Making valentines
- Delivering valentines

- Heart shapes
- Mailing valentines

**Valentine Game (Variation of Button Game).**
Use a red button, if possible. Children pretend it is a tiny valentine heart. (The teacher may wish to use a candy heart instead.)

One child has a large red button or valentine. The rest of the children fold their hands and close their eyes. The one with the button goes to each person, dropping the button into one closed hand along the way. When the child has gone to everyone in the class, someone else asks who has the button. This child asks another until the button has been found.

Insist on clear speech; for example:

Question: "Billy, do you have the valentine?"
Answer: "No, Jane, I do not have the valentine."

**Valentine Letter Game.**
(Tune: "Yankee Doodle Dandy")
I sent a letter to my love
And on the way I dropped it,
A little puppy picked it up
And put it in his pocket.

Children sit in a circle on the floor. One of them walks around the outside of the circle while they all sing the song. The child drops a handkerchief behind another child when they sing "dropped it." At the end of the song, both children, the one who dropped the handkerchief and the one who had it dropped behind him, run around the ring in opposite directions and try to reach the empty place first. The one who loses his seat then takes the handkerchief around and the verse is sung again. Try different ways of moving besides running, such as hopping around the circle, moving with two body parts, or touching the floor. Be sure to emphasize that no one *loses* in participating in games. Emphasize turns and sharing rather than winning and losing.

**Valentine Relay.** Divide the class into equal teams. Paste a large valentine heart up on a wall or chalkboard for each team.

The first child in line runs (or walks, hops, crawls) from the line to the valentine, touches the valentine (or for older children, puts his initial on it), and returns to the end of his team line (using the same movement). The next child in line repeats the process. The first group finished is the winning team. The prize: valentine candy hearts.

**Valentine's Day Delivery Game.** Formation: Single circle with a leader in the center. The leader, "Postman," calls, "I have a valentine for Mary Smith

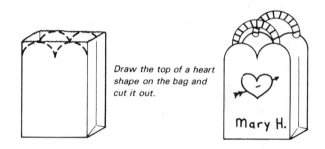

*Draw the top of a heart shape on the bag and cut it out.*

**Heart mailbag**

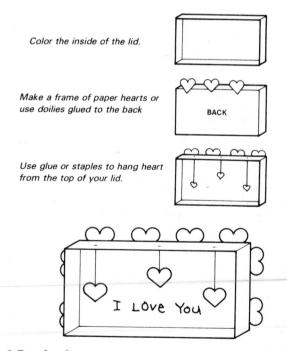

*Color the inside of the lid.*

*Make a frame of paper hearts or use doilies glued to the back*

*Use glue or staples to hang heart from the top of your lid.*

**3-D valentine**

**FIGURE 27–11 Heart mailbag and 3-D valentine.**

from Bob Brown,'' thereby naming two children in the circle. These two immediately change places while the postman tries to get one of the spaces. The child left without a space becomes the new postman. Try to play the game long enough for everyone to be postman.

---

## FINGERPLAYS AND POEMS

### Valentine Lace
Last night my yard
Was decked in lace—
Delicate, feathery snowflake lace.
Each open space
In the cypress trees,
Each snow-lined place
On the white birch bough
Forms a finely stenciled doily now.
If a crimson cardinal
Should light in the row
Of sun-flecked trees
Fluffed up with snow,
I'd have a valentine,
Splendid, bright,
Gracefully traced in red and white.

### Be My Valentine
Do you know what this is?
   (Put thumbs and forefingers together to make a heart shape)
Yes, a heart. Pretend it's mine.
   (Point to self)
I'll put it on a paper,
And make a valentine.
   (Make heart again and pretend to put it on an imaginary piece of paper on the desk or table in front of you)
Into an evelope it will go,
   (Pretend to grasp paper in one hand and slide it into imaginary envelope held in fingers of the other hand)
With address written clear.
   (Pretend to write address with imaginary pen)
Soon you'll pull it out and read:
   (Reverse pantomime for placing letter in envelope)
"To my valentine so dear."
   (Pretend to hold up a valentine and read its message)
That's you!
   (Point to someone)

**Five Pretty Valentines.** Have children hold up the correct number of fingers as they help you recite this fingerplay. Put each child's name in the blank (or as many as possible.)

Five pretty valentines waiting at the store
(Put in a child's name) bought one and then there were FOUR.
Four pretty valentines shaped just like a "V"
_____ bought one and then there were THREE.
Three pretty valentines said, "I love you."
_____bought one and then there were TWO.
Two pretty valentines—this was so much fun!
_____bought one and then there was ONE.
One pretty valentine sitting on the shelf.
I felt sorry for it, so I bought it for MYSELF!

### A Valentine's Day Song.
(Tune: "Down by the Station")
Down at the station, early in the morning,
See the happy engineer waving hello.
The wheels are all oiled and the smoke stack is cleaned out—
Puff, puff, toot, toot—he's ready to go!

Where is he going, so early in the morning?
He's loaded down with valentines and happy wishes, too.
Where is he taking them? You may have three guesses—
Puff, puff, toot, toot—to you, that's who!

**Spell-a-Name.** Write the letters of each child's name on minihearts. Scramble the hearts and let the children place them in order. When the children can arrange their first names correctly, work on the last name.

### Valentines
Valentines, valentines
How many do you see?
Valentines, valentines
Count them with me.
One for father
   (Put up thumb)
One for mother
   (Put up index finger)

**FIGURE 27–12 Spell-a-name.**

One for grandma
(Put up third finger)
One for sister
(Put up fourth finger)
One for brother
(Put up pinkie finger)
And here is one for you!
(Blow a kiss)

**Love Me—Love Me Not**
They say that daisies will not tell. (Shake head for
"No")
Of course they never do.
But when you pick their petals (Pretend to pick petals
from an imaginary display)
They tell if one you love loves you.
(Cross hands over heart)

**Lacy Hearts**
(Tune: "Jingle Bells")
Lacy hearts, candy hearts,
Flowery hearts, too.
Hearts of pink, hearts of yellow,
Hearts of red and blue.
Lacy hearts, candy hearts,
Flowery hearts, too.
Oh, what fun it is to share
Lots of hearts with you!
(Betty Silkunas)

**I Get Valentines**
(Tune: "The Farmer in the Dell")
I get valentines
From all my special friends.
I love to get, I love to give
Valentines today.
(Patricia Coyne)

**H-E-A-R-T**
(Tune: "Bingo")
To show you like your special friends,
Just give them each a heart.
H-E-A-R-T, H-E-A-R-T, H-E-A-R-T,
Each hearts says I like you!
(Debra Lindahl)

## FOOD FOR VALENTINE'S DAY

**Cherry Valentine Cake**
Ingredients:
2 cups flour
¾ cup sugar
¾ cup vegetable oil
2 eggs

1 21-ounce can cherry pie filling
2 teaspoons vanilla
1 teaspoon baking soda
½ teaspoon cinnamon
1 6-ounce package chocolate chips

Procedure:
1. Combine all ingredients and pour into two greased and floured cake pans.
2. Bake at 350°F for 40–45 minutes.

This cake is delicious frosted or unfrosted.

You might want to bake it in cupcake tins and let each child decorate their own cupcake, just as in the scene below:

> One of my activities was having children help make cupcakes and decorate them for Valentine's Day. They were a real mess, but the children really seemed to enjoy the mixing and pouring of the batter. Perhaps they aren't allowed to do such things at home. I had different-colored sugar toppings, heart candies, nuts, and pink frosting for them to decorate their cupcakes. I made the initial error of letting them see all this and they were all very eager to do the decorating *immediately*. I hate to admit to these tactics, but I told the children the room had to be in order before we could begin decorating. Their eagerness to decorate spurred them on and only a few occasional slips back to see the goodies occurred. They kept running up to me saying, "Look how I'm cleaning; can I decorate my cupcake now?" I don't know how good a teaching technique it is to hold a "fun" activity as a sort of bait to get them to clean. All I know is that it was VERY effective." (Author's log)

**Strawberry Valentine Pie.**
Ingredients:
1 graham cracker pie crust
1 8-ounce package cream cheese, softened
1 carton strawberry yogurt
1 10-ounce carton frozen, sliced strawberries, thawed

Procedure:
1. Blend cream cheese and yogurt till smooth.
2. Stir in strawberries and their syrup.
3. Pour into pie shell and place in freezer until set.

**Valentine Pretzels.**
Ingredients:
frozen bread dough

poppy or sesame seeds
salt (optional)

Procedure:

1. Thaw covered dough overnight in refrigerator, or for several hours at room temperature, until soft enough to shape.
2. On a floured surface, cut dough lengthwise into 8 strips. Cover and let rest 10 minutes.
3. Roll each strip on floured surface or between floured hands until ½ inch thick and 18 inches long.
4. Cut strips into pieces and shape the letters I LOVE YOU. Shape remaining dough into hearts.
5. Place on greased cookie sheet.
6. Brush with warm water and sprinkle with poppy or sesame seeds and salt (if desired).
7. Let rise, uncovered, in a warm place for 15 to 20 minutes.
8. Place a shallow pan of water on bottom shelf of oven. Preheat oven to 425°F.
9. Bake pretzels on center shelf 15 minutes or until golden brown.

### Honey Hearts.

Ingredients:
⅓ cup butter
¼ cup honey
⅔ cup oats
⅓ cup nonfat dry milk
4 teaspoons water
¾ cup flour
1 teaspoon baking powder
¼ teaspoon salt

Procedure:

Mix butter and honey. Add oats, dry milk, and water. Mix well. Add flour, baking powder, and salt. Mix until it is a soft dough. Roll dough ¼ inch to ½ inch thick. Cut with heart-shaped cookie cutter. Bake at 325°F for 10 to 15 minutes.

### Heart Sandwiches.

Using cookie cutters, let the children cut out hearts from pieces of soft bread. Spread the hearts with tuna, egg salad, or deviled ham. Sprinkle sprouts on top of their sandwiches, if you like. Save bread trimmings for use in puddings, or to take outside to feed to the birds. Children enjoy this activity and it can be adapted to many other special occasions by using special cookie cutters for each holiday.

### Valentine Punch.

Ingredients:
1 large can unsweetened pineapple juice
6 cups water
1 small package unsweetened punch drink mix

Procedure:

Mix ingredients together, stir, and serve with ice—a real valentine favorite with its pretty red color and delicious taste. (Makes 24 four-ounce servings or 12 eight-ounce servings)

### Valentine Gelatin Hearts.

Ingredients:
1 cup apple juice concentrate
2 cups water
2 envelopes plain gelatin
1 teaspoon unsweetened raspberry drink mix (red color)

Procedure:

1. Bring apple juice concentrate and 1 cup water to a boil in a pan.
2. Sprinkle contents from two envelopes of plain gelatin into a bowl.
3. Add drink mix.
4. Pour in heated liquid and stir until gelatin is dissolved.
5. Add 1 cup cold water.
6. Pour the mixture into a rectangular cake pan that has been sprayed with a vegetable spray. Chill.
7. When set, cut out hearts with a cookie cutter. Carefully lift the hearts out with a small pancake turner and place them on a salad plate.
8. Hearts can be served plain or placed on a lettuce leaf, spread with mayonnaise, and topped with chopped nuts.

# ADDITIONAL READINGS

**Books for Children**

Ancona, George. *I Feel.* New York: Dutton, 1977.

Budney, Blossom. *A Kiss Is Round.* New York: Dutton, 1980.

Cohen, Miriam. *Bee My Valentine.* New York: Dell, 1983.

Marshall, James. *George and Martha.* Boston: Houghton, 1972.

————.*George and Martha Encore.* Boston: Houghton, 1973.

Schwartz, Amy. *Bea and Mr. Jones.* New York: Bradbury, 1982.

Schweninger, A. *The Hunt for Rabbit's Galosh.* New York: Doubleday, 1976.

Watson, Clyde. *Catch Me and Kiss Me and Say It Again.* New York: Philomel, 1978.

Williams, Garth. *Rabbit's Wedding.* New York: Harper, 1958.

# UNIT 28
# Spring and Summer Holidays

## SPRING HOLIDAYS

**Easter.**    Easter celebrates the end of winter and the coming of spring. This is an excellent time to teach about the beauty of the renewal of life by celebrating such springtime rites as planting seeds and enjoying baby animals. Traditional Easter customs include the visit of the Easter bunny, giving baskets of candy, decorating brightly colored eggs, feasting with family and friends, and hunting for Easter eggs. The Easter bunny, Easter eggs, and the Easter egg tree are customs brought to this country from Germany.

People dressed in spring clothes attend church services or join the Easter parade, while children in the nation's capital participate in the egg-rolling race on the lawn at the White House.

**Easter Customs Around the World.**    Christians around the world celebrate Easter at churches and sunrise services. The following are some other ways people around the world celebrate this season.

*England.*    Many years ago it was the custom for the English queen or king to wash the feet of the poor on the Thursday before Easter. A queen would wash the feet of as many poor people as her age in years. This, of course, is no longer done today.

*Greece.*    People carry candles that are lighted at midnight services on Easter Eve. The worshipers leave with their lighted candles. Many believe it is good luck to keep them burning until they reach home.

*France.*    In France, the church bells are silent from Good Friday until Easter morning. Legend has it that the bells are silent because they go to Rome and come back bringing gifts. When the bells ring on Easter, children rush outside to collect the Easter eggs and candy that have fallen from the sky.

*Spain.*    Spain is famous for its long parades with religious floats and thousands of marchers. These are held the week before Easter. Some people dress in native costumes and go to fairs held on Easter or the days following. Here they enjoy dancing and visiting with friends.

*Germany.*    Many people think it is good luck to eat a green food on the Thursday before Easter. At one time, some people even believed that if they didn't eat a green salad on that day, they would turn into donkeys.

**FIGURE 28–1  Making one's own Easter decorations is a source of fun for children.**

*Australia.* The seasons for the continent down under are different from ours. While we are welcoming spring, it is fall in Australia. Many people go camping during the Easter holidays.

*Norway.* Norway has a long, five-day national holiday at Easter time. Many Norwegians enjoy skiing in the mountains. Some ski trails feature open-air chapels for worship.

*Uruguay.* In Uruguay, *Semana Criolla* (Creole Week) coincides with Holy Week. It is a special time set aside to celebrate the Uruguayan gaucho heritage. Roping and riding shows and traditional gaucho music are features throughout the week.

*Mexico.* Holy Week in Mexico is filled with special events. Thursday in Holy Week is the day on which thousands visit the altars at different beautifully ornamented churches. On the day before Easter, the ceremony of the Burning of Judas takes place, a custom observed more so in Mexico City than anywhere else in Mexico. Toys made of cardboard representing men and animals, with firecrackers attached, are sold in great quantities for this ceremony. These figures are suspended in courtyards or outside the corridors of homes. At the stroke of ten, when the church bells are heard, the figures are lighted and burned. In some streets large figures, some 6 or 7 feet high, made of straw or rags, and dressed to represent men, are hung up in the streets. These figures also contain firecrackers. There is a deafening noise when the burning of "Judas" occurs. The ritual burning is done as a reminder and condemnation of the betrayal of Jesus by Judas, an apostle and companion.

*Venezuela.* On the evening of Easter Sunday in Venezuela, Judas the Apostle is burned in effigy in an event known as *la quema de Judas.* In hundreds of communities throughout the land, the ritual execution of Judas marks a joyous end to the Lenten period. In contrast to the complex and religious devotionals of Lent, Judas burnings take place at the neighborhood level. The "Judas," as the effigy is called, is a life-sized figure stuffed with rags or straw.

At the end of parading, dancing, and group singing festivities, the "Judas" is doused with kerosene or gasoline and set on fire. Fireworks concealed inside the "Judas" go off in every direction. It is a very loud and exciting end to the Easter celebration.

*Brazil.* Just before Lent, in late February, everyone in Brazil celebrates "Carnaval" (Carnival). For four days and five nights, people fill the streets, eating, drinking, and dancing to samba music. Carnaval ends on Ash Wednesday. People from all over the world visit Rio de Janeiro, Brazil, during Carnaval. Neighborhoods (*favelas*) organize into groups called samba "schools," containing up to 3,000 dancers and musicians. They practice songs, skits, and dances for the many prizes awarded during the carnival. During Carnaval, judges vote on the dancing, floats, costumes, and music. Streetcars are decorated for the occasion. Businesses and stores close for the four days of Carnaval. But by noon on Ash Wednesday, the first day of Lent, the quiet period preceding Easter begins in Brazil.

*Vietnam.* In Vietnam, the unicorn is a symbol of springtime, similar to the bunny in the United States and Europe. The unicorn is considered by the Vietnamese to be a very shy, magical creature. The people of Vietnam celebrate a spring holiday called "Tet Nhat." During Tet Nhat, a person dressed as a unicorn dances down the street, while drums boom and cymbals clash to welcome spring. Fireworks burst in the air. People happily greet the unicorn as a symbol of the new season. Families hang money and vegetables from balconies, and the unicorn climbs poles to reach these gifts. The unicorn visits the new crops in the fields and the farm animals, bringing good luck to all living things.

*China.* "Ch'ing Ming," the celebration of trees, welcomes springtime in China. For three days before the festival, people eat only cold food so that they do not have to burn any wood. During this time, families prepare for Ch'ing Ming with quiet picnics on the grass. When the day of the festival arrives, delicious feasts are the custom in Chinese families. Another important part of this Chinese spring festival is the planting of new trees.

*India.* In India, trees are planted during a spring festival called "Kalpa Vruksha." A special young tree, which is just beginning to sprout leaves, is chosen on this festival day. Indians decorate this young tree, called the "Wishing Tree," with fruits and flowers. Children who have made wishes during the long, winter months gather under the tree. On Kalpa Vruksha, these wishes come true, and children are given presents of candy, new books, toys, and fresh fruit.

*Iran.* The first day of spring in Iran is also the first day of the new year. On the last Wednesday of the old year, each family lights a bonfire. Everyone jumps over the fire. Parties are held to celebrate the New Year and the first day of spring.

*Japan.* The day before spring in Japan, February 3, is the bean-throwing festival of "Setsu Bun." The Japanese believe that the beans will drive out the bad spirits of winter that keep spring away. The bean-throwers shout, "Out with the demons!" and "Come in good spirits!" Children play a game called "Oni Gokko." In this Japanese game, one person dresses as a spirit or *oni*. The *oni* tries to catch the other players. Sometimes the *oni* is blindfolded and must catch someone by listening to footsteps and reaching out.

Another Japanese holiday, O'bon, is important to Japanese Buddhists. It is celebrated in the middle of July or August and honors the spirits of dead friends and family. Over the three days of the O'bon festival, Japanese Buddhists welcome the spirits of the dead back into the family home for a joyful celebration. In order that all the family can be together at this time, many people return to their family homes. On the first day of the O'bon festival, the family will go out to clean and tidy the graves of their ancestors. When they return home, herbs and flowers are placed on the household shrine to welcome the spirits into the house. At each meal over the three days of O'bon, food will be set aside for the spirits.

The second day of O'bon begins with a time for thought about the fate that awaits the spirit after death. Buddhists believe people's spirits are reborn after death and go to a better or worse life, depending on the person's past behavior. Sometimes, ceremonies are performed that will give the spirits better luck in their new life. Later on the second day, people join other families for dancing and a celebration meal.

O'bon ends on the third day, when fires are lit to guide the spirits on their journey home. Sometimes, these fires are built on rafts and are left to float away on rivers or out to sea.

*Ghana.* "Apoo" is a New Year's festival celebrated in Ghana. It lasts 13 days, ending the day after the spring equinox. On each of the first 11 days of Apoo, different dances are performed: some to drive away evil, some to honor ancestral spirits, and some to bring good fortune and a rich harvest in the new year. On the twelfth day of Apoo, the shrines of the spirits are taken by procession to a river where they are washed, so they may end the old year free from the memory of any bad events.

Apoo ends with a ceremony to welcome the new year. When the festival was celebrated mainly in country villages, these ceremonies included the killing of animals as sacrifices to the spirits. Today, many of those villages have grown into towns, and the sacrifice of animals has been replaced by offerings of specially cooked vegetables like yams.

Apoo celebrations are, in one way, similar to other spring festivals like April Fools' Day. People can say what they like about each other without fear of punishment during Apoo. Traditionally, people speak out about the behavior of their government or make fun of important and powerful people, but Apoo is also a chance for people to make public any complaint they have against another person. By talking about their problems in public, people are supposed to settle their arguments and enter the new year in friendship.

*Thailand.* To celebrate spring in Thailand, people "break the ice" by throwing perfumed water during "Songkran," their national spring festival. Songkran begins when the new moon appears in the April sky and lasts for three days. Huge parades fill the streets with flowers, music, and dance. The Queen of the Water Festival marches in the parade, and participants in the Songkran parade spray perfumed water on the people who line the streets to watch.

*Zimbabwe.* In Zimbabwe, Whitsunday (what U.S. Christians call Pentecost), is celebrated on the seventh Sunday after Easter. In Zimbabwe, it is a grand holiday lasting two days. On Sunday, special church services feature old customs that the ancestors of white Zimbabweans brought to Africa with them. One of these ancient customs is to decorate churches with branches and scatter flowers on the church floors. A happy time, Whitsunday features dramas, dances, and special foods, especially sweets. Some Zimbabweans follow the custom of wearing only brand-new clothes on Whitsunday, hoping to bring good luck for the following year. Farmers believe that if the weather is good on Whitsunday, there will be a big harvest.

The Monday after Whitsunday in Zimbabwe is a school and work holiday. It is customary for many Zimbabweans to take a two-day holiday on Whitsunday Monday and Tuesday. Those who can afford it sometimes plan Whitsunday trips across the country or even into neighboring countries.

**St. Patrick's Day.** In the United States, Saint Patrick's Day is celebrated March 17, with much merrymaking. Everyone joins in the "wearing of the green." In New York, and in other large cities, children and adults line the streets to watch the St. Patrick's Day parade. People wear green hats and wave Irish flags as the marching bands pass by playing tunes such as "MacNamara's Band" and "When Irish Eyes Are Smiling." Sometimes green lines are painted down the middle of the streets, and there are always people dressed in imaginative green costumes to entertain the crowds.

**Mother's and Father's Days.** Celebrating these days with young children can contribute to an understanding and valuing of family relationships—and it is an opportunity for children to reciprocate parental affection.

Now, with so many single parents, such days take on a very special meaning to parents—as well as to children—and special sensitivity is required because of this. Be sure to avoid the assumption that all the children in your group have both parents readily available. By that time of the year, teachers usually know who serves as a surrogate parent if the natural parent is not present. They can then propose that the child make a present for that person instead. Making two cards can offer support to children whose family structure differs from those of their classmates.

**Lei Day: A Hawaiian Celebration.** May 1 is Lei Day in Hawaii, when children and adults all wear colorful "leis" (garlands of flowers) draped over their shoulders. Leis express the "aloha spirit" of Hawaii, a spirit of friendship and love. Lei Day is celebrated everywhere on the islands with lei displays and contests. For the children, there are pageants and programs that include music, singing, and hula dancing. The hula dancers, wearing leis and grass skirts, gracefully move their hips while acting out the words of songs with their hands. Dancers are usually accompanied by musicians who play guitars and ukeleles, and beat out rhythms with drums, bamboo sticks, and gourd rattles. Hula dances tell stories about beautiful things in nature like the sand and the sea, the warm trade winds, the swaying palms, and the mist-covered mountains.

**Inter-Tribal Indian Ceremonial.** In the American Southwest, a highlight of the year for Native American children is the four-day Inter-Tribal Indian Ceremonial, beginning on the second Thursday in August. Native American artists, dancers, and rodeo cowboys from more than 50 tribes gather in the town of Gallup, New Mexico, to celebrate their traditions and cultures and to perform for visitors from around the world. Events include the Ceremonial Showroom, where the finest work of Native American artists and craftspeople are displayed; and the marketplace, where weavers, potters, silversmiths, and other Native American artists are at work making items for sale. Another event is the All-Indian Rodeo, in which cowboys compete at roping, steer wrestling, and bronco and bull riding, hoping to win one of the coveted silver belt buckles that are awarded as prizes. Traditional Native American dances are also an important part of the Ceremonial. The Hoop, Deer, Buffalo, and other dances are performed by costumed dancers from many different tribes. On Saturday morning of the Ceremonial, downtown Gallup fills with the sounds of drums and bells as dancers parade through the streets along with tribal bands playing traditional and contemporary music. Sometimes children and their families dress in their native clothing and join the parade.

**Tu B'Shvat—New Year of Trees.** Jews celebrate Tu B'Shvat or the New Year of Trees, marking the beginning of spring.

Trees have always been an important symbol in the Jewish religion. They stand for what is good and noble and worthwhile in life. Every year on this day, boys and girls parade through the streets of Israel, carrying spades, hoes, and watering cans. Later they go to the fields and plant trees, amid dancing and singing. Afterward they enjoy playing active outdoor games. In Israel, trees are especially important, since the land is dry and there is seldom rain.

In other lands, Jews mark this festival by eating fruits, such as oranges, figs, or pomegranates, that grow in Israel.

**Passover.** Passover commemorates the escape of the Israelites from their bondage in Egypt and the end of a 430-year period of slavery. This Jewish feast falls sometime after the first full moon of spring.

The name *Passover,* and the festival's present meaning, refers to God's sending an angel to slay the first-born son in every Egyptian household, while "passing over" the homes of the Jews.

The traditional meal during Passover is called the "seder." Before eating the traditional dinner, the Haggadah, which is the story of the Exodus, is read. The celebration of Passover commemorates the unity of the Jews through the centuries, since there has been a spring festival in the Jewish tradition since the time when they were still wandering shepherds in the desert with no thought of a national identity.

In all spring holidays, the teacher of young children should involve them in the festivities at their level. While the children may hear the traditional stories on which these holidays are based, they may not be old enough to grasp their significance in a historic or religious sense. This does not mean that young children do not enjoy these festive times. Their involvement in the concrete, visible symbols of the holidays, such as special foods, traditional stories, games, and activities are all ways to involve them at their level. In drawing and painting activities, some topics on spring holidays are:

- Planting Trees in Israel
- Digging, Planting, Singing, and Dancing during Tu B'Shvat
- The Passover Story
- The Passover Meal
- Decorating Eggs for Easter
- Shopping for Easter
- A Beautiful Egg Tree
- A Visit from the Easter Bunny
- My Easter Basket
- Walking in the Easter Parade
- What My Mother/Father Does
- I Love Dad/Mom Because . . .
- What Is Special About My Dad/Mom
- The St. Patrick's Day Parade
- Hawaiian Dancers and Flower Garlands or "Leis"
- Native American Costumes and Dances

## ART ACTIVITIES FOR EASTER

**Decorating Eggs.** It can be difficult to control the dyeing of eggs if everyone is allowed to crowd around and slosh eggs in the dye at the same time. The best procedure is to bring to each snack table a tray with enough eggs for two per child and cups of various colored dyes from which the children may choose. When the eggs are bright enough, they can be spooned out and put in egg cartons to dry.

If an egg hunt is planned, it is necessary to hide eggs in different areas for different age children. Otherwise the fours will find all the "easy" ones immediately, and the threes will be frustrated. You may wish to separate age groups and also explain in advance that each child may find only two dyed eggs to keep and as many foil-wrapped eggs as they can locate. This works out better for everyone (except the two-year-olds, who might think that anything wrapped in foil must be litter!).

Several ideas for egg decoration are:

1. Make an interesting line design on an egg by wrapping rubber bands or string around the hard-boiled egg, dipping it in dye or paint, and removing the string when dry.
2. Stipple-design the egg with a piece of cotton or a sponge dipped in dye or food coloring; more than one color may be used. This can complete the decoration, or be the beginning of a more elaborate design.
3. Decorate eggs with ribbon, braid, sequins, little beads, or metallic foil.
4. Draw directly on eggshells with crayon, then dip the eggs in dye to create a resist effect.
5. Paint free, spontaneous designs in brilliant colors.

**Natural Dyes for Easter Eggs.**
Materials:
Coffee or tea—brown
Beets—deep red
Yellow onions—yellow
Cranberries—light red
Spinach leaves—green
Red onions—blue
Blackberries—blue
Blueberries—blue

Procedure:
1. Pick two or three colors from the above list. Make several natural dyes by boiling fruits or vegetables in small amounts of water.
2. Let the children put a cool hard-boiled egg in a nylon stocking and dip it into the dye. Keep the egg in the dye for several minutes.
3. Pull out the nylon, and check the color. If it is dark enough, remove the egg and put it on a paper towel to dry.

**Egg Instruments.**
Materials: Egg-shaped pantyhose containers, glue, permanent markers (assorted colors), materials to make a variety of sounds (such as popcorn kernels, sand, beans, paper clips, macaroni).

Procedure: Make several instruments to demonstrate various sounds. Assemble materials. Fill an egg with a noise-making material. Glue egg shut. Allow to dry. Decorate with markers. Explain to the children how various materials make different sounds. Let them guess what the sample eggs are filled with.

**Egg Portraits.** On hard-boiled eggs, make facial features with crayons or cut paper. Make ears, hair, collar, and hat with scraps of cloth, yarn, string, or paper to complete the deisgn.

Eggs can be displayed sitting in a section of an egg carton, in a bottle cap, or in a ring of construction paper.

**Pattern Eggs.** Equipment: Cardboard, fabric or wallpaper, glue. Cut out large cardboard eggs. Glue on fabric or wallpaper. Trim edges and cut each egg in half. Make six to ten different eggs. Mix up the egg halves. For a game, children sort out the egg halves and match up the egg patterns.

**Easter Bunny Basket.** Draw and cut ears from open end of flattened, white lunch bag. Add facial features to unfolded side of bag. Unfold bag and attach paper strip for handle.

**Bunny Jar.** Equipment: Baby food jars with lids, yarn pom-poms (purchased or made at home), white glue, pipe cleaners, odds and ends of buttons. Child glues pom-pom onto the lid of a baby food jar. Ears

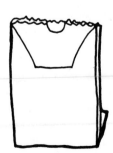 

**FIGURE 28–2 Easter bunny basket.**

**FIGURE 28–3 Bunny jar.**

**FIGURE 28–4 Egg tree.**

5. Insert a piece of string or wire through the holes, making a knot or loop at one end. If eggs are to be dyed, this must be done before removing the contents.

**Mr. and Mrs. Rabbit.** Use small, cardboard towel tubes for bodies. Decorate with construction paper. Add ears, whiskers, and a tail to complete the design.

**Cracked Eggs.** Draw a large egg on white or pink construction paper. Decorate it with crayons, magic markers, or tempera paint. Cut out the egg. Cut across the egg with a jagged line to make it look cracked. Secure halves at one corner with a brad or tack. Use scrap paper to make a chick. Glue chick to bottom half of egg.

**Easter Baskets.**
Procedure:
1. Easter baskets can be made from many different kinds of materials: paper cones or box shapes constructed from paper; plastic or waxed cardboard refrigerator containers such as margarine or cottage cheese tubs; plastic bottles cut to various shapes; milk or orange juice cartons cut down; paper baking or drinking cups. Suitable containers also include oatmeal boxes cut in half, plastic tomato racks or berry boxes, small food cartons, frozen pie tins, plastic detergent bottles cut down to a basket shape, and egg cartons cut in half.

made of pipe cleaners can then be attached. Buttons, glued on, make eyes and other features. These can be filled with candy for gifts at Easter or Christmas.

**Egg Tree (Five years and older)** Procedure:
1. Place a small branch in a vase or set it into a box of sand or plaster of Paris.
2. The tree can be trimmed with eggs cut from construction paper that has been decorated with metallic foil, tissue paper, or paper lace.
3. Hard-boiled eggs can be hung when wrapped with ribbon or string, leaving a loop at one end.
4. To blow out a raw egg, shake it a few times to loosen the membrane. Make a hole at either end, and blow steadily into one of the openings.

2. Decorate baskets with construction paper, wallpaper, ribbon, braid, discarded flowers, or feathers.
3. Interesting objects found in Easter baskets may include chicks, bunnies, and eggs modeled in clay or made of cut paper, settled in curled tissue grass.
4. String, yarn, pipe cleaners, or construction paper strips can be used as basket handles.
5. Any type of scrap materials make good decorations, so do dried macaroni, egg shells, and many other items.

## Mosaic Egg.
Procedure:
1. Cut white drawing paper into egg shape.
2. Brush surface with water.
3. Cut out small pieces of colored tissue paper. Cover egg with tissue paper scraps. (These may be torn pieces, too.)
4. Brush entire surface with water and let dry.
5. Remove tissue paper pieces. Colors in tissue will "bleed" onto egg.

## Easter Parade.
Procedure:
1. Draw figures dressed in their Sunday best, and cut them out.
2. Cut cardboard tubes into sections, and fasten them to the base of the parade figures so they can stand freely.
3. Display the Easter Parade on a table or counter top.
4. Make a background for the figures by folding construction paper in accordion folds.
5. Cut rooftops along one end to indicate a city scene.

## Chick in an Egg.
Procedure:
1. Use the upper half of an empty eggshell, leaving enough room to hold a little chick.
2. Fasten the shell to sit upright in a ring of paper and fill the shell with paper grass.
3. Chicks may be modeled in clay or made of cut paper.

## Funny Bunny.
Procedure:
1. Model a bunny from a large wad of shredded paper.
2. Wind white thread or string around to hold the shape of the body, head, legs, and tail as they are formed.
3. Ears, eyes, and whiskers can be made of cut paper glued in place.

## Easter Bunnies.
Materials: Paper, scissors, colored paper, staples, glue

Procedure:
1. Take a rectangular piece of paper and roll it into a cylinder.
2. Staple it or paste it together.
3. From another piece of paper, cut out ears and attach (paste) them to the cylinder. The ears will look more realistic if they are creased down the center before they are attached.
4. Using colored paper, add eyes, nose, mouth, eyelashes, and a tail. (Cotton balls are even better for tails!)

## Cut-Paper Bunnies and Baskets.
Have children either cut or tear colored construction paper into egg shapes. They then fill a paper basket with the colored paper eggs.

## Miniature Easter Hats. Procedure:
1. Save empty plastic cream containers from restaurants.
2. Cut small (1½ inch–2 inch diameter) circles out of colored paper.
3. Glue the cream container onto these circles.
4. A small artificial flower may be glued on for an added decoration.
5. These may also be hung on the Egg Tree, described on page 570.

## Paper Plate Bunnies.
1. Use plain, white, dinner-size paper plates.
2. Have the children cut ears, nose, eyes, mouth, and eyelashes from colored construction paper.
3. Paste the features onto the paper plate.

**FIGURE 28–5 Cut-paper bunny.**

**FIGURE 28–6 Miniature Easter hats.**

4. Punch a hole for string and hang for room decorations.

## Easter Special.
Procedure:
1. Circle Easter on the calendar. Invite children to relate the events if their families have special activities at Easter time.
2. Display a large cutout of an Easter basket.
3. Give the children large paper egg shapes of different colors.
4. On the paper eggs, the teacher can write (older children may do their own writing) Easter activities such as going to church, visiting grandparents, dyeing eggs, etc. Then the children may decorate the eggs as they wish and pin them on the basket.

## Egg Shapes.
Procedure:
1. Collect 10 or more egg shapes, plastic Easter toys, pantyhose packages, or egg cartons.
2. Mark a different numeral on the top half of each egg and the same numeral on its bottom half.
3. Separate the halves and mix them together. The

**FIGURE 28–7 Paper plate bunny.**

children make eggs by finding the matching numerals.

## Paper Bag Bunnies.
Procedure:
1. Stuff two large paper bags with crumpled newspaper, ending up with rounded shapes.
2. Partially fill two other paper bags and twist for ears.
3. Cover with layers of papier-mâché, using a flour and water paste and strips of newspaper. Be sure the strips dry between layers.
4. Cover with cotton tufts.
5. Poke holes in the rabbit's head and insert ears (also covered with papier-mâché). Add construction paper features.

## Yarn-Covered Eggs.
Obtain unused white styrofoam meat trays from the grocery store and use them to make yarn-covered eggs. Gather an assortment of colored yarn, scissors, and tape. For each child, cut an egg shape out of a white styrofoam tray or a white sheet of carboard. Cut slits around the edges of the egg shapes. Cut yarn into manageable lengths. Tape one end of a piece of yarn to the back of each egg shape and pull it through one of the slits. Let the children wind yarn around their egg shapes, each time passing the yarn through one of the slits. Encourage them to crisscross the yarn in any way they wish to create designs. When the children have finished eggs to their satisfaction, trim the ends of the yarn and tape them back.

## Color of Spring.
Procedure:
1. Cut out color pictures of spring scenes and hang them around the room.
2. Ask the children why they think these particular pictures were hung around the room today.
3. Encourage the children to see on the calendar that March 21 is the first day of spring, and that these are pictures of spring.
4. Ask volunteers to point out areas of red, blue, green, and yellow in the pictures.
5. Help the class determine which color is used most in spring pictures, and which color is second.

6. Provide time for the children to draw their own spring pictures.

## Egg Personalities.
Procedure:
1. Egg personalities can be made from hard-boiled eggs that are painted, bewigged, and dressed with cloth or paper scraps.
2. Make stands from inverted sections of an egg carton.
3. Construction-paper rings or decorated small juice cans complete the project.

# GAMES AND MOVEMENT EXPERIENCES FOR EASTER

In a discussion with the children at Easter time, make a list of feelings and objects that describe the holiday. Then have the children use movement to express these ideas. Encourage creativity. Several ideas are:

| | | |
|---|---|---|
| rabbits | nests | windy |
| eggs | spring flowers | coloring |

**Egg Roll.** Have the children curl up into balls as round as they can, and roll on the floor, trying to roll forward, sideways, and backward.

**Easter Parade.** Wearing Easter hats decorated by themselves, the children march around the room to the music of a radio or record player. Next, the children "dance" to the music. Children enjoy waving old scarves, flags, feathers, or bells as they dance. Each child can move about in her own particular way. An old pair of tap shoes adds an exciting variation.

**Everyone Do This.** Children take turns doing something active (hopping like a bunny, clapping hands, turning around) while others imitate. Everyone sings:

Everybody do this, do this, do this,
Everybody do this, just like me.

Variation: Same action but different words:

Simon says do this, do this, do this,
Simon says do this, just like me.

**Here We Go 'Round the Bunny's House.** Sung
to the tune "Here we go 'Round the Mulberry
Bush," modify the song and games as follows:

Here we go 'round the bunny's house (etc.)
This is the way we color eggs (etc.)
This is the way we dress so nice (etc.)

**In the Bunny Patch.** Sing to the tune "Paw Paw
Patch."
Let's go look for Easter eggs
Let's go look for Easter eggs
Let's go look for Easter eggs
Way down yonder in the Bunny Patch.

Picking up eggs and put 'em in my basket
Picking up eggs and put 'em in my basket
Picking up eggs and put 'em in my basket
Way down yonder in the Bunny Patch.

Little red eggs, in my basket
Little red eggs, in my basket
Little red eggs, in my basket
Way down yonder in the Bunny Patch.

**Easter Bunny Soft and White.** Sung to the tune
of "Twinkle, Twinkle, Little Star."
Easter Bunny, soft and white,
Hopping quickly out of sight.
Thank you for the eggs you bring,
At Easter time we welcome spring.
Easter Bunny, soft and white.
Hopping quickly out of sight.

---

# POEMS AND FINGERPLAYS
# FOR EASTER

### The Easter Rabbit
The Easter Rabbit keeps a very
Cheerful hen that likes to lay

Blue and red and green and yellow
Eggs for him on Easter Day.

He puts the eggs inside his basket
With a lot of other things,
Bunnies with pink ears and whiskers,
Little chicks with tickling wings.

Then on tip-toe he comes hopping
Hiding secrets everywhere,
Speckled eggs behind the mirror
Sugar bird nests in the chair.

If we saw him we would give him
Tender lettuce leaves to eat.
But he slips out very softly
On pussy-willow feet.

### The Bunny
Tall ears,
Twinkly nose,
Tiny tail,
And hop he goes!

His ears are long,
His tail is small,
And he doesn't make
Any noise at all.
(Repeat the first verse)

### Easter
I'm sure a bunny
Must remember
Everything he's told
Because his ears
Are oh, so large,
Just think how much they hold!

### The Bunny
Here is a bunny, with ears so funny
   (Fingers form ears, hands for head)
And here is a hole in the ground.
   (Hand on hip forms hole in ground)
When a slight noise he hears,
He pricks up his ears,
And jumps in the hole in the ground.

### Mr. Easter Bunny
Mr. Easter Rabbit goes hip, hop, hip.
   (Extend index and middle finger and make hand
      hop)
See how his ears flip, flop, flip.
   (Place hands on head and move them forward and
      backward)
See how his eyes go blink, blink, blink.
   (Blink eyes)
See how his nose goes twink, twink, twink.
   (Wiggle nose with finger)

Stroke his warm coat soft and furry.
  (Stroke fist)
Hip, hop, hip, he's off in a hurry
  (Extend two fingers and hop)

**Two Brave Bunnies**
Hoppity, hop, hop; hoppity, hop, hop;
Hoppity, hop, hop. (three times) (Make a bunny of
  each fist, with two fingers for ears)
"I can hop high!" cried Bunny Number one,
And he hopped and he hopped in the light of the
  sun.
  ("Hop" right hand)
"I can hop low," cried Bunny Number Two,
But she stubbed her toe on a drop of dew.
  ("Hop" left hand; make bunny "fall")
Now these bunnies hopped in the cool, fresh air
Until they saw a fox sneak out of his lair.
Then they hopped and they hopped to their home,
  sweet home,
And promised their mother no more to roam.
  (Make bunnies again and have them hop home.)

*Suggestion:* The children may name the bunnies,
voting on the most appropriate names. Two children
can act out the roles of the bunnies, repeating the
words of each. Another child may be the fox. The
class may tell and act out other ways bunnies hop,
and give them names, too.

**Wiggle Song**
(Children sitting very quietly at beginning)
My thumbs are starting to wiggle,
  (Wiggle thumbs)
My thumbs are starting to wiggle,
My thumbs are starting to wiggle,
  Around, around, around.
My hands are starting to wiggle (three times)
  (Wiggle hands)
  Around, around, around.
My arms are starting to wiggle (three times)
  (Wiggle arms)
  Around, around, around.
My head is starting to wiggle (three times)
  (Wiggle head)
  Around, around, around.
Now all of me is wiggling (three times)
  (Wiggle entire body)
  Around, around, around.

Children can suggest other parts of the body—
nose, feet, etc.—to add to the song. Read *Humbug
Rabbit,* by Lorna Balian (Abdingdon, 1974).

## COOKING EXPERIENCES FOR EASTER

**Hot Cross Buns.** Cooking hot cross buns at Easter
is an old English custom.
Ingredients:
1 cup warm milk
½ cup sugar
3 tablespoons melted butter
½ teaspoon salt
1 package dry yeast
1 egg, well beaten
3 cups flour
½ teaspoon cinnamon
½ cup raisins
½ teaspoon ground cloves
*Frosting*
½ cup confectioner's sugar
3 tablespoons milk

Procedure:
  1. Preheat oven to 400°F.
  2. Mix together milk, sugar, butter, salt, yeast, and
     egg.
  3. Add flour, cinnamon, raisins, and cloves. Mix
     well.
  4. Grease hands with margarine or oil and knead
     the dough.
  5. Cover the bowl with a cloth and let the dough
     rise in a warm place for about a half-hour.
  6. Form dough into eight round balls the size of
     your fist and place on a greased cookie sheet.
  7. Let the dough rise another half-hour.
  8. Brush the top of each bun lightly with water.
  9. Bake in a 400°F oven for 20 minutes.
 10. Mix the confectioner's sugar and 3 tablespoons
     milk to form a smooth paste. After the buns are
     done and still warm, paint a white "X" or cross
     on the top of each.

**Cole Slaw.**
Ingredients:
a small head of cabbage, grated
1 small onion, chopped fine (or 1 tablespoon dried,
chopped onion)
1 tablespoon sugar

2 tablespoons mayonnaise
salt and pepper to taste

Equipment: knife for chopping onion, grater, measuring spoons, mixing spoon, mixing bowl

Procedure:
1. Chop the onion. If dried onions are being used, simply measure the amount needed.
2. Grate the cabbage.
3. Put everything in the mixing bowl and mix well.
4. Chill before serving.

A good story to read in association with this activity is *The Tale of Peter Rabbit* by Beatrix Potter.

## Easter Bunny Salad.

Ingredients:
lettuce leaves (enough for one apiece)
pear halves (enough for one apiece)
whole cloves (enough for two eyes per child)
almond halves (enough for two ears per child)
cottage cheese (1 teaspoon per child)

Procedure:
1. Put a lettuce leaf on a plate.
2. Put a pear half upside down on top of the lettuce leaf.
3. Add 2 whole cloves for eyes and 2 almond halves for ears.
4. Add 1 teaspoon cottage cheese for a tail.

## Charoses (A Passover Treat).

Ingredients:
¼ cup finely chopped walnuts
1 finely chopped or grated apple
¼ cup grape juice
1 teaspoon cinnamon

Procedure:
Let the children try this simple version of Charoses, a Jewish Passover treat eaten during the reading of the Haggadah. Mix the above ingredients together and spread on matzoh (unleavened bread available at most grocery stores).

## Cheesy Carrots (Snack Time).

Ingredients:
yellow cheese, grated (such as cheddar, American, colby)
cream or mayonnaise

Equipment: grater, mixing bowl, mixing spoon

Procedure:
1. Let the children grate the cheese into the mixing bowl. (A blender is faster, but less fun.)
2. Mix the shredded cheese with just a little cream or mayonnaise until the mixture can be shaped with the hands.
3. Shape into tiny carrots.
4. Put a sprig of parsley on the end of each cheese carrot.

A natural follow-up to this activity is to read *The Carrot Seed* by Ruth Krauss (Scholastic Book Services, 1945).

## Green Eggs and Ham.

Ingredients:
1 teaspoon vegetable oil
1 teaspoon chopped green onions
1 teaspoon chopped green peppers
3 teaspoons chopped spinach
1 tablespoon chopped ham
1 egg
1 teaspoon milk
salt and pepper

Procedure:
1. Sauté onion, peppers, and chopped ham in a pan with a small amount of oil.
2. Stir in spinach and add the egg, which has first been mixed with the milk.
3. Add salt and pepper to taste, stirring constantly with a pancake turner. (The green onions and peppers are not necessary if your child does not care for them. Use instead green food coloring added to the egg mixture.) Makes one serving.

To make these green eggs and ham a memorable experience, read Dr. Seuss's *Green Eggs and Ham* before this cooking experience.

**Carrot Salad.**

Ingredients:

4 large carrots
½ cup seedless raisins
½ cup chopped peanuts
¾ teaspoon salt, dash of pepper
1 tablespoon lemon juice
1 cup sour cream

Materials: Knife for chopping peanuts (or a nut chopper), vegetable parer for scraping carrots, grater (or blender), measuring cup, measuring spoons, mixing bowl

Procedure:

1. Let the children chop the nuts in a nut chopper or even in a blender.
2. Wash and scrape the carrots.
3. Grate the carrots.
4. Mix everything together and serve with sour cream, or mix a few tablespoons of sour cream into the salad before serving.

Read *The Carrot Seed* for this activity, too.

**FIGURE 28–8 Shamrock person.**

## ST. PATRICK'S DAY ACTIVITIES

**Shamrock People.**  Give each child a shamrock cut out of green construction paper. Also provide black construction paper, paste, crayons, and scraps of construction paper in various colors. The shamrock becomes the body, and the black paper is cut in strips to make arms and legs. Mittens and shoes can be cut out of the other paper scraps. A face can be drawn with crayons to complete the shamrock person.

**St. Patrick's Day Cone Hats.**  Make a hat for each child to wear in your group's own St. Patrick's Day Parade.

Procedure:

1. Cut a paper plate halfway through, roll it into a cone shape to fit the child's head, and tape the edges in place.
2. Set out glue and a variety of green materials (felt-tip markers, crepe paper strips, shamrock stickers,

glitter, etc.), and let the children use these materials to decorate their hats any way they wish.
3. When the children have finished, attach green yarn to the sides of the hats for ties.

**Sprouting Leprechauns.**  Gather together paper cups, potting soil, alfalfa seeds, green construction paper, cotton balls, scissors, glue, and water.

Procedure:

1. Help the children cut or tear eye and mouth shapes out of green construction paper, then paste these shapes onto the styrofoam cups to make a face. (Use the cotton balls to make "beards.")
2. When the paste has dried, fill the cups with potting soil, sprinkle alfalfa seeds onto the soil, and moisten with water.
3. Place the leprechaun cups in a sunny spot and have the children water them each day. Alfalfa seeds sprout quickly, so it won't be long before each leprechaun has a head of green sprouting "hair." (Recycled, thoroughly washed milk cartons also work nicely for this activity.)

**FIGURE 28–9 Digging and playing in soil are excellent springtime activities.**

**Shamrock Sprouts.** You will need to start this activity at least one week before St. Patrick's Day if you want your shamrocks to be green.

Procedure:

1. Cut a shamrock shape for each child out of a piece of terrycloth.
2. Have the children place their shamrocks in aluminum pie tins, add a little water, and sprinkle alfalfa seeds all over their shapes.
3. Place the pie tin in a sunny location and have the children regularly add water to keep the shapes moist. Let them observe during the week as the seeds sprout and turn their shamrocks green.

**Go for the Gold.** For this game, you will need a coffee can, one die, gold foil or yellow construction paper, black construction paper, scissors, and tape.

Procedure:

1. Tape the black construction paper around the coffee can to make a "pot of gold."
2. Make "gold pieces" by crumpling small squares of gold foil into balls or by cutting circles out of the yellow construction paper. Put the foil balls or yellow circles into the coffee can.
3. Choose one child to be the leprechaun, and have her sit in a chair, holding the "pot of gold." Let each child in turn walk up to the leprechaun and ask, "Leprechaun, will you give me some gold?" Have the leprechaun reply, "Yes, I will when a number I'm told."
4. The child rolls the die and names the number that comes up on it. The leprechaun give the child that number of "gold pieces."
5. Continue the game until everyone has had a turn, then choose one of the children who rolled a high number to be the next leprechaun.

**Leprechaun Hat.** Procedure:

1. Fold a 12″ × 18″ sheet of green construction paper to form a triangle.
2. On the portion of the paper extending beyond the triangle, pinch the edge at the center.
3. Draw a diagonal line from that center to each upper corner of the triangle.
4. Cut along the two lines.
5. Fold and paste down the triangle flap.
6. Curl the pasted peak with the scissor blades.
7. To make leprechaun ears, trace the child's hand on folded paper. (Fingers should be close together with the thumb tucked underneath.) Cut the hand shape from the folded paper to make a pair of ears. Cut a narrow hole in the center of each ear shape.

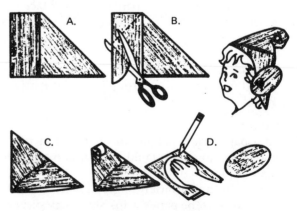

**FIGURE 28–10 Making a leprechaun hat.**

8. The children put on their hats and then slip on their "ears."

**The Greens.**

Purpose: To sharpen color discrimination.

Preparation: Circle Saint Patrick's Day on the calendar. Show and discuss the color (green) associated with this occasion.

Procedure:
1. Pin a piece of green paper on a bulletin board.
2. Have the children find green cloth and paper to cut pieces from and pin on the board. Allow the pieces to overlap to create a green collage.
3. Magazines and old wrapping paper provide good sources for "greens."
4. As a variation, use the previous three steps, but increase the level of difficulty. When the children find a green color, they must compare it with each cloth and paper piece on the board to make sure that the sample is not the same shade already displayed. If it is, then the color cannot be added to the collage.

**Saint Patrick's Day Hat.** Attach an 8″ × 10″ piece of green construction paper to a 2-inch-wide band cut to fit around the child's head. A small square may be pasted on to be a buckle ornament.

**Shamrock Posters.** Cut a shamrock shape out of heavy paper; let children decorate this with green construction-paper shamrocks, leprechauns, etc. For added effect, provide craft glue and glitter.

**Leprechaun Paper Dolls (Six years and up).** Accordian-fold strips of paper the width of the leprechaun pattern you choose. Cut out all around the pattern, except the parts on the fold, as shown in Figure 28–12.

**Shamrock Cutouts.** Follow the same procedure as in Leprechaun Paper Dolls, using a shamrock pattern instead.

**St. Patrick's Day Parade.** Using the hats made in any of the activities in this section, get each child

**FIGURE 28–11 St. Patrick's Day hat.**

dressed up to "parade" around the room for St. Patrick's Day. You may want to tie green crepe paper streamers onto the children's wrists in addition to their wearing their hats. Play a recording of Irish music (or any other marching-type music), and let the children parade around the room while playing rhythm instruments. (See Unit 17 for instructions on

**FIGURE 28–12 Leprechaun paper dolls.**

FOLD FOLD

CUT OUT LITTLE PIECE

DO NOT CUT FOLD

**FIGURE 28–13 Shamrock cut-out.**

making rhythm instruments.) If you like, you might want to tape a line of green crepe paper or yarn to the floor for the children to follow as they march.

### St. Patrick's Day Fingerplay.

On St. Patrick's Day we see shamrocks.

Count the leaflets–one, two, three. (Hold up three fingers of left hand. Count them by pointing to each one with index finger of right hand)

Like a hat with three feathers. (Hold up right hand to head, letting fingers represent feathers)

Like a coat with three buttons. (Pretend to pull imaginary coat together and button three bottons)

Like a stool with three legs. (Rest three fingers on flat surface)

Like a hat rack with three pegs. (Hold hand up with three fingers spread apart and curved)

### For St. Patrick's Day.

(Sung to the tune of "London Bridge Is Falling Down")

All the ants have worn green pants,

worn green pants,

worn green pants.

All the ants have worn green pants

for St. Patrick's Day!

Additional verses:

2. All the cats have worn green hats

3. All the ewes have worn green shoes

4. All the pigs are dancing jigs (*or* have worn green wigs)

5. All the yaks have worn green slacks

### St. Patrick's Day Song.

(To the tune of "If You're Happy and You Know It")

If you're wearing green today, dance a jig,

If you're wearing green today, dance a jig,

**FIGURE 28–14 Young children might enjoy illustrating St. Patrick's Day fingerplay.**

If you're wearing green today,

Dance a jig, then smile and say,

"Have a very Happy St. Patrick's Day"

Additional verses:

"If you're wearing green today, clap your hands."

"If you're wearing green today, spin around."

"If you're wearing green today, shout 'Hurray!' "

"If you're wearing green today, stamp your feet."

### Song of Leprechauns.

(To the tune of "Three Blind Mice")

Leprechauns, leprechauns,

Hiding here, hiding there.

They don't want us to see them play.

When they come out on St. Patrick's Day.
See them dance in their cute way,
Leprechauns, leprechauns.

## MISCELLANEOUS SPRING HOLIDAYS

### April First Fingerplay
Little bears have three feet;
   (Hold up three fingers or touch a flat surface with
   three fingers)
Little birds have four;
   (Use four fingers in same way)
Little cows have two feet;
   (Use two fingers in same way)
And girls and boys have more.
   (Use five fingers in same way)

Do you believe my story?
   (Point to "you," then point to own forehead, then
   to mouth)
Do you believe my song?
   (Point to "you," then point to own forehead, then
   to throat)
I'll tell it only once a year,
   (Hold up index finger for "once")
When April comes along.
APRIL FOOL!
   (Clap hands to express pleasure)

### Activities for Lei Day (May 1st).
*Leis.* Cut 3-inch circles, squares, and triangles out of different colors of tissue paper and poke holes in the centers. Give each child a piece of yarn about 2 feet long, with one end knotted and the other end taped to make a "needle." Let the children string the tissue paper "flowers" on their pieces of yarn to make leis. When they have finished, tie the leis around the children's necks.

*Fish puzzles.* Cut fish shapes for each child out of large index cards or white construction paper. The children can use felt-tipped pens to draw on eyes and mouths and decorate their fish shapes with colorful stripes or other designs. When they have finished, cut each child's fish into three puzzle pieces. Then let the children put their own fish back together, using the colors and shapes of the puzzles pieces as guides.

*Dancing the hula.* Hula dancers use hand movements to act out the words of songs. With the chil-

FIGURE 28–15 Acting out a poem about a rainy spring day encourages much creative movement.

dren, make up hand movements for the words rainbow, waterfall, tree, mountain, sea, flowers, bee, dancers, and me. Then recite the following poem and let the children use their hand movements to act out these words:

Rainbow over the waterfall,
Rainbow over the tree,
Rainbow over the mountain
Rainbow over me.

Rainbow over the flowers,
Rainbow over the bee,
Rainbow over the dancers,
Rainbow over me.

*Hula hand puppets.* Use brown paper lunch bags to make hula dancer hand puppets. Cut 5-inch fringes along the open ends of the sacks; pass out the flat sacks and encourage the children to draw faces on the bottom of the bag. Small flower stickers or bits of colored paper can be glued under their hula dancers' faces to make leis. Play a tape or record of Hawaiian songs (or any other appropriate music) while the children move their hand puppets to the music. The children might want to be hula dancers themselves. Let them wear their leis (made in the above activity) and use their own hand movements to act out the words of songs. They may want to wear hula skirts made from large paper grocery bags fringed and taped around their waists.

*Aloha Song*
(Tune: "Happy Birthday")
Aloha (al-low-ha) to you,
Aloha to you.
Aloha, hello,
Aloha to you.

Aloha to you,
Aloha to you,
Aloha, goodbye,
Aloha to you.

You may want to explain that "aloha" is the Hawaiian way of saying both "hello" and "goodbye." If you like, have the children place pretend leis over one another's shoulders when they sing each verse of the song. You may want to tell them that it's the custom in Hawaii to gift friends who are leaving for a long time, or who are returning, by giving them leis.

*Hawaiian coconut.*   Pass around a coconut for children to shake and examine. Pierce the eyes of the coconut with an ice pick, drain out the milk, and let each child have a taste. Place the coconut on a hard surface and break it open with a hammer. Use a strong knife to remove the meat. Peel off the brown skin and cut the meat into pieces. Then let the children help grate the coconut on the fine side of a food grater. (The meat will be easier to remove from the shell if you bake the coconut at 400 degrees for 15 minutes before breaking it open.)

*Sandpaper art.*   Give each child a piece of light blue construction paper. Let them make "beaches" by brushing glue across the bottoms of their papers and sprinkling sand on the glue (use white sand, if available). Small shells and other shapes can be glued on for the rest of the picture if they wish. Have different paint or crayon colors—green for trees, brown for stone, etc.—available to complete their beach scenes.

*Seashell fun.*   Collect an assortment of seashells, and have the children group the shells by size, kind, or color, or line them up from smallest to largest. Then let the children arrange the shells in ways they think up themselves.

**May Baskets.**
*Paper-Plate Baskets.*   Paper-plate rims can be gaily painted to create a basket as colorful inside as out. Cut away center of one plate to leave a crescent shape. Cut second plate into an equal crescent and staple to first. The upper rim forms handle. Trim with yarn bow and fill with real or paper flowers.

*Lollipop Flowers for May.*   Use pastel-colored lollipops for flowers in May baskets. Cut basket from doubled construction paper, staple bottom edges, and add a long pipe cleaner handle. Cut a flower from paper and tape or glue behind wrapped sucker. Insert stick in the basket along with paper leaves.

*Cereal Box May Basket.*   Make flowers grow from an empty cereal box. Cut away the upper two thirds of sides and the top of box. Shape upper front and back sections into handles, removing centers. Strengthen remaining basket and handles with several layers of pasted paper. Paint, then add bright flowers and leaves cut from colored construction paper.

*May Basket Fingerplay*
With my little scissors
I cut some paper strips.
    (Cutting motion with index and middle finger of right hand)
Then I wove them in and out
    (Suggest weaving by putting right index finger over and under fingers of left hand)
And pasted at the tips.
    (Pretend to dip right index finger in paste; touch it to tips of fingers of left hand)
This became a basket
Pretty and gay
    (Interlace fingers of both hands to make a basket shape)
In which to put flowers
On the first of May.
    (With right forefinger and thumb, pretend to pick flowers and put them in a "basket" suggested by slightly cupped left hand)
I twisted pipe cleaners
    (Make twisting motion with fingers)
To make a handle strong.
    (Over "basket" suggested by left hand, curve right thumb and forefinger for a handle)

And left it at your house
    (Point to someone on the word "your")
When May Day came along.

**May Day Flowers.**  Cut pictures of various flowers from magazines or flower catalogs. (You may wish to let the group do this preparation.) Then cut across each picture in an irregular line and pass out all the pieces. Each child tries to find the part that will form a complete flower, and piece it together to form the whole flower. Completed flowers may be pasted on large construction paper to form a spring poster.

**May Day Crowns.**  Cut the center out of paper plates and have the children paint the rims. When the paint has dried, the children glue small bits of crushed tissue paper on their plate rims for flowers and short strips of colored tissue or crepe paper around the edges for ribbons on their crowns. As a fun variation, have the children decorate their crowns by poking dandelions, flowers, or weeds through slits cut in their plate rims.

**May Day Nature Walk.**  Plan to "go a-Maying" with the children as part of your May Day celebration. Take a nature walk to observe the spring plants and flowers. Along the way, look for greens, dandelions, and other wildflowers the children can pick and take back for their May baskets.

**Going 'Round the Maypole.**  Make a maypole by attaching long cloth or crepe paper streamers to a pole or tree. Add flowers and colorful bows for decorations. Have the children put on their May Day crowns from the above activity and wear jingle bell bracelets around their ankles, if desired. Then let them hold onto the ends of the streamers and dance around the maypole while singing the following song:

(To the tune "Here We Go 'Round the Mulberry Bush")
    Let's dance around the Maypole today.
    Maypole today, Maypole today.
    Let's dance around the Maypole today.
    We're Kings and Queens of the May.

**Indoor Maypole.**  Make a maypole decoration by covering a long cardboard tube with green crepe paper and attaching paper flowers, bows, and ribbons. Anchor the tube in a tub of clay or playdough and place it on a chair in the center of the room. Then tie crepe paper streamers around the children's wrists and let them dance in a circle around their maypole decoration.

## MOTHER'S DAY AND FATHER'S DAY

There are a variety of small gifts that can be simply made by a child for the parent. Among these are cards made from a painting the child has done, with a message inside such as "Why I love you" or "I love you because." Or the card may describe in the child's own words some special thing he intends to do for the parent on that special day.

Handprints made in plaster of Paris are another favorite. The plaster can be tinted any color the child prefers by adding tempera to the dry plaster, but the whole process has to be done very rapidly, and some prints will have to be done more than once to obtain a clear one. (Instructions for using plaster of Paris follow later in this section.) Children also enjoy potting up small, quick-blooming plants, such as dwarf marigolds, for gifts.

**FIGURE 28–16 Mother's Day card.**

**Soap Balls.** Materials: 2 teaspoons of hot water with liquid food color and scent if desired (such as lemon or clove), ½ cup soap flakes

Procedure:
Mix hot water with food color (add scent if desired). Add colored liquid to soap flakes and mold and squeeze until it can be rolled into small balls. Or the material can be rolled out thick and cut with cookie cutters, or formed around colored, heavy cotton yarn for a bath ball.

To go with the soap balls, you can make bath salts: These are made of baking soda colored with several drops of food coloring and worked together with fingers or a spoon. These salts are nice to put in small baby food jars and give along with the soap.

**Bleach-Bottle Bookends.** Use recycled bleach bottles for this Father's or Mother's Day gift. Fill two bleach bottles or plastic detergent bottles with sand or gravel. Study the shape of each bottle. You may see a dog or cat, an elephant, or a bird in the bottle's shape. Bookends can match, or each can be a different animal. Glue on features made from colored paper, felt, yarn, assorted stickers, etc. Pipe cleaners can be added as whiskers if desired.

**Plaster of Paris Handprints.** Measure the amount of plaster needed into a disposable container and add dry tempera if desired. Pastel-colored plaster is quite pretty, and if children are free to select the color they prefer, it adds a more individual note. Add water until mixture reaches the desired thickness. To make it strong enough and avoid cracking, spread it at least 1¼ to 1½ inches thick.

Plaster of Paris *sets quickly,* so help the child pour and scrape it into a nine-inch aluminum pie plate. Shake it or tap it on the table to "settle" and smooth the mixture. When it feels warm on the bottom, which will take only a few minutes, have the child make the handprint in it. If the print is not clear and well defined, wash hand, wait a little, and try again. Allow to harden overnight.

Remember, once the chemical reaction has begun, it is not possible to thin this mixture by adding more water. Be prepared to throw out an occasional casting and do over, since the careful timing this process requires is not always possible.

**Silhouettes.** The children can give "themselves" to their parents by making silhouette patterns on newsprint. Use a filmstrip projector to cast each child's shadow on paper attached to the wall. Another child can draw the outline of the shadow. Have the youngsters cut out and decorate the silhouettes. The large "cards" can then be rolled up and tied with a ribbon and bow for attractive delivery.

**Hands Card.** Fold a piece of construction paper in half for this Mother's (or Father's) Day card. Trace both of the child's hands on the front of it. Color the hands and write the year in the bottom right-hand corner of the card. On the front of the card you may write: "You win 'hands down', Mom." On the inside of the card you might write: "You're the best Mom (or Dad) ever!" The child can sign her name, make her mark, or you may sign it for her.

**Pop-out Kiss Card.** Have the child accordian-fold a piece of ½"-wide × 5"-long stiff paper, so you have ½"-wide pleats. Cut out a pair of lips about 1½" long × 1" wide. The child will love coloring these bright red. Tape the folded paper "spring" to the right side of a folded piece of paper. Glue the lips onto the top fold. Let the child decorate the cover

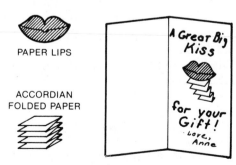

**FIGURE 28–17 Pop-out kiss card.**

of the card. Write in a special message such as, "A great big kiss for Mom/Dad." (See Figure 28–17.)

**Photo Card.** Take a photo of each child. You might want the child to hold up a sign in the picture saying, "I love you," or "Thanks for being my dad/mom."

**I Love You Cookie.** Make one giant cookie (your best recipe) and when cooled, frost it to say, "I love you, Dad/Mom." Wrap in plastic wrap and tie with yarn.

**Handprint Card.** Trace the child's hand on a piece of heavy paper. Cut it out. Tie a piece of yarn around one finger. Write, "I wanted to remember to say 'Happy Mother's (or Father's) Day.'"

**Original Artwork.** Fold a piece of typing paper in half and in half again to resemble a greeting card. Let the child draw an illustration or design on the front. Write the message the child dictates on the inside and let the child sign it, if the child desires to do so.

**Pop-out Card.** Plan the design ahead of time and draw it at the top of the inside of the card. Cut out the card, including the part that will pop up. Fold pop-out portion so that it will fold down when the card is closed and pop up when it is opened. (See Figure 28–18.)

**Litterbag.** Use a brown grocery bag. Roll or fold down the top to reinforce it. Braid two pipe cleaners for handles so that it can be hung on the dashboard of a car. Let the children decorate the bag in any way they like.

**Pencil-holder.** You will need cancelled stamps, glue, empty playdough or other cardboard "cans," and shellac.

Remove the tinfoil covering from play dough cans. Glue stamps onto the can. (The can may be painted and allowed to dry before applying the stamps.) After the glue is dry, paint the entire can with shellac for

**FIGURE 28–18 Pop-out card.**

a shiny, more permanent finish. These cans, which may be used as pencil holders, make nice gifts for Father's or Mother's Day.

**Mother's Day Songs.**
(To the tune of "Mary Had a Little Lamb")
Mommy takes good care of me,
Care of me, care of me.
Mommy takes good care of me,
Because she loves me so.

**My Special Friend**
(To the tune "Mary Had a Little Lamb")
Mommy is my special friend,
Special friend, special friend.
Mommy is my special friend.
I like the things we do.

Mom and I have lots of fun,
Lots of fun, lots of fun.
Mom and I have lots of fun.
I like to be with her.

**Mother's Day Flowers**
(To the tune "Frère Jacques")
Pick the flowers, pick the flowers.

One by one, one by one.
We'll give them to Mother,
We'll give them to Mother
When we're done, when we're done.

## My Mom's a Special Lady
(To the tune "Eensy, Weensy Spider")
My mom's a special lady,
So I hug her every day.
She give me lots of food to eat,
And takes me out to play.
My mother reads me stories
And buys me sneakers, too
I'm so very happy that I have
A mom who loves me so!

## Father's Day Songs.

### D-A-D
(To the tune "Jingle Bells")
D-A-D, D-A-D,
Dad is my best friend.
We play games, we go to the park.
The fun just never ends!
D-A-D, D-A-D,
I love to hold your hand.
It feels so good, it feels so safe
You're the best dad in this land!

### Thanks, Dad
(To the tune "Row, Row, Row, Your Boat")
Thanks, thanks, thank you Dad.
Thanks for loving me!
Hugs and kisses, hugs and kisses,
Come to you from me!

### Dad My Friend
(To the tune "Yankee Doodle")
Daddy is my special friend,
The two of us are buddies.
I always like the things we do.
I'm thankful for my daddy.

## Flowers for Mother's (and Father's) Day.
In the spring children often bring flowers to school. Lilacs, tulips, daffodils, dandelions, and flowering bushes are all a source of delight.

Prior to Mother's (and Father's) Day, the children can bring small, nonbreakable containers to school to decorate with glue and glitter, sequins, yarn, or colored paper. On Mother's (and Father's) Day, the containers are filled with miniature bouquets and a small amount of water. These make attractive gifts for proud children to present to mother and father.

This activity provides an informal opportunity for identifying cultivated and wild flowers, as well as flowering plants and weeds. It also teaches the joy of giving.

## SUMMER HOLIDAYS*

Summer in the United States is from June 22 to September 22. But summer weather is not the same for all the states. The northern states do not have high temperature readings for such a prolonged time as do the southern states, where temperatures of 80° and above occur almost daily from the middle of April to the middle of October. Therefore, each teacher should keep in mind the uniqueness of his/ her area when teaching about this season. It is difficult for young children to grasp the full meaning of the concept of "summer," but they can begin to understand some of the changes that take place at this time of year. They can also learn about some of the most common activities families enjoy together at this time and about some of the celebrations that take place during summer.

**Flag Day.** Flag Day (June 14th) is technically in spring, but since it occurs after most schools are out it is thought of as a summer celebration. Very young children cannot be expected to comprehend the history and heritage of our country. They can, however, begin to learn about some of our national symbols, such as the flag, the Statue of Liberty, the White House, the Capitol, and the Liberty Bell in Independence Hall. After hearing about the many celebrations of our country's recent Bicentennial, many children are learning much about these symbols.

On June 14, 1777, Congress adopted the flag with

---

*The first five paragraphs of this section are from *Resources for Creative Teaching in Early Childhood Education* by Bonnie Mack Flemming, Darlene Softley Hamilton, and JoAnne Deal Hicks, copyright © 1977 by Harcourt Brace Jovanovich, Inc. Reprinted by permission of the publisher.

thirteen alternate stripes of red and white representing the original thirteen states and the union represented by thirteen white stars on a field of blue. As each state was adopted another star was added to the field of blue. Our present flag has fifty stars. Betsy Ross made the first flag. Young children of three and four years of age should not be required to recite the pledge to the flag every day. However, they can learn to respect the flag and learn how to hold and carry it without letting it touch the floor. Small individual flags are best for young children, since each wants to carry one. Simply remove flags from children who are not treating them with respect.

**Independence Day.** Independence Day (July 4th) is a national holiday. Many families go to parks for picnics, to swimming pools, beaches, amusement parks, and parades and often plan to view a fireworks display after dark. This commemorates the July 4, 1776, signing of the Declaration of Independence. Independence Hall was built in 1732 and was used as a statehouse for the colony of Pennsylvania. The Declaration of Independence was signed in this hall and is on display today for all to see. The first Continental Congress met there and chose George Washington to be the first commander-in-chief of the United States Army. The Liberty Bell is now housed in the Liberty Bell Pavilion, one block from Independence Hall. It was rung for the first time on July 8, 1776, when the Declaration of Independence had its first public reading. It cracked shortly after it was hung and had to be recast. It cracked a second time in 1835. It has not been recast or rung since.

The Statue of Liberty stands on Liberty Island in New York harbor and is 150 feet high. The female figure holds a tablet in her left hand and a torch in her right hand. A symbol of freedom made by the French sculptor, Frederick Bartholdi, the statue was given to the United States by the French government in 1884. The money to build the 150-foot pedestal on which it stands was donated by thousands of Americans.

Activities for these summer holidays follow.

- On an interest center table, set out a View Master with appropriate reels: the U.S. Capitol Building, the White House, Independence Park, Statue of Liberty, and others about national parks, flowers, and monuments.

- Play the Match-Them Game: For Flag Day or July 4th, make two sets of flag cards by mounting gummed flag seals of different countries on 3″ × 5″ cards. Seals are available where stamp collecting accessories are found.

- Blow Painting: Drops of bright-colored paint blown with a straw over paper result in a fireworks-bursting-in-air effect for Independence Day.

- Read a book on summer holidays. (See Additional Readings at the end of this unit.)

- Have a patriotic parade. For Flag Day have children march to any good patriotic song, each carrying a small American flag. In the parade, stress respect for the flag. Do not allow children to abuse their flags or let them touch the ground or floor. If this is difficult to do with your group, give the children instruments while an adult or one or two children you have selected can carry the flags.

- On Independence Day, march to patriotic band music. Use drums to help the children move creatively. Have half the children beat drums while the other half move creatively:

    Walk to a drum beat
    Run to a drum beat
    Jump to a drum beat
    Hop on one foot, land on both feet
    Dance! (Bear weight first on the toes of one foot, then heal of same foot. Alternate feet. Repeat: toe, heel, toe, heel)

- With sand colored red and blue, help the children "paint" a flag, using white construction paper for the background and white stripes. Make the outline ahead of time, and have children put the glue on for one color at a time. This is fun to do if not too much stress is put on perfection. As they paint, talk with them about the meanings of the stripes and the stars.

- Make Fourth of July noise makers by putting a few rocks inside frozen orange juice cans. Wrap cans in red, white, or blue crepe paper. Close both ends with covered wire closures, such as those used to close bread wrappers. Let children have a Fourth of July parade—noisy, of course!

- Play "What Am I?" Describe our national symbols, the flag, the Statue of Liberty, the White House, the Liberty Bell, and the American eagle. Let the children take turns guessing who you are.
- On Flag Day and Independence Day decorate the snack or lunch table with red, white, and blue. Serve red, white, and blue foods.
- Make "U.S.A. Berries." You will need strawberries, blueberries, Styrofoam cups, and shredded coconut. Wash the berries. Put two strawberries and five blueberries into each cup. Sprinkle with shredded coconut. Hooray for the red, white, and blue!

## Flag Day Fingerplays.

### Flag Day
(Display a flag)
Strips of red and strips of white (Point to stripes or pretend to hold single strips in both hands. Begin with hands in front of self; separate hands as though displaying the stripes)
A square of beautiful blue (Suggest square with hands or point to union on the flag)
And on its stars, five-pointed stars—
Begin to count—one, two—(Hold up hand with fingers spread to suggest five-pointed star. Class counts stars in each row)
Each star stands for a state;
For years there were forty-eight
Now the flag has two more (Hold up two fingers)
Making a total of fifty.
Let's show that number with our hands—
Ten, twenty, thirty, forty, fifty. (Hold up both hands, drop them; repeat four times)

### I'm a Rocket
I'm a little rocket (Child crouches on heels)
Pointing to the moon
4—3—2—1—
(Said slowly)
Blast off! Zoom! (Springs and jumps into the air)

### The Space Man
Here's a space man in a rocket (Right thumb extended in air)
Safe and tight and strong (Fist closed around thumb)
Here's the launch pad where it sits, (Rest fist in palm of left hand)
So quiet, and so long,
Listen to the count down,
Soon we'll be aloft
7 6 5 4 3 3 2 1 and now watch him blast off.
(Rocket leaves hand and rises at the words "blast off")

Round and round and round he goes (Fist circles the head)
Through the atmosphere,
Now he lets his parachute out
And down he floats so near.
(Left hand opened above fist with fingers extended down to form a parachute)

### Soldiers
Five little soldiers standing in a row, (Hold up fingers of one hand)
Three stood straight (Hold three fingers straight)
And two stood so. (Bend two fingers)
Along came the captain (Extend index finger on other hand and move in front of first hand)
And what do you think?
They all stood straight, as quick as a wink. (Hold all five fingers up straight)

### Wave a Little Flag
(To the tune "I'm a Little Teapot")
Wave a little flag,
Red, white, and blue.
Our country belongs
To me and you.
So, all together we can say,
"Happy Independence Day!"

### On Independence Day
(To the tune "Mary Had a Little Lamb")
Fireworks go snap, snap, snap!
Crack, crack, crack! Zap, zap, zap!
Fireworks make me clap, clap, clap
On Independence Day!

**Make a Banner or Flag.** The banner is used universally for creating atmosphere for parades, celebrations, or special days. It is also sometimes used in religious rites and ceremonies. With the very smallest children, a project devoted to making marching flags is most rewarding. Using thin strips of wood acquired from the scrap boxes of the local lumberyards and rectangles of brown wrapping paper, each child can design her own flag, using paints or crayons, colored papers, or the materials that are normally found in scrap boxes in the art center. On certain seasonal or holiday occasions (such as Flag Day and July 4) the entire room can be decked in flags and banners representing the occasion. Each child can express in her own way the meaning of that particular holiday or season in a long, flowing banner made of brown wrapping paper, shelving paper, or ordinary white paper. The child can attach one end of the banner to a strip of wood with staples or glue and can hang the banner from the classroom ceiling or from a wire stretched from wall to wall. The child can also make banners and flags on fabrics and add the decorative elements by gluing other fabrics on to the fabric of the large piece.

### Inter-Tribal Native American Ceremonial Activities.

*Native American crafts.* Set up centers in your room so that the children can make a variety of Native American crafts.

- *Weaving.* Make a loom for each child by cutting five notches in both ends of a styrofoam food tray and stringing yarn through the notches. Tape the yarn ends to the back of the tray. The children can use the over-under method to weave short strands of yarn, feathers, and small sticks onto their looms. For younger children, make looms by cutting slits all around the edges of the styrofoam trap and taping pieces of yarn to the backs. Then let the children wind the yarn around the trays, each time passing it through one of the slits.
- *Pots.* Children can shape pots out of balls of clay and carve designs on the sides with toothpicks. Or, have them each start with a round, flat base and build up the sides by coiling "snakes" of clay on top of one another.
- *Indian necklaces.* Encourage the children to string patterns of beads made of playdough, colored straw sections, and buttons on yarn.

*Animal dancing.* At the Ceremonial, everyone enjoys watching traditional dances such as the Deer Dance and the Buffalo Dance. For your celebration, let the children try dancing like different kinds of animals while you tap out rhythms on a hand drum. Talk about how different animals move, then adapt your drumbeats to fit each animal's movements.

*Ceremonial parade.* One of the highlights of the Ceremonial is the Native American Parade in downtown Gallup, New Mexico. Let the children celebrate by having a parade, too. Provide them with drums, shakers, and bell bracelets to wear around their ankles. Play a record or tape of Native American music

(available at the library) or use any other appropriate music and let the children march around the room.

*Nature walk.* In keeping with the spirit of your Native American Celebration, take the children on a nature appreciation walk. Before the walk, discuss how Native tribes lived in harmony with nature, taking from it only what they needed to survive. Encourage the children to look for beautiful things in nature and to explore with their senses of touch, smell, and hearing. Talk about the importance of nature's creatures and how we can help protect and care for their environment. If you like, bring along a trash bag for the children to fill with any litter they find along the way.

**Decorating Classroom Windows for Summer Holidays.** Using the classroom windows is a good idea, but don't display stereotypes or copy other windows. Instead, allow the children to invent original uses for this space. There are excellent paints now available for use on glass that are easily washed away. These are good for making large paintings on the

**FIGURE 28–19 Memories of summer activities form the basis of many discussions for young children.**

windows. Windows may also be covered with thin white tissue paper, tracing paper, or acetate; children can then make beautiful designs or pictures about the summer holidays by applying transparent cellophane or paint to these areas. Occasionally, if the windows consist of small panes, each child may be assigned a single pane to design. The child may use black construction paper with areas cut out and bits of transparent paper and cellophane inserted in the open areas as one method.

# ADDITIONAL READINGS

## Children's Books—Spring Holidays

Aliki, A. *Welcome, Little Baby.* New York: Greenwillow, 1987.

Balian, L. *Humbug Rabbitt.* Nashville: Abingdon, 1974.

Bate, Lucy. *Little Rabbit's Loose Tooth.* New York: Crown, 1975.

Brown, Margaret Wise. *Runaway Bunny.* New York: Harper, 1972.

Carrick, Carol. *Rabbit for Easter.* New York: Greenwillow, 1979.

Chukovsky, Kornei. *Good Morning, Chick.* New York: Greenwillow, 1980.

Friedrich, P., and O. Friedrich. *The Easter Bunny That Overslept.* New York: Lothrop, Lee & Shepard Co., 1957.

Hartelius, Margaret A. *The Chicken's Child.* New York: Doubleday, 1975.

Krahn, F. *April Fools.* New York: Dutton, 1974.

Krauss, Ruth. *The Carrot Seed.* New York: Harper, 1945.

Milhous, Katherine. *The Egg Tree.* New York: Charles Scribner's Sons, 1950.

Parker, Kristy. *My Dad the Magnificent.* New York: Dutton, 1987.

Potter, Beatrix. *The Story of a Fierce Bad Rabbit.* New York: Western Publishing Co., 1970.

———. *The Tale of Flopsy Bunnies.* New York: Warne, 1965.

———. *The Tale of Peter Rabbit.* New York: Warne, 1969.

Sawicki, Norma J. *Something for Mom.* New York: Lothrop, 1987.

Seuss, Dr. *Green Eggs and Ham.* New York: Random House, 1960.

Seuss, Dr. *Horton Hatches the Egg.* New York: Random House, 1940.

Tudor, Tasha. *A Tale of Easter.* New York: Oxford University Press, 1941.

Zolotow, Charlotte. *Mr. Rabbit and the Lovely Present.* New York: Harper and Row, 1962.

———. *Over and Over.* New York: Harper and Row, 1957.

## Children's Books—Summer Holidays

Dalgliesh, Alice. *The Fourth of July Story.* New York: Charles Scribner's Sons, 1966.

MacDonald, Golden. *The Little Island.* Garden City, N.Y.: Doubleday, 1946.

Parsons, V. *Ring for Liberty.* New York: Golden Press, 1975.

Spier, Peter. *The Star-Spangled Banner.* Garden City, N.Y.: Doubleday, 1973.

## Books on Spring & Summer Holidays Around the World

Kalman, B., and K. Harrison. *We Celebrate Spring: The Holidays and Festivals Series.* New York: Crabtree Publishing Co., 1985.

MacDonald, M.R. *The Folklore of World Holidays: Easter Customs.* Detroit, Mich.: Gale Research, Inc., 1992.

Rosen, M. *Seasonal Summer Festivals.* New York: The Bookwright Press, 1991.

# SECTION 8
# Creative Activities Involving Seasons

# U N I T 2 9

# Autumn

Autumn is nature's last fling of the year. The landscape is brilliant with raw and muted colors ranging from bright yellow to red-orange to red, from red-brown to red-violet.

The young child is naturally sensitive to the wonders and beauty of nature: the colors and rhythm of leaves whirled by autumn winds, the texture of dried seeds and weeds, the form and color in the harvest. There are a number of things a teacher can do to enlarge children's understanding of their world and to encourage them to learn to look, feel, and think:

- Begin a collection of objects from nature for classroom use. Encourage closer observation of design in nature.
- Take children on walking trips to discover and observe the colors, shapes, and textures in trees, plants, clouds, buildings, and vehicles. Individual observation can be shared with others at "see and tell" time.

The children draw and paint the beauty of nature as they each see it, using their own feelings and ideas. Their growing visual awareness is gradually reflected in picture making, as they mature in the ability to interpret their environment. Some topics for drawing and painting are:

- Leaves in Autumn
- Birds Flying South
- A Rainy Day in Fall
- The Fall Harvest
- Raking Fall Leaves
- My Neighborhood in Autumn
- An Autumn Collage

## OBSERVATION SKILLS

The traditional beginning of school in the fall of the year is an excellent time for increasing awareness of the world around us. It starts the year off with practice in observation skills.

- Children can be taught to be more aware of their environment in only a few minutes. Discuss the fact that leaves will change color and watch together to see when it happens. Make a game of finding the largest, smallest, and most unusual colored leaf. Focus on an evergreen or pine and talk about the needles and pinecones and the fact that they stay green and don't drop off. Talk about people needing jackets and animals growing winter coats; also point out the shorter days.
- Collect leaves of different sizes and shapes. Show the children that one side is smooth and one side is rough. Have them put the rough side up and a piece of paper over it. Take a small crayon turned on its side and rub over the paper. The outline of the leaf will show through. It's fun to change colors. This can be used on any object with texture.
- Fall is also the time when apples are harvested. There are almost 10,000 varieties grown in the

591

world. A fun experiment to do with the children is to buy one of several kinds in the grocery store. See how many ways they are alike and different. Say their names. Taste a piece of each one. If you cut two pieces from each one, can the children find the ones that taste the same or different?

## AUTUMN JEWISH HOLIDAYS

The Jewish New Year, Rosh Hashanah (literally, "Head of the Year") is celebrated on the first two days of Tishri (September-October). These two days begin the most sacred period of the year, the High Holy Days, a time of deep penitence and prayer, based on the belief that in these ten days each person's fate for another year is sealed in Heaven.

Jewish tradition says that on Rosh Hashanah, God opens three books—one for the wicked, one for the good, and the third for those in-between. The good are immediately inscribed and sealed in the Book of Life, and the wicked are inscribed for death. But judgment on the third, or middle group, is suspended until Yom Kippur, giving them ten days in which to atone for whatever wrong they have done.

A traditional New Year's greeting is, "May you be inscribed and sealed for a good year." This also appears on many New Year's cards that Jewish people in the United States and other countries send to their friends and relatives.

Though these holidays are a time of penitence and seriousness, they are not a time of sadness. After the Rosh Hashanah service at the synagogue, the dinner table is festive and the spirit is happy. The menu varies from home to home according to taste, but honey and fresh fruit are traditionally included. The honey is "for a sweet year." The inclusion of fruit goes back to ancient times when Rosh Hashanah was also a harvest festival.

Yom Kippur, the Day of Atonement set by Moses nearly thirty centuries ago, brings to an end the High Holiday season. This day is the holiest, most solemn day of the Jewish year. It is a day of fasting, penitence, and prayer, most often spent in the synagogue, where services are continuous from morning to evening. It is also a day of rest and a day for those who have hurt each other during the past year to make amends. It is also considered a day for helping those less fortunate.

Sukkoth, which falls in September or October on the calendar, is the "Feast of Tabernacles." It is a tradition for boys and girls to build small huts of branches, called "sukkahs." These huts, or tabernacles, represent the huts in which Jews lived during their forty years of wandering after the Exodus from Egypt. Strictly observant Jews eat their meals in the sukkah during the holiday. (Later in this unit there are several suggestions for special Jewish foods for these fall holidays.)

Early childhood teachers will, of course, cover only the main ideas of these Jewish holidays, since the religious, more abstract ideas are difficult for young children to grasp. The symbols of these holidays may be used in art projects, such as pictures of the three books, or painting the ram's horn, another symbol for the Day of the Blowing, another name for Rosh Hashanah. (The ram's horn is said to sound man's return to the blessings of religion.)

## THE BEGINNING OF THE SCHOOL YEAR

Because fall is the time of year when many children enter school for the first time, it is important to plan these first experiences so that they are fun and not frightening for young children. Listed below are

**FIGURE 29–1 Getting acquainted with new agemates is a large part of the first days of school.**

some ideas for the first days of school in the fall that many teachers have used successfully to make these first days less anxious.

**Before the First Day of School.** Know as much as possible about each child before he comes to school; review application forms, information on parent and family background, special physical problems, and any screening or testing information provided. Other preparations are:

- Make a bulletin board welcoming all your new children featuring a bunch of large, colorful pencils made from bright construction paper. Pencils are easy to draw and make any size; make them as large as you can to fit the size of the board you are decorating. Use eraser-colored paper for the eraser, aluminum foil for the strip that holds the eraser, and wood-colored paper for the sharpened point, then color the lead point with black magic marker. Write each child's name on one of the pencils. You may want to title your board: "Welcome! What a Sharp Bunch!"

- Before your program or school year starts, write a note to each child who will be in your room. Tape a pack of gum to your notecard, then write this verse: "Would you take my gum and then not come?" Include a note to tell the child how you look forward to her coming to your room. Mention a few of the exciting things you'll be doing together. Motivate your children to be excited about coming to school before they arrive.

- Have name tags ready with each child's name. These may be laminated or made of cloth for durability. The child's bus number (if applicable) can be added on the first day. The tags could match a picture on the classroom door (for example, orange school bus tag and orange bus on the door). This will help children identify with their own room and will help place lost children in the right classroom.

- Prepare written memos and a chart with necessary information for parents, such as fees, lunch money procedures, snack-time rules, grade sponsors, dismissals, and any other school/center policies. This is especially important in day care centers and preschools where enrollment may occur throughout the year.

- Pack a resealable plastic welcome bag for new children who come into your room or program after the start of the year. You might put in it such things as crayons, any forms needing completion, a list of room rules, a picture of the class (taken in September, with copies made for just this purpose), and any information that might prove helpful to the parent. When a new child is brought to your room, grab a bag, and you're ready. The child will feel special receiving a gift the very first day! If children are moved to a new room at other times of the year, or when they "move up" into an older group, prepare a welcome bag for that occasion, too. Another nice touch is a welcome tour for the new child from a child who already knows the room.

- Have cubbies (or lockers) ready to assign to each child. This will help a child feel secure in having his own private place. These should have each child's name as well as a picture to help the child recognize his own name and cubby. Placing a different picture beside each child's cubby helps younger, non-reading children locate their cubbies. Even if a coat hook is all that is available, it is important for both organization and a child's sense of belonging that each child have a space of his own.

- At the beginning of the school year, take a Polaroid snapshot of each child, print the child's name at the bottom, and tape the picture above the child's cubby. This makes it easy for the children to locate their own cubbies and helps them learn to recognize their names. And at the end of the year, it will be fun to see how much the children have grown.

- Send a letter home or telephone each child on your enrollment list to tell him you are his teacher and how much you are looking forward to having him in your room. In day care centers and preschools this will be necessary throughout the year as individual children enroll.

**Ideas to Get You Started.** On the first day (or during the first weeks) in an early childhood pro-

**FIGURE 29–2 Learning center rules is an important part of the first part of the program year.**

gram year, plan to do the following to help both you and the children feel at home.

- Call the roll. Be sure to have some predetermined way for a child to respond, such as standing up and saying, "Good morning," a hand raised, or other ways to alert both you and the group of his presence.
- Explain the activity areas of the room and let each child choose a center. This is a good time to set limits on how many can go to each center. Explain cleanup time and the importance of putting everything back in its proper place.
- Tour the school (or center) with the children so they can become aware of their surroundings.
- Invite the principal or center director to visit the room.
- Have an activity period for clapping, walking, running, skipping, hopping, etc. Have musical activities. All such activities should help everyone relax and use large motor skills.
- For rest time children may be asked to bring mats from home if they are not furnished by the school. Soft music helps soothe children during rest time. A good rest time poem also works well.
- Prepare for lunch time. It is best to have a practice session in the morning before actually going to

lunch. This helps eliminate the confusion that may arise. A parent, extra aide, or older student can be used to help guide children through a cafeteria line.
- After lunch, plan a group activity that involves some large motor exercise. For example, let children roll balls to each other in a circle or to an interesting target in the center of the circle.
- Let children make a simple art project to hang up or take home.
- Have something to talk about to interest the children—pets, shells, etc. This is a talking time primarily for the purpose of making the children feel at home.
- Have some type of roll call system to learn children's names quickly and to make each one feel important.
- Have a card with each child's name on it and see if he can recognize his name.

## WHAT TO DO:

**1.** ☐ CUT POSTER BOARD OR OAKTAG INTO 12 SQUARES (1 FOR EACH MONTH OF THE YEAR) TO FIT SIZE OF BULLETIN BOARD.

**2.** ☐ MOUNT EACH CALENDAR PAGE ONTO CARDBOARD BOX SO IT SETS AWAY FROM BACK OF BULLETIN BOARD AND ENABLES CLOTHESPINS TO SNAP ON. GLUE BOX TO BACKBOARD.

**3.** ☐ WITH THE HELP OF A PARENT OR TEACHER, EACH CHILD WRITES HIS OR HER NAME AND BIRTH DATE ON A CLIP STYLE CLOTHESPIN AND ATTACHES IT TO CORRECT MONTH.

**4.** ☐ CLIP CLOTHESPIN(S) WITH A CANDLE DRAWN ON IT (THEM) TO A POSTERBOARD BIRTHDAY CAKE FOR CELEBRATIONS.

**5.** ☐ ADD MORE CLOTHESPINS TO CALENDAR BULLETIN BOARD FOR HOLIDAYS, TRIPS, SPECIAL EVENTS.

**FIGURE 29–3 "Happy Birthday to Us" bulletin board.**

# THIS ONE'S FOR YOU!

## CLASSROOM HELPERS: SOME SYSTEMS THAT WORK

Most teachers of young children find that a system of choosing classroom helpers is the best way to handle many daily room maintenance tasks. A system of classroom helpers not only helps accomplish these tasks, it also helps develop in the children a sense of responsibility and a pride in a job well done. Here are some systems for organizing classroom helpers that have been tried and found successful:

- Organize your helper list by writing the first name of each child on a 3" × 5" index card. Put the cards on a ring and flip them over, one at a time, when choosing classroom helpers. This way, the shy child will not be left out, and the children will learn to recognize each other's names as you read them off the cards.
- Choose a special name, such as "Mighty Ducks" for your group of children, and use the name to design a decorative helper poster. For each child, cut a picture symbolizing your group's name from wallpaper, giftwrap, or construction paper, and write the child's name on it. Glue the pictures on a wall poster. Each morning, indicate the group leader of the day by pinning a star on one of the pictures. (The leader gets first choice of where to sit at the table, helps pass the wastebasket, hand out snacks, etc.) A list of your children's names next to the poster will help you keep track of turns.
- When choosing helpers, play "Who Is It?" First, run your "magic finger" up and down a list of your children's names. Stop at a name, then give clues such as these: "My helper is a boy. He has brown hair and is wearing a blue shirt. His first name begins with a "D" and it sounds like "da." Write the initial letter of the child's name—or even the entire name—on the board. The children will love this game and will learn a great deal while playing it.
- Classroom helpers have an easier time remembering their tasks if you string clean-up cards on loops of yarn for them to wear as necklaces. Put the cards in a basket each morning and let the children choose the necklaces they want to wear that day.
- Appoint a "Door Captain." The door captain can assist in lining up the other children, counting noses and holding open all the doors that day.

- Write children's and teachers' names on the board.
- To ease the transition between home and school during the first few days of the year, place a different sticker on the floor of each child's cubby. Then give each parent several matching stickers to place, one a day, on the back of the child's hand just before coming to school. Upon arrival, the children will be eager to locate their matching stickers and will find their cubbies quickly.
- Sing songs or make up rhymes using the names.
- Cut a large gingerbread-shaped child from felt. Put him on the felt board. Tell the children that "Charlie" has just gotten up and is going to get ready for school, but he cannot decide what to wear. Maybe the children can help him. As each child says an article of clothing, pretend to put it on Charlie. When he's dressed, ask the children what else Charlie needs to do to get ready for school. Encourage the children to think of everything from brushing his teeth, to eating a good breakfast, to getting his backpack ready.
- Make a "Happy Birthday to Us" bulletin board.

- Send each parent a Sharing Time letter explaining the purposes of sharing time and giving the name of the child's assigned day to share. You might also include a few rules: The child may bring only one item to show to classmates; no toy weapons are allowed; the child does not have to participate in sharing if she chooses not to.
- Always make a few extra copies of such things as classroom newsletters, name-tag blanks, school supplies lists, and letters to parents and put them in a New Student folder. When a new child joins, it will be easier to compile the information and send it home promptly.

## ART ACTIVITIES

The following activities emphasize small and large motor skills and visual perception.

**A Tree for All Months.** Cover a bulletin board or wall area with a large tree made out of construction paper, with a lot of large limbs stretching in every direction (see Figure 29–4). Use the following suggestions to keep the tree "changing" for each month.

September—Cover the tree with multicolored leaves, numbered 1 through 30. Each day, take off a leaf (taking turns sending them home with the children). Talk about September, and what we can expect to see, hear, and feel in this month.

October—Put a few owls and cats in the almost bare tree, a big harvest moon in one corner, and numbered jack-o-lanterns. The children will enjoy decorating the tree for Halloween, and it is just as much fun to see it gradually disassembled.

November—Put fat turkeys around the tree and on the branches numbered for the days of the month. The tree has only a few brown leaves still hanging on. Compare the tree with the trees outside that are equally bare.

December—Put reindeer and Santa's sleigh under the tree. Sprinkle snowflakes on the branches and on the ground under the tree. You can fill the sleigh with presents, numbered for the days of the month.

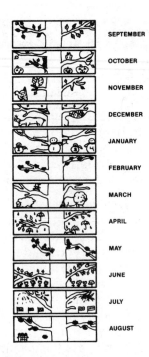

**FIGURE 29–4 A tree for all months.**

January—Snowmen stand next to the tree and some hide behind it. Each has a different-color scarf. You can talk about colors. Also talk about what animals do in the winter. Each snowman is numbered for the days of the month, ready for the children to take home.

February—Make valentines to put on the tree branches. Cover the branches with metallic hearts for an even more "glitzy" tree.

March—Lambs and lions can be made frisking around the tree. Add some fluffy clouds in the sky, a few leaf buds on the tree, with leprechauns hiding here and there. All of these have numbers for the days of the month, and are taken home by the children.

April—Add many new and green leaves to the tree. Also add a few raindrops and a rainbow in the sky. Numbered umbrellas are placed under the tree.

May—Cover the tree with pink tissue blossoms and birds with the days of the month noted on them.

June—This month finds a garden of flowers blooming under the tree. Each flower is numbered with the days of June and is ready for picking.

July—Flags are under the tree, and fireworks are above it. By this time, the children are making their own suggestions for monthly themes, and these can be incorporated into the picture.

August—The tree is covered with apples, ready for picking, rosy, and numbered. It is a natural time for including lots of apple activities (see these in later parts of this unit), cooking with apples, and even apple-head dolls. The tree has watched the children grow for a whole year, and the children have enjoyed and appreciated the changes the seasons made in the tree's life.

## Leaf People and Animals.
Procedure:
1. Have children collect autumn leaves on a class walk or on their walk to and from school.
2. They then paste the leaves to a piece of brown, red, orange, or yellow construction paper.
3. The teacher can show the children how the stem of the leaf is the first "leg" for a leaf person or animal. From that point on, the child's imaginaton aids the creation of the rest of the leaf picture.
4. After the leaf people and animals are completed, the children may want to fill in the background with crayons or chalk.

**Fall Trees.**   Use a piece of construction paper for the background. Use crayons or markers to draw a tree trunk with branches. Dip sponges in trays of orange, red, and yellow tempera. Print by pressing sponge on paper to make colorful autumn leaves. Repeat printing as many times as the child wants.

**First Day of Fall.**   Read the story of *Frederick* by Leo Lionni about mice getting ready for the long winter ahead. Take a fall stroll. Collect beautiful colored leaves as you walk. When you return, glue the leaves onto a small paper bag. Put the bag in a safe place. Next time you go walking, take the bag along and collect more fall items to use in the fall activities that follow.

**Grandparents' Day—September 14.**   Help the children make a special type of card for their grandparents. Talk about the types of "body prints" they could make—hand, foot, finger, elbow, knee, etc. Choose the ones they would like to make. Get a shallow pan and put tempera paint into it. Use white paper and carefully make the body part prints on it, using the tempera paint. When the prints are dry, write what each print is, such as "Erica's knee" or "Claire's thumb." Then make the card with the paper the children have printed.

**Johnny Appleseed Day—September 28.**   Play "Applesauce" with the child. Have the child pretend he is a big, sweet apple. First, gently shake him down from the tree and then lovingly squeeze him. As you are gently squeezing say, "Applesauce, applesauce." Do it often. It's fun. You try being the apple as he squeezes you. Then you can make *real* applesauce (recipe in food section of this unit).

*"Do You Know the Apple Man?" Song*
(Sung to the tune of "The Muffin Man")
Do you know the Apple Man,
The Apple Man, the Apple Man,
Do you know the Apple Man
Who likes to play with me?

Oh, he has a great big smile,
A great big smile, a great big smile.
Oh, he has a great big smile
And likes to play with me.

Oh, he has a bright red face,
A bright red face, a bright red face.
Oh, he has a bright red face
And likes to play with me.

Oh, he has a star inside,
A star inside, a star inside.
Oh, he has a star inside
And likes to play with me.

*Apple star prints.*   You may want to read the "Star in the Apple" story on page 604 before this activity.

Materials:
construction paper
apples
red, yellow and green tempera paint
shallow containers
sponges
paper towels
knife

Procedure:
1. Cut the apples in half crosswise. Blot the cut surfaces with paper towels and let the apples dry for about an hour.
2. Place sponges (or folded paper towels) in a shallow container and pour on the tempera paint.
3. Have the children dip the cut surfaces of the apples into the paint and then press them on their papers to make star prints.

*Apple man puppets.*
Materials:
large apple
whole cloves
toothpicks
carrot curls (optional)
tape recorder or large sheets of paper and crayons
stapler (optional)

Procedure:
1. Stick whole cloves into one side of the apple to make two eyes, a nose, and a mouth.
2. Stick toothpicks into the apple on either side of the face to make arms.
3. Use toothpicks to attach carrot curls for hair, if desired.

Let the children take turns holding the Apple Man puppet and making up stories about his adventures. Record the stories on tape for later listening. Or write down each child's story on a large sheet of paper for him or her to illustrate. If desired, staple the illustrated stories together with a cover to make an Apple Man book.

## Leaf Tree.
Procedure:
1. Find a large branch about four feet tall with many twigs on it. Stand it in a can of plaster of Paris for a firm base.
2. Children can cut, trace, or draw leaves and tie them on the twigs. They can draw freehand or trace from actual leaves. The name of the leaf can be written on each.
3. The tree itself can be reused for word games, for different seasons, and for many other kinds of activities.

**FIGURE 29–5 Leaf tree.**

## Cut-Up Puppets.
Procedure:
1. If you have a damaged or outdated copy of a book you still use with the children, cut the characters out and paste them on popsicle sticks to make puppets.
2. A few days before the book is given to the children, introduce the puppets to them. Place the puppets in a container where the children can play with them during the day.
2. After reading the book, the children can use the puppets to act out the story.

**Fall Colors.**  You know it's fall when those gaudy leaves start sticking to children's clothing. Unfortunately, those bright colors have a way of fading and drying into a crumbling brown as the season wears on. Here is a way to preserve fall color indefinitely. It will change the colors of some of the leaves, but the children will enjoy watching the magic! Purchase a bottle of glycerine at a drug store. You will need several empty jars and the leaves you collect as you take children for fall hikes.

1. Mix ⅓ cup glycerine and ⅔ cup water in a jar.
2. Crush the tips of the stems with a hammer to make it easier for the solution to be absorbed.
3. Set the leaves in the solution for a week or so.

Watch the leaves each day with the children to discover the changes that will take place. The treated leaves will stay soft for a long time. Experiment with as many different kinds of leaves as you can and see what colors result. For instance, birch leaves turn dark red, forsythia turn very dark, and magnolia leaves turn bronze.

**Corn Cobs.** Throughout the ages, in many cultures, the "cob" or empty ear of corn has itself been a doll for children. If you have access to corn cobs, dry them off, and wrap the leaves around the cob for clothes, or a use bits of cloth. You may want to add hair and a tiny face, or leave it as it is.

**Autumn Leaf Mobile.**

Materials: Twigs, leaves, string or yarn, construction paper

Procedure:

1. On a class walk or on the walk to school, have each child collect about six leaves and a small branch, about 12 inches long. A branch with a few twigs makes the best kind of mobile.
2. Under the close supervision of the teacher, have each child press the leaves between two sheets of waxed paper, using an iron on the "low" setting. This preserves the leaves.
3. When the waxed paper has cooled, the children then cut around the leaves to separate them for the mobile. The waxed paper may be left on the leaves. However, if it does not stay attached, the wax coating left by the heat application is enough to harden and preserve the leaves.
4. Children then make holes in each leaf with a needle, hairpin, or even a pencil point. Instruct children to do this carefully.
5. Children insert string or thin yarn into the holes in each of the leaves. The teacher may help in knotting the string or yarn.
6. The children then attach a piece of string or yarn (about 12 inches long) to the branch. Help the

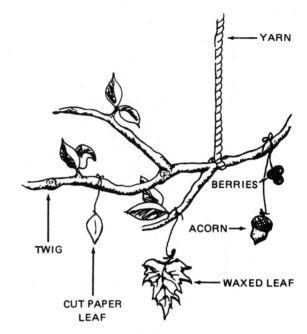

FIGURE 29–6 Leaf mobile.

children attach the string so that the branch hangs horizontally. (This is a good experiment in balance.)

7. Next, the children tie the leaves onto the branch in various places. Leaf shapes cut out of red, yellow, orange and brown construction paper can also be attached to the branch with yarn.
8. Acorns, seeds, or even berries may also be strung and attached for added color and variety.
9. Mobiles may be hung on a string across a section of the room for an attractive fall display.

**Nature Prints.** Children can make a splatter print of leaves, weeds, and grasses.

Procedure:

1. Rub a paint-filled toothbrush across a piece of wire screen, comb, or tongue blade. Create a transfer print by painting leaves and stamping them on paper.
2. Another transfer print can be made by arranging leaves, then covering them with paper. Rub over the paper with crayon. Make an overall design by

**FIGURE 29–7 Transfer print.**

moving the objects several times and repeating the rubbing. Colors may be overlapped and blended to create interesting effects.

3. For further suggestions, refer to the section on print making in Unit 12.

**Fall Field Trip.** Take the children on a neighborhood field trip. Have them pick up acorns, acorn shells, bits of grass or bark, small pine cones, etc. The next day for an art activity take an old 45 rpm record and have the children glue their finds onto the record. (Yard sales are a good source for old 45 rpm records.) Spray the decorated records with gold spray paint (in a well-ventilated area). Tape yarn or string on the back for hanging.

• When going on nature walks, give each child an empty egg carton in which to put found treasures. Or put a band of masking tape, sticky side out, around each child's wrist for holding leaves, seeds, and other small, lightweight treasures.

• Take along a shopping bag to hold miscellaneous items. Put a shoebox in the bottom of the bag to make it sturdier.

• Carry a large magnifying glass for observing nature up close.

• Bring along a bottle of hair spray to spritz delicate weeds and fluffy seed pods that the children collect.

**Weeds.** On a nice day, take the children on a walk collecting Queen Anne's lace, wild oats, goldenrod, grass, etc. The next day let each child dip these items into different colors of tempera paint, using either one or several different colors. Let dry, and then let each child take home in a plastic bag for a nice fall arrangement.

**Center of Interest Autumn Collage.** Make an arrangement with objects of nature that can be pasted easily to a flat background such as a shallow box or box lid. Sheets of heavy construction paper or cardboard are also suitable. A variety of objects (different textures, shapes, and colors) are important in creating an interesting design.

Begin the collage by placing the most important object on the background. Then arrange the other objects around it so that it remains the center of interest. A collection of autumn collages makes an attractive classroom display.

**Repeated Forms Autumn Collage.** Another nature collage can be made using seeds, pods, and other things scattered on the ground and left by the wind.

Procedure:
1. Children may classify the objects as large, small, round, straight, rough, smooth, hard, soft.
2. An egg carton is a good receptacle for small objects.
3. The objects may be arranged into a pattern of repeating forms, using contrasting shapes, textures, and colors. A group display tells the story of nature's materials.

**Fall Bouquet.** When assembling objects of nature, try making a bouquet of dried flowers, weeds, twigs, and leaves.

Procedure:
1. Select a container such as a tin can, old vase, or a paper cup. To hold objects in place, use sand, marbles, pebbles, oiled clay, play dough, or salt clay.
2. Begin the arrangement with the tallest pieces first; then use the short ones. Place objects at various

heights and angles. Use different textures, colors, and shapes. If the bouquet is to be seen from all sides it must be interesting all around.

**Papier-Mâché Harvest.** Crumple newspaper into desired shapes (fruits or vegetables). Cover each form with torn newspaper strips dipped into thin wheat paste. At least two layers of newspaper, with a generous use of paste, are needed to hold the form securely. When thoroughly dry, fruits and vegetables can be painted in brilliant colors.

**Play Store.**

Procedure:

1. A miniature store can be set up on a spare table, on some open shelves, or with a few large cartons.
2. Arrange papier-mâché fruits and vegetables in baskets and boxes from the supermarket.
3. Children can play store, buying and selling with make-believe money.

**Cut-Paper Mural.** This is another form of picture making in which each child can participate and make a contribution. Cut paper is a flexible technique that permits the child to arrange and rearrange objects on a background, grouping and overlapping them as desired.

Procedure:

1. After the topic is discussed, the children decide what they will each make, expressing their own ideas. A variety of papers may be used, such as colored construction paper, metallic foil, tissue paper, wallpaper, and illustrated magazine pages.
2. In placing objects it must be remembered that to create depth, large shapes should appear in the foreground or bottom of the picture; smaller figures are placed toward the top.
3. From time to time, children should stop working and evaluate their progress.
4. When completed, the mural glows with autumn colors. It can be used together with any of the other suggested art projects on this general topic.

**Painting with Weeds.** Some weeds can be used as brushes for painting, creating an interesting effect.

In the fall, many weeds are at maximum heights and can be collected on class walks for later use in art activities.

**Waxed Paper Pictures.** Place autumn leaves between two sheets of waxed paper, and press with a warm iron. (Shredded crayon pieces can be added before pressing for a more colorful effect.) These leaf pictures can be hung on a window or wall or used as placemats.

**Leaf Rubbings.** Place leaves under a piece of thin paper. Rub the side of an unwrapped crayon over the paper. The veins and outlines of the leaves will show up clearly. Use different colors for each leaf to create a more colorful design.

**Recycled Crayons.** Going back to school means starting fresh with bright new boxes of crayons. But what can a teacher do with the nubs left over from last year? Here are two suggestions:

*Hockey pucks.* Put the crayon bits, sorted by color, in greased muffin tins. Bake at 250° until completely melted. When the "pucks" are cooled, they can be used to make multicolored pictures and designs.

*Crayon surprise.* Shave crayons onto wax paper. Cover with a second piece of waxed paper. Using the low setting on an iron, press over the crayon sandwich so that the crayon wax melts. (*Adult supervision required at all times.*) Cut around the edge of the melted design, then hang the creations in the window as a suncatcher.

**Getting to Know You.** As the new school year begins, a good activity to help children get to know one another better is to use body outlines traced on paper in the following ways:

*Body builders.* A full-size outline of each child's body can be a starting point for many diverse activities. Cut strips from a roll of paper 1 meter (about 1 yard) wide or newsprint long enough for a child to lie full length on his or her back. Have the children pair up with partners. Partners should then take turns lying on the paper and tracing around each other with a crayon or felt-tip marker. Each child can then cut along his outline to get a body tracing. You now have the raw material for any of the following activities.

*All about me.* Have each child draw a line down the middle of his "body" and write, draw, or cut pictures from magazines to show individual likes and dislikes. You or the child can caption the two sides, "Things I like" and "Things I don't like." Follow up with a discussion of who likes what and why. Help the children understand and respect the idea that no two people have exactly the same feelings about things.

*Dress-up me.* Using crayons or markers, fill in the bodies with features and clothes. The children can first study their eyes, noses, mouths, and ears in a mirror. They can "dress" themselves either as they are dressed that day or in their own designer fashions. They may even wish to do both sides differently, one dressed up and one in play clothes. Again, use the results of this activity to discuss the similarities and differences that make everyone an individual.

*Measuring me.* The paper bodies can also be used as charts to record "vital statistics." List height and weight, of course, but also include handspan, length of nose, length of little finger, distance around the head, and so on. These life-size records could also show descriptive data, such as hair and eye color or even fingerprints.

*More me.* If time and paper permit, have the children make new tracings at a later date. This time each body should be in a frozen action pose. Then use the tracing as the basis for an action collage. Have the children search for pictures of dancers and athletes in old magazines or programs from local dance, theater, and sports groups and paste the clippings around the tracing.

*Mobile me.* Have the children make another body tracing, this time with a separate head, hands, and feet and illustrate the front and back. Tape a stick or a wire hanger across the top of the body and attach the body parts with yarn. Hang the "me mobiles" by the heads from the ceiling.

**Observing Children's Birthdays.** The purpose of observing birthdays is to honor the birthday child and mark his/her progress toward maturity (growing up is an idea dear to the hearts of most children).

Things to avoid in celebrating children's birthdays are an undue emphasis on the number of presents expected and received, and who is and is not going to be invited to the birthday party. It is also very important not to overlook a child's birthday at school, so it is wise to keep a calendar of these events. (See the "Happy Birthday to Us" bulletin board idea below.) Remember to celebrate children's birthdays that fall on holidays and other days when school is not held.

*Birthday activities.* Any activity that allows the child to assess his personal growth, such as measuring him or making a book about what he did when he was younger, is appropriate.

It helps to keep a special box that has a variety of birthday things all assembled, such as special puzzles, some stories and poems about birthdays, and games using the birthday theme. If these are kept all in one place, it is easier for you, and the children look forward to getting down the "birthday box" with great pleasure. Remember to revitalize the box at various times throughout the year; as you shop at variety stores, look for inexpensive additional birthday items.

Singling out the child by making him a special crown to wear is usually very much enjoyed; parents can be encouraged to provide a special snack—ideally one with good nutritional value that is not as costly as an elaborately decorated birthday cake.

Adults might also like to start a tradition of celebrating their own birthdays with the children by bringing a special snack to share with everyone. The children are often surprised to discover that everyone gets old—even teachers!

*"Happy Birthday to Us" Bulletin board.*
Materials: Clip clothespins (1 per child), 12 shoe boxes, glue, several pieces of oaktag or posterboard,

scissors, ruler, pencil, felt-tip markers, a long piece of paper, and a bulletin board

Procedure:

1. Cut posterboard or oaktag into 12 squares (one for each month) to fit size of bulletin board.
2. Mount each calendar page onto cardboard box so it rests away from the back of the bulletin board and enables clothespins to snap on. Glue the box to the chalkboard.
3. With the help of a parent or teacher, each child writes his name and birthday on a clip-style clothespin with a marker and attaches it to the correct month.
4. Clip the clothespins with a candle drawn on them to a posterboard birthday cake for celebrations.
5. Add more clothespins to the calendar bulletin board for holidays, trips, and special events. (See Figure 29–3.)

**What Happened?** Take photographs during a fall walk. Try to take pictures that show a sequence of events. Back in the classroom, arrange the photographs on display in sequence. Have the children think of captions for the pictures, then the story of the event, following the sequence shown in the pictures. Children who are not yet writing can dictate their captions and story to the teacher.

**Bean Necklace.**
Procedure:

1. Soak different kinds of dried beans in water with food coloring to soften and color the beans.
2. Thread a needle with heavy thread or twine. String the beans and let them dry.
3. The beans will shrink, so do not tie the necklace until they are dry.

**What's the Weather?** Ask the children to draw twin weather pictures. On the left side of the page, they can draw a familiar outdoor scene of any season of the year. On the other half of the paper, have them draw the scene as it would look at another time of year: for example, a crowded beach in summer and a lonely one in winter. After they finish their drawings, encourage the youngsters to talk about seasonal differences.

**Well-Preserved Beauty.** Here's a way to save some of the colorful beauty from autumn's fallen leaves.

Procedure:

1. Have each child choose a leaf for its color and shape and place it on a piece of tagboard.
2. Trace the outline of the leaf with a crayon or paint the area inside with a bright fall color.
3. Label the leaf. Have the children look up the leaves they cannot identify.

**Jack Be Nimble.**

Procedure:

1. The children sit in a circle, semicircle, or line.
2. Set up a block for a pretend candle. (Two or three can be set up, if desired.) The children take turns jumping over the candle(s) while every one sings:

Jack be nimble,
Jack be quick
Jack jump over the candlestick.

(Children enjoy having their own names substituted for "Jack.")

3. Variation: To give everyone a chance to be more active, have the children form a circle, holding hands, and walk around "Jack" while he jumps over the candle.

**Musical Carpets.** Use carpet or towel squares to play a cooperative version of musical chairs. The object of this game is to help everyone find a place to sit; in other words, no one is ever "out." Ask the children to arrange the squares in a circle and to stand outside the circle. Then, as you beat a drum slowly, invite children to walk slowly around the circle. When the drum stops, they find a carpet to sit on wherever they are. After everyone has found a seat, ask children to stand up and remove three squares. Again, beat on the drum while they walk around the circle. This time when you stop, some children will need to share carpets. Continue playing the game until all the children are piled together on just a few squares.

**Jump the Creek.** Two markers are separated to represent the narrow creek. The children jump over the two markers trying not to touch them. The last child over the creek gets to widen the creek for the next turn around. Any child who lands in the creek must take off his shoes and put them back on before he can reenter the game.

**The Postman Game.**
Equipment: Cards with pictures (or words) of various parts of the body and a postman's hat

Procedure: Have children sit in a circle. Place a body part card in an envelope. Choose a postman. The postman takes one envelope and hands it to any child. The child opens the envelope and moves that body part in some way. Other children raise their hands when they can identify the body part. The postman chooses a child to answer. If the body part is identified correctly, the child answering will be the new postman.

**Musical Colors.**
Equipment: Pieces of different-colored construction paper (each about 8½″ × 11″ in size), tape recorder, and a tape with any music on it

Procedure: Place the pieces of paper in a circle or line. Start the tape. When the music starts, the children walk either around the circle or down the line. The leader stops the music after a short while and each child tries to stand on the paper nearest him. Use as many pieces of paper as you have children. After the first time the music stops, remove one color and say, "Let's take yellow away now." The game is played from here on the same as musical chairs. (Variation: have the children stop with a different body part in the colored circles.)

## LANGUAGE ARTS EXPERIENCE

**Apple Story.** Have an apple ready to cut in half across the width, at the end of this story. When the apple is cut widthwise, the apple seeds look like the "star" in the story.

*The Star in the Apple*

Once upon a time there was a little boy who couldn't find anything to play with. He was tired of all his toys and asked his mother if she could please help him find something to do. She thought and thought and finally said, "Why, I know what you can do. You can go outside and look for a little red house that is round and shiny, has no doors and windows, and has a star inside." He thought it sounded like fun, and easy to find, so outside he went. He looked and looked but there was no such house to be found.

The little boy met a dog and said, "Mr. Dog, would you help me find a little house that is red and shiny, has no doors or windows, and has a star inside?" The dog said, "Surely," and they went together to find the house. (They meet a cat, a horse, a cow, and a chicken, and go through the same routine.) The whole procession at last met a little old woman who had a knife in her hand. The little boy asked her if she had seen a little house which was red and shiny, with no doors or windows, and with a star inside.

She answered, "Why, yes, come along with me and I will find it for you." The little old woman led them to a hill. Only an apple tree grew on the hill. The old woman said, "This is where the house is, little boy." The little boy and his friends looked and looked, but could not see a little red house. The old woman picked an apple and asked, "Isn't this round and shiny? It has no doors, and no windows. I wonder if there is a star inside."

With her knife, she cut the apple horizontally. There was the star! So the little boy found the little red house that is round and shiny, has no doors and windows, and has a star inside. It is an apple!

You may want to plan to do some of the apple activities on page 597 after reading this story.

## FINGERPLAYS, POEMS, AND SONGS

**Safety (Fingerplay)**
Red says STOP
  (Hold right hand in "stop" gesture)
And Green says GO.
  (Extend right arm with index finger pointed)

Yellow says WAIT;
You'd better go slow!
  (With index finger extended, wave right hand
  across body from right to left and back to right)
When I reach a crossing place
  (Cross arms at wrists)
To left and right I turn my face.
  (Turn head to left and right)
I walk, not run, across the street
  (Demonstrate walking or use index fingers to show
  walking, then running)
And use my head to guide my feet.
  (Point to head, then to feet)

**Back to School (Fingerplay)**
(Have a calendar and clockface with movable hands
ready before beginning this play.)

The calendar says September.
  (Point to the word "September" on calendar)
The clock says eight A.M.
  (Show clockface with proper time)
The school bus calls to take us
Back to school again!
  (Hold hands as though on steering wheel of bus)
When we see our friends, we'll wave
  (Wave hand and smile)
When we're in class, we will behave.
  (Fold hands in front—"good child" gesture)
We'll look at books and write our names
  (Pretend to hold an open book, and pretend to
  write in it)
And play some of our favorite games.
  (Pretend to throw a ball or jump rope)

**Falling Leaves (Fingerplay)**
Red leaves falling down
Yellow leaves falling down.
  (Move fingers in falling leaves gesture)
Over all the town.
Over all the town.
  (Make circle movements with arms)
Leaves are falling down
Leaves are falling down
  (Move fingers in falling leaves gesture)
Red leaves, yellow leaves
All are falling down.
  (Children "fall" gently down to the floor)

**The Apple Tree (Fingerplay)**
Way up in the apple tree
  (Point up)
Two little apples smiled at me.
  (Close thumb and forefinger of each hand)

I shook that tree as hard as I could
  (Grab imaginary tree and shake it)
Down fell the apples
  (Raise hands and arms high, then let fall)
M-m-m, were they good!
  (Rub tummy, satisfied smile on face)

**Five Red Apples (Fingerplay)**
Five red apples in a grocery store;
  (Hold up five fingers)
Bobby ate one, and then there were four.
  (Hold up four fingers)
Susie ate one, and then there were three.
  (Hold up three fingers)
Three red apples. What did Mary do?
Why, she ate one, and then there were two.
  (Hold up two fingers)
Two red apples ripening in the sun;
Jimmy ate one, and then there was one.
  (Hold up one finger)
One red apple, and now we are done;
I ate the last one and now there are none.
  (Hold out hands, palms up)

Variation: Substitute names of children in the group
for various verses.

**Raking Leaves (Fingerplay)**
I like to rake the leaves
  (Raking gesture)
Into a great big hump.
  (Hands make hump)
Then I go back a little way,
  (Step back)
Bend both my knees, and jump!
  (Children jump)

**Leaves Dance (Fingerplay)**
Leaves are floating softly down,
  (Waving fingers, like falling leaves)
They make a carpet on the ground.
  (Bend down, run hand close to ground)
Then swish, the wind comes whistling by
  (Stand up, raise hands above head)
And sends them dancing to the sky.
  (Dance)

**Gray Squirrel (Action Poem, Song)**
Gray squirrel, gray squirrel
Swish your bushy tail
  (Children move "bottoms" pretending to move
  "tails")
(Repeat)

Hold a nut between your paws
(Pretend to hold a nut with closed fists together)
Wrinkle up your funny nose.
(Move nose like a squirrel)
Gray squirrel, gray squirrel,
Swish your bushy tail.
(Pretend to move "tail")

**Shuffling (Action Poem)**
It's fun to shuffle on my way
(Shuffle feet)
Through rustling leaves on an autumn day.
(Shuffle feet)
The leaves aren't leaves at all to me;
(Shake head)
They are cornflakes falling from a tree.
(Pretend to munch and rub tummy)

**Trees in Fall (Action Poem)**
The elm will stretch and stretch so wide,
(Children stretch arms out wide)
It reaches out on every side.
(Still stretching—horizontally)
The pine will stretch and stretch so high
(Now stretch arms vertically)
It reaches up to touch the sky.
(Still stretching)
The willow droops and droops so low,
(Droop down)
Its branches sweep the ground below.
(Fall softly to floor)

**Come, Little Leaves (Action Poem)**
"Come, little leaves," said the wind one day.
(Beckon with index finger)
"Come over the meadows with me and play.
(Beckon with arm)
Put on your dresses of red and gold,
(Pretend to dress)
For summer is gone, and
The days grow cold."
(Rub arms to keep warm)

**One Little Leaf (Finger Play)**
One little leaf, two little leaves,
(Hold up one, then two fingers)
Three little leaves today.
(Hold up three fingers)
Four little leaves, five little leaves,
(Then fourth and fifth fingers)
Blow them all away.
(Blow on fingers, and then put them down making
them "blow" away)

**Apple Tree Adventure (Action Poem)**
As I was walking down a lane
(Walk in place)

I saw an apple tree.
(Shade eyes with hand for "I saw")
I jumped for joy and clapped my hands.
(Jump and clap lightly)
"Oh, boy!" I said. "Watch me."
(Point to self)
I marched up to that apple tree.
(March in place—mark time)
And took a flying leap.
(Leap into air, arms overhead as though grasping a
branch)
I caught a branch and hung there.
(Hands over head, fists clenched as though grasping
the branch)
Then I heard a warning cheep.
(Make appropriate bird sound)
Above my head, upon her nest, there sat a mother
bird.
(Look up, cup hands like a nest, keep above eye
level)
"Little boy," she told me,
(Bring hands down to eye level. Cup left hand,
palm up for "nest." Fit right hand over it for bird.
Move right thumb and forefinger representing
bird's bill)
"Please leave without a word. My babies will be
frightened if from the nest I stray."
(Demonstrate bird flying by keeping three middle
fingers of right hand still and flapping thumb and
little finger for wings)
So I let go and dropped down.
(Arms over head, open fists, bend knees, let hands
touch floor)
And tiptoed far away.
(Turn body, tiptoe in place)

*Note:* A child who particularly enjoys story pantomime might practice this and do it to entertain his
classmates.

**A Leaf**
If I were a leaf
(But I wouldn't be),
I'd have to be tied
To a tree, tree, tree.

I couldn't walk off
(Or skip or run),
And my nose would get burned
By the sun, sun, sun.

In summer, I'd roast,
In winter, I'd freeze.
And all through October,
I'd sneeze, sneeze, sneeze!

## Autumn Woods

I like the woods in autumn
When dry leaves hide the ground,
When the trees are bare
And the wind sweeps by
With a winsome, rushing sound.

I can rustle the leaves in autumn
And I can make a bed
In the thick dry leaves
That have fallen
From the bare trees overhead.

## Leaves

Down, Down!
Yellow and brown.
The leaves are falling
All over town.

## Fall Bird

I saw a bird the other day,
He sat upon a limb;
He looked at me, then flew away,
It was too cold for him.

He flew away where the cotton grows,
Where everything's bright, not dim;
He flew away where it never snows,
That bird upon the limb.

## Autumn Bird Song

Over the housetops,
Over the trees,
Winging their way
In a stiff fall breeze.

A flock of birds
Is flying along
Southward, for winter,
Singing a song.

Singing a song
They all like to sing,
"We'll see you again
When it's spring, spring, spring."

## Dry Leaves

Dry leaves in autumn
Go clicking down the street,
Like children playing dress up
With slippers on their feet.

## Fall Insects Sleep

What is under the grass
Way down in the ground,
Where everything is cool and wet
With darkness all around?

Little pink worms live there;
Ants and brown bugs creep
Softly round the stones and rocks
Where roots are pushing deep.

## The Little Green Frog

GUMP-BLAH! went the little green frog one day.
GUMP-BLAH! went the little green frog.
GUMP-BLAH! went the little green frog one day
And his eyes went GUMP-BLAH-GUMP!
(Stick out tongue on BLAH and blink eyes.)

## Frisky Squirrel

Whisky, frisky,
Hippity-hop
Up he goes
To the treetop!

Whirly, twirly,
Round and round,
Down he scampers
To the ground.

Furly, curly,
What a tail!
Tall as a feather,
Broad as a sail!

Where's his supper!
In the shell;
Snap, cracky,
Out it fell.

## Happy Leaves

Little *red* leaves are glad today
  (Also substitute brown and yellow)
For the wind is blowing them off and away.

They are flying here, they are flying there.
Oh little *red* leaves, you are everywhere!
  (Also substitute brown and yellow)

## I Saw a Squirrel

I saw a little squirrel,
Sitting in a tree;
He was eating a nut
And wouldn't look at me.

## Wind

I like the wind
When I play out;
It blows the leaves and me about.
I like the rain upon my nose;
Of course, it's not so good for clothes.
The sun comes out most every day;
Sometimes, you know, it hides away.

**The Milkweed**
In a milkweed cradle snug and warm
Baby seeds are hiding safe from harm.
Open wide the cradle!
Hold it high!
Come, Mr. Wind, help them fly.

**It's Raining Gold**
It's raining gold
And red and brown,
As autumn leaves
Come falling down!

---

## COOKING EXPERIENCES

**Picture Recipes.**   As children gain experience in cooking, they begin to see that specific directions are followed in recipes. It is then fun to write out recipes in picture form for children to read by themselves. To make such recipes, simply cut out pictures of ingredients and utensils from magazines or make rough drawings. The children will learn that each picture stands for a particular food or utensil. They will soon be able to tell the teacher which ingredient is used next.

A plastic set of measuring cups and spoons should be available. Each size should be a different color, to help the children learn more quickly about proper measurements. Match the color of the picture to the color of the real spoon or cup.

**Applesauce.**
Ingredients:
4 to 6 medium apples
¼ cup sugar
½ stick cinnamon (or 1–2 whole cloves, if desired)

Materials: Apple corer, vegetable peeler, cooking pot, food mill (if available)

Procedure: (if food mill is not used)
1. Peel and core the apples.
2. Cut apples into quarters, and place in pot.
3. Add a small amount of water (about 1 inch).
4. Cover the pot and cook slowly (simmer) until apples are tender. The cooked apples can then be mashed with a fork, beaten with a beater, or put through a strainer.

**FIGURE 29–8 Picture recipe for applesauce.**

5. Add sugar to taste (about ¼ cup to 4 apples), and continue cooking until sugar dissolves.
6. Add ½ stick of cinnamon (or 1 to 2 cloves) if desired.

*Note:* If a food mill is used, it is not necessary to peel and core the apples. After the apples are cooked as above, they are put through the food mill. Children enjoy turning the handle and watching the sauce come dripping out of the holes.

7. For fun, add a few cinnamon candies. What happens to the color of the applesauce? Is the flavor changed? Be sure to add them while the applesauce is still hot.

### Little People's "Bird Seed."
Ingredients:
2 cups Sugar Pops cereal
½ cup seedless raisins
½ cup butterscotch morsels
½ cup chocolate chips
½ cup salted peanuts

Procedure:
Mix all ingredients together. Great for snacks, picnics, or packed lunches on field trips.

**An Apple Snack.**   Core a whole apple. Mix peanut butter with raisins, wheat germ, or granola. Stuff the mixture into the cored apple. Eat whole or slice into wheels.

**Dried Apples.**   The adult prepares apples before this activity, peeling and cutting into triangular shapes and squares. Give each child a large needle and thread for stringing. When the string is full, tie at each end, making a necklace. Then hang string of apples in your room in the sunlight until dried out completely.

**Apple Pigs.**   Take a large, red, rosy apple and place four toothpicks in one side for legs; leave the leaf stem for a tail. Cut another, smaller apple in half. Attach one half to the "head end" of the pig's with a toothpick. The cut side of the smaller apple forms the pig's face. (See Figure 29–9.) Make eyes by inserting whole cloves or raisins; use little leaves for ears. To stop the face from turning brown, dip it in a little lemon juice or white vinegar.

### Fried Apple Pies.
Cook the apples and season with cinnamon and sugar to taste. Use canned biscuits and let children

## Apple Pig

FIGURE 29–9 Apple pig.

pat and flatten biscuits as large as they can. Have children put one teaspoon of apple mixture on each biscuit. Fold over pocketbook-style and prick edges and center with fork. Drop in hot oil and fry until brown. Sprinkle with powdered sugar.

### Vegetable Soup.
Ingredients:
1 soup bone
1 onion
1 cup peas
3 diced potatoes
½ quart tomatoes
½ cup celery diced
½ cup shredded cabbage (optional)
1 cup corn
1 cup lima beans
salt and pepper to taste
macaroni alphabet letters

Procedure:
1. Cook the soup bone in enough water to completely cover it.
2. When tender, remove meat from broth and add diced vegetables and more water if needed. Add macaroni letters.
3. Continue to cook for 20 minutes.
4. Seasoned, canned vegetables may be substituted for fresh vegetables; add just before serving. Instant vegetable soup may be used for broth, if desired. It is faster.

## Baked Apples.

Ingredients:
6 red baking apples
1 tablespoon butter
6 tablespoons sugar
1 teaspoon cinnamon
⅓ cup water
½ cup dark molasses or sorghum

Procedure:
1. Wash apples. Remove cores (teacher).
2. Place apples in a buttered, flat baking dish.
3. In center of each apple, put ½ teaspoon butter and 1 tablespoon sugar and cinnamon mixture. Combine water and molasses and pour over apples.
4. Bake at 350° for approximately 45 minutes. Baste occasionally.
5. Raisins may be added to apples, if desired.

## Pumpkin Soup.

Ingredients:
2½ cups mashed, cooked pumpkin
3 cups water
1 tablespoon chopped onion
1 tablespoon shortening
1 cup light cream or whole milk
salt and pepper to taste
1 tablespoon curry powder
dried or fresh mint

Procedure:
1. An adult or older child will need to cut the pumpkin into pieces.
2. Place these pieces in a large baking pan and pour water over slices. Bake at 325°F until very tender.
3. Cool, remove skin, and mash pumpkin through ricer or colander.
4. Chop peeled onion, and sauté in shortening until transparent.
5. Combine pumpkin pulp, water, and onion. Boil for 3 minutes.
6. Add cream or milk, salt, pepper, and curry powder. Heat, stirring constantly.
7. Fill bowls or cups for serving and sprinkle mint on top. Serves 16 children.

## Pumpkin Pudding.

Ingredients:
½ pint plus 3 tablespoons milk
¼ pound brown sugar
¼ teaspoon grated orange peel
¼ teaspoon ground ginger
scant ½ teaspoon ground cinnamon
scant ½ teaspoon salt
3 eggs lightly beaten
½ pint less 3 tablespoons freshly cooked pureed pumpkin

Procedure:
1. Preheat oven to 350°F.
2. Combine milk, brown sugar, orange peel, ginger, cinnamon, and salt in large mixing bowl. Stir thoroughly, then add the lightly beaten eggs and pureed pumpkin.
3. Beat vigorously with a spoon until the mixture is smooth. Pour it into a 1½-pint shallow greased baking dish.
4. Place the dish in a large pan in the middle of the oven and pour enough boiling water into the pan to come halfway up the sides of the baking dish.
5. Bake the pudding for about 75 minutes, or until a knife inserted in the center of the pudding comes out clean.
6. Remove the dish from the water and either cool the pudding to room temperature before serving, or refrigerate for at least three hours.

## Pumpkin Bread.

Ingredients:
15 ounces canned pumpkin
12 ounces sugar
3 ounces vegetable oil
2 eggs
1 cup flour
½ teaspoon baking powder
1 teaspoon baking soda
1 teaspoon each: salt, ground cloves, cinnamon, and allspice
½ cup each raisins and nuts (optional)
¼ cup water

Procedure:
Add sugar to oil and mix. Add eggs, pumpkin, spices sifted with flour, water, and nuts or raisins. Bake one hour at 350°F.

## Pumpkin Cookies.
Ingredients:
1 cup sugar
½ cup margarine
1 egg
8 ounces canned pumpkin
1 cup flour
½ cup each of walnuts and raisins
2 teaspoons cinnamon
1 teaspoon vanilla
1 teaspoon each baking powder and baking soda
pinch of salt.

Procedure:
Mix well, and drop on greased, flat baking sheet. Bake 8 to 10 minutes in 375°F oven. These are good as they are or may be iced if you like.

## Good Granola.
Ingredients:
1 cup oatmeal
⅓ cup wheat germ
¼ cup coconut
¼ cup sunflower seeds
¼ cup powdered milk
1 teaspoon cinnamon
2 tablespoons honey
2 tablespoons oil
1 teaspoon vanilla

Procedure:
1. Mix oatmeal, wheat germ, coconut, sunflower seeds, powdered milk, and cinnamon.
2. Add honey, oil, and vanilla. Mix well.
3. Spread on a cookie sheet. Bake at 375°F for 8–10 minutes.
4. Cool on paper towels. Good for snack or breakfast, too.

## Nutty Numbers.
Ingredients:
½ cup soft butter
1 cup flour
¼ cup honey
1 cup wheat germ
chopped nuts

Procedure:
1. Mix butter, flour, honey, and wheat germ.
2. Shape into numbers.
3. Cover with chopped nuts. Gently press nuts into the numbers.
4. Bake at 350°F for 10 minutes.

## General Vegetables Preparation.
Green or wax beans—Cut in 1-inch pieces; cook in boiling salt water 15 to 20 minutes in a covered saucepan.

Beets—Wash and cut off tops; cook beets whole without salt 30 to 60 minutes, until tender. Drain; drop in cold water; slip off skins with your fingers. Cube or quarter.

Broccoli—Cut off large stems; cook (covered) 10 to 20 minutes. Cut into bite-size pieces.

Cabbage—Shred with long sharp knife. Cook in small amount of water 5 to 15 minutes; cook red cabbage 20 to 25 minutes.

Carrots—Cut into sticks; cook 10 to 25 minutes in boiling water.

Celery—Cut into 1-inch pieces; cook in small amount of water 15 minutes.

Peas—Shell just before cooking time. Cook in small amount of water. Cover and cook until tender but not mushy.

Squash—Cut in half or pieces; remove seeds and fibers; bake 35 to 45 minutes until soft. Season with brown sugar or molasses. Cut into small pieces for tasting.

Asparagus—Wash; cut up. Cook covered in a small amount of boiling salted water for 5 to 10 minutes.

Other vegetables that might be cooked include:

| | |
|---|---|
| Lima or any beans | Peppers |
| Brussels sprouts | Potatoes |
| Cauliflower | Spinach |
| Corn on the cob | Tomatoes |
| Greens | Turnips |
| Okra | |

**Tangy Raisin Dessert.**

Ingredients:

1½ cups raisins
¾ cup water
1 large apple
1 tablespoon cornstarch
cream, whipped cream, or yogurt
½ teaspoon cinnamon
¼ teaspoon cloves
½ cup chopped walnuts or pecans

Procedure:

1. Measure raisins and water into saucepan. Cover and cook slowly for 5 minutes.
2. Wash apple; cut into small pieces. Add to raisin mixture and cook 5 minutes more.
3. Measure cornstarch into small bowl and add a little cold water. Mix thoroughly and add slowly to raisin mixture.
4. Continue cooking, stirring constantly as mixture thickens. Add cinnamon and cloves.
5. Serve warm with cream, whipped cream, or yogurt. Sprinkle with nutmeg if desired. Makes 2½ cups; serves 8 children.

**Apple Cake,**

Ingredients:

1½ cups cooking oil
3 eggs
2 cups sugar
2 teaspoons vanilla
3 cups presifted flour
1 teaspoon baking soda
2 teaspoons cinnamon
½ teaspoon salt
2 cups peeled, chopped apples
1 cup chopped walnuts

Materials: Knife for peeling and chopping apples, flour sifter, measuring cup, measuring spoons, 2 loaf pans, large and small mixing bowls, mixing spoon

Procedure:

1. Help the children peel and prepare the apples.
2. Grease the loaf pans.
3. Sprinkle a little flour in each pan and shake it until the pan is dusted with flour.
4. Measure the sifted flour into the small mixing bowl.
5. Stir in the baking soda, cinnamon, and salt.
6. In the big mixing bowl, mix the sugar, oil, eggs, and vanilla.
7. Add the flour mixture to the egg mixture and stir well.
8. Add the apples and nuts and stir gently.
9. Pour the whole mixture into loaf pans.
10. Bake for 1½ hours at 350°F. (Makes 2 loaves)

**Quick Kabobs.** Cut a banana, apple, melon, and cheese into bite-sized pieces. Put on skewer. Dip in orange juice, and roll in shredded coconut.

**Zucchini Muffins.**

Ingredients:

½ cup grated zucchini
1 egg
2 tablespoons oil
¼ cup honey
¼ teaspoon grated lemon peel
¾ cup flour
½ teaspoon baking powder
¼ teaspoon salt
¼ teaspoon cinnamon

Procedure:

1. Put grated zucchini into a bowl.
2. Add egg, oil, honey, and grated lemon peel. Mix well.
3. Then add flour, baking powder, salt, and cinnamon. Mix until smooth.
4. Put into muffin tin. Bake at 400°F for 20 minutes.

**Hot Apple Cider.** Heat cider or apple juice. Add a pinch of cinnamon or nutmeg, or both. How does it smell?

**Vegetable Dip.** Dip celery, cucumber, or carrot sticks into peanut butter, sour cream, yogurt, or cottage cheese that has been mashed with a fork.

**Rosh Hashanah Food Ideas.** In Jewish homes, the New Year is ushered in with many symbolic, special foods. Fresh apple slices dipped in honey, apple cake, and honey cake all signify wishes for a "sweet year." Sweet dishes are preferred, sour or bitter flavors avoided. The first fruits and vegetables of the fall harvest are always on the Rosh Hashanah menu. Rosh Hashanah snacks include apple slices dipped in honey, fresh fruit, and raw vegetables.

# ADDITIONAL READINGS

## Children's Books for Autumn

Ahlberg, Allan. *Each Peach Pear Plum.* New York: Viking, 1979.

Allison, Linda. *The Reasons for the Seasons.* Boston: Little, Brown & Co., 1975.

Azarian, Mary. *A Farmer's Alphabet.* Cincinnati: Godine, 1981.

Barklem, Jill. *Autumn Story.* New York: Philomel Books, 1980.

Bauer, Caroline F. *Midnight Snowman.* New York: Atheneum, 1987.

Buscaglia, Leo. *The Fall of Freddie the Leaf.* New York: Charles B. Slac, 1982.

Cleary, Beverly. *Ellen Tebbits.* New York: Dell, 1979.

Cohen, Miriam. *When Will I Read?* New York: Greenwillow, 1977.

DeRegniers, Beatrice. *May I Bring a Friend?* New York: Atheneum, 1964.

Fisher, Aileen, and Adrienne Adams (illus.). *Where Does Everyone Go?* New York: Thomas Y. Crowell, 1961.

Fox, Charles Philip. *When Autumn Comes.* Chicago: Reilly and Co., 1966.

Garnett, Eve. *A Book of the Seasons: An Anthology.* London: Oxford University Press, 1952.

Goodall, John. *Shrewbettina's Birthday.* New York: Harcourt, 1971.

Gray, Nicholas S. *Apples Stones.* New York: Hawthorn, 1969.

Hoban, Russell. *Best Friends for Frances.* New York: Harper, 1968.

Hunt, Irene. *Trail of Apple Blossoms.* Chicago: Follett, 1968.

Kane, Henry B. *Four Seasons in the Woods.* New York: Knopf, 1968.

Kessler, Ethel, and Leonard Kessler. *All for Fall.* New York: Parents' Magazine Press, 1974.

Lapp, Eleanor J., and David Cunningham (illus.). *The Mice Came in Early This Year.* Chicago: A. Whitman, 1976.

Lionni, Leo. *Frederick.* New York: Pantheon, 1970.

Lobel, Arnold. *Frog and Toad Together.* New York: Harper, 1972.

Maguire, Mack. *Hopscotch, Hangman, Hot Potato Ha, Ha, Ha. A Rulebook of Children's Games.* New York: Prentice Hall Press, 1990.

McCloskey, Robert. *On Market Street.* New York: Greenwillow, 1981.

Scheer, Julian. *Rain Makes Applesauce.* New York: Holiday, 1964.

Sterling, Dorothy. *Fall Is Here!* Garden City, N.Y.: The Natural History Press, 1966.

Stevenson, James. *Could Be Worse!* New York: Greenwillow, 1978.

Stevenson, Sucie. *Henry and Mudge Under the Yellow Moon.* New York: Bradbury Press, 1987.

Wells, Rosemary. *Timothy Goes to School.* New York: Dial, 1987.

## Children's Books About Birthdays

Bond, F. *Mary Betty: Lizzie McNutt's Birthday.* New York: Crowell, 1983.

Hoban, R. *Birthday for Frances.* New York: Harper, 1968.

Keats, Ezra J. *A Letter to Amy.* New York: Harper & Row, 1968.

Shiman, S. *A Special Birthday.* New York: McGraw-Hill, 1976.

Uchida, Y. *The Birthday Visitor.* New York: Charles Scribner's Sons, 1975.

# UNIT 30

# Winter

Young children greet winter with delight. In many areas of the country it means ice-skating and sledding, rolling snowballs to make a snowman, sliding on the ice, jumping in showdrifts, and catching snowflakes on warm mittens. In other areas, it means colder weather and shorter days, even though there is no snow. The idea of snow in winter, however, is traditional even in parts of the country where it never snows!

Winter offers many stimulating subjects for creative art activities. Children can experiment with paints to depict the gay colors of winter clothing and the active lines seen in outdoor sports. The delicate textures can be created by painting with bits of sponge, crushed paper, or old toothbrushes. White chalk also works well for winter pictures. It may be used alone, on colored paper, or in combination with crayon. Some topics for picture making are:

- Playing in the Snow
- Our Street in Winter
- Feeding the Birds
- Riding on My Sled
- We Play Safely in Winter
- Ice-Skating with My Friends
- Building a Snowman
- Dressing for Winter Weather

## LESSON PLAN IDEAS FOR WINTER AND SNOW

### Excursions.

- Walk outside to observe winter and snow characteristics
- Ice- or roller-skating rink
- Child's home, where a parent can show how to prepare for winter—furnace checked, wood for fireplace ready, etc.

- Snow removal equipment at streets department
- Sleighing at nearby hill

### Art.

- Snowmen made with cotton, then decorated with collage items
- Snowmen made with construction paper shapes—circles, squares, triangles instead of only circles, decorated with scraps of paper or other collage items
- Marshmallow-sculpture snow figures
- Snowflakes made with paper punch and tissue paper, and hung by a string from mobile or ceiling
- Fingerpaint with soap flakes or shaving cream

### Science.

- Observation and study of plants in winter with children encouraged to discover for themselves which plants stay the same all year
- Observation and study of a snowshoe rabbit, with discussion on how it changes color to match its environment in winter
- Observation of melting of icicles and snow as temperatures warm, or as they are placed over heat
- Observation of snowflakes with a magnifying glass
- Discussion of animals that hibernate for the winter
- Observation of water placed outside, with discussion of temperature as it relates to freezing and liquids, and to formation of snowflakes
- Discussion of migration of some birds before winter
- Mixing food coloring with snow
- Studying animal tracks in the snow
- Observing birds at a bird feeder
- Recognizing the differences between birds seen at the bird feeder

## Music.

- Creative movements relating to snow and different kinds of snow-storms
- Creative movements relating to jobs in winter, such as shoveling snow
- Creative movements depicting a snowman as it melts
- Creative movements of winter sports and activities—ice-skating, throwing snowballs, etc.
- Creative movements depicting birds flying around the bird feeder, eating seeds, flying in the air
- "Musical Chairs"—played with pictures of winter clothing, foods, weather, activities, places, etc., which are put on the backs of the chairs. (After the children have found their chairs. give instructions for the various categories—for example, "All who have something you wear in winter, stand up and jump to a neighbor and back again.")

## Food.

- Homemade ice cream, made with snow instead of ice for freezing. (See end of food unit for recipe.)
- Snow cones
- Chili
- Homemade soup
- Hot chocolate
- Stew (See food section for more food suggestions.)

## Visitors.

- Skier can display equipment.
- Member of ski patrol can show equipment and role-play helping a person who has been injured.
- Ice skater can show equipment.
- Snowmobiler can show equipment and snowmobile, perhaps with arrangements to take the children for a ride.

## Language Experiences.

- Slides and/or pictures of food, recreational equipment, clothing, etc., relating to winter. Items passed out to all the children, with each child telling about a specific item relating to winter.
- Sharing of vacation experiences during wintertime

- Sharing of a favorite winter activity, food, place to visit, etc.
- Stories, written or told, of most memorable winter vacation or experience
- Sharing pictures of the birds of winter (*National Geographic* and the *Audubon Society Guide to North America Birds* have beautiful photos of birds for this activity.)
- Talk about the birds' colors, sizes, and what they like to eat. A natural follow-up is to make one of the bird feeders in this unit.

## ART ACTIVITIES

Emphasis on children's creativity, use of small and large motor skills, and hand–eye coordination are the bases for the following art activities. Remember, emphasize the *process*, not the product, in all of these activities.

**Snowflakes.** The individual patterns of snowflakes vary greatly, but all have six points. Some flakes are finely cut; others are fringed like delicate feathers. (You may want to practice using newspaper first.)

Procedure:
1. Using tissue paper or other fine paper, begin by cutting a circle, then fold it in half.
2. Fold the half-circle into three parts, then in half again.
3. Make cuts along the folds but leave solid areas between, making the pattern as delicate as possible. Snowflakes can be used decoratively on a bulletin board or added to a winter mural.

**Winter on Our Street.**
Procedure:
1. Cover a table or counter top with white roll paper, a white sheet, or fireproof cotton.
2. Use discarded cardboard boxes painted or covered with construction paper to make buildings and cars.
3. Sprinkle glitter or spray snow on rooftops for a frosty effect.
4. Trees may be made of twigs stuck in clay. Arrange houses and mark streets.

## How to Make A Snowflake

Cut paper into a circle.
Fold circle in half.
Fold again along lines (a).

Fold once more along line (b).

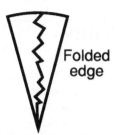

Folded edge

Cut pattern from one side.

Open out for snowflake.

**FIGURE 30–1  How to make a snowflake.**

## Torn Paper Snowman

**FIGURE 30–2  Torn paper snowman.**

### Torn Paper Snowman.

Materials: Glue, construction paper: black, white; an assortment of twigs; fabric scraps; torn pieces of black and white construction paper.

Procedure:

1. Cut large, medium, and small circles out of white construction paper (or white paper plates). Let the children glue these together onto a sheet of construction paper to form the snowman.
2. Have the children tear up white and black construction paper into small pieces. Glue the white pieces to fill up the snowman's body; use the black pieces for facial features, a hat, and any other details they want to add.
3. Glue on twigs for arms.
4. Fabric scraps may be used for other details.

### Paper Snowmen.

Procedure:

1. Large or small paper bags can be stuffed with newspaper, tied at the neck and head, and then painted. While the paint is wet, sprinkle with glitter for a frosty look.
2. The snowman's hat may be made of construction paper. A broom, shovel, and scarf may be added. Other snowmen may consist of marshmallows or cotton balls fastened together with glue or toothpicks.

### Stuffed Shapes of Winter.

Materials: Manilla paper, crayons, scissors, stapler, newspaper

Procedure:

1. Each child draws a seasonal shape.
2. Cut out two of the shape. Color in the design on one side of each shape. Staple shapes together with design facing out.
3. Leave an opening to stuff small bits of newspaper to make the shape three dimensional. Carefully staple the opening closed.
4. Hang the shapes with thread, yarn, or string

Variations: Balls, stars, snowmen, wreaths, presents, Christmas trees, etc.

**FIGURE 30–3 Stuffed shapes of winter.**

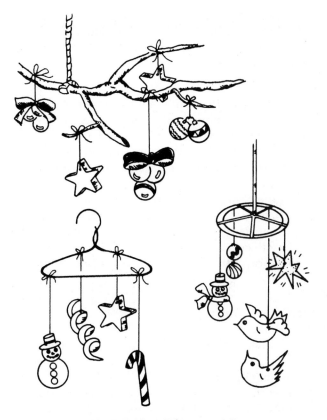

**FIGURE 30–4 Winter mobile.**

## Winter Mobile.

Procedure:

1. Mobiles may consist of two- or three-dimensional objects of paper, cardboard, or metal foil tied with string or thin wire. They can be hung from a small tree branch, coat hanger, or embroidery hoop.
2. Several objects can be made to balance a large one.
3. A winter mobile may contain icicles, snowmen, snowflakes, winter birds, or abstract shapes.
4. Add glitter or sequins to create lights and shadows as objects move with the air current.
5. In designing objects to hang, children need to think of how objects look as they turn and move. Creating a mobile helps children develop an appreciation of sculpture in motion and helps them grow in the ability to select, arrange, design, and create in space.

## Soapy the Snowman.

Procedure:

1. Pour a box of soap flakes into a large container.
2. Add water slowly until the mixture is the consistency of paste.
3. Roll into balls. Put two balls together for the body and add a smaller one for the head.
4. Toothpicks help hold the balls together. Use pipe cleaners or toothpicks for arms, and buttons for

features. After Christmas, the decorations can be removed and the balls used for hand soap.

## Indoor Snow.

Procedure:

1. Collect some snow in containers and bring it back into the classroom.
2. Mark the snow line on the container and note the difference after the snow melts. Discuss why this happens.
3. Note any pollutants in the melted snow.
4. Place some containers near the heat and others farther away from the heat. Compare the time each takes to melt. If you don't live in an area where it snows, conduct the same experiments using ice cubes.

**"Snow" Designs.** Snowlike designs can be made with a flour and water mixture.

Materials: flour and water, a plastic squeeze bottle (the kind honey is sold in), form or aluminum trays or wax paper, tempera paint or food coloring (optional).

Procedure:
1. Mix one part flour with one part water. Add food coloring or tempera paint for coloring, or leave it white. Fill the plastic bottle about half full.
2. Show the children how to squeeze the flour mixture from the bottle to make designs on the paper or trays.
3. Let the children make their own designs.
4. Variation: While designs are still wet, they may be sprinkled with silver glitter for an even more snow-like effect. Children can also add leaves, bits of grass, or even feathers before the flour mixture dries.

## Ice Cube Painting.
Procedure:
1. Use finger paint and glossy paper, but do not wet the paper as you would normally do to prepare for finger-painting.
2. Offer the children ice cubes with which to spread and dilute the paint while making designs. Children who have watched ice melt like to apply the effect in something they create themselves.

## Ice Cube Pictures.
Procedure:
1. Fill ice cube trays with water.
2. Insert a popsicle stick into each cube.
3. Freeze (outside, if possible).
4. Cover table with newspaper. Sprinkle dry tempera onto finger paint paper.
5. Rub ice cube over paint. Watch the ice melt into color.

## Snowscapes.
Procedure:
1. Press play dough into a margarine lid.
2. Stick two or three pinecones into the dough.
3. Spray the cones with snow spray.
4. Other articles can be added to the snow scene for interest.

## Snow Pictures with Cotton.
Procedure:
1. Try this idea on the day of the first snow or just after a big storm. Talk about snow and the way it piles up on roofs, trees, cars, and so on.
2. Each child then paints a picture on colored construction paper. Pictures should contain three or four large objects such as a house and trees.
3. Cotton is added to represent snow. The children will find they can roll it into small balls to make it look like snow falling, snowballs, or snowmen. Or it may be piled loosely on housetops.
4. Glue is put on the paper and the cotton laid on top of it. Children should be cautioned to keep glue away from fingers since the cotton will stick to them.

## Chalk Art.
Procedure:
1. Read the poem, "Snowstorm" to the children once. Then ask what they "saw in their minds" when they heard the poem.

### Snowstorm
I love to see the snowflakes fall
And cover everything in sight.

The lawn and trees and orchard wall—
With spotless white.

2. Read it again and ask how many others saw pictures of the scene in their minds.
3. After a short discussion of individual children's "mind pictures," they can draw the "pictures in their mind" on paper. Give each child a large (18″ × 24″) piece of dark-colored construction paper, crayons, and one piece of white chalk. Now let them draw what came to their minds when they heard this poem.

## Snow Clowns.
I watched the snow come tumbling down,
    Each flake a tiny circus clown.
They chinned themselves along the eaves,
    The clothesline made their gay trapeze.
And then they waltzed in jeweled frills,
    Upon the edge of windowsills.
They played leapfrog just everywhere,
    And ran in circles here and there.

The raindrop soldiers march and pound,
But snow clowns never make a sound.

Follow same procedure for drawing pictures as in "Snowstorm" poem.

### Snowflake Figures.

Materials: White paper, pipe cleaners, nonhardening clay.

Procedure:

1. Follow directions on how to make a snowflake on page 615 and as illustrated in Figure 30–1.
2. The figure is made from two pipe cleaners. Slits are cut in the center of the snowflake so it will slide over the figure. Glue the snowflake back together to make a skirt. A smaller snowflake makes a collar or cuffs.
3. To make the figure stand, push one foot (pipe cleaner) or both into a piece of clay. Some paper and yarn may be glued to the pipe cleaner head to make a face and hair.

### Winter Lacing Fun.

A good small motor activity, and a favorite activity for young children, is to practice lacing. Tie this activity in with winter activities by cutting out a pair of winter shapes from poster board.

Procedure:

1. Cut out two mitten shapes, two snowman shapes, two bird shapes, etc.
2. Punch holes around the edges of the shapes.
3. The children lace strands of colored yarn (taped at one end to make a "needle") through the holes. When they have finished, knot and trim the loose yarn ends on each shape.
4. Decorate their laced shapes with torn paper pieces, cotton balls, felt-tip pens, crayons, or stickers.

### Necktie Draft Catcher.

This is a fun activity as well as a useful item in the wintertime. When this snake is filled with sand and placed against the lower edge of a door on the floor, no drafts come through!

Materials: An old necktie (fat ones are best), sand, a funnel, scissors, tacky glue, red felt tongue (cut from scraps), movable eyes (found in craft stores), needle and thread

Procedure:

1. Sew the tail end of the tie closed.
2. Use the funnel to fill the tie with sand.
3. Sew the head closed across the top with tight stiches.
4. Glue on eyes and tongue. Other details may be glued on as the child desires, such as buttons, sequins, etc. (See Figure 30–6 for illustration.)

### Bird Feeders.

Winter is a wonderful time for feeding the birds. Young children are able to understand how important food is, and that birds can't always get to food they need if snow covers the ground. Even in areas where it does not snow, young children can see the bare trees, brown grass, and lack of flowers, which are all food sources for the birds. In areas where winters are very mild, children can simply help the birds more easily find food by making bird feeders. Bird feeders are easy to make and provide many learning opportunities for young children.

Hang them up near windows where children are able to observe the birds enjoying their food. Young children are keen observers of nature and will enjoy the variety of birds their feeders attract.

As winter goes on, children enjoy the daily ritual of feeding the birds and possibly putting out some water when it is freezing. Other bird feeding ideas include:

- Under supervision, even quite young children can manage to thread peanuts in shells onto a string with a large dull-tipped rug needle. Hang up these "necklaces" for the birds.
- Children can also make "bird pudding" from stale bits of bread, raisins, bird seed, and bacon rind, moistened with water and put out for the birds on special days such as Valentine's Day, St. Patrick's Day, Ground Hog Day, etc. Put the pudding out as is or put it into half a coconut shell. A small hole drilled into the coconut shell will enable you to hang it up where it can swing freely as birds land to feed.
- As spring approaches and nesting season begins, the children can hang up nesting materials like pieces of colored wool or yarn, feathers, straw, and string. Apart from being fun to watch as the birds

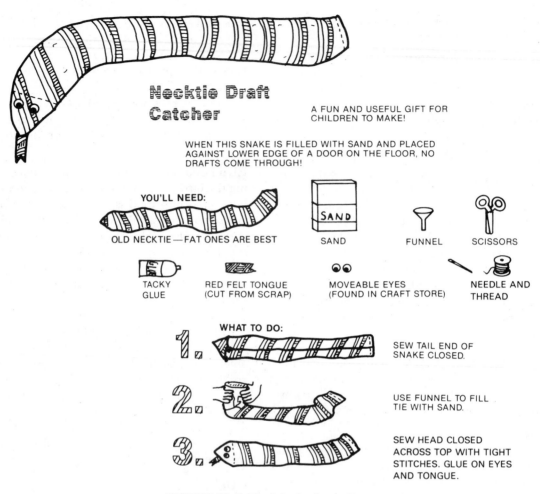

**Necktie Draft Catcher**

A FUN AND USEFUL GIFT FOR CHILDREN TO MAKE!

WHEN THIS SNAKE IS FILLED WITH SAND AND PLACED AGAINST LOWER EDGE OF A DOOR ON THE FLOOR, NO DRAFTS COME THROUGH!

YOU'LL NEED:

OLD NECKTIE—FAT ONES ARE BEST

SAND

FUNNEL

SCISSORS

TACKY GLUE

RED FELT TONGUE (CUT FROM SCRAP)

MOVEABLE EYES (FOUND IN CRAFT STORE)

NEEDLE AND THREAD

WHAT TO DO:

1. SEW TAIL END OF SNAKE CLOSED.

2. USE FUNNEL TO FILL TIE WITH SAND.

3. SEW HEAD CLOSED ACROSS TOP WITH TIGHT STITCHES. GLUE ON EYES AND TONGUE.

**FIGURE 30–5 Necktie draft catcher.**

take these things, children learn the names of the different birds and later may be lucky enough to discover a nest with some of the colored yarn they put out!

**Recycled Tissue Roll Bird Feeders.** Use empty rolls from toilet tissue or paper towel rolls (cut in half) to make simple bird feeders. Help the children spread the paper tubes with peanut butter, then roll the tubes in bird seed. Poke holes in the sides of the tubes and insert a string to hang the feeder over a window ledge or on a tree branch.

**Bird Table (Woodworking Project).** In woodworking, it is important for children to have projects simple enough to finish once started so they do not end up with many half-made things. A bird table can be made in a short time, and it is exciting for the child to watch birds feeding from it.

Materials:
One piece of wood 12″ × 12″ square, or a slice of tree trunk of similar size
Thin rope or clothesline
A hand drill with a ½-inch bit

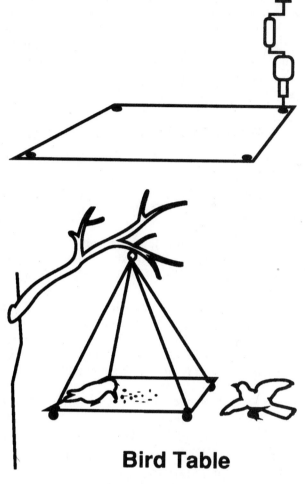

**Bird Table**

**FIGURE 30–6 Bird table.**

Procedure:
1. Sand the piece of wood until it is smooth.
2. Depending on the shape of the wood, drill three or four holes, about ¾″ from the edges. Children enjoy drilling holes with a hand-drill, so be sure to let them do this. (See Unit 13 for more information on woodworking techniques.)
3. Thread the rope through each hole.
4. Make a knot underneath the board at the end of each cord to stop the cords from slipping out. Do this for each hole.

5. Gather the cords together at the top and make a knot.
6. Hang your bird table outside the window.

## GAMES

**Freeze.** It is important for children to be able to stop and start quickly. Their locomotor skills are somewhat limited, so they need many opportunities to practice with them. This activity gives them that opportunity. At the word *freeze,* they stop and hold their position until the word *go.* Continue the game, using different body parts.

If space permits, have the children get up and move about, using those locomotor skills which are possible within the space and their abilities.

Walk!—Freeze!
Hop!—Freeze!
Run!—Freeze!
Move any other way that you can!—Freeze!

At different times, use levels (high, low), speed (fast, slow), and size (large, small).

**Chips Off the Ice Block.** Each child has a large block. Lay blocks in spaces so the children have room to move around without touching anyone.

*Exploration* (Be sure to give children time to explore.)

• Go over the block as many different ways as you can.
• Go around the block as many different ways as you can.
• Push the block with as many different parts of your body as you can.

*Exploration with limitations.*

• Place one foot on the block and move over and around it without touching it with the other foot.
• Place one hand on the block and go over and around it.
• Do the same thing with two hands on the block, or one foot and one hand.
• Sit on the block and push with your feet.

- Lie on the block and push with your hands.
- Get on the block and try to move it without using your hands or feet.
- Jump up on the block and then off.
- Jump off the block and touch the floor with your hands as soon as you land.

**Ice Cube Detectives.** Place ice cubes in paper cups. Put one cup outside; let the children place the others in different parts of the room (close to a window, close to a heater, in a refrigerator, on a table-top, etc.). Later, have the children check the cups and observe what happened to the ice. Did some cubes melt faster than others? Why? How could they make the cubes melt really fast? When all the ice has melted, pour the water into an ice cube tray and place it in the freezer. Remove the tray periodically to let the children observe the water turning back into ice. *Variation:* If there is snow in your area, use snowballs instead of ice cubes and ask the children to predict which snowball will melt fastest. Talk about their predictions and the results of this experiment.

**Ice Fishing.** Cut small fish shapes out of three different colors of construction paper. Place the shapes in a shoebox with a large hole cut in the lid. Have the children pretend that they are fishing through an ice hole in the Far North. Let them take turns reaching through the hole to "catch" the fish, then sort the fish into three piles, according to color.

**Ball Freeze Game.** In their own spaces, have the children do as many things with a ball as they can, without losing control of it. This can be done while standing or sitting. Stress keeping control of the ball. At the word *freeze,* the children stop and hold the ball in whatever position they may be.

**Snowball Through the Wreath.** Children throw "snowballs" (cotton ball, sponge, old socks made into balls) through a large Christmas wreath, suspended from the ceiling.

**Cat and Mouse (Snow) Ball.** Everyone forms one large circle. The children pass a ball around the circle with each child holding it for a second. Then, introduce a second ball. Each person passes the first ball to the next person, and then turns the other way to look for the next ball. After a few turns, make this game a winter game by having the second ball be the sun trying to shine on the snowball (other ball) and melt it.

## CREATIVE MOVEMENT ACTIVITIES

**Icicles**
We are little icicles
Melting in the sun.
Can't you see our tiny tears
Dropping one by one?

Say this poem aloud a few times until the children can repeat it with you. Then ask the children if they can be like little "icicles." How would icicles stand—straight or slouchy?

Discuss what happens to icicles in the sun. Then ask the children to show with their own bodies what happens to icicles in the sun. Reinforce the concept of the relaxed melting motions of icicles on a winter class walk. Be sure to point out some real icicles!

**Silent Snowfall.** Read this poem to the children once. Discuss how they think snowflakes "sounded" in the poem. Discuss how snowflakes would move. Read the poem again.

The snow fell softly all the night
It made a blanket soft and white.
It covered houses, flowers, and ground.
But did not make a single sound.

Now let the children move (softly, slowly) like the snowflakes in the poem.

**Skaters' Waltz.** You don't have to live in a cold climate to ice skate. Mark off an irregular shape on the classroom floor with tape to create an "ice skating pond." Let the children go "skating" in their stocking feet. A few grains of very fine sand or cornmeal sprinkled on your classroom "pond" enable the children to feel the movement and rhythm of skating as they alternately slide on either foot.

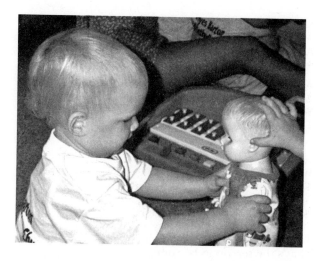

FIGURE 30–7 Winter dramatic play—getting baby dressed for outdoor activity.

**Snow Fun.** If you live in a snowy area, let the children have fun outdoors as often as possible. (Tell your plans to parents and ask them to dress the children suitably with extra mittens, scarves, etc.) Walk around in the snow, shovel paths through it, build snowmen, look for tracks in the snow, watch the snowplows at work, play "angels in the snow." If there is a hill nearby, children can go sliding on the seats of well-padded snowsuits or use big pieces of cardboard for sleds.

**Outdoor Artwork—Snow Designs.** Save the squeeze bottles that dishwashing detergent comes in. Rinse thoroughly. Fill with colored water. Let the children "draw" bright designs by squirting the colored water on the snow.

**Blow, Melt, and Trickle.** Dramatizations can be stimulated by phenomena in our everyday world. Encourage the children to pretend (by acting with their body movements) to be any of the following:

- Leaves waving in a gentle wind, a heavy wind, and then eventually flying through the air
- Snow falling softly, being made into a snowman, and then melting

- An ice cream cone or icicle melting in the sun
- Rain trickling down, running into a swift stream, the sun coming out, and a rainbow appearing
- An icy hill that is hard to walk up
- A thick fog to find one's way through

The children and teacher may think of others.

## FINGERPLAYS, POEMS, AND SONGS

**A-Sledding We Will Go**
(Sung to the tune of "A-Hunting We Will Go")

A-sledding we will go
A-sledding we will go
We'll hold on tight
And sit just right
And down the hill we go
We-e-e-e-!

**The Mitten Song**
Thumbs in the thumb place,
    (Put up thumbs)
Fingers all together!
    (Put up all fingers, together)
This is the song
We sing in mitten weather.

When it is cold,
    (Hug self with arms, in "cold" gesture)
It doesn't matter whether
    (Shake head)
Mittens are wool,
Or made of finest leather.
    (Put out hand)

This is the song
    (Keep hands up)
We sing in mitten weather:
Thumbs, in the thumb place,
    (Put up thumbs)
Fingers all together!
    (Put up all fingers, together)

**Mulberry Bush Ring Game and Song**
Here we go 'round the mulberry bush,
The mulberry bush, the mulberry bush,
Here we go 'round the mulberry bush,
All on a frosty morning.

This is the way we clap our hands,
Clap our hands, clap our hand,
This is the way we clap our hands,
All on a frosty morning.

This is the way we wash our clothes,
Wash our clothes, wash our clothes,
This is the way we wash our clothes,
All on a frosty morning.

You can then add your own verses, such as: "This is the way we scrub the floors," "this is the way we mix the bread," "this is the way we walk to school," etc. The chorus is sung as the children hold hands and dance around in a circle. The other verses are sung in a circle but with the hands free to do the actions.

### Eskimo Children at Play
Break, break, break.
Cut the snow and pile the blocks,
  (Make cutting motion with right hand. Use both
    hands to pantomime piling blocks of snow, one
    on top of the other.)
Form the high arch of the roof,
  (Show with hands an arch shape)
Scamper, scamper, scamper,
Take off your big snowshoe.
  (Make motion of removing a snowshoe)
Duck your way through the doorway
Of your cozy, warm igloo.
  (Make an igloo doorway by arching hands
    overhead. Duck head under arched hands)

### Little Groundhog (Sung to the tune of "Frère Jacques")
Little Groundhog
Little shadow
Where are you? Where are you?

Groundhog's Day is here
Spring will be here too.
Wake up you! Wake up you!

### Icy
Children particularly enjoy "acting out" this poem.

I slip and I slide
On the slippery ice
I skid and I glide,
Oh, isn't it nice!
To lie on your tummy
And slither and skim,
On the slick crust of snow
Where you skid as you swim.

### Winter
There's wind in the chimney
And snow in the air
And frost on the pane
And cold everywhere.

So wear your long leggings
And wrap up your throat
And pull on your mittens
And button your coat.

And do be careful
And don't freeze your noses
You'll need them next summer
To smell the red roses.

### Winter Morning
Winter is the king of showmen,
Turning tree stumps into snowmen
And houses into birthday cakes
And spreading sugar over the lakes.
Smooth and clean and frosty white
The world looks good enough to bite.
That's the season to be young,
Catching snowflakes on your tongue.

### Snow
Snow is snowy when it's snowing.
I'm sorry it's slushy when it's going.
                                    —Ogden Nash

### Winter Snow
O where do you come from
You little flakes of snow
Falling, falling, softly falling
On the earth below?

On the trees and on the bushes
On the mountains afar
Tell me snowflakes do you come
Where the angels are?
                                —Author unknown

### First Snow of the Season
Silently, softly, and swiftly
  (Make motion of falling snow with fingers of both
    hands)
It falls to the earth and lies
In heaps and drifts and hummocks—
  (Show heaps by motions of hands)
A wintertime surprise!

Get out your sled and boots
  (Pretend to pull a sled and put on boots)
Get out your mittens and cap,
  (Pretend to put on mittens and cap)
You can coast a long, long hour,
And then take a nice long nap.
  (Fold hands under cheek, close eyes, and pretend
    to sleep)

## Little Snowflakes

Merry little snowflakes,
Dancing in the air;
Busy little snowflakes,
Falling everywhere.

Blowing in our faces,
Falling at our feet,
And kissing all the children
As they run along the street.

## Snow

Snow makes whiteness where it falls,
The bushes look like popcorn balls.
And places where I always play,
Look like somewhere else today.

## Bed in Winter

This is a good poem to recite at rest time while the
children are on cots, and can put out their feet to
act out this poem.

At night I reach down with my feet just to see,
Then I curl up quickly instead.
For every place, except right under me,
Is terribly cold in my bed!

## Snowballs

I had a little snowball once,
It was so round and white,
I took it home with me and tried
To keep it overnight.

But when next morning I awoke,
Just at the break of day,
I went to get it and I found,
It had melted all away.

## Chasing Snowflakes

Children enjoy "chasing snowflakes" after this
poem. Gentle, soft "chasing" generally fits the poem
best. Even better—go out in a snowfall and *really*
chase snowflakes!

I had a snowman
Fat and gay.
I had him all
One winter's day.
I have him yet,
Because I took his picture
For my snapshot book!

## The Snowman

Let the children act out this poem. They especially
like wearing a top hat as a prop. Have one child play
the snowman and another the north wind.

Once there was a snowman
Who stood beside the door,
Thought he'd like to warm himself
By the firelight red,
Thought he'd like to jump upon
    The big, white bed.
So he called to the north wind—
    "Help me, wind, I pray,
I'm completely frozen, standing here
    All day."
So the north wind came along, and
    Blew him in the door,
And now there's nothing left of him,
But a puddle on the floor!

## North and South (Action Poem)

This is the first month of the year,
    (Hold up index finger for "first")
Eleven more to go.
    (Show "eleven" with ten fingers, plus one)
If you live in a north land, you have fun with snow.
    (Show "snow" falling by fluttering motions of
        fingers and hands)
Shoveling, throwing snowballs,
    (Pantomime these activities)
Playing Fox and Geese.
    (Run lightly in place)
Rolling great big snowballs to make a snowman, piece
    by piece.
    (Pantomime putting snowman together)
In southern lands, the bright sun shines
    (Make sun shape with hands held high over head)
And palm trees gently wave,
    (Rest both elbows on flat surface. Wave hands for
        "palm branches")
Even when the calendar shows a January day.
    (Point to a real calendar, or hold up one finger to
        recall that January is the first month)
Children there can swim and ski—on water, not on
    snow.
    (Pantomime swimming and water skiing)
While on the beach sand castles, made by children,
    come and go.
    (Pantomime making a sand castle. Show with wavy
        motion of arm how the high tide destroys the
        castle)

## Falling Snow

See the pretty snowflakes,
    Falling from the sky;
On the walk and housetops.
    Soft and thick they lie.

On the window ledges,
    On the branches bare;

Now how fast they gather,
Filling all the air.

Look into the garden,
Where the grass was green;
Covered by the snowflakes,
Not a blade is seen.

Now the bare black bushes
All look soft and white;
Every twig is laden—
What a pretty sight!

## A Joke
A natural follow-up to this activity is a winter walk, to see if our breath comes out like "little puffs of smoke." Try taking a picture of the puffs of smoke.

When I am outdoors in the cold,
Isn't it a joke
How my breath comes out of me
Like little puffs of smoke?

## Snow Under My Feet
A natural follow-up to this activity is a winter walk, to see if our feet make the sound, "crickery, crackery, creek."

Crickery, crackery, creek,
The snow is talking under my feet.
Ice and snow and hail and sleet,
Talk crickery, crackery, creek.

## Outside the Door
Outside the door the bare tree stands,
And catches snowflakes in its hands,
And holds them well and holds them high,
Until a puffing wind comes by.

## Ice
When it is the winter time
And I make the ice laugh
With my little feet,
"Crickle, crackle, crickle,
Crreeet, crrreeeet, crrreeet."

—Dorothy Aldis

## Winter Is Coming
Let the children play all the parts in this poem: bear, leaf, frog, bird, chipmunk, and caterpillar. It could also serve as a short play, with costumes, for a parents' meeting.

Winter is coming, and what will you do?
"Sleep," said the bear, "the cold season through."
"Float," said the leaf, "right down from the tree,

This wind in the branches is too much for me."
"Sink," said the frog, "I shall drop into bed,
In the mud of this pond I shall cover my head."
"Fly," said the bird, "the summer is old.
I am going south before it gets cold."
"Dig," said the chipmunk, "a hole in the ground.
Till spring comes again, that's where I'll be found."
"Spin," said the caterpillar, "weave a cocoon,
Tied to this twig I shall go to sleep soon."
"In the spring," said them all, "we shall start life anew,
But when winter is coming these things must we do."

## Signs of Winter
Same note as for "Winter is Coming" poem.

On a big gray cloud away up high,
Sat a soft little snowflake in the dark sky.
"I must fall," said the snowflake white.
"I must fall down to the earth tonight."

Said the big gray cloud, "Oh, please don't go.
Something might happen to you, you know."
But the little snowflake with a tear in his eye,
Said, "Good-by, good-by, I am leaving the sky."

Then off he went, and he floated down
Till he came to a quiet New Hampshire town.
And there on the hard brown earth he lay.
The next day, some children came out to play.

They said, " A snowflake has come to stay,
And winter is at last on its way.
Good-by to summer, good-by to fall,
Good-by to little leaves one and all."

That day, from the clouds came snowflake mothers
And snowflake fathers and sisters and brothers.
Oh, hundreds of snowflakes came fluttering down,
Covering rooftops all over the town.

The children laughed for they had a plan.
From mounds of snow, they would make a man.
Then all that day they worked very hard,
And they made a snowman out in the yard.

## My Zipper Suit
My zipper suit is bunny brown,
The top zips up, the legs zip down,
I wear it every day.
My daddy brought it out from town,
Zip it up, and zip it down
And hurry out to play!

## Snow
The more it snows,
The more it goes,
The more it goes,
On snowing.

And nobody knows,
How cold my toes,
How cold my toes
   Are growing

—A.A. Milne

## COOKING ACTIVITY

**Snow Ice Cream.**   Right after a snowfall, when the snow is clean, collect a pailful of snow. In a big bowl, combine a large can of evaporated milk and several cups of superfine sugar, mixing until the sugar is dissolved. Stir in one tablespoon of vanilla extract. Add large amounts of snow and stir quickly, adding more snow until the mixture looks and tastes like vanilla ice cream. (For additional activities, see Unit 26, December Holidays.)

**Snowballs.**
Ingredients:
ice cream (or ice milk)
shredded coconut
maraschino cherries

Procedure:
1. Scoop out a round ball of ice cream and place it on waxed paper that has been spread with coconut.
2. Roll until all the ice cream is covered.
3. Place in a container and freeze. Work fast! Ice cream melts!
4. Place a cherry on top and serve.

**Snowman Salad.**
Ingredients:
cottage cheese
lettuce leaves
raisins
small carrot sticks

Procedure:
Place lettuce leaves on plates and top with a round scoop of cottage cheese. Let the children make snowman faces on their scoops of cottage cheese, using raisins for eyes and mouths and carrot sticks for noses.

**Carob Milk Shake.**
Ingredients:
¾ cup milk
2 ice cubes
2 teaspoons honey
¼ cup carob powder (carob powder is similar to cocoa, but provides slightly more nutrition; it is also a substitute for those allergic to chocolate)

Procedure:
Put all ingredients in a blender and turn on high for about one minute. Serves one child.

**Frozen Pineapple Cups.**
Ingredients:
1 3-ounce package cream cheese
1 8-ounce carton pineapple yogurt
¼ cup sugar or ⅛ cup honey

Procedure:
1. Blend cream cheese, yogurt, and sugar or honey.
2. Pour into popsicle molds or in ice cube trays.
3. Freeze. Serves 6 to 8 children

Variation: Use different flavors of yogurt and other fruits.

**Orange Yogurt Popsicles.**
Ingredients:
1 small can of frozen concentrated orange juice
1 pint plain yogurt
2 teaspoons vanilla
honey to sweeten, if desired

Procedure:
1. Beat ingredients together until well blended.
2. Fill popsicle molds.
3. Freeze 24 hours. Makes 8 ½-cup servings. Other juices can be used instead of orange juice.

**Lickin' Good Fudgesicles.**
Ingredients:
2 eggs
2½ cups milk
3 tablespoons instant cocoa mix
2–3 teaspoons sugar
dash of salt
1 teaspoon vanilla

Procedure:
1. Beat eggs.
2. Add other ingredients and beat again.
3. Pour into popsicle molds.
4. Freeze. Serves 12 children.

Variations: Add chopped peanuts or other chopped nuts for extra protein and crunch. Add sliced bananas, raisins, or wheat germ.

# ADDITIONAL READINGS

## Children's Books for Winter

Bartoli, Jennifer, and Takeo Ishida (illus.). *Snow on Bear's Nose: A Story of a Japanese Moon Bear Cub.* Chicago: A. Whitman, 1976.

Bauer, Caroline Feller. *Midnight Snowman.* New York: Atheneum, 1987.

Bauer, Caroline Feller, ed. *Snowy Day Stories and Poems.* New York: Lippincott, 1986.

Branley, Franklyn M. *Snow Is Falling: A Let's-Read-and-Find-Out Science Book.* New York: Crowell, 1986.

Burton, Virginia L. *Katy and the Big Snow.* Boston: Houghton Mifflin, 1974.

Coleridge, Sara. *January Brings the Snow: A Book of Months.* New York: Dial, 1988.

Ginsburg, Mirra. *The Sun's Asleep Behind the Hill.* New York: Greenwillow, 1982.

Goffstein, M.B. *Our Snowman.* New York: Harper & Row, 1986.

Graham, Ada, and Frank Graham, Jr. *Let's Discover Winter Woods.* New York: Golden Press, 1974.

Gundersheimer, Karen. *Happy Winter.* New York: Harper, 1982.

Hader, Berta, and Elmer Hader. *The Big Snow.* New York: Macmillan, 1948.

Handforth, Thomas. *Mei Li.* New York: Doubleday, 1938.

Hutchins, Pat. *The Wind Blew.* New York: Macmillan, 1974.

Keats, Ezra, J. *Snowy Day.* New York: Viking, 1962.

Lawson, Robert. *The Tough Winter.* New York: Penguin, 1979.

Lewis, C. S. *The Lion, the Witch, and the Wardrobe.* New York: Macmillan, 1968.

Lionni, Leo. *Frederick.* New York: Pantheon Books, 1966.

Minarik, Else Holmelund. *Little Bear.* New York: Harper & Row, 1978.

Ormerod, Jan. *Moonlight.* New York: Lothrop, 1982.

Rockwell, Anne, and Rockwell, Harlow. *The First Snowfall.* New York: Macmillan, 1987.

Rogers, Jean. *Runaway Mittens.* New York: Greenwillow, 1988.

Tejima, Keizaburo. *Fox's Dream.* New York: Philomel, 1987.

Tresselt, Alvin. *The Mitten.* New York: Lothrop, 1964.

Tresselt, Alvin, and Roger Duvoisin (illus.). *White Snow, Bright Snow.* New York: Lothrop, Lee & Shepard, 1947.

Wilder, Laura Ingalls. *The Long Winter.* New York: Harper & Row, 1953.

# UNIT 31

# Spring

The gradual coming of spring brings many signs of beauty, such as the color and texture of flowers in the sunlight and the pattern of delicate leaves against the sky. Children can share their experiences during a class discussion or they can bring in objects of nature for closer observation. Objects may include a bouquet of dandelions, a piece of moss, some pussy willows, or a budding tree branch. These discoveries motivate children to learn by stimulating their curiosity about the world around them and arousing new interests and ideas.

In picture making, children can express their feelings and understanding of the beauty of spring and summer in many ways. Some topics include:

- Spring Flowers
- Walking on a Windy Day
- Flying Kites
- Birds in Spring
- Planting Seeds in the Garden
- Playing Outdoors in Spring
- Helping with Spring Cleaning
- My New Spring Clothes
- Insects, Worms, and Caterpillars in Spring

## LESSON PLAN IDEAS FOR SPRING

You may find the following ideas helpful as you plan your spring activities for the young children in your group.

### Spring Excursions.

- Garden shop
- Spring walk
- Farm, to see baby animals or crops being planted
- Nursery
- Greenhouse
- Gardens that are being planted
- Place where children might be flying kites
- Home where spring repair and cleanup are in progress
- Park for a picnic

### Art.

- Flowers made from egg cartons, with pipe-cleaner stems placed in a clay base in a paper cup
- Flower pictures made with squares of crepe paper formed over a pencil or crayon and then glued onto paper
- Seed collages
- "Painting" with water—children are given buckets, brushes, and water to "paint" the outside of the building, sidewalks, etc.
- Pictures of blossoming trees, with the blossoms made of popcorn or crushed tissue paper
- Kites and pinwheels made and then decorated
- Egg-carton bugs made and decorated

### Music.

- Pretending to dance in the wind, as a growing flower, as a drop of rain
- Creative movements depicting growing plants, baby animals, rainstorm, flying kite, windy day, skate-boarding, golfing, fishing
- Seed shakers, made with different kinds of seeds in the shakers so that children can listen to the different sounds made by the various kinds of seeds
- Songs and fingerplays about spring

### Food.

- Fresh strawberries
- Fruit salads
- Fresh vegetable salads
- Picnic lunch

## Visitors.

- Adults to bring in gardening tools and other items used in planting spring garden or caring for yard in spring
- Farmer to come in and explain and demonstrate what he does
- Weather forecaster
- Construction worker
- Someone to bring in newborn animals

## Science.

- Planting an outdoor garden or planting seeds in small flower pots for windowsill observation of growing process
- Planting seeds—vegetable or flower—in the classroom
- Observation of the stages of growth of a plant, such as a fruit tree, during the spring
- Seeds such as beans and alfalfa sprouted and eaten
- Study and observation of kinds of flowers—colors, shapes, smells, and growth patterns noted
- Study and observation of leaves; leaf collection made by pressing leaves and mounting them in a scrapbook
- Study and observation of animal babies—their names, the sounds they make, what they eat, whether they are dependent on their mother
- Study of birds and what they do in the spring

## Language Experiences.

- Slides and/or pictures of spring scenes; discussion, perhaps with each child, describing one
- Objects or pictures having something to do with spring, with children encouraged to tell about them (include recreation equipment, clothing, foods, etc.)

# ART ACTIVITIES

## Spring Flowers.
Procedure:
1. Paper can be rolled, twisted, fringed, curled, or folded into a desired flower shape.
2. Suitable papers include newsprint, construction paper, tissue paper, metallic foil, cellophane, gift wrapping. Discarded materials are also useful, such as paper cupcake liners, small frozen pie tins, paper cups, toweling tubes, egg cartons.
3. Stems can be made from pipe cleaners, toothpicks, wire, tongue depressors, paper drinking straws, Popsicle sticks.
4. Small discarded flower pots, egg cartons, plastic bottles, juice cans, or rolled corrugated cardboard can be used for flower containers. They can be covered with paper or painted.
5. Use paper flowers in decorative ways, such as a flower show, store, or garden in a bulletin board display or three-dimensional exhibit.

## Spring Flowers.
Materials: An iron, paper, crayons

Procedure:
1. Fold the paper in half, then open it.
2. On one side of the fold, the children draw flowers: a single flower or a bouquet.
3. When finished, they refold the paper, with the flower drawing on the inside, and bring it up to the teacher for ironing.

*Note:* While children are working, set up an ironing station. On a desk, near an outlet, place several layers of newspaper, a magazine, or other paper. When ironing, place a piece of paper over the child's folded paper to prevent crayons from soiling the iron. The heat of the iron on the crayon creates an impressionistic-like flower picture.

4. These can be used for greeting cards or cut out and put on a class flower mural.

## More Spring Flowers.
Materials: Paper, felt-tip pens or black crayons, watercolors

Procedure:
1. Another technique for making spring flowers is to use felt-tip pens and watercolor. The idea here is to outline the flower with a felt-tip pen (preferably) or a black crayon.

2. Then fill in with watercolors and *do not* try to keep within the lines.

**Cherry Blossoms.** Children can decorate a wall or bulletin board with bright cherry blossoms.

Procedure:
1. Cover the wall or board with light blue construction paper.
2. Draw branches across the blue paper.
3. Give each child a supply of pink facial tissue or pink colored art tissue paper. Have the children tear the tissue into small pieces.
4. The children then spread small circles of glue on the branches and press bits of tissue onto the glue to create fluffy blossoms.

This activity can be done on separate sheets of paper for individual cherry blossom creations. *Variation:* Peach-colored tissue can be used for peach blossoms; white tissue can be used for dogwood blossoms.

**Spring Murals.**
Materials: Paper, coloring materials, scissors, glue or staples, 8½″ × 11″ pieces of paper for each child.

Procedure:
1. The children can create a mural using the above techniques or other simple methods. First, discuss with them which things are to be included (for example, birds, butterflies, insects, flowers, trees, grass).
2. Have the children decide which items they are going to prepare.
3. The children work at their own desks and cut out their finished pictures.
4. The pictures are then glued onto a larger paper.

**Tissue Paper Flowers.**
Procedure:
1. Cut pattern through many layers of tissue paper.
2. Make a small slit in the center of flower.
3. Push through a 6″ length of florist wire.
4. Attach flower centers to top end of wire.
5. Push tissue flower up tight against centers.
6. Wrap wire with florist tape adding leaves as you tape.
7. Ruffle layers of tissue, softly shaping petals.

**Caterpillars.**
Materials: A pair of black or brown cloth garden or knit gloves, 10 bright-colored pipe cleaners, 10 buttons (about ¾ inch in diameter) for faces—use brown for black gloves, black for brown gloves, 20 ¼-inch dots for eyes (any bright color)

Procedure:
1. Wearing one glove, coil pipe cleaners around each finger. Extend coil beyond end of finger to make caterpillar wiggly and to free fingertips for pulling on and off gloves.
2. Secure with needle and thread.
3. Bend over end of each pipe cleaner to make bigger surface. Place button on end. Bend pipe cleaner so button face can be seen when fingers

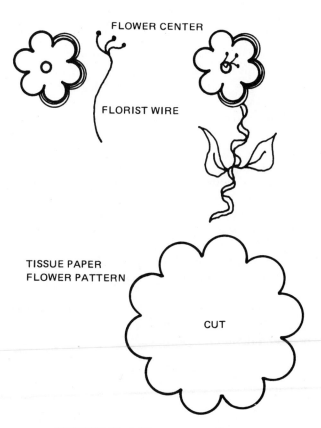

**FIGURE 31–1 Tissue paper flowers.**

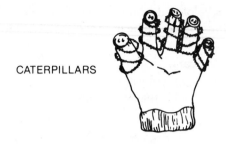

CATERPILLARS

**FIGURE 31–2 Caterpillars.**

are upright and extended forward (see Figure 31–2).

4. Repeat with the other gloves. Place dot over button holes for eyes. Glue buttons in place and let dry.

## Butterflies.

Procedure:

1. Fold a sheet of paper in half, then open it and place generous spots of paints on one side of the paper.

**FIGURE 31–3 Brush-painted butterfly.**

2. Fold the blank side over the wet, painted area and press.
3. Cut or tear the paper into a desired shape while folded. Open and allow to dry.
4. Add a body and antennae with cut paper. Wings may be cut in lacy designs. Then fill the open area with various colors.

**Balloon Bees.** A fun activity to celebrate the return of the birds and mostly the bees.

Materials:
yellow balloons
black felt-tip markers
circle stickers

Procedure:

1. Blow up the balloons. The children can help with this, but an adult will usually need to assist.
2. The children create "bees" by drawing stripes around their yellow balloons with black felt-tip markers.
3. Put on circle stickers for eyes, or draw eyes on the bees with the markers.
4. When the children have finished, let them toss their balloon bees up and down in the air and "buzz" around the room.

## Birds.

Procedure:

1. Draw the body and head on one piece of paper and cut it out.
2. Repeat the design on the other side.
3. Colorful wings and tail feathers can be folded, curled, or fringed, and then attached to the body.
4. Another bird can be made by folding a piece of paper in half and cutting a half-circle with the center along the fold.
5. Cut along the fold about halfway, and fold back pieces to form the wings.
6. Add a design in crayon or cut paper.
7. Use sequins, glitter, and metallic foil when making birds and butterflies to create unusual textural effects.
8. Display birds singly or group them on a tree branch inserted in a box. Butterflies may be added to the exhibit.

**Egg Carton Critters—Caterpillars, Snakes, Alligators.** See Appendix E for instructions on making caterpillars, snakes, and alligators from egg cartons.

**Miniature Garden.**
Procedure:
1. Suitable containers are frozen pie tins, a discarded dish or bowl, empty tin cans, cheese cartons, or cut-down plastic bottles covered with colored paper or metallic foil.
2. Fill containers with soil and plant whatever seeds are available, such as grass seed, lentil beans, and carrot seeds for the tops.
3. Add a few small stones or pebbles for texture.
4. Add a small clay turtle, frog, or bird; or make a cut-paper butterfly or ladybug fastened to a stick.

**Toy Kites.**
Procedure:
1. Begin with a piece of 12″ × 18″ construction paper, or use newsprint if a larger size is desired.
2. After the design is made in crayon or paint, the paper can be folded and stapled with all corners toward the center in a diamond shape.

**FIGURE 31–4 Spring and planting seed—a natural combination.**

3. Strips of masking tape may be criss-crossed on the back for reinforcement and a string may be fastened in the center.
4. A tail can be added using several bow ties of cloth or paper tied to a length of string.
5. Smaller kites make colorful room decorations when used on bulletin boards or strung across open areas.

**Windswept.**
Procedure:
1. Spread newspaper on the floor.
2. Give each child a full sheet of white or pastel construction paper.
3. Place the papers on the newspaper.
4. Put a dab of red, yellow, blue, and white tempera paint on each paper.
5. Give each child a small piece of cardboard.
6. The children push, pull, turn, and twist the cardboard through the paint puddles to create windswept strips and patches of color.
7. Do this activity outside for the best results.

**Blow Painting.**
Procedure:
1. Place sheets of typing paper on a flat surface.
2. Give each child a small amount of watery tempera paint in a container and a plastic spoon.
3. The children spoon a very *small* puddle of tempera on the paper.
4. They use a straw to blow the paint in various directions, creating a variety of patterns.
5. To create interesting wind patterns, have the children experiment with blowing gently, hard, and so forth.

**Decorate a Spring Shirt.** Have each child, using fabric crayons, color a spring picture on a white or light-colored T-shirt. Iron with newspaper over the picture and the ironing board. The picture will stay on indefinitely.

**Windy-Day Painting.**
Procedure:
1. Wet white construction paper with water.
2. Give each child a small amount of red, yellow,

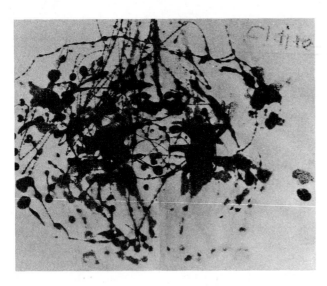

**FIGURE 31–5 A windy-day painting.**

blue, and white *dry* tempera and several small strips of cardboard.

3. The children use the cardboard strips to paint a windy day by quickly brushing the dry tempera onto the wet surface. Encourage the children to mix and blend the colors.

4. Wind motion can be used to create unusual effects with the strips. Push, pull, and twist the paint over the surface.

**Shaving Practice.** Spread shaving cream on unused styrofoam meat trays, cookie sheets, trays, or just on the table tops. Children can practice writing numbers, letters, names, or just have fun drawing anything they want. You can clap a rhythm while they make marks for each clap they hear, and then go back and count them.

**Peekers.**
Procedure:
1. Mount pictures of familiar objects (elephant, rabbit, dog, airplane, orange, etc.)
2. Help children identify the pictures.
3. Take three pieces of cardboard, each large enough to cover the pictures. Cut a few small holes in one piece of cardboard, medium-size holes in the next, and large holes in the third cardboard.
4. Place the cardboard with the small holes over a selected picture.
5. A child guesses what the picture is from the parts seen through the holes. If the child can't guess correctly, place the cardboard with the medium-size holes over the picture, and if necessary, use the cardboard with the large holes.

**Bird Mobiles.**
Procedure:
1. Each child cuts the body of a large bird from oak tag or a double thickness of construction paper.
2. The tail and wings are made by folding pieces of paper like fans. The tail is one fan stapled to the body. The wings are a single fan pinched in the middle to make both wings.
3. To attach, cut a hole in the body and push the wings through.
4. The birds are strung and hung from the ceiling, a wire, or a large tree branch set in plaster of Paris.
5. Air currents in the room will keep the birds moving.

**FIGURE 31–6 Bird mobile on string.**

**FIGURE 31–7 Bird and butterfly mobile on branch.**

6. For a variation, attach cut-paper birds to a twig (with string), and tie on cut-paper leaves. Hang with yarn as a mobile.

### Easy Three-Dimensional Flowers (Five years and older).
Procedure:
1. Cut colored construction paper into squares of different sizes. Each square can be made into a three-dimensional flower.
2. To make one flower, for example, fold the square in half two times and cut around the outside edges (those with no folds) to create a circle.
3. Fringe the rounded edge and unfold.
4. The flower can then be decorated with crayon lines, spots, or other touches.
5. Now cut from the outside to the center on one fold.
6. Overlap one side over the other and paste.
7. A pipe cleaner with one end folded over may be pushed down through the center for a stem.
8. Small boxes filled with sand and painted or decorated make attractive flowerpots.

*Note:* Another cut-paper flower activity is shown in Figure 31–9.

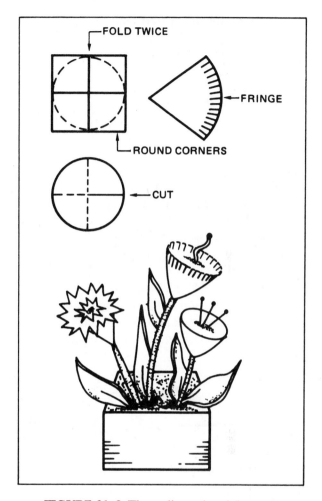

**FIGURE 31–8 Three-dimensional flowers.**

**FIGURE 31–9 Cut-paper toothpick flowers in egg carton.**

## Back Packs from Recycled Detergent Boxes.

Materials:

large empty detergent boxes
scissors
construction paper
crayons or felt-tipped pens

Procedure:

1. Cut the top off the detergent box.
2. Punch holes to string heavy soft yarn through the box (see Figure 31-10).
3. Paste a piece of construction paper on the front of the box so the child can decorate the box. Have the children color and decorate their back pack with felt tip pens, crayons, glued-on bits of cloth, paper, etc.
4. Loop the straps over the child's arms to hold the pack on.

Children can carry their favorite toys and dolls in the back pack. They are also great to take along on a spring walk for storing nature's treasures found along the way!

**FIGURE 31–10 Back pack from recycled detergent box.**

## Stand-up Painted Faces.

Procedure:

1. Small children can easily roll a piece of paper to form a cylinder. Let them start with paper about 12″ × 12″.
2. Paste the edges and fasten, pressing from the inside to make the paste hold securely.
3. Stand the cylinder on end.
4. Paint eyes, nose, mouth, teeth, glasses, freckles, cheeks, ears, hair, mustache, and any other features desired. Do not forget to paint the back of the head.
5. Cut-paper shirts, collars, and ties can also be added.
6. Each child will have an individual "face" and will be pleased that it is three dimensional.

**Paper Butterflies.** Have children draw butterflies (or use the butterfly patterns in Figures 31–11 and 31–12). Use finger paint, regular tempera paint, or crayons to decorate the butterflies.

**Magazine Flowers.** Cut out the top of flower shapes from color pictures in glossy magazines. Simple, round shapes are good. Children glue the flower shapes to a piece of colored construction paper or manila paper. The stems and leaves as well as the background can then be colored in.

## Cupcake Liner Flowers.

Procedure:

1. Use multicolored cupcake pan liners to make flowers.
2. Glue the liners to a piece of construction paper.
3. Decorate the centers of the flowers by gluing on (with white glue) bits of colored paper, popcorn, sawdust, etc., for a textured effect.
4. Color on the stems and leaves, or glue on cut-paper pieces.

**Paper Plate Clown Faces.** Use a white paper plate for the clown's face. Paste on cut-paper features for eyes, hair, nose, and mouth.

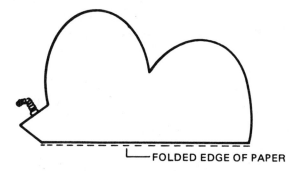

FOLDED EDGE OF PAPER

**FIGURE 31–11 Butterfly pattern—beginning.**

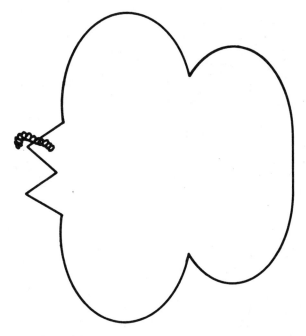

**FIGURE 31–12 Butterfly pattern—end.**

**FIGURE 31–13 Magazine flowers.**

## A Rainbow in Your Room.

Procedure:

1. Make a rainbow in the classroom. All that is needed is a glass of water and a sunny day. (Be sure to use a clear glass. The wider the mouth, the better.)

2. When the glass is placed in sunlight, there should be a rainbow where the shadow would fall.

**FIGURE 31–14 Paper plate clown face.**

3. What is made is a simple prism, which can be used in lessons about the color spectrum. Point out to the children that a rainbow forms outdoors when drops of water in the air act as prisms.

## Spring Is Spring.

Procedure:

1. Discuss the look, feel, sound, and smell of spring and the other seasons as they happen.
2. How do the children know that it is spring in their neighborhood? By the green grass and pussy willows? Mud? Reruns on television? Different clothes? Baseball?
3. Divide the bulletin board into four areas: "My Eyes See Spring," "I Feel Spring," "I Hear Spring," "My Nose Knows It Is Spring." Have the children draw pictures to illustrate each theme.

## Window Gardens.

Procedure:

1. Draw outlines of stems and leaves on the windows and ask each child to add a flower.
2. Have the children work out their patterns on paper or on the chalkboard first.
3. Have each child use a black crayon to trace the outline on top of a stem on the window.
4. Mix thick tempera paint in various colors with detergent, so the paint will stick to the window, and have the children fill in their outlines.
5. Keep plenty of rags on hand for cleanup.

## Flying Fish.

Materials: A strip of paper 11″ × 1½″ (any thin paper will do), scissors, pencil, ruler, felt-tip pen

Procedure:

1. Cut a slit about half way through the strip of paper, about 3″ from each end of the paper strip.
2. Decorate the strip in bright colors.
3. Roll the strip around and slide slits into each other.
4. Pinch lightly in the center.
5. Reach up and "drop" the flying fish in the air. It will twirl down.

## Egg Carton Zoo.

Many innovations in art come from the use of discarded materials. Parts of egg car-

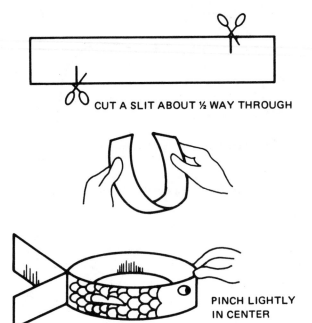

CUT A SLIT ABOUT ½ WAY THROUGH

PINCH LIGHTLY IN CENTER

**FIGURE 31–15 Flying fish.**

tons can be used to create real and imaginary animals for a "big city zoo."

Procedure:

1. Begin by cutting the cartons into separate parts to use either the inside or the outside of the egg cup.
2. Turn a cup upside down to make the body and legs of an animal.
3. Make the head with construction paper or use part of another cup and attach with glue.
4. Paint the features and body.
5. Add paper ears, horns, or hair.
6. The project can be extended to include little trees made of twigs and stuck in clay, painted "pools" for the animals, and rocks can be made of crumpled paper.

## Magical Mystery Paints.

Here's an art project with a touch of mystery.

Procedure:

1. Have the children place waxed paper over drawing paper and use sharp pencils to make pictures or designs.

2. The wax will be "invisibly" transferred to the drawing paper.
3. Attractive drawings magically appear when the children brush on watercolor paints. (Since the lines of the pictures will appear the same color as the drawing paper, it is best to use dark paint on white paper.)

**A Marvelous Mess.** Was there a mess left after some of your more successful art projects? Here's a way to turn the leftovers into another fun time for the children.

Procedure:
1. Collect the colorful bits from each art project—glitter, hole-punched paper, fine-colored gravel, paper, cloth scraps.
2. When you have a good selection, roll out a large sheet of craft paper on the floor.
3. Place one large puddle or several small puddles of glue on the paper. Spread the glue.
4. Have the children place their leftover scraps wherever they want on the paper.
5. Sprinkle the finished design generously with glitter or confetti.

**Pipe Cleaner Dancers.**
Procedure:
1. Obtain extra-fluffy pipe cleaners.
2. Shape them into dancing figures. (This is a good activity to do when a dancer visits the class.)
3. Dip the characters into a mixture of one cup soap powder and four tablespoons plastic starch, and sprinkle with glitter.
4. After they dry, hang them as mobiles.

**Recycled Paint.** Scrape the dried paint from containers used at the easel and save them. Squeeze glue onto construction paper, making any kind of design. Sprinkle with paint chips. Shake off the excess.

**Sawdust Sculpture.**
Procedure:
1. Mix wheat paste and water to a thick consistency.
2. Add sawdust until the mixture can be formed into a ball.

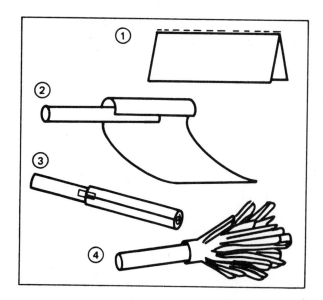

**FIGURE 31–16 Pom-poms.**

3. Give each child a lump of the mixture to mold into any shape.
4. Dry the shapes for two or three days. They can be painted with tempera.

**Pom-Poms.**
Procedure:
1. Fold a sheet of tissue paper lengthwise.
2. Paint a 1″ border of paste near the end of an empty paper towel cylinder.
3. Wrap the folded tissue around the end of the cylinder.
4. Tape the wrapped tissue in place.
5. Fringe the end of the tissue by cutting slits about ¼-inch apart.
6. Have the children shake their pom-poms to music.
7. Play recorded selections that suggest wind sounds.

**Dyeing Tips.** When dyeing macaroni by shaking it in a plastic bag with food coloring, add a few drops of rubbing alcohol instead of water. The alcohol produces brilliant colors and helps the macaroni dry quickly. And it won't make the macaroni sticky the way water does.

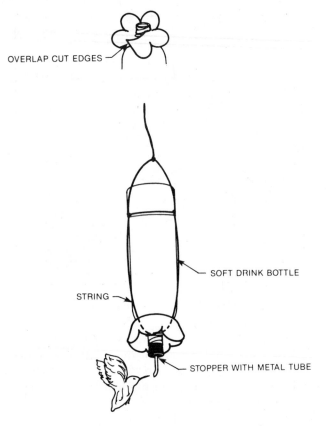

OVERLAP CUT EDGES

STRING

SOFT DRINK BOTTLE

STOPPER WITH METAL TUBE

**FIGURE 31–17 A hummingbird bottle.**

**Bird's Nest.** You can set out a supply of nesting materials in spring whether you have a nesting box or not. Nesting materials should be placed in a protected spot so that the rain won't saturate them and the wind won't blow them away. Use a container such as a large coffee can with a hole cut in its plastic lid. Set it on a window ledge or tack it to a post. Place a selection of the items listed below inside the can. Make certain that the thread, yarn, and string are cut in pieces no longer than four inches. If the pieces are longer, the birds may tangle themselves in them.

Some good nesting materials are: straw, lichen, shredded paper, scraps of cloth (in strips), cotton, string, yarn, thread, unraveled rope, feathers.

### A Hummingbird Bottle.

Materials: Stopper with metal tube through it (available at pet store), soft drink bottle, 1 cup water, ½ cup sugar, red construction paper, cellophane tape, string

Procedure:
1. Buy the stopper at a pet shop. Choose one that fits a plastic soft drink bottle.
2. Boil the water and stir in the sugar until it disappears. Then cool the mixture.
3. Pour the cooled syrup into the bottle and put on the stopper.
4. Cut a flower out of the red construction paper (see Figure 31–17). Make a slit between two of the petals.
5. Place the flower around the neck of the bottle. Overlap the edges of the petals, then tape them together.
6. Find a place to hang the bottle upside down. It may drop some syrup, so hang it over a place that won't be hurt by dripping sugar.
7. To hang the bottle, tie string around the neck and near the bottom. Next, tie a long piece of string from the neck loop to the bottom loop on one side of the bottle. Lift it loosely over the top of the bottle, then tie it to the bottom loop and on down to the neck loop on the other side of the bottle.

## OUTDOOR ACTIVITIES AND GAMES

**Playground Adventures.** Special trips can be planned for young children without ever leaving the school grounds! The following "trips" are only three possibilities for learning experiences in the school play yard. You will have many more of your own, once you start thinking about all the possibilities!

*A buggy trip.* A trip to Bugland, U.S.A., requires no special passport or traveler's checks. The only luggage required is hula hoops, magnifying lenses, and the five senses. Transportation to Bugland on your school play yard is on hands and knees.

Lay the hula hoops in the grass. Small groups of children explore the area inside the hoop using their magnifying lenses, searching for signs of bug life. The size, shape, color, and movement of the bugs are observed. Children listen for the sound of the bugs. Bugs can be collected for further study in an empty jar or oatmeal box. Remind the children that bugs can be fun to watch, but should be let go after a short while. Some children may want to draw pictures of the bugs they found.

Large sheets of easel paper allow the children to make paintings of Bugland as they saw it.

A bug maze can be mapped out on the grass using rope or on the blacktop using tape or colored chalk. The children crawl or "fly" through the maze as bugs.

*Bear country.*   To prepare for a trip to Bear Country, children bring a stuffed bear to school the day before the trip. Prior to the children's arrival on trip day, the teacher hides the bears in the playground under sliding boards, in the trees, on swings, behind playhouses, and in the bushes. On the signal, children hunt for their own bear.

A rolled-up gym mat makes a high mountain for the children to climb over as they sing, "The Bear Went Over the Mountain." They crawl forward and backward and roll over the mountain.

A large blanket and picnic basket filled with tea and honey on crackers are needed for the teddy bears' picnic. (Use apple juice in place of tea.) Another blanket can be set up under a shady tree for children to enjoy stories about the Berenstein Bears and Winnie the Pooh.

The outdoor setting of Bear Country is perfect for acting out the story of The Three Bears. Children act out the bears eating porridge, going on a walk in the woods, Goldilocks arriving at the bear's house, trying the porridge, sitting on the chairs, and sleeping on Baby Bear's bed.

Soap flakes and water can be mixed in the water table outside and molded into small bears. After the bears are dry, they are used at bath time at home.

*Safety land.*   This is a land created by children and teachers. It can be inside, but preferably outside. Lines are taped or painted on the ground for simple maps showing roads and intersections. Large appliance boxes are painted to simulate houses, school, police station, toy store, restaurant, and a hospital for safety abuses that end in injury. A box laid on its side with both ends open acts as a tunnel or a bridge over a body of water. Inexpensive toy traffic signs can be purchased or built and placed appropriately throughout Safety Land. Using the school's bikes and big wheels or those brought from home, children travel around Saftey Land following traffic rules.

Have one child act as a police officer after you have discussed the job of a traffic officer and why traffic rules are important. The day's snack can be served from Safety Land's fast-food restaurant drive-in window. Reading speed limit signs helps with number recognition. Visual perception and large motor skills are developed as children drive around Safety Land.

**Musical Bees.**   For something just right for the springtime, try this version of musical chairs. You will need a chair for each child, music, construction paper, crayons or felt-tip markers, and tape. Each child draws a picture of a flower on a piece of construction paper. Tape one picture on each chair and place the chairs back-to-back in a double line. Set up music, if necessary. The children pretend that they are bees and that the chairs are flowers. Start the music and have the children "buzz" around the line of chairs. When you stop the music, have each child sit down on the chair by which he is standing. Continue as long as the children are interested.

**FIGURE 31–18 Spring activities are outdoor activities!**

**Together Outdoors.** In the spring, plan some outdoor activities together with the children. You may want to try some of the following:

*Seeds.* Plant some seeds, and watch them grow. Remember, younger children are impatient for action, so select a seed variety that germinates quickly.

*Shadows.* Draw a shadow, and watch how it changes. Trace a shadow with a piece of chalk, and watch how the shadow changes during the day.

*Wind.* On a windy day, catch a bag of wind in a clear plastic bag. Ask the children what they see inside the bag.

*Fly a kite.* With young children a pinwheel is easier and more interesting, as it is closer and quicker to respond to the wind.

*Lifestudy.* Observe living things. Follow the path of an ant, find a worm, or catch a snail. Watch how an insect changes its path or climbs over an obstacle such as a small twig. Feed the birds; have the children note how different food attracts different birds.

**Paper Plate Sail.** For a fun spring name-recognition activity, give each child a small paper plate on which you have written his name. Using whatever art media you prefer, children draw a picture or design on the other side of the plate. On a nice day, take the children outside and line them up at a starting point. You go down the field and toss their plates at random, name side up. At a signal, the children race to find their own plates. First child back to you is the winner. Repeat several times to give them both name recognition practice and exercise.

**Zoo Game.** Every child should have a hoop. Each child places his hoop on the ground and stands inside it, and then pretends the hoop is a cage at the zoo and he is inside the cage. He can be many different animals by placing body parts in different animal positions in the cage, such as an elephant, kangaroo, giraffe, bear, gorilla, etc.

**Jump Rope Games for Beginners.** Spring weather brings out the jump ropes. Sounds of jump rope jingles fill the air. Young children join in the chanting, but many cannot join in the jumping since it requires skills that young children have yet to master. Even turning the rope can present problems!

There are a variety of games that can help young children develop the necessary skills and coordination for jumping rope activities. Not only are some children less agile than others, but some lack the body strength to endure such activities. Weak hearts and poor lung strength may also be the culprits. Rope jumping can help improve these areas. Remember to start out at a level that's very basic, and then build on the child's accomplishments.

*Follow the tracks.* Cut footprints from adhesive-backed paper and make patterns for children to follow on the floor. Children must either jump with two feet or hop with one foot as indicated by the number of "feet" on the floor. Make several versions, ranging from easy to more difficult.

*Spinning exercises.* Cut a length of rope (about six or seven feet) for each child. Let the child hold it forward in one hand and turn it. Then, have the child jump along as he rotates the rope beside him. The child will eventually pick up the rhythm. Do the same on the opposite side.

*High water, low water.* Two children hold the end of a rope about 10 to 12 feet long. The rope starts out resting on the ground. Each child in line jumps over it. It is then raised about two inches after all have had a turn. If a child touches the rope, he is out. The game continues until there is one child left.

*Rope swing.* Two children take the ends of the rope. The rope is held about four inches from the ground. The children swing the rope slowly from side to side, but not too far. Each child in line jumps over the rope without touching it or he is out. After the line goes through, the rope is swung a little farther, and the game continues until there is one child left.

*Over the waves.* The rope is held by children. The turner at one end makes waves in the rope by moving his arm up and down. Each jumper must jump over the waves without touching.

**Physical Development Games.** The objectives of the following activities are to improve large motor (muscle) coordination, to develop good sportsmanship, and to have fun!

*Balloon balance.* Ask the children to find a partner and give each pair one balloon. Invite children to find different ways they can balance the balloon between them without using their hands! Once they have it balanced, ask them to try walking around the area without dropping the balloon. After children have done this for a while, beat a drum as a signal for them to try balancing the balloon in a different way. Allow them to try different ways for as long as they seem interested in the game.

*Untying the knot.* The first time you play this game, you might want to try it with four children at a time. Invite the other children to be a cheering squad for the participants and to offer suggestions to them. Ask participants to stand in a circle and to reach across it to hold hands with different children to make a knot. Then, while still holding hands, invite them to twist and turn and duck under arms to unravel the knot. With some luck, they can unravel themselves into a circle of children again.

*Body designs.* In this game, the children work with their friends to create a giant body design. Before you go outside, discuss designs and show children some designs. Choose a beginning place and an ending place by drawing lines in the ground or making lines with sticks. Ask all the children to stand at the beginning and tell them that when you beat a drum three times, it's time for them to run to the end line and pose with their friends as if they are a human design. It might help children create a design if you suggest a theme, such as a happy, scary, sad, or even funny design. Emphasize the importance of interacting with one another.

*Windy.* A table tennis ball is placed at the center of a table. Each player attempts to blow the ball off opponent's end of table by being as windy as possible.

*Floating clouds.* A white balloon is used as a "cloud." Inflate the balloon and tie. Make cloud float in the air by striking it underneath with hands.

*Blow balloon, go balloon.* Blow up balloon. When teacher says, "Go," release balloon. Watch how far the balloon will fly. Blow more air into the balloon and more wind will be released, making balloon fly farther.

*Catch the wind.* Two children hold opposite sides of the open end of a large trash bag. Walk or run into the wind to make the bag inflate.

*Windmill exercise.* Stand with arms extended outward. Move arms forward and backward in small circles, larger circles, and giant circles.

*April Fool's fun.* Have a "Backwards Day" to celebrate either April Fool's Day or just spring in general. Discuss with the children what backwards or doing things in the opposite way, means. You might suggest that they wear their clothes backwards, put their socks on backwards, walk backwards, or anything else that sound like fun for this "Backwards Day."

*Caterpillars walk.* Have the children form a "caterpillar" by lining up in a row on their knees. Ask each child to hold onto the back or the legs of the person in front of him or her. Then have the children crawl together in a line by taking steps first with their right knees, then with their left knees, etc. Sing the song below as the children take their "caterpillar walk."

(To the tune of "Frère Jacques")
Caterpillar, caterpillar,
Crawl, crawl, crawl; crawl, crawl, crawl.
Crawling on the ground,
Crawling all around.
Crawl, crawl, crawl; crawl, crawl, crawl.

You may want to follow up this active game with a quiet activity such as making egg-carton caterpillars. See Appendix E for instructions.

**Wind Words.**   Read "The Wind," by Robert Louis Stevenson. Create a windy day with an electric fan. Or take the children outside on a windy day. Have them close their eyes and feel the wind in their faces and at their backs. Hold up a strip of tissue and watch its movements. Encourage the children to call out words that describe how the wind feels to them and how it moves.

**Spring Has Come.**   Sing the Japanese folk song, "Haru Ga Kita," from *Expressing Music/New Dimensions in Music,* by Robert A. Choate and others (American Book, 1940). For a follow-up activity, have the children paint pictures of spring coming to the hills, to the city, or to a village.

### March Wind
The March winds roars loudly,
"Winter can't stay!"
Wind murmurs through branches
While Sun warms the day.

Wind purrs through the treetops
And as branches sway,
Wind whispers this secret,
"Spring's not far away!"

—Billie M. Phillips

Let the children act out this poem.

# ACTION SONGS, POEMS, AND FINGERPLAYS

### Bumblebee Song
(To the tune of "Jingle Bells")
Bumblebee, bumblebee,
Landing on my nose.
Bumblebee, bumblebee,
Now he's on my toes.
On my arms, on my legs,
On my elbows.
Bumblebee, oh, bumblebee,
He lands and then he goes!

Have the children touch the various parts of the body mentioned in the song as they sing the song.

### The Fuzzy, Fuzzy Caterpillar
(To the tune of "Eeensy Weensy Spider")
The fuzzy, fuzzy caterpillar
Curled up upon a leaf,
Spun her chrysalis
And then fell fast asleep.
While she was sleeping,
She dreamed that she could fly.
And later when she woke up,
She was a butterfly!

### Circus Day
The circus is coming. Hurrah! Hurray!
   (Clap hands, jump up and down, to express joy)
I'm going to see the parade.
   (Pretend to be standing on sidelines, move head as though watching the parade go by)
I'm going to walk through the sideshow.
   (Pretend to walk along, looking on both sides in amazement)
And have some pink lemonade.
   (Pretend to sip a drink through a straw)
There'll be galloping horses,
   (Pantomime riding a galloping horse)
And comical clowns.
   (Pretend to be a clown or point and laugh as though looking at a clown)
And ladies on elephants in beautiful gowns.
   (Pretend to be a lady riding an elephant or wave to one)
There'll be jugglers and tight-rope walkers
   (Pantomime these activities)
And men on the flying trapeze.
   (Pretend to watch, looking up, showing anxiety, etc.)
There'll be wonderful lion tamers
   (Pretend to be a lion tamer with a chair and a whip)
And the sawdust will make me sneeze.
   (Pretend to sneeze)
"Peanuts, popcorn, candy!" the eager vendors will say.
   (Say the quoted words as a vendor says them)
And "Teedle-doo-dum-dee-aya" the circus band will play.
   (Pretend to play a band instrument)
Oh, the circus is coming! Hurray! Hurray!
   (Repeat gestures of delight)

### About a Tree
Here is a tree so tall and strong.
   (Rest elbows on table. Hold forearms upright close together)
It took a long time to grow.
   (Indicate a "long time" by stretching arms wide)

Patches of sunshine come through its boughs and
   shine on the ground below.
   (Make circle with thumb and index finger of each
   hand. Move hands here and there as though
   directing sunlight to areas on the ground)
The leaves of the tree stir in the breeze.
   (Resume tree position of arms. Wave fingers for
   "leaves")
The trunk bends in a "blow."
   (Bend arms representing tree trunk as though hit
   by a gale)
Squirrels leap from limb to limb
   (Keep left arm and hand as the tree. Use fingers of
   right hand for "squirrels." Make them "leap" on
   the left fingers)
While birds fly high and low.
   (Make a bird with each hand—three middle fingers
   together, thumbs and little fingers flapping like
   wings. "Fly high and low")
I like to climb from branch to branch
   (Use arms overhead to represent an upward crawl
   movement)
Or sit in a leafy nook,
   (Arch arms overhead to represent the "nook")
And watch the birds and squirrels play
   (Show birds flying and squirrels climbing or
   leaping)
While seeming to read a book.
   (Hold imaginary book in both hands)

**The Birds**
Here's the nest, (Cup hands together to show nests)
   and here's Mama bird (each child lifts one finger to
   show Mama bird)
Wondering about
A noise she heard.

Here's the daddy. (Each child lifts a finger of the
   other hand for Daddy)
Watch him squirm; (Wiggle that finger)
He is looking
For a worm.

The baby birds (Open hands and lift fingers to show
   baby birds)
Will grow up some day;
Then they will all
Fly away. (Flutter fingers and move hands outward as
   the birds fly away)

**Ten Little Caterpillars**
Ten little caterpillars climbing on a vine;
One climbed too high; then there were nine.
Nine little caterpillars crawled out the garden gate;
One got stuck, and then there were eight.
Eight little caterpillars resting on a stone;

One slipped off, and seven were alone.
Seven little caterpillars humped across some sticks;
One got scratched; then there were six.
Six little caterpillars eat to stay alive;
One wiggled away; then there were five.
Five little caterpillars crawling on the ground;
A big foot went "plop" and they weren't around.
Four little caterpillars climbing up a tree;
One tumbled down; then there were three.
Three little caterpillars wondering what to do;
Along came a bird; then there were two.
Two little caterpillars resting in the sun;
One curled up in a leaf; then there was one.
One little caterpillar resting all alone;
One day became a butterfly; now she has flown!

**Good-Bye Winter**
Good-bye winter, good-bye winter,
Good-bye winter, we wish you'd go away.

Good-bye snow!
Good-bye slush!
Good-bye puddles!
Good-bye snowsuits!
Good-bye cold wind!

Come back springtime.
Come back springtime.
Come back springtime.
We wish you'd come to stay.

Come back green grass!
Come back flowers!
Come back birdies!

**Who Has Seen the Wind?**
Who has seen the wind?
Neither you nor I (Shake head sideways)
But when the trees bow down their leaves (Bow)
The wind is passing by (Move arms)

**Bubbles, Bubbles**
Bubbles, bubbles, large and small (Make large, then
   small circle)
Sailing through the air.
I reach out to catch one (Pretend to catch bubble)
and POP (Clap hands)
It isn't there!

**Blow a Bubble!**
Blow a bubble (Blow and form circle with hands)
Catch a bubble (Pretend to catch a bubble)
Look, what do I see? (Pretend to look in bubble)
It looks just like me! (Point to self)

**Fuzzy Wuzzy Caterpillar**
Fuzzy wuzzy caterpillar
Into a corner will creep (Children may creep)

He'll spin himself a blanket
And then go fast asleep (Children curl up)
Fuzzy wuzzy caterpillar
Wakes up by and by (Children awaken and dance
    about)
To find he has wings of beauty,
Changed to a butterfly!

### It's Raining

I wear a rubber raincoat
To cover up my clothes,
And some shiny, new black rubbers
To cover up my toes.

I hold a green umbrella
As I walk along to school,
And the raindrops make some splashes
In the little, muddy pools.

### Rain

Rain is falling down,
Rain is falling down.
Pitter, patter,
Pitter, patter,
Rain is falling down.

### A Kite

I often sit and wish that I
Could be a kite up in the sky,
And ride upon the breeze and go
Whichever way I chanced to blow

### Kite Days

A kite, a sky, and a firm breeze,
And acres of ground away from trees,
And one hundred yards of clean, strong string
On boy, O boy! I call that spring!

### No Drop of Rain

It rained on Anne,
It rained on Fran,
It rained on Arabella,
    But—
It did not rain on Mary Jane
She had a HUGE umbrella!

### Dandelions

Oh, dandelion, as yellow as gold,
What do you do all day?
"I wait and I wait in the tall green grass
Till the children come out to play."

Oh dandelion, as yellow as gold,
What do you do all night?
"I wait and I wait in the tall green grass
Till my yellow hair turns white."

And what do the little children do
When they come out to play?
"They pick me up in their hands
And blow my white hair all away!"

### Who Likes the Rain?

"I," said the duck, "I call it fun,
For I have my little red rubbers on.
They make a cunning three-toed track
In the soft cool mud. Quack! Quack! Quack!"

"I," cried the dandelion, "I.
My roots are thirsty, my buds are dry."
And she lifted her little yellow head
Out of her green and grassy bed.

"I hope 'twill pour! I hope 'twill pour!"
Croaked the tree toad at his gray back door.
"For with a broad leaf for a roof
I am perfectly weatherproof."

Said the brook, "I welcome every drop;
Come, come, dear raindrops, never stop
Till a great river you make of me.
Then I will carry you to the sea."

### Mud

Mud is very nice to feel
All squishy-squash between the toes!
I'd rather wade in wiggly mud
Than smell a yellow rose.

Nobody else but the rosebush knows
How nice mud feels between the toes.

### The Wind

Who has seen the wind?
Neither I nor you;
But where the leaves hang trembling,
The wind is passing through.

Who has seen the wind?
Neither you nor I;
But when the trees bow down their heads,
The wind is passing by.

### Clouds

If I had a spoon
As tall as the sky,
I'd dish out the clouds
That go slip-sliding by.

I'd take them right in
And give them to cook,
And see if they tasted
As good as they look.

**Little Wind**
Little wind, blow on the hilltop,
Little wind, blow down the plain;
Little wind, blow up the sunshine,
Little wind, blow off the rain.

**Clouds**
White sheep, white sheep,
   On a blue hill,
When the wind stops,
   You all stand still.
When the wind blows
   You walk away slow.
White sheep, white sheep,
   Where do you go?

**Windy Wash Day**
The wash is hanging on the line,
And the wind's blowing—
Dresses all so clean and fine,
Beckoning
And blowing.

Stockings twisted in a dance,
Pajamas very tripping,
And every little pair of pants
Upside down
And skipping

**The Wind**
I saw you toss the kites on high
And blow the birds about the sky;
And all around I heard you pass,
Like ladies' skirts across the grass—
   O wind, a-blowing all day long,
   O wind, that sings so loud a song!
I saw the different things you did,
But always you yourself you hid.
I felt you push, I heard you call,
I could not see yourself at all—
   O wind, a-blowing all day long,
   O wind, that sings so loud a song!
O you that are so strong and cold,
O blower, are you young or old?
Are you a beast of field and tree,
Or just a stronger child than me?
   O wind, a-blowing all day long,
   O wind, that sings so loud a song!

**The Storm**
From my bed so safe and warm,
I like to listen to a storm.

Thunder rumbling grand and proud,
Is louder than the rain is loud.

Bang it goes (like little boys)
But lightning doesn't make a noise.

Bright and quick and sudden though
It can cut the dark in two—

For just a second in its light,
My chair is red, my curtains white.

**I Am a Tall Tree**
I am a tall tree
I reach toward the sky
   (Both hands reach upward)
Where bright stars twinkle
And white clouds float by
   (Look upward, arms sway)
My branches toss high
As the wild winds blow
   (Arms wave wildy)
Now they bend forward
Loaded with snow
   (Arms out front swaying)
I like it best
When I rock birdies
To sleep in their nest.
   (Continue swaying while forming nest)

At the end of the poem, place hands at the side of
the head and close eyes.

**Rain**
The rain is falling all around,
It falls on field and tree,
It rains on the umbrellas here,
And on the ships at sea.

**The Secret**
We have a secret
   Just we three,
The robin and I,
   And the sweet cherry tree.
The bird told the tree,
   And the tree told me,
And nobody knows it,
   Just we three.

But of course, the robin
   Knows it best
Because he built the nest,
   I shan't tell the rest.
And laid the four little
   Somethings in it
I'm afraid I shall tell it
   Every minute.

But if the tree and the robin
   Don't peep,
I'll try my best
   The secret to keep
Though I know when the little
   Birds fly about,
Then the whole secret
   Will be out.

## Rain Song

The sky has shut its big blue eye,
   The trees are wet with seeping.
Oh, where's the bright and laughing sky?
   Sleeping,
      Sleeping,
         Sleeping.
Nothing but the river sings,
   Not a bee is humming.
Oh, where's the sun with yellow wings?
   Coming,
      Coming,
         Coming.

## Tulips

(Attach tulip shapes to each fingernail—red ones on
   the little fingers, purple on the fourth fingers, and
   so on)

In Holland the beautiful tulips grow.
   (Hold both hands on flat surface in front of you,
   palms up, as though looking at nails)
Red and purple, white, yellow, pink.
   (Show little fingers first, fourth fingers next, and so
   on, until all "tulips" are visible to the children in
   front of you)

Each flower is like a cup.
   (Put forearms together for a flower stem; cup hands
   for blossom)
Someday I think I'll take a drink.
   (Pretend to drink from cupped hands)

## Kites

"I can go higher than you,"
Boasted a dragon-shaped kite.
   (Make a rotating upward motion with the right arm
   and hand)
"But I am stronger than you,"
Answered a box-shaped kite.
   (Make a box with both hands)
"Well, I am prettier than you,"
Said a round-faced kite in the sky.
   (Make a circle with both hands)
"But I have a longer tail than you,"
Was a dainty kite's reply.
   (Make a streaking motion through the air with left
   hand)

The last little kite flew out of sight.
He didn't talk. He didn't boast.
   (Shake head in a negative motion)
He just did things.
   (Raise the right hand higher and higher; drop both
     hands to rest in lap)

## Pussy Willow

I have a little pussy
And her coat is silver gray,
She lives out in the meadow
And she never runs away.

She always is a pussy,
She'll never be a cat,
Because she's a pussy willow,
Now what do you think of that?

## Caterpillar

Fuzzy, wuzzy, creepy, crawly,
Caterpillar funny—
You will be a butterfly
When the days are sunny.

## Tenants

I printed a "For Rent" sign
For all the world to see.
Dad set it on the birdhouse
Up in the maple tree.
The robins liked the birdhouse
Lived there the summer long.
And paid their rent each morning
By singing us a song!

## Butterfly

Up and down the air you float,
Like a little fairy boat.
   I should like to sail that sky
   Gliding like a butterfly.

## Wind on the Hill

No one can tell me,
   Nobody knows,
Where the wind comes from,
   Where the wind goes.

It's flying from somewhere,
   As fast as it can,
I couldn't keep up with it,
   Not if I ran.

But if I stopped holding
   The string of my kite,
It would blow with the wind
   For a day and a night.

But then when I found it,
   Wherever it blew,

I should know that the wind
    Had been going there too.

So then I could tell them
    Where the wind goes . . .
But where the wind comes from
    Nobody knows.

### From Seed to Seed

See the little seed I brought
    (Hold up imaginary seed between left thumb and
    forefinger)
I'll dig a hole and plant it
    (Dig hole with right hand for trowel; "plant" seed
    with left hand)
I'll smooth the earth with little pats
    (Do so, using both hands on flat surface)
And water it with care
    (Pretend to hold watering can in right hand)
The sun will shine on it
    (Make "sun" with one or both hands held high)
And one day I will see
A tiny green shoot
    (Use right forefinger to represent the shoot)
Then a leaf or two
    (Bring right thumb up beside forefinger; bring up
    middle finger)
And finally a flower
    (Make circle of left thumb and forefinger; hold it
    above right forefinger)
It will nod in the breeze
    (Keeping the "flowers" just formed, wave it back
    and forth)
I will smell its perfume
    (Bend head over "flower" and sniff)
Then the petals will fall
    (Let fingers of left hand represent petals and flutter
    downward)
Soon the seeds will scatter
    (Let fingers of right hand be seeds; flutter fingers
    away from self)
Someday there will be more flowers.
    (Lift all ten fingers to represent flowers)

### Rope Jumping

Jumping rope is lots of fun.
Turn the rope. Here I come!
    (Jump lightly in place)
Hop, hop; clap, clap, clap.
    (Hop lightly on both feet; clap hands)
Hop, hop; tap, tap, tap.
    (Hop lightly; tap with right toe)
Right foot hop; left foot hop.
Spin around like a top.
    (Suit actions to words)

Hop, hop; banana-peel slide.
    (Hop lightly; slide, wave arms for balance)
Hop, hop, carabao ride.
    (Hop lightly; bucking bronco pantomime)
Hop, hop; pineapples prick.
    (Hop lightly; pantomime pricking finger, put it in
    mouth to ease hurt)
Hop, hop, sugar-cane lick.
    (Hop lightly; pretend to hold a length of sugar cane
    and lick the end of it)

## FOOD ACTIVITIES

**Limeade.**    Cut a lime in half. Squeeze juice. Pour juice into glass. Add ⅓ cup water and one teaspoon honey; stir. Add two ice cubes and drink.

**Sunshine Salad.**    Mix ½ carton plain yogurt with one teaspoon honey. Put one slice pineapple in each dish. Put one tablespoon yogurt mixture in the middle of the pineapple slice. Eat the sunshine!

**Rainy Day Sandwich.**    To liven up a rainy day, try *ironing* a sandwich. Make up cheese sandwiches as you normally would for grilling. Butter the outsides and wrap each sandwich in tin foil. Iron both sides of the sandwich with an iron (1 to 2 minutes each side). Older children may help with the ironing. *(Extreme caution is advised when using potentially hazardous appliances with young children.)*

**Flower Power.**    Pick or buy broccoli and cauliflower. Wash and pull off leaves into separate florets. Steam. Sprinkle with salt and pepper or Parmesan cheese.

**Spinach Wrappers.**    Pick or buy fresh, raw spinach. Wash thoroughly. Mix one tablespoon cream cheese, three shelled, broken peanuts. Spread mixture on a spinach leaf. Roll and hold with a toothpick. (Soften cream cheese before making this snack; a four-ounce package will serve six children.)

**Stuffed Tomato Snacks.**    Pick or buy cherry tomatoes. Wash. Slice off the tops. Scoop out the seeds and pulp. Fill with cottage cheese. Sprinkle with sunflower seeds. Note: Large cherry tomatoes are easier to stuff.

**Pineapple Pick-ups.**   Slice off the top of a fresh pineapple. Cut in half, then in fourths. Slice off the rind and the core. Remove any "eyes." Slice the pineapple quarter lengthwise, then crosswise. Pick them up with toothpicks and dip in crushed bran flakes.

**Snacks-on-a-Stick.**   Have the children spear bite-sizes cubes of cheese, fruit, or vegetables on straight pretzels. They are fun to make and fun to eat.

**Moving Celery.**   Cut cleaned celery into small pieces, 2″ to 3″ in size. Fill them with peanut butter or egg salad. Put carrot wheels on the side with toothpicks to make a car. Put a sail on one with a toothpick. Make several "cars" and hook them together to make a celery "train." Children will come up with many more "moving" ideas.

**Orange Yogurt Drink.**
Ingredients:
¼ cup orange juice concentrate
½ cup plain yogurt
½ cup milk

Procedure:
Blend ingredients together in a blender. A banana can be substituted for the yogurt. Recipe is enough to two servings.

**Juice Jumble.**   Squeeze the juice out of one grapefruit and one orange. Mix the two juices. Drink over ice.

**Frozen Fruit Slush.**
Ingredients:
1½ cups fresh orange juice (5 to 6 oranges)
¾ cup fresh lemon juice (4 to 5 lemons)
1½ cups mashed ripe banana (1 to 2 bananas)
½ cup honey
1 quart milk

Procedure:
1. Roll oranges and lemons on cabinet or table. Cut in half, squeeze juice, and measure into bowl.
2. Peel and mash bananas.
3. Add banana, honey, and milk to juices and mix well.
4. Pour the mixture into the ice cube trays and place in freezer.

5. When partially frozen, remove, turn into bowl, and beat quickly, but do not let mixture melt.
6. Return to trays and freeze until solid. A double recipe can be frozen in an ice cream freezer. Serves 16 children.

**Carrots and Honey.**
Ingredients:
honey
carrot sticks
sesame seeds

Procedure:
Put small amounts of honey into paper cups and add sesame seeds. Let the children dip carrot sticks into the honey for a sweet "bee snack." (If desired, use apple slices or orange segments instead of carrot sticks.)

**Carrots and Apples.**
Ingredients:
2 cups sliced carrots
1 cooking apple
2 tablespoons brown sugar or honey
2 tablespoons margarine
¼ teaspoon salt
½ teaspoon cinnamon

Procedure:
1. Slice carrots and parboil until almost tender.
2. Core and dice apple.
3. Add apple and other ingredients and cook until apple is tender. Serves 6 to 8 children.

**Banana Rounds.**
Ingredients:
4 medium bananas
½ cup yogurt
3 tablespoons honey
⅛ teaspoon nutmeg
⅛ teaspoon cinnamon
¼ cup wheat germ

Procedure:
1. Peel bananas and slice into rounds.
2. Measure spices, wheat germ, and honey. Mix with yogurt and bananas.
3. Chill. Serves 8 children.

# ADDITIONAL READINGS

## Children's Books About Baby Animals, Hatching, and Pets

Bridge, Linda McCarter. *Cats: Little Tigers in Your House.* Washington, D.C.: National Geographic Society, Books for Young Explorers, 1974.

Ets, Marie Hall. *Play with Me.* New York: Viking Press, 1955.

Hall, Derek. *Elephant Bathes.* New York: Alfred A. Knopf, 1985.

Hughes, Shirley. *Out and About.* New York: Lothrop, 1988.

Hutchins, Pat. *Where's the Baby?* New York: Greenwillow, 1988.

Keats, Ezra Jack. *Pet Show.* New York: Macmillan Co., 1974.

Rinard, Judith. *Helping Our Animal Friends.* Washington, D.C.: National Geographic Society, 1985.

Selsam, Milicent. *All Kinds of Babies and How They Grow.* New York: Scholastic Book Services, 1971.

Stein, Sara. *Cat.* San Diego: Harcourt Brace Jovanovich, 1985.

Ward, Lynd. *The Biggest Bear.* New York: Scholastic Book Services, 1975.

## Children's Books About Insects, Spiders, and Earthworms

Bason, Lillian. *Spiders.* Washington, D.C.: National Geographic Society, Books for the Young Explorers, 1974.

Brandt, Keith. *Insects.* Mahwah, N.J.: Troll Associates, 1985.

Caudill, Rebecca. *A Pocketful of Cricket.* New York: Holt, Rinehart and Winston, 1964.

Conklin, Gladys. *I Like Butterflies.* New York: Holiday House, 1958.

————. *I Like Caterpillars.* New York: Holiday House, 1960.

————. *We Like Bugs.* New York: Holiday House, 1962.

Cornelius, Carol. *Isabella Wooly Bear Tiger Moth.* Chicago: Children's Press, 1978.

Fischer-Nagel, Heiderose. *Life of the Ladybug.* Minneapolis: Carolrhoda Books, 1986.

Florian, Douglas. *Discovering Butterflies.* New York: Charles Scribner's Sons, 1986.

Goudey, Alice. *Butterfly Time.* New York: Charles Scribner's Sons, 1964.

Graham, Margaret Bloy. *Be Nice to Spiders.* New York: Harper & Row, 1967.

Podendorf, Illa. *The New True Book About Insects.* Chicago: Children's Press, 1981.

Pollock, Penny. *The Spit Bug Who Couldn't Spit.* New York: G.P. Putnam's Sons, 1982.

Sabin, Francene. *Amazing World of Ants.* Mahwah, N.J.: Troll Associates, 1982.

Selsam, Milicent. *Terry and the Caterpillars.* New York: Harper & Row, 1962.

Stang, Judy. *The Pet in the Jar.* Racine, Wis.: Western Publishing, 1974.

Stevens, Carla. *Catch a Cricket.* New York: Young Scott Books, 1961.

Wonder Starters. *Butterflies.* New York: Wonder Books, 1972.

## Children's Books About Birds, Fish, and Amphibians

Bernard, George. *Common Frog.* New York: G.P. Putnam's Sons, 1979.

Cole, Joanna. *Hungry, Hungry Sharks.* New York: Random House, 1986.

Day, Jennifer. *What Is a Bird?* New York: Golden Books, 1975.

Florian, Douglas. *Discovering Frogs.* New York: Charles Scribner's Sons, 1986.

————. *Discovering Seashells.* New York: Charles Scribner's Sons, 1986.

Gans, Roma. *When Birds Change Their Feathers.* New York: Thomas Y. Crowell, 1980.

Heller, Ruth. *Chickens Aren't the Only Ones.* New York: Grosset and Dunlap, 1981.

Kaufman, John. *Birds Are Flying.* New York: Thomas Y. Crowell, 1979.

Myers, Arthur. *Sea Creatures Do Amazing Things.* New York: Random House, 1981.

Ryder, Joanne. *Snail in the Woods.* New York: Harper & Row, 1979.

Sabin, Louis. *Reptiles and Amphibians.* Mahwah, N.J.: Troll Associates, 1985.

Santrey, Laurence. *Birds.* Mahwah, N.J.: Troll Associates, 1985.

Selsam, Milicent. *Plenty of Fish.* New York: Harper & Brothers, 1960.

# UNIT 32

# Summer

Summer is a time for growing. Young children are very aware of the ever-new earth around them. See with the children the many features of the summer:

- The tiny world of ants
- The large and tiny wildflowers
- The colors and shapes of the clouds
- The rainbow after a summer shower
- The ladybug crawling up a flower stem

Experience with the children all these things and many more during the summer. Talk with the children about them. This will help them develop and extend their world in the wide open space of summertime.

## LESSON PLAN IDEAS FOR SUMMER

### Excursions

- Beach or swimming pool for wading
- Picnic
- Backyard garden
- Zoo
- Outdoor walk to see summer characteristics
- Farm
- Breakfast outing

### Art.

- Painting with weeds for brushes
- Blot painting with white paint to represent clouds on gray or blue paper that represents the sky
- Flowers made out of nut cups, using pipe cleaners for stems; stems placed in clay base in paper cup
- Sponge painting of sunrise or sunset
- Collage of summer—sand, shells, rocks, pebbles, grass
- Painting rocks
- Child-made hats decorated for a summer outdoor parade
- Painting with water outside
- Having an art show of the children's work

### Science.

- Study and observe shadows
- Study, observe, and grow seeds and plants
- Study and observe ants, caterpillars, spiders
- Study the life cycle of a frog
- Study and observe flowers, clouds, and sunlight and its effect on growing plants

### Music.

- Shadow dancing behind screen or sheet
- Creative movements relating to summer activities—fishing, swimming, throwing a frisbee, etc.
- Creative movements interpreting sprinkler, fountain, waterfall
- Creative movements representing sun rising or setting
- Creative movements interpreting growth of a seed into a plant and the wilting of a plant in the summer's heat and its perking up when watered
- Creative movements interpreting animals seen in summer—birds, butterflies, insects, etc.
- Marching parade with or without rhythm instruments

### Food.

- Homemade ice cream
- Marshmallows and hot dogs cooked over a grill on the playground or at a park
- Fresh fruits in salads, on toothpicks, blended for drinks
- Sandwiches and other picnic snacks, even if the picnic is outside the classroom on the grass or at a nearby home or park
- Fruits dried in the sunshine, and eaten a day or two later

652

- Flavored ice pops, slush, or other frozen treats
- Gelatin squares with fresh fruits

### Visitors.

- Lifeguard
- Farmer
- Gardener
- Artist
- Florist or flower arranger
- Person who enjoys fishing
- Golfer
- People to share vacation experiences
- Ice-cream vendor

### Language Experiences.

- Slides and/or pictures of summer scenes, with children discussing them
- Objects or pictures of food, recreational equipment, clothing, etc., relating to all seasons—items passed out to children, with each child who has something relating to summer telling about it
- Sharing of vacation experiences
- Sharing of a favorite summer activity, food, place to visit, etc.
- Stories—written, told, or taped—of most memorable summer vacation or experience

## ART ACTIVITIES FOR SMALL MOTOR DEVELOPMENT

**Grass Rubbings.** Place different grasses on a piece of paper. Place a second piece of paper over the grasses. Rub with crayon or chalk so impressions of grasses are visible. (Grasses can be collected by children from around school or home.)

**Garbage Mobile.** Collect trash from around school (children should help). Clean what can be cleaned up. Make a mobile or a Garbage Monster. (Caution the children not to pick up broken glass, tin cans, etc.)

**Walnut Smile/Sad Faces.**
Procedure:
1. Save walnut half-shells.
2. Make a knot in the center of a piece of yarn.

(Make sure the yarn is longer than the size of the child's head.)
3. Set the knot between two walnut shells, and glue them together.
4. When the glue has dried, use nail polish to paint a smiley face on one side and a frown on the other side of the walnut shells. Children can show their moods by exhibiting either the smile or the frown side of the walnut.

**Paper Plate Fish.** Cut a pie-shaped wedge out of a white paper plate. Staple the wedge to the plate for the fish's tail. Give the children bits of shiny colored foil, of colored construction paper, fabric pieces, and anything else decorative to paste onto their paper plate fish. Crayons and felt-tip markers can also be used to put more decorative details on their fish. (See Figure 32-1.)

**Pinwheels.** Follow directions in Unit 26 (Figure 26–13) for making pinwheel ornaments. Substitute wallpaper samples (oilcloth) for regular paper so pinwheels will be strong enough for outdoor use. Hold the pinwheel together with a straight pin, stuck through the pinwheel center and into a pencil eraser.

**Three-Dimensional Water Pictures.** For a summer art activity, use manila drawing paper for a back-

**FIGURE 32–1 Paper plate fish.**

ground and paste light blue construction paper on it for waves.

Procedure:
1. First cut the blue paper in a wave shape.
2. Then glue it in a few places, allowing it to "bump out" in other places, to create the effect of real waves.
3. The children can fill in the rest of the water scene with crayons, markers, or cut-paper designs.

**Accordian Pictures.** For an interesting effect, have the children accordion pleat (or fan) their colored pictures. It provides an unusual three-dimensional effect.

**Sandy Pictures.** Get a piece of blue construction paper. Use white glue to draw a sandy beach. Sprinkle on sand. Use white shoe polish to make tips of waves, other details. Cut paper figures from scraps, if desired, and glue to the picture.

**End-of-the-Year Fun.** Why not have a hose and sprinkler party? Ask each child to bring a bathing suit and make arrangements to have a hose and sprinkler available. On the first warm day during the final weeks of school, have a splash party.

**Footprints in the Sands.** Try a foot mural. Spread out a long roll of wrapping paper. Have the children take off their shoes and socks and trace around their feet with magic markers. Label each pair of feet with the child's name.

**Footprint Activities.** Summertime is barefoot time, a time for experiences that involve our whole bodies—especially our feet. Try these fun and learning foot-oriented activities:

- Play some toe-tapping music. Children lie on the floor and "direct" the music with their feet. This is also good exercise for the legs.
- Hold feet-painting sessions. Tape newspapers to the floor for easy cleanup, then spread and securely tape newsprint or mural paper to the floor. At one end of the mural paper, place large trays or pans with sponges saturated in a mixture of tempera and liquid detergent. Have at least two or three colors, each in its own pan. At the other end, place a tub of soapy water and plenty of old towels. Children first color their feet by stepping on the sponges. They then walk and dance on the mural paper, painting with their feet. They can experiment with all sorts of strokes, using any part of their feet for different effects. Enhance their painting movements by playing soothing music while they footpaint. When children are finished painting, have them step into the soapy water, wash the paint off, step out onto a towel, and dry. Join your children in this activity—you'll love the feel of paint between your toes, and they'll love sharing the experience with you.
- Inspire imaginative movement activities. Tell children to pretend they're walking through a room that has six inches of peanut butter all over the floor. Discuss how that would differ from walking through mashed potatoes, butter, whipped cream, or ketchup. Spread popcorn on the floor and experience walking barefoot through it. Then describe how it feels.
- Encourage children to tell you about these foot-related experiences. Take down their stories for them to illustrate, or tape their descriptions to enjoy later.

**Potato Porcupine.** Slice off the top of an Irish potato. Carve out a hole, leaving plenty of meat on the walls. Insert four toothpicks as legs. Make eyes by attaching two small white paper circles. Fill cavity with earth (or moist cotton), sprinkled with grass seed. Keep watered for about 10 days until Porky's spines sprout.

**Animal Pins.** Sew or glue a safety pin on back of circle of fake fur or velvet. Decorate with felt.

**Tub or Pool Toys.** Use one rectangular sponge for a base. Use another sponge from which you will cut other shapes. Glue these shapes onto the base sponge to create various animals and boats. (See Figure 32–3.)

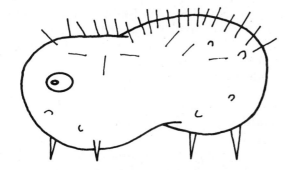

**FIGURE 32–2 Potato porcupine.**

**Children's Outdoor Art Show.** What could be more fun on a summer day than an outdoor art show? In addition to displaying the children's work on tables, walls, and portable easels, include some of these ideas:

- Pictures drawn with colored chalk on the sidewalk
- Colorful string or yarn woven in a fence
- Large sculptures created with giant discards
- Pictures hung from a line with clothespins
- Areas where children can draw or paint while their art show is in progress.

**Tie Dye.**
Materials:
large pan of warm water
marbles
rubber bands
pieces of old sheets, undershirts, or cloth squares to use as a scarf
liquid dye

Procedure:
1. Fill a large pot one-third full of warm water. Add the liquid dye and stir. The brightness of the color will depend on how much dye you add.
2. Show children how to tie dye by placing marbles inside the cloth and fastening them with a rubber band. (Adults may need to tighten the rubber bands.) Tie several marbles into the cloth at different places, then quickly dip the cloth in the dye.
3. Remove the rubber bands and show the children that the area under the rubber band is not dyed.
4. It's best to do this activity outdoors to avoid spilling the dye on the carpet or furniture. (See Figure 32-4.)

**Bubble Painting.** Enhance your summer art program with bubble painting. Make bubble solution by pouring ⅔ cup of liquid detergent into a gallon container, add 1 tablespoon food coloring and enough water to fill the container; let the solution sit for a few hours before using. Put in clear jars or glasses,

A TUGBOAT     A BUNNY     A SEA MONSTER

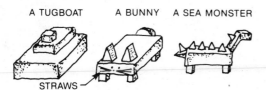

STRAWS

THEY'LL NEVER SINK!

**FIGURE 32–3 Tub or pool toys.**

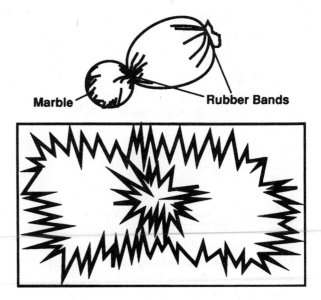

Marble     Rubber Bands

**FIGURE 32–4 Tie dyeing.**

and add liquid food coloring or tempera in primary colors. Form secondary colors by mixing. Experiment with further color mixtures. Compare the bubbles you can make with these colored solutions to bubbles made with plain solution. Make an interesting spatter design by blowing the colored bubbles over absorbent paper.

Variation: Prepare a dark painting mixture with liquid poster paint and bubble solution. Place this in a cereal bowl. With a soda straw, blow bubbles until they fill the bowl, reaching barely above the edge of the bowl. Carefully place a light sheet of construction paper over the top of the bowl; bubbles will pop on the paper and leave a circular design. If you get a spatter print, you blew the bubbles too high out of the bowl. Be sure you *blow* on those straws—you don't want to drink "soap soda." Just to be sure, poke a small hole at the top of the straw to prevent accidental sipping.

**Dandelion Sponge Prints.**
Materials:
light blue construction paper
sponges
thick yellow tempera paint
thin white tempera paint
green crayons
scissors
paper towels
shallow containers

Procedure:
1. Cut sponges into circle shapes.
2. Place folded paper towels in shallow containers and pour on tempera paints.
3. Use a green crayon to draw "stems" on sheets of light blue construction paper. Make one sheet for each child, or let children draw their own stems.
4. Let the children dip circle sponge shapes into yellow and white paint. Then have them press the shapes onto their papers at the tops of the stems to create dandelions. The children may use green crayons to add leaves if they wish.

**Children's Outdoor Art Show.** What could be more fun on a summer day than an outdoor art show? In addition to displaying the children's work on tables, walls, and portable easels, include some of these ideas:

• Pictures drawn with colored chalk on the sidewalk
• Colorful string or yarn woven in a fence
• Large sculptures created with giant discards
• Pictures hung from a line with clothespins
• Areas where children can draw or paint while their art show is in progress.

## GAMES

**Water Games.** Take advantage of the warm summer weather, the outdoors, and the young child's fascination with water to introduce and reinforce basic concepts through water play learning games.

Water games will provide both fun and educational achievement for the young child. These activities will also aid in gross motor skills while enhancing perceptual and cognitive abilities. But since skill

**FIGURE 32–5 A day at the pool with mom and dad— summer activity in the doll corner.**

levels vary, be sure to choose an activity that can be a successful experience for the child.

### Table Tennis Balls.

- Place a dozen table tennis balls in an egg carton and spray them with assorted colors of enamel paint. Give each child a plastic straw and let them practice blowing the balls across the water. Structure the activities according to the abilities of the children.
- Make flash cards to match the colors of the table tennis balls. Hold up the card and have the child pick out the matching ball with a slotted spoon (from the water).
- Write numbers (or draw shapes) on the balls. Using a ladle, slotted spoon, or tongs, have the children pick out specified balls.

### Outdoor Car Wash.
Have an outdoor "car wash." Provide the children large paintbrushes and buckets of water and let them "wash" the riding toys.

### Easy Sandboxes.
Even if your outdoor area is small, or if cats live in your neighborhood, your children can still enjoy a sandbox. Fill a baby bathtub with sand and set it outside on a small table. The sand can be used either dry or wet, and the tub can be stored indoors when not in use.

### Sponges.

- Provide sponges in different sizes, colors, and shapes. First, play games to reinforce these concepts; then use the sponges to discover absorption and evaporation. Which sponge holds the most water? Have children guess and then squeeze the water from two different-sized sponges into separate cups and see the results.
- Place two identical sponges in the pool until saturated. Remove one and place it in the sun until it is dry. Have children find the floating sponge that matches and then compare the sizes.

### Sink or Float.

- Place a variety of items in a paper bag. Have each child pull out an item. Ask her if it will sink or float.

To find out, let her toss the item into the water tub. Include a piece of Ivory soap, a foil pan, cork, pencil, and other interesting items.

- Fill several clear plastic containers with colored water—a quarter full, half full, and full. Float the containers in the tub. Ask the children, "Find the one that is half full, less than half full . . ." Ask what would happen if children removed the lids. Let the children find out!
- Float a plastic measuring cup (or a milk carton with the top cut off) in the water. Set out colored, nested measuring cups. Have children "estimate" how much water they can pour into the cup before it sinks—one red cup (⅓ cup) or one green cup (½ cup) . . .

### Boats.
Children can make their own play boats by using pieces of styrofoam decorated with crayon and felt-tip pen designs. Make a mast for each boat by poking a pipe cleaner through the center of each piece of foam. Bend the end of the pipe cleaner up and under so the mast will stay in place. Attach construction paper sails to the pipe cleaners, and let the children have fun floating and racing their boats in a large tub of water.

### Poker Chips.
Scatter poker chips in the water. Ask children to find a red one; a red one and a blue one; two white ones; four of the same color. This activity could be extended by having children place the retrieved chips on clear contact-covered sheets that contain the same number and color of chips. Children will enjoy fishing them out with their hands, but kitchen tools can also be used.

### Tossing Games.
Soft balls, sponges, Nerf balls, or sponge toys when tossed at a water target are challenging activities that involve hand–eye coordination and spatial awareness. The targets might be different-sized tubs of water, rings, or tubes floating in the pool, or tubs of water set at different distances.

Be sure to also allow plenty of time for unstructured use of your water environment so children can explore, experiment, and create their own fun games that will automatically be good learning experiences.

**Special Days of Summer.**   As the summer wears on, use a theme to give new pep to the summer program. Choose a theme such as "Animal Day," and each child becomes an animal for that day. Snacks can be animal crackers, songs can be about animals, stories about animals can be read, and art activities on the same theme can be done. Other ideas for theme days are color days, black-and-white day, bird day, insect day. The ideas are as limitless as your and the children's imagination.

**Raindrops Are Falling.**   Have the children sit in a circle on the floor with their eyes closed and one hand open behind their backs. Appoint one child to be the "rainmaker," to carry a "raindrop" pebble or button around the circle and drop it into the hand of one of the other children, who then jumps up and tries to tag the rainmaker. If the rainmaker can reach the safety of the vacated seat, the chaser becomes the next rainmaker; otherwise, the rainmaker must take another turn.

**Balloon Throw.**   Everyone stands behind a chalk line and sees how far they can throw an inflated balloon. A mark is made where the balloon first touches the floor, and the child's initial is put on it. The player who throws the balloon the farthest is the winner.

**How Many Fingers.**   To review the numbers one to five, play this guessing game. The person chosen to be "it" is blindfolded or closes his eyes. The rest stand at their seats. At a signal from the leader, everyone stretches a number of fingers. "It" tries to guess the number of extended fingers, calling the number aloud. The object is to see how few guesses "it" needs. After five turns or when "it" has guessed correctly, this child chooses a new "it."

**One-Pin Bowling.**   A milk carton makes a good bowling pin. Any size ball is satisfactory for this activity, but stress the point that the ball must be rolled smoothly to the pin. Each child has five rolls. Scores are kept. Groups of three children work well in playing this game—one bowls, one keeps score, and one sets the pin. Then players change places so another can bowl.

**On My Way to School.**   The children are seated in a circle or at their desks. A player starts the game by imitating something that might be seen on the way to school, such as a paper boy, a dog, an airplane, or anything else that can move. The leader says, "On my way to school, I saw . . ." and then dramatizes what was seen. The player who guesses correctly becomes the new leader and the game continues.

**Inchworm.**   Have the children begin in a kneeling position and push themselves up, so their weight is supported on both their hands and feet. They then move both hands forward at the same time, supporting themselves on their toes. After their hands are repositioned, tell the children to bring their feet forward together, while they support their weight on their hands.

**Bike Race.**   Set up a mini-racecourse on the playground or sidewalk and let the children have a "trike race." Place empty cardboard boxes along the course for the children to go around or in between, riding their tricycles on the course one at a time. Explain that the purpose of this kind of race is not to go faster than someone else but to follow the course and finish it. For a festive touch decorate the trikes with crepe paper streamers.

**Moving Music.**   Play selections from the record "Creative Movement and Rhythmic Explorations," by Hap Palmer (Education Activities). Encourage the children to move as they think the lyrics indicate. Or play any song the children can move to without demonstration.

**Balloon, Feather, and Bubble Chasing.** Balloons and very light feathers can be batted into the air with the hands or fists, then chased and caught. Children can also run after bubbles, trying to pop them before they get away.

**Duck Game.**   While the children sit in a group, choose one to be the Mother (or Father) Duck and have that child leave the room. Choose two or three other children to be the Baby Ducks, and have all the children lower their heads and cover their mouths with their hands. Have the Mother Duck return and walk around the group saying "Quack, quack." As she does so, the Baby Ducks make peeping sounds. When the Mother Duck thinks that a child is one of her ducklings, she taps that child on the shoulder. If the Mother Duck guesses correctly, the Baby Duck raises her head. When the Mother Duck has found all of her babies, select new players and start the game again.

*Variation:* Follow the same procedure to play baby frogs, baby chicks, baby birds, or even baby snakes.

**Fun with Dandelions.** When you and the children are out on a summer nature walk, pick dandelions. Then show them how to do one or more of the following:

- Using your thumbnail, slit the sides of dandelion stems down to the ends. Dip the stems in water to make "curls" and wear them tucked over your ears.
- Hold a dandelion in your fist and use your thumb to flip off the flower head. (Save the flowers to make a "floating garden" in a bowl of water.)
- Start a dandelion chain by slitting the stem of one dandelion and pulling the stem of another dandelion through the slit. Continue the process until you have a long chain.
- Blow seeds from the dandelion tops.
- Encourage children to think of other fun things they can do with their dandelions.

**A Trip to the Zoo.** Children and animals go together. What better way to celebrate this special relationship than taking a trip to the zoo! The following section contains some helpful information on planning, preparations, and follow-up activities to make an excursion to the zoo a rewarding learning experience for young children.

*Planning.*

- Make a few calls to find out what zoos or farms are available in your area. Find out what time each is open; the hours, the cost, and what services they offer to groups of children. Try to choose one with zoo animals, a "petting zoo" area, a picnic area, restrooms, and a playground.
- Plan on a date, send permission forms home, work out safe transportation, and decide ahead of time what to do if the weather does not cooperate.
- Involve the children in helping to plan the snack or picnic lunch menu for your trip. Food eaten away from school somehow tastes much better!

*Preparation.*

- Take a trip (with or without the children) to the children's room of your local library to look up zoo (or farm) animals in the card catalog. Choose books, posters, films, filmstrips, or records to use before and after your trip. Spend up to a week examining these materials with the children. They will learn a little about the animals they will see and can think of some questions about them too. (See the end of this unit for books on visiting the zoo.)
- The day before the trip, ask the children to list the animals they think they might see there. Write the words for them, and give them each a copy to bring along. During the visit, many preschoolers can circle the names or the pictures of the ones they see.
- The children might enjoy making their own nametags in the shape of their favorite animal to wear during the trip.

*The trip.*

- After checking the weather forecast, get ready with appropriate outdoor gear, an overflowing picnic basket, a first aid kit, a list of emergency telephone numbers for each child, nametags, and an instant camera. If more than one vehicle will be used, be sure that the adult in charge of each group has the names and emergency numbers of the children in his care, understands what car rules are to be enforced, and has a map to follow in case the cars lose one another.
- On the way to the zoo, try singing. "Old MacDonald Had a Zoo!"
- When you arrive, take a slow walk around half the zoo. (Pre-plan by knowing the layout and preparing your route.) Talk about the names of the ani-

# THIS ONE'S FOR YOU!

## SUMMER OUTINGS HINTS

- When going on summer outings, have each child wear a name tag with your school's name, address, and telephone number on it.
- If you're taking a summer outing to a place where there will be lots of other people, plan to carry a helium-filled balloon or wear a brightly colored hat or scarf on your head so your children can easily spot you in the crowd. Carrying an opened umbrella also does the trick.
- For quick and easy cleanups on your outing, take along some diaper wipes.
- If you're going on your summer outing by car, guard against hurt fingers by having the children put their hands on top of their heads before you close the car doors.
- To help keep track of children on summer outings, arrange to have them dress in matching t-shirts or matching colors.
- Don't forget to take a camera and a tape recorder when you go on an outing. Later, the photos and recorded tapes will provide a good review of what the children learned.

mals, the sounds they make; the sights, sounds, and smells of the zoo; the sizes, colors, and designs on animals; the number of legs, antlers, babies, and so on.

- Assign one adult chaperone to take instant snapshots of the animals that impress the children the most. These will be especially valuable when you get back to school.
- After you've covered half the zoo, find the picnic area for snack or lunch (hopefully near the playground). Spread yourselves out to exercise, eat, and relax.
- Next, go to the "petting zoo" area. Here you can pat and feed lots of very friendly, but often assertive, animals. It is a good idea for an adult to go in first to check out the mood of the animals.

Understand that some children may be reasonably (or unreasonably) cautious about getting eye-to-eye with some animals, so respect their decisions. It might help to have the children enter in small groups, so that the animals won't get overstimulated.

- If the zoo has a train, monorail, or bus, take a final trip around the whole zoo to rediscover where you

have been and what you have seen before you leave the zoo.

*Follow-up activities.*

- Sort through the photos you took and encourage the children to help put them in order, tell stories about them, and put their drawings and words together with the photos to make an "experience story," mural, or class book.
- Over the next few days, continue to read zoo animal books and reexamine the posters, records, or films you used before your trip. Children love repetition and will now have real experiences to relate to the audio-visual materials.
- Be sure to allow lots of opportunities for follow-up activities in all areas of the curriculum. Make zoo animal–shaped cookies for snacks, do creative movement activities about animals, have a paper-bag animal parade, tape-record children's accounts of the trip. Set up the dramatic play area as a "petting zoo," with stuffed animals or paper-bag animal costumes, or even as the bus you rode to the zoo, and encourage the children to make

thank-you cards to give to parents who accompanied them on the trip.

**Balloon Instruments.** Make some balloon instruments for an interesting addition to your music activities.

- Rub and thump inflated and tied balloons.
- Put pebbles, paper clips and beans in different balloons, inflate, tie, then shake for great rattling noises.
- Blow up balloons and hold necks closed, then let air out, stretching the necks to make interesting noises.
- Put together a band to play a combination of rubs, thumps, rattles, and squeaks to accompany a song played on the piano or a simple recorder.
- And don't forget, balloons are perfect for "pop" music, too!

**Flower Pot Bells.** Create interesting musical instruments by making several flowerpot bells in different sizes. Bells can be hung in a row from the low branch of a tree or from a broomstick placed horizontally over the backs of two chairs. One bell may hang by the door and visitors can ring it when they come in.

Materials:
clay flowerpot (uncracked)
two wooden beans (larger than hole in the base of the pot)
piece of strong string or shoelace, about three times as long as your pot is high

Procedure:
1. Thread one of the beads on one end of the string and make a knot to stop the bead from slipping off. Measure the height of your flowerpot and

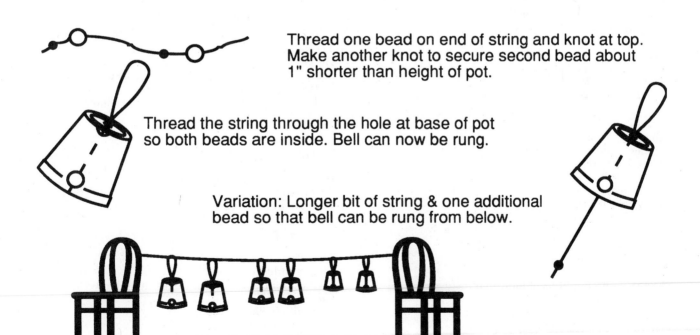

Thread one bead on end of string and knot at top. Make another knot to secure second bead about 1" shorter than height of pot.

Thread the string through the hole at base of pot so both beads are inside. Bell can now be rung.

Variation: Longer bit of string & one additional bead so that bell can be rung from below.

FIGURE 32–6 Flower pot bell.

make another knot to secure a second bead about one inch shorter than the height measurement of the pot.

2. Thread the string through the hole at the base of the flowerpot so that both beads are inside. The bell can now be rung. (Big pots will make the bell ring with a deep sound. The smaller the pot, the higher the sound.)

3. Make a loop with the rest of the string so that you can hang your bell. If the hole in the bead is large enough to take a double thickness of string, make the loop as shown.

*Variation:* Use a longer bit of string and one additional bead so that the bell can be rung from below. Only use one bead for each bell. By hitting the bells with a spoon, you can play a tune.

---

## POEMS, FINGERPLAYS, AND SONGS

**The Earth**
The earth must be a lady;
She likes to change her clothes,
In winter time she loves to wear
The very whitest snows.
In spring she goes about in green,
In summer, flowers bold,
And in the fall she's very grand,
All dressed in red and gold.
    —Hansi Chambers

**Air**
Air, air—air.
Where? Where? Where?
I can't see it.
I can't feel it.
But I *know* it's there.
    —M. Terwilliger

**Thunder**
Black clouds are giants
Hurrying across the sky
And they slip out bolts of ligntning
As they go racing by.
When they meet each other,
They shake hands and thunder
How-do-you-do
How-do-you-do
HOW-DO-YOU-DOOOOO!

**Fog**
The fog comes
On little cat feet.
It sits looking
Over harbor and city
On silent haunches
And then moves on.
    —Carl Sandburg

**Whickety-Whack**
Wind is a train
That goes so fast
You hold your hat
When it whizzes past.

Whickety-whack,
The wind goes by,
Whisking its car
Across the sky.

Whooshing past,
On a magic track,
Switching rails,
And swishing back!

**The Moon's the North Wind's Cooky**
The moon's the North Wind's cooky
He bites it, day by day,
Until there's but a rim of scraps
That crumble all away.

The South Wind is a baker
He kneads clouds in his den,
And bakes a crisp new moon that . . . greedy
North . . . Wind . . . eats . . . again!
    —Vachel Lindsay

**The Tire**
I'll play that I'm a tire
And take a breath just so;
Pretend that I am filled with air
From my head down to my toe.
And then when I am very full,
I'll let it go like this:
Softly . . . slowly . . . softly . . .
 "Sssssssssss."

**Tiny Tim**
I had a little turtle
 (Put thumbs and index fingers together)
His name was Tiny Tim.
I put him in the bathtub
To see if he could swim.
 (Make swimming motions with arms)
He drank up all the water
 (Head back, hands to mouth in drinking gesture)

He ate up all the soap
  (Chewing gesture)
He woke up in the morning
With bubbles in his throat.
  (Wave fingers in air from mouth up to above head)

### Picnic-time (Action Poem)
Here's a tree in summer
(Hold a piece of grass with seed head in your hand)

Here's a tree in winter
(Slide your hand up the grass and pull off the seed
  heads, leaving grass bare)

Here's a bunch of flowers
(Hold out seed heads in other hand)

And here's the April showers
(Sprinkle the seed heads on the ground)

### Birds Fly
Tie scraps of colored ribbon or cloth around each
finger and the thumb of one hand. The ends should
not be too long, as they should give the effect of
wings.

Here is Mr. Bluebird.
Fly, Mr. Bluebird.
  (Wiggle the little finger: Color—blue)
Here is Mr. Cardinal.
Fly, Mr. Cardinal.
  (Wiggle fourth finger: Color—red)
Here is Mr. Oriole.
Fly, Mr. Oriole.
  (Wiggle middle finger: Color—orange)
Here is Mr. Hummingbird.
Fly, Mr. Hummingbird.
  (Wiggle index finger: Color—green)
Here is Mr. Blackbird.
Fly, Mr. Blackbird.
  (Wiggle the thumb: Color—black)
The birds fly and sing
For now it is spring.
  (Wiggle all fingers)

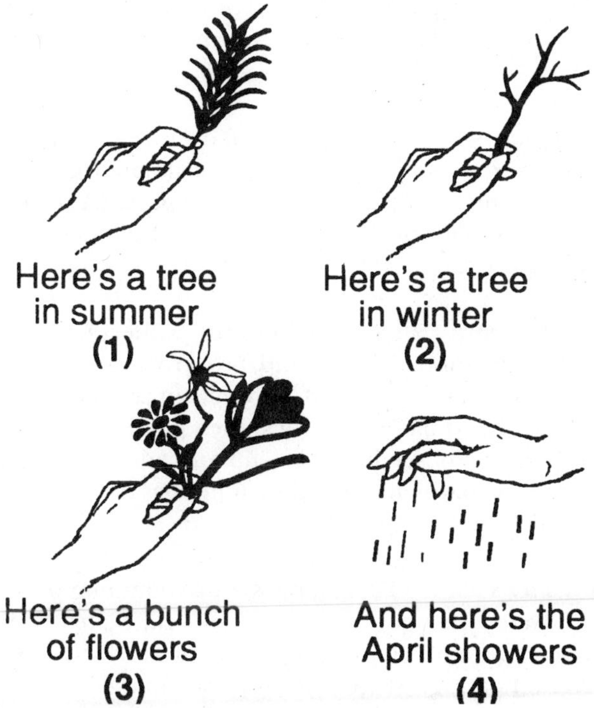

Here's a tree
in summer
(1)

Here's a tree
in winter
(2)

Here's a bunch
of flowers
(3)

And here's the
April showers
(4)

**FIGURE 32–7 The seasons (action poem).**

### Birds Flying
Up, up in the sky, the little birds fly
  (Fingers flying like birds)
Down, down in the nest, the little birds rest
  (Hands form nest)
With a wing on the left, and a wing on the right
  (Hands on each hip)
Let the little birds rest all the long night.
  (Head to one side like tucking under wing)

### Winkie
Winkie, the elephant, walks and walks
  (Arms in front to make a "trunk")
Never making a sound.
She moves her trunk from side to side
And it never touches the ground.

### Little Turtle
There was a little turtle
  (Make small circle with hands)
Who lived in a box
  (Hands form box)
He swam in a puddle
  (Hands swim)
He climbed on the rocks
  (Fingers climb up)
He snapped at a mosquito
  (Snap fingers)

He snapped at a flea
(Snap fingers)
He snapped at a minnow
(Snap fingers)
He snapped at me.
(Snap fingers)
He caught the mosquito
(Clap hands)
He caught the flea
(Clap hands)
He caught the minnow
(Clap hands)
But he didn't catch me!
(Shake head no, no, and point to self)

**Ten Red Balloons**
Ten red balloons flying in the air
(Put 10 fingers in the air and wave them back and forth)
One went POP!
(Clap hands)
and nine were there.
(Put nine fingers in the air)
Nine red balloons flying in the air
(Wave them)
One went POP!
(Clap hands)
and eight were there.
(Put eight fingers in the air)
Eight red balloons flying in the air
(Wave them)
One went POP!
(Clap hands)
and seven were there.
(Put seven fingers in the air; Continue counting down to . . .)
One red balloon flying in the air
(Put one finger in the air)
It went POP!
(Clap hands)
and NONE were there.
(Open hands, palms up to show "all gone")

**Dandy Lady**
(Sung to the tune of "Mary Had a Little Lamb")
Little Dandy Lady,
Lady, Lady,
Little Dandy Lady
Was quite vain, they say.

She had hair of yellow,
Yellow, yellow.
She had hair of yellow
And loved to dance all day.

As she grew older,
Older, older,
As she grew older,
Her hair all turned to gray.

Now when she dances,
Dances, dances,
Now when she dances,
Her hair all blows away!
—Jean Warren

Repeat, substituting the word "dandelion" for "Dandy Lady" and changing "she/her" to "he/his."

## EATING OUTDOORS

Eating outside is a welcome change in the daily routine for both young children and adults. The following are some simple ways to enjoy the outdoors, as well as a meal!

**Plan a Picnic.** *A hobo hike.* Put lunch in a bandana (square piece of sheet that children have tie-dyed or colored with fabric crayons) and tie it to a stick.

*A parade to the park.* Let children select outfits from the dress-up box, select an instrument from the musical cupboard, and march to the park. (A strong senior member of the band can pull the lunch in a wagon at the end of the parade.)

*A beach party.* Serve lunch to the bathers who are seated on towels in the sand box. You can have a snowcone stand nearby. (Children can put ice cubes in heavy handmade cloth sack, then pound sack with a hammer. Put ice in paper cup and add powdered drink mix to which only a little water has been added to make the "syrup.")

*At water's edge.* Fill several plastic swimming pools with water. In one, float the drinks (in sealed containers) for the children's lunch. In another, have several floating fish (cut from plastic margarine tub tops, numbered with permanent marker). Fasten paper clips to the fish and let children cast poles with magnet "bait" into the water to find out which group they'll eat their tuna fish sandwiches with. After lunch, let children feed the ducks (plastic water toys) in the third "pond." They'll love throwing Styrofoam packing "popcorn" into the water.

*A teddy bear picnic.* Pack up teddy bears (or other favorite stuffed animals) and lunch in backpacks made by decorating a covered cereal box or heavy grocery sack and stapling on or threading through straps.

*Begin the day with a big surprise.* If you serve breakfast in your program, have children pick their food from the "breakfast tree." Hang it with small boxes of dry cereal (the kind that kids can eat from), bananas, and individual cartons of milk. If you don't have breakfast at your center, you can serve the same meal for lunch as a special treat.

*A garden party.* Let children clean, peel, and cut vegetables outside. While some of the children are doing this, others can be making dips by combining sour cream and onion soup mix. Serve the dip in individual cups so germs won't be passed if children double dip.

Remember eating out doesn't have to mean a fancy restaurant. What it really means is a change!

## COOKING EXPERIENCES

### Juicy Summer Drink.
Ingredients:
1 quart carbonated water or soda water
1 quart of your favorite fruit juice, such as apple, orange, pineapple-grapefruit, cranberry, or lemon

Procedure:
Mix together two liquids and serve in glasses filled with ice.

### Cheese and Cucumber Sandwiches.
Ingredients:
1 cucumber, thinly sliced
1 4-ounce package cream cheese (softened)
4 slices bread

Procedure:
1. Spread two slices of bread with cream cheese.
2. Top with cucumber slices.
3. Place remaining slices of bread on top to make sandwiches.

### Ice Pops.
Ingredients:
1 cup hot water
2 cups lemonade
1 package gelatin

Procedure:
1. Mix and pour ingredients into ice pop mold or ice cube trays.
2. Put in freezer until solid. Experiment with different-flavored ingredients.

### Watermelon Ice Pops.
Ingredients:
1 cup seedless watermelon chunks
1 cup orange juice
1 cup water

Procedure:
1. Blend ingredients together in a blender.
2. Pour into ice pop holders or small paper cups.
3. Place in freezer. When partially frozen, insert popsicle sticks or small plastic spoons into the cups for handles. Continue freezing.
4. Pour hot water over the bottom of cup to remove frozen ice pop.

### Frozen Pinapple Buttermilk.
Ingredients:
1 quart buttermilk
½ to ¾ cup honey
1 20-ounce can crushed pineapple, drained
¼ cup lemon juice or juice of 1 lemon
grated rind of 1 lemon

Procedure:
1. Measure all ingredients and mix together thoroughly.
2. Freeze in freezer tray until almost solid.
3. Put in bowl and beat until light and fluffy.
4. Return to freezer tray for at least 1 more hour.

5. Pour in glasses. Makes about 1½ quarts. Serves 16 children. Variations: use orange or lime instead of lemon. Use 20-ounce can of other fruit of your choice.

**Homemade Ice Cream.**
Ingredients:
4 eggs
1 cup honey
7 cups milk
3 cups whipping cream
1 tablespoon vanilla
½ teaspoon salt

Procedure:
1. Beat eggs well.
2. Add other ingredients and mix together.
3. Freeze in ice cream freezer. Makes 3 to 4 quarts.

**Cantaloupe Cooler.**
Ingredients:
1 cup cantaloupe chunks
¼ cup apple juice concentrate
1 cup milk

Procedure:
Mix in a blender for a sweet, foamy drink. Makes four 4-ounce servings.

**Snow Cones.** Place crushed ice in a paper cup. Make a mixture of apple or orange juice concentrate diluted one-to-one with water. Pour ¼ cup diluted concentrate over the ice. Children suck on the flavored ice.

**Daylight Delights 1.**
Ingredients:
1 orange or 1 cup orange juice
¼ cup milk
½ teaspoon vanilla
2 tablespoons sugar or 1½ tablespoons honey
6 ice cubes

Procedure:
1. Peel, section, and remove seeds from orange.
2. Put orange sections in blender and blend.

3. Add milk, sugar or honey, and vanilla. Blend until mixture is smooth.
4. Add ice and blend. Serves 2 to 3 children.

**Daylight Delights 2.**
Ingredients:
1 cup orange-grapefruit or pineapple-grapefruit juice
½ banana
½ cup plain yogurt
¾ teaspoon sugar or 1½ tablespoon honey
4 ice cubes

Procedure:
Put all ingredients in blender and blend until smooth. Serves 2 to 3 children.

**Dandelion Eggs.**
Ingredients:
milk
margarine
dandelion greens
eggs

Procedure:
1. Have the children help pick and wash some very young, tender dandelion greens (leaves only not stems or flowers).
2. Pat the greens dry with paper towels and tear into little pieces.
3. Mix eggs with milk and scramble them in melted margarine.
4. Just before the eggs become firm, add dandelion greens. Continue cooking until the eggs are done.
5. If desired, sprinkle on grated cheddar cheese when adding the greens. (Dandelion greens are non-toxic and high in nutritive value.)

**French Toast.**
Ingredients:
2 eggs
½ teaspoon salt
⅔ cup milk
½ teaspoon vanilla
1 tablespoon butter
4 slices bread

Materials: Measuring spoons, mixing bowl, egg beater, large frying pan, spatula

Procedure:
1. Melt the butter in the frying pan over low heat.
2. Put eggs, milk, salt, and vanilla in mixing bowl.
3. Beat well with an egg beater.
4. Soak slices of bread in the mixture.
5. Brown the bread in the frying pan.
6. Use a spatula to turn the bread over so that it will brown on both sides.
7. Sprinkle with sugar and cinnamon or serve with maple syrup.
8. This makes servings for four people.

(Maurice Sendak's *In the Night Kitchen,* Harper and Row, 1970 is a good story to read with *any* cooking activity.

## Hawaiian Toast.
Ingredients:
4 slices white bread
2 eggs
1 cup pineapple juice (if fresh pineapple is used, save the top to grow later)
½ teaspoon salt
8 slices bacon
4 slices pineapple

Materials: Measuring spoons, measuring cup, spatula, egg beater, mixing bowl, paper towels, large frying pan (preferably electric)

Procedure:
1. Cook the bacon in a frying pan until crisp.
2. Use a spatula to turn the bacon over so that it will be crisp on both sides.
3. Drain the bacon on paper towels.
4. Put the eggs, pineapple juice, and salt into a mixing bowl.
5. Beat well with egg beater.
6. Soak bread in the mixture.
7. Brown the toast in bacon fat in a frying pan.
8. Turn with a spatula to brown on both sides.
9. Put toast and bacon on plates.
10. Fry the pineapple slices in a frying pan.
11. Put one slice of pineapple on each piece of toast.

## Zoo Sandwiches.
Ingredients:
several slices of bread
cream cheese
cream (use 1 tablespoon cream for a 3-ounce package of cream cheese)
food coloring

Materials: animal cookie cutters, mixing bowl, measuring spoons, mixing spoon, table knife

Procedure:
1. Put the cream cheese and cream into a mixing bowl.
2. Mix together with a mixing spoon until the cream cheese is soft.
3. Add a few drops of food coloring (if desired), and stir well.
4. Cut out the bread with animal cookie cutters.
5. Spread on the cream cheese mixture with a knife.
Variation: Try spreading whole wheat bread with honey and peanut butter.

## Orange Crush.
Ingredients:
1½ cups orange juice
1 pint soft vanilla ice cream
orange slices, cherries

Materials: Knife for slicing oranges, measuring cup, mixing bowl, mixing spoon, 3 glasses

Procedure:
1. Let the children slice the oranges.
2. Put ice cream and orange juice in the mixing bowl.
3. Stir with the mixing spoon until smooth.
4. Pour into glasses.
5. Decorate each glass with orange slices and cherries.

## Fruit Kabobs.
As fresh fruit becomes reasonably priced in the summer, children enjoy eating it, cut into bite-sized pieces and threaded with three or four other chunks on a toothpick or stick pretzel.

## Little Pizzas.

Ingredients:
1 English muffin for each child
cheddar cheese (or American, colby, or mozzarella)
tomatoes
salad oil
oregano

Materials: Knife for slicing tomatoes and cheese, and a cookie sheet

Procedure:
1. Heat oven to 400°F.
2. Have the children help slice the tomatoes and cut the cheese into strips.
3. Split each muffin in half.
4. Put the halves on the cookie sheet.
5. Put a slice of tomato on each one.
6. Put some cheese on top of the tomatoes.
7. Sprinkle a few drops of oil on each.
8. Sprinkle with a bit of oregano.
9. Bake in the oven for about 6 or 7 minutes.

## Pancake People/Animals.

Ingredients:
ready-mixed pancake batter
raisins
syrup

Materials: Electric frying pan, mixing bowl, mixing spoon, measuring cups

Procedure:
1. Mix batter, adding water as directed on the package.
2. Pour enough batter in the frying pan to make a medium-sized pancake.
3. Drop a small amount of batter at the top of this pancake to make ''ears'' on both sides.
4. Flip over the pancake to complete cooking.
5. Place raisins for eyes, nose, and mouth.
6. Some animals to try: elephant, cat, dog. Simple, round pancakes can be made into ''faces'' by decorating with raisins.

## Peach Yogurt.

Ingredients
1 cup diced, peeled peaches
¼ cup apple juice concentrate
1 cup plain yogurt

Procedure:
Blend together in a blender. Makes four small servings.

## Peach Crisp.

Ingredients:
1 cup oatmeal
½ cup presifted flour (children should do the sifting)
½ cup brown sugar, well packed
½ teaspoon salt
½ cup melted butter
1 teaspoon lemon juice
4 cups peeled, sliced peaches
ice cream (vanilla or peach)

Materials: Knife for peeling and slicing peaches, flour sifter, measuring cup, measuring spoons, mixing bowl, mixing spoon, glass baking dish, small pan for melting butter

Procedure:
1. Help the children sift the flour and prepare the peaches.
2. Melt the butter over low heat.
3. Heat the oven to 350°F.
4. Put oatmeal, flour, sugar, and salt into a mixing bowl.
5. Mix well with a mixing spoon.
6. Pour in melted butter and beat into the mixture.
7. Butter a glass baking dish.
8. Spread the sliced peaches on the bottom of the dish.
9. Sprinkle peaches with lemon juice.
10. Spread oatmeal mixture over the peaches.
11. Bake for 30 minutes or until brown.
12. Serve with ice cream (or liquid cream).

A good story to use for a supplement to this activity is Roald Dahl's *James and the Giant Peach.*

# ADDITIONAL READINGS

## Books About Zoos and Zoo Animals

Bahr, Robert. *Blizzard at the Zoo.* New York: Lothrop, 1982.

Bridges, William. *Zoo Babies.* New York: Morrow, 1953.

Buchenholz, Bruce. *Doctor in the Zoo.* New York: Viking Press, 1974.

Caras, Roger. *Going to the Zoo with Roger Caras.* New York: Harcourt, Brace, Jovanovich, 1973.

Crammond, Joan. *Zoo.* North Pomfort, Vt.: David & Charles, 1973.

Durrell, Gerald Malcolm. *A Bevy of Beasts.* New York: Simon & Schuster, 1973.

Grosvenor, Donna K. *Zoo Babies.* Washington, D.C.: National Geographic Society, 1978.

Hewett, Joan. *Watching Them Grow: Inside a Zoo Nursery.* Boston: Little, Brown, 1979.

Jacobsen, Karen. *Zoos.* Chicago: Children's Press, 1982.

Livingston, Bernard. *Zoo; Animals, People, Places.* New York: Arbor House, 1974.

Marshak, S. *Babies of the Zoo.* Progress Publishers (USSR), 1975.

Oana, Katherina. *Zoo Fun Book.* Akron, Ohio: Carson-Dellosa Publishers, 1985.

Paige, David. *Behind the Scenes at the Zoo.* New York: Beginner Books, 1962.

Pienkowski, Jan. *Zoo.* New York: W.S. Heineman (David & Charles), 1985.

Rinard, Judith. *Zoos Without Cages.* Washington, D.C.: National Geographic Society. 1981.

Schick, Alice. *Zoo Year.* Philadelphia: Lippincott, 1978.

Tongren, Sally. *What's for Lunch: Animal Feeding at the Zoo.* New York: GMG Publishers, 1981.

Tremper, Andra, and Linda Diepert. *What's New at the Zoo, Kangaroo?* Carthage, Ill.: Good Apple, 1982.

## Children's Books for Summer

Adamson, Joy. *Elsa.* New York: Pantheon Books, 1963. An extraordinary true story of lion cubs in the "wild," yet friends of humankind.

Anglund, Joan Walsh, *Spring Is a New Beginning.* New York: Harcourt, Brace & World, 1963. This delightful book defines spring.

Bernstein, Margery. *The Summer Maker. An Ojibway Indian Myth.* New York: Charles Scribner's Sons, 1977. An easy-to-read retelling of the Ojibway Indian myth about the creation of summer.

Beskow, Elsa. *Pelle's New Suit.* New York: Harper and Row, 1929. The story of how wool from a lamb becomes a suit for a little boy, who is surprised that he has grown bigger.

Brown, Marc. *D. W. All Wet.* New York: Joy Street, 1988.

Brown, Marcia. *Three Billy Goats Gruff.* New York: Harcourt, Brace, Jovanovich, 1957.

Burnett, Frances Hodgson. *The Secret Garden.* Milwaukee: Raintree Publications, 1978. A spoiled little girl visits the home of her equally spoiled cousin out in the Yorkshire moors. Mary and Colin despise each other initially, but gradually overcome their differences and develop a strong friendship.

Carle, Eric. *One, Two, Three to the Zoo.* Cleveland: Collins, William, and World, 1968. Each double-page spread contains a numeral and corresponding number of zoo animals.

Carlstrom, D. *Better Not Get Wet, Jesse Bear.* New York: Macmillan, 1988.

Clifton, Lucille, and Brinton Turkle (illus.). *The Boy Who Didn't Believe in Spring.* New York: E.P. Dutton, 1973. Two city boys are reluctant to believe in spring until they discover two signs of spring in a vacant lot that convince them of the season.

Colby, C.B. *Big Game: Animals of the Americas, Africa, and Asia.* New York: Coward, McCann and Geoghegan, 1967. Pictures of some famous big game animals with simple text.

Cosgrove, Margaret. *Eggs and What Happens Inside Them.* New York: Dodd, Mead and Co., 1966. A look at what happens inside eggs.

Daugherty, James. *Andy and the Lion.* New York: Penguin Books, 1970.

Delaney, M.C. *The Marigold Monster.* New York: E.P. Dutton, 1983. A fantastic book for children because it is a fun story full of colorful, interesting pictures. Also included in the story are jokes that children love.

Enright, Elizabeth. *Thimble Summer.* New York: Holt, Rinehart and Winston, 1938. (Newberry Medal) This book describes life on a Wisconsin farm.

Epple, Anne O. *Beginning Knowledge Book of Ants.* New York: Macmillan, 1969.

———. *Beginning Knowledge Book of Fossils.* New York: Macmillan, 1969. Two books that introduce children to ideas about ants and fossils.

Ets, Marie H. *Play with Me.* New York: Viking Press, 1955.

Factor, June. *Summer.* New York: Viking Kestrel, 1988.

Fatio, Louise. *The Happy Lion.* New York: McGraw Hill, 1954.

Fisher, Aileen. *We Went Looking.* New York: T.Y. Crowell, 1968. A glimpse of wild creatures as they really are.

Flack, Marjorie. *Tim Tadpole and the Great Bullfrog.* New York: Doubleday, 1959.

Fox, Charles Philip. *When Spring Comes.* Chicago: Reilly and Co., 1966. An environmental approach to spring, using photographs of wildlife to illustrate the changes in nature at spring.

————. *When Summer Comes.* Chicago: Reilly and Co., 1966. Excellent photographs showing signs of nature in summer.

Freeman, Don. *Come Again, Pelican.* New York: Viking Press, 1961.

Freschet, Bernice, and Roger Duvoisin (illus.). *The Web in the Grass.* New York: Charles Scribner's Sons, 1972. A spider spins a delicate web one spring. Describes the silent, busy beauty of the spider's life. A good book for incorporating science into read-aloud time.

Garelick, May. *Where Does the Butterfly Go When It Rains?* New York: Scholastic Book Service, 1970.

Getz, Arthur. *Hamilton Duck's Springtime Story.* New York: Western Publishing Co., 1974.

Graham, Kenneth. *The River Bank* from *The Wind in the Willows.* New York: Charles Scribner's Sons, 1977. This book is the first chapter of *The Wind in the Willows,* but with pictures added. It is a story about friendship and describes a river outing that Rat and Mole take.

————. *The Wind in the Willows.* New York: Charles Scribner's Sons, 1977. Mole and Rat meet on a spring day at the riverbank when Rat is spring cleaning his home. They later meet Badger and Otter and have many adventures together as a foursome. This is a children's classic; it would be good to read aloud to a class.

Green, Carol. *The Truly Remarkable Day.* St. Louis: Concordia, 1974.

Gunthorp, Karen. *The Wonderful Ball.* New York: Doubleday, 1968.

Hammond, Winifred. *The Riddle of Seeds.* New York: Coward, McCann, and Geoghegan, 1965, A story of seeds and their importance in the world.

Helmrath, Marilyn Olear, and Bartlett, Janet. *Bobby Bear in the Spring.* New York: Oddo Publishing, 1968. Tells about the first day of spring and helps children become acquainted with what nature does during spring.

Hess, Lilo. *Animals That Hide, Imitate and Bluff.* New York: Charles Scribner's Sons, 1970. This story tells and shows (in photographs) how camouflage enables many animals to survive.

Hutchins, Pat. *Rosie's Walk.* New York: Macmillan, 1971. Rosie walks around the barnyard unaware she is being followed by a sly and greedy fox.

Johnson, Crockett. *Time for Spring.* New York: Harper & Brothers, 1979. A little girl anxiously awaits springtime, but cannot help wondering where her snowman will go when winter ends. Story deals with the consistency of the seasons and cycle of the year. Illustrations are in black and white, but enjoyable.

Kay, Helen, and Helen Cooney (illus.). *City Springtime.* New York: Hastings House Publishers, 1957. A young farmboy compares signs of spring in the city to the ones he knows so well at his home in the country. Delicate illustrations and a busy story.

Kohn, Bernice. *Chipmunks.* Englewood Cliffs, N.J.: Prentice-Hall, 1970. A story of chipmunks, told through words and pictures.

La Fontaine, Jean de. *The Lion and the Rat.* New York: Watts, 1963.

Langstaff, John, and Feodor Rojankovsky. *Over in the Meadow.* New York: Harcourt, Brace, Jovanovich, 1971.

Larrick, Nancy. *Piping Down the Valleys Wild.* New York: Dell, 1982. This collection of verse for children contains poems about spring and all the seasons.

Leisk, David Johnson. *Will Spring Be Early? or Will Spring Be Late?* New York: Thomas Y. Crowell, 1959. A silly groundhog mistakes an artificial flower for a real one and tells everyone that spring is coming.

Lenski, Lois. *On a Summer Day.* New York: Henry Z. Walck, 1953. This cute book contains a song for summer and has rhyming verses about play between a girl and her brother on a summer day.

Lionni, Leo. *Swimmy.* New York: Pantheon Books, 1963. A clever fish enjoys all the sea has to offer and cooperates with other fish in order to survive.

Lovelace, Maud Hart. *Betsy-Tacy.* New York: Harper and Row, 1979. Set in 1910, this book gives a lively account of a little girl's summer in Minneapolis. Betsy has a big imagination that frequently gets her in big trouble, but she is a very appealing character. There is a whole series of "Betsy" books, and the illustrations by Lois Lenski are a real bonus.

McCloskey, Robert. *Blueberries for Sal.* New York: Penguin Books, 1976.

Mari, Iela, and Engo, Mari. *The Chicken and the Egg.* New York: Pantheon Books, 1970. Wordless book, beautifully illustrating the hatching of a chick.

Newberry, Clare Turlay. *Widget.* New York: Harper and Row, 1958. A naughty kitten is rescued by his mother.

Patent, Dorothy Hinshaw. *All About Whales.* New York: Holiday, 1987.

Posell, Elsa. *The Beginning Knowledge Book of Seashells.* New York: Macmillan, 1969. A child's introduction to seashells.

Rey, H.A. *Curious George.* Boston: Houghton Mifflin, 1973. The tale of an adventurous monkey named George.

Robbins, Ken. *Beach Days.* New York: Viking Kestrel, 1987.

Sauer, Peter. *Seashell Towns.* New York: Coward, Mc-

Cann, and Geoghegan, 1968. A description of snails, mussels, and barnacles.

Schima, Marilyn. *Something Grows*. Englewood Cliffs, N.J.: Prentice-Hall, 1969. The story of how each seed is special; how living seeds are able to change and grow until they are like the plant or animal from which they came.

Schwartz, Elizabeth, and Charles Schwartz. *When Water Animals Are Babies*. New York: Holiday House, 1970. Accurate drawings in soft colors; describes wide variety of ways that water mothers care for their young.

Selsam, Millicent. *All Kinds of Babies*. New York: Scholastic Book Service, 1967. Picture book about baby animals.

Sendak, Maurice. *Pierre*. New York; Harper and Row, 1962.

Steig, William. *Amos and Boris*. New York: Farrar, Straus, & Giroux, 1971. Amos, a mouse, and Boris, a whale, learn about each other's worlds and share a lasting friendship based on reciprocity and love. Wonderful, large illustrations, perfect for read-aloud time in the classroom.

————. *Sylvester and the Magic Pebble*. New York: Simon and Schuster, 1970. Family love demonstrated through a donkey named Sylvester.

Stevenson, James. *The Worst Person in the World at Crab Beach*. New York: Greenwillow, 1988.

White, E.B. *Charlotte's Web,* New York: Harper and Row, 1952, and *The Trumpet of the Swan,* New York: Harper and Row, 1973. Both stories begin in the spring time and follow the ''growing up'' periods of Wilbur and Lewis, respectively. These are great ''read aloud'' books. (A third E.B. White book, very popular among elementary school children, is *Stuart Little*). Illustrated by Garth Williams.

Wong, Herbert, and Matthew Vessel. *Our Terrariums*. Reading, Mass.: Addison-Wesley, 1969. The excitement of catching and caring for an animal is expressed in this story.

————. *Pond Life: Watching Animals Grow Up*. Reading, Mass.: Addison-Wesley, 1970. Two boys observe aspects of pond ecology—how animals grow and how animal parents treat their young.

Yeoman, John. *The Bear's Water Picnic*. New York: Atheneum, 1987.

Zion, Gene, and Margaret Bloy Graham (illus.). *The Summer Snowman*. New York: Harper & Row, 1955. Peter has a big surprise for everyone on July 4.

Zolotow, Charlotte. *Summer Is. . . .* New York: Thomas Y. Crowell, 1967. Simple book with nice illustrations about the different things associated with each season.

# Appendix A
# Fine and Gross Motor Skills*

## BY TWO YEARS

### Gross Motor.

- Walks forward (average age 12 months)
- Walks backward (average age 15 months)
- Walks upstairs with help (average age 17 months)
- Moves self from sitting to standing (average age 18 months)
- Seats self in small chair (average age 18 months)
- Uses rocking horse or rocking chair with aid (average age 18 months)

### Fine Motor.

- Builds tower of two blocks (average age 15 months)
- Builds tower of three or four blocks (average age 19 months)
- Places pellet in bottle (average age 15 months)
- Places blocks in cup (average age 15 months)
- Places four rings on peg or large pegs in pegboard (average age 18 months)
- Imitates vertical line stroke (average age 20 months)
- Turns pages of book, two or three at a time (average age 21 months)

## BY TWO AND ONE-HALF YEARS

### Gross Motor.

- Kicks ball forward (average age 20 months)
- Jumps in place (average age 23 months)

---

*90% of children at specific age level will have acquired skill.
Adapted from Gesell, Arnold; Ilg, Frances L.; Ames, Louise Bates; and Rodell, Janet Leonard. *Infant and Child in the Culture of Today: The Guidance of Development in Home and Nursery School.* New York: Harper and Row, 1974.

- Runs (stiffly) (average age 2 years)
- Hurls small ball overhand, one hand, without direction (average age 22 months)
- Pedals tricycle (average age 2 years)

### Fine Motor.

- Builds tower of six cube blocks (average age 23 months)
- Imitates circular motion with crayon, after demonstration (average age 2 years)
- Turns pages of book, one at a time (average age 2 years)

## BY THREE YEARS

### Gross Motor.

- Walks up and down stairs without adult help, but not alternating feet (average age 22 months)
- Walks four steps on tiptoe (average age 2¼ years)
- Jumps from bottom step (average age 2 years)
- Walks backward 10 feet (average age 28 months)
- Broad jumps 24–34 inches (average age 2½ years)
- Balances on one foot one second (average age 2½ years)

### Fine Motor.

- Imitates vertical line from demonstration (average age 22 months)
- Imitates vertical or horizontal line (average age 2½ years)
- Imitates V stroke from demonstration (average age 2½ years)
- Strings four beads in two minutes (average age 2½ years)
- Folds paper (average age 2½ years)
- Builds tower of seven or eight cubes (average age 2¼ years)

## BY THREE AND ONE-HALF YEARS

**Gross Motor.**

- Walks on tiptoe 10 feet (average age 3 years)
- Balances on one foot five seconds (average age 3¼ years)

**Fine Motor.**

- Imitates bridge of three blocks from demonstration (average age 3 years)
- Copies circle from picture model (average age 3 years)
- Imitates cross from demonstration (average age 3 years)
- Closes fist, wiggles thumb (average age 35 months)
- Picks longer of two lines (average age 3 years)

## BY FOUR YEARS

**Gross Motor.**

- Hops, preferred foot (average age 3½ years)
- Walks up stairs, one foot on each step, holding rail (average age 3½ years)
- Walks downstairs, one step per tread (average age 3½ years)
- Throws ball with direction (average age 3½ years)
- Balances on toes (average age 3½ years)
- Jumps over rope 8″ high (average age 3½ years)
- Swings on swing independently (average age 3½ years)
- Jumps from height of 12 inches (average age 3½ years)
- Holds standing balance, one foot advanced; eyes closed, 15 seconds (one of two tries by 4 years)

**Fine Motor.**

- Buttons up clothing (average age 3 years)
- Cuts with scissors (average age 3¾ years)
- Touches point of nose with eyes closed (by age 4, two of three tries)

- Puts 20 coins in a box, separately (by age 4, one of two tries)

## BY FOUR AND ONE-HALF YEARS

**Gross Motor.**

- Balances standing on one foot, five seconds (average age 3¼ years)
- Does forward somersault with aid (average age 3½ years)
- Catches ball in arms, two of three tries (average age 4)
- Catches bounced ball (average age 4 years)
- Heel to toe walk (average age 3¾ years)
- Jumps from height of 2½ feet (average age 4 years)

**Fine Motor.**

- Copies cross from picture model (average age 3¾ years)
- Draws a man, three parts (average age 4 years)
- Copies square from demonstration (average age 4 years)

## BY FIVE YEARS

**Gross Motor.**

- Balances on one foot for 10 seconds (average age 4½ years)
- Hops on nonpreferred foot (average age 4½ years)
- Bounces ball two times successively with one hand (average age 4½ years)
- Catches large bounced ball, two of three tries (average age 4 years)
- Somersaults forward without aid (average age 4¾ years)
- Balances on tiptoes for 10 seconds, one of three tries (by age 5 years)
- Jumps over cord at knee height, feet together, one of three tries (average age 4½ years)
- Walks heel to toe (average age 4¾ years)
- Walks heel to toe, backward (average age 4¾ years)
- Walks 2″ × 4″ balance beam, 3″ off floor, without falling (average age 4½ years)

**Fine Motor.**

- Draws man, three parts (average age 4 years)
- Builds pyramid of six blocks after demonstration (average age 4½ years)
- Clenches and bares teeth (by age 5 years)
- Draws diamond after demonstration (average age 4½ years)
- Copies square from picture model (average age 4¾ years)
- Ties any knot that holds with lace (average age 5 years)

# Appendix B
# Language Development Objectives and Activities for Infants and Toddlers*

| LEVEL | OBJECTIVE | ACTIVITY |
|---|---|---|
| Birth to 1 month | 1. To develop intimacy and awareness of communication based on personal contact.<br>2. To introduce the concept of oral communication.<br>3. To introduce verbal communication.<br>4. To stimulate interest in the process of talking. | 1. Whisper into the child's ear.<br><br>2. Coo at the child.<br><br>3. Talk to the child.<br>4. Let the child explore your mouth with his or her hands as you talk. |
| 1 to 3 months | 1. To develop oral communication.<br>2. To develop auditory acuity.<br>3. To develop the concept that different people sound different.<br>4. To develop the concept of oral and musical communication of feelings. | 1. Imitate the sounds the child makes.<br>2. Talk to the child in different tones.<br>3. Encourage others to talk and coo to the child.<br>4. Sing songs of different mood, rhythms, and tempos. |
| 3 to 6 months | 1. To develop the concept of positive use of verbal communication.<br>2. To stimulate excitement about words.<br>3. To develop the concept that words and music can be linked.<br>4. To develop the ability to name things and events. | 1. Reward the child with words.<br><br>2. Talk expressively to the child.<br>3. Sing or chant to the child.<br><br>4. Describe daily rituals to the child as you carry them out. |
| 6 to 9 months | 1. To develop use of words and reinforce intimacy.<br>2. To develop the concept that things have names. | 1. Talk constantly to the child and explain processes such as feeding, bathing, and changing clothes.<br>2. Name toys for the child as the child plays, foods and utensils as the child eats, and so on. |

FIGURE B–1 Language development: Objectives and activities for infants and toddlers (Adapted from Tarrow and Lundsteen, 1981, pp. 21–22)

*Adapted from Tarrow & Lundsteen, 1981, pp. 21–22.

| LEVEL | OBJECTIVE | ACTIVITY |
|---|---|---|
| | 3. To develop the concept that there is joy in the written word.<br>4. To develop the concept that language is used to describe. | 3. Read aloud to the child, enthusiastically.<br>4. Describe sounds to the child as they are heard. |
| 9 to 12 months | 1. To develop the concept that body parts have names.<br>2. To reinforce the concept that things have names.<br>3. To stimulate rhythm and interest in words.<br>4. To stimulate experimentation with sounds and words. | 1. Name parts of the body and encourage the child to point to them.<br>2. Describe the name things seen on a walk or an automobile trip.<br>3. Repeat simple songs, rhymes, and fingerplays.<br>4. Respond to sounds the child makes, and encourage the child to imitate sounds. |
| 12 to 18 months | 1. To develop the ability to label things and follow directions.<br>2. To expand vocabulary and lay the foundation for later production of sentences.<br>3. To reinforce the concept of names and the ability to recognize names and sounds.<br>4. To encourage verbal communication.<br>5. To reinforce the concept of labels and increase vocabulary. | 1. Line up various objects and, naming one, ask the child to get it.<br>2. Act out verbs ("sit," "jump," "run," "smile," etc.)<br>3. Use animal picture books and posters of animals.<br>4. Let the child talk on a real telephone.<br>5. Describe things at home or outside on a walk or an automobile trip. |
| 18 to 24 months | 1. To stimulate imitation and verbalization.<br><br>2. To improve the ability to name objects.<br><br>3. To encourage repetition, sequencing, and rhythm.<br>4. To develop auditory acuity, passive vocabulary, and the concept of language constancy.<br>5. To stimulate verbalization, selectivity, and–eventually–descriptive language.<br><br><br>6. To stimulate conversation. | 1. Tape-record the child and others familiar to the child, and play the tapes back for the child.<br>2. On a walk around the home or neighborhood with the child, point out and name familiar objects.<br>3. Play counting games, sing songs, and tell and retell familiar stories.<br>4. With the child, listen to the same recording of a story or song over and over.<br>5. Cut out of magazines and mount on stiff cardboard: pictures of foods, clothing, appliances, etc. Have the child identify them as you show them. Use memorable descriptions: "orange, buttery carrots"; "the shiny blue car."<br>6. With the child, prepare and eat a make-believe meal. |

**FIGURE B–1 (cont.)**

| LEVEL | OBJECTIVE | ACTIVITY |
|---|---|---|
| 24 to 36 months | 1. To practive descriptive language and build vocabulary. | 1. Keep a box of scraps of materials and small objects. Have the child select objects, using words to describe them ("fuzzy," "big," "red," etc.) |
| | 2. To encourage verbalization, repetition, comprehension, and speaking in sentences. | 2. Ask the child: "Show me the floor," ". . . the door," etc. When the child points, say "Here's the floor," etc., and encourage the child to imitate you. |
| | 3. To develop the concept of written symbols. | 3. Label the child's possessions. Use the child's name repeatedly: "Mike's bed," "Mike's toy chest." |
| | 4. To encourage specific and descriptive language. | 4. Ask "Which one?" when the child gives a single-word description; and expand on the child's language. (E.g., Child: "Cookie." You: "Yes; this is a ginger cookie.") |
| | 5. To increase understanding of the relation between spoken and written language, and to stimulate the use of both. | 5. Call to the child's attention familiar brand names or identifying symbols on products, buildings, and so on. |

**FIGURE B–1  (cont.)**

# Appendix C
# Basic Program Equipment for an Early Childhood Center

## INDOOR EQUIPMENT

The playroom should be arranged into well-planned areas of interest, such as the housekeeping and doll corner, block building, etc. This encourages children to play in small groups throughout the playroom, engaging in activities of their special interest, rather than attempting to play in one large group.

The early childhood center must provide selections of indoor play equipment from all the following areas of interest. Selection should be of sufficient quantities so that children can participate in a wide range of activities. Many pieces of equipment can be homemade. Consider the age and developmental levels of the children when making selections.

### Playroom Furnishings.

- Tables—seat four to six children (18″ high for three-year-olds, 20″–22″ high for four- and five-year-olds)
- Chairs–10″ high for three-year-olds, 12″–14″ high for four- and five-year olds
- Open shelves—26″ high, 12″ deep, 12″ between shelves
- Lockers—12″ wide, 12″ deep, 32″–36″ high

### Housekeeping or Doll Corner.

| Item | Number Recommended for 10 Children |
|---|---|
| Dolls | 3 |
| Doll Clothes | Variety |
| Doll beds—should be large enough for a child to get into, bedding | 1 |
| Doll high chair | 1 |
| Small table, four chairs | 1 set |

| Item | Number Recommended for 10 Children |
|---|---|
| Tea party dishes | 6-piece set with tray |
| Stove—child size, approximately 24″ high, 23″ long, 12″ wide | 1 |
| Sink—child size, approximately 24″ high, 23″ long, 12″ wide | 1 |
| Refrigerator—child size, approximately 28″ high, 23″ long, 12″ wide | 1 |
| Pots and pans, empty food cartons, measuring cups, spoons, etc. | Variety |
| Mop | 1 |
| Ironing board and iron | 1 |
| Clothespins and clothesline | 1 |
| Toy telephones | 2 |
| Dress-up box—men's and women's hats, neckties, pocketbooks, shoes, old dresses, scarves, jewelry, etc. | Variety |
| Mirror | 1 |

### Art Supplies.

| Item | Number Recommended for 10 Children |
|---|---|
| Unprinted newspaper 18″ × 24″ | 1 ream |
| Colored paper—variety | 3 packages |
| Large kindergarten crayons | 10 boxes |
| Tempera paint—red, yellow, blue, black, white | 1 can each |

679

| Item | Number Recommended for 10 Children |
|---|---|
| Long-handled paint brushes—making a stroke from ½″ to 1″ wide | 10–12 |
| Easels | 1 |
| Finger paint paper— glazed paper such as shelf, freezer, or butcher's paper | 1 roll |
| Paste | 1 quart |
| Blunt scissors | 10 |
| Collage—collection of bits of colored paper, cut-up gift wrappings, ribbons, cotton, string, scraps of fabric, etc., for pasting | Variety |
| Magazines for cutting and pasting | Variety |
| Clay—playdough, homemade dough clay | 50 pounds |
| Cookie cutters, rolling pins | Variety |
| Smocks or aprons to protect children's clothes | 10 |

## Block Building Area.

| Item | Number Recommended for 10 Children |
|---|---|
| Unit blocks—purchased or home-made (directions are available) | 276 pieces, 11 shapes |
| Factory scraps | Variety |
| Large, light-weight blocks | Variety |
| Small wooden or rubber animals and people that can live in block houses | Variety |
| Small trucks, airplanes, cars, and boats | 12 |
| Medium airplanes | 3 |
| Medium boats | 2 |
| Medium-sized trucks—12″ to 24″ | 3 |

## Music Corner.

- Record player
- Suitable records—activity and listening records
- Rhythm instruments
- Dress-up skirts and scarves for dancing

## Manipulative Toys.

| Item | Number Recommended for 10 Children |
|---|---|
| Wooden inlay puzzles— approximately 5 to 20 pieces | 6 |
| Color cone | 1 |
| Nested blocks | 1 |
| Peg boards—variety of shapes and sizes | 1 |
| Large spools and beads for stringing | 2 sets |
| Toys that have parts that fit into one another | 2 |
| Lotto games | 2 |
| Dominoes | 1 |

## Books and Stories (20–30 Books).

A carefully selected book collection for the various age levels should include the following categories:

- Transportaion, birds and animals, family life
- Community helpers, science, nonsense rhymes
- Mother Goose rhymes, poems, and stories (library books enrich the collection)
- Homemade picture books
- Collection of pictures classified by subject

## Nature Study and Science.

- Aquarium or fish bowls
- Magnifying glass, prism, magnet, thermometers
- Growing indoor plants, garden plot
- Additional material such as stones, leaves, acorns, birds' nests, caterpillars, worms, tadpoles, etc.

## Woodworking Center.

Basic woodworking operations are:

- Sanding
- Gluing

- Hammering
- Holding (with a vise or clamp)
- Fastening (with screws)
- Drilling
- Sawing
  Materials for a woodworking center include:
- Sturdy workbench (or table)
- Woodworking tools: broad-headed nails ¾″ to 1½″ long, a C-clamp or vise (to hold wood), flat-headed hammer weighing about 12 ounces for beginning woodworking experiences, later a claw hammer may be added, 14″ saw with ten teeth to the inch
- Soft white pine lumber scraps (it is difficult to drive nails into hardwood); plywood is not suitable either. Packing boxes of soft pine can be disassembled and used for hammering work.

**Sand Play.** In an outdoor sand area, sand should be confined so it does not get scattered over the rest of the playground. The area should be large enough so several children can move about in it without crowding each other. A 10″ to 12″ ledge around a sandbox can serve as a boundary and at the same time provide children with a working surface or a seat. If sand is about 6″ to 8″ below the top of the ledge, it is less likely to spill onto the playground. Sand should be about 18″ deep so children can dig or make tunnels. Four or five inches of gravel on the bottom of the sandbox provides drainage.

Basic equipment: Ordinary plastic or metal kitchen utensils—cups, spoons, pails, shovels, sifters, funnels, scoops, bowls

**Water Play.** Water play can be either an indoor or an outdoor activity, depending upon the climate. Clear plastic water basins can be used for water play. When they are on a stand with wheels, they can be moved easily to any area of a room. When these plastic containers are used, children have the advantage of being able to see through the sides and the bottom. If a table stands on a carpeted floor, a plastic runner can be used to protect the carpet, and spillage will not be a serious housekeeping problem.

Materials: Clear tubing, sponges, strainers, funnels, corks, pitchers, and measuring cups. For added interest, rotary beaters, spoons, small bowls, plastic basters, and straws.

## OUTDOOR EQUIPMENT

The outdoor play equipment should be grouped according to use. For example, plan for both active and quiet play; allow for free areas for use of wheel toys. The following is a list of basic outdoor play equipment for the day care center:

- Jungle gym or other climbing structure
- Large and small packing boxes
- Slide
- Swings with canvas seats
- Wagons and wheelbarrows
- Pedal toys—tricycles, cars, etc.
- Mounted steering wheels
- Sandbox with spoons, shovels, pails, etc.
- Tile or open barrels set in concrete
- Balls
- A variety of salvage material, such as rubber tires, tire tubes, lengths of garden hose, ropes, and cardboard boxes, will enrich the play.

Many activities, such as housekeeping play and art activities, at times should be transferred to the outdoor area.

Use the checklist below to evaluate your playground setup:

_____ There are clear pathways and enough space between areas so that traffic flows well and equipment does not obstruct the movement of children.

_____ Space and equipment are organized so that children are readily visible and easily supervised by adults.

_____ Different types of activity areas are separated. (Tricycle paths are separate from swings, sand box is separate from the climbing area.)

_____ Open space is available for active play.

_____ There is some space for quiet play.

_____ Dramatic play can be set up outdoors, as space is available.

_____ Art activities can be set up outdoors.

_____ A portion of the play area is covered for use in wet weather.

_____ A storage area is available for play equipment.

_____ A drinking fountain is available.

_____ The area has readily accessible restrooms.

# Appendix D
# Room and Yard Organization, Exhibitions, and Displays

## ROOM AND YARD ORGANIZATION*

**Large Cardboard Cartons.**   Puppet theaters, post offices, and stores are easily constructed by slicing or sawing out a rectangular portion in the top half of the front section of a large carton. When folded to the inside, the flap can be cut back to the desired width for a stage or shelf. The flap is supported by a dowel or a length of heavy cord strung from one side of the box to the other. Leftover latex wall paint is ideal for painting these large structures. This type of paint conceals advertising, does not smear when dry, and can be washed off a brush or child's hands with water. Use old postage stamps, greeting cards, and envelopes if this is to be a post office. Paper tickets, signs, money (bottle tops, etc.) can be used if the structure is to be a theater.

**Cable Spools.**   Empty cable spools are fun additions to the outside play area. A slat can be removed from the core creating a hiding place for the children or a climbing device. Two or three spools may be secured one on top of another with a plumber's pipe inserted through the center of each; a second pipe can be sunk in concrete close enough to the structure to be used as a fire fighter's pole. A rope ladder attached to the top spool adds to the climbing challenge.

**Cardboard Boxes.**   To create a table easel from a large cardboard box, measure one side the equivalent length of the bottom and mark. Cut diagonally across from this mark to the bottom corner on both

*These suggestions are taken from Jean W. Quill's *A World of Materials*, Washington, D.C.: National Association for the Education of Young Children, 1969.

sides. This produces a sturdy cardboard triangle that serves as a table easel once two slits have been made for clothespin clips at the top. The children themselves will be able to remove or replace newsprint for paintings.

The same triangular arrangement covered with a piece of flannel makes a nontipping flannel board for children's and teacher's use. A show box containing flannel board figures may be stored beneath the triangle for the child's convenience. It can be used for retelling stories or reworking number experiences in small groups or as a solitary, self-selected activity.

**Wooden Crates.**   During cantaloupe season, grocery stores will supply empty cantaloupe crates. These are durable and good for school use. At a minimal cost, these crates may be transformed into a stove, sink, sofa, work bench, or locker arrangement. To form a solid front, it is necessary only to tap the wooden slats loose, add a few additional slats, and replace side by side. To create a stove, individual pie tins can be turned upside down to simulate gas burners. These are especially effective when painted black to look like "grating." Painted bottle tops add stove controls. A spool set on top of a scrap of wood and painted silver makes a faucet; the entire "sink" may cost little more than the price of the required pan. Many leftover aluminum foil pans are suitable for this purpose. The ends of the cantaloupe crates make sturdy frames for children's drawings or trays for the doll corner or science table.

**Window Shades.**   The discarded portion of the rollers make good instruments. Several roofing washers or bottle caps can be secured on a nail driven into the roller segment. This results in an effective shaking instrument.

**Wooden and Plastic Soft-Drink and Milk Crates.** These crates, sometimes available at a small charge, are excellent substitutes for commercial hollow blocks. Paint them bright colors with latex paint. A set of casters on one crate can produce a durable wagon for hauling friends or blocks. Set the casters far enough in to allow stacking at those times when the crates are not in use. They also make excellent "cubby holes" for storage.

**Boats.** At the beginning or end of the boating season, some rowboats may be destroyed or abandoned as no longer seaworthy. These boats are often donated by marina managers to a school or playground, if transportation is provided by the school. When stored safely, these boats can be made into useful playground equipment.

**Junked Tires.** Used tires, hung either horizontally or vertically, make excellent swings. Inflated tubes can be rolled from place to place, bounced on, and used for various movement games.

**Ice Cream Containers.** A circular, spatter-paint screen may be created from the three-gallon containers discarded by ice cream stores or restaurants. Cut the bottom from one of these containers, leaving only a narrow edge to which the edges of a circular piece of screen may be glued. A matching narrow circle, cut from another piece of cardboard, placed over the first and glued down, will secure the screen. A paint-dipped toothbrush is scraped across the screen; any object placed beneath will leave a design on the paper on which it is resting. The carton should be cut down to leave approximately one quarter of its original length; this gives a satisfactory height for spatter painting.

Ice cream containers can also be converted to wastebaskets, space helmets, and diver's masks. To make the latter, simply remove an area from an upside-down carton large enough for the child's face to appear. Allow the child to paint in a choice of colors. Ice cream containers can also be used as storage space, when bolted together.

**Sawdust.** Sawdust is available from the lumber mill for use in making sawdust clay. Simply mix a small amount of wallpaper paste in water and add sawdust until a pliable consistency has been reached. This clay hardens over a period of time.

## EXHIBITIONS, DISPLAYS

It is stimulating and educational for children to see their work displayed. Whether the purpose of the exhibit is to introduce new ideas and information, to stimulate interest in a single lesson, to show the children's work, or to provide an overview of their work, the subject of the exhibition should be directly related to the children's interest. Exhibits should be changed often to be of educational and decorative value.

### Labels.

- Make large, bold letters that can be easily read.
- Keep titles brief. Descriptive material should be in smaller letters.
- Label children's work with their names as a means of creating pride through recognition of their work.
- Vary the material in making letters. In addition to paper letters, labels can be made of paint, ink, crayon, chalk, cloth, fancy papers, string, rope, yarn, and other three-dimensional materials.

### Color.

- Choose a basic color scheme related to the visual material displayed. Seasonal colors can be used, such as warm colors for fall (yellow, orange, red), cool colors for winter (blue, blue-green, gray), and light and cool colors for spring (colors with yellow in the mixture, such as yellow-orange).
- Use colors for mounting that are more subdued than the materials mounted. This may be accomplished by using lighter color, darker color, or grayer color.
- Select a bright color for accent, as in bands or other pleasing arrangements on the larger areas of gray, lighter, or darker colors.
- Create a contrast to emphasize or attract attention. Intense color makes a visual impact, such as orange against black.

- Use both light and dark color values.
- Create color patterns that lead the eye from area to area.

**Balance.** Balance can be achieved formally or informally. To create formal balance, the largest piece of work may be placed in the center with similar shapes on either side. Informal balance is more interesting, subtle, and compelling. Material may be grouped in blocks of different sizes, colors, or shapes, and still be balanced. Margins of the bulletin board should be wider at the bottom.

**Unity.** Unity in design is the quality that holds the arrangement together in harmony.

- Ideas can be unified with background paper, lettering, strips of construction paper, yarn, or ribbon.
- Repetition of similar sizes, shapes, colors, or lines can help to create harmony.
- Shapes can be arranged to lead the eye from one part of the board to another.
- One large unusual background shape helps unify the design.
- Avoid cluttering the display; items placed at all angles destroy the unity.

**Variety.** Variety in arrangement prevents monotony. Use interesting combinations of color, form, line, and texture.

**Emphasis.** Emphasis is the main idea or center of interest. This can be achieved by using larger letters, a brighter color, a larger picture, an unusual shape, texture, or a three-dimensional object. Other material should be grouped into subordinate areas.

**Line.** Line is used to draw the eye to a specific area, suggest direction, action, and movement, and to hold the display together. Use thick or thin lines; solid, dotted, or dashed lines. Diagonal lines are used to show action, zigzag lines suggest excitement; slow-moving curves are restful. Lines may be painted, cut from paper, or formed with string, yarn, ribbon, or tape.

**Texture.** Texture may be created with a variety of materials:

- Paper and cardboard—textured wallpaper, sandpaper, metallic foil, egg containers, corrugated cardboard
- Fabrics—netting, flannel, burlap, fur, felt, carpet remnants, assorted felt scraps
- Miscellaneous—chicken wire, metal screen, sheet cork

### Three-Dimensional Effects.

- Pull letters or objects out to the head of the pin.
- Staple a shallow box to the board as a shelf to hold lightweight three-dimensional items.
- Mount a picture on a box lid and fasten it to the board.
- Use shallow boxes as buildings, animals, and people.
- Pleat a strip of paper in an accordion fold with pictures attached.
- Use paper sculpture—strips of paper can be twisted, curled, folded, rolled, fringed, perforated, or torn. Puppets, animals, birds, flowers, people, abstract forms, and masks can also be made.
- Use three-dimensional materials in displays—Styrofoam, egg cartons, paper plates, paper cups, soda straws, cupcake cups, paper lace, toweling tubes, and other discarded materials.
- Use objects from nature—branches, shells, bark, driftwood, feathers.

### Background Materials.

- Display paper, tissue paper, burlap, corrugated cardboard, construction paper
- Egg carton separators, blotters, textured wallpaper, shelf paper

### Display Boards for Two-Dimensional Work.

- Standard cork boards or sheet of plywood to which cork tiles have been glued.
- Builder's wall board with wood strip nailed to the top with hooks for hanging.
- Thick cardboard that will hold pins.

- A pasteboard box open for standing on a table or the floor, depending on size.
- A folding screen made from an old crate or packing box.
- Wide strips of binding tape attached along a blank wall; pin pictures to tape.
- Wire stretched across an empty space with pictures attached to it.

## MORE ON BULLETIN BOARDS

The most immediate evidence of an art program is the display of children's artwork. A teacher's creative approach to display is an extension of the art program in the physical environment. Bulletin boards are the most frequent form of display. Consider the "fairy tale" below:

> Once upon a time there was a carpenter who was building a classroom. When he was on the very top of his ladder, a hammer fell and crashed into the wall, making a very large hole. The carpenter did not know what to do since he had no materials left to repair the wall. Suddenly he had an idea! He found a 4′ × 8′ slab of cork and hung it over the hole. Then he tacked wood strips around the edges and said, "I am well pleased." He named his creation "Bulletin Board."

The dictionary defines a bulletin board as "a board on which bulletins and other notices are posted." Teachers often have other definitions for this term: (1) a surface that must be covered before the first day of school and before parents' night; (2) a board that is always three inches wider than the paper just cut for it; and (3) a rectangle that has a width never sufficient for the number of letters needed to be pinned across it.

Whatever your definition, a bulletin board is much more than a board on which notices are posted. It is a visual extension of a learning experience, a visual form of motivation, and a reflection of a curriculum area. Because bulletin boards are a visual phenomenon, teachers should be concerned about their content and appearance.

Thirty spelling papers, or fifteen identical paper pumpkins hanging up like someone's laundry do not constitute a good bulletin board. Mimeographed pictures, commercial cardboard turkeys, and corrugated cardboard trim are *not* visually appealing and certainly are not reflections of the children whose interest you are trying to catch.

A display designed for the eye is also designed for the mind. Children are very much attuned to symbols. Television commercials, billboards, posters, and cereal boxes attest to the impact of images. Bulletin boards should attract constructive attention. Stereotypical smiley faces and dog-eared paper letters with a thousand pin holes will not do it. Ideas and paper fade. Stereotyped versions of an upcoming holiday do absolutely nothing for children's art development.

For an early childhood teacher, one of the best solutions is to display the children's artwork. Art is a visual extension of the child and her own unique ideas and expression. It is the result of the child's own experience and serves as a motivation for others and the child herself. Any subject can be the theme for an effective bulletin board, but one rule of thumb is that all boards should be student oriented and entice student participation. Boards that ask questions, have games to play, or have objects to be handled can be fun *and* valuable learning experiences.

Eye-catching photographs (of the children, if possible) and short stories, poems, and cartoons are exercises for both the eye and mind. Whatever the mode, the key is visual impact. In order for a bulletin board to be a learning experience, it first must get the child's attention. Bright colors, bold design, legible, catchy, succinct phraseology, and relevant themes are vital to bulletin boards by, for, and about the children.

Try some of these suggestions for improving your bulletin boards:

- Take advantage of interest in the World Series or other big sports events for a variety of projects. Find bulletin board space for newspaper clippings, pictures of heroes and heroines, posting of scores and relative standings. Have the children write reports or draw pictures of games they are interested in. Make up graphs with scores for each team. Vary these activities according to the level of the children's interest and abilities.

- If you have a bulletin board too big to cope with, cut it down to size by covering it with wallpaper samples, outlining each sample with black construction paper in a kind of giant patchwork quilt effect. Each child can use one of these squares as a personal bulletin board. Or you could use each of the squares to depict a different aspect of one main theme: symbols of Christmas, kinds of animals, favorite people, etc.
- Be sure all your bulletin boards and other kinds of displays are at the children's eye level.
- When your classroom closet is awash with caps and mittens, why not bring their splashy colors and designs into the open with a self-portrait mural for a bulletin board? On a strip of butcher paper, draw a circle for each child. Have the students add features to turn these circles into self-portraits. Two lines looping down from each face become instant arms. Finally, have each child draw her own hat and mittens on the heads and hands. Encourage the young artists to copy the actual styles, colors, and designs of their own apparel as exactly as possible. This mural not only makes a colorful bulletin board, but also helps you easily identify the owners of any stray clothing.

**Display Areas for Three-Dimensional Work.**

- Use tops of cupboard or built-in shelves.
- Build shelves with boards supported by cigar boxes or brick, used permanently or temporarily.
- Attach a shelf of wood or particleboard underneath a bulletin board.
- Cigar boxes nailed together make display shelves.
- Dioramas are especially useful where exhibit space is limited.
- A card table can be used for temporary exhibits, then folded up when not in use.
- If obtainable, a small showcase is valuable for displaying museum-type objects.
- Cardboard boxes fastened to bulletin boards make a display place for light-weight objects.
- Use driftwood as an interesting display for weaving and jewelry.
- Puppet display rods can be made with a board and some dowel sticks.
- Mobiles are attractive display devices. Coat hangers can also be used.
- Cover cardboard or cigar boxes and use them as bases for displaying art objects.
- Use pegboard with brackets.

# Appendix E
# Recycled Materials

Creative teachers find that art possibilities abound everywhere, including a new look at old, discarded materials. For example, in the teaching suggestions below, one kind of discarded item—gallon milk containers—provides a wealth of storage, display, and equipment possibilities.

## TEACHING SUGGESTIONS: EMPTY CONTAINERS FULL OF PROMISE

When that plastic gallon milk container is out of milk, it's full of potential for classroom implements you can make yourself. Scoops, funnels, sorting trays, display or storage containers, and carrying baskets are just waiting to be cut out.

Outline the area you wish to cut with a felt-tip marker and use a sharp knife or a small pencil-type soldering iron to do the cutting. (If you use the iron, be sure to work in a ventilated area and avoid the fumes.)

The containers are so readily available you can afford to experiment with a few to find just the shapes you're after. Here are directions for some basic cuts to get you started:

- Scoop—Cut away the handle and part of the side below it. The container's handle instantly becomes

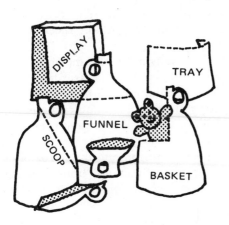

the scoop's handle, while the section below becomes the scoop itself.
- Sorting trays—Cut off the bottom or the entire side opposite the handle to make trays of varying depths. These are perfect for sorting small objects, such as pebbles or shells, or for examining small amounts of sand or soil.
- Funnel—Cut the handle a few centimeters from the top. Then cut around the base of the handle to make the funnel's body from the curved section of the jug. The top of the handle becomes the spout. For a larger funnel, just cut the bottom from the container and use the top as the spout.
- Carrying basket—Cut away the upper portion of the side opposite the handle. The children then carry the jug by the handle and use it to transport all kinds of items.
- Display or storage container—Cut the bottom off the jug just below the handle. You'll end up with a square container about 3″ deep, perfect for displaying or storing the specimens that students collect on their outings.

## EQUIPMENT FOR MOVEMENT ACTIVITIES FROM RECYCLED MATERIALS

A valuable addition to the movement program in the early childhood classroom is equipment made from recycled materials. For example, empty plastic gallon milk jugs can be used as safe game goals, pins for indoor/outdoor bowling games, or cut out for scoops (see Figures E–1 and E–2) to toss yarn or other light balls in classroom movement activities.

Old pantyhose can be used to make light child-sized rackets for great hand–eye coordination practice in racket games. These rackets are especially good for young children as they are light enough to handle and yet sturdy enough to hit a yarn, Nerf, or plastic ball.

Using recycled materials has an obvious cost ben-

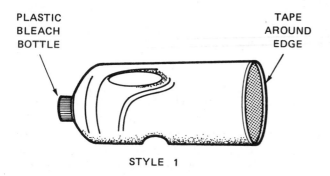

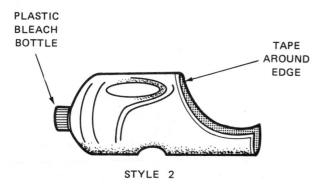

**FIGURE E–1 Equipment using recycled materials: scoops.**

**FIGURE E–2 Plastic scoop and yarn ball.**

efit in addition to demonstrating the importance of conservation to young children. Young children can possibly use these same materials at home for their own play experiences.

Even better, you can enlist parent participation and involvement in the program by asking parents to donate recycled materials to make movement equipment. Perhaps parents and children together could even get involved at home in making some of the equipment for the class's use, such as yarn balls or pantyhose rackets.

## OTHER IDEAS FOR RECYCLING MATERIALS

Just as recycled materials were used for making movement equipment in Unit 16, these same "dis-cards" can be valuable art materials. Both conservation and creativity can be practiced in ways like these:

- Be a scavenger. (But remember that the word is "scavenger," not beggar or receiver of junk goods.)
- Begin your scavenger hunt by making a list of the equipment and supplies that you feel you might find in your community at little or no cost.
- Search for your treasures in attics, basements, garages, thrift or Goodwill Industry stores, and at garage sales.
- Ask parents to contribute to the needs of creative children, or send a "want ad" home being specific about what you need. Your ad may read something like this:

PLEASE SAVE
-yarn and ribbon scraps
-large empty spools
-shirt cardboards
-leftover wallpaper
-men's shirts—we will turn them into smocks
-juice cans with smooth edges
-plastic squeeze bottles
-bits of fabric, trim
-buttons, old jewelry

THEY WILL BE USED BY YOUR CREATIVE CHILD(REN) IN THE EARLY CHILDHOOD PROGRAM.

- Check with wallpaper and carpet dealers. Wallpaper dealers will sometimes give you their old sample books, and carpet dealers will often sell their sample swatches for a very small sum. These carpet swatches are useful as sit-upons, as rugs for houses the children build, as colorful mats under items on display, and as working mats for use under table toys.
- Trim the bristles from 1"-wide house painting brushes to about 1" in length and use these in place of more expensive easel brushes.
- Gather paper from a variety of sources:

Be a bag grabber. Collect plain paper bags. Cut them open and use them for painting, crayoning, etc.

Save old newspapers for easel painting. Bright tempera (water color) paint on a newsprint background makes a very attractive and interesting work of art.

Check with your community or local newspaper office. They may donate or sell newsprint or old newspapers to you at a minimal cost.

Other materials listed in Figure E–3 can be valuable in the art center.

**Sandbox Toys from the Kitchen.** From the cupboard—use plastic storage containers such as scoops,

The materials listed below can be valuable instructional tools in the art program as well as in other curriculum areas.

1. Empty plastic containers—detergent bottles, bleach bottles, old refrigerator containers. These can be used for constructing scoops, storing art materials, etc.
2. Buttons—all colors and sizes. These are excellent for collages, assemblages, as well as sorting, counting, matching, etc.
3. Egg shells. These can be washed, dried, and colored with food coloring for art projects.
4. Coffee or shortening can lids and cans themselves. These can be covered with adhesive paper and used for the storage of art supplies, games, and manipulatives materials.
5. Magazines with colorful pictures. These are excellent for making collages, murals, and posters, too.
6. Scraps of fabric—felt, silk, cotton, oil cloth, etc. These can be used to make "fabric boards" with the name of each fabric written under a small swatch attached to the board, as well as for collages, puppets, etc.
7. Yarn scraps. These can be used for separating buttons into sets; also for art activities.
8. Styrofoam scraps.
9. Scraps of lace, rick rack, or decorative trim.
10. Bottles with sprinkler tops. Excellent for water play and for mixing water as children finger paint.
11. Wallpaper books of discontinued patterns.
12. Paper doilies.
13. Discarded wrapping paper.
14. Paint color cards from paint/hardware stores.
15. Old paintbrushes.
16. Old jewelry and beads.
17. Old muffin tins. These are effective for sorting small objects and mixing paint.
18. Tongue depressors or ice cream sticks. Counters for math, good for art construction projects, stick puppets, etc.
19. Wooden clothespins. For making "people," for construction projects, for hanging up paintings to dry.

**FIGURE E–3 Beautiful junk list.**

molds, or buckets. Foam cups are good scoops or molds. A plastic flowerpot with drainage holes can be a sifter.

Cut an egg carton into individual egg cups for molds.

Make an egg-carton sifter by cutting the lid off an egg carton and cutting the egg cup section in half the short way. In the bottom of each cup, poke a hole. The holes may be the same size or of varying sizes.

**Egg Carton Ideas.** Egg cartons can be used for a multitude of projects. Some of the following may be fun for the children to try:

*Caterpillars.* An upside down egg carton, taped shut (or use only the egg cup half); decorate with markers, crayons, and bits of felt for details (such as antennae, mouth, eyes).

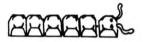

*Flowers.* Use egg cups stuck on pipe cleaners as flowers. Add color and details as you please.

*Traffic signal.* Use three egg cup sections, painted red, yellow, and green. Paste on tongue depressor. Can be used in wheel toy area, block area, dramatic corner, etc.

*Crazy glasses.* Cut egg carton in paired sections, making two joined cup sections. Cut off the top part to make glasses.

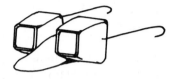

*Snakes.* Cut separate cup sections from egg carton. Using a large carpet needle and yarn, join the cup sections into a snake form. You may want to add features with markers, crayons, pieces of scraps glued on, etc.

*Alligator.* Use the cup side of the egg carton, turning it upside down for the "bumpy" alligator back. Add a long snout and tail, cut out from the top section of the egg carton. Decorate with markers, crayons, glue on all kinds of features with fabric scraps, bits of felt, etc.

*Christmas bell.* Single egg cup. Punch hole in top for pipe cleaner "clanger." Put a small button or wooden bead on end of pipe cleaner for clapper.

*Egg carton turtle.* Cut a large circle from colored construction paper. Glue on single egg cups for "bump" on turtle's back. Add head, feet, and tail by gluing on scrap pieces of cloth or construction paper.

*Easter basket.* Cut four adjoining egg cups from bottom of the egg carton. This would make three baskets from one egg carton. Paint or crayon as desired and staple on handle (or punch a pipe cleaner into the side for a handle).

*Spider.* Attach pipe cleaner "legs" to single egg cup. Add eyes and any other features desired, with crayons, markers, glued-on scrap pieces of cloth or felt.

*Table games.* Cut out single egg cups for table games: color each cup a different color (or put a different letter or number on each). Match the egg cup to a board with the matching color (letter or number).

 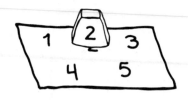

**Miscellaneous Projects from Scraps.**

- Giant paper clip chains. Link large paper clips for "necklaces," "ropes," etc.

- Walnut shell turtle

- Walnut shell boat (small lump of clay holds the toothpick sail)

- Thread spool animals

- Clothespin animals

- Clear contact paper and tissue window pictures. Cut a piece of clear contact paper. Child arranges colored tissue over sticky side. Top with clear contact paper. Makes a beautiful, durable stained-glass window hanging. Also could be used for alphabet, scenes, poems, etc.

**Paper Plate Projects.** Commercial paper plates now come in a variety of shapes and sizes. The porous, noncoated variety are the least expensive and absorb the paint well. A stapler is used to assemble most of the following:

1. Stick puppets

2. Turkey

3. Lacers  made with long shoe strings

4. Collage base  plate and platter sizes

5. Pumpkin  painted orange

6. Turtle  painted green

7. Fish

8. Bill holder  or wall flower holder

9. Elephants

10. Snowman

11. Rabbit

12. Clocks  with brad hands

13. Shamrock  painted green; two plates back to back

14. Heart  from two plates back to back, cut and stapled

15. Fish bowl covered with plastic wrap

16. Balloon bunny hats

17. Paper plate faces or Jack-O-Lanterns

18. Spinner games 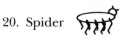 with soup size plates

19. Owl

20. Spider  painted black

21. Octopus

22. Dancing man on string or elastic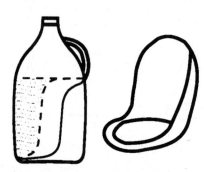

23. Bunny

24. Butterfly

25. Pig

26. Ladybug

- Doll infant seat. Cut top off round plastic bottle, leaving the round basket. Punch hole on each side. Smooth all edges, or cover with plastic tape. The seat can be colored, covered with fabric, or decorated with nursery decals. Holes are used to put string through to hold the infant seat on a chair for "feeding" times. Tie the infant seat onto a chair when it's time to "feed the baby."

# Appendix F
# Criteria for Selecting Play Equipment for Young Children

1. *A young child's playthings should be as free of detail as possible.*
   A child needs freedom to express himself by creating his own childlike world; too much detail hampers him. Blocks are the best example of "unstructured" toys. Blocks, construction sets, and other unstructured toys and equipment such as clay, sand, and paints allow the imagination free rein and are basic playthings.

2. *A good plaything should stimulate children to do things for themselves.*
   Equipment that makes the child a spectator, such as a mechanical duck, may entertain for the moment but has little or no play value. The equipment provided for play should encourage children to explore and create or offer the opportunity for dramatic play.

3. *Young children need large, easily manipulated playthings.*
   Toys too small can be a source of frustration because the child's muscular coordination is not yet developed enough to handle the smaller forms and shapes. A child's muscles develop through his play. A child needs equipment for climbing and balancing.

4. *The material from which a plaything is made has an important role in the play of the young child.*
   Warmth and pleasurable touch are significant to him. The most satisfactory materials have been established as wood and cloth.

5. *The durability of the plaything is of utmost importance.*
   Play materials must be sturdy. Children hate to see their toys break. Axles and wheels must be strong to support a child's weight. Some materials break so readily that they prove to be very expensive.

6. *The toy must "work."*
   What frustration when a door or drawer won't shut, wheels get stuck, or figures won't stand up. Be sure parts move correctly and that maintenance will be easy.

7. *The construction of a plaything should be simple enough for a child to comprehend.*
   This strengthens his understanding and experience of the world around him. The mechanics, too, should be visible and easily grasped. Small children will take them apart to see how they tick.

8. *A plaything should encourage cooperative play.*
   As we seek to teach children to work and play together, we should supply the environment that stimulates such play.

9. *The total usefulness of the plaything must be considered in comparing price.*
   Will it last several children through several stages of their playing lives?

# Appendix F

*What are some good toys and play materials for young children?*
*All ages are approximate. Most suggestions for younger children are also appropriate for older children.*

| Sensory materials | Active play equipment | Construction materials | Manipulative toys | Dolls and dramatic play | Books and recordings | Art materials |
|---|---|---|---|---|---|---|
| **2-year-olds and young 3s** | | | | | | |
| Water toys: food coloring, pumps, funnels<br>Sand toys: containers, utensils<br>Harmonica, kazoo, guitar, recorder<br>Tools for working with clay | Bicycle<br>Outdoor games: bocce, tetherball, shuffleboard, jump rope, Frisbee | More unit blocks, shapes, and accessories<br>Props for roads, towns<br>Hollow blocks<br>Brace and bits, screwdrivers, screws, metric measure, accessories | More complex puzzles<br>Dominoes<br>More difficult board and card games<br>Yarn, big needles, mesh fabric, weaving materials<br>Magnets, balances<br>Attribute blocks | Cash register, play money, accessories, or props for other dramatic play settings: gas station, construction, office<br>Typewriter | Books on cultures<br>Stories with chapters<br>Favorite stories children can read<br>Children's recipe books | Watercolors, smaller paper, stapler, hole puncher<br>Chalkboard<br>Oil crayons, paint crayons, charcoal<br>Simple camers, film |
| **Older 3s and 4-year-olds** | | | | | | |
| Water toys: measuring cups, egg beaters<br>Sand toys: muffin tins, vehicles<br>Xylophone, maracas, tambourine<br>Potter's clay | Larger 3-wheeled riding vehicle<br>Roller skates<br>Climbing structure<br>Rope or tire swing<br>Plastic bats and balls<br>Various sized rubber balls<br>Balance board<br>Planks, boxes, old tires<br>Bowling pins, ring toss, bean bags and target | More unit blocks, shapes, and accessories<br>Table blocks<br>Realistic model vehicles<br>Construction set with smaller pieces<br>Woodworking bench, saw, sandpaper, nails | Puzzles, pegboard, small beads to string<br>Parquetry blocks<br>Small objects to sort<br>Marbles<br>Magnifying glass<br>Simple card or board games<br>Flannel board with pictures, letters<br>Sturdy letters and numbers | Dolls and accessories<br>Doll carriage<br>Child-sized stove or sink<br>More dress-up clothes<br>Play food, cardboard cartons<br>Airport, doll house, or other settings with accessories<br>Finger or stick puppets | Simple science books<br>More detailed picture and story books<br>Sturdy record or tape player<br>Recordings of wider variety of music<br>Book and recording sets | Easel, narrower brushes<br>Thick crayons, chalk<br>Paste, tape with dispenser<br>Collage materials |
| **5- and 6-year-olds** | | | | | | |
| Water and sand toys: cups, shovels<br>Modeling dough<br>Sound-matching games<br>Bells, wood block, triangle, drum<br>Texture matching games, feel box | Low climber<br>Canvas swing<br>Low slide<br>Wagon, cart, or wheelbarrow<br>Large rubber balls<br>Low 3-wheeled, steerable vehicle with pedals | Unit blocks and accessories: animals, people, simple wood cars and trucks<br>Interlocking construction set with large pieces<br>Wood train and track set<br>Hammer (13 oz. steel shanked), soft wood, roofing nails, nailing block | Wooden puzzles with 4–20 large pieces<br>Pegboards<br>Big beads or spools to string<br>Sewing cards<br>Stacking toys<br>Picture lotto, picture dominoes | Washable dolls with a few clothes<br>Doll bed<br>Child-sized table and chairs<br>Dishes, pots, and pans<br>Dress-up clothes: hats, shoes, shirts<br>Hand puppets<br>Shopping cart | Clear picture books, stories, and poems about things children know<br>Records or tapes of classical music, folk music, or children's songs | Wide-tip watercolor markers<br>Large sheets of paper, easel<br>Finger or tempera paint, ½" brushes<br>Blunt-nose scissors<br>White glue |

# Index